NORTHERN NECK WILLS, INVENTORIES & OTHER RECORDS 1800 – 1825

•

Probate, Estate, Guardianship & Chancery Records for the Virginia Counties of Westmoreland, Richmond, Northumberland & Lancaster

NORTHERN NECK WILLS, INVENTORIES & OTHER RECORDS 1800 – 1825

•

Probate, Estate, Guardianship & Chancery Records for the Virginia Counties of Westmoreland, Richmond, Northumberland & Lancaster

By
Robert K. Headley, Jr.

Genealogical Publishing Co., Inc.

Published by Genealogical Publishing Company
3600 Clipper Mill Rd., #260
Baltimore, Maryland 21211

Library of Congress Catalog Card Number 2013955987
ISBN 978-0-8063-1985-8

Made in the United States of America

To my daughters

Sarah and Amy
&
my grandson
Joshua

CONTENTS

INTRODUCTION

Probate records are a rich source of genealogical, social, historical, and even linguistic data. They can illuminate family relationships and attitudes. They can provide windows on the times when they were produced. Sometimes they can even suggest the ways the people of that time spoke. [1]

This book started out when I planned to abstract all the wills of Westmoreland County; so many had been missed or abstracted incorrectly by previous abstractors. But, gradually, I moved to the mostly untouched wills of the early nineteenth century. The Northern Neck, despite being divided into several counties, must be considered as a single unit. Families from one county easily spill over into neighboring counties. I therefore decided to include records from the four lower Northern Neck counties: Westmoreland, Richmond, Northumberland, and Lancaster. I also decided to include wills, inventories and appraisements, divisions of estates, guardianship records, and chancery court records. Few of the early 19th century probate or estate records from these counties have been published. The county records for the Northern Neck during the first quarter of the 19th century are fairly complete and, with a few exceptions, easy to read. The Richmond County records are written in especially clear attractive hands, perhaps a legacy of the long-time 18th century county clerk Sir Marmaduke Beckwith. Lancaster County wills between 1795 and 1800 contained in Will Book 28 but not included in ALCW have been abstracted as have a small group of Westmoreland County wills discovered after Fothergill completed her WWCV. Since Lewis and Booker provided very full abstracts of Northumberland County wills and inventories up to 1816, I have included herein only those recorded after that year. A few wills missing from published abstracts have also been added. I was surprised at the number of references to marriages that are not recorded in the published marriage records and to the number of wills that appear to be missing. Many of the chancery cases from Westmoreland, Northumberland and Lancaster counties have been checked and have provided much valuable information.[2]

The user of this book should be warned that there are many pitfalls to using abstracts such as are contained herein; names may be transcribed incorrectly or whole lines or names may be missed. One should always check the original

---

[1] Examining the way a word was spelled can provide information about how that word was pronounced at the time in this area. For example, note the various spellings of family names such as: Purcell or Pursley; Hardwick, Hardich, Hadridge; Mothershead or Modiset; and Claughton or Clayton. The spelling of 'joiner' as 'giner' suggests how at least one person pronounced the word.

[2] The chancery cases are wonderful sources of all manner of information for the Northern Neck from the mid 1750s up to the late 1800s. The Richmond County cases are not available yet online but have been microfilmed; we can only hope they are made available soon. Selected cases for Westmoreland County have been abstracted by Elizabeth Nuckols Lee and published by New Papyrus Publishing. (see Select Bibliography).

records. There is no substitute for original records and even the sources consulted for this book have not been completely mined for genealogical data.

I have profited greatly from earlier published works which are listed in the bibliography. I have also, as always, profited by discussions with my friend Robert W. Barnes and my wife Anne. The Interlibrary Loan Department of the University of Maryland McKeldin Library did yeoman service in obtaining microfilm copies of various Virginia county records. All errors of interpretation or abstracting are entirely mine, and I will appreciate corrections.

Robert K. Headley, Jr.
University Park, Maryland
2013

METHODOLOGY

The wills and other records have been abstracted to include any information which I believe may have genealogical or historical value including, but not limited to, names of spouses, names of children, grandchildren, siblings, parents, nieces and nephews, and friends. I have also included the names of any African-Americans mentioned in the records.[3] Likewise any tracts of land and the manner in which it was acquired are included. In some instances I have included the exact wording where it seemed to me useful, for example where the writer of the will described a person or a person's circumstances or made some interesting specific bequest. I have not usually included bequests of household or kitchen furniture or clothing, but I have usually noted such items as ships, weaving implements, medical instruments, and tools of various sorts which may provide clues to occupations. I have also indicated sums of money left to legatees. In an effort to save space I have resorted to a number of abbreviations which may be found listed at the end of this book. Any words or numbers which I could not read are indicated by [?] or [*1 wd. unclear*]; words that I have made guesses at are enclosed in square brackets, e.g., John [SMITHSON]. Surnames are in upper case letters.

CAVEAT – The records abstracted herein are taken from microfilms. For the most part they are very clear. Having said this, there are problems. The abstracts are subject to errors by the abstractor, a line might have been skipped, a name might have been missed, or a date might have been wrong. I admit that I had some difficulty in reading some of the handwriting; it was especially difficult to distinguish between capital L and capital S. Ms and Ns gave the usual difficulty. Names of slaves, since many were unusual nicknames or were rare, offered some problems. I have endeavored to crosscheck the information in published sources where possible, but despite my best efforts, errors have certainly occurred. The sources of all the abstracts have been provided. These should be consulted in every case.

The abstracts are organized alphabetically by the name of the deceased followed by the date the record was written or ordered, the date the document was probated or recorded and then the abstract of the record – this is the anchor abstract. Any additional information gleaned from other records is included in a section of notes which follows the citation of the original source. Place names have been annotated where possible.

Below are samples of abstracts of the various kinds of documents which appear in this book.

---

[3] Hopefully these names, which sometimes include ages and relationships, will be helpful to genealogists researching African-American families. Furthermore, family relationships can often be traced through one or more generations by comparing the names of the slaves that they owned.

1. **Will:** name of testator; date will was written; date will was probated; parish of residence [if given]; county of probate; details of will; witnesses; codicil [if any]; additional information such as relinquishments [if any]; source; notes.

   Example: DOULIN, Joseph. [m], 12 Aug 1822. NC; all est. to wife as long as she remains my wid. for her use & the use of my children until they arrive to the age of 21 or marry; at wife's death or marriage, son Joseph DOULIN to have land and Negro boy Solomon; rest of est. to be eq. div. among sons Thomas & William and daus. Elizabeth L. DOULIN & Lucy C. DOULIN and a newborn baby not yet named; wife & Richard COCKARILL to have management of est.; WITS: Chas. L. BELL, Jn. FLYNT, Linezey DAVIS, Elisha H. GILL, Jos. WALKER; [court believed that the exors. named would not qualify as such & appointed the sheriff Sam. DOWNING to be administrator with the will annexed]

2. **Inventory:** name of deceased; date of court order for inventory, date inventory was made or presented in court; date inventory was recorded; county of inventory; value of inventory [if given]; names of any persons mentioned; any interesting items included in inventory.

   Example: NEWTON, Willoughby, PO 1812, T 3 Jan 1813; 24 Apr 1815. WC, INV, [m], includes a large number of books (among which are Cicero's Life, 15-vol History of England, Fuller's Pharmacopoeia, Love's Art of Surveying, a French dictionary, Elements of Agriculture, Dictionary of English & Latin Phrases) and Negroes Billy Blundell (aged 45), Ned (35), Dick (30), Marquis (30), [Oaks] Billy (40), Charles (45), [?]ey (70), Winney (55), Zara (55), Betty (65), Dinah (55, disabled), Rachel (50), Nancey (13), Winney (11), Cordelia (10), Rose (9), Franky (6), Becky (22), James (13), Ellick (9), Letty (1), Lucy (22), George (12), John (10), Margaret (4), Jeffrey (2), Letty (35), Winney (6), James (5), [Akey] (4), Charles (2), Betty (27), Sam (21), Felicia (4), Joe (2).

3. **Division of Estate:** name of deceased; date of court order for division, date division was made; date division was recorded; names of heirs and certain specific legacies such as slaves, land, ships, and books.

   Example: HULL, John; PO 13 Mar 1820, T 14 Oct 1822; [m]. NC; DIV of est., after allotting to Martha HULL her dower & thirds (152 ac & slaves Ben, Judy & child Lewis, Charlotte), amongst the heirs Paul HULL (55 ac & Anthony), Samuel S. HULL (60 ac & Ezekiel), John HULL (53 ac & Eliza), Peter HULL (54 ac & Willoughby), Broadie S. HULL (53 ac & Young Judy & Adam) & Thomas HULL (53 ac & Joseph).

4. **Court Orders:** county court orders can confirm the identities of heirs or provide the names of missing children or spouses:

   Example 1: NC, 13 Feb 1809; It appears to the court that Sarah E. BALL wife of the Rev. David BALL, James EWELL son of Ann EWELL deceased, Alice P. MONCURE wife of John MONCURE, Thomas GASKINS, Richard H. GASKINS, Martha HULL wife of John HULL, John E. GASKINS, and Mary HULL the wife of Thomas G. HULL are the children, grandchild, and legal representatives of Col. Thomas GASKINS deceased.

Example 2: RC, Oct 1809; Ordered that John DUDLEY and Sarah G. his wife and Griffin and Thomas DUDLEY, children of Mary G. DUDLEY deceased daughter of said Griffin and first wife of said John DUDLEY, and Jeremiah GARLAND which said Sarah and Jeremiah are children of said Griffin GARLAND and who together with the plaintiffs and Griffin and Thomas DUDLEY constitute the heirs of Griffin GARLAND.

5. **Guardianship Records:** these may identify spouses and children who are not named in wills or other records. These may also give clues to subsequent spouses or relatives as in the cases of Ann POPE the wid. of Elijah POPE married (2) Charles DAMERON in 1819 and that same year Charles DAMERON was appointed guardian of Ann POPE the orphan of Elijah and James BARTLETT orphan of Elisha BARTLETT who chose his brother Joel as his guardian. It also often happened that a young woman would marry her guardian. Since an orphan older than 14 could choose his or her guardian, but one under 14 had a guardian appointed by the court, these records can provide rough guides to the ages of the orphans.

Example 1: RC, 5 Jun 1820; Fanny DUDLEY orphan of John DUDLEY chose Fleet B. PLUMMER as her guardian and PLUMMER was appointed guardian of William DUDLEY orphan of John DUDLEY. Here we can surmise that Fanny was over 14 and that William was younger.

Example 2 : RC, 5 Aug 1810; Ann BISPHAM widow of Robert BISPHAM and Thomas STOWERS are appointed guardians of Maria and Ann BISPHAM orphans of Robert BISPHAM

6. Chancery Court Cases: cases in chancery court involve disputes usually over money, land, or slaves. Many cases were suits to obtain payment of debts. The more interesting ones were between sets of heirs in disputes over an inheritance. These often recited chains of land ownership or named heirs of persons who died intestate. A few chancery cases involved women who asked for relief from their husbands' cruel treatment. A chancery case file might contain as few as three documents or as many as several hundred. Some of the documents that may be included in chancery case files are statements of the complainants and the answers of the defendants, orders to appear in court, wills, deeds, receipts, accounts, court orders, and plats. The chancery cases for Lancaster, Westmoreland, and Northumberland counties have been scanned and are available online from the Library of Virginia website. Sadly, the Richmond County cases have only been microfilmed and are not available online.

Example 1: NC, 1808; William CONNOLLY d. intest. leaving a wid. Hannah, who mar. (2) Rich. LITTRELL, and the following children: Sally (who mar. Francis VANLANDINGHAM), Milly (who mar. John MOTHERSHEAD), Betsy (who mar. Jeremiah JONES), Peggy (who mar. HALL and had four children: Fanny, Ann, William & unknown), and George.

Example 2: NC; Hiram CORBELL d. intest. in 1826 leaving as his only heirs and next of kin: Judith SHEARMAN, Martin and Peter CORBELL (bros.) and Gawin and Eliz. CORBELL inf. children of John CORBELL the dec'd bro. of Hiram.

Example 3: LC; William DAVIS d. intest. leaving a wid., Amy, and three children: Elizabeth (who mar. Andrew CHILTON, LC, bond 23 Dec 1788), Judith (who mar. George DOGGETT, LC, bond 19 Jan 1795), and Richard; his wid., Amy, mar. (2) Joseph KEM (LC, before 19 Aug 1785) and had three children by him: Burgess Kirk, Susanna (d.s.p. 1806) and Molly Thompson (d.s.p. 1808); William DAVIS was entitled to a considerable est. under the will of Elizabeth YERBY who d. in 1772; Amy the wid. of William DAVIS was the grdau. of George and Elizabeth WOODBRIDGE) YERBY and prob. the dau. of George YERBY; Judith (DAVIS) DOGGETT brought suit against her husband George saying that she had lived with him for about two years but that he treated her badly and she was obliged to separate herself and her two young children from her husband

The Probate Process

It may be helpful to discuss the process that an estate went through upon the death of the testator. If an executor or executors were named in the will, upon the testator's death, that person or those persons went to court to begin the probate process and to receive an order to prepare an inventory (or inventory and appraisement) of the estate. If no executor was named or none came forward, the court appointed an administrator. The inventory was returned to the court from a few days after the order to several years later. There may be several inventories if additional property was discovered following the presentation of the first inventory or if the decedent had property in another county or state. Inventories may contain the date the inventory was ordered, the names of the men who made the inventory, the date the inventory was made, the date it was presented in court, the date it was recorded, the items inventoried, and the value of the estate. Although most inventories were recorded within a year of the date they were ordered, some of them were recorded several years after the death of the decedent. An extreme case is the inventory of the estate of John WRIGHT of RC which was recorded in December 1824, 30 years after it was ordered. The property included in the inventory ranged from slaves, livestock, household and kitchen furniture to plantation equipment and debts due the estate. Many inventories included the total value of the estate. During the period 1800 through 1825, the changeover from pounds, shilling and pence to dollars and cents was taking place so that values in earlier inventories usually were given in the earlier system while values in later inventories were in dollars and cents. Rarely values were given in both systems.

Sometimes an estate or portions of an estate, especially land and slaves, had to be divided among several heirs. In such cases the court would appoint commissioners to make this division. Divisions can be very helpful if the decedent did not leave a will or did not name all his or her heirs in the will. When a piece of land was not large enough to divide into useful shares, a court case might be instituted to have it sold and the proceeds divided among the heirs.

A man could appoint guardians for his children in his will. In some cases, at the death of a spouse the surviving spouse was appointed guardian to his or her children. If neither parent were living or unable to provide for all the children, the court could appoint guardians. If the children were older than 14, they could chose their own guardians. Children were considered infants and required guardians until they reached 21. The guardian was responsible for overseeing the infant's estate and had to present a yearly accounting to the court.[4]

The records abstracted in this book provide numerous interesting statistics. Estate values were given in pounds as late as 1824, but they began giving way to dollar values after 1809. The largest number of inventories was recorded in 1815 when there were 62; the fewest, 14, were recorded in 1823.[5] The average yearly number of inventories for the four counties included in this book was 30.

The average value of estates which were valued in pounds was £504. The five largest estates were:

Maj. William CLAUGHTON, NC, £9068
John TURBERVILLE, WC, £8258
James PARK, WC, £4901
William REDMAN, WC, £4423
John FAWCETT, RC, £4262

The average value of estates valued in dollars was $2,133, but most were far less than this. The five largest estates were:

John COCKARILL, NC, $39,893
William A. WASHINGTON, WC, $26,793
Severe GALLE, LC, $24,873
Joseph B. DOWNMAN, LC, $22,439

---

4 For an exhaustive study of children and the law including aspects of guardianship, see: Holly Brewer, *By Birth or Consent. Children, Law, & the Anglo-American Revolution in Authority*, University of North Carolina Press, Chapel Hill, 2005. The law governing guardians may be found in Shepherd, Vol. I, pp. 103-106.

5 The large number in 1815 was apparently due to the unusually large number of deaths from an epidemic of some upper respiratory disease which swept through parts of the Northern Neck between 1814 and 1816. For more on this epidemic, see "Pandemic in Northumberland County, 1814-1816," Richard C. Bush III, Ph.D., *BNCHS* Vol. XXXVI, 1999:87-100. Bush believes that the epidemic killed possibly 12 percent of the adult population in Northumberland County.

William CHOWNING, LC, $16,700

The value of the slaves belonging to the estate of Landon CARTER was $43,550, but the total value of his large estate was not recorded.

The average number of slaves among slaveholders was 13. The five largest slaveholders were:

Landon Carter, RC, more than 233 slaves
Walker TOMLIN, RC, 152
Joseph B. DOWNMAN, LC, 137
James B. BURWELL, RC, 119
William A. WASHINGTON, WC, 95
Robert MITCHELL, RC, 86

Out of 1178 inventories abstracted here, slightly more than half (51.5%) included slaves.

Twenty men owned some kind of watercraft. The most common of these was the schooner. The following men owned vessels:

Nicholas CARTER, LC, schooner "George Wythe"
John COURTNEY, RC, fishing boat
William DAWSON, LC, schooner
Leroy DOBYNS, RC, boat
Samuel EFFORD, RC, vessel ?
Peter R. GARLAND, RC, schooner "Lively"
Davenport HAYNIE, NC, canoe
William HUTT, WC, sloop
John F. INGRAM, LC, schooner "Dolphin"
Catesby JONES, NC, brig and schooner "Betsy"
Polly JONES, NC, one small schooner, one large schooner
Thomas KENT, NC, schooner "Ann"
Alfred KIRKHAM, NC, sloop "More Grog"
Timothy McNAMARA, LC, schooner
Henry NUTT, LC, schooner "William & Henry"
Henry B. SEBREE, LC, schooner
Thomas SHORT, LC, schooner "Eagle"
George THOMPSON, WC, ferry boat
William A. TRAVERS, NC, schooner
William WINDSOR, WC, schooner "Philicity"

Thirty-six inventories contain a significant number of books. A surprising item found in three inventories was buffalo. The inventory of Thomas PULLEN (NC, 1814) contained a "buffalow heifer," the inventory of James THOMAS (NC, 1807) contained a "buffelow steer," and the inventory of Alexander YOUNG (WC, 1810) contained a "brown buffalo cow & calf."

PROBATE AND ESTATE RECORDS

ADAM, John; PO 20 Jul 1807; 19 Oct 1807. LC; INV, £34.10.9. (LC EB 27:21)
ADAMS, Amy; 27 Apr 1807; 5 Feb 1809
RC; WILL; all land to son William and at his death to his heirs; pers. prop. to be sold and proceeds to be eq. div. between 3 sons: William, Charles & Henry; bro. Edmund DAVIS exor; WITS: Jn SMITH, Edmund DAVIS, Mary TILLORY; her inventory valued at £25.3.0. was rec. on 3 Sep 1810. (RC WB 9:375, 403)
ADAMS, William; T 24 May 1804; 5 Jun 1809. RC; INV, £16.4.11. (RC WB 9:348)
ALDERSON, Betsy; 24 Sep 1810; 7 Jan 1811
RC, NFP; WILL; land in RC & Negroes to be eq. div. between 4 bros. James, John, William, & Jerry ALDERSON & 2 sis. Jane NORTHEN & Saryan BAKER; bro. Jerry to keep all money due me from him; bros. James & William & friend John M. YERBY exors; WITS: Jn. HADDEN, Winny HADDEN, Wm. BAKER; [Cod: to bro. John ALDERSON all money due me from him; same wits; 24 Sep 1810]. (RC WB 9:382)
[Betsy ALDERSON was a dau. of James (d. RC 1785) & Sarah Ann ALDERSON; *see below*]
ALDERSON, Frances; T. 15 Jun 1816; 1 Jul 1816
RC; INV, [m], Daniel FLINN admr. (RC WB 9:531)
[Frances ALDERSON must be the Fanny ALDERSON named in the div. of slaves of James ALDERSON in Dec 1815; *see below*]
ALDERSON, James; PO 5 Sep 1808; 1 May 1809
RC; DIV of slaves among Peter NORTHEN (rec'd Winney, Joe), Jeremiah "Jerry" ALDERSON (Milly, Sam), John BAKER (Judah & child Isaac, Fanny), heirs of Bryant PHILLIPS (Robbin, Old Rachel), Elizabeth ALDERSON (Daniel), William ALDERSON (Adam), John ALDERSON (Michael, Davy), James ALDERSON (George, Old Judah). (RC AB 3:216)
[Jas. ALDERSON in his will (RC 2 Jun 1782 - 2 May 1785) named his children Jas., Jn., Eliz., Wm., Jeremiah, Jane NORTHEN, Sarah Ann STONE and Anne Walker and his wife Sarah Anne (RC WB 7:472); the births of several children to Jas. & Sarah Ann ALDERSON are recorded in the NFPR:Reubin (1755), Jenny (1756), Sarah Ann (1759), Ann (1762), Jas. (1764), Jn. (1766), Wm. (1769) and Jeremiah (1774) (NFPR:1); Peter NORTHEN mar. Jane ALDERSON (dau. of James & Sarah Ann ALDERSON) ca. 1773; Sary Ann ALDERSON mar. (1) Thos. STONE, RC, bond 20 Jun 1780 and (2) Jn. BAKER, RC, bond 26 Dec 1786 (MRC:6, 148, 196)]
ALDERSON, James; PO Mar 1815, T 1 May 1815; 6 Jun 1815
RC; INV, [m], includes the following slaves (in WC): Dick, Jude, George, Paramous (a boy); appraisement of the Negroes (in WC) belonging to James ALDERSON dec'd for the life of Mrs. Jane ALDERSON who was Jane BABER: boy Dunkin, Pricela & child Lucy, Anna, [Carb] (a boy), Ned (a boy), girl Matilda in WC; $504.00. (RC WB 9:477)
[James ALDERSON mar. Jane BABER, the wid. of Dabney BABER, WC, bond 23 Jun 1814 (MLBWC:1)]
ALDERSON, James; PO 11 Apr 1815; 5 Dec 1815
RC; DIV of proceeds from sale of certain slaves conveyed by James ALDERSON dec'd to Polly FLINN and others; proceeds of $840.95 were div. into 5 parts and allotted to Daniel FLINN in right of his wife Polly, Sally ALDERSON, Eliza ALDERSON, Nancy ALDERSON & Fanny ALDERSON. (RC AB 3:366)

ALDERSON, James; PO Nov 1816 [*sic*]; T 2 Jan 1816; Rec 7 Jul 1817
RC; DIV of Negroes; Lot 1 (Dick) drawn by Nancy ALDERSON, Lot 2 (George) drawn by E. ALDERSON, Lot 3 (Perimus) drawn by William ALDERSON, Lot 4 (Matilda & Jude) drawn by R. ALDERSON, Lot 5 (Ann & child Amey) drawn by D. FLINN, Lot 6 (Balaam) drawn by L. JACKSON the Negroes Matilda & Jude, Ann & child Amey & boy Balaam were the Negroes belonging to [BABER's] est, the first husband of Mrs. ALDERSON the wid. consequently they are only life est. and were valued at one third. (RC AB 3:427)
[Daniel FLINN mar. Polly M. ALDERSON, RC, bond 9 May 1808; Luke JACKSON mar. Sally ALDERSON, RC, bond 3 Jun 1815 (MRC:70, 101)]

ALDERSON, James; Jan 1822
RC; Mary ALDERSON orphan of James ALDERSON chose Presley HUDSON as her gdn. (RC OB 25:227)
[Presley HUDSON, of NC, mar. Eliza W. ALDERSON, RC, bond 30 Jan 1818 (MRC:99)]

ALDERSON, Jeremiah; PO 7 Oct 1816; 25 Jan 1819
RC; INV; $9893.74, includes the following Negroes: Sipps, Frank, Lewis, Turner, Traverse, Abraham, Anthony, John, Mitchell, Dianna, Sarah, Hannah, Ellen, Betty, Winny, Dianna, Fanny, Esther. (RC WB 9:649)
[This is prob. Jer. ALDERSON, the son of Jas. & Sarah Ann ALDERSON, b. NFP 31 May 1774 (NFPR:1); Jonathan P. ROBINSON aptd. gdn. to Sam. & Margaret ALDERSON orphans of Jer. ALDERSON, 1 Jan 1821 (RC OB 25:98); Robt. WEIR was chosen gdn. by Geo. N. ALDERSON orphan of Jer. ALDERSON, 7 Jan 1822 (RC OB 25:231); settlement of Robt. WEIR's gdnship. acct. of Geo. N. ALDERSON orphan of Jer. ALDERSON, 3 Oct 1825 (RC OB 27:7, 188); settlement of Jonathan P. ROBINSON's gdnship. acct. of Sam. B. & Marg. J. ALDERSON orphans of Jer. ALDERSON, 6 Mar 1826 (RC OB 27:44)]

ALDERSON, William; 5 Jul 1819
RC; Wm. ALDERSON admr. to Jas. ALDERSON, Sr., dec'd hath been absent and without the limits of this state for more than 7 years and no account having been heard of him ... Presley HUDSON to admin. his est. (RC OB 24:357)
[Suit, Daniel FLINN & Polly his wife, Luke JACKSON & Sally his wife and Rich. ALDERSON vs. Presley HUDSON admr. of Wm. ALDERSON and Nancy ALDERSON an inf. (RC OB 24:363)]

ALEXANDER, Angus; 21 Aug 1804
LC; Peter TANKERSLEY and Samuel L. STRACHAN & Betsy his wife who was Betsy T. ALEXANDER are admrs. of Angus ALEXANDER. (LC OB 1804-05:174)
[Angus and Hannah were children of Jesse ALEXANDER; Hannah d. unmarried in 1800; Angus d. leaving a wid, Betsy and a son Robt. (LC CC 1810-007; NC CC 1816-002; NC RB 16:122); Angus ALEXANDER mar. Betsey T. POLLARD, LC, bond 20 Nov 1797 (MLBLC:1); Sam. L. STRAUGHAN mar. Betsy T. ALEXANDER, wid., NC, bond 30 Jul 1804 (MLBNC:95)]

ALEXANDER, Ewell; T 9 Oct 1810; 8 Jul 1811
NC; INV, $111.23; includes Negroes boy Robert, Nancy, girl Polly. [INV was recorded twice]. (NC RB 19:75)
[A Euel ALEXANDER had been dead more than 3 mos. by 10 Sep 1810 when the sheriff was ord. to sell his perishable est. (NC OB 1807-11:209)]

ALEXANDER, Ewell; PO 13 Dec 1819; 9 Sep 1822

NC; distribution of est. in the hands of Royston BETTS admr. of Ewell ALEXANDER to Richard POOLEY gdn. to James, [Sydnor] and Kitty ALEXANDER orphans of Ewell ALEXANDER (on 14 Mar 1820) and Giles WEBB admr. of William S. ALEXANDER dec'd (on 14 Aug 1822). NC RB 23:218)

[There were at least two Ewell ALEXANDERs; one was the son of Rawleigh ALEXANDER (d. NC 1804) (NC RB 17:228) and the other was the son of Thomas & Fanny ALEXANDER, born 3 Feb 1784 (SSPR:6); Rich. POOLEY aptd. gdn. of Wm., Jas., Kitty & Sydnor ALEXANDER orphans of Ewell ALEXANDER, NC 13 Dec 1819 (NC OB 1816-20:418); for more on Ewell and Rawleigh ALEXANDER see NC CCs 1810-017 and 1812-001]

ALEXANDER, Rawleigh; PO 8 Oct 1804; 14 Jul 1806

NC; INV, £812.12.5; includes Negroes Will, Jack, Siller, Betty & child, Nancy & child (in dispute), girl Hannah, boys Spencer, Sam & Peter, girl Peggy, boys Joe & Daniel; PO 14 Jan 1805, Div of est. among the heirs: John ALEXANDER (rec'd Will), Lucy ALEXANDER (rec'd Betty), Thomas ALEXANDER (rec'd Mitchell), Rawleigh ALEXANDER (rec'd Hannah), Isaac EDWARDS (rec'd Spencer), Salley ALEXANDER (rec'd Sam), Ewell ALEXANDER (rec'd Daniel), Elizabeth ALEXANDER (the wid; rec'd Jack). (NC RB 17:447)

[In his will (NC 23 Jul 1803-8 Oct 1804) Rawleigh ALEXANDER names his wife, and probable children Lucy, Sally, Euel, Thos., Rawleigh, Jn., Polly, Betty, Vincent & Jesse D. (NC RB 17:228); Isaac EDWARDS mar. Mary ALEXANDER, NC, bond 4 Nov 1799 (MLBNC:34)]

ALEXANDER, Rawleigh; T 30 Oct 1804; 8 Sep 1806

NC; articles of agreement between Eliz. ALEXANDER (wid. of Rawleigh ALEXANDER) and Ewell ALEXANDER, Isaac EDWARDS, Thos. ALEXANDER, Lucy ALEXANDER, Sally ALEXANDER, Jn. ALEXANDER, and Rawleigh ALEXANDER; Eliz. agrees to take a proportionable part of her dec'd husband's est. with said heirs provided that the heirs give her choice of Negro man Jack. (NC RB 17:461)

ALEXANDER, Thomas; 9 Jun 1823

NC; Euel ALEXANDER aptd. gdn. of Judith & Thos. ALEXANDER orphans of Thos. ALEXANDER. (NC OB 1820-25:300)

ALFORD, Zachariah; PO 18 Jun 1804, T 12 Feb 1806; 22 Apr 1806

LC; DIV of cash & bonds; possessed Peter H. MILLER as gdn. of Nathan ALFORD, Abel ALFORD & Lucy ALFORD with £50.2.9 in cash & £16.15.9 in bonds. (LC EB 24:340)

[Chancery suit: Jn. ALFORD, complt., against Margaret ALFORD, Sam. ALFORD. Jn. O. BRADLEY & Eliz. his wife, Nathan ALFORD, Abel ALFORD, and Lucy ALFORD; Eliz. BRADLEY, Nathan, Abel & Lucy ALFORD are inf. under 21 (LC Orders V 1802-03:138); Nathan ALFORD orphan of Zachariah ALFORD chose Peter H. MILLER as his gdn. and the sd. MILLER is aptd. gdn. of Abel & Lucy ALFORD orphans of Zachariah ALFORD, LC 18 Jun 1804 (LC OB 1804-05:150); acc. to MLBLC:7, Jn. BRADLEY mar. Eliz. ALFRED dau. of Robt. & Margaret ALFRED, LC, bond 2 Apr 1800; on the mot. of Jn. ALFORD one of the heirs of Zachariah ALFORD ... it appearing to the court that the land of which Zachariah ALFORD d. seized & possessed is not of the value of $100 to each of his reps. and the sd. Zachariah d. intest., ord. that Jn. O. BRADLEY & Eliz. his wife who was Eliz. ALFORD, Sam. ALFORD, Nathan ALFORD, Abel ALFORD,and Lucy ALFORD children & heirs of sd. Zachariah ALFORD which sd. Nathan, Abel, and Lucy are infants by Margaret ALFORD their gdn. ad litem be summoned to show cause why the land of sd. decedent should not be sold, 21 Sep 1802 (LC Orders V 1802-03:207; LC CC 1804-003); Lucy ALFORD orphan of Zach. ALFORD chose Moses ROBINSON as her gdn. and settlement of the gdnship. acct. of Peter H. MILLER with sd. Lucy, 16 Sep 1811 (LC Orders 24:47)]

ALFORD, Zachariah; PO 20 Jan 1800; 18 Feb 1800. LC; INV, $364.15.(LC EB 24:110)

ALLEN, William; PO 11 Mar 1811; 9 Dec 1811. NC; INV, [m]; Charles DAMERON admr. (NC RB 19:136)

ALLGOOD, John; 3 Sep 1777; 8 Dec 1807
WILL; late of RC but now a soldier in the Continental Army; sis. Sarah ALLGOOD £12; sis. Winefred ALLGOOD £12; sis. Catharine ALLGOOD £10; sis. Catharine extx; WITS: Benj. BRAMHAM, Jn. HOW, Geo. HOW Jr. (RC WB 9:316)
[This is probably John ALLGOOD the son of William & Mary Ann ALLGOOD, b 12 May 1751 in NFP; Wm. & Mary Ann ALLGOOD had other children whose births are rec. in the NFPR: Edward, 19 Oct 1741; Eliz., 26 Aug 1745; Winny, 17 Mar 1747 (NFPR:3)]

ALLISON, Rebecca; 26 Apr 1821; 2 Jul 1821
RC; WILL; sis-in-law Mary Dorinda ALLISON; niece Rebecca ALLISON; Lucy Smith BRAMHAM; my Negro woman Winney to be free if she should comply with the law by leaving the state, if not, to be able to choose her master or mistress; remaining est. to be sold and proceeds eq. div. between nephews Richard Lawson HIPKINS, Samuel William HIPKINS, and niece Rebecca Allison HIPKINS; friend Vincent BRAMHAM ex; WITS: W[m]. SETTLE, Sophia C. CREWDSON. (RC WB 9:706)
[Rebecca & Catherine ALLISON were daus. of Hen. & Bathsheba (LAWSON) ALLISON; Catherine ALLISON mar. (1) William JACKSON (d. RC 1794) RC, bond 7 May 1792 and (2) Samuel William HIPKINS, RC, bond 8 Sep 1797 (RC WB 9:9, 10, MRC:3, 95, 101)]

ALLOWAY, Isaac; 3 Aug 1801; 7 Feb 1803
NFP, WC; WILL; wife Mary Anne part of the land w/o the house stands including them [sic] & joining to Col. Walker TOMLIN's land beginning down the Indeng [sic] Town Gut; son John all lands after wife's death; Caty ALDERSON (and her 3 children: John, William, & Polly); dau. Elizabeth ALLOWAY; Molly WALE (and her 2 children: Peggy & Polly); Jane DAVIS; Fillis SAMPSON; wife, son John & William NEWSOM exors; WITS: Chas. BAILEY, A. NEALE, C. L. DOBYNS. (RC WB 9:204)
[Isaac ALLOWAY, son of Gabriel ALLOWAY (d. RC 1760), mar. (2) Mary Ann HAMMOND in RC, bond 29 Jul 1797; Caty ALDERSON was Isaac's dau. who mar. Jery ALDERSON in RC, bond 17 May 1791; Molly WALE was a dau. who mar. Timothy WALE in RC, bond 26 Sep 1792 and Jane DAVIS was a dau. who mar. Thos. DAVIS in RC, bond 5 May 1798 (RC WB 6:192, MRC:51, MWO:12, 14, 104, 362)]

ALLOWAY, Isaac; 7 Feb 1803
RC; INV; £1222.18.8 1/2; includes the following Negroes: Solomon, Hannah, Betty & child Ned, Phillis, James, Landon, Winney, Lewis, Esther, Jessy, Simon. (RC WB 9:209)

ALLOWAY, Isaac; PO 7 Feb 1803; 4 Apr 1803. RC; DIV; Lot 1 to Mrs Maryann ALLOWAY, Lot 2 to Isaac ALLOWAY's est. (RC AB 3:102)

ALLOWAY, Isaac; T 24 Sep 1805; 7 Oct 1805

RC; DIV at Totuskey Bridge of the balance of an account (settled 6 Jul 1804 by an order of RC Court) in the hands of William NEASOM ex. of the sd. dec'd among: John ALLOWAY, Thomas S. DAVIS, Thomas S. DAVIS in right of his former wife, Vincent REYNOLDS, Peggy WALES & Polly WALES. (RC AB 3:149)

[Vincent REYNOLDS mar. Eliz. ALLOWAY, RC, bond 28 Dec 1803 (MRC:168-169); Miller:158 locates Totuskey Bridge in RC where Little Totuskey Creek joins the main branch below Richmond Hill.]

ALLOWAY, Mary Ann; 10 Jun 1818; 2 Sep 1822

NFP, RC; WILL; Negro man Bob to niece Susan ENGLISH; Negro boy Sam to Peter Thompson ENGLISH son of niece Susan ENGLISH; I lend to niece Patty DOGGETT the following Negroes: Hannah, Godfrey, Joanna, Matilda, & Mary who are to be eq. div. between her children at her death; rest of property to be sold to pay debts; friends John PLUMMER & Coleman DOGGETT exors; WITS: Jn. G. WHITE, Sam. WILLIAMS, Aldea A. GLASCOCK. (RC WB 10:1)

[This is Mary Ann HAMMOND who mar. Isaac ALLOWAY, RC, bond 29 Jul 1797 (MRC:3); Mary Ann was prob. a dau. of Jn. & Eliz. HAMMOND of RC; the births of the following children to a Jn. & Eliz. HAMMOND are rec. in the NFPR: Lucy, 1734; Jane, 1736; Jane, 1741; Winny, 1744; Thos. & Ann, 1746; Martin, 1748; Mary Ann & Lucy, 1750; Betty, 1753; Caty, 1755; Janey, 1763; John, 1764; Eliz. 1768; Judith, 1771 (NFPR:82, 83, 84); in his will (RC 12 Feb 1771 - 4 Mar 1771), Jn. HAMMOND named his children Thomas, Absolom, Susannah CONNELL, Jean LEE, Ann, Mary Ann, Betty & Caty (RC WB 7:78); Caty HAMMOND mar. prob William ENGLISH bef. 17 Feb 1775 (MWO:125); Susannah HAMMOND mar. Davis CONNELL, RC, bond 7 Mar 1757 (MWO:84)]

ALMOND, Ann; PO 14 Sep 1808 [sic], T 17 Dec 1801; 11 Jan 1808

NC; INV, £319.11.6; includes Negroes Jesse, girl [Jinsey], boys William, James, Davis & Edmund. (NC RB 17:598)

[This is Ann the wid. of John ALMOND (d. NC, 1795) (*see below*); in her will (NC 15 Aug 1801 - 14 Dec 1801) Ann ALMOND named Jean HARDING, Hannah MORRISON, Jn. HUMPHRIS, Geo. HUMPHRIS, Nancy WOOD, Winnifrit BERRY, Winney PICKREN and Winney CARPENTER (NC RB 16:313); acc. to NC CC 1821-001 Jos. WOOD the father of Jn., Jos., Wm. & Nancy WOOD was the only bro. of Ann ALMOND]

ALMOND, John; PO 14 Jun 1802, T 18 Jun 1802; 13 Sep 1802

NC; DIV of est. between Thomas BETTS (rec'd Negroes Sarah & child Edmund, Jensee, David) and Nancy WOOD orphan of Joseph WOOD (rec'd Negro James). (NC RB 16:446)

[This is prob. Jn. ALMON[D] who mar. Anne HUMPHRIS (wid. of Jn. HUMPHRIS Sr.) in NC, lic. 12 Apr 1783 (MWO:15) and named his wife Ann, Jos. WOOD, Jobe SYMS, John (son of Thos. CROWTHER) and Rawley ALEXANDER in his will (NC 25 Jan 1792-14 Sep 1795) (NC RB:15:203)]

ALVERSON, Frederick; T 15 Dec [1812]; 25 Jan 1813. WC; INV, £112.14.0. (WC RI 9:355)

[There are 2 marriages rec. for a Frederick ALVERSON in WC, (1) to Caty DOULMAN, bond 23 Apr 1800 and (2) to Nancy CARROLL, dau. of Jn. CARROLL (d. WC 1810) bond 5 Mar 1810 (see below; MLBWC:1); admin. on the est. of Frederick ALVERSON granted to Ann ALVERSON, 26 Oct 1812 (WC Orders 1810-13:273); Patsy & Polly ALVERSON chose William GUTTRDGE as their gdn. and GUTTRIDGE was aptd. gdn. to John

ALVERSON, 26 Jun 1820 (WC OB 1819-23:162); Wm. GUTTRIDGE is gdn. of Patsy, Polly & Jn. orphans of Fred. ALVERSON, 28 Feb 1825 (WC OB 1823-27:147)]

ALVERSON, Mary; 1 Aug 1811; 23 Dec 1811
WC; WILL; grson. Bucknell ALVORSON; youngest son Jeremiah ALVORSON; eldest dau. Elender HILL; grdau. Frances ALVORSON a single woman & she is to be extx; WITS: M. DOVE, Nathaniel LEFAVOUR, Jas. KNASH. (WC DW 22:241)
[This is Mary MOORE the dau. of Wm. MOORE (d. WC 1796); she mar. [fnu] ALVERSON bef. 26 Sep 1792 (MWO:15)]

ANDERSON, Hiram; 9 Feb 1824
NC; on the mot. of William R. FALLIN & Alice his wife ord. that Willis ANDERSON, Edward ANDERSON, Sally ANDERSON, Christopher ANDERSON, Nancy ANDERSON and Linsey & James ANDERSON heirs of Hiram ANDERSON show cause why lands of Hiram ANDERSON should not be sold and proceeds div. among heirs. (NC OB 1820-25:350)
[Edw., Willis, Jas., Linsey, Nancy, Alice and Christopher were siblings, the children of Wm. ANDERSON (d. NC 1819) (*see below*); Alice, who mar. Wm. R. FALLIN, had d. bef. 1829 leaving a son Chas. FALLIN her only heir (NC CCs 1830-003 and 1831-001); Wm. R. FALLIN mar. Alice ANDERSON, NC, bond 3 Feb 1820 (MLBNC:37); Nancy P. ANDERSON, ward of Willis ANDERSON, mar. Jn. PEARSON, NC, bond 12 Feb 1824 (MLBNC:80; NC OB 1820-25:393)]

ANDERSON, Izates; 25 Jul 1823; 8 Sep 1823
of Cherry Point, NC; WILL; tombstone to be placed on the grave of my half-sister Jane WILDY and also another on mine; H. OPIE & F. BATES to write the inscription to deter the young woman from living & dying an old maid and the young man from living and dying a bachelor; tract of land called the Brick House and [Negroes] Isaac his wife Diner & their two children Polly & Grace to Elizabeth A. ANDERSON; land where I live to Col. Samuel BLACKWELL for the use of my nephew John ANDERSON; Sall & child Hannah, the younger [Soock] & Jim an old man to nephew John ANDERSON; Peter, Winney & George to Izates COLES; Negro boy Jim to Heirod BETTS; young fellow Vincent to James & Mir[i]am HUGHLETT's youngest child whatever its name may be; Ciller & her youngest dau. & youngest son to Sally & James WILDY which is more than I was to do by contract if I should die without issue or lawful heir; my Negro woman Hannah to have $20 for 5 years for herself & her youngest child Peter, at the expiration of that time she is privileged to choose a home say master or mistress among my kindred for herself & son; Isaih having been faithful he hath the privilege [to] choose a home among the kindred of his late mistress or myself; my man Jack I give the same privilege as Isaih; $100 in bonds to Heli WILDY; $100 in bonds to Betsy WILDY dau. of Heli WILDY; Negro girl Winney to Jane WILDY dau. of Heli WILDY; Nancy D. CLAUGHTON; $50 to Mrs. E. LELAND wife of B. M. LELAND; $50 to cousin Nancy TRAVERS; all other Negroes & prop. not willed or devised to be eq. div. between my nephew John ANDERSON & niece Elizabeth Ann ANDERSON; William HENDERSON, William ROUTT & John MIDDLETON exors; [no wits, but will proved by oaths of James SMITH, William [JETT] & Willis W. HUDNALL; John MIDDLETON relinquished his right of executorship on 13 Oct 1823; Wm. HENDERSON & Wm. ROUTT relinquished their right of

executorship & certif. was granted Wm. HENDERSON to obtain letters of admin. with the will annexed]. (NC RB 23:362)

[Izates ANDERSON was a son of John & Judith ANDERSON born in SSP 7 Feb 1779 (SSPR:5,4); in his will (NC 1780 - 13 May 1782) Jn. ANDERSON named his wife Judith and his children Walter, Marina, and Izates (NC RB 11:176); in her will (NC 8 Oct 1810 - 14 Dec 1812), Judith ANDERSON named her dec'd husband Jn. and his sons Izates & Walter (NC RB 19:282); div. of the Negroes Siller and her 2 children, Jerry & Alice, bequeathed by Izates ANDERSON to Sally & Jas. A. WILDY children of Wm. WILDY dec'd, 13 Jun 1825 (NC OB 1825-30:16); Izates ANDERSON died on 11 Aug 1823; his tombstone exists near Cherry Point; his friends Hierome L. OPIE and Fleming BATES had the tombstone inscribed as he requested: "In other relations of life he might have been equally praiseworthy, but he died a bachelor having never experienced the comfort of beng a husband or father. This situation he found so comfortless that in his last will he directed this stone to be placed over his remains, with an inscription warning all young men from imitating an example of celibacy, which had yielded to himself no other eventual fruits but disappointment and remorse." (NNVHM Vol. IX, No. 1, p. 841)]

ANDERSON, Izates; PO 13 Oct 1823 T 14 Nov 1823; 12 Sep 1825
NC; INV, [m]; includes the following Negroes: James, Isaac, Peter, Moses, Isiah, Jack, Vincent; boys Stephen, George, Jim, [Ike], old Hannah & son Peter, Diner & two children, Sally & child, Sarah, girl Hannah, Rachel & child, Siller & two children, Winney WILDY, [Emsey], Ginney, Winney HARRISON. (NC RB 24:326)

ANDERSON, John Jr.; T 17 Feb [1815]; 14 Aug 1815. NC; INV, $104.75. (NC RB 20:175)

ANDERSON, Judith (Mrs.); PO 1[2] Dec 1812, T 6 Apr 1813; 12 Jul 1813
NC; INV, Iz[ates] ANDERSON, ex., $210.24. (NC RB 19:420)
[Judith ANDERSON of SSP, wid. of John ANDERSON (*see above*)]

ANDERSON, Sarah [14] Mar 1825; 11 Apr 1825
NC; WILL; Negro man Mott & rest of est. due me from my father's est. to bro. [Artha.] ANDERSON; [no ex. named]; WITS: Thos OLDHAM, [?] MOORE, Fanny MOORE. (NC RB 24:187)
[Sarah ANDERSON was the dau. of William ANDERSON (d. NC 1819) (*see below*)]

ANDERSON, Walter; PO May 1816; 12 Jan 1818. NC; INV, [m]. (NC RB 21:315)
[Walter ANDERSON in his will (NC 20 Nov 1815-13 May 1816) names children John and Elizabeth, bro. Izates ANDERSON & Elizabeth COLES (NC RB 20:458); Izates ANDERSON aptd. gdn. of Jn. ANDERSON orphan of Walter ANDERSON, NC 11 Nov 1822 (NC OB 1820-25:246); Jn. ANDERSON orphan of Walter ANDERSON chose Wm. JETT as gdn. and sd. JETT is aptd. gdn. of Eliz. A. ANDERSON orphan of Walter, NC 8 Sep 1823 (NC OB 1820-25:322)]

ANDERSON, William;
NC; William ANDERSON d. intest. in 1812 leaving three children: James, John, and Sally. (NC CC 1821-009)

ANDERSON, William; 26 Jan 1819; 11 Oct 1819
NC; WILL; tract of land between William BARNES & Charles KENT & Negro girl Hariot to dau. Alice ANDERSON; warehouse tract & tract of land joining my mill that I purchased of Capt. William ROUTT to son Willis ANDERSON; tract known as [Barren] Neck to son Hiram ANDERSON; my

forest tract that I now live on & the tract lying between George WINSTEAD & Fallon BARNES to son Edward ANDERSON [above are 4 eldest children]; tract of land called the Latin Schoolhouse Tract south of the Cherry Point Road to son Lindsey ANDERSON 60 ac. more or less valued at $600; 50 ac. of land on Cherry Point Road by the corner of the meat house valued at $500 to son Christopher ANDERSON; 50 ac. of land where my dwelling house is adjacent land of son Christopher, William [S.] GARNER, William & Richard FALLIN near Jack's Bridge valued at $700 to son James ANDERSON; Negro man [Motty] to dau. Sally ANDERSON; two Negro men Ephraim & James to dau. Nancy ANDERSON; my mill & tract of land between Willis JONES & Samuel DAWSON to be sold to pay debts; the overplus to be eq. div. among five youngest children; friends Izatus ANDERSON, Richard STREET & John MIDDLETON exors; WITS: Jn. HALL, Geo. WINSTEAD, Chas. KENT. (NC RB 22:133)

[Wm. ANDERSON mar. (1) Nancy BARNES and (2) Nancy ASHBURN, NC, bond 11 Sep 1797; by his first wife he had four children: Jn., Sam., Alice & Willis; by his second wife he had eight children: Hiram (b. 1799), Edw. (b. 1801), Lindsey (b. 1802), Sally (b. 1804), Christopher (b. 1805), Nancy (b. 1807), Jas. (b. 1809), Nathan (b. 1812) (see Register of Wicomico Baptist Church in BNCHS vol. III no. 1:45); Alice ANDERSON aptd. gdn. of Lindsey, Christopher & Jas. ANDERSON orphans of Wm. ANDERSON; Willis ANDERSON aptd. gdn. of Sally H. and Nancy ANDERSON orphans of Wm. ANDERSON, NC, 8 Nov 1819 (NC OB 1816-20:403); Sally ANDERSON orphan of Wm. ANDERSON chose Jas. W. RICE as her gdn., NC 14 May 1821 (NC OB 1820-25:94)]

ANDERSON, William; T 17 Nov 1819; 12 Jun 1820. NC; INV, $2770.04; includes Negroes: James, Molly, Ephraim, Billy, Harriett. (NC RB 22:300)

ANDERSON, William; 17 Nov 1819; 9 Aug 1824. NC; INV of bonds & accts due est., [m]. (NC RB 24:18)

ANGEL, Robert; 16 Dec 1811

LC; settlement with Baker ANGEL the acct. of his gdnship. with Samuel & Josiah ANGEL orphans of Robert ANGEL. (LC Orders 24:54)

[This is prob. the Robt. ANGEL who mar. Sally ANGEL, NC, bond 3 Apr 1792 (MLBNC:2)]

ANNADALE, William; 25 Jan 1797; 24 Aug 1801

WC; WILL; wife Ann; two children Samuel & Fanny; wife to be extx; WITS: Presley NEALE, Jos. MARMADUKE. (WC DW 20:236)

[Frances and Sam. C. ANNADALE orphans of Wm. ANNADALE chose Sam. CARTER their gdn., WC 26 Nov 1804 (WC Orders 1804-07:167)]

ANNADALE, William; T 28 Sep 1801; 28 Sep 1801

WC; INV, £443.1.6; includes Negroes Rachel & 3 children, Angor, Nelly & 2 children. (WC RI 8:138)

ANNANDALE, Thomas; 3 Apr 1792; Sep 1792

WC; WILL; wife Penelope; dau. Flora Muse ANNANDALE; [no ex. named]; WITS: [?] CARTER, Robt. HALL, Umphrey MOTHERSHEAD. (WC Unrec Wills 1755-1800 #41))

[Thos. ANNADALE mar. Penny MOTHERSHEAD, WC, bond 23 Jan 1790 (MLBWC:1)]

ARMES, John; 26 Jan 1793; 17 Feb 1795

LC; WILL; all land & two Negroes Sally & Hannah to bro. Walter ARMES; friend William BISCOE ex; WITS: Hen. TOWLES, Wm. CHOWNING, Geo. BISCOE. (LC WB 28:10)

ARMES, Walter; 2 Dec 1818; 15 Mar 1819
LC; WILL; use of whole est. to wife during her life or widowhood; at her death est. to be eq. div. between 2 children Narcissa & Polly; dau. Roxalana has received a Negro woman; Col. John CHOWNING ex; WITS: Wm. OLDHAM, A. J. PALMER, Wm. GEORGE. (LC WB 28:196)
[Walter ARMES seems to have had 2 wives, (1) Nancy HARDING, LC bond 7 May 1804 and Betsey O. TARKLESON, LC bond 21 Dec 1807 (MLBLC:1); Jos. R. PURSELL aptd. gdn. to Polly ARMES orphan of Walter ARMES, 17 Oct 1825 (LC OB 26:146)]

ARMES, Walter; T 28 May 1819; 21 Jun 1819. LC; INV, $269.47 1/2; includes [Negro] Letty. (LC EB 27:485)

ARMES, Walter; 4 Dec 1820
RC; Roxy ARMS orphan of Walter ARMS chose Jos. R. PURCELL as her gdn. (RC OB 25:92)
[Roxy ARMS mar. Jos. R. PURCELL, RC, bond 4 Dec 1820 (MRC:164)]

ARMES, William; T 26 Dec 1786; 20 Oct 1795
LC; INV, £539.0.3; includes Negroes: Robin, Davy, George, Anthony, Letty, Mary, Rose. (LC EB 24:50)
[This may be the u/i husband of Jane MYERS dau. of Thos. MYERS Sr. (d. LC bef. 7 May 1794) (LC WB 22:462, WB 28:16)]

ARMISTEAD, Winifred; [m]; 5 Jan 1801
RC; INV in the counties of Spotsylvania & Richmond; includes the following slaves in Spotsylvania Co: Domine (man), Rachel (old woman) and the following slaves in Richmond Co: Winey & her youngest son Henry Carlos, her [other] sons: Billy, Dominy, George; Jenny & child Rachel Madelane. (RC WB 9:140)
[This is Winifred PEACHEY, dau. of Wm. PEACHEY, who mar. Henry ARMISTEAD, RC, bond 14 Apr 1774 (MRC:4); see also will of Sam. PEACHEY (RC WB 9:26) where he names his "cousin" Mrs. Winifred ARMISTEAD; Hen. & Winifred ARMISTEAD had at least one child, Wm. Burgess ARMISTEAD, b. 10 Nov 1775 (NFPR:6)]

ARMISTEAD, Winifred; T 3 Dec 1800; 5 Jan 1801
RC; DIV of est. between: Miss Eliza A. ARMISTEAD & Miss Alice P. ARMISTEAD; each girl received slaves, books, furniture & china worth $788.48. (RC AB 3:40)

ASBURY, Henry; 12 Jun 1813; 6 Dec 1813
RC; WILL; Negro girl Dianna to grson. William H. SANFORD; Negro girl Lucy to grdau. Susanna M. L. ASBURY; Negro girl Milly to grson. Richard ASBURY and also all my lands in Loudoun Co. when he arrives to the age of 14; Negro girl Delily to grson. Thomas H. ASBURY; Negro girl Hann[ah] to grdau. Elizabeth ASBURY; $100 to grdau. Anne Lyne MOTHERSHEAD; $20 to dau. Anne BISPHAM; $100 to son Henry KELLY son of Mary KELLY; Mary ASBURY (widow of my son William ASBURY) to have, hold & occupy the plant. w/o I now live and also the following Negroes: Tom, Dick, Phill, & Judy for the maintenance and education of her three children; after her death land to descend to grson. Thomas H. ASBURY & Negroes Tom, Dick, and Phill to be eq. div. between my three grchil. Thomas H. ASBURY, Richard ASBURY and Elizabeth ASBURY; Negro Judy & her increase to be eq. div. between Betsy CRASK, Pattey CRASK, Sarah CRASK, Polly Lyne CRASK and Anne CRASK daus. of Bethiah CRASK; dau. Bethiah CRASK to have use of the following Negroes: Luce, Sinah, & Levina and after her death to be eq. div. between her 5 children: Betsy CRASK, Pattey CRASK, Sarah

CRASK, Polly Lyne CRASK, & Anne CRASK; remainder of est. to be sold and after debts are paid, Mary ASBURY the wid. of son William ASBURY to have the interest arising from the balance of the money until her three children Thomas H. ASBURY, Richard ASBURY, & Elizabeth ASBURY shall arrive to the age of 18 to help maintain & school them; when they reach 18 the money to be eq. div. between them; friends James DOZIER and Thomas STOWERS exors; WITS: Thos. Moore BRAGG, Rich. READ, Rich. BULGAR, Mary RUST, Margaret BRAGG [STOWERS & DOZIER refused to qualify as executors but DOZIER became administrator with the will annexed]. (RC WB 9:437)

[Hen. ASBURY had three wives, (1) Ann LYNE, dau. of Thos. & Mary LYNE, bef. 17 Feb 1792; (2) Sally Maulden KELLY, dau. of James KELLY Sr., RC, bond 17 Feb 1792, and (3) Sally MOXLEY. wid., WC, bond 9 Apr 1796 (MWO:18); Nancy or Ann ASBURY mar. Robert BISPHAM, RC bond 11 May 1804 (MRC:19); Bethiah CRASK was a dau. of Henry ASBURY; she mar. (1) Richard SANFORD in RC in 1790 and (2) Wm. CRASK of WC in RC in 1797 (MWO:93, 310)]

ASBURY, Henry; PO Dec 1813; 7 Mar 1814

RC; INV, $4378.73, included the following Negroes: Sam, Barbara, girl Diana, Lucy, girl Lavina, boy Simon, boy Phill, boy Dick, girl Judah, old man James, girl Hannah, girl Milly, girl Delia, child Sophia, girl Lucy, boy Tom. (RC WB 9:452)

ASBURY, Thomas; 3 Aug 1818

RC; Richard N. MARINER was gdn. to Susan W. ASBURY the orphan of Thomas ASBURY. (RC OB 24:239)

ASBURY, William; 4 Jun 1827

RC; settlement of William BISPHAM's acct. of his gdnship. of Thomas H. ASBURY orphan of William ASBURY. (RC OB 27:164)

[This may be the Wm. ASBURY who mar. Mary MUSE, dau. of Thos. MUSE, WC, bond 14 Apr 1806 (MLBWC:2)

ASHBOURNE, George; 15 May 1815

LC; Judith ASHBOURNE aptd. gdn. of James Booth ASHBOURNE, Polly Dodson ASHBOURNE & William ASHBOURNE orphans of George ASHBOURNE. (LC Orders 24:229)

[Judith ASHBOURNE is Judith DODSON who mar. Geo. ASHBOURNE, LC, bond 2 Dec 1802 (MLBLC:1)]

ASHBURN, George C.; 8 Jan 1827

NC; on the mot. of Edward BARNES in his own right and as atty. in fact for George & Elizabeth BARNES, ord. that [Cyril M. EDWARDS], John & Steptoe ASHBURN, William BRICKEY & Elizabeth his wife, John PEARSON & Ann his wife, James, Christopher and Linszey & Edward ANDERSON be summoned to show cause why lands of George C. ASHBURN should not be sold; it appeared to the court that Linsey ANDERSON was not an inhabitant of the state. (NC OB 1825-30:138)

[Geo. C. ASHBURN mar. Anna R. BARNES, NC, bond 16 May 1825; Jn. PEARSON mar. Nancy P. ANDERSON, ward of Willis ANDERSON, NC, bond 12 Feb 1824 (MLBNC:2, 80); Wm. BRICKEY Jr. mar. Eliz. ASHBURN, RC, bond 3 Jan 1820 (MRC:24);]

ASHBURN, Thomas Sr.; T 20 Apr 1815; 12 Aug 1816. NC; INV, $177,3[8]. (NC RB 21:45)

[Thos. ASHBURN mar. Rachel HEADLEY, dau. of Hen. & Temperance (SELF) HEADLEY, RC, bond 23 Dec 1795 (MWO:18); Thos. & Rachel

ASHBURN had at least five children whose births are rec. in the SSPR: Wm. (b. 1796), [Sal]ley (b. 1798), Hen. (b. 1800), Betsy (b. 1802) and Neddy or Teddy (b. 1805) (SSPR:7); the est. of Thos. ASHBURN was ord. to be admin. by Rachel ASHBURN, NC, 13 Mar 1815 (NC OB 1811-1816:288); Rachel ASHBURN aptd. gdn. of Wm., Betsy, Edw., Eliz., Jas., & [Roya] ASHBURN orphans of Thos. ASHBURN, NC, 10 Jun 1816 (NC OB 1816-20:52); on the mot. of Wm. ASHBURN, ord. that Jn. SHIRLEY & Milly his wife, Edw., Elisa, Jas. & Roxey ASHBURN be summoned to show cause why lands of Thos. ASHBURN should not be sold, 11 Dec 1826 (NC OB 1825-30:134)]

ASKINS, W.; [m]; [31 Jul 1823]
WC; INV, $3343.81; includes Negroes Anthony, Ned, Randal, John, Polly (young woman), Maria (young woman) & William her child, Rachel, Betsy her child, Rose (young woman) & her children Ellen & William, Frankey & her children Jim, Jerry, Fanny & Phil; chargeables Old Hannah, Billy, Barbara & Sarah; 3 small children Delphia, Miranda, Zara. (WC RI 11:427)
[This is prob. William ASKINS who mar. Sally BEALE, dau. of Sam. BEALE in WC in 1812 (MLBWC:2)]

ATWELL, Francis; T 15 Nov 1821; 25 Mar 1822. WC; INV, [m]. (WC RI 11:159)
[This is prob. Francis ATTWELL who mar. Fanny McCAVE, WC bond 5 Apr 1796 (MLBWC:3); Jn. ATTWELL (d. WC 1770) names a son Francis and a bro. Francis in his will (WC Apr 1770-26 Jun 1770) (WC DW 25:72)]

ATWELL, William; T 18 Dec 1806; 26 Jan 1807
WC; INV, $327; includes Negroes Hannah, boy Bill, girls Fanny & Harriott, boys Daniel & Henry. (WC RI 9:10)

AUSTIN, David; T 30 May 1800; 2 Jun 1800
RC; INV; includes the following slaves: Ned, Patty (girl), Amey (woman), Simon (small boy), Eliza (woman), Billy (small boy), Winey (woman), Maria (young girl), Guy (small boy), Watt (alias Peter NELSON), Charles (Winey's son). (RC WB 9:133)
[David AUSTIN, in his will, RC, 31 Dec 1798-7 Apr 1800, named his sons Chatman, Orville, Thos., David, & Warner (RC WB 9:127); Wm. HAMMOCK was gdn. of Warner AUSTIN orphan of David AUSTIN, 2 Apr 1821 (RC OB 25:113)]

B[E]AVENS, John; 16 Oct 1814; 19 Feb 1816
LC; WILL; ex. to sell 53 3/4-ac. tract of land & discharge all just claims against me & give remainder to my bro. Williamson WEBLING; friend Thomas RIVEER ex; WITS: Raw. DUNAWAY, Thaddeus GOODRIDGE, Betsey RIVEER. (LC WB 28:174)
[John BEAVENS was prob. a son of Sarah BEAVENS who must have been a wid. when she mar. Wm. WEBLIN, Jr. in LC, bond 17 Mar 1789 (MLC:79); A poss candidate for Sarah's previous husband and the father of John is Thos. BEVANS whose est. was appraised in 1786 by Jas. NEWBY, Johnson RIVEER & Wm. WEBLIN (LC WB 22:133)]

BABER, Claibourn; T 13 Dec 1810; Jan 1812
WC; INV, £204.17.2; includes Cate & child Anthony, boy Dick, girl Felicia, Daniel, Henry; Benedict M. CRABB was acting for Hannah BABER admx. (WC RI 9:307)
[Acc. to an 1841 chancery suit in WC, Claibourn BABER mar. Hannah C. CRABB, WC, in 1803; he d. leaving 2 children Jane (who died an infant) & Amanda who mar. Wm. PORTER and had died bef 1841; his wid. Hannah mar. Geo. C. [sic] MOTHERSHEAD in WC, bond 15 Jan 1816. (WCCP:44; MLBWC:47); on the mot. of Geo. G. MOTHERSHEAD ord. that he and his

wife Hannah who was admx. of Claibourne BABER settle up their admin. on his est., 24 Nov 1823 (WC OB 1823-27:19); Hannah C. MOTHERSHEAD (who was Hannah C. BABER) wife of Geo. G. MOTHERSHEAD is the mother of Amanda BABER, 24 Aug 1824 (WC OB 1823-27:117)]

BABER, Dabney; 21 Apr 1810; 24 Sep 1810
CP, WC; WILL; wife Jane to enjoy whole est. and at her death to be eq. div. between the children of my bro. Claibourn BABER & Peter BABER; wife sole extx; WITS: Wm. RICE, Mary P. CRABB. (WC DW 22:135)
[Dabney BABER mar. Jane CRABB, WC, bond 14 Dec 1809 (MLBWC:3, WCCP:44); Jane BABER mar. (2) James ALDERSON, WC, bond 23 Jun 1814 (MLBWC:1)]

BABER, Dabney; T 13 Dec 1810; Jan 1812
WC; INV, £301.10.0, includes Negroes Siller, child Moriah, Joe, Ann, child Matilda, boy Duncan. (WC RI 9:311)

BACCHUS, John; 10 May 1801; 26 Mar 1804
WP, WC; WILL; dau. Elizabeth SIMMS; Hannah HORTON rest of est. and she to be extx; WITS: Thos. MUSE, Harrison BURGESS. (WC DW 21:16)

BAILEY, Charles; 6 May 1816; 20 May 1816
LC; WILL; land to be sold; Negroes to be hired out until either of daus. should marry or come of age & then to be eq. div. between two daus. Judy B. & Nancy O. BAILEY; Rich. PAYNE & Jn. HATHAWAY exors.; WIT: Wm. BROWN. (LC WB 28:177)

BAILEY, Hugh; 19 Sep 1803; 18 Jun 1804
LC; WILL; to wife Sally BAILEY all the est. which I received of her, that is the Negroes Charles, Alice, Travis, & Polly etc. during her widowhood, the life of her mother or my dau. Frances [C.] BAILEY or the child she now goes with arrive to the age of 21 or marry; in case of mother's death the Negroes to be div. between Frances BAILEY & the child my wife now goes with; if wife should remarry & have children, one half of est. to go to son John BAILEY; after wife's death land & Negro Samuel to go to son John and also $30 to school son; wife Sally BAILEY & friends William [S.] BALL, John CHOWNING Jr., & bro. Charles BAILEY exors; WITS: Jas. ROBB, Thos. SHEARMAN. (LC WB 28:82)
[Hugh BAILEY mar. Salley M. SHEARMAN, LC, bond 18 May 1801 (MLBLC:2); Jn. S. CHOWNING aptd. gdn. to Jn. BAILEY orphan of Hugh BAILEY, 20 May 1816 (LC Orders 24:300); acct. of Chas. BAILEY's gdnship. with Jn. BAILEY orphan of Hugh BAILEY, 18 Aug 1817 (LC Orders 24:384); Wm. CALLAHAN aptd. gdn. to Jn. BAILEY orphan of Hugh BAILEY, 21 Sep 1818 (LC OB 25:19)]

BAILEY, Hugh (Capt.); PO 18 Jun 1804; 18 Feb 1805
LC; INV, £357.12.0; includes Negroes: Alce, Lemuel, Travers, Polly. (LC EB 24:305)

BAILEY, Hugh (Capt.); T Jan 1806; 10 Sep 1806
LC; list of Negro slaves held by Sarah M. BAILEY wid. of Hugh: Travis (9 years), Polly (5). (LC EB 24:346)

BAILEY, Jeremiah G.; T 31 Dec 1796; 26 Aug 1805
WC; INV, £2109.11.3; includes Negroes: Michael, Ben, Isaac, Harry, Davey, Billey, Ned, Tom, Solomon, Sampson, Ned, [Leasar], Reuben, Charles, Criss, Winney & Sally, Aggey, [?] & [Assey], [?], Peggy & Jesse; Lett, [Sidwall] & Hannah; Cloe, Dinah & Suckey; Nance, Lett & Sampson; Joe; George, Daniel, Winney, Milley, Marget, James, Bill, Luce, Nance, Lindsay, James; DIV (PO Nov 1803, T 23 Aug 1805) of est. among: Mrs. Susannah BAILEY as dower;

Fanney BAILEY; Stephen BAILEY; Sydnor BAILEY; John BAILEY; Jere BAILEY; Robert BAILEY; William BAILEY; Susanna M. BAILEY. (WC RI 8:570)

[Jeremiah Garland BAILEY mar. Susannah SYDNOR, RC, bond 13 Aug 1774 (MRC:6); in his will (WC 2 Mar 1791 – 25 Oct 1791) Jeremiah G. BAILEY left his est. to be eq. div. among all his children and child unborn; wife has land n RC; son Stephen is one of his exors. (WWCV:192); an inv. & app. of his RE dtd 19 Oct 1797 showed 400 ac. and a water grist mill worth a total of £1220; he d. in 1791 leaving a wid. and children Frances, Stephen, Sydnor, Jn., Jeremiah Garland, Robt., Wm. and a dau. born after his death Susanna Mitchel (WC CC 1800-008); Jeremiah G. BAILEY's wid., Susannah, died about 1825 leaving a large est. in RC; a chancery suit filed in WC in 1845 names her children as: Sydnor, Stephen, Robert, John L. and Frances P. BAILEY; Frances P. mar. Peter P. COX, WC, bond 18 Sep 1796 and had a child, Fleet E. COX. (WCCP:73, 84, 85; MLBWC:16)]

BAILEY, John; PO 22 Dec 1795; 17 Oct 1796

LC; DIV of est. among wid. Mrs. Judith BAILEY (her dower, includes Negroes [Mansir], Dick, Alice, Esther, Nan), Charles BAILEY (Rose & child), Hugh BAILEY (Lemael), Caty BAILEY (Joe), Jesse BAILEY (Sarah), William CARPENTER (James), Judith BAILEY (Daniel), Thomas SHEARMAN (Ned). (LC EB 24:35)

[Jn. BAILEY mar. Judith BRENT, LC, bond 17 Jun 1765 (MLBLC:2); Wm. CARPENTER mar. Sally BAILEY, LC, 18 Aug 1794 (MLBLC:11); Thos. SHEARMAN mar. Molly BAILEY, LC, bond 7 Jun 1794 (MLBLC:67); Jesse & Judith B. BAILEY orphans of Jn. BAILEY chose Wm. CARPENTER as their gdn., 18 Oct 1802 (LC Orders V 1802-03:211)]

BAILEY, John; PO 20 Dec 1802, T 1 Jul 1803; 19 Sep 1803

LC; sale of Negroes and DIV of proceeds among: William CARPENTER gdn. for Judith BAILEY, Thomas SHEARMAN for Caty BAILEY, Hugh BAILEY, Charles BAILEY, Jesse BAILEY, Caty BAILEY, Beverly DANIEL. (LC EB 24:249)

BAILEY, Stephen; [m]; 26 Feb 1816

WC; WILL; wife Ellen to have the place w/o I now live bounded as follows: beginning at the creek opposite the west end of mother's dwelling house & running up a valley to the main road leading from Yeocomoco ware-houses to Yeocomoco Church thence up the sd. road to the line of John BAILY thence with his line to the line of Jeremiah JEFFRIES thence with the line of JEFFRIES to the creek thence down the creek to the beginning containing by estimation 150 ac; wife also to have one third part of my Negroes and one half of the proceeds of my mill; est. to be kept together for benefit of children who are to receive their parts when 21 or marry; bros Sydnor, John & Robert to have management of est. & children and to bind out my sons to some trade; land which I now hold under lease from Mr. NEWTON to be given up to Mr. William ASKINS if he should think proper to take it and exonerate me of such lease; [no ex. named]; [no WITS]; WC DW 23:160)

[Stephen BAILEY mar. Ellen LAWSON, dau. of Jn. & Eleanor (PIERCE) LAWSON, WC, bond 15 Nov 1797 (MWO:22, 222, 347)]

BAILEY, Susanna M.; PO Nov 1803, T 16 Feb 1804 [29 May 1804]

WC; INV & DIV of the PE of Susanna M. BAILEY; included Negroes Ben & Lucy, Nancy, Jessey, Peggey, James, Lucy; £438; DIV among: Robert BAILEY, Jere. G. BAILEY, Peter P. COX, Stephen BAILEY, John BAILEY and Sydnor BAILEY; each claimant rec'd £73. (WC RI 8:425)

[Susanna M. BAILEY was a dau. of Jeremiah & Susanna (SYDNOR) BAILEY (*see above*)]

BAILEY, William; PO Nov 1803, T 23 Aug 1805; 26 Aug 1805
WC; DIV among: Susanna M. BAILEY, Robert BAILEY, Peter COX, Stephen BAILEY, Sydnor BAILEY, John BAILEY, [J.] [G.] BAILEY. (WC RI 8:564)
[Wm. BAILEY was the son of Jeremiah G. & Susanna (SYDNOR) BAILEY & bro. (or b-i-l) of the devisees (*see above*); Peter P. COX mar. Fanny BAILEY, WC bond 18 Oct 1796 (MLBWC:16)]

BAINE, Baldwin; 9 Nov 1807; 9 Nov 1807
NC; late of Amherst [Co.] lately dec'd, bachelor, left behind him at the time of his death John LANSDELL who mar. Jemima BAINE one of the sisters of the sd. decedent, the sd. Jemima being still alive, and Nancy SAMPSON, the wid. of Joseph SAMPSON, another of the sisters of Baldwin BAINE; John LANSDELL, in right of his wife, and Nancy SAMPSON are next of kin and entitled to eq. proportions of the est. of Baldwin BAINE; LANSDELL & SAMPSON appoint Jesse LANSDELL, son of John & nephew of SAMPSON, as their attorney. (NC RB 17:579)

BAKER, Corban (Dr.); PO Dec 1814 & 15, T 1 Jan 1816; 8 Sep 1817
NC; WILL; house & lot belonging to the heirs of Corban BAKER dec'd was rented out for $24 a year; bonds for 1/3 were payable to & delivered to James SMITH; commissioner Richard CLAUGHTON retained bonds for the other 2/3 subject to future order of the court. (NC RB 21:242)
[Dr. BAKER's wid. Eliz. B. BAKER and his children Virginia H. and Walter C. were named in a CC in 1815 (NC CC 1815-030, CC 1820-22); as of Nov 1809 it was believed that Eliz. B., Virginia & Walter BAKER were not inhabitants of Virginia (*Richmond Enquirer*, 9 Jan 1810, p. [4]; NC CC 1820-022), however a Walter BAKER was listed as the head of a household in Jefferson Co., Va. in the 1810 census; the est. of Corban BAKER was admin. by Jos. DESHIELDS, 11 Dec 1809 (NC OB 1807-1811:145)]

BAKER, John; 14 Sep 1814; 4 Apr 1815
NFP, RC; WILL; Negro boy George to son William BAKER; Negro boy Isaac to son Samuel BAKER; Negro girl Fanny to dau. Nancy NEASOME; Negro girl Lucy to dau. Sarah BAKER; house w/o she now lives & 1 ac. of adjoining land to sis. Milly BAKER during her life; land w/o I now live to be sold & money eq. div. between my children William, Samuel, Sarah BAKER & Nancy NEASOME; sons William & Samuel & Samuel NEASOME exors; WITS: Hen. M. DOBYNS, Jeremiah ALDERSON. (RC WB 9:470)
[This may be the Jn. BAKER who mar. Sary Ann STONE, dau. of James ALDERSON & wid. of Thos. STONE, RC bond 26 Dec 1786 (MRC:6); Nancy BAKER mar. Sam. W. NEASOM, 12 Sep 1811 (MRC:145, MWO:23)]

BAKER, John; PO Nov 1815, T 9 Nov 1815; 6 Feb 1816
RC; DIV of est. among: Samuel W. NEASOM (Negro Bryant), Sarah BAKER (David & Lidia), Samuel BAKER (Daniel & George). (RC AB 3:370)

BAKER, Nancy; 3 Feb 1806; 7 Apr 1806
RC; WILL; niece Alice ALDERSON; Sarah Anne BAKER; Lucy GARNER; Milly BAKER; niece Catherine ALDERSON; friends John BAKER & William ALDERSON exors; WITS: Jas. ALDERSON, Jeremiah ALDERSON, Chas. SWANN. (RC WB 9:278)
[This is prob. Nancy BAKER the dau. of Wm. BAKER (d. RC 1782) who named children Samuel, Winifred HARFORD, John, Lucy, Nancy, Caty, Betty, Billington, Barbara & Milly in his will (RC 26 Jan 1780-7 Oct 1782);

Eliz. BAKER mar. Wm. ALDERSON, RC bond 29 Apr 1789 (RC WB 7:406, MRC:1)]

BAKER, Nancy; [m]; 2 Feb 1807. RC, INV, £88.4.2 or $294.03, includes Negro girl Philis. (RC WB 9:303)

BAKER, Samuel; PO Dec 1798; 2 Jun 1800
RC; INV, £131.3.0; includes the following slave: Newman. (RC WB 9:131)
[Poss. Samuel BAKER son of Wm. & Ann BAKER, b. 28 Jan 1758 (NFPR:8)]

BALDERSON, Ebenezer; 28 Oct 1825; 7 Nov 1825
RC; WILL; all land & pers. est. to wife Ann BALDERSON during her life; after wife's death all land to son John BALDERSON, nevertheless as this portion is more than it is in my power to give to any other of my sons or daus, I oblige him to pay all my just debts out of my whole est.; at wife's death all pers. est. to be sold and eq. div. among my seven children: James P. BALDERSON, Lucy BALDERSON, [Eliza] BALDERSON, Polly BALDERSON, Elizabeth BALDERSON, Uriah BALDERSON, & Leonard BALDERSON; son John BALDERSON & dau. Nancy J. COATS wife of Samuel COATS shall have no part of my pers. est.; son James P. BALDERSON ex; WITS: Enoch FINCH, Jn. BALDERSON, Berryman BALDERSON. (RC WB 10:90)
[Ebenezer BALDERSON, named afer his paternal grandfather who was the immigrant ancestor of the Virginia BALDERSONs, was the son of Gilbert BALDERSON; he was born around 1771 and mar. Anne CLARK, WC bond 19 Dec 1791 (RC DB 15:77, MLBWC:4)]

BALDERSON, Gilbert; 18 Nov 1804; [m]
RC; WILL; sons Ebenezer, John, William, Gilbert Hardwick & Berryman; wife Ann; Ebenezer & William BALDERSON exors; WITS: Daniel MARMADUKE, Jn. KELLY, Abraham WHITE. (RC unrecorded wills)
[This unrecorded will was located by James F. Lewis in a bundle marked "Unrecorded Deeds & Wills" in the RC Courthouse; Gilbert BALDERSON was also the father of 3 daus, Frances who mar. Vincent EDMONDS, RC, bef. 22 Nov 1815, Nancy who mar. Jn. BEDDOWS, RC, bef. 22 Nov 1815, and Sally Jarvis who mar. Berryman REAMY, RC, bond 15 Apr 1791 (RC DB 20:75; MRC:14, 62, 166)]

BALL, (Mrs.); [m]; 2 Sep 1805
NC; INV, list of the dower Negroes & their ages: Daniel (56), Esther (45), Rhoda (42), Bob (43), Dominy (30), Elijah (26), Phebe (27), Nancy (21), Lindsey (5), William (5), Billy (7), Bond (2), Robin (1), Judy (1), Bacchus (born 26 Apr 1805), Tom (3), Venus (16, who was by mistake allotted as a dower Negro). (NC RB 17:302)

BALL, Catharine; PO May 1812; 5 Aug 1812. RC; INV, $200.80. (RC WB 9:409)
[This is Catherine the wid. of Chaney BALL (*see below*)]

BALL, Chaney; PO 2 Dec 1811; 1 Jun 1812. RC; INV, £14.4.0. (RC WB 9:407)
[Chaney BALL mar. Catherine BUNYAN, RC, bond 9 Jan 1805 (MRC:8); Jos. DALE aptd. gdn. to Eliz. W. BALL orphan of Chaney BALL, 1 Sep 1823 (RC OB 26:108); settlement of Rich. WEBB's gdnship. acct. of Eliz. [W.] BALL orphan of Chaney BALL, 5 Sep 1825 (RC OB 27:5)]

BALL, Cyrus (Maj.); PO 18 Dec 1820, T 20 Dec 1820; 20 Mar 1821
LC; INV, $4348.[04]; includes Negroes Joe, Matilda, Hannah, Rose, [Annis], Sarah, Lucinda, Nelly, Sam, Tom, Hannah, Anna, Gabriel, Randal, Shadrack; all of the Negroes except Anna, Gabriel, Randal & Shadrack were mortgaged to R. W. DOWNMAN by deed dtd. 17 Aug 1817. (LC EB 29:81)

[Cyrus BALL mar. Fidelia DOWNMAN, dau. of R. W. DOWNMAN, LC bond 2 Nov 1807 (MLBLC:2)]

BALL, David; PO 11 Nov 1811; 13 Feb 1815
NC; INV, [m]; includes Negroes Peter, Anthony, Robin, Moses, Shadrick, James, Daniel, Spencer, Betty, Sukey & child, Judith, Sarah, Suckey, Molley, Sarah, Letty, Winney, Margery, Pleasant, Matilda, Nancy (slaves were appraised at $3708.32). (NC RB 20:26)

BALL, David; T 22 May 1816; 11 Nov 1816
NC; INV, includes the following Negroes: Shadrick (an old man), Daniel (an old man), Harry, Billy, Ben, Solloman, Willoughby, Billy Jun., [Lazurus], Frankey, Lewis, Moses, [?], Sellar, Peggey, Chriss, Mina, Anna, Mary, [Westtey], Martin, Delia, Winney, Rose, Hannah, [Clarkey], Patty, Sally, Beck, Patty, Abraham, Leroy, Harriett, Griffin, Letty, Susan, Jesse. (NC RB 21:100)
[Sarah E. BALL aptd. gdn. of Hannah G. BALL, David BALL, Thos. BALL, Betsy BALL, Harriet BALL, Wm. BALL & Rich. BALL orphans of the Rev. David BALL, NC, 10 Jun 1816 (NC OB 1816-20:51)]

BALL, David (Rev.); PO 14 Mar 1825, T 2 May 1825; 13 Jun 1825
NC; sale of Negro girl Pleasants to Moses LUNSFORD for Seth LUNSFORD for $184 and distribution of proceeds among David [S.] BALL, Thomas G. BALL, William W. BALL, Richard H. BALL, Hilkiah BALL in right of his wife Hannah G. BALL, John HALE in right of his wife Sally HALE who was Sally BALL, Elizabeth A. BALL & Harriett S. BALL. (NC RB 24:237)
[This is prob. the Rev. David BALL, who was at one time rector of All Hallows Parish, Worcester Co., Md. He mar. Sarah E. McADAM, dau. of Thos. GASKINS (d. NC 1800) and wid. of Geo. Thos. McADAM (MWO:24); while the wife of Hilkiah BALL is identified in this rec. as "Hannah G.," there is a rec. for the marriage of Hilkiah BALL to a Harriet BALL, dau. of David BALL, NC, bond 11 Nov 1811 (MLBNC:4)]

BALL, Elizabeth; PO 8 Apr 1816, T 13 May 1822; 13 May 1822
NC; INV, [m]; includes Negroes woman Pleasant, Alice, girl Nancy. (NC RB 23:137)

BALL, Elizabeth (Miss); T 17 Sep 1809; 8 Sep 1817
NC; Supp. INV, $6414.62; includes the following Negroes worth $6,306: Ned (an old man), Joe, Peter, Henry (a young man), Phill (a lad), Ishmael, [Paisley] (a lad), Tom (a boy), Boy (a boy), Luke (a boy), James (a lad), Moses (a boy), Jesse (a boy), George (a small boy), Letty, Rachel, Winney, [Happy] (a young woman), Becky (a young woman), Marilla (a young woman), Hannah (a young woman), Letty (a young woman), Fanny (a girl), Winney (a girl), Frankey (a girl), Polly (a girl), [Cathey] (a girl). (NC RB 21:253)

BALL, George; PO 9 Nov 1801, T 14 Nov 1801; 9 Sep 1805
NC; INV, £715.18.6; includes Negroes Jesse, Peter, Nel & child, Beck, Mimah, Jenny, Patt, Lett, Winney, boy Daniel. (NC RB 17:305)

BALL, George; 22 Aug 1819 - 18 Oct 1819
LC; WILL; my mulatto woman Anna to have her freedom and the house and lot w/o she now lives during her life; son Hilkiah BALL to purchase 2 Negro girls, one for my grdau. Elizabeth BALL & one for my grdau. Jane BALL; if he complies, I give to him all the land I die possessed of; if he refuses to comply, all my land to go to two grdaus.; rest of est. to son Hilkiah BALL; son Hilkiah ex.; WITS: Jos. BALL, Thos. G. RAINS. (LC WB 28:198)

BALL, Hannah; d. intest.; several of her children including Lucy wife of George BLACKWELL, Joseph BALL, David BALL, Grace the wife of William

NELMS and Jane the wife of George BALL were named in a suit to sell land and div. the proceeds (NC CC 1809-012)
[Hannah was the wid. of Jos. BALL who in his will (NC 17 Apr 1777 – 8 Feb 1779) named his wife Hannah and children Geo., Jos., David, Jn., Wm., Jesse, Sam., Jane, Hannah, and dau. NELMS (NC RB 10:423)]

BALL, James; 5 May 1824 - 16 Jan 1826
CCP, LC; WILL; to son Joseph BALL tract of land known as Ditchley in NC containing 447 ac; to son William Lee BALL 75 ac. on a branch of Deep Creek in LC; to son James Kendall BALL 500 ac. part of my Moratico Tract and now known as Edgewood; to dau. Frances Ravenscroft now the wife of Capt. William D. McCARTY 365 ac. in LC known as the Forest Quarter; land where I now live known as Bewdley containing 580 ac. to be eq. div. between my grsons Atherall & Joseph Pierce BALL (Atherall to have the part on which the dwelling house stands); if either grson. dies before age 21 the survivor to get the whole tract; if neither grson. lives to age 21, tract to go to grson. William Lee BALL; d-i-l Mary BALL to have the use of one third of sd. land; to son James Kendall BALL 530 ac. adj. him being the balance of my tract in the fork of Moratico Creek also my water grist mill & the marsh with the priviliges thereto belonging on the branch of the creek below Moratico Mill supposed to contain 11 ac; ex. to sell land on Moratico Swamp and one of the 4 shares which I hold in the James River Co. and apply the money to the education of my grsons. Atherall, Joseph P. & William L,; my sons & s-i-l William D. McCARTY consented to take the land in Middlesex Co. & 150 ac. in LC adj. the land of Richard SELDON & other prop. in lieu of £1000 left my children at the death of his dau. Fanny my late wife by her father Rawleigh DOWNMAN Esq.; land called Westham in Middlesex Co. to my sons Joseph, James K. BALL & the children of my dec'd son William Lee BALL; the land in LC to William D. McCARTY for the balance of my dau's part of the sd. legacy left her by her grfath Rawleigh DOWNMAN dec'd; sons Joseph & James exors; [no wits listed, but will proved by oaths of Jn. CHOWNING & Jos. W. CHINN]. (LC WB 28:260)
[Maj. James BALL mar. Fanny DOWNMAN, dau. of Rawleigh DOWNMAN (d. LC 1781) bef. 10 Mar 1781 (MWO:25); Frances Ravenscroft BALL, dau. of Jas. BALL, mar. (1) Humphrey F. CARTER, LC, bond 22 Nov 1815 and (2) Wm. D. McCARTY, LC, bond 23 Oct 1818 (MLBLC:11, 50); Ditchley, which once belonged to Richard LEE, is located in NC near the end of State Route 607 between Dividing Creek and Prentice Creek; Bewdley was located in LC near the mouth of Deep Creek; Morattico Creek is located in southeastern RC (Miller:10, 40, 103)]

BALL, James Jr.; PO 16 Jun 1800, T 30 Jul 1800; 20 Oct 1800
LC; INV, £300.9.4 1/2; includes Negroes: Mima, Winny, Joseph, Caleb, Williamson; DIV of est. among: Stokley TOWLES for Augustine GREEN, Thomas TAYLOR for W. BALL, Richard SELDEN for John GORDON, John BALL. (LC EB 24:124)
[Ann BALL, dau. of Col. Jesse BALL (*see below*), mar. Augustine GREEN bef. 15 Sep 1800; Augustine & Ann GREEN were living in Culpeper Co. by Oct 1800. (MWO:155)]

BALL, James W.; 8 Nov 1794; 17 Feb 1795
LC; WILL; use of all est. & the following Negroes to wife Ann BALL: Adam, [plasterer] Joe, Siller & Nancy; at wife's death or marriage, exors. to sell land I purchased of Capt. Richard SELDEN on the east side of Bradley's Swamp together with the water grist mill & proceeds eq. div. amongst my daus.

Mary Wallace, Ann, Judith Epham & Sarah BALL; at wife's death or marriage use of all remainder of est. to son Cyrus; my Negro Joshua to be maintained & supported with good and sufficient clothing & victuals during his life & not be subject to the orders or control of any person except my wife; late father Richard BALL; wife Ann, Col. James BALL, John TANKERSLEY & Spencer BALL exors; COD dtd. 12 Nov 1794: my est. shall make to Jeduthan MOORE a lawful right & title to 15 ac. of land which my late father sold to Richard CUNDIFF & for which no deed was ever given; further COD dtd. 15 Nov 1794: gives exors. right to dispose of pers. est; [no wits listed, but will proved by oaths of Wm. CHOWNING & Severn GALLE]; LC WB 28:11)

[James Wallace BALL mar. Anne BALL, LC bond 31 May 1779 (MWO:25); Ann BALL orphan of Jas. W. BALL chose Stokeley TOWLES as her gdn., 16 Dec 1799 (LC Orders 21 1799-1801:70); Judith E, BALL orphan of Jas. W. BALL chose Jas. BALL as her gdn., 18 Dec 1809 (LC Orders B23 1808-11:139)]

BALL, James Wallace; PO 17 Feb 1795; 17 Feb 1801

LC; INV, [m]; includes Negroes: Joshua, Pluto, Old Kitt, Peter, Perthshire, Will, Adam, Planter Joe, Sawyer Joe, Frank, Daniel, Argyle, James, [Mores], Tom, Syphax, Jack, George, Charles, Armistead, Phillis, Beck, Sophana, Zelpha, Sukey, Nelly, Sillar & child, Nanny & child, Levinia, Lucinda, Tab, Dianna, Lucy, Peggy, Rebecca. (LC EB 24:135)

BALL, James W.; PO 19 Jun 1815; 17 Nov 1817

LC; DIV of est. among: Sarah BALL, William L. LEE, Robert S. HIPKINS, Mary Wallace Ball TOWLES, Stokley TOWLES, Cyrus BALL; INV; includes Negroes: Phillis (age 70), Joseph, Jack, Old Moses, Matilda, Hannah, Duke, Sucky, Lucy, Milly, Beck, Frederick, Rose, Alice, Sam, Nance, Fanny, Jeffery (infant), Lavinah, Cate, [Criss], Winny, Moses, Jude, Perrymus, Lewis, James. (LC EB 27:395, 397)

[Wm. L. LEE mar. Judith E. BALL, LC bond 27 Dec 1809; Robt. HIPKINS mar. Ann BALL, LC bond 22 Jan 1800; Stokely TOWLES mar. Mary W. BALL, LC bond 21 Jan 1799 (MLBLC:38, 47, 74)]

BALL, Jesse; PO Jan 1797 T 17 Jan 1797; 21 Feb 1797

LC; DIV of est. among his orphans Ann GREEN & William BALL; William BALL & Augustine GREEN each received £173. (LC EB 24:59)

BALL, Jesse C.; T 20 Oct 1800; 19 Jan 1801

LC; INV, £30; includes only Negro boy Billy aged 14 entitled to his freedom at 21. (LC EB 24:131)

BALL, Joseph; PO Jan 1792, T 10 Jan 1792; 10 Jun 1793

NC; DIV of est. of Jesse & Samuel BALL orphans of Joseph BALL dec'd in the hands of Hannah BALL dec'd their late gdn. and possess John BALL their present gdn. with the same; slaves were allotted to Jesse BALL: James, Fanny (who was formerly in the lot of the sd. John BALL who agreed that she was the prop. of Jesse BALL in the room of a Negro girl Nancy formerly drawn in the lot of Jesse & Samuel BALL which slave Nancy the sd. John BALL now has), Anthony, Meshack & Molly; to Samuel BALL: Barbara, Sarriphal & young child, Francis, Abraham & Uphama. (NC GA 1788-1824:76)

BALL, Joseph; PO 10 Oct 1808, T 19 Oct 1808; 8 Jan 1810

NC; INV, [m]; includes Negroes Tom, Harry, Oliver, George, David, old woman Agatha, Darky & child, Fanny, Levina, Matilda & child, Peggy & 2 children, Hannah, Sukey, Hiram, Jacob, Griffin, William, Henry, Richard, Polly, Rose, Matilda, Alford, Sharper, Jesse, Edmund, Esther, Sarah, Judith,

Harrison, Charity, Stephen, Abraham, Sally, Fielding, Adam, Daniel, Patty, Cloe, Alice, Marena, Samuel, Louisa. (NC RB 18:269)
[In his will (NC 14 Mar 1808-13 Jun 1808) Jos. BALL named his wife Sarah and children Margaret Steptoe BALL & Joseph BALL; his bro. David BALL was one of his exors. (NC RB 17:633)]

BALL, Joseph; PO 10 Oct 1808, T 19 Oct 1808; 12 Mar 1810
NC; INV, £2855.5.11; includes Negroes Tom, Harry, Oliver, George, David, Old Agatha, Darky & child, Fanny, Levina, Matilda & child, Peggy & 2 children, Hannah, Sukey, Hiram, Jacob, Griffin, William, Henry, Richard, Polly, Rose, Matilda,Alford, Sharper, Jesse, Edmond, Esther, Sarah, Judith, Harrison, Charity, Stephen, Abraham, Sally, Fielding, Adam, Daniel, Patty, Chloe, Alice, Morena, Samuel, Louisa. (NC RB 18:344)

BALL, Joseph; PO 13 Jan 1817, T 10 Feb 1817; 10 Mar 1817
NC; allotment and div. of Negroes belonging to Joseph BALL dec'd between John L. CHINN who mar. Margaret S. BALL & Joseph BALL heirs of sd. Joseph BALL; Lot 1 (George, Sam, [T]oliver, lad Jacob, boy Hiram, Patty & child, Cloe & child, girls Salley & Susan, Matilda, Salley) to John L. CHINN; Lot 2 (William, Sharper - a lad, Edmond - a lad, Alice & child, Pharney & child, woman Sarah, Levina, Aggy, Lucy - a girl, Mima - a girl) to Joseph BALL. (NC RB 21:154)
[Chas. LELAND was gdn. of Marg. S. BALL and Jos. BALL orphans of Jos. BALL, NC, 9 Jan 1815 (NC OB 1811-15:269); The first wife of Jn. L. CHINN was Margaret S. BALL, NC, bond 11 Jul 1816; he mar. (2) Lucy E. LELAND, NC, bond 12 Feb 1821 (MLBNC:17)]

BALL, Joseph; PO 11 Dec 1820, T 2 Jan 1821; 8 Jan 1821
NC; DIV of slaves belonging to the est. of Joseph BALL dec'd lately held as dower by Sally BALL dec'd between John L. CHINN (received Tom, Esther & child Peggy, Mitchell, Abraham, Charity & Solomon) & Joseph BALL (received Sucky & child Emmily, Adam, Areana & child Fanny, Bob & Judy). (NC RB 22:451)

BALL, Lettice; T 29 Dec 1788; 19 Feb 1798
LC; INV, [m]; includes Negroes: Ruben, Ben, Mary, Daphney, Lucy, Daniel, Sinah & child, Lucinda, Sally, Adam. (LC EB 24:69)

BALL, Richard; 12 Oct 1807
NC; Edward ROGERS & Sally his wife, John CORBELL & Nancy his wife, George W. BALL by Edward ROGERS his gdn. and Sanford LOWE & Lucy his wife were heirs of Richard BALL. (NC OB 1807-11:3)
[Edw. ROGERS mar. Sally BALL, ward of Rich. BALL, NC, bond 5 Jun 1804 (MLBNC:89); Jn. CORBELL mar. Nancy BALL, NC, bond 28 Dec 1805 (MLBNC:21); Sanford LOWE, wid., mar. Lucy BALL, ward of Edw. ROGERS, NC, bond 28 Apr 1807 (MLBNC:70)]

BALL, Richard (Capt.); T 25 Jan 1805; 10 Sep 1810
NC; INV, [m]; includes slaves Tigner [PINN], James TUXON, Davy, Humphry, Jacob, Philes, Judith. (NC RB 18:460)
[Davy, Dick, Steward, Lila & Jenny TUXEN, children of Betty TUXEN were registered as free persons, 7 Nov 1820 (RC OB 25:83)]

BALL, Sarah; 15 May 1815; 13 Nov 1820
NC; WILL; to nephew Charles Henry LELAND son of my late bro. Charles LELAND my Negro girl Louisa; to my niece Lucy LELAND my Negro boy Alfred; to my nephew Samuel A. M. LELAND my Negro boy Dick; to my nephew Henry Towles LELAND my Negro girl Susannah; to my nephew Lucious Cary LELAND my Negro girl Mary; nephew Richard Hall BRENT;

s-i-l Joseph BALL; d-i-l Margaret S. BALL; £20 to niece Mary L. BRENT dau. of my niece Eliza L. BRENT; remainder of est. to my nephew John D. LELAND; cousin Henry GASKINS ex; [COD] 6 Jun 1817; any former will in favor of my nephew John D. LELAND to be void except with respect to my Negro Griffin which I shall give him; all the other prop. with the money in Henry Lee GASKINS' hands $250 left to him in my former will I now desire may be eq. div. between my bro. Charles LELAND's 3 youngest sons: Samuel, Henry & Lucious LELAND; WIT: Eliz. Lee BRENT. (NC RB 22:431) [This is Sarah LELAND who mar. Jos. BALL, wid., NC, bond 15 Jan 1807 (MLBNC:4); in his will (NC 3 Feb 1815-14 Mar 1815) Chas. LELAND only named his sisters Lucy LELAND, Sarah BALL, and Mary CRALLE (NC RB 20:33)]

BALL, Sarah; PO 13 Nov 1820, T 5 Dec 1820; 14 Jan 1822
NC; INV at Point Pleasant, $3788.56; includes Negroes Griffin (legacy to J. D. LELAND), Alfred (legacy to Lucy LELAND), Dick (legacy to S. A. M. LELAND), Louisa (legacy to C. H. LELAND), Susan (legacy to H. T. LELAND), Mary (legacy to Lucius LELAND), Matilda, Delia. (NC RB 23:63)

BALL, Thomas (Dr.); PO 9 Mar 1824; 14 Jun 1824
NC; DIV of slaves; to Patrick SPILLER in right of his wife the slaves Criss (young woman), girl Caroline, Polly (young woman), Eliza (her child), Anthony (old man), Billy; to Thomas BALL the slaves Betty, Jesse, Hannah, Joe, Fanny, Criss (old woman), Sally, Harriott, [Bessick], Criss, Betty, Sally; Patrick SPILLER was Dr. to the following slaves sold: Delia, Linszey, Jinney, Albert, James, Isaac.; we have thought proper to allot the whole of the account because the debts were contracted by Mrs. SPILLER before marriage, we conceive for the mutual benefit of mother and son & because Mr. SPILLER has paid debts of a considerable amount since marriage of a similar nature such as taxes, blacksmith's account, etc. (NC RB 23:518) [Dr. Thos. BALL mar. Louisa EDWARDS, dau. of LeRoy EDWARDS, NC, bond 26 Mar 1800 (MLBNC:4); in his will, NC, 15 Nov 1814-12 Dec 1814, Thos. BALL names his wife Louisa, his bros. Joseph & Wm. BALL, his nephew Helkiah BALL, and his son Thomas (NC RB 19:574); Patrick SPILLER mar. Louisa BALL, dau. of LeRoy EDWARDS & wid. of Dr. Thos. BALL, NC bond 21 Feb 1818 (MLBLC:4, 94)]

BALL, Thomas P.; 10 May 1813; 5 Feb 1816
LC; WILL; wife Eliza B. BALL entire est.; if any heirs, they are to inherit an eq. proportion of est; Col. James BALL exor; WITS: Thos. P. SMITH, Jn. L. [BEVAN], Robt. NUTT. (RC WB 9:503)
[Thos. P. BALL of LC mar. Eliz. B. GARLAND, RC, bond 9 Mar 1811 (MRC:8)]

BALL, William; T 25 Mar 1816 [1817]
NC; INV, $3613.[8]5; includes the following Negroes: James, George, Williamson, Peter, James, Joe, Ben, Old Joe, Malinda & child Betsy, Grace, Happy, Alice, Patty, Siller, Rachel. (NC RB 21:288)
[Jos. BALL was aptd. gdn. of Luke, Delia & Lydia BALL orphans of Wm. BALL, NC, 11 Nov 1816 (NC OB 1816-20:101) but it is not certain if it is this William]

BALL, William Lee; T 1 Jun 1824; 17 Jan 1825
LC; INV, $584[4].61; includes Negroes Tom, Tab & child, girl Celia, Sally, Fanny, boy Isaac. (LC EB 29:381)
[Wm. Lee BALL Esq., a native citizen of this county, died in Washington where he was attending to his duties as a member of Congress, 16 Mar 1824

(LC OB 26:31); Lettice Lee BALL chose Jos. BALL for her gdn. and sd. Jos. BALL aptd. gdn. for Fanny D. & Wm. Lee BALL orphans of Wm. Lee BALL, 20 Jun 1825 (LC OB 26:127); Chas. MARSHALL and Judith S. his wife who was Judith S. BALL (dau. of Wm. L. BALL, dec'd), [m] HALE and Olivia D. his wife who was Olivia D. BALL (dau. of Wm. L. BALL, dec'd). and Mary BALL (wid. & rel. of Wm. L. BALL, dec'd) declare that Wm. L. BALL d. intest. in 1824 leaving Mary, the wid., and the following children: Judith S., Olivia D., Lettice L., Fanny, Atharell, Jos. P. and Wm. L. and ask that a tract of his land in LC be div. (LC CC 1825-005); Olivia D. BALL mar. Francis T. HALE of Fauquier Co., LC, bond 16 Dec 1824 (MLBLC:34)]

BALL, Williamson; PO Dec 1796; 2 Sep 1805
INV of Negroes in Frederick County: Daniel, Nelson, Sam, Molly (little), Sally, Charlotte, Stephen, Patrick, Big Molly, Suckey, Peter, Pleasant, Charity, Mary, Alse, Lenah, Moses, Rosetta, Richard, Tom, £907.0.0. (RC WB 9:259)

BALL, Williamson; 6 Jun 1808. RC, INV, [m]. (RC WB 9:326)

BALL, Williamson; PO 1 Dec 1800, T 8 Jan 1801; 6 Feb 1809
RC; DIV of slaves among Harrison BALL (carpenter Jerry, Ned's family, carpenter Ned, Janet Ned's wife, Kitty, Pleasant, Sally, Lucretia, Jane, Jeremiah; Hannah's family, Hannah, Peg Hannah's dau, Charles, William, Mary; Betty's family, Betty, Easter, Marcus, Daniel; Manuel, Winney, David, Jane David's wife, Moses, Beck, Judy, Charity, Nancy, Beck, Old Pleasant, Elisha), Col. Walker TOMLIN in right of his wife Priscilla (Tom, Old Sam, Molly, Suckey, Peter, Pleasant, Charity, Mary), Newman B. BARNES in right of his wife Lucy H. (Young Sam, Young Molly, Sally, Charlotte, Stephen, Patrick, Fanny, Peggy), Judith SHORT (Daniel, Sinah, Tabitha, David, Suckey, Nelson) & Margaret Williamson BALL (James, Alice, Leanna, Richard, Moses, Rosetta, Jacob). (RC AB 3:211)
[Col. Walker TOMLIN mar. (2) Priscilla BALL, dau. of Capt. Williamson & Priscilla (CHURCHILL) BALL, RC bond 9 Dec 1788; Newman Brockenbrough BARNES mar. Lucy Harrison BALL between 1786 & 1800; John SHORT mar. Judith BALL, RC bond 7 Apr 1785 (MRC:10, 186, 218)]

BANKHEAD, James; Oct 1797
WC; acc. to a chancery suit begun in Oct 1797, James BANKHEAD mar. Christian [MILLER] and had at least three children: Elizabeth (mar. Thomas MAGRUDER), James & Jennett; James and Jennett were born after 1776. (WC CC 1804-029)
[Eliz. BANKHEAD was born at Port Royal, Caroline Co., Va. on 5 Nov 1778 and died at Charlottesville on 19 Aug 1849. She mar. Thos. MAGRUDER of Prince George's Co., Md. (http://www.rootsweb.ancestry.com/~vaogc/A_8_1_6.html, accessed 23 Mar 2012)]

BANKHEAD, Stewart; PO 24 Jun 1805, T 16 Jul 1805 [26 Aug 1805]
WC; INV, £3361.6.6; includes Negroes Winney & 2 children, Eve & child, Suckey, Jenny & 1 child, Cate & 1 child, Dinah, Sarah dau. to Dinah, Polly 3 sons & 1 dau, boy Ned, Charles, Willis, Mason, Milly & 2 children, Hannah dau. to Milly, Dolly dau. to Milly, James, Thomas, Adam, Will, Betty & child, Winney, Emeline, Sarah, girl Peggy, Lucy, Eliza, boy James, Henry, John, [Dummore], Nancy, John son to ditto [sic], [Thay], Humphrey, Old Hannah, Milley. (WC RI 8:568)

BANKHEAD, Stewart; PO Nov 1813; 18 Jul 1817
WC; Chancery suit, Elizabeth HIPKINS, complt. vs Robert G. ROBB & Eve his wife who was wid. & admx. of Stewart BANKHEAD and Eliza

BANKHEAD child of sd. Stewart defendants; commissioners sold at Mattox Bridge on 12 Jan 1814 the following Negroes belonging to the est. of Stewart BANKHEAD: James Jr., Willis, Joshua, Joseph, James (an old Negro), Adam, Polly & Robert her child, [Lizza] (about 16), George (about 10), Alexander (about 7) for $3661.91; proceeds applied to pay off debt to HIPKINS. (WC RI 10:106, OB 1814-18:330)
[Robt. G. ROBB mar. Eve BANKHEAD, WC bond 1 Mar 1808 (MLBWC:59)]

BANKHEAD, Stewart; PO 1808, T 20 Jan 1818; 26 Jan 1818
WC; settlement of accts; Dr. E. Lawson WARING mar. Miss Eliza BANKHEAD the only child of Stewart BANKHEAD; balance due from the est. to the admx. Eve ROBB formerly Eve BANKHEAD of £1737.6.6. (WC RI 10:230)
[Eppephroditus Lawson WARING mar. Eliz. BANKHEAD, WC, bond 30 Oct 1817 (MLBWC:73)]

BANKHEAD, William; 1 Mar 1788; Jun 1788
WC; WILL; physician; land on north side of Mattox Cr. which I now live on to son Stewart (who is under age); £500 to dau. Nelly BANKHEAD; if both children die without issue, est. to be eq. div. among children of brothers & sisters; bro. John BANKHEAD & friend Beckwith BUTLER exors; WITS: Archd. CAMPBELL, Peter JETT, [N.] MONROE. (WC Unrec Wills 1755-1800 #34)
[Jn. BANKHEAD Gent. qualified as ex. in Oct 1788]

BARECROFT, George & Susanna; 13 May 1805; 10 Jun 1805
NC; INV & DIV of est. between Thomas T. ATWELL (rec'd Manuel, Jacob, Bill, Fanny, Charles, Levina & Luce) and Willoughby N. BERRYMAN (rec'd Rachel, Vincent, Nancy & child Thornly, Winney & Willis; also div. of land on the Warehouse Road. (NC RB 17:273)
[Charlotte BARECROFT, dau. of George, mar. (1) [fnu] CLARK, bef. 22 Nov 1788 and (2) Thos. ATTWELL, NC, bond 10 Feb 1800 (MWO:77, MLBNC:3); Newton Willoughby BERRYMAN [sic] mar. Jane Presley BARECROFT, dau. of Susanna BARECROFT, NC, bond 1 Dec 1792 (MLBNC:8)]

BARECROFT, Mottrom; PO 11 Jun 1804, T 1 Sep 1804; 8 Oct 1804
NC; settlement of William BARECROFT's acct. of his admin. of the est. of Mottrom BARECROFT dec'd and DIV of balance among legal reps: William BARECROFT, William WINSTEAD, Richard H. BARECROFT, Alice BARECROFT, Thomas BARECROFT, Mottrom BARECROFT, James SMITH & Thomas SELF for the benefit of his children. (NC RB 17:226)
[This is apparently Mottrom BARECROFT who mar. Alice SELF, dau. of Thos. SELF, bef. 1758 (MWO:34); the births of 10 children to Mottrom & Alice BARECROFT are rec. in the SSPR: Keziah (17 Nov 1758), Caty (17 Apr 1761), Wm. (8 May 1763), Jeanne (20 Feb 1766), Thos. (17 Apr 1768), Mottrom (20 Mar 1771), Alice (12 Oct 1773), Nancy (21 Nov 1775), Martha (2 Mar 1778), & Rich. Haynie (9 Feb 1781) (SSPR:17, 18, 21); Wm. WINSTEAD, wid., mar. Nancy BEARCROFT, NC bond 26 Dec 1800; Jas. SMITH, wid., mar. Jane BEARCROFT, NC bond 2 Jan 1797 (MLBNC:92, 111); Thos. SELF, son of Jas. & Margaret SELF, mar. Keziah BEARCROFT, dau. of Mottrom & Alice BEARCROFT, NC, 17 Jan 1781 (MWO:315)]

BARKER, Milly; 2 Jul 1827
RC; copy of order of Spencer Co. Court, Kentucky, evidencing the apt. of Thomas BARKER as gdn. to Mary Ann BARKER infant heir of Joseph REDMAN was admitted to record; Mary Ann BARKER was the child of Milly BARKER dec'd wife of Thomas BARKER. (RC OB 27:173)

BARNES, Alexander; T 29 January 1805; 9 Jun 1806
NC; INV, includes Negroes Pithanio & child Ephriam, Hannah & child Lawson, girls Jude & Elizah, boy Joe. (NC RB 17:426)
[The est. was admin. by Jane O. BARNES & Oliver STOTT (NC Min. Book 1801-1805); Thos. ROCK mar. Jane O. BARNES, NC, bond 13 Oct 1806 (MLBNC:88); Thos. ROCK to settle the acct. of his former wife, Jane O. who was Jane O. BARNES of her admin. of Alex. BARNES and of Thos. & Jane's gdnship. of Polly the dau. of sd. Alex. BARNES, 15 Mar 1827 (NC OB 1825-30:171); *see also* NC CC 1827-003]

BARNES, Charles; PO 7 Apr 1800; 1 Jun 1807. RC; INV, £254.8.1. (RC WB 9:308)

BARNES, Edward; PO 8 Feb 1808, T 11 Feb 1808; 10 Oct 1808
NC; INV, £133.9.8; includes Negroes James & Rebecca. (NC RB 18:47)
[Edw. BARNES, wid., mar. Griffithello CLAUGHTON, dau. of Jn. CLAUGHTON (d. NC, 1796), NC, bond 15 Nov 1806; Griffithello (CLAUGHTON) BARNES mar. (2) Lewis LAMKIN, Jr., NC, bond 29 Oct 1811 (MLBNC:65, NC OB 1811-15:51)]

BARNES, Edwin; PO 13 Apr 1801; 12 Oct 1801. NC; INV, [m]; includes Negro Sally. (NC RB 16:296)

BARNES, Edwin; 9 Feb 1824
NC; on the mot. of [?] BARNES & Edw. BARNES for himself and as gdn. of Elisa & Geo. BARNES orphans of Sam. G. BARNES ord. that Eliz. BARNES and Holland & Elisa WINSTEAD show cause why the lands of Edwin BARNES dec'd should not be sold and the proceeds div. among his heirs. (NC OB 1820-25:350)
[On the motion of Alex. NEWSOM & Jane his wife, Jas. DODSON & Betsy his wife, Edw. BARNES in his own right and as gdn. & next friend of Geo. & Eliza BARNES and Austin BARNES it is ord. that Sam. BARNES, Wm. BARNES & Mary BARNES & Edw. BARNES childrn & heirs of Merideth BARNES dec'd and Holland & Eliz. WINSTEAD children & heirs of Nancy WINSTEAD dec'd be summoned to show cause why the lands of [Harriet] BARNES should not be sold and proceeds distributed, NC 15 Mar 1825 (NC OB 1820-25:456); in his will (11 Oct 1799 - 13 Apr 1801) Edwin BARNES named his wife Hannah, son Ostain, daus. Jane Booth BARNES and Herett Garner BARNES but does not name the rest of his children (NC RB 16:241); Alex. NEWSOM mar. Jane BARNES, ward of Hannah BARNES, NC, bond 11 Feb 1813 (MLBNC:77); Jas. B. DODSON mar. Eliz. BARNES, NC, bond 8 Nov 1824 (MLBNC:30)]

BARNES, Edwin; PO 12 Jan 1824, T 8 Mar 1824; 8 Mar 1824
NC; DIV of slaves agreeable to the will among: Meredith BARNES (rec'd Amos), Nancy WINSTEAD's orphans (rec'd Sally & Milley), Betsy BARNES (rec'd Isaac & Lucinder), and Samuel G. BARNES's orphans (rec'd Mariah & Silva); div. of slaves belonging to Samuel G. BARNES among: Eliza BARNES (rec'd Mimy & child, Sarah & Charlotte), Meredith BARNES (rec'd Thornton, Julet & Maria), Edward BARNES (rec'd Spencer, Ginney & Silve). (NC RB 23:432)
[This record seems to be for Edwin BARNES of SSP who, in his will (NC 11 Oct 1799-13 Apr 1801) named wife Hannah and children Ostain, Jane Booth, and Herett Garner. (NC RB 16:241); the births of Sam. Garner (1778), Meredith (1781), Ostin (178?), Morton (1787), and Ann Edwards (1790) to Edwin & Hannah BARNES are rec. in the SSPR (SSPR:21, 22, 23); Wm. WINSTEAD, wid., mar. Nancy BARNES, NC bond 6 Feb 1809; Hannah BARNES gave her consent as to Nancy (MLBNC:111)]

BARNES, Henry; PO 14 Jan 1805; 14 Apr 1807
NC; DIV of est. among heirs [not named], Lot 1 (Siner, Tomsey), Lot 2 (Salley & child, Amy). (NC RB 17:519)

BARNES, John; 11 Oct 1824; 20 Dec 1824
LC; WILL; all the money due me from Joseph DALE to my bro. Samuel BARNES; rest of money due me to Ann LUNSFORD; bro. Samuel ex; money given to Ann LUNSFORD not to come into my brother's hand; WITS: Jn. GRESHAM, Sarah CHOWNING. (LC WB 28:254)

BARNES, John; PO 20 Dec 1824, T 13 Dec 1825 [sic]; 17 Jan 1825
LC; INV, $60.50; includes legacy to Ann LUNSFORD. (LC EB 29:389)

BARNES, Peter; 23 Dec 1824
RC; Lewis TUNE, adm. with the will annexed, has paid Joannah, Mary, Sally, and Caty TUNE four of the legatees of Peter BARNES, dec'd, the sum of $40. (RC AB 4:302)
[Joannah, Mary, Sally, and Caty TUNE were daus. of Samuel and Sarah TUNE, *see below*]

BARNES, Peter M.; T 21 Jan 1821; 14 Feb 1827. NC; INV, $725.50. (NC RB 24:149)
[Alex. DODSON aptd. gdn. to Alice BARNES orphan of Peter M. BARNES, 14 May 1827 (NC OB 1825-30:164)]

BARNES, Richard M. F.; 5 Feb 1827
RC; Chancery suit; Claiborn W. GOOCH & Maria R. R. his wife who was Maria R. R. BARNES, Lucy A. BARNES, Arthur L. BARNES and William A. WRIGHT & Charlotte his wife who was Charlotte BARNES, pltfs., vs. Thomas R. BARNES in his own right and as admr. of Richard M. F. BARNES dec'd, deft. (RC OB 27:132)
[This is Rich. BARNES Jr., the son of Rich. BARNES & Lucy ROANE (dau. of Col. Wm. ROANE & Sarah UPSHAW), who mar. Rebecca ROANE; Rich. & Rebecca had six children: Lucy who mar. Philip BRANHAM, EC, 26 Apr 1827, Maria who mar. Claiborn W. GOOCH, Essex Co., 14 Oct 1818, Charlotte who mar. Wm. A. WRIGHT, EC, 10 Jan 1827, Thomas, Rich., and Arthur (Lenora Higginbotham Sweeny, "The Upshaw Family of Essex" in *Genealogies of Virginia Families from the William and Mary College Quarterly Historical Magazine*, 1982, Baltimore:The Genealogical Publishing Co., p.284)]

BARNES, Samuel; 2 Nov 1819
RC; Newman, Thomas, John & Samuel were identified as infant children of Samuel BARNES living at the time of his death; it appears that other children of Samuel BARNES were Chas. BARNES and Traverse BARNES; Catherine the wife of Christopher CHINAULT and Polly the wife of Edw. DAVIS were children of Chas. BARNES. (RC Orders 1809-10:18; OB 24:385)
[Newman, son of Sam. & Betty BARNES, was b. in 1789 (NFPR:11); Christopher CHINAULT mar. Catherine BARNES, RC, bond 13 Dec 1791 (MRC:35); Edw. DAVIS mar. Polly BARNES, RC, bond 28 Dec 1797 (MRC:49)]

BARNES, Samuel G.; T 15 Jan 1815; 13 Sep 1819
NC; INV, [m]; includes Negroes Mimah, girls Charlotte & Cyner, boy Spencer. (NC RB 22:123)
[Samuel G. BARNES was a son & heir of Edwin BARNES; he was b. on 13 Dec 1778 in SSP (SSPR:21); he mar. Hannah ASHBURN, NC, bond 4 Feb 1799 (MLBNC:5); Wm. ANDERSON was aptd. gdn. of Edw., Sally, Geo., and Elisa BARNES orphans of Sam. G. BARNES, NC, 11 Apr 1815 (NC OB 1811-

15:310); Meredith BARNES aptd. gdn. of Edwin, Sally H., Geo., and Eliz. BARNES orphans of Sam. G. BARNES NC 13 Dec 1819 (NC OB 1816-20:415)]

BARNES, [Tarlton]; 18 Mar 1823; 14 Apr 1823
NC; WILL; whole est. to wife Nancy; wife & Meredith BARNES exors; wife to be gdn. to all my children; wits: Thos. COOKMAN, Sam. BRUMLEY, Winnefred LEWIS. (NC RB 23:293)
[This is prob the man identified as "Fallon Barnes" in MLBNC:5 who mar. Nancy BRUMLEY, NC, bond 10 Dec 1810; this bond is listed between Stephen Barnes & William Barnes and may have been a typo for "Tallon Barnes." A Tallon BARNS, the son of Wm. & Winney BARNS, was born in SSP 18 Mar 1786 (SSPR:22); Fleet read the first name as "Fallon," but all these variants are certainly for Tarlton which actually appears in later records; Sam. BRUMLEY aptd. gdn. to Vincent & Jane BARNES (orphans of Tarlton BARNES), 12 May 1828 (NC OB 1825-30:258, 360)]

BARNES, Tarlton; T 20 May 1823; 12 Jul 1824
NC; INV, $85.65; includes Negro girls Mahalia & Phillis. (NC RB 24:9)

BARNES, Vincent; T 9 Oct 1816; 15 Apr 1817
NC; INV; $1293.64; includes the following Negroes: Siller, Griffin, Pattey, Phillis. (NC RB 21:170)
[In his will (NC 3 Feb 1816-11 Mar 1816) Vincent BARNES names his father Wm. BARNES, his bros. Talton BARNES & Wm. BARNES Jr., and his sis. Hanny BARNES; Meredith & Hannah BARNES witnessed his will (NC RB 20:389)]

BARNES, William Jr.; 12 Mar 1816; 8 Dec 1817
NC; WILL; to son William Fleet Barnes BROWN the whole of my est; reserves a maintenance for wife; if son dies without heirs est. to go to bro. Stephen BARNES' children: Suckey, Nancy, Eliza & Jane; ex. to furnish Negro Old Alice with a barrel of corn a year & a house to live in; John GRINSTEAD ex.; WITS: Sam. BARNES Sr, Wm. BARNES; [Betsy BARNES renounces all rights etc. accruing to her under the will of her husband William BARNES Jr., 13 Apr 1818; WITS: Th. TOWLES, F. BATES]; NC RB 21:300, 399)
[Wm. BARNES Jr. was a son of Wm. BARNES and bro. of Vincent, Tarlton & Hanny BARNES.(NC RB 20:389); he was no doubt the Wm. BARNES, wid., who mar. Eliz. BROWN, NC bond 13 Aug 1809 (MLBNC:5)]

BARNES, William Jr.; T 22 Dec 1817; 13 Dec 1819
NC; INV, $1102.50; includes Negroes Jack, Polly. (NC RB 22:169)

BARNETT, Henry; PO 24 Nov 1806; 25 Mar 1808
WC; INV, £570.12; includes Negroes Sawney, Glasgow, Jerry, Nancy & child, [Jimmey]. (WC RI 9:41)
[This may be the Hen. BARNETT who mar. Alleymenty CARROLL, WC bond 31 Jan 1791 (MLBWC:4); Sally BARNETT orphan of Hen. BARNETT chose Mary BARNETT as her gdn.; Geo. GLASCOCK was gdn. of Jos., [Hen.], Nancy, & Alice BARNETT orphans of Hen. BARNETT, 28 Aug 1809 (WC Orders 1807-10:398)]

BARNETT, Henry; 22 Nov 1819
WC; Richard BARNETT aptd. gdn. to William BARNETT orphan of Henry BARNETT. (WC OB 1819-23:92)

BARNETT, Mary; 28 Mar 1808
WC; George GLASCOCK was gdn. of William, Alice & Joseph BARNETT orphans of Mary BARNETT. (WC Orders 1807-1810:150)

BARNETT, Mary; 21 Jan 1822

LC; admin. of the est. of Mary BARNETT dec'd granted to John BARNETT. (LC OB 25:278)
[This is prob. Molly HAYDON, dau. of Lucy HAYDON, who mar. Jn. BARNETT, LC, bond 11 Feb 1811 (LC OB 25:278); Jn. BARNETT aptd. gdn. to his children Jn., Peter & Sally, 18 Mar 1822 (LC OB 25:282)]

BARRETT, George; 2 Feb 1816; 1[8] Nov 1817
NC; WILL; lend to my wife Nancy BARRETT all my est. for her comfortable subsistance during her life; lend to my son James BARRETT after the death of my wife all my land & plant. w/o I now live & two Negroes Isaac & Rachel; if son dies without heirs land to be sold & money eq. div. between sons Walter & George BARRETT; to dau. Nancy HARCUM one Negro girl Lucy; son Walter one Negro boy Stephen; son George one Negro boy [Umpha]; rest of Negroes to be eq. div. between three children Nancy HARCUM, Walter BARRETT & George BARRETT; sons Walter & George to be bound to some trade that they choose; friend Henry L. GASKIN & nephew Thomas HUDNALL exors; WITS: Spencer GASKINS, Chas. MARSH; [admin. granted to Ann BARRETT]. (NC RB 21:278)
[Geo. BARRETT, wid., mar. Nancy BARRETT, NC bond 26 Sep 1791 (MLBNC:5); Nancy BARRETT, dau. of Geo. BARRETT, mar. Leroy HARCUM. NC, bond 28 Jun 1815 (MLBNC:46); Walter BARRETT orphan of Geo. BARRETT chose Wm. HUDNALL as his gdn., NC, 9 Nov 1818 (NC OB 1816-20:300)]

BARRETT, George; T 10 Nov [1818]; 14 Feb 1820
NC; INV, $6946.53 1/2; includes Negroes Ned, Tom, Isaac, Humphrey, Harry, Siner, Polly & child [Sally], Polly & child [Zachy], Matilda, [Claresy], Siller, Hannah, Eddy, Darky, Rachell. (NC RB 22:201)

BARRETT, George; PO 9 Nov 1818, T 10 Mar 1819; 14 Feb 1820
NC; DIV of Negroes and est. acct. balance held by Leroy HARCUM admr. among Leroy HARCUM (rec'd Tom, [Claricy], Harrey, Siller, Hannah, Eddy), Walter BARRETT (rec'd [Ned], [Sener], Polly & child Sally, Matilda, Polly & child Zachry) & James BARRETT (rec'd Humphrey, Darky). (NC RB 22:209)

BARRETT, John [m]; 28 Feb 1804. WC; INV, £150.4.8. (WC RI 8:371)
[Wm. BARRETT orphan of Jn. BARRETT chose Tarpley BRYANT as his gdn., WC 27 Sep 1804 (WC Orders 1804-07:88)]

BARRETT, John; T 13 Mar 1815; 26 May 1817. WC; INV, $27.41 1/2. (WC RI 10:105)

BARRETT, Milley [m]; 9 Jan 1815
NC; settlement of admin. acct. of Mrs. G. BARRETT at her house and DIV of est. of Milley BARRETT dec'd; George BARRETT rec'd Negro Ned, William DORETY rec'd Samuel, Joseph PALMER's heirs rec'd Winey & child Sharlott; INV, T. 26 Oct 1814, $1323.47 1/2, includes Negroes Ned, Sam, Winny & child Charlotte, Lucy. (NC RB 19:602, 603)
[Millicent or Milley BARRETT was the sis. of Caty BARRETT, a dau. of Jn. BARRETT, who mar. James HARCUM bef. 5 Jan 1788; Caty HARCUM in her will (NC 1 Oct 1814-12 Dec 1814) names her children Leroy, Betsy DAUGHITY, Sally HUDNALL, and James & her sis. Millicent; Betsy HARCUM mar, Wm. DAUGHITY, NC bond 11 Jan 1808; Jos. PALMER mar. Sally BARRETT, NC bond 22 Mar 1791 (MLBNC:26, 79; MWO:164; NC RB 19:572)]

BARRETT, Susanna; 10 May 1804; 2 Jul 1804

NFP, RC; WILL; nephew George GLASCOCK; Richard Martin GLASCOCK; 6 nieces: Judah Ball HUNT, Eliz. HUNT, Sarah HUNT, Judah SMITHER, Fanny Carter HUNT, & Sarah SMITHER; sisters Judah HUNT & Sarah SMITHER; friends George HUNT & Richard SMITHER exors; WITS: Vincent HOWARD, Rich. T. HUNT. (RC WB 9:237)
[Susanna (b. 1751), Judith (b. 1756) and Sarah (b. 1761) were daus. of Geo. & Judith (BALL) GLASCOCK; the births of these 3 and their siblings are rec. in the NFPR (MWO:149, NFPR:70-71); Judith mar. Geo. HUNT (RC, bond 19 Sep 1778) & Sarah mar. Rich. SMITHER (RC, bond 17 Jan 1793) (MWO:192, 326)]

BARTLETT, Elisha; 10 May 1803; 4 Jul 1803
RC; WILL; dau. Pennelapy; all lawful children [nfi]; sons John & Isaac exors; WITS: Jas. SCATES, Bartlett SCATES. (RC WB 9:216)

BARTLETT, Elisha; 4 Jun 1804. RC; INV. (RC WB 9:236)

BARTLETT, Elisha; 6 Sep 1820; 6 Nov 1820
RC; WILL; land & plant. to son Joel BARTLETT; all my children to live together so long as they can agree & if not, dau. Johannah BARTLETT to have a house built on one part of my plant.; all my movable property to be eq. div. among my children: Johannah BARTLETT, Maria BARTLETT, Sarah BARTLETT & James BARTLETT; son James to be well schooled; WITS: Lemuel G. SANDY, Saml. LYELL, Jn. CASH; RC WB 9:675)
[Elisha BARTLETT was the son of Thos. BARTLETT of LP (d. RC 1783) (RC WB 7:432); he mar. (1) Leah SCATES, dau. of Jos. (d. RC 1795) & Sarah SCATES, RC, bond 9 Feb 1791 and (2) Eliz. JONES, wid, RC, bond 6 Aug 1795 (MRC:11); Elisha & Leah had at least 3 children born in LP: Jehu (b. 1791), Joanna (b. 1794), and Joel (b. 1796) (NFPR:11); Joel BARTLETT mar. Sally WILSON, WC, bond 24 Dec 1821 (MLBWC:5); Jas. BARTLETT orphan of Elisha BARTLETT chose Joel BARTLETT as his gdn., 6 May 1822 (RC OB 25:283)]

BARTLETT, Elisha; T 17 Nov 1820; 7 May 1821. RC; INV, $477.90 1/2. (RC WB 9:703)

BARTLETT, John; PO Feb 1816; 7 Oct 1816. RC; INV, [m]. (RC WB 9:540)
[This is prob. Jn. BARTLETT of LP; the births of three children to Jn. & Eliz. BARTLETT are rec. in the LPR: Eliz., 14 Mar 1792, Penelope Wilson, 13 Jul 1794 and John, 28 Nov 1796 (NFPR:11); Jas. JENKINS mar. Frances BARTLETT, WC, bond 1 Jan 1817 (MLBWC:34); Wm. KENDALL mar. Penelope BARTLETT, WC, bond 18 Nov 1816 (MLBWC:37); Jn. BARTLETT having died seized of a small tract of land in RC of not more than 100 ac. and having left the following children: Suckey, Jas., Thos., Frances, Eliz., Penelope, Jn. & Matthew who are of age, Wm. Kendall, Hen. & Louisa who are infants ... ord. that the aforesd. children together with Jas. JENKINS husband of Frances, Wm. L. MOTHERSHEAD who mar. Eliz. & Wm. KENDALL husband of Penelope be summoned to show cause why land should not be sold, 3 Feb 1823 (RC OB 26:25); Louisa BARTLETT mar. Elijah SCATES, RC, bond 5 Feb 1827 (MRC:181; RC OB 27:152)]

BARTLETT, Joseph; PO Nov 1814, T 13 Dec 1814; 25 Sep 1815. WC; INV, [m]. (WC RI 10:23)
[Jos. SUTTON aptd. gdn. to Jn. BARTLETT orphan of Jos. BARTLETT, 26 Jun 1815 (WC OB 1814-18:157)]

BASYE, Betsy; 7 Jan 1823; 19 Dec 1825
LC; WILL; all prop. & money to be eq. div. between my children: Polley, Caty, Judeth, Milley & Isaac; [no ex. named]; WITS: Raw. DUNAWAY,

Judith ROGERS, Ann BISCOE, W. BASYE, Judith SAMPSON. (LC WB 28:257)
[This is Betsy (CUNDIFF) BASYE, wid. of Elismond BASYE (*see below*)]

BASYE, Elismond; 18 Mar 1820; 19 Jun 1820
LC; WILL; all est. to wife Betsy BASYE as long as she remains my widow; if she marries she is to have only one third; wife to educate my 3 children Judah, Milly & Isaac; son John to have $200 less than the rest of my children having given him that amount already; rest of est. to be eq. div. among all children: [Anney], John, Polly, Caty, Judah, Milly & Isaac; wife extx; WITS: Raw. DUNAWAY, Wm. PULLIN, Geo. MYERS. (LC WB 28:205)
[Elismond BASYE mar. Betsy CUNDIFF, LC, bond 27 Aug 1793 (MLBLC:3)]

BASYE, Elismond; T 3 Jan 1821; 16 Jul 1821
LC; INV, $3215.17; includes Negroes Isaac, Lee, Jerry, Joe, Solomon, John, Daniel, Phillis, Fanny, [Cande], Maria, Sarah, Charlotte. (LC EB 29:109)

BASYE, Isaac; 7 Apr 1824 - 8 May 1826
NC; WILL; to two sons William BASYE & Joseph BASYE all the land I hold on the S side of my mansion house (being [on] a branch making into the Great Wicomico River including the land I purchased from John CUNDIFF) to be eq. div.; my three daus. Sally HARDING, Elizabeth BASYE & Rebecca M. BASYE to hold & enjoy during their lives all my lands on the N side of the aforesd. branch including my mansion house & the lands I purchased of Edmond BASYE; to three daus. my three Negro girls Mahala, Charlotte & Ann and my three Negro boys Willie, Elijah & Hampton, my dau. Sally to have first choice; to son William a Negro man Isaac; to son Joseph a Negro man Adam; grson. Thomas BASYE, son of William, a small [Negro] boy David; to grdau. Sally Ann BASYE, dau. of Joseph, a Negro girl Pleasant; sons William BASYE & Joseph BASYE exors; WITS: Thos. BROWN, Robt. FORESTER, Thornton SAMPSON [admin with the will annexed granted to Wm. BASYE, 8 May 1826]. (NC RB 24:70)
[Isaac BASYE mar. Sally POPE, dau. of Geo. POPE, NC, lic. 22 Dec 1772 (MWO:31); Sally BASYE, dau. of Isaac BASYE, mar. Jn. HARDING, NC, bond 9 Jan 1799 (MLBNC:45)]

BASYE, Jesse; Jesse BASYE was the father of Elismond, Judith (who mar. Thos. WEBB), Mary (who mar. Epaphroditus FIELDING), Elizabeth (who mar. George SAMPSON) and Jesse BASYE who were complts. against Caty BETTS (the wife of Jordan BETTS) and the wid. of Moses SUTTON and [fnu] PITMAN; the complts. state that Moses SUTTON as the gdn. of Elismond BASYE took possession of the est. of Jesse BASYE; they wish the est. of SUTTON to be sold and the proceeds div. (NC CC 1812-020)
[Caty PITMAN, wid., mar. Moses SUTTON, wid., NC, bond 11 Jan 1793; Caty SUTTON, wid., mar. Jordan BETTS, NC, bond 2 Feb 1809 (MLBNC:9, 96); Judith BASYE mar. Thos. WEBB, LC, bond 30 Sep. 1786 (MLBLC:78)]

BAYNE, Matthew; 2 Jan 1802; 25 Jan 1802
WC; INV of a part of the est. of Matthew BAYNE which has been recovered by law of Henry GLASS since the first INV was returned: Winney, Flora, Rachel, [Mary], Polly, Jeany, Anthony; Peter & William born since the [first inv.]; £290.0.0. (WC RI 8:156)

BAYNE, Matthew; PO Nov 1803, T 1 Jan 1804; 26 Nov 1804
WC; DIV of Negroes; Lot 1 to Elizabeth M. BAYNE: Sue, Jenny, Rose, Harry; Lot 2 to Richard BAYNE: Aaron, Minney, Rachael, William; Lot 3 to Martha BAYNE: Joshua, Dafney, Fill, Florah, Peter; Lot 4 to John BAYNE: Bet & child Mariah, Winney, Moses, Polley, Anthony. (WC RI 8:512)

[This is prob. the Matthew BAYNE who mar. Caty HARRISON, wid., WC, bond 31 Auf 1789 (MLBWC:5); on the mot. of Rich. PAYNE ex. of Matthew BAYNE ord. to settle sd. PAYNE's acct. as ex. and possess Jn. PAYNE gdn. of Jn. and Rich. BAYNE with their parts of Matthew BAYNE's ext., 25 Apr 1799 (WC Orders 1799-1801:2); Rich, PAYNE aptd. gdn. of Martha BAYNE orphan of Matthew BAYNE, 26 Aug 1799 (WC Orders 1799:1801:102); a chancery suit to div. land involved Jn. & Rich. BAYNE infants under 21 by Jn. PAYNE their gdn. and Martha BAYNE by Rich. PAYNE her gdn. against Geo. BRUCE and Eliz. his wife who was Eliz. BAYNE, 25 Jan 1808 (WC Orders 1807-10:128, 268; Orders 1810-13:69; CCs 1804-030, 1808-007)]

BEACHAM, [Abraham]; PO 11 May 1807, T 3 May 1807; 13 Jul 1807
NC; DIV of Negroes; Lot 1 (Nancy & George) to George L. BEACHAM, Lot 2 (Letty & Betty) to Abraham BEACHAM, Lot 3 (Fanny & Hannah) to James BEACHAM, Lot 4 (Sally, Jane, James & Bryan) to Elizabeth L. FORTT. (NC RB 17:560)

BEACHAM, A[braham]; PO 12 Apr 1808; 8 May 1809
NC; DIV of est. recovered by a decree in favor of Eliza L. [FORTT], George L. BEACHAM, Abraham BEACHAM & James BEACHAM by their next friend Eliza L.; after deducting expenses attending the said prosecution and three others against Thomas BEACHAM, George L. BEACHAM and Samuel L. BEACHAM for the recovery of sundry Negroes of them the sum of £330.13.4, £248.0.0 which we did possess Abraham BEACHAM with in right of himself and as attorney for Eliza L. FORTT to William CLAUGHTON and as attorney from Sary BEACHAM who was attorney from George L. BEACHAM to receive of sd. CLAUGHTON on acct. of sd. decree we also did possess William CLAUGHTON as gdn. of James BEACHAM with the sum of £82.13.4 which sum appeared to be each claimant's distributable part. (NC RB 18:145)
[Thos., Geo. & Sam. L. were sons of Abraham & Leasure (WEST) BEACHAM (MWO:32); Geo. BEACHAM d. unmarried and intest. without issue in 1814 entitled to 1/3 of the price of 1200 ac. in Harrison Co. as per the will of his father (NC CC 1817-007); the births of 7 children to Abraham & Leasure BEACHAM are rec. in the SSPR: Eliza (1755), Jn. West (1758), James (1767), Isaac (1771), Geo. Leasure & Griffin (1774), Sam. Lamkin (1778) (SSPR:15, 16, 17, 18, 20, 21); Abraham & Leasure had at least 1 other child, Wm., as shown in the will of their grand father Jn. WEST (NC 4 Jan 1759-10 Dec 1759) (NC RB 5:156); *see also NC CC 1807-003*]

BEACHAM, Daniel; PO 8 Oct 1810, T 3 Jan 1811; 14 Jan 1811
NC; DIV of Negroes at house of Capt. Thomas BEACHAM; Lot 1 (Dick, Mima, Alfred) to Molley F. BEACHAM, Lot 2 (Isaac, Mary, Daniel & Isaac [sic]) to Bushrod M. BEACHAM, Lot 3 (Abram & Jane) to Daniel W. BEACHAM. (NC RB 18:517)
[Polly F. BEACHAM, orphan of Dan. BEACHAM, chose Geo. L. BEACHAM her gdn., NC, 10 Feb 1812 (NC OB 1811-15:43)]

BEACHAM, George L.; [m]; 14 Apr 1817. NC; INV, $125.18 3/4. (NC RB 21:176)
[George Leasure BEACHAM (and his twin Griffin, who prob. died young) was a son of Abraham and Leasure (WEST) BEACHAM; he was b. in SSP, NC, on 10 Oct 1774 (SSPR:20)]

BEACHAM, George L.; PO 15 Oct 1817, T 7 Mar 1818; 9 Mar 1818
NC; Chancery suit; Thomas BEACHAM complt. against George L. BEACHAM, William COUNCILMAN & Elizabeth his wife, Abraham & James BEACHAM, which sd. George, Elizabeth, Abraham & James are

children of William BEACHAM dec'd, Alice L. G. B. TURNER only child of Elizabeth TURNER dec'd, Thomas TARPLEY and Jane L. his wife, which Jane L. is the only child of John W. BEACHAM dec'd, Bushrod McF. & Daniel W. BEACHAM only children of Daniel BEACHAM dec'd and Harriett R. BEACHAM only child of Samuel L. BEACHAM defts; Griffin EDWARDS appointed gdn. to Harriett R. BEACHAM an infant under 21; lands belonging to George L. BEACHAM in Harrison, Lewis and Northumberland (in Mondays Neck) counties to be div. among complt. & defts. as follows: to Thomas BEACHAM one eq. sixth part, to George L. BEACHAM, William COUNCILMAN & Elizabeth his wife, Abraham & James BEACHAM one eq. sixth part, to Alice L. G. B. TURNER one eq. sixth part, to Thomas TARPLEY & Jane L. his wife one eq. sixth part, to Bushrod McF. & Daniel W. BEACHAM one eq. sixth part, and to Harriett R. BEACHAM one eq. sixth part; div. of tract of land in Mondays Neck on main road leading to Mondays Point; Lot 1 (half of the tract) to William HENDERSON (who purchased the right of the heirs of John W. BEACHAM, Daniel BEACHAM and the heirs of Elizabeth TURNER dec'd; Lot 2 (the one third of the other half) to Harriett R. BEACHAM [*1 wd unclear*] of Samuel L. BEACHAM dec'd; Lot 3 (the one third as above) to the heirs of William BEACHAM; Lot 4 (the one third as above) to Thomas BEACHAM. (NC RB 21:372; CC 1817-007)

BEACHAM, Parker; 10 Dec 1827
NC; on the mot. of Mary LEWIS, ord. that Griffin HEADLEY, Ruth BEACHAM, Susan BEACHAM, William COOKMAN & William HUDSON heirs of Parker BEACHAM be summoned to show cause why the lands of sd. Parker BEACHAM should not be sold. (NC OB 1825-30:223)
[Parker BEACHAM mar. Susanna DOUGLAS, dau. of Jn. & Susanna DOUGLAS, bef. 22 Nov 1763; the births of several of their children are rec. in the SSPR: Mary & Eliz. (1763), Ruth (1766), Susanna (1768), Mary (1771), Jn. (1775), Wm. Trussell & Martha Hall (1778) (MWO:32); Mary BEACHAM mar. Jeremiah LEWIS, NC, 1784 (MWO:226); Griffin HEADLEY mar. Martha H. BEACHAM with the consent of Parker & Susanna BEACHAM, NC, bond 12 Jan 1803 (MLBNC:52)]

BEACHAM, Samuel L.; PO 11 Nov 1807, T 13 Nov 1807; 12 Mar 1810
NC; INV, £592.12.9; includes 1 steel mounted gun, 1 large musket, one brass mounted gun and 1 old gun, several books including a dictionary, *Everyman's Own Lawyer*, *Letters on Ireland*, and Knox's *Sermons* and Negroes Siller, boys Mitchel, George & Asman, girl Amey (died before the sale of Negroes), Monk, Rachel, old man James, boy Peter, Harry. (NC RB 18:341)
[Samuel Lamkin BEACHAM was a son of Abraham and Leasure (WEST) BEACHAM; he was b. in SSP, NC, on 17 Sep 1778 (SSPR:21); he had been dead over 3 mos. as of 10 Nov 1807 when the sheriff of NC was ord. to admin. his est. (NC OB 1807-11:12); on 14 Mar 1814 the court ord. that Thos. E. NUTT be allotted the dower of his wife Alice [sic] K. in the est. of her late husb. Sam. L. BEACHAM (NC OB 1811-15:222, but in a later record Thos. E. NUTT's wife is named Mary K. (NC OB 1811-15:345)), marriage bonds show that Sam. L. BEACHAM mar. Mary K. EDWARDS, NC, bond 7 Feb 1801 and Thos. E. NUTT mar. Mary K. BEACHAM, wid., NC, bond 22 May 1812 (MLBNC:6, 78); Harriet BEACHAM orphan of Sam. L. BEACHAM chose Griffin EDWARDS as her gdn., NC, 9 Sep 1816 (NC OB 1816-20:86)]

BEACHAM, Thomas; PO Jul 1789; 15 Dec 1789

NC; settled Parker BEACHAM's acct. of admin. of the est. of Thomas BEACHAM & div. £30.2.0 among: Salley BEACHAM, John BEACHAM, Nancy T. BEACHAM. (NC GA 1788-1824:39)

BEACHAM, Thomas (Capt.); T 29 Jun 18[??]; 10 Nov 1823
NC; INV; includes Negroes old Negro man [nfi], Polly & child, boy Joe, girl Winney and several books among them *Discipline of the Methodist Church*, Wesley's & Whitfield's sermons, and 2 hymn books. (NC RB 23:373)

BEACHAM, Trussell; PO 13 Apr 1801; 12 Oct 1801. NC; INV, £2.19.7 1/2. (NC RB 16:291)
[Trussell BEACHAM was a son of JN. BEACHAM (d. NC 1784) (NC RB 12:273); he mar. Molly CLAUGHTON, wid. of Thos. CLAUGHTON (d. NC 1783), on 15 Oct 1784 (MWO:32)]

BEACHAM, William; William BEACHAM was the son of Abraham and Leasure BEACHAM and the father of Elizabeth L. FORTT, George L. W. BEACHAM, Abraham BEACHAM and James BEACHAM (NC CC 1807-003; *see also Abraham BEACHAM above*)

BEALE, Alfred; 18 Mar 1813; 4 Oct 1813
RC; WILL; dau. Susan Fauntleroy Tomlin the whole of the Negro slaves which I got by her mother my first wife & also Negro man Joe & also chest of drawer made by Tarpley McCARTY; dau. Alice Olivia slaves I got by my marriage with her mother my late wife Millian; rest of est. to be eq. div. between 2 daus.; suit of clothes to my father's servant William; my father Richard BEALE & friends Bartholomew McCARTY, Joseph B. DOWNMAN & Rawleigh W. DOWNMAN exors; WITS: Feriol LEMOINE, Geo. W. DOWNMAN, Jn. RICE. (RC WB 9:432)
[An Alfred BEALE mar. Susanna F. TOMLIN, RC, bond 2 Mar 1805 (MRC:12)]

BEALE, Charles; 1 Mar 1816 - 1 Jul 1816
RC; WILL; bros. James BEALE, Reuben BEALE & George BEALE all right, title & interest to the Chestnut Hill tract I hold in reversion and which is now in the possession of my mother to be eq. div. among them; sisters Mildred EWELL, Eliza BEALE, Marion HAMILTON and Winnefred T. BEALE my interest in the dower Negroes which my mother has in her possession; niece Fanny FOUSHEE my interest in the slaves which George CHRISTOPHER now holds and which were the property of my late bro. William C. BEALE; nephew Thomas E. FOUSHEE land I hold in reversion in WC and which was the property of my late bro. William C. BEALE; rest of property to my mother; bros. James & George BEALE exors; WITS: Benj. REYNOLDS, Hen. PACKET, Wm. RICHARDS. (RC WB 9:529)
[Chas. BEALE was a son of Thos. (d. RC 1799) & Sinah BEALE of Chestnut Hill, LP, RC. (RC WB 9:123); Mildred BEALE mar. Jesse EWELL, RC, bond 12 Nov 1799, Marion or Maria BEALE, dau. of Sinah BEALE, mar. Wm. B. HAMILTON, RC, bond 9 Jul 1803. (MRC:66, 85)]

BEALE, Eliza; PO [Nov] 1815, T 1 Dec 1821; 3 Dec 1821
RC; DIV.; distrib. of surplus of the est. to Sinah BEALE, Reuben BEALE, Mildred EWELL, Maria HAMILTON, Winifred BROOKE, Fanny FOUSHEE, Geo. BEALE, each to receive $17.18 1/2; and Ann H. BELFIELD to receive $8.59. (RC AB 4:20)
[Fanny BEALE, dau. of Thos. BEALE, mar. Francis FOUSHEE of NC on 21 Oct 1798, RC, bond 19 Oct 1798 (MRC:71)]

BEALE, George; T 10 Sep 1822; 2 Dec 1822

RC; INV, [m]; includes Negroes: Jerre, Ben, Ben [sic], Will, Betty, Betty (young girl, infirm). (RC WB 10:11)

BEALE, James; 17 Dec 1817; 6 Jan 1818
RC; WILL; I lend my sis. Mildred EWELL my Negro boy Moses, after her death to her son Jesse EWELL; sis. Maria HAMILTON my Negro boy [Troalous]; I lend my Negro woman Molley to Mrs. Ann CHRISTOPHER for 4 years and then she is to have her freedom; Edwin REYNOLDS son of Alice REYNOLDS $150; sis. BELFIELD; bro. George BEALE; $300 in hands of exors. for Fanny & Thomas [P.] FOUSHEE to be put out at interest which they are to receive until age 21 when they are to receive the principal; nephew Robert BEALE; nephew Jesse EWELL; $100 to Julia RICHARDS; all remaining property to be eq. div. among sisters Mildred EWELL, Mariah HAMILTON & bro. George BEALE; bro. George & Mr. George CHRISTOPHER exors; WITS: Robt. FAUNTLEROY, Robt. REYNOLDS, Cath. EVANS. (RC WB 9:597)

BEALE, Jesse B.; PO May 1810; 4 Nov 1817. RC; INV, £364.13.9. (RC WB 9:574)

BEALE, Reuben [m]; 24 Nov 1823
WC; DIV of lands of Reuben BEALE dec'd in RC & also the lands in WC descended to the heirs in right of their mother who was Eliza T. TURBERVILLE from their uncle Maj. John TURBERVILLE; Lot 1 (413 3/4 ac. in WC part of the Narrows adj Geo. CHRISTOPHER near the bridge) to Robert BEALE, Lot 2 (balance of the Narrows Tract containing 463 3/4 ac) to Felicia Corbin BEALE, Lot 3 (tract in RC known as Clear View & a small tract with a mill seat known by the name of the Vestry House & 17 ac. a part of the Chestnut Hill Tract & also 1106 ac. a part of the Hickory Hill Tract allotted to the above named heirs in the div. of the est. of the late Maj. John TURBERVILLE) to John Turberville BEALE. (WC RI 11:377)
[Reuben BEALE, bro. of Wm. C. BEALE, mar. Eliza Taylor TURBERVILLE, WC, bond 28 Apr 1800 (MLBWC:5); Reuben BEALE was aptd. gdn. to his children Robt., John T., and Felitia C., RC 2 Sep 1816 (RC OB 24:38, 70); Robt. BEALE is gdn. to Jn. T. and Felicia C. BEALE orphans of Reuben BEALE, 7 Mar 1825 (RC OB 26:282); settlement of Robt. BEALE's gdnship. acct. with his ward Jn. T. BEALE orphan of Reuben BEALE, 2 Oct 1826 (RC OB 27:118); settlement of Robt. BEALE's gdnship. accts. with his wards Jn. T. BEALE & Felicia C. BEALE orphans of Reuben BEALE, 5 Mar 1827 (RC OB 27:146)]

BEALE, Reuben; PO 22 Dec 1823; 23 Feb 1824
WC; DIV of slaves; Lot 1 (Solomon, Sam, Stephen, Patty & infant, Alice & infant, Washington, Judith & Lucy) to John Turberville BEALE, Lot 2 (Daniel, Dick, [Philice], Winny & infant, Sally & infant, Alice, Fanny, Old Rachel) to Felicia Corbin BEALE, Lot 3 (Billy, George, Patty, Ewell, Joshua, Old Billy & Old Prue, Lavina & infant William) to Robert BEALE Jr. (WC RI 11:385)

BEALE, Richard; 25 Feb 1819; 6 Sep 1819
NFP, RC; WILL; Negroes Betty, Martin, Vincent & Sary to dau. Lucinda MOSS also every article of property I possess upon this earth; after her death I give it to be eq. div. between my two grandchildren Harriet A. MOSS & Richard H. MOSS, except Bill who is to be free; friends Henry M. DOBYNS & Warner L. TAPSCOTT & dau. Lucinda MOSS exors; [no WITS]. (RC WB 9:626)
[Richard BEALE mar. Alice Griffin COLSTON, dau. of Chas. COLSTON bef. 27 May 1785 (MWO:33); Lucinda BEALE mar. (1) John A. MOSS, RC, bond 5 Oct 1808 and (2) Wm. McCARTY, RC, bond 20 Sep 1820 (MRC:124, 139); the

land which Rich. BEALE died seized in right of his wife Alice Griffin was div. among: Townsend D. PEYTON & Harriet his wife, Lucinda MOSS and Alice Olivia BEALE (RC OB 24:351)]

BEALE, Samuel Sr.; 2 May 1811; 22 Jan 1816
CP, WC; WILL; wife Alice BEALE to have use of land & plant. w/o I now live until her youngest child now living with her arrive to the age of 21 or until that period of time the better to enable her to raise her children and then the law to provide; tho in case she die before that time the profits of the same to go to the support of the three youngest children until they arrive to 21; sd. land & plant. to go to son Thomas BEALE after my wife's period of time are out; moveable property to be eq. div. among rest of my children including John Beale HARRIS & Ewell Beale HARRIS excepting my son Samuel BEALE; $8 to be deducted out of Anna HAMMOCK's part for property already had; wife & son John Beale HARRIS exors; WITS: Wm. MOORE, Hen. BEALE, Stephen OLIVE. (WC DW 23:142)
[Samuel BEALE mar. Alice HARRIS (who must have been a wid. at the time), WC, bond 9 Oct 1792 (MLBWC:5); Anna BEALE, dau. of Sam. BEALE, mar. Jn. HAMMOCK, RC, bond 26 Jun 1799 (MRC:85)]

BEALE, Samuel; T 6 Feb 1816; 24 Jun 1816. WC; INV. [m]. (WC RI 10:75)

BEALE, Samuel [Jr.] [m] May 1809 - 24 Apr 1815
CP, WC; WILL; all land to two daus. Sarah BEALE & Polly; Sarah to have all that part that I bought of George GARNER except 5 ac. which is to be taken off adjoining the lands formerly MIDDLETON's which 5 ac. and the remaining part of my lands I give to my dau. Polly with this proviso that if either dau. should die without heir or should not arrive to the age of 21, the whole to the survivor; if both daus. die without heirs or not arrive to 21, all lands to go to my bro. Robert BEALE; friend Thomas STOWERS ex; WITS: Thos RIGMAIDEN, Franc[i]s MOORE, [Habern] MOORE, Jeremiah JONES. (WC DW 23:95)
[Walter SELF aptd. gdn. to Polly BEALE orphan of Sam. BEALE Jr., 22 May 1815 (WC OB 1814-18:125)]

BEALE, Sinah; 26 Nov 1816; 5 Feb 1817
RC; WILL; tract called Stony Hill which was willed to me by my late son Charles BEALE & my interest in the land at Chestnut Hill which fell to me by my late dau. Eliza BEALE; Negro woman Betty to dau. Winifred T. BEALE; daus. Mildred EWELL, Maria HAMILTON & Winifred T. BEALE all my interest in the dower Negroes at Chestnut Hill which I hold by the death of my late children Jesse B. BEALE & Eliza BEALE also my part of the Negroes which the sd. Eliza BEALE had in possession at her death; sons James BEALE, Reuben BEALE & George BEALE my interest in the Negroes now in the possession of George CHRISTOPHER which was held in reversion by my late children Thomas S. BEALE, Jesse B. BEALE & Eliza BEALE; $50 each to grandchildren Fanny B. FOUSHEE & Thomas [E.] FOUSHEE; rest of est. to be eq. div. among children Mildred EWELL, James BEALE, Reubin BEALE, Maria HAMILTON, Winifred T. BEALE, & George BEALE; sons James BEALE & Reuben BEALE exors; WITS: Hen. PACKETT, Geo BROOKE, Austin BROCKENBROUGH RC WB 9:544)
[Sinah BEALE was the wid. of Thos. BEALE (d. RC 1799) and dau. of Col. James BALL of LC (MWO 33; RC WB 9:123); Miller:151 locates Stony Hill in RC between Singerly and Rappahannock Church]

BEALE, Thomas I.; PO Jan 1808; 5 Jul 1808

RC; INV; £707.7.0, includes Negroes: man Isaac, woman Jenny & 2 children Molly & Jacob, Beck, Amy, boy Tom, boy [Warney], woman Betty & 2 children Beckey & Lewis, girl Merilla, girl Suckey, girl Fanny, old man Warney. (RC WB 9:332)

BEALE, William C.; T 5 Feb 1803; 25 Apr 1803
WC; INV, £570.4.0.; inludes Negroes Billy (carpenter), Richard (carpenter), James, [Colchester], Aggy, Isabella (child), John (carpenter), Nanny (old). (WC RI 8:210)

BEALE, William Currie; 26 Nov 1802; 24 Jan 1803
WC; WILL; land on Ragged Point adj. land of heirs of Richard JACKSON to wife Ann during her life then to be div. between bros. Charles & George BEALE; if either bro. should die before he comes of age his portion to go to friend Thomas BELFIELD of RC; Negro man Farnham to wife and after her death to be freed; wife also to have Negroes Mary, Old Nanny & Little Nanny; friend Francy FOUSHEE of WC to receive half the profits for 7 years of the mill that belonged to my father for repairing her; Thomas ENOS; neighbor Thomas HUTT; wearing clothes to servant Farnham; bro Reubin BEALE & friends Willoughby NEWTON, John PEAKE, & Thomas HUTT exors; WITS: Solomon REDMAN, Wm. McKENNEY. (WC DW 20:413)
[Wm. Currie BEALE was the son of Thos. BEALE of LP, RC (d. RC 1799) and bro. of Thos. S., James, Reuben, Jesse B., Chas., Geo., Robt. T., Fanny, Anne H., Mildred, Eliza, Maria and Winifred T. (RC WB 9:123); his wid., Ann BEALE, mar. Geo. CHRISTOPHER, WC, bond 18 Jul 1803 (MLBWC:13); additional info. on this family is found in a WC CC (WCCP:53, 75); Miller (p. 131) locates Ragged Point in WC on Coles Neck east of Lower Machodoc Creek]

BEAN, George; PO 13 Mar 1809, T 24 Mar 1809; 8 May 1809. NC; INV, [m]. (NC RB 18:147)

BEAN, George; 8 May 1809
NC; George BEANE, John BEANE, Lydia BEANE, August PITMAN who mar. Peggy BEANE, Vincent THOMAS who mar. Sukey BEANE and Richard BEANE are heirs of George BEANE dec'd. (NC OB 1807-11:102)
[Augustine PITMAN mar. Peggy BEANE, NC, bond 1 Mar 1802 (MLBNC:82); Vincent THOMAS mar. Sukey BEANE, LC, bond 24 May 1808 (MLBLC:73); lands which Geo. BEANE died seized in right of his wife Susanna to be sold (NC OB 1807-11:113)]

BEAN, George; PO 12 Jun 1809; 14 May 1810
NC; sale of lands which George BEAN died seized in right of his wife Susanna BEAN dec'd; 50 ac. sold to John BEAN for $106 and each claimant possessed with a bond (John BEAN excepted); claimants were George BEAN, Vincent THOMAS who mar. Sukey BEAN, Augustine PITMAN who mar. Peggy BEAN, William PITMAN who mar. Lydia BEAN, George BEAN gdn. for Richard BEAN, and John BEAN. (NC RB 18:392)
[Wm. PITMAN mar. Lidda R. BEAN, LC, bond 24 Nov 1809 (MLBLC:60, 73)]

BEAN, William B.; PO 13 Mar 1809, T 24 Mar 1809; 8 May 1809
NC; INV, [m], includes parcel of "giner's" tools. (NC RB 18:146)

BEANE, Edward; PO 16 Aug 1824; 17 May 1825
LC; INV, [m]; includes Negroes Richard, Spencer, Sinah, boys Joe, Harry, and Tom. (LC EB 29:436)
[Silas BEANE chose Geo. E. BEANE as his gdn., 17 Jan 1825; on the mot. of Ro. E. BEANE ord. that Nicholas P. BUCHAN who mar. Polly BEANE, Geo.

BEANE, Edw. BEANE & Silas BEANE be summoned to show cause why the land of which Edw. BEANE died seized should not be sold and the proceeds div. among his heirs, 17 Jan 1825 (LC OB 26:96, 97); Nicholas P. BUCHAN mar. Polly BEANE, LC, bond 5 Feb 1816 (MLBLC:10)]

BEANE, John; 6 Jun 1805; 21 Oct 1805

LC; WILL; sons Thomas & Opie BEANE; wife Leannah BEANE to have choice of two Negroes; Negro girl Mary to dau. Molly LOCKE; Negro girl Sally to dau. Judith CLARKE; Negro girl Sinah to son Edwin BEANE; dau. Milly HUTCHINGS; at wife's death whole est. to be eq. div. among my eight children: Peter, Molly, John, Edwin, Judith, Milly, Thomas & Opie; sons Peter & John, Jos. LOCKE and Rich. HUTCHINGS exors; WITS: Thos. CARTER, Thos. HUTCHINGS. (LC WB 28:91)

[Molly BEANE mar. Jos. LOCKE, LC, bond 6 Jul 1785; Milly BEANE mar. Rich. HUTCHINGS, LC, bond 17 Dec 1791 (MLBLC:41, 48); Judith BEANE mar. Gardner CLARK, LC, bond 3 Nov 1795 (MWO:77); Opie BEANE was b. 28 Mar 1780 and mar. Sally H. CROWDER (b. 12 Dec 1787) dau. of Eliz. CROWDER, NC, bond 23 Nov 1805 (MLBNC:7, BNCHS vol. IV, no. 1:49)]

BEANE, Peter; 5 Dec 1820 - 16 Aug 1824

LC; WILL; my land & plant. called Mosquito to son Thomas J. BEANE if he has an heir, but if he does not, land & plant. to grson. Peter Henry BEANE; son Thomas J. also to have my Negro boy Henry; $500 for the education of grson. Peter Henry & he is to have Negro woman Dolley; Negro woman Rose to grdau. Ann C. CHILTON; balance of est. to be eq. div. between Leanna CHILTON during her life & at her death to her heirs, my son Peter & my grson. Peter Henry; small piece of land on Carter's Creek containing about 10 ac. lately sold to me by [William] H. GEORGE & Bailey GEORGE to son Peter; [no ex. named]; [no wits listed]; [when will was presented the court's opinion was that it was not the legal will of Peter BEANE; Henry C. LAWSON, gdn. to Peter H. BEANE prayed an appeal to the Superior Court of LC which was allowed; the case, Henry C. LAWSON against Thomas J. BEANE & Cyrus CHILTON, was heard on 10 Sep 1824, and the lower court's judgment was reversed; sd. will was ord to be recorded on 20 Sep 1824]. (LC WB 28:253)

[Leanna BEANE mar. Cyrus CHILTON, LC, bond 18 Jun 1804 (MLBLC:13)]

BEARCROFT, Mottrom; PO 2 Nov 180[?]; 12 Dec 1803. NC; INV, [m]. (NC RB 17:87)

BEARCROFT, Thomas; PO 9 Dec 1811, T 1 Jan 1812; 14 Dec 1812. NC; INV, [m]. (NC RB 19:277)

BEATLEY, Ahira; PO 12 Dec 1808, T 14 Jan 1809; 13 Feb 1809

NC; Jesse WALKER's acct. of guardianship of the sd. dec'd and DIV of est. among the heirs: W. G. BEATLEY, Sally BEATLEY, James BEATLEY, Rodham [sic] BEATLEY, Rushworth BEATLEY, Elias & Elizabeth EDWARDS, Frances BEATLEY, [Butcher] BEATLEY. (NC RB 18:116)

[Ahira BEATLEY was the dau. of Wm. & Eliz. BEATLEY, (see below); the heirs of Hira [sic] BEATLEY were named as: Elias EDWARDS & Eliz. his wife, Francis BEATLEY, Butcher BEATLEY, Waidy G. BEATLEY, Sally BEATLEY, James BEATLEY, Rushworth BEATLEY, and Rhoda BEATLEY, NC, 12 Dec 1808 (NC OB 1807-11:75); see also NC CC 1809-004]

BEATLEY, Elizabeth; PO 9 May 1808, T 17 May 1808; 13 Jun 1808. NC; INV, [m]. (NC RB 17:638)

[This is the wid. of Wm. BEATLEY, *see below*]

BEATLEY, Frances; PO 13 Apr 1818; 14 Dec 1818. NC; INV, [m]. (NC RB 21:556)

BEATLEY, Francis; 8 Feb 1819
NC; Jn. ROBINSON aptd. gdn. of James BEATLEY orphan of Francis BEATLEY. (NC OB 1816-20:329)
[This is prob. the Francis BEATLEY who mar. Eliz. ROBERTSON, NC, bond 20 Nov 1806 (MLBNC:7)]

BEATLEY, John; T 8 Jun 1803; 13 Jun 1803
NC; William TIGNOR rec'd £10 and one cow & calf in full for his wife Sally's proportional part & legacy of her father's (John BEETLY) dec'd est. (NC RB 17:9)
[Wm. TIGNOR, wid. mar. Sarah BEATLEY, NC, 8 Dec 1800 (MLBNC:101)]

BEATLEY, John; PO 14 Jan 1811; 8 Jun 1812. NC; INV, [m]. (NC RB 19:196)

BEATLEY, William; PO 10 Jan 1804, T 1 Feb 1804; 13 Feb 1804
NC; INV, £255.13.1; includes Negroes Chloe, boy Spencer. (NC RB 17:117)

BEATLEY, William; PO 10 Jan 1804, T 1 Feb 1804; 13 Feb 1804
NC; DIV of est. among the wid. Elizabeth BEETLY, Francis BEETLY, William B. BEETLY, Elizabeth BEETLY, James BEETLY, Wady BEETLY, Sally BEETLY, [Ahira] BEETLY, Rhoda BEETLY, Rusha BEETLY; the wid. rec'd her dower of £85.4.4 1/2 and each heir rec'd £18.18.8 3/4. (NC RB 17:118)
[In her will (NC 7 Oct 1807-15 Mar 1808) Eliz. BEATLEY named only dau. Rhoda and son Rushia (NC RB 17:612); Ahira BEATLEY chose Jesse WALKER her gdn. and he was also gdn. of Rhoda & Rusha BEATLEY; Sally BEATLEY chose Thos. W. GOFF as her gdn., NC 12 Oct 1807 (NC OB 1807-11:2)]

BEATLEY, William B.; PO 10 Nov 1823; 8 Mar 1824. NC INV. (NC RB 23:435)

BECKWITH, Jonathan; 4 Aug 1824 - 6 Sep 1824
RC; WILL; to [Sillar] MAIDEN & her two sons, Landen & Mattimore, the lot w/o Christopher MOZINGO lives containing 10 or 12 ac. together with the annual rents as they shall become due from Betty HALL & sisters for the land on which they live; as I am giving Col. John BELFIELD a sum of money for which he has a deed of trust on my land and as I wish to give Barnes BECKWITH the remainder of my land, all the remaining part of my pers. prop. to be sold; to Barnes BECKWITH all the remaining part of my land & my gold repeating watch, which is an old family piece, provided that he pay David GREENLAW the money I borrowed of him; Col. John BELFIELD & Barnes BECKWITH exors; WITS: Sam. TEMPLEMAN, Wm. BURGESS, Thos. SPENCE, Jn. FERGUSON; [BELFIELD refused to be ex. & Barnes BECKWITH lived in a remote part of the state; Joshua REAMY was appointed curator of the est]. (RC WB 10:47)

BECKWITH, Jonathan (Sir); PO Feb 1797; 6 Jul 1801
RC; INV; includes the following slaves: Davy, Dido, Salley & her child Aphia, Patience & her child Daniel, Patience, Sarah, Coleman, Silvia, Winney, Phoebe, David, James, Billey, Willoughby, Jacob, Tom, Fanny & infant, Alice & her child, Daniel son of Fanny, Jerry, Sarah & child Patty, Ruffin, Harriet; Negroes for which a suit is now pending in the High Court of Chancery, Alexander HOOE & others against BECKWITH & others: Moses, Humphrey, Aaron, Joe, Kitt, Old Joe, Bett, Old Betty. (RC WB 9:153)

BECKWITH, Jonathan; PO 6 Sep 1824; 2 Aug 1825
RC; INV, [m]; includes two Negroes Kit (a shoemaker) & Peter BUTTON. (RC WB 10:81)

BELFIELD, Ann H.; PO 5 Mar 1824; 5 Jul 1824
RC; sale of slaves Sucky & Sophy late the prop. of Mrs. Ann H. BELFIELD & the slaves Daniel & Martha in which the sd. Ann H. BELFIELD & her dau.

Mrs Alice C. WOOLLARD held a joint interest and a div. among the legal distributees of sd. Ann H. BELFIELD who were John W. BELFIELD, Joseph BELFIELD, Thomas M. BELFIELD, David C. BELFIELD, Samuel B. KELSICK, Alice C. WOOLLARD, Ann C. BOUGHTON & John E. DAINGERFIELD infant child of Elizabeth Mildred DAINGERFIELD who was Elizabeth Mildred BELFIELD. (RC AB 4:130))
[Ann Harwar (BEALE) BELFIELD was the wid. of Thos. BELFIELD (1745-1804) whom she mar. in RC, bond 25 Oct 1780; Sam. B. KELSICK mar. Jane C. BELFIELD, dau. of Thos. & Ann Harwar (BEALE) BELFIELD, RC, bond 13 May 1800; Wm. DAINGERFIELD mar. Eliz. M. B. BELFIELD, RC, bond 20 Dec 1814; Ann C. B. BELFIELD mar. Anderson BOUGHTON, RC, bond 2 Oct 1821 (MRC:15-16, 21, 48, 111)]

BELFIELD, John; 26 May 1801; 5 Oct 1801
RC; WILL; wife Ruth; sons Sydnor, Thomas; daus. Mary SMITH, Elizabeth CHINN dec'd & her children; grsons John Wright son of Thomas BELFIELD, Joseph son of Thomas BELFIELD, Thomas Merriwether son of Thomas BELFIELD & John son of Sydnor BELFIELD; son Sydnor & friend John CAMPBELL exors; WITS: R. [?] MITCHELL, Dan. LARSON, Benj. N. GARLAND, Moore FAUNTLEROY, Wm. SMITH, Martha SMITH; RC WB 9:158))
[Jn. BELFIELD (1725-1801) mar. Ruth SYDNOR, 5 Apr 1744; he was the son of Capt. Thos. Wright & Mary (MERIWETHER, COLSTON) BELFIELD; bride was the dau. of Anthony & Eliz. (DEW) SYDNOR (MWO:35)]

BELFIELD, John; 7 Jun 1802
RC; INV; £2773.1.0; includes the following slaves: Old General, Joe, Harry, Abram, Billy, James, Adam, Charles, Joe, Harry, Charles, Adam, Dick, Daniel, Jere, Patrick, Billy, Eve, Betty, Sinah, Phebe & two children Eve & Winny, Peggy & child Frank, [Alice] & child Polly, Nelly & two children [Jenny] & John, Molly & child Alice, Lucy & child Sarah, Nancy, Sukey, Patt, Lett, Yellow Patty, Hannah, Milly, Molly, Caty, Grace. (RC WB 9:176)

BELFIELD, Thomas; PO Sep 1804; 2 Jun 1806
RC; INV, £1475.8.0; includes the following Negroes: Old Betty, Old Sarah, Kate, Lucy & child, Joyce & child, Lett & child, Lett, Bett, Milly, Sophia, Willoughby, Jim, Daniel, Will, George, Bob, Isaac, Jimmy, Adam, Cyrus, Robin, Polly, Sarah. (RC WB 9:280)

BELFIELD, Thomas; PO 5 Jan 1824, T 16 Feb 1824; 7 Jun 1824
RC; DIV of slaves; to John W, BELFIELD (Lucy, age 22); to Samuel B. KELSICK (Daniel, 55; Martha, 7); to John E. DAINGERFIELD (Cyrus, 28); to Anne C. BOUGHTON (Henry); to Joseph BELFIELD (Lett, 35; William infant of Lett); to Thomas M. BELFIELD (Polly, 25); to David C. BELFIELD (Frances, badly grown; Henrietta, 5; Willoughby, 68); to Alice C. WOOLLARD (Sarah, 25; Maria, infant of Sarah). (RC AB 4:123))
[Jane C. BELFIELD, dau. of Thos. & Ann Harwar (BEALE) BELFIELD, mar. Sam. B. KELSICK, RC, bond 13 May 1800 (MRC:111); Anne C. B. BELFIELD, dau. of Thos. & Ann Harwar (BEALE) BELFIELD mar. Anderson BOUGHTON, RC, bond 2 Oct 1821 (MRC:21); Alice Corbin BELFIELD, dau. of Maj. Jn. & Mary (BECKWITH) BELFIELD, mar. (1) Peter R. GARLAND, RC, bond 9 Aug 1806 and (2) Wm. J. WOOLLARD, RC, bond 17 Apr 1813 (MRC:75, 235); Maj. John BELFIELD was a son of Capt Jn. & Ruth (SYDNOR) BELFIELD and a bro. of Thos. BELFIELD (MRC:245); on the mot. of Jn. W. BELFIELD, Jos. BELFIELD, Thos. M. BELFIELD, David C. BELFIELD, Alice C. WOOLLARD and Ann C. BOUGHTON and Jn. E.

DAINGERFIELD gdn. of Jn. E. DAINGERFIELD who is an inf. child of Eliz. M. DAINGERFIELD who was Eliz. M. DAINGERFIELD [sic], ord. that Jn. W. JONES sell Sucky & Sophia two slaves late the property of Mrs. Ann H. BELFIELD the mother of Jn. W., Jos., Thos. M., David, Alice and Ann C. BELFIELD, 3 Mar 1824 (RC OB 26:171); Eliz. M. B. BELFIELD mar. Wm. DAINGERFIELD, RC, bond 20 Dec 1814 (MRC:48)] DUPLICATED

BELL, Charles; 18 Feb 1805

LC; Thomas BELL, James BELL, Nathaniel ANDERSON & Mildred his wife formerly Mildred BELL, Elizabeth LEE formerly Elizabeth BELL, Ann GAMBLE formerly Ann BELL, & James BELL [sic] pltfs. against Charles BELL in chancery to div. the lands of Charles BELL dec'd. (LC OB 1804-05:283, Orders B23 1808-11:121)

[A chancery suit in LC explains this case: Charles BELL died without children in LC in 1791; in his will he named his wife Eliz. and brothers Jas. and Thos.; the children of Thos. are Thos., Jas., Mildred, Eliz., Ann and Chas. and they are entitled to all the lands of Chas. BELL (LC WB 20:198, CC 1809-008)]

BELL, Charles; PO 21 Dec 1813; [17 Jan 1814]

LC; INV; includes Negroes: Dinah, Nancy, Charles, Hannah & child Anthony, David, Fanny, Maria. (LC EB 27:165)

BELL, Charles; 25 Aug 1825; 7 Nov 1825

RC; WILL; son James L. BELL when 21; dau. Alice F. BELL when 21 or marries; dau. Elizabeth N. BELL when 21 or marries; son William D. BELL when 21 or marries; son Thornton P. BELL when 21 or marries; to wife Elizabeth BELL the use of my est. both real and pers. during her life or widowhood; if she marries to have her lawful dower; after wife's death est. to be eq. div. among my children: Charles L. BELL, Bartholomew BELL, James S. BELL, Alice F. BELL, Elizabeth N. BELL, William D. BELL, & Thornton P. BELL; I loan to my grson. William M. BELL an eq. part of my est. with the rest of my children except my land & mill which I desire to remain for the support and schooling of my small children until the youngest is 18; wife Elizabeth & son Charles exors; WITS: Rodham CLARKE, Thos. FRANCE, Malinda A. LAMKIN. (RC WB 10:88)

[This is prob. the Rev. Charles BELL who mar. Betsy GARLAND (wid. of Wm, GARLAND and dau. of Jas. & Alice (FORRESTER) LEWIS), RC, bond 5 Jan 1807 (MRC:16, 75)]

BELL, Elizabeth; 13 Aug 1812 - 21 Dec 1813

CCP, LC; WILL; should I die in this county or anywhere else convenient my body to be carried to Christ Church there to be interred by my husband; [Negroes] Pegg, Billy, Sukey, Peter, James, Mary, Warner, Harriett, Jane, Letty & Leroy & Mima Pegg's children to niece Elizabeth BROWN; [Negroes] Lucy, Deanna, & Sally to nephew Thomas HULL; to Thomas GASKINS [Negro] Anna; [Negro] Nathan to Richard GASKINS; to Sally BALL (Parson BALL's dau) [Negro] [Louannah]; [Negro] Easter to niece Sally LEE (dau. of my sis. LEE); my Negro girl Patty to my sis. LEE during her life & at her death I give the same to Molly LEE dau. of Kendall LEE; [Negro] Fanny to Sally LEE dau. of Richard LEE; [Negro] Lindsey to Kendall LEE's son Kendall; stock of cattle to be eq. div. between Elizabeth BROWN & Thomas HULL; Richard LEE, Richard GASKINS, Thomas BROWN; WITS: O[liver] TOWLES, Thos. GASKINS; [COD dtd. 22 Aug 1812: Jn. HULL, Thos. BROWN & Rich. GASKINS exors]. (LC WB 28:144)

BELL, Elizabeth; PO 21 Dec 1813; 20 Jun 1814

LC; INV, $4685.1 1/2; includes Negroes: Peter, Billy, Joe, Anthony, Adam, Lucy, Anna, Easter, Lavina, Nathan, Sally, Patty, Eliza, Fanny, Lindsay; admrs. with the will annexed were Thomas WEST, Thomas BUTLER, Enoch GEORGE. (LC EB 27:177)

BELL, Elizabeth; T 21 Dec 1813; 18 Sep 1815
LC; INV; includes Negroes: Joe, Anthony, Adam, Lucy, Sally, Eliza, Anna, Lavina, Nathan. (LC EB 27:255)

BELL, John; 6 Aug 1820 - 11 Sep 1820
NC; WILL; wife Elizabeth BELL; Negro girl Sarah to dau. Elizabeth Y. BUSH; s-i-l Thomas BUSH; rest of est. including house, land & Negroes to be sold and proceeds eq. div. between wife and 4 daus: Sally DOZIER, Nancy [ALFARD], Molly HEANIE & Tomzie THOMAS; each dau. to have $15 per year until they have their full parts; friend Eppa NORRIS ex; WITS: Thos. LUNSFORD, Cyrus REVERE, Jn. M. BEAN, Thos. BEAN; Eppa NORRIS relinquished his right of executorship and was granted a certificate for obtaining letters of admin. on the est. with the will annexed. (NC RB 22:402) [Eliz. Y. BELL, dau. of Jn. BELL, mar. Thos BUSH, NC, bond 18 Feb 1817; Sally S. BELL mar. Thos. DOZIER, wid., NC, bond 23 Mar 1815; Molley BELL mar. Jas. HAYNIE, wid., NC, bond 17 Jun 1813; Tomsey BELL, of Wic. Par., mar. Geo. THOMAS, NC, bond 22 Dec 1813 (MLBNC:14, 32, 49, 99)]

BELL, John; PO 11 Sep 1820; 12 Feb 1821
NC; INV, $506.06 1/4; includes Negroes boy Dick, girl Sarah. (NC RB 22:463)

BENNEHAN, Richard; 4 Jan 1814 - 4 Jul 1814
RC; Nunc. will; depositions by C. TAPSCOTT, James ALDERSON, Archelus DALE, Joseph DALE, and Charles PALMER; whole est. to wife [Catherine] for her own & family's enjoyment; wished son Dominick to be sent to school in LC; some money on hand to be used to purchase Thomas WILLIAMS' land; money owed James TUNE for a barrel of corn; James TUNE & Maj. John M. YERBY owed him for walnut planks for coffins; Rawley W. DOWNMAN should have management of est. & affairs. (RC WB 9:462) [Rich. BENNEHAN mar. Catherine OLDHAM, dau. of Wm. OLDHAM, RC, bond 17 Jan 1796 (MRC:16); Overton CARPENTER & Ann his wife, Edw. SAUNDERS & Maria his wife and Dominick BENNEHAN, complts., against Cath. BENNEHAN admx. of Rich. BENNEHAN dec'd def., 6 Feb 1826 (RC OB 27:34); Overton CARPENTER of LC mar. Ann BENNEHAN dau. of Cath. BENNEHAN, RC, bond 13 Dec 1815; Edw. SAUNDERS Jr. mar. Maria BENNEHAN, RC, bond 5 Dec 1825 (MRC:33, 180)]

BENNETT, Henry; 28 Jan 1811
WC; ord. that George GLASCOCK gdn. of the orphans of Henry BENNETT pay out of the orphans' respectively: out of Joseph BENNETT $20, out of William BENNETT $10, out of Alice BENNETT $5; Joseph & Alice's parts to be paid to Mary BENNETT and William's part to be paid to William JEWELL for their support in 1809. (WC Orders 1810-13:75)

[BENNETT], Henry; 22 Dec 1806
WC; Geo. [GLASCOCK] aptd. gdn. of John, Sally, Richard, Alice, Nancy, William and Joseph the orphans of Henry [BENNETT]. (WC Orders 1804-07:466)
[*This man's name is not clear to me; but it looks like BENNETT and is almost certainly the Hen. BENNETT in the preceeding item*]

BERKLEY, John; 14 Oct 1790 – 27 Mar 1792
WC; WILL; all lands to son John; wife Ann; dau. Molly; mother Margaret; wife, mother, and friends Lewis SMITH and William NELSON exors.; WITS:

Jn. THOMSON, Isaac STONE, Chas. WICKLIFF; John BERKLEY's est. was appraised PO 27 Mar 1792; the app. of £888.15.6 was recorded on 30 Sep 1794. (WC CC 1817-011)

[Jn. BERKLEY is the son of Wm. and Peggy BERKLEY; in his will (WC 2 Nov 1769 – 28 Jul 1772), Wm. BERKLEY named his wife Peggy and son Jn. (WC DW 15:217); Wm. BERKLEY was the ex.of Margaret BERKLEY the gdn. of Wm and Polly BERKLEY (WC CC 1817-011); Mary (= Polly, Molly) BURKLEY mar. Geo. G. BOON, WC, bond 29 Nov 1805 (MLBWC:7)]

BERKLEY, Peggy; 30 May 1801; 23 Mar 1807

WP, WC; WILL; grson. William BERKLEY slaves: Martin, Joe, Big Peter & Little Peter, Keziah, Hanna, all Keziah's children also all livestock; none of Negroes to be hired out of the neighborhood; Thomas MUSE, Charles WICLIFF, & Daniel CARMICHAEL exors; WITS: Dan'l CARMICHAEL, Jas. JETT, Thos. LENDRUM; WC DW 21:322)

[This is prob. Peggy the wid. of Wm. BERKELEY (d. WC 1772) and mother of Jn. BERKELEY, *see above* (WC DW 14:201, DW 15:217)]

BERRICK, Charles [H.]; 1 Oct 1804. RC; INV. (RC WB 9:245)

[a Chas. BERRICK mar. Eliz. CLARKE, RC, bond 26 Jan 1795 (MRC:16)]

BERRICK, David; 6 Nov 1816

RC; Chancery suit, Reuben BERRICK, Catherine BERRICK, David BERRICK, Newby BERRICK, Sarah P. BERRICK, & Elizabeth BERRICK against George BERRICK & Thomas BERRICK infants of George BERRICK dec'd, Ann Griffin BERRICK orphan of Charles F. BERRICK to show cause why the lands of David BERRICK the Elder should not be sold. (RC OB 24:56)

BERRICK, George; 1 May 1820

RC; George BERRICK orphan of George BERRICK chose John LYELL as his gdn. (RC OB 25:6)

BERRYMAN, Newton; 1 Jul 1809 - 24 Dec 1810

WC; WILL; son William BERRYMAN all lands given to me in my father's will; my little unfortunate child Winefred to the care of my son William; land I purchased of Samuel JACKSON called Green Hill & the land I bought of Henry LEE and other property, Negroes excepted, to be sold and the money arising with all Negroes to be eq. div. among rest of my children: Newton BERRYMAN, [Walter] BERRYMAN, Henry BERRYMAN, & Catherine BERRYMAN; bro. Thomas N. BERRYMAN, James HARVEY, & son William exors; WITS: Sam. BAKER, Ritchie ALSOP, Francis KEYES, Ja. HARVEY, J. STEWARD. (WC DW 22:170)

[Newton BERRYMAN is the son of Wm. BERRYMAN (d. WC 1784) (WC DW 16:210, 17:25); Catherine BERRYMAN dau. and orphan of Newton BERRYMAN chose Thos. N. BERRYMAN her gdn.; Newton BERRYMAN aptd. gdn. of Hen. BERRYMAN, also an orphan of Newton BERRYMAN, 23 Sep 1811 (WC Orders 1810-13:171)]

BERRYMAN, Newton; T 10 Jan 1811; Jul 1811

WC; INV, [m]; includes Negroes Phillip, Milly, David, Mary, Nelly & child, Willis, Polly, [Lindy], Aaron. (WC RI 9:272)

BERRYMAN, Newton; PO Feb 1814, T 18 Mar 1814; 28 Mar 1814

WC; INV, $528.66; includes Negroes Milley, girl Melindy, boy Robbin. (WC RI 9:411)

BERRYMAN, Sarah; 4 Mar 1819 - 29 May 1821

WC; WILL; deceased son Richard BERRYMAN took with him to Kentucky a Negro girl belonging to me named Charlotte which Negro it is believed will not be recovered without recourse to law, money to defray expense of a suit for that purpose and bringing her here to be deducted from the money due me in Kentucky for the hire of Negroes, the balance together with my Negroes Fleming & Flora and her offspring I give to be eq. div. amongst the children of Richard BERRYMAN; to grson. George GLASCOCK when 25 or marries my Negroes Saunders, Grace, Polly & her child Sophia, Peggy & her child Alfred, and Charlotte with [her] offspring; friends George GLASCOCK Sr., William NELSON & James DOUGLAS exors; WITS: Francis SELF, Catharine [ENNIS]. (WC DW 24:171)

BERRYMAN, Walter; 3 Nov 1814; 27 Feb 1815

WC; WILL; My sister will keep this until she sees me again, and, if I never return, the property that I left at home will be divided between my sister Catharine & bro Henry to their satisfaction without selling any of the Negroes. [no ex. or wits] [proved by oath of Alicks BERRYMAN]. (WC DW 23:64)

[Walter BERRYMAN is prob. the son of Wm. BERRYMAN (d. WC 1784); in WWCV:178 he is called "Waters" (WC DW 16:210, 17:25)]

BERRYMAN, Walter; T 13 Apr 1815; 24 Apr 1815

WC; INV, £237.6.0; includes Negroes Nell & daus. Jenny, Winney, Sally & Emily. (WC RI 9:434)

BERRYMAN, Willoughby N.; PO 12 Dec 1808; 8 Jan 1810

NC; DIV of Negroes (valued at £944) between Jane P. BERRYMAN (rec'd Dick, Sinah, Winney, Rachel, Thornly, Stephen, Willis, Nanny) and George W. BERRYMAN (son of the dec'd; rec'd Jacob, Vincent, Joe, Tabby, Isaac, Phebe, James, Bob, Silvey). (NC RB 18:284)

[Jane Presley BARECROFT, dau. of Susanna BARECROFT, mar. Newton Willoughby BERRYMAN, NC, bond 11 Dec 1792 (MLBNC:8); Jane P. the wid. of Will. N. BERRYMAN mar. Jn. B. STEELE, NC, bond 22 May 1813 (MLBNC:95, NC OB 1811-15:246, NC CC 1825-004)]

BERRYMAN, Willoughby N[ewton]; T 16 Dec 1807; 14 Mar 1810

NC; INV, $4103.28 2/3; includes Negroes Dick, Jacob, Thornley, Vincent, boys Joe, Stephen & Willias, Rachel, Sinah, Nan, Phebe, Tabby, Winney, small girl Chloe, Silva. (NC RB 18:355)

BERRYMAN, Willo[ughby] N.; PO 8 Apr 1822, T 28 Aug 1822; 12 May 1823

NC; INV of slaves includes Sinah, Jacob, Dick, boy Nace, girl Winnefred. (NC RB 23:299)

BETTS, Betsey & Jorden; 24 Mar 1818; 27 Mar 1818

NC; D of G; livestock & furniture to Hannah WILKINS, Ann WILKINS & Walter W. WILKINS; WITS: Thos. LUNSFORD, Jn. BROWN. (NC RB 21:390)

BETTS, Thomas; 20 Oct 1821 - 11 Jul 1825

NC; WILL; to dau. [Heney] TAYLOR 100 ac. tract of land in Cockarell's Neck called The Great House; at her death to go to grsons. Thomas B. TAYLOR & Frederick TAYLOR; if grsons. die without issue land to go to son Herod BETTS; to grdau. Mary Ann GRIFFETH 20 ac. tract from Burrough's line up to Polly COCKARELL's Cove with liberty to cut wood off any other land for the purpose of firewood during her life & for her mother Sarah GRIFFETH; dau. Sally GRIFFETH; to son Telus BETTS $15; to son Thomas Didimus BETTS $50 per annum; remaining part of est. to son Herod BETTS; son Herod, William APPLEBY & Benedict & Samuel BURGESS exors; WITS: Wm. NELMS, Wm. W. APPLEBY, R. B. COVINGTON Jr.; two COD dtd. 20 Oct 1821: two Negroes Sinar & Winney to grsons Thomas & Frederick TAYLOR & all HHF to son Herod BETTS; same WITS. (NC RB 24:281)

[Heney] TAYLOR is prob. Henrietta BETTS who mar. James R. TAYLOR, bond NC 30 Mar 1813 (MLBNC:98); Sarah BETTS of NC mar. Thos. GRIFFITHS of Baltimore on [18] Jun 1816 (*Baltimore Patriot & Evening Advertiser*, 19 Jun 1816, p. [2])]

BETTS, Thomas [m]; 12 Dec 1825
NC; WILL; I give my Negro woman Mary her freedom after sd. Thomas BETTS decease also all the land below the spring called Blundon's which is supposed to be five ac. adj John BLUNDON; WITS: Sam. BURGESS, Hiram DAVIS. (NC RB 24:375)

BEVANS, Thomas; PO 20 Jan 1820; 21 Jul 1800
LC; INV, £93.11.3; includes 'George;' DIV of est. to Thomas RIVEER gdn. of John BEVANS orphan of Thomas. (LC EB 24:113)
[Jn. BEVANS orphan of Thos. BEVANS chose Thos. REVEER as his gdn., 20 Jan 1800 (LC Orders 21 1799-1801:72)]

BISCOE, Hannah; T 4 Dec 1815; 19 Aug 1816. LC; INV. (LC EB 27:348)
[This is Hannah BLAKEMORE prob. the dau. of Edward BLAKEMORE of CCP, LC (d. 1777) and the wid. of Wm. BISCOE (d. LC 1812, see below) whom she mar. in LC, bond 2 Dec 1780 (LC WB 20:108, WB 22:214; MWO:40)]

BISCOE, John; 17 Nov 1823
LC; Eppa NORRIS aptd. gdn. to Henry L. BISCOE orphan of John BISCOE. (LC OB 26:2)

BISCOE, Thomas; 19 Jun 1820
LC;; admin. de bonis non of the est. of Hannah BISCOE unadministered by Thos. BISCOE granted to Jn. HUTCHINS; settlement with Kitty BISCOE admx. of Thomas BISCOE who was admr. of Hannah BISCOE. (LC OB 25:140)

BISCOE, William; 28 Dec 1798 - 20 Apr 1812
LC; WILL; whole est. to wife Hannah during her life or widowhood; if any of children come of age or marry, wife to lend them part of est; after wife's death or marriage tract of land w/o I now live to son John BISCOE; Negro girl [Vina] to dau. Sally Newton BISCOE; Negro girl Easter to dau. Elizabeth Lawson BISCOE; Negro girl Prue to dau. Molley BISCOE; all my sons to be bound to such trades as my exors. may think proper as soon as they arrive to a convenient age; wife & friends John CHOWNING & Edward BLACKMORE exors; Negro boy Perrimos to youngest child [dau] not yet christened born since the writing of this will; [no wits, but will proved by oathes of Jn. CHOWNING Jr. & Merryman PAYNE. (LC WB 28:130)
[Wm. BISCOE mar. Hannah BLAKEMORE, LC, bond 2 Dec 1780 (MLBLC:5); Eliz. L. & Polly BISCOE chose Edw. BLACKMORE as their gdn. and sd. BLACKMORE is aptd. gdn. of Nancy BISCOE orphan of Wm. BISCOE, 16 Oct 1815 (LC Orders 24:264, OB 25:108); Robt. BISCOE aptd. gdn. to Nancy BISCOE orphan of Wm. BISCOE, 19 Jul 1819 (LC OB 25:71)]

BISCOE, William; T 19 Jul 1821; 20 Aug 1821. LC; INV; John BISCOE admr. (LC EB 29:117)

BISHOP, Isaac; 27 Dec 1815 - 5 Feb 1816
RC; WILL; mother Elizabeth AYERS of the state of New Jersey; after her death to be eq. div. between Lucien B. HAINES and Ann Matilda HAINES; remainder of est. to Lucien B. HAINES and Ann Matilda HAINES; Sarah HAINES to be guardian to Lucien B. and Ann Matilda; if Sarah HAINES is pregnant; the posthumous child to receive an eq. proportion or one third of

my est; Sarah HAINES & William SETTLE exors; WITS: Vin. SHACKLEFORD, Thos. DOBYNS. (RC WB 9:502)

BISHOP, Isaac; T. 12 Jan 1816; 4 Mar 1817. RC; INV, [m]. (RC WB 9:549)

BISPHAM, Robert; 26 May 1810 - 6 Aug 1810

RC; WILL; bro. William BISPHAM tract of land I bought of Col. Vinct. REDMAN & where Charles R. THOMPSON now resides; sis. Margaret BISPHAM $1,000 in bonds & tract of land w/o John HOLT now lives after the death of John & his wife Jane; Negroes Frankey & her 2 children Nancy & Lucy; wife Ann to have house plant. & mill; after wife's death house & mill to go to 2 daus. Maria & Ann equally; tract called "Epping" to daus. Maria & Ann; rest of est. to be held by wife and go to daus. Maria & Ann at her death; [no ex.named]; WITS: Chas. R. THOMPSON, Vincent REDMAN, Jas. JENKINS, Shelton WILLSON, Pheby LAYCOCK, Thos. JONES. (RC WB 9:373)

[Robt. BISPHAM mar. Nancy ASBURY, RC, bond 11 May 1804 (see MRC:19 where there is additional info on Robt. BISPHAM); Ann BISPHAM wid. of Robert and Thos. STOWERS were aptd. gdns. to Maria and Ann BISPHAM orphans of Robt. BISPHAM, RC, 5 Aug 1810 (RC Orders 1809-10:66); Maria BISPHAM orphan of Robt. BISPHAM chose Jn. W. BELFIELD as her gdn. and sd. John is also aptd. gdn. to Ann BISPHAM orphan of Robt., 6 Aug 1821 (RC OB 25:183); report of settlement of the gdnship. accts. of Maia & Ann BISPHAM orphans of Robt. BISPHAM ord. to be rec., 5 Jun 1826 (RC OB 27:80); Ann BISPHAM mar. Marcus C. HARVEY and Maria BISPHAM mar. Jn. SPENCE (WCCP:14, 21; RC OB 26:106)]

BISPHAM, Robert; PO 3 Sep 1810; 2 Sep 1811

RC; INV, [m], includes Negroes: Billy, Sam, Abram, James, James, Davey, Sam, General, Dick, John, Ludwell, Bill, Aron, George, General [sic], Joan, Beck, Milly, [Milly], Betty, Betty, Mary, Charlotte, Stafford, Portia, Sarah, Louisa, Delphia, Sophia, Charieta, Sophia, Maria, Frankey, Nancey, Lucy. (RC WB 9:395)

BLACKERBY, Caty; 17 Mar 1821; 14 Jul 1823

NC; WILL; $20 to son Thomas BLACKERBY; son William BLACKERBY (if he should come to live in this county again); son Joseph W. BLACKERBY; son Richard BLACKERBY; dau. Caty BLACKERBY; dau. Sally ANGEL; dau. Elizabeth BLACKERBY; James BROWN; dau. Sally DAMERON; legacies to Joseph & Richard to be left in the hands of James BROWN; friend William HUDNALL ex; WITS: Spencer GASKINS, Seth LUNSFORD. (NC RB 23:331)

[This is Catherine HAYDON, dau. of Ezekiel HAYDON (d. NC 1788) and wid. of Wm. BLACKERBY (*see below*) whom she mar. in NC on 17 Mar 1784 (MWO:41, NC RB 14:196); Sally Glascock BLACKERBY, dau. of Wm. BLACKERBY, mar. Jn. ANGEL Jr., NC, bond 2 Feb 1802 (MLBNC:2); I do not understand two daus. named Sarah, however a Sary BROWN mar. Jn. DAMERON, NC, bond 7 Feb 1792 with Wm. BLACKERBY sec. (MLBNC:25)]

BLACKERBY, Thomas; 12 Oct 1818;

NC; Judith BLACKERBY orphan of Thomas BLACKERBY chose William STIMSON as her gdn. (NC OB 1816-20:294)

BLACKERBY, William; PO 14 Oct 1816; 10 Mar 1817

NC; Joseph & Richard BLACKERBY by Catharine BLACKERBY their gdn. & next friend, Catharine BLACKERBY by Williamson WIBLIN her gdn. & next friend & Williamson WIBLIN & Alice his wife who was lately Alice BLACKERBY pltfs. against Frances K. MUSE, John ANGELL & Sally his

wife and Elizabeth BLACKERBY & Thomas BLACKERBY & William BLACKERBY defts.; defts Thomas & William are infants under 21 and Seth LUNSFORD appointed gdn. to defend them; ordered est. of William BLACKERBY dec'd to be div. among the pltfs & defts. acc. to the will & their several interests therein; est. divided as follows: Lot 1 (old Negro man [Offer]) to Thomas BLACKERBY; Lot 2 (Negro boy James) to Joseph BLACKERBY; Lot 3 (old Negro man Spencer and girl Mirna) to William BLACKERBY; Lot 4 (Negro man Jesse) to [Richard] BLACKERBY. (NC RB 21:164; CC 1816-008)
[In his will, recorded twice in NC, 8 Sep 1802-10 Apr 1815 & 7 Feb 1812-1 Apr 1815, Wm. BLACKERBY named his wife Caty, daus. Frances K. MUSE, Alice BLACKERBY, Sally ANGELL, Eliz. BLACKERBY, and Caty BLACKERBY and sons Thomas, Joseph, William, and Richard (NC RB 20:52, 54); Williamson WIBLIN mar. Ailece BLACKERBY, NC, bond 14 Aug 1815 (MLBNC:108)]

BLACKERBY, William; PO 12 Jun 1815; 12 Jan 1818. NC, INV, $1871.82. (NC RB 21:327)

BLACKERBY, William; PO 8 Jan 1816, T 20 Jan 1816; 12 Jan 1818
NC; laid off and allotted Catharine BLACKERBY her dower and thirds in the est. of her dec'd husband William BLACKERBY; she received the Negroes Betty & child, Isaac, and old man Spencer. (NC RB 21:336)

BLACKERBY, William; PO 16 Oct 1816, T 12 Nov 1823; 12 Jan 1824
NC; DIV of balance of his est. left in the hands of his wid. Mrs. Catharine BLAKERBY dec'd; Lot 1 (Negro Isaac) to John ANGELL. Lot 2 (Negro woman Betty) to Elizabeth BLAKERBY, Lot 3 (Negro Mary) to William MUSE, Lot 4 (Negro girl Lucy & boy Anthony) to Catharine BLAKERBY. (NC RB 23:405)

BLACKWELL, George; 13 Sep 1820 - 14 Aug 1821
NC; WILL; all prop. that I got by her in Maryland & Virginia to wife Nancy BLACKWELL; also land where I now live to wife during her life; after wife's death land to go to sons George B. BLACKWELL & Thomas BLACKWELL; my forest plant. to son Thomas; wife to give son Thomas a good education; wife & bro. Samuel BLACKWELL exors; [no wits, but will proved by oaths of Samuel BLACKWELL & Garrett HUGHLETT; wife & Samuel BLACKWELL relinquished their executorship and Benedict BURGESS granted certif. for obtaining letters of admin. with the will annexed]. (NC RB 22:621)
[This is prob. Geo. BLACKWELL who mar. Nancy COTTRELL, NC, lic. 13 Jan 1772 (MWO:41)]

BLACKWELL, George; PO [4 Jun] 1821; 12 Aug 1822
NC; INV; includes Negroes Daniel, Isaac, Judah, Margaret & child, girl Betty (appraised for the life of Nancy BLACKWELL). (NC RB 23:199)

BLACKWELL, Hiram; 3 Jul 1822; 14 May 1823
NC; WILL; wife to have use of whole est; all land on the right hand of the road leading down Brereton's neck to son John BLACKWELL; all land on left hand of the road leading down Brereton's Neck to son William BLACKWELL; if son John should die before age 21, his land to go to son William and son William's portion of land to go to son Samuel; other four children Sally W. HUDNALL, Elizabeth S. BLACKWELL, Samuel BLACKWELL, & Virginia A. N. BLACKWELL; all children to have a good education particularly my sons John, William & Samuel that they should at least understand the English grammar and Latin & then to study law or

phisic whichever they may choose; ex. to be gdn. of children; bro. Samuel BLACKWELL ex; [no wits, but will proved by oaths of Thos. H. JETT & Fleming BATES]. (NC RB 23:314)
[Hiram BLACKWELL mar. Eliz. HAYNIE, dau. of Salley HAYNIE, NC, bond 10 Mar 1801 (MLBNC:10); Sally W. BLACKWELL, dau. of Hiram, mar. Wm. B. HUDNALL, NC, bond 23 Nov 1821 (MLBNC:56); Miller:15 identifies Brereton's Neck as "probably the southern portion of present Bull Neck" on the Chesapeake Bay]

BLACKWELL, Samuel; T 27 Feb 1800; 14 Apr 1800
NC; INV, [m]; includes Negroes Molly, Vena, Dinah & child, Nell & child, Mima, Maria, Solloman, Mily, Suky, George, Tom, Sue, Old James. (NC RB 16:83)
[Sam. BLACKWELL mar. Catharine DOWNING, dau. of Thos. DOWNING (d. NC 1799), lic. 2 Nov 1786 (MWO:41, NC RB 16:23); the est. of Sam. BLACKWELL was ord. to be adm. by Catharine BLACKWELL & Thos. DOWNING, NC, 11 Feb 1799 (NC Fiduciary Bonds 1797-1801:[m]); Cath. BLACKWELL mar. (2) Edwin NELMS, NC, bond 7 Jan 1803 (MLBNC:77, CC 1804-014)]

BLACKWELL, Samuel; PO Dec 1803; 14 May 1810
NC; allottment to Capt Edwin NELMS his wife's pers. part of the est. & her thirds of the real est. of her husband Samuel BLACKWELL dec'd; NELMS rec'd Negroes Molley, Leviah, Solomon, Suck, Patt, land in the forest near Col. Thomas D. DOWNING and a third part of the mill known as Blackwell's Mill on the north side of Great Wiccocomoco River and the third part of the mill seat on the head of Little Wiccocomoco River. (NC RB 18:378)
[The use of the earlier form Wiccocomoco was dying out in favor of Wicomoco around this time. Catherine BLACKWELL, wid, mar. Edwin NELMS, NC, bond 7 Jan 1803 (MLBNC:77)]

BLAKEMORE, Edward; 10 Feb 1816; 15 Nov 1819
LC; WILL; Negroes Charles, Ned & Milly to son William BLAKEMORE; Negroes [Agg] & [Genge] to dau. Molly HUTCHINGS; my Negro Prescilla I lend to dau. Molly; Negro Hannah to dau. Lucinda WAYMAN; land & plant. to son William BLAKEMORE; if my mother should return to live in my house I have obliged myself to give her two rooms & a closet; Negro girl Winny to grdau. Sally Chowning BLAKEMORE; Negro boy Edmond to grson. John Edward BLAKEMORE; son William & friend John CHOWNING exors; WITS: Wm. WARWICK, J. CHOWNING. (LC WB 28:199)
[Molly BLAKEMORE mar. Rich. HUTCHINGS, LC, bond 16 Aug 1813 (MLBLC:41); Lucinda BLAKEMORE mar. Jn. WAYMAN, LC, bond 11 Sep 1805 (MLBLC:78)]

BLAND, James; T 24 Oct 1799; 24 Nov 1800
WC; INV, £548.17.6; DIV of Negroes: Dower Negroes: Nelly, Matilda; Olivia BLAND's Lot: George, Lavina, Peggy; J. BLAND's Lot: Michael, Sally. (WC RI 8:105)
[This is prob. the James BLAND who mar. Ursula GORDON, a wid., WC, bond 12 Feb 1788 (MLBWC:7); Jn. GORDON aptd. gdn. of Jas. BLAND inf. orphan of Jas. BLAND, 24 Jun 1799 (WC Orders 1799:1801:15); Thos. [?] aptd. gdn. of Jas. BLAND orphan of Jas. BLAND, 25 Sep 1809 (WC Orders 1807-10:402)]

BLUFORD, Spencer M.; T 22 Mar 1814; 13 Feb 1815. NC; INV, [m]. (NC RB 20:12)

[Spencer Morgin Beckly BLUFORD was the son of George & Lette BLUFORD; he was born in SSP, NC 22 Oct 1771 (SSPR:17) and mar. Catharine CORNISH, NC, bond 13 Oct 1794 (MLBNC:11); Acc. to the SSPR and NC CC 1809-014, Spencer M. B. BLUFORD was one of four children and heirs of George BLUFORD; the others were William, George (b. to Geo. & Eliz., 1763) and Nancy (b. to Geo & Eliz., 1765); another child, Giles b. to Geo. & Eliz. in 1768 must have died young (SSPR:17)]

BLUNDELL, John; 19 Nov 1791 - 10 Sep 1792

NC; WILL; my 2 Negro women Milley & Lettey to have their freedom after serving 2 years from this ensuing Christmas & their increase if any from this time; Negroes Winney & her child George & Solomon to wife Betsey BLUNDELL; wife to have the use of Negro children Moses, Charlot, Henry, & Rose until they arrive to 25 then they & their increase shall have their freedom; rest of est. including that given me by deed from William HAYES & wife dtd. 12 Oct 1789 to wife; wife extx; WITS: Jos. CONWAY, Thos. GILL, Robt. CONWAY. (NC DCO:289)

[The surname BLUNDON often occurs as the variant BLUNDELL; this is apparently John BLUNDON who mar. Eliz. KEEVE, dau. of Beverly KEEVE, in NC bet. 1769 and 1791 (MWO:44); the slave Charlotte whom BLUNDELL freed at 25 with her increase brought suit in NC claiming that Geo. GILL had sold her and her child to PICKETTS who intended to remove them from NC; the court ruled that Charlotte and her child were free as of 8 Jul 1806 and GILL was charged with the court costs (NC CC 1806-013); *see also John BLUNDON below*]

BLUNDELL, Thomas; 27 Jan 1815 - 26 May 1821

CP, WC; WILL; to dau. Elizabeth MARMADUKE wife of Vincent MARMADUKE the following Negroes now in their possession: Orrange, Siller & her three children, Anne, Heaby, & Humphrey; to two grdaus. Martha & Anne OMOHUNDRO the Negroes Maria & her children now in the possession of their father Thomas OMOHUNDRO & Negro Patty to be eq. div. between them when 21 or they marry; wife Sarah to have the use of the residue of my est. during her life; after wife's death I give to my grson. Elliott STONE (under 21), son of Presley STONE, two Negroes Harry & Juliett; daus. Anne OMOHUNDRO & Elizabeth MARMADUKE; s-i-l Thomas OMOHUNDRO ex; WITS: Rich. T. BROWN, Jn. HUNTER, Susan P. HUNTER. (WC DW 24:170)

[Betsy BLUNDELL mar. Vincent MARMADUKE, WC, bond 26 Jan 1803; Nancy B. BLUNDELL mar. Thos. OMOHUNDRO, WC, bond 16 Jan 1808; Presley STONE mar. Fanny Baker BLUNDELL, WC, bond 25 Aug 1796 (MLBWC:43, 52, 68)]

BLUNDON, John; PO Sep 1792, T 13 [Dec] 1792; 8 Apr 179[3]

NC; APP; includes Negroes: Solomon, child George, Winney, Milley & Letty (said in BLUNDON's will to be free at Christmas '93, if so each is worth £3, if not £25), Moses, Charlotte, Rose, & Harry (said in Blundon's will to be free at 25 years old, if so Moses is worth £15, if not £30, if so Charlotte is worth £12 if not £24, if so Rose is worth £6 if not £12, if so Harry is worth £12 if not £20). (NC DCO:320)

[*See also John BLUNDELL above*]

BLUNDON, Samuel; PO 14 Aug 1815, T 27 Sep 1815; 9 Oct 1815

NC; INV, $1631.20; includes Negroes Phillis, boys Simon, Peter, & Solomon, girl Sarah, boy George. (NC RB 20:276)

BLUNDON, Samuel; PO 12 Nov 1821, T 7 Nov 1821 [sic]; 10 Dec 1821

NC; commissioners appointed to sell Negroes Phillis, Sarah & George late the prop. of Samuel BLUNDON dec'd; Negroes were sold for $320 & balance was div. among the legal reps: Samuel M. BLUNDON, Samuel WEBB who mar. Piney BLUNDON, Samuel WEBB as gdn. to Seth BLUNDON (orphan of Wesley BLUNDON dec'd), and Thomas TIGNOR as gdn. to Lucy & Elijah BLUNDON. (NC RB 23:52)
[Sam. L. BLUNDON aptd. gdn. of Pinney BLUNDON orphan of Sam. BLUNDON, NC, 9 Oct 1815 (NC OB 1811-15:381); Sam. WEBB wid. mar. Piony [sic] BLUNDON, NC, bond 20 Aug 1820 (MLBNC:106); Lucy BLUNDON chose Thos. TIGNOR as her gdn. and the sd. Thos. is aptd. gdn. of Seth BLUNDON orphans of Sam. BLUNDON, NC 11 Jun 1821 (NC OB 1820-25:116); on the mot. of Sam. M. BLUNDON and Sam. WEBB who mar. Piney BLUNDON in his own right and as gdn. to Seth BLUNDON orphan of Wesley BLUNDON and of Thos. TIGNOR gdn. of Lucy & Elijah BLUNDON orphans of Sam. BLUNDON ... to sell Negroes late the prop. of Sam. BLUNDON dec'd, NC 12 Nov 1821 (NC OB 1820-25:146)]

BLUNDON, Samuel; PO 11 Oct 1824; 4 Mar 1825. NC; INV, [m]. (NC RB 24:185)

BLUNDON, Samuel; PO 14 Mar 1825, T 11 Apr 1825; 11 Jul 1825
NC; sale of Negroes Isaac & girl Dealia and div. of proceeds between David [McDONALD] in right of his wife who was Lucy BLUNDON and Thomas TIGNOR gdn. for Elijah BLUNDON; each rec'd $200.45. (NC RB 24:271)
[Lucy BLUNDON mar. David McDONALD, NC, bond 3 Feb 1825]

BLUNDON, Wesley; 11 Mar 1822
NC; Jn. HULL aptd. gdn. of Seth BLUNDON orphan of Wesley BLUNDON. (NC OB 1820-25:180)
[Westley BLUNDON, son of Sam. BLUNDON (d. NC 1815), mar. Sally BLUNDON, NC, bond 24 Oct 1807 (MLBNC:11); Seth BLUNDON mar. Charlotte CORBELL, NC, bond 31 Dec 1828 (MLBNC:11)]

BLUNDON, William; PO 14 Sep 1807; 9 Jan 1809
NC; INV, £168.6.8 3/4; includes Negroes Winny, girl Alice. (NC RB 18:90)

BOATMAN, William; [m] 1812; [16] Nov 1812
LC; WILL; 1 shilling to son John BOATMAN; 1 shilling to grdau. Sally WEBB; the mean profits of the balance of my est. to be eq. div. between my three children: William, Betty Y. & Milly Y. BOATMAN; my afflicted dau. Milly Y. BOATMAN to have the house lot; my son John & grdau. Sally WEBB have already received their full portions of my est. in my lifetime; friends Armistead A. PALMER & William YERBY exors; WITS: Geo. ROBERTSON, Wm. NEWBY, Edw. PINCKARD, Jn. HILL. (LC WB 28:136)
[This is prob. Wm. BOATMAN who mar. Sarah YERBY, dau. of Jn. & Eliz. (YERBY) YERBY, LC, bond 18 Jan 1781 (MWO:44); Molly BOATMAN mar. Thos. WEBB, LC, bond 16 Feb 1795 (MLBLC:78)]

BOATMAN, William; T 26 Nov 18[12]; 15 Feb 1813
LC; INV; includes Negroes Aaron, Sarah. (LC EB 27:149)

BODMAN, Caleb; PO 9 Jan 1815; 13 Nov 1815
NC; INV, $1847.00 1/2; includes Negroes Peggy & child Sally, lad Isaac, boy Moses. (NC RB 20:307)

BOND, Alice; 4 Jan 1796; 20 Jun 1796
LC; WILL; whole est. to mother Mrs. Sarah BOND; at mother's death est. to go to sis. Caty; sis. Caty BOND & friend Henry TOWLES exors; WITS: Hen. TOWLES, William[son] NORRIS. (LC WB 28:4)
[Alice BOND was a dau. of John & Sarah BOND and sis. of Mary, Catherine and Frances BOND (LC WB 20:154)]

BOND, Alice; PO 26 Jun 1796; 17 Oct 1796
LC; INV, £430.3.6; includes Negroes: Daniel, Fielding, Murray, Letty & child Winny, Milly, Jesse, Sam. (LC EB 24:31)

BOND, Caty; 13 Jan 1806; 15 Jun 1807
LC; WILL; use of 25 Negroes to niece Mary Bond EDMONDS during her life; if niece marries, her husband is not to have any right to dispose of any of the Negroes; if niece dies without any heirs, Negroes to go to my sis. Frances GARLAND; after sister's death use of Negroes to go to niece [Alcy] Martin GARLAND; Mrs. Elizabeth SYDNOR; Mr. Anthony SYDNOR; £20 each to the two daus. of Anthony SYDNOR: Sarah & Elizabeth Chowning SYDNOR; neither of the brothers of niece Mary Bond EDMONDS to have anything to do with my est; Stokeley TOWLES, James TOWLES, Anthony SYDNOR, & James CARTER exors; WITS: Jas. CARTER, Chattin DUNAWAY. (LC WB 28:100)
[This is Catherine BOND the dau. of Jn. & Sarah BOND and sis. of Mary, Alice, & Frances BOND (LC WB 20:154); her sis. Frances mar. at least 3 times (1) Jn. WORMELEY, LC, bond 19 Aug 1784; (2) Nathaniel BURWELL, LC, bond 20 Apr 1786; and (3) Griffin GARLAND, wid., LC, bond 16 Mar 1791 (MLBLC:10, 29, 80); in MWO:60 the wife of Nathaniel BURWELL was incorrectly identified as a dau. of Ralph WORMELEY.]

BOND, Caty; PO 15 Jun 1807, 26 Jun 1807; 18 Jun 1808
LC; INV at the house of Frances GARLAND; includes Negroes: Hannah, Phill, Abraham, Grace, Winny, Richard, Walt, Isaac, Jacob, Joseph, Lucy, Milly, Mary, Dolly, [Manay], Shadrack, Sam, Dinah, Prue, Billy, Nicholas, Harriot, Cynderella, Ludwell, Sinah. (LC EB 27:25)

BOND, John; PO 20 Oct 1801, T 17 Dec 1801; 18 Jan 1802
LC; INV at Mount Pleasant, £120; includes Negroes Dick, Agga, Hannah & child Sinah; & DIV of est. among: Griffin GARLAND, Mary EDMONDS, Caty BOND. (LC EB 24:166)
[Jn. BOND (d. LC intest. bef. 1764) mar. Sarah SHARP, wid. of Thos. SHARP, LC, bond 22 Jun 1753 (MWO:45); Sarah was the sis. of Robt. EDMONDS (d. LC 1750); she and Thos. SHARP had five children: Eliz., Sarah, Thomasin, Elias, and Ann (LC WB 15:33, 132); the est. of Jn. BOND was div. in 1779 among the wid. Sarah, and children Mary EDMONDS, Alice BOND, Catherine BOND, and Frances BOND (LC WB 20:154); Miller:105 identifies Mount Pleasant tracts in WC, RC and NC, but not in LC]

BOND, Sarah;
LC; WILL; being aged and infirm; my whole est. to my dau. Caty BOND & she is to be extx. with friend Henry TOWLES as ex. (LC WB 28:48)
[Sarah was the wid. of (1) Thos. SHARP and (2) Jn. BOND whom she mar. LC, bond 22 Jun 1753 (MLBLC:45)]

BOND, Sarah; [m]; 21 Jun 1802. LC; INV, [m]. (LC EB 24:197)

BOOTH, John; PO 13 Jan 1800; 9 Jun 1800
NC; INV of est. presented by Rodham BOOTH the ex, £300.3.6; includes Negroes Solomon, boy Sam, old Negro wench. (NC RB 16:132)
[This is Jn. BOOTH of SSP whose will (NC 26 Dec 1798-9 Dec 1799) names his wife Winnifred and his 7 children by his last wife: Rodham, Joseph, Thaddious, Frederick, Nancy, Anthony Sydnor and William Raughly and his other dau. Elizabeth Dale and sons James, George, and John (NC RB 16:44); the births of four children to Jn. & Winnifred BOOTH are rec. in the NFPR: Jn. BOOTH, bastard son of Jn. BOOTH & Winnefrit HUDSON (b. 16

May 1767), Nancy Rowbuck (b. 25 Nov 1787), Judith Robuck (b. 23 Aug 1790), Anthony Sidnor (b. 21 May 1792) (NFPR:18, 19, 22, 23); Rodham BOOTH was named as a nephew in the will of Rodham HUDSON (NC 28 Mar 1791-13 Feb 1792) (NC RB 14:523)]

BOOTH, Joseph; 8 May 1815
NC; Joseph BOOTH was aptd. gdn. of Wm., Hiram, Walter and Harriet his children. (NC OB 1811-15:318)
[Jos. BOOTH mar. (1) Sally RICE, NC, bond 26 Dec 1803 and (2) Nancy ROUTT, NC, bond 27 Dec 1815 (MLBNC:11; he was prob. appointed gdn. to his children when his first wife died.)

BOUGHTON, Anderson; T 13 Mar 1823; 1 Mar 1824. RC; INV, $500.23 1/2. (RC WB 10:33)
[Anderson BOUGHTON mar. Anne C. B. BELFIELD, RC, bond 2 Oct 1821 (MRC:21)]

BOURKE, Richard; 21 Jul 1801
LC; Rebeckah BOURKE orphan of Richard BOURKE chose John OSBOURNE as her gdn. (LC Orders 21 1799-1801:282)
[Rebecca BOURKE, dau. of Marcy BOURKE, mar. Jn. OSBOURNE, LC, bond 21 Jul 1801 (MLBLC:57)]

BRADBERRY, William; PO 16 Mar 1812, T 16 Apr 1812; 20 Jul 1812. LC; INV, $43.28. (LC EB 27:112)
[Wm. BRADBURY mar. Eliz. McTYRE, LC, bond 6 Dec 1811 (MLBLC:7)]

BRAGG, Elizabeth; 31 Sep 1811 - [m] Mar 1812
CP, WC; WILL; First, whereas my Negro man Tom was formerly appraised to 60 pounds, and it will appear by my papers & accounts that I have long since paid debts for my husband's est. to more than the amount thereof as was considered by the persons who was appointed to allott me my dower and who refused to divide the sd. Negro man Tom in consideration of the money which I had paid for the est, and whereas the sd. Negro man Tom has been a faithful servant to me and has been the chief means of my support down to my old and infirm state, in consideration whereof I wish to give him his freedom and liberty after my decease in order to effect which and to compel my children to comply with this my wish, in the first place I give & bequeath unto Beckham THOMAS in trust for the benefit of my sd. Negro man Tom all the est. of every kind that I die possessed of to be applied to the only use and behoof of the sd. Negro man Tom, but it is especially to be understood that if William HALL who married Rebecca my dau. and Martha STONE my other dau. shall on my death secure to the sd. Negro man Tom his freedom & liberty so that he shall not be molested therein, then the property above devised to Beckham THOMAS as trustee for my sd. Negro man Tom, I give and dispose of in the following manner: household furniture & livestock to Martha STONE & eldest dau. Rebecca HALL; William STONE; if William HALL in right of his wife Rebecca or Martha STONE refuses to comply with my will as it respects the freedom & liberty of my sd. Negro man Tom, Beckham THOMAS shall take possession of my whole est. as trustee & apply it as first directed; Samuel TEMPLEMAN ex; WITS: Sam. TEMPLEMAN, Polly STONE. (WC DW 22:247)
[There is a mar. bond dtd. 22 Dec 1790 for Martha BRAGG dau. of Eliz. BRAGG, and Jn. PINSTONE; Wm. HALL was sec. (MLBWC:54)]

BRAGG, William; PO Sep 1818, T 5 Feb 1820; 7 Feb 1820

RC; DIV of land among Henry BRAGG, Mr. BURGESS, Sarah BRAGG, Sally BRAGG, T. M. BRAGG, Patty BRAGG, Elizabeth BRAGG, J. BRAGG, W. H. BRAGG. (RC AB 3:677)

[Wm. & Ruth BRAGG had at least two children whose births are recorded in the LPR: Thos. Moore BRAGG (b. 1791) and Betsey BRAGG (b. 1796) (NFPR:19); Ruth BRAGG was aptd. gdn. to her children: Eliz., Henry C., Letty R., Polly K., & Sarah BRAGG, RC, 4 May 1818 (RC OB 24:203); on the mot. of Hen. BRAGG, ord. that Wm. R. BRAGG, Thos. M. BRAGG, Wm. BURGESS & Nancy his wife, Jas. CRASK & Eliz. his wife, Ishmael BRAGG, Letty BRAGG, Polly BRAGG & Sarah BRAGG be summoned to show cause why dower Negroes of Ruth BRAGG, late wid. of Wm. BRAGG, should not be sold; Letty, Polly & Sarah are infants, 6 May 1822 (RC OB 25:289); heirs & distributees of Wm. BRAGG are: Wm. R. BRAGG, Thos. M. BRAGG, Wm. BURGESS & Nancy his wife, Jas. CRASK & Eliz. his wife, Ishmael BRAGG, Letty, Polly, Sarah and Hen. BRAGG, 2 Dec 1822 (RC OB 26:13; OB 27:22); Williamson HALL mar. Mary BRAGG, RC, bond 26 Mar 1825 (RC OB 27:22; MRC:85)]

BRAGG, William (Capt.); PO 1808; 1 May 1809. RC, INV, [m]. (RC WB 9:344)

[BRAIDY], Betsey; PO Oct 1797; 17 Feb 1800. LC; INV, £11.6.6. (LC EB 24:109)

BRAMHAM, Benjamin Jr.; 19 Dec 1812 - 7 Mar 1814

LP, RC; WILL; 3 Negroes Ellin, Hudson & Adam to 3 grchildren Elenor BRAMHAM, Mary BRAMHAM, & Nancy BRAMHAM; Negro boy Hiram to son Vincent BRAMHAM in trust for dau. Frances MOXLEY without her husb having any right to the same; land & plant. w/o I live & also my mill & adjoining land which I purchased of John REYNOLDS to son Vincent; 3 Negroes Hester, Dennis, & Charlotte to grdau. Mary B. RICE; rest of est. not before given I give to my children: Vincent BRAMHAM, Ailce DEMERITT, Mary GARLAND, & Nancy NEALE; son Vincent ex; [no wits named]. (RC WB 9:447)

[Fanny BRANHAM mar. Daniel MOXLEY, WC, bond 12 Feb 1807 (MLBWC:48); Alice BRAMHAM mar. Jn. DEMERITT, RC, bond 10 Feb 1767 [sic] (MRC:53); Jn. CHANDLER aptd. gdn. to Ellen, Mary & Nancy BRAMHAM, orphans of Benj. BRAMHAM, Jr., 5 Apr 1818 (RC OB 24:201); slaves Ellen, Hudson & Adam devised by will of Benj. BRAMHAM Sr. to be div. between Rich. O. JEFFRIES in right of his wife Eleanor Ann, Mary S. BRAMHAM & Ann BRAMHAM equally, 4 Jan 1825 (RC OB 26:268); Eleanor Ann BRAMHAM mar. Rich. Orlando JEFFRIES, RC, bond 16 Dec 1824 (MRC:103)]

BRAMHAM, Benjamin Jr.; T 28 May 1825; 2 Aug 1825

RC; DIV of slaves devised by the will of Benjamin BRAMHAM to Elenor Ann, Mary Stuart & Ann Stuart BRAMHAM; the devisees were requested to meet at Richmond Courthouse on 28 May 1825 to carry out the div, but they could not attend; commissioners were chosen by Jemima S. BRAMHAM gdn. to Mary S. & Ann S. BRAMHAM and Richard O. JEFFRIES who has mar. Eleanor Ann BRAMHAM to make the div; Ann S. BRAMHAM rec'd Hutson & Robert; Richard O. JEFFRIES rec'd Anne & John; Mary S. BRAMHAM rec'd Harriet & Adam. (RC AB 4:197)

[This is Benj. BRAMHAM, Jr. who mar. Jemima Sanford MOXLEY, dau. of Jos. MOXLEY of WC, RC, bond 7 Mar 1797 (MRC:23); Jn. CHANDLER aptd. gdn. to Ellen, Mary & Ann orphans of Benj. BRAMHAM, 24 Nov 1817 (WC OB 1814-18:356); Eleanor A. BRAMHAM & Mary BRAMHAM orphans of Benj, BRAMHAM chose Jemima S. BRAMHAM and the sd. Jemima is also aptd. gdn. of Ann BRAMHAM orphans of sd. Benjamin, 3 Dec 1821 (RC OB 25:215); Richard Orlando JEFFRIES mar. Eleanor Ann BRAMHAM, RC, bond 16 Dec 1824 (MRC:103)]

BRANHAM, Benjamin; [m]; 22 Sep 1822. WC; INV; includes Negroes Bill, Kate, (WC RI 11:262)

BRANN, Nick; PO Apr 1798, T 15 Nov 1798; 9 Sep 1799. NC; INV, £107.2.6. (NC RB 16:1)
[Rebeeck BRANN refused to admin. on her husband, Nicholas BRANN's est., and Benedict LAMKIN admin. it (NC Fiduciary Bonds 9 Apr 1798 abstracted in Lewis & Booker, 1964, p. 49)]

BRANN, Stephen; PO 14 Feb 1814, T 25 Feb 1814; 14 Mar 1814. NC; INV, [m]. (NC RB 19:533)
[Stephen BRANN's est. was admin. by Thos. BRANN (NC OB:213)]

BRANN, Thomas; PO 5 Jan 1824; 1 Mar 1824. RC; INV, $186.50. (RC WB 10:31)

BRANN, Vincent; PO 1 Jul 1799; 1 Jun 1801. RC INV; £14.14.0. (RC WB 9:148)

BRANNAN, Spencer; 28 Jul 1800 - 7 Dec 1807
RC; WILL; all est. to wife Caty; at wife's death or remarriage to sister's son William DARBY; friends Richard NASH & William BRYAN exors; [no wits named]. (RC WB 9:317)
[Spencer BRANNAN mar. Caty MARTIN, RC, bond 22 Dec 1794 (MRC:23)]

BRANSON, Newyear; PO 28 Sep 1818; 28 Feb 1820
WC; INV, [$2996.05]; includes Negroes Charity & child Eliza, boy Friday, girl Mariah. (WC RI 10:454)
[Newyear BRANSON mar. Fanny BRINNON, WC, bond 11 Oct 1810 (MLBWC:8)]

BRENT, Ann; 9 May 1794 - 19 Jan 1795
LC; WILL; my Negro woman [Venus] to dau. Judith SULLIVANT; grdau. Judith KENT; est. of bro. John YERBY; Negro girl Betty (dau. of Negro woman [Venus]) to grdau. Jane KENT; dec'd husband Thomas BRENT; Negro woman Rachel to be eq. div. among four of husband's children George BRENT (dec'd), Thomas BRENT, Vincent BRENT & Anna KENT (dec'd); my son Vincent BRENT ex; WITS: Newton BRENT, Thos. JAMES, [Ramey] PALMER, Amy YOPP; [will was finally proved 16 Feb 1795]. (LC WB 28:8)
[This is Ann YERBY, dau. of Thos. & Hannah YERBY, who mar. Thomas BRENT, LC, bef. 20 Mar 1756; Judith BRENT mar. Jos. SULLIVAN bef. 21 Feb 1782 (MWO:50, 337)]

BRENT, Charles; PO 17 Feb 1817, T 1 Mar 1817; 18 Mar 1817
LC; DIV of Negroes among legal heirs: George BRENT gdn. of Charles S. BRENT, Kenner BRENT, John HUBBARD gdn. of James K. BRENT. (LC EB 27:370)
[Geo. BRENT Jr. aptd. gdn. to Kenner BRENT orphan of Chas. BRENT, 22 Aug 1815, 15 Jul 1816 (LC Orders 24:250, 322); Jas. K. BRENT orphan of Chas. BRENT chose Jn. HUBBARD as his gdn., 18 Sep 1815 (LC Orders 24:259); Geo. BRENT Jr. relinquished his gdnship. of Chas. S. BRENT orphan of Chas. BRENT whereupon Jas. K. BRENT aptd. his gdn., 20 Dec 1819 (LC OB 25:102)]

BRENT, Charles; PO 17 Feb 1817, T 1 Mar 1817; 18 Mar 1817
LC; DIV of slaves among his legal heirs: George BRENT gdn. of Charles S. BRENT (received Peter & Mary), Kenner BRENT (received Betty), John HUBBARD gdn. of James K. BRENT (received George & Harry). (LC EB 27:374)

BRENT, Eleanor; 17 Jul 1807; 20 Jul 1807
LC; renounces benefit she might claim by the will of her late husband William BRENT & asks court to appoint commissioners to allot her dower in his land; WITS: Geo. ARMES, Benj. DOGGETT, Hugh BRENT Jr. (LC EB 27:18)

BRENT, Eleanor; 27 Oct 1819 - [21] Feb 1820
LC; WILL; dau. Elizabeth DOGGETT to have one heifer of black cattle & also one share of the rest of my est; dau. Eleanor MITCHELL & her dau. Fanny M. MITCHELL; dau. Elizabeth SHEARMAN; Mary Juliett [STOTT], Frances E. B. [MITCHELL] & Fanny M. MITCHELL; Addaline B. [BRENT]; remainder of est. to son James BRENT Jr.; son James ex; WITS: David BUCHAN, Wm. GRESHAM, Thos. LUNSFORD. (LC WB 28:203)
[This is Eleanor the dau. of Sam. BRUMLEY & wid. of [fnu] STOTT who mar. Wm. BRENT, LC, bond 20 May 1779 (LC WB 20:232; MLBLC:8, *see below*); the first dau. Eliz. may be the Eliz. STOTT who mar. Benj. DOGGETT, LC, bond 19 Dec 1791 (MLBLC:21); Eleanor B. BRENT mar. Jas. MITCHELL, LC, bond 13 Dec 1809 (MLBLC:52)]

BRENT, Eliza ; 12 Apr 1814; 17 Oct 1814
LC; WILL; my two Negroes Hannah & Sinah to friend Thomas JAMES; at his death to my bro. Thomas JAMES [sic]; one fourth of my part of my mother's third of my father's est. to my bros. John HUNT, James BRENT, Richard Hall BRENT & Mary Lee BRENT & the other fourth to my nephew James Brent DEGGE; bro. John HUNT ex; WITS: David H. JAMES, Eliza HUNT, Eliza B. GEORGE. (LC WB 28:150)

BRENT, George; T 31 May 1815; 18 Sep 1815
LC; INV; includes Negroes: Charlotte, Mariah. (LC EB 27:251)

BRENT, George; 23 Jan 1821; 16 Feb 1824
LC; WILL; land & plant. to dau. Frances BRENT as long as she remains single; if she marries land to son George BRENT; Negro boy Bill to dau. Frances; girl Winney to grdau. Sarah Ann POLLARD; remainder of Negroes & pers. est. to be eq. div. between daus. Frances BRENT & Catharine POLLARD; £10 a year for 5 years to son Newton BRENT; son George [P.] BRENT & s-i-l James POLLARD exors; WITS: Eliz WADDEY, Jane A. ROBERTSON. (LC WB 28:243)
[Geo. BRENT served for 3 years in the Va. State Line during the Revolutionary War; his son Newton was dec'd without heirs by 1833; his son Geo. P. was a resident of Orange Co., Va. by 1833 (VS1776 II:592); Catherine Payne BRENT mar. James POLLARD, LC, bond 28 Sep 1818 (MLBLC:60)]

BRENT, George Jr.; T 23 Mar 1818; 20 Apr 1818
LC; settlement of est.acct. & DIV of est. among George BRENT, Kenner BRENT in right of his wife Elizabeth who was Elizabeth E. BRENT, Elias E. BRENT and William H. BRENT. (LC EB 27:417)
[Kenner BRENT mar. Eliz. BRENT, LC, bond 29 Jan 1816 (MLBLC:8); Elias E. BRENT & Wm. H. BRENT orphans of Geo. BRENT chose Geo. BRENT as their gdn., 16 Dec 1816 (LC Orders 24:343)]

BRENT, Hugh; PO Apr 1805; 1 Jul 1805
RC; INV, £135.12.6; "supposed to be dead;" includes following Negroes: Isaac, Winney, girl Hannah. (RC WB 9:255)

BRENT, Hugh; PO 19 Feb 1810, T 3 Mar 1810; 18 Jun 1810
LC; INV, includes Negroes: Nanny, Tom, Ned, Charles, Patty, [?], Matilda. (LC EB 27:72)

BRENT, Hugh (Capt.); PO 1 Jan 1820; 19 Mar 1821
LC; DIV of slaves: Fanny, Sarah, Jack, Ralph, Frank, girl Betty, girl Sally, girl Caty, boy Solomon, boy Ezekiel, boy Juby, girl Margarett, Harry, [Churchill], girl [Elisia]; widow's dower (Frank, Caty, Solomon, Harry, Elisia), James BRENT (Jack), William BRENT (Ralph, Fanny), Hugh BRENT (Betty, Ezekiel), Judith N. BRENT (Churchill, boy Juby), Kenner BRENT (girls Salley, Margaret & Sarah). (LC EB 29:69)
[This is prob. Hugh BRENT who mar. Alice MARTIN dau. of Wm. MARTIN, RC, bond 30 Nov 1799 (MWO:49); Judith N. BRENT orphan of Hugh BRENT chose Alice BRENT as her gdn. and sd. Alice is aptd. gdn. to Hugh, Wm. and Kenner BRENT also orphans of Hugh, 17 Jan 1820 (LC OB 25:106); Thos. L. LAWSON aptd. gdn. to Hugh & Kenner BRENT orphans of Hugh BRENT, 20 Mar 1822 (LC OB 25:291)]

BRENT, James; 17 Sep 1804
LC; Eliz. the wife of Thomas JAMES was the extx. of James BRENT. (LC OB 1804-05:228)
[Jas. BRENT mar. Eliz. HUNT, LC, bond 25 May 1780 (MLBLC:7); in his will (LC 13 May 1791 - 17 Dec 1792) Jas. BRENT named his wife Eliz., sons Jas. & Wm., daus. Susannah, Sarah Nutt, Mary and Eliz., and an unborn child (LC WB 22:357); Thos. JAMES mar. Eliz. BRENT, wid., LC, bond 7 Sep 1795 (MLBLC:42); Spencer GEORGE (admr. of Susanna GEORGE), Jn. HURST (ex. of Eliz. BRENT), Jn. T. DEGGES & Mary his wife, Sarah N. JAMES and Jas. BRENT (claiming by purchase instead of Wm. BRENT, dec'd) which sd. Susanna, Eliz., Mary, Sarah N. and Wm. were children and devisees of Jas. BRENT the Elder (LC CC 1820-066)]

BRENT, James; T 23 May 1815; 19 Jun 1815. LC INV. (LC EB 27:204)

BRENT, James K.; T 31 Jan 1823; 17 Feb 1823
LC; INV, [m]; includes Negroes Perseus, Argail, George, Harry, Mary. (LC EB 29:249)

BRENT, John; 19 Apr 1811 - 20 May 1811
LC; WILL; all est. to my friend Spencer GEORGE & also all my interest in the est. late belonging to Isaac DEGGE dec'd of LC which I claim in right of my late wife Ann BRENT who was Ann DEGGE & also all my interest in my uncle's est. late of RC; Spencer GEORGE ex; WITS: Robt. MEREDITH, Caroline MEREDITH, Gracy EDMONDS. (LC WB 28:122)
[Jn. BRENT mar, Ann DEGGS [sic], LC, bond 8 Jun 1796 (MLBLC:7)]

BRENT, Judathan; 17 Jul 1826
LC; on the mot. of Addison BRENT ord. that [Allenon] BRENT, Middleton BRENT, [Alcinda] BRENT, Allison BRENT, Addison BRENT, Cinderilla BRENT, [Celia] BRENT and [Disna] BRENT heirs of Jeduthan BRENT dec'd be summoned to show cause why the land of the sd. decedent should not be sold and the proceeds div. among his legal reps. (LC OB 26:195)
[James D. Wilkinson in "'Fit Objects of Charity': Community, Race, Faith, and Welfare in Antebellum Lancaster County, Virginia, 1817-1860," *Journal of the Early Republic*, Vol. 21, No. 1 (Spring, 2001), pp. 64-65 notes that Jeduthan BRENT was arraigned several times in LC for petty crimes. Wilkinson identifies several of his children as Middleton, Cinderilla, Addison, Alcinda, Celia, and Allington; Jeduthan BRENT mar. Molly BRENT, LC, bond 15 Sep 1779 (LCVMB:6)]

BRENT, Kenner; PO 19 Dec 1803; 17 Sep 1804
LC; INV; Hugh BRENT is the surviving ex; includes Negroes: Travis, Nelly & child, one old woman; est. was div. among: Hugh BRENT, Martin BRENT,

Joseph STEPHENS, George STEPHENS and Thomas JAMES ex. of James BRENT, Nancy BRENT extx of Newton BRENT, George BRENT, F. MAXWELL, Sarah BERRYMAN, George GLASCOCK (the last 6 received half shares). (LC EB 24:296)
[Jos. STEPHENS mar. Charlotte BRENT, LC, bond 15 Mar 1782; Geo. STEPHENS of Orange Co., Va. mar. Priscilla BRENT, LC, bond 15 Oct 1787; Thos. JAMES mar. Eliz. BRENT, wid., LC, bond 7 Sep 1795; Jn. MAXWELL mar. Frances BRENT, LC, bond 16 Feb 1775 (MLBLC:42, 51, 70)]

BRENT, Margaret S.; PO 18 Apr 1808, T 3 May 1808; 20 Jun 1808. LC; INV, Hugh BRENT admr. (LC EB 27:30)

BRENT, Newton; 31 Jan 1795; 21 Jul 1795
LC; WILL; to wife Nancy Steptoe all my est; wife to raise & educate my children; wife is expected to be now pregnant, if she has a son I devise my land on Rappahannock River purchased of William [LAWSON] to him when he is 21; daus. to live with their mother until they marry or reach age 21; if wife has a son he is to be bound out & a young Negro lad or man be bound out with him; if wife marries she is to have one third of my land & all my houses at Fleet's Bay Neck; bro. George BRENT & friend James HENRY exors; WITS: Eliz. BRENT, V. BRENT, Augustus CARTER. (LC WB 28:18)
[Newton BRENT mar. Ann Steptoe LAWSON, dau. of Thos. LAWSON, LC, bond 14 Apr 1779 (MLBLC:8, MWO:50); Ann Steptoe (LAWSON) BRENT mar. (2) Rich. GLASCOCK, LC, bond 5 Sep 1800 (MLBLC:33); Rich. GLASCOCK mar. Ann S. BRENT wid. of Newton BRENT who was aptd. gdn. of Lettice, Peggy & Nancy BRENT orphans of Newton,15 Dec 1800 (LC Orders 21 1799-1801:201); Lettice L. BRENT orphan of Newton BRENT chose Elias EDMONDS as her gdn., 15 Jun 1801; Geo. BRENT & Hugh BRENT aptd. gdns. of Margaret Steptoe & Ann Newton BRENT orphans of Newton BRENT, 20 Jul 1801 (LC Orders 21 1799-1801:266, 273); Lettice L. BRENT mar. Thos. G. ROBERTSON, LC, bond 11 Dec 1801 (MLBLC:63; LC Orders V 1802-03:10); settle the acct. of Hugh & Geo. BRENT of their gdnship. of Ann & Margaret BRENT orphans of Newton BRENT, 15 Dec 1806 (LC Orders D22 1805-08:274); Margaret BRENT orphan of Newton BRENT chose Jn. KENT as her gdn., 21 Dec 1807 (LC Orders 22D 1805-08:431); settlement with Hugh BRENT of the acct. of his gdnship of Ann N. BRENT orphan of Newton BRENT, 16 Dec 1811 (LC Orders 24:54); report of the settlement of Hugh BRENT's gdnship. of Ann N. INGRAM formerly Ann N. BRENT, 21 Sep 1812 (LC Orders 24:117); Jn. INGRAM mar. Ann N. BRENT, LC, bond 12 Aug 1811 (MLBLC:41)]

BRENT, Newton; 20 Jun 1795; 21 Sep 1795
LC; INV, £557.7.6; includes Negroes: lad Haydon, George, Spencer, Kendal, John, William, Milly & child, Betty, Esther, Nancy, Sally. (LC EB 24:47)

BRENT, Newton; PO 20 Oct 1800; 17 Sep 1804
LC; DIV of the est. among: the widow KENDALL, John HUNT in right of his wife Lucinda, Robert M. ROBERTSON in right of his wife Janey, Margaret BRENT, Letty BRENT, Ann N. BRENT. (LC EB 24:293)
[Jn. HUNT mar. Lucinda BRENT, LC, bond 20 Jun 1796; Robt. M. ROBERTSON mar. Jane Newton BRENT, LC, BOND 28 JAN 1800 (MLBLC:40, 63)]

BRENT, Vincent; 27 Apr 1799 - 16 Sep 1799
LC; WILL; to wife Margaret Steptoe use of all my land in Fleet's Bay Neck; to son Charles the place I purchased of Gilson BERRYMAN known as Poplar Neck including the reversion of the land now held by Mrs. Sarah

BERRYMAN as her dower together with my 3 Negroes Mose, Jesse & Fanny, the rent from John HUNT ($60); all my land in Fleet's Bay Neck to my son Arthur when he arrives of age or marries; the land I purchased of Capt. Thomas LAWSON to be eq. div. between my 3 daus: Katherine Lawson, Ann Steptoe & Sarah Newton; my 3 Negroes Thomas, Elliot & Mary should remain in the possession of Capt. Thomas LAWSON during his life; friend William YERBY to be gdn. to my son Charles & ex. of my will; WITS: Leroy NUTT, Ann [S.] BRENT, Lettice LAWSON, Thos. JAMES, Jn. HUNT. (LC WB 28:30)

[Hugh BRENT aptd. gdn. of Sarah BRENT orphan of Vincent BRENT and Thos. JAMES aptd. gdn. of Arthur BRENT orphan of Vincent BRENT, 18 Apr 1808 (LC Orders 22D 1805-08:461); Cath. L. BRENT orphan of Vincent BRENT chose Hugh BRENT as her gdn. and Ann S. BRENT orphan of Vincent BRENT chose Jas. BRENT as her gdn., 20 Jun 1808 (LC Orders 22D 1805-08:477); settlement with Thos. JAMES the acct. of his gdnship. with Arthur BRENT orphan of Vincent BRENT, 21 Oct 1811 (LC Orders 24:48); settle Jas. BRENT's gdnship. of Ann S. BRENT orphan of Vincent BRENT & possess Hugh BRENT her present gdn. with her est., 16 Dec 1811 (LC Orders 24:54); Sarah BRENT orphan of Vincent BRENT chose Sam. M. SHEARMAN as her gdn., 16 May 1814 (LC Orders 24:186); Arthur BRENT orphan of Vincent BRENT chose Jas. BRENT as his gdn., 19 Sep 1814 (LC Orders 24:188); Arthur BRENT orphan of Vincent BRENT chose Hen. C. LAWSON as his gdn., 19 Dec 1814 (LC Orders 24:210); Vincent BRENT mar, Margaret S. LAWSON, LC, bond 24 Jun 1786 (MLBLC:8); Poplar Neck is in southeastern LC between Dymer Creek & Tabb's Creek near Fleets Bay (Miller:127)]

BRENT, William; 3 Jan 1798 - 15 Dec 1806

LC; WILL; Negro boy Tom to son Hugh BRENT at the death of his mother; Negro girl Judith to dau. Eleanor B. BRENT; Negro girl Jane to dau. Fanny BRENT; Negro girl Lucy to dau. Elizabeth BRENT; wife Ellen to have use of entire remainder of est. during her life or widowhood for support of herself & my four younger children; land & plant. to son James BRENT after wife's death; four younger children: Elleanor Brumley, Elizabeth, Fanny, & James BRENT; if son Hugh interrupts or disturbs wife or four younger children all bequests & legacies to him are revoked; son James to be bound out until 21; friends Rawleigh W. DOWNMAN, Richard MITCHELL & Joseph CHINN exors; WITS: Geo. SYDNOR, Wm. SETTLE, Raw. CHINN, Edw. BLACKEMORE, Jas. SUTTON, Raw. DAVENPORT. Geo. M. MITCHELL, Jn. GRESHAM; COD dtd. 9 Oct 1805: If son Hugh BRENT should become dispossessed of the est. he holds under the will of William BRUMLEY dec'd & for which there is now a suit in Chancery pending I give my grson. William Brumley BRENT my Negro boy Daniel and to my grson. Albert Hugh BRENT my Negro girl Nancy & boy Charles; my still to my son James BRENT; WITS: Raw. DAVENPORT, Geo. M. MITCHELL, Jn. GRESHAM. (LC WB 28:96)

[Wm. BRENT mar. Eleanor, the dau. of Sam. BRUMLEY and wid. of [fnu] STOTT, LC, bond 20 May 1779 (LC WB 20:232; MLBLC:8); Hugh BRENT was named as nephew in the will of Wm. BRUMLEY (LC 13 Feb 1788-21 Jan 1793) (LC WB 22:358); Frances & Jas. BRENT, orphans of Wm. BRENT, chose Rawleigh DOWNMAN as their gdn., 21 Dec 1807 (LC Orders 22D 1805-08:431)]

BRENT, William; T 27 Dec 1806; 16 Feb 1807

LC; INV, £160?.7.9.; includes Negroes: Jerry, Peter, James, Harry, Daniel, Dominy, Charles, Aron, Manuel, Joe, Winny, Hannah, Lydda & child [Dilsy], Patty & child Anthony, Jude, Lucy, [Alie], Mary, Nancy, Grace, Matilda, Eva, Adam, Nelson. (LC EB 27:3)

BRENT, William; PO 20 Jul 1807; 15 Feb 1808
LC; DIV of est. among: the widow, James BRENT, Fanny BRENT, Elizabeth BRENT, Ellen BRENT; also laid off the widow's dower in the land located near the Poor House Field & adj William BOATMAN, the road to Williamson JONES', Pinckard's tavern (formerly the prop. of George M. MITCHELL) and the road to Lancaster Courthouse. (LC EB 27:27)

BRENT, William; PO 19 Sep 1808; 15 Jan 1810
LC; DIV of the est. presented by Rawleigh W. DOWNMAN admr. with the will annexed among: Ellen BRENT (the widow), James D. BRENT in right of his wife Fanny & Rawleigh W. DOWNMAN gdn. to James BRENT orphan of the sd. dec'd, Henry MITCHELL in right of his wife Elizabeth. (LC EB 27:67)
[Hen. M. MITCHELL mar. Elizabeth BRENT, LC, bond 7 Dec 1808 (MLBLC:52); Eliz. mar. (2) Thos. SHEARMAN, LC, bond 17 Dec 1817 (MLBLC:67)]

BRENT, William; PO 15 Feb 1813; 19 Jun 1815. LC INV. (LC EB 27:201)

BRENT, William; PO 21 Feb 1820, T 23 Feb 1820; 18 Sep 1820
LC; INV, $171.95; DIV of dower slaves allotted to Eleanor BRENT of the est. of her dec'd husband William BRENT among his legatees: James D. BRENT (Nelson, Peter, Molly) who mar. Fanny BRENT, James BRENT (Robin, James), Thomas SHEARMAN (Matilda, Hannah) who mar. Elizabeth MITCHELL formerly Elizabeth BRENT, James MITCHELL ([Delsa], Alice) who mar. Elenor BRENT. (LC EB 29:40)
[James D. BRENT mar. Fanny BRENT, LC, bond 16 Jan 1809 (MLBLC:8)]

BRENT, William; 21 Jan 1822
LC; ord. that Alice BRENT, Isaac BRENT, Thomas L. LAWSON & Judith his wife, Hugh BRENT & Kenner BRENT be summoned to show cause why the real & personal est. of which William BRENT died seized should not be sold and the proceeds divided. (LC OB 25:279)
[Thos. L. LAWSON mar. Judith N. BRENT dau. of Alice BRENT, LC, bond 28 Nov 1821 (MLBLC:47); see also Capt. Hugh BRENT above]

BRENT, William; PO 21 Jan 1822, T 20 Sep 1822; 20 Jan 1823
LC; INV, $470; includes [Negroes] Ralph & Fanny. (LC EB 29:247)

BRENT, William; PO 17 Dec 1821, T 12 Jan 1823; 17 Nov 1823
LC; sale of Negro Charles for $450 and div. of proceeds under the will of William BRENT among James MITCHELL who mar. E. B. BRENT, Elizabeth SHEARMAN who was Elizabeth BRENT, James D. BRENT who mar. Fanny BRENT and James BRENT Jr. (LC EB 29:302)

BRENT, William; 17 May 1824
LC; Eliz. L. McNAMARA is aptd. gdn. to Richard & Mary BRENT. (LC OB 26:39)
[This is prob. Wm. BRENT who mar. Eliz. L. HALL, LC, bond 19 Aug 1809; Eliz. L. (HALL) BRENT mar. (2) Timothy McNAMARA, LC, bond 20 Nov 1820 (MLBLC:8, 50)]

BREWER, James; T 3 Dec 1818; 22 Mar. 1819. WC; INV, [m]. (WC RI 10:362)

BREWER, John; 12 Nov 1802; 25 Apr 1803.

WP, WC; WILL; whole est. to wife [Ellender] and she to be extx.; WITS: Nathaniel MOTHERSHEAD, Chas. MOTHERSHEAD, Wm. MOTHERSHEAD. (WC DW 20:458)

BREWER, John; PO 28 Feb 1820; 26 Jun 1820

WC; DIV of est; John NEALE shall retain out of the sum to be divided $14 to be paid John BREWER in addition to his distributable part of the est. as a compensation to him a great coat loaned to the intestate many years since; est. div. among: Mrs Ann BREWER for her dower, John NEALE's children by Elizabeth BREWER, Samuel BREWER, John BREWER, Alexander BREWER, Sarah CARTER, Haney JEWELL, Robert BREWER, James RAMEY, William CARPENTER, Richard BREWER, Thomas BREWER. (WC RI 11:10)

[Jn. NEALE mar. Eliz. BREWER, WC, bond 1 Sep 1790; Jn. CARTER mar. Sary BREWER, WC, bond 15 Feb 1798; Jas. REAMY mar. Lucy BREWER, LC, bond 25 Nov 1817; Haney BREWER mar. Jas. JEWELL of RC, WC, consent of Haney BREWER dtd. 13 May 1808; Wm. CARPENTER mar. Catherine BREWER, LC, bond 7 Jan 1818 (MLBWC:11, 12, 35, 50, 57)]

BRIDGMAN, Eunice; T 29 Dec 1821; 8 Jul 1822

NC; William BRIDGMAN & William LEDFORD in right of his wife have agreed to div. the est. of Eunice BRIDGMAN dec'd eq. between them; William LEDFORD rec'd Polly & child Lucy Sank; William BRIDGMAN rec'd Solloman. (NC RB 23:184)

[Eunice KESTERSON, the dau. of Eliz. KESTERSON, mar. Jos. BRIDGEMAN, NC, bond 22 Dec 1788 (NC RB 19:139, MLBNC:12)]

BRIDGMAN, Joseph; 13 Feb 1815

NC; Thos. H. JETT was aptd. gdn. of Fleet H., Sally, Harriet and Joseph BRIDGMAN orphans of Joseph BRIDGMAN. (NC OB 1811-15:280; OB 1820-25:391)

[Jos. BRIDGMAN in his will (NC 23 Jan 1815 - 13 Feb 1815) named his sons Fleet H. & Jos. and his daus. Harriet & Sally; Thos. H. JETT was his ex. (NC RB 19:624); Wm. W. APPLEBY aptd. gdn. of Sarah BRIDGMAN orphan of Jos. BRIDGMAN, 12 Feb 1827 (NC OB 1825-30:142)]

BRINNON, Elizabeth; PO 27 Jan 1806; 26 Jan 1807

WC; INV, $1157; includes Negroes Mag (age 47), Milley, William, Susanna, Prue, Reubin, Sam, Lucy. (WC RI 9:9)

[Eliz. BRINNON, the dau. of Jn. (d. WC 1778) & Hannah BRINNON, d. intest. in 1805 leaving the following heirs: sisters of the whole blood Ann, the wife of David CRENSHAW, who d. in 1807 and Hannah the wife of Jn. NORWOOD Sr., a neice Eliz. C. the wife of Nath. SPRIGGS, the grandchildren of Jn. BRINNON Sr., Nancy & Susanna BRINNON by their gdn. Mrs. Fanny BRINNON, and Owen, Jn., Sally, Fanny Jr., Hannah, Geo., and Ewell the children of her bro. Geo. BRINNON (WC CC 1810:004)]

BRINNON, George; PO Aug 1799; 27 Jun 1803

WC; INV, £279.12.8; includes Negroes Ben (infirm in his limbs), girl Rose, girl Jane, boy Dennis, girl Sarah. (WC RI 8:235)

[Geo. BRINNON was the son of Jn. BRINNON (d. WC 1778); in his will (WC 1 Jan 1798 - 25 Mar 1799) Geo. named his sons Geo., Nel [sic], dau. Sally, and bro. John; he did not identify his wife (WC DW 16 :292, DW 17:145, DW 19:377; WC CC 1810-004 identified his children as: Owen, Jn., Sally, Fanny Jr., Hannah, Geo., and Ewell]

BRINNON, George; PO 23 Mar 1807, T 10 Mar 1811; Oct 1811

WC; settlement of acct. of John B. STEEL who mar. Leannah BRINNON wid. & extx of George BRINNON. (WC RI 9:298; CC 1817-016)

BRINNON, John Jr.; 25 Oct 1819
WC; Nancy BRINNON, orphan of John BRINNON Jr. chose Thomas STOWERS as her gdn. (WC OB 1819-23:87)

BRINNON, John Sr.; [m]; 25 Apr 1812
WC; INV, [m], includes Negroes Lucy & infant son, Pindar, Benjamin (cripple), boy James, girl Charity, boy Laurence, girls Patty, Milly & Jenny, Cupid (man about 27 to be free at 31), [General] (man about 18, to be free at 31), Lucy (woman about 15, to be free at 21), Meredith (boy, to be free at 31). (WC RI 9:328)
[Jn. BRINNON was prob. the son of Jn. BRINNON (d. WC 1778) and the bro. of Geo. BRINNON (d. WC 1799) (WC DW 16:292, DW 17:145, DW 19:377)]

BRINNON, John Sr.; 10 Aug 1805 - 26 Jul 1819
WC; WILL; wife and step-dau. Elizabeth BRINNAN to receive a genteel & comfortable support & maintenance out of my est. and may reside in my mansion house during their lives; all my lands & three Negroes Jenny, James, & one other to grdau. Nancy BRINNAN; residue of my slaves after the death of my wife & step-dau. to grdau. Susannah A. BRINNAN; 20 shillings to dau. Elizabeth C. SPRIGGS; to each of the three oldest children of Nathaniel SPRIGG[S] which he had by his last wife Elizabeth C. SPRIGGS the sum of £50; friend Robert SANFORD of WC ex; WITS: Thos A, SORRELL, Jn. NORWOOD, Wm. H. COLLINSWORTH. Wm. CARPENTER; [will was proved in Nov 1805 but sent for further proof]. (WC DW 23:499)
[Jn. BRINNON Sr. was the son of Jn. (d. WC 1778) & Hannah BRINNON; Jn. BRINNON in his will (WC rec. 30 Jun 1778) named his wife Hannah, dau. Ann CRENSHAW, grdaus. Hannah & Ann RICE, dau. Hannah HOLLAND, dau. Eliz. BRINNON and sons Jn. & Geo. (WC DW 16:292, DW 17:145); A court case in WC named many descendants of Jn. & Hannah BRINNON: Jn. NORWOOD Sr. & Hannah his wife, Nathan SPRIGGS & Eliz. his wife, Nancy & Susanna BRINNON inf. under 21 by Fanny BRINNON wid. their gdn., Owen BRINNON, Jn. BRINNON, Fanny BRINNON, Sally BRINNON, Geo. BRINNON, Ewell BRINNON & Hannah BRINNON inf. under 21 by David CRENSHAW their gdn. complts. vs. David CRENSHAW to sell a Negro and div. the proceeds, 23 Jul 1810 (WC Orders 1807-10:555; WC CC 1810-004); Ann BRINNON mar. David CRENSHAW, bef. 30 Jun 1778 (MWO:94); Hannah BRINNON mar. (1) [Youell] HOLLAND bef. 30 Jun 1778 and (2) Jn. NORWOOD (MWO:183); Nathan SPRIGGS mar. Eliz. C. BRINNON, WC, bond 26 Aug 1795 (MLBWC:67); Susan BRINNON orphan of Jn. BRINNON Jr. chose Jn. S. WILKINSON as her gdn., 28 May 1821 (WC OB 1819-23:26)]

BRINNON, Youel; T 10 Dec 1804; 23 Sep 1805
WC; INV, $116.22; includes blacksmith tools valued at $27.58. (WC RI 8:582)
[This is prob. the Youel BRINNON who mar. Sarah McKENNEY, WC, bond 27 Oct 1792 (MLBWC:8)]

BRISCOE, Daniel; PO Mar 1801 & Mar 1802; 25 Apr 1803
WC; DIV of est; to William BUTTON gdn. to Lucy BRISCOE Negro Charlotte; to Stephen JOHNSON who mar. Elizabeth BRISCOE Negro Nancy; to William DEATLEY gdn. to Patsy BRISCOE Negro [Sybrie]; to William DEATLEY who mar. Elenor BRISCOE Negroes Delilah & Maria; in addition houses & lots in Leedstown and nearby land were sold for

£160.12.0 & the Negroes were appraised at £250 for a total of £400.13.0 to be div. among Daniel BRISCOE's four daus. (WC RI 8:211)
[Daniel BRISCOE of the Town of Leeds, WC, in his will (WC 2 Apr 1789-27 Apr 1790) named his wife Eliz., and 5 children: Jn., Eliz., Ellen, Martha, and Lucy (WC DW 18); Wm. DEATLEY mar. Ellen BRISCOE, LC, bond 2 Mar 1801 (MLBLC:19); Wm. DEATLEY was aptd. gdn. of Patsy BRISCOE orphan of Dan. BRISCOE, WC, 23 Nov 1801 (WC Orders 1801-04:192); *see also WC CCs 1801-04 and 1802-020*]

BRISCOE, James; PO 23 May [1803], T 26 Nov 1803; [m]
WC; INV, £332.10.3; includes Negroes Will, Sarah & child Jack, Davy, Ben, [Siday]. (WC RI 8:513)

BRISCOE, James; 1 [Jun 1797] - Nov 1797
WP, WC; WILL; whole est. to wife Mary; after wife's death Negro girl Jude to dau. Susanna BRISCOE; after wife's death remaining est. to be sold and the money arising therefrom divided as follows: dau. Susanna BRISCOE one sixth and remainder to be eq. div. amongst my grandchildren; friend Beckwith [BUTLER} and bro. Capt. Reuben BRISCOE exors; WITS: [?] MARKS, [?] MARKS. (WC Unrec Wills 1755-1800 #44)

BRISCOE, Reubin; 24 Nov 1817
WC; Eliza BRISCOE orphan of Reubin BRISCOE chose Nath. KING as her gdn. (WC OB 1814-18:350)
[Reuben BRISCOE mar. prob. twice, (1) Betsey THORP, WC bond 29 Jun 1790 and (2) Ann B. JOHNSON, dau. of Sam. JOHNSON, WC bond 19 Dec 1803 (MLBWC:9)]

BROCKENBROUGH, Austin; 1 Mar 1810 - 22 Apr 1810.
WP, WC; WILL; son Champe BROCKENBROUGH use of all my lands w/o I now live known as Bloomsbury & use of my Negro servants for his natural life & no longer; after his death to go to his eldest son, but if son dies without a son, est. to be kept together for the benefit of all the daus. of son Champe until the youngest arrives at 18; grson. Austin BROCKENBROUGH son of Rev'd John BROCKENBROUGH to be educated and paid £500 when 21; £400 to dau. Elizabeth ELLIOTT; 10 Negroes I gave to dau. Jane on her marriage to Mr. Thomas PRATT was all I ever intended for her; friends Baldwin Mathews LEE & William ROBINSON Esq. & son Champe exors; WITS: Ballaile FITZHUGH, Jas. BROWN, Jn. PAYNE; WC DW 22:82)
[Col. Austin BROCKENBROUGH mar. Lucy CHAMPE, dau. of Col. Jn. CHAMPE of KGC, WC, 1761 (MWO:52); Champe BROCKENBROUGH mar. Sarah Skinker BOWIE, WC, bond 24 Nov 1795 (MLBWC:9); by 1833, Champe had died and his wid. Sarah was a resident of Caroline Co.; one of the children of Champe & Sarah BROCKENBROUGH was Catherine Augusta who mar. Thos. B. TURNER of Jefferson Co., Va; Catherine died in Jun 1832 leaving children Carter Bushrod Washington TURNER & Catherine Augusta Brockenbrough TURNER (WCCP:28); The Rev. Jas. ELLIOTT mar. Eliz. BROCKENBROUGH -- identified incorrectly as dau. of Arthur BROCKENBROUGH -- WC, bond 20 Nov 1792 (MLBWC:22); on the mot. of Austin BROCKENBROUGH, ord. that Sarah BROCKENBROUGH, wid. of Champe BROCKENBROUGH, Sally Champe BROCKENBROUGH, Mary BROCKENBROUGH & Augusta BROCKENBROUGH, children of sd. Champe BROCKENBROUGH be summoned to show cause why admin. de bonis non with the will annexed of Austin BROCKENBROUGH shall not be taken (WC OB 1823-27:160); Miller:12 locates the Bloomsbury Tract in RC on Cobham Park Neck]

BROCKENBROUGH, Austin; [T 24 May 1810]; 23 Mar 1812
WC; INV, £2115,5,3; includes Negroes Daniel (aged 37), Dublin (37), Tom (40), Sam (35), Joshua (21), Jonathan (51), Simon (35), Charles (33), Will (22), Daniel (55), Jack (65), Stephen (66), James (69), Grace (22), Mary (40), Nancy (55), Sal (50), Lucy (25), Winefred (60), John (6), Betsey (5, a cripple), Winnefred (3), Peter (1). (WC RI 9:319)

BROCKENBROUGH, John; 23 Dec 1811
WC; Champ BROCKENBROUGH aptd. gdn. of Austin BROCKENBROGH orphan of John BROCKENBROUGH. (WC Orders 1810-13:191)

BROCKENBROUGH, William; PO Oct 1802; 7 Feb 1803
RC; INV; [m], includes the following Negroes: Jack, Milly, Mina & child Harison, Nelly, Dick, Henry, Charles, George, Lett, Solomon, Marcus, Eve, Pegg, Kate. (RC WB 9:206)

BROMLEY, Sarah; 17 Nov 1795 - 21 Dec 1795
LC; WILL; Negro man Fortin to sis. Hannah BAILEY; at sister's death [Fortin] to niece Molly WILLIAMS; Betsy NEWBY dau. of John NEWBY dec'd; niece Ann NEWBY; niece Jane NEWBY; Sarah McCARTY; Betty dau. of Winney; Nan[c]y; Betty & Jinney; my mare Nancy Dameron to William BAILEY; Hugh BRENT; nephews James NEWBY, Oswald NEWBY; sis. Ellen BRENT; Molly LUCKHAM; 3 barrels of corn to Negro man [Fortin]; Negro man Immanuel to be hired out; nephew Oswald NEWBY ex; WITS: Rawleigh TAPSCOTT, Cyrus NEWBY. (LC WB 28:22)
[This is Sarah NEWBY, dau. of Hen. (d. LC 1741) & Mary (d. LC 1762) NEWBY, who mar. Wm. BRUMLEY bet. 1741 and 1761 (MWO:56); her sis. Hannah NEWBY mar. Wm. BAILEY, LC, bet. 1741 and 1761 (MWO:22); there is no mention of a sis. Ellen in either the will of her father or mother (LC WB 13:265, WB 16:181)]

BROMLEY, Sarah; PO 21 Dec 1795, T 5 Jan 1796; 18 Apr 1797
LC; INV, £92.6.[5]; includes Negro man Fortune. (LC EB 24:62)

BROMLEY, William; 21 Jan 1793; 19 Jun 1797
LC; INV, £749.7.6; includes Negroes: Tom, Ned, Manuel, Charles, David, Guy, Manuel, Fortune, Winney, Nan, Betty & child Fanny, Jenny, Charles, Polly, Betty & child Tom, Betty, Haley. (LC EB 24:64)

BROOKE[S], Edmond; 7 May 1809 - 18 Dec 1809
LC; WILL; to wife Caty all est. during her life or widowhood; at wife's death or marriage est. to be eq. div. between three daus: Polly, Caty & Fanny; friends John LUNSFORD & John C. HINTON exors; WITS: Alex. NASH, Polly HILL. (LC WB 28:112)
[Frances BROOKES orphan of Edmund BROOKES chose Jesse KENT for her gdn., 18 Dec 1809 (LC Orders B23 1808-11:141)]

BROOKE[S], Henry; 25 Nov 1815 - 18 Dec 1815
LC; WILL; son Humphry BROOKE[S]; all of est. after paying debts to dau. Nancy; friend Spencer GEORGE ex; WITS: Spencer GEORGE, Chattin DUNAWAY. (LC WB 28:172)
[Thos. NEWGENT aptd. gdn. to Nancy [N.] BROOKE orphan of Hen. BROOKE, 21 Oct 1816 (LC Orders 24:339)]

BROOKES, Edmond; PO 18 Dec 1809; 19 Feb 1810
LC; INV, $133.23; includes Negroes: old woman Hannah, David. (LC EB 27:71)

BROOKES, Henry; PO 18 Dec 1815, T Dec 1815; 19 Feb 1816. LC ; INV. (LC EB 27:279)

BROWN, Charles; PO 8 Feb 1802, T 20 Feb 1802; 14 Jun 1802. NC; INV, [m]. (NC RB 16:405)

BROWN, Elizabeth; 3 Dec 1811; 27 Jan 1812
WC; WILL; to bro. John BROWN a Negro man Guy & also a woman Hannah; WITS: Jn. PURSLEY, Jos. BROWN. (WC DW 22:246)

BROWN, Ellen; 6 Sept 1810 - 20 Mar 1815.
CCP, LC; WILL; grdaus. Betsy Hurst DAMERON, Fanny Winder BROWN; daus. Sally CURTIS, Mary DAMERON; [no ex. named]; WITS: Geo. P. OLIVER, Judith YERBY. (LC WB 28:159)
[Sally BROWN mar. (1) Thos. DAMERON, LC, bond 26 Apr 1794 & (2) Nicholas CURTIS, LC, bond 10 Oct 1797; Molly BROWN, dau. of Eleanor BROWN, mar. Jn. DAMERON, LC, bond 25 Sep 1794 (MLBLC:19)]

BROWN, George McAdam; T 14 Nov 1812; [m]
NC; INV, [m]; includes a large number of books including Voltaire's *History of the War of 1741*, 3 vols. of *Tom Jones*, 1 vol. of *Diseases of Women*, *Institutions of Scottish Law*, Euclid's *Elements*, *Method of Studying Divinity*, the *Virginia Gazette* from Aug 1736 to Jul 1740, *History of Jamaica*, *Mercantile Penmanship*, and 12 vols of Greek & Latin books; [beginning on p. 299 of NC RB 20 is an account of the sales of BROWN's estate which includes many people who bought his books; among the purchasers were Thomas D. DOWNING who bought Swift's works, *Tom Jones*, a vol. of the *Tattler*; Thomas MILLER who bought *Moral Philosophy*, a vol. of the *Guardian*, and 2 vols. of Stern's works; Fleming BATES who bought Voltaire's *History of the War of 1741* and the *Practice of Physick*; John MIDDLETON who bought 4 vols of Kersley's Travels & Young's *Night Thoughts*; Thomas BROWN bought 30 vols. of Latin & French books and 12 vols. of Greek & Hebrew books)]. (NC RB 19:317, RB 20:299)
[Geo. McAdam BROWN was the son of Wm. BROWN, d. LC, 1797 (LC WB 28:26); he was born 8 Jan 1773 (Broun Family Records in NCHS); he was named as nephew in the wills of Martha McADAM (NC 16 Jul 1791-13 Jan 1794) and her bro. Geo. Thos. McADAM (NC 11 Apr 1793-15 Apr 1794) (NC RB 15:9, 35)]

BROWN, John; 19 Apr 1813
LC; Bartholomew & Vincent BROWN orphans of John BROWN chose Thomas FLINT as their gdn. (LC Orders 24:148)

BROWN, John; 2 Jun 1811; 2 Jan 1815
RC; WILL; use of est. to wife Elizabeth BROWN during her life; at her death plant. w/o I now live to son John BROWN he paying his bros. £50 to be eq. div. amongst them; if son John die before reaching lawful age, land to go to son Septimus BROWN; if either son should fail to pay £50 as above, land to be eq. div. amongst my sons; four daus. Caty BROWN, Polly BROWN, Betsy BROWN, & Sally BROWN; wife & James THOMAS exors; WITS: Chas. LAMKIN, Geo. DAVENPORT. (RC WB 9:462)
[Vincent BROWN orphan of Jn. BROWN chose Thaddeus BROWN as his gdn., 15 May 1815 (LC Orders 24:226)]

BROWN, John B.; 20 Feb 1804; 26 Mar 1804
WC; Nunc. will; gave his bro. Jeremiah BROWN his watch, horse, saddle & bridle and after his death his wearing apparel; rest of est. after debts paid to be eq. div. between bro. and sis. GREGORY; WITS: Ebenezer MORSE & Jeremiah G. BAILEY. (WC DW 21:21)

BROWN, John B.; PO Mar 1804, T 20 Apr 1804; 24 Nov 1806. WC; INV, £14.9.0. (WC RI 9:6)

BROWN, John T.; 28 Jun 1819
WC; Thornton CONNELLEE aptd. gdn. to Mary BROWN orphan of John T. BROWN. (WC OB 1819-23:61)
[This is prob. the Jn. T. BROWN who mar. Eliz. HENAGE, WC, bond 21 Dec 1813 MLBWC:9)]

BROWN, Margaret "Peggy"; 28 Apr 1801; 22 Jun 1801
WC; WILL; mother Anne OWINGS entire est. and she to be extx; WITS: [Durant Germain BUTTS], Kessey JOHNSTON. (WC DW 20:219)

BROWN, Presley; T 3 May 1811; 17 Jun 1811. LC ; INV, £6.12.9. (LC EB 27:87)

BROWN, Spencer; PO 16 Jul 1810, T 13 Nov 1810; 17 Dec 1810. LC INV. (LC EB 27:76)

BROWN, Spencer; PO 18 Nov 1811, T 28 Feb 1812; 20 Apr 1812
LC; DIV balance of admin. acct. among his children: Betsey, William, Fanny, Winny, Jane, Esther & Milly BROWN & his grson. Samuel ANGELL. (LC EB 27:110)

BROWN, William; 22 Oct 1797 - 18 Dec 1797
LC; WILL; whole of my land to son George McAdam BROWN on condition that he lays no claim to any of the Negroes nor any other part of my est; my other est. to my other four children Ann S. BROWN, Thomas BROWN, Harriet BROWN & Edwin BROWN; Col. James BALL, Col. Henry TOWLES, Joseph B. CHINN, Cyrus PINCKARD & my two sons George McAdam & Thomas BROWN exors; WITS: Thos. CARTER, Thos. BALL, M.D., Sam. YOPP. [will was finally proved 15 Jan 1798]; LC WB 28:26)
[Wm. BROWN mar. Janita (or Janetta) McADAM, dau. of Dr. Jos. & Sarah Anne McADAM, NC 22 Oct 1771 (MWO:55)]

BROWN, William; 12 Mar 1810; 19 Mar 1811
LC; WILL; to wife one third of whole est.; at wife's marriage or death her third to go to my three children; all my est. to be eq. div. between my children Leroy BROWN, Thomas BROWN & William BROWN; land may be sold when son Leroy is 21; friend William YERBY ex; WITS: Nathan SPRIGGS, Sally CIRTIS, Molley DAMERON. (LC WB 28:118)

BROWN, William; PO 8 May 1815, T 20 Nov 1815; 11 Dec 1815
NC, INV; his est. included cash rec'd from Thomas TOWLES Esq., paymaster in the 37th Regt. Virginia Militia, for services rendered by BROWN in the last war - $21.25; total est. was valued at $31.80. (NC RB 20:320)

BROWN, William; 19 Jun 1819
LC; Susanna BROWN wid. of William BROWN, Ann BROWN, Griffin BROWN & Lawson BROWN inf. orphans of sd. William BROWN by Thomas [COATS] their gdn. to show cause why slave of which sd. William BROWN d. seized & possessed should not be sold. (LC OB 25:70)
[This is Wm. BROWN who mar. Susan COATS, LC, bond 1 Jan 1817 (MLBLC:9); settlement. of Wm. BROWN with Nancy & Griffin BROWN his wards & an acct. & rep. of the settlement of Thos. COATS admr. of the est. of Wm. BROWN, 18 Sep 1820 (LC OB 25:162)]

BRUCE, Andrew; 2 Sep 1799; 7 Jan 1802.
RC, INV; includes Negro woman Betty, boy Moses, girl Sal, small boy George. (RC WB 9:172)
[This is prob. the Andrew BRUCE who mar. Rebecca BRAGG, RC, 5 Feb 1798 (MRC:27)]

BRUCE, George; [m]; 2 Feb 1816

RC; WILL; debts to be paid & balance of est. to go to 2 children; James SCATES, John BAYNE & Richard BAYNE exors; WITS: Rich. COLLINS, Ruben MARKS. (RC WB 9:502)
[Acc. to a fairly complicated and confusing CC filed in WC in 1830 (WCCP:47), the two children of Geo. BRUCE are Pamelia (who mar. Rich. H. CARVER) and Cordelia (who mar. Wm. PAYTON, WC, bond 28 Jun 1824) (MLBWC:53); Rich. BAYNE aptd. gdn. to Cordelia & Pamela BRUCE orphans of Geo. BRUCE, 23 Jun 1817 (WC OB 1814-18:313; OB 1823-27:165)]

BRUCE, George; 1 Jul 1816
RC; INV, [m], included slaves Aaron, Rose & her 3 children Aaron, Minna, & Mary, Jane & her 2 children Joseph & Maria. (RC WB 9:535)

BRUCE, William; 31 May 1800; 7 Feb 1803
RC; INV; £584.17.10; includes the following Negroes: man George, man Peter, boy Harry, girl Dinah, girl Winney, girl Frank, Darcas & child Nancy, boy Joe, boy Moses. (RC WB 9:206)

BRUMLEY, Samuel; 10 Oct 1808
NC; motion of Vincent LEWIS to allot to Winifred LEWIS her dower in the lands of her late husband Samuel BRUMLEY. (NC OB 1807-11:67)
[Sam. BRUMLEY mar. Winifred EIDSON, NC, bond 11 Nov 1797; Vincent LEWIS mar. Winifred BRUMLEY, wid., NC bond 26 Sep 1808 (MLBNC:13, 68)

BRUMLEY, Samuel; PO 14 Dec 1813, T 7 Mar 1818; 14 Dec 1818
NC; WILL; land adj. Jones Mill Pond containing about 49 ac. belonging to Nancy BARNES, Samuel BRUMLEY & Lewis BRUMLEY orphans of Samuel BRUMLEY dec'd was sold to Samuel BRUMLEY for $160 and div. among heirs. (NC RB 21:555)
[Nancy BRUMLEY mar. Tallon (Tarlton) BARNES, NC, bond 19 Dec 1810 (MLBNC:5); Thos. BELL, gdn. of Lewis BRUMLEY, asked the court to ord. the sale of a tract of land in NC adj. Jones MIll and div. the proceeds into 3 parts for Tarlton BARNES and Nancy his wife, Sam. BRUMLEY, and Thos. BELL as gdn. of Lewis BRUMLEY, NC, 14 Dec 1813 (NC OB 1811-15:206); Tarlton BARNES who mar. Nancy BRUMLEY, Sam. BRUMLEY and Thos. BELL gdn. of Lewis BRUMLEY asked the court to ord. Jas., Wm., and Betsy BRUMLEY, orphans of Sam. BRUMLEY, to show cause why certain lands they inherited from their father should not be sold, NC, 15 Feb 1814 (NC OB 1811-15:218); Thos. BELL aptd. gdn. of Eliz. & Wm. BRUMLEY orphans of Sam. BRUMLEY, NC, 13 May 1816 (NC OB 1816-20:41); Miller:76 locates Jones Mill in NC in the vicinity of Lodge Creek and the South Yeocomico River]

BRYAN, John; T 26 Dec 1818; 9 Aug 1819
NC; INV, $1371.10 1/2; includes Negroes Arch & boy Adderson. (NC RB 22:92)

BRYANT, Alexander; 28 Sep 1816; 8 Apr 1817
RC; WILL; wife Betty all est; at her death to be eq. div. amongst all my children except my son Thomas BRYANT unless he pays the money that I am his security for otherwise I give him only 10 shillings; wife Betty, son Alexander BRYANT and s-i-l Chichester DOBYNS exors; WITS: Luke JACKSON, Elinor S. BRYANT, Jn. WROE. (RC WB 9:553)
[Alex. & Betty BRYANT were also the parents of Lucy T. BRYANT b. 3 Jan 1802 (NFPR:27); Chichester DOBYNS mar. Fanny L. BRYANT, RC, bond 25 Dec 1811 (MRC:54); Alex. BRYANT, compl., vs. Hen. MISKELL & Hannah his wife, Jn. WROE & Eliz. his wife, Chichester DOBYNS & Fanny his wife,

Thos. BRYANT, Lucy BRYANT & Alfred BRYANT, 3 Jul 20 (RC OB 25:41); Alfred BRYANT orphan of Alex. BRYANT chose Alex. BRYANT as his gdn., 6 Nov 1820 (RC OB 25:75); Hen. MISKELL mar. Hannah BRYANT, RC, bond 12 Sep 1798 (MRC:133); Jn. WROE mar. Betsy B. BRYANT, RC, bond 12 Jun 1813 (MRC:236)]

BRYANT, Ellender; 10 Nov 1812; 14 Feb 1820
NC; WILL; tract of land in NC & tract of land in RC named Buck Ordinary to son Thomas BRYANT; Thomas WAY & William WAY exors; WITS: Thos. FALLIN, Jn. FRANCE Sr., Betsy FRANCE. (NC RB 22:212)
[Buck or Buck's Ordinary was located in RC near Marvin Grove Camp (Miller:17)]

BRYANT, James; PO Jun 1803, T 23 Jul 1803; 28 Feb 1804. WC; INV, £48.15.9. (WC RI 8:376)

BRYANT, John; 17 May 1801 - 6 Jul 1801
NFP, RC; WILL; wife Eleanor; youngest son Thomas (under 21); son William S.; son William exor; WITS: Luke HANKS, Rich. BENNEHAN. (RC WB 9:155)
[Jn. BRYANT mar. Eleanor SMOOT dau. of Wm. SMOOT of SSP, NC bef 28 Aug 1782 (NC RB 14:630; RC WB 7:475)]

BRYANT, John; PO Jun 1801; 7 Oct 1805
RC; INV, £209,18,6, includes Negro fellow Ned. (RC WB 9:273)

BRYANT, John; PO 6 Feb 1817; 22 Feb 1817
RC; allotted to Richard DOWNMAN in right of his wife Elizabeth the wid. of John BRYANT dec'd her dower in the pers. prop. of sd. dec'd: Polley & Kitty (one third of the est). (RC AB 3:494)
[Rich. DOWNMAN mar. Eliz. BRYANT, wid., RC, bond 4 May 1816 (MRC:59; RC OB 1816-20:59)]

BRYANT, John; T 15 Jun 1815; 7 Jul 1817
RC; INV, $1693.23, includes the following Negroes: Jeremiah, Polley, Pheba, Elizabeth, Sarah & Polley. (RC WB 9:562)

BRYANT, John; T 19 Jul 1817; 1 Dec 1817
RC; at Farnham Church, DIV of est. of John BRYANT between Richard WALL gdn. for M. S. BRYANT & William SAUNDERS gdn. of Harriet [P.] BRYANT & Newton BRYANT. (RC AB 3:496)
[Harriet M., Newton, and Maria BRYANT were orphans of John BRYANT (RC OB 24:112, 238); Maria S. BRYANT orphan of Jn. BRYANT chose Wm. SAUNDERS as her gdn., 1 May 1820 (RC OB 25:6)]

BRYANT, John; PO 28 Oct 1816; 23 Feb 1818. WC; INV, $183.17 1/2. (WC RI 10:245)

BRYANT, Jonathan; 12 Oct 1815; 6 Nov 1815
RC; WILL; son Lewis D. BRYANT; son Jesse BRYANT; dau. Judith DOUGLAS; son John BRYANT; Thomas HALE to have $1.00; balance of est. to sons John & Lewis D.; son Reuben BRYANT; Griffin HEADLEY & John BRYANT exors; WITS: Griffin HEADLEY, Eliz. BRYANT. (RC WB 9:486)
[Judith or Judah BRYANT mar. Jn. DOUGLAS, RC, bond 23 Dec 1801 (MRC:58)]

BRYANT, Joseph; 20 Jan [1808]
NFP, RC; WILL; 50 ac. of land to be sold if required; whole est. to wife Elizabeth; at wife's death or remarriage est. to be div. among 4 children: Patty T. BRYANT, Samuel BRYANT, Richard J. BRYANT & Joseph BRYANT; wife & bro. John BRYANT exors; WITS: Robt. JEFFRIES, Rawleigh BRYANT, Job THRIFT. (RC WB 9:318)

[The land of Jos. BRYANT was div. among Geo. TUNE and Patty his wife who was Patty BRYANT, Sam. BRYANT, Rich. BRYANT, and Jos. BRYANT, RC, 2 Mar 1819 (RC OB 24:314); Geo. D. TUNE mar. Patty F. BRYANT, RC, bond 11 Dec 1815; she was prob. his 2nd wife (MRC:219); see also RC OB 24:314]

BRYANT, Joseph; 6 Jun 1809. RC; INV, [m]. (RC WB 9:355)

BRYANT, Joseph; 22 Aug 1810; 6 Mar 1815
NFP, RC; WILL; wife Frances BRYANT use of whole est. during her life; Negro boy Bill to son Samuel BRYANT; dau. Sally GORDON; dau. Fanny LEWIS; dau. Violet BROOKS; dau. Winney BRYANT; William FORRESTER, Samuel BRYANT, & William LEWIS exors; WITS: Famous FICKLIN, Thos. BRYANT, Polly BRYANT. (RC WB 9:464)
[Sally A. BRYANT mar. Jn. GORDON, RC, bond 28 Feb 1809; Fanny BRYANT mar. Wm. LEWIS of NC, RC, bond 23 Aug 1809; Violett BRYANT mar. Wm. H. BROOCKE, RC, bond 1 Jan 1808 (MRC:25, 79, 119)]

BRYANT, Joseph; T. 16 Feb 1815; R. 6 Feb 1816
RC; INV, $1010.31, includes 4 small Negroes: Lucy, Sally, George, John. (RC WB 9:504)

BRYANT, Joseph; [T 11 Nov 1816]; 6 Jan 1817
RC; John GORDON who mar. Sally BRYANT, William LEWIS who mar. Fanny BRYANT, Vilot BROOKS who was Vilot BRYANT and Winefred BRYANT all heirs of Joseph BRYANT dec'd desired to have the balance of the est. of sd. Joseph BRYANT divided; the balance was $248.80, in the hands of Samuel BRYANT the ex. (RC AB 3:374)

BRYANT, Joseph; PO 4 Apr 1815, T 6 May 1815; 6 Jan 1817
RC; DIV. of Negroes which Joseph BRYANT died seized & possessed of agreeable to an agreement entered into by William LEWIS (rec'd. Sally a girl), John GORDON (rec'd.George a boy), William H. BROOKS (rec'd.John a boy) (in right of their wives) & Winifred BRYANT (rec'd.Lucy a girl). (RC AB 3:383)

BRYANT, Joseph; T 16 May 1816; 6 Jan 1818. RC; INV, $222.93. (RC WB 9:598)

BRYANT, Joseph; PO 2 Mar 1819; 4 Oct 1819
RC; DIV of land (187 ac) among George TUNE in right of his wife Patty who was Patty BRYANT, Samuel BRYANT, Richard BRYANT, Joseph BRYANT. (RC AB 3:668)

BRYANT, Joseph; PO 6 May 1816; Dec 1819. RC, INV, $220.53. (RC WB 9:640)

BRYANT, Rawleigh; 8 Dec 1800 - 6 Apr 1801
RC; WILL; son Joseph home plant. w/o I now live containing 62 1/2 ac; son John all remaining land; 5 children: Joseph, Samuel, Rawleigh, John & Winney DOTSON; my Negroes to have liberty to make their choices of a master among my children & they that choose to go to shall have 3 years credit to pay for them; sons Joseph & John exors; WITS: Jn. WILSON, Wm. DODSON, Letty DOTSON. (RC WB 9:147)
[Jas. B. DODSON mar. Winifred BRYANT, RC, bond 1 Jan 1795 (MRC:57)]

BRYANT, Rawleigh; T 20 Dec 1800; 7 Dec 1801
RC; INV; £182.3.11; includes Negro Hannah & boy child Joe, girl Ellin. (RC WB 9:161)

BRYANT, William; 29 Dec 1814; 6 Mar 1815
RC; WILL; Negro girl Moriah to dau. Sally; Negro girl Winney to dau. Nancy; plant. w/o I now live to son John; balance of est. to be eq. div. among 3 children Sally, Nancy & John; Thaddeus BRYANT exor; WITS: Wm. LEIGHTON, Wm. W. BROOKE, Luke HANKS. (RC WB 9:466)

BRYANT, William; T. 21 Feb 1815; R. 6 May 1816. RC; INV, [m]. (RC WB 9:517)

BRYANT, William L.; PO 6 Jul 1818; 7 Sep 1818. RC; INV, $1525.00. (RC WB 9:607)

BUCHAN, William; 18 Jan 1802

LC; David BUCHAN orphan of William BUCHAN chose Martin SHEARMAN as his gdn. and settle the gdnship. acct. of Spencer HINTON with [Davey] BUCHAN. (LC Orders V 1802-03:4)

[Wm. BUCHAN mar. Catherine HINTON, LC, bond 9 Oct 1779 (MLBLC:10); Catherine HINTON was prob. the dau. of Jn. POPE (d. NC 1776) and wid. of Fleet HINTON whom she mar. in LC, bond 17 Nov 1768 (MLBLC:38, MWO:181, NC RB 10:1); Cath. (POPE, HINTON) BUCHAN d. in LC bef. 1793 leaving the following heirs: Nicholas Pope BUCHAN, Wm. GOODRIDGE, David BUCHAN and Spencer CURRELL (LC WB 22:430); Lucy HINTON, a dau. of Cath. BUCHAN, mar. Spencer CURRELL, LC, bond 17 Jun 1793 (MLBLC:18); Cath. Martin HINTON mar. Wm. GOODRIDGE of Orange Co., LC, bond 17 Dec 1793 (MLBLC:33)]

BULGER, John; 16 Sep 1814; 4 Mar 1816

RC; WILL; all est. to wife Mary BULGER during her widowhood or natural life; if she does not marry, at her death to be eq. div. among all my children except my son Thomas who under the will of his grandmother sets up a claim to the land w/o I now live, but if son Thomas relinquishes all claims against my est. and will agree to an eq. div. of the sd. land among his brothers, then I desire that after the death of my wife my est. shall be eq. div. among the whole of my children; wife to be sole extx.; WITS: Thos. JONES, Danl. MARMADUKE, Jas. SCATES. (RC WB 9:511)

BURCH, Jilson B.; 3 Aug 1800; 6 Apr 1801

NFP, RC; WILL; wife Lucy; dau. Eliza; wife & friend Bartho. McCARTY exors; WITS: B. McCARTY, Jas. GORDON. (RC WB 9:145)

[Jilson or Gilson BURCH was the son of Baynum BURCH who d. intest. and bro. of Ann Baynum BURCH (WC CC 1795-007); Jilson BURCH mar. Lucy MORGAN, RC, bond 4 Sep 1797; their dau. Eliza was born 21 Mar 1798 (MRC:30; NFPR:28)]

BURGESS, Joseph; 6 Mar 1806; 22 Sep 1806

WC; WILL; whole est. to wife Molly; after her death to be eq. div. among six children: Daniel, John, Harrison, Sally, Nancy & [Lemuel]; wife extx; WITS: Wm. Storke JETT, Eliz. SMITH, Mary NELSON. (WC DW 21:269)

BURN[S], Edward; 24 Jun 1822

WC; William CARPENTER aptd. gdn. to the orphans of Edward BURNS: Elizabeth, William, Nancy and George BURNS. (WC OB 1819-23:429)

[This is Edw. BURN who mar. Milley SPURLING, WC, bond 3 Apr 1819; she was prob. his 2nd wife; his first was Nancy CARPENTER whom he mar. in WC, bond 5 Jun 1797 (MLBWC:10); Milley BURNS aptd. gdn. to Edw. BURNS orphan of Edw. BURNS (WC OB 1819-23:429); Wm. CARPENTER, gdn. of Geo. BURNS an inf. of about 6 years of age and unfit to be bound out; it appears to the court that profits of the est. are insufficient to maintain him so Wm. CARPENTER is authorized to make use of the principal to the amount of $15, 27 Jan 1823 (WC OB 1819-23:512)]

BURWELL, James B.; 2 Sep 1811 - 4 Nov 1811

RC; WILL; two thirds of the 2 tracts of land called the Folly & Samfords purchased of William CLEMENTS dec'd shall be fully complied with as expressed in the deed of trust & also all the pers. prop. purchased at the sale of my grandmother Lucy SMITH shall be fully complied with as expressed

in the deed of trust; uncle Bacon BURWELL all that part of my real est. on the right of the main road leading from Winchester to Martinsburg in the counties of Frederick & Berkley and also 1000 pounds to be paid to my aunt Rachel EMMERSON of Tennessee; remainder of my est. in Frederick, Berkley & Richmond cos. to my friend John R. F. CORBIN & all monies due & to become due either by bonds or otherwise chargeable with 500 pounds to be paid to Francis SMITH, chargeable with 100 pounds to be paid to Thomas [P.] SMITH & chargeable with a handsome gold watch to be purchased for Mary CLEMENTS the dau. of my aunt Lucy CLEMENTS; all land in Northampton Co to the 3 children of my uncle James BURWELL: [Gavin,] Nancy & James; body servant Squire to have as much land allotted to him as the law requires & provides for the establishing [of] his liberty & to remain in trust to John R. F. CORBIN; [no ex. named]; WITS: Thos. J. SCHRIMGER, David BARRICK; will was contested by Lucy CLEMENTS & Bacon BURWELL; probate finally granted 5 Nov 1811, but BURWELL & CLEMENTS appealed to the Superior Court. (RC WB 9:401)
[James B. BURWELL is the son of Nathaniel BURWELL of York Co. & Eliz. SMITH, dau. of John & Lucy SMITH (MRC:31, RC WB 9:72); Lucy, another dau. of Jn. & Lucy SMITH, mar. Wm. CLEMENTS, RC, bond 9 Apr 1788 (MRC:40); Squire PALMER, man of color, emancipated by this will, was permitted to reside in RC, 6 Jan 1818 (RC OB 24:177); acc. to <http://www.singletonfamily.org/getperson.php?personID=I269260&tree=1>, accessed 13 Jun 2012, Bacon BURWELL was the son of James & Priscilla (MERCHANT) BURWELL; he was born in York Co. in 1774 and died before 1830]

BURWELL, James B.; PO Mar 1812; 2 Mar 1813
RC; INV, $12,545.70, includes following slaves: Traverse, Bob, Billy, Philip, Sam, Charles, Billey, Peter, Ben, Lee, Nancy & child Daniel, Doll, Mary & 2 children Amea & Peter, Easter & 2 children Lucy & Mary, Milly, Nancy No. 21, Isaac, Isaac 2nd, Gabriel, Robin, Bartlett, Charles, Dennis, Prince, Betty, Harry, Billy & Judith, Lucy & child Betsey, Rachel & 3 children Abram, Cornelius, & Joseph, Letty & 3 children Patty, Aaron, & Fanny, Rachel & child Arianna, Suckey & 5 children Polly, Sally, Ned, Fanny, & Hannah, Easter, Susan No. 32; inv of est. in Frederick Co; includes following slaves: Julius, Lewis, Randal, Major, Robin, Franky, Peter & his wife Patty, Polly, Harry, Amy, Nancy, Betty, Kitty, Lucy, Bartlet, Bartlet [sic], Christine, Isaac, Mary Ann, Tempe (no value), George, Sally, Abram, Ambrose, Daniel, George, Little [Lien], Betty, Peter, Marcus, Janney, Janney [sic], Marcus, James, Jacob, Patty, Letty, Caty, Lidia, Lewis, Sucky, Paul, John, Bob, John, Patty, Cynthia, Simon, Nancy, Jacob, Lucy, John, Judith, Grace, Moses, John, Solomon, Dinah, Billy, Carter, Sally, Marie, Dinah, Ambrose, Billy, James (of no value). (RC WB 9:420)

BURWELL, Nathaniel; 13 May 1784 - 15 Feb [1813]
LC; WILL; all plant. & lands in LC & following slaves: York, Bob, Shoemaker Bob, Jack, George, Isle of Wight ,[Sey], Jacob, Little Jacob, Frank, Kitt, Betty, Anthony, Phillis, Sue, Joshua, Ben, Billy, Amos, Frank, Mary, Ann, Aggy, Grace, Sally, Molly, Venus, Rachel, Delphia, Zenith, Natt, Little Natt, Sarah, Mary, Letty, Fanny, Andrew, Billy, Marlow, [Amaryllis], Hannah, Phill, Little Zenith to wife Mary BURWELL; £500 to each of my daus. Jane, Sarah, Frances & Arianna six mos. after the death of my wife to be raised out of the sale of my plant. & slaves above; Negro girl Betsy to dau. Frances; Negro girl Suckey to dau. Arianna; remainder of est. to son Robert Charles BURWELL; wife Mary & Philip GRIMES Esq. & Dr. William BALL exors; WITS: Ann

[MOSTYN], Wm. BRENT; [the two wits. were dead when the will was probated, but their handwriting was proved by the oaths of Jn. M. GILMOUR & Jn. M. SMITH]. (LC WB 28:138)

BUSH, James; 15 Aug 1791 - 20 Jul 1812

LC; WILL; all est. to wife during her life or widowhood; at wife's death or marriage land and plant. to son Thomas BUSH; rest of est. after wife's death or marriage to be eq. div. among all my children; wife Fanny & bro. Peter BUSH exors; WITS: Wm. GOODRIDGE, Rawleigh RAINES, Wm. RAINES. (LC WB 28:131)

[James BUSH mar. Fanny JARRETT (poss. the wid. of Thos. JARROT), LC, bond 8 Mar 1782 (MLBLC:10; LC WB 20:241)]

BUTLER, James; 17 May 1810

NC; James BUTLER having been dead more than 3 months and no one applied for administration of his est.; the sheriff ord. to sell his perishable estate. (NC OB 1807-11:185)

BUTLER, John; 28 Mar 1808

WC; John SMITH was the gdn. of Nancy BUTLER, orphan of John BUTLER, who mar. William B. SMITH. (WC OB 1807-10:151)

[Nancy BUTLER mar. Wm. B. SMITH, WC, bond 1 Apr 1806 (MLBWC:66)]

BUTLER, Thomas; mar. Frances "Frankey" MOXLEY dau. of Joseph MOXLEY, WC, bond 3 Dec 1787 (MLBWC:11, CC 1801-018)

BUTLER, Thomas; 26 Sep 1808

WC; Overseers of the Poor to bind Thomas BUTLER orphan of Thomas BUTLER to James DOZIER (a carpenter). (WC Orders 1807-10:201)

BUTLER, Westley; 27 Nov 1826

WC; Frances BUTLER aptd. gdn. to Henry M., Catherine T., Samuel C. F., Frances T. A., & Robert W. BUTLER orphans of Westley BUTLER. (WC OB 1823-27:334)

[Wesley BUTLER mar. Frances T. CRASK, WC, bond 24 Nov 1813 (MLBWC:11)]

CADDEEN, Richard; 17 Nov 1791; 23 Jun 1806

CP, WC; WILL; wife Mary all that belongs to her by our marriage and one Negro man James; son John CADDEEN 1 shilling; dau. Sarah HALL 1 shilling; dau. Hannah BUTLER 1 shilling; son Thomas CADDEEN 1 shilling; dau. Ann COLLINSWORTH 1 shilling; grdau. Betty Caddeen BRENNON 1 shilling; wife to be extx; WITS: Wm. MOOKLAR, Wm. P. TEBBS, Peter [GALLAGHER], Sam. CRABB, Dan. TEBBS, Thos. ATTWELL. (WC DW 21:255)

[Rich. CADDEEN mar. Mary BENNETT, wid., WC, bond 3 Feb 1787 (MLBWC:11); Mary BENNETT may have been the wid. of Daniel BENNETT (d. WC, 1785) (MWO:37); Wm. COLLINSWORTH mar. Nancy CADDEAN, WC, bond 26 Oct 1789 (MLBWC:15); Dick, a mulatto belonging to Thos. STOWERS was charged with the rape of Mary CADDEEN, wife of Rich., but he was found not guilty, WC 23 Oct 1804 (WC Orders 1804-07:95)]

CAMPBELL, Archibald; 24 Jun 1774 - 25 Apr 1775.

WP, WC; WILL; desires the following advertisement be published in Edinburgh & Glasgow public papers: In October 1741 a certain young man, Archibald CAMPBELL, came over from Scotland to Virginia being obliged to leave several small debts he had contracted there unpaid, most of those debts he had accepted bills for according to the Scotch form but was never applied to for the discharge of them, the sd. Archibald CAMPBELL being lately dead in the County of Westmoreland in the sd. Colony of Virginia, we

his exors. hereby give notice to his several creditors ... to apply to us properly for their respective [*1 word unclear*] that we may do therein what is necessary; exors. to recover from John BERRYMAN the money principal & interest due from him to me upon mortgage and invest it in the purchase of land for my two sons Alexander & John CAMPBELL; wife Hannah third part of lands purchased of BOWCOCK & TRIPLETT & one third of lands to be purchased with money from John BERRYMAN & also one third part of my slaves; son Archibald CAMPBELL lands I bought of Thomas BOWCOCK & John TRIPLETT; rest of est. to be eq. div. among my several children: Archibald, Alexander, Mary Stuart & John CAMPBELL; if either son should succeed to the est. of Ascogh in Scotland it is then my will that the lands devised herein to such son be eq. div. among my other sons; wife, Alexander ROSE, Thomas JETT, Daniel McCARTY, Daniel FITZHUGH, Dr. James BANKHEAD, Joseph FOX & William BANKHEAD exors. and guardians to children; son Archibald to be sent to William & Mary to be educated & brought up for the service of the established church and to be an ex.of my will when he is 21; WITS: Wm. BERNARD, Wm. [PIPER], Peter JETT; [attested copy of the will was presented at court on 23 Nov 1812 by John CAMPBELL and it appearing that the book in which the original was recorded as well as the original itself has been lost the sd. copy together with the certificate of the clerk thereon indorsed was ord. to be recorded]. (WC DW 22:385)
[This is the Rev. Archibald Campbell, of Argyleshire, Scotland, who was minister of Washington parish, Westmoreland county, and of Round Hill Church, KGC, from 1754 to 1774. He mar. (1) Rebecca RAWLINGS, dau. of Jn. & Mary RAWLINGS bef. 1754 and (2) Hannah McKAY (or McCOY), dau. of the Rev. Wm. & Barbary McKAY of KGC, RC, bond 23 Jan 1760; He died in 1774 (*Virginia Gazette* 4 Aug 1774, MRC:32, MWO:64); acc. to Nelson:306, The Rev. CAMPBELL was b. in Scotland, attended school in Aberdeen and Edinburgh, and mar. (1) Rebeca GRYMES and (2) Hannah McCOY; he served Washington Parish, WC between 1753? and 1774; for more on Archibald CAMPBELL, see Meade, Vol. 2:159-162]

CAMPBELL, Charles; PO 11 Mar 1816, T 12 Aug 1816; 13 Aug 1816
NC; sale of land which Charles CAMPBELL died seized & possessed & DIV of proceeds as a result of suit by Thomas JONES ex. & John CAMPBELL against Pryce, Pinkey, Thomas, Nancy & James CAMPBELL. (NC RB 21:65) [On the motion of Thos. JONES & Betsy his wife and Jn. CAMPBELL ord. that Pryce CAMPBELL, Pinky CAMPBELL, Thos. CAMPBELL, Nancy CAMPBELL and Jas. CAMPBELL show cause why the lands of Chas. CAMPBELL should not be sold (NC OB 1816-20:5); Thos. JONES mar. Eliz. CAMPBELL, NC, bond 7 Mar 1815 (MLBNC:62); This is prob. Charles CAMPBELL one of the sons of Pryse CAMPBELL (d. NC 1800) (NC RB 16:147); see also Jn. CAMPBELL below]

CAMPBELL, James; PO 18 Jun 1804; 17 Sep 1804. LC; INV. (LC EB 24:277)

CAMPBELL, John; T 15 Mar 1817; 14 Jun 1819. NC; INV, $118.67. (NC RB 22:61)

CAMPBELL, John; PO 14 Jun 1819, T 11 Aug 1819; 13 Sep 1819
NC; allottment of balance after settlement of est. by Royston BETTS Jr. admr; on 11 Sep 1819 the following people acknowledged receipt of the balance of $70.96 1/2: Thomas JONES, John BEACHAM, James CAMPBELL, Thomas CAMPBELL, Price CAMPBELL, William WALKER. (NC RB 22:113)
[Wm. WALKER mar. Nancy CAMPBELL, NC, bond 8 Jan 1818 (MLBNC:62, 105)]

CAMPBELL, Pryse; T 20 Jan 1800; 14 Jul 1800. NC; INV, £30.12.6. (NC RB 16:154)
[In his will (NC 24 Apr 1800-14 Jul 1800) Pryse CAMPBELL named his wife Sarah and his 2 eldest children James and Charles (NC RB 16:147)]

CANNON, William; PO 1793; 15 Oct 1798
LC; INV, £137.15.3; includes servants: Harry & Sarah both to serve until 23. (LC EB 24:81)
[Jn. D. EVERETT aptd. gdn. to Sally CANNON orphan of Wm. CANNON, 16 Jun 1800 (LC Orders 21 1799-1801:124); settle the gdnship. acct. of Jeduthan PULLEN with Sally & Jane CANNON orphans of Wm. CANNON lately his wards and possess Wm. [CLAUGHTON] their present gdn. with their estates, 15 Feb 1802 (LC Orders V 1802-03:12); Sally CANNON orphan of Wm. CANNON chose Wm. W. HUNTON as her gdn., 16 Sep 1805 (LC Orders D22 1805-08:54); settlement of gdnship. accts. of Wm. CLAUGHTON with Sally CANNON now Sally HUNTON dau. & orph. of Wm. CANNON and possess Wm. W. HUNTON with her est., 16 Dec 1805 (LC Orders D22 1805-08:100); settlement with Jeduthan PULLEN the acct. of his gdnship. of Sally & Jane CANNON orphans of Wm. CANNON, 15 Apr 1811 (LC Orders 24:13)]

CANNON, William; 19 Jan 1801; 15 Jun 1801. LC ; INV, £217.8.6. (LC EB 24:147)

CARPENTER, Griffin; 2 Dec 1821; 18 Mar 1822
LC; WILL; all my est. to wife Peggy CARPENTER during her life or widowhood; after wife's death or marriage est. to the heirs of my bro. Hiram CARPENTER; bro. Hiram ex; WITS: C[hichester] TAPSCOTT, Jn. HANKS, Eliz. HANKS, Mariah HAMMACK, Jas. STOTT. (LC WB 28:226)
[Griffin CARPENTER mar. Margaret C. NEWGENT, LC, bond 19 Jul 1819 (MLBLC:11)]

CARPENTER, Hiram; 18 Oct 1824
LC; Lucy CARPENTER aptd. gdn. to Lucy P. & Ann M. G. CARPENTER orphans of Hiram CARPENTER. (LC OB 26:77)
[Heirom CARPENTER mar. Lucy POLLARD, LC, bond 29 Aug 1814 (MLBLC:11)]

CARPENTER, John; 19 Feb 1818; 17 Jul 1820
LC; WILL; land I live on & land in RC to wife Ellen CARPENTER during her life; land in forest which I purchased of Richard STOTT's heirs, Ann WARWICK & John DUNAWAY with following Negroes Sucky to son William C. CARPENTER; after death of wife, land I live on & land in RC with Negroes Little Winn[ey], boy Anderson & girl Hannah to son Overton CARPENTER; Negroes Lucinda, [Jeffery], Maddison, Fanny & Samuel to dau. Olivia NORRIS; to grson. Henry L. BISCOE all to Negroes which I loaned his mother Jane BISCOE: Anna; John BISCOE the father of my sd. grson. to have the use of Negroes; Negro boys David & Richardson I lend to my grson. but they are never to be put into the possession of his father; son William C. CARPENTER & s-i-l John NORRIS exors; [no wits listed, but will proved by oaths of Jn. [SEWARD], Chichester TAPSCOTT & Raw. DUNAWAY]. (LC WB 28:206)
[Jn. CARPENTER mar. Ellen CARTER, LC, bond 18 Mar 1784; Jn. NORRIS mar. Olivia CARPENTER, LC, bond 17 Jun 1816 (MLBLC:11, 55); div. of that portion of the life est. devised by Jn. CARPENTER to his wife Ellen into three eq. parts (except the Negroes) between Jn. NORRIS, Wm. C. CARPENTER and Overton CARPENTER; and the Negroes to be div. in the same manner except one fourth which is to be delivered to the sd. Ellen

CARPENTER to be retained for her life and afterwards to Hen. L. BISCOE, 20 Aug 1822 (LC OB 25:323); *see also LC CC 1822-002*]

CARPENTER, John (Capt.); PO 1820, T 6 Sep 1820; 17 Sep 1821
LC; INV, $5444.8[1] 1/2; includes Negroes James, Adam, Aaron, Daniel, Young James, Dominy, David, Richardson, Nelly, Milly, Winny & infant Sally, Alice, Easter, Sinah, Eliza, [Kelly]. (LC EB 29:121)

CARPENTER, Margaret C.; 10 Jul 1824; 6 Sep 1824
RC; WILL; to Betsey HANKS; to Nancy HAZZARD; balance of prop. to bro. George C. NEWGENT; if NEWGENT die without issue remaining prop. to go to children of my father by his last wife, Robert & Elizabeth NEWGENT; friend Ewell HANKS ex; WITS: D[ominick] [BENNEHAN], Ewell HANKS. (RC WB 10:48)
[This is Margaret C. (NEWGENT) the wid. of Griffin CARPENTER who d. in LC in 1822 (LC WB 22:226, MLBLC:11); Margaret CARPENTER the wid. of Griffin CARTER [sic] relinquishes all manner of benefits or provisions made for her in the will of her dec'd husband, 16 Sep 1822 (LC OB 25:330)]

CARPENTER, William; 10 Nov 1818; 15 Feb 1819
LC; WILL; land & plant. w/o I now live to son Griffin CARPENTER; Negro man Dick & girl Jude to son Hiram CARPENTER; I lend to my grdau. Sarah Ann BISCOE my Negro girl Bett at the time of her marriage; balance of est. to be eq. div. between my 2 sons Griffin & Hiram; 2 sons exors; WITS: C[hichester] TAPSCOTT, Jn. SEWARD, Robt. CHINN, Robt. WOODDY, Thos. NEWGENT. (LC WB 28:195)

CARPENTER, William; PO 15 Feb 1819; 17 Dec 1821
LC; INV, [m]; includes legacies to G. CARPENTER, Sarah Ann BISCOE, H. CARPENTER and the Negroes Hannah, Juliet, Joe, [Amanda], Hannible, Anna, Dick, Judith. (LC EB 29:144)

CARROLL, John; 7 Dec 1809; 26 Feb 1810
CP, WC; WILL; to my dau. Nancy CARROLL [Negro] named Guy during Miss Nancy MORSE's natural life; dau. Elizabeth CARROLL Negro named Susan; son John CARROLL Negro boy Robbin; rest of est. to be eq. div; my Negro woman Jenney shall be at liberty from the time of my life until death [sic]; [no ex. named]; WITS: Thos. BUTLER, William RICE Sr., Wm. RICE, Henry GREGORY, [fnu] McGUIRE. (WC DW 22:57)
[Nancy CARROLL mar. Frederick ALVORSON, WC, bond 5 Mar 1810 (WCCP:12, MLBWC:1)]

CARROLL, John; PO 26 Feb 1810; 27 Aug 1810
WC; INV, £451.5.3; includes Negroes Jenney, Suckey, Robert. (WC RI 9:191)

CARTER, [fnu]; 21 Jul 1823
LC; Catherine M. CARTER chose Mary B. CARTER for her gdn. and Mary B. CARTER is aptd. gdn. to [Elias] J. CARTER. (LC OB 25:390)
[Catherine M. CARTER mar. Wm. BRENT, LC, bond 20 Nov 1823 (MLBLC:8)]

CARTER, Abner; PO 22 Dec 1813; 28 Feb 1814
WC; INV, $1821.85; includes Negroes Aaron, Anney, Sarah Sr., Sarah Jr. (WC RI 9:409)

CARTER, Augustine; 22 Oct 1811; 16 Dec 1811
LC; WILL; being within one day of 71 years of age; debts of about $14 to James KESTERSON & about $5 to George P. OLIVER; debts due me: John M. SMITH about £10, est. of Vincent GARLAND dec'd of RC (Samuel KELSICK dec'd sec to his bond) £38, Mr. Joseph CARTER inspector $8, Mrs. Elizabeth GEORGE wid. of William GEORGE about $7, from the Messrs. LUNSFORD

storekeepers. some few dollars; all my prop. some at house of Charles WEBB, some at Edward BLACKMORE's & some at my bro. James CARTER's; half of my prop. to go Charles WEBB for his kindness to me to be eq. div. between him & the poorest man living in LC (the judges of the poorest man Captains William & John CHOWNING, Porteus TOWLES & Maj John CHOWNING or any 3 of them); Charles WEBB & Merryman CHILTON exors; WITS: Wm. LUNSFORD, Moses LUNSFORD. (LC WB 28:124)
[This is Augustine CARTER the son of Dale CARTER (d. LC 1776) (LC WB 20:100)]

CARTER, Augustine; T 11 Jan 1814; 19 Feb 1816
LC; DIV of est. between Charles WEBB dec'd & the poorest man in LC which person was to be chosen by Col. CHOWNING & ourselves, but Col. CHOWNING having taken administration on the est. of Charles WEBB dec'd was unwilling to express an opinion. We therefore give it as our decided opinion that William SMITH is the most indigent and necessitous man of our acquaintances in LC and is under sd. CARTER's will entitled to one half of his est. Col. CHOWNING who was ex. of Augustin CARTER having produced to us the account of sales of sd. est. and his acct. against it with proper vouchers thereto, we find that there is $50.11 in sd. CHOWNING's hands, $25.05 1/2 is due to William SMITH; /s/ Wm. CHOWNING, Porteus TOWLES, Jn. CHOWNING. (LC EB 27:278)

CARTER, Carmen; T 6 Nov 1823; 15 Mar 1824. LC; INV, [m]. (LC EB 29:319)
[This is prob. Carmen PULLEN, the wid. of Jn. CARTER (d. LC, 1822) (see below)]

CARTER, Charles (Dr.); 19 Dec 1825
LC; Jos. C. CABELL aptd. gdn. to Parke Farley CARTER orphan of Charles CARTER. (LC OB 26:155)
[Died at the Sweet Springs on Oct. 12, Miss Rebecca Parke Farley CARTER, daughter of the late Dr. Charles & Mrs. Elizabeth L. CARTER of Corrotoman, Lancaster Co., Va. Buried in Nelson Co. by her grandmother, the late Mrs. Judge TUCKER, at Edgewood, the residence of her adopted parents, Mrs. Joseph C. & Mrs. Mary W. CABELL (*American Beacon & Norfolk & Portsmouth Daily Advertiser*, date missing, but prob. Oct. 1839); she is buried in the Edgewood Cabell Family Cemetery, Warminster, Nelson Co., Va. where her death date is given as 11 Oct 1839; a petition by Lelia (SKIPWITH, CARTER) TUCKER printed in Loren Schweninger, ed., *Southern Debate Over Slavery, Vol. 2 Petitions to Southern County Courts 1775 - 1867*, Urbana & Chicago: Univ. of Illinois Press, 2008, pp. 169-171, provides information on the family of Rebecca Parke Farley CARTER; Lelia dau. of Sir. Peyton SKIPWITH mar. (1) Geo. CARTER in 1784 and had two children Charles and Mary Walker; Geo. CARTER d. intestate in 1788 and Lelia (SKIPWITH) CARTER mar. (2) St. George TUCKER in 1791; Chas. CARTER was the father of Rebecca Parke Farley CARTER; Mary Walker CARTER mar. Joseph C. CABELL]

CARTER, Charles B.; 1 Jan 1800; 4 Apr 1808
RC; WILL; debt due to Charles JONES for building a mill for me (which began operation on 10 Apr 1794); ex. to collect outstanding debts esp. £1000 due from Landon CARTER ex. of Robert W. CARTER which was left my wife by her father & £800 due from John TAYLOE of Mount Airey; money to be used to buy good piece of land on Rappahannock or Potomac river; all lands in RC and WC to be sold and money from this to be used to buy good

land on same rivers; sd. lands to be settled with my Negroes and cultivated for wife and children during their minority; 800 ac. tract known as Nantepoison Neck now occupied by E. CURRIE; at her death to be settled with the necessary number of my Negroes and stocks for the maintenance of my wife, Ann Beale CARTER; at her death land and Negroes to be eq. div. between 2 sons John Hill CARTER & Charles CARTER (both under 21); dau. Winefred Beale CARTER when 21; if either son has the capacity to receive a liberal education he is to be sent to the best & most approved seminary on the American continent; if sons prefer the more laborious mechanical professions which by the bye are generally most profitable such as house carpenter, joiner or carriage building they should have three of the likeliest Negro boys that may be in my est. bound with them to assist them in carrying on their trade; books to be div. between my sons provided they have each a turn for reading, otherwise to be sold; Negroes to be well clothed, fed and comfortably lodged and treated well; blooded filly which I purchased & the one I am to have of Mr. John TAYLOE to be kept in my est. as blood mares; friends Edward CARTER of Prince William, Landon CARTER, & John TAYLOE, both of RC, and Thomas L. LEE of Loudoun exors; [no wits]. (RC WB 9:322)

[Chas. B. CARTER mar. Ann Beale CARTER, dau. of Robt. Wormeley & Winifred (BEALE) CARTER, RC, bond 5 Apr 1796 (MRC:33); Jn. Hill CARTER is gdn. to Mary & Eliz. CARTER orphans of Charles B. CARTER, 7 May 1821 (RC OB 25:120); Nantepoison or Antipoison Neck is located in LC between Tabbs Creek and Antipoison Creek fronting on Little Bay (Miller:2)]

CARTER, Charles B. Esq.; T 15 Dec 1819; 3 Jul 1820

RC; allotted Mrs. Ann B. MOFFETT the following slaves as her dower of the Negroes of Charles B. CARTER dec'd: Dick, Phillip, Anderson, John, Griffin, Reed, Robert, Robin, Harry, Phil, Boughten, Matilda & her [5] children, Catherine & her 6 youngest children, Lucy, Alice & her 3 children, Diana, Priscilla & her 3 children, Rebecah & her 5 children, Martha, Marjory & her 6 children, Winney & her 3 children, Abby & her 5 children, Ellen & her child. (RC AB 3:695)

[Ann B. CARTER, wid. of Charles B. CARTER, mar. Wm. MOFFETT bef. 1 Dec 1817 (RC OB 24:162)]

CARTER, Daniel; 6 May 1794; 20 Oct 1794

LC; WILL; wife Rachel CARTER; weaver's loom to dau. Betsey; son Ambrose; est. bequeathed to wife to be eq. div. among my 3 children Ambrose, John & Betsey after death or marriage of wife; wife & friend George CAMPBELL exors; WITS: Rawleigh TAPSCOTT, Jn. LUCKHAM, Betty CAMPBELL. (LC WB 28:6)

CARTER, Edward; [m]; 20 Jul 1795

LC; INV, [m]; includes Negroes: Daniel, Rose, Dinah, George, Bett, Peter. (LC EB 24:43)

[Jn. LUNSFORD was aptd. gdn. of Thos. CARTER orphan of Edw. CARTER, 17 Jun 1799, but it may not be this Edw. CARTER (LC Orders (21) 1799-1801:1; OB 1804-05:1, 332); settle Jn. LUNSFORD's gdnship. acct. of Thos. CARTER orphan of Edw. CARTER (LC Orders 21 1799-1801:200; Orders B23 1808-11:77; Orders D22 1805-08:101; Orders 24:57)]

CARTER, Edward; [m]; 20 Jul 1795

LC; INV, [m]; includes Negroes: Daniel, Rose, Dinah, George, Bett, Peter. (LC EB 24:43)

[Jn. LUNSFORD was aptd. gdn. of Thos. CARTER orphan of Edw. CARTER, LC 16 Jan 1804, but it may not be this Edw. CARTER (LC Orders W 1804-05:1)]

CARTER, Elizabeth; T 6 Mar 1795; 21 Sep 1795. LC; INV, £62.7.9; includes Negro Stephen. (LC EB 24:48)

CARTER, George; PO 16 Dec 1793; 17 Oct 1796
LC; INV, £293.19.4; includes Negroes: Spencer, Sarah & child, Isabel, boy Harry, girls Sinah, Milly & Fanny. (LC EB 24:30)

CARTER, George; 16 Dec 1806
LC; CC; Hierom & Peggy CARTER, infants, by Geo. ROBINSON & his wife Sarah, pltfs., against William GIBSON admr. of Geo. CARTER; Geo. CARTER, Robert MARSH & Nancy his wife and are made complts. and Wm. GIBSON as gdn. of Caty B. CARTER, Nicholas CARTER & Dale CARTER are made defts. (LC Orders D22 1805-08:278)
[Geo. CARTER, Nancy MARSH, Judith, Hierom, Peggy, Caty B., Nicholas & Dale CARTER are children of Geo. CARTER (NC CC 1810-003); Sally the wid. of Geo. CARTER mar. (2) Geo. ROBINSON (LC CC 1819-038); Robt. M. MARSH of NC mar. Ann CARTER, RC, bond 22 Oct 1805 (MRC:128)]

CARTER, George; 21 Feb 1815; 26 Jan 1816.
WP, WC; WILL; whole of my property to wife Letty CARTER; if wife marries, property to be div. as follows: wife to have 4 Negroes of her choice; balance of Negroes to be div. between children, "that is to say John S, Carter [sic], Frankey, [Presly], William; wife is now pregnant; Negroes Henry & Clary to be sold; wife & her bro. Thomas STOWERS exors; WITS: Jn. NEALE, Rich. NEALE, Jacob MILLER. (WC DW 23:151)
[Geo. CARTER mar. Lettice STOWERS, RC, bond 5 Jan 1792 (MWO:66)]

CARTER, Humphrey; PO Sep 1816; 19 Nov 1821
LC; INV, [m]; includes Negroes Dick, Charles, Davey, [Osison], Tunnell, Harry, Lewis, James, Willis, Aaron, Solomon, Armistead, Stokeley, Davy (young), Tom, Ellyson, Butler, Milly, Abigal, Letty, Easter, Aggy, Maria, Phillis, Charlotte, Amanda, George and a number of books; his only child named was Frances Ann CARTER. (LC EB 29:124, 140)

CARTER, Humphrey [F.]; PO 16 Nov 1818, T 30 Dec 1818; 18 Jan 1819
LC; Frances R. McCARTY late Frances R. CARTER (wid. of Humphrey P. CARTER) was assigned her thirds of her late husband's pers. est. which included the Negroes: Lewis, Davy, Charles, Thomas, Ellyson, Stokeley, Milly, Maria & child James, and Amanda; total slaves appraised at $4425; out of this total James K. BALL gdn. of Frances [A.] CARTER was paid $8.66 2/3. (LC EB 27:453)
[Humphrey F. CARTER mar. Frances Ravenscroft BALL, dau. of James BALL, LC, bond 22 Nov 1815; Frances Ravenscroft (BALL) CARTER mar. (2) Wm. D. McCARTY, LC, bond 23 Oct 1818 (MLBLC:11, 50); Jas. K. BALL aptd. gdn. to Frances Ann CARTER orphan of Humph. F. CARTER, 16 Nov 1818 (LC OB 25:24)]

CARTER, Humphry F.; T 16 Nov 1821; 19 Nov 1821
LC; settlement of admin. acct. of William Lee BALL in the presence of James K. BALL gdn. of Frances Ann CARTER only child of Humphry F. CARTER dec'd and William D. McCARTY who mar. Frances R. CARTER wid. of sd. Humphry who was the only child & heir of Joseph CARTER dec'd; Humphry F. CARTER had administered the est. of Joseph CARTER Sr. and at his death William L. BALL took administration de bonis non; the two estates were blended into the same acct. (LC EB 29:140

CARTER, James; PO 20 Jan 1800; 21 Jul 1800
LC; INV; includes only Negro Mingo valued at £10. (LC EB 24:114)

CARTER, James Jr.; PO 16 Mar 1813, T 3 May 1813; 18 Apr 1814
LC; INV $392.91 1/2 & allotment of dower to the wid, Mary B. CARTER. (LC EB 27:172

CARTER, John; 23 Dec 1821; 18 Mar 1822
LC; WILL; to son Rawleigh CARTER the Negroes loaned him: Isaac, Joseph, James, Lucy & her 3 young children; use of my land & the following Negroes: Joshua, Griffin, Joe, Mitchell, Spencer, John, Moses, Joshua, Nella, Cate, Aggy, Delia, Betty & Polly to wife Carmin during the time she lives my widow for her support & the support & education of my 3 young children Robert CARTER, John CARTER, & Joseph CARTER; Negro man Billy to be sold; wife & son Rawleigh exors; WITS: Spencer GEORGE, Jn. WADDEY, Alley GASKINS. (LC WB 28:223)
[Jn. CARTER mar. Carmin PULLEN, LC, bond 24 Dec 1816 (MLBLC:12); Carmin CARTER aptd. gdn. to Robt., Jn. and Jos. CARTER orphans of Jn. CARTER, 21 Oct 1822 (LC OB 25:335)]

CARTER, John; PO 18 Mar 1822, T 10 Apr 1822; 20 May 1822
LC; INV; includes Negroes Joshua Sr., Griffin, Mitchell, Joshua Jr., Spencer, Joe, John, Polly, Nelly, Moses, Kate, Aggy, Delia, Betty, Billy (sold); Negroes willed to R. CARTER: Isaac, Silvy, Josias, Lucy, James, Washington, Maria, Elizabeth. (LC EB 29:197)

CARTER, John; 17 Apr 1824; 4 Oct 1824
RC; WILL; all my land to my three sons Daniel CARTER, Fenner CARTER, & Jack S. CARTER to be eq. div. after death of wife Polly CARTER; rest of est. after debts paid to be eq. div. between two daus. Lucy CARTER & Elizabeth CARTER after wife's death; William GUTRIDGE ex; WITS: Enoch FINCH, Thos. FONES, Austin HINSON. (RC WB 10:48)

CARTER, John; T 15 Oct & [23] Dec 1824; 2 May 1825. RC; INV, $196.09 3/4. (RC WB 10:76)

CARTER, John M.; PO 17 May 1824, T 21 Jun 1824; 19 Jul 1824
LC; INV, $484.20; includes [Negroes] Samuel, Julian and a Latin dictionary and grammar. (LC EB 29:344)

CARTER, Joseph; [m]; 16 Feb 1824
LC; INV, $11,564; includes Negroes Thoma, Samuel, Harry, James, Peter, George, Davy, Moses, Young Peter, Jesse, Nelson, Isaac, Philip, Jenny, Patty, Lucinda & child Julia Ann, Mary, Lavina & child Rose, Felicia, Mariah, Harriet, Lucy, Sarah, Old Robin, Charles (deformed & expense). (LC EB 29:304)

CARTER, Joseph Jr.; 26 Nov 1815; 18 Dec 1815
LC; WILL; use of all my est. to wife Frances Everett; if wife marries she is to have one third; wife to educate my children William Henry, John Miller, Robert Alexander & Fanny in as well [and] liberal a manner as I have educated my three elder children Joseph Addison, Warren & Polly; dau. Lettice to be sent to school 8 months of the ensuing year; if wife dies before younger children receive their schooling, exors. to educate them; friends Rawleigh DUNAWAY & Ralph EDMONDS counselors to advise my exors; sons Joseph Addison CARTER & Warren CARTER exors; WITS: Nathan SPRIGGS, Sarah D. SPRIGGS. (LC WB 28:171)
[Jos. CARTER, Jr., wid., mar. Fanny HUTCHINGS, dau. of Jn. (d. LC 1784-85) & Sarah HUTCHINGS, LC, bond 1 Jun 1797 (LC WB 22:56, 210; MLBLC:12); Lettice L. CARTER orphan of Jos. CARTER Jr. chose Jos. A.

CARTER as her gdn., 17 Nov 17 (LC Orders 24:397); Frances E. CARTER mar. (2) Rawleigh DUNAWAY, LC, bond 27 Apr 1818 (MLBLC:24); commission to lay off and assign unto Frances E. DUNAWAY her dower in the slaves of her late husband Jos. CARTER; Warren CARTER chose Jos. A. CARTER for his gdn. & the sd. Jos. A. CARTER is aptd. gdn. to Wm. H., Frances M., Jn. M., & Robt. A. CARTER orphans of Jos. CARTER, 21 Dec 1818 (LC OB 25:32)]

CARTER, Joseph Jr.; PO 20 Jul 1818, T 29 Dec 1818; 18 Jan 1819
LC; slaves assigned to Frances E. CARTER the wid. & rel: Thomas, James, Moses, Jesse, Phill, Lucinda & child Juliann, Felicia, Old Lucy, Samuel, Peter (old), David, Nelson, Jenny, Lavina & child Rose, Maria, Sarah, Harry, George, [1 word unclear] Peter, Isaac, Patty, Mary, Harriott, Robin; slaves were appraised at $10050.01; the widow's dower consisted of: George, [1 word unclear] Peter, James, Felicia, Phill, Samuel, Lucy, Lucinda & child Juliann (worth a total of $3350). (LC EB 27:452)

CARTER, Joseph Jr.; PO 21 Dec 1818, T 19 Mar 1819; 20 Dec 1824
LC; DIV of slaves (except widow's dower which was assigned her at a former time) amongst his legatees: John LUNSFORD in behalf of his wife Lettice (Tom & Harriet), John M. CARTER (Sam & Julian), Warren CARTER (Harry & Maria), William H. CARTER (Moses & Sarah), Frances M. CARTER (Jesse & Mary), William H. ROGERS in behalf of his wife Mary P. (Isaac & Levina & child Rose), Joseph A. CARTER (Lucinda, Charles-deformed, Felicia). (LC EB 29:368)
[Jn. LUNSFORD mar. Lettice L. CARTER, LC, bond 17 Nov 1817; Wm. H. ROGERS mar. Mary Page CARTER, LC, bond 9 Dec 1813 (MLBLC:49, 65); *see also LC CC 1819-045*]

CARTER, Landon; PO 7 Jan 1822; 2 Dec 1823
RC; list of slaves allotted to Mrs. Mary B. CARTER, wid. of the late Landon CARTER Esq. of Sabine Hall: Joe (blacksmith, 40), Elias (striker for blacksmith, 20), George (brick layer, 24), James Saunders (carpenter, 45), Billy (house servant, 22), Jesse (18), Watt Jr. (23), Cato (28), Benjamine (25), Harry (from Clifton, 19), Bartley (16), John (from Clifton, 15), Nassau (14), Billy (from Sabine Hall, 14), Tom (weaver, 46), John (from Sabine Hall, 20), Moses (13), Tom (from Bluff Point, 42), Tom (son of weaver Tom, 10), Peter (from Bluff Point, 7), Thos. (son of Suckey, 5), Judy (from Sabine Hall, 16), [Sally] (19), Sukey (34), Adeline (2), Nanny (33), Anne (2), Lazarus (3), Serena (5), Becky (1), Nelly (45), Franky (18), Judy (16), Sarah (12), Criss (21), Susan (1), Billy (16), Austin (9), Willis (4), Betty (house maid, 19), Ellen (7), Louisa (2), Moses (5), Polly (18), Simon (60), Rich, (5), Eliza (13), Joe (deformed, 38), John Wiggins (60), Sally (10), Grace (25), Billy (wheelwright, 60), Nanny (called Big Nanny, 50), Dinah (3), Simon (1), Sukey (45), Moses (50), Fanny (20), Anderson (5), Beck (45), John Neale (55), Billy (58), Billy (3); the following are chargeable slaves: Polly, Betty, Jack (miller), Franky, Beck, Billy (an idiot), Peggy (from Loudoun) & Sarah (from Bluff Point); following slaves assigned to Mrs. CARTER: Billy (40 years old), Patty (38), Reuben (20), Betsy (9), Lewis (3), Mary (2), Spencer (a cook, 55), Hen. (scullion, defective in one foot, 20), Molly (18); the six following lots were allotted to Elizabeth CARTER (Shadrac, blacksmith, 40; Chas., 20; Enock, 17; Tom, 38; Wm., 14; Tolly, 10; Marry Anne, 27; Aggy, 5; Sarah, dau. of Franky, 20; David, 1; Billy, gardner, 50; Penny, 10, Zachariah, 8; Caroline, 21; Adderson, 1; Archibald, 48; Lydia, 8; Sally, 5; Elvia, 8), to Williamson B. TOMLIN in right of his wife Anne TOMLIN who was Anne CARTER (Bidwell,

carpenter, 22; Billy Willis, 28; Godfrey, 28; Anthony, 36; Wm., 19; Talbot, cook, 48; Beck, 24; Edmund, 1; Beck, Matt's wife, 37; Easter, 2; Matt Sr., 47; Charlotte, 5; Louisa, 13; Louisa, 13; Betty, 9; Wm., 10; Bibby, 25; Fanny, 1; Simon, 2); to Landon CARTER (Absylum, carpenter, 32; Billy, 27; Ralph, 35; Washington, 16; Jos., 12; Geo., 40; Betty, called Little Betty, 30; Fanny, 2; Jenny, 32; [?], [sitified, 6; Alice, 20; Thos., infant; Nancy, 24; Levy, deaf, 13; Rebecca, 7; Dolly, 11; Nelson, [5]; Lucy, 50; Mann, 58; Jenny, 1; Franky, 2); to Mary L. CARTER (Peter, carpenter, 40; Phill, striker for blacksmith, 24; David, 35; Jerry, 17; Rich., 12; Randal, 40; Nelly, 30; Peggy, 5; Franky, 21; Beck, 1; Betsy, 39; Adelaide, 2; James, 30; Judy, 27; Franky, 3; Natt, 57; Bob, 4; Franky, 7; Harry, carpenter, 60); to Frances A. CARTER (Ralph, striker for blacksmith, 24; Lazarus, 28; Reed, 32, Jacob, 20; Anxious, 14; Anthony, 13; Betty, sickly, 24; [Betty], 2; [Nelly], 20; Sally, infant; Polly, 24; Spencer, 2; Fanny, 16; [Olivay], 4; Isarel, 48; Charlotte, 11; Lucy, 3; Willmouth, 8); to John A. G. CARTER (Henry, blacksmith, 30; Phill, 24; Moore, 17; George, 38; Barnaba, 26; Henry, 8; Suckey, 21; Alice, 1; Sarah, 4; Luncinda, 12; Venus, 40; George, 1; Molly, 19; Anna, 18; Nelly, 22; Letty, 2; Mary, infant; Chochena, has but one eye, 16; Cate, 6; Phill, cooper, 70); following is a list of slaves advanced to Robert W. CARTER by his father with their ages & values when advanced: Samuel, 36; Jane, 30; Agga, 4; Delia, 2; Franky, 35; Elisa, 5; Mary, infant; Jane, 38; Judy, 6; Maria, 15; Henry, 3; Sally, 2; Dolly, 27; Arabella, 3; Ralph, infant; Alexander, 5; Cate, 8; Cress, 7; Mary, 4; Peggy, 4; Easter, infant; Molly, 13; Alice, 17; Franky, 41; Jonathan, 19; Joseph, 3; Jenny, 27; Jacob, 1; Traverse, 9; Celia, infant; John, 14; Nanny, 17; Israel, 14; Peter, 9; James, 60; Bob, 11; total value of slaves which Landon CARTER died possessed $43,550; RC AB 4:140)

[Williamson Ball TOMLIN mar. Ann C. CARTER, RC, bond 5 May 1819 (MRC:218); Mary L. CARTER & Frances A. CARTER orphans of Landon CARTER chose Chas. CARTER as their gdn. and the sd. Chas. is aptd. gdn. of Jn. A. G. CARTER another of the orphans; Landon CARTER orphan of Landon CARTER chose Robt. W. CARTER as his gdn., 1 Jan 1821 (RC OB 25:97); CC, Mary B., Eliz. L., Robt. W. & Williamson B. TOMLIN & Ann his wife, compl. vs. Landon, Mary L., Frances A. and Jn. A. G. CARTER infants by Jn. T. LOMAX their gdn. to show cause, 2 Sep 1822 (RC OB 25:336); Mary L. CARTER mar. Wm. Alex. ELIASON, 27 Jun 1825 (MRC:64); Jn. A. G. CARTER orphan of Landon CARTER chose Robt. M. CARTER as his gdn., 2 Jan 1826 (RC OB 27:29); Frances A. CARTER mar. Hen. R. DULANY, RC, bond 7 Apr 1827 (MRC:60)]

CARTER, Martin; 18 Sep 1815
LC; Overseers of the Poor to bind out Edward CARTER orphan of Martin CARTER to Eppa LAWSON. (LC Orders 24:259)

CARTER, Nicholas; PO 15 Dec 1817; 20 Apr 1818
LC; INV, $313.06 1/3; includes half the schooner "George Wythe"; LC EB 27:415)
[Wm. H. GEORGE aptd. gdn. to Cath. CARTER orphan of Nic. CARTER, 19 Jan 1818 (LC OB 24:412)]

CARTER, Peter; T Oct 1817; 9 Mar 1818. NC, INV, $283.50. (NC RB 21:378)

CARTER, Samuel; PO Sep 1808; 26 Feb 1810. WC; INV, [m]; includes Negroes Dick & Milley. (WC RI 9:166)

CARTER, Samuel; WC; made a will and did not alter it before his death prior to 1819; in his will he gave all his est. to his natural son Samuel Carter CRENSHAW son of Peggy CRENSHAW who was a sis. of the whole blood

of Jane CRENSHAW; Peggy also d. before 1819 leaving no other children; Samuel Carter CRENSHAW went to sea at least seven years before 1819 and has not been heard of since; admin. on his est. granted to John HARVEY. (WC CC 1819-003)
[Sam. CARTER's will, which was supposed to be included in WC CC 1819-003, has not been located.]

CARTER, Spencer; PO 17 Jan 1803; 21 Feb 1803. LC ; INV. (LC EB 24:229)
[Thos. CARTER aptd. gdn. to Dale CARTER orphan of Spencer CARTER and Chatham CARTER orphan of sd. decedent chose Thos. CARTER as his gdn., 17 Jan 1803 (LC Orders V 1802-03:257)]

CARTER, Spencer; PO 18 June [1804]; 17 Dec 1804
LC; DIV of £93.3.7 among: Mrs Ann CARTER (the wid.), Thomas CARTER (gdn. of Dale CARTER), [Chatham] CARTER, John FLOWERS in right of his wife Sarah. (LC EB 24:299)
[Spencer CARTER, wid., mar. Ann CONWAY, wid., NC, bond 23 Dec 1792 (MLBNC:16); Jn. FLOWERS Jr. mar. Salley CARTER, LC, bond 16 Mar 1801 (MLBLC:28)]

CARTER, Thomas; 21 Jan 1816; 17 Jun 1816
LC; WILL; friend Mrs. Judath LAWRY; friend John LAWRY; half-sisters in Kentucky Frances ROBB and Judah ROBB; friends Joseph A. CARTER & John LAWRY exors; WITS: Humphry F. CARTER, Thos. NEWGENT, Warren CARTER. (LC WB 28:178)
[Frances & Judah ROBB were prob. daus. of James ROBB who mar. Judith CARTER, wid., LC, bond 7 Jan 1794 (MLBLC:63)]

CARTER, Thomas; PO 17 Jun 1816, T 27 Jun 1816; 21 Jul 1817
LC; INV, $863.50; includes Negroes: Betty & child John, Harry, Scillar, Dick. (LC EB 27:388)

CARTER, Thomas; 15 Nov 1818; 16 Feb 1824
LC; WILL; all est. except the land which was my father's to wife Judith; at wife's death est. to be eq. div. between my two children Dale CARTER & Harriett CARTER; if both children should die before their mother, est. to be eq. div. between my daus. Rebecca & Lucasta CARTER; if these daus. die without heirs est. to be eq. div. between children of Joseph DALE & Robert D. PALMER; tract of land that was my father, Harry CARTER's, to daus. Rebecca & Lucasta; wife Judith & friends James TOWLES & James KIRK exors; [no wits listed but will proved by oaths of Raw. DUNAWAY & Jas. BRENT]; LC WB 28:247)
[This is prob. Thos. CARTER who mar. Judah PALMER, LC, bond 18 Nov 1799 (MLBLC:12)]

CARY, Hannah; T Jan 1803; 25 Mar 1804. WC; INV. (WC RI 8:384)
[Hannah CARY qualified as admx. of Geo. CARY, WC, 23 Mar 1801 (WC Orders 1801-04:26)]

CAVENDER, Sturman; [m] Dec 1810; 25 Feb 1811
WC; Nunc. will made by Sturman CAVENDER on [m] day of Dec 1810 during his last sickness at the habitation of Wm. CARPENTER where he had resided during the year 1810; all est. to dau. [Jenney] CAVENDER;; admin. with the will annexed granted to Wm. CARPENTER. (WC DW 22:186)
[Thos. CAVENDER in his will (WC 23 Nov 1786 – 28 Mar 1796) named his wife Sally Sturman CAVENDER; is it possible that she was Sally STURMAN and that one of their children was Sturman CAVENDER? (WC DW 19:157)]

CAVENDER, Thomas; 28 Apr 1823

WC; on the mot. of Younger HOLLIDAY, ord. that William CARPENTER settle his admin. of the est. of Thomas CAVENDER and his gdnship. of Jane HOLLIDAY his wife who was Jane CAVENDER dau. of Thomas. (WC OB 1819-23:553)
[This is prob. the Thos. CAVENDER who mar. Sarah SCINNER, WC, bond 16 May 1809 (MLBWC:12)]

CHAMPION, James; PO 12 Apr 1819; 8 Nov 1819
NC; INV, $496; includes Negroes Eve & boy Davy; DIV of est. held by admr. Richard H. GASKINS between Richard H. GASKINS as gdn. to William T. CHAMPION (Negro Eve) & George JONES who mar. Elizabeth CHAMPION (Negro boy David). (NC RB 22:153)
[Geo. JONES, wid, mar. Eliz. CHAMPION, wid, NC, bond 19 Jul 1815 (MLBNC:61)]

CHAMPION, William T.; PO 15 [?] 1799; 13 Jun 1803
NC; INV, [m]; includes Negroes Fielding, Job, Eave, Sharlotte, Judith, Nancey, Old Billey. (NC RB 16:554)

CHAMPION, William T.; PO 13 Nov 1809, T 11 Jan 1810; 11 Jun 1810
NC; allottment of dower in land (on Harvey's Creek) and Negroes Charlotte & Mariah to the wid. Elizabeth CHAMPION; as gdn. to James & William T. CHAMPION, she also rec'd Negroes Jobe, Eve, Nanny, David & Mischick. (NC RB 18:407; OB 1807-11:131))
[This is Wm. T. CHAMPION who mar. Betsey INGRAM, dau. of Capt. Geo. INGRAM, NC, bond 24 Jul 1795 (MWO:71); the est. of Wm. T. CHAMPION was ord. to be admin. by Eliz. CHAMPION & Roger W. HUGHLETT with Josias INGRAM, Hen. HURST and Thos. HARVEY, sec. (NC Fiduciary Bonds 1797-1801); Wm. CHAMPION orphan of Wm. CHAMPION chose Jn. INGRAM as his gdn., 11 Mar 1816 (NC OB 1816-20:18); Eliz. JONES wife of Geo. JONES and mother of James CHAMPION late a pvt. in Capt. Cumming's co. of the 4th Inf. of the US and William T. CHAMPION the bro. of sd. James are the only heirs at law of the sd. James CHAMPION, NC 13 Jul 1819 (NC OB 1816-20:368); Harveys Creek is located in NC in Harveys Neck; it flows into Ingram Bay (Miller:63)]

CHARLETON, Richard; T 19 Feb 1807; 25 Apr 1808. WC; INV, £75.18.6. (WC RI 9:47)

CHASTAIN, Elizabeth; PO Jun 1801, T 27 Oct 1801, [m] 1801
WC; INV, £45.0.0; includes Negro Frank. (WC RI 8:145)
[This is prob. Eliz. RUST, wid., who mar. Lewis CHASTAIN, WC, bond 23 Jul 1793 (MWO:72)]

CHILTON, Andrew; 14 Nov 1819 - 17 Jan 1820;
LC; WILL; use of all my est. to wife Elizabeth except my military land; after wife's death or marriage, plant. w/o I now live to my two sons [Hiram Davis] & William CHILTON reserving to my 2 daus. Sarah & Mary CHILTON homes on sd. plant. during their single lives; my military land to be sold; after wife's death rest of est. to be eq. div. between my daus. Sarah & Mary and the heirs of my son [Hiram] reserving to [Hiram] the use of his heir's part during his life; wife extx.; WITS: Benj. WADDEY, B[enj.] M. WALKER. (LC WB 28:202))
[Andrew CHILTON served 3 years as a private in the Continental Line during the Revolutionary War (VS1776 II:622); he mar. Eliz. DAVIS, LC, bond 23 Dec 1788 (MLBLC:13); Andrew CHILTON deposed that he served as a private in Capt. Butler's company 5th Regt. of the Virginia Line; that he enlisted on 25 Dec 1778 and remained in the service until the end of the war

and that he was in need of assistance from the country, 19 May 1818 (LC Orders 24:433); Andrew CHILTON d. 17 Nov 1819 (PR1835:714); the file under Andrew CHILTON's name accessed at <http://www.revwarapps.org/> indicates that he d. on 15 Nov 1819 and that his wife Betsy d. on 15 May 1839 leaving three children: Rich. D. CHILTON, Hiram CHILTON (who d. leaving children Rich. & Margaret CHILTON) and Mary CHILTON.]

CHILTON, Andrew; PO 20 Jan 1820; 18 Sep 1820;
LC; INV, $794.50; includes Negroes Barbary, boy James. (LC EB 29:40)

CHILTON, Charles; d. intest.; his admrs. were Thomas CHILTON & Joseph BLACKWELL; he had formed a partnership in trade as merchants in Fauquier Co. with his bros. Thomas, William, and John; Thomas CHILTON d. intest. and his est Curriomen in WC fell to his nephew Orrick CHILTON, q.v., William CHILTON d. leaving three children: Orrick, William, and Susannah; Orrick d. intest. leaving a wid., Felicia, and two children Sarah Orick who mar. Steptoe PICKETT and Felicia Ann Corbin. (WC CC 1811-003)

CHILTON, Edwin; PO 17 Jan 1814, T 7 Feb 181[4]; 21 Feb 1814
LC; INV, $129.86 3/4. (LC EB 27:170))
[Edwin CHILTON mar. Betsey CHILTON, LC, bond 24 Nov 1804 (MLBLC:13); Eliza who mar. Chattin DUNAWAY LC, bond 22 Aug 1815 was the wid. of Edwin CHILTON (MLBLC:23, LC Orders 24:259); Chattin DUNAWAY aptd. gdn. to Cyrus & Polly CHILTON orphans of Edw. CHILTON, 16 Oct 1815 (LC Orders 24:264); Cyrus CHILTON orphan of Edwin CHILTON chose Eliz. DUNAWAY for his gdn. and sd. Eliz. is aptd. gdn. of Polly [S.] CHILTON, 20 Nov 1820 (LC OB 25:172)]

CHILTON, George; 18 Oct 1803 - 16 Apr 1804
LC; WILL; to mother Phebe CHILTON one Negro fellow Moses; at mother's death prop. to be eq. div. among bros John CHILTON & William CHILTON, my nephew Robert FORESTER, my niece Nancy FORESTER & my two nieces Alice & Milly ROBINSON; bro. John CHILTON to be gdn. to Alice & Milly ROBINSON & that their father Epa ROBINSON have nothing to [do] with it at all; bro. John CHILTON ex; WITS: Jos. POPE, Nancy CHILTON. (LC WB 28:78)
[Geo. CHILTON was the son of Jn. & Pheby CHILTON and bro. of Wm. & Jn. CHILTON (LC WB 22:138); his sis. Mildred mar. Epaphroditus ROBINSON, LC, bond 22 Jul 1785 (MLBLC:63)]

CHILTON, George; PO 20 Jun 1804, T 13 Jul 1804; 16 Jul 1804
LC; INV, £112.7.0; includes one unidentified Negro man. (LC EB 24:273)

CHILTON, Jesse; 28 May 1793; 19 Jan 1795
LC; WILL; Negro boy Tom & girl Leah to son Jesse; five Negroes Aaron, Jack, child Abraham, Ruth, & girl Fanny to dau. Alice; four Negroes Charles, Isaac, [Suck] & [Dinah] to dau. Ann; nine [sic] Negroes Anthony, Cyrus, Dennis, Sam, Adam, Eve, [Tamar] & [Jean] to son Cyrus (under 21); Capt. John CHOWNING, William WADDY, Joseph CARTER Sr. & Joseph CARTER Jr. exors; WITS: Wm. GEORGE, Merryman PAYNE, Oswald NEWBY, William BISCOE. (LC WB 28:9)
[Jesse CHILTON mar. Ann (NEWSUM) SMITH, dau. of Robt. NEWSUM & wid. of Jn. SMITH (d. LC 1765), LC, bond 19 Nov 1767 (MWO:73); Jesse CHILTON was the gdn. of Cyrus CHILTON orphan of Jesse CHILTON, 17 Apr 1804 (LC OB 1804-05:66); Alice CHILTON mar. Hen. TOWLES Jr., LC, bond 21 May 1795 (MLBLC:74)]

CHILTON, Jesse; PO 19 Jan 1795; 20 Jul 1795
LC; INV, £882.13.3 1/2; includes Negroes: Leah, Tom, Aaron, Jack, Abram, Ruth & child, Fanny, Charles, Isaac, [Suck], [Dinah], Anthony, Cyrus, Dennis, Samuel, Adam, Eve, Tamar, Jean, Mary. (LC EB 24:41)

CHILTON, Jesse; 11 Feb 1811; 21 May 1811
LC; WILL; wife Judy CHILTON to have use of whole est. during her life; to son Fauntleroy Nutt my Poplar Neck Plant; if he should die before age 21 or marries my son Robert Newsom should have sd. land; to son Robert Newsom the plant. w/o I now live; dau. Sally Nutt first choice of my Negroes; daus. Louisa Ann & Cordelia; to my three daus. three other Negroes to be chosen out of my est. by William NUTT or in case of his death by my wife; children: Sally, Fauntleroy, Robert, Louisa Ann & Cordelia; wife extx; WITS: Edw. BLACKAMORE, Porteus TOWLES. (LC WB 28:120)
[Jesse CHILTON, son of Jesse & Ann (NEWSUM, SMITH) CHILTON, mar. Judith NUTT, dau. of Moseley & Sarah (GARLINGTON) NUTT, NC, bond 22 Dec 1796 (MWO:73); Sally CHILTON orphan of Jesse CHILTON chose Judith CHILTON as her gdn., 17 Jan 1814 (LC Orders 24:175); Chas. J. YERBY aptd. gdn. to Robt. & Delia CHILTON orphans of Jesse CHILTON, 18 Aug 1817 (LC OB 24:382); Fauntleroy GEORGE aptd. gdn. to Delia & Robt. GEORGE orphans of Jesse GEORGE, 20 May 1822 (LC OB 25:300)]

CHILTON, Jesse; T 8 Dec 1817; 15 Mar 1819
LC; INV, $1203.58 1/2; included slaves: Charles, John, Rob, Jesse, Griffin, Arch, Henry, Lewis, Tom, [Marten], William, Young Tom, Alice & child Delia, Old Dick, Long Hannah & child Stokeley, Hannah, Lavina & her child Emma, Lucinda, Malinda (blind), Sally, Rachel, Leah; slaves appraised at $6435.27. (LC EB 27:467)

CHILTON, John; PO 12 Oct 1812, T 23 Oct 1812; 12 Apr 1813
NC; INV, $977.31 1/2; includes $79.25 in cash in the house and Negroes Moses, & Aaron. (NC RB 19:365)

CHILTON, John; T 17 Mar 1819; 28 Feb 1820. WC; INV, $94.35. (WC RI 10:446)

CHILTON, Orrick; [m]; 29 May 1804
WC; INV, £966.10.0; includes [Negroes] Sarah, Jonathan, Nancy, George, Izard, Sukey, Calia, Jo, Maria, Joan, Jerry, Sally, Jesse [the first 13 slaves are annotated "victuals and cloaths"]; Cate, Thomas, Absolom, Patience, Hannah, Charity, Vincent, Milly, Jenny, Moll, Caroline, Polly, James, Hannah, Judy, Tom, Guy, Ben, Ozmyn, Monkey, Billy younger, Billy house servant, Jack, Old Will, Jim blacksmith, Boatswain, Daniel, Old Sukey, Young Sukey, Cloe, Little Daniel (purchased of Thos. HILL and by information from Gerard McKENNY we learn that he cannot be sold but by the consent of the exors. of Jos. PEIRCE and is bound under Mr. CHILTON's purchase from HILL to serve until he arrives to the age of 31 years, supposed 3 years old), Nelly (under the same incumbrance and by information from Mr. McKENNY to serve until she arrives to the age of 21 years, supposed age 16 years); Grachen (man slave), Robin, Billy, Beverley (man), Mary, Dick (her child), Burgess (her child), Dinah, Jerry (her child), Lucy, George (her child), Frankey (her child), Caty (her child), Hannah (her child), Marylla (girl), Patty (girl). (WC RI 8:414)
[Orick CHILTON mar. Felicia CORBIN, WC, bond 19 Dec 1791 (MLBWC:13); Felicia CHILTON and Jn. MAUND were aptd. gdns. of Sally and Felicia CHILTON orphans of Orick CHILTON, WC, 28 Oct 1801 (WC Orders 1801-04:182); Felicia CHILTON, wid. of Orick, seems to have mar. Jn. CHILTON bef. 27 Feb 1805 (WC Orders 1804-07:201); Geo. CHRISTOPHER

was aptd. gdn. of Sally and Philicia orphans of Orick CHILTON, WC 24 Mar 1806 (WC Orders 1804-07:386); Chancery suit; Thos. CHILTON & Jos. BLACKWELL admrs. of Chas. CHILTON dec'd vs. Jn. CHILTON admr. de bonis non of Orrick CHILTON, Steptoe PICKETT and Sarah Orrick his wife who was Sarah Orrick CHILTON & Felicia Ann Corbin CHILTON infant & coheir of Orrick CHILTON by Geo. CHRISTOPHER her gdn. to recover $4428.28 with interest from 15 Apr 1808 from sale of land, 26 Aug 1811 (WC Orders 1810-13:165); Steptoe PICKETT mar. Sarah O. CHILTON, WC, bond 7 Jan 1811 (MLBWC:53); ord. to settle Geo. CHRISTOPHER's adm. acct. on the est. of Felicia CHILTON and also his gdnship. acct. of the orphans of the sd. Felicia CHILTON and div. the est. conveyed in trust to him for their benefit eq. between the sd. orphans: Sarah ORRICK now the wife of Steptoe PICKETT and Felicia Ann Corbin CHILTON, 29 Oct 1811 (WC Orders 1810-13:184)]

CHILTON, Orrick; 23 Jul 1804; 24 Nov 1806
WC; INV of residue of est, £144.0.0; includes [Negroes] Colchester, Dinah's child Jerry inventoried, Henry not inventoried born since, Esau & Jacob children of Mary; Robin (an old man 60 years old). (WC RI 9:8)

CHILTON, Stephen; PO 16 Oct 1820; 19 Feb 1821
LC; INV; includes Negroes Sally, Mary, William, Isaac. (LC EB 29:56)

CHILTON, Stephen; T 1 Jan 1821; 19 Feb 1822
LC; DIV of $662.23 (proceeds from selling 4 Negroes) among Stephen CHILTON gdn. to Mary W. Y. CHILTON & Amanda W. Y. CHILTON, Elizabeth DUNAWAY gdn. to Polly Y. CHILTON & Cyrus CHILTON and Griffin CHILTON gdn. to John M. DOGGETT. (LC EB 29:171)

CHILTON, Stephen [Jr.]; 15 Jan 1821
LC; Stephen CHILTON aptd. gdn. to his children Mary W. & Amanda W. CHILTON. (LC OB 25:187)

CHILTON, Stephen Sr.; 20 Sep 1820; 16 Oct 1820
LC; WILL; all my land, the land I heired from my bro. William CHILTON & the land I live on to my son Griffin CHILTON; balance of est. to all my grchil. Cyrus CHILTON & Polly L. CHILTON, Mary W. B. Y. CHILTON & Nanny CHILTON, and John DOGGETT son of Samuel DOGGETT; son Griffin & friend Bidkar GEORGE exors; WITS: Jas. CARTER, Jn. DOGGETT, Bidkar GEORGE. (LC WB 28:209)
[Stephen CHILTON Sr. was the son of Stephen CHILTON (d. LC, 1761) (LC WB 16:180)]

CHILTON, William; T 15 Sep 1795; [2 Sep 1795]. LC; additional INV, £2. (LC EB 24:49)

CHILTON, William; 5 Apr 1804; 18 Feb 1805
LC; WILL; upper half of the land I now possess to bro. Stephen CHILTON; sis. Sarah Ann DYE; lower half of land I now possess it being the part w/o my dwelling house now stands to cousin Jemima GEORGE; friends Chattin DUNAWAY & James CARTER exors; WITS: Jas. CARTER, Chattin DUNAWAY, Jas. CARTER Jr. (LC WB 28:88)
[William CHILTON & Sarah Ann DYE were children of Stephen CHILTON (d. LC, 1761) (LC WB 16:180)]

CHILTON, William; PO 18 Feb 1805, T 20 Feb 1805; 16 Apr 1805
LC; INV, £55.16.9. (LC EB 24:314)

CHINN, Bartholomew Esq.; PO 20 Apr 1801, T 5 Sep 1801; 20 Jun 1802
LC; INV, £2058,5,4; includes a number of books and the following Negroes: Dominy, Young Daniel, Stephen, Aaron, [Sheaper], Moses, Bob, Old Daniel,

Tom carpenter, Bass, Dinah, Ellen, Phebe, Nancy, [Amine], Esther, Rhoda, Shadrack, Venus, Harry, [Janie], [Molly], [Betty], Sylvia, Betty, Lindsey. (LC EB 24:190)

CHINN, Bartholomew; PO 21 Dec 1801; 15 Feb 1802

LC; DIV of slaves among: the wid. Mrs. Olivia CHINN, Rawleigh W. DOWNMAN, Joseph CHINN, John M. SMITH, Eliza NUTT, John Y. CHINN. (LC EB 24:183)

[Bartholomew CHINN, son of Jn. CHINN of CCP (d. LC 1791), mar. Olivia DOWNMAN, dau. of Jos. Ball DOWNMAN, LC, bond 8 Jun 1799 (LC DW 22:292, 443; MWO:74); Rawleigh W. DOWNMAN mar. Bartholomew's sis. Priscilla CHINN, LC, bond 25 May 1783 (MWO:114); another of Bartholomew's sisters, Eliz. CHINN, mar. Wm. NUTT, LC, bond 6 Dec 1798 (MWO:267); his 3rd sis. Sarah CHINN mar. John Mathews SMITH, LC, bond 20 Sep 1791 (MWO:323); Bartholomew CHINN d. intest. without issue leaving a wid., Olivia, who mar. Jos. BALL of Ditchley, NC; he also left the following bros. and sisters: Priscilla (the wife of Rawleigh W. DOWNMAN), Jos. CHINN, Jn. Y. CHINN, Sarah Y. (the wife of Jn. M. SMITH) and Eliz. (the wid. of Rich. SELDEN); by 1825 Raw. W. DOWNMAN had survived Priscilla, Sarah Y. had survived Jn. M. SMITH but was dead, Jos. CHINN had died; the dower slaves in 1802 were named as: Nancy, Pheeby, Billy, Venus, Elijah, Bob, Esther, Betty, Old Daniel, Dominy, Rhoda, and Lindsey and were worth a total of £566; by 1825 the dower slaves were: Nancy and her children Tom, Robt., Sylvia, Eliza, Ralph, and Sarah Ann; Wm.; Bacchus; Bond; Hannah and Eve children of Phoebe who had died; Elijah; Bob; Ethan; Betty and her children Saunders, Amina and an unnamed infant; Dominy and Rhoda and her children Lindzey and Judy; Venus and Daniel had died; Tom the son of Nancy had run away; Olivia, the wid., had died and the remaining heirs wish to div. the dower slaves; the div. was made on 1 Feb 1825 as follows: Lot 1 (Esther, Wm., Ralph, Betty and her dau. Tab) drawn by Jn. Y. CHINN as admr. of Sarah Y. SMITH; Lot 2 (Rhoda, Bacchus, Julia, Eliza) drawn by Mrs. Eliza SELDEN; Lot 3 (Bob, Lindsey, Hannah, Nancy and child Sarah Ann) drawn by Jn. Y. CHINN; Lot 4 (Domina, Robin, Sylvia, Amina) drawn by Jn. Y. CHINN as admr. of Jos. CHINN; Lot 5 (Elijah, Bond, Eve, Saunders) drawn by Raw. W. DOWNMAN (LC CC 1825-006)]

CHINN, Bartholomew; [m]; 11 Aug 1818

NC; Negroes who are the issue of the dower Negroes of Olivia CHINN who mar. Joseph BALL and who were born since the marriage: Hannah (b. 10 Apr 1807), Eliza (30 Sep 1807), Eve (9 Oct 1808), [Lelivia] (Apr 1810), Ralph (1812). (NC RB 21:417)

[Olivia CHINN was Olivia DOWNMAN , dau. of J. B. DOWNMAN, who mar. (1) Bartholomew CHINN, LC, bond 8 Jun 1799 (MLBLC:13)]

CHINN, Joseph; PO 21 Dec 1795; 20 Jun 1796

LC; DIV of est. among: John CHINN, Rawleigh William DOWNMAN in right of his wife Priscilla, John Mathew SMITH in right of his wife Sarah, Joseph CHINN, Elizabeth CHINN, Bartholomew CHINN, Rawleigh CHINN; each lot was valued at £94.12.0. (LC EB 24:13)

[This is Jos. the son of Jn. CHINN of CCP, LC (d. 1791); his est. is being divided among his siblings and their spouses (LC WB 22:292)]

CHINN, Joseph; 7 May 1799; 19 Dec 1803

CCP, LC; WILL; whole est. to wife Elizabeth during her life or widowhood; to son John Leroy the plant. called Sion House on the Rappahannock River in RC containing 930 ac; if son die before age 21 or has no issue, plant. to go to son Joseph William; to son Joseph William the plant. w/o I now live containing 1020 ac; if son Joseph William die before age 21 or has no issue, plant. to go to son John Leroy; all right, title & interest in & to my claim of that part of the land in Kentucky to be eq. div. between my two sons John Leroy & Joseph William; if both sons die before age 21 or have no issue, real est. to be eq. div. between bro. John Yates CHINN & his heirs; pers. est. to be div. between my brothers & sisters: Priscilla DOWNMAN, John Y. CHINN, Sarah Y. SMITH and Elizabeth NUTT; John Yates CHINN, Richard MITCHELL, Martin SHEARMAN, & Joseph CARTER Jr. exors; WITS: John M. SMITH, Robt. CHINN; COD dtd. 3 Mar 1800; Negro boys David & Billy to son John Leroy & [Juba] & Daniel to son Joseph William. (LC WB 28:73) [Jos. CHINN was the son of Jn. CHINN (d. LC 1791); he mar. Elizabeth GRIFFIN, dau. of Maj. Leroy & Judith (BALL) GRIFFIN, RC bond 18 Jul 1792 (LC WB 22:318; MWO:75); Eliz. (GRIFFIN) CHINN mar. (2) Jn. SEWARD, LC, bond 3 Sep 1806 (MLBLC:66); chancery suit, Jn. SEWARD & Eliz. his wife who was Eliz. CHINN, wid. & rel. of Jos. CHINN, and Jn. Leroy & Jos. Wm. CHINN sons and only children of Jos. CHINN, pltfs, against Jn. Y. CHINN ex. of Jos. CHINN to settle admin. acct., 22 Aug 1809 (LC Orders B23 1808-11:93); Jn. SEWARD aptd. gdn. to Jos. W. CHINN orphan of Jos. CHINN, 21 Apr 1817 (LC OB 24:359); (*see also LC CC 1811-032 and Bartholomew CHINN above*)]

CHINN, Joseph; PO 19 Dec 1803; 20 Feb 1804
LC; INV presented by John Y. CHINN ex., [m]. (LC EB 24:260)

CHINN, Joseph; 17 Jan 1825, T 1 Feb 1825; 22 Mar 1825
LC; as the result of a suit in LC Court between John Y. CHINN in his own right and as admr. of Joseph CHINN dec'd and as admr. to Sarah Y. SMITH and Elizabeth SELDON against Rawleigh W. DOWNMAN admr. of Priscilla DOWNMAN dec'd, the following slaves were div. into five lots: Nancy & her children Tom, Robin, Silvia, Eliza, Ralph & Sarahann, William, Bacus, Bond, Hanah & [Eve] children of Phoebe who is dead, Elijah, Bob, Esther, Betty & her children Saunders, Ammana & an infant name unknown, Domminy & Rhoda & her children Lindsey & Judy; one lot was allotted to each of the parties to the suit. (LC EB 29:422, OB 26:94-95)
[Eliz. SELDON is prob. Eliz. CHINN, the dau. of Jn. CHINN (d. LC 1791) and sis. of Jos. & Bartholomew CHINN who mar. (1) Wm. O. NUTT, LC, bond 6 Dec 1798 and (2) Rich. SELDEN, LC, bond 14 Jun 1803 (see above and MLBLC:66)]

CHINN, Rawleigh; 31 May 1798; 17 Jun 1799
LC; WILL; all pers. est. to bro. [Bart.] and "if I should not return, [bro. to] protect from injury and insult my Fanny;" bro. [Bart.] ex.; WITS: Jn. P. MATTHEWS, Thos. T. MONTAGUE, Jn. M. SMITH. (LC WB 28:30)
[This must be Rawleigh CHINN, son of Thos. & Sarah (MITCHELL) CHINN, who mar. (1) Fanny TARPLEY, RC, bond 30 Jan 1775 and (2) Eliz. SHEARMAN, LC, bond 8 Feb 1797 (MWO:75)

CHINN, Robert; 8 May 1820; 19 Mar 1821
LC; WILL; to niece Matilda Ann Elizabeth JEFFRIES the wife of John F. B. JEFFRIES my tract of land w/o I now live & my Negro woman Lucy & her 3 children Judah, Peter & Anna; my woman Cate for her faithful service together with her children Henry & Addison [*several lines unclear*] shall live on my quarter in the sd. land together with her children and be furnished annually by the sd. Matilda with 8 barrels of corn & 100 weight of pork; Henry & Addison to be taught to read write & cipher as far as the rule of

three in arithmatic and immediately thereafter to have them sent to Baltimore and have Henry bound to a shoemaker until full age & Addison bound to a taylor if it can be effected under reasonable terms; if Henry lives to age 21, niece to pay him $[600] and if Addison to live to same age, niece to pay him $500; my Negro boy Allen to Richard M. SYDNOR of Frederick County; niece Matilda A. E. JEFFRIES is to care for my unfortunate son John & she and her heirs are charged to have my sd. son John during his life furnished with good strong clothing suited to the season supported with good wholesome diet & decent lodging & taken care of; rest of est. to niece; friends John F. B. JEFFRIES & William B. MITCHEL exors.; WITS: Aug. NEALE, Thos. SYDNOR Jr., Lemuel YERBY; COD., same date, increase of female slaves to niece; any children of my woman Cate to be free and emancipated. (LC WB 28:213)
[Cate CARTER emancipated by will of Robt. CHINN, 16 Jul 1821 (LC OB 25:232); court decided not to allow Cate CARTER to remain in the county, 20 Aug 1821 (LC OB 25:237)]

CHITWOOD, George; 21 Jun 1793; 20 Jul 1801
LC; WILL; use of my est. to wife Judy; at wife's death est. to be eq. div. among my children; my plant. that I now live on to son William; if he should die, plant. to go to son George; rest of est. to be eq. div. amongst children Susannah, Elizabeth, George, Nancy, and Alcey; wife extx; WITS: Jn. CHOWNING, Thos. POTTS, Edw. PAYNE, Thos. CHOWNING. (LC WB 28:53)
[Geo. CHITWOOD was prob. a son of Wm. CHITWOOD (d. LC 1788); he was named as one of the exors. of William's will (LC 27 Apr 1788 - 21 Jul 1788) (LC WB 22:183); the will of Geo. CHITWOOD was presented in court by Judith CHITWOOD the extx. and ord. to settle with her the acct. of Geo. CHITWOOD with the est. of Wm. CHITWOOD of which he is the ex. and possess Jn. RICE gdn. of Jn. & Wm. CHITWOOD orphan of Wm. with the est. of the sd. Wm., 20 Jul 1801 (LC Orders 21 1799-1801:274)]

CHITWOOD, George; T 22 Nov 1806; 16 Feb 1807
LC; INV, £220.19.5; includes [Negroes] Pleasant & Nancy. (LC EB 27:2)

CHITWOOD, William; 15 Jun 1801
LC; John and William CHITWOOD orphans of William CHITWOOD chose John RICE as their gdn. (LC Orders 21 1799-1801:266)

CHOWNING, Catharine; T 12 Aug 1817; 17 Nov 1817
LC; INV; includes her interest in a suit depending in the Chancery District Court of Fredericksburg, Blakey's admr. et al. v. Newby's admr. & her interest in a suit in LC Court in chancery between Blakey's admr. et al. & Chowning's admr. (LC EB 27:398)
[Acc. to LC CC 1817-003, Ann BLAKEY, Catherine CHOWNING and Lucy STREET were daus. of Wm. CHOWNING of Middlesex Co.]

CHOWNING, Catharine; PO 21 Dec 1818, T 31 Dec 1818; 18 Jan 1819
LC; DIV of proceeds of sale of 3 slaves (John, Eliza, Priscilla) among John CHOWNING, James CHOWNING, James TOWLES, William J. PAYNE, Kitty KESTERSON & John CHOWNING gdn. of Edwin & Matilda DOBYNS. (LC EB 27:449)
[This Catharine was the wid. of Jn. CHOWNING, *see below*]

CHOWNING, John; 24 Jul 1811; 18 Sep 1815
LC; WILL; all est. to wife Catherine CHOWNING during her life; to son John CHOWNING after wife's death the land w/o I now live & the land I bought of Martin GEORGE; to son James CHOWNING the land I bought of

John M. GILMOUR called The Hills after wife's death; to son Thomas CHOWNING my plant. in Middlesex Co. that I bought of John ROBINSON called Green Branch after wife's death; if son Thomas should die before coming of age or marrying sd. plant. to be sold and the money eq. div. amongst my daus.; after wife's death remainder of est. to be div. as follows: one seventh part each to sons John, James, Thomas & daus. Lucy DOBYNS, Felicia TOWLES, Betsy CHOWNING & one seventh part in the hands of my exors. in trust for the support & maintenance of my dau. Kitty KESTERSON's family until the death of either James KESTERSON or Kitty KESTERSON; if dau. Kitty should die first legacy to be div. eq. amongst such children as she may leave; if she has no children her seventh to return to my est; wife Catherine, sons John & James & s-i-l James TOWLES exors; [no wits listed, but will proved by oaths of Porteus TOWLES, Wm. CALLIHAN & Wm. T. YERBY]. (LC WB 28:167)
[Christian L. DOBYNS mar. Lucy CHOWNING, LC, bond 11 Dec 1809; Jas. KESTERSON mar. Kitty CHOWNING, LC, bond 16 Apr 1804; Jas. TOWLES mar. Felicia CHOWNING, LC, bond 8 Oct 1807 (MLBLC:21, 45, 74); Eliz. CHOWNING orphan of Jn. CHOWNING chose Jas. TOWLES as her gdn., 20 Nov 1815 (LC Orders 24:266)]

CHOWNING, John (Capt.); T 11 Oct 1815; 20 May 1816
LC; INV, $10,880.56 3/4; includes Negroes: Sam, Moses, James, [Simas], Captain, Samuel, Tom, John, Cyrus, Reubin, [Lena], Harry, Phill, Davy, Young Harry, Elliott, Charles, Old James, Armistead, Bristol, Rose, Mary & child Arena, Dilcy & child Harriott, Charlott & child Rhoda, Sylva & child Cate, Daphne, Sucky, Judy, Annie, Betty, Sally, Young Sally, Young Annie, Fanny, Philais, Dinah, Polly; DIV of slaves among: Lucy DOBYNS (lapsed by her death), John CHOWNING, John CHOWNING as trustee for Kitty KESTERSON (wife of James KESTERSON), James CHOWNING, Thomas CHOWNING (lapsed by his death), James TOWLES in behalf of his wife Felicia, William J. PAYNE in behalf of his wife Betsy; John CHOWNING as gdn. to Edwin & Matilda DOBYNS, T 29 Dec 1815. (LC EB 27:318, 325)

CHOWNING, John [S.]; T 24 Nov 1818; 15 Nov 1819. LC; INV, [m]. (LC EB 27:505)
[Hannah CHOWNING aptd. gdn. to Caroline, Sarah, Thos., Anne & Jn. CHOWNING orphan of Jn. S. CHOWNING, 17 Dec 1821 (LC OB 25:271); Hannah CHOWNING is admx. of Jn. [S.] CHOWNING, 21 Jan 1822 (LC OB 25:279); on the mot. of Caroline Jane CHOWNING by Raw. DUNAWAY her next friend for the sale and division of the part of the upper plant. on Corotoman which descended from Wm. CHOWNING dec'd to the heirs of Jn. [S.] CHOWNING dec'd, Sally G, Thos., Ann C. P. & Jn. [S.] CHOWNING appealed by Hannah CHOWNING their gdn. ... ord. that the land be sold, 20 Aug 1822 (LC OB 25:323); Corotoman is probably the Corotoman River in south central LC (Miller:35)]

CHOWNING, Thomas; PO 19 Jun 1798; T 25 Oct 1798; 17 Jun 1799
LC; INV, £549,19, includes Negroes: Simon, Winny, Fanny, Dinah & child Milly, Rodham, John, Sam, Elias, Sarah. (LC EB 24:95)
[Thos. CHOWNING mar. Sally RICE, NC, bond 4 May 1796 (MLBNC:17); Wm. CHOWNING aptd. gdn. of Wm. Hackett CHOWNING orphan of Thos. CHOWNING, 18 Oct 1802 (LC Orders V 1802-03:214); Wm. CHOWNING was gdn. of Wm. Hackett CHOWNING orphan of Thos. CHOWNING, LC 17 Sep 1804 (LC OB 1804-05:220; Orders B23 1808-11:147); lay off & assign to Sally POTTS her dower in the est. of her late husband

Thos. CHOWNING and possess Wm. CHOWNING gdn. of Wm. Hackett CHOWNING orphan of the sd. decedent with his part of the sd. est. being the residue, 18 Oct 1802 (LC Orders V 1802-03:217); Sally CHOWNING mar. Jn. POTTS, LC, bond 13 May 1802 (MLBLC:61); settlement of Wm. CHOWNING's gdnship. acct. with [Millicent] CHOWNING orphan of Thos. CHOWNING, 19 Sep 1808 (LC Orders D22 1805-08:488)]

CHOWNING, William (Capt.); PO 17 Nov 1821, T 21 Dec 1821; 21 Jan 1822
LC; DIV of Negroes belonging to the est. after allotting to Mrs. Tomsy CHOWNING her dower in sd. Negroes (Old Charles, Hiram, Jack, Billy, Charlotte, Sinah, Fanny, Young Sam, Phoebe, Hagar); heirs were the heirs of Elizabeth SYDNOR dec'd (Grace, Mimy, Godfrey, Aggatha, Aaron, Charlotte, Daniel), William CALLAHAN (Alice, Hagar, Dennis, James, Lucy, Maria, Daniel, Billy, Letty, Sam), William C. CALLAHAN (Harry, Esther, Charles), William SETTLE (Pricilla & child Phebe, John, Martha, Mimy), Jane GEORGE (Phoebe, Sophia, Lewis, Laurah, Arrena, Lindsey, Sam, Susanna), John BAILY (Lazarus, Ned, Simon), William BLACKMORE (Judith, Stafford, Lucy & child), heirs of John S. CHOWNING (Eve, Henry, Hannah, [Nedry], Dennis, Lindsey, Harriet, George), John GRESHAM ([Lorahamah], Kizziah, Vilette, Patrick, George, Simon), Sally CHOWNING (Letty, Joe, Dick, Winney, Harry, Soloman, Abigail). (LC EB 29:188)
[Wm. CHOWNING mar. Thomasin SHARPE, dau. of Thos. & Sarah SHARPE, LC, bond 28 Dec 1764 (MWO:76, MLBLC:14); Wm. CHOWNING was the father of Sally, Mary, Eliz., Nelly, Tomsy, Jn. S., Margaret, Frances, and Jane CHOWNING Anthony SYDNOR mar. Eliz. CHOWNING, LC, bond 7 Jan 1788; Wm. CALLAHAN mar. Nelly CHOWNING, LC, bond 30 Nov 1796; Wm. SETTLE mar. Mary CHOWNING, LC, bond 13 Feb 1819; Wm. BLAKEMORE mar. Tomza CHOWNING, LC, bond 29 Nov 1801; Jn. GRESHAM mar. Margaret CHOWNING, LC, bond 19 Oct 1807; Hugh BAILEY mar. Frances CHOWNING, LC, bond 8 Jan 1798/9; Eliz. & Anthony SYDNOR were the parents of Fortunatus, Wm., Thos Sharp, Eliz, Chowning, and Sarah; Nelly & Wm. CALLAHAN were the parents of Wm. C.; Jn. S. and Hannah CHOWNING were the parents of Caroline, Sally, Thos., Ann E. P., and Jn. S.; Frances & Hugh BAILEY were the parents of Jn (who laft for parts unknown) (LC CC 1823:008, MLBLC:2, 5, 10, 34, 66, 71)]

CHOWNING, William; T 15 Dec 1821; 21 Oct 1822
LC; INV, $16,700.28 1/2; includes Negroes [Junow], Susanna, George, Ned, Hiram, Jack, Old Charles, John, Young Charles, Samuel, Fanny, Phebe, Young Samuel, Charlotte, Billy, Easter, Lucy & child Sinah, Stafford, Lazarus, Mima, Martha, Old Sinah, Hagar (on expence), Grace, Mimy, Godfrey, Agathy, Aaron, Charlotte, Daniel, Alice, Hagar, Dennis, James, Lucy, Maria, Daniel, Billy, Zelly, Sam, Harry, Priscilla & child Phebe, Phoebe, Sophia, Lewis, [Zaurah], [Ane??], Lindsey, Judith, Eve, Henry, Hannah, Mary, Dennis, Lindsey, Harriott, Leanahamah, Keziah, Vilet, Partrick, George, Simon, Letty, Joe, Dick, Winney, Harry, Solomon, Abigail. (LC EB 29:231)

CHOWNING, William H.; PO 16 Dec 1816; 17 Mar 1817
LC; DIV of est. among: William CHOWNING, John MILLS in right of his wife Lucy, Winifred LITTRELL, Jonathan ABBAY in right of his wife Margaret, Richard ROUT, Peter C. RICE. ; LC EB 27:357)
[Jonathan ABBAY mar. Peggy ROUT, NC, bond 18 May 1791; Rich. LITTRELL mar. Winifred F. (ROUT) STANLEY, wid. of Thos. STANLEY and sis. of Anthony S. ROUTT, NC, bond 16 Jul 1796 (MLBNC:69, 95;

MWO:229, 330); Peter C. RICE mar. Jane ROUTT, dau. of Katherine ROUTT, NC, bond 11 Dec 1793 (MLBNC:1, 69, 86)]

CHRISTIAN, Humphrey F.; 6 Jun 1812; 8 Nov 1819

NC; WILL; a pvt. in the 5th US Regt. of Infantry; all the claims I may have on the government for my military service accrued or to accrue to nephew Humphrey F. CARTER and he is to be ex; WITS: F. BATES, Jn. L. CHINN. (NC RB 22:138)

[Humphrey F. CHRISTIAN and Rawleigh C. CHRISTIAN (*below*) are prob. sons of Francis H. CHRISTIAN of NFP, RC; their sis. Nancy mar. Jos. CARTER, RC bond 14 Dec 1782 and is almost certainly the mother of Humphrey F. CARTER(NFPR:31, MWO:68)]

CHRISTIAN, Rawleigh C.; 2 Jan 1812; 15 Feb 1813

LC; DIV of slaves conveyed to Catherine C. CHRISTIAN, Rawleigh C. CHRISTIAN (in behalf of William CHRISTIAN), Rhodam BOOTH in right of his wife who was Elizabeth F. CHRISTIAN, and Thomas ARMSTRONG in right of his wife who was Ann R. CHRISTIAN by Rawleigh C. CHRISTIAN & Elizabeth his wife by deed of 2 Jan 1812. (LC EB 27:141)

[Rod H. BOOTH mar. Eliz. F. CHRISTIAN, NC, bond 11 Apr 1808; Thos. ARMSTRONG mar. Ann Richardson CHRISTIAN, NC, bond 17 Jul 1810 (MLBNC:2, 11); Raw. C. CHRISTIAN served as a pvt. in the Virginia Line during the Rev. War; he was about 74 when placed on the pension roll in Mar 1819; he d. 14 Jul 1828 (PR1835:725)]

CHRISTOPHER, [Robert]; PO 14 Nov 1821; 11 Feb 1822

NC; as a result of a suit, John CHRISTOPHER, pltf., against George, Mary & Sally CHRISTOPHER, infants, defts., commissioners appointed to sell land of Robert CHRISTOPHER dec'd; land was div. into two tracts, Home Tract & Forest Tract; John CHRISTOPHER, one of the heirs, bought both tracts; after commission was deducted each heir was entitled to $142.37 1/2. (NC RB 23:96)

[Robt. CHRISTOPHER mar. Sally L. WAY, NC, bond 21 Dec 1797; Jn., Geo., Mary and Sally are children of Robt. and Sally L. CHRISTOPHER; Sally L. (WAY) CHRISTOPHER mar. (2) Edmund R. JEFFRIES, wid., NC, bond 10 Jan 1818; Sally (WAY, CHRISTOPHER) JEFFRIES did not have any children by Edmund JEFFRIES and d. in 1821 (MLBNC:17, 60; NC CC 1821-006)]

CHRISTOPHER, Dolly; PO 12 Sep 1803; 11 Jun 1804. NC; INV, £56.2.5. (NC RB 17:170)

[*see Dorothy CHRISTOPHER below*]

CHRISTOPHER, Dorothy; 12 Dec 1803, T 2 Jan 1804; 9 Apr 1804

NC; DIV of est. among her heirs: Thomas CHRISTOPHER rec'd Dick; Winney CHRISTOPHER rec'd Sook; Thomas ALEXANDER rec'd Levinah. (NC RB 17:134)

[This is Dorothy or Dolly FLEET who mar. Jn. CHRISTOPHER (*see below*), LC, bond 19 Jul 1781 (MLBLC:14); the birth of Wm. Fleet to Jn. & Dolley CHRISTOPHER is rec. on 3 Mar 1782 in the SSPR (SSPR:34)]

CHRISTOPHER, John; PO 13 Sep 1802, T 1 Jan 1803; 9 Apr 1804

NC; allottment to Thomas ALEXANDER who mar. Mary the dau. of John CHRISTOPHER dec'd the sd. Mary's proportion of the est. and to Dorothy the wid. of the sd. John her dower (rec'd Negroes Dick, Sook & child Lavina); Thomas ALEXANDER rec'd Thornton, Charlotte; Thomas CHRISTOPHER rec'd Nelson; and Winney CHRISTOPHER rec'd Sarah and Manuel. (NC RB 17:133)

[Thos. ALEXANDER mar. Mary E. CHRISTOPHER, NC, bond 2 Feb 1802 (MLBNC:1)]

CHRISTOPHER, John Sr.; 17 Jul 1821; 8 Oct 1821

SSP, NC; WILL; plant. where I now live to grson. Thomas CHRISTOPHER; tract of land in NC adj. lands of DOWNING & LAMKIN known by the name of Blinco's & Oldham's a part of which my father purchased of a James BLINCO & the balance I purchased of Nathaniel OLDHAM to grson. John CHRISTOPHER; Negro woman Sarah to the children of my grdau. Mary ALEXANDER of Kentucky; grdau. Winifred FULKS to have the use of my Negro girl Mary until my great grson. John FULKS is 21 at which time he is to have girl Mary; tract of land near Coan Mill adj. William MITCHELL to dau. Nelly [S.] MITCHELL; son George CHRISTOPHER; son William CHRISTOPHER of Kentucky; Negro girl Mahala to friend Washington HAYNIE; after debts paid rest of est. to be eq. div. among son George CHRISTOPHER, grdaus Elizabeth MITCHELL & Nancy MITCHELL, my grsons. William C. MITCHELL & John MITCHELL, my grdaus. Sally CHRISTOPHER & Mary CHRISTOPHER & my grson. George CHRISTOPHER (daus. & son of Robert CHRISTOPHER); son George & friends Royston BETTS & George RICE exors; WITS: Elisha FALLIN, Griffin LAMKIN, Yarrett HUGHLETT. (NC RB 23:3)

[Jn. CHRISTOPHER mar. Mary Ellen DAWKINS, dau. of Peter DAWKINS, bef. 9 Nov 1756 (MWO:76); the births of 6 children to Jn. & Mary Ellen CHRISTOPHER were rec. in the SSPR: Jn. (b. 9 May 1759), Thos. (b. 20 Mar 1762), Wm. (b. 1 Feb 1767), Peter (b. 28 Feb 1771), Peter (b. 20 Jun 1777), and Nelly Shoop (b. 14 Nov 1780) (SSPR:29, 30, 31, 34); Winifred CHRISTOPHER mar. Chas. L. FULKS, who was prob. the grson. of Jn. FULKS (d. NC 1810), NC, bond 3 Sep 1811 (MLBNC:40, NC RB 18:351); acc. to a deed in 1799, Wm. BETTS commonly called Wm. CHRISTOPHER (and wife Ellen) and Jn. BETTS of Woodford Co., Ky. commonly called Jn. CHRISTOPHER were sons of Jn. CHRISTOPHER (NC RB 16:4)]

CHRISTOPHER, Robert; PO 9 Mar [1818]; 9 Nov 1818

NC; INV, $2459.41 1/2; includes following Negroes: Peter, Richard, Letty, Judith, Winnefred, Jerry, Siner, Sarah. (NC RB 21:534)

CHRISTOPHER, Robert; PO 13 Sep 1818; 9 Nov 1818

NC; allotted to Edmund R. JEFFRIES & Sally his wife the sd. Sally's dower thirds in the est. of Robert CHRISTOPHER dec'd and div. of the est. among the heirs; Sally's dower includes Negroes Peter, Dick, and Letty; Lot 1 drawn by John CHRISTOPHER (received Jude), Lot 2 drawn by Sally CHRISTOPHER (received Winny), Lot 3 drawn by George CHRISTOPHER (received Jerry), Lot 4 drawn by Mary CHRISTOPHER (received Siner & Sarah). (NC RB 21:540)

[Robt. CHRISTOPHER mar. Sally L. WAY, NC, bond 21 Dec 1797; Sally mar. (2) Edmund R. JEFFRIES, wid., NC, bond 10 Jan 1818 (MLBNC:17, 60); Sally CHRISTOPHER chose Edmund R. JEFFRIES as her gdn. and he was aptd. gdn. of Mary & Geo. CHRISTOPHER orphans of Robt. CHRISTOPHER, NC, 11 May 1818 (NC OB 1816-20:247); Jn. CHRISTOPHER orphan of Robt. CHRISTOPHER chose Wm. [WAY] as his gdn. NC, 11 May 1818 (NC OB 1816-20:249); Sally & Mary CHRISTOPHER chose Jn. CHRISTOPHER as their gdn. and the sd. Jn. CHRISTOPHER is aptd. gdn. of Geo. CHRISTOPHER, NC 13 Nov 1820 (NC OB 1820-25:67); on the mot. of Jn. CHRISTOPHER in his own right and as gdn. of Sarah, Mary & Geo. CHRISTOPHER orphans of Robt. CHRISTOPHER and Nelly MITCHELL gdn. of Eliz., Nancy, Wm. and Jn. MITCHELL ord. that Geo. CHRISTOPHER ex. of Jn. CHRISTOPHER to show cause why certain Negroes should not be sold, NC 12 Nov 1821 (NC OB 1820-25:149); Polly & Mary CHRISTOPHER chose Wm. JETT as their gdn. and the sd. JETT is aptd. gdn. of Geo. CHRISTOPHER orphans of Robt. CHRISTOPHER, NC 11 Mar 1822 (NC OB 1820-25:180); master commissioner to settle Wm. JETT's acct. of his gdnship. of Mary CHRISTOPHER now the wife of Jas. A. SNEAD, 13 Mar 1827 (NC OB 1825-30:153); Mary CHRISTOPHER mar. James Allanelia SNEAD, RC, bond 17 Jul 1826 (MRC:192); NC CCs 1820:007 and 1821:006 provide information on Robert CHRISTOPHER's family]

CHRISTOPHER, Robert; PO 12 Nov 1821; 10 Jun 1822
NC; on motion of John CHRISTOPHER in his own right & as gdn. of Sarah, Mary & George CHRISTOPHER orphans of Robert CHRISTOPHER and Nelly S. MITCHELL gdn. to Elizabeth, Nancy, William & John MITCHELL ord. that John CHRISTOPHER be summoned to appear at the next court and show cause why the Negroes included in the residuary clause of the will of John CHRISTOPHER dec'd shall not be sold and the proceeds div. among his sd. legatees; commissioners appointed to sell the Negroes Isaac, James, Peter, Nancy & infant, Nelly & child Jessee, Sally & Jane late the prop. of John CHRISTOPHER; proceeds of $1372.82 after commission deducted were div. among George CHRISTOPHER in his own right, Nelly S. MITCHELL as gdn. for Betsy, Nancy, William & John MITCHELL, and John CHRISTOPHER as gdn. for Sarah, Mary and George CHRISTOPHER orphans of Robert CHRISTOPHER dec'd. (NC RB 23:170)
[Nelly S. MITCHELL was Nelly S. DAWSON who mar. Rich. MITCHELL, NC, bond 9 Jan 1799 (MLBNC:74); she was prob. Nelly Shoop CHRISTOPHER dau. of Jn. & Mary Ellen CHRISTOPHER (*see above*); she may have mar. (1) David DAWSON who d. around 1797-1798 (NC Fiduciary Bonds 1797-1801); see also NC CCs 1820-007 and 1821-006)]

CHURCH, James; 21 Jun 1824
LC; Overseers of the Poor to bind James CHURCH to John D. WALKER to learn the art of a waterman. (LC OB 26:49)
[There are two marriage records in LC for Wm. CHURCH who may be the father of James: (1) to Betsey Johnson DAVIS, bond 17 Aug 1801 and (2) to Ollin GUNDRY, bond 12 Jan 1809 (MLBLC:14)]

CLARK, Catharine; PO 7 Mar 1815; R. 6 May 1816. RC; INV, [m]. (RC WB 9:521)

CLARK, Charles; 14 Oct 1795
NC; D of G; gift of slaves to his children; dau. Elizabeth to receive Winney and George SLOVIN; dau. Susanna to receive William CARTER and Drusilla; and son Charles M. B. to receive James SORRILL and John SORRILL; the following children were born to Charles and Cynthia CLARKE: Jane, b. 6 Jul 1772; Eliz., b. 18 Apr 1775; Susanna Hancock, b. 25 Mar 1779; Septimus, b. 10 Sep 1781; Jn. Rogers, b. 17 Nov 1784 and Chas. Marmaduke Berkley, b. 16 Aug 1787; Eliz. CLARKE mar James SHACKLEFORD (NC CC 1802-016; SSPR:34, 35)

CLARK, Charles; PO 9 Dec 1799, T 13 Jan 800; 13 Jan 1800
NC; allottment of dower to Betty CLARK; includes Negroes James & Margery and £7. (NC RB 16:48)
[This may be Chas. CLARK who mar. Betty DEAT[L]EY, wid., RC, bond 16 Jul 1792; Betty DEAT[L]EY was prob. Betty SMITHER, sis. of Lancelot SMITHER, who mar. (1) Wm. DEATLEY, RC, bond 14 Jan 1788 (MRC:37, 53; MWO:77)]

CLARK, James; PO Oct 1803; 29 May 1804
WC; INV, £156.3.9; includes Negro Harry. (WC RI 8:420)
[Thos. CLARK aptd. gdn. of Youel CLARK orphan of Jas. CLARK, 26 Jun 1809 (WC Orders 1807-10:362)]

CLARK, Randall; 2 Sep 1816
RC; Nancy CLARK was appointed gdn. to her children William, John, Hempsell, Josiah, Eliza, Fanny & Sally, orphans of Randall CLARK, dec'd. (RC OB 24:38, 290)
[Randolph CLARKE, wid., mar. Nancy DAVIS, ward of Wm. CLAUGHTON, NC, bond 16 Jun 1801 (MLBNC:18); Randall (or Randolph) CLARK served as a pvt. in the 20th Regiment of Infantry in the War of 1812; he d. on 21 Jan 1815 (PR1835:1835)]

CLARK, Robert; 2 May 1801; 20 Sep 1802
WCP, LC; WILL; I leave to be sold of my est. a fellow named Manuel; money left over after paying debts to purchase 30 or 40 ac. of land for my wife & children to live on; wife Judith to have all est. as long as she lives or remains unmarried; at her death or marriage land to be sold; son Robert to have good schooling so far that he may be fit for bisnes [sic]; two daus. to have learning to read & write; wife & children to have the benefit of the Negroes at my mother's at her death; Negro fellow Harry to be sold or hired out; exors. to get homes for Negroes that are to be hired out as they think best, not to hire them out at public; Rawleigh DUNAWAY, Thomas FLINT, Thomas [RAVEER] exors; WITS: Jas. REVEER, Alex. ROBINSON, Chas. BELL. (LC WB 28:63)
[Robt. CLARK mar. Judith WILKINSON, NC, 20 May 1786 (MLBNC:15); settlement with Geo. PITMAN the acct. of his gdnship. with Robt. CLARK orphan of Robt. CLARK, 16 May 1814 (LC Orders 24:188); in a RC deed dtd 28 Aug 1799, Robt. CLARK and Judah his wife of NC sold land Robt. inherited from his father Jn. CLARK to Jn. FRANCE (RC DB 17:319)]

CLARK, Robert; PO 20 Sep 1802, T 5 Oct 1802; 19 Dec 1803
LC; INV, £342.13.0; includes Negroes: Emanuel, Jenny, Dinah, James, Moses, Milly. (LC EB 24:251)

CLARK, Robert; PO 15 May1809, T 26 Dec 1809; 17 Feb 1812
LC; INV & DIV of the proportional est. of Nancy CLARK infant dec'd among the legal reps: her mother, surviving bro. & sis. [*The names Thos. TAYLOR, Elisamond BASYE & Wm. YERBY are written in the right margin but not further identified; they may be the ones preparing the inv. and making the div.*]. (LC EB 27:103)

CLARK, Robert; PO 13 Feb 1815, T 30 Jan 1815 [sic]; 12 Feb 1816
NC; INV, [m]. (NC RB 20:356)
[The est. of Robt. CLARK was ord. to be admin. by Sam. CLARK, NC, 13 Feb 1815 (NC OB 1811-1816:281)]

CLARK, Robert; 13 Aug 1815; 18 Mar 1816
LC; WILL; Negroes Sinah, Dinah, Janey & boys Spencer & Harry to sis. Judith THRALL (wife of John THRALL); at sister's death Negroes to go to niece Nancy THRALL; William POLLARD, Capt. Henry Chinn LAWSON & Joseph SHEARMAN exors; WITS: Mark TOWELL, Lighanna HAYDON. (LC WB 28:176)
[Jn. THRALL mar. Judith CLARK, LC, bond 17 Dec 1810 (MLBLC:73)]

CLARK, Robert; PO 18 Aug 1817, T 27 Oct 1817; 20 Apr 1818
LC; INV, $438.25; includes Negroes Dinah & June. (LC EB 27:422)

CLARK, Samuel; T 30 Jan 1823; 10 Nov 1823

NC; INV; includes Negroes Jude, Sarah & child Silva. (NC RB 23:372)

CLARK, Susanna; T. 9 Feb 1815; 6 Feb 1816. RC; INV, $273.37 1/2. (RC WB 9:508)

CLARK, Thomas; 30 Dec 1800; 6 Sep 1802
RC; INV, [m]; includes the following Negroes: Jerry, Patt, Dinah & child, Sue & child, Simon, [Maria], Hannah, Immanuel. (RC WB 9:179)

CLARK, Thomas; PO Jan 1801, T 17 Apr 1801; 6 Sep 1802
RC; DIV of slaves and pers. est; wid. Susannah CLARK allotted her dower and residue div. among the children: Elizabeth CLARK, Jane CLARK, Thomas CLARK, Robert CLARK, Richard CLARK, Charlotte CLARK. (RC AB 3:89)
[Thos. CLARK mar. Susanna NUTT, dau. of Winifred NUTT, bef. 26 Apr 1788 (MWO:78); the births of several of the children of Thos. & Susannah are rec. in RC, Sahary (b. 26 Apr 1788 in NFP), Richard (b. 15 Apr 1791 in LP), Eliz. (b. 28 Feb 1795 in LP) and Thos. (b. 9 Jun 1800 in LP) (NFPR:32)]

CLARK, Thomas Sr.; PO Apr 1801, T 13 Apr 1801; 6 Jul 1801
RC; DIV of est. among Susannah CLARKE administrative [sic] of Thomas CLARKE Jr., dec'd, William CLARKE Sr, Judith CLARKE, John FRENCH, & Reuben CLARKE. (RC AB 3:47)
[MRC:73 records the marriage of John "FRANCE" to Frances CLARKE, bond 1 Feb 1794; however in this document, his name is given as John "FRENCH."]

CLARK, William; 4 Jun 1802; 6 Jun 1803
FP, RC; WILL; wife Lucy; son Rodham all lands; daus. Susannah, Lucy, Sally; son Samuel what was left by his grfath William LANSDELL; wife & Mr. George CHRISTOPHER exors; WITS: Jn. HUGHES, Robt. CLARK, Wm. CLARK Sr. (RC WB 9:214)
[In his will (NC 28 Aug 1788 - 4 Feb 1791) Wm. LANSDELL of SSP names his wife Sarah, grdaus. Betsy SUTTON & Sally Lansdell SUTTON, grsons. Wm. SUTTON & Sam. CLARK (NC RB 14:414)]

CLARK, William [m]; 18 Jan [1812]
LC; list of dower slaves held by Joanna ROBERTSON formerly Joanna CLARK wid. of William CLARK in the est. of sd. CLARK: Sarah (age 33), Daniel (12), Peter (10), Spencer (8), Harry (6), /s/ Moses ROBERTSON, Joanna ROBERTSON. (LC EB 27:130)

CLARK, William; PO 3 Jan 1814; 7 Mar 1814
RC; INV, [$]1385.04, included the following Negroes: Sarah, Winney, girl Judy, girl Sillah, boy Wesley. (RC WB 9:449)

CLAUGHTON, Hannah; PO 10 Jun 1805, T 11 Jun 1805; 8 Jul 1805
NC; INV, £421.17.0; includes Negroes Vincent, Lucy, Sinah, Stephen, Jerry, James. (NC RB 17:293)
[This is Hannah COX, dau. of Mary COX, who mar. James CLAUGHTON, NC, lic. 1 Jun 1767 (MWO:78); James CLAUGHTON, in his will (NC 28 Oct 1783 - 10 Jul 1797) named his wife Hannah, daus. Sally, Molly Presley, Alice, Susanna Hardwick, and son John (NC RB 15:399); Hannah CLAUGHTON, in her will (NC 2 Apr 1802-10 Jun 1805) named her daus. Hannah, Molly Presley WRIGHT and Alice COX; her sons-in-law, Wm. WRIGHT & Thos. M. COX were her exors. (NC RB 17:288); the births of 6 children to James & Hannah CLAUGHTON are rec. in the SSPR: Peter (b. 25 Jul 1768), Sally (b. 29 Oct 1770), Eliz. Cox (b. 11 Jan 1773), Eliz. (b. 29 Jul 1778), Ailcey (b. 7 May 1781), & Hannah (b. 4 May 1785) (SSPR:30, 31, 32, 34);

Wm. WRIGHT mar. Polly P. CLAUGHTON, NC, bond 23 May 1796; Thos. McF. COX mar. Alice CLAUGHTON, NC, bond 5 Jul 1799 (MLBNC:22, 112)]

CLAUGHTON, James; 18 Mar 1820

NC; Eliza CLAUGHTON orphan of James CLAUGHTON chose John HUGHLETT as her gdn. (NC OB 1820-25:2)

CLAUGHTON, John; PO 11 Nov 1805, T 7 Dec 1805; 14 Jul 1806

NC; INV, £373.2.6; includes Negroes Hannah & child Mahala, girls Luezer, Miriam, Philis, Drucilla, & Terraza; DIV of Negroes among his reps. on 7 Jun 1806: Pemberton CLAUGHTON (rec'd Hannah & child Mahala), Griffithello CLAUGHTON (rec'd Luizer), Jane Griffin CLAUGHTON (rec'd Miriam & Terraza), William G. CLAUGHTON (rec'd Phillis & Drucilla). (NC RB 17:440, 444)

[In his will (NC 21 Jan 1796-11 Jul 1796) Jn. CLAUGHTON names his wife Nancy, and his sons John Lewis & Pemberton, and daus. Griffethello, Ann Pemberton & Jeane Griffin (NC RB 15:290); the births of 5 children to Jn. & Nancy CLAUGHTON are rec. in the SSPR: Griffithello (b. 7 Sep 1783), Ann Pemberton (b. 25 Dec 1785), Jn. Lewis (b. 16 Aug 1787), Pemberton (b. 16 Mar 1789) & Jean Griffin (b. 12 Apr 1792) (SSPR:32, 34, 35); Griffithello CLAUGHTON mar. (1) Edw. BARNES, wid., NC, bond 15 Nov 1806 and (2) Lewis LAMKIN Jr., NC, bond 29 Oct 1811 (MLBNC:4, 65); Ann CLAUGHTON mar. at least twice, (1) Wm. G. LANGLEY, of St. Mary's Co., Md. who d. c. 1806, St. Mary's Co., Md, 19 May 1805 and (2) Thos. BELL Jr., NC, bond 22 Aug 1808 (NC CC 1820-019, MLBNC:8; <http://www.rootsweb.ancestry.com/~mdstmary/mrgs/mrg_l.htm> accessed 22 Sep 2012); Jane G. CLAUGHTON in her will (NC 27 Sep 1813 – 14 Dec 1813) named her bro. Pemberton CLAUGHTON and her inf. nephew Phillip LANGLEY (NC RB 19:464)]

CLAUGHTON, John; PO 8 Feb 1808; 8 Feb 1808

NC; DIV of Negroes belonging to Jn. CLAUGHTON between Fanny [H.] GRINSTEAD & Susan CLAUGHTON his daus.; Susan CLAUGHTON rec'd Stephen, James, Young Silvey, Emanuel, Old Surfey, John, Sam & Rose; Mrs. Fanny GRINSTEAD rec'd Joe, Ginney, Young Surfey, Bob, Old Aggy, Jerry & Fanny. (NC RB 17:609; OB 1807-11:15)

[Fanny [H.] GRINSTEAD may be the Fanny K. CLAUGHTON who mar. Jn. GRENSTEAD, St. Mary's Co., Md., 25 Jun 1807 (<http://www.mdgenweb.org/stmarys/mrgs/mrg_c.htm> accessed 15 Jun 2012)

CLAUGHTON, Nancy; PO 11 Nov 1805, T 7 Dec 180[5]; 14 Jul 1806

NC; INV, [m]. (NC RB 17:440)

[This is prob. Nancy the wid. of Jn. CLAUGHTON; her est. was ord. to be admin. by Wm. CLAUGHTON, NC, 9 Dec 1805 (NC Minute Book 1805-1807:69)]

CLAUGHTON, Pemberton; T 22 Nov 1814; 14 Jul 1817

NC; INV, $566.57 1/2; includes the following Negroes: [Leazure] (a man) & Sam (a boy). (NC RB 21:206)

[Pemberton CLAUGHTON mar. Ann L. TURNER, NC, bond 27 Apr 1814 (MLBNC:18); in his will (NC 18 Jul 1814 - 12 Sep 1814) Pemberton CLAUGHTON named his wife Ann L. and the child she might have been pregnant with (NC RB 19:566); Ben. TURNER aptd. gdn. of Eliza P. TURNER orphan of Pemberton CLAUGHTON, NC, 12 Jan 1819 (NC OB 1816-20:319); Jn. P. TAPSCOTT aptd. gdn. of Eliz. P. CLAUGHTON orphan of Pemberton CLAUGHTON, NC 14 Jun 1824 (NC OB 1820-25:388)]

CLAUGHTON, Pemberton; T 22 Nov 1814; 6 Mar 1819
NC; INV, $566.57 1/2; include Negroes [Leazure] & boy Sam. (NC RB 22:16)

CLAUGHTON, Peter; 5 Jan 1807
RC; INV; orphan of Richard CLAUGHTON; inv. taken by Rich. CLAUGHTON his guardian; [m]. (RC WB 9:301)

CLAUGHTON, Richard; PO Sep 1802; 2 Jun 1806
RC; INV, [m], includes the following Negroes: Abraham, Bill, Nell, Mary. (RC WB 9:284)

CLAUGHTON, Richard; 13 Dec 1819; 12 Feb 1821
NC; Chancery suit; Richard CLAUGHTON in his own right & as next friend to Priscilla L. JONES, John W. & Eliza JONES children & heirs of Eppa JONES & Sally his wife, Eliza CLAUGHTON, John H., Esther & Ann CLAUGHTON children & heirs of James CLAUGHTON dec'd, Emily McCLANAHAN, Leroy & Jane McCLANAHAN children of Peter G. McCLANAHAN & Jenny his wife, William BENNETT & Phoebe his wife, William CLAUGHTON & Nancy CLAUGHTON against Hiram CLAUGHTON; committee appointed to sell Negro Abraham late the prop. of Richard CLAUGHTON (and assigned to Nancy CLAUGHTON dec'd as her dower) & div. proceeds among the heirs; Abraham sold for $150; $142.50 div. into 8 eq. parts for: Richard CLAUGHTON, Hiram CLAUGHTON, William BENNETT & Phoebe his wife, Nancy CLAUGHTON, William McCLANAHAN, Eppa JONES' children, James CLAUGHTON's children & Peter G. McCLANAHAN's children (the sd. Abraham was purchased by Richard CLAUGHTON); on 1 Feb 1820 R. CLAUGHTON acknowledged receipt of $17.81 1/4 for the sale of Abraham as his proportion of the amount of the sale and the same amount as admr. of William CLAUGHTON dec'd and $11.88 the proportion of John W. & Elizabeth H. JONES to whom he was gdn. (NC RB 22:471; OB 1816-20:405)
[This is Rich. CLAUGHTON who mar. Priscilla LEWIS, dau. of Jas. & Priscilla (RANDOLPH) LEWIS, NC, lic. 23 Nov 1774 (MWO:79); the births of 2 children to Rich. & Priscilla CLAUGHTON are rec. in the SSPR: Sally Lewis (b. 26 Aug 1775) & James (b. 19 Nov 1777) (SSPR:31, 117); Epaphroditus JONES mar. Sally Lewis CLAUGHTON, dau. of Rich. CLAUGHTON, RC, bond 14 Dec 1798 (MRC:108); see also RC DB 18:256]

CLAUGHTON, William (Maj.); T 12 Oct 1808; 12 Oct 1812
NC; INV, $9067.53; includes Negroes Cesar, Jacob, Spencer, Big Adam, George, Matt, Big Bill, Sam, Little Bill, Emanuel, boys Job, Little Adam, Sall, Betty & child Hannah, girl Miram, girl [Vicey], boy Joe, old man Harry, woman Crease, girls Dinah & Leah, Sarah & child Winney, boy John, girl Phillis, Milley & child Charlotte, girl Melinda, boys William, Charles, & Sampson, girl Harriett, boy Henry, boy Jack, Harvey (blacksmith). (NC RB 19:266)
[This is Wm. CLAUGHTON who mar. Catherine ROUTT, NC bond 25 Jun 1803 (MLBNC:18); he d. intest. leaving two children: Betsy wife of Sam. SMITHER and Kitty CLAUGHTON; he had land on Cherry Point, Mattapony Neck and Monday's Neck which was ord. to be div. (NC CC 1819-004); Catherine CLAUGHTON, wid. of Wm. CLAUGHTON, was aptd. gdn. to Eliz. & Cath. orphans of William CLAUGHTON, NC 13 Sep 1808 (NC OB 1807-11:64); Wm. ROUTT was aptd. gdn. to Betty and Kitty CLAUGHTON, orphans of Wm. CLAUGHTON, NC 14 Oct 1811 (NC OB 1807-11:17)]

CLAUGHTON, W[illiam]; PO 10 May 1819, T 28 Dec 1819; 10 Jan 1820

NC; DIV of slaves held by William ROUTT, gdn, between Betsy CLAUGHTON now the wife of Samuel SMITHER (received Salley, Jack, Charles, Joe, Sam, George, Dennis, Phillis & child, Melinda, Lear & 2 children, Winney, Milly, Mary) & Kitty CLAUGHTON (received Cesar, Mottrom, Job, Williamson, John-foolish, Young Cesar, [Longene], Betty, [Cresa], Dinah, Miriam & child, Sarah & 2 children, [Vica], Charlotte). (NC RB 22:200)

[Based on the names of the slaves, this is Maj. Wm. CLAUGHTON who d. c. 1808; his est. was ord. to be admin. by Catharine CLAUGHTON & Peter C. RICE, NC, 13 Sep 1808 (NC OB 1807-1811:106); Sam. SMITHER mar. Eliz. CLAUGHTON, NC, bond 29 Mar 1819 (MLBNC:93); at the time of his death, Wm. CLAUGHTON possessed tracts of land on Cherry Point, Mattapony Neck and Monday's Neck; following a suit in chancery by Sam. SMITHER and his wife Eliz., the NC court ordered the lands surveyed and div. eq. between Wm. CLAUGHTON's two children: Eliz. and Cath. "Kitty" (NC CC 1819-004)]

CLAYTOR, Richard; PO Dec 1800, T 16 Dec 1800; 5 Jan 1801
RC; DIV of £19.8.5 in the hands of Ann B. CLAYTOR extx. among: William QUISENBERRY, Joseph [MOXLY], William GUTRIDGE, John CLAYTOR. (RC AB 3:41)

[Rich. CLAYTOR mar. Ann B. BRAGG, wid., RC, bond 7 Oct 1793 (MRC:40); Ann B. CLAYTOR, wid. of Richard, mar. Jn. KELLY, Jr., RC, bond 2 Mar 1801 (MRC:111); Wm. Randolph CLAYTOR and Eliza Hamilton CLAYTOR were children of Rich. CLAYTOR (WC Orders 1801-04:216); Wm. QUISENBERRY mar. Ann CLATOR, bef 2 Oct 1797 (MWO:291); Jos. MOXLEY mar. Caty CLAYTOR, WC, bond 22 Oct 1787 (MLBWC:48); Wm. GUTRIDGE mar. Mary CLATOR bef. 2 Oct 1797 (MWO:158); Acc. to RC AB 2:345, Ann, Caty and Mary CLATOR were daus. of Mary CLATOR; *the name of this family has been transcribed as CLAYTON in several earlier works, however, it looks much more like CLAYTOR in this record*]

CLEMENTS, William; 23 Dec 1805; 2 Feb 1807
RC; WILL; est. in Georgia to be sold for benefit of wife; any est. in Kentucky & Virginia to wife; friend Henry ROBERTSON of Hanover, friend Frances SMITH of Essex, & friend Thomas P. SMITH of RC exors; WITS: Jn. WROE, Jas. B. BURWELL, Thos. P. SMITH. (RC WB 9:304)

[This is prob. Wm. CLEMENTS who mar, Lucy SMITH, RC, bond 9 Apr 1788 (MRC:40)]

CLEMONDS, Charlotte; 1 Jun 1807; 15 Jun 1807
LC; WILL; all land in LC to friend Hugh BRENT & he is to be ex; WITS: Jesse HAMMOND, Augustine HUGHLETT, Martin HUGHLETT. (LC WB 28:101)

CLUSKEY, Thomas; PO Feb 1813; 23 Aug 1813. WC; INV, £[70].11.3. (WC RI 9:376)

COATES, James; T 18 Feb 1825; 5 Apr 1825. RC; INV, [m]. (RC WB 10:69)

COATES, Rawleigh; T 4 Jan 1815; 17 Jul 1815
LC; INV; includes slaves: Liddy & child Joseph, Harry, Marier, Spencer, Aggy, Lilay, Lewis. (LC EB 27:241)

COATES, Rawleigh; [m]; 16 Jun 1817
LC; DIV of est. among: Thomas COATS, William BROWN as gdn. to his children Nancy & Griffin, Thomas COATS as gdn. to Susan COATS, Thomas COATS as gdn. to Catharine GARNER; each heir received $305. (LC EB 27:382)

[Susanna COATES orphan of Raw. COATES chose Thos. COATES as her gdn., 20 Feb 1815 (LC Orders 24:218); Wm. BROWN mar. Susan COATS, LC, bond 1 Jan 1817 (MLBLC:9)]

COCKARELL, Thomas; 19 Aug 1822
LC; court certifies that Sally LEWIS who was Sally COCKARELL, Betsy COCKARELL & Nancy COCKARELL are sisters and only heirs at law of Thomas COCKARELL dec'd. (LC OB 25:321)
[Sally B. COCKARILL mar. Chas. LEWIS, wid., NC, bond 11 Jan 1816 (MLBNC:68)]

COCKARILL, Jane; 21 Sep 1812
LC; Jane COCKRILL died intest.; no person will administer; sheriff to dispose of est. (LC Orders 24:119)

COCKARILL, John; PO 14 Nov 1814; 10 Jun 1816
NC; INV, $39,893; includes Negroes lad Absolom, Lemmon, James, Samuel, Jack, Emanuel, Spencer, Bob, Anthony (a small lad), Liley & young child James, George (a lad, Liley's child), David (a small lad), Rachel (a small girl), Judith & child Mitchel, Aggy (a small girl, Judith's child), Eliza (a small girl, Judith's child), Fanny (a yellow Negro woman), Siner & child Jerry, Mary (a small girl, Siner's child), Steptoe (a small boy, Siner's child), Winney, Simon (a small boy, Winney's child), girl Salley, Jenny (small woman), [Fably] (a small girl, Jenny's child), Jubee (a small boy, Jenny's child), Aggy (a small girl, Jenny's child), Joe TRACY, Frank (old Negro fellow), Tom (yellow Negro fellow), Ann (young Negro woman), Fanny (young Negro woman), Simon (a lad), Polley (girl), Rachel (young girl), Parker, Isaac (young fellow), Jenney (old woman); COCKARILL's exceptionally large inv. appears to be the contents of a store and included, among various other items, were many kinds of cloth and 1/2 lb. of opium. (NC RB 20:486)

COCKARILL, John; PO 8 Mar 1819; [12 Jun 1820]
NC; DIV of land belonging to the heirs of John COCKARILL in Bruenton's Neck among: Lot 1 (103 ac.) to John N. COCKARILL by Hiram HARDING gdn., Lot 2 (100 ac.) to Thomas BLACKWELL, Lot 3 (100 ac.) to Hiram HARDING; the Flood Point Tract was divided as follows: Lot 1 (32 + 25 ac) to John C. SUTTON by his gdn. Hiram HARDING, Lot 2 (58 + 55 ac) to Thomas BLACKWELL, Lot 3 (58 + 85 ac) to John N. COCKARILL. (NC RB 22:347)
[Jn. COCKARILL had three children: Eliz. N., Peter P., and Millicent B. (NC CC 1819-009); Hiram HARDING mar. Millicent B. COCKRELL, ward of Jas. SUTTON, NC, bond 24 Apr 1815 (MLBNC:45); Eliz. N. SUTTON, with the consent of Jn. COCKARILL, mar. (1) Jas. SUTTON Jr., NC, bond 1 May 1811; she mar. (2) Thos. BLACKWELL, wid., NC, bond 17 Sep 1819 (MLBNC:10, 96); Bruenton's or Bruington's Neck is loc. in the Fairields Dist., NC; Flood Point is also loc. in the Fairfields Dist. on the north side of the Little Wicomico River (Miller:17, 51)]

COCKARILL, Littleton; PO 13 [Aug] 1821, T 29 Oct 1821; 14 Jul 1823 NC; INV. (NC RB 23:335)
[Littleton COCKRELL was b. 14 Jun 1760 the son of Jn. COCKRELL; he mar. (1) Winifred HARCUM, 1780 and (2) Mary (Molly) TRACEY, NC, bond 5 Aug 1793; by his first wife he had four children: Hetty, Edw., Jas., and Pinny who mar. Matthew HUDSON, wid., NC, bond 28 Nov 1815; by his second wife he had seven children: Leven; Jn. who mar. Judith WHEELER, NC, bond 22 Dec 1817; Thos. who mar. Hannah BALL, NC, bond 20 Dec 1824; Lyttleton who mar. Eliz. (TIGNOR) HAYNIE, wid., NC, bond 16 Feb 1825;

Rebecca who mar. Valentine HARCUM, wid., NC, bond 19 Sep 1815, Robt., and Sally (BNCHS vol. VIII, no. 1:50; MLBNC:18, 54); Rebecca COCKRELL orphan of Littleton COCKRELL chose Valentine HARCUM as her gdn., NC, 11 Sep 1815 (NC OB 1811-15:373)]

COCKARILL, Peter P.; T 16 Dec 1817; 12 Jun 1820
NC; INV, [m]; includes Negroes: Moses, Joe, Manuel, Sam, Isaac, Jesse, Lemuel, Winney, Simon, Jane, Matilda, Hannah, Spencer, Fanny (old woman), Judith, Eliza, Mitchell, Dennis, Lucy, Molly, Winny (Black) and a number of books. (NC RB 22:302)
[Peter P. COCKARILL is the son of Jn. COCKARILL and bro. of Eliz. N. & Milicent M. COCKARILL (NC CC 1819-009); Peter B. [sic] COCKARILL mar. Sarah HUDNALL, NC, bond 5 Apr 1813 (MLBNC:18); his name is given as "Peter B." in MLBNC, but it is clearly "Peter P." in NC RB 22]

COCKARILL, Peter P.; PO 8 Dec 1817, T 30 Dec 1817; 12 Jun 1820
NC; DIV of slaves in the est. which included Moses, Joe, Manuel, Sam, Isaac, Jesse, Lemuel, Winney, Simon, Jane, Matilda, Hannah, Spencer, Fanny (old woman), Judith, Eliza, Mitchell, Dennis, Lucy, Polly, Winney (black); the third allotted to Mrs. Sally C. COCKARILL wid. includes Manuel, Jesse, Winney, Matilda, Jane, Hannah; William HARDING Jr., the current husband of Sally COCKARILL, acknowledged receipt of the balance due on the allottment. (NC RB 22:327)
[Wm. HARDING mar. Sarah C. COCKARILL, wid. of Peter, NC, bond 10 Aug 1818 (MLBNC:46); Hiram HARDING was aptd. gdn. of Jn. N. COCKARILL orphan of Peter P. COCKARILL, NC, 8 Dec 1817 (NC OB 1816-20:210)]

COCKARILL, Presley; 16 Oct 1809
LC; Presley COCKRELL died intestate; sheriff to take his est. (LC Orders B23 1808-11:117)
[Jn. COCKARILL, Betsy COCKARILL & Nancy COCKARILL orphans of Presley COCKARILL chose Chas. LEWIS for their gdn., 17 May 1819, (LC OB 25:53)]

COLE, William; PO 28 Feb 1820, T 2 Mar 1820; 26 Jun 1820
WC; INV & DIV; to William COLE (Silvia & Fanny), to Elizabeth COLE (George & Violett), to Nancy COLE (Amy & Tom), to John COLE (Charlott & Sesar), to Hannah COLE (Lavinia & child Peter). (WC RI 11:8)

COLEMAN, Thomas; 29 Mar 1810; 7 May 1810
RC; WILL; son Thaddeus COLEMAN when 21, 2 Negroes Sam & George, books & dwelling plant. & tract of land w/o I now live; if son die before age 21 all est. to be eq. div. between my children: Lucy FULKS, Sarah WALKER, Mary STOTT, Thomas, Robert & James COLEMAN; [Negroes] Simon & Jane to dau. Sarah; Negro man Abram to grson. John ROUTT; $1 to Betsy ROUTT, $1 to Richard COLEMAN; rest of est. to be eq. div. among all my children except Richard COLEMAN, Thaddeus COLEMAN, & Betsy ROUTT; Negro woman Milley to have choice of master or mistress among my children to whom the balance of my est. is given; friend Thomas STOWERS of WC, Mr. Thomas WALKER & William FORRESTER exors; WITS: Thos. [HEARNE], Fred. BOOTH, Fanny EDWARDS, Rawleigh HAZZARD. (RC WB 9:369)
[Thos. COLEMAN mar. (1) Betty CONNOLLY c. Jul 1758 and (2) Ann STOWERS in 1790; Lucy COLEMAN mar. Wm. FULKS, RC, bond 4 Feb 1779; Sarah COLEMAN mar. Thos. WALKER, RC, bond 27 Apr 1793; Mary COLEMAN mar. Oliver STOTT, RC, bond 28 Jan 1797; (MWO:82, 140, 335,

364); the births of 9 of Thos. COLEMAN's children are rec. in the NFPR: Lucy (b. 1 Mar 1759), Rich. (b. 22 Apr 1761), Betty (b. 26 Jan 1763), Thos. (b. 30 Jun 1770), Robt. (b. 15 Aug 1772), Sarah (b. 19 May 1775), James (b. 4 Jan 1778), Molley (b. 23 Apr 1780) and Thaddeus (b. 21 May 1791); the first 8 are children of Thos. & Betty while the last is a son of Thos. & Ann; these births are also rec. in the SSPR as is the birth of another child, Charity Ann (21 Feb 1793) to Thos. & Ann and the death of Betty COLEMAN on 14 Dec 1788 in her 49th year (NFPR:33; SSPR:32, 34, 36, 131)]

COLEMAN, Thomas; T 12 Jul 1810; 4 Feb 1811
RC; INV, £529.2.1, includes Negroes: George, Sam, Abram, Simon, Jane, Milly, James, John & Jane [sic]. (RC WB 9:385)

COLEMAN, Thomas; 26 Feb 1816
WC; Robert LONG aptd. gdn. to Rebeckah COLEMAN orphan of Thomas COLEMAN. (WC OB 1814-18:205)

COLES, Edward; PO 13 Sep 1802, T 1 Jan 1806; 8 Dec 1806
NC; DIV of slaves agreable to his will among the wid., Rhoda, (rec'd Moses, Simon, Job, James, Stephen, Sarah, Easter, Patty, Polly, Pleasant), [John] COLES (rec'd William, Phillis, Pamelia, Frederick), Elizabeth COLES (rec'd Levy, Luannah, Mary, Sam), Nancy COLES (rec'd Abell, Judah, Lily, Milly, [Bask] & Cate), Edward COLES (rec'd David, Agey, Fanny, Tab), Richard P. COLES (rec'd Ben, Kendall, Nancy, Caroline). (NC RB 17:485)
[In his will (NC 6 Sep 1793 - 12 Oct 1801) Edw. COLES named his wife Rodah, sons Jn., Edw. & Rich. Presley and his daus. Eliza, Francinah & Nancy (NC RB 16:287); Edw. COLES mar. Rhoda NELMS in 1778 (MWO:82)]

COLES, Edward; PO 14 Nov 1814, T 3 Jan 1815; 13 Nov 1815
NC; DIV of est. among the heirs; John COLES (rec'd Negroes Simon, Patty, Armstead & [Shurya]), Ann COLES (rec'd Polly, Sarah, Warner & Mahala), Edward COLES (rec'd Stephen, Alfred & Jery), Richard P. COLES (rec'd Job, Ann & Robert), John COTTRELL (rec'd Moses, [Grance] & Pleasant). (NC RB 20:298)
[Jn. COTTRELL mar. Eliza COLES, NC, bond 12 Mar 1812 (MLBNC:21); in her will (NC 8 Oct 1812 - 13 Mar 1815) Eliz. COTTRELL wife of Jn. COTTRELL named her bros. Jn., Edw. & Rich. P. COLES and Ann COLES (her sis.) (NC RB 20:16)]

COLES, Elizabeth; 22 Jan 1819; 12 Apr 1819
NC; WILL; nephews John COLES, Edward COLES, Richard P. COLES; niece Ann BISCOE; nephew John ANDERSON & Elizabeth ANDERSON $100 to be eq. div. when they come of age; $25 to the buildings of the new Methodist Meeting House; nephew Edward COLES ex; WITS: Mathew HUDSON, Jos. COLES. (NC RB 22:29)
[Ann COLES mar. Jn. BISCOE, wid., NC, bond 31 Dec 1816 (MLBNC:9)]

COLES, John; 12 Sep 1825
NC; settle Mary COLES' (now BURGESS) acct. of her admin. of the est. of Jn. COLES and allot her her dower. (NC OB 1825-30:41)
[This is prob. the Jn. COLES who mar. Mary CONWAY, NC, bond 8 Jan 1818; Mary (CONWAY) COLES, wid., mar. Sam. BURGESS, wid., NC, bond 6 Jul 1825 (MLBNC:14, 19); Edw. COLES aptd. gdn. of Robt. E. COLES orphan of Jn. COLES, 10 Dec 1827 (NC OB 1825-30:225); *NB: it is not certain that the two Jn. COLES are the same person*]

COLES, Richard; PO 13 Nov 1809, T 29 Dec 1809; 10 Jun 1811

NC; INV, £1675; includes Negroes Joseph, Lott, Daniel, Isaac, William, Peter, boys Samuel, Lazarus, Solomon, Philip, Moses, and James, Sarah & 2 children Grace & Let, Rachel & 2 children Hiram & Charles, girl Claracee, boy Ned, girls Nely & Sally Ann, [Candere] $ 2 children [Lidge] & Noah, girls Polly & Lucy, old women Grace & Letty, boy George. (NC RB 19:60)

COLES, Richard; PO 12 Apr 1819 [14 Feb 1820]
NC; INV & DIV, Negroes $11,475, rest of est. $417; includes Negroes Grace, Lazerus, James, Lucy, Phillip, Edward, Elijah, Stephen, [Emsy], Ann, Lott, Sollomon, Moses, Hiram, Charles, John, Thomas, Sarah, Nelly, Sally, Gracey, Rachel, Mary, [Mathey], Juliet, Mariah, Bill, Polly, Milley, Hannah; total vaule for Negroes $11,475; DIV of Negroes to: Molly WILDAY (Phillip), Joseph COLES (James & [Emsy]), Richard COLES (Lazarus & Ann), Izatus COLES (Lucy & Stephen), Sally CROCKET (Elijah & Edward), heirs of Edward COLES: John COLES (Lott, Rachel, Bill, Nelly), John BISCOE (Moses, Mary, Hannah, Sarah), Edward COLES (Hiram, Polly, Milly, Thomas, Juliet), Richard P. COLES (Sollomon, John, Mathey, Mariah), Rhoda A. C. COTTRELL (Charles, Sally, Gracey). (NC RB 22:232)
[Molly (or Mary) COLES mar. Jos. WILDAY, NC, bond Sep 1817 (MLBNC:110); Ann COLES mar. Jn. BISCOE, wid, NC, bond 31 Dec 1816 (MLBNC:9)]

COLES, William; PO 8 Dec 1806, T 8 Apr 1807; 13 Jul 1807
NC; INV, £433.10.6; includes Negroes Epp, Sam, Peter, George, James, Solomon, Massey & child Rachel, Jane, girl Sally, Susannah, girls Sharlotte & [Terah], Winne. (NC RB 17:548)

COLES, William Jr.; PO 14 Aug 1815; 11 Mar 1816
NC; INV; includes Negroes George, James, Sharlot & child Peter, boy Adam, girl Catey, boy Tignor, Eave, child Grace, child Huldy, child Rachel, Winey, Susan, [Jenny]. (NC RB 20:382)

COLES, William Jr.; PO 14 Aug 1815, T 4 Dec 1815; 11 Mar 1816. NC; INV, $68.50. (NC RB 20:385)

COLES, William Jr.; T 4 Dec 1815; 14 Dec 1818. NC; INV, $69.50. (NC RB 21:556)

COLES, William Sr.; PO 11 Dec 1815, T 21 Dec 1815; 11 Mar 1816
NC; DIV of est. in the hands of the admr. Joseph COLES among Joseph COLES, Molley COLES, Richard COLES, Izates COLES, Thomas HAYES admr. of Robert CROCKET (each rec'd $10.27 1/4); a second div. of the est. in the hands of Joseph COLES names the same heirs and adds that Thomas HAYES admr. of Robert CROCKET rec'd the money for Sally CROCKET dau. of Robert; the Negroes of the est. of William COLES Jr. were div. among his heirs: Molley COLES (rec'd George, Rachel, Winney), Izates COLES (rec'd Sharlot & child Peter, Adam, Susanna), Richard COLES (rec'd [Cave], George, Tignor), Thomas HAYES admr. of Robert CROCKET (rec'd James, Caty, Huldy). (NC RB 20:378, 379)
[Wm. COLES of SSP in his will (NC 30 May 1806-8 Dec 1806) named his wife Sarah and children William, Joseph, Mary, Richard, Izates & Judith (NC RB 17:493); Robt. CROCKETT, wid., mar. Judith COLES, NC, bond 10 Dec 1812; Mary COLES, nfi, gave consent for Judith (MLBNC:23)]

COLLINS, Bagwell; T 23 Apr 1810; 11 Jun 1810
NC; INV, $6.26; included coopers tools. (NC RB 18:407)
[Bagwell COLLINS dead more than 3 mos. and his est. ord. to be admin. by the sheriff, NC, 12 Feb 1810 (NC OB 1807-1811:154)]

COLLINS, Christopher J.; PO 24 Nov 1823; 23 Feb 1824

WC; INV by Daniel PAYNE admr, $4155.04; includes slaves Bil, Moses, Henry, Vincent, Davey, Henry, Barbary, Hannah, Milly, Fanny, Charlotte, Jenney (old), Sarah Ann & child. (WC RI 11:453)
[Christopher J. COLLINS mar. Eliz. Washington LINDRUM, dau. of Thos. LINDRUM, WC, bond 21 Apr 1806 (MLBWC:14)]

COLLINS, Elizabeth; 21 Aug 1803; 20 Feb 1804
LC; WILL; all my land in Middlesex Co. to [Isom] WILLIAMS; to Bailey CHOWNING son of Henry CHOWNING dec'd $60 provided he returns from sea, but if he does not return, $60 to sis. Hannah PARRON; Betsy WILLIAMS & Caty WILLIAMS; Lucy STREET; Ann A. CHOWNING; Mariah STREET; Nancy WILLIAMS dau. of sis. Hannah PARRON; sister's three daus: Betsy WILLIAMS, Caty WILLIAMS, & Mariah PARRON; John CHOWNING ex.; WITS: Jn. CHOWNING Jr., Thos. STREET. (LC WB 28:75)

COLLINSWORTH, John; 28 Aug 1810
WC; Chancery suit, John B. STEEL gdn. of William & Elizabeth STEEL and William FRANKLIN gdn. of Thomas FRANKLIN complts. vs. Charles SANFORD & Sabina his wife admx. of John COLLINSWORTH, 28 Aug 1810. (WC Orders 1810-13:33)
[Jn. COLLINSWORTH mar. Sebinah WEAVER, WC bond 3 Jun 1790 (MLBWC:14); he d. intest. in 1793 leaving his wid. and one child, Nancy, who d. in 1795; he had two sisters of the whole blood, Sarah who d. in 1799 and Nancy who d. in 1788; Sarah mar. Jn. B. STEEL and had two children Wm. and Eliz. N.; Nancy mar. Wm. FRANKLIN and had one child Thos. (WC CC 1821-017); Jn. Brown STEEL mar. Sarah COLLINSWORTH, WC, bond 31 Jan 1788 (MLBWC:67); Wm. FRANKLIN mar. Ann COLLINSWORTH, WC, bond 30 Oct 1786 (MLBWC:24); Sabina COLLINSWORTH mar. (2) Jn. ROSE, WC, bond 12 Oct 1795 and (3) Chas. SANFORD, WC, bond 22 Sep 1800 (MLBWC:60, 61); in her will (WC 23 May 1790 - 28 Dec 1790) Sarah COLLINSWORTH (who may have been Jn. COLLINSWORTH's mother) named Jn. COLLINSWORTH, Wm. STEEL and Thomas son of Wm. FRANKLIN (WC DW18)]

CONALLY, Harrison; PO 11 Dec 1815; 13 May 1816
NC; DIV; Negro boy Daniel belonging to the est. sold at Lancaster Court House to R. W. DOWNMAN for $400; proceeds div. among: John CONALLY, Williamson CONALLY, Elizabeth CONALLY, Elizabeth EFFORD, Peter BEAN admr. of William CONALLY dec'd, & Ellison CURRIE gdn. of Nancy HILL; BEAN & CURRIE rec'd $38 for their wards; the others rec'd $76 each. (NC RB 20:440)
[The est. of Harrison CONOLLY was ord. to be admin. by Jn. CONOLLY, 10 Jul 1815 (NC OB 1811-1816:349); Eliz. EFFORD is prob. Betsy CONOLLY who mar. Lewis EFFORD, NC, bond 29 Dec 1807 (MLBNC:35)]

[CONALLY], Harrison; PO 10 Jul 1815; 12 Feb 1816
NC; INV at the house of George CONOLLY, $341.25; includes Negro boy Daniel. (NC RB 20:338)
[The est. of Harrison CONOLLY was ord. to be admin. by Jn. CONOLLY, NC, 10 Jul 1815 (NC OB 1811-1816:349)]

CONNALLY, John; PO 14 Jul 1800; 14 Oct 1805
NC; INV, [m]; includes Negroes David, Dianah, Sue, Hannah ([under] a conditional bill of sale), Levinah, Cate, Fanney, Daniel; DIV of est. among Mrs. Mary CONERLEY (rec'd David), George CONERLEY (rec'd Dinah), Betsy CONERLEY (rec'd Sue), John CONERLEY (rec'd Hannah), William CONERLEY (rec'd Levina), James HILL (rec'd Cate), Williamson

CONERLEY (rec'd Fanney), Harrison CONERLEY (rec'd Daniel). (NC RB 17:336, 339)
[This births of the following children to Jn. & Mary CONNALLY are rec. in the SSPR: Harrison (b. 2 Nov 1780), George (b. 13 Aug 1782), Jn. (b. 14 Mar 1785), Betsy (b. 6 Apr 1787) & Williamson (b. 8 Jul 1789) (SSPR:28, 34, 35); James HILL may be the man who mar. Nancy CONNALLY, NC, bond 21 Dec 1786 (MWO:180) *although the marriage seems too early for a child of Jn. & Mary; see also Mary CONNALLY below*.]

CONNALLY, Mary; PO 12 Dec 1814; 13 Feb 1815
NC; INV, $132.63 1/2. ; NC RB 20:4)
[This is Mary the wid. of Jn. CONNALLY; in her will (NC 17 Dec 1808 - 9 Jan 1815) she names her dau. Elizabeth HEREFORD and her son Williamson CONNOLLY (NC RB 19:585)]

CONNELLEE, William Y.; PO Jun 1809; 7 Aug 1809. RC, INV, £44.8.9. (RC WB 9:360)

CONNOLEY George; PO 9 Jan 1815; 13 Feb 1815
NC; INV, $652.78 1/2; includes Negroes Judith, Diner, Harry. (NC RB 20:1)

CONNOLLEE, Daniell; 27 Apr 1809; 2 Oct 1809
RC; Nunc. will; Ruth R. BRAGG visited Daniel CONNALLEE who was very sick & weak who said that he desired his son Hudson CONNALLEE should have his Negro man Tom & that his wife should be maintained from his est. & that the rest of his est. should be eq. div. amongst all his children, 29 Apr 1809; Molly CONNELEE said basically the same, 29 Apr 1809. (RC WB 9:365)
[a Daniel CONNELLEE mar. Jane NEWMAN, RC, bond 8 Apr 1791 (MRC:43)]

CONNOLLY, George; PO 13 Oct 1817; 9 Jul 1821
NC; land bel. to George CONNOLLY dec'd sold to Williamson CONNOLLY; William CONNOLLY brought suit in chancery against John, James, Peggy, Elizabeth & Nancy CONNOLLY children & heirs of George CONNOLLY (as they were infants under 21, John CONNOLLY was appointed their gdn.) and land was ord to be sold. (NC RB 22:586)
[This is George the son of Jn. & Mary CONNALLY who was b. in SSP 13 Aug 1782 (SSPR:34); he is prob. the same Geo. who mar. Betsy SUTTON, NC, bond 14 Mar 1803 (MLBNC:20); Wm. & Jn. CONNOLLY chose Jn. ROGERS as their gdn. and the sd. ROGERS is aptd. gdn. of Jas., Peggy, Eliz., & Nancy CONNOLLY orphans of Geo. CONNOLLY, NC 9 Jul 1821 (NC OB 1820-25:118); Williamson CONNOLLY aptd. gdn. to Jn., Peggy, Betsy, & Nancy CONNOLLY orphans of Geo. CONNOLLY, 13 Nov 1826 (NC OB 1825-30:127)]

CONNOLLY, James; PO Dec 1796; 20 Feb 1797
LC; INV, £175.4.3; includes Negroes: Old Sawney, Winny, Charlotte. (LC EB 24:57)
[Peter BEANE aptd. gdn. to Nancy CONNOLLY orphan of James CONNOLLY, 17 Feb 1800 (LC Orders 21 1799-1801:79)]

CONNOLLY, Peggy; PO 17 Feb 1823, T 21 Feb 1823; 15 Mar 1824
LC; INV, $33.33. (LC EB 29:313)
[Admin. on the est. of Peggy CONNOLLY dec'd granted to Daniel P. MITCHELL; Albert CONNOLLY chose Dan. P. MITCHEL as his gdn.; on the mot. of Dan. P. MITCHELL ord. that Addison CONNOLLY, Jas. CONNOLLY, Janetta CONNOLLY, Dan. P. MITCHELL as gdn. of Albert CONNOLLY and Nancy CONNOLLY children & heirs of Peggy

CONNOLLY be summoned to show cause why the land of Wm. CONNOLLY dec'd should not be sold and the proceeds divided, 17 Feb 1823 (LC OB 25:352)]

CONNOLLY, William; 10 Nov 1806
NC; William CONNOLLY died intest. leaving a wid. Hannah, who mar. (2) Rich. LITTRELL, and the following children: Sally (who mar. Francis VANLANDINGHAM), Milly (who mar. John MOTHERSHEAD), Betsy (who mar. Jeremiah JONES), Peggy (who mar. HALL and had four children: Fanny, Ann, William & unknown), and George. (NC CC 1808-002)
[Jn. MOTHERSHEAD mar. Milly CONNOLLY, RC, bond 5 Dec 1785; Peggy CONNOLLY mar. Rich. HALL, RC, bond 4 Oct 1789; Jeremiah Nash JONES mar. Betty CONNOLLY, RC, bond 7 Sep 1795 (MRC:84, 108, 139); Sally, who was the wid. of Edmond WALKER at the time, mar. (2) Francis VANLANDINGHAM, NC, bond 17 Nov 1795 (MWO:360)]

CONWAY, [Edward]; PO 14 Feb 1814, T 14 May 1814; 9 Jan 1815
NC; possessed Thomas J. HAYES with his ward, Cuthbert CONWAY's est. in the hands of Benedict BURGESS admr. of Edw[ard] CONWAY dec'd, to wit, the following Negroes Mark, Sally, girl Bety, boy Hiram and $227.24 1/2. (NC RB 19:604)

CONWAY, Edwin; T 22 Dec 1812; 9 May 1814
NC; INV, $[4242]; includes Negroes James, Peter, Mack, Tom, Adam, Silva, Rose, Old Suckey, Old Nancy, Letty, Polly, Old Rose, Simon, Salley, Salley and her child John, Mariah, Austin, Harriett, Hiram, Bettey, Joe. (NC RB 19:543)

CONWAY, Edwin; PO 11 Jan 1813, T 22 Mar 1814; 9 May 1814
NC; DIV of est. among the heirs; allotted the wid. (Suckey CONWAY) her third part of the Negroes (James, Joe, Tom, Silva, Harriet, Suckey, Polly, Old Rose) valued at $1414; allotted each child's part, valued at $944, to James CONWAY (Adam, Mariah, Austin, Rose, Letty), Cuthbut C. CONWAY (Mack, Sally, Bettey, Hiram), Edward C. CONWAY (Peter, Simon, Salley & child John); Edwin CONWAY's land near Little Wicomico River also divided among above heirs. (NC RB 19:546)
[Cuthbert CONWAY orphan of Edw. CONWAY chose Benedict BURGESS as his gdn., NC 13 Oct 1819 (NC OB 1816-20:396)]

CONWAY, James; 14 Feb 1823; 7 Apr 1824
NC; WILL; est. to wife Margaret B. CONWAY; if wife should have an heir 9 months from this date, I give all my est. to the sd. child; if wife should not have an heir 9 months from the date of this will all my est. including my right in the third Negroes of Susannah CONWAY which she holds for life to John HUDNALL; wife Margaret extx; WITS: Royston B. COVINGTON Sr., Ann WADDEY; [on 6 Apr 1824 the will was offerred for proof by Steptoe TAYLOR & its validity contested by Cuthbert CONWAY & Edward CONWAY by the sd. Cuthbert his next friend & the same being proved in the usual form by Royston B. COVINGTON & Ann WADDEY; sundry other witnesses thereto were sworn & examined and the court not being advised what judgment to give in the premises takes time to consider thereof till tomorrow ... and after mature advisement the court is of opinion & doth decide that the same be established as the true last will of the sd. James CONWAY...the extx. in the will named renounced her right of executorship and on the motion of Steptoe TAYLOR who has intermarried with the sd. extx. a certificate is granted him for obtaining letters of administration]. (NC DCO:461)

[James CONWAY mar. Margaret B. HUDNALL, wid. of Jn. HUDNALL (d. NC 1820), NC, bond 18 Jul 1822; Steptoe TAYLOR mar. Margaret B. CONWAY, wid, NC, bond 12 Feb 1824 (MLBNC:20, 99)]

CONWAY, James; T 1 Feb 1824; 14 Jun 1824
NC; INV, includes Negroes Lazarus and boy Marke. (NC RB 23:535)

CONWAY, Joseph; T 9 Jan 1816; 8 Apr 1816
NC; INV, $8356; includes Negroes Doctor (age 50), Solomon (45), John (36), Presley (17), James (20), Shedrick (18), Penop (14), Bacchus (14), Williamson (3), Harrison (4), George (2), Moses (1), Isaac (1), Thomas (infant), Sally (70), Bet (65), Peggy (60), Phamy (27), Charlotte (25), Sally (24), Grace (24), Alice (24), Violet (14), Joannah (12), Miriam (4), Peggy (2), Judah (infant). (NC RB 20:434)

CONWAY, Robert; PO 12 Jan 1801, T 20 Jan 1801; 14 Jun 1802
NC; DIV of est. among John LACKY & Mary his wife late Mary CONWAY (rec'd her dower Spencer, Ned, Juanna & child Silla, Hannah, Peter), Fanny CONWAY (rec'd Jacob, Peggy), Robert CONWAY (rec'd Nancy, Martha & Sally), Thomas CONWAY (rec'd Winny, Polly & Solloman), Molly CONWAY (rec'd Gabriel & Patty), Elliza CONWAY (rec'd Gabriel & Patty [sic-must be in error], Kitty CONWAY (rec'd Darky & Lucy). (NC RB 16:381)
[Robt. CONWAY served as a captain in the navy and 3 years in the Continental Line during the Revolutionary War; he d. intestate leaving the following children: Thos., Robt., Francis [sic], Eliza, and Catherine; Thos. d. intestate leaving children: Jane, Mary, Hannah and Senica (VS1776 I:469); Jn. LACKEY mar. Mary CONWAY, wid., NC, bond 24 Sep 1799 (MLBNC:65); Dan. MUSE, son of Dan. MUSE, mar. Frances CONWAY, NC, bond 22 May 1801 (MLBNC:76); on the mot. of Eliza SUTTON, Cath. NELMS, Robt. CONWAY & Frances his wife in their own right and the sd. Robt. as gdn. to Sam. BURGESS orphan of Mary BURGESS & Wm. MIDDLETON admr. of Thos. CONWAY, ord. sale of the slaves of Robt. CONWAY dec'd lately held in dower by Mary LACKEY formerly Mary CONWAY wid. of sd. Robt., 11 Nov 1828 (NC OB 1825-30:317); Cath. CONWAY, ward of Thos. CONWAY, mar. Peter NELMS, wid., NC, bond 19 Nov 1812, Eliza CONWAY mar. Wm. SUTTON (wid.), NC, bond 9 Aug 1822 (MLBNC:77, 97); *see also NC CCs 1818-004 and 1821-017*]

CONWAY, Walker; T 8 Jan 1800; 17 Feb 1800
LC; DIV of est. in Stafford Co. between: John M. CONWAY & Richard H. GASKINS (legal rep. of Agnes S. GASKINS formerly Agnes [J.] CONWAY). (LC EB 24:108)

COOKMAN, Ezekiel; T. 16 Dec 1812; 6 May 1816
RC; INV, $546.58; RC WB 9:524)
[Ezekiel COOKMAN was a son of Rice COOKMAN (d. NC 1794) (NC RB 15:118)]

COOKMAN, George; PO 14 Dec 1813, T 23 Dec 1813; 14 Feb 1814
NC; INV, $210.66 3/4. (NC RB 19:532)
[The est. of Geo. COOKMAN was ord. to be admin. by Ann COOKMAN, NC, 13 Dec 1813 (NC OB 1811-1816:207); a Geo. COOKMAN mar. Nancy HEADLEY, dau. of Wm. & Jean (DOUGLAS) HEADLEY, NC, bond 2 Jan 1795 (MWO:87); the births of the following children to Geo. & Nancy COOKMAN are rec. in the SSPR: Polly Sydnor (b. 30 Apr 1796), Eliz. Hollon (b. 21 Jan 1798), Jn. (b. 4 Jul 1800), Ledey Pue (b. 28 Sep 1802), Jenny Singer (b. 30 Jan 1805), Jeremiah (b. 20 Mar 1807) (SSPR:32, 33)]

COOKMAN, Solomon; 14 Dec 1813

NC; David J. TELLIS asked the court to ord. the sale of Negro Jesse, late the property of Solomon COOKMAN and div. the proceeds between himself and Susanna TELLIS gdn. of Thos. COOKMAN. (NC OB 1811-15:206) [Solomon COOKMAN was the son of Rice COOKMAN (d. NC, 1794); he received Negro Jesse in his father's will (NC RB 15:118); Solomon COOKMAN mar. Susanna KNOTT, NC, bond 30 Nov 1791 (MLBNC:21); Rodham TELLIS, wid., mar. Susanna COOKMAN, wid., NC, bond 13 Feb 1804 (MLBNC:99)]

CORBELL, Austin; 23 Nov 1817; 12 Jan 1818

NC; WILL; land & all I possess to eldest bro. William CORBELL; if he dies without heir land & est. to youngest bros. Peter CORBELL & [Gelberd] CORBELL; [no ex. named]; WITS: [Wady] G. BEETLEY, Jas. S. ELLISTON. (NC RB 21:359)

[Austin, Martin, Peter, Gilbert, Hiram, Jn. and Judith CORBELL were children of Wm. CORBELL Sr. who in his will (NC 8 Nov 1814 – 15 Nov 1814) named his 4 youngest sons Austin, Martin, Peter & Gilbert; Jn. d. leaving children Gawin and Elizabeth; Hiram d. in 1826 intestate; Judith mar. (1) Sam. M. BLUNDON and (2) Geo. R. SHEARMAN, NC, bond 2 Oct 1822 (NC RB 20:92; MLBNC:91; NC CCs 1817-011, 1819-010)]

CORBELL, Gilbert; T 9 Jan 1800; 9 Jun 1800

NC; INV, [m]; includes Negroes Nancy, girls Sarah, Mime & [Scinex], Isaac, Chloe. (NC RB 16:116)

[Gilbert CORBELL was the son of Wm. CORBELL Sr. (d. NC, 1814) (NC RB 20:92); he mar. Ann DOCKSEY, wid., NC, bond 31 Dec 1792 (MLBNC:21)]

CORBELL, Hiram;

NC; Hiram CORBELL d. intest. in 1826 leaving as his only heirs and next of kin: Judith SHEARMAN, Martin and Peter CORBELL (bros.) and Gawin and Eliz. CORBELL inf. children of John CORBELL the dec'd bro. of Hiram (NC CC 1826-005)

CORBELL, Richard; PO 11 Dec 1820, T 15 Feb 1821; 11 Jun 1821

NC; DIV of real est. of which Richard CORBELL died seized it being that part of the tract allotted to the sd. Richard's wid. as her dower near the head of a cove known at this time as Humphlett's Cove and adj land Edward HUMPHLETT & William HARDING Jr.; land was div. between Briney CORBELL (dau. of sd. Richard) & Mottrom PICKERING (grson. of sd. Richard). (NC RB 22:576)

CORBELL, Richard S.; PO 12 Oct 1801, T 7 May 1802; 13 Sep 1802

NC; DIV of est. (which included Negroes Joe, Molley, girl Rose, girl Patty, girl Judith and child Ciller); possessed the wid. with her third (the man Joe); the wid. rec'd Molly & child as gdn. to her dau. Sabrina CORBELL and she rec'd Patty & Judith as gdn. to her son Richard S. CORBELL; John CORBELL rec'd girl Rose as gdn. to Julia CORBELL; we find due in div. of Negroes from Judith CORBELL gdn. to Jn. CORBELL gdn. £6.13.4 appears to be in the hands of Loftis JONES D.S. from the sale of a Negro girl Sinah from the est; in the DIV of land, the wid. rec'd tract on Cockarill's Cr. (NC RB 16:439) [This is prob. Rich. Smith CORBELL, son of Jn. & Sarah CORBELL, b. in SSP 12 Jan 1763 (SSPR:30); Rich. S. CORBELL, wid., mar. Judith RICE, dau. of Isaac RICE, NC, bond 8 Jul 1790 (MLBNC:21, NC RB 19:463); Judith (RICE) CORBELL mar. (2) Edw. HUMPHLETT, NC, bond 21 Sep 1803 (MLBNC:58); Juliet or Julia CORBELL, dau. of Rich. S. CORBELL, NC, bond 4 Feb 1807 (MLBNC:109)]

CORBELL, Richard S.; PO 15 Oct 1805, T 11 Jan 1806; 8 Dec 1806

NC; DIV of est. among his next kin; possessed Julit [sic] CORBELL with Negro Judah & one third of the land on Cockarill's Creek and Sabrina CORBELL with Negro Patty & two thirds of the land on sd. creek. (NC RB 17:486)

CORBELL, William; T 18 Nov [1816]; 9 Dec 1816

NC; INV, [m]; includes the following Negroes: man Solomon, woman Criss. (NC RB 21:115)

[Hiram CORBELL was aptd. gdn. of Martin, Peter and Gilbert orphans of Wm. CORBELL, NC, 9 Jan 1815 (NC OB 1811-15:272)]

CORBIN, Gawin; 8 Sep 1822; 15 Jun 1823

LC; WILL; to George L. CORBIN one cent; dau. [Sally J. BOWEN] who went off to Kentucky with John S. [BOWEN]; I do hereby liberate and set free Anna [LONE] alias Anna MERCER and all her children and grandchildren, her two youngest Jane and Robert are my children and [further] for them and for their support ... tract of land on Tabb's Creek and Long Cove and silverware and china; son John; grson. William (son of son Gawin) one half of the Negroes; friend Capt. KIRK residue of land and est. and gold watch; mentions est. due him from est. of Reuben TURNER late of Caroline Co.; any money unappropriated from TURNER's est. to Armistead Hill CURRIE; family pictures and looking glass to Mary B. J. CURRIE; Armistead CURRIE, Edwin DAINGERFIELD, James KIRK, William S. DOGGETT and William SUTTLER exors; WITS: Jas. THRALL, Jn. B. L. REEVES, Benj. GEORGE [*This is a long will in which CORBIN rails against Geo. L. CORBIN and his wife because he says they treated him very badly during a period when he was bed-ridden; it was brought to court on 19 May 1823, but not recorded until the following month.*] (LC WB 28:228)

[Mary Bathurst Jones CORBIN, dau. of Gawin CORBIN, mar. Armistead CURRIE, LC, date of bond missing (MLBLC:19); George L. CORBIN mar. Sarah D. SPRIGGS, LC, bond 8 Dec 1817 (MLBLC:16); on the mot. of Geo. L. CORBIN ord. that Jn. R. F. CORBIN, Armistead CURRIE who mar. Mary B. CORBIN, Geo. L. CORBIN, Wm. CORBIN son of Gawin CORBIN, Ann Eliz. ANDERSON, Mary ANDERSON and Lettice ANDERSON children & grandchildren of Gawin CORBIN be summoned to show cause why a part of the land of which Gawin CORBIN died seized should not be sold and the proceeds divided, 18 Oct 1824 (LC OB 26:77)]

CORNELIUS, William; 19 May 1801

LC; William CORNELIUS and Sarah his wife who was Sarah CORNELIUS are admrs. of William CORNELIUS. (LC Orders 21 1799-1801:243)

[*It appears that this record may be in error as a later entry in the same order book indicates that it was Wm. WILLIAMS who mar. Sarah CORNELIUS the admx. of Wm. CORNELIUS (LC Orders 21 1799-1801:343)*; Wm. WILLIAMS mar. Sarah CORNELIUS, LC, bond 17 Dec 1798 (MLBLC:80)]

COTTRELL, John; 23 Mar 1804

LC; Hiram BLACKWELL was gdn. of Nancy COTTRELL orphan of John COTTRELL. (LC OB 1804-05:74)

[NC CC 1808-004 suggests that Jn. COTTRELL, Alice the wife of Samuel TILLERY, Leannah the wife of Robt. DAVIS and Nancy COTTRELL are children of Jn. COTTRELL; Leannah COTTRELL mar. Robt. DAVIS, NC bond 25 Jul 1806 (MLBNC:27); *It is not certain that the Nancy above is the same person as the Nancy or Ann COTTRELL who mar. Wm. ROGERS*; Nancy COTTRELL mar. Wm. ROGERS, NC, bond 10 Jul 1820 (MLBNC:89); settle Royston BETTS acct. of his admin. of the est. of Ann ROGERS formerly Ann

COTTRELL, 13 May 1828 (NC OB 1825-30:261); the est. of Jn. COTTRELL was div. among Thos., Leannah, Alice, Nancy and Jn. COTTRELL; Peter COCKARELL was gdn. to Alice, Jn. and Nancy COTTRELL; Alice COTTRELL mar. (1) Sam. TILLERY in 1805 and (2) Jeremiah OLDHAM, wid., NC, bond 28 Nov 1810 (NC CC 1817-001; MLBNC:78)]

COURTNEY, George; 13 May 1807; 27 Jun 1808
CP, WC; WILL; land and plant. to be eq. div. between two sons William & George; rest of est. to be eq. div. among all my children: William, Betsy, Sally & George; Sally & George to be schooled; [Edmund] JEFFRIES & son William exors; WITS: Sam. BEALE, Jeremiah JEFFRIES, Wm. ROBINSON; WC DW 21:430)
[This is prob. Geo. COURTNEY who mar. Ann JEFFRIES, WC, bond 2 Jan 1787 (MWO:90); Betsy & Sally COURTNEY orphans of Geo. COURTNEY chose [Redmond] R. JEFFRIES as their gdn., 25 Oct 1809 (WC Orders 1807-10:436)]

COURTNEY, John; 18 Nov 1806; 1 Feb 1807
LP, RC; WILL; sons Leonard & John 30 ac. each; rest of land to wife; after her death to sons; daus. Nancy & Catey; large sein & fishing boat to son Leonard; blacksmith tools to son John; dau. Maria; William FRANKLIN exor; WITS: Abner HOWE, Eppa WEATHERS. (RC WB 9:313)
[Leonard COURTNEY mar. Mary ALDERSON, RC, bond 4 Nov 1812 (MRC:45)]

COURTNEY, John; PO Jun 1807; 3 Oct 1808. RC; INV, £145.5.5. (RC WB 9:340)

COVINGTON, Royston B.; 12 Sep 1821; 10 Jan 1825
NC; WILL; plant. called White's where Jesse MOORE now lives containing 75 ac. & Negro Cate UMPHRY to dau. Rebeccah R. GARNER; plant. called [Sprie's Hill] where Mr. WILKINSON now lives containing 75 ac. & Negro woman Ann CASSITY [& Dinah] to dau. Sally W. CRITCHER; 20 ac. on Horn Harbor Creek I leave to my Negro man Moses during his life & I give him his freedom; remainder of est. to son Royston B. COVINGTON; son Royston ex; WITS: Nathan WHEETLEY, Rich FLYNT, Wm. KESTERSON. (NC RB 24:144)
[Royston B. COVINGTON seems to have had two wives: (1) Eliz. DAVENPORT, NC, bond 18 Mar 1788 and (2) Judith HUGHLETT, NC, bond 8 Jun 1796 (MLBNC:22); Rebecca R. COVINGTON mar. Wm. GARNER, NC, bond 12 Feb 1812; Sally W. COVINGTON mar. Jn. CRITCHER, NC, bond 9 May 1817 (MLBNC:40); Miller:69 locates Horn Harbor stream in east central NC]

COVINGTON, Thomas D.; PO 8 Nov 1819; 12 Feb 1821
NC; INV, $1894.75; includes Negroes Numan, Dick, boy Samuel, Pleasant, Caralin, Fame, Lilia, Matildah. (NC RB 22:476)
[Jos. COLES mar. Mary COVINGTON, wid., NC, bond 19 Sep 1820 (MLBNC:19); allot to Jos. COLES & Polly his wife her dower & thirds in the est. of her former husband Thos. D. COVINGTON, NC 9 Dec 1822 (NC OB 1820-25:256)]

COVINGTON, Thomas D.; PO 8 Nov 1819; 10 May 1824
NC; INV; includes Negroes Caroline, Fannie, [Lilea], Samuel, [Numan], Richard, Pleasant. (NC RB 23:469)

COWARD, William; d. in late 1792 or early 1793; in his will (WC 17 Oct 1792 – 27 Jan 1793) named his wife Mary and Elizabeth THRAILKILL, Letty THRAILKILL, and Letty HALL; Letty HALL mar. Lindsey COLE; Mary THRAILKILL d. in 1794. (WC CC 1805-020)

[Letty HALL mar. Lindsey COLE, WC, bond 17 Jan 1799; HALL's name is given as HUTT in WWCV and as HULL in MWO; it is clearly HALL in the CC. (WC DW 19:77, MWO:82)]

COX, Alice R.; PO 1 Mar 1812; 14 Aug 1815
NC; DIV of land adj. to the house tract of Hiram L. OPIE known as the Brick House Cove made at Gill's in Cherry Point; land was div. among Pemberton CLAUGHTON, William R. FALLIN & Richard [M.] FALLIN. (NC RB 20:177) [NC CCs 1798-001, 1810-006 and 1812-015 shed additional light on this record: Sally and Mary G. NEALE are children of Rich. NEALE; Sally mar. Pemberton CLAUGHTON, NC, bond 3 Sep 1796 (MLBNC:79); Mary G. "Molly" mar. Chas. FALLIN, NC, bond 8 Dec 1794 (MWO:128); Alice R. "Alcey" NEALE, another dau. of Rich. NEALE, mar. as her last husband Wm. P. COX (she was the wid. Thos. A. TRAVERS when she mar. COX in 1800 (MLBNC:22); Alice and Wm. P. COX d. intestate; land of COX to be div. among Pemberton CLAUGHTON and Wm. R. & Rich. M. FALLIN sons of Chas. & Mary G. FALLIN; One Brick House tract was identified by Miller:15 as being located on the Potomac River in NC 8 miles northeast of Heathsville.]

COX, Fleet; 23 May 1799; [m]
WC; WILL; son Presley on day of marriage or when 21 home plant. w/o I now live adj. Wm. MIDDLETON & Job SELF and smith's shop with tools, distillery with stills, worms, & tubs, water grist mill and land purch. from Jn. SELF; son Fleet on day of marriage or when 21 the Brick House Tract w/o my grandfather Presley COX lived, also land w/o James [*1 wd. unclear*] lives and tract purch. from B. B. SMITH; son Downing on day of marriage or when 21, land in Yeocomico Neck purch. of Jn. C[?] & Peter RUST [*portion missing and remainder unclear*]; WITS: Phillip PEAD, Dan. BARKER, Jn. BARKER. (WC DW 20:8)
[Jas. COX aptd. gdn. of Fleet COX orphan of Fleet COX and Presley COX aptd. gdn. of Downing COX orphan of Fleet COX, 25 Oct 1809 (WC Orders 1807-10:433, 434); Downing COX orphan of Fleet COX chose Jas. COX as his gdn., 24 Jun 1816 (WC OB 1814-18:247)]

COX, Fleet; T Nov 1800; 26 Nov 1810
WC; INV, £848.0.6, Negroes were valued at £1744.2.0; includes Negroes Old Charles, Florah, Absalom, James & Nelson (children of Florah), Young Nell, Hannah, Suckey, Bill, Wormley, Tasker, Frank, Charles & David Ashton (children of Young Nell), Old Sukey, Henney, Vincent & Chichester (children of Old Sukey), Henry, Fanny, Peter, Joe & Lucey (children of Fanny), Beck, Lucy, Daniel & Eliza (children of Beck), Nancy, George, Mary, Old George, Old Mary, Lee Hall Mary, Tom, Willoughby, Young Sam, Scipio, Blacksmith Sam, Old Lett; slaves were div. among: Polly COX, Downing COX, Presley COX, Sally COX, Fleet COX; Presley COX was gdn. to Downing COX & James COX was gdn. to Fleet COX. (WC RI 9:204)
[Downing COX orphan of Fleet COX, who has attained the age of 14, chose Fleet COX as his gdn. and the former ord. appointing Presley COX has gdn. is repealed, 27 Feb 1815 (WC OB 1814-18:98)]

COX, Fleet; [m]; 28 Jul 1817
WC; INV. $3359.85, includes Negroes Sam, Achia, Joe, Rebeckah, Eliza, Nancy. (WC RI 10:112)

COX, Fleet; 22 Sep 1819; 17 Mar 1822

LC; WILL; wife's dau. Nancy George HU[GH]LETT; wife Mary COX; at wife's death est. to dau. Elizabeth Jane FLEET; [no ex. named]; WITS: Jn. T. DEGGE, Leanna TREACLE. (LC WB 28:227)

COX, Fleet Sr.; 24 May 1816; 27 May 1816

WC; WILL; Richard KNOTT; £200 to sis. Polly COX; £50 to sis. Sally PAYNE; use of whole est. remaining to my bro. Downing COX provided he should not sell or distress any of my servants or sell the whole or any part of my lands; bros. Presley & Downing; sis. Polly COX & Sally PAYNE; friends William MIDDLETON & Benedict LAMKIN exors; WITS: Benedict WRIGHT, Job SELF, Walt SELF, Fleet SELF. (WC DW 23:175)

[Fleet COX Sr. was a son of Fleet COX (d. WC after 1799) (WC DW 20:8); Sally COX mar. Daniel PAYNE, WC, bond 15 Nov 1815 (MLBWC:53)]

COX, George; PO 10 Feb 1800, T 18 Mar 1800; 12 Jan 1801

NC; INV, £275.12.6; includes Negroes Sampson, Lett, boys Frederic, Tom & Cesar, girl Anna. (NC RB 16:208)

COX, James; [m]; 9 Mar 1812

NC; DIV of lands; Lot 1 (60 ac) to Peter COX, Lot 2 (25 ac. with improvements) to Carlos COX, Lot 3 (65 ac) to James A. COX, Lot 4 (53 1/3 ac.) to Peter COX, Lot 5 (53 1/2 ac) to Carlos COX, Lot 6 (53 1/3 ac) to James A. COX; James ALDERSON, surveyor. (NC RB 19:157)

[*See also NC CC 1811-018*]

COX, James Jr.; PO 12 Nov 1811; 13 Jan 1817

NC; William COX for himself and as gdn. of Peter & James COX children of James COX pltfs. against Charles COX orphan of James COX Jr. by Elizabeth [COX] his gdn. & Polly, Dandridge & Sally COX children of Peter COX dec'd by Sally COX their gdn. defts. appointed the subscribers to make sale of the lands called Harry Hogan which James COX Sr. dec'd died seized; land was purchased by Hiram L. OPIE for $301. (NC RB 21:136; OB 1807-11:277)

[Harry Hogan is a point of land in NC on the South Yeocomico River; the name first appears in a 1707 deed as "Harry Hokin Neck;" it has variants Arehokin and Harrihokin (see Miller:63)]

COX, James Sr.; T Mar 1815; 15 Aug 1815

NC; INV of est. which came to the hands of John HULL, sheriff of NC, [m]; includes Negroes old men Solomon, Jack, & Willoughby, Harry, Phill, Barnes (or Jacob), Letty, Dinah, Winny, boys Wheeler & Bob, Stephen, Edie & her 3 children Judy, Dick & Sally, Fillis & her 2 children William & Mary, old man Dick (Edie's husband); the last two women and their children and Dick the husband of Edie went off to the British. (NC RB 20:194)

COX, Jane; 20 Apr 1804; 7 Apr 1807

SSP, NC; WILL; sis. Judith ANDERSON; Negro boy Bill purchased from Capt. Henry TRAVERS to my nephew Izates ANDERSON; est. acquired since the APP of the est. of my dec'd husband Peter COX to be eq. div. between sis. Judith ANDERSON, Molly BETTS the wife of Thomas BETTS, Sally COLES the wife of William COLES & Izates ANDERSON; livestock to nephew William COX & Peter COX son of my nephew James COX; nephews Walter & Izates ANDERSON exors; WITS: Sarah SMITH, Jas. ENGLISH. (NC DCO:426)

[This is Jane HARDING, dau. of Wm. & Sarah HARDING, who mar. (1) Parish GARNER, 1765 and (2) Peter COX, 1771; her sis., Judith mar. (1) Jos. WILDEY, 1757 and (2) Jn. ANDERSON, 1774; Sally COLES was a dau. of

Judith & Jos. WILDEY; she mar. Wm. COLES in 1778 (MWO:15, 82, 91, 143, 376)]

COX, Jane; PO 7 Apr 1807, T 23 Nov 1807; 2 Sep 18[08]
NC; INV, [m]; includes Negro boy Bill; Negro woman Eve; a sorrell horse legacy to Izates ANDERSON and a riding mare, a gray [mare] & a lady's saddle legacies to Judith ANDERSON. (NC DCO:444)

COX, John; 5 Aug 1800; 22 Dec 1800
WC; WILL; wife Sally; if wife is with child, est. to go to child; bro. James COX (under 21); nephew Presley COX and Presley's bro. Fleet COX; friends Peter COX, James COX and Thomas [*1 wd. unclear*] DOWNING to be exors; WITS: Walt. JONES, Eliz. GLASCOCK, Nancy GUYTHER. (WC DW 20:173) [Sally COX, wid. of Jn. COX, mar. Beverly ROBINSON, WC, bond 25 Jan 1803 (MLBWC:59; WC Orders 1801-04:351)]

COX, Peter P.; 6 Oct 1818; 28 Feb 1820
WC; WILL; son Fleet COX the tract of land called Mount Sion that I bought of George [WHITELOCK], also the land my father gave me called Cherry Point which joins that I bought of WHITELOCK, and also the land I bought of Ellyson CURRIE & John PECK the exors. of Dr. Walter JONES together with the mill I have lately built and also the money due me from the state of Philip GRYMES of Middlesex which will pay for the land I bought of CURRIE & PECK and also the following Negroes: Davy, Stella & her two daus. Fanny & Maria, Megg & her three children Betsy, James, & Aron, Nasaw, Bill, Stephen & old Franky at Cherry Point; son Fleet to pay his sis. Sally Graham $1000 when she is 21 or marries; son Fleet is also to relinquish all right etc. to land that I sold to his uncle Stephen BAILEY which I got in right of his mother; dau. Mary Elizabeth the following Negroes: old Daniel, Charlotte, Hannah & her four children (Nancy, Suckey, Nelly & Emanuel), Mima (Nancy's dau) & Grace and also my forest plant. on which John [MESSICK] now lives which was given to me by my father and the land that I bought of Samuel WALKER; dau. Sally Graham the following Negroes: old Franky, Simon, [Sinna], Willoughby, Sarah, Louisa (dau. of Hannah), Lucy and Anna (dau. of Nancy) and also tract of land I bought of Thomas TUCKER; son Peter Presley (under 18) the following Negroes: Michael, Isaac, Edmond, Sally and her child Daniel, Nelly, James (whom I bought of Charles ASKINS), Henry (Hannah's son), Nancy & her youngest child Scilla and old Jeany and also the plant. on which I live called Federal Hill including the place where Robert BAILEY now lives and also the place where John [ROCK] now lives also the tract I bought of John BAILEY called Rust's and the tract w/o [Mrs WARDSBY] now lives; my overseer & friend Daniel MEALY may live at Federal Hill; bro. James COX, son Fleet COX & two nephews William MIDDLETON & John MIDDLETON & two friends John MURPHY & Robert BAILEY exors. & guardians of my children; WITS: Robt. MURPHY, Rich. THOMPSON, Jn. MEALY; COD. 20 Dec 1819 - dau. Sally Graham has died & her legacies redistributed; WITS: Robt. MURPHY, Gordon [FORBES], Rich THOMPSON. (WC DW 24:40)
[Peter Presley COX was the son of Fleet COX (d. WC, 1791) (WWCV:192); Cherry Point is located in NC between the Yeocomico River and the Glebe (Miller:25)]

COX, Presley; 25 Jun 1797; 18 Jun 1798
LC; WILL; I am going away by water and if any accident happens to me so that I never return again, I give all I have to my beloved wife Betsy COX after paying what is owing from me. I desire Mr. William BLACKERBY if he

will settle my business and if he [w]ont some other man my beloved wife Betsy COX choses. This my last will and desire. WIT: Wm. COX; [will proved by the oaths of Wm. BLACKERBY & Peter TANKERSLEY]; LC WB 28:29)

[Presley COX mar. Betsy THOMAS, NC, bond 4 Jun 1794 (MWO:91)]

COX, Presley; PO 18 Jun 1798; 20 Apr 1801. LC ; INV, $187.94. (LC EB 24:139)

COX, Presley; 28 Jan 1824; 28 Jun 1824

WC; WILL; plant. to be kept together & worked; wife Sarah Ricarda to have one third of proceeds from selling grist mill; other two thirds to be used for schooling and expenses of children Richard L. COX, Mary E. COX & Sarah L. COX until they marry or arrive of age; Locust Farm to be included in wife's thirds for a home during her life or widowhood; son Richard L. COX to have all the land left me by my father Fleet COX & the land I purchased of Peter P. COX likewise the land I purchased of William GILBERT with my water grist mill; to dau. Mary E. COX half the land I purchased of Daniel PAYNE & Polly COX & all my interest in the est. of Robert MITCHELL; to dau. Sarah L. COX half the land I purchased of Daniel PAYNE & Polly COX and all my interest in the land where Peggy [BUNN] now lives; if children die without issue wife is to have the Negroes Judy & her child Cornelius, Lewis, [Debrious] & Sophia, Robert S. BAILEY is to have land left me by my father Fleet COX & the land I purchased of William GILBERT and all the remaining Negroes; BAILEY is not to move any of the Negroes out of the neighborhood and is to use them with the greatest humanity and should any of them become infirm he shall furnish them with a house & garden, provision & clothes & treat them well in every aspect, William MIDDLETON Jr. to have all the land I purchased of Peter P. COX & the land I purchased of Daniel PAYNE & Polly COX; wife Sarah Ricarda extx; WITS: Jn. COX, Jn. ROCK, Dan. MEALEY. (WC DW 25:56)

[Presley COX was a son of Fleet COX of WC (WWCV:20); he mar. Sally Ricarda LEE, WC, bond 8 Jun 1815 (MLBWC:16)]

COX, William; 20 Apr 1801

LC; settlement of gdnship. acct. of Presley COX with Fleet COX orphan of William COX. (LC Orders 21 1799-1801:231

COX, William P.; 17 May 1810; 14 Oct 1811

NC; WILL; Negroes Andrew, Pegg and Nancy to be sold to pay debts; wife Sally to receive Negroes Mark, Bob, Molly, Rawleigh, Silvy, Mima, and Nelson during her widowhood; dau. Ann McFarlane COX; bro. Thos. McFarlane COX; bro. Thos. McFarlane COX and Peter P. COX exors; WITS: Sam. CRALLE, Jn. WEYMOUTH, Peter P. COX. (NC RB 19:102)

[Sam. CRALLE aptd. gdn. of Wm. P. COX & Ann COX orphans of Wm. P. COX, NC 11 May 1818 (NC OB 1816-20:252)]

CRABB, Benedict; 3 Nov 1806; 24 Nov 1806

WC; WILL; sis. Mary [R.] YEATMAN Negro man Isaac & girl Cate; sis. Sarah R. CRABB Negro boy Paul; nephew Philip John A. CRABB Negro boy Bill; bro. William M. CRABB; rest of est. to be eq. div. among Mary R. YEATMAN, Sarah R. CRABB & William M. CRABB; friend Henry [L.] YEATMAN exor; WITS: Willis GARNER, Thos. STOWERS, Habron MOORE; WC DW 21:294)

[Benedict CRABB was a son of Jn. (d. WC 1799) & Eliz. CRABB of CP, WC (WC DW 19:372)]

CRABB, Benedict; PO Sep 1805; 22 Aug 1809

WC; INV, [m]; DIV of est. among widow Mary P. CRABB (who received her dower and the Negroes Siller and the girl Frank), William P. CRABB (received Negro boy John), Claiborn BABER (girl Philicia), Benedict M. CRABB (Lucy), Molly P. CRABB (boy Osman) & Jenney CRABB (girl Maria). (WC RI 9:57)
[Claiborn BABER mar. Hannah C. CRABB, WC, bond poss. 1803 (MLBWC:3)]

CRABB, Benedict; PO 24 Nov 1806; 23 May 1814
WC; INV, $956.13; includes Negroes Isaac, Bill, Paul, Cate. (WC RI 9:426)

CRABB, Benedict M.; T 15 May 1815; 22 Feb 1819
WC; INV, [m]; includes Negroes James, Dinah, Haney, John, Maria, Lucy. (WC RI 10:352)

CRABB, Daniel; PO Sep 1800; 23 Jul 1804. WC; INV, £71.3.6. (WC RI 8:434)
[Ann GILL mar. Dan. CRABB, Sr., WC, bond 24 Aug 1795 (MLBWC:16); Sam. CRABB aptd. gdn. of Jn. CRABB orphan of Dan. CRABB, 28 Apr 1800 (WC Orders 1799-1801:207); Ann CRABB, wid. of Dan. CRABB was next friend to Rich. and Gerard CRABB orphans of Daniel, WC, 28 Sep 1801 (WC Orders 1801-04:165, 203)]

CRABB, William Middleton; d. intest. leaving siblings Mary, who mar. (1) [Daniel] BENNETT, WC bef. 23 Jan 1775 and (2) Rich. CADDEEN, WC, bond 3 Feb 1787, John, Elizabeth, Benedict, Jane Middleton, and Lettice CRABB; they were the children of John CRABB who in his will (23 Jan 1775 – 27 Apr 1779) named his daus. Elizabeth Rogers Middleton, John, Benedict, Mary Bennett, Jane Middleton RUST, Lettice and William Middleton. (WC CC 1805-016, DW 16:63, DW 17:149, MWO:37, MLBWC:11)
[Jane Middleton CRABB mar. [Jn.] RUST bef. 23 Jan 1775 (MWO:306)]

CRABB, William P.; PO 26 Dec 1808, T 21 Feb 1809; 24 Jul 1809
WC; INV, $737,09; includes Negroes Levinah & child, Ben, John. (WC RI 9:145)

CRAINE, James; [m]; 11 Sep 1809
NC; Thomas D. DOWNING certifies that he was well acquainted with the family of the late James CRAINE and that Maria now the wife of Edwin C. BROWN was the dau. and only child of James CRAINE who d. when she was an infant; Maria was born in Feb or Mar 1787. (NC RB 18:216)
[Settlement of gdnship. acct. of Eliz. LOVELL (a pensioner) with Maria CRAINE orphan of Jas. CRAINE, 20 Jan 1800 (LC Orders 21 1799-1801:74)]

CRALLE, Ann; T 18 Dec 1822; 12 May 1823; NC; INV. (NC RB 23:298)

CRALLE, John; PO 11 Jan 1813; 8 Feb 1813
NC; the wid. Mary CRALLE was allotted her dower in the real est. which is that part of the est. usually called the Point bounded by the lands of the late John CRALLE Jr. and Coan River; also allotted her the following slaves: Lewis, Griffin, Arthur, Bob, Isaac, Caleb, Phebe, Martha, Siller, Polly, James, & Charlotte. (NC RB 19:325)
[The est. of Jn. CRALLE was ord. to be admin. by Sam. McCURDY & Jos. DESHIELD, NC, 11 Jan 1813 (NC OB 1811-1816:141)]

CRALLE, John; T 15 & 21 Jan 1813; 11 Apr 1815
NC; INV, $10,887; includes 10 yoke of oxen and Negroes London, Ben, Lewis, Griffin, Bill, Armstead, Arther, Stephen, Tom, Isaac, Rob, Jacob, George, Jack, Samuel, Matt, Simon, Caleb, Martha & children Charlott & James, Milly & young child Louise, Matilday, Nancy, Betty, Siller, Dinah, Polly, Betty (weaver), Phoebe, Letty. (NC RB 20:60)

CRALLE, John Sr.; PO 8 Nov 1812 & 14 Jan 1814, T 24 Mar 1815; 8 May 1815

NC; settled est.acct. of admin. of Joseph DESHIELDS & Samuel McCURDY in the est. of John CRALLE Sr. dec'd; balance of $1382.95 which was div. between the sd. McCURDY in right of his wife Hannah McCURDY dau. & distributee of the sd. CRALLE, Mary CRALLE wid. of sd. dec'd, the heirs of John CRALLE Jr., and to the heirs of Mary F. WILLIAMS' grandchildren & distributees of John CRALLE Sr. (NC RB 20:111)

CRALLE, John Sr. (Capt.); PO 15 Sep [1813]; 14 Mar 1814
NC; DIV of slaves among his heirs; Lot 1 (London, Stephen, George, Simon, Bettey, Milly, & Tom; young children Louisa & Lindsay; slaves rec'd in advancement Rachel, Grace, Charlott, Sally, & Nancy) drawn by Dr. Samuel McCURDAY in right of his wife Hannah McCURDY; Lot 2 (Armstead, [Sam], Mottrom, Jack, Matilda & Betty - weaver; slaves rec'd in advancement Joe, Jack, Will, Peter, Solomon) drawn by John CRALLE, William CRALLE, Mottrom CRALLE, Kenner CRALLE, Septimus CRALLE & Richard CRALLE heirs of John CRALLE Jr.; Lot 3 (Ben, Jacob, Sam, Nancy, Letty, [Dinar]; slaves rec'd in advancement Jesse, Bill, Milly & Winny) drawn by John WILLIAMS, Joseph C. WILLIAMS, William WALKER in right of his wife Catherine and William FICKLIN in right of his wife Elizabeth H. heirs of Molly WILLIAMS; the last lot was subdivided among the respective claimants as follows: No. 1 (Ben) drawn by John WILLIAMS; No. 2 (Jacob & Letty) drawn by the undersigned [commissioners] for William FICKLIN; No. 3 (Nancy) drawn by Joseph C. WILLIAMS; No. 4 (Sam & Dinah) drawn by William WALKER. (NC RB 19:531)
[Hannah Kenner CRALLE, dau. of Jn. & Sarah CRALLE, was b. 31 Jul 1778 (SSPR:31); she mar. (1) Jos. HUDNALL, Jr., wid., bond 27 Aug 1795 and (2) Dr. Sam. McCURDY, NC, bond 21 Aug 1801 (MLBNC:55, 72); Mary Kenner CRALLE mar. Jos. WILLIAMS, NC, 17 Jun 1777 (MWO:378); Jn. CRALLE orphan of Jn. CRALLE, Jr. chose Nancy CRALLE his gdn. and she was also aptd. gdn. to Wm., Mottrom, Kenner, Septimus & Rich. CRALLE also orphans of Jn. CRALLE Jr., NC, 8 Nov 1813 (NC OB 1811-15:202); Jas. C. WRIGHT aptd. gdn. to Sept. & Rich. CRALLE orphans of Jn. CRALLE, 12 Aug 1828 (NC OB 1825-30:295); *see also NC CCs 1813-002 and 1825-009*]

CRALLE, Mary; 17 Nov 1821; 11 Feb 1822
NC; WILL; to niece Mary LEE: Betty, Dominick, Robert, Joseph, John, Molley, Eliza, Dianna, Grace, Charlotte, Martha and other prop. requiring of my niece that she will not exact any service of the aforementioned Betty mother to the other Negroes willed to her or of her child Martha; I do furthermore wish that Betty may be retained in the family for the purpose of better providing for her children; to my relation Mary L. LEE dau. of my niece Mary LEE my Negro girl Nancy now living with her mother; my relation Sarah E. LEE dau. of my niece Mary LEE; to my relation Henry Towles LELAND son of my late bro. Charles LELAND my Negro boy Isaac; to my relation Lucius C. LELAND son of my late bro. Charles LELAND my Negro girl Harriott; Negro woman Mary & her 2 children Lydia & David to my relation John B. LELAND son of my late nephew John L. LELAND, if he should die under age or without heir they should be eq. div. between my nephew B. M. LELAND's 2 daus. Ann Maria LELAND & Salley Moore LELAND and the dau. of Leroy P. LELAND, Mary LELAND; my Negro woman Maria & her 3 children Polley, Edy & Thomas to my relations Judith Smith LELAND & Mary J. LELAND daus. of my nephew B. M. LELAND; my riding carriage & Negro woman Letty to my nephew B. M. LELAND requiring that she may live where she pleases and not to exact any service

from her also to provide for her should she need it; $25 to the wid. of my late friend the Rev. Samuel STRAUGHAN; remainder of est. to my niece Maria EUSTACE; nephew B. M. LELAND & friend Izates ANDERSON exors; WITS: Rebeccah TRAVERS, Dounda TRAVERS. (NC RB 23:102)
[Mary CRALLE is prob. Mary LEE the dau. of Thos. LEE (d. LC 1759) and his wife Lucy; Lucy LEE, wid. of Thos. mar. (2) the Rev. Jn. LELAND of NC, LC, bond 20 Jan 1762; among others, Thos. LEE named his dau. Mary LEE in his will (LC 1 Dec 1758 - 10 Mar 1759); Jn. LELAND was aptd. gdn. of Mary LEE; Jn. LELAND in his will (NC 1 Feb 1778 - 14 Apr 1778) named his wife Lucy, daus. Sarah, Martha NUTT, Mary HAYNIE, Susannah, Anne Henrietta, and Lucy and sons John and Charles (NC RB 10:285); Mary LELAND mar. (1) Jn. HAYNIE, NC, lic. 26 Dec 1770 and (2) Jn. CRALLE, NC, bond 18 Feb 1793; Chas. LELAND, whom Mary names as her bro. had at least four children: Hen. Towles, Lucius C., Lucy & Sam. A.; Jn. LELAND, the bro. of Chas., had at least four children: Jn. L., Baldwin M., Maria & Leroy P. (NC RB 10:42; RB 13:120; RB 20:33; LC WB 16:52, WB 17:15; MWO:92, 174, 225)]

CRASK, Elizabeth; 4 Jan 1818; 3 Mar 1818
RC; WILL; money due from father's est. to be eq. div. between two youngest sisters Polly CRASK & Ann CRASK; two youngest sisters also to have my part of my mother's est. left by my grandfather Henry ASBURY to my mother Bethiah CRASK; WITS: Jonathan BECKWITH, Rich. N. MARINER, Polly JENKINS, Polly JONES, Margaret BRAGG. (RC WB 9:602)
[Eliz. was the dau. of Wm. CRASK and Bethiah (ASBURY) SANFORD (MWO:93); *see Wm. CRASK (d. 1816) below*]

CRASK, Elizabeth; 7 Feb 1820
RC; Thos. M. BRAGG, William [R.] BRAGG, William BURGESS who mar. Nancy BRAGG, Ishmael BRAGG, Henry BRAGG, Letty BRAGG, Molly BRAGG and Sarah BRAGG are heirs of Elizabeth CRASK who was Elizabeth BRAGG. (RC OB 24:401)
[Eliz. BRAGG mar. James CRASK, WC, bond 17 Mar 1819 (MLBWC:16); Thos. Moore BRAGG mar. Margaret BISPHAM, RC, bond 3 May 1813 (MRC:22); on the mot. of Thos. M. BRAGG, one of the heirs of Eliz. CRASK who was Eliz. BRAGG, ord. that Wm. R. BRAGG, Wm. BURGESS who mar. Nancy BRAGG, Ishmael BRAGG, Hen. BRAGG, Letty BRAGG, Polly BRAGG & Sarah BRAGG heirs of sd. Eliz. be summoned to show cause why land of sd. Eliz. should not be sold, 2 May 1820 (RC OB 25:11)]

CRASK, Griffin; 10 Sep 1810; 24 Nov 1817
WC; WILL; Negro woman Dinah & boy Meridith & weaving loom to dau. Hannah; Negro boy Vincent & girl Sary Ann to dau. Francis THORNTON; Negro boy David to son John CRASK; Negro Lewis to dau. Elizabeth GUTRAGE during her life and at her death to her son Griffin Thornton & her dau. Sary Ann Crask; Negro boy William Henry and [boy] James Thornton to son George CRASK; John PAYNE Sr. & son John CRASK exors; WIT: Thos. MUSE; COD leaving any remaining money to be eq. div. among his 5 children; WIT: Thos. MUSE, W, BUTLER, Alice BUTLER. (WC DW 23:313)
[Eliz. CRASK mar. Jn. GUTRIDGE, WC, bond 8 May 1804 (MLBWC:27)]

CRASK, Griffin; T 17 Dec 1817; 26 Jan 1818
WC; INV. [m]; includes Negroes girl Maria, boys Richard & Henry, Diner, Meridith, Vincent, lad Lewis, boys David & Thornton. (WC RI 10:302)

CRASK, James; PO 2 Jun 1794; 1 Dec 1800
RC; INV, £243.4.[4]; includes the following slaves: Newman, Esther. (RC WB 9:139)

CRASK, Joel; 27 Aug 1814; 27 Feb 1815
WC; WILL; now at camp in Dumfries, Prince William Co; expecting to go into action in some short time, the enemy being not far distant; wife Nancy all my est; WITS: Sam. LAMKIN, Wm. [?], Sam. RYALS, Thos. W. CLARK. (WC DW 23:60)
[Joel CRASK, son of Jas. CRASK (d. RC, 1794), mar. Ann Hunter PAYNE, dau. of James & Ann (HUNTER) PAYNE, 9 Jan 1810; Ann H. (PAYNE) CRASK mar. (2) Osmond JOHNSON, WC, bond 16 Feb 1821 (MLBWC:36, RC WB 8:170); Descendants of John Payne, Sr. at URL <http://familytreemaker.genealogy.com/users/g/e/m/Jennifer-S-Gemmelladams/FILE/0004text.txt> accessed 24 Jan 2012)]

CRASK, John; [9 Apr 1806]; 2 Jun 1806
RC; Nunc. will; George CAVENDER deposed that John CRASK departed this life on Tuesday 8th instant at his own house and that during his last illness, on Sunday evening last the 6th of April, the sd. CRASK called on the sd. CAVENDER and Nancy his wife in the presence of part of his family but in a voice so low from sickness that he is not sure CRASK was heard by any person but the sd. George and Nancy and said that his wife should have the use of his property with liberty to dispose of it at her death as she thought proper; [Nancy CAVENDER made essentially the same deposition]. (RC WB 9:289)

CRASK, Marks; 28 Mar 1815
WC; George G.MOTHERSHEAD aptd. gdn. to James CRASK orphan of Marks CRASK. (WC OB 1814-18:108)
[This is apparently the Marks CRASK, bro. of Joel CRASK, who mar. (1) Mary PAYNE, WC, bond Dec 1808 and (2) Caty COLLINS, WC, bond 1 Jan 1810 (MLBWC:17); he is named Mark in the will of his father, Jas. CRASK (d. RC, 1794) who also named another son Joel (RC WB 8:170)]

CRASK, William; 11 Mar 1816; 28 Oct 1816
CP, WC; WILL; $60 to son Richard CRASK; $40 to dau. Nancy CRASK; dau. Elizabeth CRASK; dau. Martha CRASK; $34 to dau. Sarah CRASK; $34 to dau. Polly L. CRASK; $34 to dau. Ann CRASK; son Richard CRASK ex; WITS: WM. OMOHUNDRO, Thos. OMOHUNDRO, Wm. H. SANFORD. (WC DW 23:216)
[Thos. M. BRAGG aptd. gdn. to Eliz. CRASK orphan of Wm. CRASK, 27 Jan 1817 (WC OB 1814-18:275); Rich. CRASK aptd. gdn. to Polly & Ann CRASK orphans of Wm. CRASK, 27 Nov 1817 (WC OB 1814-18:353)]

CRAWFORD, Andrew; 24 Jun 1799
WC; Nelly CRAWFORD is the only and sole heir of Andrew CRAWFORD. (WC Orders 1799-1801:32)

CREWDSON, Henry; 6 Jun 1825
RC; Louisa CREWDSON orphan of Henry CREWDSON chose John G. CREWDSON as her gdn. (RC OB 26:311)
[This is prob. the Hen. CREWDSON who mar. Sophia Carter GARLAND, RC, bond 26 Mar 1799; Sophia (GARLAND) CREWDSON died in Fredericksburg in Mar 1824 (MRC:46)]

CRITCHER, George; 5 May 1816
RC; Sally CRUTCHER, wid. of George, aptd. gdn. to her children Vincent, George & Richard CRUTCHER. (RC Orders 1814-16:108)

[Geo. CRUTCHER mar. Sally HADON, RC, bond 18 Jan 1809 (MRC:47)]

CRITCHER, George; 5 Jun 1821
RC; Henry M. DOBYNS said on oath that Sarah CRITCHER was the wid. of George CRITCHER and that Richard, George & Vincent CRITCHER are the only legitimate heirs of sd. George and that they are infants under 16. (RC OB 25:162)

CRITCHER, John; 17 Nov 1806; 24 Nov 1806
WC; WILL; son John land w/o I now live and all land belonging to me excluding those that are not already given by deed of gift to him & his sis. Susanna and half of slaves; other half of slaves to dau. Susanna; friends George GARNER, Thomas STOWERS, & Stephen BAILEY exors; WITS: Thos. LITTLE, Wm. BEALE, Wm. KINDRICK, David WARDROBE. (WC DW 21:283)
[This is prob. the Jn. CRITCHER who mar. Lettice GARNER, WC, bond 22 Jun 1792 (MLBWC:17); Geo. GARNER was aptd. gdn. of Susanna & Jn. CRITCHER, orphans of Jn. CRITCHER, 24 Nov 1806 (WC Orders 1804-07:463); Thos. STOWERS aptd. gdn. of Jn. & Susanna CRITCHER orphans of Jn. CRITCHER, 26 Jun 1809 (WC Orders 1807-10:362)]

CRITCHER, John; T 20 Dec 1806; 26 Oct 1807
WC; INV, £616.18.6; includes Negroes Isaac, [Bray], Judy (an old woman), Beck, Betty & her child, girls Nancy & Hannah, boy Tom. (WC RI 9:33)

CROCKETT, Robert; PO 13 Feb 1815, T 17 Feb 1815; 13 Feb 1815
NC; INV, [m]; includes Negroes William, William [sic], Esther, Haylie, Sally & child, boy John, Lucey, Abigall, Old Sarah. (NC RB 20:10)
[In his will (NC 5 Sep 1814-13 Feb 1815), Robt. CROCKETT named his wife Judah and dau. Sally CROCKETT (NC RB 19:622); Thos. J. HAYES was aptd. gdn. of Sally CROCKETT orphan of Robt. CROCKETT, 13 Oct 1817 (NC OB 1816-20:188); Leroy HARCUM aptd. gdn. of Sally CROCKETT orphan of Robt. CROCKETT, 9 Jun 1828 (NC OB 1825-30:280)]

CROWDER, E.; [m]; 9 Dec 1811. NC; INV, [m]. (NC RB 19:137)

CROWDER, Isaac H.; PO 14 Nov 1814, T 23 Nov 1814; 14 Mar 1815
NC; INV, $551.25; includes Negroes Emanuel, Nanny. (NC RB 20:28)
[Isaac was a son of Jesse & Eliz. CROWDER (*see below*); in his will (NC 4 Aug 1814-14 Nov 1814), Isaac H. CROWDER named his sis. Sally BEANE, bro. Thos. CROWDER, sisters Mary and Nancy CROWDER (NC RB 20:77); Sally BEANE is prob. Sally H. CROWDER, dau. of Eliz. CROWDER, who mar. Opie BEAN of LC, NC, bond 23 Nov 1805 (MLBNC:7)]

CROWDER, Jesse; T [26] Oct 1802; 11 Apr 1803
NC; INV, [m]; includes Negroes Thomas, Jack, Nanny, boys Danniel, Emanuel, Bille, and Benjamin, Rachel, Polly, Liddy, Lucy. (NC RB 16:530)
[Jesse CROWDER mar. Eliz., dau. of Isaac & Winifred HURST (d. NC 1805) bef. 16 Feb 1788; in his will (NC 30 Mar 1802-11 Oct 1802) he named his wife Eliz., sons Thos., Isaac Hurst & daus. Salley Hurst, Eliz. Hurst, & Nancy (NC RB 15:37, RB 16:466, RB 17:352); Thos. CROWDER was gdn. of Isaac, Eliz. & Nancy CROWDER orphans of Jesse CROWDER; Thos CROWDER was also granted admin. on the est. of Eliz. CROWDER, NC 14 Jan 1811 (NC OB 1807-10:226); Eliz. CROWDER's will was proved NC 11 Feb 1811 (NC OB 1807-11:227); Nancy CROWDER orphan of Jesse CROWDER chose Opie BEANE as her gdn., 19 Dec 1814 (LC Orders 24:209)]

CROWDER, Jesse; 12 May 1828
NC; on the mot. of William CROWDER, ord. that Jesse, John, Thomas, Sally & Betsy CROWDER heirs of Jesse CROWDER be summoned to show cause

why the lands of Jesse CROWDER should not be sold; William CROWDER aptd. gdn. to Jesse & John CROWDER orphans of Jesse CROWDER. (NC OB 1825-30:256)

CROWDER, Joshua; PO 19 Sep 1800; 19 Dec 1803. LC; INV, £34.18.6. (LC EB 24:258)

CROWDER, Thomas; 5 Jan 1803; 18 Jan 1813
LC; WILL; mean profits of whole est. to use of my sis. Nancy HUBBARD; at her death whole est. to Moses WEBB commonly called Moses CROWDER; friends William YERBY & William BLACKERBY; WITS: Jn. W. REVERE, Thos. YERBY, W. T. YERBY. (LC WB 28:138)
[Nancy CROWDER dau. of Jn. CROWDER mar. Amos HUBBARD, NC, bond 2 Feb 1791 (MLBNC:54)]

CROWTHER, John; PO 15 Nov 1814, T 26 Nov 1814; 13 Feb 1815
NC: INV. (NC RB 19:608)
[The est. of Jn. CROWTHER was ord. to be admin. by Stephen CROWTHER, 15 Nov 1814 (NC OB 1811-1816:259)]

CROWTHER, Robert; [m]; 12 Sep 1803
NC; INV, £212.13.0. (NC RB 17:59)
[The est. of Robt. CROWTHER was ord. to be admin. by Jesse CROWTHER, NC, 10 Jan 1802 (NC Minute Book 1801-1805:143)]

CROWTHER, Robert; PO 12 Aug 1816; 13 May 1817. NC; INV, [m]. (NC RB 21:192)

CROWTHER, Thomas; PO 8 Jan 1816; 13 May 1816. NC; INV, [m]. (NC RB 20:449)

CROWTHER, William; 8 Feb 1813
NC; by Feb 1813, CROWTHER had been dead more than 3 months, and the sheriff was ord. to sell his perishable property. (NC OB 1811-15:144)

CUNDIFF, Benjamin; [m]; 11 Jan 1802
NC; DIV of est. among David PALMER (rec'd Negroes Charles & Ben), Benjamin CUNDIFF (rec'd Negroes Duke (& tools) & boy Spencer), Miss Milley CUNDIFF (rec'd Negroes Emanuel & Dianah--£5 was deducted for keeping old Negro Sarah), Henry CUNDIFF (rec'd Negroes Bell & Treasy). (NC RB 16:335)
[This is prob. Benj. CUNDIFF who mar. Alcy (or Alley) McTYRE, LC, 15 Oct 1795 (MWO:96); David PALMER mar. Nancy CUNDIFF bef. 3 Jun 1785 (MWO:271)]

CUNDIFF, Henry; T 9 May 1803; 12 Dec 1803
NC; INV, [m]; includes Negroes Jesse, Daniel, Ephraim, George, Winney, Dorcas, Nancy, Mimey, girls Teresy, Synthia & Lucey, boy Jack; also set of surveying instruments. (NC RB 17:97)
[The est. of Hen. CUNDIFF was ord. to be admin. by Wm. DAVENPORT & Rich. LUNSFORD, 13 Dec 1802 (NC MB 1801-1805:141); Wm. SYDNOR was aptd. gdn. to Hen. & Thos. CUNDIFF orphans of Hen. CUNDIFF, NC 12 Feb 1816, but it is not certain that the father is this Hen. CUNDIFF (NC OB 1816-20:9)]

CUNDIFF, John; PO 18 Nov 1812; 21 Feb 1814
LC; INV at the house of Thomas CARTER, $16.00. (LC EB 27:171)

CUNDIFF, Richard; PO 20 Jun 1803; T 16 Aug 1803; 20 Feb 1804
LC; DIV of est. among: Molly CUNDIFF, Betsy B. PALMER, John CUNDIFF, Nancy CUNDIFF, Richard CUNDIFF, Elismond BASYE; the court appointed surveyor James ALDERSON laid off the following tracts: 102 ac. together with the mansion house for Molly CUNDIFF; 125 ac. part of the mansion

plant. adj. to land of Thos. TAYLOR for John CUNDIFF; 135 ac. the lower lot of the mansion plant. adj the bridge that leads to the mill for Nancy CUNDIFF; 30 1/4 ac. together with the grist mill for Betsy B. PALMER; 119 ac. known as Everit's for Elismond BASYE; 85 ac. part of the sd. Everit's tract adj Elismond BASYE to Richard CUNDIFF. (LC EB 24:263)

[Molly CUNDIFF orphan of Rich. CUNDIFF chose Jn. CUNDIFF as her gdn., 19 Sep 1803 (LC Orders V 1802-03:437); Elismond BASYE mar. Betsy CUNDIFF, LC, bond 27 Aug 1793 (MLBLC:3); on the mot. of Eliz. [BASYE] & Jn. CUNDIFF ord. that Thos. ROCK & Nancy his wife, Sam. STONHAM & Betsy his wife & Mary SAMPSON, Jn. SAMPSON Jr., Nancy SAMPSON, Eliza SAMPSON, [Betsy] SAMPSON & Judith SAMPSON be summoned to show cause why the lands of which Rich. CUNDIFF died seized & possessed should not be sold and the proceeds divided, 17 Aug 1824 (LC OB 26:65); Mary, Jn. & Nancy SAMPSON and Eliz., Betsy & Judith SAMPSON are infants under 21 and Jn. SAMPSON is aptd. their special gdn. to defend them in this suit, 17 Nov 1824 (LC OB 26:87); Nancy CUNDIFF mar. (1) Thos. PULLIN, 11 Feb 1813 and (2) Thos. ROCK, wid., 23 Sep 1817 (MLBNC:84, 89); Molly CUNDIFF mar. Jn. SAMPSON, NC, bond 20 Apr 1808 (MLBLC:65)]

CUNDIFF, Richard; T 20 Dec 1820; 21 May 1821. LC ; INV, [m]. (LC EB 29:91)

CUNDIFF, Thomas; 11 Dec 1826
NC; DIV of Negroes belonging to the est. of Elisa D. CUNDIFF, dec'd, an infant, between her mother Sally PATTERSON and her bro. Henry F. CUNDIFF. (NC OB 1825-30:134)

[Thos. CUNDIFF, ward of Wm. SYDNOR, mar. Sally DOWNING, dau. of Betsy DOWNING, NC, bond 10 Dec 1821; Sally (DOWNING) CUNDIFF mar. (2) Eli PATTERSON, NC, bond 5 Jul 1826 and (3) Thos. S. SYDNOR, wid., NC, bond 12 Mar 1828 (MLBNC:25, 80, 98); Thos. S. SYDNOR aptd. gdn. of Hen. F. CUNDIFF orphan of Thos. CUNDIFF, 11 Dec 1826 (NC OB 1825-30:135); ord. to div. Betsy CUNDIFF's part of the slaves which were allotted to Mrs. Sally CUNDIFF now Mrs. SYDNOR wife of Thos. S. SYDNOR as her dower in the slaves of her dec'd husband Thomas CUNDIFF between the sd. Thomas S. SYDNOR and his wife and Henry F. CUNDIFF and also allot to sd. SYDNOR & wife her dower in the slaves belonging to the est. of her dec'd husband Eli S. PATTERSON, 13 May 1828 (NC OB 1825-30:262)]

CURLEY, David; PO Dec 1813, T 4 Jan 1814; 28 Mar 1814. WC; INV, $295.34. (WC RI 9:416)

CURRELL, Amey; 2 Dec 1803; 2 Feb 1804
LC; WILL; Negro girl Charlotte to dau. Judith TOWLES; to grson. William FORD son of Daniel FORD balance of est; if he has no heirs est. to be eq. div. among grchildren: Henry TOWLES, Stockley TOWLES, Sally LELAND, James TOWLES, Fanny TOWLES, Thomas TOWLES & Oliver TOWLES all children of my dau. Judith TOWLES; [no ex. named]; WITS: Sam. M. SHERMAN, Mary SNOW. [will was further proved on 20 May 1811]. (LC WB 28:119)

[Amey CURRELL was the wid. of Henry or Harry CURRELL (d. LC 1785) who named his son Gilbert, his bro. Nicholas and his grson. Wm. FORD in his will (LC 4 Dec 1782-17 Jun 1785) (LC WB 22:77); she was poss. AMY BRENT, dau. of Geo. BRENT (d. LC 1748), who mar. (1) James HAYNES Jr.bef. 6 Jul 1748 (MWO:172); Judith TOWLES was Judith HAYNES, dau. of James & Amy HAYNES, who mar. Hen. TOWLES, LC, bond 1 May 1768

(MWO:355); Daniel FORD mar. Eliz. F. CURRELL, dau. of Hen. CURRELL, LC, bond 27 May 1773 (MLBLC:28)]

CURRELL, Edward; PO 19 Jan 1818; 19 Oct 1818. LC ; INV, $5604.50. (LC EB 27:438)

[This may be Edw. CURRELL who mar. Eliz. SYDNOR, LC, bond 10 Apr 1890 (MLBLC:18); Nancy C. CURRELL orphan of Edw. CURRELL chose Lawson HATHAWAY as her gdn., 16 Nov 1818 (LC OB 25:24); Edw. & Jn. CURRELL orphans of Edw. CURRELL chose Benj. GEORGE for their gdn., 17 Jul 1826 (LC OB 26:195); Eliz. CURRELL aptd. gdn. to Catherine & Judith CURRELL, 21 Aug 1826 (LC OB 26:202); on the mot. of Zamoth GEORGE ord. that Edw. CURRELL, Jn. CURRELL, Wm. CURRELL, Sally CURRELL, Judith CURRELL, & Cath. CURRELL be summoned to show cause why a certain tract of land in Fleets Island of which Edw. CURRELL died seized should not be sold and the proceeds div. among his heirs, 21 Aug 1826 (LC OB 26:203); Miller:51 locates Fleets Island at the extreme southeast end of LC.]

CURRELL, Gilbert; 8 Dec 1799; 20 Feb 1804

LC; WILL; whole est. to my mother Amy CURRELL; at mother's death est. to descend to nephew William FORD son of Daniel FORD; if nephew dies unmarried whole est. to be eq. div. between my niece Francis TOWLES, James TOWLES & my godson Thomas TOWLES; [no ex. named]; WITS: Wm. CORNELIUS, Mary SNOW, Lindsay PULLEN, Gilburd SPILMAN. (LC WB 28:76)

[Gilbert CURRELL was the son of Henry & Amy CURRELL, *see above*; Gilbert CURRELL d. possessed of an est. on which no person will admin; sheriff to sell est., 14 Jun 1807 (LC Orders D22 1805-08:361)]

CURRELL, Nicholas; 6 May 1801; 15 Jun 1801

LC; WILL; my Kentucky land and Negroes Patty & all her children, Kendall, Spencer, Hanna, Rachal, Richard & Lettice to my son James CURRELL; to son-i-l Thomas LEE all the Negroes that he has that formerly belonged to me; Negroes Oliver, Sarah, Lavina, Susanna, Eliza, Patty, Hiram, Ailce, Henry, Mariner, Spencer, and Samuel, Henry, Daniel, Fielding, David & Agatha to dau. Ann BALL; Negroes Robin, Solomon & Sarah to grdau. Margaret Steptoe LAWSON; Negroes William, Thomas, & Henry to grdau. Ann Currell LEE; Negro girl Mary to grdau. Margaret Steptoe BALL; my 3 old Negroes Hannar, James, & Esther to be free and in case they should not be able to maintain themselves, they shall be maintained out of my est.; 2 sons-in-law Joseph BALL & Thomas LEE and Capt. Henry C. LAWSON exors; WITS: Geo. FORD, Hen. LAWSON, Lawson HATHAWAY. (LC WB 28:49)

[Thos. LEE mar. Eliz. CURRELL, LC, bond 1 Feb 1780 (MLBLC:47); Jos. BALL, wid., mar. Ann [CURRELL] (given as Ann "CANELL" in MLBLC), LC, bond 25 Jan 1797 (MLBLC:3)]

CURRELL, Robert; 16 Dec 1796; 19 Jun 1797

CCP, LC; WILL; wife Molly CURRELL; two children Elizabeth Heard CURRELL & Julius Caesar CURRELL; if son Julius Caesar CURRELL should get a sufficient deed to the real est. from Robert C. JACOB he is to give £100 to Elizabeth H. CURRELL; if children & wife die withouth heirs est. to descend to Harry LIGHTBURNE's children: Stafford LIGHTBURNE, Henry LIGHTBURNE, Sarah LIGHTBURNE, Robert LIGHTBURNE & Alice LIGHTBURNE; friends Lawson HATHAWAY, Vincent BRENT & James

POLLARD exors; WITS: Lawson HATHAWAY, Wm. CURRELL, Wm. HATHAWAY. (LC WB 28:24)
[Robt. CURRELL was the son of Geo. CURRELL, d. LC, 1788 (LC WB 22:183); Capt. Hen. LIGHTBURNE mar. Eliz. CURRELL, dau. of Geo. CURRELL, LC, bond 26 Dec 1771 (MLBLC:48); Wm. HATHAWAY aptd. gdn. of Julius Cesar & Eliz. CURRELL orphans of Robt. CURRELL, 21 Jul 1800 (LC Orders 21 1799-1801:127); Eliz. CURRELL orphan of Robt. CURRELL chose Martin SHEARMAN as her gdn., 16 Jun 1806 (LC Orders D22 1805-08:192)]

CURRELL, Sarah; 7 Jul 1806; 17 May 1813
LC; WILL; after debts paid I lend the whole of my prop. to my son Isaac CURRELL & Dolly his wife; after their deaths sd. prop. to be eq. div. among grchil. Elizabeth CURRELL, James CURRELL, Polly CURRELL, Alice CURRELL & Isaac CURRELL; grson. James CURRELL ex.; Hen. C. LAWSON, Jos. SHEARMAN. (LC WB 28:144)

CURRELL, William; 17 Nov 1801; 16 Feb 1802
LC; WILL; my watch to my father Isaac CURRELL and at his death to my bro. Isaac CURRELL; my Negro woman Lucy to my bro. Isaac; bro. James; sis. Polly CURRELL; sis. Elizabeth CURRELL; sis. Alcy CURRELL; [no ex. named]; WITS: Lawson HATHAWAY, Jn. W. REVERE. (LC WB 28:60)

CURRIE, David; PO Oct 1797; 1[6] Jul 1798
LC; INV, £401.10.0; includes Negroes: Anthony, Willoughby, Lucy, boys Spencer & William, girls Grace & Patty, boys Isaac & William. (LC EB 24:77)

CURTICE, Hillary; PO 8 Dec 1800, T 30 Dec 1800; 8 Jun 1801
NC; DIV of est. among the legatees: Lucy E. CURTICE (rec'd Negroes George Jr., Matildy, Mitchell & legacy Negro Isabel agreeable to will), William YERBY testamentary gdn. to Cyrus CURTICE (rec'd Negroes Sam, Spencer, Dennis), Thomas CURTICE (rec'd Negroes John, Ailse, Malinda), William YERBY as testamentary gdn. to William CURTICE (rec'd Old George & shoe tools, Cate, James, Violet). (NC RB 16:255)
[Hillary CURTIS (or CURTICE) mar. at least twice; (1) Eliz. DOGGETT, dau. of Elmore DOGGETT, LC, bond 17 May 1771 and (2) Nancy ROBUCK, wid., NC, bond 12 Jul 1790 (MWO:97)]

DABNEY, Benjamin; WC; mar. Sarah the dau. of the Rev. Thomas SMITH (WC CC 1791-002)

DAINGERFIELD, William; T 7 Dec 1818; 7 Feb 1820
RC; INV; $5557.49, includes the following Negroes: Ceasar, John, James, Isaac, Ambrus, Caty, Betsey, Patty. (RC WB 9:656)

DAMERON, Bartholomew; PO 12 Mar 1810; 12 Apr 1813
NC; INV, £44[0].10.0; includes Negroes Peter, Travis, Rachael, Moses, Levina, Stephen, Beck. (NC RB 19:370)

DAMERON, Charles; 11 Feb 1828
NC; Sally DAMERON aptd. gdn. to William, Isaac & Elizabeth DAMERON orphans of Charles DAMERON. (NC OB 1825-30:234)
[This is prob. the Chas. DAMERON who mar. Sally Webb THOMAS, NC, bond 10 Sep 1810 (MLBNC:25)]

DAMERON, George; PO 11 Feb 1805; 14 Apr 1806
NC; INV, includes Negroes Charles, Judah, Molly, Sukey, Fanny, Frank, Israel, Clarkey & child Polly, Archibald, Mahala, David, Fanny & child Milton, John, Spencer, Daniel, Billey, Phill, Matilda, Winney, Charlotte; Richard BERRYMAN admr. (NC RB 17:386)

DAMERON, George; PO 11 Feb 1805, T 1 Jan 1806; 12 Dec 1808

NC; INV, £834.15.0; includes Negroes Charles, Judah, Sukey, Molly, Fanny, Frankey, Israel, Archibald, Clerkey & child Patty, Mahala, David, Charlotte, Fanny & child Milton, John, Spencer, Daniel, Billy, Phill, Matilda, Winny; DIV of est. among legal reps, PO 10 Jun 1805, Lot 1 (Fanne & child Milton, Billy, Mahala, John, Phill, Old Sukey) to Thomas DAMERON, Lot 2 (Winney, Clerkey & child Patty, Archibald, David, Charles, Judah, Frankey) to Robert DAMERON, Lot 3 (Israel, Charlotte, Matilda, Daniel, Spencer, old Molly & Fanny) to Alice DAMERON. (NC RB 18:62, 63)
[In his will (NC 19 Feb 1801-12 Oct 1801), Geo. DAMERON names his wife Mary Ann, his sons Geo. W., Thos. & Robt., his dau. Alice GIDDEINGS and his grson. Geo. D. GIDDEINGS (NC RB 16:289); Geo. DAMERON was a son of Col. Thos. & Ann (BALL) DAMERON, he mar. Mary Ann JONES, dau. of Chas. JONES, NC, 1756 (MWO:99); Alice DAMERON mar. Wm. GIDDINGS, NC, bond 12 May 1794 (MLBNC:42); it is not clear why Alice is called Alice DAMERON in the est. div.]

DAMERON, George; PO 8 Jan 1810, T 19 Jan 1810; 12 Mar 1810
NC; INV, £31.5.11 1/2. (NC RB 18:338)

DAMERON, George; 9 May 1826
NC; on motion of William BURTON & Sally his wife, ord. that Alexander, Nancy, Christopher & Catherine DAMERON be summoned to show cause why the land of George DAMERON should not be sold. (NC OB 1825-30:88)
[Wm. S. BURTON mar. Sally S. DAMERON, NC, bond 23 Feb 1825 (MLBNC:14)]

DAMERON, Jesse; 15 Dec 1806
LC; Elizabeth DAMERON orphan of Jesse DAMERON chose Spencer GEORGE as her gdn. (LC Orders D22 1805-08:274)

DAMERON, John; 15 Jan 1803; 21 Feb 1803
LC; WILL; James BROWN not to have anything to do with my est. or any part that my dau. Sally DAMERON shall have; WIT: Wm. BROWN. (LC WB 28:65)

DAMERON, Rachel; 7 Mar 1794; 17 Oct 1796
LC; WILL; dau. Hannah WEBB; dau. Jemima WEBB; dau. Hannah & bro. Lott PALMER exors; WITS: Lott PALMER, Betty PALMER, Dale PALMER. [Following this will is this notation: "NB: The following wills as far as [the] 23d folio [inclusive] were first recorded in an old half-bound book by no means proper for a record book, but being the only book in the ofice at that time I was obliged to make use of it, but now being supplied by the court with a proper book I have caused the said wills to be transcribed. /s/ Henry Towles cl. curiae."]; LC WB 28:5)
[Rachel DAMERON seems to be the wid. of (1) Travers WEBB (d. LC bef Jul 1779) and (2) Jn. DAMERON (d. LC 1782) (LC WB 20:143, 244)]

DAMERON, Rachel; T 3 Dec 1796; 19 Dec 1796. LC; INV, £14.3.6. (LC EB 24:39)

DAMERON, Thomas; 21 Feb 1803
LC; Wm. BLACKERBY aptd. gdn. to Sally DAMERON orphan of Thomas DAMERON. (LC Orders V 1802-03:260)

DAMERON, Thomas; 8 Feb 1808
NC; Thomas DAMERON aptd. gdn. to his children Mary Ann, Elizabeth, Willis & Margaret S. DAMERON. (NC OB 1807-11:22)
[On the mot. of Jas. BRENT, ord. that Willis DAMERON, Isaac BRENT & Mary his wife who was Mary DAMERON, Margaret BRYANT who was Margaret DAMERON, Wm. DAMERON & Caroline DAMERON and Ralph EDMONDS atty. in fact for Jas. P. ELLIS who mar. Jane BERRYMAN and

gdn. to Jas. BERRYMAN and also as atty. in fact for [*1 wd unclear*] BERRYMAN who is gdn. for the other children of Rich. BERRYMAN summoned to court, 18 Nov 1823 (LC OB 26:5); on the mot. of Ralph EDMONDS atty. in fact for the heirs of Rich. BERRYMAN, ord. that Isaac BRENT & his wife Mary, Jas. BRENT & Eliz. his wife, Willias DAMERON, Margaret S. BRYANT, Wm. DAMERON & Caroline DAMERON be summoned to show cause why lands of which Thos. DAMERON d. possessed should not be sold and proceeds div. among legal heirs, 17 May 1824 (LC OB 26:39, 60); Isaac BRENT mar. Mary Ann DAMERON, LC, bond 8 Mar 1819 (MLBLC:7); Jn. BRYAN[T] mar. Margaret L. DAMERON dau. of Thos. DAMERON, LC, bond 7 Jan [m] (MLBLC:10; Rich. BERRYMAN mar. Ann Steptoe DAMERON, dau. of Thos. DAMERON Jr., NC, bond 29 Apr 1802 (MLBNC:8))]

DAMERON, William; 10 May 1821; 9 Jul 1821
SSP, NC; WILL; all land w/o he now lives to son Luke DAMERON; all land where he now lives to son William DAMERON; all my land on the side of the road next to Presley HUDSON to son John DAMERON; use of my land w/o I now live & land I purchased of Presley COX to wife; at wife's death land to son Bartholomew DAMERON; land w/o Christopher DAWSON now lives to William LEWIS; Negro Prissey & child Sarah to my dau. Fanny; Negro girl Milley to grdaus Eliza & Mary RICHARDSON; Negro boy Spencer to son Bartholomew; Negro James to son John; rest of est. to son Bartholomew; son John DAMERON & friend Thomas BELL exors; WITS: Luke DAMERON, Rich. JEWELL. (NC RB 22:585)
[Molley D. DAMERON, dau. of Wm. DAMERON, mar. Edw. Garner RICHARDSON, NC, bond 20 Dec 1809; Wm. LEWIS mar. Nancy DAMERON, dau. of Wm. DAMERON, NC, bond 29 Dec 1812 (MLBNC:69, 86); heirs of Wm. DAMERON, including Jn. C. DAMERON & Susanna his wife, Luke DAMERON Jr. & Polly his wife, Wm. DAMERON Jr. and Lucinda his wife, Wm. B. LEWIS & Nancy his wife, Frances DAMERON and Bartholomew DAMERON all of NC, sold an 18-ac. tract of land in NC to Presley HUDSON, 24 Dec 1821 (NC RB 23:61)]

DARBY, Eliza Churchill; [m]; 2 Oct 1809
RC; INV of est. in hands of John DARBY gdn. includes Negroes Harry, Little Lucy & 2 children; Lucy youngest, Jesse, Arianna, Venus & child; Fanny, Henry, Ke[s]iah & child, Johanna; Joice & child, Betty, Molly & child, Mira; Cate & 5 children, Sarah & 3 children; Alice & 4 children, Peggy & 3 children; "Where I have mentioned a woman & many children is because they are hired out in that way, and the names of them all are not known by me, no other property has ever come to my hands belonging to my daughter and ward nor has she any other property to my knowledge except the reversionary right to eight [sic] or a thousand acres of land in Middlesex which may never come into my hands as guardian. There is also a suit depending in chancery against the admr. of her former guardian T. CHURCHILL to compell him to acct. for seven years hire of the above Negroes. What sum may be due I am not able to say." Aug 1809, /s/ Jno. DARBY; various Negroes were hired out at Jackson's Store in Middlesex Co in Jan 1807 and at Bowler's in EC in Jan 1808 & Jan 1809, and at Montigue's Tavern in EC in Jan 1811 (RC AB 3:225, 259)

DAVENPORT, Ann; 16 Oct 1817; 19 May 1822
LC; WILL; whole of my prop. to my four grchil. Nancy BARRACK, Betsey PAYNE, John PAYNE & Judith PAYNE; prop. to remain in the hands of

Newby BARRACK until Betsey PAYNE, John PAYNE & Judith arrive to the age of 21 or marry; 1 shilling only to dau. Betsey PINKARD; 1 shilling only to dau. Judith HAZZARD; [Newby] BARRACK ex; WITS: Thos. G. ROBERTSON, Wm. [BROWN], Cyrus [MASON], Jesse BAILEY. (LC WB 28:227)

[Newby BARROCK mar. Nancy PAYNE dau. of Edw. PAYNE, LC, bond 22 Dec 1814; Alex. HAZZARD mar. Judith DAVENPORT, LC, bond 19 Dec 1796 (MLBLC:3, 37)]

DAVENPORT, Daniel D.; 21 Jul 1817

LC; D of G, Daniel D. DAVENPORT to his children: Joseph H., Elizabeth F. & Harriett Ann DAVENPORT. (LC OB 24:381)

[This is Dan. D. DAVENPORT who mar. Sarah HUDNALL, LC, bond 15 Dec 1806 (MLBLC:20)]

DAVENPORT, David; PO 16 Jan 1815, T 14 Mar 1815; 19 Feb 1816

LC; INV; includes Negroes: Fairy & child Spencer, Rose, boy Rawleigh. (LC EB 27:285)

DAVENPORT, Elizabeth; 21 Nov 1821; 14 May 1822

NC; WILL; s-i-l Thomas S. SYDNOR; nephew William BLACKWELL (son of my bro. Thomas BLACKWELL); son Steptoe TAYLOR; son Steptoe ex; WITS: Mary HUGHLETT, Mary SULLIVAN; [Steptoe TAYLOR relinquished his right of executorship and was granted a certificate for obtaining letters of admin. with the will annexed]. (NC RB 23:156)

[This is Eliz. Steptoe BLACKWELL who mar. (1) Moses TAYLOR, NC, bond 38 Aug 1791 and (2) Wm. DAVENPORT, wid., NC, BOND 28 Nov 1815 (MLBNC:26, 99; *see also* Moses TAYLOR *below*); Thos. S. SYDNOR mar. Fanny E. TAYLOR, NC, bond 25 Oct 1817 (MLBNC:98)]

DAVENPORT, Frances; PO 6 Mar 1815; 4 Nov 1817. RC; INV, $117.25. (RC WB 9:575)

[This is prob. Frances DOBYNS, dau. of Daniel DOBYNS of NFP (d. RC, 1784), who mar. Jos. DAVENPORT, RC, bond 2 Sep 1782 (MWO:101)]

DAVENPORT, John; 30 Sep 1818; 14 Dec 1818

NC; WILL; use of all est. to wife Polley K. DAVENPORT; if she should die my widow; I give the same to son William B. DAVENPORT provided he does not die a minor; if son die a minor, my two plants. "David Haynie's" & "New Buildings" to William BLACKWELL son of Thomas BLACKWELL; rest of land & two Negro boys Charles & Imanuel to friend Steptoe TAYLOR; should wife remarry I give her all the Negroes that came by her that I now hold (except Betty & [Maricha]) & one third of my lands for life; Betty & [Maricha] to son William for his education & maintainance until he comes to 21; friends Hiram BLACKWELL & Samuel BLACKWELL exors; WITS: Thos. HUGHLETT, Sam. PROSSER, Sam. BLACKWELL; NC RB 21:564)

[Jn. DAVENPORT mar. Mary K. HUDNALL, NC, bond 11 Sep 1815 (MLBNC:26); Steptoe TAYLOR mar. Mary K. DAVENPORT, wid. of Jn., NC bond 30 Mar 1819 (MLBNC:99); Steptoe TAYLOR aptd. gdn. of Wm. B. DAVENPORT orphan of Jn. DAVENPORT, NC 18 Dec 1819 (NC OB 1816-20:417)]

DAVENPORT, John; T 6 [Jan] 1814; 14 Jun 1824

NC; INV; includes Negroes James, Joseph, [*1 wd. unclear*], Mark, Abraham, Hiram, Massey (girl), Harry, Charles, Manuel, Charlotte, Mahala, Adeline, Polly, Letty, Marecha, Phillis (old woman), Robert (old man), Spencer, Betty,

Nancy, Steptoe, Lewis, Caroline, Grace (old woman), Hannah (old woman), Simon. (NC RB 23:502)

DAVENPORT, Joseph; [m]; 4 Nov 1817
RC; INV, £676.9.0; includes the following Negroes: Lucy, Runey, Isaac, Judea, Solomon, Rose, Easter, Charles, Sam, Lucinda, Winney, Rachel. (RC WB 9:576)

DAVENPORT, Nancy; 23 Jan 1821; 2 May 1825
RC; WILL; I lend my Negro man Joshua to my dau. Sally S. DAVENPORT; dau. Betsy H. DAVENPORT; rest of prop. to be eq. div. among children of son William H. DAVENPORT, son David F. DAVENPORT's son Richard O. DAVENPORT, dau. Fanny T. DUNAWAY's dau. Nancy O. DUNAWAY, my son Linzy O. DAVENPORT, my dau. Sally S. DAVENPORT, my dau. Betsy H. DAVENPORT; William FORESTER & Henry PRIDDY exors; WITS: Edw. C. PITMAN, Ann J. PRIDDY. (RC WB 10:71)
[Nancy DAVENPORT was prob Nancy FORRESTER, dau. of Robt. FORRESTER Sr. (d. RC 1783), who mar. Opie DAVENPORT (b 29 Apr 1752; son of Wm. & Eliz DAVENPORT), RC, bond 13 Dec 1781 (MWO:101); the births of 2 of Opie & Nancy DAVENPORT's children are rec. in the NFPR: Wm. Heale Forester DAVENPORT, b 4 Mar 1783 & Suckey Norris DAVENPORT, b 11 Nov 1787 (NFPR:40); Fanny T. DAVENPORT mar. Wm. DUNAWAY of LC, RC, bond 7 Sep 1811 (MRC:49, 61)]

DAVENPORT, Opie; 6 Dec 1799; 3 Sep 1800
NFP, RC; WILL; use of whole est. to wife Nancy DAVENPORT; after her death or remarriage Negro boy Sam to son William H. DAVENPORT; Negro boy Jery to son David DAVENPORT; Negro boy Ned to dau. Nancy O. DAVENPORT; Negro girl Darkey to dau. Fanny T. DAVENPORT; Negro boy James to son Linsey O. DAVENPORT; Negro girl Cate to dau. Betsy H. DAVENPORT; wife & friends William FORESTER & William DAVENPORT exors; WITS: Geo. HUNT, Richard T. HUNT. (NC DCO:403)
[Opie DAVENPORT was the son of Wm. & Eliz. (HEALE) DAVENPORT; he was b. in NFP 29 Apr 1752; Wm. DAVENPORT in his will (RC 11 Jul 1771-11 May 1772) names his wife Eliz. and children Wm. Fortunatus, Rawleigh, Opie, Judith GEORGE and Eliz. TUNE and grson. Wm. OLIVER (NFPR:40, RC WB 7:108, MWO:101); Thos. FALLIN of LC mar. Nancy Opie DAVENPORT, RC, bond 1 Jul 1803 (MRC:67)]

DAVENPORT, Opie; T 17 Jan 1810; 7 Jul 1817
RC; allotment of dower to wid. Nancy DAVENPORT & div. of residue among William H. DAVENPORT (received Negro boy David), Fanny F. DAVENPORT (received girl Liviny), David F. DAVENPORT (legacy boy Jerry), Thomas FALLIN (legacy boy Ned), Lindsey O. DAVENPORT (legacy boy), Salley S. DAVENPORT (legacy boy), Betsey H. DAVENPORT (legacy woman Cate), ; RC AB 3:424)

DAVENPORT, William; 24 Jan 1818; 13 Apr 1818
NC; WILL; to wife Elizabeth [S.] DAVENPORT the house in which I now live and the adj. land as far as the public road leading from Northumberland Courthouse to Wico[comico] Church, half of my water grist mill & one third of my Negroes during her life; after wife's death the land & mill to son John DAVENPORT; Negroes devised to wife to be eq. div. between son John DAVENPORT & dau. Nancy JETT; to wife the field called "Esther's" as it now stands enclosed which field adjoins the lands of George SAMPSON & after her death to son John DAVENPORT; rest of land in NC; to dau. Nancy JETT all land in RC; to nephew William BLACKWELL son of Thomas

BLACKWELL a Negro boy Moses son of Winnefred; wife, son John & son-in-law William JETT exors; WITS: Sam. BLACKWELL, [Hiram] BLACKWELL, Thos. BLACKWELL. (NC RB 21:401)
[Wm. DAVENPORT, wid., mar. Eliz. Steptoe TAYLOR, wid. of Moses TAYLOR, NC, bond 28 Nov 1815; Eliz. Steptoe BLACKWELL mar. Moses TAYLOR, wid., NC, bond 8 Aug 1791; Wm. JETT, wid, mar. Nancy DAVENPORT, NC, bond 4 Dec 1815 (MLBNC:26, 61); Moses TAYLOR d in NC in 1797 leaving his wid. and 3 children: Geo. B., Steptoe, & Fanny TAYLOR (NC RB 15:371)]

DAVENPORT, William H.; T Feb 1821; 6 May 1822. RC; INV, [m]; RC WB 9:727)
[This is prob. Wm. Heale Forester DAVENPORT, son of Opie & Nancy DAVENPORT, b. NFP 4 Mar 1783 (NFPR:40); he mar. Eliz. P. DAVENPORT, RC, bond 15 Apr 1809 (MRC:49); Eliza P. DAVENPORT aptd. gdn. of Margaret, Juliet & Wm. DAVENPORT orphans of Wm. H. DAVENPORT, 2 Jul 1821 (RC OB 25:179)]

DAVIS, Bartley; 22 May 1821
LC; Daniel P. MITCHELL aptd. gdn. of Janetta, Ailcey & Jesse DAVIS orphans of Bartley DAVIS. (LC OB 25:215)
[Bartley DAVIS mar. Nancy DODSON, LC, bond 11 May 1799 (MLBLC:20)]

DAVIS, George; 17 Dec 1804
LC; Ephraim Saunders DAVIS orphan of George DAVIS chose Holland DAVIS for his gdn. (LC OB 1804-05:269)

DAVIS, Hannah; 23 May 1799; 16 Sep 1799
LC; WILL; I lend to my dau. Janetta two Negroes [Nasse] & Betty; if dau. die without issue prop. lent to her to be eq. div. between my two nieces Gracey B. NELMS & Hannah H. NELMS; friend Capt. William NELMS ex; WITS: Wm. YERBY, Milly FENDLY, Jean BALL. (LC WB 28:35)
[Hannah is the wid. of Wm. DAVIS (d. LC, 1799) *see below*]

DAVIS, Hugh; 9 Dec 1756; 26 Jul 1757
WC; WILL; planter; all land to son Peter DAVIS; dau. Ann Bayley DAVIS; wife Elizabeth; friends Richard LEE & [Mr.] FLEET exors. (WC DW 13:156)
[omitted by Fothergill in WWCV; this must be the Hugh DAVIS who mar. Eliz. BAILEY, dau. of Wm. BAILEY (d. WC 1748/49) bef. 24 Feb 1746/47 (MWO:102)]

DAVIS, John; d. intest. in the 1790s leaving a wid. and five children (John, Ann, Winny, Sally and Elizabeth); his wid. Elizabeth d. in 1804; Ann DAVIS mar. Randal CLARK, wid., NC, bond 16 Jun 1801; Winny mar. John HAYDON; Elizabeth mar. Robert GILLESPIE, NC, bond 24 Apr 1790 (MLBNC:18, 42; CC 1805-024)

DAVIS, John; [m]; 7 Oct 1805
RC; INV, £363.16.6, includes the following Negroes: Nan, Traverse, Leanna, Daniel. (RC WB 9:259)

DAVIS, John; T 21 Mar 1818; 14 Sep 1818. NC; INV, [m]. (NC RB 21:474)

DAVIS, Rodham; PO 14 Oct [1805], T 24 Apr [1806]; 9 Feb 1807
NC; Elizabeth DAVIS, the wid, allotted her thirds in the pers. est. of her husband (£115.10.11 1/4 from the est. sale and Negro Winney, also the store house, granary except the yard & garden is eq. to one third of the real est. – the dwelling house, kitchen, cornhouse, deary [sic], garden & yard commencing from the north end of the granary and running in a straight line from thence to the near corner of the garden is equal to the other two

thirds); she was also to pay £10 to the gdn. of the orphan of Rodham DAVIS. (NC RB 17:505)
[Rodham DAVIS operated a general store located in present-day Village; the store was later rented out by his heirs to Col. William HENDERSON; an account book of Rodham DAVIS is in the Library of Virginia; his est. was ord. to be admin. by Martin SISSON, NC, 14 Apr 1806 (NC Minute Book 1805-1807:95); Rodham DAVIS' wife is named Patty in a deed of 7 Jun 1800, this was Patty SISSON, dau. of Geo. SISSON, whom he mar in RC, bond 11 Aug 1798; Elizabeth was his second wife, Betsy ENGLISH, whom he mar. in RC, bond 2 Jan 1805 (NC RB 16:122, MRC:51)]

DAVIS, William;
LC; William DAVIS d. intest. leaving a wid., Amy, and three children: Elizabeth (who mar. Andrew CHILTON, LC, bond 23 Dec 1788), Judith (who mar. George DOGGETT, LC, bond 19 Jan 1795), and Richard; his wid., Amy, mar. (2) Joseph KEM (LC, before 19 Aug 1785) and had three children by him: Burgess Kirk, Susanna (d.s.p. 1806) and Molly Thompson (d.s.p. 1808); William DAVIS was entitled to a considerable est. under the will of Elizabeth YERBY who d. in 1772; Amy the wid. of William DAVIS was the grdau. of George and Elizabeth (WOODBRIDGE) YERBY and prob. the dau. of George YERBY; Judith (DAVIS) DOGGETT brought suit against her husband George saying that she had lived with him for about two years but that he treated her badly and she was obliged to separate herself and her two young children from her husband (LC CCs 1812-016, 1813-003; LC WB 18:42, WB 20:38, WB 22:104, 143, 294; MLBLC:73, 111; MWO:388)

DAVIS, William; 27 Jun 1798; 16 Sep 1799
LC; WILL; all est. to wife Hannah DAVIS until dau. Janetta comes to age 21 or marries and then [dau] is to have only as much as my wife can spare; at wife's death all est. to dau. Janetta; if dau. die without heirs her est. to be eq. div. among my sister Molly JONES's children in Worcester Co on the Eastern Shore [of] Maryland; wife extx. & my bros-i-l Joseph BALL & David BALL should join their sis. as exors.; WITS: David BALL Jr., Jean BALL, Mill[y] FENLY; [COD dtd. 2 Apr 1799: I further desire as there is little prospect of my dear wife living to raise my dau. Janetta that Capt. William NELMS & his wife shall take my dau. Janetta to bring up & raise until of age for which kindness I give unto the sd. NELMS & wife my top chaise & white horse forever, likewise my Negro woman Betty CASSITY & her 3 children Jack, James & Anthony to go with my dau; if the sd. Betty CASSITY should have children in the time Capt NELMS' dau. Hannah Hanye NELMS should have them; at daughter's marriage or reaching age 21 it is my desire that Betty CASSITY shall be free forever; Negro man Abel to be sold; [same wits]. (LC WB 28:33)
[Wm. DAVIS mar. Hannah BALL, LC, bond 2 Nov 1793 (MLBNC:27); Wm. TAYLOR aptd. gdn. of Janetta DAVIS orphan of Wm. DAVIS, 20 Jun 1803 (LC Orders V 1802-03:372); acct. of Wm. TAYLOR with Janetta DAVIS orphan of Wm. DAVIS; Edw. P. BALL mar. Janetta DAVIS, 18 Dec 1809 (LC Orders B23 1808-11:139); Edw. P. BALL mar. Janetta DAVIS, ward of Wm. TAYLOR, NC, bond 2 Oct 1809 (MLBNC:3)]

DAVIS, William; PO 16 Sep 1799; 15 Jun 1801
LC; INV, [m]; includes Negroes Able, [Nara], Daniel, Fanny & young child, Betty CASSADY, Betty, Beck, Daniel son of Betty CASSADY, James, Antony. (LC EB 24:148)

DAVIS, William;

LC; d. intest. before 1810; his wife was Elizabeth and he had the following children: Thomazine (who mar. Peter MASON, LC, bond 26 Aug 1789), Betsy Johnson (who mar. William CHURCH, LC, bond 17 Aug 1801), Alice (who mar. Philip DIDLICK), William (who was the father of Janetta, see below), Bartley (who was the father of Sally, Janetta, Alice, Billy and Jesse), Judith (who mar. Alexander ELLIOTT, LC, bond 17 Jun 1794), and Sally (who mar. William WILDER, LC, bond 18 May 1786) (LC CC 1811-022; MLBLC:14, 20, 51, 79)

[Acc. to the above-cited CC, the husband of Sally DAVIS was Stuart or Steret WILDER, but he is identified as William in the marriage bond; Sally and her husband Wm. or Stuart (or poss. William Stuart WILDER) were not residents of Virginia in 1810]

DAVIS, William; 19 Dec 1808

LC; on the mot. of Alexander ELLIOT, admr. of Wm. DAVIS, it appearing to the court that the slaves of which sd. decedent d. seized & possessed cannot be div. in kind among his legal reps., ord. that Stewart WILDER, Peter MASON, Nancy DAVIS wid. of Bartley DAVIS, William CHURCH, and Philip [DEDLICK] be summoned to show cause why his slaves should not be sold. (LC Orders B23 1808-11:8)

[Peter MASON mar. Nancy DAVIS, LC, bond 19 Jan 1788; Bartley DAVIS mar. Nancy DODSON, LC, bond 11 May 1799, Wm. CHURCH mar. Betsey Johnson DAVIS, LC, bond 17 Aug 1801 (MLBLC:14, 20, 51)]

DAVIS, William;

NC; William DAVIS d. intest. in 1821 leaving his only children William Lee, Sally, Mahala Lellum, John Beacham, and Joseph; Leroy DAVIS was aptd. the gdn. ad litem to Sally, Mahala, John and Joseph in a suit to have land belonging to William sold (NC CC 1823-009)

DAWKINS, Jesse; PO 13 Jul 1801; 12 Jul 1802. NC; INV, £24.11.3. (NC RB 16:422)

[The est. of Jesse DAWKINS was ord. to be admin. by Letty DAWKINS, 13 Jul 1801 (NC MB 1801-1805:38); Jesse DAWKINS was the son of Penley DAWKINS of SSP (d. NC 1783) (NC RB 12:70)]

DAWSON, Christopher; T 2 Oct 1816; [m]. NC; INV, $151.50. (NC RB 21:80)

DAWSON, John; PO 9 Dec 1805, T 17 Dec 1805; 14 Apr 1806. NC; INV, £119.8.4. (NC RB 17:398)

DAWSON, John; PO 13 Jan 1806, T 8 Oct 1808; 10 Oct 1808

NC; allotted to Molly DAWSON her dower of the land of John DAWSON dec'd, the home house & land adj Samuel CRALLE & William HEADLEY; also div. the est. among his heirs which was £16.1.4 1/4 each except those cut off in the will of the sd. John DAWSON. (NC RB 18:47)

[In his will (NC 4 Jan 1804 - 9 Dec 1805) John DAWSON named his wife Molly, children Christopher, Jane - 2 shillings each, two elder sons George & John 2 shillings div. between them, son William, children Samuel, Molley N., Ben, Thomas (NC RB 17:357)]

DAWSON, John; 13 May 1822

NC; Judith DAWSON aptd. gdn. of David DAWSON orphan of Jn. DAWSON. (NC OB 1820-25:201)

[This is prob. the Jn. DAWSON who mar. Judith Pickron EDWARDS, NC, bond 11 Jul 1816 (MLBNC:28); Judith (EDWARDS) DAWSON, wid., mar. (2) Talbot CROWTHER, wid., NC, bond 16 Dec 1824 (MLBNC:24)]

DAWSON, William; PO 1813; 20 May 1816

LC; INV, $276.50; includes one schooner boat worth $70. (LC EB 27:317)

DEGGE, Isaac; T 6 Mar 1812; 15 Jun 1812
LC; INV of the unadministered est, $2436.34; includes Negroes: Nat, Peter, Jenny, Giles, Solomon, Billy, Chriss, Nanny, Patty; DIV of Negroes PO 17 Feb 1812 among: John DEGGE, Christopher GALE, William DEGGE, Ann [BOSS]. (LC EB 27:111, 112)
[*The surname variants DEGGE and DEGGES occur in just about equal numbers; no attempt has been made to standardize them here.*]

DEGGE, John; T 15 Feb 1813; 15 Feb 1813
LC; INV of dower Negroes of Mrs. Dorothy MITCHELL who was formerly Mrs. Dorothy DEGGE & mar. Richard MITCHELL which Negroes the sd. Richard & Dorothy MITCHELL consented to give up to the heirs of John DEGGE: Lot 1 (Nancy, Lucinda the child of Nancy, Addison child of Nancy, Maria, Joseph) to John F. DEGGE, Lot 2 (Sally, girl Harriott, boy Leroy) to William DEGGE, Lot 3 (Polly & her son Griffin, Lewis son of Polly, girl Sukey, boy Talbert) to Bidkar GEORGE who mar. Mary DEGGE. (LC EB 27:139)
[Rich. MITCHELL mar. Dolly DEGGE(S), LC, bond 22 Jul 1800; Capt. Bedkar GEORGE mar. Mary DEGGE, LC, 5 May 1812 (MLBLC:30, 52); Mary DEGGE orphan of Jn. DEGGE chose Jos. CARTER as her gdn., 18 Dec 1809 (LC Orders B23 1808-11:140); settlement with Jos. CARTER Jr. the acct. of his gdnship. of Mary DEGGE orphan of Jn. DEGGE, 21 Mar 1811 (LC Orders 24:12, 60)]

DEGGE, John (Capt.); PO 20 Oct 1800, T 13 Feb 1804; 17 Sep 1804
LC; dower in the est. of Capt. John DEGGE for his wife Dolly MITCHELL was laid off; the tract of land was adj. Peter BEANE, Chatten DUNAWAY, Griffin GARLAND, John MILLER, & Francis ROBB; the Negroes and bonds were div. among: the wid., Polly DEGGES, John DEGGES, William DEGGES; Richard MITCHELL was an admr. in right of his wife. (LC EB 24:288)

DEGGE, William; 14 May 1802; 20 Jun 1803
CCP, LC; WILL; dau. Lucy K. DEGGE to be sufficiently supported on profits from sale of est.; if dau. Lucy K. DEGGE should die before she marries or reaches age 20, est. to be eq. div. between Jane DEGGE, Elizabeth LIPSCOMB, Catharine C. MITCHELL, & Catharine BRENT; set of silver teaspoons to dau. Lucy K.; large bible to Jane DEGGE; friend Daniel P. MITCHELL ex; WITS: Spencer GEORGE, Jn. BRENT. (LC WB 28:70)
[Catharine C. DEGGE mar. Daniel P. MITCHELL, LC, bond 1 May 1800 (MLBLC:52); Lucy K. DEGGE orphan of Wm. DEGGE chose Jas. TOWLES as her gdn., 16 Jan 1815 (LC Orders 24:213)]

DEGGE, William; PO 20 Jun 1803; 16 Apr 1805
LC; INV, $571.[?].3; includes Negroes Daniel, Sukey, Hannah, Old Patty, girl Aggy, girl [Rose], boy Harry. (LC EB 24:316)

DEGGES, Isaac; 20 Sep 1802
LC; settle with John BRENT & Ann his wife who was Ann DEGGES and Mary DEGGES the extx. of Isaac DEGGES who was the ex. of John PEARSON the accts. of the sd. Isaac DEGGES with he est. of sd. John PEARSON. (LC Orders V 1802-03:190)
[This is Isaac DEGGE[S] who mar. Mary DEGGE[S], RC, bond 31 Dec 1772 (MRC:53); in his will (LC 18 Jul 1792 - 15 Jul 1793) Isaac DEGGES named his wife Mary DEGGES, his relations Mary Tunstall DEGGES & her sis. Ann DEGGES, and Simon the son of bro. Wm. DEGGES (LC WB 22:385); Jn. BRENT (wid.) mar. Ann DEGGES, LC, bond 8 Jun 1796 (MLBLC:7)]

DEGGES, John; 16 Jan 1804

LC; Chancery suit; Rich. MITCHELL & Dolly his wife who was Dolly DEGGES gdns. of John [T.] DEGGES, William DEGGES and Polly DEGGES orphans of John DEGGES. (LC Orders W 1804-05:3)

[Rich. MITCHELL mar. Dolly DEGGES, LC bond 22 Jul 1800 (MLBLC:52); Rich. MITCHELL aptd. gdn. of Jn. T. DEGGES & Wm. DEGGES & Polly DEGGES orphans of Jn. DEGGES, LC 17 Sep 1804 (LC OB 1804-05:224)]

DEMERITT, Alice; 6 May 1823; 8 Sep 1823

NC; WILL; Negroes Robin, Sinah, Albert, Penny, Hannah & Henry and George the son of Penny to dau. Nancy B. DUNGAN and also all the prop. which I purchased of her husband David DUNGAN in his lifetime; Negroes Delphia, Bob, Daniel, George & James to the children of my dau. Elenor HUTT; Negro girl Fanny to grdau. Ann BELL; Negro girl Charlotte to great grdau. Ann BELL, dau. of Ann BELL; Negro children Celia & Jenny to grchildren Elizabeth HUTT & Ann HUTT; Negro girl Milley to be sold & proceeds eq. div. among grdau. Ann BELL, grdaus. Elizabeth Mary HUTT & Elenor Ann NUTT, Elizabeth Bennett BELL & my grson. Thomas Griffin HUTT son of Richard HUTT; $100 to the children of my grdau. Winnefred HAMMOCK wife of John HAMMOCK to assist in educating them; any residue to be eq. div. between dau. Nancy B. DUNGAN, the children of dau. Elenor HUTT and grson. Thomas Griffin HUTT; faithful old slave Winney to have choice of her home at the end of every year to live with either of my daus. Nancy B. DUNGAN or Elenor HUTT or either of my grdaus. and to be supported and well treated by whomsoever she may select; nephew Augustine NEALL, Thomas BELL & William BELL exors; WITS: Jn. FULKS, Sydnor T. HUDSON, Vin BRAMHAM; admin. with the will annexed granted to Thomas BELL [10] Nov 1823. (NC RB 23:360)

[Alice DEMERITT was Alice BRAMHAM, dau. of Benj. BRAMHAM, who mar. Jn. DEMERITT (d. 1797, *see below*), RC, bond 10 Feb 1767 (MRC:53); Nancy Bramham DEMERITT, sis. of Benj DEMERITT, mar. David DUNGAN, LC, 21 Jul 1793 (MWO:118); Eleanor DEMERITT mar. Gerard HUTT, RC, bond 12 Dec 1804 (MRC:100); Winifred S. DEMERITT, dau. of Molly DOBYNS and Benj. DEMERITT, mar. Jn. W. HAMMOCK, RC, bond 10 Jul 1815 (MRC:86)]

DEMERITT, Alice; [?]; 10 Jan 1825

NC; INV; includes the following Negroes: Robin, Sinah, Albert, Penny, Henry, George, Hannah, Delphia, Bob, Daniel, boys George & James, girls Fanny & Charlotte, Sam, girls Celia & Jenny, Milly, old woman Winney; ex. of her est. was Thomas BELL. (NC RB 24:125)

DEMERITT, Elizabeth; 25 Jun 1805; 7 Oct 1805

RC; WILL; sis. Mary WHITE all interest etc. in an undivided tract of land containing about 150 ac. in LP which fell to me by the death of my father John DEMERITT; sis. Ellen HUTT; friend and b-i-l [David] DUNGAN; three sisters Mary WHITE, Nancy DUNGAN, Ellen HUTT; nieces Elizabeth Gilbert DUNGAN and Nancy Bramham DUNGAN; b-i-l David DUNGAN ex.; WITS: Eliz. WOOLLARD, Alice DEMERRITT, Vincent BRAMHAM. (RC WB 9:262)

[This is Elizabeth the dau. of Jn. and Alice (BRAMHAM) DEMERITT, *see Alice DEMERITT above and Jn. DEMERITT below*]

DEMERITT, John; PO Dec 1796; 18 Dec 1797

LC; INV, £796.8.0 1/2; includes Negroes: Thadeus, Jack, Jenny, Rachel, Nero, Phillis, Lydia, Sylvia, Jacob, Spencer, Cilla, old Jenny; DIV of est. among: the

wid. Alice DEMERITT, Ellenor DEMERITT, Benjamin DEMERITT, Eliza DEMERITT, Griffin WHITE in right of his wife Mary, Dr. DUNGAN in right of his wife Nancy. (LC EB 24:67, 72)
[*See Alice DEMERITT, above, for information on the marriages of the children of Jn. and Alice (BRAMHAM) DEMERITT;* Griffin WHITE mar. Mary DEMERITT, LC, bond 31 Dec 1793 (MLBLC:79)]

DEMERITT, John; PO [6] Jan 1817 [sic]; 8 Dec 1818
RC; land which DEMERETT died seized & possessed was sold for $350 and proceeds div. among the distributees: Gerard HUTT in right of his wife Ellianor, Nancy DUNGAN in her own right, John W. HAMMOCK in right of his wife Winifred, John G. WHITE in his own right, Richard B. HUTT in right of his wife Alice B.; John G. WHITE & Alice B. HUTT (Hierome F. WHITE being dead) are the only heirs of Mary WHITE dec'd who was entitled to 2 shares one in her own right & one under the will of Betsy DEMERETT. (RC AB 3:649)
[Gerard HUTT & Eleanor his wife summoned Nancy DUNGAN, Jn. G. WHITE, Hierome F. WHITE (orphan of Mary WHITE), Rich. B. HUTT & Alice his wife, and Jn. W. HAMMOCK and Winefred his wife to show cause why the lands of Jn. DEMERITT should not be sold and the proceeds div. among the heirs, 7 Oct 1816 (RC OB 24:45); David DUNGAN & Nancy B. his wife who was Nancy B. DEMERITT, Griffin WHITE & Polly his wife who was Polly DEMERITT and Jn. CARPENTER gdn. of Eliz. and Ellenor DEMERITT brought suit against Benj. DEMERITT admr. of Jn. DEMERITT dec'd in LC in 1800 (LC CC 1800-010); David DUNGAN mar. Nancy Branham DEMERETT, sis. of Benj. DEMERETT, LC, bond 19 Jul 1793; Griffin WHITE mar. Polly DEMERITT, LC, bond 31 Dec 1793 (MLBLC:23, 79)]

DEMERITT, Molly; 23 Dec 1823; 6 Dec 1824
RC; WILL; Negro boy Edmund to my grson. Napoleon B. HAMMOCK; if grson. die before marriage or age 21, Negro to go to grdau. Augusta M. HAMMOCK; Negro girl Eliza to grdau. Augusta M. HAMMOCK; Negro woman Phillis to be eq. div. between sd. grson. Napoleon & grdau. Augusta; if both sd. grson. & sd. grdau. die without heirs, Negroes Edmund, Eliza & Phillis to go to children of dau. Winifred S. HAMMOCK by her present husband John W. HAMMOCK or by any future husband; [no ex. named]; [no WITS]. (RC WB 10:53)
[Molly DEMERET, the wid. of Benj. DEMERET, was Mary DOBYNS who mar. Benj., RC, bond 14 Aug 1797 (MRC:53); Jn. W. HAMMACK mar. Winefred DEMERITT, dau. of Molly DEMERITT, RC, bond 10 Jul 1815 (MRC:86); Molly & Benj. DEMERITT had two children, Alice and Winefred; Benj. DEMERITT had died bef. Jul 1818 (RC OB 24:235)]

DENTON, William; PO 15 Jan 18[10]; 16 Apr 1810. LC; INV, [m]. (LC EB 27:71)

DICKESON, Elijah; 27 Feb 1815
WC; it appears to the court that Elijah DICKESON has been dead more than 3 mos. and no one has applied for admin.; sheriff to admin. est. (WC OB 1814-18:96)

DISHMAN, Philip; PO May 1815; 26 Jun 1815. WC; INV, $158.[9]1. (WC RI 9:458)

DISHMAN, William; 23 May 1810; 23 Jul 1810
WP, WC; WILL; small tract in KGC on the head of Mattox Creek devised to me by my father to son James DISHMAN; all land down in WC to son William DISHMAN that is the tract w/o I now live, the tract purchased of Isaac ROBUCK, and the tract purchased of Joseph FOX; dau. Ann BRYANT

Negroes Sarah & her 4 children: Bill, Anthony, Nelly & David & a Negro boy Benjamin; grdau. Ann Monroe MASSEY a Negro boy Simon; dau. Mary MASSEY; rest of est. to be eq. div. between sons James & William; son James & William exors; WITS: Jos. FOX, Geo. PINCKARD, Chris. HOLLINS, Jn. BAILEY. (WC DW 22:106)

DISHMAN, William Sr.; PO 26 Nov 1810; 25 Apr 1814
WC; DIV of est; to surviving son James DISHMAN (Negroes William, Charles, Frederick, Leydia, Ann, Dennis); to est. of his son William DISHMAN (Davey, Aaron, Anthony, Rachel, [F]anny, Caroline. (WC RI 9:421)

DIX, Thomas E.; PO 1 Mar 1813; 1 Mar 1813. RC; INV, $723.29. (RC WB 9:417)

DOBYNS, Abner; 25 Mar 1802; 1 Nov 1802
RC; WILL; dau. Molly DEMERITT a widow; son Abner land & plant. w/o I now live; son Charles my forest plant. with all the land I bought from Col. Thomas B. GRIFFIN's exors. & also the land I bought from Col. John TARPLEY known by the name of Hendren's & Osgriffin's; sons Abner & Charles exors; WITS: Thaddeus FORRESTER, Washington GLASCOCK, Rich. DOWNMAN. (RC WB 9:197)
[Mary (Molly) DOBYNS mar. Benj. DEMERRIT in RC, b. 14 Aug 1797 (MWO:106)]

DOBYNS, Abner; 1 Mar 1803; 5 Dec 1803
RC; WILL; land & plant. to bro. Charles; asks bro. to pay sis. Molly DEMERRIT £150; bro. Charles ex.; wits: Daniel DOBYNS Jr; Sam. PALMER. (RC WB 9:224)

DOBYNS, Abner; PO 2 Dec 1822, T 30 May 1823; 7 Jul 1823
RC; DIV of land; wid. would not take her third in the land; all land was sold (tract containing 100 ac. sold to Edward J. NORTHEN for $101.50 & tract containing 63 2/3 ac. sold to Edmond NORTHEN for $71); proceeds div. among George H. DOBYNS, Parthania DOBYNS, Peggy DOBYNS, Amanda DOBYNS, [Armineous] DOBYNS, Brunetta DOBYNS, Leroy DOBYNS, Polly DOBYNS, Arretta DOBYNS. (RC AB 4:60)
[This is prob. Abner DOBYNS, Jr. who mar. Winifred NORTHEN, dau. of Geo. & Margaret (JONES) NORTHEN, RC, bond 14 Nov 1798 (MRC:54); Winifred DOBYNS, wid. of Abner, mar. (2) Wm. NEWSOM, RC, bond 6 Feb 1818 (MRC:145); Thos. DOBYNS aptd. gdn. to Brunetta W. & Leroy W. DOBYNS orphans of Abner DOBYNS, 4 Nov 1822 (RC OB 26:2); Geo. H., Leroy W., Parthana, Margaret, Amanda F., [Manus], Brunetta W., Polly M., Arretta L. DOBYNS, the last 8 named being infants by Thos. DOBYNS their gdn. to defend them, complts., vs. Wm. NEASOM and Winifred his wife, 2 Dec 1822 (RC OB 26:10); Parthenia DOBYNS mar. Jos. P. KELSICK, RC, bond 18 Dec 1824 (MRC:111); Margaret N. DOBYNS mar. Thos. JESPER, RC, bond 24 Dec 1827 (MRC:106); acc. to RC OB 28:160, Winifred (DOBYNS) NEWSOM was a resident of Spencer Co., Ky by Aug 1833; George H. DOBYNS was a resident of EC, Va., and Arretta DOBYNS had died; Winifred was identified as the mother of Arretta, Parthenia, Margaret N. and Mary M. DOBYNS; that same document stated that Elijah SWOPE mar. Mary M. DOBYNS, however acc. to MRC:200, Elijah SWOPE mar. Brunetta W. DOBYNS, RC, bond 5 Feb 1828]

DOBYNS, Abner; PO 2 Dec 1822, T 7 Mar 1823; 7 Jul 1823
RC; sale & div. of Negroes belonging to the est. of Abner DOBYNS after deducting the wid's dower; wid. rec'd old woman Nanny, Felicia & child Fanny; remaining Negroes Bob, Joe, Anna, Solomon, Janetta, Sarah, & Jerry

sold for $1528 which was div. among: George H. DOBYNS, Parthenia DOBYNS, Peggy DOBYNS, Arminda F. DOBYNS, Armenious DOBYNS, Brunetta DOBYNS, Leroy W. DOBYNS, Arretta S. DOBYNS, and Polly M. DOBYNS; each rec'd $169.77 7/9. (RC AB 4:58)

DOBYNS, Abner; T 11 Dec 1822; 5 Sep 1825
RC; INV, [m]; includes Negroes worth $1875: [Nanny], Bob, Joe, Felicia & child Fanny, Solomon, Anna, Janetta, Sarah, Jerry. (RC WB 10:85)

DOBYNS, Charles; 23 May 1812; 2 Nov 1812
RC; WILL; wife to possess all est. until son Sydnor Lawson Rowland comes of lawful age; son Sydnor Lawson Rowland my plant. w/o I now live & also my plants in the forest known by the name of Hendron's and Griffin's when 21; if son die before 21 or without heirs land to wife; wife to be extx; WITS: Thos. P. SMITH, Chr. L. DOBYNS, Edmund N. NORTHEN. (RC WB 9:413)
[Chas. DOBYNS, son of Abner DOBYNS (d. RC, 1802), mar. Sarah L. DOBYNS, dau. of [Leroy] DOBYNS, RC, bond 5 Feb 1806 (MRC:54); Sarah L. (DOBYNS) DOBYNS mar. (2) Thos. P. SMITH, RC, bond 15 Nov 1815 (RC OB 24:221, 230; MRC:191)]

DOBYNS, Charles; PO 7 Dec 1812; 4 Nov 1817. RC; INV, $1013.00. (RC WB 9:569)

DOBYNS, Christian; 18 Sep 1815
LC; John CHOWNING aptd. gdn. to Edwin & Matilda C. DOBYNS children of Christian DOBYNS. (LC Orders 24:259)
[Christian DOBYNS mar. Lucy CHOWNING, LC, bond 11 Dec 1809 (MLBLC:21)]

DOBYNS, Leroy; 29 Oct 1820; 6 Aug 1821
RC; WILL; ex. to sell all land I purchased of John DAVIS, the land I bought of Joshua STONE & the dower right in the land I purchased of Molly [STOTT] and the proceeds kept in the hands of my ex. for the schooling of my grandchildren now living; to Susan STONUM for her kindness & attention to me; son William DOBYNS my boat; grson. John Lawson DOBYNS; rest of est. to be kept by ex. and given to daus. & grandchildren as he thinks proper; friend Warner L. TAPSCOTT ex; WITS: Jas. H. RUST, Margaret [N.] JESPER. (RC WB 9:708)
[Leroy DOBYNS was the son of Wm. & Rebecca (MISKELL) DOBYNS; he was b. in NFP 25 Dec 1756 (NFPR:46, MWO:109); he mar. Lucy LAWSON, RC, bond 16 Sep 1782; they had at least 5 children: Christopher, Wm., Sarah, Rebecca & Alice (MRC:55)]

DOBYNS, William; 8 Feb 1804; 2 Sep 1805
NFP, RC; WILL; wife Susannah all land on the south side of the road leading from Farnham Church to Farnham Bridge, after her death to son Leroy; son Leroy all land purchased of Edward DOBYNS; grson. Abner DOBYNS tract of land purchased of William TAYLOR containing 100 ac; wife also to receive land purchased of Jonathan WILLIAMS, after her death part of sd. land lying on the north and northwest side of the road leading from Richmond Courthouse to Farnham Church to grson. Jesse DOBYNS, residue of sd. tract to friend John DAVIS son of Bob; d-i-l Sarah DOBYNS land purchased of William MISKEL & Jesse MORRIS during her widowhood & after lands to go to grson. Thomas DOBYNS; desires that his "old woman" shall enjoy her freedom and my est. shall maintain her at the expense of 40 shillings per annum; grson. Joshua STONE; s-i-l Luke JACKSON; grson. Jesse DOBYNS land I got by his grmother; grson. Henry M. DOBYNS;

grsons Leroy DOBYNS & Chichester DOBYNS; son Leroy & wife exors.; WITS: Jn. SMITH, Daniel DOBYNS Gent. (RC WB 9:256)
[Wm. DOBYNS mar. Susanna DAVIS, RC, bond 11 Dec 1790 (MRC:56); Luke JACKSON mar. Ann DOBYNS, RC, bond 28 Feb 179[4], MRC:101]

DOBYNS, William; PO Sep 1805; 4 Feb 1811
RC; INV, £1583.18.2, included 28 Negroes: Tom, Cesar, Moses, Jerry, Ned, George, Sam, Winney, Patty, Jane, Rose & 2 children, Violet, Judith, Yellow Patty, Betty, Hannah, Easter, Nelly, Rachel, Polly, Mary, Fanny, Edmond, Solomon, Peg, Daniel. (RC WB 9:398)

DOBYNS, William; PO Sep 1805, T 13 Dec 1805; 4 Feb 1811
RC; DIV of est. among Susanna DOBYNS, the wid, (Caesar, Edmond, Black Patty, Solomon, Tom, Winny), Leroy & Chichester DOBYNS (Moses, Hope & her 2 children Violet & Willoughby, Easter, Rachel), Leroy DOBYNS (Sam, Polly, Judith, Mary); the following slaves were div. between Leroy DOBYNS Jr. & Chichester DOBYNS: Leroy DOBYNS Jr. (Moses, Rachel, Violet) and Chichester DOBYNS (Easter, Rose & child Willoughby); divisions were also made to Thomas DOBYNS & Jesse DOBYNS. (RC AB 3:247)

DOBYNS, Winifred; 16 Apr 1798; 2 Sep 1801
FP, RC; WILL; at my death my Negro woman Esther to have full freedom & liberty from all bondage & bonds of slavery; all my Negroes Daniel, Billy, Richard, & Esther's offspring from this time til my death and any other est. which I now possess to the Reverend Henry TOLER of WC, Cople Parish; the Reverend Henry TOLER, the Reverend Samuel TEMPLEMAN & Ransdell PIERCE all of WC exors; WITS: Jemima DAVIS, Peggy DAVIS, Ann FAUNTLEROY; PO 2 Sep 1801, APP of est; includes Negroes Daniel, Billy, Dick; recorded 3 Apr 1802. (NC DCO:402)

DOBYNS, Winnefred; 26 May 1801; 1 Feb 1802
NFP, RC; WILL; husband Abner; mentions their mar. contract of 5 Jan 1784; after husband's death est. to be div. as follows: nieces Betty B. WILLIAMS & Caty WILLIAMS, children of sis. Betsy TAPSCOTT, child of bro. David WILLIAMS, nephews David H. TAPSCOTT, James M. TAPSCOTT, Samuel WILLIAMS, d-i-l Molly DEMERITT (during her widowhood), s-i-l Abner DOBYNS; Negro whom she possesses by virtue of her sis. Sarah B. WILLIAMS' will dtd. 1 Apr 1786; [no exors]; WITS: Polly TAPSCOTT, Betsy TAPSCOTT, Caty BUNYON. (RC WB 9:162)
[This is Winnefred WILLIAMS dau. of Sam. & Betty Anne WILLIAMS born on 30 Mar 1752 in NFP; their mar. bond was dtd. 5 Jan 1783 (RC DB 15:105, RC WB 7:273, 538; NFPR:46, 47, 202; MRC:54); Betsy TAPSCOTT was Betsy WILLIAMS who mar. Chichester TAPSCOTT, MWO:342); *see also Molly DEMERITT above.*]

DOBYNS, Winnefred; PO 7 Oct 1805, T 30 Oct 1805; 4 Dec 1809
RC; DIV of slaves bequeathed to be div. between E. C. WILLIAMS who mar. John C. ROY (Molly) & Catharine WILLIAMS (Charity). (RC AB 3:231)
[Elizabeth Corrie WILLIAMS, dau. of Thaddeus & Catharine (CORRIE) WILLIAMS, mar. John Corrie ROY of King & Queen Co, bond dtd. 29 Nov 1804. (MRC:174)]

DODD, John; 16 Jul 1819; 28 Feb 1820.
CP, WC; WILL; wife Elizabeth DODD to be extx; Harriett SANFORD now living with [her] aunt Peggy SANFORD; remainder of est. to wife; at wife's death, half of her Negroes & property to return to Rodham SANFORD (under 21) now living with me; sd. Rodham SANFORD asked to stay with

wife and take care of her; WITS: Jn. R. McNEIL, Sam. MOTHERSHEAD, Jos. DODD. (WC DW 24:37)

[Jn. DODD mar. Eliz. SANFORD, WC, bond 24 Dec 1791 (MLBWC:19)]

DODD, John; PO 27 Mar 1820, T 14 Oct 1820; 25 Dec 1820
WC; INV, $1216.66; includes Negroes Rachel & child, Thomas, Miriah, Taylor. (WC RI 11:11)

DODD, Quesenbury; d. intest. leaving a son Daniel DODD and a dau. Jenny who mar. Thomas POOR. (WC CC 1805-006)

[Thos. POOR may have been a son of Chas. POOR who d. in WC in 1799 (WC DW 20:5)]

DODSON, Abraham; 1 Apr 1822
RC; Alexander DODSON of legal age made oath that Bartholomew DODSON is heir at law of Abraham DODSON a soldier who died in the service of the US. (RC OB 25:276)

[Abraham DODSON of RC enlisted on 8 Aug 1812 as a pvt. in the company of Capt. Jn. RITCHIE of the US Artillery for 2 years and he died at Sackett's Harbor on 29 May 1814 [sic; the battle at Sackett's Harbor, NY took place on 29 May 1813], 6 May 1822 (RC OB 25:286)]

DODSON, Charles; 27 Apr 1801; 2 Apr 1802
RC; WILL; being well stricken in years; dau. Judith ROCK; son Alexander; son Rawleigh's five children Abraham, Betty, Patty, Austin and Bartholomew; daus. Joanna, Franky BRYANT, Elizabeth ELMORE, Ruth CORNISH; sons James B., Charles; grchil. Ruth (mar. Thomas FRANCE), Thomas and Catherine children of John DODSON; son Charles DODSON and Richard SMITHER exors; WITS: William STUCKEY, Mary STUCKEY and Mary B. STUCKEY; this will was probated in the Superior Court for the District of Richmond, Westmoreland, Lancaster and Northumberland counties; the inv. of his est. ordered 2 Apr 1802 by the District Court of NC and taken on 12 Apr 1802 revealed a net worth of £618.2.6 and included the following slaves: Criss and her two boy children, Betty, Lucy, George, Fanny, girl Jenny, boy Eppa, girl Molly, boys Tom, Isaac and Billy, and girl Criss; the Negroes were div. as follows: Judith ROCK rec'd Molly; James B. DODSON rec'd Tom; Charles DODSON rec'd Fanny; Joseph DODSON rec'd Betty; John DODSON's children rec'd Criss and two children; Alexander DODSON rec'd Betty and Criss; Rawleigh DODSON's five orphans rec'd Lucy; George ELMORE rec'd Eppy and William CORNISH rec'd Isaac. (LC CC 1808-001)

[Judith ROCK was the wife of Francis ROCK of LC who d. in late 1793 or early 1794 (*see below*); Wm. CORNISH mar. Ruth DODSON, RC, bond 17 Sep 1791 (MRC:44); Ruth CORNISH filed suit against her husband William for cruel and barbarous treatment in 1804; a decree nisi for divorce was issued in Aug 1805 (LC CC 1809-006)]

DODSON, Charles; PO 2 Apr 1802, T 12 Apr 1802; 8 Jun 1812
NC; INV, £618.2.6; includes Negroes Criss & 2 boy children, Betty, Lucy, George, Fanny, girl Jinny, boy Eppa, girl Molly, boys Tom, Isaac & Billy, & girl Criss; after legacies for Alexander DODSON, Joannah DODSON, and Rawleigh DODSON's five children, est. div. among James B. DODSON, Judith ROCK, Charles DODSON, Joseph BRYANT, John DODSON's 3 children, Alexander DODSON, Rawleigh DODSON's 5 children, George ELMORE, & William CORNISH (each rec'd £49.5.2 3/4). (NC RB 19:208)

DODSON, Charles; 19 Jul 1812; 16 Nov 1812

LC; WILL; wife Maryann to have use of plant. in RC until my youngest child shall come to age of 21, then the aforesd. plant. to son Charles DODSON for his paying to my est. £40; I lend to my wife my Negro boy Tom during her life; rest of est. after debts are paid to be eq. div. amongst my children: Nancy DAVIS, Judith ASHBOURN, Polly PITMAN, Elizabeth R. TAFF, Peggy BRADSBERRY, Richard DODSON, Joseph DODSON, & John DODSON; wife to have an equal share with children; friend John CHOWNING ex; WITS: Thos. SHEARMAN, Wm. DUNAWAY, Baker ANGELL. (LC WB 28:138)
[Nancy DODSON mar. Bartley DAVIS, LC, bond 11 May 1799; Judith DODSON mar. Geo. ASHBURNE, LC, bond 2 Dec 1802; Polly DODSON mar. Wm. PITMAN, LC, bond 11 Jan 1809; Eliz. DODSON mar. Jn. TAFF, LC, bond 26 Dec 1808; Peggy DODSON mar. Jas. BRADBERRY, LC, bond 19 Sep 1808 (MLBLC:1, 7, 20, 60, 72)]

DODSON, Charles; T 29 Dec 1812; 17 May 1813. LC; INV; includes Negro boy Tom. (LC EB 27:152)

DODSON, Charles; PO 20 Mar 1815, T 1 Apr 1815; 15 Jun 1818. LC; INV, $325. (LC EB 27:428)

DODSON, James; 29 Sep 1814; 4 Dec 1815
RC; WILL; whole est. to wife Elizabeth during her life or widowhood; if she marries she is to be thirded and the balance to be eq. div. among my 4 children: Sally, John, James & Matilda; [no exors]; WITS: Jn. DAWSON, Rawleigh DODSON; Wm. RICE. (RC WB 9:490)
[Jn., Jas., & Matilda DODSON who are infants of Jas. DODSON, Jr. dec'd by Thos. W. BRYANT their next friend, compl. brought suit against Jn. ROUTT & Sally his wife, 1 Oct 1821 (RC OB 25:197); Jn. ROUTT, of NC, mar. Sarah DODSON, RC, bond 16 Oct 1820 (MRC:174)]

DODSON, James B.; T 5 Nov 1818; 6 Dec 1819
RC; INV; $7172.71 1/4, includes following Negroes: Harry, Ezekiel, Sarah, Fanny, Criss, [Jenney], Charlotte, Patty, Margaret, Maria. (RC WB 9:631)

DODSON, James B.; PO 6 Apr 1819, T 28 Dec 1819; 1 May 1820
RC; allotted to Elizabeth STOTT, who was the wid. of James B. DODSON dec'd, her dower in the slaves belonging to the est. of sd. decedent: Ezekiel, Fanny, Charlotte; the remaining slaves were sold at Farnham Church on 28 Dec 1819; the proceeds were div. into 10 eq. parts and allotted to: Richard ELMORE, Rawleigh DODSON, Thomas W. BRYANT gdn. of the heirs of James DODSON Jr. dec'd (Sally DODSON, John DODSON, James DODSON & Matilda DODSON), Richard RICE, Alfred DODSON, Richard DODSON, William FORRESTER (gdn. of Lot DODSON); John TODD was later mentioned as one of the parties in the division. (RC AB 3:683, 685)
[Rich. ELMORE mar. Catherine DODSON, spinster, RC, bond 17 Dec 1794; Rich. RICE, of NC, mar. Sally DODSON, spinster, RC, bond 13 Oct 1801; Jn. TODD mar. Matilda DODSON, RC, bond 23 Dec 1812 (MRC:65, 169, 216); RC, 8 Dec 1818, Eliz. DODSON wid. of James B. DODSON was allotted 1/3 of the value of his RE and the remander was div. into 10 parts: (1) Rawleigh DODSON, (2) Rich. ELMORE & Catherine his wife, (3) Wm. DODSON, (4) Rich. RICE & Sally A. his wife, (5) Thos. BRYANT & Fanny his wife, (6) Jn. TODD & Matilda his wife, (7) Alfred DODSON, (8) Rich. DODSON, (9) Lot DODSON, (10) the heirs of James DODSON a son of James B. DODSON: Sarah, Jn., Jas., & Matilda (RC OB 24:292)]

DOGGETT, [fnu]; 15 Mar 1824

LC; Coleman DOGGETT aptd. gdn. to Elizabeth, Peggy, Polly & Randall DOGGETT. (LC OB 26:28)

DOGGETT, Benjamin; PO 16 Jul 1811, T 3 Dec 1811; 15 Feb 1813
LC; INV; includes Negroes: Manuel, Sarah, Amany, Bob, Peggy. (LC EB 27:144)

DOGGETT, Benjamin; T 1 Jan 1812; 15 Feb 1813
LC; DIV of Negroes among the wid. (her dower), Ben DOGGETT, William DOGGETT, Josiah DOGGETT, Hugh DOGGETT. (LC EB 27:147)
[Wm. & Benj. DOGGETT orphans of Benj. DOGGETT chose Anne J. PALMER as their gdn.; Rich. HUTCHINGS aptd. gdn. to Hugh DOGGETT orphan of Benj. DOGGETT; Coleman DOGGETT is aptd. gdn. to Josiah DOGGETT orphan of Benj. DOGGETT, 16 Dec 1811 (LC Orders 24:55); Hugh DOGGETT orphan of Benj. DOGGETT chose Jas. BRENT [Jr.] as his gdn., 19 Sep 1814 (LC Orders 24:199)]

DOGGETT, Clement; PO 12 Jun 1820; 10 Jul 1820. NC; INV, [m]. (NC RB 22:370)

DOGGETT, James; PO 15 Oct 1821; 15 Jul 1822
LC; INV, [m]; includes Negroes boys Tom & Page, Winney, boy child Spencer. (LC EB 29:214)

DOGGETT, John; 17 Aug 1803; 22 Apr 1806
LC; WILL; whole est. to wife Judith DOGGETT; wife to raise & educate children; if wife remarries she is no longer to enjoy any part of my est; after wife's death or marriage all land w/o I now live to my son John Longwith DOGGETT; if he should die without heirs sd. land to my second son William DOGGETT; my Negro girl [China] to dau. Judith Pinkard DOGGETT but she is not to have possession of her legacy until she comes of age or marries; Negro boy Joe to son William; when son John L. comes of age or marries he is to have one of my Negroes; wife Judith extx; WITS: Wm. MEREDITH, Augustine GEORGE, Martin GEORGE; [will was finally proved on 15 Nov 1824]. (LC WB 28:251)
[Jn. DOGGETT mar. Judith LONGWITH, LC, bond 17 Aug 1795 (MLBLC:22); Judith DOGGETT orphan of Jn. DOGGETT chose Jos. SHEARMAN as her gdn., 16 Dec 1816 (LC Orders 24:344)]

DOGGETT, John; T 21 Aug 1806; 10 Sep 1806
LC list of Negroes devised to Judith DOGGETT for and during her life or widowhood by John DOGGETT her late husband: James (about 45), Patt (about 36), Sally (about 13), Charlotte (about 12), Joe (about 8), China (about 5), Nanny (about 4). (LC EB 24:346)

DOGGETT, John; PO 22 Apr 1806, T 11 Jun 1806; 15 Sep 1806
LC; INV of personal est; includes Negroes James, Patty, Charlotte, Sally, [Chrisa], Nancy, Joe. (LC EB 24:370)

DOGGETT, John; 27 Mar 1824; 19 Dec 1825
LC; WILL; my home plant. to son Cyrus; my upper plant. to son David S.; the bed & bed stand with 2 pair of sheets, 2 pair of pillow cases, 2 blankets, one best white & one checkered cotton & one yarn fringed counterpanes & 2 best bed quilts & one small painted oval table that stand in the back chamber or preacher's room (so called) remain there for the accommodation of preachers of the gospel; Negroes Charles, Reuben, Suckey & Beckey to son Cyrus who is to treat them with humanity; Negroes Venus, Eliza & Lewis to dau. Sarah; Negroes Rosanna, Spencer & Dorcas to dau. Mary S.; Negroes Henry, Miranda, Winney & Judith to son David S. who is to treat them with humanity also all my law books; $30 to Jane SUTTON for her particular

attention to my family affairs; balance of est. to be eq. div. amongst my daus. Sarah & Mary S. and my son David S.; exors. to hold in trust all the est. devised to dau. Sarah until she settles her admin. acct. on the est. of her dec'd husband; son Cyrus to be gdn. to son David; under the existing laws of this state as it is impracticable to emancipate slaves to remain herein it is my request of my sons that should the laws of our land permit slaves to be granted their freedom at any time during their life time that they set free and at full liberty the following slaves: Reubin at the age of 40 if practicable and the others Suckey, Becky, and Judeth as soon as practicable; friend John CHOWNING and son Cyrus exors; WITS: Bidkar GEORGE, Eliz. T. KIRK, Frances SIMMONDS, Eliz. C. EDWARDS. (LC WB 28:257)

DOGGETT, John G.; PO 17 Feb 1812, T 9 Jul 1813; 17 Mar 1817. LC; INV, $120.91. (LC EB 27:366)

DOGGETT, John S.; 19 Nov 1823; 16 Jul 1824
LC; WILL; all my est. to bro. William DOGGETT; all est. which I am to have at my mother's death given me by my father according to my father's will to my bro. William; [no ex. named]; WITS: Jn. PAYNE, Geo. KIRK, Polly [L.] WILDER. (LC WB 28:244)

DOGGETT, Judith; PO 10 May 1813, T 21 May 1813; 11 Jul 1814
NC; INV, [m]; includes Negroes Isaac, George, Patrick. (NC RB 19:557)
[The est. of Judith DOGGETT was ord. to be admin. by Jn. M. ROBB, NC, 10 May 1813 (NC OB 1811-1816:167)]

DOGGETT, Nancy; 20 Jul 1804; 16 Apr 1805
LC; WILL; Negro Winny to bro. James DOGGETT; rest of est. to sis. Milley DOGGETT; [no ex. named]; WITS: Jn. COWARD, Lucy COWARD; [certif for letters of admin. granted to Jas. DOGGETT]. (LC WB 28:89)

DOGGETT, Nancy; PO 16 Apr 1805; 16 Jun 1806
LC; INV, $527.82; includes Negroes: boy Charles, Winney; James DOGGETT admr. (LC EB 24:340)

DOGGETT, William; 25 Sep 1795; 19 Oct 1795
LC; WILL; son Benjamin DOGGETT the place w/o he now lives being a purchase made by him & paid for by myself together with 1 shilling; son George DOGGETT the place on the eastern branch of Corotoman as per a deed granted to him together with 1 shilling; dau. Hannah DOGGETT; son James DOGGETT the plant. w/o I now live (exclusive of the purchase from STEPTOE); son Coleman DOGGETT land I purchased of STEPTOE between my sd. plant. & Kilmarnock; James POLLARD, Martin SHEARMAN & Peter TANKERSLEY exors; WITS: Jn. HUTCHINGS, Jn. WATTS Sr., Jn. WATTS Jr. (LC WB 28:21)

DOGGETT, William; 5 Jun 1801; 20 Jul 1801
LC; WILL; Negro Ben to bro. John DOGGETT; Negro Tab to sis. Lucy HAYDEN; remaining pers. prop. to be eq. div. between bro. & sis; John DOGGETT & Ezekiel HAYDEN exors; WITS: J. M. GILMOUR, Griffin HAYDEN. (LC WB 28:54)
[Lucy DOGGETT, dau. of Wm. DOGGETT, mar. Ezekiel HAYDEN, LC, bond 30 May 1788 (MLBLC:36)]

DOGGETT, William G.; 18 May 1801
LC; Wiliam BLACKERBY gdn. of John DOGGETT orphan of William G. DOGGETT. (LC Orders 21 1799-1801:234, Orders V 1802-1803:431, OB 1804-05:86)
[Jn. G. DOGGETT orphan of Wm. DOGGETT chose Benj. PALMER as his gdn., 22 Mar 1808 (LC Orders 22D 1805-08:458); settlement with Wm.

BLACKERBY gdn. to Jn. G. DOGGETT dec'd orphan of Wm. DOGGETT dec'd & possess Priscillah DOGGETT wid. & admx. of the sd. Jn. G. DOGGETT with his est., 21 Sep 1812 (LC Orders 24:121); Jn. G. DOGGETT mar. Siller PALMER, LC, bond 22 Mar 1808 (MLBLC:22)]

DOLEMAN, John H.; PO 25 Mar 1816; 23 Mar 1819
WC; INV, $1971.75; includes Negroes Nel, Rose, girl Felishe, boys Tom, Edmond & George. (WC RI 10:364)
[Jn. H. DOLEMAN mar. Frances Bayne VIGAR, WC, bond 10 Jun 1805 (MLBWC:20); Acc. to a CC filed in WC in 1835, John H. DOLEMAN died in Sep 1815; he left at least 5 children: Jacob V. DOLEMAN, Laurence P. DOLEMAN (d. in Sep 1834), James DOLEMAN (killed by lightning in Jun 1826), Henry DOLEMAN (drowned in Apr 1828) & William DOLEMAN (d. 1816); his wid. Fanny, remarried Rich. CRASK, WC, bond 19 Nov 1818 (WCCP:34, MLBWC:17; WC OB 1819-23:98)]

DOLEMAN, Sanford; 28 Jun 1824
WC; William DOLEMAN and Thomas DOLEMAN on oath proved that Elizabeth DOLEMAN is the sis. of Sanford DOLEMAN who about 1812 enlisted as a soldier under Capt. James BANKHEAD in the late war and that he has no other sis. or bro. or child now living. (WC OB 1823-27:94)

DOLEMAN, Thomas; 23 Jan 1818; May 1818
WC; DIV of Negroes belonging to DOLEMAN's est: Josiah HAZARD as legal representative of Thomas DOLEMAN, Jr. has drawn one Negro girl [?] and a small girl Sally; Elizabeth DOLEMAN drew a Negro girl named Patty & a woman Minny. (WC DW 23:385)
[Betsy DOLEMAN orphan of Thos. DOLEMAN chose Andrew MONTGOMERY as her gdn., 25 Mar 1816 (WC OB 1814-18:213)]

DOLEMAN, William; PO 22 Aug 1803; 27 Aug 1810. WC; INV, £61.7.3. (WC RI 9:190)
[Thos. DOLEMAN aptd. gdn. of Jn. DOLEMAN orphan of Wm. DOLEMAN, 22 May 1809 (WC Orders 1807-10:288); Wm. CARPENTER aptd. gdn. of Jn. DOLEMAN orphan of Wm. DOLEMAN and the Overseers of the Poor are to bind Jn. DOLEMAN to CARPENTER as an apprentice to the wheelwright & carpenter trade, 25 Oct 1809 (WC Orders 1807-10:438); Overseers of the Poor to bind Jn. DOLEMAN orphan of Wm. DOLEMAN to Jn. NORWOOD boot maker, 22 Jul 1811 (WC Orders 1807-10:158)]

DOUGLAS, [Judith]; 17 Jul 1826
LC; Reubin, William S., & John W. DOUGLAS chose Thomas DOUGLAS for their gdn. and sd. Thomas is aptd. gdn. to Frances, Polly, Lucy, [Gordon], John, James, & Malinda DOUGLAS. (LC OD 26:196)
[These orphans may be children of Judith DOUGLAS since a commission to settle her est. with sheriff Rawleigh W. DOWNMAN was appointed on the following day, 18 Jun 1826 (LC OB 26:197)]

DOULIN, Joseph; [m]; 12 Aug 1822
NC; WILL; all est. to wife as long as she remains my wid. for her use & the use of my children until they arrive to the age of 21 or marry; at wife's death or marriage, son Joseph DOULIN to have land and Negro boy Solomon; rest of est. to be eq. div. among sons Thomas & William and daus. Elizabeth L. DOULIN & Lucy C. DOULIN and a newborn baby not yet named; wife & Richard COCKARILL to have management of est; WITS: Chas. L. BELL, Jn. FLYNT, Linezey DAVIS, Elisha H. GILL, Jos. WALKER; [court believed that the exors. named would not qualify as such & appointed the sheriff Sam. DOWNING to be administrator with the will annexed]; NC RB 23:205)

[Joseph DOULIN mar. Eliz. GILL, NC, bond 16 Aug 1796; Eliz. and Lucy GILL were daus. of Wm. GILL and Sally HARCUM (dau. of Elisha HARCUM; NC, lic. 15 Feb 1774); Lucy GILL mar. Jas. TRACIE, NC, bond 9 May 1796 (MLBNC:30, 102, MWO:149; NC CC 1800-06)]

DOULIN, Joseph; 14 Jun 1824
NC; INV; includes Negroes John, [Fanne], Vaner, girl Hannah, boys James & Solomon, girls Rose, Nancy & Charlotte, boy Jacob. (NC RB 23:480)

DOWNING, Betty; PO 11 Jan 1808; 12 Feb 1810
NC; DIV of est. among heirs; Lot 1 (Negroes [Hance], Polley, Tabitha, Peggy) to the heirs of Capt. John DOWNING, Lot 2 to Capt. John DOWNING (Rachel, Barshaba, Tilley, Juna). (NC RB 18:327)

DOWNING, Charles; PO 10 Dec 1804, T 4 Feb 1805; 11 Feb 1805
NC; DIV of Negroes among Edward DOWNING (rec'd Willoby), Nancy DOWNING (rec'd Will), Hannah SHEARMAN (rec'd Daniel & Moley), John DOWNING of Louisa [Co.] (rec'd Isaac & Nancy), John [B.] KENNER (rec'd Pleasant & her two children Mima & Sillah); also div. of land near Hull Mill Creek and Pickrens or Mile Branch. (NC RB 17:245)
[Hannah SHEARMAN is Hannah the dau. of Jn. & Hannah (FALLIN) DOWNING who mar. Martin SHEARMAN in NC in 1783 (MWO:317); in her will (NC 2 Dec 1813 - 8 Apr 1816) Hannah SHEARMAN named her nephew Jn. D. KENNER, niece Eliz. KENNER, nephew Jn. DOWNING, and niece Hannah DOWNING; her bro. Jn. DOWNING was one of the exors. (NC RB 20:422); Jn. B. KENNER mar. Sarah DOWNING, dau. of Jn. & Hannah (FALLIN) DOWNING, NC, lic. 11 Oct 17[77] (MWO:212)]

DOWNING, Richard; 18 Feb 1823; 11 Mar 1823
NC; WILL; all est. to mother Elizabeth DOWNING; sisters Sally & Betsy; bro. George DOWNING should be furnished with such articles of clothes & other accessories which he may from time to time require; old man Peter to be free and have a certain piece of land w/o he lives beginning at the Deep Hole and adj land of Bridgar HAYNIE; Negro boy Aaron to Maria & Betsy DOWNING daus. of Edward DOWNING; Negro boy Lewis to Jane DOWNING dau. of Edward DOWNING and she is to be under the direction & control of Capt. John MIDDLETON until she marries or arrives to the age of 21; piece of land near the courthouse & place where the old shop stood & a piece of land near Boyd's Run; cousin John MIDDLETON; cousin John MIDDLETON ex; WITS: Thos. S. SYDNOR, Jn. D. BETTS, Lee TAYLOR. (NC RB 23:288)
[div. the lands of Rich. DOWNING between his heirs Sally CUNDIFF and Betsy HARDING, 8 May 1826 (NC OB 1825-30:82); Sally DOWNING, dau. of Betsy DOWNING, mar. Thos. CUNDIFF, ward of Wm. SYDNOR, NC, bond 10 Dec 1821 and Eliz. R. DOWNING, dau. of Betsy DOWNING, mar. Jn. H. HARDING, NC, bond 5 Apr 1825 (MLBNC:25, 45)]

DOWNING, Sarah; PO 9 Jul 1792, T 18 Jul 1792); [m]. NC; INV, [m]. (NC RB 16:77)
[Sarah DOWNING named her dau. Hannah (who mar. Rich. M. BALL, NC, bond 30 Nov 1798) in her will (NC 25 Jun 1792 – 9 Jul 1792), Edw. DOWNING was her ex.; NC CC 1809-007 revealed that she had another dau., Sarah who mar. Winder KENNER, NC, bond 11 Oct 1799 (NC RB 14:577, MLBNC 4)

DOWNING, Septimus; 3 Oct 1821; 12 Nov 1821
SSP, NC; WILL; mother Elizabeth DOWNING to have the use of whole est. as long as she shall live; at her death plant. w/o I now live to my bro.

Richard DOWNING also tract of land adj BLACKWELL, CHRISTOPHER, WALKER, EDWARDS & LAMKIN and known as Everett's and the following slaves Isaac, Jerry, Solomon, Grace & Matilda; to sis. Salley DOWNING two slaves Chloe & her child Bob; to sis. Betsy DOWNING 2 slaves Nancy & Sarah; to friend Joseph BASYE my 2 houses & lots near Northumberland Courthouse adj lands of HUGHLETT, BASYE & DOWNING; friend John MIDDLETON; bro. Richard DOWNING, my uncle Samuel DOWNING & friend John MIDDLETON exors; WITS: W. BASYE, Jas. HAYNIE, Rich. KNOTT. (NC RB 23:20)

[Septimus DOWNING was the son of Thos. Dameron & Eliz. DOWNING (d. NC 1816) see below]

DOWNING, Thomas (Capt.); T 17 Dec 1799; 13 Jan 1800

NC; INV, [m]; includes Negroes Peter, Rosa, Shadrack, David, Little Peter, Moses, Joe, Harry, Darky, Jerry & Cloe, Meshack, Phillis, Peter, Bill, Big George, Simon, Jude & child Mima, Old Jude, Mima, John, Paul, [Len], Manuel, James, Aga, George, Esop, Sinah & child Peg, James [KEY], Jery, Lucy, Little Peter (Cord's child), Rubin, Easter & child Sinah, Jess, Winny, Nancy, Mary, Tignor, Hannah, Isaac, Lila, Fran, Pleasant & child Daniel, Sue, Sarah, Ailce, Silla. (NC RB 16:40)

DOWNING, Thomas (Capt.); T 21 Jan 1800; 14 Apr 1800

NC; DIV of est. among: Maj. T. D. DOWNING (rec'd Negroes Peter, Roda), Mrs. Catharine BLACKWELL (rec'd Negroes Darkey, Jenny [black], Meshack, Phillis, Peter, Bill & Big George, Simon, Jude & child Mima, old Jude, Mima), Edward DOWNING (rec'd Negroes Shadrack, David, Little George -- drawn by division James, Hannah, Isaac, Lila, Fanny, Aga, Reuben, Sarah), Samuel DOWNING (rec'd Negroes Moses, Joe, Harry -- drawn by division, Ailcey by legacy, Manuel, Sinah & child Peg, James KEY, Jery, Sue, Pleasant & child Daniel, Lewis), Sarah DOWNING (rec'd Negroes John, Paul, Len, Silla by legacy, George, Easter & child Sinah, Jess, Winny, Nancy, Mary, Tignor, Peter, Lucy). (NC RB 16:84)

[In his will (NC 27 Aug 1799 - 9 Dec 1799) Thos. DOWNING named his sons Thos. D., Edw., and Sam. and daus. Catharine BLACKWELL, Eliz. COX and Sarah DOWNING (NC RB16:23)]

DOWNING, Thomas D. (Col.); T 7 Nov 1816; 8 Sep 1817

NC; INV, [m]; includes the following Negroes: Domini, Will, Spencer, Nell, Bill, Johnston, Maria, Ned, Isaac, Sarah, Jerry, Grace, Chloe, Tilley, Nancy, Solomon, Peter (preacher), Clem, Charlotte, Aaron, Lewis, Tabby, Ellen, David, Hannah, Bathsheba, Adam, Mima, Jacob, Rodham, Griffin, Cordelia, Susanna, Alice, Young Peter, Daniel, Juno, Henry, Patty, Matilda, Pleasant, Elijah, Martin, Siller, Cate, Cordelia (infant) (NC RB 21:250)

DOWNING, Thomas Dameron; 29 Mar 1816; 8 Jul 1816

SSP, NC; WILL; all est. to wife Betsey DOWNING as long as she lives a widow in my name and that she gives up to my children hereafter named as they come of age or marry two thirds of the est; if wife die or marry est. to be div. as follows: to my three sons George, Septimus & Richard DOWNING the fishing shore in Brereton's Neck; to my three daus. Sarah, Betsy & Mary the residue of my land in Brereton's Neck also the land which my father purchased of William ALEXANDER adj the land w/o Capt. [Mat] LAMKIN now lives to be eq. div. between them; to son George DOWNING tract of land w/o Daniel GILL now lives & the following Negroes: Dommony, Will, Spencer, [Nell], Bill, Johnson, Mariah, & Ned; to son Septimus the land I now live on near Northumberland Courthouse adj the tract of land I purchased of Rawleigh ALEXANDER dec'd and also one tract of land which my father purchased of [?] EVERETT & also another tract of land w/o George [COLES] formerly lived adj the aforesaid tract called Everett's with the following Negroes: Isaac, [Jerry], Grace, Sarah, Chloe, [Tilla], Nancy & Solomon; to son Richard DOWNING four tracts of land, one I purchased of Edwin TOWNSEND, two I purchased of my bro. Edward DOWNING and a tract of woodland adj the est. of Bennet [JONES] dec'd which I purchased of William [BRYANT] with the following Negroes: Peter, [Clem], [Charles], [Aaron], [Lewis] & [?]; to dau. Sarah DOWNING the following Negroes: David, Hannah, Bathsheba, Ellen, Adam, [Minney], and Jacob; to dau. Betsy DOWNING the following Negroes: Rodham, Griffin, Cordelia, Susanna, [?], Peter, Daniel, & [?]; to dau. Mary the following Negroes: Henry, Pattey, Matilda, Pleasant, Elijah, Martin, and Saller also $50; wife Betsy DOWNING, bro. Samuel DOWNING, sons George & Septimus & friends Peter P. COX, James COX, & John MIDDLETON exors; WITS: W. BASYE, Jas. SMITH, Royston BETTS Jr. (NC RB 21:27)

[Thos. Dameron DOWNING, son of Thos. & Sarah Ann (ROGERS) DOWNING, mar. Eliz. COX, dau. of Fleet COX (d. WC 1791), 5 Apr 1787 (MWO:114); Thos. D. and Eliz. DOWNING had the following children: Thos. Fleet (b. 1789, d. 1808), Jn. Calvin (b. 1790, d. 1796)), Geo. (b. 1792), Jas. (b. 1794, d. 1798), Jos. (b. 1796, d. 1801), Septimus (b. 1797, d. 1821), Rich. (b. 1800. d. 1823), Sarah (b. 1802), Betsey (b. 1806, d. 1838), and Mary (b. 1809, d. 1817); Thos. D. DOWNING d. 28 Apr 1816 (BNCHS vol. IV, no. 1:61-62); Miller:15 identifies Brereton's Neck as prob. the southern portion of present Bull Neck on the Chesapeake Bay in NC]

DOWNING, Winnifred; PO 8 Apr 1816, T 20 Apr 1816; 13 May 1816
NC; INV, $502; includes Negro Solomon. (NC RB 20:442)

DOWNMAN, Elizabeth; 16 Aug 1817; 1 Dec 1817
NFP, RC; WILL; Negroes James, Abraham & Frank (a woman) to son William DOWNMAN; Negro men Will & Walter to son Richard DOWNMAN; Negroes Sally, Alice (and her son Billy) & Milly to dau. Elizabeth GLASCOCK wife to my son-in-law Washington GLASCOCK; slaves Tabb, Daingerfield, Paramus, & Peter to be held by exors. for benefit of my dau. Eleanor B.; slaves Eve, [Ame??], Betty & Carlus to be held by exors. for the benefit of my grson. John D. GLASCOCK; grson. Rawleigh W. DOWNMAN son of my son William; granddau. Frances C. DOWNMAN dau. of my son William; grand dau. Elizabeth GLASCOCK dau. of my s-i-l Washington; granddau. Elizabeth DOWNMAN dau. of my son Richard; two sons William & Richard DOWNMAN exors; WITS: Wm. PALMER, Robt. GLASCOCK, Jos. GLASCOCK. (RC WB 9:600)

[This is apparently Eliz., the dau. of Wm. GLASCOCK, who mar. Rawleigh DOWNMAN, RC, bef. 1784 (MRC:59); Eliz. DOWNMAN, dau. of Rawleigh DOWNMAN, mar. Washington GLASCOCK, RC, bond 18 Dec 1805 (MRC:78)]

DOWNMAN, Joseph B.; 21 Sep 1801; 15 Feb 1802
LC; DIV of slaves among: Mrs. Olivia DOWNMAN, Judith DOWNMAN, Mrs. Olivia CHINN, Jospeh B. DOWNMAN, Margaret DOWNMAN, Sarah DOWNMAN, Capt. William MONTAGUE, Harriot Jane DOWNMAN, George M. DOWNMAN, James Welmot Payne DOWNMAN, William DOWNMAN. (LC EB 24:180)

DOWNMAN, Joseph B.; Filed 19 Nov 1805; 10 Sep 1806

LC; list of slaves held for life under the will of Joseph B. DOWNMAN by Olivia DOWNMAN relict of sd. DOWNMAN: Harry (age 42), Tom (40), George (now dead), Perrimus (31), Randolph (28), Emanuel (26), Isaac (22), Robin (21), Bass (20), Betty (41), Amy (26), Penelope (26), Hetty (now dead), Wilmouth (23), Ellen (19), Sciller (13); increase of the female slaves: Peggy (3), Mary (3), Charlotte (now dead). George (1), Clifford (9 mos), Bridgett (9 mos). (LC EB 24:344)

DOWNMAN, Joseph B.; PO 19 Nov 1817; 20 Apr 1818
LC; INV of pers. est. in Stafford Co, $3654.17 1/2; includes Negroes (worth $6011.80): [Isabel], Milley, Sally & child Charlotte, Nancy, Lucinda, Louisa, Rachel, George, Eliza, James (about 30, now run away). (LC EB 27:418, 420)

DOWNMAN, Joseph B. Esq.; PO 21 Oct 1799, T 26 Dec 1799; [21] Jul 1800
LC; INV, at Morattico, $22,438.58, includes a number of named horses and 2 groupings of Negroes, (1) Carpenter Davy, George, John, Isaac, Tom, Isaac, Davy, Shadrack, Betty, Esther, Penny, Leanna, Wilmoth & child Elizabeth, Fanny, Sillah, Nanny, Jessa, Lindsay, Grace, Old Moses, Dominy, Manuel, Will, Randall, Robin, Hercules, Winny, Tab & child Louisa, Milly, [Hetta], Amy, [Lyda], Mima, Mary, Patt, Eppy, Charlotte, Little Harry, Perrymus, Robin, Marcus, Bass, Daniel, Fielding, Judy, Cate, Violet & child Nelly, Amine, Ellen, Sarah, Winny, Adam, Hannah, Old Harry, Little Moses; (2) James, Hill, Abram, Jerry, Chichester, Bond, Abel, Duke, Holland, Old Daniel, Old Nanny, Old Hannah, Lydda, Nanny, Lucy, Chriss, Aggy & child Jesse, Alce & child Judy, Sall, Mariah, Sinah, Joshua, Dick, Tom, Simon, Elijah, [Joe], Ezekiel, Baccus, George, Jenny, Bell & child [David], [?], Esther, Letty & child [Jonathan], Levina, Lucinda, Zenah, Sarah, Anna; in Stafford Co T on 9 Dec 1799, £1788.10: Old Rachel, George, Eppy, Tom, Peter, Dinah, Nan, Charlotte & child Judy, Rachel & child Daphne, Tab & child James, Jane, [Win], Hannah, Sarah, Ben, John, David, Will, Catharine, Eve, Bett, Cylla, Henry, Anthony, Helen, Mary, Clara, Penelope, Rebecca, [Mariah] & child Maria, James. (LC EB 24:114)

DOWNMAN, Joseph Ball; 12 Aug 1799; 21 Oct 1799
LC; WILL; use of land & plant. w/o I now live to wife Olivia DOWNMAN; my Negro carpenter David & his wife Judy to wife; my land & plant. in Stafford Co. known as the Little Falls to son Joseph Ball DOWNMAN; my land & plant. in LC called the Forest Quarter together wth my land & tenements adj thereto to son George William DOWNMAN; if child wife is now pregnant with should be a son, sd. child should have the land & plant. I now live on; if the child be a girl I give the sd. land & plant. to my son George William DOWNMAN; my tract of land in Culpeper Co. on Hazel River & my tract in Fauquier Co. on Summer Duck Run to be sold and proceeds used to pay debts; my daus. Olivia Chinn, Frances, Sarah, Margaret, Millian, Judith & Harriott Jane; bro. Rawleigh William DOWNMAN & friend Col. James BALL exors; WITS: Alice PRENTICE, Rebecca LANKTON, Wm. KIRKHAM, Dan. SCURLOCK. (LC WB 28:35) [Jos. Ball DOWNMAN was the son of Rawleigh DOWNMAN (d. LC 1781) (LC WB 20:188); Olivia DOWNMAN, dau. of Jos. Ball DOWNMAN, mar. Bartholomew CHINN, LC, 8 Jun 1799 (MWO:74); Frances DOWNMAN orphan of Jos. B. DOWNMAN chose Raw. Wm. DOWNMAN as her gdn., 16 Feb 1801 (LC Orders 21 1799-1801:210); Olivia DOWNMAN aptd. gdn. of Harriet Jane & Jas. Wilmott Payne DOWNING orphans of Jos. B. DOWNMAN; Sarah DOWNMAN orphan of Jos. B. DOWNMAN chose Jas. BALL as her gdn. and sd. Jas. BALL is also aptd. gdn. of Millian & Judith

DOWNMAN; Wm. MONTAGUE aptd. gdn. of Wm. DOWNMAN orphan of Jos. B. DOWNMAN; Margaret DOWNMAN orphan of Jos. B. DOWNMAN chose Rawleigh W. DOWNMAN as her gdn. and sd. Rawleigh W. DOWNMAN is aptd. gdn. of Jos. B. DOWNMAN, 21 Sep 1801 (LC Orders 21 1799-1801:322); Wm. MONTAGUE mar. Frances DOWNMAN, LC, bond 17 Mar 1801 (MLBLC:53); chancery suit: Wm. MONTAGUE & Frances his wife, Jos. BALL & Olivia his wife, Sarah DOWNMAN, Wm. DOWNMAN by Jas. BALL his gdn., Geo. W. DOWNMAN by Wm. MONTAGUE his gdn., Harriet J. DOWNMAN & Jas. W. P. DOWNMAN by Olivia DOWNMAN their gdn., pltfs. against Rawleigh W. DOWNMAN ex. of Jos. B. DOWNMAN and as gdn. of Margaret & Jos. B. DOWNMAN, defts., to settle the est. of Jos. B. DOWNMAN and div. the amount among the legatees,19 Mar 1806 (LC Orders D22 1805-08:118, 137); Millian DOWNMAN mar. Alford BEALE of RC, LC, bond 13 Jun 1810; Margaret DOWNMAN mar. Wm. B. MITCHELL, LC, bond 30 May 1815; Harriet Jane DOWNMAN mar. Jos. B. DOWNMAN, LC, bond 6 Jan 1816 (MLBLC:3, 23, 53); acc. to LC CC 1826-006 concerning the disposition of the land in Fauquier & Culpeper cos. the children of Jos. B. DOWNMAN the Elder were named as: Margaret (who mar. Wm. B. MITCHELL), Olivia (who mar. Jos. BALL), Frances (who mar. Wm. MONTAGUE), Millian (who mar. Alf. BEALE), Judith, Harriet Jane (who mar. Jn. B. DOWNMAN), Jos.B. the Younger, Geo. W., Jas. W. P. and Sarah; Frances, Millan and Jos. B. the Younger were dec'd by 1826; Wm. D. MONTAGUE was the only child of Frances & Wm.MONTAGUE; Alice Olivia was the only child of Millian & Alfred BEALE, and Jas. F. was the only child of Olivia & Jos. BALL (see also LC OB 26:196)]

DOWNMAN, Judith; PO 21 Apr 1806; 15 Jun 1807
LC; INV of est. presented by Joseph BALL her admr., £907.16.8; includes several named books and the Negroes: Ezekiel, Joe, Lindsey, Cate & child, Esther, Winney, Zena, Eliza WIGGENS, Louisa, Tab; PO 19 Jan 1807 DIV of est. among: Capt. William MONTAGUE in right of his wife Frances, Harriet J. DOWNMAN, Sally DOWNMAN, William DOWNMAN, Joseph BALL in right of his wife Olivia, James W. P. DOWNMAN, Mrs. Olivia DOWNMAN, Margaret DOWNMAN, George W. DOWNMAN, Joseph B. DOWNMAN. (LC EB 27:16)
[This is Judith, the dau. of Jos. B. & Olivia DOWNMAN.]

DOWNMAN, Rawleigh; 27 Dec [1811]; 6 Apr 181[2]
RC; Nunc. will; on 2 Feb 1812 Richard DOWNMAN deposed that on 27 Dec last he was at the house of Mr. Rawley DOWNMAN (his father) who wished his land eq. div. in 3 parts & that he wished his 3 daus. to take choice agreeable to their ages, that is that the eldest should have first choice; Rawleigh DOWNMAN d. on 1 Feb 1812. (RC WB 9:404)

DOWNMAN, Traverse; 4 Mar 1801); [m]
NFP, RC; WILL; £100 cash now in my house to be delivered to elders James GREENWOOD of Essex, Brian PHILLIPS of Richmond, Henry TOLER & Samuel TEMPLEMAN of Westmoreland whom I appoint trustees for the purpose to be divided by them according to their best judgment among the most faithful laborious Baptist ministers of the Gospel who have neglected their worldly interest to make full proof of their ministry and any poor suffering private members of the Baptist churches who shall be pious and orderly; sis. Nancy; bro. Rawleigh; tract of land purchased of William COLESON and all my est. to be div. in 5 eq. parts: sis. Nancy, sis. Frances,

bro. Rawleigh; one part to be eq. div. between the children of my sis. Elizabeth SYDNOR dec'd, sis. Priscilla DAVIS which shall be eq. div. between the surviving heirs of her body; bro. Rawleigh & Elder Brian PHILLIPS exors; WITS: Jas. ALDERSON, Dan. DOBYNS Sr., Lawson DOBYNS, C. CHINAULT. (RC WB 9:157)
[Traverse DOWNMAN, the son of Jas. & Lucy (SYDNOR) DOWNMAN, was born 20 Jan 1760 (NFPR:52); Elizabeth DOWNMAN, dau. of Jas. & Lucy (SYDNOR) DOWNMAN, who was incorrectly identified as a dau. of Robt. & Eliz. DOWNMAN in MWO:340, mar. Anthony SYDNOR bef. 1777 (MWO:340); Priscilla DOWNMAN, dau. of Jas. & Lucy (SYDNOR) DOWNMAN, was born 5 Mar 1762 (NFPR:52); she mar. Jesse DAVIS, RC, bond 14 Dec 1789 (MWO:102)]

DOWNMAN, Traverse; T 13 Oct 1801; 7 Jun 1802
RC; INV; £643.19.11; includes the following Negroes: Jupiter, Rody, Archable, Susannah & her child Billy, Milly & her child Isaac, Simon, Prince, Sam. (RC WB 9:174)

DOWNMAN, Traverse; PO Oct 1801, T 15 Dec 1801; 7 Jun 1802
RC; DIV of slaves of Travers DOWNMAN among: the reps. of Anthony SYDNOR dec'd., Ann DOWNMAN, Fanny DOWNMAN, Rawleigh DOWNMAN, reps. of [Jesse] DAVIS. (RC AB 3:87)

DOWNMAN, Traverse; PO 2 Dec 1811, T 31 Dec 1811; 6 Jan 1812
RC; DIV of Negroes between the heirs of Priscilla DAVIS dec'd. agreeable to the will of Traverse DOWNMAN: Lot 1 (Susannah & girl Sally) to Sophornia DAVIS, Lot 2 (girl Cate) to Fred DAVIS, Lot 3 (boy Prince) to Samuel DAVIS, Lot 4 (boy Sam) to Hiram DAVIS, Lot 5 (boy Billy) to Thomas L. DAVIS. (RC AB 3:263)

DOWNMAN, William; 2 Mar 1819
RC; Wm. DOWNMAN aptd. gdn. to his children: Frances Eliz., Rawleigh Wm., Milly Ball, and Judith Pane. (RC OB 24:318)
[Frances E. DOWNMAN mar. Wm. M. MISKELL, RC, bond 23 Mar 1832 (MRC:134), Judith P. DOWNMAN mar. Ewell HANKS, RC, bond 6 Feb 1834 (MRC:86)]

DOZIER, J. Smith; PO 24 Mar 1823, T 13 Jan 1824; 23 Feb 1824
WC; INV, $391.58 1/3; Allen S. DOZIER admr; includes Negro Henry (age 18). (WC RI 11:385)

DOZIER, James; 26 Dec 1808
WC; Allen S. DOZIER was gdn. of Smith DOZIER who was prob. the orphan of James DOZIER. (WC Orders 1807-10:251)
[This is James Smith DOZIER who mar. Molly HUTT, dau. of Gerard & Caty HUTT, WC, bond 17 Jan 1780 (MWO:115); on the mot. of Allen S. DOZIER, Nancy S. DOZIER, Frances H. DOZIER, Nelson R. DOZIER & Smith DOZIER children & distributees of James Smith DOZIER were summoned to court to show cause why the land of James Smith DOZIER should not be sold, 27 May 1812 (WC Orders 1810-13:248)]

DOZIER, Joseph; 2 Aug 1797; Jun 1799
WC; WILL; sis. Elizabeth Walker DOZIER to receive Negro woman Betty; rest of est. to bro. Thomas DOZIER except for six pounds in gold or silver to be given to Negro girl Fanney belonging to Thomas BEALE in RC at the age of 15; Thomas DOZIER ex.; [*WITS unreadable*]. (WC Unrec Wills 1755-1800 #45)

DOZIER, Joseph; 3 Dec 1814; 23 Dec 1816

WC; WILL; son Walker DOZIER to continue at my father's where he now is; wife Sally DOZIER to have every thing that was hers before we were married; dau. Amelia C. DOZIER to have whole of wife's est. after death of wife; [no ex. named]; WITS: M. M. MARMADUKE, Jn. McCLANNAHAN. (WC DW 23:234)

[Jos. DOZIER was a son of Thos. DOZIER, Sr. (*see below*); he mar. Sally MUSE, WC, bond 16 Sep 1811 (MLBWC:20)]

DOZIER, Richard; 24 Dec 1814; 2 Nov 1818

RC; WILL; all land & est. to dau. Polly DOZIER except for one bed which I give to my son Josep[h] DOZIER if my dau. be willing; dau. Polly to have the same power to manage my affairs as if she was qualified by law as extx; WITS: Sarah P. TUNE, Reuben BRANN, Betsy BRANN. (RC WB 9:610)

DOZIER, Richard T.; PO 19 [Dec] 1808; 19 Jun 1809. LC; INV, £29.18.[14]. (LC EB 27:51)

[Rich. T. DOZIER mar. Nelly NORRIS, LC, bond 1 Jan 1808 (MLBLC:23)]

DOZIER, Thomas; T Jun 1822; [?] Feb 1823. WC; INV, $123.57. (WC RI 11:334)

DOZIER, Thomas Sr.; 21 Jan 1822; 6 May 1822

WC; WILL; lend unto my wife Nancy DOZIER all my est. during her life & at her death, I give to my son Joseph DOZIER's widow Sarah DOZIER six shillings; to dau. Mary DOZIER the house I now live in with 55 ac. of land adjoining sd. house; to son Martin P. DOZIER the old house plant. & all the balance of my land; my sis. Elizabeth W. DOZIER to live with my daughter Mary DOZIER; WITS: Jn. ANTON, Jn. SUTTON, Martha SUTTON. (WC DW 24:299)

[Nancy DOZIER extx. of will of Thos. DOZIER Sr., 27 May 1822 (WC OB 1819-23:400)]

DOZIER, Vincent; T 18 Sep 1822; 23 Feb 1824. WC; INV; includes Negroes Sam, Lavina. (WC RI 11:383)

DRAKE, Rose; [m]. WC; INV; £582.8.6.; includes Negroes Gilbert, Cyras, Peg, boy Abraham, Daniel (this Negro claimed by Mrs. DAVIS). (WC RI 8:19[4])

DRAKE, Rose; PO Nov 1801; 28 Nov 1803

WC; settlement of the admin. acct. of Thomas LARKIN on the est. of Rose DRAKE; it appears by the foregoing settlement on the part of Samuel TEMPLEMAN admr. of John DRAKE whose est. is interested in the settlement aforesaid it was suggested by TEMPLEMAN that all the cattle which Rose DRAKE died possessed of was the prop. of John DRAKE his intestate and upon having the matter fully explained we are of the opinion that they ought to be considered the prop. of Rose DRAKE in as much as John DRAKE his intestate received a Negro from his father's est. which exonerated any claim for the cattle as appeared by an agreement between John DRAKE & his bros & sisters at the time they made a friendly settlement & division among themselves. On the part of the sd. Samuel TEMPLEMAN who conceived he was doing his duty in like manner he objected to the admrs. giving up the horses on the plant. of the sd. Rose DRAKE at the time of his death, so Thomas DAVIS who claimed them in right of his wife Sarah DAVIS & upon consideration we are of opinion that the horses claimed by the sd. DAVIS are not the prop. of Rose DRAKE & we believe them to be the prop. of sd. DAVIS. 31 Oct 1803; DIV of est. of Rose DRAKE among: John DRAKE's est: Gilbert & Cyrus; John BOWEN in right of his wife: Daniel; Thomas DAVIS in right of his wife; Abram; Thomas LARKIN in right of his wife: Peggy, Davy (child), Reuben. (WC RI 8:366)

[Jn. DRAKE, son of Rose, d. in WC 1798; in his will he named his mother Rose, his wife Anne, his son Francis Thomas, and his sisters Sarah DRAKE, Leannah LARKIN, and Rachel BOWEN (WC DW 19:353); Jn. BOWEN mar. Rachel DRAKE, dau. of Rose DRAKE, WC, bond 5 Feb 1787; Thos. DAVIS mar. Sally DRAKE, dau. of Rose DRAKE, WC, bond [1799] (MLBWC:7, 18); Thos. LARKIN mar. Leannah DRAKE, WC, bond 29 Nov 1784 (MWO:220)]

DUDLEY, John; T 7 Jul 1815; 2 Apr 1821. RC; INV, $1054.65 3/4. (RC WB 9:698)
[Frances & William were children of Jn. DUDLEY (RC OB 24:1816-20:15); Fanny DUDLEY orphan of Jn. DUDLEY chose Fleet B. PLUMMER as her gdn., and he was aptd. gdn. of Wm. DUDLEY also an orphan of Jn. DUDLEY, 5 Jun 1820 (RC OB 25:28, 29); Rawleigh DOWNMAN ex. of Jas. D. SYDNOR, pltf., vs. Griffin DUDLEY, Thos. DUDLEY, Fanny DUDLEY & Wm. DUDLEY heirs of Jn. DUDLEY dec'd, 7 Mar 1822 (RC OB 25:270); Wm. DUDLEY orphan of Jn. DUDLEY chose Griffin G. DUDLEY as his gdn., 7 Mar 1825 (RC OB 26:284); Griffin DUDLEY is a son and admr. of Jn. DUDLEY, 5 Sep 1825 (RC OB 27:2)]

DUDLEY, Landon; PO 20 Feb 1815, T 2 Mar [1815]; 18 Dec 1815. LC; INV. (LC EB 27:275)
[This is apparently the Landon DUDLEY who was head of a household in NC in 1810; Jn. ROGERS aptd. gdn. of Peggy, Jas., Thos., Wm., & Anna DUDLEY orphans of Landon DUDLEY, 19 Feb 1816 (LC Orders 24:283); Joel RIVEER aptd. gdn. to Peggy DUDLEY orphan of Landon DUDLEY, 16 Feb 1818 (LC Orders 24:415); Jn. ROGERS gdn. of Thos. DUDLEY orphan of Landon DUDLEY authorized to bind out Thos. DUDLEY to Joel REVEER, 21 Sep 1818 (LC OB 25:19); Joel REVEER aptd. gdn. to Thos., Jas. and Ann DUDLEY orphans of Landon DUDLEY, 21 Jul 1823 (LC OB 25:390)]

DUDLEY, Polly ; PO 19 Feb 1816; 19 Mar 1816. LC ; INV, $77.50. (LC EB 27:288)
[Polly was a dau. of Jas. REVERE, *see below* (LC Orders 24:430)]

DUFF, William; PO 6 Jan 1818; 1 Mar 1824. RC; INV, $29.25; includes one fiddle. (RC WB 10:34)

DUNAWAY, Ann; 18 Jul 1811; 16 Sep 1811
LC; WILL; dau. Molly C. BAILEY; George D. BAILEY; Elizabeth Opie DUNAWAY; rest of prop. to be eq. div. among my children Opie DUNAWAY, Molly C. BAILEY & William DUN[AW]AY; [no ex. named]; WITS: Charles BAILEY, Judith NEWGENT, Sarah DOWNMAN, Margaret DOWNMAN; [certif granted Opie DUNAWAY to obtain letters of admin]. (LC WB 28:123)
[This is Ann DAVENPORT who mar. Sam. DUNAWAY, LC, bond 18 Dec 1778 (MLBLC:24); in his will (LC 8 Apr 1789-15 Jun 1789) Sam. DUNAWAY named his wife Ann and children Geo. Davenport, Opey, Molly Chowning, Sam., Jn., and Wm. (LC WB 22:210); Mary Chowning DUNAWAY, dau. of Sam. & Nancy DUNAWAY, born 18 Mar 1781, mar. Chas. BAILEY, LC, bond 2 Apr 1802 (MLBLC:2)]

DUNAWAY, Ann; PO 16 Sep 1811, T 5 Oct 1811); [15 Feb 1813]. LC ; INV; includes slave Adam. (LC EB 27:143)

DUNAWAY, Elizabeth; 3 Dec 1801; 21 Dec 1801
LC; WILL; to bro. James L. NORRIS my land that my father George NORRIS gave me which contains 150 ac. provided that he shall give up his right & title of the land that his father left him to his bro. John NORRIS; bed & furniture to my mother; WITS: Presley SANDERS, Hannah NORRIS, Nancy NORRIS; LC WB 28:57)

[In MWO:117 the Eliz. NORRIS who mar. Geo. C. DUNAWAY was identified as prob. a dau. of Jn. NORRIS (d. LC 1789), but it is clear from this document that she was a dau. of George NORRIS; see also LC CCs 1805-022 and 1806-001 for more on the 150 ac. and the NORRIS and DUNAWAY families]

DUNAWAY, George C.; PO 21 Jul 1800, T 25 Jul [1800]; 18 Jan 1802. LC ; INV, $118.99. (LC EB 24:168)

DUNAWAY, John; 1 Jun 1814; 17 Oct 1814
LC; WILL; land I now live on containing 152 ac. which I originally bought from Reuben MITCHELL, Joseph SHEARMAN & Richard TAPSCOTT also my Negro Siller & her youngest child David to son John DUNAWAY; use of my plant. in RC w/o he now lives containing 54 ac. to son Samuel DUNAWAY; at son Samuel's death land to go to grson. George Washington DUNAWAY; Negro girl Julia to dau. Fanny DUNAWAY; Negro girl Judy to dau. Lucy BARRICK; Negro girl Hannah to dau. Betsey DUNAWAY; rest of est. to be eq. div. between my children: John DUNAWAY, Fanny DUNAWAY, Peggy PERCIFULL, Lucy BARRICK, & Betsey DUNAWAY & my grson. John Joseph DUNAWAY; son John ex; WITS: C[hichester] TAPSCOTT, Nicholas GEORGE, Wm. B. MITCHELL. (LC WB 28:149)
[Margaret DUNAWAY mar. Jn. Y. PERCIFULL, LC, bond 11 Apr 1812; Lucy DUNAWAY mar. Wm. BARROCK, LC, bond 23 Nov 1813; (MLBLC:3, 58); Reubin BARRACK aptd. gdn. to Jn. Jos. DUNAWAY orphan of Jn. DUNAWAY, 20 Feb 1815 (LC Orders 24:215)]

DUNAWAY, John; T 2 Mar 1815; 15 May 1815
LC; INV; includes Negroes: Sillah, Juliet, Jude, Hannah. (LC EB 27:200)

DUNAWAY, Mary; 23 May 1800; 15 Feb 1808
LC; WILL; to son Chattin DUNAWAY my Negro man Harry; to dau. Judy NUGEN[T] my Negro woman Alice; rest of est. to be eq. div. amongst my children: Nancy DUNAWAY, Chattin DUNAWAY & Milly CARTER; son Chattin DUNAWAY & s-i-l Martin CARTER exors; WITS: Jn. CHOWNING, Jn. CHOWNING Jr. (LC WB 28:105)
[Judith DUNAWAY mar. Thos. NUGENT, LC, bond 15 Oct 1798; Milly DUNAWAY mar. Martin CARTER, LC, bond 16 Feb 1786 (MLBLC:12, 56)]

DUNAWAY, Milly; 17 Mar 1818
LC; on the mot. of William CURRELL & Polly his wife & Thomas NEWGENT & Fanny his wife, ord. that James LAWRY, Lucy LAWRY & John LAWRY Jr. inf. children of John LAWRY be summoned to show cause why the lands of Milly DUNAWAY who was Milly HILL should not be sold; John LAWRY aptd. gdn. to his inf. children; on the mot. of William CURRELL & Polly his wife & Thomas NEWGENT & Fanny his wife, ord. that James LAWRY, Lucy LAWRY & John LAWRY Jr. inf. children of John LAWRY be summoned to show cause why the lands of Fanny PITMAN who was Fanny HILL should not be sold; John LAWRY aptd. gdn. to his inf. children. (LC Orders 24:421)
[This is Milly HILL, dau. of Eliz. HILL (d. LC 1796) q.v., who mar. Chattin DUNAWAY, LC, bond 14 Dec 1791 (MLBLC:23); Thos. NEWGENT mar. Fanny LAWRY, LC, bond 15 May 1815; Jn. LAWRY mar. Betty HILL, LC, bond 24 Dec 1791 (MLBLC:49, 54); Frances HILL mar. Thos. PITMAN, LC, bond 6 Jan 1791 (MLBLC:60)]

DUNAWAY, Presley; PO 7 Feb 1814; 1 Jul 1816. RC; INV, $238.25. (RC WB 9:539)
[Presley DUNAWAY mar. Alice DOBYNS, RC, bond 25 Dec 1811 (MRC:61)]

DUNAWAY, Samuel; PO 16 Sep 1811, T 5 Oct 1811; 15 Feb 1813
LC; INV of the est. unadministered by Joseph DAVENPORT dec'd his ex; includes Negroes: Armestead, Isaac, Abraham, James, Sarah, Winney & her child Hannah, Patty & her child Seller, Jesse, Billy, Penny, Lucy; DIV of slaves among: Opie DUNAWAY, Charles BAYLIE in behalf of his wife & William DUNAWAY. (LC EB 27:142, 144)
[*see* Ann DUNAWAY *above*]

DUNAWAY, Thomas; 21 Jan 1799; 19 Jan 1801
LC; WILL; to wife Susanna DUNAWAY whole est. during her life; at wife's death, land & plant. containing 80 ac. & Negro man Henry to my son Rawleigh DUNAWAY; daus. Caty, Ellen, & Axsah DUNAWAY to enjoy a home with my wife and son as long as they remain unmarried; at wife's death whole est. to be eq. div. among my four children: Rawleigh, Caty, Ellen, & Axsah; son Rawleigh ex; WITS: Rawleigh TAPSCOTT, Thos. REVEER, Thaddeus GOODRIDGE. (LC WB 28:47)
[Thos. DUNAWAY, of CCP, LC, mar. Susannah FINDLEY, dau. of Jn. FINDLEY, bef 21 Jan 1779 (MWO:117)]

DUNAWAY, Thomas; PO 20 Jul 1801; 20 Apr 1802
LC; INV, £471.11.8; includes Negroes: Mary, Ruth, Easther, Siller, Ben, Will, Matilda, Hannah. (LC EB 24:186)

DUNAWAY, William; 14 Mar 1798; 19 Jun 1798
LC; WILL; all est. to mother Mary DUNAWAY except my gun to my bro. George DUNAWAY; uncle John CHOWNING ex.; WITS: Edw. BLAKEMORE, Jn. CHOWNING. (LC WB 28:29)
[Mary DUNAWAY was a dau. of Chattin CHOWNING (d. LC 1771) (LC WB 20:28)]

DUNTON, William; 21 May 1810
LC; Sarah DUNTON was wid. & admx. of William DUNTON and along with William, Catherine & Thomas an heir of sd. William. (LC Orders 23B 1808-11:182)
[Wm. DUNTON mar. Sarah GEORGE, dau. of Benj. & Cath. GEORGE, LC, bond 8 Apr 1794 (MLBLC:23); *see also LC CC 1810-008*]

DYE, Sarah Ann; 16 May 1814
LC; Sarah Ann DYE, lately a pensioner residing in this county, died on 31 Dec 1813; she was gdn. to Sarah Chilton DYE. (LC Orders 24:187)
[Sarah Ann DYE was the dau. of Stephen CHILTON and sis. of Wm. CHILTON, *see above*]

ECKLES, Solomon; 18 Mar 1778; 25 Mar 17[??].
CP, WC; WILL; all land made over to me by John MOORE to son William ECKLES alias SPENCE; rest of est. to be eq. div. between son William ECKLES alias SPENCE and d-i-l Elizabeth SPENCE and s-i-l Thomas SPENCE; son to have three year's schooling and d-i-l to have one year; son and d-i-l to be schooled and brought up by David AUSTIN until son is 16 and dau. is [*several words unclear*]; if son die before age 21, land to go to sis. Hannah HALL alias ECKLES; trusty friends Dan. BAILEY & Jn. MOORE exors; WITS: Dan. BAILEY, Vincent BAILEY, [Jas.] BAILEY; NB: Fiddle is given to William ECKLES alias SPENCE. (WC Unrec Wills 1755-1800 #32)
[Will was proved by oath of Vincent BAILEY and lodged for further proof; there is a record for the mar. of Hannah ECKLES to Bennett McGUY, WC, bond 1 Dec 1787 (MWO:241)]

EDMONDS, Elias; 20 Dec 1802

LC; Polly EDMONDS orphan of Elias EDMONDS chose Caty BOND as her gdn. (LC Orders V 1802-03:250)
[Elias EDMONDS was a merchant who had a store in Kilmarnock (LC CC 1819-010); Polly Bond EDMONDS, orphan of Elias EDMONDS, chose Anthony SYDNOR as her gdn., 21 Sep 1807 (LC Orders D22 1805-08:403)]

EDMONDS, Elias; 18 Nov 1816
LC; Jn. HALL aptd. gdn. of Susan EDMONDS orphan of [Elias] EDMONDS. (LC Orders 24:341)
[Susanna EDMONDS was the wid. of Elias EDMONDS who d. intest. on 2 May 1816; one of his sons Ralph EDMONDS qualified as his admr.; Elias left 10 other children: Frances F. GLASCOCK (who by 1820 was a wid.), Janette P. WADDY wife of Benj. WADDY, Susanna HALL wife of Addison HALL, Elias, Jn. W. A., Wm., Robt., Eliz., Philip, and Margaret M. EDMONDS (LC CC 1820-064); on the mot. of Benj. WADDEY & Janetta P. his wife, Addison HALL & Susan his wife, Elias EDMONDS, Jn. [M.] A. EDMONDS, Wm. EDMONDS & Frances F. EFFORD ord. that Ralph EDMONDS, Jn. A. EDMONDS, Eliz. EDMONDS, Robt. EDMONDS, Philip EDMONDS & Margaret M. EDMONDS heirs of Elias EDMONDS dec'd be summoned to show cause why the lands of which Elias EDMONDS died seized should not be sold and the proceeds div. among his legal reps., 21 Aug 1826 (LC OB 26:202-203); Benj. WADDEY mar. Janette P. EDMONDS, LC, bond 27 Nov 1817 (MLBLC:76); Addison HALL mar. Susan EDMONDS, LC, bond 1 Jan 1817 (MLBLC:34); *do not confuse* Elias EDMONDS *with* Elias EDWARDS or Ellis EDWARDS of NC]

EDRINGTON, Christopher; 31 Jan 1803; 22 Apr 1805
WC; WILL; friend James [D.] DISHMAN choice of merchandise on hand at time of death at a credit of eq. payments of 9, 18, 24 & 30 months; whole of property to son William P. EDRINGTON & he to be supported during his minority; bro. Edmund EDRINGTON entitled to 1/3 of any profit on my business since 1 April last & also to a sum eq. to £50 per annum for his services in my business; former servant & faithful friend Negro Daniel $50 12 months after my decease; if son die before age 21 or without issue, £100 to niece Mary Diggs ASHMORE, £100 each to sisters Susanna STEWARD, Frances BERRYMAN, & Catherine PORTER, £500 to bro. Edmund EDRINGTON; residue after this distribution to be eq. div. between bro. & sis. Elizabeth EDRINGTON; bro. Edmund & friend James D. DISHMAN exors; WITS: Rich. THOMPSON, [S. Jos.] Slaughter BROWN, Wm. THOMPSON. (WC DW 21:168)
[Christopher EDRINGTON was a nephew of James DEGGES (d. WC 1778) (WC DW 16:21, DW 17:168)]

EDRINGTON, Christopher; [m]; 22 Jul 1805
WC; INV, includes Negroes: Reubin, Tom, Solomon, Ben, Patty. (WC RI 8:556)

EDSOR, Joseph; 4 Jul 1779; [m]
WC; WILL; sis. Katharine REED; nephew John QUESENBURY when he comes of age; friend Daniel McCARTY ex; WITS: Jn. CARR, Eliz. GRANGER. (WC Unrec Wills 1755-1800 #18)

EDWARDS, Elias; PO 13 Mar 1809, T 16 Mar 1809; 12 Mar 1810
NC; INV, [m]. (NC RB 18:337)
[Eliz. EDWARDS was apt. gdn. of Eliz. N. EDWARDS orphan of Elias EDWARDS, NC, 8 May 1815 (NC OB 1811-15:318); there are two marriages recorded for an Elias EDWARDS of NC: (1) to Jane PICKRON, dau. of Geo.

PICKRON, NC, bond 9 Mar 1793 and (2) to Eliz. BEETLEY, NC, bond 17 Mar 1804 (MLBNC:33)]

EDWARDS, Ellis; 5 Jul 1818; 4 Dec 1818
NC; WILL; dau. Lucy EDWARDS; dau. Rebeckah B. EDWARDS; dau. Polly M. EDWARDS; son Haynes P. EDWARDS; son Broday EDWARDS; son Griffin EDWARDS; Elizabeth CURTIS; son William EDWARDS; Hannah M. EDWARDS [my grchild.] $25 to be left in the hands of my dau. Lucy EDWARDS; rest of est. to be eq. div. between my children: Lucy EDWARDS, Rebeckah EDWARDS, Griffin EDWARDS, Haynes EDWARDS, Brody EDWARDS, & Polly EDWARDS; son Haynes EDWARDS & Royston B. COVINGTON exors; WITS: Royston B. COVINGTON, Thos. TIGNOR. (NC RB 21:544)

EDWARDS, Ellis; PO 14 Dec 1818, T 12 Feb 1819; 4 Jun 1819
NC; INV, $302.49 3/4; DIV of est; the heirs are: Griffin EDWARDS, Hayns EDWARDS, Brawdus [sic] EDWARDS, Thomas TIGNOR, Rebeccah B. EDWARDS, Polly M. EDWARDS. (NC RB 22:56)
[Thos. TIGNOR mar. Lucy EDWARDS, NC, bond 29 Sep 1818 (MLBNC:101)]

EDWARDS, George; PO 14 Feb 1803; 13 Sep 1803. NC £126.1.10 1/2. (NC RB 17:47)

EDWARDS, George; 13 Nov 1826
NC; Griffin EDWARDS aptd. gdn. of Royston, Opie & Nancy EDWARDS orphans of George EDWARDS. (NC OB 1825-30:126)
[On the mot. of Griffin EDWARDS & Jos. EDWARDS, ord. that Royston, Opie & Nancy EDWARDS children & heirs with sd. Griffin & Jos. of Geo. EDWARDS be summoned to show cause why lands of sd. Geo. should not be sold, [9] Jul 1827 (NC OB 1825-30:188)]

EDWARDS, John; PO 12 Jan 1801; 9 Feb 1801. NC; INV, £23.19.6. (NC RB 16:222)

EDWARDS, John; T 19 Apr 1815; 1[5] May 1815
LC; INV; includes Negroes: Jack, Simon, George, Daniel, [Seacer], Mitchell, Isaac, Isbelle, [Diner], Winney, Lucy, children [sic], Spencer, Anthony, Jessee, Peggy, Judy, Moses, Matilda, Sharlot, James, Lee, Fanny, Levina, Edmond, Jinny, Aggy, Cato, Betty, Isaac, Anny, Sam. (LC EB 27:195)
[David EDWARDS orphan of Jn. EDWARDS chose Geo. P. OLIVER as his gdn., 15 Apr 1816 (LC Orders 24:297); Bidkar GEORGE aptd. gdn. to Eliz. EDWARDS orphan of Jn. EDWARDS, 20 May 1816 (LC Orders 24:300); Moses LUNSFORD aptd. gdn. to Mary EDWARDS orphan of Jn. EDWARDS, 21 Jun 1819 (LC OB 25:66)]

EDWARDS, John; 21 Aug 1820
LC; on the mot. of Rich. Davis EDWARDS ord. that Enoch GEORGE gdn. of Jn., Roxa, Lucy & Susan KEMM heirs of Lucy KEMM & Bidkar GEORGE gdn. of Betsy EDWARDS be summoned to show cause why the land of which Mary S. EDWARDS orphan of Jn. EDWARDS died seized should not be sold for the purpose of a division with the exception of the dower of Moses LUNSFORD & wife. (LC OB 25:153)
[Moses LUNSFORD mar. Margaret EDWARDS the wid. of Jn. EDWARDS, LC, bond 11 Jun 1819 (MLBLC:49; LC OB 25:153)]

EDWARDS, Judith; T 21 Nov 1807; 10 Oct 1808
NC; INV, [m]; includes Negroes Judah, girls Polly, Nancy, & Mariah, boy Sam. (NC RB 18:42)

EDWARDS, Lancelot L.; PO 12 Mar 1812, T 8 Jun 1812; 10 Aug 1812

NC; Chancery suit, Thomas HARVEY against Lucy, Leroy, Sally, Richard & Samuel EDWARDS infants and only children of Lancelot L. EDWARDS; Richard EDWARDS appointed gdn. to the defts.; defts. ord to pay the complt. $97.48 with interest from 13 Mar 1810, $41 with interest from 13 Jan 1811 & the costs of the suit; also ord. that water grist mill and ac. of land be sold and the bond taken be payable to the complt. for the amount of his claim and any balance paid to the defts; mill was sold to Edwin NELMS for $286; HARVEY rec'd $160.85. (NC RB 19:233)
[Lancelot L. EDWARDS mar. Nancy W. HUDNALL, dau. of Lucy HUDNALL, NC, bond 19 Oct 1798 (MLBNC:34); In her will (NC 18 Aug 1810-14 Jun 1813), Lucy HUDNALL named her grchildren Lucy Ann, Sally Hudnall, Elizabeth Sally, Leroy, Richard, and Sam EDWARDS (NC RB 19:399); Rich. EDWARDS was aptd. gdn. of Lucy, Leroy, Sally, Rich., and Sam. orphans of Lancelot L. EDWARDS, NC, 14 Jun 1813 (NC OB 1811-15:176); Lucy Ann EDWARDS orphan of Lancelot EDWARDS chose Hiram BLACKWELL as her gdn., NC, 8 May 1815 (NC OB 1811-15:315); Wm. JETT was aptd. gdn. of Leroy, Sally, Rich. & Sam. EDWARDS orphans of Lancelot EDWARDS, NC, 11 Mar 1816 (NC OB 1816-20:11); master commissioner to settle Wm. JETT's acct. of his gdnship. of Rich. & Sam. EDWARDS orphans of Lan. L. EDWARDS, 12 Jun 1826 (NC OB 1825-30:92)]

EDWARDS, Leroy; PO 13 Oct 1800; 12 Apr 1802
NC; INV, [m]; includes Negroes Daniel, Marcus, Betty & child Criss, Aggatha, Harry. (NC RB 16:359)
[Leroy EDWARDS served for "nine months and 7 years as a captain during the Revolutionary War" (VS1776 I:180); in his will (NC 24 Dec 1799-13 Oct 1800), Leroy EDWARDS named his dau. Louisa EDWARDS, his wife Molly, his bro. Griffin EDWARDS and his nephew Rich. EDWARDS; his military lands in the Western Country were to be eq. div. between his bro. & nephew; he freed his Negro man James (NC RB 16:181); Patrick SPILLER mar. Louisa the only child of Leroy EDWARDS dec'd, late a capt. in the army of the Rev., 13 Mar 1826 (NC OB 1825-30:69); Louisa EDWARDS mar. (1) Dr. Thos. BALL, NC, bond 26 Mar 1800 and (2) Patrick SPILLER,NC, bond 21 Feb 1818 (MLBNC:4, 94)]

EDWARDS, Leroy; PO 12 Jan 1801; 13 Jun 1803
NC; allotted to Mary EDWARDS her dower in the est. of her late husband (included lower lot of [tendable] land and the upper lot of wood land, 17 apple trees at the north end of the orchard & one third of the peach orchard & Negro Daniel). (NC RB 16:555)

EDWARDS, Lucy; PO 21 Apr 1817, T Jan 1818; 19 Jan 1818. LC; INV, $273.64 1/4. (LC EB 27:402)

EDWARDS, Presley, William & Martin; PO 13 Mar 1815, T 18 Mar 1815; 11 Apr 1815
NC; INV, Presley EDWARDS' est. cash $12.50; William EDWARDS' est. cash $18.50 & Negro girl Maria; Martin EDWARDS' est. Negroes Judith & young child Elizabeth, girl Nancy, girl Lucy; allotment of Negroes among the heirs of the dec'd Presley, William & Martin EDWARDS: Ellis EDWARDS (Negro woman Judith & her young child Elizabeth), David HAYNIE (girl Nancy, girl Lucy), Peggy WOOD's children (girl Maria). (NC RB 20:56)
[David HAYNIE, wid., mar. Eliz. EDWARDS, NC, bond 3 Feb 1794 (MLBNC:48)]

EDWARDS, Presley, William & Martin; PO 13 Mar 1815, T 7 May 1816; 13 May 1816

NC; DIV of est. of Presley, William & Martin EDWARDS dec'd among the legal reps. viz. we find that as a former div. has been made on the est. of Steptoe EDWARDS supposed to be dead & since has returned and we find the est. of Presley, William & Martin EDWARDS to be a balance in the hands of the admr. of $48.75 and two Negro girls Nancy & Maria; est. was div. among Steptoe EDWARDS (whole share $179.50), Ellis EDWARDS (half share), David HAYNIE (half share), Robert EDWARDS, Peggy WOOD & John MASON (half share). (NC RB 20:444)
[Presley, Wm., Martin, & Steptoe EDWARDS were sons of Judith EDWARDS (d. NC 1805) (NC RB 17:91)]

EDWARDS, Richard; PO 13 Feb 1815; 11 Mar 1816
NC; INV, [m]; includes $45 cash found in house, a number of books and Negroes Moses, Jo, Nelly; on p. 374 is an acct. of the sales of EDWARDS' est. which provides names of those who bought his books; William JETT bought *The Turkish Spy, The Jewish Spy,* and the *Spectator*; John BOOTH bought a testament and an English dictionary; Thomas DOWNING and Fleming BATES also bought books. (NC RB 20:370, 371, 374)
[In his will (NC 3 Jan 1815-13 Feb 1815) Rich. EDWARDS named his dau. Eliz. Salley EDWARDS, Charlotte P. WOOD (who rec'd $30 annually on the 1st day of January for 10 years) and his uncle Leroy EDWARDS (NC RB 19:623); the *Turkish Spy* no doubt refers to the eight-volume work *Letters Writ by a Turkish Spy Who Lived Five and Forty Years Undiscover'd at Paris* which were published in English between 1691 and 1694. The first volume was probably written by the Italian Giovanni Paolo Marana. *The Jewish Spy* or *Lettres juives* is a novel written between 1738 and 1742 probably by the Marquis d'Argens. *The Spectator* was the daily periodical of Joseph Addison and Richard Steele published in 1711, 1712 and 1714]

EDWARDS, Richard; 10 May 1819; William EDWARDS aptd. gdn. of Richard, Alice, Molly, and Leroy EDWARDS orphans of Richard EDWARDS. (NC OB 1816-20:353)

EDWARDS, Robert (Capt.); PO 13 Dec 1802, T 21 Dec 1802; 12 Apr 1803
NC; INV, £11[8]5.17.0; includes Negroes old man Bob, Dinah, Lewis, Hannah, child Grace, Betty, Milley, Fanny, Nanny, child James, Sharlotte, Sarah, Solomon, Nacca, Bill, Sam, Betty, Ezekiel, Peter, Aggy, Juliet, Harriet, Robert, Lucy. (NC RB 16:539)

EDWARDS, Robert; PO 9 Jul 1816; 14 Oct 1816. NC; INV, [m]. (NC RB 21:90)

EDWARDS, Robert; PO 9 Sep 1816, T 20 Sep 1816; 13 Jan 1817
NC; allotted Jane EDWARDS her thirds part of the est. of her late husband Robert EDWARDS; also allotted Jane EDWARDS ($75.[38]), Walter EDWARDS ($50.52 1/8), Elias EDWARDS ($50.52 1/8), & Rebecca EDWARDS ($50.52 1/8) their parts of the est. of $225.36 in the hands of George EDWARDS admr. of Robert EDWARDS dec'd. (NC RB 21:140)
[Robt. EDWARDS, wid, mar. Jane B. WOOD, NC, bond 18 Apr 1815; Walter & Elias EDWARDS orphans of Robert EDWARDS chose Wm. JETT as their gdn., Rebecca EDWARDS chose Ellis GILL as her gdn. NC, 9 Sep 1816 (NC OB 1816-20:87); Sam. DOWNING aptd. gdn. of Robt. A. EDWARDS orphan of Robt. EDWARDS, NC 8 Jul 1822 (NC OB 1820-25:221), but it is not clear if this is the same Robt. EDWARDS as the above]

EDWARDS, Thomas; 15 Dec 18[07]; 12 Jan 1818
RC; WILL; use of all est. to wife during her life; to dau. Sally B. EDWARDS for her great attention to me in my sickness my Negro boy Jack; my fishing shore land to remain in possession of my wife till after 1817 & from that time

I give to my son Joseph [C.] EDWARDS the use of the sd. land exclusive of the fishing shore until the death of his mother; after her death I leave the sd. fishing shore land & the fishing shore attached thereto to be eq. div. between my two daus. Anne Mariah EDWARDS & Sally B. EDWARDS; after wife's death I leave the plant. w/o I now live to my son Joseph C. EDWARDS; two small Negroes Lucy & Mary to wife; son Joseph ex.; WITS: Cyrus SUTTON, Reeves OWENS. (NC RB 21:344)

EDWARDS, Thomas (Capt.); PO 12 Jan 1818; 18 Aug 1818
NC; INV, $4249; includes the following Negroes: Mitchel, Randall, Armstead, Jack, Ned, Dominick, Jude, Margary, Pheby, Alberd, Luce, Mary. (NC RB 21:469)

EDWARDS, William (Capt.); PO 24 Aug 1807; 23 Nov 1807
WC; INV, [m]; includes Negroes Judah, Sarah, Philitia, Natt, James, Sall, George, Henry, Jenny, Sophia. (WC RI 9:35)

EDWARDS, William; 7 Jan 1812; 17 Feb 1812
LC; WILL; land & plant. w/o I now live & Negroes Burgess & Fanny (now in the possession of Thomas KENT of NC) to son John EDWARDS; son Dale C. EDWARDS; Negro woman Judith & her 3 children James, Polly & Chidister to dau. Frankey EDWARDS; use of my Negro woman Letty to son James EDWARDS; use of Negro woman Sharlotte to son Cyrus EDWARDS; Negro girl Mahala to be sold to pay debts; friend James TOWLES & James CARTER exors; WITS: Jas. CARTER, Chattin DUNAWAY. (LC WB 28:125)

EDWARDS, William; PO 17 Feb 1812, T 11 Mar 1812; 20 Jul 1812
LC; INV; includes Negroes: James, Birgess, Letty, Judith, Sarah, Charlotte, Matilda, James, Polly, Chichester. (LC EB 27:113)

EDWARDS, William; PO 17 Nov 1812, T 30 Nov 1812; 21 Dec 1812
LC; DIV of est. among the legatees according to his will: Fanny EDWARDS, Cyrus EDWARDS, John EDWARDS. (LC EB 27:130)

EDWARDS, William; PO 28 Sep 1812, T 20 Oct 1812; 23 May 1814
WC; DIV of proceeds from sale of Negroes among Thomas, Susan, Alice & Lucy EDWARDS & Elliott PORTER who mar. Frances EDWARDS orphans of the sd. William EDWARDS; each received $128.10. (WC RI 9:424; Orders 1810-13:268)
[This is the Rev. Wm. EDWARDS who mar. Frankey POPE; Elliott PORTER mar. Frances EDWARDS, dau. of Frankey EDWARDS, WC, bond 5 Feb 1807 (MLBWC:55); Elliott PORTER aptd. gdn. of Thos., Susan, Alice, and Lucy EDWARDS orphans of Wm. EDWARDS, 24 Dec 1810 (WC Orders 1810-13:74); Thos. and Susan EDWARDS orphans of Wm. EDWARDS chose Rich. L. BATTIN as their gdn., 23 Dec 1811 (WC Orders 1810-13:190); Rich. BATTIN aptd. gdn. of Alice & [Lucy] EDWARDS orphans of Wm. EDWARDS, 27 Dec 1813 (WC Orders 1810-13:379); the confusing CC Edwards &c vs Edwards &c, WC, 1846-01 B15 prob. contains information on this family (WCCP:65)]

EDWARDS, William; PO 26 Feb 1816, T 18 Jun 1816; 24 Jun 1816
WC; settlement of the gdnship. acct. of Richard BATTIN on the estates of Richard EDWARDS, William EDWARDS, Alice EDWARDS & Lucy EDWARDS orphans of William EDWARDS. (WC RI 10:79; OB 1814-18:247)
[Rich. BATTIN was the gdn. of Eliz., [Thos.], Susan, Rich., Wm., Alice & Lucy EDWARDS orphans of Capt. Wm. EDWARDS; his wid. was Fanny EDWARDS, 26 Sep 1808 (WC Orders 1807-10:198)]

EFFORD, George; PO 8 Jul 1816, T 7 Mar 1818; 14 Dec 1818

NC; Thomas BELL gdn. of John, William & Zachariah EFFORD heirs of George EFFORD who died intestate; land belonging to sd. George EFFORD sold to Samuel BROMBLEY for $106 to be div. among heirs. (NC RB 21:554; OB 1816-20:61)

EFFORD, John; PO Jan 1789, T 24 Jan 1789; 9 Feb 1789
NC; DIV of slaves; to William EFFORD, son of John EFFORD, Negro Job; to Hannah EFFORD Negroes Ussee & Cate; to Elizabeth EFFORD Negro girl Lucy; to Lewis EFFORD Negro woman Sarah; to Catharine EFFORD Negro woman Phillis; to Anne EFFORD Negro woman Rachael. (NC GA 1788-1824:12)
[Jn. EFFORD apparently had two wives, (1) Mary [GARNER], dau. of Parish GARNER (d. NC 1761) & sis. of Sam. & Wm. Parker GARNER, whom he must have mar. bef. 1767 and (2) Catrine HAYNIE, dau. of Hezekiah HAYNIE, whom he mar. c. 1775; Mary was the mother of Wm. (b. 1767), Hannah, and Eliz. (b. 1771); Catrine was the mother of Lewis, Nancy (b. 1778), and Catrine; Catrine (HAYNIE) EFFORD mar. (2) Wm. WALKER bef. 1789; NC CC 1796-003 makes it clear that Catrine HAYNIE was the wid. of Jn. EFFORD bef. she mar. Wm. WALKER; Hannah EFFORD mar. Wm. BRYANT, RC, bond 7 Jan 1792 (SSPR;47, NC RB 5:482, RB 10:126, CC 1796-003; MRC:29)]

EFFORD, John; PO 14 Apr 1800; 9 Jun 1800. NC; INV, [m]. (NC RB 16:131)

EFFORD, Lewis; 13 Feb 1815, T 2 Mar 1815; 14 Mar 1815. NC; INV, $329.79 1/2. (NC RB 20:29)

EFFORD, Lewis; 13 Sep 1819; 13 Nov 1820
NC; Chancery suit; Janetta EFFORD by Samuel ASHBURN her next friend against Eliza & Olivia EFFORD infants of Lewis EFFORD dec'd by Richard C. LITTRELL their gdn.; commission appointed to sell a tract of land belonging to the infant heirs of Lewis EFFORD dec'd; the heirs Janetta EFFORD, Olivia EFFORD & Eliza EFFORD each received $53.83 1/3 cents. (NC RB 22:430; NC CC 1819-003)
[Jn. ROGERS aptd. gdn. of Janetta, Olivia & Eliza orphans of Lewis EFFORD, NC 9 Jul 1821 (NC OB 1820-25:118)]

EFFORD, Richard; T 13 May 1824; 2 Aug 1824. RC; INV, $12.63. (RC WB 10:45)
[This is prob. Rich. EFFORD who mar. Frances F. GLASCOCK, wid., RC, bond 6 Feb 1821 (MRC:63)]

EFFORD, Samuel; 24 Nov 1824; 2 May 1825
RC; WILL; plant. & all prop. to wife during her life; after her death to be eq. div. between four of my children: Nancy EFFORD, John B. EFFORD, Polly Lucinda EFFORD, & Fanny D. EFFORD; my plant. I give to my son Samuel & also my [vessel] I desire him to have; son Samuel EFFORD Jr. ex; WITS: Jas. H. RUST, Jn. W. WOOLLARD, Cath. W. WOOLLARD. (RC WB 10:72)

ELLIOTT, Alexander; 14 May 1812; 17 Apr 1818
LC; WILL; after debts are paid balance of est. to wife Judith ELLIOTT during her life; at wife's death to son Robert D. ELLIOTT; if there is enough money son Robert to have one year of schooling; friends George [GRESHAM], Thomas TAYLOR & Thomas FLINT exors; WITS: David F. DAVENPORT, Burgess BROWN. (LC WB 28:189)
[Alex. ELLIOTT mar. Judith DAVIS, LC, bond 17 Jun 1794 (MLBLC:26)]

ELLISTON, John S[hapleigh]; 31 Jan 1801; 9 Feb 1801
NC; D of G; for good will and affection gives following Negroes: Pharo, Ben, Armstead, Silla, Patty & Mary and future increase to his children John S.

ELLISTON, Thomas, James, Philip, Judith and Sally ELLISTON; WITS: Wm. NELMS, Griffin EDWARDS, Jn. DAUGHITY. (NC RB 16:223)
[In his will (NC 16 Jan 1807-9 Mar 1807) John Shapleigh ELLISTON names the following legatees: dau. Sally ELLISTON, son James ELLISTON, and grson. Winder WILDY; he directed that his Negro woman Hannah should not be compelled to live with any person as a hireling without her consent; son James to live with John COCKARILL; Jn. COCKARILL, Hely WILDY & Robt. CROCKETT exors; WITS: Wm. NELMS, Wm. HARCUM (NC RB 17:507)]

ELLISTON, John S[hapleigh]; T 18 Mar 1807; 14 Aug 1815
NC; INV, [m]; includes Negroes Letty, boys Reubin & Vincent, Hannah. (NC RB 20:172)

ELLISTON, Mary; PO 11 Jan 1813, T 22 Jul 1813; 13 Sep 1813. NC; INV, $106.62. (NC RB 19:438)
[In her will (NC 24 Aug 1812 - 11 Jan 1813) Mary ELLISTON named her nephews Cudberth E. S. CONWAY and Edw. C. CONWAY, their uncle Rich. CONWAY, and her sis. Sukey CONWAY; she also emancipated her Negro fellow Tom (NC RB 19:302); Tom, a free man of color emancipated by the will of Mary ELLISTON, was permitted to reside in NC, 13 Apr 1818 (NC OB 1816-20:242); Edw. CONWAY, wid., mar. Susanna ELLISTON, NC, bond 16 May 1798 (MLBNC:); Mary & Susanna ELLISTON were children of Cuthbert and Mary "Molly" CONWAY and sisters of Jn. S., Cuthbert, Hannah S., Ann, and Betty Shapleigh ELLISTON (SSPR:46, 47; NC CCs 1814-010, 1815-015)]

ELMORE, George; 1 May 1815. RC; INV, $99.99. (RC WB 9:473)

ELMORE, John; T 18 Apr 1808; 27 Mar 1809. WC; INV, £53.2.0. (WC RI 9:130)

ELMORE, Richard; T 17 Mar 1813; 1 Mar 1824. RC; INV, [m]. (RC WB 10:35)
[This must be the Rich. ELMORE who mar. Catherine DODSON, RC, bond 17 Dec 1794 (MRC:65); Olivia N. ELMORE orphan of Rich. ELMORE chose Thos. W. BRYANT as her gdn., 7 Apr 1823 (RC OB 26:42); Nancy ELMORE, orphan of Rich. ELMORE chose Thaddeus ELMORE as her gdn., 1 Mar 1824 (RC OB 26:155); Sally ELMORE, Fred. ELMORE, Rich. ELMORE, Thaddeus ELMORE, who are all 21 years, and Hen., Olivia, Nancy, Jas., Rawleigh & Lucy ELMORE the last six being infants by Wm. FORESTER their gdn., compl. against Cath. ELMORE, def., 4 May 1824 (RC OB 26:194); Cath. ELMORE aptd. gdn. to Sally, Jas., Rawleigh & Lucy ELMORE orphans of Rich. ELMORE, 4 Oct 1824 (RC OB 26:235)]

ELMORE, William; 25 Sep 1807; 5 Dec 1808
NFP, RC; WILL; use of est. to wife Fanny ELMORE; at her death or remarriage, son Robert to have land & still; son William ELMORE $50; rest of est. to be div. between younger children [Katharine] & John ELMORE; wife Fanny & John BRYANT & William FORRESTER admins; WITS: Jas. B. DODSON, Rawleigh DODSON. (RC WB 9:341)
[Wm. ELMORE mar. Frances CLARK, RC, bond 9 Apr 1793 (MRC:65); Kitty ELMORE orphan of Wm. ELMORE chose Moses LUNSFORD as her gdn., NC 12 Jan 1819 (NC OB 1816-20:320)]

ELMORE, William; PO 5 Dec 1808; 1 May 1809. RC; INV, [m]. (RC WB 9:347)

ENGLISH, William; T 10 Apr 1800; 1 Jun 1801. RC INV; $120.53. (RC WB 9:147)

ESKRIDGE, Burditt; 20 Mar 1815; 26 Feb 1816
WC; WILL; all worldly property to wife Ann ESKRIDGE during her life; after her death plant. w/o I now live to son Vurnon [sic] ESKRIDGE; all my Negroes to be eq. div. between son Burrell and two daus. Verrinea &

Elizabeth; [no ex. named]; WIT: Jas. H. MOTHERSHEAD; [will proved by Wm. L. MOTHERSHEAD & Thos. POOR]. (WC DW 23:149)
[Burdett ESKRIDGE mar. Ann WASHINGTON, WC, bond 31 Dec 1800 (MLBWC:22)]

ESKRIDGE, William; 29 Jan 1823; 11 Aug 1823
NC; WILL; one third of est. to wife Ann ESKRIDGE; after wife's death her third to be eq. div. between three children Robert Edwards ESKRIDGE, Elizabeth Baker ESKRIDGE & Mary Cedar ESKRIDGE; plant. w/o I now live in Hack's Neck containing 230 ac. to son Robert E.; plant. known by the name of Welsh Neck containing 140 ac. to dau. Ann Haynie WILKINSON (wife of James WILKINSON); slaves belonging to Mrs. Mary CRALLE formerly Mrs. Mary HAYNIE; wife & Samuel DOWNING exors; WITS: W. BASYE, Rich. HUDNALL Jr., Winder K. ELLISTON; [Ann ESKRIDGE & Samuel DOWNING relinquished their right of execution & Ann ESKRIDGE was granted certificate to obtain letters of admin. on the est. of the sd. dec'd with the will annexed]. (NC RB 23:352)
[Wm. ESKRIDGE mar. Ann EDWARDS, dau. of Robt. EDWARDS, NC, bond 16 Nov 1797 (MLBNC:36); Ann H. ESKRIDGE, dau. of Wm. ESKRIDGE, mar. James WILKINSON, NC, bond 27 Sep 1817 (MLBNC:110); Royston B. COVINGTON mar. Mary C. ESKRIDGE, NC, bond 26 May 1826 (MLBNC:22); settlement of Yarrett HUGHLETT's gdnship of Mary C. ESKRIDGE now the wife of R. B. COVINGTON, 10 Sep 1827 (NC OB 1825-30:202); Miller:61 locates Hack Neck in the Fairfields District of NC]

ESKRIDGE, William; PO 8 Dec 1823; 14 Jun 1824
NC; DIV of slaves worth $2975; one third (Tignor, Solomon, Mose, Charlotte, Nace) allotted to Mrs. Ann ESKRIDGE the wid; Lot 1 ([Phanie] & 2 children Henry & Hiram) to Yarrett HUGHLETT who mar. Elizabeth ESKRIDGE a dau, Lot 2 (John, Kendall, Liston) to Mary ESKRIDGE another dau, Lot 3 (Lewis, Bill, Betty) to Robert ESKRIDGE the only son. (NC RB 23:478)
[Yarrett HUGHLETT mar. Eliz. ESKRAGE [sic], NC, bond 28 May 1823 (MLBNC:57)]

EUSTACE, John; PO 14 Aug 1815; 11 Mar 1816
NC; INV, includes Negroes Gerry, Isaac, Spencer, Crosky, Harry, Caty & child Polly, Darky, Alice, children Lewis & Joney, Nancy, Maria & child Billy, a bible and Murray's Dictionary. (NC RB 20:399)
[Jn. EUSTACE mar. Maria LELAND, LC, bond 24 Jun 1808 (MLBLC:26); the est. of Jn. EUSTACE was ord. to be admin. by Maria EUSTACE and Maria EUSTACE was aptd. gdn. of Wm. Conway EUSTACE orphan of Jn. EUSTACE, NC 14 Aug 1815 (NC OB 1811-1816:355)]

EUSTACE, William; 10 [Jan] 1803; 11 Jul 1803
NC; INV, £3400.1.0; includes Negroes old Daniel, Betty, Joshua, Jesse (blacksmith), [Lues], George, David, Harry, Arch, Joe, Jerry, Daniel Jr., Bill (house), Emberson, Sall, Esther & child (Anthony in the arms), Voilet & child (Alice in the arms), Patt & child (Silvey in the arms), Clary & child (Winney in the arms), Molley, Darkey, Patty, Keziah, Sukey, Fanny, [Kitty], Dinah, Winny, Mariah, Lucy, Jenny, Esther, Darkey, Patience, Rebeckah, Letty, Nanny, Isaac, Charles, Emanuel, Josiah, Nick, John, James, Spencer, Arch (old), Stephen, Charles, Isaac, James, Peter, Reuben, Spencer, [Konoko], Croskey, Norah, Fanney, Harrah, Peggy, Ta[b]. (NC RB 17:14)

EUSTACE, William; PO 9 Mar 1807, T 1 May 1807; 10 Aug 1807
NC; allotted Mary S. EUSTACE, wid. & rel of William EUSTACE, what we supposed to be one third part of the tract w/o the sd. William dec'd lived at

the time of his death; beginning a few paces north of the old blacksmith's shop on the main road leading from the Baptist Meeting House to Kilmarnock ... thence up the meanders of the Little Mill Swamp to Kilmarnock ... including the whole of the land on the west side of the road and we also allot to her by consent of the parties all the dwelling house except the room at the south end commonly called the parlor, the room above the parlor, the cellar under it and the closet attached to it likewise the two largest bedrooms up the stairs of the main house and the closets under under the stairs and also all the out houses except the following: the long barn, the shead of the small barn, one half of the dairy and one half of the meat house, one corn house, the house at the south end of the dwelling house and Daniel's house commonly called the Wheelwright Shop, also one half of all the fruit trees and one half of the garden on the north side and also one half of the tract called the Brickhouse Tract of the Woodland Part (on Dick's Branch adj Geo. W. YERBY & Jack HUTCHINGS) and the south side of the field below the hill (on which stands the dwelling house) near the Locust Point and a branch of Dymers Creek and also one third of the mill and the following Negroes: Esther, Molly, Emanuel, Joe, Polly & child, Charles, Jenny, Kezziah, Pegg & child, Joshua, Suck, Emberson, Harry, Old Daniel, James, Sall & Mary; est. also div. among William EUSTACE's children: John EUSTACE (rec'd Mariah, Alice, Spencer, Darkey, Old Darkey, Jerry, Croskey, [Haney], Isaac & Archey, William EUSTACE (rec'd Tab, Rhuben, Beck, Daniel, Fanny, Charles, Dinah & Stephen), Ann EUSTACE (rec'd Archey, Violett, Clary & child, [Patience], George, Spencer, Nanny, House Billy & Nancy), Agatha EUSTACE (Luis, John, Letty, Josiah, Silvy, Winny, Peter, Isaac & Esther & child). (NC RB 17:566)

EUSTACE, William; 20 Feb 1815; 18 Apr 1815
LC; WILL; third of est. to wife Harriet EUSTACE; balance of landed est. & my mill to be eq. div. between sons John & William EUSTACE; Negro woman Dinah to dau. Maryann EUSTACE (under 18); wife & bro. John EUSTACE exors; WITS: J. K. BALL, Jn. HUTCHINGS, Mary S. EUSTACE. (LC WB 28:160)
[Harriett EUSTACE aptd. gdn. to Mary Ann, Jn., & Wm. EUSTACE orphans of Wm. EUSTACE, 18 Apr 1815 (LC Orders 24:223); Jn. PAYNE mar. Harriott EUSTACE, the wid. of Wm., LC, bond 29 Apr 1818 (MLBLC:58, LC OB 25:36, 75); *see also LC CC 1820-057*]

EUSTACE, William; PO 17 Apr 1815, T 10 Aug 1815; 21 Aug 1815
LC; INV; includes Negroes: Charles, Rheuben, Peter, Atwell, Solomon, Stephen, Fanny, Tabatha, Dinah, Becka, Polly. (LC EB 27:247)

EUSTACE, William; PO 18 Nov 1823; 17 Mar 1824
LC; DIV of slaves at Kilmarnock; Reuben, Kissiah, Peter & Fanny to John PAYNE in right of his wife & also PAYNE is to receive from the balance of the heir's $26.66 the balance of the Negroes after deducting the legacy for Mary Ann EUSTACE leaving Beck & Atwell cannot be divided in coin. (LC EB 29:334)

EVANS, Peter; 26 Sep 1788; 6 Jun 1803.
LP, RC; WILL; wife house & land, after her death to William HARRIS son of Susanna HARRIS; desires that William HARRIS should be a joiner; James KELLY Sr, James KELLY Jr, & Williamson HALL exors; WITS: Jn. KELLY, Wm. PACKETT, Jas. KELLY Jr., Williamson HALL. (RC WB 9:216)

EVANS, Solomon (Capt.); T 20 Jul 1822; 12 Sep 1824. NC, INV, $799.49. (NC RB 24:42)

[On the mot. of [Lovey] EVANS, ord. that Zepporah, Robt., Eliz. A. D., Rich., & Jos. D. EVANS children and heirs together with sd. Lovey of Solomon EVANS dec'd be summoned to show cause why lands of sd. Solomon should not be sold, [9] Jul 1827 (NC OB 1825-30:185); Susan EVANS aptd. gdn. to Eliza Ann, Rich., and Jos. D. EVANS orphans of Sol. EVANS; allot to Susan EVANS her dower in the lands of her late husband Sol. EVANS, 13 Aug 1827 (NC OB 1825-30:191, 192); Sol. EVANS mar. Susanna DAVENPORT, RC, bond 8 Jun 1815 (MRC:66)]

EVERETT, John D.;
John D. EVERETT d. in 1772 leaving children Charles and Thomas EVERETT and a pregnant wife who soon after gave birth to John D. EVERETT; Thomas EVERETT d. shortly after his father under the age of 21 (LC CC 1801-011)

EWELL, James (Maj.); 31 Jan 1792; 15 May 1797
LC; WILL; to dau. Sally Conway EWELL the Negroes mentioned in the deed of gift recorded in Lancaster court; all my lands to son James EWELL; my two sisters Mary & Ann EWELL; dau. Sally Conway EWELL to be brought to Virginia as soon as convenient; William & John CHOWNING to be allowed to sell masts & other timber off my land; Col. Thomas GASKINS of NC & Col. James EWELL of Prince William Co. and my friend Richard SELDEN of Lancaster exors; Wm. CHOWNING, Hen. TOWLES, W. DAVIS, Thos. CHOWNING; COD: in case my dau. Sally C. EWELL shall be prevented by her relations or any other person or persons in South Carolina so that she does not return to this state within 2 years after my decease she shall have no further or other part of my est. except the Negroes in the deed of gift above entioned; if my dau. shall not comply with my will as expressed in the preceding clause, I give my son James EWELL all the Negroes devised to her; WITS: Hen. TOWLES, Tunstall WILDEY, [Homer] WEBB. (LC WB 28:23)
[This is the James EWELL who mar. Sarah Ann CONWAY, LC, bond 7 Jul 1783 (MLBLC:26); acc. to the Ewell Family Bible, James EWELL was the son of Solomon EWELL and was born 4 Jul 1754 and died in Prince William Co. on 13 Apr 1797; his first wife, Sarah Ann CONWAY was born 17 Dec 1767; James EWELL mar. (1) Sarah Ann CONWAY (b. 17 Dec 1767, d. 31 Oct 1784) on 12 Jul 1783 and (2) Ann Lee GASKINS (d. 30 Nov 1790) on 23 Oct 1786; he had three children: Sarah Conway, b. 14 Oct 1784, James b. 1789, and Thomas Gaskins, b. 13 Nov 1790]

EWELL, James (Maj.); PO 15 May 1797; 21 Jan 1799. LC; INV, £126.7.5. (LC EB 24:89)

EWELL, James (Maj.); PO 15 May [1797], T 8 Aug 1797; 18 Jul 1803
LC; INV in Prince William Co., £933.2.[6]; includes Negroes: Williamson, George, Ezekiel, [Henna], Sinah & child Tom, Zachariah, Marianne, Harry, Dennis, Charlotte & child Sally, Elijah, Lucinda, Hagar, Ben, Billy, Alice, Amy; INV in Culpeper Co., £65.10.6; includes Negroes: Ben, Billy, Amy, Ailce. (LC EB 24:244)

FALLIN, Charles; PO Dec 1787, T 29 Dec 1787; 13 Apr 1789
NC; DIV of est. among Mrs. Sarah FALLIN, wid. of William FALLIN dec'd, together with the sd. deceased's orphans & Rodham LUNSFORD who mar. a dau. of the sd. deceased who received Stephen, Mima & child Jane, Aaron, Ailcey, Daniel, Peter an old man to be supported; Miss Sally FALLIN who received Solomon, Judah & child Letty, Winney, Esther, China; Capt. John FALLIN who received Sam, Moses, Phillis, Solomon, Charlotte; Joseph

HUDNALL & Elizabeth his wife dau. of the sd. Charles FALLIN received Joshua, Pharoah, Nancy, Darcus, Francis. (NC GA 1788-1824:19)

FALLIN, Charles; T 20 Nov 1805; 8 Sep 1806
NC; INV, £850.10.2 1/2; includes Negroes Toney, Sam, James, Phillis & child Charlotte, girl Ciller, boys Shadrach, Mace, Jerry, & Solomon, old woman Judah. (NC RB 17:460)
[Wm. and Rich. FALLIN were named orphans of a Charles FALLIN in a CC in 1808; their gdn. was Pemberton CLAUGHTON (NC CC 1810-006)]

FAUNTLEROY, Ann; 8 Aug 1808; 3 Oct 1808
NFP, RC; WILL; all my land in Naylor's Hole Neck purchased of Mr. Joseph FAUNTLEROY & half of my household property to my ex. to be held in trust for my dau. Ann THOMPSON during her life & after her death to her children; dau. Elizabeth FAUNTLEROY Negroes Harry, Suckey, [Pheby] & her 3 children: Patrick, Amey, & Sally; my servant Aaron to my friend Elder Henry TOLER as long as he may think proper to hold him in servitude & desire that he should after serving him so long that he the said Aaron be liberated; son Joseph FAUNTLEROY to be exor; WITS: Alice JONES, B. McCARTY. (RC WB 9:338)
[This is Ann BELFIELD who mar. Griffin Murdock FAUNTLEROY, c. 1770 (*see below*); Ann FAUNTLEROY mar. Chas. R. THOMPSON, RC, bond 28 Dec 1797 (MRC:208); Miller:109 locates Naylors Hole on the Rappahannock River above Cat Point Creek.]

FAUNTLEROY, Griffin M.; PO Dec 1798, T 31 Dec 1798; 3 Jun 1799
RC; DIV of the slaves relinquished by Ann FAUNTLEROY of the est. of Griffin M. FAUNTLEROY dec'd; Lot 1 (Prince, Hannah, Tom) allotted to Thomas YERBY; Lot 2 (John Blue, Little Sam, Molly, Susanna) allotted to Elizabeth FAUNTLEROY; Lot 3 (Young Humphrey, Nancy, Sally, Patt, Henry) allotted to Polly FAUNTLEROY; Lot 4 (General, Kate, Little Tom, child John) allotted to Charles R. THOMPSON; Lot 5 (Guy, Aaron, Rachell, Jacob) allotted to Joseph FAUNTLEROY; Lot 6 (Little Billy, Peter, Judy, Willoughby) allotted to Belfield FAUNTLEROY. (RC AB 3:8)
[Thos. YERBY mar. Peggy FAUNTLEROY, RC, bond 4 Sep 1786 (MRC:239)]

FAUNTLEROY, Griffin M.; PO Oct 1808, T 29 Dec 1808; 3 Jan 1826
RC; DIV of est. including land & plant. called Mars Hill & land & plant. called Hard Bargain on the north side of Farnham Creek and lands in Naylors Hole Neck; it was agreed between William FORBES who claimed the half to which Belfield FAUNTLEROY was entitled by purchase & Joseph FAUNTLEROY that the sd. Joseph FAUNTLEROY should hold & possess the plant. called Mars Hill as his full moity of the lands of the sd. Griffin M. FAUNTLEROY and the plant. called Hard Bargain on Farnham Creek & the plant. in Naylors Hole Neck should be held and possessed by the sd. William FORBES as claiming under the sd. Belfield FAUNTLEROY; the slaves were allotted as follows: to Joseph FAUNTLEROY (Billy, Bob, Betty & child Arthur), to John M. YERBY in behalf of Peggy YERBY's est. (Isaac, Patty, Lucy & child Anna, John Lucy's boy), to Charles R. THOMPSON (Frank, Young Joe, Milly, Doll), to William FORBES as claiming from Belfield FAUNTLEROY (Bradley, Rachel & child William, Sally, John, Old Joe), to Elizabeth FAUNTLEROY (James, Harry, Nelly, Betsy), to John CAMPBELL (Sam, Winney, Young Billy, Sinah); the slaves in Lot 3 were claimed by John CAMPBELL as purchased from Charles R. THOMPSON and those in Lot 4 were claimed by William FORBES under the same right

that he claimed the land, as the portion of Belfield FAUNTLEROY. (RC AB 4:210)

[Griffin Murdock FAUNTLEROY, son of Wm. FAUNTLEROY, mar. Ann BELFIELD, dau. of John & Ruth (SYDNOR) BELFIELD, c. 1770 (MRC:68); Miller:94 locates Mars Hill in RC four miles north of Farnham]

FAUNTLEROY, Henry; 6 May 1822

RC; Robert FAUNTLEROY made oath that Henry FAUNTLEROY was [a] captain and served in the Revolutionary War and was slain in battle ... on 28 Jun 1778 at Monmouth in New Jersey, that the sd. FAUNTLEROY left no will ... was never mar., that Moore FAUNTLEROY was heir at law, his eldest bro., ... and that Robert FAUNTLEROY, Henry S. TURNER & Edward H. CARTER are lawful heirs of Moore FAUNTLEROY. (RC OB 25:280)

[Wm., Moore, Jn., Griffin, Jos. and Robt. were bros. of the whole blood of Hen. FAUNTLEROY; Griffin had d. by Jul 1801 leaving six children: Peggy, Eliz., Jos, Belfield, Maria who mar. Jn. CAMPBELL and Ann who mar. Chas. R. THOMPSON; Jn. and Wm. had also d. by Jul 1801; Jn. left three children: Louisa who mar. Peter TEMPLE, Wm. and Letty; Wm. left no issue (NC CC 1801-012)]

FAUNTLEROY, John; PO 5 Feb 1798; 7 Oct 1805

RC; INV at Lion House; [m], includes the following Negroes: Tom, Margery, Edward, Newton, Dick, John, Aaron, Somerset, Bob, George, Jack, Aaron, Lydia & child, Betty, Winney & child, Winney, Sarah, Moses, James, Henry, Frederick, Suckey, Daniel. (RC WB 9:266)

FAUNTLEROY, John; T 5 Jun 1800; 7 Oct 1805

RC; INV at the plant. in Naylor's Hole Neck, £1602.12.9, includes the following Negroes: David, Kate, Phillis, Peter, John (child), Winny, Jack, Peggy, Joe, Betsy (child), Sinah, Isaac (child), Nancy, Moses, James, Jimmy, Nancy, Billy, Liverpool, Billy, Jacob, Patty, Bobb, Robin, Jimmy, David, Philip (child). (RC WB 9:275)

FAUNTLEROY, Moore; 15 Dec 1801; 5 Apr 1803

RC; WILL; bro. Robert; nephew Henry S. TURNER all my coat-of-arms china; the female children of the dec'd Daniel WILSON; the blind free Negro Billy LEWIS 40 shillings per annum; at the end of 1802 all Negroes to have their freedom if it can be effected, if it cannot ... they are to be hired in the county and not to be removed out against their consent; the money arising from their hires, half to them at the end of the year in proportion as they hire, the other half the Negroes to be clothed out of; nephew Edward Hill CARTER; bro. Robert & nephew Henry S. TURNER exors; [no wits]. (RC WB 9:211)

[Moore FAUNTLEROY was the son of Wm. FAUNTLEROY of Naylor's Hole (d. RC 1793). Hen. S. TURNER was the son of Moore FAUNTLEROY's sis. Jane who mar. [Thos.] TURNER; Edw. Hill CARTER was prob a son of his sis. Apphia who mar. Jn. Champe CARTER in RC bond 4 Feb 1782. (RC WB 8:162; MWO:68, 359)]

FAUNTLEROY, William H.; P 1 Apr 1805; 3 Jun 1805

RC; INV, £1170.0.[?], includes the following Negroes: Isaac, John, Winefred & child Franky, Polly, Sarah, Isaac, Darcas & child Molly, Sarah, Robin, John, Winny & 4 children: Sukey ([6]), Charles (4), Molly (2), & James (an infant), Dick. (RC WB 9:252)

FAWCETT, John; 18 Feb 1802; 5 Apr 1802

RC; WILL; Joseph SCATES the land I purchased of Thomas WRIGHT & John BULGER & 100 ac. I purchased of George Lee TURBERVILLE; Thomas

JONES Sr; James KELLY Jr; servant Priss & her Sam to have their freedom & also land purchased of John MITCHELL; servants Grace, Judith, & little Billy to be freed & have land; Anne KELLY (formerly Anne CLAYTOR); should Anne KELLY or James SCATES claim or interfere with the small piece of land I now live on, my will & desire is that they shall have none of the above legacies; remainder of est. to nephew Robert BISPHAM; John HOULT the tract of land w/o he now lives during his life; friends James KELLY Jr, James SCATES & nephew Robert BISPHAM exors; WITS: Elisha BARTLETT, Jas. JENKINS, Jn. HOULT, Isaac BARTLETT. (RC WB 9:164)
[Jos. SCATES mar. Patty HINSON, dau. of James HINSON, RC, bond 6 Mar 1797; Jn. FAWCETT was a bondsman; Anne B. CLAYTOR mar. Jn. KELLY Jr. [sic], RC, bond 2 Mar 1801 (MRC:111, 181); Anne (CLAYTOR) KELLY was dec'd by Jun 1815 (RC OB 1814-16:40)]

FAWCETT, John; PO Apr 1802; 7 Feb 1803
RC INV; £4261.15.2; includes the following Negroes: Abram, James, Sam, General, Aron, Sam CRANK, Willoughby, Isaac, boy Billy, James, Alek, Lewis, John, Kate, Joan & child Stafford, Nanny & child Dick, Betty, Betty & two children Billy & Louisa, Charlotte, Judith & Billy, Priss & son Sam, Grace & son Ludwell, girl Molly, girl Barbara, Milly, Philicia, Old Beck, Mary & two children Lett & infant, Frank & child Nancy, Milly & two children Eve & Portia, Jane & four children Eve, Reuben, Polly & Simon. (RC WB 9:199)

FAWCETT, John; 5 Oct 1818
RC; Priscilla FAWCETT and her son Samuel rec'd land in the will of John FAWCETT. (RC OB 24:270)
[This must be the servant Priss & her Sam who were to have their freedom & also land purchased of John MITCHELL (*see above*)]

FEAGINS, Margett; 7 May 1800; 1 Jun 1801
RC; WILL; widow; sons William, John; grson. Peter MORGAN; daus. Hannah, Winnifred; children John, Hannah & Winnifred exors; WITS: Robt. JEFFRIES, Judith FRANCE, Thos. HOGAN, Wm. MOORE. (RC WB 9:150)

FEAGITT, James; PO 23 Sep 1805; 25 Aug 1806
WC; INV, £67.15.10. (WC RI 8:619)
[Wm. SETTLE aptd. gdn. of Polly, Ellin & Alice FEAGIT the orphans of Jas. FEAGIT, 23 Nov 1807 (WC Orders 1807-10:123); on the mot. of Benedict WALKER atty. for Mary FIGGET orphan of Jas. FIGGET and Geo. WINSTEAD who mar. Nelly FIGGET, ord. to settle the gdnship. acct. of Wm. SETTLE who was gdn. for the sd. Mary, Nelly & Alice FIGGET, 26 May 1817 (WC OB 1814-18:298)]

FEAGITT, Thomas; 9 Dec 1800; 26 Jan 1801
WP, WC; WILL; dau. Eliz. FEAGITT & son Henry FEAGITT; unborn child; wife Tilday [Matilda]; son Spence FEAGITT my tailor's tools; son John FEAGITT; son Thomas FEAGITT; wife & son Spence to be exors; WITS: Chas. C. MOTHERSHEAD, Jn. MOTHERSHEAD, Mary POPE . (WC DW 20:179)
[Thos. FIGGOT [sic] mar. Matilday COLEBROOK, WC, bond 30 Aug 1793 (MLBWC:[23]]]

FEAGITT, Thomas; T 20 Oct 1801; 25 Jan 1802. WC; INV, £60.7.3. (WC RI 8:148)

FERGUSON, Robert; 17 Oct 1807; 28 Nov 1825
WC; WILL; of Mulberry Grove, Charles Co., Md; various assets to John CAMPBELL & other surviving partners of John Glassford & Co; my [merine ?] bro. John MURPHY of WC in Virginia; land and Negroes given me by the

late John BALLANTINE as a portion with his daughter Elizabeth; £20 sterling charged by Henry RIDDELL of Glasgow for cost and charges of the iron works of a threshing machine; I give to the present children of the said John MURPHY in the following proportions, to my nephews John B. MURPHY and Robert MURPHY the sum of £10 sterling to each in good plain silver watches; to my four lovely nieces whom I equally regard, I give the remainder but on account of the names they bear not in equal proportions, to my niece Elizabeth Ferguson MURPHY I give one third part; to my niece Jane Crosbie MURPHY I give one third part and the remaining third part to be equally divided between Ann MURPHY and Sally MURPHY when they shall respectively arrive at the age of 16 or day of marriage; in the year 1802 I borrowed of my bro. John MURPHY the sum of £750.7.6 sterling money of Great Britain for which I have passed my bonds to him dated 3 May 1802; this money was to enable me to pay for a part of my land called Rogers Refuge in part of which bond I have paid for board & schooling of his sons John and Robert – Robert FERGUSON – at Charlotte Hall; I give to my old servant Charity HILL during her natural life the occupation and use of the houses wherein she now lives and six acres of ground around them on that side of the main road whereon they stand; I likewise give her priviledge to take water from the springs on the land which I bought of Theophilus WATHEN; I also give and bequeath unto said Charity HILL the sum of $60 current money yearly to be paid her on every New Year's day, the first payment to be paid on the first New Year's day after my death and on every New Year's day after during her life; I give and bequeath to Alexander HILL the son of said Charity HILL the sum of $1,000 current money; I hereby emancipate and set free my Negro slave Tom or Thomas and if this mode of emancipation be not sufficient I will and direct that my residuary legatee hereafter named do execute a proper deed of emancipation and put the same on record; but if any law should pass in this state compelling Negroes so set free to leave the state as is the law in Virginia, Tom shall not be emancipated but my residuary legatee shall permit him to work for himself when he pleases and yearly pay him the sum of 16 dollars the first payment to be made as directed for Charity HILL; I hereby emancipate and set free my Negro woman Mary or Molly who I bought of William Sydebothom of Bladensburg and for Molly's faithful services to me I further bequeath and give to her the sum of $8.00 to buy clothes for the first year after my death; I hereby emancipate and set free my Negro boy Will or William the son of Sarah born the 4th day of October 1798 when he shall arrive at the age of 21 years; if this mode of emancipation be not sufficient residuary legatee shall do for Molly and Will as I have directed to be done for Tom; I give and bequeath to Will the sum of $8.00 yearly for 3 years after my death if Will chooses to learn a trade this will assist to clothe him; I give and bequeath to bro. William FERGUSON in [Moniaive], Scotland the sum of £300 sterling money of Great Britain; I also give and bequeath to my said bro. William all the money I have heretofore remitted to him and which stands charged to his account on my said ledger.; I do this [that] he may therewith provide for his son in Scotland if he thinks proper – Robert FERGUSON; I give and bequeath to my nephew James FERGUSON the sum of $6,000 current money of the United States; I will and direct that my executors do convey the fee simple estate of my lands in Durham Parish called Middleton and Christian Milford containing 1288 acres more or less or by whetever names they may be called and are now in the occupation of Samuel HAISLIP unto my nephew Robert FERGUSON merchant in Baltimore and I give and bequeath to said Robert FERGUSON my old gold watch which he has long been in possession of; I will and direct that my executors do convey the fee simple estate of my lands called Rogers Refuge, Moores Folly, Moores Branch, Hawkins Barrons, Hawkins Addition, Come by Chance, and Grays [Syciemi] and any other lands I am possessed of in Port Tobacco Parish by whatever name they may be called unto my nephew John FERGUSON his heirs and assigns conditioned that he the said John FERGUSON pay unto his bro. James FERGUSON $6,000 as bequeathed by me to him, that he pay to William FERGUSON his father the sum of £300 sterling bequeathed to him as above, that he pay to Alexander HILL $1,000 as bequeathed to him and that he pay to Negroes Molly and Will the legacies bequeathed to them and that he pay the annuities bequeathed to Charity HILL and Negro Tom and that he take care of Negro William my old servant as long as he may live and that he pay all my just debts; but if the said John FERGUSON shall refuse to accept of these lands and the residue of my personal estate on these conditions then and in that case my said executors shall sell the residue of my personal estate or any part thereof and so much or many of my said lands in Port Tobacco Parish as will pay my debts the legacies and annuities aforesaid and shall convey the fee simple estate to the purchasers thereof always allowing Charity HILL to hold her life estate and priviledges in land and houses devised to her and when said payments are made and performed, my executors are hereby directed to convey the fee simple estate of the remainder of said land to said John FERGUSON and his heirs and I hereby empower my said executors the majority of them the survivors or survivor of them so to do; remainder of PE to nephew John FERGUSON; I do expect that the balance due to me by the firm of Henderson, Ferguson, and Gibson as will appear by the books kept by me for transactions in their affairs will pay the balance which may owe to the firm of Henderson, Riddle & Campbell of Glasgow for losses in the partnership with them but if it should fall short the balance must be paid by my said nephew John FERGUSON as any other debt due by me; bro. John MURPHY of Virginia, nephews Robert FERGUSON and John FERGUSON and friend Thomas MUNDELL of Prince George's County to be exors. WITS: Jn. BARNES, Jn. MATTHEWS, Jn. J. JENKINS; brought to court in Charles Co., Md 8 May 1813. (WC DW 25:216)

[What appears to be a somewhat different will for Robert FERGUSON is to be found at <http://dna.cfsna.net/GEN/MD/RobertFergusson.html> accessed 26 Jan 2013; Robt. FERGUSON Sr., a native of Scotland and Chief Judge of the Orphans Court, d. at Mulberry Grove, Charles Co., Md. on 1 Sep 1812 (*Maryland Gazette* 17 Sep 1812); Moniaive is a village in Dumfries and Galloway, Southwest Scotland; a Charity HILL was head of a household of 3 "other free" in Charles Co., Md. in 1800 and of 6 "other free" and 2 slaves in 1810 (<http://freeafricanamericans.com/Hailey-Jones.htm> accessed 26 Jan 2013]

FICKLIN, Ann; 31 Jan 1824; 7 Feb 1825

NFP, RC; WILL; all est. to be eq. div. between my bros. Christopher D. FICKLIN, Leroy D. FICKLIN, & sis. Sally FICKLIN; if sis. Sally die without heir, her share to be eq. div. between two bros.; bros. to be exors; WITS: Jn. A. MISKELL, Peter S. NORTHEN. (RC WB 10:68)

[Ann FICKLIN was a dau. of Famous FICKLIN (*see below*)]

FICKLIN, Famous; PO Dec 1815; 7 Sep 1818. RC; INV, $3374.00. (RC WB 9:604)

[Famous FICKLIN mar. Eliz. DEATLEY, dau. of Christopher DEATLEY of FP (d. RC 1795), bef. 27 Sep 1793 (MWO:131); Acc. to MRC:69, citing a Fredericksburg District Court suit, Famous FICKLIN left a wid. and six children: John D., Leroy D., Christopher D., Ellen (who predeceased her husband Wm. F. DAVIS), Sally, and Nancy; a 5 May 1819 RC record confirms this adding that Francis C., Bowler D. and Jas. F. A. DAVIS were children of Ellen DAVIS (RC OB 24:339)]

FICKLIN, Famous; T 20 May 1816; 6 Dec 1819
INV, RC; $2374.27, includes following Negroes: Lucy & 2 children (Harry & Daniel), Phoeba & child Lidia, George (a boy), Aaron (a boy), Rose (a girl), James (a boy). (RC WB 9:628)

FIELD, George; [m]; 23 Sep 1805
WC; WILL; wife Sibellah [P.] FIELD all est; if she remarries, all est. to only dau. Mary Elizabeth FIELD; entitled to half the profits arriving from the Clerk's Office of Westmoreland Co. until 1 Jan 1806; old Negro man Will should not be removed from the neighborhood where he now lives but be hired out (convenient to his wife) for the benefit of my est; exors. to sell all lands in Kentucky for benefit of wife & dau; father-in-law Thomas SPENCE & bro. Daniel FIELD exors; no wits. (WC DW 21:204)
[Sibellah P. FIELD was a dau. of Thos. SPENCE (d. WC 1822; *see below*); she mar. (2) Wm. M. WALKER, WC, bond 22 Jul 1807 (MLBWC:73); Wm. M. WALKER qualified as gdn. of Mary FIELD orphan of Geo. FIELD, 27 Jun 1808 (WC Orders 1807-10:175); Mary Eliz. FIELD mar. Thos. S. DAVIS, WC bond 6 Feb 1819 (MLBWC:18; WC OB 1819-23:167)]

FIELD, George; T 22 Jan 1808; 25 Jan 1808. WC; INV, £195.18.6; includes Negroes Martin & Sam. (WC RI 9:38)

FINDLA, John; 16 Jun 1803; 19 Sep 1803
LC; WILL; wife Sally FENDLA use of all est; at wife's death or marriage my land to son Elias FENDLA; balance of est. to be eq. div. between three children: Siller Lee FENDLA, Sally George FENDLA, & James FENDLA; wife exts; WITS: Wm. KIRK, Thad. PULLEN, Jn. K. SCHOFIELD. (LC WB 28:71)
[Jn. FENDLA mar. Sally Lee SCHOFIELD, LC, bond 15 Aug 1787 (MLBLC:27)]

FINDLA, John; PO 19 Sep 1803; 20 Feb 1804. LC; INV, £[79].16.0. (LC EB 24:266)

FISHER, James; 4 Nov 1825; 23 May 1825
WC; WILL; Betty SANDERS; John F. ANDERSON; James F. ANDERSON; the use & benefit of my houses, land & one moiety of six Negroes (Alexander, Harry, Henry, Hannah, her 2 children William & John) to my sis. Peggy ANDERSON & her husband William ANDERSON; after death of sis. & her husband my houses, land & the one moiety of the Negroes to be eq. div. between my 3 nephews John F. ANDERSON, William P. ANDERSON, & James F. ANDERSON; WITS: Uriah E. HEAD, Ritchie ATKINS, Leannah HEAD. (WC DW 25:183)
[Peggy FISHER mar. Wm. ANDERSON, WC, bond 4 Feb 1811 (MLBWC:1)]

FISHER, Thomas; T 31 Aug 1810; 25 May 1812. WC; INV, £98.14.6. (WC RI 9:332)

FITZHUGH, George; 24 Oct 1810; 25 Jan 1811
WP; WC; WILL; dau. Frances Tabb FITZHUGH; wife Mary use of the est. I purchased of William STORKE Esq. in KGC known as Bellisle; to go to dau. Frances Tabb FITZHUGH at wife's death; bro. Francis FITZHUGH, sons-in-law John Gibbon STUART & John B. S. FITZHUGH, & friend Younger

JOHNSTON exors; WITS: Thos. MAGRUDER, Sophia BLAND, Jas. DEATLEY. (WC DW 22:173)

[Geo. FITZHUGH mar. Mary STUART, KGC, bond 17 Jul 1797 (KGCVM:5)]

FITZHUGH, George Esq.; [m]; 27 Oct 1817 [sic]

WC; INV. [m]; includes a number of books and Negroes Old James (age 90), Abram (60+), Ben (50), Jack (45), Nat (40), Warner (36), Peyton (24+), Jerry (20), Henry (18), Set[h] (16), Tom (14+), Carter (13), Joise (60+), Suky (28), William (12), Jack Willis (10), Bartley (8), Phill (6), Henderson [sick] (1), Maria (23+), Jessy (5+), Jacob (2+), Caroline (17), Cress (70), Jenny Bird (21+), Willis (7+). (WC RI 10:291

FLANNERY, Michael; [m]; 13 May 1817; NC, INV, [m]. (NC RB 21:190)

[The est. of Michael FLANERY was ord. to be admin. by Israel PEYTON, 13 Dec 1813 (NC OB 1811-1816:205); Michael & Rebecca FLANNERY of Alexandria manumitted a slave named Joe on 4 Jul 1806 (District of Columbia Circuit Court Records M:177); M. FLANNERY advertised his 700-ac. farm with about 100 "fine wool sheep" on Coan River in NC in May 1815 (*Alexandria Daily Gazette Commercial & Political* 15 May 1810, p. [3]); acc. to an Arlington Co. CC of 1817, Rebecca married Michael FLANNERY "many years ago" and believed him to be a native of Ireland who had come to this country when he was very young; he d. around 1814 leaving no children (Arlington Co., Va. CC 1817-008)]

FLANNERY, Rebecca; 20 Apr 1816; 24 Apr 1816

NC; of Alexandria; D of G to her children Eliza K. TURNER & Charles F. TURNER the following Negro slaves: James, Isaac, [Tom], Rhody, Winney, Jesse, Betty, Rose, Dinah, Molly, [Milly], Amy, Sarah, [Pensy] & all her increase, Mary & all her increase, Sinah, Rachel, Peter, Rhody, Davy, Nancy, Lucy & all their increase; WITS: Joshua REDDLE, Mountjoy BAYLY, Geo. DENEAL; rec in NC 8 Jul 1816. (NC RB 21:25)

[Rebecca FLANNERY was a dau. of Rodham KENNER (d. NC, 1819), *see below*; she was prob. mar. first to Charles TURNER who was the father of Eliza and Charles (NC Minute Book 1801-05:145)]

FLEET, John; 17 Feb 1800

LC; Chancery suit: Henry HINTON, John SMALLWOOD & Lucy his wife, Mary INGRAM, John INGRAM, Richard INGRAM, Benjamin & Lucy INGRAM by Thomas INGRAM their father & next friend, Thomas NOLLIN and Mary E. his wife, Thomas NOLLIN gdn. of Holland HAYNIE and Joseph HAYNIE, Catherine, Elizabeth, William & Nancy CHRISTIAN by Rawleigh CHRISTIAN their father and next friend, Mary WADDEY, Henry HINTON & Nancy his wife, complts. against John FLEET regarding slaves sold by FLEET to HINTON. (LC Orders 21 1799-1801:78; CCs 1800-012, 1822-005)

[Jn. FLEET d. in LC in 1793 named his wife Mary, son Jn., daus. Eliz. CHRISTIAN, Dolly and Judy FLEET; and Jn., Mary, Lucy, Rich., Ann & Benj. INGRAM in his will written on 12 Jul 1792 (LC WB 22:385); Jn. SMALLWOOD mar. Lucy FLEET, LC, bond 16 Jun 1781 (MLBLC:68), Thos. INGRAM mar. Sarah FLEET, LC, bond 16 Apr 1772 (MLBLC:41); Hen. HINTON mar. Anna FLEET, LC, bond 23 Jun 1766 (MLBLC:58)]

FLEET, John; 7 Feb 1800; 19 Jan 1801

LC; WILL; all my est. to my friend Martin SHEARMAN & he is to be ex; WITS: Gilbert CURRELL, Robt. HILL, Hugh BRENT. (LC WB 28:48)

FLEET, Mary; 28 Nov 1794; 16 Sep 1799.

CCP, LC; WILL; all est. to son John FLEET; [no ex. named]; WITS: Martin SHEARMAN, Chas. INGRAM. (LC WB 28:33)
[This is prob. Mary EDWARDS, who mar. Jn. FLEET, LC, bond 29 May 1746 (MLBLC:27), *see above*]

FLEMMING, James; 12 Dec 1814; 20 Mar 1815
LC; WILL; son William FLEMMING; son James FLEMMING; son John FLEMMING; dau. Judith; [no ex. named]; WIT: Geo WEBB. (LC WB 28:158)
[Polly FLEMING aptd. gdn. of Patsy FLEMING orphan of James FLEMING, 19 Feb 1816 (LC Orders 24:284); Judith FLEMING orphan of Jas. FLEMING chose Wm. FLEMING as her gdn., 17 Jun 1816 (LC Orders 24:313); Jas. FLEMMING mar. Molly ASHBOURNE, LC, bond 2 Nov 1813 (MLBLC:27)]

FLETCHER, Mayes; PO 10 Oct [1808], T 13 Oct 1808; 9 Jul 1810
NC; INV, [m]. (NC RB 18:423)
[Mayes FLETCHER mar. Molley LUNSFORD, dau. of Jos. LUNSFORD, NC, bond 17 Jul 1789 (MLBNC:38); in his will (NC 5 May 1808-10 Oct 1808), Mayes FLETCHER of WicP named his wife Polley and daus. Milley & Molley (NC RB 18:50)]

FLINT, David; T [?] Sep 1807; 12 Oct 1807. NC; INV, £75.8.6. (NC RB 17:581)
[David FLINT, prob. a son of Jn. & Chloe FLINT, mar. Betsy SCHOFIELD, dau. of Thos. SCHOFIELD, NC, bond 7 Jan 1797 (MWO:134); The est. of David FLINT was ord. to be admin. by Eliz. FLINT, 14 Sep 1807 (NC MB 1805-1807:256)

FLINT, John; PO 21 Apr 1795; 17 Oct 1796
LC; INV, £153.19.16; includes Negroes: Letty, Jenny [the est. of John FLINT was appraised side by side with the est. of Richard FLINT]; DIV of estates of Richard & John FLINT among Ann FLINT, Winny FLINT, Thomas FLINT, Mary FLINT. (LC EB 24:33)
[Jn. and Rich. FLINT were prob. sons of Thos. FLINT who in his will (LC 17 Mar 1783-17 Apr 1783) named his wife Priscilla and children Molly, Rich., Thos., and Jn. (LC WB 20:257)]

FLINT, Richard; PO 21 Apr 1795; 17 Oct 1796
LC; INV, £150.18.4.; includes Negroes: Moses, Rose; [the est. of John FLINT was appraised side by side with the est. of Richard FLINT]; DIV of estates of Richard & John FLINT among Ann FLINT, Winny FLINT, Thomas FLINT, Mary FLINT. (LC EB 24:33)

FLINT, Thomas; 15 Mar 1815; 21 Aug 1815
LC; WILL; first choice of a Negro girl to dau. Priscilla M. FLINT on the day of marriage or when she arrives to 21 years; second choice of a Negro girl to dau. Mary N. FLINT on the day of marriage or when she arrives to 21 years; to child wife is now pregnant with if a dau. to have third choice of a Negro girl; Negro boy Aaron to son Thomas O. FLINT when 21; Negro boy Spencer to son William P. FLINT when 21; if wife gives birth to a son he is to have Negro boy Moses when 21; wife to have all my land & Negroes Nancy, Polly, Caty, Daniel, Jack, Harriett, Caroline, Mahala, Jenny & Brittania, the prop. that I heir by the death of my dau. Sarah A. FLINT now in the hands of Mr. Prichard NEWBY & the money due from the estates of Edward NEWBY & Oswald NEWBY dec'd; at wife's death or marriage all my land to be eq. div. between my sons Thomas, William & the one wife is now pregnant with if it be a son; friends William L. BALL, Joseph B. DOWNMAN, Richard HUTCHINGS & Rawleigh DUNAWAY exors; WITS: Raw. DUNAWAY, Moses ROBINSON, Feriol LEMOINE, Jane DAVENPORT. (LC WB 28:166)

[Thos. FLINT was prob. a son of Thos. FLINT who in his will (LC 17 Mar 1783-17 Apr 1783) named his wife Priscilla and children Molly, Rich., Thos., and Jn. (LC WB 20:257); Rich. WALL aptd. gdn. of Mary N. FLINT orphan of Thos. FLINT, 15 Mar 1819 (LC OB 25:41); Mary N. FLINT orphan of Thos. FLINT chose Geo. L. CORBIN as her gdn. and sd. CORBIN aptd. gdn. to [Edw.] R. FLINT also an orphan of Thos., 20 Dec 1819 (LC OB 25:100, 348); Thos. C. FLINT, Wm. P. FLINT and Priscilla M. FLINT by Rich. NORRIS their gdn. and Edw. R. FLINT and Mary N. FLINT by Rich. WALL their gdn. brought suit against Rawleigh DUNAWAY admr. with the will annexed of Thos. FLINT for a div. of slaves; Lot 1 (Daniel & Nancy) drawn by Margaret FLINT; Lot 2 (Jack) drawn by Wm. FLINT, Lot 3 (Frances) drawn by Oswald FLINT, Lot 4 (Brittania) drawn by Edw. FLINT and Lot 5 (Hannah & Caty) drawn by Mary FLINT, LC 1 Jan 1824 (LC CC 1823-007)]

FLINT, Thomas; T 25 Nov 1815; 20 May 1817
LC; INV; includes Negroes: Nancy, Patty, Caty, Harriet, Daniel, Jack, Mahala, Jenny, Franky, Aaron, Spencer, Moses, Brittanna; Rawleigh DUNAWAY admr; INV of est. of Thomas FLINT after the death of his relict made 3 Dec 1816. (LC EB 27:378)

FLINT, Thomas; PO 19 Jul 1819; 17 Apr 1820
LC; settlement of the administration acct. of Rawleigh DUNAWAY on the est. of Thomas FLINT and after the death of Mrs. FLINT; est. div. among the children of Thomas FLINT: Margaret, Mary, Thomas, William, & Edward (each rec'd $116.17). (LC EB 21:20)
[Rich. WALL aptd. gdn. of Edw. R. FLINT orphan of Thos. FLINT, 16 Nov 1818 (LC OB 25:24); settle with Raw. DUNAWAY his admin. acct. of the est. of Thos. FLINT and the acct. of his transactions in renting & receiving the rents of the land of which Thos. FLINT d. seized and that the slaves & prop. of the sd. Thos. FLINT after the choice of a Negro girl each is made by Priscilla M. & Mary FLINT be sold ... so that Rich. NORRIS may receive the part due his ward and Rich. WALL the part due his ward, 19 Jul 1819 (LC OB 25:71)]

FLINT, Thomas; 12 Mar 1828
NC; Rich. FLINT, George ROBINSON & Catherine his wife and Emily FLINT are heirs of Thomas FLINT. (NC OB 1825 - 30:249)
[Geo. ROBINSON mar. Cath. FLYNT, ward of Thos. FLYNT, NC, bond 20 Dec 1825 (MLBNC:87)]

FLOOD, William (Dr.); PO 22 May 1815; 28 Aug 1815
WC; settlement of est. accts. of Walter JONES in his capacity as ex. of Dr. William FLOOD (who died in or about 1789), gdn. & next friend of Elizabeth, William P. & Nicholas FLOOD children of the sd. dec'd; est. was div. among William P. FLOOD, Elizabeth FLOOD (now ORR) & to Walter JONES in right of his wife Alice (who was half sis. to William P., Elizabeth & Nicholas FLOOD). (WC RI 9:500)
[Elizabeth FLOOD mar. Benjamin G. ORR in NC, bond dtd. 31 Dec 1789; Walter JONES was the sec. (MLBNC:79); *see also the will of Dr. Nicholas FLOOD (RC WB 7:310)*]

FLYNT, John; 6 Aug 1819; 15 Sep 1819
NC; use of all est. to wife Nancy FLYNT; at wife's death or marriage land between the land of Joseph WALKER & Robert CONWAY dec'd to son Thomas FLYNT and also $168 to make him equal with my son Richard FLYNT to whom I give the land w/o I now live; balance of est. after wife's death or marriage to be eq. div. between my 3 daus. Catharine, Emily &

Eliza FLYNT; friend William W. APPLEBY ex; WITS: Jn. LANSDELL Sr., Linzey DAVIS, Wm. [WILDEY]; [COD:] If son Thomas should die with[out] a lawful heir, the land to be my son Richard FLYNT's and vice versa. (NC RB 22:119)

[There are 2 marriage records for a Jn. FLYNT in NC; the first is to Frankey HARCUM, dau. of Ellis HARCUM, bond 11 Jun 1792 and the second is as a wid. to Nancy DOGGETT, bond 1 Apr 1796 (MLBNC:38); Thos. FLYNT aptd. gdn. of Cath., Amey [sic], and Eliza FLYNT orphans of Jn. FLYNT, NC 8 Mar 1824 (NC OB 1820-25:355); Jn. FLYNT served as a carpenter in the Virginia State Navy (BNCHS vol. XII, no. 1:57); Catherine FLYNT mar. Geo. ROBINSON (given as ROBERTSON in VS1776 III:1130), NC, bond 20 Dec 1825 (MLBNC 87); Emily FLYNT mar. Nathaniel MOORE, wid., NC, bond 20 May 1829 (MLBNC:75); Thos. FLYNT is gdn. of Kitty, Eliza & Emmy FLYNT and admr. of the est. of Jn. FLYNT, 13 Mar 1826 (NC OB 1825-30:69); Eliza FLYNT mar. Joel ROBINSON, NC, bond 28 Jan 1830 (MLBNC:87)]

FORBES, William; 23 May 1809

WC; Priscilla MITCHELL aptd. gdn. of Louisa L. and Robert M. FORBES orphans of William FORBES. (WC Orders 1807-10:300)

[This may be the Wm. FORBES who mar. Hannah GORDON, WC, bond 30 Dec 1795 (MLBWC:[23]); Priscilla MITCHELL was presumably Priscilla CARTER, dau. of Robt. & Frances (TASKER) CARTER, who mar. Robt. MITCHELL, Mar 1782 (MWO:247); Geo. WHITLOCK aptd. gdn. of Gordon FORBES, Wm. FORBES & Ann FORBES orphans of Wm. FORBES, 25 Sep 1809 (WC Orders 1807-10:402); Valentine BONTY, who had a certificate from the Registrar of Wills in the District of Columbia, was gdn. to Wm. FORBES orphan of Wm. FORBES, 28 Oct 1816 (WC OB 1814-18:267); Robt. FORBES orphan of Wm. FORBES chose Gordon FORBES as his gdn., 5 Dec 1825 (RC OB 27:19); on the mot. of Gordon FORBES gdn. of Robt. M. FORBES to div. the slaves to which Robt. M. FORBES & Louisa C. FORBES are entitled under the will of Robt. MITCHELL, 2 Jan 1826 (RC OB 27:33)]

FORBUSH, William; PO 14 Nov 1810, T 19 Dec 1810; 11 Feb 1811

NC; allotted John ROBINSON his wife's dower of her late husband William FORBUSH which totaled $450 and included Negroes Moses & boy George; $14.25 was due to the orphans of William FORBUSH. (NC RB 18:523)

[Wm. FORBUSH mar. Catharine HARCUM, NC, bond 19 May 1792; bride was prob. a dau. of Thos. & Sarah HARCUM (MWO:135); Leroy HARCUM was chosen gdn. by Wm. & Thos. FORBUSH and was aptd. gdn. of Hiram & Geo. FORBUSH orphans of Wm. FORBUSH, NC, 9 Dec 1816 (NC OB 1816-20:111); Wm. FORBUSH aptd. gdn. of Thos., Hiram and Geo. FORBUSH, NC, 13 Jul 1818 (NC OB 1816-20:271); John ROBINSON, wid, mar. Katharine (HARCUM) FORBUSH, wid, NC, bond 8 Sep 1809 (MLBNC:87)]

FORBUSH, William; PO 14 Dec 1818; 8 Nov 1819

NC; DIV of est.; each heir to receive $630; to William FORBUSH Negroes Sarah & Vincent; to Thomas FORBUSH Negroes Nancy & Thomas; to Hiram FORBUSH Negroes Sam & James; to George FORBUSH Negroes Mary & Spencer. (NC RB 22:156)

FORD, George; PO 1 Nov 1805; 21 Apr 1806

LC; INV, £162.7.11; includes Negroes: Jane, girl Charlotte, Spencer. (LC EB 24:338)

[Rich. FORD aptd. gdn. of Jane White FORD & Geo. FORD orphans of Geo. FORD, 21 Oct 1805 (LC Orders D22 1805-08:62)]

FORRESTER, Griffin; PO 15 Apr 1800, T 19 May 1800; 9 Jun 1800

NC; INV, £249.8.0; includes Negroes Nance, Salle, Betty, boy Isaac. (NC RB 16:115)

FORRESTER, Griffin; T 20 Apr 1811; 14 Oct 1811
NC; INV & DIV of est; Molly TIFFY who was Molly FORESTER admr. of Griffin FORESTER rec'd widow's thirds (included Negroes Isaac, Lucy, Old Betty); William H. FORESTER (rec'd Sally & Mariah), Robert FORESTER (rec'd Jacob & Nancy), Polly G. HALL (rec'd Young Betty & Rachel). (NC RB 19:105; OB 1807-11:232)
[Griffin FORRESTER, son of Robt. & Bridget FORRESTER, mar. Mary "Molly" (WALKER) SHIVERAL, wid. of Allen Long SHIVERAL, NC, bond 22 Apr 1790 (MWO:136, 319); in his will (NC 1 Feb 1798-12 May 1800), Griffin FORRESTER named his wife Molley and three children Molley Griffin, Robt., & Wm. Howe (NC RB16:94); Molly (WALKER, SHIVERAL) FORRESTER mar. (3) Austin TIFFEY, wid., NC, bond 9 Jun 1803 (MLBNC:101); Polly Griffin FORESTER mar. Benj. HALL, NC, bond 24 Jan 1810 (MLBNC:44)]

FORRESTER, Griffin; PO 13 Jan 1812, T 13 Jul 1812; 13 Jul 1812
NC; DIV of Negroes among Molly TIFFY (the wid.) rec'd Isaac, Benjamin HALL rec'd Lucy & Betty, Robert FORESTER rec'd Sally, Mariah & Nancy, William H. FORESTER rec'd Jacob & Rachel. (NC RB 19:224)

FORRESTER, James; PO 15 Nov 1814; 11 Sep 1815. NC; INV, £64.19.3 3/4. (NC RB 20:209)

FORRESTER, Robert; PO 7 Apr 1800, T 5 Sep 1801; 5 Oct 1801
RC; DIV of land; 100 ac. with houses allotted to Charles FORRESTER & James FORRESTER, Robert FORRESTER to have 84 ac. out of the plat known as Everett's on the west end of sd. land adj William ELMORE, Griffin FORRESTER's orphans to have out of the plat formerly Everett's on the east end of sd. land adj William FORRESTER & George ELMORE; remainder of est. was div. among: Alice LEWIS, James FORRESTER, Robert FORRESTER, Fanny DAVIS, Bridgett FORRESTER, Griffin FORRESTER's orphans. (RC AB 3:64)
[Alice FORRESTER mar. James LEWIS, RC, bond 25 Aug 1772; Fanny FORRESTER mar. (1) Elias HUMPHRIES, RC, bond 12 Aug 1783 and (2) Bartley DAVIS, RC, bond 5 Nov 1795 (MRC:49, 100, 118)]

FOSTER, Benjamin; 8 Feb 1819
NC; Benjamin FOSTER late of this county, enlisted in the service of the US and has since departed this life in the service and has left as next of kin & heir at law only one paternal half bro., Edward FOSTER, now residing in NC and a minor; it also appears that Ezekiel FOSTER, late of NC, who enlisted in the service of the US hath also departed this life and hath left as next of kin and heir at law only the following persons: one bro. of the whole blood the aforesd. Edward FOSTER and one maternal half bro. Lemuel BELL both residents of NC. (NC OB 1816-20:327)

FOSTER, Ezekiel; 12 Jan 1819; Edward FOSTER orphan of Ezekiel FOSTER chose William JETT as his gdn. (NC OB 1816-20:323)

FOWLER. Timothy; 18 [m] 1808; 6 Feb 1809
RC; WILL; dau. Elizabeth B. FOWLER bed & furniture that came to her by her mother; balance of est. to be eq. div. between wife Sally FOWLER & dau. Elizabeth B. FOWLER; Capt. Clement SHACKLEFORD & Mr. Ephraim BEAZLEY exors; WITS: Benj. BROUGHTON, Newby BARRICK. (RC WB 9:344)

[Timothy FOWLER mar. Sally SHACKLEFORD, RC, bond 7 Dec 1807 (MRC:72)]

FOWLER, Timothy; PO Feb 1809; 4 Nov 1817. RC; INV, £68.17.6. (RC WB 9:593)

FOX, Caty; 4 Feb 1803; 26 Jul 1819

WC; WILL; whereas at the death of my mother [Anjelitte] FOX, by the act of Assembly directing descents, I became entitled to a reversionary right of a child's part in that tract of land my father now occupies, I therefore give my reversion in the sd. tract to my sis. Susanna FOX; bro. Joseph FOX Jr. ex; WITS: [Jn.] FOX, Jenny PIPER. (WC DW 23:503)

[Catherine "Caty" FOX was one of seven children of Capt. Jos. FOX and Anjalettah WROE (*see below*)]

FOX, Joseph; 8 Sep 1804; 22 Oct 1804.

WP, WC; WILL; dau. Lucettah HARVEY Negro girl Kate; rest of est. to be eq. div. between dau. Susannah FOX & son Joseph FOX, [Jr.]; son Joseph exor.; WITS: Jn. F. PRICE, Thos. WROE Jn.; Fielding OWEN. (WC DW 21:113)

[This is Capt. Jos. FOX, son of Capt. Jos. FOX and Susanna SMITH of Louisa Co., Va. He mar. Anjeletta WROE and had seven children: Jos. FOX (d. 1823) mar. Mary HIPKINS, Eliz. FOX mar. Sam. BAKER, Jane FOX mar. Jn. PIPER, Catherine FOX (d. 1819), Ann FOX mar. Wm. WROE, Lucettah FOX mar. Jas. HARVEY and Susannah FOX mar. Robt. SANFORD, For an extensive article on the Fox Family, see Geo. H. S. King, "Memorial to Henry Fox, Gentleman of 'Huntington,' King William County, Virginia," *Tyler's Quarterly Historical and Genealogical Magazine* vol. XXI (1940) 217-290. Lucette FOX mar. James HARVEY, WC, bond 18 Mar 1793 (MLBWC:29); Susannah FOX mar. Robt. SANFORD, WC, bond 20 Jul 1807 (MLBWC:62); Lucinda HARVEY mar. Thos. MUSE, WC, bond 22 Jun 1820 (MLBWC:49); Jenny FOX, dau. of Jos. FOX, mar. Jn. PIPER, WC, bond 13 May 1788 (MLBWC:54); Susannah BAKER mar. Thos. FOWKE, WC, bond 26 May 1814 (MLBWC:[23])]

FOX, Joseph; T 7 Nov 1804; 23 Jan 1809

WC; INV, £809.15.10; includes Negroes Billy, John, [Sipro], Thomas, Betty, Lucy, girls Nelly & Catey; est. div. between Susannah FOX & Joseph FOX. (WC RI 9:66)

FOX, Joseph; 14 May 1823; 22 Dec 1823

WC; WILL; to sis. Susanna SANDFORD all my lands & houses in WC & the slaves Old Harry & his wife Lizzy & my servant Aaron; also land in Kentucky under the care of Maj. William BOON to my sis. Susanna SANDFORD; to my niece Rebecca E. ROWE a Negro girl named Calferney; to nephew Milton A. HARVEY my book case with all my books & my servant Aaron at the death of my sis; Negro Harry & his wife Lizzy to my nephew William PIPER at the death of my sis; residue of Negroes to be eq. div. among my nephews & nieces as follows: Octavious A. HARVEY, Milton A. HARVEY, Marcus C. HARVEY, Joseph F. HARVEY, John James HARVEY, Jane Elizabeth HARVEY, Ann Eliza HARVEY, Lucinda MUSE, William PIPER, Buttler BAKER, Anjalettah P. BAKER & Susanna FOOKE; at sister's death land to be sold and proceeds div. among 12 nephews & nieces; family burying ground to be reserved and fenced in; nephew Milton A. HARVEY ex; COD: 6 Oct 1823, Negro girl Caroline to Eliza Jane MUSE eldest dau. of Thomas [S.] MUSE; [no wits]. (WC DW 25:4)

[This is Jos. FOX the son of Capt. Jos. FOX and Anjalettah WROE (*see above*)]

FRANKLIN, William; T 27 Mar 1812; 26 Apr 1813. WC; INV, $418.74. (WC RI 9:324)

FULKS, John; PO 12 Mar 1810, T 17 Mar 1810; 9 Sep 1811
NC; INV, £599.0.10 1/2; includes Negroes woman Pleasant, Winney, boys James, Bob & [Lewis], Fanney, girl Sary. (NC RB 19:94)
[In his will (NC 2 Dec 1809-12 Mar 1810) Jn. FOLKS named his dau. Eliz., and grsons Chas. L., Jn., and Wm. FOLKS (NC RB 18:351)]

FULKS, William; PO 9 Apr 1810; 13 Mar 1811
NC; William FULKS having been dead more than 3 months and no one applied for administration of his est.; no est. could be found to administer. (NC RB 19:12; OB 1807-11:170)

FULKS, William Sr.; PO 11 Nov 1811; 9 Mar 1812. NC; INV, $25.12 1/2. (NC RB 19:154)
[The est. of Wm. FULKS was ord. to be admin. by Chas. L. FULKS, 11 Nov 1811 (NC OB 1811-1816:27)]

GALLE, Severe; PO 16 Feb 1801; 20 Jul 1801
LC; INV, $24,873.44 1/2; includes Negroes: Hannah & child David, girl Lishia, Mima, boy [Lewis], Donnil, girl Rose, girl Mariah, Robin, boy Jack, Peter, Abram, boy James, girl Sally, young boy Moses, old boy Moses. (LC EB 24:152)
[Severe GALLE, a wealthy LC merchant, mar. Alcey [T.] CONWAY, LC, bond 7 Oct 1799; Nottingham renders this name as "Severn GALLE" but it is clearly "Severe" in several records; in the mar. lic bond, 18 Mar 1802, for his dau. to Leroy NUTT, the dau's name is given as "Alcy T. GALLO," but in the index it is "Alcy T. GALLS." (MLBLC: 29, 56, 91); certificate granted Alice T. GALLE & Jn. GALLE to obtain letters of admin. on the est. of Severe GALLE on 16 Feb 1801 (LC Cancery Case 1803-002); Alcy T. GALLE aptd. gdn. of Alcy M. GALLE orphan of Severe GALLE; ord. to div. the est. of Severe GALLE and lay off and assign unto Alice T. GALLE wid. & rel. her dower in the lands and possess the sd. Alcy T. GALLE with the est. of Alcy M. GALLE orphan of sd. decedent her ward, 21 Dec 1801 (LC Orders 21 1799-1801:361, 364); Leroy NUTT and Alice T. his wife who was Alice T. GALLE admx. of Jn. GALLE admr. of Severe GALLE, LC 23 May 1804 (LC OB 1804-05:131); settle with Alcy T. NUTT formerly Alcy T. GALLE the acct. of her gdnship. of her ward Alice M. GALLE, 17 Feb 1812 (LC Orders 24:57)]

GALLE, Severe; PO 21 Dec 1801; 20 Apr 1802
LC; DIV of slaves between Mrs. Alice T. GALLE & Miss Alcy M. GALLE. (LC EB 24:187)

GALLE, Severe; PO 21 Dec 1801, T Apr 1802; 17 Dec 1804
LC; dower of the wid. Alcy T. GALLE laid off by Benjamin N. GARLAND. (LC EB 24:301)

GALLOWAY, James B. (Dr.); T Jul 1813; 21 Dec 1813
LC; INV; includes a large number of accounts. (LC EB 27:158)
[James B. GALLOWAY mar. Ann F. SMITHER, LC, bond 9 Dec 1812 (MLBLC:29)]

GARLAND, Elizabeth; [m]; 5 Jan 1807
NFP, RC; WILL; Negro fellow Sam to sis. Milly PALMER; after sis. death to her son George G. PALMER; Negro woman Amey to bro-in-law William PALMER; bro. William GARLAND's 3 children: Sophia GARLAND, Charine GARLAND, & Mary GARLAND; Negro women Rachell & Martha to sis. [Hany] GARLAND; Negro boy John Travers to sis. [Hany] GARLAND's son Robert G. GARLAND; 2 daus. of sis. Milly PALMER: Elizabeth G. PALMER & Hennarita PALMER; Negro girl Mary to Eliz. G. PALMER; Negro girl Lifa to Hennarita PALMER; bro. William's dau. Betsy

EVANS £20; friend [Bryan] N. GARLAND & bro-in-law William PALMER exors; WITS: Eliz. JONES, Easter READE. (RC WB 9:301)
[Eliz. GARLAND was a dau. of Geo. GARLAND of LP, RC who in his will (RC 24 Mar 1797 - 3 Dec 1798) named his wife Mary and children William, George Taylor, Elizabeth, Melia, Sarah & Henrietta (RC WB 9:99); Melia GARLAND, dau. of Geo. GARLAND, mar. Wm. PALMER Jr., RC, bond 5 Feb 1798 (MRC:153)]

GARLAND, George; PO Feb 1799; 7 Jul 1806
RC; DIV of slaves among: Elizabeth GARLAND, George [T.] GARLAND, William PALMER, Henrietta GARLAND, William GARLAND. (RC AB 3:160)

GARLAND, Griffin; 10 Sep 1804; 19 Apr 1809
RC; WILL; to be buried in the family burying ground as near as possible to my dear wife & children heretofore departed this life; land of Phil ROSE of North Carolina which came to me from my son William Griffin GARLAND is not my property but his; yellow girl Phelitia otherwise called Philitia PARROT dau. of Rose I purchased under execution of the est. of Mr John WORMELY shall live with my dau. Alice Martin GARLAND until she, Philitia, arrives to the age of 18 (she being born 20 Dec 1797) during which time she shall be treated as a free born orphan & to have two years schooling or otherwise taught to read and write and at the age of 18 my dau. Alice shall pay her the usual freedom dues as apprentices receive; at the age aforesaid the sd. Philitia PARROT shall be liberated and free; in case my dau. Alice Martin should die before Philitia comes to the age of 18, she shall live with either of my other daus. as she may choose until age 18 during which time she shall not be carried out of the four lower counties on the Northern Neck; all est. I had with her to wife Frances GARLAND if she abides by will including the man Aaron, woman Easter, and all her children; after wife's death Negroes to go to dau. Alice Martin GARLAND; wife to also have man Dick and woman Rose; son Jeremiah GARLAND; land in Buckingham Co. sold to Capt. Lewis [WILKINSON] of that county; bridge I built over the little creek of Totuskey & tract of land on which I now live purchased of Capt. Samuel KELSICK to son Jeremiah GARLAND; son Benjamin GARLAND; daus. Sarah Gwynn & Betsy Brereton GARLAND; son Peter Rust GARLAND; first wife Mary a dau. of Peter RUST; children I had of first wife: Benjamin Newton, William Griffin, Jeremiah, Peter Rust and William Griffin YERBY son of my dau. Elizabeth; Negro boy Phil PARROT commonly called Parrot and a Negro boy Phil JOHNSON both sons of man Phil [Jeremiah GARLAND granted certificate to obtain probat; *this is a very long complicated will and should be examined very carefully*]. (RC WB 9:718)
[There are at least 3 marriages for a Griffin GARLAND, 2 in RC and 1 in LC; (1) to Mary Colston SMITH, dau. of Wm. SMITH, RC, bond 27 Jul 1781, (2) to Sarah PLUMMER, RC, bond 11 Sep 1785, and (3) to Frances BURWELL, wid. of Nathaniel BURWELL, LC, bond 16 Mar 1791 (MWO:141); Griffin GARLAND had at least nine children: Benjamin N., Peter R. (mar. Alice C. BELFIELD, RC, bond 9 Aug 1806), William G., Mary Griffin "Polly" (mar. Jn. DUDLEY, RC, bond 14 Jan 1793), Jeremiah, Elizabeth Rust (mar. Geo. YERBY, RC, bond 11 May 1790), Elizabeth B. (mar. Thos. P. BALL, of LC, RC, bond 9 Mar 1811), Sally (mar. Jn. DUDLEY), and Alice Martin (mar. Enoch GEORGE, LC, bond 20 Sep 1808) (MRC:60, 75, 238; MLBLC:30; RC

Orders 1814-16:45, LC OB 26:166); NB: It looks like Jn. DUDLEY mar. (1) Mary G. GARLAND and (2) her sis. Sarah]

GARLAND, Griffin; T 2 Dec 1823; 5 Jan 1824

RC settlement of ests. of Griffin GARLAND dec'd (Jeremiah GARLAND admr) & Benjamin N. GARLAND dec'd (William FORRESTER admr); the following people were heirs & distributees: the admr. of Peter R. GARLAND dec'd, the children of sd. Peter R. GARLAND (John B. & Benjamin N. GARLAND), Joseph JANEY & Adelaide his wife, Spencer GEORGE admr. of Enoch GEORGE who was the admr. of Alice, Griffing DUDLEY & Thomas DUDLEY children of Mary G. the first wife of John DUDLEY, Griffin DUDLEY as the admr. of John DUDLEY, and William G. YERBY the only child of Betsy. (RC AB 4:92)

[Jn. DUDLEY mar. Mary Griffin 'Polly" GARLAND, RC, bond 14 Jan 1793 (MRC:60)]

GARLAND, Jeremiah; 25 Dec 1815; 1 Jan 1816

RC; WILL; all est. to wife until son Griffin GARLAND becomes of age; Negro Bob is a runaway; if wife is pregnant, half of my est. loaned her after my son becomes of age should be left to the child now in the womb; if wife is not pregnant, at her death whole of est. to son Griffin; friends [Hillkiah] BALL & Robert BAILEY exors; WITS: Horace WELLFORD. (RC WB 9:500)

[Robt. BAILEY aptd. gdn. to Griffin & Jeremiah B. GARLAND orphans of Jeremiah GARLAND, 2 Apr 1827 (RC OB 27:150, 152)]

GARLAND, Mary; PO 5 Feb 1816; 2 Apr 1816

RC; DIV of dower Negroes of Mary GARLAND dec'd., wid. of George GARLAND, into 4 eq. parts: George T. GARLAND (infant) (Tom), George T. GARLAND (boy George), William GARLAND's heirs (Negro boys Henry & Martin), William PALMER (Thaddeus & Winny); the 2 Negroes allotted to William GARLAND's children were sold & the proceeds div. among: John GARLAND in behalf of his wife Sophia, Elizabeth EVANS, Caty GARLAND, Polly GARLAND (each received $181.81 1/4). (RC AB 3:372)

[This is Mary WRIGHT who mar. Geo. GARLAND, RC, bond 27 Oct 1796 (MRC:75); Wm. PALMER, Jr. mar. Melia GARLAND, RC, bond 5 Feb 1798 (MRC:153); Jn. GARLAND mar. Sophia GARLAND, RC, bond 21 Dec 1810 (MRC:75)]

GARLAND, Mary; PO 1 Jan 1816; 3 Nov 1824

RC; DIV of Negroes into 5 eq. parts: Vincent BRAMHAM (received Abram), Nancy NEALE (John), James RICE & Mary his wife (Tony), children & grandchildren of Benjamin BRAMHAM Jr. dec'd (Sinah & child Ben), Alice DEMERET (Milly); Sinah & child Ben were sold and the proceeds div. among the children & grandchildren of Benjamin BRAMHAM Jr. dec'd as follows: to Ellen BRAMHAM, Mary BRAMHAM & Nancy BRAMHAM each one fourth part, to Nancy MOXLEY one half of one fourth part & to James MOXLEY one half of one fourth part. (RC AB 4:151)

GARLAND, Peter R.; 8 Oct 1807; 8 Dec 1807

RC; WILL; new house to be finished in degrees and the expenses to be paid out of my son John's est; Negroes Will, Robin, Steven to wife during her widowhood; Negroes Charles Siner, Charles Isaac, Pat & her son Henry to son John [Belfield] after the death of his mother-in-law; Negroes Moses Nancy, Billey Nancy, Letty Cupid to youngest son not yet christened; Negroes [*portion unclear*] to my son John J. G.; [Negroes] Pat & David to wife they serving her during 20 years; bro. Benjamin N. GARLAND ex. & gdn. to

my two sons, after his death, bro. Jeremiah GARLAND [to be ex. & gdn.]; WITS: Alice M. GARLAND, Geo. DAVIS. (RC WB 9:315)
[Peter R. GARLAND was a son of Griffin GARLAND; he mar. Alice C. BELFIELD, RC, bond 9 Aug 1806 (MRC:75); however, acc. to a rather confusing RC record, Winifred the only child and heir of Maj. Jn. BELFIELD mar. Peter R. GARLAND, and died on or about 5 Jun 1812 leaving one child, John B. GARLAND (RC OB 24:216); in Oct 1809, Jn. B. and Benj. N. GARLAND were named as infant children of Peter R. GARLAND dec'd and his wid. Alice B. (RC Orders 1809-10:25); settlement of Moore F. BROCKENBROUGH's gdnship. acct. of Jn. B. GARLAND orphan of Peter R. GARLAND, 5 Sep 1825 (RC OB 27:1)]

GARLAND, Peter R.; PO 5 Dec 1808, T 6 Jan 1809; 6 Feb 1809
RC; DIV of slaves between Benjamin N. GARLAND as gdn. to John B. GARLAND (Young Charles, Old Charles, Sinah, Nancy & child Patty) and Alice C. GARLAND gdn. to Benjamin N. GARLAND an infant (Moses, Isaac, Letty, Young Sinah, Harry); Stephen a likely boy but at present so afflicted as to be rendered uncertain whether he will ever be of any value remains as the est. of Peter R. GARLAND subject in future to a division should he recover. (RC AB 3:214)

GARLAND, Peter R.; T 18 Dec 1807; 4 Nov 1817
RC; INV, £1395.12.1, includes the following Negroes: Charles, Sinah, Charles, Patt & young child Joe, Sinah, Isaac, Harry, Moses, Nancy, Letty, Henry, Stephen, Robert, Will and the schooner "Lively." (RC WB 9:589)

GARLAND, Vincent; 27 Jan 1816; 5 Mar 1816
RC; WILL; small tract of land which I possess near Richmond Courthouse containing 53 and a half ac. also my interest in my mother's dower land should be sold together on a credit of 6 months and just debts paid out of the proceeds; plant. w/o I now live to son James GARLAND, but wife Elizabeth GARLAND shall have the use of the sd. plant. during her widowhood; if she should remarry, son James to have whole & sole possession of sd. plant.; whole pers. est. to be kept together for use of wife & her three children: James, Elizabeth & Felicia; if wife remarries, est. to be eq. div. among my three children; Vincent SHACKLEFORD & bro. Daniel GARLAND to be exors; WITS: Geo. MILES, Geo. Y. GARLAND, Thos. DOBYNS. (RC WB 9:512)
[This is prob. Vincent GARLAND, Jr. who mar. Betsey JACKSON, RC, bond 4 Jan 1808 (MRC:75); Eliz. (JACKSON) GARLAND mar. (2) Jn. PLUMMER, RC, bond 13 Jul 1819 (RC OB 24:375, 419; MRC:159); Wm. PLUMMER aptd. gdn. of Jas. V. GARLAND, Eliza GARLAND & Felitea GARLAND orphans of Vincent GARLAND, 4 Dec 1820 (RC OB 25:94); Eliz. & Jas. GARLAND orphans of Vincent GARLAND chose Wm. GARLAND as their gdn., 5 Jun 1826 (RC OB 27:79)]

GARLAND, William; PO Dec 1805; 4 Feb 1806
RC; INV, £344.14.6, includes the following Negroes: Suck & child Eliza, Clem, David. (RC WB 9:277)

GARLAND, William; PO 7 Aug 1816, T 17 Aug 1816; 4 Mar 1817
RC; DIV of proceeds of sale of Negroes Suckey & Clem belonging to the est. of William GARLAND dec'd & held by Mary GARLAND his wid. as dower among John GARLAND in behalf of his wife Sophia, Elizabeth EVANS in her own right, Catharine "Caty" GARLAND (ward of John PLUMMER), Polly GARLAND. (RC AB 3:411)

[Jn. GARLAND mar. Sophia GARLAND, RC, bond 21 Dec 1810; Eliz. GARLAND mar. Francis EVANS, RC, bond 12 Nov 1803 (MRC:66, 75,76)]

GARLAND, William Jr.; PO Oct 1805; 2 Jun 1806
RC; INV, £282.14.0, includes the following Negroes: Han[n]ah (afflicted), girl Fanny, boy Stephen. (RC WB 9:281)

GARLICK, Mary; [28 Aug] 1776
WC; son William GARLICK; [grson.] Lewis Bennett GARLICK; WITS: Edw. GILL, [?] [DANKS]. (WC Unrec Wills 1755-1800 #17)
[*NB: This will is very difficult to read and the names must be regarded as tentative.*]

GARLINGTON, William; PO 13 Jun 1803, T 20 Sep 1803; 13 Jun 1808
NC; INV, [m]; includes Negroes Darkey, Agga, Sam, Isabel, [Isaac], Levina, Argle, Tabba, Dick, Diannah; PO 9 Jul 1804 Lucy GARLINGTON allotted her dower in the lands and one third of the Negroes; residue of est. div. among John NORRIS & Susannah his wife (rec'd 61 ac. of land & Negro Armistead). Lucy GARLINGTON (rec'd 38 ac. of land & Negro Argle), Nancy GARLINGTON (rec'd 38 ac. of land & Negro Tabba), Polly GARLINGTON (rec'd 27 ac. of land & Negro Levina), William GARLINGTON (rec'd 27 ac. of land & Negro Darkey); Negro Armistead was born since the appraisement of the est. (NC RB 17:628, 629)
[This is prob. Wm. GARLINGTON who mar. Lucy CURRELL, dau. of Geo. CURRELL (d. LC 1788), LC bond 8 Nov 1877 (MWO:142); the est. of Wm. GARLINGTON was ord. to be admin. by Lucy GARLINGTON, NC, 13 Jun 1803 (NC Minute Book 1801-1805:167); Jn. NORRIS mar. Susanna GARLINGTON dau. of Lucy GARLINGTON, NC, bond 8 Aug 1803 (MLBNC:78); on the mot. of Robt. J. DAMERON gdn. of Wm. GARLINGTON ord. that Jas. L. NORRIS gdn. of Jas. NORRIS show cause why lands which Lucy GARLINGTON died seized should not be sold, NC 14 Nov 1821 (NC OB 1820-25:156; *see also* NC CC 1820-013)]

GARLINGTON, William; PO 11 Dec 1815, T 15 Jul 1816; 9 Sep 1816
NC; Negro boy Patrick belonging to the est. of William GARLINGTON dec'd was sold & proceeds were div.among the heirs: William GARLINGTON, Enoch H. POTTS, Nancy GARLINGTON, Lucy GARLINGTON, William GARLINGTON gdn. of John H. [?]. (NC RB 21:67)
[Enoch Hill POTTS mar. Polly GARLINGTON, NC, bond 9 Aug 1813 (MLBNC:83)]

GARLINGTON, William; 15 Nov 1817; 12 Jan 1818
NC; WILL; I lend my land & Negroes to wife Maryann J, GARLINGTON until son William is 21; wife & friend William HARDING exors; [no WITS]. (NC RB 21:309)
[Wm. GARLINGTON mar. Mary Ann J. GIDDINGS, NC, bond 11 Jul 1816 (MLBNC:40)]

GARLINGTON, William; PO 9 Feb 1818; 9 Nov 1818
NC; INV, $84[3].22; includes Negroes Matilda & Diana. (NC RB 21:517)

GARNER, Ann; 23 Apr 1819; 22 May 1820
WC; WILL; land I got from my father I lend to my sis. Jane WROE during her life; the Negroes which came to me by the death of my father to be eq. div. between Benedict WRIGHT, William WRIGHT, Benedict LAMKIN Jr. & Jeremiah MIDDLETON reserving that portion of Negroes that may fall to Jeremiah MIDDLETON to his mother OLDHAM during her life; to Martha OLDHAM dau. of Nathaniel OLDHAM one Negro woman Peggy with her five children & one Negro man Harry; to Hannah WRIGHT dau. of William WRIGHT one Negro woman Judy & her [two] children; to Mary WRIGHT

dau. of William WRIGHT a Negro woman [Sarafine] & her son George; to William WRIGHT Sr. my old man Sampson; to William WRIGHT son of William WRIGHT the tract of land w/o I now live; Suckey MORGAN; Sally BRANN; Jane WRIGHT dau. of William WRIGHT; Martha OLDHAM wife of Nathaniel OLDHAM; rest of my est. to be eq. div. between William WRIGHT Sr., Benedict WRIGHT, Jane WRIGHT & my sis. Martha OLDHAM; William MIDDLETON & William WRIGHT Sr. exors; WITS: Eliza WRIGHT, Sam. TEMPLEMAN, Sally BRANN, Jn. BAILEY. (WC DW 24:68)

[Ann GARNER was a dau. of Benedict MIDDLETON who d. in WC in 1785; she had the following siblings: Elizabeth (mar. 1. Francis WRIGHT, WC, bef 1782 & 2. Geo. LEWIS, WC, bef 1786), Jane (mar. [fnu] WROE), Hannah, & Martha (mar. Nathaniel OLDHAM, WC, 1793); Anne mar. George GARNER (WC, 1790) (WC DW 16:355. MWO:142, 226, 267)]

GARNER, Cathrine; 27 Sep 1785; [m]

WC; WILL; Negro Charlotte & boy [Sanney] to son George; Negro woman [Alce], her dau. Jane and boy [Aksy] to son Vincent; Negro Silva & boy Glasgow lent to dau. Elenor (if she should die without heirs Negroes to go to son George's eldest son); Negro Sarah and her dau. Levina to dau. Elizabeth; Negro girls Nance, Judith & Susanna to dau. Lettice; Negro girl Sina to grson. Willis GARNER; grchildren Hanna & Sally GARNER and Thomas & Cathrine GARNER; sis. Mary HALL; Negro Marriah to have the liberty to live with which she chooses of her young masters; son George ex.; WITS: Geo. RUST, Robt. Bladen CARTER, Wm. JONES, Jn. [HAYNE], Thos. [?RKEY]. (WC Unrec Wills 1755-1800 #33)

[This is Catherine the wid. of Bradley GARNER who named his wife Catherine, sons Geo., Vincent, Benj. & Jeremiah, his daus. Eleanor, Lettice, Hannah COX and Elizabeth and his grandchil. Thos. & Catrin [PRITCHETT] in his will (WC 13 Oct 1769 - 26 Jun 1770); Thos. & Catrin [PRITCHETT] were prob. chil. of Rodham PRITCHETT of Prince William Co., Va. (WC DW15:63)]

GARNER, Elizabeth; [m]; 10 Feb 1800. NC; INV, [m]. (NC RB 16:63)

GARNER, Jeremiah; 23 Sep 1794; Jun 1796

CP, WC; WILL; whole est. to wife Deborah; at her death to be eq. div. among her children: Letty Sandy, Molly Taylor, Leonard Dozier and the child she is now big with; wife extx.; WITS: Jas. GRANT Jr., Jas. GRANT Sr., David WARDROBE. (WC Unrec Wills 1755-1800 #42)

[Jeremiah GARNER mar. Deborah MOSS, WC, bond 5 Nov 1793 (MLBWC:24); Deborah (MOSS) GARNER seems to have mar., prob. (3), James C. SELF, WC, bond 10 Apr 1795 (MLBWC:64); since Deborah MOSS mar. Jere. GARNER in 1793 and he died just two years later, she must have had a previous husband who was prob. the father of some of her children.]

GARNER, Jesse; PO Dec 1814; 4 Dec 1815. RC; INV, [m]. (RC WB 9:494)

[Griffin GARNER, poor orphan of Jesse GARNER, bound to Chichester DOBYNS, shoemaker, complained of ill treatment, 7 Dec 1825 (RC OB 27:26, 31)]

GARNER, Mary; 4 Feb 1823; [21] Jul 1823

LC; WILL; all my land in this county containing 100 ac. to my six daus. Polly GARNER, Elizabeth GARNER, [Nancy] GARNER, [Caty] GARNER, Jane GARNER, & [Sally W.] GARNER; [no ex. named]; WITS: Thos. CARTER, Opie BEANE, Jn. WATTS. (LC WB 28:236)

GARNER, Presley; T 22 Oct 1818; 14 Dec 1818. NC; INV, $234.00. (NC RB 21:551)

GARNER, Presley; 26 Nov 1821
WC; Elizabeth GARNER orphan of Presley GARNER chose Catherine GARNER as her gdn. and Catherine is aptd. gdn. of Catherine, James, Ann & Willis also orphans of Presley. (WC OB 1819-23:335)
[Presley GARNER mar. Caty ASKINS, WC bond 17 Dec 1805 (MLBWC:24)]

GARNER, Reuben; PO 22 Dec 1800; 26 Jan 1801. WC; INV, £55.18.9. (WC RI 8:107)
[Reuben GARNER mar. Ann TUPMAN, WC, bond 23 Jan 1799 (MWO:143)]

GARNER, Thomas; PO 18 Jan 1805; 17 Jun 1805. LC; INV, [m]. (LC EB 24:318)

GARNER, Thomas; T 3 May 1814; 16 Jun 1817
LC; INV, $111.09. (LC EB 27:386)
[Thos. COATES aptd. gdn. to Catharine GARNER orphan of Thos. GARNER, 20 Feb 1815 (LC Orders 24:218)]

GARNER, Vincent; 27 Aug 1810
WC; gdnship. acct. of Charlotte PITMAN's gdnship. of William GARNER orphan of Vincent GARNER. (WC Orders 1810-13:22)
[Lottey GARNER, wid. of Vincent GARNER, mar. (2) Lee PITMAN, WC, bond 7 Dec 1795 (MWO:284)]

GARNER, William; PO 17 Apr 1815, T 22 Apr 1815; 16 Jun 1817
LC; INV, $1292.56 1/2; includes Negroes: Tom, Sarah, George, Ben, Fanny; J. CHOWNING admr. with the will annexed; DIV of est. among: Mary COATS who was Mary GARNER, Thomas COATS in behalf of his ward Catharine GARNER, William GARNER; each heir received $426.54 1/3. (LC EB 27:387, 388)
[Molly GARNER mar. Rich. COATES, LC, bond 2 Nov 1813 (MLBLC:15)]

GARNER, William; 17 Aug 1825; 28 Nov 1825
WC; WILL; wife Rebecca R. GARNER; wife is not to charge dau. Olivia C. GARNER any board except when necessary to board her out to educate her; half of my est. to wife and other half to dau. Olivia; if wife Rebecca should not be alive at the death of Olivia I give the Negroes that came by my mother and those that came by my wife namely Bil, Sillar, Judy, Robert, Leah, Affia, [Cagy], Mima, Charles, Sila, Polly, Grandason, Henry, Fanny, Daniel, Edmond, Harriett, Steptoe, Ann, Jane, Matilda, Mary, Umphrey, Albert, Letty, Umphrey and Cate to be div. between John CRITCHER & William GARNER son of Willis GARNER; if dau. Olivia should die before age 18 or after leaving no heirs and her mother Rebecca should be alive at that time, I give to my wife the Negroes before named and the balance of my est. to John CRITCHER & William GARNER son of Willis GARNER to be eq. div. after death of wife who is to have the use of it during life; wife, John CRITCHER & Robert BAILEY exors; WITS: Thos. STOWERS, Allen S. DOZIER, Jn. THOMAS. (WC DW 25:225)
[Wm. GARNER mar. Rebecca R. COVINGTON, dau. of Royston B. COVINGTON (d. NC, 1825, *see above*), NC, bond 12 Feb 1812 (MLBNC:40); Jn. CRITCHER mar. Sally W. COVINGTON, WC, bond 9 May 1817 (MLBNC:23); commissioners aptd. to div. the landed est. of Wm. GARNER between D. B. TRAVERS who mar. the wid. of sd. Wm. and Olivia GARNER, 26 Mar 1827 (WC OB 1823-27:356); acc. to CC in WC, Rebecca C. TRAVERS &c vs. Adm. of Olivia C. GARNER &c, 1853-13, B28, Wm. GARNER d. in 1825 leaving his wid. Rebecca R. GARNER (the dau. of Royston B. COVINGTON) and dau. Olivia C. GARNER; his wid. mar.

Devereaux B. TRAVERS, WC, bond 1 Nov 1826 and had 2 daus. Rebecca C. & Eliz. D. TRAVERS; Rebecca R. (GARNER) TRAVERS d. in 1829; Olivia C. GARNER d. in 1834 (WCCP:130; *see also NC CC 1837-012*)]

GARNER, William [S.]; T 27 Jul 1818; 10 Jan 1820
NC; INV, $467.29; includes Negro Betty. (NC RB 22:196)
[Wm. S. GARNER mar. Ann KEENE, NC bond 10 May 1815 (MLBNC:40); Ann GARNER aptd. gdn. of Sam. N. GARNER orph of Wm. S. GARNER, NC 12 Jul 1819 (NC OB 1816-20:370)]

GARNER, William P.; PO 8 Oct 1798, T 17 Jan 1799; 15 Oct 1799
NC; INV, [m]; includes Negroes Harry, Bill, Roger, Jerry, Antony, Darby, Reubin, Will Sr., Moses, Natt, Jeffery, Griffin, Harry Jr., David, Spencer, George, Hannah, Ruth, Betty, Betty [sic], Betty (yellow), Sinah, Sillar, Winney, Jane, Clarisa, Lucy. (NC RB 16:16

GARNER, William P.; PO 14 Sep 1801, T 18 Sep 1801; 12 Oct 1801
NC; DIV of land among Lucy GARNER, the wid. (rec'd her dower in the home plant. beginning at the lower landing on the side of the cove, the peach orchard) and Parish GARNER (rec'd the apple orchard and the lower part of the plant). (NC RB 16:301)
[Wm. P. GARNER mar. Lucy NELMS, NC, lic. 25 Jan 1772 (MWO:143); in his will (NC 14 Sep 1798-8 Oct 1798) Wm. Parker GARNER named his wife Lucy and sons Parish, Sam. & Wm. Spelman (NC RB 15:529)]

GARNER, Williamson; PO 29 Oct 1807; 19 Dec 1808. LC; INV, £44.10.0. (LC EB 27:44)

GARNER, Willis; 23 Jan 1826
WC; Overseers of the Poor to bind out Robert, William, Lyddia, Susan & Middleton orphans of Willis GARNER. (WC OB 1823-27:238)
[There are two marriages recorded for Willis GARNER in WC, (1) to Magdaline CRABB, sis. of Daniel CRABB in 1803 and (2) to Frances LAMKIN, bond 25 Nov 1805 (MLBWC:24, 25); Frances G. GARNER mar. Wm. S. BEALE, WC, bond 29 Dec 1823, Susan R. GARNER mar. Peter L. SELF, WC, bond 31 Mar 1838, Lydia E. B. GARNER mar. Peter B. GALLAGHER, WC, bond 15 Jun 1837 (MLBWC:6, 24, 64); acc. to WC CC 1841-001, the heirs of Willis GARNER were Mary Ann GARNER (extx. of Willis B. GARNER), Robt. E. GARNER (of Philadelphia), Wm. S. BEALE & Fanny his wife, Peter L. SELF & Susan his wife, Peter B. GALLAGHER & Lydia B. his wife, Middleton GARNER, and Hannah A. BEALE and Mary BEALE (infants by Hen. BEALE, Jr. their gdn.); Willis B. GARNER was also a son of Willis GARNER; Hannah A. & Mary BEALE must have been children of Frances (LAMKIN, GARNER) BEALE]

GARTON, Anthony; 5 Oct 1794; 16 Feb 1795
LC; WILL; wife Lettice GARTON; wife's children; wife Lettice & John WHEELER to have one fourth of all the crop that is made on the plant; grson. James GARTON son of William GARTON; [no ex. named]; WITS: Gilbert CURRELL, Armistead CURRIE. (LC WB 28:10)
[Anthony GARTON mar. Lettice WHEELER, LC, bond 20 Apr 1786 (MLBLC:29)]

GARTON, Anthony; PO [10] Feb 1795; 21 Dec 1795. LC; INV, [m]. (LC EB 24:51)

GARTON, Benjamin; 9 Nov 1795; 15 Feb 1796
LC; WILL; all my land to wife Mary; at wife's death or marriage land to go to son Samuel GARTON; sons Benjamin, & Uriah GARTON; dau. Nancy GARTON 1 shilling and no more; land that is to fall to me by my father's

will to go to son John GARTON; [no ex. named]; WITS: Gilbert CURRELL, Thos. N. LAWSON. (LC WB 28:3)

[Benj. GARTON mar. Molly REEVER, LC, bond 19 Jan 1788 (MLBLC:29); he was the son of Benj. GARTON who, in his will (LC 22 Sep 1793-21 Oct 1793), named his son. Benj., dau. Judith CLEMONS wife of Jn. CLEMONS, d-i-l Mary GARTON, grdau. Sarah CORNELIUS wife of Wm. CORNELIUS and their son Jn. B. CORNELIUS, Leviney LAWSON, and Ann, Betty & Judith HILL daus. of Rachel CROWTHER (LC WB 22:397); Sam. GARTON orphan of Benj. GARTON chose Hugh BRENT as his gdn., 19 Dec 1808 (LC Orders B23 1808-11:7)]

GASKINS, Edwin; PO 11 Nov 1811; 8 Jun 1812

NC; INV, [m]; includes Negroes boy Bartley, girls Edey & Jane. (NC RB 19:205)

[The est. of Edwin GASKINS was ord. to be admin. by Epaphroditus NORRIS, NC, 11 Nov 1811 (NC OB 1811-1816:24)]

GASKINS, Edwin; PO 11 Dec 1815, T 10 Jan 1816; 11 Mar 1816

NC; DIV of est. among following children: Sally GASKINS (rec'd Bartley), Edwin GASKINS (rec'd girl Jenney), and Thomas GASKINS (rec'd girl Edy). (NC RB 20:385)

GASKINS, Henry L.; 15 Sep 1816; 9 Mar 1818

NC; WILL; I lend to my wife Judith GASKINS all that part of any plant. w/o I now reside to the northward of the ditch between Thomas WHEELER & myself, the sd. ditch begins near a pond or marsh on the river shore & runs nearly a west course to near the house where George DAMERON now resides; following Negroes also to wife: [John], Pleasant, Emmy & her three sons Sam, Solomon & Harry & $500; son Henry L. GASKINS all that part of my land attached to the tract w/o I now reside to the southward of the above mentioned ditch which includes Sandy Point, the place w/o Thomas WHEELER now resides & contains about 200 ac. & the sd. $400 is to be returned sd. Thomas WHEELER at the expiration of his lease; to son Henry L. GASKINS all that part of my plant. w/o I now reside to the north of sd. ditch; to son Charles L. GASKINS all that tract of land on the bay shore near Smith's Point that I purchased of Col. Thomas D. DOWNMAN & containing about 343 ac. dry land & marshes; to son William Henry GASKINS all that small tract of land at Wico[mico] Church containing about 30 ac. part of the land I purchased of James SUTTON dec'd and $1500; the tract of land I purchased which belonged to Lancelott HALL dec'd containing about 62 ac, my store house at North[umberland] Courthouse that I purchased of Edward C. BROWN and all my interest in the house & lot near Lancaster Courthouse that belongs at this time to William HARDING & myself which we purchased of Ball LELAND to be sold; to the rest of my children not herein mentioned $2000 cash half to be paid in Negroes; rest of est. to be sold and money eq. div. among all children; wife Judith & son Henry L. exors; WITS: Thos. TAYLOR, Lee TAYLOR, Chas. YERBY, Jo. BALL Jr. (NC RB 21:370)

[Hen. L. GASKINS mar. Judith BALL, dau. of David BALL Sr., NC, bond 31 Aug 1795 (MLBNC:41); master commissioner to settle Hen. L. GASKINS' acct. of his admin. of the est. of Hen. L. GASKINS and also the sd. Henry's gdnship. of Sally L., Hannah B., Ann E., Chas. L., Wm. H., Judith B., Thos., Fred., & Jn. GASKINS orphans of Hen. L. GASKINS, 15 Nov 1825 (NC OB 1825-30:50, 96); Chas. L. GASKINS orphan of Hen. L. GASKINS, chose Wm. HUDNALL as his gdn., 15 Nov 1825 (NC OB 1825-30:53)]

GASKINS, Henry Lee; T 20 Oct 1818; 13 Dec 1819
NC; INV, $12,216.75 1/2; includes Negroes Moses, Robbin, Hannibal, Billy, Joshua, Plato, John, Peter, Daniel, Sam, Solomon, Harry, Jesse, Moses, Anthony; Emma, Silvea & child, Sinah, Patty, Judith, Martha, Betty. (NC RB 22:175)

GASKINS, Henry L.; PO 14 Dec 1818, T 30 Dec 1819; 14 Feb 1820
NC; DIV of slaves; Lot 1 (Old Moses, Joshua, Anthony) to Sally L. GASKINS, Lot 2 (Hannibal, Sinah) to Thomas GASKINS, Lot 3 (Billy, Judith) to Judith B. GASKINS, Lot 4 (Plato, Betty) to Ann E. GASKINS, Lot 5 (John, Patty) to Hannah B. JENKINS, Lot 6 (Silvia & child John, Peter) to Frederick B. GASKINS, Lot 7 (Daniel, Young Moses, Jesse) to John GASKINS. (NC RB 22:230)

GASKINS, John; PO 10 Dec 1795; 9 Feb 1801
NC; DIV of est. among legal reps: Lot 1 to John GASKINS (Lemoine, Emanuel, Phillis, Letty, Silva, Easter, Hannah, Peggy, Humphra, Sam, Winney, Hannah's eldest child up the country), Lot 2 to Edward DIGGS (Solomon, Joe, Billy, Silva, Jude, Hannah up the country, Lidda, Agga, Jude, Dick, Mima, Hannah's two youngest children up the country). (NC RB 16:225)
[Edw. DIGGES of York Co. mar. Eliz. GASKINS, the dau. of Thos. GASKINS (d. NC 1785), NC, lic. 8 Jun 1775 (MWO:108)]

GASKINS, Joseph; PO 12 Aug 1811, T 23 Aug 1811; 9 Dec 1811. NC; INV, [m]. (NC RB 19:131)
[The est. of Jos. GASKINS was ord. to be admin. by Rich. H. GASKINS, NC, 12 Aug 1811 (NC OB 1811-1816)]

GASKINS, Thomas; PO 13 Oct 1800, T 23 Dec 1800; 13 Dec 1802
NC; INV; includes Negroes Emanuel, Old Emanuel, Old George, Peter, James, Sam, George LEWIS, Old David, Old Joe, Aron, Anthony, Robin, Old Winney, Judah, Mimy, Lucy, Betty WIGGINS, Chloe, Betty, Patty, Hannah, Ester, Dye, Old Sarah, Stephen, Solomon, David, Peter, Jack, Jery, John WIGGINS, David (son of Lucy), Isaac, Frederick, Nancy WIGGINS, Judah, Lucinda, Lucy, Silva, Darkey, Sally, Anna; DIV of est. among Richard H. GASKINS, Thomas GASKINS, and Hannah GASKINS. (NC RB 16:497)

GASKINS, Thomas; PO 14 Mar 1815; 8 Sep 1817
NC; INV, $4354.90; includes the following Negroes: Sam, [Keers], Emanuel, Lucy, Mary, Anna, Patty, [Sady], Old Sarah, Yellow Lucy, Esther, Moses, Sam, Anthony, David, Charles, Winney, Silvy, James, Elijah, Billy. (NC RB 21:248)

GASKINS, Thomas; 9 Nov 1818; Hannah H. GASKINS orphan of Thomas GASKINS chose Richard H. GASKINS as her gdn. (NC OB 1816-20:300)

GASKINS, Thomas; PO 14 Nov 1821; 8 Jul 1822
NC; David BALL & Hannah his wife complts. against Richard H. GASKINS & Ann his wife, Sarah, Elizabeth, Alice & Fanny GASKINS defts.; Richard H. GASKINS aptd. gdn. to Sarah, Elizabeth, Alice & Fanny GASKINS who are infants; commissioners & surveyor appointed to lay off and assign to Richard H. GASKINS & Ann his wife the sd. Ann's dower in the lands [of Thomas GASKINS dec'd] and div. the remainder among the the complts. and defts.; land was located near the main road leading from Ball's Neck to Wiccomoco Church & was surveyed 11 May 1822. (NC RB 23:181)
[David BALL mar. Hannah the dau. of Thos. GASKINS and niece of Sarah E. BALL, NC, bond 9 Nov 1818 (MLBNC:3, NC CC 1821-008); Rich. H. GASKINS, wid., mar. Ann GASKINS, wid., NC, bond 28 Jul 1815

(MLBNC:41); Hannah, Sarah, Eliz., Alice & Fanny are children of Thos. GASKINS (NC CC 1821-008); Miller:5 locates Ball Neck [sic] in the Wicomico District of NC between Cloverdale Creek on the north and Ball Creek on the south fronting on the Chesapeake Bay]

GASKINS, Thomas Col.; 13 Feb 1809
NC; court recognizes that Sarah E. BALL wife of the Rev. David BALL, James EWELL son of Ann EWELL dec'd, Alice P. MONCURE wife of John MONCURE, Thomas GASKINS, Richard GASKINS, Martha HULL the wife of John HULL, John E. GASKINS and Mary HULL the wife of Thomas G. HULL are the children, grchild, and legal reps. of Col. Thomas GASKINS, dec'd. (NC OB 1807-11:78)
[In his will (NC 12 Mar 1800-14 Apr 1800) Thos. GASKINS named his wife Hannah, eld. son Thos., nephew Thos PINCKARD, niece Alice C. PINCKARD, second son Rich. H., son Jn. Eustace, dau. Sarah E. BALL and her husb. Rev. David BALL, grson. Jas. EWELL, dau. Martha HULL and husb. Jn. HULL, dau. Mary HULL and husb. Thos. G. HULL (NC RB 16:79); Thos. GASKINS (son of Col. Thos. and Sarah GASKINS) mar. Hannah HULL (dau. of Rich. & Eliz. HULL), NC, 4 Sep 1767 (MWO:145); Nancy Lee GASKINS mar. Jas. EWELL, NC, bond 13 Oct 1788 (MLBNC:37); Alice Peachy GASKINS mar. Jn. MONCURE, NC bond 14 Feb 1792 (MLBNC:74); Martha GASKINS mar. Jn. HULL, NC, bond 21 Oct 1797 (MWO:191); Mary GASKINS mar. Thos. Gascoyne HULL, NC, bond 24 Feb 1800 (MWO:192)]

GASKINS, William; PO 12 Sep 1803; 12 Dec 1803. NC; INV, £43.3.0. (NC RB 17:100)

GASKINS, William; PO 12 Sep 180[3], T 3 Nov 1803; 8 Jun 1807
NC; DIV of land; one half being the part next to David BALL Jr. allotted to John LEDFORD & Elizabeth his wife; also laid off the widow's dower out of the sd. LEDFORD's part and the other half where the dwelling house stands to Jane H. GASKINS; Negroes Ann & Jesse to Jane H. GASKINS and Judy & Sally to John LEDFORD & his wife. (NC RB 17:528)
[The est. of Wm. GASKINS was ord. to be admin. by Thos. HAMMOND, NC, 12 Sep 1803 (NC Minute Book 1801-1805:182); Jn. LEDFORD mar. Eliz. GASKINS, NC, bond 14 Dec 1801 (MLBNC:67)]

GAVIN, John; T 18 Oct 1805; 24 Nov 1806. WC; INV, £41.6. (WC RI 9:6)

GAYLE, Christopher; T 6 Mar 1812; 15 Jun 1812
LC; INV, $627.08; includes Negroes Peter & Billy and $9.08 due in division of Negroes from John DEGGE's heirs; Daniel P. MITCHELL admr. (LC EB 27:111)
[GAYLE rec'd a portion of the est. of Simon DEGGES, LC 30 Mar 1780 (LC WB 20:178)]

GEOFF, Thomas W.; [?]; 12 Jun 1820. NC; INV, [m]. (NC RB 22:330)
[Thos. W. GEOFF, wid., mar. Millicent C. WORNOM, (poss. the wid. of Wm. WORNOM), bond 30 May 1816 (MLBNC:42)]

GEORGE, Balaam; PO 11 Oct 1802; 10 Jan 1803. NC; INV, £60.11.2 1/4. (NC RB 16:512)
[Balam or Balah GEORGE, son of Wm. & Nancy GEORGE mar. Bettey RICE, dau. of Isaac & Sarah RICE, NC, bond 13 Jun 1793 (MWO:145); Balaam and Eliz. GEORGE had two children: Jn. (b. 1797) and Emily (b. 1801) (*see Register of Wicomico Baptist Church in BNCHS vol. III no. 1:46*)]

GEORGE, Betsey; T 17 Apr 1806; 10 Sep 1806
LC; list of slaves held by Betsey GEORGE wid. & rel of Daniel GEORGE: Dinah (age 50), Addison (14). (LC EB 24:347)

[This is prob. Eliz. READ, dau. of Nicholas READ, who mar. Daniel GEORGE, LC, bef. 19 Nov 1777 (MWO:145)]

GEORGE, Betsy Waters; 15 Jul 1799

LC; on the mot. of John TAPSCOTT admr. of Betsy Waters GEORGE, ord. that Charles CURTICE, Bailey George BRENT, Hannah BRENT and Lucy BRENT heirs of sd. Betsy Waters GEORGE be summoned to show cause why the est. of sd. Betsy Waters GEORGE should not be sold. (LC Orders (21) 1799-1801:12)

[Betsy Waters GEORGE was a dau. of Juduthan GEORGE (d. LC 1788) (LC WB 22:164)]

GEORGE, Daniel; 20 Jun 1803

LC; INV, £240.19.[?], includes Negroes Ambros, Alice, Aderson, Dinah; DIV of est. among: widow Mrs. Elizabeth GEORGE, William GEORGE, [and poss. one other unidentified heir]. (LC EB 24:237)

GEORGE, Daniel; T 17 Apr 1806; 10 Sep 1806

LC; list of dower slaves held by Betsy GEORGE wid. of Dan GEORGE: Dinah (age 50), Addison (14). (LC EB 24:347)

GEORGE, Daniel; PO 16 Feb 1824, T 13 Mar 1824; 15 Mar 1824

LC; DIV of dower slaves belonging to the est. of Daniel GEORGE that Elizabeth GEORGE died seized and possessed between Hannah H. KELLEY (Old Dinah, Isaac, Polly) and Jane GEORGE gdn. of William H. and, Warren GEORGE (Fanny & her child Siller). (LC EB 29:312)

GEORGE, Elizabeth; [m] 1820; 17 Dec 1821

LC; WILL; niece Mary PITMAN; son Spencer; son Bidkar; dau. Elizabeth MITCHELL; d-i-l Ann CURTIS; grson. Spencer [G.] MITCHELL; three children of dec'd dau. Rebecca M. [THRALL]; son Spencer ex; WITS: Jas. CARTER, Moses LUNSFORD. (LC WB 28:221)

[This is Eliz. the wid. of Spencer GEORGE (d. LC 1800) *see below*; Eliz. GEORGE mar. Daniel P. MITCHELL, LC, bond 24 Feb 1808; Capt. Bidkar GEORGE mar. Mary DEGGE, LC, 5 May 1812 (MLBLC:30); Ann GEORGE, dau. of Spencer GEORGE, mar. Chas. CURTIS, LC, bond 21 Nov 1789; Rebecca M. GEORGE mar. Thos. THRALL, LC, bond 1 Feb 1809 (MLBLC:19, 52, 74)]

GEORGE, Elizabeth; [3] Dec 1819; 20 Oct 1823

LC; WILL; plant. w/o I now live containing about 25 ac. to my dau. H[annah] KELLEY as long as she lives; at her death plant. to be eq. div. between my grchildren William [H.] GEORGE & Warren GEORGE the children of my son William GEORGE dec'd; use of my Negroes Alice & Harry to my dau. Hannah [H.] KELLEY; at her death Negroes to be eq. div. between my grchildren John R. KELLEY, Mahala Y. KELLEY & Williamson KELLEY; grson. John Read KELLEY; [no ex. named]; WITS: Raw. DUNAWAY, Mary SNOW, Wm. WARWICK, Wm. OLDHAM, Thos. D. GEORGE. (LC WB 28:239)

[This is Eliz. GEORGE the wid. of Dan. GEORGE, *see above*; Hannah H. GEORGE mar. (1) Ezekiel TAPSCOTT and (2) Jas. KELLEY, LC, bond 25 Jan 1799 (MLBLC:44; http://familytreemaker.genealogy.com/users/l/o/n/Nakia-L-Long/WEBSITE-0001/UHP-0008.html and familytreemaker.genealogy.com/users/l/o/n/Nakia.../PDFBOOK1.pdf accessed 13 Dec 2012)]

GEORGE, Elizabeth L.; 5 Jun 1814; 19 Dec 1814

LC; WILL; $50 due me from Maj. John BISCOE for the rent of land for the year 1809 to be eq. div. amongst my 3 youngest children: Wickliff, Keturah & Araman; rest of est. after debts paid to be eq. div. amongst my children: Polly NEALE, Rebeckah M. THRALL, Luther GEORGE, Calvin GEORGE, Wickliff GEORGE, Keturah GEORGE & Araman GEORGE; Col. John CHOWNING ex; WITS: Thos. BISCOE, Humphrey F. CARTER. (LC WB 28:152)
[This is Eliz. Linton (ARMS) GEORGE wid. of Wm. GEORGE (*see below*); Polly GEORGE mar. Presley NEALE, LC, bond 29 Jan 1812; Rebecca M. GEORGE mar. Thos. THRALL, LC, bond 1 Feb 1809 (MLBLC:54, 74)]

GEORGE, Elizabeth L.; PO 19 Dec 1814, T 10 Jan 1815; 21 Nov 1815. LC INV. (LC EB 27:272)

GEORGE, Ellen; 28 Aug 1807; 20 Jun 1808
LC; WILL; all est. to son Harrison GEORGE; full proportion of est. already given to dau. Ellen THRALL & sons [Zamoth] GEORGE & Rawleigh GEORGE; [no ex. named]; WITS: Jn. GAINES, Thos. MASON, Jas. POLLARD. (LC WB 28:109)
[Ellen GEORGE was the wid. of Martin GEORGE (*see below and LC CC 1811-034*)]

GEORGE, Enoch; T 4 Aug 1823; 18 Aug 1823
LC; INV, $1096.73 [1/2]; includes [Negro] Felicia. (LC EB 29:287)
[Enoch GEORGE aptd. gdn. to his children Benj., Griffin, and Warren GEORGE, RC, 2 Nov 1818 (RC OB 24:271)]

GEORGE, Fortunatus; T 6 Nov 1822; 20 Jan 1823. LC; INV, [m]; includes [slave] Mina. (LC EB 29:242)

GEORGE, Fortunatus; PO 21 Oct 1822, T 29 Nov 1822; 20 Jan 1823
LC; sale of Negro Mima belonging to the est. of Fortunatus GEORGE dec'd and div. of proceeds among the heirs: to Mrs Patty GEORGE (Lawson GEORGE & Enoch GEORGE's bond for her dower), Patty GEORGE as gdn. to Alice T., Enoch, Harrison & Caty GEORGE, to Richard BARECRAFT in right of his wife Judith who was Judith GEORGE, to Thomas N. GEORGE, to Lawson GEORGE (who purchased above Negro). (LC EB 29:199, OB 25:335)
[Rich. H. BARECROFT mar. Judith GEORGE, NC, bond 6 Jul 1816 (MLBNC:6); Patty GEORGE aptd. gdn. to Ailcey, Enoch, Harrison and Caty GEORGE, 18 Nov 1822 (LC OB 25:338)]

GEORGE, Frances; PO 19 Mar 1821; 16 Jul 1821
LC; sale of Negro boy Henry and child Davy for $135 to John MEREDITH and div. of proceeds among: Wesly KIRK, Jonathan PULLIN's gdn, William FALLIN's gdn, Nancy B. PULLIN's gdn. & William GEORGE gdn. to Frances GEORGE (each one rec'd $25.38). (LC EB 29:115)

GEORGE, Henry; 20 Nov 1810
LC; on the mot. of John LEDFORD, ord. that William & Martin GEORGE heirs of Henry GEORGE be summoned to show cause why slaves of sd. Henry GEORGE should not be sold. (LC Orders B23 1808-11:225)
[Jn. LEDFORD mar. Judith M. GEORGE, LC, bond 30 Nov 1807 (MLBLC:47)]

GEORGE, Henry; PO 21 Jan 1811; 15 Apr 1811
LC; DIV of est. among: George GRESHAM, Mrs. GEORGE, Martin GEORGE. (LC EB 27:85)

GEORGE, Isaac; 16 Oct 1818

LC; Fleet COX allowed to use $26 of the est. of his wards Newton Lee & Moses GEORGE orphans of Isaac GEORGE for their support the present year. (LC OB 25:25)

[This is prob. the Isaac GEORGE who mar. Winney BROWN dau. of Spencer BROWN, LC, bond 11 Oct 1808 (MLBLC:30)]

GEORGE, James; PO 9 Jul 1810, T 28 Jul 1810; 8 Oct 1810

NC; INV, £17.8.3. (NC RB 18:473)

[In his will (NC 14 May 1810-9 Jul 1810) James GEORGE of WicP left all his est. to Jane BELL (NC RB 18:420)]

GEORGE, [Jane]; 20 May 1816

LC; Fleet COX aptd. gdn. to Moses & Leroy GEORGE orphans of [Jane] GEORGE. (LC Orders 24:301)

GEORGE, Jemima; 17 Feb 181[1]; 18 Dec 1815

LC; WILL; to dau. Betsey Hunton GEORGE my land & plant. during her life; if she should die without heirs, land & plant. to my uncle Stephen CHILTON; remainder of est. to dau. Betsey Hunton GEORGE; if she dies without heirs, remainder of est. to the children of my sis. Mary PALMER; sis. Mary PALMER to have my silk bonnet; friends William NEWBY & Capt. John BEANE exors; WITS: Jas. CARTER, Moses GEORGE, Joel KENT. (LC WB 28:173)

GEORGE, Jemima; T 21 Dec 1815; 20 May 1816. LC; INV. (LC EB 27:310)

GEORGE, Jesse; PO 18 Oct 1797; 15 Apr 1799

LC; laid off widow's dower & div. est. among: Frances GEORGE, Alice M. GEORGE, Bailey GEORGE in virtue of his wife Ann M. GEORGE, Sally GEORGE. (LC EB 24:92)

[Jesse GEORGE mar. [Mary] MEREDETH dau. of Jn. MEREDETH of CCP, LC bef 27 Mar 1784; Bailey GEORGE mar. Nancy M. GEORGE, LC, bond 21 Mar 1797 (MWO:145, 146); Mary (MEREDETH) GEORGE prob. mar. (2) Thos. CURRELL, LC, bond 17 Dec 1801 (MLBLC:18); on the mot. of Robt. C. WAIDE ord. to settle the adm. acct. of Mary CURRELL (late GEORGE) with the est. of Jesse GEORGE and div. the est. of sd. Jesse GEORGE among his legal reps. and possess the sd. Robt. C. WAIDE with his wife's proportion thereof, 19 Apr 1802 (LC Orders V 1802-03:60); Sally GEORGE orphan of Jesse GEORGE chose Spencer GEORGE he gdn. and sd. Spencer is aptd. gdn. of Fanny Harding GEORGE orphan of sd. decedent, 21 Feb 1803 (LC Orders V 1802-03:263); Robt. C. WAIDE mar. Alice M. GEORGE, LC, bond 23 Dec 1801 (MLBLC:76)]

GEORGE, Jesse; [m]; 19 Dec 1803

LC; settled accts. of Mary GEORGE now Mary CURRELL admx. of Jesse GEORGE and allotted the wid. her dower and div. remainder of est. among Bailey GEORGE in right of his wife Nancy M. GEORGE, Robert C. WAIDE in right of his wife Alice M. GEORGE, Sally GEORGE and Frances GEORGE. (LC EB 24:258)

[Bailey GEORGE mar. Nancy GEORGE, LC, bond 21 Mar 1797 (MLBLC:30); Mary GEORGE mar. Thos. CURRELL, LC, bond 17 DEc 1801 (MLBLC:18)]

GEORGE, John; PO 10 Sep 1821, T 23 Sep 1821; 12 Nov 1821

NC; INV, $10.24; includes box of shoemaker's tools. (NC RB 23:35)

GEORGE, Judith; 10 Mar 1795; 21 Apr 1795

[CCP], WILL; LC; all land that I bought of Nathaniel GORDON to be eq. div. between my dau. Elizabeth M. STEPTOE, Nancy H. GEORGE, Landon GEORGE & Linsey GEORGE; my seven Negroes Ned, Sarah, Easter, Nancy, Sarah, David & Mahaly also to be eq. div. among children; son Bailie

GEORGE not to inherit any part of my est; friends John STEPTOE, Martin SHEARMAN & James POLLARD exors; WITS: Wm. GIBSON, Wm. KIRK; [The name Nancy H. GEORGE was interlined before signing]; LC WB 28:14) [Eliz. Martin GEORGE mar. (1) Jn. STEPTOE, LC, bond 12 Dec 1786 and (2) Jos. SHEARMAN, LC, bond 7 Apr 1807 (MWO:331; MLBLC:67); Nancy H. GEORGE mar. Wm. POLLARD, LC, bond 21 Aug 1797 (MWO:284)]

GEORGE, Judith; 30 Jun 1802; 16 Dec 1805
LC; WILL; son Martin GEORGE; son Augustine GEORGE; to dau. Judith M. GEORGE Negro man Humphrey; bro. William GIBSON & friend William MEREDITH exors; WITS: Jn. GIBSON, Sally M. GIBSON. (LC WB 28:93)

GEORGE, Judith; PO 23 Jan 1806, T 23 Jan 1806; 17 Aug 1812. LC; INV. (LC EB 27:117)

GEORGE, Landon; T 22 Jan 1811; 21 May 1811. LC; INV; includes Negroes: Philis, Sally. (LC EB 27:95)
[Landon GEORGE d. intest leaving Bailey GEORGE, Eliz. the wife of Jos. SHEARMAN and Ann H. the wife of Wm. POLLARD his siblings as next of kin (LC CC 1811-008); Judith GEORGE of CCP in her will named Landon as one of her children (*see above*)]

GEORGE, Lazarus; PO Jan 1797, T 24 Jan 1797; 20 Feb 1797
LC; DIV of est. which includes Negro Old Harry among William GEORGE, John GEORGE, Elizabeth GEORGE, Lucy HUBBARD, Judith GEORGE & Robert GEORGE. (LC EB 24:60)

GEORGE, Martin; PO 17 Oct 1808, T 29 Nov 180[8]; 19 Jun 1809
LC; sale of dower slaves held by the wid. Ellen GEORGE and div. of est. among: John THRALL in right of his wife, John THRALL in right of Leroy HUBBARD & Charles JAMES heirs of Joseph HUBBARD dec'd, [Zamoth] GEORGE, Harrison GEORGE, William GEORGE's heirs, Tarpley GEORGE's heirs. (LC EB 27:50)
[Ellen GEORGE mar. Jn. THRALL, LC, bond 2 Feb 1780 (MLBLC:73); Jos. HUBBARD mar. Rebecca GEORGE, LC, bond 21 Sep 1780 (MLBLC:39)]

GEORGE, Martin; PO 16 Feb 1818; 18 May 1818. LC; INV, $127.32. (LC EB 27:424)

GEORGE, Martin; PO 19 Jan 1818; 17 Aug 1818. LC INV. (LC EB 27:436)

GEORGE, Moses; 19 Aug 1816
LC; ord. that Samuel GEORGE, Milly DUNTON, Molly COX, Rebeckah FOSTER & Milton Brooks HUGHLETT by Bidkar GEORGE now aptd. his gdn. and Moses GEORGE & Leroy GEORGE by Fleet COX their gdn. be summoned to show cause why land of which Moses GEORGE died seized & possessed intestate should not be sold for a distribution of the proceeds among the sd. reps. of sd. Moses GEORGE. (LC Orders 24:325)
[Dan. DUNTON mar. Milly GEORGE, LC, bond 15 Jul 1799 (MLBLC:23]

GEORGE, Nicholas; PO 20 Dec 1791, T 30 Dec 1791; 19 Jul 1796
LC; DIV of Negroes among Frances GEORGE (rec'd Negroes Daniel, Frank, Toney, Old Kate, Mima, Charles, Dinah, Dennis), William GEORGE (Cuff, Joe), Frances TAPSCOTT (Harry, Sarah), Nicholas GEORGE (Duke), Catharine GEORGE (Winney, Moses) & Thomas GEORGE (Young Kate, Rose); Nicholas GEORGE one of the legatees died prior to the div. (LC EB 24:25)
[This is Nicholas GEORGE who mar. Frances CONNELLY, LC, bond 10 Jun 1762 (MWO:146); in his will (LC 28 Sep 1781-22 Jul 1785), Nicholas GEORGE named his sons Wm., Thos., Nicholas and Gilbert, his daus. Catharine & Frances (LC WB 22:87. 109, 132); Frances GEORGE, dau. of Nicholas &

Frances (CONNELLY) GEORGE, mar. Rich. TAPSCOTT, LC, bond 14 Aug 1789 (MWO:343)]

GEORGE, Nicholas; 3 Jan 1815; 21 Jan 1822
LC; WILL; cousin Samuel DUNAWAY; cousin's son George DUNAWAY; $30 to Jiles EUBANK[S]; cousin Rawleigh DUNAWAY; [no ex. named]; WITS: Jn. KEMM, Jas. KEMM, Caty R. KEMM. (LC WB 28:222)

GEORGE, Nicholas Lawson; 12 May 1794; 15 Feb 1796
LC; WILL; all est. to wife Sukey GEORGE; at wife's death est. to be eq. div. amongst all my children; bro. Martain GEORGE; son Benjamin GEORGE; b-i-l Ezekiel TAPSCOTT & John TAPSCOTT to overlook the Negroes for their sis. with respect to their work in cropping; b-i-l Ezekiel TAPSCOTT & John TAPSCOTT and friend Lott PALMER exors; WITS: Jn. LONGWORTH Jr., Ezekiel TAPSCOTT. (LC WB 28:2)
[Nicholas Lawson GEORGE mar. Susanna TAPSCOTT, LC, bond 17 Apr 1783 (MLBLC:31); [Edney] GEORGE orphan of Nich. L. GEORGE chose Sam. M. SHEARMAN as his gdn, 16 Dec 1805 and Fortunatus GEORGE was aptd. gdn. to Judith, Jn. & Eppa GEORGE orphans of Nicholas L. GEORGE, 16 Dec 1805 (LC Orders D22 1805-08:99); settlement of Fortunatus GEORGE's acct. of his gdnship. of Jn. GEORGE orphan of Nicholas GEORGE; Jn. GEORGE then chose Sam. M. SHEARMAN as his gdn. 18 Jan 1808 (LC Orders 22D 1805-08:435); admin. on the estates of Judith and Edney GEORGE granted to Jn. GEORGE, 19 Feb 1816 (LC Orders 24:285)]

GEORGE, Nicholas L[awson]; PO 15 Feb 1796; 20 Jun 1796
LC; INV, £153.4.0; inludes Negroes George, Simon, Lisha. (LC EB 24:15)

GEORGE, Nicholas L[awson]; PO 21 Oct 1805; 16 Dec 1805
LC; exors. John & Ezekiel TAPSCOTT; possessed Benjamin GEORGE, one of the children of Nicholas, with his portion of the est.; mention of Betsy W. GEORGE dec'd and Fortunatus GEORGE but their relation to Nicholas is not clear. (LC EB 24:335)

GEORGE, Rawleigh; PO 17 Oct 1808, T 29 Nov 1809; 19 Jun 1809
LC; DIV of proceeds of sale of est. among the legal reps; John THRALL, John THRALL in right of L. HUBBARD, [Henry C. LAWSON] [*portion unreadable*], Hugh BRENT in right of Harrison GEORGE, Harrison GEORGE in right of his mother dec'd, William GEORGE's heirs, Tarpley GEORGE's heirs, Zamoth GEORGE; div. of proceeds of land sale among: John THRALL in right of his wife, John THRALL in right of L. George, John THRALL in right of H. GEORGE, John THRALL in right of Leroy HUBBARD, Charles JAMES in right of his wife, Harrison GEORGE in right of his mother, William GEORGE's heirs, Tarpley GEORGE's heirs. (LC EB 27:51)
[Charles JAMES mar. Sally HUBBARD, LC, bond 7 Jan 1804 (MLBLC:42); on the mot. of Jn. THRALL adm. of Rawleigh GEORGE ord. that Martin GEORGE, Wm. Hen. GEORGE, Caty GEORGE, Thos. GEORGE, Jesse GEORGE, Michael GEORGE, Tarpley GEORGE, Benj. GEORGE, Zamoth GEORGE, Eliz. GEORGE, Zamoth GEORGE Jr., Harrison GEORGE, and Chas. JAMES in right of his wife Sarah and Leroy HUBBARD the heirs and legal reps. of Rawleigh GEORGE be summoned to show cause why land and slaves of which Rawleigh GEORGE died seized & possessed should not be sold, 20 Jun 1808 (LC Orders 22D 1805-08:479)]

GEORGE, Spencer; 18 May 1792; 20 Oct 1800
CCP, LC; WILL; all est. to wife Elizabeth during her life or widowhood; after her death or remarriage land & plant. w/o I now live to son Spencer GEORGE & he is not to sell land to anyone except his bro. Bidcah GEORGE;

land & plant. I purchased of Capt. John DEGGES to son Bidcah GEORGE; half of my still to son Spencer and the other half to son Bidcah; Negro Siller to dau. Ann CURTICE during her life and at her death Negro to go to her dau. Elizabeth Hunton CURTICE; Negro girl Sarah to dau. Elizabeth GEORGE; Negro girl Rose to dau. Rebeckah Martin GEORGE; the use of my chamber to my two daus. Elizabeth & Rebeckah GEORGE during the time they remain single; remainder of est. to be eq. div. between all my children: Spencer, Bidcah, Ann CURTICE, Elizabeth GEORGE & Rebeckah M. GEORGE; wife, son Spencer & friend James CARTER exors; WITS: Jas. CARTER, Jas. DOGGETT, Chas. BAILEY. (LC WB 28:45)
[Ann GEORGE, dau. of Spencer GEORGE, mar. Chas. CURTIS, LC, bond 21 Nov 1789 (MLBLC:19); Eliz. & Rebecca GEORGE orphans of Spencer GEORGE chose Eliz. GEORGE as their gdn., 20 Oct 1800 (LC Orders 21 1799-1801:164)]

GEORGE, Spencer; PO 20 Oct 1800, T 16 Dec 1800;
LC; INV, $3764.?5; includes Negroes: Solloman, [Nellon], Charles, Winney, Sarah, Siller, Rose, Stephen, David, Philip, Armstead, Rachel, Charlotte, Maria, Isaac, [Nellie], Sinah. (LC EB 24:202)

GEORGE, Spencer; 6 Mar 1823; 19 Jan 1824
LC; WILL; use of one third of my est. to my wife Mary GEORGE while she remains my widow; plant. that I now live on to my son James B. GEORGE; plant. w/o my father lived to son Spencer GEORGE; son Bidkar; dau. Elizabeth B. STEPHENS; dau. Rebecca M. GEORGE; son Warren W. C. GEORGE half the money due me in Culpeper Co. for my right in the est. of Mrs. Sarah Ann NEWBY dec'd together with half of all monies rec'd as his mother's proportion of the estates of Elizabeth H. MILLER dec'd & Ann M. MILLER dec'd; son Charles D. GEORGE; sons Warren & Charles are under 21; late departed wife Sarah E. GEORGE; present wife now pregnant; son James B. GEORGE ex. and he is to council with Mr. E. CURRIE; [no wits listed, but will proved by oaths of Raw. DUNAWAY & James KIRK]; LC WB 28:241)
[Spencer GEORGE mar. (1) Sarah E. MILLER, LC, bond 15 Apr 1815 and (2) Mary PITMAN, LC, bond 9 Jul 1822 (MLBLC:31); Eliz. B. GEORGE mar. Geo. STEPHENS, LC, bond 25 Jan 1819 (MLBLC:70)]

GEORGE, Spencer; PO 20 Jan 1824; 18 May 1825
LC; allottment to Mary GEORGE of her dower in the est. of Spencer GEORGE dec'd includes Negroes Lucy, Daniel, Peggy, Winny, George. (LC EB 29:439)

GEORGE, Spencer (Maj.); PO 19 Jan 1824, T 28 Jan 1824; 21 Feb 1825
LC; INV, [m]; includes Negroes Charles, Maria & child Winny, Charlotte, Siller & child Ralph, Peggy, Winny, Letty, Henry, Armstead, Emanuel, Daniel, George, Madderson, Brittania, Florinda, Jane; DIV of slaves PO 20 Dec 1824 among Rebecca M. GEORGE (Charlotte, Florinda), George P. STEPHENS in right of his wife Elizabeth who was Elizabeth GEORGE (Maria, Winny), Charles D. GEORGE (Prescilla, Ralph), Bidkar GEORGE (Jenny, Maddison), Warner W. C. GEORGE (Armstead, Britania) made on 28 Dec 1824. (LC EB 29:393, 402)
[Spencer GEORGE chose Jas. B. GEORGE as his gdn. and sd. Jas. is aptd. gdn. to Rebecca M., Warren W. C. & Chas. D. GEORGE, 19 Jan 1824 (LC OB 26:16); Acc. to the George Family Bible in the LVA, Maj. Spencer GEORGE Jr. (d. 22 Dec 1823) mar. (1) Susanna BRENT (d. 13 Dec 1815), 24 Nov 1796 and (2) Sarah E. [MILLER] (d. 15 Jan 1822) LC, bond 15 Apr 1815; he had the

following children: Eliz. Brent b. 2 Jan 1798; James Brent, b. 1 Jun 1800; Sally, b, 26 Feb 1803, d. 26 Feb 1803; Spencer, b. 30 Apr 1804; Susan Nutt, b. 27 Sep 1806, d. 5 Aug 1808; Bidkar, b. 12 Jul 1809; Walter, b. 22 Dec 1811, d. 7 Feb 1814; Rebecca Mary, b. 3 Dec 1813; unnamed, b. 10 Dec 1815, d. 13 Dec 1815; Warren William Corbin, b. 6 Jul 1817; Charles Drury, b. 29 Aug 1819; Elizabeth Brent GEORGE mar. Geo. STEPHENS, 27 Jan 1819; Spencer GEORGE mar. Mary PITMAN, 10 Jul 1822; James Brent GEORGE mar. Mary N. FLINT, 5 May 1824; Warren William Corbin GEORGE mar. Eliz. W. PALMER dau. of Sally PALMER, 29 Sep 1836]

GEORGE, Tarpley; Dec 1801; 18 Jan 1802
LC; INV, [m], John STEPTOE admr. (LC EB 24:167)
[Tarpley GEORGE was the son of Martin GEORGE; he mar. Eliz. JAMES, dau. of Wm. JAMES (d. LC 1779), LC, bond 15 Feb 1790 (MWO:146)]

GEORGE, Thomas M.; PO 21 Nov 1814, T 16 Feb 1815; 19 Jun 1815
LC; DIV of balance of est. in the hands of Joseph CARTER, the admr., among the legal reps: Joseph CARTER Jr. one of the admrs. of William GEORGE the bro. of Thomas, Frances G. KIDD, sis. of Thomas, Samuel JESSE in right of his wife Catharine who was another sis. of sd. Thomas. (LC EB 27:223)
[Frances G. KIDD was Frances GEORGE, dau. of Frances GEORGE and wid. of Rich. TAPSCOTT who mar. Benj. KIDD, wid., LC, bond 1 Aug 1798 (MLBLC:45, 73); Sam. JESSE mar. Catherine GEORGE, dau. of Frances GEORGE, LC, bond 2 Dec 1793 (MLBLC:43)]

GEORGE, William; 17 Sep 1810
LC; it appearing to the court that the lands of which William GEORGE died seized & possessed in this county are not of the value of $100, ord. that dower in the sd. lands be assigned unto Sarah HARMAN who was Sarah GEORGE the wid. of sd. dec'd. (LC Orders B23 1808-11:219)
[This must be Wm. GEORGE, wid., who mar. Sarah WILDER, LC, bond 9 Nov 1796 (MLBLC:32); Sarah (WILDER) GEORGE mar. (2) Daniel H. HARMAN, LC, bond 22 May 1805 (MLBLC:35)]

GEORGE, William; PO 8 Feb 1813, T 16 Feb 1813; 14 Jun 1813
NC; INV, $118.80. (NC RB 19:393)
[The est. of Wm. GEORGE was ord. to be admin. by Giles EUBANK, NC, 8 Feb 1813 (NC OB 1811-1816:145)]

GEORGE, William; PO 18 Oct 1819; 20 Dec 1819
LC; INV, [m]; includes Negroes: Ambrose and [Dinah]; Jane GEORGE was admx. (LC EB 27:510)
[This is prob. Wm. GEORGE who mar. Jane HATHAWAY, LC, bond 6 Jan 1816 (MLBLC:32)]

GEORGE, William [Sr.]; T 22 Mar 1816; 17 Apr 1817
LC; INV; includes Negroes: Portious, Daniel, Moses, Suckey, Dinah, Nelley. (LC EB 27:369)

GEORGE, William; 16 Jul 1810
LC; on the mot. of Geo. THRALL, ord. that Martin, William Henry, Caty, Thomas, Jesse, Michael & Tarpley GEORGE by Martin SHEARMAN gdn. of Jesse, Michael & Tarpley, heirs of William GEORGE dec'd be summoned to show cause why lands of William GEORGE should not be sold. (LC Orders B23 1808-11:205)
[Sarah [HAMMON] aptd. gdn. to Jesse, Michael Wilder, & Tarpley GEORGE orphans of Wm. GEORGE, 18 Jul 1808 (LC Orders 22D 1805-08:480); Overseers of the Poor to bind out Michael GEORGE orphan of Willam GEORGE the son of Martin GEORGE to Martin SHEARMAN, 19 Jun 1809

(LC Orders B23 1808-11:80); Martin SHEARMAN aptd. gdn. to Jesse W. & Tarpley GEORGE, 16 Jul 1810 (LC Orders B23 1808-11:206); Jesse, Michael W. & Tarpley GEORGE orphans of Wm. GEORGE chose Moses LUNSFORD as their gdn., 20 Oct 1817 (LC Orders 24:395)]

GEORGE, William; PO 21 Jan 1811; 17 Feb 1812

LC; laid off dower of Elizabeth L. GEORGE, wid. & rel, & DIV of slaves among: Elizabeth L. GEORGE, Luther GEORGE, Thomas THRALL, Keturah GEORGE, Catherine GEORGE, Armon GEORGE, Wickliff GEORGE. (LC EB 27:102)

[Wm. GEORGE mar. Eliz. Linton ARMS, LC, bond 2 Jul 1785 (MLBLC:32); Thos. THRALL mar. Rebecca Martin GEORGE, LC, bond 1 Feb 1809 (MLBLC:74); on the mot. of Thos. THRALL who mar. Rebecca Martin GEORGE one of the orphans of Wm. GEORGE son of Nicholas dec'd, ord. to assign unto Eliz. L. GEORGE wid. of sd. Wm. GEORGE her dower; Thos. THRALL aptd. gdn. to Calvin, Luther, Wickliff, Kitty and Arman GEORGE orphans of Wm. GEORGE in the div. of sd. dec'd's lands, 15 Oct 1810 (LC Orders B23 1808-11:223); Calvin GEORGE orphan of Wm. GEORGE chose Jn. CHOWNING Jr. as his gdn. and he is to be bound to Thos. THRALL to learn the trade of shoe & boot making, 21 Jan 1811 (LC Orders B23 1808-11:236); Luther GEORGE orphan of Wm. GEORGE chose Jn. CHOWNING as his gdn., 15 Apr 1811 (LC Orders 24:14); Eliz. GEORGE aptd. gdn. to Wickliff, Keturah, Catherine GEORGE orphans of Wm. GEORGE, 20 May 1811 (LC Orders 24:15); Luther GEORGE orphan of Wm. GEORGE son of N. with the consent of his gdn. Jn. CHOWNING to be bound to Robt. BLAKEY as an apprentice to learn the trade of a carriage maker and [shop] joiner, 20 Apr 1812 (LC Orders 24:68); Wickliff GEORGE orphan of Wm. GEORGE chose Presley NEALE as his gdn., 17 Oct 1814 (LC Orders 24:201); Wickliff GEORGE orphan of Wm. GEORGE chose Porteus TOWLES as his gdn., 21 Nov 1814 (LC Orders 24:205); Thos. ARMSTRONG aptd. gdn. to Armon GEORGE orphan of Wm. GEORGE, 21 Nov 1814 (LC Orders 24:206)' Porteus TOWLES aptd. gdn. to Keturah GEORGE orphan of Wm. GEORGE, 19 Dec 1814 (LC Orders 24:211); ord. that Rebecca M. THRALL, Polly L. NEALE & Luther GEORGE & Calvin GEORGE by Jn. CHOWNING their gdn., Keturah GEORGE & Wickliff GEORGE by Porteus TOWLES their gdn. & Armon GEORGE by Thos. ARMSTRONG his gdn. be summoned to show cause why the slaves of Wm. GEORGE dec's held for life by his wid. Eliz. L. GEORGE dec'd may not be sold, 19 Dec 1814 (LC Orders 24:211); Armon GEORGE orphan of Wm. GEORGE chose Calvin GEORGE for his gdn., 20 Apr 1818 (LC Orders 24:427); Polly GEORGE mar. Presley NEALE, LC, bond 29 Jan 1812 (MLBLC:54); this Wm. GEORGE was a son of Nicholas GEORGE, *see also LC CC 1821-005*]

GEORGE, William; PO 20 Feb 1815; 21 Dec 1818

LC; DIV of proceeds of sale of slaves held for life by his wid. among Polly L. NEALE, Rebecca M. THRALL, John CHOWNING gdn. of Calvin GEORGE, John CHOWNING gdn. of Luther GEORGE, Porteus TOWLES gdn. of Wickliff GEORGE, Porteus TOWLES gdn. of Kitturah GEORGE, Thomas ARMSTRONG gdn. of Armon GEORGE; the commissioners placed their commission of $55 in the hands of Porteus TOWLES gdn. for Kitturah GEORGE for the benefit of Kitturah since she had lost her property by the British. (LC EB 27:445)

[Settlement with Jn. CHOWNING the acct. of his gdnship. with Calvin & Luther GEORGE orphans of Wm. GEORGE, 19 Aug 1816 (LC Orders 24:325)]

GEORGE, William S.W.; 22 Jul 1815; 18 Mar 1816
LC; WILL; use of whole est. to wife Behethaland GEORGE during her widowhood; at wife's death est. to be eq. div. among my children; all sons to be bound to trades; friends John BISCOE & William PAYNE exors; WITS: Spencer BROWN, Wm. L. WATTS. (LC WB 28:175)
[Wm. GEORGE mar. Behethelam N. PAYNE, dau. of Jn. PAYNE (d. LC 1788), LC, bond 11 Apr 1806 (MLBLC:32, LC WB 22:193); S. W. apparently stands for "son of William" to distinguish this Wm. GEORGE from several other Wm. GEORGEs. Bethaland GEORGE aptd. gdn. to Rich. [sic] N. B. and Helkiah GEORGE orphans of Wm. GEORGE son of Wm., Edw. GEORGE son of Wm. GEORGE chose [Wm. George J. PAYNE] as his gdn., 17 Mar 1817 (LC OB 24:353); ord. that Isaac M. GEORGE who is not an inhabitant of this county appear to answer a bill filed in LC court; Nelly GEORGE, Thos. D. GEORGE, Edw. H. GEORGE, Hilkiah P. GEORGE, Bridget N. B. GEORGE & Barbary D. GEORGE are also to be summoned to show cause why the lands of which Isaac MERCER died seized should not be sold, 19 Nov 1821 (LC OB 25:260-261); acc. to LC CC 1828-020, William GEORGE the son of William GEORGE married three times: (1) Molly, the dau. of Isaac MERCER, (2) Barbara and (3) Behethelam and had four children, Lucy T., Isaac M., Jesse and Nellie, by Molly, two children, Thos. D. and Edw. H., by Barbara, and three children, Hilkiah P., Bridget N. B. and Barbara D., by Behethelam; an additional child, Luther, is named in LC CC 1828-018; Wm. GEORGE mar. (1) Molly MERCER dau. of Isaac MERCER (d. LC 1780), LC, bond 2 Dec 1782 and (2) Barbara DOBYNS, LC, bond 18 Aug 1794 (MLBLC:32); acc. to MLBLC Wm. GEORGE's first wife was "Molly MINER" and other transcriptions give her name as "Molly MORRIS;" CC 1828-020 corrects this to Molly the dau. of Isaac MERCER; Lucy T. GEORGE mar. Thos. D. DAVENPORT; there were eight Isaac GEORGEs listed in the 1820 census; two of them, one in Henry Co., KY and one in Sumner Co., TN, are poss. candidates for the above Isaac]

GEORGE, William S.W.; PO 17 Jan 1820; 22 Nov 1820
LC; no est. unadministered on by the sd. William GEORGE S.D. except $143.01 which sum was found in the hands of Jane GEORGE [admx] of William GEORGE S.D. dec'd who was admr. of William GEORGE S.W.; it will be found by reference to the will of William GEORGE S.W. that he devised his est. to his wife during her widowhood who has it in possession. (LC EB 29:49)

GEORGE, [Zamoth]; 18 Nov 1817
LC; John BEANE aptd. gdn. to Betsy H. GEORGE orphan of [Zamoth] GEORGE. (LC Orders 24:397)

GIBERNE, Isaac William; T [7] Apr 1801; 7 Sep 1801. RC INV; [m]; RC WB 9:155)
[This is the Rev. Isaac William GIBERNE, rector of LP, RC; he was born in England poss. around 1728 and ordained in 1758; he came to Virginia in 1759 and mar. Mary (FAUNTLEROY) BEALE, dau. of Maj. Moore & Margaret FAUNTLEROY and wid. of Chas. BEALE (*see below*). For more on GIBERNE, see Nelson 2001:173-178, 310]

GIBERNE, Mary; 28 Apr 1819; 5 Jun 1820

RC; WILL; all of est. real & personal (except specific legacies below) to nephew Charles L. CARTER son of Landon CARTER in Prince William Co; I lend unto John MORTIMER son of Dr. Charles MORTIMER one Negro woman Beck & her dau. Jenny until his dau. Marianne arrives at lawful age or marries at which time she is to have Beck and Jenny; to William BROCKENBROUGH son of Dr. BROCKENBROUGH formerly of Tappahannock one Negro man named Godfrey; to Mrs. Hannah MILES (formerly Hannah HOWE) whose father was John HOWE one Negro boy named Harry; to David GASKINS a free Black man now residing in RC a small bay mare, a cow & calf, & £10 in money in gratitude for the many services which he has rendered me; whereas several years ago, a Negro man named Davy CARRINGTON purchased of me his son a Negro boy called Davy who has remained in my possession, and whereas I promised the sd. Davy CARRINGTON that in case he should not take the sd. boy from me before my death, I would emancipate the sd. boy by my will; in conformity therefore to my sd. promise, I hereby will that the sd. boy Davy shall be and remain free immediately from and after my decease; to Davy the son of Davy CARRINGTON before named £5 in cash; Jerry my manservant to be emancipated and set free after my decease; I have been informed that the 72 ac. formerly deeded to Caroline and Clementina WEBB daus. of Jeremiah WEBB was taken by the sd. Jeremiah in his own name, therefore it is my will & desire that the sd. 72 ac. shall be the property of the sd. Caroline & Clementina and I now bequeath the same accordingly; nephew Charles L. CARTER to be ex.; WITS: Wm. Y. STURMAN, W. R. JEFFRIES, Sam. WILLIAMS, Wm. THRIFT. (RC WB 9:660)
[This is Mary, dau. of Maj. Moore & Margaret (MICOU) FAUNTLEROY and wid. of (1) Chas. BEALE and (2) Rev. Isaac William GIBERNE (MRC:77); Hannah HOWE mar. Geo. MILES, RC, bond 24 Apr 1817 (MRC:132)]

GIBSON, James (Dr.); T 24 Mar 1815; 17 May 1819
LC; INV, $439.58 2/3; includes several lots of books. (LC EB 27:475)

GIBSON, John; 8 Apr 1815; 19 Feb 1816.
LC; WILL; all est. to son Albert GIBSON; if son should die before 21 or marriage the prop. that came by his mother to return to her relations & remaining prop. to be eq. div. among my brothers & sisters; son to be liberally educated; I appoint sisters Sally & Polly GIBSON to the care of my son; bro. William GIBSON & friend John HALL exors; WITS: Lawson HATHAWAY, Jn. HALL, Ephraim SPRIGGS. (LC WB 28:175)
[This is prob. the Jn. GIBSON, son of Wm. GIBSON Sr. (d. LC 1812) *see below*, who mar. Molly HUNTON, LC, bond 27 Jul 1803 (MLBLC:32); Albert GIBSON, orphan of Jn. GIBSON chose Jn. HALL as his gdn., 16 Dec 1822 (LC OB 25:346)]

GIBSON, William (Col.); PO 15 Jun 1812, T 18 Jun 1812; 19 Jun 1815
LC; INV; includes Negroes: Spencer, Eady, Roxy, Austin, Rob, Sam, Winney, Nace, Addison, David, James, Fanny, Manuel, Page, Harry, Spencer, Dinah, Betty, James, Nathan, Mariah, Amanda, Moses. (LC EB 27:202)

GIBSON, William Sr.; 18 Nov 1811; 15 Jun 1812
LC; WILL; plant. where I now live to wife Sally GIBSON during her life & that plant. to be a home for my two daus: Sally M. GIBSON & Molley K. GIBSON; at wife's death plant. to be sold and after debts are paid money to be eq. div. among all my children; Negro girl [Maria] to dau. Sally M.; Negro girl Amanda & $50 to dau. Molley K.; Negro Moses to son William GIBSON; rest of est. to be eq. div. among my children: John GIBSON, Sally M.

GIBSON, Molley K. GIBSON, & William GIBSON; son James GIBSON to have no other part of my est. except in the sale of the plant; son[s] John & William GIBSON & friend John HALL exors; WITS: Clarissa HALL, Betsey T. STRAUGHN, Judith M. HUNTON; [COD dtd. 12 Jan 1812; wife to have one third of my Negroes & other pers. prop; WITS: Ralph EDMONDS, Ephriaim SPRIGGS, Jn. HALL] (LC WB 28:132)

GIDDINGS, William; PO 8 Nov 1802; 9 Jul 1804
NC; INV, [m]; includes Negroes Ben & Venus. (NC RB 17:184)
[This is prob. the Wm. GIDDINGS who mar. Alice DAMERON dau. of Geo. DAMERON (d. NC 1801), NC, bond 12 May 1794 (MWO:148); Alice (DAMERON) GIDDINGS, wid., mar. Sam. DAMERON, wid., NC, bond 3 Jan 1804 (MLBNC:26; NC CC 1805-020); Jn. HURST was aptd. gdn. of Geo. [L.], Mary Ann J., and Sarah GIDDINGS orphans of Wm. GIDDINGS, NC, 14 Feb 1814 (NC OB 1811-15:212); Geo. D. GIDDINGS, Mary Ann Jones GIDDINGS, and Sary Ann Scott GIDDINGS are children of Alice GIDDINGS; Alice (DAMERON, GIDDINGS) DAMERON mar. (3) Jn. DAVIS, NC, bond 30 May 1810 (LC CC 1820-009; MLBNC:27); Jas. HURST was gdn. to Sarah GIDDINGS until his death in early 1819; Sarah mar. Sam. HUGHLETT, NC, bond 20 Jan 1821 at which time she was the ward of Jn. INGRAM (NC CC 1833-002, MLBNC:57)]

GILBERT, Hannah; 9 Jul 1800; 22 Dec 1800.
CP, WC; WILL; son William GILBERT girl named Alice GARNER; land to be div. among Youell, Samuel & Nancy GILBERT; sons Samuel & Youell exors; WITS: Jas. C. KNOTT, Mary COLE, Mary KNOTT. (WC DW 20:172)
[Hannah GILBERT was prob the dau. of Sam. & Magdalen HARRISON and the wid. of Wm. GILBERT (d. WC 1788) who named children Wm., Nancy, Samuel & Uel (Youell) as well as an unborn child in his will (WC DW 16:314, 17:43, 18:)]

GILL, Eli; T 21 Feb 1815; 13 Nov 1815. NC; INV, [m]. (NC RB 20:297)
[This is prob. the Eli GILL who mar. Alice WHE[E]LER, NC, bond 12 Jan 1807 (MLBNC:42); in his will (NC 31 Jan 1815-13 Mar 1815) Eli GILL named his son Royston and his bro. Elisha H. GILL (NC RB 19:626); Jas. FORBUSH aptd. gdn. of Royston GILL orphan of Eli GILL, NC 8 Jul 1822 (NC OB 1820-25:220)]

GILL, George; 14 Feb 1820
NC; Fanny GILL orphan of George GILL chose Leroy HARCUM as her gdn. (NC OB 1816-20:423)
[This is prob. the Geo. GILL of SSP who in his will (NC 28 Sep 1812 - 8 Feb 1813) named his wife Fanny GILL, his eldest son Hiram M. GILL, and his other children Fanny Muse GILL, James Reed GILL and William George GILL (NC RB 19:329)]

GILL, John; 14 Feb 1825
NC; Thomas B. GILL chose William W. APPLEBY as his gdn. & the sd. APPLEBY is also aptd. gdn. of John M. & Nancy GILL orphans of John GILL. (NC OB 1820-25:442)

GILL, Thomas; PO 14 Oct 1816; 10 Sep 1821
NC; INV of Negroes: Leroy, Marina, Winne, Isaac, Patty, Fanny & Martin, Aggy (worth total of $1875.00); DIV among: Peggy GILL, Lucy GILL, Nancy GILL, Lucrecy SWAN, Sally GILL, Ellis GILL's heirs, Elisha GILL. (NC RB 22:628)
[Jos. DOULIN aptd. gdn. of Margaret & Lucy GILL orphans of Thos. GILL, NC, 14 Oct 1816 (NC OB 1816-20:95)]

GILL, Thomas; PO 11 Feb 1822, T 9 Mar 1822; 11 Mar 1822
NC; Chancery suit; Lindsey DAVIS & Sally his wife, James FORBUSH & Lucretia his wife, Elisha H. GILL, Marcellus PITTS & Margaret his wife & Daniel H. HAYNIE & Lucy his wife (which sd. Sally, Lucretia, Elisha, Margaret & Lucy are the only surviving children of Thomas GILL, dec'd), pltfs., against Thomas, John M. & Nancy GILL (only children of John GILL dec'd & infants under 21) and Royston GILL (infant under 21 & only child of Eli GILL dec'd) which sd. John & Eli GILL dec'd were sons of the sd. Thomas GILL, defts., commissioners appointed to sell land of Thomas GILL dec'd; land was sold to Griffin LAMKIN for $755 and after commission was deducted $717.25 was div. among legal reps: Linzy DAVIS & Sally his wife, James FORBUSH & Lucrecie his wife, Elisha GILL, Marcellus PITTS & Margaret his wife, Daniel HAYNIE & Lucy his wife, Thomas GILL, John GILL, Nancy GILL, & Royston GILL; each legal rep. was entitled to $102.46 1/4. (NC RB 23:110; CC 1822-005)
[Lindsey DAVIS, wid., mar. Sally GILL, NC, bond 12 Jun 1820 (MLBNC:27); Lucretia GILL mar. (1) Jos. SWANN, NC, bond 14 Feb 1814 and (2) Jas. FORBUSH, NC, bond 22 Jan 1817 (MLBNC:38, 97); Margaret GILL mar. Marcellus PITTS, NC, bond 9 Dec 1820 (MLBNC:82)]

GILL, William; mar. Sally HARCUM dau. of Elisha HARCUM, NC, lic. 15 Feb 1774; he d. c. 1780 leaving his wid., Sally who admin. his est., and daus. Betsy who mar. Joseph DOULIN, NC, bond 16 Aug 1796 and Lucy, who mar. James TRACY, NC, bond 9 May 1796; Sally (HARCUM) GILL mar. (2) Capt. Joshua COCKRELL c. 1787 and bore him a son; James TRACY was dead by Mar 1798 (NC OB 1773-1783:405; MLBNC:30, 102; MWO:81, 357; CC 1800-006)

GILL, Winder; 14 Feb 1820
NC; Winder GILL orphan of Winder GILL chose Richard GILL as his gdn. (NC OB 1816-20:423)

GILMOUR, Helen; 21 Nov 1826
LC; sheriff to dispose of est. of Helen GILMOUR, dec'd. (LC OB 26:219)

GILMOUR, John M.; T 9 Jul 1813; 21 Feb 1814
LC; INV; includes Negroes: John, Sam, Harry, Aaron, Frank, Nancy, Caroline, Felicia. (LC EB 27:168)

GILMOUR, John M.; 6 Jul 1799; 21 Mar 1814
LC; WILL; all my est. to wife Cordelia until my son William GILMOUR shall come to age 21; if wife is with child and has a son, est. to be eq. div., if she has a dau, dau. to have £1000; to my mother my blessing & a mourning ring; Merryman PAYNE & Leo STAMPER exors; WITS: Wm. BROWN, Matthew NEALL; Merryman PAYNE & Leonard STAMPER relinquished their right of executorship 17 Jul 1813; the wid. & rel Cordelia GILMOUR renounced all benefits by the sd. will on 21 Mar 1814. (LC WB 28:147; LC EB 27:184)
[Jn. M. GILMOUR mar. Cordelia BALL, LC, bond 30 Jun 1796 (MLBLC:33); Wm. GILMOUR orphan of Jn. M.GILMOUR chose Rawleigh W. DOWNMAN as his gdn., 15 Nov 1813 (LC Orders 24:170)]

GILMOUR, Robert; PO 17 Apr 1815, T 8 Jun 1815; 19 Mar 1816. LC ; INV; includes Negro man Harry. (LC EB 27:286)

GLASCOCK, Ann S.; [m]; 15 Jun 1801
LC; appointment of gdn; "To the Worshipful Court of Lancaster, my two children by my first husband Mr. Newton BRENT, Margaret & Ann, are without a guardian at present other than myself in consequence of the death of Mr. Richard G. GLASCOCK; and owing to my impaired health, I cannot

take upon myself the burthen of their maintenance and tuition. I have therefore applyed to Mr. Elias EDMONDS for that purpose who has agreed to become their guardian. I address you in this way as expressive of my wish that he may be vested with such power. I am your worships most obt. " /s/ Ann S. GLASCOCK; WITS: Lettice L. BRENT, Margaret STEPTOE, Ann NEWTON. (LC EB 24:146)
[Ann Steptoe LAWSON mar. Newton BRENT, LC, bond 14 Apr 1779; she mar. (2) Richard GLASCOCK, LC, bond 5 Sep 1800 (MLBLC:8, 33)]

GLASCOCK, Ann S.; PO 18 Jan 1802; 17 Sep 1804
LC; DIV of slaves allotted to Ann S. GLASCOCK late Ann S. BRENT dec'd as her dower of the est. of Newton BRENT dec'd as also the balance due the sd. Newton BRENT's est. in the hands of George BRENT the surviving ex. among the legatees of the sd. Newton BRENT: John HUNT in right of his wife Lucinda, Robert M. ROBERTSON in right of his wife Jane, Thomas G. ROBERTSON in right of his wife Letty, Margaret S. BRENT, Nancy N. BRENT (allotted to her gdn. Hugh BRENT). (LC EB 24:292)
[Jn. HUNT mar. Lucinda BRENT, LC, bond 20 Jun 1796; Robert M. ROBERTSON mar. Jane Newton BRENT, LC, bond 28 Jan 1800; Thos. G. ROBERTSON mar. Lettice L. BRENT, LC, bond 11 Dec 1801 (MLBLC:40, 63)]

GLASCOCK, Ann S.; T 10 Jul 1801; 17 Dec 1804. LC; INV, [m]. (LC EB 24:299)

GLASCOCK, Milton Syms; 1 May 1815
RC; WILL; son Aldea Amazon only exor; $1000 & Negro girl Molly to dau. Amelia Ann Hinson upon her marriage; $1000 & Negro girl Lucinda to dau. Evalina Syms upon her marriage; Negroes Solomon, Big Fanny, Little Fanny & Peggy, Island Field garden & lot back of the garden & dwelling house to wife during her life; [no wits]; RC WB 9:471)
[Milton Syms GLASCOCK, son of Rich. GLASCOCK (d. RC 1801, *see below*) mar. Sally Meredith YERBY, RC bond 10 Nov 1790 (MRC:78); Aldea A. GLASCOCK mar. Mary B. SMITH, RC, bond 8 Oct 1822 (MRC:78); Evelina S. GLASCOCK mar. Rich. B. HUTT of WC, RC, bond 21 Jan 1819 (Ann T. GLASCOCK, mother of the bride [sic], gave her consent) (MRC:100); Amelia A. T. GLASCOCK mar. Jn. G. WHITE, RC, bond 7 Dec 1816 (MRC:230)]

GLASCOCK, Richard; 8 Dec 1799; 1 Jun 1801
RC; WILL; sons: Milton Syms, Richard Chichester; daus: Mary Chichester, Ellen Ball, Eliza D., Emma Downer, Melissa; the order in which the legacy is to be paid is as follows: son Richard Chichester, dau. Ellen Ball, dau. Mary Chichester, dau. Eliza, dau. Melissa, dau. Emma Downer; [no ex. named]; WITS: Ezekiel LEVY, Peter BEANE; COD: 21 May 1800, mentions Elizabeth the wid. of son Syms C. GLASCOCK the use of the northeast wing of dwelling house also the use of the garden in common during her widowhood. (RC WB 9:149)

GLASCOCK, Richard M.; T. 9 Mar 1815; 5 May 1817
RC; INV, $3495.00, included Negroes Kesiah & child, Kitty & child, Jeremy, Billy, Elijah, Nancy, Sally, Nelly & child, boy Shadrack, Betty a young woman, young Sally, Tabby, old George Burn, old Suckey a charge. (RC WB 9:554)
[Frances F. GLASCOCK, the wid. of Rich. M. GLASCOCK, mar. (2) Rich. EFFORD, RC, bond 6 Feb 1821 (MRC:63)]

GLASCOCK, Susannah; 11 Dec 1804; 1 Jul 1805.
Farnham Par., RC; WILL; daus. Winifred, Priscilla, Nancy HARDING; sons Washington, Robert, Thomas, & Joseph; sons Washington, Robert & Thomas

exors; WITS: [Milton] S. GLASCOCK, Rich. MITCHELL, Hannah MITCHELL. (RC WB 9:255)
[Susannah GLASCOCK was the the dau. of Robt. & Hannah (BALL) MITCHELL & wid. of Jn. GLASCOCK (d. RC 1796) (RC WB 9:49; MWO:150); Nancy GLASCOCK mar. Jas. HARDING, RC, bond 13 May 1794 (MWO:164)]

GLASCOCK, William; PO 8 Jul 1793, T 13 Jul 1793; 10 Nov 1823
NC; INV of slaves of the est. includes Charles, George, girls Hannah, Nancy, Winney & Lucy. (NC RB 23:377)

GOAD, Bernard; 25 Apr 1814
WC; it appears to the court that Bernard GOAD d. intestate; sheriff to administer his est. (WC OB 1814-18:73)
[This might be the man identified as Barnett GOOD who mar. Eliz. WEAVER, WC, bond 14 May 1806 (MLBWC:25)]

GOLDSMITH, John; PO 1807; [26 Feb 1810]
WC; DIV of est. to Mrs. Juliett GOLDSMITH (her dower, Negroes James, Anjalettah, George), Capt. Henry MICOU who married Harriett GOLDSMITH one of the daus. of John GOLDSMITH (Negroes Lessey, Melvell, Bill, Sophiah, Albert, Amanda); £366.13.4 was to be div. among 4 children (nfi, but apparently including Harriett). (WC RI 9:178)
[Dr. Jn. GOLDSMITH mar. Julia ARNOLD, alias LOVELL, dau. of Jn. LOVELL, WC, bond 17 Jan 1788 (MWO:151); John H. MICOU mar. Harriet GOLDSMITH, KGC, 7 Feb 1804 (*VMHB* Vol. 10, No. 4, p, 435)]

GOLDSMITH, William; 4 May 1809; 27 Aug 1810
New Orleans, [letter dtd.] May 4th 1809, Dear Mother, Take up my pen to let you no that I am well at present and hope that these few lines lines wil find you well and all the rest of the family well this countlery [*sic*] a very warm climate and is very sickly. I have sene a grate many hardships since I left you. I left Cape Henry the 6th of February and arived in this place first of April after grate difficultys in a storm at sea eight & forty hours and thought when we would sink in a moment [2 *words unclear*] of God we were saved. I hardly expect ever to return again and is my mind for my wish for my sister namely to have my property after your death. I am now in haste and must bid you a due. Give my love to all my inquirein friends. I rote to you from Norfolk. Give my love Juliana. You may tell cozen [*1 word unclear*] that Ned is in this place sends his love to him and his and hopes to be in this fal. This is a very rich country and everything is very high. If this shud ever com to hand I hope you will right without delay and direct to to 5st. If life last I shall return immediately. Give my love to my sisters & brothers and believe me to be your affectionate son. /s/ William GOLDSMITH; the aforegoing letter from Wm. GOLDSMITH to Julia GOLDSMITH his mother ... was admitted to record. (WC DW 22:116)
[Apparently Wm. GOLDSMITH was a son of Dr. Jn. and Julia (LOVELL) GOLDSMITH (*see above*)]

GOODE, Nancy C. & Rebecca DAUGHETY; PO 12 Sep 1808, T 22 Sep 1808; 10 Oct 1808
NC; DIV of est. of Nancy C. GOODE & Rebeca DAUGHETY in the hands of James DAUGHETY their gdn. & father; [Rawleigh] GOODE husband of Nancy C. GOODE possessed with his part of Negroes (Winnefred, child John [BOEN], Cloe, Jean, Winnefred, Jesse); possessed Rebecah DAUGHETY with following Negroes in the hands of James DAUGHETY her gdn. (boy Manuwell, Nancy DOWNING, Pegy, Peter). (NC RB 18:42)

GOODRIDGE, Richard; PO 18 Jan 1802; 20 Sep 1802
LC; INV, £1416.5.2; includes Negroes [Robin], Anthony, George, Saul, Daniel, Charles, Isaac, Jery, Letty, [Mitilda], Lewis, [Fielding], [Ruby], Jane & child, Martin, Milinda & child David, Siller, Dinnes, Hannah. (LC EB 24:209)

GOODRIDGE, Richard ; 5 May 1801; 18 Jan 1802
LC; WILL; to son William GOODRIDGE my Negroes Roben, George, James, Hannah, Sarah, Spencer, Young Sam, and Anthony; to son Thaddeus GOODRIDGE my land I now live on & the land called Peavine & that called Campbells & my Negroes Old Sam, Daniel, Charles, Isaac, Jerry, Letty, Matilda, Lewis, Fielding, Rueben; if son Thaddeus should die without heir, the land to go to my son William & the balance to be eq. div. between my surviving cildren; to dau. Sarah LANSDELL my Negroes Judy, Jenny & Martin; at dau's death the Negroes to go to her children Thomas & Nancy LANSDELL; to dau. Mary HARDING my Negroes Fanny, Dorcas, & Milindy; at dau. Mary's death Negroes to go to her children Samuel & Rebecca HARDING; son William ex; WITS: Rawleigh RAINES, Susanna HUNTON. (LC WB 28:57)
[Benj. LANSDELL, Jr. mar. Sarah GOODRIDGE, NC, 1778 (MWO:220); Cyrus HARDING of NC mar. Mary GOODRIDGE, dau. of Rich. GOODRIDGE, LC, bond 13 Sep 1791 (MLBLC:35); Rich. MITCHELL mar. Nancy LANSDELL, NC, bond 23 Dec 1807 (MLBNC:74); the slaves devised by Rich. GOODRIDGE to Thos. & Nancy LANSDELL were to be div. between Rich. MITCHELL who mar. Nancy LANSDELL and the admrs. of Thos. LANSDELL dec'd (NC OB 1811-15:312)]

GOODRIDGE, Thadday; PO 21 Oct 1816, T 22 May 1818; 20 Jul 1818
LC; INV, $680.13 1/2; DIV of est. among legatees William GOODRIDGE, the heirs of Benjamin LANDSDALE who mar. Sally GOODRIDGE & the heirs of Cyrus HARDING who mar. Molly GOODRIDGE; Sally & Molly were daus. of Richard GOODRIDGE dec'd. (LC EB 27:430)
[This is Thaddeus son of Rich. GOODRIDGE (*see above*); on the mot. of Wm. GOODRIDGE suggesting that the land whereof Thaddeus GOODRIDGE died intestate and which descends to his heirs at law will not on a divison amount to $100 to each heir, it is therefore ord. that Thos. E. HARDING & Rebecca his wife who was Rebecca HARDING, Polly HARDING, Rich. MITCHELL & Nancy his wife who was Nancy LANSDELL, Jn. M. LANSDELL & Thos. LANSDELL children of Thos. LANSDELL dec'd be summoned to show cause why the sd. land should not be decreed to be sold, 20 Jan 1817 (LC Orders 24:346); Thos. E. HARDING mar. Rebeckah K. HARDING ward of Wm. HARDING, NC, bond 25 Sep 1815, NC, bond 23 Dec 1807 (MLBNC:46)]

GORDON, Ann; PO 21 Jan 1811; 18 Mar 1811
LC; INV of bonds in the est. of Ann GORDON unadministered by James [H.] GORDON. (LC EB 27:78)

GORDON, Ann; 29 Mar 1818; 8 Jun 1818
NC; WILL; to niece Ann MONROE following Negroes: Henry, Maria, Sucky, Sucky [sic], & Robin & all my interest in the Thicket Tract; to sis. Betsy the following Negroes: Bob, Philles, Harriet, Emmanuel, Eliza, John & Matty; [no ex. named]; WITS: Isaac HAYNIE, Mary HAYNIE, Eliza L. BRENT. (NC RB 21:419)

GORDON, James; 11 Feb 1792; 20 Oct 1794

LC; WILL; whole of est. to wife Ann; children Mary Smith, James Harrison, John Matthews, Ann Smith & Addison [sic]; wife extx; WITS: Wm. LEE, Wm. WHYTE, Thos. TAYLOR. (LC WB 28:7)

GORDON, John; 15 Dec 1800; 26 Jan 1801

WC; WILL; req. that wife consent to sell 100 ac. adj. her bro. in Hack's Neck & money used to pay debts; wife's daughter; sis. Elizabeth Sally GORDON money due from Orrick CHILTON to purchase plant. commonly called "Gordonsville" formerly bel. to his dec'd mother; dau. Nancy (under 18); bro. George GORDON; friend Wm. FORBES & bro. George GORDON exors. and guardians of dau.; WITS: Elihu HALL, Jn. YEATMAN Sr., Jn. YEATMAN Jr. (WC DW 20:177)

[Miller:58 identifies Gordonsville as the site of a proposed town and locates it in LC near Merry Point]

GORDON, John; T 26 Mar 1801; 27 Apr 1801

WC; INV, £860.18.3; includes following Negroes: Jack, James, Daniel, Willoughby, Molly & children, Charlotte & boy [Lemmon], Suckey, Winney. (WC RI 8:121)

GORDON, John;

NC; WILL; wife to have choice of any three Negroes, son William to have Font Hill est.; daus. Ann, Mary, Betsy; wife Ann and son William exors; Joseph Jones MONROE shall neither directly or indirectly have any connection or agency with any atom belonging to the property I have now devised in January 1803; Sally MONROE to have one ring of value of $20 as a manifestation of my love for her; WITS: Shapleigh WADDY, Shapleigh Neale WADDY, John GRAHAM; probate granted to Wm. GORDON, 10 Oct 1803 (NC CC 1821-007)

[Several suits instituted against the heirs and heiresses of Jn. GORDON are detailed in the above-cited CC which also contains GORDON's will and several deeds; as of 1821, Mary and Elizabeth GORDON were residents of Alexandria; Joseph Jones MONROE was a bro. of President James MONROE; he mar. Sarah "Sally" GORDON, NC, bond 27 Oct 1801 as his second wife (MLBNC:74, <http://genealogical-gleanings.com/monroe-joseph.htm> accessed 14 Nov 2012)]

GORDON, John; PO 12 Dec 1803; 14 Oct 1805

NC; INV, [m]; includes Negroes Peter, boys Kendal & Alfred, Barbara, Judah, Rachall, girl Massa, Charlotte & child, girl Henna, Will WIGHAM, old woman Betty, girl Bina, Old Le[tt]y, Old Tim, Old Daniel, boy Joe, old woman Win Pin, Sarah & child, girl Pleasant, woman Bina, girl Louisa, boy Gilbert, girl Letticia, old woman Grace, Winney & child, girls Mary, Emilia & Polley, Phillis & child, girl Harriett, boy Emanuel, Jane & child, boy Jacob, Tom, Webb, Jane (Webb's wife), Milley, Bob, Jesse, miller Jack, Job (sailor); property appraised in Hack's Neck: Billey, Toney, Old Tom, Cate, Tabb & child, Winney, Judah & child, Sale & child Adam, boy Job, girls Anne & Esther, boy Sam, girl Polley; William GORDON ex. (NC RB 17:327)

GORDON, John; PO 12 Dec 1803; 10 Nov 1809

NC; INV, [m]; includes Negroes Peter, boys Kendal & Alfred, Barbara, Judah, Rachel, girl Massa, Charlotte & child, girl Henna, Will WIGHAM, old woman Betty, girl [Bina], Old Letty, Old Tim, Old Daniel, boy Joe, old woman Win Pin, Sarah & child, girl Pleasant, woman [Bina], girl Louisa, boy Gilbert, girl Lettecia, old woman Grace, Winney & child, girls May, Emelia & Polley, Phillis & child, girl Harriett, boy Emanuel, Jane & child, boy Jacob, Tom, Webb, Jane (Webb's wife), Milley, Bob, Jesse, Miller Jack. Job sailor;

property appraised in Hack's Neck: Billey, Toney, Old Tom, Cate, Tabb & child, Winney, Judah & child, Sall & child Adam, boy Job, girls Anne & Esther, boy Sam, girl Polley. (NC RB 18:249)

[GORDON, John] (Col.); PO 9 Jul 1804; 10 Feb 1806
NC; DIV of tract in Hack's Neck among Ann GORDON, John GRAHAM, Peter P. COX & Sarah his wife & Ransdell PIERCE & Nancy his wife; div. was by a line drawn from a large white oak by the road side to Little Wicco[moco] River which being done, the western part adjoining the land Col. GORDON purchased of BREWER was drawn by Ann GORDON & the part adjoining Edmonds Cove by the other parties each containing 139 acres ... one half of which 139 acres drawn by the joint parties was drawn by the said John GRAHAM by virtue of his mother's will Mary Eliz. GRAHAM dec'd which was the lower part on the river, the upper part being the right of the heirs of Spencer H. GRAHAM dec'd. (NC RB 17:385)
[Jn. GORDON, Jr. mar. Sarah GRAHAM, dau. of Jn. & Mary Eliz. (HACK) GRAHAM, NC, bond 11 Jan 1797; Sarah (GRAHAM) GORDON mar. (2) Peter Presley COX of WC in 1802 (MWO:152); Ransdell PIERCE mar. Ann GRAHAM, another dau. of Jn. & Mary Eliz. (HACK) GRAHAM, LC, bond 1 Dec 1794 (MWO:281)]

GORDON, William; T 18 Feb 1825; 1 Aug 1825. RC; INV, $123. (RC WB 10:80)

GRAHAM, Mary E.; PO 12 Nov 1804, T 19 Dec 1804; 8 Jul 1805
NC; DIV of half of tract of land called Welch Neck into 2 lots; Lot 1 (upper part of the land adj the main road leading down Hack's Neck) drawn by Capt. Shapleigh WADDY for Messrs. Ransdell PIERCE, John GRAHAM & Peter P. COX and Lot 2 (lower part of the tract where the houses stood formerly occupied by John EDMONDS). (NC RB 17:296)

GREEN, Jemima; 7 Mar 1796; Nov 1796
WP, WC; WILL; half my land to [dau.] Mary Minton GREEN; other half to son Austin GREEN [*portion torn*]; dau. Nancy GREEN; son Richard GREEN; dau. [??th] GREEN; [no ex. named]; WITS: Jas. [FISHER], Thos. [PRI??LEY]. (WC Unrec Wills 1755-1800 #43)

GREEN, Sarah; 29 Dec 1800; 26 Jan 1801
WC; WILL; land and all property to two daus. Mary & Lucetty; son Chas. GREEN to be ex; WITS: Rich. DRAKE. (WC DW 20:179)
[Wm. GREEN mar. [Sarah] BURCH, dau. of Baynham BURCH, WC, bef. 27 Apr 1779 (MWO:155); Lucetty GREEN who was about 22, dau. of Sarah GREEN, mar. Jesse GREEN, WC, bond 16 May 1798 (MLBWC:26)]

[GREEN], Ellis; PO 8 Jun 1818; 11 Nov 1822. NC; INV. (NC RB 23:250)

GREENLAW, William Sr.; 4 Jan 1811; 25 Feb 1811
WC; WILL; wife Mary; after wife's death lands to be eq. div. between sons William GREENLAW Jr. & David GREENLAW; dau. Betsey GREENLAW Negro girl Adaline; [*portion unclear*] FRANKLIN dau. of William FRANKLIN; rest of est. after debts paid to be div. into 6 eq. parts: one part to children of my dau. Philadelphia by William FRANKLIN, one part to the children of dau. by [J.] LEWIS & Thomas SANDY, one part to William GREENLAW; one part to my dau. Betsey; one part to David GREENLAW; and one part to dau. Polley SETTLES; William GREENLAW Jr. & David GREENLAW exors; WITS: Sam. TEMPLEMAN, Elizar OMOHUNDRO, Thos. FRANKLIN. (WC DW 22:180)
[Wm. GREENLAW, Sr. of WC mar. Mary OLDHAM, dau. of Wm. OLDHAM, bef. 1778 (MWO:155); Philadelphia GREENLAW mar. Wm. FRANKLIN, 1 Feb 1795 (MWO:138); Ann GREENLAW mar. (1) Jn. LEWIS,

RC, bond 14 Aug 1786 and (2) Thos. SANDY, WC, bond 16 Mar 1792 (MWO:227, 309); Mary "Polly" GREENLAW mar. Wm. SETTLE, WC, bond 8 Aug 1798 (MWO:316); on the mot. of David GREENLAW, commissioners aptd. to div. the land of Wm. GREENLAW dec'd between Wm. GREENLAW & David GREENLAW; admin. on the est. of Mary GREENLAW is granted to David GREENLAW, 25 Jul 1825 (WC OB 1823-27:194, 195)]

GREENLAW, William; PO 25 Feb 1811, T 16 Mar 1811; 25 Mar 1811
WC; INV, [m]; includes Negroes Harry, Winney, girls Louisa & Adeline. (WC RI 9:228)

GREGORY, James; 22 Jul 1805
WC; Chancery suit; Daniel Thomas GREGORY plft. sued Catherine GREGORY, wid. of James, James GREGORY, George GREGORY, John GREGORY, Joseph GREGORY, Robert ANTHONY and his wife Lettice, Sarah HOWELL and Ann Carr GREGORY to div. est. [of James GREGORY]; Catherine GREGORY received 40 ac. and Daniel Thomas GREGORY received 12 ac. on the head of Carter's Mill Pond. (WC Orders 1804-07:285; CC 1805-021)
[Jas. GREGORY, in his will (WC 3 Mar 1791 - 27 Mar 1792) named his wife Cath. Carr, son Dan. Thos., and children George Carneby, James, Joseph Carr, John, Lettice ANTHONY, and Sarah Carr HOWELL wife of Jn. HOWELL (WWCV:193; WC Orders 1799:1801:118); Robt. ANTHONY mar. Lettice GREGORY, WC, bond 1 Dec 1788 (MLBWC:16); Jn. HOWELL mar. Sarah Carr GREGORY, WC, bond 24 Jan 1789 (MLBWC:186)]

GREGORY, James; 30 Jul 1810; 26 Nov 1810.
CP, WC; WILL; Molly BILLINS one cow named Friday & calf; wife Nancy land & improvements thereon; after wife's death or remarriage to bro. Daniel T. GREGORY; bro. Daniel exor; WITS: Gerard HUTT, Nancy GREGORY, James GREGORY Jr. (WC DW 22:162)
[Molly BILLINS is prob. the Molly BILLINGS who mar. Geo. GREGORY, WC, bond 2 Feb 1811 (MLBWC:26)]

GREGORY, James; 28 May 1821
WC; Isabella GREGORY is the wid. of James GREGORY. (WC OB 1819-23:251)
[Jas. GREGORY mar. Isabella TEMPLEMAN, WC bond 5 Mar 1812 (MLBWC:26)]

GREGORY, James; PO 22 Oct 1821, T 1 Nov 1821; 27 Dec 1824. WC; INV, $77.42. (WC RI 11:492)

GRESHAM, George; 10 Nov 181[3]; 21 Feb 1814
LC; WILL; whole est. to wife Mary GRESHAM during her life or widowhood; at wife's death or marriage tract of land on Rappahannock River which I purchased of William BRENT to son William GRESHAM; land & plant. w/o I now live to son James GRESHAM; £500 each to daus. Betsey & Polly; balance of est. to be eq. div. between my 4 children: William, James, Betsey & Polly; wife Mary & friend Col. John CHOWNING exors; WITS: C[hichester] TAPSCOTT, Jas. BRENT. (LC WB 28:146)
[This is prob. the Geo. GRESHAM who mar. Mary JAMES, LC, bond 25 Apr 1798 (MLBLC:34); Betsy GRESHAM orphan of Geo. GRESHAM chose Mary GRESHAM for her gdn., 17 May 1819 (LC OB 25:53)]

GRESHAM, George; T 28 May 1814; 20 Jun 1814

LC; INV; includes Negroes: Joe, Lewis, Guy, Elijah, John, Joe (boy), Fanny, Sarah, Mariah, Natus, Lavina, Aaron, Elick, Isaac, Solomon, Spencer, [Adaline], Sarah (small girl). (LC EB 27:181)

GRESHAM, George; T 12 Oct 1821; 19 May 1823
LC; valuation of slaves George, Joe, Davy, Ellick per request of Mary GRESHAM the extx. who advanced the sd. slaves to Charles PALMER who mar. Betsey GRESHAM one of the daus. of George GRESHAM. (LC EB 29:263)
[Chas. PALMER mar. Eliz. GRESHAM, LC, bond 8 Jun 1819 (MLBLC:57)]

GRIFFIN, Leroy; 4 Jul 1825
RC; Thomas SYDNOR made oath that the late Elizabeth SEWARD wife of John SEWARD, formerly the wid. of Joseph CHINN was the dau. of the late Leroy GRIFFIN and sis. of the whole blood of the late Judith GRIFFIN who died intestate and without issue of her body having never been married, that the late Thomas PINCKARD was the only child of the late Ann C. PINCKARD who was a sis. of the half blood of the sd. Elizabeth SEWARD and Judith GRIFFIN, the sd. Ann being a dau. of the late Leroy GRIFFIN by his first marriage; Vincent BRAMHAM and Rawleigh DOWNMAN said essentially the same. (RC OB 26:324; OB 27:99)
[Maj. Leroy GRIFFIN mar. (1) Alice CURRIE, LC, bond 28 Jul 1764 and (2) Judith BALL, LC, bond 3 Nov 1772; he was the father by his first wife of Ann Corbin who mar. Thos. PINCKARD and by his second wife of Eliz. GRIFFIN who mar. Jos. CHINN and Judith GRIFFIN (MRC:82; RC WB 7:211); Judith GRIFFIN d. intest. (LC CC 1797-007)]

GRIGGS, Henry; PO Mar 1805, T 15 Jul 1805; 26 Aug 1805
WC; INV, £269.6.0; includes Negroes Cyrus, Peter, Louisa. (WC RI 8:560)

GRINSTEAD, Richard; PO 9 Jun 1806, T 23 Jun 1806; 14 Jul 1806
NC; INV, £917.17.0; includes Negroes James, Solomon, boys Bill & Jerry, Rose & child, gearls [sic] Rose & Siller. (NC RB 17:444)

GRINSTEAD, Richard; PO 12 Jan 1817, T 9 Nov 1818; 9 Nov 1818
NC; Div. of est. among: Lot 1 to John GRINSTEAD (received Jerry & Rose), Lot 2 to John GRINSTEAD [sic] (received Seller & Mott), Lot 3 to John & Sally TIFFEY orphans of Austin TIFFEY (received Sam & Ann). (NC RB 21:530)
[In his will (NC 1 Jan 1806-9 Jun 1806), Rich. GRINSTEAD of SSP named his wife Wine, sons John & Rich., and grchildren Jn. TIFFEY & Salle TIFFEY (NC RB 17:413); Austin TIFFEY mar. Becke GRINSTEAD, dau. of Rich. GRINSTEAD, NC, bond 25 Apr 1796 (MLBNC:100)]

GROVES, George; PO 10 Apr 1821; 10 May 1825
NC; INV, $1136.87; includes Negro woman Winney. (NC RB 24:212)
[This is prob. the Geo. GROVES who mar. Lucinda CARTER, NC, bond 14 Feb 1814 (MLBNC:44)]

GUNDRY, John; 16 Nov 1818
LC; Overseers of the Poor of the Middle District to bind out John & Elizabeth GUNDRY orphans of John GUNDRY. (LC OB 25:24)

GUTRIDGE, Henry; 5 [Sep] 1803. RC; INV. (RC WB 9:220)
[Poss. the Hen. GUTRIDGE who mar. Sally Sneed MORTON, WC, bond 28 Oct 1790 (MWO:158)]

GUTRIDGE, Thomas; 8 Apr 1815; 24 Apr 1815
WC; Nunc. will; Lawrence BALLINGS & John RYALS swore that Thos. GUTRIDGE who died at his own house on this 8th day of April 1815 called on them to bear witness to his last will and desire on the 4th of sd. month

while in his deathbed and declared that all of his property should be given to his wife Sarah GUTRIDGE and his two daus. Nancy GUTRIDGE & Rebecca GUTRIDGE. (WC DW 23:94)
[James GUTRIDGE, one of the children of Thos., filed an exception to this will, 24 Apr 1815 (WC OB 1814-18:114)]

GUTRIDGE, Thomas; T 31 May 1815; 26 Aug 1816. WC; INV, [m]. (WC RI 10:84)

HABERN, Mary; 28 Nov 1809; 2 Apr 1810
RC; WILL; Sarah HABERN dau. of Charles HABERN; grson. [George] HABERN, grson. John HABERN, grdau. Nancy HABERN, dau. Mary HABERN, son Charles HABERN; rest of est. to grdau. Lucy HABERN; WITS: Chas. BELL, Jn. HUGHES, Rich. DOZIER. (RC WB 9:366)

HACKNEY, Benjamin; [m]; [m]
WC; DIV of Negroes; to James HACKNEY: Lucy & 3 children, Peter, Edmund; to Elizabeth BOTELER: Juno & 2 children, Liddy, John, Dick; to Meredith M. HACKNEY: Easter, Milley, Bob, Phill, Harriott, Fanny, Ben, Sam, Peggy, Baldwin, Eliza, Frank; total value for all 3: £986.0.0. (WC RI 8:514)

HACKNEY, Benjamin; 20 Oct 1802; 22 Nov 1802
WC; WILL; son Meredeth HACKNEY to have following Negroes: Ester's children, Rachel's children & Sam and silver watch; all remaining slaves to be div. between son James HACKNEY and dau. Elizabeth BUTLER; sons James & Meredeth to be exors; WITS: Chas. [R.] THOMPSON, Wm. C. CHANDLER, [Y.] SETTLE. (WC DW 20:402)
[Eliz. HACKNEY mar. (1) Benj. PHILPOTT, of Frederick Co., Md., RC, bond 25 Oct 1786; she must have mar. a BUTLER or BOTELER after PHILPOTT's death (MWO:280)]

HAGGOMAN, John; PO 15 Feb 1800; 20 Jul 1801
LC; INV, [m]; includes Negroes: Daniel, [Grandy], Will, Ne?on, Tamer, Cate, Mary, small girl Amy. (LC EB 24:155)
[Mary Ann HAGGOMAN (wid. & rel. of Jn. HAGGOMAN) aptd. gdn. to Eliz., Sarah, Ann, Jn. & Molly HAGGOMAN orphans of Jn., 15 Dec 1800 (LC Orders 21 1799-1801:200)]

HAGGOMAN, John & Mary Ann; T 5 Jun 1817; 9 Jun 1817
NC; sale of slaves (Will, Cate & Sam) belonging to the est. of John & Mary HAGGAMAN & proceeds payable to distributees [nfi]. (NC RB 21:196)
[Lucy P. LELAND was the admx. of the est. of Jn. HAGGOMAN, NC, 13 Jan 1817 (NC OB 1816-20:118); Jn. HAGGOMAN and Mary HAGGOMAN chose Baldwin M. LELAND as their gdn., NC, 13 Jan 1817 (NC OB 1816-20:119)]

HAGGOMAN, Mary Ann; PO 9 Feb 1818, T 11 May 1818; 8 Jun 1818
NC; settlement of Baldwin M. LELAND's acct. of the est. of Mary Ann HAGGEMAN dec'd and div. among the heirs: John HAGGEMAN (minor), Baldwin M. LELAND, Leroy P. LELAND, Arthur LEE & Griffin LAMKIN. (NC RB 21:423)
[Baldwin M. LELAND mar. Eliz. HAGGOMAN, dau. of Mary Ann HAGGOMAN, LC, 1806; Leroy P. LELAND mar. Ann G. HAGGOMAN, LC, bond 10 Feb 1807 (MLBLC:48); Griffin LAMKIN mar. Mary HAGGEMONS [sic], NC, bond 8 Feb 1817 (MLBNC:65)]

HALE, Benjamin R.; T 7 Oct 1815; 13 May 1816. NC; INV, [m]. (NC RB 20:448)
[This is prob. Benj. HALE, the son of Jn. and Ruth (SELF) HALE, who mar. Peggy BRYANT, dau. of Lydia BRYANT, RC, bond 31 Aug 1795 (MRC:83, NC RB 18:113, 291); Lewis & Booker (1964:153) read this man's name as

"Benjamin H.," but it is clearly "Benjamin R." in this record; the est. of Benj. R. HALE was ord. to be admin. by Chas. L. FULKS, NC, 14 Aug 1815 (NC OB 1811-1816:358)]

HALE, John; T 22 Jan 1810; 14 May 1810. NC; INV, £72.4.0. (NC RB 18:386)

HALE, John; PO 4 Aug 1813; 12 May 1817. NC; INV, $89.87 1/2 (NC RB 21:183)

HALL, Anne; 1 Nov 1800; 2 Feb 1807.
LP; RC; WILL; all est. to daus. Susan, Elizabeth & Sarah; one cent each to son Robert, William H. HALL, Mary YEATMAN, & Martha JENKINS; daus. Susan, Elizabeth & Sarah HALL exors; WITS: Vincent REDMAN, Jonathan BECKWITH, Wm. BRAGG, Mary SULLON. (RC WB 9:306)

HALL, Austin (or Astin); 8 Mar 1819
NC; Jane HALL orphan of Astin HALL chose Peter HALL as her gdn. (NC OB 1816-20:333)
[Austin HALL mar. Jane WALKER, Jul 1787; they had six children: Peter (b. 1788), Stephen (b. 1790), Nancy (b. 1794), Griffin (b. 1797), Jane (b. 1802) and Priscilla (b. 1806) (see Register of Wicomico Baptist Church in *BNCHS* vol. III no. 1:47); Priscilla HALL orphan of Astin HALL chose Jn. GEORGE as her gdn., 11 Mar 1822 (NC OB 1820-25:176)]

HALL, George H.; PO 13 Nov 1815; 8 Jan 1816
NC; settlement of Samuel DAWSON's acct. of his admin. of the est. and allowed Stuart R. PURSELL & Nancy his wife her dower ($43.74); the balance due to Robert HALL orphan of George H. HALL the sum of $87.49 which Elijah WILLIAMS his gdn. is to be possessed; PURSELL & wife were also allotted Nancy's dower in the land near land of John HUGHES; two lots of land were allotted to Robert HALL. (NC RB 20:331)
[The est. of Geo. H. HALL was ord. to be admin. by Sam. DAWSON, NC, 10 May 1813 (NC OB 1811-1816:170); Geo. H. HALL mar. Nancy FERGUSSON, NC, bond 26 Dec 1810; Stuart R. PURCELL, wid., mar. Nancy HALL, wid. of Geo. HALL, NC, bond 21 Dec 1814 (MLBNC:44, 85; NC OB 1811-15:375); Elijah WILLIAMS was aptd. gdn. of Robt. HALL orphan of Geo. HALL, NC, 13 Nov 1815 (NC OB 1811-15:386); Sam. DAWSON was aptd. gdn. of Robt. HALL, NC, 13 Jan 1817 (NC OB 1816-20:116)]

HALL, John; [m]; 14 Apr 1794
NC; INV of the est. of John HALL orphan of John HALL dec'd; includes 2 tracts of land (75 ac. & 60 ac); his gdn. was William HALL. (NC GA 1788-1824:124)
[This is John HALL the son of Jn. HALL & Hannah BUTLER (dau. of Jn. & Sarah BUTLER); Jn. the son of this Jn. mar. Clarissa POLLARD, NC, bond 30 Nov 1796 (MWO:160; NC RB 15:544; MLBNC:44)]

HALL, John; PO 10 Oct 17[8]6; 8 Oct 1804. NC; INV, £14.4.3. (NC RB 17:216)

HALL, John; 1814
NC; John HALL d. intestate around 1814 leaving a wid. Martha and six sons: John (eldest), Brodie, Thomas, Peter, Samuel S. and Paul. (NC CC 1820-002)

HALL, John; T 28 Nov 1821; 11 Feb 1822. NC; INV, $757.28 1/2; includes old man Jack. (NC RB 23:98)

HALL, Martin; PO 10 Feb 1823, T 19 Feb 1823; 10 Mar 1823
NC; Chancery suit; Axy HALL, Nancy HALL & Polly HALL by Thaddeus BROWN their next friend, pltfs, against Henrietta HALL deft., Robert DAVIS apptd gdn. to Henrietta HALL, an infant; land which Martin HALL died seized & possessed sold to Samuel C. PRITCHETT. (NC RB 23:279; CC 1823-006)

[Thaddeus BROWN aptd. gdn. to Axy, Henrietta, Nancy & Polly HALL orphans of Martin HALL, NC 13 Jan 1823 (NC OB 1820-25:262)]

HALL, Nancy; PO 11 May 1812, T 18 May 1812; 8 Jun 1812
NC; INV, $628; includes Negroes Rachel & George. (NC RB 19:195)
[The est. of Nancy HALL was ord. to be admin. by Astin HALL, NC, 11 May 1812 (NC OB 1811-1816:72)]

HALL, Richard; 16 Dec 1811
LC; Richard HALL died intestate leaving property of small value and no person will administer; sheriff ord. to dispose of est. (LC Orders 24:53)

HALL, Robert; Aug 1802; 23 May 1803
WC; INV, [£487.15.0]; includes Negroes Betsy & child Cyrus, Nancy & child, boy Lenard, girl [Phick], girl Sarah, boy Immanuel. (WC RI 8:229)

HALL, Steven; PO 14 Mar 1814, T 16 Apr 1816; 14 May 1816. NC; INV, [m]. (NC RB 20:476)

HALL, Steven the Elder; 9 Nov 1819; 18 Mar 1820
NC; Chancery suit, Richard KNOTT & Mary KNOTT, Eliza WALKER & Hendley H. WALKER by Richard KNOTT their next friend, Thomas HALL, John HALL, Jeremiah HALL, Thomas HALL, John ROBINSON & Nancy his wife who was Nancy HALL, Peter HALL, Stephen HALL, Griffin HALL, John GEORGE & Nancy his wife who was Nancy HALL, William HAYNIE & Jane his wife who was Jane HALL & Priscilla HALL by Peter HALL her next friend, Ann HALL, Alfred HALL & Elizabeth HALL by Benedict WALKER their next friend against John DAVIS & Elizabeth his wife who was Elizabeth WINSTEAD, William LUMKIN & Sarah his wife who was Sarah WINSTEAD,[Maria] COLEMAN, John WALKER & Nancy his wife who was Nancy WINSTEAD, Rebecca WINSTEAD, Catharine BEDFORD, Samuel WINSTEAD, Stephen WINSTEAD, Cotance WINSTEAD, Charles WINSTEAD, Alexander WINSTEAD & Thomas WINSTEAD; land in question was sold to Benedict WRIGHT for $800; after court costs deducted $750 remained and was divided into 5 eq. shares, to the children of Rodham HALL [of the] whole blood in right of their grandmother Elizabeth KNOTT one fifth and in right of their father one other fifth, to the children of Austin HALL to one half share or the half of one fifth part, to the children of Thomas HALL the same, [to] the children of John HALL the same, to the children of Stephen HALL the same, to the children of Caty WINSTEAD the same & to the children of Molly KNOTT the same. (NC RB 22:249)

HALL, Steven the Elder; PO 18 Dec 1819; 18 Mar 1820
NC; DIV of proceeds of sale of Negro Dennis among: Lunsford HALL, Leasure HALL, Presley HALL, James HALL, Rodham HALL, Austin HALL, Thomas HALL & Caty WINSTEAD (now dead); to Rodham HALL's heirs: Ann HALL, Alfred HALL & Elizabeth HALL (they rec'd $47.96 1/2); to Austin HALL's heirs: Peter HALL, Steven HALL, John GEORGE, Griffin HALL, William HAYNIE & Priscilla HALL (they rec'd $47.96 1/2); to Thomas HALL's heirs: Thomas HALL, Jeremah HALL & John ROBINSON (they rec'd $47.96 1/2); to Caty WINSTEAD's (sister of the half blood to the dec'd) heirs: John DAVIS (or DAVEY), William LUMKIN, Maria COLEMAN, John WALKER, Rebeccah WINSTEAD, Catharine BEDFORD, Samuel WINSTEAD, Stephen WINSTEAD, Cotance WINSTEAD, Charles WINSTEAD, Alexander WINSTEAD & Thomas WINSTEAD. The aforesd. Lunsford HALL, Leasure HALL, [Presley] HALL & James HALL are all dead, of age, unmarried, & without issue surviving; the following persons as is hereafter set forth their legal heirs: Elizabeth KNOTT (formerly Elizabeth

HALL) their mother but now dead leaving the children of her son Rodham HALL her only heirs: Ann HALL, Alfred HALL, & Elizabeth HALL; heirs of Molly WALKER (sis. of the half-blood of the dec'd): Richard KNOTT, Mary KNOTT, Elis W. WALKER; Steven HALL & Elizabeth WILKINS children of Steven HALL (bro. of the half blood of the dec'd); Thomas HALL & John HALL heirs of John HALL (bro. of the half blood to the dec'd); Peter HALL, Steven HALL, John GEORGE, Griffin HALL, William HAYNIE & Priscilla HALL heirs of Austin HALL (bro. of the half-blood of the dec'd); Thomas HALL, Jeremiah HALL & John ROBINSON heirs of Thomas HALL (bro. of the half blood of the dec'd). (NC RB 22:243)
[Wm. HAYNIE mar. Jane HALL, ward of Peter HALL, NC, bond 24 Mar 1819 (MLBNC:50); Catharine HALL married Cottance WINSTEAD (b. NC bet. 1748 and 1755, d. Person, North Carolina, 1806), the son of Sam. WINSTEAD & Sarah JONES; they had 12 or poss. 14 children b. bet. 1772 and 1795: Eliz., Sally, Nancy, Mary, Sam., Stephen Hall, Cottance, Chas., Alex., Thos., Rebecca and Katharine (<www.cemetarian.com/media/Winstead.pdf> accessed 5 Aug 2012 and <http://www.angelfire.com/ms/mollygal/wga44.html> accessed 5 Aug 2012); a Cotance WINSTEAD was the head of a household in Caswell Co., North Carolina in the 1790 census]

HALL, William H.; 18 Apr 1818; 26 Oct 1818
WC; WILL; $100 to wife Rebecca HALL; I lend unto my wife all the land that I hold in WC and RC except 50 ac. in WC & 50 ac. in RC and nine Negroes: Lewis, Jane, Charles, Moses, Joe, [Amey], Malindy, Hannah & George ... and my still & stilling materials in part as follows that is provided my son William Bragg HALL will keep the still in good repair he may still for his neighbors and have the hire for the sd. repair including casks & stands; wife to board & school my three children Samuel three years, Sally three years, & James H. HALL six years; granddau. Ann FRANKLIN one Negro girl Patsy; dau. Martha HALL a Negro girl Malinda; son Robert HALL a Negro boy Moses & $40; son William B. HALL a Negro boy George & my still after the death of my wife & half of my land lying in WC after the marriage or death of my wife and he is to have 50 ac. when he becomes 21; son Henry HALL all the land that I purchased of John SISSON, Charles BARNES, & Thomas NEALE after the marriage or death of my wife; wife to give son Henry 50 ac. when he reaches 21; dau. Elizabeth HALL a Negro woman Amey; Samuel HALL a Negro boy Joe & $50 to be reserved for him until he becomes 21; dau. Sally HALL a Negro girl Hannah & $50; son James H. HALL one half of land where I live in WC on the north side of sd. plant, one Negro Charles & $100; James MONTGOMERY & wife exors; WITS: Elliott PORTER, Thos. FRANKLIN, Harriet FRANKLIN, M. M. MARMADUKE. (WC DW 23:420)
[Thos. FRANKLIN mar. Nancy HALL, prob. a dau. of Wm. H. HALL, WC, bond 27 Dec 1810 (MLBWC:24)]

HALL, William H.; T 26 Feb 1819; 23 Aug 1819
WC; INV, $4889.83; includes Negroes Lewis, Jane, Charles, Amey, Malinda, Moses, Joe, Hannah, Patsey, George. (WC RI 10:412)

HAMILTON, Anne; 7 Jan 1778; 1 Feb 1802.
LP, RC; WILL; late husband Gilbert whose will was dtd. 31 Aug 1765; son John Tayloe tract of land w/o I now live; son Robert tract of land in Orange Co, [Va]; daus. Anne EDWARDS, Janet CARTER, Elizabeth & [Eupheme]; friends Mr. Thomas LAWSON & Robert W. CARTER exors; WITS: Mary BEALE, Jn. BEALE, Will BEALE Jr.; COD: 7 Jul 1781; dau. [Eupham] to

receive additional legacy; WITS: Landon CARTER, Robt. GRAHAM, Janet CARTER; first brought to court by Robt. HAMILTON on 2 Aug 1784 & ord to lie for further proof; finally proved on 1 Feb 1802. (RC WB 9:163) [Gilbert HAMILTON mar. Ann BEALE in NFP on 4 Nov 1732; he died in LP, RC c. 1768 leaving his entire est. to his wife Anne (NFPR:78, RC WB 7:7); Anne HAMILTON mar. Rich. EDWARDS, RC, bond 14 Mar 1764 (MRC:63)]

HAMILTON, Thomas B.; 20 Aug 1821
LC; Thomas B. HAMILTON declared in open court that he had migrated in the state from Hallifax [*sic*] and that his occupation is a teacher of grammar. school and that he intends to reside in the state; he shall be entitled to all the rights, privileges and advantages of a citizen of the state. (LC OB 25:236)

HAMMACK, Benedict; 20 Aug 1805; 2 Jan 1815
NFP, RC; WILL; all my land to wife Sarah HAMMOCK during her life; after her death part of land where I formerly lived from the bottom to the out lines to son John HAMMOCK; residue where I now live to son Louis HAMMOCK; son Louis & daus. should live with their mother while unmarried; wife & son William HAMMOCK exors; WITS: Jas. LAMBERT, Wm. CLARKE, Geo. SISSON; [when Louis HAMMOCK (William HAMMOCK being dead) brought will to court all wits were dead so Martin SISSON & Rich. DOZIER (who was present at the signing of the will) swore will was Benedick HAMMOCK's; wife relinquished her exorship & Louis was appointed exor]. (RC WB 9:463)
[The births of 3 children to Benedick & Sarah HAMMOCK are rec. in the NFPR: Sarah b. 6 Nov 1771, Molley b. 22 Jan 1777 and a second Sarah b. 25 May 17[??] (NFPR:79)]

HAMMACK, Benedict; PO 2 Jan 1815; 4 Sep 1820
RC; INV, [m], includes Negro woman Frank & mulatto girl Tildy. (RC WB 9:665)

HAMMACK, William; 6 Jul 1818
RC; Richard B. HUTT was aptd. gdn. to Maria, Polly, William and Sophia HAMMACK to receive the proceeds of the sale of the lands of William HAMMACK, dec'd. (RC OB 24:228)
[Based on a chancery suit between Wm. HAMMACK, Maria HAMMACK, Molly HAMMACK and Sophia HAMMACK, infants by Sam. TEMPLEMAN their next friend, against Eliz. HAMMACK, Chapman AUSTIN & Nancy his wife and Jn., Thos., and Betsy AUSTIN, and Jn. W. HAMMACK, Tobias PURCELL, Thos. DOBYNS and Rich. EFFORD aptd. to sell land which Wm. HAMMACK d. seized and possessed, 6 Oct 1817 (RC DB 21:66); settlement of Rich. B. HUTT's acct. of his gdnship. of Polly, Sophia & Wm. HAMMACK orphans of Wm. HAMMACK, 2 Jun 1823 (RC OB 26:63); Maria HAMMACK mar. Turner HANKS, RC, bond 4 Dec 1823 (MRC:87)]

HAMMOND, Thomas; T 16 Mar 1804; 17 Sep 1804
LC; INV, £258.8.8; includes Negroes Frank, Solomon, boy Jack, girl Ellen. (LC EB 24:291)

HAMMOND, William; T 14 Jan 1814; 4 Oct 1819. RC; INV, $47.87 1/2. (RC WB 9:627)

HAMMONDS, Jesse; 3 May 1824; 21 Jun 1824
LC; WILL; est. to wife Nancy; at her death whole est. to dau. Nancy; if dau. die without heirs, est. to bro. James HAMMONDS; [no ex. named]; WITS: Jn. MEREDITH, Thos. DUNTON; [COD dtd. 21 May 1824 revokes legacy to bro. James; same wits.]. (LC WB 28:250)

[Jesse HAMMOND mar. Nancy CHILTON, LC, bond 10 Jun 1802 (MLBLC:35)]

HAMMONDS, Thomas; 19 Apr 1803; 20 Jun 1803
LC; WILL; whole est. to wife during her widowhood; to son Thomas HAMMONDS my plant.; 10 shillings to son Charles HAMMONDS; remainder of est. to be eq. div. amongst my children Sally SPRIGGS, [Alcey] HAMMONDS, Lewis HAMMONDS, & [Huldy] HAMMONDS; if son Thomas die without heir plant. given him to go to son Lewis HAMMONDS; [no ex. named]; WITS: Jn. HALL, Fortunatus GEORGE, Benj. GEORGE; [Nancy HAMMOND the widow admx]; LC WB 28:69)
[Sarah HAMMOND mar. Ephraim SPRIGGS, LC, bond 18 Jan 1802 (MLBLC:69); Nancy HAMMONDS aptd. gdn. of Lewis & Huldy HAMMONDS orphans of Thos. HAMMONDS, 18 Feb 1805 (LC OB 1804-05:275); Alcy HAMMONDS orphan of Thos. HAMMONDS chose Nancy HAMMONDS as her gdn., 19 Feb 1805 (LC OB 1804-05:284)]

HANKS, Luke; 1 Sep 1817
RC; Ewell, John, Levina, Sally, and Turner HANKS were orphans of Luke HANKS; Foushee TEBBS was gdn. to Ewell, John & Levina. (RC OB 24:141)
[Luke HANKS was the son of Turner and Sarah HANKS, born 17 May 1771 (NFPR:86); Luke HANKS mar. Levina STOTT, dau. of Jn. STOTT, RC, bond 4 Jan 1792 (MRC:87); Ewell HANKS mar. Sally C. STOTT, RC, bond 4 Jan 1814 (MRC:86); Turner HANKS mar. Maria HAMMACK, RC, bond 4 Dec 1823 (MRC:87)]

HARCUM, Caty; PO 12 Dec 1814, T 31 Mar 1815; 8 May 1815
NC; INV, $411.50; includes Negro Sam. (NC RB 20:121)
[Caty HARCUM, dau. of Jn. BARRETT, mar. James HARCUM bef. 5 Jan 1788; in her will (NC 1 Oct 1814-12 Dec 1814) she named her son Leroy, dau. Betsy DAUGHITY, sis. Millicent BARROTT, grdau. Ann HUDNALL, dau. Sally HUDNALL, and son James (MWO:164; NC RB 19:572)]

HARCUM, Cuthbert; PO 11 Nov 1805, T 27 Nov 1805; 13 Jun 1808
NC; INV, £200.8.9, & DIV of pers. est; includes Negroes Daniel and girl Charlotte. (NC RB 17:632)
[Cuthbert HARCUM, son of Elisha & Margaret (BERRY) HARCUM, mar. Elinor COVINGTON, dau. of Eliz. Betts COVINGTON, NC, lic. 22 Feb 1774 (MWO:163)]

HARCUM, Elisha; PO 13 Apr 1801, T 24 Apr 1801; 8 Feb 1802
NC; INV, £482.17.0; includes Negroes Tom, Jacob, Field, Sukey, Chloe, Polly. (NC RB 16:339)
[In his will (NC 18 Feb 1800-9 Feb 1801) Elisha HARCUM, age 71, left his whole est. to his grson. Lee P. HARCUM (NC RB 16:211)]

HARCUM, Ellen; PO 13 Apr 1801, T 24 Apr 1801; 8 Feb 1802
NC; INV, £170.13.6; includes Negroes Will, boy Rodham, Sinah & child Polly. (NC RB 16:340)

HARCUM, James; PO 15 Nov 1814; 8 May 1815
NC; INV, $3266.37; includes Negroes Richard, Antoney, Joseph, Spencer, Peter. (NC RB 20:118)
[In his will (NC 4 Apr 1810-15 Nov 1814) Jas, HARCUM names his wife Katherine, sons Leroy & James, and daus. Betsy DAUGHITY, Sally HUDNALL & grdau. Sally DAUGHITY (NC RB 20:83); Sally HARCUM, dau. of Jas., mar. Thos HUDNALL, NC, bond 7 Dec 1808 (MLBNC:55); Betsy HARCUM, dau. of Jas., mar. Wm. DAUGHITY, NC, bond 11 Jan 1806 (MLBNC:26)]

HARCUM, James; PO 9 Jan 1815; 13 May 1816
NC; DIV of est. among the legal reps: William DAUGHITY, Thomas HUDNALL, James HARCUM, Leroy HARCUM; each rec'd $64.91. (NC RB 20:442)

HARCUM, John; PO 11 Dec 1815, T 28 Dec 1815; 12 Feb 1816
NC; INV, [m]. (NC RB 20:339)
[Jn. HARCUM mar. Rhoda AIRS, NC, bond 28 Aug 1806 (MLBNC:46); in his will (NC 18 Oct 1814 - 11 Dec 1815) Jn. HARCUM named his wife Rode, son Skelton and daus. Sarah, Betsy & Roxy (NC RB 20:322); his wid. Rhoda mar. Jn. DOGGET by 10 Jun 1816 (NC OB 1816-20:54)]

HARCUM, Mary; PO 11 Jun 1805, T 30 Jan 1806; 10 Feb 1806
NC; INV at the house of Capt. Edward ROGERS, [m]. (NC RB 17:379)
[The est. of Molly HARCUM was ord. to be admin. by Edw. ROGERS, NC, 11 Jun 1805 (NC Minute Book 1805-1807:20)

HARCUM, Phil J[aculin]; 28 Apr 1818; 11 May 1818
NC; WILL; to dau. Mary Elizabeth HARCUM one Negro girl [Herma]; to dau. Jane HARCUM one Negro girl Easter; to five children William Polk HARCUM, Cuthbert HARCUM, Mary Elizabeth HARCUM, Joseph HARCUM, & Jane HARCUM all monies due me and all land in Virginia and Maryland to be eq. div; wife Nancy HARCUM extx.; WITS: Sam. BLACKWELL, Jn. LANSDELL Jr. (NC RB 21:417)
[Wm. P. HARCUM & Cuthbert HARCUM chose Leroy HARCUM their gdn. and the sd. Leroy is aptd. gdn. of Mary E. & Jos. HARCUM orphans of Phil J. HARCUM, NC 9 Sep 1822 (NC OB 1820-25:235); Wm. P. HARCUM aptd. gdn. of Cuthbert, Mary E. & Jos. H. HARCUM orphans of Phil J. HARCUM, 13 Nov 1826 (NC OB 1825-30:125); NB: It is not clear why Cuthbert was apparently old enough to chose his own gdn. in 1822, but had one appointed by the court in 1826.]

HARCUM, Phil J[aculin]; PO 11 Jan 1819; 12 Aug 1822
NC; INV; includes Negroes Isaac, Daniel, Judith, George, Stephen, Rolland, Aaron, Peter, Margaret, Henry (legacy), Easter (legacy), child Betty. (NC RB 23:204)

HARCUM, Thomas; PO 13 Apr 1801; 14 Dec 1801
NC; INV, £404.16.6; includes Negroes Sippey, Isack, Tilley & child Simon, Sarah, William, Daniel, Mara. (NC RB 16:305)
[In his will (NC 2 Mar 1800 - 13 Apr 1801) Thos. HARCUM named his daus. [Nancy], Rebecca, [Katherine], and Jean and his sons Thos. J. & Valentine; his wife & bro. James were exors. (NC RB 16:230]

HARCUM, Thomas; PO 11 Jan 1813, T 12 Jan 1813; 9 Aug 1813
NC; INV, $718.03; includes Negroes Isaac, boys Peter & Isaac; Div of est. in the hands of James HARCUM ex. on 15 Jul 1813 among John ROBINSON, Richard MORRISON, Thomas J. HARCUM, Vallentine HARCUM, Jane HARCUM, and Winder GILL's children in the hands of the ex. (each heir received $109.54). (NC RB 19:430)
[Rebecca HARCUM, dau. of Sally C. HARCUM, mar. Rich. MORRISON, NC, bond 3 Dec 1803; Winder GILL, wid., mar. Nancy HARCUM, dau. of Thos. HARCUM, NC, bond 3 Nov 1792 (MLBNC:43, 75)]

HARCUM, Valentine; 13 Jul 1818
NC; Catherine ROBINSON aptd. gdn. of Eliza HARCUM orphan of Valentine HARCUM. (NC OB 1816-20:268)
[Valentine HARCUM was the son of Thos. HARCUM (d. NC 1801) (NC RB 16:230); Catherine ROBINSON is prob. a sis. of Eliza HARCUM; she mar. (1)

Wm. FORBUSH, NC, 19 May 1792 and (2) Jn. ROBINSON, wid., NC, bond 8 Sep 1809 (MLBNC:38, 87); Thos. HARCUM aptd. gdn. to Eliza HARCUM orphan of Valentine HARCUM, 11 Aug 1828 (NC OB 1825-30:292)]

HARCUM, William; PO 14 Mar 1814, T 21 Feb 1815; 11 Mar 1816
NC; INV, $1340.72; includes Negroes Silva & child Milly, boys Steptoe & Manuel, girls Jane & Siner. (NC RB 20:391)
[In his will (NC 25 Jan 1807-14 Mar 1814) Wm. HARCUM, of SSP, named his sons Sam. & Hiram (NC RB 19:533)]

HARCUM, William; PO 14 Aug 1820, T 30 Dec 1820; [m]
NC; DIV of est. among Samuel HARCUM who relinquished his part of the est. for support of his brothers & sisters, except his proportion of the Negroes; William HARCUM orphan of William HARCUM dec'd has received $92.32 more than he is entitled to which is due to his sis. Mary out of his proportion of the Negroes; allotted to Samuel HARCUM Negroes Silvy, boy Manuel; to Mary HARCUM Negro boy Stephen; to William HARCUM Negro girl Jane; Samuel, Mary, William & Hannah were orphans of William HARCUM; their gdn. was William HUDNALL. (NC GA 1788-1824:445)
[Mary HARCUM chose Sam. HARCUM her gdn. and the sd. Sam. was aptd. gdn. of Hannah and Wm. HARCUM orphans of Wm. HARCUM, NC 14 Feb 1820 (NC OB 1816-20:423)]

HARDING, Cyrus; PO 13 Nov 1806, T 31 Dec 1806; 9 Jun 1807
NC; INV, [m]; icludes Negroes Peter, Richard, Fanney, Millinda, Darcus, Henry, Dennis, Hannah, Hannah (younger), David, Siller, Rose, Easter, Jerry, Daniel. (NC RB 17:544)
[Cyrus HARDING, in his will (NC 16 Jan 1805-9 Jun 1806) named his two youngest children Polly & a child not yet baptised (NC RB 17:415); Wm. HARDING was aptd. gdn. to Rebecca, Polly and Nancy HARDING the orphans of Cyrus HARDING, NC, 11 Jan 1813 (NC OB 1811-15:139)]

HARDING, Hopkins; PO 14 Dec 1812, T 7 Jan 1813; 14 Jun 1813
NC; INV, [m]; includes Negroes Tom, Isaac, Daniel, Joshua, Stephen, Emanuel, Suckey, Violet, Sinah, Lucy, George, Rachael, Sarah, David, Charles, Mary, James, Levina, Solomon, Matilda, Spencer, Mariah. (NC RB 19:390)
[In his will (NC 12 Oct 1812-14 Dec 1812) Hopkins HARDING named his wife Jemima, grdaus. Polly & Nancy (daus. of dec'd son Cyrus), grdau. Rebeccah, dau. Lucy PITMAN (wife of Edw.), d-i-l Sally HARDING (wid. of son Jn. HARDING), grson. Jn. H. HARDING, grsons. Hiram HARDING, Cyrus HARDING, & Thos. E. HARDING, niece Hannah H. CARTER, and son Billey (NC RB 19:278); Lucy HARDING, dau. of Hopkins & Jemimie HARDING, b. 20 Feb 1788, mar. Edw. C. PITMAN, NC, bond 4 Sep 1810 (MLBNC:82)]

HARDING, Samuel; 15 Jun 1819; 11 Dec 1820
NC; WILL; whole est. to sis. Jane HARDING; at her death land I now live on to grand nephew William JETT; Negroes Mira & Bob to grand nephew Joseph JETT; Negroes Young Milley & her children & boy William to grand nephew John H. JETT; grand nephew to make provision for Old Milley; grand nephew William JETT ex.; WITS: Wm. DAUGHITY, Jas. DAUGHITY, Jn. SULLIVAN. (NC RB 22:447)

HARDING, William; 11 Mar 1786; 12 Jun 1786
NC, WILL; children James, William, Thomas, Sarah. Ann Esther, Alcey and Milly; all land to son James who is under 21; friends Jas. COX and Peter

COX exors.; WITS: Jn. HARFORD, Sarah SMITH, Chas. Wm. KESTER (NC RB 13:198)
[Lewis & Booker 1964:114 give Ann Easter's name as two names Ann and Easter, but NC CC 1803-012 proves that Ann Easter is one name; Ann Easter mar. Hen. H. TRAVERS, Sarah HARDING mar. Wm. B. TRAVERS and Alice HARDING mar. Edw. BARNES (NC CC 1803-012)]

HARPER, John; T 15 Feb 1799; 24 Mar 1800. WC; INV; £15.13.9. (WC RI 8:43)
[This may be the Jn. HARPER who mar. Hannah Harrison WAUMOTH, WC, 8 Jul 1790 (MWO:166)]

HARRIS, Agnes; 28 Nov 1814
WC; on the mot. of Youell RUST alias HARRIS ord. to div. the est. of Agnes HARRIS. (WC OB 1814-18:90)

HARRIS, Hugh; 23 Oct 1802; 6 Jun 1803
RC; WILL; son George; wife Sally; mentions plant. & water grist mill; daus. Peggy & Nancy SISSON (& her children); children of Frances KENNAN; mentions plant. purchased of Randall WALKER [ ]; wife, son George & friend George MISKELL exors; WITS: Jonathan BRYANT, Parker BEACHAM, Jas. PULLEN. (RC WB 9:215)
[Hugh HARRIS mar. Sally HALL, wid., RC, bond 23 Feb 1785; Geo. Henry HARRIS, son of Hugh & Sally HARRIS, was b. 20 Nov 1789 (NFPR:88); Fanny HARRIS mar. Jn. KENNAN of Frederick Co., RC, bond 19 Feb 1798; Nancy SISSON is prob. Nancy HARRIS who mar. (1) Giles SYDNOR, RC, bond 7 Apr 1795 and (2) Martin SISSON, RC, bond 10 Apr 1802 (MRC:88,112, 188, 201)]

HARRIS, Hugh; 16 Feb 1804); [7] Jul 1806. RC, INV, £776.17.0. (RC WB 9:293)

HARRIS, James; PO 19 Oct 1801; 21 Jul 1807
LC; DIV of est. among: Miss Molly HARRIS, [Juriah] HARRIS, John HARRIS. (LC EB 27:20)
[Juriah HARRIS orphan of James HARRIS chose Joseph CARTER Jr. as gdn., 21 Sep 1801 (LC Orders 21 1799-1801:325)]

HARRIS, John; PO 17 Jun 1805; 21 Jul 1807
LC; DIV of est. among: Miss Molly HARRIS, Juriah HARRIS. (LC EB 27:20)

HARRIS, John; 4 Jul 1825
RC; upon the mot. of Rebecca HARRIS wid. & extx. of John HARRIS, Colin McRAE & Judith his wife (formerly HARRIS), William A. PATTERSON & Ann his wife (formerly HARRIS), Delia HARRIS, Louisa HARRIS, Matilda HARRIS, Mary HARRIS, Camilla HARRIS, and Francis HARRIS, and Hypatia McRAE dau. of the late Hypatia McRAE (formerly HARRIS) the last six by Rebecca HARRIS their mother and next friend they being minors. (RC OB 26:324)
[This seems to be Jn. HARRIS who was b. in Powhatan Co., Va. on 13 Oct 1758 and d. in Chesterfield co., Va. in 1816; he mar. Rebecca BRITTON, in Chesterfield Co. in 1794 and they had 12 children: Desapyhen (b. 1795), Hiram (b. 1796), Hypatia (b. 1798), Ann O. (b. 1799), Judith J. (b. 1801), Delia (b. 1802), Louisiana (b. 1804), Caroline Matilda R. (b. 1806), Philip Francis (b. 1808), Caroline Matilda (b. 1810), Mary Elizabeth (b. 1812) and Camilla (b. 1814) (data extracted from Harris-Hunters-L on Ancestry.com, at <http://archiver.rootsweb.ancestry.com/th/read/HARRIS-HUNTERS/1998-10/0909867129> accessed 2 Jan 2012)]

HARRIS, Sarah; 16 Feb 1804); [7] Jul 1806. RC; INV, £178.19.7. (RC WB 9:294)
[This is prob. Sally the wid. of Hugh HARRIS (*see above*)]

HARRISON, George; 21 Jan 1800

LC; settlement of the gdnship. acct. of Jonathan PULLEN with Alice G. EVERETT who was Alice G. HARRISON orphan of George HARRISON and possess John D. EVERETT with her est. (LC Orders 21 1799-1801:77) [Jn. D. EVERETT mar. Alice G. HARRISON, LC, bond 1 Jan 1800 (MLBLC:26); Betsy G. HARRISON orphan of Geo. HARRISON chose Jn. D. EVERETT as her gdn., 16 Jun 1800 (LC Orders 21 1799-1801:124)]

HARRISON, Jeremiah; 24 Dec 1788; 3 Apr 1793
Berkeley Co; WILL; all est. and my parts of the estates of my father Samuel HARRISON, my mother Magdaline HARRISON, my bro. William HARRISON & my sis. Ann STONES to be eq. div. between John CRABB Sr. of Ragged Point Neck & John Harrison SMITH son of Elizabeth SMITH rel of Spencer SMITH of Yocomoco Neck; friends John CRABB & Daniel CRABB exors. & trustees to see that John Harrison SMITH [is] well raised and [has] as much schooling as his portion can afford him; [no WITS]. (NC DCO:319)
[This is Jeremiah HARRISON the son of Sam. (d. WC 1764) & Magdalene (d. WC1786) HARRISON (WC DW 14:280, 16:314, 17:43); Ann HARRISON, dau. of Sam. HARRISON mar. Wm. STONE bef. 3 Apr 1793 by which time she was dec'd (MWO:334); Ragged Point is located in WC on Coles Neck (Miller:131); Yeocomico Neck is also in WC on the Potomac Riv. between Bonum Cr. & the Yeocomico Riv. (Miller:175)]

HARRISON, Jeremiah; PO 3 Apr 1793, T 10 Aug 1793; 3 Sep 1799. [WC]; APP, £34.10.10. (NC DCO:358)

HARRISON, John R.; 5 Apr 1821; 12 Nov 1821
NC; WILL; Charlot and all the rest of my Negroes to be free if it be consistent to law and those that are under the age of 21 years cannot be lawfully free then I do give to all that are 21 years and upwards their freedom & the young Negroes that is under that age I give in the care of Charlot their mother to raise them until they arrive to 21 & then for them to be free; I give to Charlot $200 to support her children that are under age; $200 to James TREAKLE; rest of est. to Alsy T. STRAUGHAN; WITS: Wm. HARDING Jr., Rich. NELMS, Cyrus SUTTON; first I leave Capt. Edward COLES to administer. Second William W. APPLEBY. (NC RB 23:41)

HARRISON, John R.; PO 12 Nov 1821, T 20 Nov [1821]; 11 Aug 1823
NC; INV; includes Negroes Charlet, Winston, [Famsy] & child, girl Pattey, boy Roston. (NC RB 23:343)

HARRISON, Lovell; PO 28 Feb 1815, T 7 Mar 1815; 22 May 1815
WC; INV, $817.16; includes Negro man Isaac. (WC RI 9:450)

HARRISON, William; 17 Sep 1778); [m]
CP, WC; WILL; all est. that I got by or with her at the day of marriage to wife Abigail; mother Magdalene HARRISON; friend William MIDDLETON & wife Abigail exors.; WITS: Vincent PENDERGRASS, Rhodam [BOOTH]. (WC Unrec Wills 1755-1800 #35)
[Wm. HARRISON was the son of Sam. & Magdalen HARRISON; Sam. HARRISON in his will (WC 11 Aug 1763 - 31 Jul 1764) named his sons Wm. & Jeremiah, his daus. Ann & Hannah; wife Magdalene & father Geo. HARRISON dec'd; Magdalen HARRISON in her will (WC 16 Dec 1775 - 27 Jun 1786) named her son Jeremiah and dau. Hannah GILBERT and [dec'd] husband Sam. HARRISON. (WC DW 14:280; DW 16:314; DW 17:43)

HARRISON, William; 3 Feb 1800; 6 Apr 1801

RC; WILL; wife Jean; bro. James HARRISON my part of my father's lands w/o my mother now lives; wife & bro. Daniel exors; WITS: H[en.] W. HEADLEY, Patsy DUFF. (RC WB 9:146)

HART, Reuben; 4 Mar 1823
RC; Overseers of the Poor of LP ord. to bind out James HART orphan of Reuben HART to Joshua REAMY. (RC OB 26:34)

HARTLY, George; PO 13 Jan 1800, T 20 Feb 1801; 13 Apr 1801. NC; INV, £17.2.0. (NC RB 16:229)

HARVEY, Elizabeth; 24 Jan 1817; 13 Oct 1817
NC; WILL; to my son James HARVEY a Negro woman Polly & her child Solomon; to son Thomas HARVEY the whole of my administration for my executorship of my husband's est; the balance of my est. to be eq. div. among all my children; friend Thomas W. HUGHLETT with my son Thomas HARVEY exors; WITS: Cyrus SUTTON, Eliz. CARTER. (NC RB 21:264)
[Eliz. HARVEY seems to be the wid. and admx. of Thos. HARVEY (*see below*) who d. in NC between 1815 and 1817 (NC CC 1820-010); a Thos. HARVEY mar. Eliz. HUDNALL, dau. of Lucy HUDNALL,NC, bond 9 Dec 1793 (MLBNC:47)]

HARVEY, James; 21 Mar 1811; 24 Apr 1815
WP, WC; WILL; son Octavious HARVEY one Negro boy named Thornton in lieu of a boy left my sd. son by his aunt SMITH named Frederick; residue of est. I lend to my wife Lusettah HARVEY; friend Joseph FOX ex; WITS: Chris. J. COLLINS, G. PAYNE. (WC DW 23:91)
[Jas. HARVEY mar. Lucette FOX, WC, bond 18 Mar 1793 (MLBWC:29); Jas. FOX aptd. gdn. of Lucinda, Jos. F., Ann E., Jas. J. & Eliz. J. HARVEY orphans of Jas. HARVEY, 26 Feb 1816 (WC OB 1814-18:205)]

HARVEY, James; T 14 Nov 1816; 26 Nov 1821
WC; INV, $2408; includes Negroes Able, Cate, Patty, Betsey dau. to Cate, Henry & Aaron sons to Cate. (WC RI 11:130)

HARVEY, Onesiphorus; PO 8 Oct 1798, T 1 Dec 1798; 11 Jul 1808
NC; DIV of est. among Thomas HARVEY (rec'd Solomon, Sarah & girl Betty), Alice HARVEY (rec'd Amos & Sarah), Onesiphorus HARVEY (rec'd Mime & child Patte, girl Fanne & boy Jess), [Jamie] HARVEY (rec'd Isaac, boy Solomon), Winifred HURST (rec'd woman Sarpher, girl Judith), Judith YERBY (rec'd boys James & Daniel); INV, [m]; includes Negroes Solomon, Isaac, Amos, Sarah, Sarpher, Mime & child Patte, Hannah, Rose, Harry a lad, James a lad, boys Daniel & Solomon, Judith (Sarpher's child), Judith, Fanne, Sarah, & Jesse (Mime's children), girls Huldy & Bettey. (NC RB 18:3, 4)
[In his will (NC 25 Sep 1797-8 Oct 1798) Onesiphorus HARVEY, Sr. named the orphans of Chas. YEARBY, Thos. HURST, sons Thos. & Onesiphorus, daus. Judah YEARBY, Winifred HURST, Jonna & Alice and wife Sarah (NC RB 15:525); Winifred HARVEY mar. Thos. HURST, son of Kemp & Sukey (TAYLOR) HURST, NC, 28 Jun 1792 (MWO:194); Judith YERBY is prob. the wid. of Chas. YERBY (d. NC 1794) (NC RB 15:100)]

HARVEY, Sukey; T 10 Mar 1825; 10 May 1825
NC; INV, $1070.96; includes the following Negroes: Frederick, Anna, boy Elijah. (NC RB 24:203)

HARVEY, Thomas; T 4 Nov 1817; 9 Mar 1818
NC; INV, $10,641.62 1/2; includes following Negroes worth $8600: Solomon, Moses (old man), Young Moses, Israel, Isaac (boy), David (boy), Sam (boy), Isaac (boy), Reuben (boy), Moses (boy), Old Winney, Siller & child, Sukey & child, Betty & child, Sally & child, Milley & child, Milly (girl), Nelly (girl),

Nancy (girl), Phillis (girl), Sarah (girl), Letty (girl), Judith (girl), Ginny (girl), Delia (girl), [Charly] (girl), Winney (girl), Betty (girl), Garry (boy). (NC RB 21:375)

[Thos. HARVEY orphan of Thomas HARVEY chose Wm. HARDING as his gdn., NC, 11 Aug 1817 (NC OB 1816-20:164); Sally HARVEY orphan of Thos. HARVEY chose Thomas H. HARVEY as her gdn., NC 14 Jun 1819 (NC OB 1816-20:363); Thos. H. HARVEY aptd. gdn. of Jas. & Lewis G. HARVEY orphans of Thos. HARVEY, NC 12 Jul 1819 (NC OB 1816-20:373); Eliz. [A.] HARVEY chose Thos. H. HARVEY as her gdn. and the sd. Thos. H. HARVEY is aptd. gdn. of Mary HARVEY orphans of Thos. HARVEY, NC 14 Aug 1820 (NC OB 1820-25:49)]

HATHAWAY, Elizabeth; PO 18 Mar 1817; 17 Jul 1820. LC; INV, [$499.21 1/2]. (LC EB 29:29)

HATHAWAY, Lawson; 24 May 1815; 20 Sep 1819

LC; WILL; Negro woman Cate to wife Elizabeth HATHAWAY; if wife does not survive her sd. husband having no other issue by him nor any other surviving husband, then after my death my est. shall be accountable for the sum of £500 to be disposed of agreeable to the marriage contract; land to be sold and proceeds eq. div. among living descendants; son Lawson HATHAWAY; dau. Elizabeth [ROGERS] has £5 legacy from Capt. James KIRK; dau. Sarah DEGGE; £5 each to grchil legal heirs of William HATHAWAY; friends William KIRK & Henry C. LAWSON exors; WITS: Arch. ANDERSON, Thos. MASON, Nich. P. BUCHAN, Jn. EDMONDS, Jn. HUNT. (LC WB 28:197)

[Lawson HATHAWAY mar. Eliz. KING, dau. of Wm. KING, LC, bet. Dec 1781 and Dec 1784 (MWO:171); Sary HATHAWAY mar. Jn. DEGGES, LC, bond 1 Dec 1801 (MLBLC:21)]

HATHAWAY, Lawson; PO Oct 1819; 19 Jun 1821. LC; INV, $237.21 1/4. (LC EB 29:101)

HATHAWAY, Thomas; 6 Nov 1802; 21 Feb 1803

LC; WILL; wife Elizabeth HATHAWAY to have use of my plant; at wife's death plant. to be sold & money eq. div. among all my children; wife to have use of following Negroes in lieu of her dower: Manuel, Jesse, Phill, Dick, Pegga & Siller; $20 to be deducted out of my son John HATHAWAY's & dau. Judith ROGERS' parts for bed & furniture they have received; balance of est. to be eq. div. among children; wife Elizabeth to be gdn. to my following children: Sally HATHAWAY, William HATHAWAY, Nancy HATHAWAY & George HATHAWAY; friends John CHOWNING, Joseph CARTER Jr., William BISCOE & Peter BEANE exors; WITS: Martin SHEARMAN, Geo. CAMPBELL, Jas. NORRIS Jr. (LC WB 28:65)

[This is prob. Thos. HATHAWAY who mar. Eliz. KIRK, dau. of Jas. KIRK (d. LC 1776-1777), LC, bond 18 Nov 1772; Judith HATHAWAY mar. Chas. ROGERS, LC, 10 Mar 1796 (MWO:171, 302)]

HATHAWAY, Thomas; PO 21 Feb 1803; 15 Sep 1806

LC; DIV of est. among: Thomas HATHAWAY, Mrs. Judith ROGERS, George HATHAWAY, Miss Sally HATHAWAY, Miss Nancy HATHAWAY, [William] HATHAWAY, John HATHAWAY. (LC EB 24:372)

HATHAWAY, Thomas; PO 17 Jan [1805]; 15 Sep 1806

LC; INV, £944.18.8; includes Negroes Manuel, Phil, Dick, Peggy, Jesse, Sciller, Solomon, Davy, Porteus, Chris, Mima, Polly, Nanny, Grace, Blair, Milly. (LC EB 27:371)

HATHAWAY, Thomas; PO 20 Jun 1808, T 5 Jul 1808; 18 Jul 1808

LC; INV, £131.8.; includes Negro Solomon. (LC EB 27:38)

HATHAWAY, Thomas; 13 Sep 1807; 16 Jul 1810
LC; WILL; use of all est. to wife until dau. Elizabeth Kirk is 21 then dau. is to have whole est; if dau. should die, est. to go to wife Jane HATHAWAY; wife extx; WITS: Porteus TOWLES, Fanny TOWLES; [certif granted to Jane HATHAWAY & William CALLAHAN for obtaning letters of admin. 20 Jun 1808] (LC WB 28:108)
[This is poss. Thos. HATHAWAY who mar. Jincy [sic] CHOWNING, 1804 (MLBLC:36); Wm. GEORGE son of [D.] aptd. gdn. to Eliz. HATHAWAY orphan of Thos. HATHAWAY, 17 Mar 1817 (LC OB 25:353)]

HATHAWAY, William; 19 Dec 1808
LC; William HATHAWAY orphan of William HATHAWAY bound out by the Overseers of the Poor for the Upper District of LC to William CALLAHAN. (LC Orders B23 1808-11:6)

HAYDON, Armistead; 23 Dec 1814; 15 May 1815
LC; WILL; to be buried on the family farm; to wife Nancy all that portion of my est. that I received by intermarriage with her; also to wife use of residue of est. including woman [Tab] & her son Spencer [H.H.] during her life; after wife's death residue of est. to be eq. div. among all my brothers which descended by my father & mother; wife extx; [no wits listed]; [will was remanded to LC Court to be recorded from the Superior Court of LC]. (LC WB 28:163)
[Armistead HAYDON mar. Nancy P. HAYDON, LC, bond 3 Apr 1810 (MLBLC:36)]

HAYDON, Armistead; PO 15 Apr 1822, T 26 Apr 1824; 17 May 1824
LC; sale of Negro the prop. of Armistead HAYDON for $263.20; div. of proceeds among John BARNET, Abner HAYDON & Ezekiel HAYDON. (LC EB 29:334)
[Molly HAYDON, dau. of Lucy HAYDON, mar. Jn. BARNETT, LC, bond 11 Feb 1811 (MLBLC:3)]

HAYDON, Ezekiel; 20 Dec [1808]; 17 Jul 1809
LC; WILL; use of land w/o I now live to wife Lucy HAYDON during her life or widowhood; at wife's death or marriage, plant. to go to son Armistead; if Armistead should die without male heirs, land should go to son Ezekiel; Negro boy Tom to son Armistead; after wife's death or marriage other Negroes & all PE to be eq. div. between Abner, Mary, Judith, Shapley & Ezekiel; wife & Dr. Thomas BALL exors; WITS: Griffin HAYDON, Rich. HAYDON, Thos. BALL M.D. (LC WB 28:110)
[Ezekiel HAYDON was the son of Jn. (d. LC, 1773) & Mary (d. LC, 1787) HAYDON (LC WB 20:64, WB 22:173, 174); he mar. Lucy DOGGETT, dau. of Wm. DOGGETT, LC, bond 30 May 1788 (MLBLC:36); Nathan SPRIGGS aptd. gdn. of Ezekiel HAYDON orphan of Ezekiel HAYDON, 16 Jan 1815; Lucy HAYDON must have died just before this date since admin. on her est. was granted at that time (LC Orders 24:212); on the mot. of Nathan SPRIGGS gdn. of Ezekiel HAYDON orphan of Ezekiel HAYDON ord. that .. lay off & assign to Nancy HAYDON late the wid. her dower in his hands, 19 Feb 1816 (LC Orders 24:284); settlement of Nathan SPRIGGS' gdnship. acct. with Ezekiel HAYDON orphan of Ezekiel HAYDON, 15 Jun 1818 (LC OB 25:3); ord. that Abner HAYDON, Ezekiel HAYDON by Nathan SPRIGGS his gdn., Jn., Peter & Polly BARNETT be summoned to show cause why the lands of which Nancy P. HAYDON died seized should not be sold for a division, 21 Jan 1822 (LC OB 25:278)]

HAYDON, Ezekiel; PO 17 Jul 1809, T 30 Dec 1809; 19 Feb 1810
LC; INV, $1341.22; includes Negroes: Tabby, boy Tom, girls Lucy, Sarah, Peggy, boy Jacob, old woman Peggy. (LC EB 27:69)

HAYDON, Ezekiel; PO 13 Jan 1812, T 26 Sep 1812; 12 Oct 1812
NC; INV, includes Negroes Tom, Spencer, Daniel, Young Daniel, Billey, Markanthony, Mesheck, Ephraim, Sarah, Mary, Young Tom, Moses, Lucinda, Sukey, Shadrick, [Olwen], Salley; est. which amounted to $500.12 1/2 was div. among Charles HAYDON, George HAYDON, William BLACKERBY, heirs of Thomas HAYDON dec'd. (NC RB 19:253)

HAYDON, George; PO 8 Dec 1823, T 23 Dec 1823; 12 Apr 1824
NC; DIV of Negroes; Joshua, Milley, Lee, Stokely, Jane & Suky allotted to Elizabeth HAYDON the wid. as her dower; James, Polly, Felicia to Thomas B. HAYDON; Davy, Mahala, Lucy to Willis HAYDON; Shadrack, Mary, Mariah to Judith B. HAYDON; the widow's dower in land on the road from Hudnall's Mill to Wicomico Church was also laid out. (NC RB 23:439) [Miller:70 locates Hudnall's Mill in NC south of the Great Wicomico River near the head of Mill Creek]

HAYDON, George; T 22 Oct 1823; 12 Sep 1824
NC; INV, $4143.45; includes the following Negroes worth $3585: Joshua, Joe, Shadrick, Mary, Milly, Mahala, Maria, Lucy, Felicia; boys Stokely, James, Stephen, Davy, Lee, Polly [sic]; young women Sukey, Sally; girls Jane, Mary. (NC RB 24:36)

HAYDON, Griffin; 16 Dec 1816
LC; Edw. BEANE aptd. gdn. to Helkiah & Dorinda HAYDON orphans of Griffin HAYDON. (LC Orders 24:343)

HAYDON, John; 15 Jun 1820; 8 Oct 1823
NC; WILL; tract of military land which descended to me by the death of my sons Jesse & Thomas HAYDON to my son Robert; use & benefits of the land I now live on to my sons Willis & Warner HAYDON; sis. Leannah HAYDON & my dau. Polly HAYDON to have a place of [abidance] on my sd. land during their single lives which places I have pointed out to my friend John SIMMONDS; sons Willis & Warner to equally enjoy benefits of my orchard; three youngest children Willis, Warner & Elizabeth; balance of est. to be eq. div. among my children Robert, Polly, Matilda, Willis, Warner & Elizabeth; Griffin EDWARDS Sr. & John SIMMONDS exors; WITS: Ralph EDWARDS, Cyrus PINCKARD; probate granted Griffin EDWARDS 10 Nov 1823. (NC RB 23:367)
[Jesse HAYDON, was a pvt. in the 5th U.S. Regiment of Infantry, when he dictated his will (NC 6 Jun 1812-13 Sep 1813) (NC RB 19:440); Jn. HAYDON was the father and heir at law of Jesse HAYDON formerly of NC who enlisted in the service of the US in 1812 for 5 years and later died in the service; 11 Mar 1816 (NC OB 1816-20:20)]

HAYDON, Judith & Shapley; PO 16 Jan 1815, T 20 Feb 1815; 21 Aug 1815
LC; DIV of proceeds of sale of slave Sarah belonging to est. of Judith HAYDON dec'd to Richard PAYNE for $310 & DIV of proceeds (after deducting 5% commission) among Nancy HAYDON admx. of Armistead HAYDON, Nathan SPRIGGS gdn. of Ezekiel HAYDON, John BARNETT, Abner HAYDON & DIV of proceeds of sale of slave Peggy belonging to the est. of Shapley HAYDON dec'd among Nathan SPRIGGS gdn. to Ezekiel HAYDON, John BARNETT, and Abner HAYDON. (LC EB 27:246)

HAYDON, Lucy; T 25 Jan 1815; 16 Oct 1815. LC INV. (LC EB 27:259)

HAYDON, Thomas; PO Oct 1797; 15 Oct 1798

LC; INV, [m]; includes Negroes: Ephraim, Cyrus, Rachel, Fanny. (LC EB 24:80)

HAYDON, Thomas; PO 18 Dec 1815, T 15 Jan 1816; 18 Mar 1816
LC; DIV of proceeds of sale of slave Harrow among the following heirs Nancy HAYDON, Charles HAYDON, Moses LUNSFORD gdn. of Brunetta HAYDON, & heirs of Griffin HAYDON. (LC EB 27:288)
[Nancy P. HAYDON orphan of Thos. HAYDON chose Judith HAYDON as her gdn. and sd. Judith is aptd. gdn. to Chas., Osmond, Monroe and Brunetta HAYDON orphans of sd. Thos., 19 Jan 1801 (LC Orders 21 1799-1801:205); chancery suit: Willis HAYDON, Griffin HAYDON & Rich. HAYDON, complts., against Nancy Payne, Chas., Osmond, Monroe and Brunetta by their gdn. Judith to sell a mill, 19 Jan 1801 (LC Orders 21 1799-1801:207; CC 1801-015); Brunetta HAYDON orphan of Thos. HAYDON chose Moses LUNSFORD as her gdn., 19 Jun 1815 (LC Orders 24:235)]

HAYDON, William; T 4 Jan 1796; 18 Jul 1796. LC ; INV, £18.10.3. (LC EB 24:24)
[Wm. BROWN aptd. gdn. to Wm. HAYDON orphan of Wm. HAYDON, 16 Sep 1799 (LC Orders (21) 1799-1801:46); Jn. & Wm.HAYDON named as heirs of Wm. HAYDON who is prob. this Wm. HAYDON, 20 Jun 1803 (LC Orders V 1802-03:372)]

HAYDON, William O.; PO 15 Jan 1821, T 24 Jan 1821; 19 Feb 1821
LC; INV, [$1661]; includes Negroes Tom, Winney, Delia, Alice, James. (LC EB 29:68)

HAYDON, William O.; PO 1821, T Jan 1822; 18 Mar 1822
LC; DIV of proceeds from selling 5 Negroes & 2 tracts of land among 7 heirs: Elias FENDLEA, Denis DAMERON, Thomas M. OWENS gdn. to George D. HAYDON, Polly HAYDON, Harriot HAYDON, Lucy HAYDON, Hierom HAYDON. (LC EB 29:182; OB 25:242, 257)
[Elias FENDLA mar. Winna C. HAYDON, LC, bond 24 Nov 1815; Dennis DAMERON mar. Eliz. HAYDON, LC, bond 9 Dec 1816 (MLBLC:19, 27); Thos. M. OWENS aptd. gdn. to Geo. D., Harriott, Lucy M., Polly & Hierom HAYDON, 17 Dec 1821 (LC OB 25:274); Harriott HAYDON mar. Thos. N. GEORGE, LC, bond 19 May 1823 (MLBLC:31, LC OB 25:379)]

HAYES, George; 8 Oct 1827
NC; Max. HAYNIE aptd. gdn. to Eliz. HAYES orphan of George HAYES. (NC OB 1825-30:209)
[Allot to [Jem.] HAYES now the wife of Jn. WHEELER her thirds of the slaves of the est. of her late husband Geo. HAYES, 14 Jan 1828 (NC OB 1825-30:229, 291)]

HAYES, James; T 10 Apr 1815; 12 Jun 1815
NC; INV; est. included only a debt of $22.37 due from the U[nited] States for military services; his admr. was Thomas J. HAYES. (NC RB 20:138)
[The est. of Jas. HAYES was ord. to be admin. by Thos. J. HAYES, NC, 11 Apr 1815 (NC OB 1811-1816:311)]

HAYES, Nancy; 25 Apr 1816; 10 Jun 1816
SSP, NC; WILL; all my est. to my two sis. [Milifred] HAYES & Treasy HAYES; Leroy HARCUM ex; WITS: Leroy HARCUM, Wm. [DOWNTUN], Sisson CONWAY. (NC RB 21:13)
[The name of the first sis. is clearly "Milifred," but this must be an error for "Millicent" who mar. Hiram HAYNIE, NC, bond 23 Sep 1822 (MLBNC:49)]

HAYES, Peter; PO 13 Jan 1806, T 18 Jan 1806; 10 Feb 1806. NC; INV, £42.8.6. (NC RB 17:380)

[The est. of Peter HAYES was ord. to be admin. by Maximillion HAYNIE, NC, 13 Jan 1806 (NC Minute Book 1805-1807:72)]

HAYES, Thomas; PO 15 Nov 1814, T 2 Jan 1815; 13 Feb 1815
NC; INV, [m]; includes Negroes Cesar, Aggee & child Hiram, boy Morris. (NC RB 19:627)

HAYES, Thomas J.; 21 Jan 1819; 8 Nov 1819
NC; WILL; whole est. to be used & enjoyed by wife Elizabeth HAYES; if wife remarries she is to have one third of est; dau. Ann; friend Leroy HARCUM ex; WITS: Sam. BLACKWELL, Matthew HUDSON; Leroy HARCUM refuses executorship & wid. is granted certificate for obtaining letters of admin. with the will annexed. (NC RB 22:152)

HAYES, Thomas J.; 1819; 14 May 1821
NC; INV, [m]; includes Negroes Zacharias, Edward, Sippio, Lucy. (NC RB 22:527)

HAYES, Thomas J.; PO 14 May 1822, T 30 May 1822; 10 Jun 1822
NC; settlement of account with Jordan LEWIS & Elizabeth his wife who was Elizabeth HAYES admx. of Thomas J. HAYES dec'd; balance of $269.06 div. among wid. and two others [nfi]. (NC RB 23:168; OB 1820-25:205)
[Jordon LEWIS mar. Eliz. HAYES, wid., NC, bond 10 Dec 1821 (MLBNC:68)]

HAYES, Thomas J.; PO 8 Jul 1822, T 10 Sep 1822; 9 [sic] Sep 1822
NC; allotment of dower in the lands of her late husband, Thomas J. HAYES, to Elizabeth the wife of Jordan LEWIS. (NC RB 23:262)

HAYES, Treasy; 6 Dec 1820; 14 May 1821
SSP, NC; WILL; all est. to sis. Milisent HAYES; friend Leroy HARCUM ex; WITS: Betsey CURTES, Leroy HARCUM; [Leroy HARCUM relinquished his executorship] (NC RB 22:543)
[Treasy or Tracey HAYES was the dau. of Thos. HAYES (d. NC 1808) (NC RB 18:64)]

HAYNIE, [fnu]; 13 Aug 1827
NC; Nancy HUMPHLET aptd. gdn. of Mary HAYNIE orphan of [fnu] HAYNIE. (NC OB 1825-30:192)
[Nancy HAYNIE mar. Edw. HUMPHLETT, NC, bond 27 Nov 1823 (MLBNC:58)]

HAYNIE, Abner; 12 Oct 1812
NC; Isaac BAILEY aptd. gdn. of Margaret HAYNIE, orphan of Abner HAYNIE. (NC OB 1811-15:119)
[Abner HAYNIE mar. Nancy NEWSOM, NC, bond 5 Dec 1797 (MLBNC:47); the est. of Abner HAYNIE was ord. to be admin. by Hen. HAYNIE, NC 14 Oct 1811 (NC OB 1811-15:20); Wm. SMITHER was gdn. of Catesby HAYNIE and Lindsay HAYNIE orphans of Abner, NC, 9 May 1815 (NC OB 1811-15:322)]

HAYNIE, Alexander; T 23 Nov 1824; 10 May 1825. NC; INV, $507.47. (NC RB 24:223)

HAYNIE, Ann; PO 13 Oct 1819, T 27 Dec 1819; 18 Mar 1820
NC; INV, $1666; includes Negroes John, Isaac, Ann & child, Jemiah, Phillis (old). (NC RB 22:248)

HAYNIE, Ann N.; PO 18 Sep 1797; 17 Dec 1798
LC; INV, £255, includes Negroes worth £255: George, Simon, Aggy, Joe. (LC EB 24:84)

HAYNIE, Bridgar; PO 10 Oct 1803, T 25 Jan 1804; 9 Apr 1804
NC settlement of Martin & Bridgar HAYNIE's acct. of their admin. of the est. of Bridgar HAYNIE dec'd and div. among Nancy HAYNIE, Martin

HAYNIE's children, Bridgar HAYNIE, Matthew LAMKIN who mar. Mary HAYNIE, Washington HAYNIE, Hancock HAYNIE, Elizabeth HAYNIE & Chichester HAYNIE. (NC RB 17:132)
[Bridgar HAYNIE was the son of Jn. & Sarah HAYNIE; in his will (NC 7 Nov 1783 - 13 Jun 1791) Jn. HAYNIE names his daus. Ann, Mary & Sally and sons Martin, Bridgar, Washington, Hancock, and wife Sarah (NC RB 14:440); in her will (NC 22 Aug 1800-9 Feb 1801) Sarah HAYNIE names her sons Bridgar, Washington, Hancock, and Chichester and daus. Ann and Eliz. (NC RB 16:222); Matthew LAMKIN mar. Mary HAYNIE, NC, bond 5 Dec 1796 (MLBNC:66); see also NC CC 1806-016]

HAYNIE, Bridgar; 13 Nov 1820
NC; Harriett & Martin HAYNIE chose Royston BETTS Jr. as their gdn. and sd. BETTS is also aptd. gdn. of Priscilla & Lucy HAYNIE orphans of Bridgar HAYNIE; NC OB 1820-25:64)
[Bridgar HAYNIE, orphan of Bridgar HAYNIE chose Hancock HAYNIE as his gdn., NC 13 Nov 1820 (NC OB 1820-25:65); on the mot. of Martin HAYNIE one of the heirs of Bridgar HAYNIE, ord. that Roys. BETTS, Jas. HAYNIE, Edw. OLDHAM, Sally HAYNIE, Bridgar HAYNIE, Priscilla & Lucy HAYNIE be summoned to show cause why the lands of Bridgar HAYNIE should not be sold, 12 Dec 1825 (NC OB 1825-30:56); Royston BETTS Jr. mar. Ann C. HAYNIE, dau. of Bridgar HAYNIE, NC, bond 18 Dec 1811; Edw. OLDHAM, wid., mar. Sally HAYNIE, NC, bond 1 Feb 1819 (MLBNC:9, 78)]

HAYNIE, Bridgar; T 21 Nov 1820; 8 Oct 1821
NC; INV, [m]; includes slaves James, Billey, Fanney. (NC RB 23:7)

HAYNIE, Davenport; 30 Jul 1821; 11 Mar 1822
SSP, NC; WILL; all land & pers. est. to Ann HAYNIE as long as she remains my wid.; my canoe to my eldest son Jurdan HAYNIE; my land to stand for the benefit of my wife & small children until my youngest lawfully begotten child shall arrive to the age of 21; friend Hiram DAVIS ex.; WITS: Wm. HUGHLETT, Nathan MOORE, Jn. WOOD, Sam. HUGHLETT. (NC RB 23:113)
[Davenport HAYNIE seems to have been mar. twice; (1) to Lucy SPENCE dau. of Nancy RICHARDSON, NC, bond 17 Dec 1800 and (2) to Nancy PICKERING, ward of Jos. MORRISON, NC, bond 5 Feb 1818 (MLBNC:48); Nancy (PICKERING) HAYNIE mar. (2) Joseph JONES, NC, bond 31 Dec 1822 (MLBNC:62); lay off and allot to Jo. JONES and Nancy his wife the sd. Nancy's dower in the est. of Davenport HAYNIE, 12 Jun 1826 (NC OB 1825-30:95)]

HAYNIE, Davenport; PO 12 Nov 1821; 10 May 1824. NC INV. (NC RB 23:444)

HAYNIE, David; PO 12 May 1823; 10 May 1824. NC INV. (NC RB 23:443)

HAYNIE, Elias; T 21 Dec 1818; 12 Jul 1819. NC; INV, [m]. (NC RB 22:74)
[Thos. FRENCH aptd. gdn. of Polly, Max., & Jas. HAYNIE orphans of Elias HAYNIE, NC 13 Nov 1820 (NC OB 1820-25:68)]

HAYNIE, Elizabeth; PO Jan 1816; T 20 Jan 1816; 20 Mar 1817
NC; INV, $150; includes Negro woman Fanny. (NC RB 21:169)

HAYNIE, Hannah; PO 10 Dec 1821; 10 Mar 1823. NC; INV. (NC RB 23:282)

HAYNIE, Henry; 13 Dec 1819
NC; Margaret HAYNIE orphan of Henry HAYNIE chose Catesby HAYNIE as her gdn. (NC OB 1816-20:415)
[In his will (NC 1 Mar 1815 - 13 Mar 1815) Hen. HAYNIE named his wife Judith, his sons Jn., Henderson, Hiram, Burgess and daus. [Susaner]

Margaret HAYNIE, Nancy HAYNIE, and Susannah HAYNIE (NC RB 20:23); this is prob. the Hen. HAYNIE who mar. Judith HAYNIE, NC, lic. 5 Dec 17[77] (MWO:173); Hiram HAYNIE chose Henderson HAYNIE as his gdn. and the sd. Henderson HAYNIE is aptd. gdn. of Nancy, Susanna & Burgess HAYNIE, NC 13 Jan 1823 (NC OB 1820-25:261)]

HAYNIE, Hezekiah; 8 Feb 1829
NC; Dolly HAYNIE aptd. gdn. to Thornton & [Benedict] HAYNIE orphans of Hezekiah HAYNIE. (NC OB 1825-30:355)

HAYNIE, Holland; 13 May 1823
NC; on the mot. of Jesse HAYNIE ord. that Rebecca HAYNIE and Betsy EDWARDS be summoned to show cause why lands of which Holland HAYNIE died seized should not be sold and the proceeds div. between sd. Jesse, Rebecca & Betsy heirs of Holland HAYNIE. (NC OB 1820-25:290)
[Holland HAYNIE was the son of Jacob HAYNIE (d. NC bef. 1805) and bro. of Jesse and Rebecca HAYNIE; he mar. Wilalmira WEBB, MC, Va., 17 Sep 1781 (NC CC 1812-010, Lewis & Booker 1964:80, MWO:173)]

HAYNIE, Jacob; PO 9 Apr 1805; 9 Sep 1805
NC; INV,£28.15.2 & £17.19.3; assest wid. with her dower and Jesey HAYNIE with his part of the est. (NC RB 17:323)
[Est. of Jacob HAYNIE was ord. to be admin. by Maximillian HAYNIE, 9 Apr 1805 (NC MB 1801-1805:[m], Lewis & Booker 1964:80)]

HAYNIE, Lucy; [m]; 8 Apr 1822. NC; INV, [m]. (NC RB 23:132)

HAYNIE, Martin; PO 14 Mar 1803, T 22 Mar 1803; 15 Oct 1804
NC; INV, [m]; includes Negroes Philis & young child Isaac, boy Jessee, girl Milley, girl Anna, boy John. (NC RB 17:218)

HAYNIE, Martin; PO 14 Feb 1820; 18 Mar 1820
NC; DIV of est. amongst: to Peter HALL who mar. Mary HAYNIE a dau. of sd. Martin: Yellow John, Jemima, Phillis (an old woman); to Patsy HAYNIE: Jonas, Ann & child. (NC RB 22:249)
[Peter HALL mar. Mary T. HAYNIE, NC, bond 20 Dec 1815 (MLBNC:45); Patsy HAYNIE orphan of Martin HAYNIE chose Peter HALL as her gdn., NC, 13 Oct 1817 (NC OB 1816-20:182)]

HAYNIE, Molley; PO 14 Jun 1814, T 23 Jun 1814; 11 Jul 1814. NC; INV, $140.89 1/2. (NC RB 19:563)

HAYNIE, Nancy; 19 Oct 1820; 11 Dec 1820
SSP, NC; WILL; dau. Nancy HAYNIE; dau. Betsy HAYNIE; dau. Millison HAYNIE; [dau.] Hannah HAYNIE; dau. Rodah HAYNIE; son Samuel HAYNIE; Hiram HAYNIE & Leroy HARCUM exors; WITS: Leroy HARCUM, Sam. HARCUM. (NC RB 22:448)
[Nancy HAYNIE was the wid. of Rich. HAYNIE, whom she had mar. in 1783 (MWO:175) and the dau. of Thos. & Millicent HARCUM; Millicent (d. NC 1802) named Nancy and her children Nancy, Betsy, Rhoda & Millicent in her will (NC RB 16:440); Hannah HAYNIE orphan of Rich. HAYNIE chose Sam. HARCUM as her gdn., NC 12 Aug 1822 (NC OB 1820-25:225)]

HAYNIE, Presley; PO 13 Aug 1824, T 31 Aug 1824; 9 Nov 1824
NC; sale of land whereof Presley HAYNIE & Levi HAYNIE his son died seized & possessed to Henry HAYNIE for $50.37 and a half cents; balance div. among Millicent HAYNIE, Jane HAYNIE, Betsy, Sally & Eliza HAYNIE; the wid. was Alice HAYNIE. (NC RB 24:73)
[Presley HAYNIE mar. Alice HAYNIE, NC, bond 2 Nov 1804 (MLBNC:50)]

HAYNIE, Stephen; T 12 Nov 1813; 11 Jul 1814

NC; INV, $1324.89; includes Negroes Old Betty, Ciller, boy John, child Emney. (NC RB 19:562)
[Stephen HAYNIE mar. Mary Ann COPPEDGE, NC, bond 25 Oct 1793 (MWO:175); in his will (NC 15 Aug 1812-14 Jun 1813) Stephen HAYNIE of WicP, named his wife Maryann, bros. Cyrus & Hiram HAYNIE, and sisters Hannah HAYNIE, Judith HAYNIE, Lucy HAYDON and Maryann TIGNOR (NC RB 19:400)]

HAYNIE, Stephen; 10 Nov 1817; Rodham HAYNIE was aptd. gdn. of Martin, Joseph, Jefferson, Winney, and Louisa HAYNIE orphans of Stephen HAYNIE. (NC OB 1816-20:197)

HAYNIE, Stephen; T Nov 1817; 14 Dec 1818. NC; INV, $150.02. (NC RB 21:566)

HAYNIE, Stephen; [m]; 12 May 1823. NC; INV, $113.56. (NC RB 23:305a)

HAYNIE, Thornton; PO 13 Feb 1815, T 13 Feb 1815; 9 Oct 1815
NC; INV, $55.98; includes Negro woman Jennie. (NC RB 20:268)

HAYNIE, Thornton; PO 13 Nov 1815; 11 Dec 1815
NC; possessed Hannah HAYNIE, wid. of Thornton HAYNIE, with her part of his est. and have div. the est. (amounting to $587.41) among the heirs of the dec'd due from the admr. Haynie WILKINS: Rabesh HAYNIE, Hezekial HAYNIE, Catharine HAYNIE (rec'd Negro Jemima), Jacob HAYNIE, Emzy HAYNIE. (NC RB 20:316)
[Thornton HAYNIE mar. (1) Nancy SMITH, NC, bond 27 Dec 1794 and (2) Hannah WILKINS, NC, bond 15 Sep 1801 (MLBNC:50); Hannah HAYNIE wid. of Thornton was aptd. gdn. to his orphans Cath., Jacob and Lindsay, NC, 9 Oct 1815 (NC OB 1811-15:379)]

HAYNIE, Walter; PO 14 Sep 1801, T 22 Oct 1802; 13 Dec 1802
NC; INV & DIV of est. (none of the reps. named), £544.14.9 3/4; includes Negroes Sarah, Joseph, Bob, Darkey, Patty, William, Ned, Spencer, Salley, Morris, Winney & Mariah. (NC RB 16:490)
[In his will (NC 27 Mar 1801-14 Sep 1801) Walter HAYNIE of SSP named Sam. HAYNIE (son of Rich. HAYNIE), his mother Hannah COCKARILL, Hanah HAYNIE (dau. of Wm. HAYNIE), Stephen HAYNIE, Nancy HAYNIE (wife of Rich. HAYNIE), grmoth. Millicent HARCUM, Sally HARCUM (wid. of Thos. HARCUM), Thos. J. HARCUM, uncle James HARCUM, bro. Jn. COCKARILL, Millicent HAYES (wife of Thos. HAYES), Valentine HARCUM (son of Thos. HARCUM), Fanny HAYNIE, and sis. Lucy COCKARILL (NC RB 16:282)]

HAYNIE, Wilalmira W.; 28 Nov 1821; 2 Dec 1822
RC; WILL; to son William Dandridge HAYNIE that part of my land w/o I now live & on which the dwelling house stands agreeable to a plat & division which I have heretofore had made commonly called (and is) the lower part of the plant. adj. the lands of Vincent BRAMHAM, Fanny DOWNMAN, B. McCARTY, Tomlin's & Mars Hill Tract containing 242 & a quarter ac. & one Negro woman Cate; to dau. Delia Griffin DESCHAMPS that part of my land w/o she now resides which was laid off & surveyed by Benj. M. GARLAND on the SE side of the Beaver Run containing 174 & a quarter ac.; after dau's. death land to her children: Lewis H. DESCHAMPS, Virginia DESCHAMPS & Mary Susan DESCHAMPS; to grdaus. Wilalmira Lucy WALKER & Elizabeth Ann WALKER that part of my land to the N side of the Beaver Dam Run containing 174 & a quarter ac. & also one Negro woman Pleasant; son William Dandridge HAYNIE ex.; WITS: Aug. NEALE, Jn. SHADDOCK; COD dtd. 14 Jan 1822: after debts paid residue of est. to be given to son Dandridge W. HAYNIE [sic]; land given to dau. Delia Griffin

DESCHAMPS should be given to my grson. Lewis H. DESCHAMPS; whatsoever I have given to my grdaus. Wilalmira L. & Elizabeth Ann WALKER is to be given to them at marriage or age 18; WITS: Jn. DARBY, Harriet HILL, Charlotte P. TARPLEY; 2nd COD dtd. 9 Aug 1822: desk formerly given son William to go to dau. Delia G. DESCHAMPS; son William D. HAYNIE to pay grdaus Wilalmira Lucy & Elizabeth Ann WALKER $50 each; WITS: Miskell SAUNDERS, Frances Ann TARPLEY. (RC WB 10:8)

[This is Wilalmira WEBB, dau. of Wm. & Winifred Griffin (TARPLEY) WEBB of RC, who mar. Holland HAYNIE in MC, 17 Sep 1781 (MWO:173); in MWO:173, a second husband, Cap. James MONTAGUE, was given for Wilalmira (WEBB) HAYNIE; however MONTAGUE was the second husband of her mother, Winifred WEBB; Delia Griffin HAYNIE mar. Jos. DESCHAMPS, RC, bond 20 Dec 1809 (MRC:53)]

HAYNIE, William; T 16 Feb 1811; 13 Jul 1812. NC; INV, [m]. (NC RB 19:225)
[The est. of Wm. HAYNIE was ord. to be admin. by Thos. H. JETT, NC, 11 Feb 1811 (NC OB 1807-11:230)]

HAYNIE, William D.; 4 Oct 1824
RC; Chancery suit; Delie G. DESCHAMPS & John CLARK & Willalmira his wife compl. against Elizabeth WALKER, infant, to div. the RE of William D. HAYNIE allotting to Mrs. Delia G. DESCHAMPS one half and the other half to be eq. div. between John CLARK & wife and Elizabeth WALKER. (RC OB 26:235)
[Delia G. DESCHAMPS is the sis. of Wm. D. HAYNIE; Willalmira CLARK & Eliz. WALKER are nieces, 2 Nov 1824 (RC OB 26:243); Delia Griffin HAYNIE, dau. of Capt. Holland & Wilalmira (WEBB) HAYNIE, mar. Jos. DESCHAMPS, RC bond 20 Dec 1809 (MRC:53); Mira HAYNIE, another dau. of Capt. Holland & Wilalmira (WEBB) HAYNIE, mar. Thos. WALKER, RC, bond 27 Dec 1803 (MRC:223); Almira L. WALKER mar. Jn. CLARK, RC, bond 28 Jan 1823 (MRC:38)]

HAYS, Armistead; PO 15 May 1815; 18 Sep 1815
LC; INV, $461.59; includes Negroes: Tabatha, boy Spencer, boy Joshua. (LC EB 27:250)

HAYWOOD, John; 15 Sep 1818; 2 Nov 1818
RC; WILL; all est. to William REUICK and he is to be ex.; WITS: Geo. R. THRIFT, Jn. EFFORD, Polly THRIFT. (RC WB 9:618)

HAZARD, Elias; 28 Dec 1813; 4 Dec 1820.
RC; WILL; of LC; Negro woman Prue to [Rocksy] ARMS; wife Mary HAZARD my Negroes Nancy, Milly & Charles; bro. Thomas HAZARD; friends John CARPENTER & Rawleigh DUNAWAY exors; WITS: Rawleigh DUNAWAY, Martin GEORGE, Jn. KEMM, Jas. KEMM; RC WB 9:677)
[Elias HAZARD mar. Mary ROGERS, LC, bond 10 Dec 1792 (MWO:176)]

HAZARD, Henry; PO 6 Nov 1809; 2 Apr 1810. RC; INV, £80.5.6. (RC WB 9:367)

HAZARD, James; 2 Sep 1822
RC; Nancy R. & Henry HAZARD chose Ellen HAZARD as their gdn. and sd. Ellen is aptd. gdn. of William HAZARD orphans of James HAZARD. (RC OB 25:333)
[Jas. HAZARD mar. Ellen STONUM, dau. of Wm. STONUM, RC, bond 25 Dec 1800 (MRC:91)]

HAZARD, Joseph; PO 2 Jan 1815; 5 Jun 1815. RC; INV, $143.49 1/2. (RC WB 9:476)

HEAD, Isaac; 4 Mar 1816; 27 Oct 1817.

WP, WC; WILL; all property to wife Rachael HEAD as long as she remains single; if she marries she is to have a child's part; at wife's death all children to have an eq. part of est; dau. Molly OLIFF; dau. Sally RYALS; grson. Langhorne Dade HEAD to have half of the property that his mother Molly OLIFF (OLLIVE) shall receive; wife & Daniel CARMICHAEL exors; WIT: Jn. NEALE, Enoch FINCH. (WC DW 23:333)

[Polly HEAD mar. Reubin OLIVE, WC, bond 18 Nov 1806 (MLBWC:51); acc. to MLBWC:58, Sally HEAD mar. Jn. RIDDLES, but her husband's name in this will is clearly RYALS]

HEAD, Isaac; T 6 Nov 1817; 28 Sep 1818. WC; INV. $817.47. (WC RI 10:295)

HEADLEY, Anna M.; 7 Aug 1826

RC; Thomas H. HEADLEY admr. of Anna M. HEADLEY to settle his admin. acct. (RC OB 27:97)

[This is Anna M. GARLAND wid. of Hen. W. HEADLEY, *see below*]

HEADLEY, George; 14 Aug 1826

NC; admin. on the est. of George HEADLEY granted to Randall HEADLEY. (NC OB 1825-30:106)

[Randall HEADLEY aptd. gdn. to Fanny & Henry HEADLEY orphans of Geo. HEADLEY; Wm. HEADLEY aptd. gdn. to Jane & Geo. HEADLEY [also orphans of Geo.], 11 Feb 1828 (NC OB 1825-30:235)]

HEADLEY, Henry Sr.; 26 Apr 1814; 6 Jun 1814

RC; WILL; wife Letty HEADLEY; after her death to grson. Richard S. HEADLEY; $1 each to daus. Rachel ASHBURN, Sally STEPHENS, & Moley STEPHENS & son Eppa HEADLEY; rest of est. to son William HEADLEY; son Eppa HEADLEY & Richard HEADLEY exors; Wit: Griffin HEADLEY. (RC WB 9:460)

[Hen. HEADLEY, the son of Hen. & Ann (PUGH) HEADLEY, mar. (1) Temperance SELF, dau. of Wm. SELF, and (2) Letty (BRYANT) DODSON, wid. of Rawleigh DODSON (MWO:110, 176); Rachel HEADLEY mar. Thos. ASHBURN, RC, bond 23 Dec 1795 (MWO:18); Sally HEADLEY mar. Wm. STEPHENS, NC, bond 23 Dec 1806 (MLBNC:95)]

HEADLEY, Henry W.; 19 Jan 1820 - 1 May 1820

RC; WILL; son Robert P. HEADLEY his choice of my plants., my Negro man Squire & Negro woman Rose; son Thomas H. HEADLEY 2nd choice of my plants., my Negro man Palmer & woman Let; dau. Sarah Lucinda HEADLEY my plant. called Appleby's together with the land owned by Betty HILL also the land lying on Totuskey which I purchased of PRITCHARD, also the land I purchased of YOUNG & wife; Negro man Solomon & Negro women Peg & Lydia; son Littleton W. HEADLEY Negro girl Deale & boy Henry; son Staunton G. HEADLEY Negro boy George & girl Patt; dau. Maria Louisa HEADLEY Negro boy Emanuel & child Fanny (now an infant); wife Ann Maria HEADLEY the plant. called Cherry Lain and after her death to be eq. div. between her three children Littleton W., Staunton G., and Maria Louisa also Negro man Peter, Kate & girl Apphia; friend Col. William MIDDLETON & Richard DURRETT exors; WIT: Geo. T. GARLAND; Robert P. HEADLEY qualified admon. with the will annexed 4 Sep 1820. (RC WB 9:658)

[Henry Wiatt HEADLEY, son of Robert & Eliz. HEADLEY, mar. (1) Rebecca Willoughby PLUMMER, RC, bond 17 Apr 1794 and (2) Anna Maria GARLAND, RC, bond 1 Jan 1803 (MRC:92); Sarah Lucinda HEADLEY orphan of Hen. W. HEADLEY chose Jos. PALMER as her gdn., 6 Nov 1820 (RC OB 25:74); Rich. B. PLUMMER mar. Sarah L. HEADLEY, RC, bond 7

May 1821 (MRC:159; RC OB 25:166); Thos. H. HEADLEY orphan of Hen. HEADLEY chose Rich. B. PLUMMER as his gdn., 1 Oct 1821 (RC OB 25:199); Robt. P. HEADLEY, Thos. H. HEADLEY & Rich. B. PLUMMER compl. against Littleton HEADLEY, Staunton HEADLEY & Maria Louisa HEADLEY, infants, defts., in chancery to div. the land of Hen. W. HEADLEY into 5 eq. proportions; Rich. B. PLUMMER not allowed to partake because he did not have a possession in deed or his late wife during the coverture, 2 Mar 1824 (RC OB 26:166); Alex. BRYANT aptd. gdn. to Littleton W., Staunton G., & Maria L. HEADLEY orphans of Hen. W. HEADLEY, 6 Feb 1826 (RC OB 27:37, 144); Miller:25 locates Cherry Lain in RC between Emmerton and Farnham]

HEADLEY, Luke; T 10 Mar 1794; 14 Apr 1794

NC; DIV of est. of Luke HEADLEY's children in the hands of sd. HEADLEY their gdn; £29.19.10 to be div. among Richard, Sarah & Rebecca HEADLEY. (NC GA 1788-1824:124)

[Luke HEADLEY, son of Hen. & Ann (PUGH) HEADLEY, mar. Mary Warrick LUTTRELL, dau. of Rich. LUTTRELL (d. 1786), bef. 24 Apr 1781 (MWO:176)]

HEADLEY, Samuel; 11 Feb 1828

NC; Benj. DAWSON aptd. gdn. to Elizabeth & William HEADLEY. (NC OB 1825-30:235)

[Eliz. and Wm. were orphans of Sam. and Sarah (COURTNEY) HEADLEY; Benj. DAWSON was the husband of Sam. HEADLEY's sis. Fannie Hall HEADLEY]

HEADLEY, William; PO 12 Apr 1813, T 12 Apr 1813; 14 Jun 1813

NC; INV, $3341.04; includes Negroes [Margary], Nanc[e] & child, Ellen, Tom, Nann, Bill, Sarah, Harriot, John, Bill, [Lett]. (NC RB 19:409)

[Wm. HEADLEY, son of Hen. & Ann (PUGH) HEADLEY, mar. Jane DOUGLAS, dau. of Jn. & Susanna DOUGLAS; in his will (NC 5 Sep 1811 - 12 Apr 1813) he named his wife Jane, sons Randall, Wm., Geo. H., & Sam., and daus. Nancy COOKMAN, Susannah DAWSON, Peggy JONES, Alcey LEWIS, Jane HUDSON, Maggy D. & Fanny (MWO:177, NC RB 19:371)]

HEATH, Chloe; 26 Jun 1818; 10 Nov 1823

NC; WILL; being advanced in years & desirous to leave my temporal concerns [*portion unclear*] to afford as little difficulty to my successors as possible have adopted the following plan to exhibit to all whom it may concern the manner in which the personal property allotted me as my dower as the widow of my former husband William GLASCOCK has been distributed and disposed of, viz., between 25 & 30 years past Dellah, Nancy, [Winney] & Manuel the child of Hannah have died & Hannah & child Nancy and Lucy & child Lindsey I did on or about the year 1809 deliver to my grchildren by William & George GLASCOCK my son; and that George a slave died during the present year, and lastly that Charles the only slave attached to my before-mentioned dower not herein before mentioned is now alive & in my possession; WITS: Thos. BROWN, Rich. CUNDIFF; [receipt from Joseph SANFORD dtd. 4 Mar 1809; received of Chloe HEATH 4 Negroes Hannah (about 26) & her child Nancy (about 10), Lucy (about 23) & her child Lindsey (about 6) who were allotted to her in the division of the est. of her first husband William GLASCOCK which sd. Negroes the sd. Chloe HEATH doth now deliver into the possession of [*1 word unclear*] Joseph SANFORD of Halifax Co who doth agree ... to take the sd. Negroes to the county of Pittsylvania & there be eq. div. between the legal reps. of her

son dec'd sons William GLASCOCK & George GLASCOCK]. (NC RB 23:377)
[This is Chloe HUGHLETT, dau. of Jn. & Esther (COLES) HUGHLETT, who mar. (1) Wm. GLASCOCK, NC, lic. 14 Jan 1771 and (2) Capt. Jn. HEATH bef. 29 Aug 1793 (MWO:150, 177); in his will (NC [m] - 11 Mar 1776) Wm. GLASCOCK of WicP named his wife Chloe and his sons William & John and noted that his wife was pregnant (NC RB 9:634a); Eliz. C. HEATH, dau. of Chloe HEATH, mar. James CLAUGHTON, NC, bond 27 Jul 1801 (MLBNC:18)]

HEATH, Chloe; 11 Oct 1823; 10 Nov 1823
NC; WILL; to dau. Elizabeth Cole CLAUGHTON 3 Negroes Moses, Lexy, & Lindsay and the use of my plant. w/o I now live during her life; at her death I give sd. plant. to my grson. John Heath CLAUGHTON and also 2 Negroes Isaac & Caroline; to dau. Esther Cole CLAUGHTON 2 Negroes Shadrick & young Letty; to grdau. Ann CLAUGHTON 2 Negroes Florinda & Daniel; I wish it to be clearly & distinctly understood that neither my grandchildren by sons William & George GLASCOCK nor my granddau. Elizabeth H. LAMPKIN are in any wise to benefit or share any interest in my estate of any description as I have previously given and delivered over to them all their respective portions that I intend to give; bro. Thomas W. HUGHLETT & dau. Elizabeth C. CLAUGHTON & Thomas BROWN exors; WITS: Thos. BROWN, Thos. CURTIS, Jn. W. MITCHELL; HUGHLETT, CLAUGHTON & BROWN relinquished their right of executorship and Thomas W. HUGHLETT was granted a certificate for obtaining letters of admin. with the will annexed. (NC RB 23:375)

HEATH, Chloe; T 12 Dec 1823; 8 Mar 1824
NC; INV, $3611.60 1/2; includes Negroes Isaac (younger), Moses (younger), Roxy (young woman), Criss & child Joe, boy Shadrick, girl Florindy, boy Lindzey, old woman Caty, boy Daniel, girls Letty & Caroline, boys Fortune & Munrow, old women Jane & Letty. (NC RB 23:433)

HEATHCOTE, John; 6 Apr 1814; 9 Apr 1814 (in Baltimore)
of Baltimore, Md; WILL; all real & landed est. in Great Britain to William HEATHCOTE my natural son by Margaret BANK; by a former will executed in Great Britain, I have sundry legacies bequathed and among them, a legacy to my natural dau. Maria HEATHCOTE by the sd. Margaret BANK, now I hereby revoke the sd. devise to my sd. dau. and in lieu thereof I do hereby give to her £30,000 to be paid her in England; to Michael & John HEATHCOTE, the sons of my bro. George HEATHCOTE, £2,500 each; to George EKWALL of London £5,000; to Hugh Williams EVANS £5,000; to Samuel F. MERITT $700 and also the sum of $700 a year in lieu of all wages during the time he has been in my employ; to William PALEY $1,000 over and above all wages that may be due him; to John SUTHERLAND $500 over and above all wages due him; residue of est. to son William HEATHCOTE; to Edward DAY $1,000 over and above all wages that may be due him; if any merchandise or goods arrive in North America after my decease, I give the goods and merchandise to my trusty friend Edward DAY; to Edward DAY & Hugh Williams EVANS all my est. in North America; William COOKE Esq, Robert OLIVER, Hugh Williams EVANS, & Edward DAY exors; WITS: Wm. GIBSON Jr., Sarah BAYTON, Jos. HARRIS. (WC DW 24:220)
[John HEATHCOTE was a merchant in Baltimore. In 1796, Heathcote & Dall were listed in the Baltimore City Directory as merchants at 74 Baltimore St.;

HEATHCOTE was named as an ex. of the will of James DALL dtd. 14 Mar 1808. He died in Baltimore on 6 Apr 1814; he was about 64. (Baltimore Co Wills 8:354, 9:438, *Federal Gazette and Baltimore Advertiser* 6 Apr 1814)]

HENDLEY, John; T. 13 Nov 1805; 6 Oct 1806. RC; INV, £152.2.9. (RC WB 9:299) [NB: The index to WB 9 calls this man "John Headley," but in the will transcript it is clearly "Hendley."]

HENDLEY, Thomas; Thomas HENDLEY d. intest. bef. Jan 1800 leaving a wid. Sarah who mar. (2) William W. APPLEBY (NC bond 24 Feb 1800), sisters Mary and Ann who mar. Josiah TIGNOR and bros. John and William (NC Fiduciary Bonds 1797-1801 cited in Lewis & Booker 1964:50, NC CC 1806:023; MLBNC:2)

HENRY, Edward; PO 10 Mar 1818 T 21 Dec 1819;
NC; commission laid off 200 ac. of land exclusive of marsh as the dower of Mrs. Elizabeth PATTERSON late Edward HENRY's widow at the head of Smith's Creek; comm. met at the house of George PATTERSON late the residence of Edward HENRY dec'd and assigned to the sd. George PATTERSON in right of his wife Elizabeth W. who was Elizabeth W. HENRY her dower in the land & Negroes whereof Edward HENRY died seized; they assigned her the following Negroes: Peggy, Sally, Dinah, Philip, Jacob, Ezekiel, Harriet, Isaac & also 200 ac. (NC RB 22:425; CC 1818-003) [Edw. HENRY was prob. the son of James HENRY (d. NC 1805) (NC RB 17:320); his est. was ord. to be admin. by Eliz. W. HENRY, 13 Mar 1815 (NC OB 1811-1816:287); Eliz. W. HENRY was aptd. gdn. of Mary Catherine, Sarah S. and Edw. Hugh HENRY orphans of Edw. HENRY, NC, 8 May 1815 (NC OB 1811-15:313); Eliz. W. HENRY, wid, mar. Geo. PATTERSON, NC, bond 21 Dec 1816 (MLBNC:80; NC OB 1816-20:126, *American Beacon & Commercial Diary*, 27 Dec 1816, p. [2]); Geo. PATTERSON and his wife gdns. of Mary C. HENRY, Sarah S. B. HENRY & Edw. H. HENRY, NC 9 Nov 1824 (NC OB 1820-25:429); Mary C. HENRY mar. Valentine Y. CONWAY (NC CC 1826-003); Mrs. Eliz. W. PATTERSON wife of the Rev. Geo. PATTERSON and member of the Baptist Church died in NC on 2 Oct 1823 age 34 (*Richmond Enquirer* 4 Nov 1823, p. [3]); the only Smith Creek in Miller (p. 147) is located near Farnham Creek in RC]

HENRY, Edward; PO 13 Mar 1815, T 24 May 1815; 11 Sep 1815
NC; INV, $7603.40 2/3; includes Negroes Jacob, Bill, Caleb, Isaac, Abell, Tom, [Eleanor], Liah, Phillip, Aggatha, Old Dinah, Abba, Mahala, Pegga, Salley, Mariah, Ezekiel, Patrick, Milley, Daniel, Phillis, Bettey, [Ketty], Presley, Shadrick, David, Rachel, Ader, Harriett, Martha, Arthur, Jack, Roxy. (NC RB 20:213)

HENRY, Edward; PO 10 Mar 1820; 13 Nov 1820
NC; Chancery suit, George PATTERSON & Elizabeth his wife (wid. of Edward HENRY) against Mary, Sarah, & Edward H. HENRY infant children of Edward HENRY dec'd; commission appointed to lay off & assign to George PATTERSON & Elizabeth his wife in right of the sd. Elizabeth W. her dower & thirds in the land & slaves of which the sd. Edward HENRY died seized & possessed. (NC RB 22:425, NC CC 1818-003)

HENRY, Edward; T 5 Apr 1824; 6 Sep 1825
NC; INV; includes Negroes: Abel, Isaac, B M Shadrack, Jack, Philip, Presley, Daniels, Arthur, Davy, Peg, Milley, Sully, Mariah, Martha, Renah, Kitty, Dinah, [Adah] & her 4 children, Leah & 3 children, Harriet & child, Agga & child, Anna. (NC DCO:462)

HENRY, James; [m], T 15 Sep 1807; 14 Mar 1810

NC; DIV of Negroes between Edward HENRY, rec'd Charles, Jack, Caleb, Abel, Jacob, Bill, Solomon, Keah, Shadrick, Tom, Abigail & child, Zeno & 2 children, Rachall, N. ROGERS, Ader & child, Peg & child, Isaac, Leah (child of Abigail), Davy (child of Menly), Winnifred (child of Nan), Jude (child of Menly), Davy, Roxalana, Arthen, Sarah, Anthony; total value £2070 and John HENRY, rec'd Abraham, Agnes, Stephen, George, James, Miles, Phillip, Abraham Jr., Keah, Marthey, Ned, Agnes, Fann, Hannah, Arthen, Fanney, Lilley, Adin, Randolph, Leah, Cate, Juliet, Patience, Moses, Washington, Anthony, Menly, 2 children of Menly, total value £2070. (NC RB 18:359) [In his will, (NC 9 Mar 1801 - 9 Sep 1805) Jas. HENRY named wife Sarah, son Edward HENRY, Jn. WISE (of Accomack, who mar. his dau. [nfi] and had two children, Geo. & Jn. WISE, by her), grdau. Maria EUSTACE (dau. of his s-i-l Hancock EUSTACE of Stafford Co.), dau. Eliz. MONCURE (wife of Wm. MONCURE), Jas. & Charles Scarburgh HENRY (sons of his dec'd son Sam. H. HENRY), and son Jn. HENRY (NC RB 17:320)]

HESTER, Joseph; PO 14 Jan 1805; 8 Jul 1805. NC; INV, £37.15.6. (NC RB 17:297) [The est. of Jos. HESTER was ord. to be admin. by Moses GEORGE & Peter BEANE, 14 Jan 1805 (NC MB 1801-1805:[m]; he was prob. mar. twice: (1) Winny CHAMPION, NC, lic. 11 Oct 1771 and (2) J. Cloey WHEELER, NC, bond 29 Jan 1793 (MWO:178); acc. to NC CC 1800-009 Jos. HESTER kept a small store near the home of Thos. DAMERON in NC]

HILL, Britain; PO 19 Sep 1796, T 12 Oct 1796; 20 Feb 1797.
LC; INV, £358.3.0; includes Negroes: George, Old Jane, Ellen, Winifred & child James, [Doria] & child Delphia, Lazarus, Polly, Venus & child Ruben and a 179 ac. plant. on the eastern branch of Corotoman formerly the property of George DOGGETT & the following Negroes which were "those that were recovered of James [SIMMON's] representatives by James HILL's representatives and the heirs of James HILL dec'd, which is the heirs of Britain HILL dec'd being of full age requested of us to blend the two estates together and make a division of the whole amongst them according to law": Lewis, George, Joshua, Abigail, Jane, Cate; DIV of est. among: John LAWRY, Thomas PITMAN, Chattin DUNAWAY. (LC EB 24:58)
[Jn. LOWRY mar. Betty HILL, LC, bond 24 Dec 1791 (MWO:230); Thos. PITMAN mar. Frances HILL, LC, bond 6 Jan 1791 (MLBLC:); Chattin DUNAWAY mar. Milly HILL, dau. of Britton HILL, LC, bond 14 Dec 1791 (MWO:117)]

HILL, Elizabeth; 6 Feb 1794; 18 Jul 1796.
CCP, LC; WILL; to grdau. Polly Simmonds LAWRY a small Negro girl not under 10 part of the est. of my father & mother now in dispute in LC; remainder of est., if got, to my 3 children: Brittain HILL, Milly DUNAWAY, & Elizabeth LAWRY; dau. Frankey PITMAN to have no part at all; son Brittain HILL, Chattin DUNAWAY & John LAWRY exors; WITS: Jn. DEGGES, Jas. CARTER. (LC WB 28:4)

HILL, Eppa; 19 Mar 1822; 20 Jan 1823
LC; WILL; use of all my land to wife during her life; at her death land to be sold & proceeds to be eq. div. between all my children: John M. HILL, Humphrey C. HILL, James Monroe HILL & Milly HILL; wife Mary C. HILL; vessal to be kept at work until she is sold; wife & friend Bidkar GEORGE exors; WITS: Addison CONNALLY, Leah HINTON; [will finally proved 15 Sep 1823]; LC WB 28:236)

[Eppa HILL mar. Polly Chowning CARTER, LC, bond 13 Feb 1817 (MLBLC:38); Cyrus HAZARD aptd. gdn. to Jn. M., Humphrey C. and Jas. M. HILL orphans of Eppa HILL, 21 Aug 1826 (LC OB 26:202)]

HILL, Eppa; PO 23 Jan 1823; 18 Mar 1823. LC; INV, [m]. (LC EB 29:254)

HILL, Eppa; PO 20 Jan 1823, T 2 Jun 1823; 20 Oct 1823
LC; settlement with Addison HALL admr. of Eppa HILL dec'd & HILL's admin. of the est. of Milly HILL dec'd leaves a balance due from sd. Eppa HILL of $158.58 out of which sum Eppa HILL is entitled to one share ($22.65 3/7); remainder was div. as follows: Eppa HILL by virtue of a conveyance from William HILL, Leroy & Sally PITMAN children of Betsy HILL, Royston HUGHLETT who mar. Lucy HILL, Thomas P. HILL, Clarissa DOGGETT, child of Polly HILL, and Nancy N. HILL; A. J. PALMER gdn. for Nancy HILL & Clarissa DOGGETT acknowledged receipt of $45.30 6/7 from Addison HALL admr. of Eppa HILL for their part of the est. of Milly HILL. (LC EB 29:291)
[Lucy HILL, dau. of Mary HILL, seems to have been the wid. of [fnu] POLLARD when she mar. Royston HUGHLETT, LC, bond 19 Mar 1818 (MLBLC:40)]

HILL, James; PO 17 Oct 1796; 20 Feb 1797
LC; INV & DIV of est, £543.7.0; includes Negroes Old Lazarus, Tabb & child Bett, Darius & child Delphia, Amy & child [Ciller], George, Winny & child James, Abigail, Ellen, Jane, Polly, Jude; div. among: the widow, John LAWRY, [Chattin] DUNAWAY, Britain HILL. (LC EB 24:56)
[The children of Jas. HILL were Eliz. who mar. Jn. LOWRY (LC, bond 24 Dec 1791), Milly who mar. Chattin DUNAWAY (LC, bond 14 Dec 1791) and Brittain HILL (LC CC 1796-011; MWO:117, 230)]

HILL, James; 9 May 1802; 16 Dec 1805
LC; WILL; use of whole est. to wife Nancy during her life; after wife's death whole est. to dau. Nancy; friend Joseph CARTER Jr. ex; WITS: Jn. MILLER Sr., Edmond BROOKE, Job CARTER. (LC WB 28:92)
[This is prob. James HILL who mar. Nancy CONNALLY, LC, bond 21 Dec 1786 (MLBLC:38); Overseers of the Poor to bind out Nancy HILL orphan of James HILL to Mrs. Cordelia GILMAN (LC Orders B23 1808-11:73); Nancy HILL orphan of Jas. HILL chose Ellyson CURRIE as her gdn., 20 Mar 1815 (LC Orders 24:218); Nancy HILL orphan of Jas. HILL chose Jas. HILL as her gdn., 15 Jul 1816 (LC Orders 24:322)]

HILL, John; PO 15 Jan 1816, T 22 Jan 1816; 20 May 1816
LC; INV; includes Negroes: Kitt, Daniel, Isaac, Linsey, Siller, Easter. (LC EB 27:333)

HILL, John; PO 16 Dec 1816, T 26 Apr 1817; 20 May 1817
LC; after settling Mary HILL's admx. account, $334.51 was div. among legal heirs: James TOWLES in right of William HILL, Leroy & Salley PITMAN orphans of William PITMAN, Griffin DOGGETT, Eppa HILL, Mary HILL gdn. to Lucy P. HILL, Mary HILL gdn. to Thomas P. HILL, Mary HILL as gdn. to Milley HILL, Mary HILL as gdn. to Nancey N. HILL. (LC EB 27:378)
[Lucy & Thos. HILL orphans of Jn. HILL chose Mary HILL for their gdn. and sd. Mary HILL is aptd. gdn. to Milly & Nancy HILL also orphans of sd. dec'd, 19 Feb 1816; ord. that Mary HILL, Wm. HILL, Eppa HILL, Wm. PITMAN father & natural gdn. of his children Leroy & Sally, Lucy HILL, Thos. HILL, Milly HILL & Nancy HILL by the sd. Mary HILL their gdn. be summoned to show cause why the slaves of which Jn. HILL died seized & possessed should not be sold, 19 Feb 1816 (LC Orders 24:285); Nancy N.

HILL orphan of Jn. HILL chose Armistead PALMER as her gdn., 19 Nov 1821 (LC OB 25:260); see also LC CC 1816-005]

HILL, John; 23 Jun 1817
WC; Mahala & Eleanor HILL orphans of John HILL chose William GUTTRIDGE as their gdn. (WC OB 1814-18:316)

HILL, Joseph P.; PO 7 Nov 1825; 5 Dec 1825
RC; INV, $330; includes one unidentified Negro woman. (RC WB 10:99)

HILL, Mary; 3 Oct 1818; 19 Nov 1821
LC; WILL; son Eppa HILL; Negro boy Isaac to son Thomas P. HILL (under 21), dau. Lucy P. HUGHLETT; daus. Milly HILL & Nancy N. HILL; son Eppa HILL & friend Bid GEORGE; WITS: Bidkar GEORGE, Janetta CARTER, Chloe LUNSFORD, Leah HINTON, Lucy SIMMONDS. (LC WB 28:220)
[This is Mary the wid. of Jn. HILL, *see above*; admin. of the est. of Milly HILL dec'd granted to Eppa HILL; settlement with Mary HILL of her gdnship. with Milly HILL; on the mot. of Eppa HILL ord. that Mary HILL, Wm. HILL, [Clary] DOGGETT, Lee M. PITMAN and Lucy PITMAN by Eppa HILL their gdn., Mary HILL gdn. of Thos. P. HILL & Nancy N. HILL be summoned to show cause why the slaves of which Milly HILL died seized & possessed should not be sold for a division of the proceeds, 16 Jul 1821 (LC OB 25:233, 262)]

HILL, Mary; PO 20 Nov 1821, T 2 Jan 1822; 18 Mar 1822
LC; sale of Negroes Daniel, Malinda and Anna for $909; after commission of $54.54 was deducted, $854.45 was div. among Eppa HILL, Eppa HILL as gdn. to Leroy M. PITMAN & Sally PITMAN orphans of Elizabeth HILL who mar. William PITMAN, Eppa HILL as admr. of Milly HILL dec'd, Thomas TOWLES as gdn. to John & Henry TOWLES orphans of James TOWLES dec'd by virtue of a conveyance from William HILL to James TOWLES of all his interest in the real & personal est. of John TOWLES dec'd, Armistead J. PALMER as gdn. to Clary DOGGETT & Nancy HILL, Royston HUGHLETT who mar. Lucy HILL, Thomas P. HILL. (LC EB 29:185)

HILL, Mary; T 27 Dec 1821; 16 Sep 1822. LC; INV, [m]. (LC EB 29:229)

HILL, Mary; PO 30 Jan 1823, T 2 Jun 1823; 20 Oct 1823
LC; settlement with Addison HALL admr. of Eppa HILL dec'd the acct. of sd. dec'd's admin. of the est. of Mary HILL dec'd; balance due from Eppa HILL of $144.05 and having by the will of Mary HILL, Eppa HILL is entitled to one fourth part ($36.01 1/4); also entitled to shares are Nancy HILL, Thomas P. HILL, and Royston HUGHLETT who mar. Lucy HILL; Milly HILL another legatee died before Mary HILL. (LC EB 29:293)

HILL, Milly; PO 16 Jul 1821, T 20 Aug 1821; 20 Aug 1821
LC; INV consists of $140.5[9] in the hands of Mary HILL her gdn. (LC EB 29:118)

HILL, Robert; 17 Sep 1804
LC; Thomas BOND aptd. gdn. of Richard HILL orphan of Robert HILL; Kitty the wife of Thomas BOND is the wid. of Robert HILL. (LC OB 1804-05:222)
[Thos. BOND mar. Kitty HILL, bond 14 Jun 1804 (MLBLC:6)]

HINDS, Rachel; 3 Feb 1817
RC; died intestate; sheriff to admin. her small est. (RC OB 24:67)
[Wm. L. LEE was aptd. gdn. to Polly HINDS orphan of Rachel HINDS, RC, 5 Jan 1818 (RC OB 24:170); LEE was still gdn. of Polly HINDS, 7 Mar 1822 (RC OB 25:257)]

HINDS, Thomas; PO 2 Dec 1811; 4 Nov 1817. RC; INV, $286.89. (RC WB 9:587) [This is poss. Thos. HINDS who mar. Sarah WARNER, RC, bond 3 May 1779 (MRC:94)]

HINSON, Joshua; 2 Jan 1812; 4 Apr 1814.
LP, RC; WILL; tract of land called Mozingo's joining Reamy & the land called Wicks & Beckworth's to son William HINSON; tract of land bought of Daniel [CARMICLE's] family called Wicks to son James HINSON; tract formerly called Benson's joining William GUTRIDGE & William HINSON to son Presley HINSON; tract of land over the mill joining SISSON, REAMY & William HINSON to dau-in-law Mary HINSON widow of my son John HINSON during her life or widowhood; at her death to son Austin; tract of land I now live on formerly called Beckworth's & the mill to dau. Ann HINSON; at her death to be div. between my 2 grsons & grdau. [Yelley] HINSON, George HINSON, & Caty HINSON; £10 to dau. Sarah JONSON; dau. Mary HINSON; grdau. Lucy HINSON; grdau. Cata HINSON; dau. Ann HINSON; son James HINSON; sons William HINSON & James HINSON & friend Aleck SANDERS exors; WITS: Wm. MARKS, [Cata] HINSON, Elijah M. OLLIVE, Jn. A. S. HEAD; [further proved by oath of Jn. A. S. HEAD, 4 May 1818]. (RC WB 9:454)

HINSON, Joshua; PO 4 Apr 1814; 5 Jun 1815. RC; INV, £86.8.6. (RC WB 9:475)

HINSON, Mary; 2 Jul 1821
RC; Overseers of the Poor of LP to bind out Thomas HINSON orphan of Mary HINSON to his uncle William HINSON. (RC OB 25:178)

HINTON, Henry; 1 Aug 1821; 19 Nov 1821
LC; WILL; manor plant. I now live on & Negroes Robbin, George, Jesse the Elder, Lucy, Hannah, & Charles to wife Ann HINTON during her life or widowhood; wife also to have anything coming to me from the est. of John FLEET Jr. late of LC; balance of prop. to be eq. div. among my children Sarah F. STOTT, Molly HINTON, Dorothy PIERCE, and Archibald; tract of land in the Island beginning at the head of the White Marsh & running down to the little island cove & Negro fellow Jesse to son William HINTON; heirs of dau. Alice ROBBINS who was Alice HINTON & intermarried with Jesse ROBBINS should have $1 except my grson. Henry ROBBINS whom I wish to have $20 towards his schooling; grson. Jasper STOTT ex; WITS: Thos. INGRAM, Jasper STOTT, Ann CURRELL, [*1 word unclear*], Chas. INGRAM. (LC WB 28:218)
[Hen. HINTON mar. Anna FLEET, LC, bond 23 Jun 1766; Sarah F. HINTON mar. Wm. STOTT, LC, bond 19 Apr 1797; Alice Burgess HINTON mar. Jesse ROBINS, LC, bond 21 Apr 1800 (MLBLC:38, 63, 70)

HINTON, Mary; 31 Dec 1821; 19 Jan 1824
LC; WILL; all est. including that from the will of dec'd father Henry HINTON to be eq. div. between nephews Jasper & William H. S. STOTT; nephew Jasper STOTT ex; WITS: Griffin CHILTON, Jos. STOTT; [will further proved 15 Mar 1824]. (LC WB 28:248)
[Mary HINTON was the dau. of Hen. HINTON (*see above*)]

HINTON, Richard; PO 19 Feb 1816, T 22 Feb 1816; 18 Mar 1816
LC; DIV of slaves among Anne HINTON (Negroes Molly & Dinah), Bartley JAMES as gdn. to William S. INGRAM orphan & heir at law of his mother who was full sis. to the sd. dec'd (Negro Ann), Elizabeth L. JAMES (Negro Joe), Richard TOWELL (Negro Fortune). (LC EB 27:289)

[a Susanna HINTON, dau. of Ann HINTON, mar. Jn. F. INGRAM, LC, bond 13 Dec 1802; Betsy L. HINTON mar. Jn. JAMES, LC, bond 29 Apr 1811; Rich. TOWELL mar. Sally HINTON, LC, bond 24 Sep 1811 (MLBLC:41, 42, 74)]

HINTON, Spencer; 26 Feb 1811; 17 Jun 1811.

CCP, LC; WILL; I lend whole est. to Nicholas Pope BUCKHANN son of Catherine BUCKHANN; if Nicholas Pope BUCKHANN has an heir he is to have whole est; if he has no heir Richard HINTON Jr son of Richard HINTON Sr. to have my manor plant. which I purchased of John EDWARDS; [no ex. named]; WITS: A. CURRIE, Jos. LOCKE, Arch. ANDERSON, Geo. L. CORBIN, Peter BEANE Sr., Fleet CURRELL, Mathias JAMES. (LC WB 28:116)

[This is prob. Spencer HINTON the son of Sam. HINTON of CCP (d. LC, 1771) (LC WB 20:20); Catherine HINTON mar. Wm. BUCHAN, LC, bond 9 Oct 1779 {MLBLC:10)]

HINTON, Spencer (Capt.); PO 17 Jun 1811, T 26 Jul 1811; 21 Oct 1811.

LC; INV; includes Negroes: Charles, Sam, Middleton. (LC EB 27:94)

HINTON, Thomas; PO 17 Feb 1794; 21 Feb 1797

LC; allotment of dower to Elizabeth HINTON the wid. of Thomas, £216.18.2; includes Negro man Harry. (LC EB 24:55)

HINTON, William; PO 22 Dec 1795; 17 Oct 1796. LC; INV, £99.9.6. (LC EB 24:29)

HINTON, William; 18 Aug 1802

LC; Thomas DANCE & Sarah his wife, Anthony SYDNOR & Elizabeth his wife, Matthias JAMES & Judith his wife, Philip POINDEXTER & Mary his wife, George C. POINDEXTER & Ann his wife, and Richard HINTON, complts., against Lawson HATHAWAY admr. of William HINTON; the court made the following findings and ord. that the pltfs. recover £900: (1) that Henry FLEET made his will on 26 Nov 1735 and gave the use of certain Negroes and their increase to Rebecca BANTON during her life and then to Samuel HINTON; (2) that Henry FLEET d. bef. 11 Feb 1735 when his will was proved; (3) that Rebecca BANTON possessed the slaves and that they passed on to Samuel HINTON at her death; (4) that Samuel HINTON d. in 1771 leaving a son Richard as his heir at law and several other children named in his will made on 3 Apr 1771; (5) that Samuel HINTON devised one half of the aforesd. Negroes to his wife during her lifetime; (6) that the wife of Samuel HINTON d. in 1799; (7) that Robert the son of Samuel HINTON d. in 1779 intestate leaving the following children: William his eldest son and heir, Sarah now the wife of Thomas DANCE, Elizabeth now the wife of Anthony SYDNOR, Judith now the wife of Matthias JAMES, Mary now the wife of Philip POINDEXTER, Ann now the wife of George C. POINDEXTER and Richard HINTON; (8) that William HINTON d. in 1792. (LC Orders V 1802-03:237)

[Thos. DANCE mar. Sally HINTON, LC, bond 4 Jun 1785 (MLBLC:19); Anth. SYDNOR mar. Eliz. HINTON, LC, bond 1 Jan 1788 (MLBLC:71); Matthias JAMES mar. Judith HINTON, LC, bond 20 Jan 1790 (MLBLC:42); Hen. FLEET, of CCP, in his will named his mother Eliz. FLEET, Sam. HINTON, Rebecca BANTON, Thos. EDWARDS, David PUGH, Wm. MUGG; nephews Geo. & Jn. FLEET, and godson Rich. EDWARDS (LC WB 12:358); in her will (LC 1 Oct 1750 - 15 Feb 1754), Rebeckah BANTON named Wm. BOND, Rich. EDWARDS, Wm. HINTON, Hen. HINTON, Robt. DUDLEY's dau. Ann & Mary COX living in WC (LC WB 15:303); Sam. HINTON in his will (LC 3 Apr 1771 - 21 Jun 1771) named his sons Rich., Wm., Spencer, Hen, Sam. and Fleet HINTON and his wife Eliz. (LC WB 20:20); on the mot. of Rich.

TOWELL who mar. Sally HINTON orphan of Wm. HINTON to examine the acct. of Lawson HATHAWAY with the est. of Wm. HINTON, 15 Jun 1812 (LC Orders 24:89)]

HINTON, William; PO 21 Oct 1805, T 27 Dec 1805; 20 Jun 1808
LC; INV, £736; Negroes Jesse, Spencer, Phil, [?], Charles, Letty, Jenny, Charity, Amy, Esther, Judy & child Letty, [Beck] & child Ellen; DIV of est. between: Nancy HINTON & Richard B. HINTON. (LC EB 27:30)
[Rich. [B.] HINTON orphan of Wm. HINTON chose Martin SHEARMAN as his gdn., 15 Sep 1800 (LC Orders 21 1799-1801:157); settle the gdn. acct. of Hen. HINTON with Nancy & Rich. B. HINTON orphans of Wm. HINTON, 20 Sep 1802 (LC Orders V 1802-03:188, 255); Sarah HINTON orphan of Wm. HINTON chose Martin SHEARMAN as her gdn., 21 Apr 1807 (LC Orders D22 1805-08:322); Susanna HINTON, dau. of Ann HINTON, mar. Jn. F. INGRAM, LC, bond 13 Dec 1802 (MLBLC:41); on the mot. of Sally HINTON orphan of Wm. HINTON by her gdn. Martin SHEARMAN ord. that Rich.[B.] HINTON, Eliz. HINTON & Susanna INGRAM the other children & reps. of sd. Wm. HINTON be summoned to show cause why the slaves of Wm. HINTON should not be sold, 14 Jun 1807 (LC Orders D22 1805-08:361); a Wm. HINTON mar. Ann SYDNOR dau. of Anthony & Eliz. SYDNOR of NC bef. 15 Mar 1785, but it may not have been this Wm. HINTON (MWO:181)]

HIPKINS, William A.; 24 Nov 1818
WC; settle the acct. of Peggy HIPKINS now Peggy MILLER on the est. of William A. HIPKINS and allot her her dower. (WC OB 1814-18:428)
[Wm. A. HIPKINS d. intest c. 1806 leaving a wid. Peggy, who mar. (2) James MILLER (WC bond 23 Dec 1808), and three children: Ann Benger, b. 6 Mar 1802, who mar. John Taylor THORNTON (son of John Taylor THORNTON & Susan KENNER), Elizabeth, who d. young without heirs, and William A. who was born posthumously (WC CC 1820-008); Wm. Aug. HIPKINS mar. Margaret MARTIN dau. of Capt. Jacob MARTIN, WC, bond 10 Jun 1799; Margaret mar. (2) Jas. MILLER, WC, bond 23 Dec 1808 (MLBWC:31, 45); Wm. HIPKINS orphan of Wm. A. HIPKINS chose Jn. [T.] THORNTON as his gdn., 24 Mar 1823 (WC OB 1819-23:529); see also <www.wikitree.com/genealogy/Thornton-Descendants-781> accessed 20 Aug 2012.]

HODGE, Catharine; Oct 1821; 23 Sep 1822
WC; WILL; Mrs Elizabeth [*1 word unclear*] Jane ASHTON; Jane Christian JETT; my uncle William Storke JETT; uncle to be ex; WITS: Geo. D. ASHTON, Margaret A. HODGE, M. A. HARVEY. (WC DW 24:379)
[Catherine HODGE was the dau. of Sucky JETT (d. WC 1822) (*see below*)]

HODGE, Catharine (Mrs.); T 27 Sep 1822; 26 May 182[3]
WC; INV; includes Negroes Tom, Adam, Eliza, Winny, Lewis, George, Evalina. (WC RI 11:361)

HOGAN, Christopher D.; 19 Oct 1817; 5 Nov 1817
NFP, RC; WILL; plant. to be rented out & my Negro boy George to be hired out until my son Richard J. HOGAN comes of age; rest of est. to be sold and after debts are paid remainder to be eq. div. between two children Richard J. HOGAN & Sally T. HOGAN; land to be eq. div. between two children when son comes of age; children to have sufficient schooling; my relations to have the refusal of keeping my children; Richard STREET ex.; WITS: Jeremiah LEWIS, Edmund R. JEFFRIES, Jn. DAWSON. (RC WB 9:566)

[Christopher D. HOGANS [sic], son of Travis & Salley HOGAN, was b. 4 Jan 1791 (NFPR:97); he mar. (1) Eliz. JACKSON, grdau. of Eliz. JACKSON,RC, bond 24 Apr 1810 and (2) Polly L. HOGAN, RC, bond 7 Jan 1813 (MRC:95)]

HOGANS, Fanny; 28 Jan 1806; 7 Jul 1806

RC; WILL; all my proportion and part of the est. that is coming to me by the will of my father, Thomas HOGANS dec'd, to bro. Travers E. HOGANS; nieces Fanny C. HOGANS & Nancy HOGANS; bro. Travers ex; WITS: Martin SISSON, Thos. HOGANS. (RC WB 9:290)

[Fanny HOGAN, the dau. of Thos. & Nanny HOGAN, was b. 15 Sep 1775 (NFPR:97)]

HOLBURNE, William; 6 May 1809; 5 Nov 1810

RC; WILL; all worldly substance except servant Dick whom I emancipated in 1804 & articles specifically bequeathed to be sold at auction to pay debts; respected friend & benefactor John TAYLOE of Mt. Airy $1,000; nephews Thomas & John ANSLOW £50 recommending them to be friends & act like brothers; young female friends Henrietta Hill TAYLOE, Rebecca P. TAYLOE, Sarah WASHINGTON, dau. of William Augustine WASHINGTON, & my god dau. Betsy [Maeria] of [Rangefield] near Dumfries all my house & table linen to be eq. div. "between 'em;" mahogany chest of drawers to Catharine TAYLOE as from her godmother my sis. to whom it belonged; godson William H. TAYLOE my silver pint can; my old friend George MURREN formerly of RC; £400 Irish sterling in my hand belonging to the est. of my friend Hugh MOLLOY formerly of Frankford near Balliboy, Kings Co., Ireland, agreable to his wish, I leave as follows: to his son Michael MOLLOY, same address, £100; to Mary YOUNG mother to the sd. Michael £40 same address; to Richard [SCISSARS] £100 same address; to the children or other heirs of William SCULLY same address committed to the care of Thomas McCONNICK or in the case of his absence to Matthew CROSBY, same address; £40 to Eleanor MOLLOY the relict of Michael DUNN, Red Gate near Tullamore, Kings Co., Ireland; £30 to Mary TRACEY sis. to the sd. E. M. to be addressed to the care of Alexander CUMMING Esq., Banagher, Kings Co.; £80 & remainder of est. to my 2 godsons William H. TAYLOE of Mount Airy & [William] Holberne GALLAGHER of Dumfries; friend James GALLAGHER; friends John TAYLOE Esq. of Mount Airy, Anthony [BUCK] of Fredericksburg, Thomas T. PAGE of Neabsco, Prince William Co., & George MURREN to be exors; WITS: Ephraim BEZLEY, Jas. B. JONES, Newby BARRICK, Rich. BEAZLEY; [added at end of will, "I shall probably have to make some alterations & observations in this will which it requires should it please God to allow me time so to do."]. (RC WB 9:376)

[For more on HOLBURNE, see <http://adglossar.com/William_Holborne> accessed 29 June 2012]

HOLBURNE, William; T 7 Nov 1810; 7 Jan 1811. RC; INV, £1201.04.0, includes Negro man Harry. (RC WB 9:383)

HOLBURNE, William; T 7 Nov 1810; 3 Aug 1819

RC; INV taken at Mt. Airy, RC, $1328.79 [a second inv. for HOLBURNE was taken at Neabsco, Prince William Co., on 30 Nov 1810 with the value of $200.25] (RC WB 9:624)

HOLLIDAY, Frances; T 20 Dec 1824; 12 Sep 1825

NC; INV, [m]; includes Negro man Jo. (NC RB 24:319)

[Wm. ROCHESTER aptd. gdn. of Sally F. HOLLIDAY orphan of Frances HOLLIDAY, 11 Jul 1825 (NC OB 1825-30:25)]

HOLLIDAY, Richard; PO 13 Feb 1815, T 13 May 1815; 12 Feb 1816. NC; INV, [m]. (NC RB 20:355)

HORN, Elizabeth; 15 Apr 1815; 16 Sep 1816
LC; WILL; tract of land I now live on containing 128 ac. to grson. Thomas Martin OWENS; [no ex. named]; WITS: Opie BEANE, Jn. TOMMUS, Betsey GARNER, Nancy GARNER. (LC WB 28:180)

HORNSBY, James; T 8 Jul 1818; 9 Nov 1818. NC; INV, $158.81. (NC RB 21:532)
[This may be the James HORNSBY who mar. Rachel WEBB, NC, bond 25 May 1803 (MLBNC:54)]

HOULT, John; 4 Mar 1810 - 7 Dec 1812
RC; WILL; after death of wife, Jane, balance of est. to dau. [Theasia] Nancy; if wife should remarry est. to children; [no ex. named]; WITS: Margaret BISPHAM, Ann BISPHAM, Thos. M. BRAGG. (RC WB 9:414)
[Jn. HOULT (or HOLT) mar. Jane BALDERSON, prob a sis. of Gilbert BALDERSON and dau. of Ebenezer & Frances BALDERSON, in WC, bond 26 Jan 1787; the births of two children to Jn. & Jane HOULT are recorded in the LPR: Jane Ridgway, 20 Jan 1797 & Thriza, 11 Sep 1799; the second dau's name was also recorded as Thirza; she mar. Jn. SPILMAN, WC, bond 3 May 1815 (NFPR:98; MWO:184; MLBWC:67)]

HOW, Thomas; 2 Apr 1804; RC INV. (RC WB 9:232)
[Thos. HOW seems to have been a son of Geo. HOW, of LP, who d. in RC in 1794 (RC WB 9:12)]

HOW, Thomas; 5 Apr 1818
RC; Mason SANDY was aptd. gdn. of Fanny HOW, orphan of Thomas HOW. (RC OB 24:202)
[This is prob. the Thos. HOW who mar. Ann M. SANDY dau. of Jn. SANDY, RC, bond 1 Jan 1796 (MRC:98); a Fanny HOW, ward of Geo. MOTHERSHEAD, mar. Simon BROWN, RC, bond 6 Sep 1820 (MRC:26)]

HOWELL, John; Nov 1802; 25 Mar 1803
WC; INV, £53.16.6.; includes Negro boy Dick. (WC RI 8:198)
[This is apparently Jn. HOWELL who mar. Sally GREGORY, WC, bond 24 Jan 1789 (MLBWC:32); Thos. GREGORY was aptd. gdn. to Molly and Thos. HOWELL orphans of Jn. HOWELL, 24 Sep 1804 (WC Orders 1804-07:87); Thos. SCUTT mar. Mary HOWELL dau. of Jn. HOWELL & Sally HOWELL; Jn. HOWELL d. intestate, 24 Oct 1814 (WC OB 1814-18:80); Thos. SCUTT mar. Molly HOWELL, WC, bond 9 Aug 1813 (MLBWC:64)]

HUBBARD, Charles; [11] Feb 1794; 15 Jun 1795;
CCP, LC; WILL; son John HUBBARD; plant. w/o I now live & whole est. to wife; at wife's death or marriage est. except land, to be eq. div. among all my children then found alive; land to son John; wife extx; WITS: Jn. DOGGETT, Sam. YOPP, Sarah BRENT, [Lorimer] CHOWNING. (LC WB 28:16)

HUBBARD, Charles; PO 15 Jun 1795, T 12 Aug 1795; 17 Oct 1796
LC; INV, £125.18.0; includes Negroes: [Serine], Anne. (LC EB 24:31)

HUBBARD, Joseph; 21 Dec 1801
LC; Sally HUBBARD orphan of Joseph HUBBARD chose Spencer GEORGE her gdn. (LC Orders 21 1799-1801:362)

HUBBARD, Judith; PO 17 Nov 1807; 21 Dec 1807. LC; INV, £16.19.10. (LC EB 27:23)
[This must be Judith the wid. of Wm. HUBBARD (*see below*)]

HUBBARD, William; 7 Oct 1796; 18 Sep 1797
LC; WILL; all est. to wife Judith HUBBARD; at wife's death or marriage est. to be div. as follows: all land & old Negro man Solomon to son Warner

HUBBARD; my man Robin to my dau. Chloe; friend William EDWARDS ex; WITS: WITS: Sam. YOPP, Maryann YOPP, Nancy NUTT. (LC WB 28:24) [Wm. HUBBARD mar. Judith YOPP, prob. dau. of Wm. YOPP (d. LC, bef. Apr 1787), LC, bond 3 Jan 1785 (MWO:187); Jn. [M.] REVERE aptd. gdn. of Warner HUBBARD orphan of Wm. HUBBARD, 28 Oct 1807 (LC Orders 22D 1805-08:414)]

HUBBARD, William; PO Oct 1797; 18 Jun 1798
LC; INV, £131.9.6; includes Negroes: Robin, old man Solomon. (LC EB 24:75)

HUDNALL, Ann; T 30 Nov 1811; 9 Mar 1812
NC; INV, $1265; her est. seems to have been div. among William HUDNALL, Ann HUDNALL, Richard HUDNALL, Thomas HUDNALL, Jane DAVENPORT & Warner HUDNALL. (NC RB 19:166, 167)
[This is Ann or Nanne the wid. of Rich. HUDNALL (d. NC 1804) (*see below*); in her will (NC 6 Apr 1811 - 8 Jul 1811), Ann HUDNALL of WicP named her daus. Ann & Jane HUDNALL and sons Rich., Thos., & Warner HUDNALL, and grdau. Ann BRYAN (NC RB 19:81); Jane HUDNALL mar. David F. DAVENPORT, NC, bond 7 Aug 1811 (MLBNC:26); the Negroes Spencer, Sam, Lear, Jas., Betty, Jasper & Rachel were ord. to be sold and the proceeds div. among Wm. HUDNALL, Rich. HUDNALL, Thos. HUDNALL, Warner HUDNALL, Ann HUDNALL, Hen. HURST, David F. DAVENPORT, Hancock HAYNIE and Hen. HURST as gdn. to Jn. BRYAN, NC, 10 Feb 1812 (NC OB 1811-15:41)]

HUDNALL, Ann; T 1 Jan 1813; 14 Jun 1813
NC; INV, $1242.47 1/2; includes Negroes Joe, Winney, Rose, Sophia. (NC RB 19:394)

HUDNALL, John; 21 Jun 1819; 14 Feb 1820
NC; WILL; Negroes Zacharias, George, Suckey, Easter, Grace, Peter, Jenney, Griffin, Richard, Joshuway, Randal, Hanah, Dinah, the plant. w/o I now live & my water grist mill to wife Margaret B. HUDNALL; at wife's death or remarriage plant. & mill to be sold, but land not to be sold until youngest child is 21; four children; if all children die before reaching lawful age or without heirs, all property to friend Capt. William HUDNALL; Capt William HUDNALL ex; WITS: Royston B. COVINGTON, Jn. LANSDELL Jr., Haynes EDWARDS; [Wm. HUDNALL relinquished his right of executorship & Margaret B. HUDNALL renounced the provisions made for her by the sd. will; admin. with the will annexed granted Wm. HARDING 14 Aug 1820]; NC RB 22:210)
[Jn. HUDNALL mar. Margaret B. WADDY, NC, bond 11 Sep 1809 (MLBNC:55); Margaret HUDNALL deed to her children Eliz., Margaret & Jn. HUDNALL, NC 10 Feb 1823 (NC OB 1820-25:264); Margaret B. (WADDY) HUDNALL mar. (2) Jas. CONWAY, NC bond 18 Jul 1822 and (3) Steptoe TAYLOR, NC bond 12 Feb 1824 (MLBNC:20, 99)]

HUDNALL, John; PO 14 Mar 1820, T 22 Nov 1820; 17 Dec 1820
NC; INV, [m]; includes Negroes Zachariah, Joshua, Kendall (? for the life of Mrs. ?), boy George, Easter, child Lucazey, child Griffin, Grace, Dinah, Suckey, Richard, Hannah, boy Peter; PO 13 Nov 1820 the following Negroes were allotted to Margaret B. HUDNALL as her third of the Negroes of the est. of John HUDNALL: Zachary, Easter, girl Louisa, boy Griffin, boy Peter. (NC RB 22:444, 446)

HUDNALL, Joseph; PO 8 Dec 1817; 13 Jul 1818
NC; Negroes belonging to the est. of Joseph HUDNALL div. into two lots; Lot 1 (Rachel, Hiram, Alfred, Griffin, [*name unclear*], Sally, Walter, Harriet,

Malinda) drawn by Sally COCKARILL and Lot 2 (Charlotte, Robert, Mahala, Adeline, Nancy, Steptoe, Lewis, Abraham, Grace, Caroline) drawn by John DAVENPORT. (NC RB 21:458)
[Sarah HUDNALL mar. Peter B. COCKARILL, NC, bond 5 Apr 1813; Jn. DAVENPORT mar. Mary K. HUDNALL, NC, bond 11 Sep 1815 (MLBNC:18, 26)]

HUDNALL, Joseph Jr.; PO 9 Jun [1800], T 1 Jul 1800; 8 Feb 1802
NC; INV, includes Negroes Jenny, Jenny's child John, girl Matilda, Hannah & young child Jesse, girl Amey, boy Robert, girl Peggy, girl Milly, boy Joe, girl Betty, Moses, James, Lucy & child Cooper, boy Isaac, girl Hannah, boy Tom, boy Solomon. (NC RB 16:340)

HUDNALL, Joseph Jr.; PO 13 Jun 1803, T 3 Oct 1804; 8 Oct 1804
NC; DIV of est. among the wid. & "childering;" Samuel McCURDY who mar. Hannah K., the wid, rec'd one third part that included Negroes Moses, Lucy, Tom, Solloman & Cooper and a tract of land on the Wicomico River adj. Lanslot L. EDWARDS & SMOOT; McCURDY also rec'd Negroes Jacob, Mark, Emanuel, William, Hannah, Betty, Nancy, Hannah, Jane, Matildey, [Merutsey], Lucey, Milley, Peggy, Betty, Joseph, Jesse, Ammey & Henery and residue of land as gdn. to Sally C. HUDNALL & Polley K. HUDNALL orphans of Joseph HUDNALL. (NC RB 17:220)
[Jos. HUDNALL, wid., mar. Hannah K. CRALLE (dau. of Jn. CRALLE), NC, bond 27 Aug 1795 (MLBNC:55); Hannah K. HUDNALL, wid., mar. (2) Sam. McCURDY, NC, bond 21 Aug 1801 (MLBNC:72); *see also NC CC 1806-011*]

HUDNALL, Joseph Jr.; PO 13 Jan 1806, T 8 Feb 1806; 10 Feb 1806
NC; John CRALLE Sr. possessed with all the est. of Joseph HUDNALL Jr. dec'd which is now in the hands of Samuel McCURDY who was a joint admr. on HUDNALL's est. in right of his marriage with his wife Hannah who was an admr. on the est. of the sd. dec'd; CRALLE rec'd the following Negroes: Mark, Jacob, Nanny, Hannah, Hannah THOMAS [sic], Jane, Amy, Milly, Peggy, Emmanuel, Joe, William, Jessee, Betty, Betty Jr., Matilday, Rachael, Lucy, Henry, Tom, Solomon, Cooper, Lewis & Moses. (NC RB 17:382)
[*It is not clear whether one of the slaves is named "Hannah THOMAS" or this is two slaves, "Hannah" and "Thomas"*]

HUDNALL, Richard; PO 13 Feb 1804; 9 Apr 1804
NC; INV, [m]; includes Negroes Ned, Spencer, Sam, Harry, James, Lear, Betty, Jasper, Rachel, Mimey, Sarah, Joshua, Lucy, Nelson, Winny, Joseph, Rose, Sophia, Sinah, Jack, David, Fanny, Charles, Rawley, Thomas, Spencer, Betty, Aaron, Polly. (NC RB 17:146)
[Rich. HUDNALL mar. Nancy BARRETT, dau. of Wm. BARRETT of WicP, NC, 16 Jun 1769 (MWO:188); in his will (NC 14 Jan 1803 - 13 Feb 1804) Rich. HUDNALL of WicP named his daus. Betsy PARROTT, Judith HURST, Nancy HUDNALL, & Jenny HUDNALL, his grchildren Jn. & Nancy BRYAN, his sons William, Rich., Thos., & Warner and his wife Nanny (NC RB 17:129); a CC of 1812 pitted Rich., Thos., Warner, and Ann HUDNALL (children of Rich. HUDNALL the Elder, Hen. HURST (who mar. Judith HUDNALL), David F. DAVENPORT (who mar. Jane HUDNALL), Hancock HAYNIE (who mar. Ann BRYAN a grdau. of Rich. HUDNALL), and Jn. BRYAN (a grson. of Rich. HUDNALL) against Wm. HUDNALL to sell slaves willed by Rich. HUDNALL the Elder to his wife (NC CC 1812-017) (*see also Ann HUDNALL above*)]

HUDNALL, Richard; PO 8 Dec 1811; 9 Mar 1812

NC; INV, [m]; his est. seems to have been div. among William HUDNALL, Henry HURST, [m] HUDNALL, Richard HUDNALL, Thomas HUDNALL, Jane DAVENPORT, Warner HUDNALL, Nancy HAYNIE & John BRYAN; HAYNIE & BRYAN rec'd half shares. (NC RB 19:164)
[Hen. HURST mar. Judith HUDNALL, dau. of Rich. HUDNALL, NC, bond 4 Jan 1796; Jn. BRYAN mar. Becky HUDNALL, NC, bond 24 May 1791 (MLBNC:14, 58)]

HUDNALL, Thomas; PO 10 Sep 1792, T 23 Oct 1792; 11 Jul 1808
NC; INV, includes Negroes Daniel, Tom, Moses, Jean RICH, Charlotte's child Betsie, Cate & child Samson, girl Barbara, Sall; Robin, Moses, Spencer, Joseph, Charles, John, William, Jesse, Sally (and sucking son), boy Spencer, girl Mima, [Sanah], Agga, [Nama], Miller, Isaac, [Lilah] & child Sam, Jacob, Pleasant, Phoebe, Solomon, Hannah, Reubin, [Nela] & child Nela, Sukey, James, William, Winnie, Massie, Darka, Silva, Nancy, Burgiss, Luce & child Polly, Daniel, Fanny, Winnie, Lewis, Aaron, Molly & young child a girl, Hester, [Nacie], Hany. (NC RB 18:11)
[The est. of Thos. HUDNALL was ord. to be admin. by Lucy HUDNALL & Thos. HARVEY, NC, 10 Sep 1792 (NC OB 1790-1795:264); a Negro named Solomon, who claimed to have belonged to Mrs. Lucy HUDNALL of NC, was jailed as a runaway in Baltimore Co., Md. in Feb 1815; he was described as about 32 years old and about 6' 6 1/2" (*Baltimore Patriot & Evening Advertiser*, 24 Feb 1815, p. [1])]

HUDNALL, Thomas; PO 14 Oct 1794, T 29 Dec 1794; 11 Jul 1808
NC; DIV of est. among the wid. Lucy HUDNALL her dower (Daniel, Agga, Harry, John, Lucy, Polly, Aaron, Jervis, Fanny, Molly, Jean, Silva, Burges, Solomon, Winnie); Thomas HARVEY & Elizabeth his wife (rec'd Darke, Polly, Spencer, Moses, Nelly, Sally, Nelly, William, James, Sukey, Massie, Winnie, Jacob, Pheby); Sally W. HUDNALL dau. of Thomas HUDNALL dec'd (rec'd Charlotte, Emanuel, Bettie, Joe, Moses, Sally & child, Vanah, Grace, Mima, Sally, Old Jane, [Rubin], Nancy); Nancy W. HUDNALL dau. of Thomas HUDNALL dec'd (rec'd Milly, Agga, Isaac, Robin, Jesse, Lilah, Sam, Mariah, Cate & child, Sampson, Barbara, Pleasant, Nanny, Hannah). (NC RB 18:14)
[Thos. HUDNALL mar. Lucy WEBB, dau. of Giles WEBB of SSP, NC, lic. 14 Aug 1770 (MWO:188)]

HUDNALL, Thomas; PO 10 Nov 1824; 13 Dec 1824
NC; INV, $2241.70; includes following Negroes: Argyle (old man), Joseph, David, Elijah (boy), Sinah, Silvy (girl), Rachel & child Harriett. (NC RB 24:75)
[Wm. HUDNALL aptd. gdn. of Virgia HUDNALL orphan of Thos. HUDNALL, NC 10 May 1824 (NC OB 1820-24:375)]

HUDNALL, Thomas & Lucy; 7 May 1814; 9 May 1814
NC; Elizabeth HARVEY who was Elizabeth HUDNALL dau. of Thomas & Lucy HUDNALL and Richard EDWARDS who mar. Sally W. HUDNALL dau. of sd. Thomas & Lucy and the sd. Richard EDWARDS as gdn. to the orphans of Lancelot L. EDWARDS who mar. with Nancy HUDNALL dau. of the sd. Thomas & Lucy, all of NC, appoint Thomas CONWAY their attorney to sell a slave Solomon alias Solomon WATSON who was jailed in Baltimore. (NC RB 19:545)
[Eliz. HUDNALL mar. Thos. HARVEY, son of Onesephorous & Sarah HARVEY, NC bond 9 Dec 1793; Rich. EDWARDS mar. Sally W. HUDNALL, NC, bond 13 Jul 1798 (MWO:122, 170)]

HUDNALL, Warner; [n.d.]; 20 Mar 1815

WicP, NC; WILL; Negro man Peter to be sold & Negroes Tom, Spencer & Betty to be hired out; money along with yearly product of the mill to pay debts; all my est. to my wife Susan HUDNALL; at wife's death or marriage unless she has a lawful heir of my body I desire my est. to be divided as follows: to my wife all the prop. that I got by her that has not been disposed of except Siller who I give to my niece Judith HURST; to my bro. Thomas HUDNALL my half of the mill now owned [by] him and myself; to my bro. Richard my Negro man Tom; to my sis. Jane DAVENPORT the Negro girl Betty; to my cousin Thomas HUGHLETT my Negro boy Spencer; to my niece Nancy HAYNIE two thirds of the tract of land I purchased of Robert M. ROBERTSON the other third I give to my nephew John BRYAN; bro. Thomas ex; [no wits listed, but proved by the oaths of Wm. HARDING & Jos. BALL]. (LC WB 28:156)

[Warner HUDNALL mar. Suckey LATTIMORE, NC, bond 8 Jun 1812 (MLBNC:56); Jane HUDNALL mar. David F. DAVENPORT, NC, bond 7 Aug 1811 (MLBNC:26)]

HUDNALL, Warner; PO 26 Mar 1815, T 30 [?] 1815; 18 Dec 1815
LC; INV, $3010.43; includes Negroes: Peter, Joshua, Spencer, Mary & child (*not named*), Letty & child Rodham, Betty, boy Cornelius, girl Chloe, girl Pricilla. (LC EB 27:274)

HUDNALL, William; PO 12 Sep 1808, T 31 Oct 1808; 8 May 1809
NC; allottment of land of William HUDNALL dec'd as result of a suit in chancery between Thomas HUDNALL complt. against John HUDNALL & William HUDNALL by Thomas HARVEY their gdn. defts.; Upper Lot (150 ac) adj Edward CONWAY to Thomas HUDNALL, Middle Lot (102 ac) on Mill Swamp to William HUDNALL, Lower Lot containing the houses & mill (90 ac) to John HUDNALL. (NC RB 18:139; OB 1807-11:65; NC CC 1809-015)

HUDSON, John C.; PO 9 Dec 1799, T 25 Feb 1800; 9 Jun 1800
NC; proceeds of sale of est. amounted to £5.19.3 due to his five oldest legatees each: Elizabeth DAWSON, Sally BROWN, Robert HUDSON, Jemimah DAMERON, & Milley WILKINS and a balance due four of the youngest legatees namely John C. HUDSON, Samuel HUDSON, Molly C. HUDSON & Nancy HUDSON of £8.1.7 1/2 and also the sum of £10.1.7 1/2 due the other two younger legatees each namely Thomas T. HUDSON & Presley HUDSON which amounts we have left in the hands of the ex. John C. HUDSON to possess the legatees when the bonds are on demand. (NC RB 16:95)

[John Corbin HUDSON was a son of Robert & Easter HUDSON; he mar. Jemima, the dau. of William & Jean SELF; Milly HUDSON mar. Dan. WILKINS, NC, bond 16 Feb 1792 (MWO:189, 376); in his will (NC 27 Feb 1795 – 14 Sep 1795) Jn. C. HUDSON named his wife Jemimah, sons Robt., Jn. C., Sam., Thos. T. and Presley and daus. Sally BROWN, Jemimah DAMERON, Milley WILKINS, Eliz. DAWSON, Molly C. HUDSON, and Nancy S. HUDSON (NC RB 15:197)]

HUDSON, Sarah; PO 28 Feb 1815, T 8 Mar 1815; 28 Mar 1815. WC; INV, £83.12.10. (WC RI 9:433)

HUGHES, John; PO 12 Jan 1818, T 7 Mar 1818; 30 Apr 1818
NC; Chancery suit; Thomas BELL pltf. against John, James, Lucy & Benjamin HUGHES defts.; defts. are infants under 21 and Sally HUGHES, wid. of John HUGHES, appointed gdn; land which John HUGHES died seized & possessed, subject to dower, sold to William B. LEWIS for $351; bonds distributed. (NC RB 21:400)

[Jn. HUGHES d. intest. leaving a wid. and the following children: Wm., Jn., Jas., Lucy, and Benj. (NC CC 1818-010); Sally HUGHES aptd. gdn. of Lucy and Benj. HUGHES orphans of Jn. HUGHES, NC 11 May 1819 (NC OB 1816-20:359); Jn. HUGHES orphan of Jn. HUGHES chose Jn. FULKS as his gdn., NC 9 Aug 1819 (NC OB 1816-20:377); Jas. HUGHES orphan of Jn. HUGHES chose Wm. DAMERON as his gdn., NC 18 Mar 1820 (NC OB 1820-25:2)]

HUGHLETT, Ephraim; 12 Dec 1810; 18 Mar 1811
LC; WILL; all est. to my two youngest children Nancy George HUGHLETT & Addison HUGHLETT; if they die without heirs or before age 21, est. to descend to wife Molly and children [Boston] HUGHLETT, Beady HUGHLETT, Moses HUGHLETT, Siller HUGHLETT, [Romy] HUGHLETT, [?] HUGHLETT, & Milly HUGHLETT; as for my sons [sic] Augustine HUGHLETT, Martin HUGHLETT & Mary Cottrell, I have already given them their full proportion; [no ex. named]; WIT: Wm. POLLARD; [certif. granted Spencer GEORGE to obtain letters of admin.]. (LC WB 28:113)
[Ephraim HUGHLETT mar. Molly GEORGE, LC, bond 28 Dec 1806; he may be the same Ephraim HUGHLETT who earlier mar. Barbara SPILMAN, LC, bond 21 May 1801 (MLBLC:39); Spencer GEORGE aptd. gdn. to Nancy George HUGHLETT & Addison HUGHLETT orphans of Ephraim HUGHLETT, 19 May 1812 (LC Orders 24:79)]

HUGHLETT, Ephraim; T 29 Mar 1811; 15 Apr 1811
LC; INV; includes Negroes: [Sukey] & child Hiram, [?]. (LC EB 27:82)

HUGHLETT, Ephraim; T 29 Mar 1811; 16 Dec 1811
LC; INV, [m]; includes Negroes: Sukey & child Hiram, David. (LC EB 27:97)

HUGHLETT, Ephraim; PO 19 May 1812, T 6 Jul 1813 [sic]; 17 May 1813
LC; DIV of est, Lot 1 (Sukey) to Nancy George HUGHLETT, Lot 2 (Hiram) to Addison HUGHLETT, Lot 3 (David) to Molly HUGHLETT, wid; Spencer GEORGE was gdn. to Nancy G. & Adderson HUGHLETT. (LC EB 27:153)

HUGHLETT, Ephraim; 10 Mar 1817. Samuel HUGHLETT aptd. gdn. of Hiram, Chatham, William & Octavius HUGHLETT orphans of Ephraim HUGHLETT. (NC OB 1816-20:127)

HUGHLETT, John; PO 13 Jan 1806;
NC; DIV of est. among: William HUGHLETT (rec'd Spencer), Mary C. HUGHLETT (rec'd Joseph), John HUGHLETT (rec'd Peter), William SMITHER (rec'd Daniel), Ailcey HUGHLETT (rec'd Robert). (NC RB 17:488)
[Wm. SMITHER mar. Betsy HUGHLETT, NC, bond 26 May 1801; he may have also mar. (2) Alice HUGHLETT, NC, bond 1 Feb 1815 (MLBNC:93)]

HUGHLETT, John; T 23 Jul 1796; 8 Jun 1801
NC; settlement of William HUGHLETT & Norman APPLEBY dec'd now in the hands of George BARRETT ex. of John HUGHLETT dec'd; the total amount of William HUGHLETT's est. was £166.19.0 1/4; George CANNADY's children claim against Norman APPLEBY's est. in the hands of William HUGHLETT dec'd was £28.10.0; widow HUGHLETT's thirds £30.15.1 1/4; Bridgar HAYNIE's part for two children Nicholas & Samuel HUGHLETT; James SYMS part [for] his wife Cloah HUGHLETT. (NC RB 16:259)
[James SIMS, wid, mar. Chloe HUGHLETT, dau. of Wm. HUGHLETT, NC, bond 7 Feb 1792 (MWO:320)]

HUGHLETT, John; T 8 Sep 1810; 10 Sep 1810
NC; John HUGHLETT acknowledges his receipt of £291.10.11 in full for all claims against Thomas W. HUGHLETT his former gdn. on acct. of his

father's est. and also on acct. of his grandfather John HUGHLETT's est. (NC RB 18:468)

HUGHLETT, John; [m]; 10 Dec 1821
NC; WILL; plant. where I now live to kinsman Hollon HUGHLETT provided he will let my aunt Molley BARRETT have a home with him during her single life if it be her choice; balance of est. after debts paid to be eq. div. between Hollon HUGHLETT & Richard HUGHLETT; friend Thomas HUGHLETT ex; WITS: Isaac EDWARDS, Benj. LANSDELL. (NC RB 23:54)

HUGHLETT, Nicholas; T 10 Jan 1804; 10 Sep 1804
NC; Elizabeth HUGHLETT gdn. of William HUGHLETT against James SIMS & Chloe his wife & Samuel HUGHLETT upon a summons; lands of Nicholas HUGHLETT sold to Samuel HUGHLETT. (NC RB 17:203)
[Nicholas HUGHLETT was the son of Wm. HUGHLETT (d. NC, 1794) (NC RB 15:64)]

HUGHLETT, Roger W.; 14 Oct 1816;
NC; Chancery suit, William J. McCLANAHAN & Chloe his wife, Thomas HUGHLETT, Eliza HUGHLETT by her gdn. & next friend Ann HUGHLETT & Judith & George HUGHLETT by their gdn. & next friend Ann HUGHLETT which sd. Chloe, Thomas, Elizabeth, Judith & George are the only children of Roger W. HUGHLETT dec'd, against Ann HUGHLETT rel. & wid. of Roger HUGHLETT dec'd; commissioners appointed to allot to Ann HUGHLETT wid. of Roger W. HUGHLETT her dower in the land of her dec'd husband and div. the residue among the children of the sd. dec'd. (NC RB 22:295; CC 1816-011)
[Roger Winter HUGHLETT mar. Ann INGRAM, dau. of Geo. INGRAM, NC, bond 12 May 1790 (MLBNC:56); the est. of Roger W. HUGHLETT was ord. to be admin. by Ann HUGHLETT, NC, 9 Jan 1814 (NC OB 1811-1816:269); Chloe HUGHLETT mar. Wm. J. McCLANAHAN, wid., NC, bond 18 Mar 1813 (MLBNC:71)]

HUGHLETT, Roger W.; PO 7 Jan 1815, T 31 Oct 1816; 14 Jul 1817
NC; APP & DIV of Negroes among the heirs after allotting the wid. her dower as follows; Lot 1 (Patty) to the wid. Elizaeth HUGHLETT; Lot 2 (boy James) to Thomas HUGHLETT; Lot 3 (boy Bob) to Judith HUGHLETT; Lot 4 (boy Joe & girl Fanny) to George HUGHLETT; Lot 5 (boy Rawleigh, Delia & [Eirsila]) to William J. McCLANAHAN. (NC RB 21:199)

HUGHLETT, Roger W. ; PO Jan 1814, T 18 Jan 1814; 11 Sep 1815
NC; INV, [m]; includes Negroes old woman Betty, Kendall, Judah, Sinah, Patty, James, Bob, Delia, Betty, Joe, Fanny, Rawleigh; Ann HUGHLETT admr. (NC RB 20:222)

HUGHLETT, Thomas; 19 Jul 1770, 8 Oct 1770
NC; WILL; plantation w/o I now live to be eq. div. between two sons Winter and Thos.; dau. Huldy born before wedlock; wife to have her son Thos. HUGHLETT's part of the land; rest of est. to be eq. div. between all my children (NC RB 8:76)
[A NC chancery suit provides additional details on Thos. HUGHLETT's descendants; he left two sons, Winter HUGHLETT by a former wife, Elizabeth, and Thos. HUGHLETT by his last wife, prob. Winifred; he also left two daus. by his last wife, Hannah who mar. Thos. FLEMING and Winifred who mar. Jn. RANKINS; Winter HUGHLETT, who d. in NC in 1795, left his wife, Eliz., his est. during her life or widowhood and the plant. w/o he lived to his son Thos.; not mentioned by name in Winter

HUGHLETT's will were his children Margaret who mar. Benj. LANSDELL Jr., NC, bond 22 Nov 1800, and Eliz. who mar. Benj. WALKER, NC, bond 5 Mar 1798(NC RB 15:185; MLBNC:66, 104; NC CC 1820-023)]

HUGHLETT, William; 10 Jan 1820
NC; Richard HUGHLETT orphan of William HUGHLETT chose Thomas HUGHLETT as his gdn. (NC OB 1816-20:419)
[This is prob. the Wm. HUGHLETT who mar. Eliz. WALKER, sis. of Jn., Leannah, Benj. and Thos. WALKER, NC, bond 29 Jan 1799 (MLBNC:57, NC CC 1810-007); MLBNC:61 gives the husband of Leannah WALKER as "Benjamin JONES" however his name is given as "Bennett JONES" in NC CC 1810-007; their marriage apparently took place in St. Mary's Co., Md with bond dtd. 14 Feb 1799; Ewell BEALE mar. Betsy HUGHLETT, wid., NC, 24 May 1818 (MLBNC:6); allot to Ewell BEALE & Eliz. his wife the sd. Elizabeth's dower & thirds of the est. of her late husb. Wm. HUGHLETT, NC 14 Feb 1820 (NC OB 1816-20:427); *see also Jn. WALKER below*.]

HUGHLETT, Yarrett; PO 9 Feb 1801, T 7 Mar 1801; 13 Apr 1801
NC; INV, £51.11.9. (NC RB 16:230)
[In his will (NC 2 Oct 1800 - 9 Feb 1801) Yarrott HUGHLETT named his wife Betsy, his two daus. Cloey & Fanny and noted that his wife was pregnant (NC RB 16:216)]

HULL, John; PO 13 Mar 1820, T 14 Oct 1822
NC; Chancery suit; John HULL complt. against Broadie, Thomas, Peter, Samuel S. & Paul HULL children of John HULL dec'd defts; Richard H. GASKINS apptd gdn. to the defts who are infants; after assigning her dower and thirds to Martha HULL the wid. of sd. John HULL in the real & pers. est. of the sd. John, the sd. est. was div. into 6 fair & eq. proportions for the heirs; Martha HULL (rec'd 152 ac. and the slaves Ben, Judy & child Lewis, & Charlotte), Paul HULL (rec'd 55 ac. & Anthony), Samuel S. HULL (rec'd 60 ac. & Ezekiel), John HULL (rec'd 53 ac. & Eliza), Peter HULL (rec'd 54 ac. & Willoughby), Broadie S. HULL (rec'd 53 ac. & Young Judy & Adam) & Thomas HULL (rec'd 53 ac. & Joseph). (NC RB 23:232); DIV of est, after allotting to Martha HULL her dower & thirds (152 ac. & slaves Ben, Judy & child Lewis, Charlotte), amongst the heirs Paul HULL (55 ac. & Anthony), Samuel S. HULL (60 ac. & Ezekiel), John HULL (53 ac. & Eliza), Peter HULL (54 ac. & Willoughby), Broadie S. HULL (53 ac. & Young Judy & Adam) & Thomas HULL (53 ac. & Joseph). (NC RB 23:233)
[Jn. HULL mar. Martha GASKINS dau. of Thos. GASKINS, NC, bond 21 Oct 1797 (MLBNC:57); the NC Court recognized Jn. HULL, Thos. G. HULL, Brodie S. HULL & Eliz. who mar. Dabney HERNDON as the only heirs of the late Col. Jn. HULL and that Col. HULL was the heir at law of Edwin HULL (NC OB 1807-11:148); Martha HULL aptd. gdn. of Peter, Paul & Sam. S. HULL orphans of Jn. HULL, 13 Mar 1826 (NC OB 1825-30:69); Thos. R. G. HULL d. in 1826 (NC CC 1826-004); NC CC 1811-019 shows that Jn. HULL held a water grist mill in coparcenary with Thos. G. HULL, Brodie S. HULL and Eliz. HULL; NC CC 1820-002 adds that Jn. HULL d. intest. c. 1814 leaving a wid, Martha, and six sons: Jn., Brodie, Thos., Peter, Sam. S., and Paul of whom Jn. was the eldest.]

HULL, John (Maj.); T 5 Apr 1815; 8 May 1815
NC; INV, $3636.71; includes Negroes John, Ben, Willoughby, Old Chloe, Judith, Charlott; Eliza, Anthony & Joe left by Mrs. E. BELL in dispute. (NC RB 20:103)

HUMPHLET, Edward; 17 Jan 1825; 14 Mar 1825

SSP, NC; WILL; half my est. to wife Nancy HUMPHLET; I lend to Sabrina CORBELL the other half of my est. during her life; wife to have management of Sabrina CORBELL & her part of the est; [no exors. named]; WITS: Sam. HARCUM, Eliz. HAYNIE, Millicent HAYNIE; [Nancy HUMPHLET qualified as extx.]. (NC RB 24:182)
[Edw. HUMPHLETT mar. Nancy HAYNIE, NC, bond 27 Nov 1823 (MLBNC:58); Sabrina CORBELL is prob. the dau. of Rich. S. CORBELL of NC (*see above*)]

HUMPHREY, Richard; [m]; 25 Mar 1811. WC; INV, [m]. (WC RI 9:231)

HUMPHRIES, George; 13 Dec 1816; 13 May 1817
NC; Nunc. will; George HUMPHRIES who died on 8 Dec 1816 at his residence in NC, in his last illness was at his residence about the day before his death being then in his perfect senses & memory called Shapley P. GILL & Rebecca WHEELER to take [notices] that he left to Thomas JAQUES the Negro girl [Merina] which was Jessee MORRISSON's as well as all the rest of the est. which was sd. MORRISSON's upon his the sd. JAQUES paying to the widow of him, the sd. George HUMPHRIES, the sum of $70 [?] the sd. JAQUES having kept & raised the aforesaid Negro girl from a child; [Nancy HUMPHRIES the widow & Winifred HUMPHRIES, child of the decedent were summoned to court; the widow consented]. (NC RB 21:193; OB 1816-20:148)
[Geo. HUMPHRIES mar. (1) Molley PICKREN, bond 25 Apr 1800, (2) Hatha MORRISON, bond 24 Dec 1804 and (3) Nancy WHEELER, bond 14 Feb 1814 (NC MLB:57)]

HUMPHRIES, John; PO 13 Jan 1812; 10 Feb 1812
NC; allotted Sarah Ann HUMPHRIES her dower of land descended to her by the death of her late husband John HUMPHRIES; land adj to Thomas HUGHLETT. (NC RB 19:147)
[*See Sarahann HUMPHRIES below*]

HUMPHRIES, Joseph; 9 Nov 1818
NC; Matthew LAMKIN aptd. gdn. of Betsy, Thomas, Winny & John HUMPHRIES orphans of Joseph HUMPHRIES. (NC OB 1816-20:303)
[Jos. HUMPHRIS d. intestate about 1818 leaving four children: Betsy, Thos., Winney and Jn. (NC CC 1822-009); Nath. WILSON was aptd. gdn. of Jos. HUMPHRIES orphan of Jos. HUMPHRIES; Frances HUMPHRIES was the wid., NC 8 Mar 1819 (NC OB 1816-20:335); Frances was Fanny WILSON, dau. of Nath. WILSON, the second wife of Jos. HUMPHRIES whom he mar. in NC, bond 17 Aug 1815 (MLBNC:57); Sam. HUGHLETT aptd. gdn. of Jos. HUMPHRIES orphan of Jos. HUMPHRIES, NC 15 Aug 1820 (NC OB 1820-25:52); Leroy DAVIS aptd. gdn. of Jos. HUMPHRIES orphan of Jos. HUMPHRIES, NC 9 Jun 1823 (NC OB 1820-25:305); Thos. ROCK aptd. gdn. to Thos. & Winifred HUMPHRIES orphans of Jos. HUMPHRIES, 12 Mar 1827 (NC OB 1825-30:147); Max. HAYNIE aptd. gdn. to Thos. & Winifred HUMPHRIES orphans of Jos. HUMPHRIES, 13 Aug 1827 (NC OB 1825-30:193); settlement of Matthew LAMKIN's acct. of his gdnship. of Jn. HUMPHRIES orphan of Jos. HUMPHRIES, 12 Nov 1828 (NC OB 1825-30:321)]

HUMPHRIES, Sally; PO 12 Apr 1813, T 8 May 1813; 14 Jun 1813
NC; INV at the house of Elizabeth HUGHLETT, [m]. (NC RB 19:405)

HUMPHRIES, Sarahann; 31 Jul 1820; 11 Sep 1820
NC; WILL; to grdau. Elizabeth HUMPHRIES trunks (and all that is in them) at Royston BETTS & at Hiram HAYNIE's; grson. John HUMPHRIES;

Royston BETTS Jr to qualify as admr.; money that Mathey LAMKIN Sr owes me to be eq. div. betwixt grdaus. Elizabeth HUMPHRIES & Winifred HUMPHRIES and grsons. John & Thomas HUMPHRIES; WITS: Wm. H. PICKERING, John N. HURST. (NC RB 22:403)
[This is the wid. of Jn. HUMPHRIES above]

HUNGERFORD, Anne; 7 May 1800; 24 Nov 1800
WC; WILL; 4 [sic] grsons.: Thomas, John & William when of age; housewoman Winney to be liberated; son John; son John ex; WITS: [H.] HOOE, Anthony PEYTON, Wm. JETT, Rich. CLARK. (WC DW 20:165)
[This is no doubt Anne Birkett PRATT the dau. of Jn. & Marg. PRATT, wife of Thos. HUNGERFORD and mother of Thos. HUNGERFORD (*see below*); she was b. 26 Oct 1718 and d. 8 May 1800 and is buried in the Hungerford Cem, Leedstown, Va.; the name of the missing grson. was Henry (*for details on interments in the Hungerford Cem. see* <http://www.rivahresearch.com/westmorelandcty/vitals/resources/cemetery/secondtier/leedstowninterm.htm>]

HUNGERFORD, Anne; [m]; 26 Jul 1802
WC; INV; includes Negroes George, Danniell, Scipio, boys Jack & Arthur, Winney, Lucy, girls Winney, Lucy & Fanney. (WC RI 8:170)

HUNGERFORD, Thomas; 2 May 1803; 24 Jun 1803
WC; WILL; bro. John Pratt HUNGERFORD to take possession of whole est. pay debts and div. rest eq. among sons Thomas, John Washington, Henry & William HUNGERFORD; bro. John Pratt HUNGERFORD & son Thomas HUNGERFORD to be exors.; no wits. (WC DW 20:468)
[Thos. & Brig. Gen. Jn. Pratt HUNGERFORD (1761 – 1833) were sons of Thos. & Anne Pratt HUNGERFORD; both are buried in the Hungerford Cem., Leedstown, Va. (*see above*)]

HUNTER, John; 25 Mar 1811
WC; Nancy and Sally HUNTER orphans of John HUNTER chose John McCLANAHAN as their gdn. (WC Orders 1810-13:89)
[This is Jn. HUNTER who mar. Molly MARMADUKE, dau. of Vincent MARMADUKE, (*see below*)]

HUNTER, Muscoe G.; T 25 Aug 1818; 24 Nov 1818
WC; INV, $15,648.81; includes Negroes Davy, Rachael, Mary, Fanny, Bartlett, Delphy, Marinda (an infant, female), Maria, Esther, John, Charles, Jesse, Polly, Ned, Rachael, John, Mingo, Tabby, Patty, Esther, Peggy, Daniel, Abbey, Julia (an infant, female), Rose, Nancy, Franky, James, Jerry, Caroline, Billy, Anthony, Dick, Charles (old), Wyat, Moses (old), Moses, Randolph, old Hannah & old Franky (past labour). (WC RI 10:320)

HUNTER, Muscoe G.; PO 22 Jul 1822, T 2 Jan 1824; 26 Apr 1824
WC; INV, $3585; includes Negroes Anthony, Ned, Randal, John, Polly (young woman), Maria (young woman) & William her child, Rachel, Betsy her child, Rose (young woman) & her children Ellen & William, Frankey & her children Jim, Jerry, Fanny & Phil; chargeables Old Hannah, Billy, Barbara & Sarah; 3 small children Delphia, Merinda, Zara. (WC RI 11:[419])

HUNTON, Alexander; PO Dec 1795, T 12 Jan 1799; 3 Jun 1799
RC; DIV of PE £217.15.0; there were originally 13 children and each was allotted £16.5.2, but 2 of the children had died; the proceeds of the sale of land in Albemarle Co., £23.3.7, were also to be divided among 11 claimants, but 3 of the children had also died; none of the claimants was identified. (RC AB 3:14)

[Alexander HUNTON mar. Betty GOODRIDGE, dau. of Wm. GOODRIDGE, bef 12 Nov 1759 (MWO:193); in his will (RC 28 Apr 1789 - 5 Oct 1789) Alexander HUNTON named 13 children: Robert, William, John, George, Thomas, Alexander, Mary, Betty, Susannah, Sally, Nancy, Caty & Lucy (RC WB 8:58); the births of 6 children to Alex. & Betty HUNTON are rec. in the NFPR: Robt. b. 12 Nov 1759, Mary b. 6 Feb 1764, Betty b. 21 Apr 1765, Thos. b. 27 Jan 1767, Nanny b. 25 May 1774 and William [Reu] b. 25 Jul 1776 (NFPR:101); suit in chancery, Wm. NEWBY admr. of Eliz. NEWBY, Susanna HUNTON, Cyrus NEWBY & Ann his wife who was Ann HUNTON and Wm. W. HUNTON, complts., against Alex. HUNTON & Thos. WILLIAMS exors. of Alex. HUNTON dec'd; 18 Mar 1802 (LC Orders V 1802-03:51, Orders W 1804-05:61, LC CC 1804-013); Cyrus NEWBY, son of Jas. NEWBY (d. LC 1791), mar. Nancy HUNTON, RC, bond 21 May 1796 (MWO:261); Wm. NEWBY mar. Betty HUNTON, RC, bond 22 Apr 1791 (MRC:145)]

HUNTON, Elizabeth; 22 Nov 1792; 21 Jul 1800
LC; WILL; all my land in LC being between the land of C[ol.] John FLEET & Elizabeth HINTON [sic] Jun. containing 8 ac. to son Henry HUNTON; [no ex. named]; WITS: Severe GALLE, Geo. CHRISTOPHER. (LC WB 28:42)

HUNTON, John W.; PO 17 Dec 1821; 17 Mar 1823. LC; INV, [m]; includes Negro Nelson. (LC EB 29:252)

HUNTON, John Wren; 20 Jan 1806
LC; Wm. POLLARD aptd. gdn. to Lucy Pollard, Jn. Wren & Polly [Bisive] HUNTON orphans of Jn. Wren HUNTON. (LC Orders D22 1805-08:108)
[This is prob. Jn. W. HUNTON who mar. Mary POLLARD, dau. of Jas. POLLARD, LC,bond 15 May 1794 (MLBLC:40)]

HUNTON, Judith M.; 3 Jul 1818; 21 Sep 1818
LC; WILL; whole est. to be div. into 5 eq. parts (except legacies hereafter mentioned) among the following persons: Thomas Y. HUNTON, Elizabeth W. McCARTY, John W. HUNTON, Albert GIBSON & the children of my sis. Frances BRENT dec'd; my bro. Thomas Y. HUNTON to have my Negro woman [Eady] & her child Mary; sis. Elizabeth W. McCARTY to have my Negro man Emanuel; Negro man Harry & all remainder of est. to be sold & proceeds eq. div. among John W. HUNTON, Albert GIBSON & the children of my sis. Frances BRENT; niece Elizabeth [M.] [*1 word unclear*]; bro. John W, HUNTON's proportion to be put in the hands of friend Benjamin WADDEY and used for bro's support; nephew Albert GIBSON's part of my est. to remain in the hands of my ex. until he is 21 or marries; the proportion of my dec'd sis. Frances BRENT's children to be placed in the hands of their father James BRENT; bro. Thomas Y. HUNTON ex; WITS: Thos. [L.] P. JAMES, B[enj.] M. WALKER, Jasper STOTT. (LC WB 28:190)
[Frances HUNTON mar. James BRENT, LC, bond 17 Jun 1805 (MLBLC:8); Elizabeth W. HUNTON mar. Sydnor McCARTY, RC, bond 27 Sep 1809 (MRC:124); Albert GIBSON was the son of Jn. GIBSON who mar. Molly HUNTON (*see above*)]

HUNTON, Judith M.; T 21 Nov 1818; 18 Jan 1819
LC; INV, $1750; includes Negroes: Harry, Manuel, Eady & child Mary; Thomas G. HUNTON admr. with the will annexed. (LC EB 27:449)

HUNTON, Judith M.; PO 15 Mar 1819, T 20 Mar 1819; 17 May 1819
LC; DIV of est. among: Thomas Y. HUNTON, Elizabeth W. McCARTY, James BRENT in right of his children, Thomas Y. HUNTON with Albert GIBSON's part, & Benjamin WADDEY with John W. HUNTON's part. (LC EB 27:482)

HUNTON, Thomas; PO 20 Dec 1802; 20 Jun 1803
LC; DIV of Negroes: Peter, Daniel (yellow), Manuel, Daniel (young), Winny, Lilly, Sally, Violet, Lucy, Armstead, Mary & child Sally, Patty, Ralph, Daniel (look up), Harry, Billy, Jesse among: Mary B. HUNTON, Judith M. HUNTON, John W. HUNTON, Fanny HUNTON, Elizabeth W. HUNTON, Thomas Y. HUNTON. (LC EB 24:240)
[Frances HUNTON orphan of Thos. HUNTON Jr. chose Jn. M. YERBY as her gdn., 21 Sep 1801 (LC Orders 21 1799-1801:325); Molly HUNTON orphan of Thos. HUNTON chose Wm. GIBSON as her gdn., 18 Oct 1802 (LC Orders V 1802 - 03:212); Eliz. HUNTON orphan of Thos. HUNTON chose Wm. GIBSON as her gdn. and sd. GIBSON is aptd. gdn. to Jn. HUNTON orphan of the sd. decedent, 20 Dec 1802 (LC Orders V 1802-03:250); Fanny HUNTON orphan of Thos. HUNTON chose Jn. GIBSON as her gdn., 19 Dec 1803 (LC Orders V 1802 - 03:507); Thos. Y. HUNTON orphan of Thos. HUNTON chose Geo. W. YERBY as his gdn., 19 Dec 1808 (LC Orders B23 1808-11:7); Jn. HUNTON orphan of Thos. HUNTON chose Thos. Y. HUNTON as his gdn., 18 Feb 1811 (LC Orders B23 1808-11:237)]

HUNTON, Thomas; PO 16 Dec 1811, T 27 Dec 1811; 16 Mar 1812
LC; DIV of est. among: John HATHAWAY as gdn. to John PASQUETT, John HATHAWAY in behalf of his wife Jane & John NEWBY. (LC EB 27:108)
[Jn. NEWBY mar. Eliz. HUNTON, LC, bond 30 Dec 1772 (MLBLC:54)]

HUNTON, Thomas Y.; T 12 dec 1820; 19 Feb 1821
LC; INV, $3935.49; includes Negroes James [Crissily], [?], Edy, Letty, Mary Ann, Polly, [Sam], Daniel, Mary, Adam, Bell, Matilda. (LC EB 29:57)

HURST, James; 14 Jun 1819
NC; Patrick SPILLER is aptd. gdn. of [Thwaites], [Levi], James, Ann, Frazer, and Louisa HURST orphans of James HURST. (NC OB 1816-20:363)
[James HURST mar. Susanna SPILLER, dau. of Benj. SPILLER and Ann FRAZER of LC, as her 2nd husband around 1807; her first husband was James' bro. Warner HURST whom she mar. in LC, bond 15 Oct 1801; their children are also given as: James Kemp, Thwaits L., Ann Frazer, and Maria Louisa suggesting that Levi and Frazer may be middle names (<http://spotisadog.wordpress.com/2010/06/23/more-on-benjamin-c-spiller-and-children/> accessed 11 Nov 2012]

HURST, John; 15 Oct 1811; 14 Aug 1820
NC; WILL; plant. I now live on that I bought of Ana GORDON to my son John N. HURST & also the plant. I bought of Chas. ROGERS on the Herrin Creek; if son dies without heirs the two sd. plants. to my dau. Elizabeth H. HURST; to dau. Elizabeth H. HURST the plant. I bought of Lucy HUDNALL containing 110 ac.; but if son John dies without heirs I give this plant. to my dau. Susannah HURST; to dau. Susannah the plant. I bought of Winnefred WEBB containing 110 ac; to Joseph RICHARDSON & Noah RICHARDSON I leave a support out of my est. until they are old enough to be bound out; rest of est. to be eq. div. between 3 children: John N., Elzabeth H. & Susannah; friends Royston B. COVINGTON, William HUDNALL, Samuel BLACKWELL & Thomas HARVEY exors; WITS: Royston B. COVINGTON, Wm. L. LEE, Thos. BETTS, Thos. HUDNALL; [COVINGTON relinquished his right of executorship &; admin. with the will annexed granted to John N. HURST 10 Jun 1822]. (NC RB 22:377)
[Jn. [N.] HURST orphan of Jn. HURST chose Thos. H. JETT as his gdn., NC 13 Nov 1820 (NC OB 1820-25:63); Eliz. H. HURST orphan of Jn. HURST chose Leroy HARCUM as her gdn., NC 11 Dec 1820 (NC OB 1820-25:72);

Miller:37, 65, 66 identifies three Herring Creeks, one was an early name for Nomini Creek, one was poss. another name for Cubitt Creek--in northeast NC between Hull Neck and Mob Neck--, and one was in RC]

HURST, Joseph; PO 10 Dec 1798, T Jan 1799; 10 Feb 1800
NC; INV of PE in the hands of Capt. John HURST the admr, £257.0.0; includes Negroes Spencer (about 36), girl Pleasant (about 14), [Meashie] (about 18). (NC RB 16:61)
[The est. of Jos. HURST Sr. was admin. by Hen. HURST, NC, 10 Dec 1798 (NC Fiduciary Bonds 1797-1801]

HURST, Joseph; PO 10 Dec 1798, T 1 Jan 1799; 10 Feb 1800
NC; DIV of est. among John HURST, Judith CORBELL (includes Negro Spenser), Henry HURST (includes Negro lad Meashick), Richard HURST (includes Negro girl Pleasant). (NC RB 16:62)
[Judith Nutt HURST, dau. of Jos. & Winifred (NUTT) HURST, mar. Peter CORBELL, bef. 13 Dec 1784 (MWO:88)]

HURST, Thomas; PO 10 Jan 1803; 9 Apr 1804. NC; INV, £25.5.5. (NC RB 17:159)

HURST, Thomas; PO 8 Jun 1801; 10 Feb 1806. NC; INV, £221.19.0. (NC RB 17:376)

HURST, Thomas; PO 11 Dec 1815, T 12 Nov 1817; 8 Jun 1818
NC; Chancery Suit; Thomas HUDNALL & Susan his wife & Winefred HURST, pltfs. against John N. HURST, Thomas K. HURST, Kemp HURST, Isaac W. HURST, Elizabeth [K.] HURST & Jane H. HURST children of Thomas HURST; defts are infants under 21; land of Thomas HURST was div. as follows: entire tract of land on the mill creek to Thomas HUDNALL & Susan his wife and Hudnall is to pay $6.13 to each of the other heirs. (NC RB 21:425; CC 1815-004)
[Jas. HURST was aptd. gdn. of Jn. N. & Thos. K. HURST orphans of Thos. HURST; Thos. HUDNALL was aptd. gdn. of Kemp & Isaac W. HURST orphans of Thos. HURST, and Winifred HURST was aptd. gdn. of Eliz. K. and Isaac W. HURST orphans of Thos. HURST, NC 9 Oct 1815 (NC OB 1811-15:380); Thos. HUDNALL mar. Susan T. HURST, NC, bond 27 Jun 1815 (MLBNC:55); Kemp HURST orphan of Thos. HURST chose Jn. N. HURST as his gdn., NC 10 May 1819 (NC OB 1816-20:354); Thos. K. HURST aptd. gdn. Kemp HURST orphan of Thos. HURST, NC 11 Sep 1820 (NC OB 1820-25:57)]

HURST, Thomas; T 23 Oct 1815; 14 Sep 1818
NC; INV, $4611.98; includes the following Negroes: Jesse, Argile, Harry, Darkes, Hannah, Rachael, Sukey, Mimy, Siner (child), Polly, Phoebe, Silvey, Moses, Plato. (NC RB 21:495)

HURST, Warner; 8 Feb 1819
NC; Patrick SPILLER aptd. gdn. of Chatham and Warner HURST orphans of Warner HURST. (NC OB 1816-20:329)
[Chatham C. and Warner HURST were grsons. of Thos. HURST (d. NC 1807) (NC RB 17:514); Warner HURST orphan of Warner HURST chose Wm. F. RUST as his gdn., NC 10 May 1824 (NC OB 1820-25:372); Chatham HURST mar. Ann E. GASKINS, ward of Jn. D. LELAND, NC bond 24 Sep 1825 and Warner HURST mar. (1) Eliz. K. HURST, ward of Wm. HARVEY, NC, bond 10 Oct 1825 (MLBNC:58)]

HURST, Winifred; PO 9 Dec 1805; 12 Oct 1812
NC; INV, [m]; includes Negroes Hannah, Cate, Harry, Charles, Billy, [Betey], Marck. (NC RB 19:258)
[This is prob. Winifred (SHEARS) HURST the wid. of Isaac HURST whom she mar. in NC in Mar 1757 (MWO:193); in her will (NC 29 Dec 1804 - 9 Dec

1805) Winnifred HURST named her son Isaac HURST and grdau. Sally H. CROWDER, her dau. Eliz. CROWDER was extx. (NC RB 17:352)]

HURST, Winifred; 7 Jan 1817; 14 Jul 1817
WicP, NC; WILL; two daus. Elizabeth [K.] HURST & Jane H. HURST; dau. Sukey T. HUDNALL; rest of est. to be eq. div. between daus. Elizabeth & Jane; dau. Sukey T. HUDNALL to have the management of two daus. Elizabeth & Jane; friend Thomas W. HUGHLETT & my s-i-l Thomas HUDNALL exors; WITS: Jn. BRYANT, Jane DAVENPORT, Susan HUDNALL. (NC RB 21:211)
[This is Winifred (HARVEY) HURST the wid. of Thos. HURST, *see above*.]

HURST, Winifred; PO 14 Jul 1817; 13 Oct 1817. NC; INV, $640.4[1]. (NC RB 21:260)

HUTCHINGS, John; T 19 Dec 1815; 19 Feb 1816
LC; INV; includes Negroes: Will, Bettey, Pattey, Joe, Dinah, Jerry, Isaac, Billy. (LC EB 27:280)

HUTCHINGS, John; [m]; 20 Sep 1819
LC; DIV of est. to Elizabeth HUTCHINGS, the wid., to Nancy HUTCHINGS (a child), to George H. HUTCHINGS (a child), to Elizabeth HUTCHINGS (a child) and to Lucy HUTCHINGS (a child). (LC EB 27:500)
[This is prob. Jn. HUTCHINGS who mar. Eliz. TANKERSLY, LC, bond 17 Mar 1794 (MLBLC:40); Eliz. HUTCHINGS Jr. orphan of Jn. HUTCHINGS chose Eliz. HUTCHINGS as her gdn. and sd. Eliz. is aptd. gdn. to Lucy HUTCHINGS also an orphan of sd. Jn., 17 Aug 1818 (LC OB 25:9)]

HUTCHINGS, Richard; 4 Nov 1819; 20 Dec 1819
LC; WILL; whole of est. to wife Mary HUTCHINGS as long as she remains my widow; the land which I now live [on] & what prop. I have already given to son John HUTCHINGS; his sisters to be entitled to a home as long as they remain single; prop. that I got by my present wife to be div. between her three children Edward E., Robert N. & Elizabeth; balance of est. to be eq. div. among my children Richard, Hugh, Janetta, Milley, Opie, Leannah, Maryann & Thomas; sons John, Richard & Hugh exors; WITS: Thos. G. ROBERTSON, Ann BISCOE, Edw. PAYNE; [COD] dtd. 5 Nov 1819; if wife & her children claim prop. now in the hands of Edward BLAKEMORE, I revoke 1st & 3rd clauses & give her only her third; WITS: Edw. PAYNE, Ann BISCOE. (LC WB 28:201)
[Rich. HUTCHINGS mar. Molly BLAKEMORE, dau. of Edw. BLAKEMORE (d. LC, 1819), LC, bond 16 Aug 1813 (but she was prob. not his first wife; if the mar. bond says that Rich. HUTCHINGS mar. Molly BLAKEMORE and Edw. BLAKEMORE names his dau. Molly HUTCHINGS in his will made in 1816, who was the father of her three children Edw. E., Robert N. and Elizabeth? Is it possible that Mary HUTCHINGS was not Molly BLAKEMORE but a second or third wife?) (MLBLC:41; *see above*); there is an earlier marriage bond for a Rich. HUTCHINGS who mar. Milly BEANE, LC, bond 17 Dec 1791 (MLBLC:41)]

HUTCHINGS, Richard; PO 17 Jan 1820; 21 Aug 1820
LC; INV, $4221.03 [?]; includes Negroes Jessee, Samuel, Edmond, George, James, Billy, Becky, Amy, Rose. (LC EB 29:38)

HUTCHINGS, William; T 2 Mar 1811; 18 Sep 1815. LC INV. (LC EB 27:250)

HUTCHINSON, [fnu]; 19 Feb 1821
LC; Willis DAMERON aptd. gdn. to John, Fanny & Sally HUTCHINSON. (LC OB 25:191)

[Frances HUTCHINSON mar. Jn. S. TREAKLE, LC, bond 13 Jun 1828 (MLBLC:75)]

HUTCHINSON, Hill W.; John SULLIVAN who d. intest. leaving a wid., Mary, but no children was the uncle to Hill W. HUTCHINSON who was his next of kin; SULLIVAN's wid. Mary mar. (2) Chas. WEBB, LC, bond 6 Jun 1795 (LC CC 1797-009; MLBLC:78)
[A Jn. SULLIVAN mar. Mary NICHOLS, LC, bond 2 Jul 1779; Hill W. HUTCHINSON mar. Molly PEARSON, LC, bond 8 Jan 1805 (MLBLC:41, 71)]

HUTT, Gerard; 7 Dec 1773; [m].
CP, WC; WILL; to be buried in my own garden; Negro Ben to son John HUTT at age 21; Negro [W]ill to son Ger. HUTT at age 21; Negro boys Joe & James to son Thomas HUTT at age 21; Negro girl Judy to dau. Molly [HUTT] at age 21 or day of marriage; Negro girl Joan to son Nimrod HUTT at age 21; Negro girl Sall to son William [?] HUTT; various tracts of land to sons; dear wife [Katy] HUTT; friends Joseph LANE & Thomas EDWARDS & wife exors; WITS: Alexander McGUIRE, Wm. BROWN, Gerad [sic] McKENNY, [Andrew READ]. (WC Unrec Wills 1755-1800 #12)
[This is Gerard HUTT III son of Gerard II & Mary HUTT; he mar. Catherine (Caty) SPENCE, WC, 16 Aug 1760 (see: <http://freepages.genealogy.rootsweb.ancestry.com/~genroots1/gerardhutt3.htm> and <http://ohiohutts.freeservers.com/gerrard3.htm> accessed March 2012)]

HUTT, Thomas; 21 Jul 1805; 23 Sep 1805
WC; WILL; all est. to wife until son Richard B. HUTT is 21; land where my dwelling house stands bounded by the Spring Branch, Robinson's, near my school house, and Nomony Creek to the mouth of Mill Creek to wife and after her death to son Richard; mill to son Richard; rest of land to be eq. div. among other children; Negro man Peter and Molly HUBARD to stay with wife as long as she remains unmarried; friends Samuel TEMPLEMAN, Ransdell PIERCE, & Thomas SPENCE exors; no wits. (WC DW 21:203)
[Thos. HUTT mar. Mary STURMAN, WC, bond 4 Sep 1792 (MLBWC:33); Nomony or Nomini Creek flows into the Potomac from east central WC; Miller lists 3 Mill Creeks, but none seem to be this one (Miller:99, 111)]

HUTT, Thomas; PO 24-28 Nov 1814, T 3 Mar 1815; 27 May 1816
WC; DIV of est. among the wid. Maria HUTT (incl. slaves Joe, Jack, Judith, Sam), Richard B. HUTT (incl. slaves Dennis. Lydia), Stella HUTT (incl. slave Rachel), Thomas HUTT (incl. slaves Jack & Sam), William HUTT (incl. slaves Sarah & Matthew), Gerard HUTT (incl. slave Hannah). (WC RI 10:55)

HUTT, Thomas; [m]; 27 May 1816
WC; INV, $3351.78; includes Negroes Hubbard & child Joe, Jack (5 years old), Judy (12), Sam (10), Lydia (about 50), Rachel (about 2), Jack, Hannah, Denis, Sam, Sarah, Matthew. (WC RI 10:67)

HUTT, Thomas; 26 Aug 1817
WC; William Y. STURMAN aptd. gdn. to Thomas W. HUTT orphan of Thomas HUTT, but Thomas W. HUTT is apparently of age to choose a gdn. himself and STURMAN is also his choice. (WC OB 1814-18:345)

HUTT, William; 18 Nov 1799; 23 Dec 1799
WC; WILL; debts of store kept at Nomini Ferry with Gerrard HUTT and others to be paid; half of sloop to James son of Dan. NEALE; Negroes Peter, Phillis, Matthew, [Old Tom,] Old Jane and [Patunee] to be set free after my death; Negro boy Charles to continue w/ James FEGGIT to learn tailor's

trade then to be free; Negroes Long Dick, Lett, Sambo, Miller Sam, and Jenney to be sold for 3 years and then set free; Negroes Sam, Dennis, Jack, Hannah, and Rose to be sold for seven years and then set free; Negroes Yellow Hannah, Black Hannah, Judy, Sarah, Yellow Judy to be sold for seven years then to be free; Negroes Joe, Young Jack, Young Dick, and Daniel to be sold for 10 years then to be free; Negroes Jerry, Milley, Nancy and Lavina to be sold for nine years then to be free; Negroes Bess, Little Dick, Venus, Bill Hitt, Luisa and Bridgett to be sold for 14 years then to be free; relation Thos. HUTT of WC son of Gerrard HUTT Sr. plant. w/o I now live and the new mill; Corbin HUTT & Gerrard HUTT sons of Gerrard HUTT Jr. tract of land and old mill; land adj. new mill where Presley McKINNEY now lives to Benj. PORTER son of Dan. PORTER; any remainder to Rich. HUTT son of Thos. HUTT; exors. Wm. EDWARDS, Thos. HUTT, Sam. TEMPLEMAN; WITS: Thos. SPENCE, Jn. McCLANAHAM, Jn. LYELL, Presley McKINNY
COD: voided the half of the sloop given to James NEALE and also what is given to Rich. HUTT son of Thos. HUTT to be given to Allen DOZIER, Nelson DOZIER, and James S. DOZIER. (WC DW 20:66) [Nomini Ferry was located in WC at the site of the present Nomini Bridge which takes Route 202 across Nomini Creek (Miller:111)]

HUTT, William; PO Dec 1799; Mar 1801
WC; INV, $3162.27; includes the following Negroes: Long Dick (time of servitude 3 years), Lett (3 yrs), Sambo (3 yrs), Miller Sam (3 yrs), Jenney (3 yrs), Sam (7 yrs), Dennis (7 urs), Jack (7 yrs), Hannah (7 yrs), Rose (7 yrs), Yellow Hannah (7 yrs), Black Hannah (7 yrs), Judah (7 yrs), Sarah (7 yrs), Yellow Judah (7 yrs), Joe (10 yrs), Young Jack (10 yrs), Young Dick (10 yrs), Daniel (10 yrs), Jerry (9 yrs), Milley (9 yrs), Nancy (9 yrs), Lavina (9 yrs), Bess (14 yrs), Little Dick (14 yrs), Venus (14 yrs), Bill (14 yrs), Kitt (14 yrs), Luisa (14 yrs), Bridgett (14 yrs). (WC RI 8:116)

INGRAM, John F.; T 6 Dec 1805; 15 Dec 1806
LC; INV, £207.3.6; includes Negro man [Guy], boy Armistead and a schooner "Dolphin."; LC EB 27:1)
[Wm. G. INGRAM orphan of Jn. INGRAM chose Lawson HATHAWAY as his gdn., 19 Oct 1818 (LC OB 25:21); *NB: it is not certain that Wm. G. is the son of the Jn. INGRAM whose inv. was taken in 1805.*]

INGRAM, Thomas; 17 Apr 1797; 18 Apr 1808
LC; WILL; wife Molly INGRAM use of all my est; if wife marries, whole est. to be eq. div. between my six children: Thomas INGRAM, Charles INGRAM, George INGRAM, William Francis INGRAM, Betsy INGRAM & Chloe INGRAM; friends Henry [HINTON] & Martin SHEARMAN; WITS: W. DOGGETT, Hen. L. NUTT, Rawleigh TAPSCOTT, Eliza HILL, Fanny HILL. (LC WB 28:105)
[Thos. INGRAM, wid., mar. Molly WADDY, dau. of Jas. & Lucy (CHILTON) WADDY, NC, bond 12 Apr 1790; Geo. INGRAM, Eliz. W. INGRAM and Chloe INGRAM orphans of Thos. INGRAM chose Geo. [T.] WADDY as their gdn., 16 Apr 1810 (LC Orders 23B 1808-11:178)]

INGRAM, Thomas; T 30 Mar 1810; 16 Apr 1810. LC; INV, $10.59. (LC EB 27:72)

INGRAM, Thomas; T 22 Dec 1813; 13 Feb 1815
NC; INV, $1766.63; includes Negroes Winney (about 36 years old), Milan[y] (about 12), Nancy (about 12), Darkey (about 7), Mary (about 4), Eady (about 2). (NC RB 19:613)

[The est. of Thos. INGRAM was ord. to be admin. by Wm. HUDNALL, NC, 13 Dec 1813 (NC OB 1811-1816:207)]

INSLEY, George Slocum (alias George SLOCUM); [m]; 12 Feb 1810; NC. INV, [m]. (NC RB 18:322)

[The est. of Geo. SLACUM was ord. to be admin. by Lewis LAMKIN, Jr., NC, 12 Feb 1810 (NC OB 1807-1811:152)]

ISLES, Absolom; 18 Jan 1802

LC; Elizabeth the wife of John ANGEL was Elizabeth ISLES admx. of Absolom ISLES. (LC Orders V 1802-03:6)

[Jn. ANGEL mar. Betsey ISLES, LC, bond 8 Oct 1801; Betsey was the wid. of Absolom ISLES whom she mar. in LC, bond 15 Apr 1794 (MLBLC:1, 42)]

JACKSON, Christopher; T 16 Sep 1799; 28 Apr 1800. WC; INV; £126.10.9. (WC RI 8:55)

[This may be Christopher M. JACKSON son of Christopher D. (d. WC 1749) & Magdalene (COX, RUST) JACKSON (d. WC 1767) (WC DW 11:154, 14:513, MWO:197)]

JACKSON, Daniel; 30 Oct 1814; 7 Mar 1815

RC; WILL; land to wife Nancy during her life; at her death to 3 small children; Negro man Paucious to son George; Negro girl Sarah to 3 small children; Negroes Will & Sam to stay on plant. with wife; Foushee G. WEBB and Martin SISSON exors; WITS: Luke JACKSON, Humphrey POPE. (RC WB 9:469)

[This may be the Daniel JACKSON who was prob a wid. when he mar. Ann BRICKEY, prob the wid. of Jarrard BRICKEY, RC, bond 20 Aug 1814 (MRC:24, 101; Thos. J. SCRIMGER aptd. gdn. to [Winefred] & Dan. JACKSON orphans of Dan. JACKSON, 5 Feb 1821 (RC OB 25:106); settlement of Merideth HUDSON's, dec'd, acct. of his gdnship. of Geo. JACKSON orphan of Dan. JACKSON, 6 Aug 1821 (RC OB 25:187)]

JACKSON, Newman; 9 Jan 1815; 27 Feb 1815

WC; WILL; heirs of son Thomas JACKSON all the property that I lent sd. Thomas when he was married; balance of my est. to be eq. div. between my son Newman B. JACKSON and my dau. Polly JACKSON; son Newman B. JACKSON ex.; WITS: Garrod B. GARNER, Thos. DOLMAN. (WC DW 23:67)

JACKSON, Richard; PO 26 Feb [1816]; [m]

WC; DIV of tract of land known as Wilton containing 446 ac; Lot 1 to Richard R. JACKSON; Lot 2 to Peter P. COX in right of his wife Elizabeth; Lot 3 to Peter P. COX in right of his wife Eleanor [sic]; Lot 4 to Charles R. THOMPSON in right of his wife Mary; Lot 5 to Rebecca R. THOMPSON; James COX in right of his wife Hannah; [land was located on Jackson's Creek]. (WC DW 23:188)

[Peter P. COX mar. Eleanor JACKSON, WC, bond 17 Aug 1808; Chas. R. THOMPSON mar. Mary JACKSON, dau. of Rebecca JACKSON, WC, bond 25 Jan 1792; Jas. COX mar. Hannah JACKSON, WC, bond 12 Jun 1804 (MLBWC:16, 71); see also entry for "Wilton" in Miller; Jackson Creek is located in East central WC (Miller:75, 173]

JACKSON, Samuel; PO 7 Jan 1811; 4 Feb 1811

RC; DIV of slaves between Christopher D. HOGAN & Elizabeth his wife who was the dau. of Samuel JACKSON (Nanny, Daniel, Charlotte) & William JACKSON orphan of Samuel JACKSON (Patt, Joe, George, Nanny). (RC AB 3:244)

[Christopher D. HOGAN, son of Travis HOGAN, mar. Eliz. JACKSON, RC, bond 24 Apr 1810; Eliz. JACKSON was the bride's grandmother and legal gdn. (MRC:95)]

JACKSON, Thaddeus; 3 Feb 1802; 22 Nov 1802.
CP, WC; WILL; wife Elizabeth; daus. Elizabeth BRYANT, Peggy COLE, Polly JACKSON; WITS: Lewis HILLYARD, Robert HUDSON, Mathew LAMKIN. (WC DW 20:405)
[Thaddeus JACKSON was a son of Christopher D. (d. WC 1749) & Magdalene (COX, RUST) JACKSON (d. WC 1767) and bro. of Christopher M. JACKSON (WC DW 11:154, 14:513, MWO:197); he mar. Eliz. FLEMING bef. 7 Jan 1767 (MWO:198); Eliz. JACKSON mar. Jos. BRYANT, RC, bond 25 Feb 1793 (MRC:28); Peggy JACKSON mar. Wm. COLE, NC, bond 30 Nov 1798 (MLBNC:19)]

JACKSON, Thomas; 25 Aug 1817
WC; Richard BULGER aptd. gdn. to William & Elizabeth JACKSON orphans of Thomas JACKSON. (WC OB 1814-18:337)
[Thomas JACKSON mar. Polly BROWN, WC, consent of Polly BROWN dtd 23 Sep 1809 (MLBWC:34); Polly (BROWN) JACKSON mar. (2) Richard BULGER, WC, bond 7 Jun 1815 (MLBWC:10)]

JACKSON, Vincent; PO Dec 1805, T 21 Jan 1806; 2 Jun 1806.
RC. DIV of slaves amongst his 4 children: John JACKSON, Vincent JACKSON, Elizabeth JACKSON & Thomas JACKSON. (RC AB 3:158)
[This is Vincent JACKSON who named his son William and four children by Elizabeth ALLGOOD: John, Vincent, Tom, and Betty, in his will (RC 11 Dec 1791-6 Feb 1792) (RC WB 8:137, MWO:198); Jn. JACKSON was a resident of Frederick Co., Va. by Jan 1801 (RC DB 18:253); Elizabeth JACKSON mar. (1) Vincent GARLAND, RC, bond 4 Jan 1808 and (2) Jn. PLUMMER, RC, bond 13 Jul 1819 (MRC:75, 159; RC DB 19:86; OB 27:4, 12); Thos. JACKSON was a resident of Georgetown in the District of Columbia by May 1819 (RC DB 20:681)]

JACKSON, William; PO Dec 1794; 6 Feb 1816
RC; INV, £723.8.0, includes the following Negroes: Jane & her child Julia, Sady, Old Luke, Young Luke, Buster, Nausaw, Jim, Frankey, Patty, Levina, Lucy & her young child, Glasgow, Polly, Tom, Easter, Nanny, Mariah. (RC WB 9:580)
[Wm. JACKSON d. leaving his wife Catherine pregnant; she gave birth to Catherine William Henry JACKSON after her husband's death (the posthumous child was not Henry Allison as given in WRC:178; he must have been a child who d. before William's death); Cath. (ALLISON) JACKSON mar. (2) Sam. W. HIPKINS, RC, bond 8 Sep 1797 (MRC:95); Cath. W. H. JACKSON mar. Wm. Younger WEATHERS, RC, bond 27 Jun 1814 (MRC:225)]

JACOB, Robert Clark; 17 Jun 1822
LC; on the mot. of George HAYWOOD & Ann his wife, John W. HALL & Susan his wife, John KING & Sarah his wife, William [*1 word unclear*], Thomas [L.], Margaret P. and Rebecca B. [WALTERS], Elizabeth JACOB, Margaret T. EVANS, Thomas H. KELLUM & Elizabeth his wife, Ann S. & Charlotte H. JACOB, ord that Peter S. BOWDOIN & Susan his wife be summoned to show cause why a tract of land called Cherry Point in LC belonging to the heirs of Robert Clarke JACOB should not be sold and the proceeds divided. (LC OB 25:310)

[Margaret T. EVANS, Eliz. KELLAM, Susan BOWDOIN, Ann S. JACOB, and Charlotte JACOB are children of Col. Robt. A. JACOB (d. 1808, Northampton Co.) and his wife Eliz. HACK of Accomack Co. (www.arlisherring.com, accessed 11 Mar 2012)

JAMES, Bartley; 6 Feb 1818; 16 Feb 1818
LC; WILL; Negro man Adam, woman Mary & her dau. Lina to wife Sarah Nutt JAMES; I lend the balance of my est. to my wife during her life or widowhood; at wife's death or marriage Negro girl Fan to go to grdau. Amy HUBBARD & balance of est. to be eq. div. amongst grchil. that my dau. Polley may have; [no ex. named]; WITS: A. WEST, Geo. P. OLIVER, A. [PENQUITE], Jn. J. DEGGE. (LC WB 28:186)
[This is Bartley or Bartlett JAMES, son of Bartlett JAMES and his 2nd wife Eliz. WAUGH. Bartley JAMES mar. (1) Amy YOPP, LC, bond 16 Feb 1795; (2) Salley N. BRENT, LC, bond 19 May 1817 (MLBLC:42); he may have had another wife, Susanna INGRAM who was mar. to a Bartlet JAMES, LC, bond 23 Jun 1812; Polly B. JAMES mar. Jesse HUBBARD, NC, bond 5 Jan 1814 (MLBLC:39); LC CC 1799-003 provides information on Bartlett or Bartley JAMES and his family; acc. to this case, Walter JAMES (d. LC, 1799) was the father of an earlier Bartlett JAMES who mar. (1) Eliz. HATHAWAY (dau. of Wm & Sarah HATHAWAY and sis. of Lawson HATHAWAY), LC, bond 20 Dec 1763 and (2) Eliz. WAUGH, LC, bond 17 Jan 1771. Bartlett and Eliz. (1) were the parents of John and Nancy JAMES (mar. Achilles BARNETT, Fauquier Co., bond 11 Oct 1788); Bartlett and Eliz. (2) were the parents of Bartlett, Eliz. (mar. Wm. KENT, LC, bond 13 Jul 1795) and Mary (mar. Geo. GRESHAM, LC, bond 25 Apr 1798); John JAMES, Jr. who d. intestate of smallpox in 1788 and while in the final stages of his illness and allegedly not in his senses was induced to sign a will by a relative Wm. JAMES and his uncle Lawson HATHAWAY; the will left his est. to his sis. Ann and step-mother Elizabeth; his half siblings sued and each received one fifth of his est. (LC WB 20:31, 43, 80, 145, 156, WB 22:199; MLBLC:34, 45; King 2001:46); a Lawson Achilles BARNETT (1791 – 1864) is buried in the Barnett Cemetery near Shelby in Madison Co., Va.; he must be a son of Nancy JAMES & Achilles BARNETT)<the-millers.org/history/Barnett_Cemetery/barnett_cemetery.htm> accessed 22 Jul 2012)]

JAMES, Bartley; PO 16 Feb 1818; 21 Jun 1819. LC; INV, $3290.[4?]. (LC EB 27:484)

JAMES, Benjamin;
LC; Benjamin JAMES d. intest. between 1800 and 1810 leaving his sisters Mary, wife of Fleet CURRELL, and Elizabeth GEORGE, his mother Sarah JAMES, and his bro. Charles JAMES. (LC CC 1810-002)
[Benj. JAMES was poss. a grson. of Walter JAMES (d. LC 1779) (LC WB 20:156); Mary JAMES mar. Fleet CURRELL, LC, bond 6 Dec 1796; Eliz. JAMES mar. Tarpley GEORGE, LC, bond 15 Feb 1790 (MLBLC:18; MWO:146); in MWO on p. 146 it was stated that the Eliz. JAMES who mar. Tarpley GEORGE was a dau. of Walter JAMES; this is not correct; she was prob. his grdau.]

JAMES, Benjamin; PO 29 Nov 1808, T 29 Nov 1808; 19 Dec 1808
LC; INV of est. unadministered by Charles JAMES; one Negro man [?] @ $340. (LC EB 27:43)

JAMES, Berryman Jr.; PO 19 Dec 1803; 16 Jul 1804
LC; INV, £116.7.0; included a chest of joiner's tools and a Negro boy Isaac; Charles JAMES admr. (LC EB 24:277)

JAMES, Catharine; PO 12 Feb 1804; 11 Jun 1804
NC; INV at the house of Mary W. JAMES, £123.19.6 (1/2 of this value is the est. of the dec'd); includes Negro Richard. (NC RB 17:165)
[In her will (NC 10 Jul 1803-10 Oct 1803) Catharine JAMES of WicP named her sis. Mary Waters JAMES (NC RB 17:69)]

JAMES, Elizabeth (Mrs.); PO 31 Dec 1795; 20 Jun 1796. LC; INV, £65.16.6. (LC EB 24:16)

JAMES, John [Sr.]; 27 Oct 1814; 18 Apr 1815
LC; WILL; all est. to son John JAMES except the legacy given to my mother Mary JAMES; if son should die without issue or before age 21 use of all est. to wife Betsy L. JAMES; at wife's death land to bro. William M. JAMES; balance of est. to be eq. div. between my 4 sis: Margaret MASON, Mary K. GEORGE, Betsy P. JAMES, & Nancy JAMES; wife & friends Henry C. LAWSON & William POLLARD exors; WITS: Jas. GIBSON, Lawson HATHAWAY, Wm. JAMES. (LC WB 28:161)
[Jn. JAMES mar. Betsy L. HINTON, LC, bond 29 Apr 1811 (MLBLC:42); Margaret JAMES mar. Thos. MASON, LC, bond 1 Oct 1790; Mary K. GEORGE mar. Zamoth GEORGE, prob. as his 2nd wife, LC, bond 8 Apr 1805 (MLBLC:32, 51)]

JAMES, John Sr.; PO 18 Apr 1815, T 16 Jun 1815; 20 Nov 1815
LC; INV; includes Negroes: Billy, Lidda, boy James, boy Elijah, girl Apha. (LC EB 27:263)

JAMES, John Sr.; PO 18 Mar 1822; 20 May 1822
LC; sale of 4 Negroes (James, Rocksey, John, Margaret) belonging to the est. of John JAMES Sr. and paid over to Thomas JAMES the balance ($411.32) which is divided among the said James' heirs: Thomas JAMES, Thomas MASON, William M. JAMES, Betsey JAMES, Nancy JAMES, John JAMES Jr.'s admx, Polly K. GEORGE (each heir rec'd $58.76). (LC EB 29:195)

JAMES, Mary; 18 Dec 1821; 21 Jan 1822
LC; WILL; daus. Elizabeth & Nancy JAMES; rest of est. to be eq. div. amongst the balance of my children namely my d-i-l Elizabeth L. JAMES, William M. JAMES, Thomas JAMES, Mary K. GEORGE,and my s-i-l Thomas MASON; Hiram CARPENTER ex; WITS: Thos. N. LAWSON, Hiram CARPENTER. (LC WB 28:223)
[This must be Mary the wid. of Jn. JAMES, Sr.; *see above*]

JAMES, Mathias; T 7 Jan 1817; 21 Jul 1817
LC; DIV of slaves among his children: Polly JAMES, William JAMES, Letty JAMES, Richard JAMES; each child received $260. (LC EB 27:389)
[This is prob. the Matthias JAMES who mar. Judith HINTON, LC, bond 20 Jan 1790 (MLBLC:42); Polly & Rich. JAMES orphans of Matt. JAMES chose Edw. CURRELL as their gdn., 16 Dec 1816 (LC Orders 24:344); Fleet CURRELL aptd. gdn. to Letty JAMES orphan of Mathias JAMES, 20 Jan 1817 (LC OB 25:347); Polly JAMES orphan of Math. JAMES chose Rich. JAMES as her gdn. and sd. Rich. is aptd. gdn. to Letty JAMES also an orphan of sd. Math., 19 Oct 1818 (LC OB 25:21); Polly JAMES chose Jas. POLLARD as her gdn., 17 Sep 1821 (LC OB 25:250)]

JAMES, Robert; 17 May 1813
LC; Judith JAMES aptd. gdn. to Thomas Opie & Janetta JAMES orphans of Robert JAMES. (LC Orders 24:153)

JAMES, Sherard; T 18 Mar 1814; 28 Mar 1814

WC; INV, [m]; includes Negro Harry one half of whom belongs to the est. & the other to Abner JAMES; admin. with the will annexed granted to James DEATLEY. (WC RI 9:419)

JAMES, Sherard (Sherrod); 2 Mar 1813; 26 Jul 1819
WC; WILL; all est. to wife Frances JAMES during her widowhood; at her death to be eq. div. between my two children which I had by my sd. wife; bro. Abner JAMES ex.; WITS: Thos. N. BERRYMAN, Chris. J. COLLINS, Thos. JAMES. (WC DW 23:512)
[Sherrod JAMES mar. Fanny DEATLEY in WC, bond 30 Nov 1809 (WC MLB:34); Jas. DEATLEY aptd. gdn. to Sherard JAMES inf. son of Sherard JAMES & Abner JAMES moved the court to sell a slave named Harry who belonged equally to Abner & Sherard JAMES, 22 Oct 1821 (WC OB 1819-23:324); Thos. JAMES aptd. gdn. to Sherod JAMES orphan of Sherod JAMES, 26 Apr 1824 (WC OB 1823-27:42)]

JAMES, Thomas; PO 8 Sep 1800; 13 Jul 1801. NC; INV, £120.3.6. (NC RB 16:273)

JAMES, Walter; 1 Jul 1807; 23 Nov 1807
WP, WC; WILL; son Abner JAMES, son Sherod JAMES, nephew William [J.] JETT; dau. Elizabeth; wife Sarah rest of est; after wife's death est. to be eq. div. among following children: Lucy JAMES, Elizabeth JAMES, Mary JAMES, Thomas JAMES, Maria JAMES, Margaret JAMES, & Eliza JAMES; two oldest sons Abner & Sherod exors; WITS: Thos. BERRYMAN, Jas. PEYTON, Jas. FISHER; [COD adds wife as an extx.] (WC DW 21:397)
[On the mot. of Geo. BARRICK & Maria his wife ... and [since] it appears to the court that Eliz. JAMES is an inf. under 21 and that certain lands which descend from Walter JAMES are not of sufficient value to give each devisee $300, ord. that Lucy JAMES, Wm. J. JETT & Eliz. his wife, Mary JAMES, Thos. JAMES, Margaret JAMES and the sd. Eliz. JAMES be summoned to show cause why the land should not be sold, 28 Jul 1823 (WC OB 1819-23:581); Geo. G. BARROK mar. Maria JAMES, WC, bond 11 Feb 1820 (MLBWC:4)]

JAMISON, Walter; PO 19 Jun 1809; 17 Jul 1809
LC; INV, $804.0.8 1/3; includes Negroes: Billy, Polly, Patsy. (LC EB 27:62)

JAQUES, William [Hill]; Hill JAQUES, Thomas JAQUES and Jordan HAYNIE & Nancy his wife sued Elizabeth JAQUES, admx. of William JAQUES, in a CC beginning in Oct 1812 (NC CC 1817-013)
[Wm. H. JAQUES, wid., mar. Betty WHITE, lic. 29 May 1791 (MWO:199); Betty Fallin WHITE was a dau. of Simon WHITE (d. NC 1791-1792) (NC RB 14:512); Nancy JACQUES mar. Jordan HAYNIE. NC, bond 24 Oct 1792 (MLBNC:49); Nancy must have been the child of Wm. JAQUES and his first wife who was also named Elizabeth; the births of Mary (12 Feb 1770), Ann (10 May 1774) and Hill (28 Sep 1776) to Wm and Eliz. JAQUES are recorded in the SSPR (SSPR:145); the est. of Hill JAQUES was admin. by Thos JAQUES, 13 Feb 1815 (NC OB 1811-1816:282)]

JEFFRIES, Edmund R.; 11 Feb 1828
NC; Jeremiah JEFFRIES aptd. gdn. to James & Alice JEFFRIES orphans of Edmund R. JEFFRIES. (NC OB 1825-30:234)
[Edmund R. JEFFRIES, wid., mar. Sally L. CHRISTOPHER, wid. of Robt. CHRISTOPHER, NC, bond 10 Jan 1818 (MLBNC:60)]

JEFFRIES, Elizabeth; PO 12 Oct 1812, T 31 Oct 1812; 14 Jun 1813
NC; INV, $139.31. (NC RB 19:403)
[The est. of Eliz. JEFFRIES was ord. to be admin. by Robert D. PALMER, NC, 12 Oct 1812 (NC OB 1811-1816:117)]

JEFFRIES, Jeremiah; 8 Dec 1802; 24 Apr 1809.
CP, WC; WILL; all est. to sis. Jane JEFFRIES & she is to be extx; WITS: [Timothy] HARRINGTON, Dan. MATHANEY, David WARDROBE. (WC DW 21:492)

JEFFRIES, Joseph; PO 13 Feb 1809, T 21 Dec 1809; 9 Jul 1810
NC; INV, [m]. (NC RB 18:422)
[The est. of Jos. JEFFRIES was ord. to be admin. by Wm. HARDING, NC, 13 Feb 1809 (NC OB 1811-1816:80)]

JEFFRIES, Sally; 17 Apr 1801; 28 Mar 1803
WC; WILL; all est. except cloth to bro. Jeremiah JEFFRIES; cloth to be div. between sisters; bro. to be exor.; WITS: Rich. BENNETT, Jeremiah JEFFRIES Jr., Danl. GARNER. (WC DW 20:438)

JENKINS, John Barker; 25 Oct 1809
WC; Richard OMOHUNDRO aptd. gdn. of [Sally] JENKINS, Thomas JENKINS, and Richard JENKINS orphans of John Barker JENKINS. (WC Orders 1807-10:435)
[Two marriages for a Jn. B. JENKINS are rec. in WC: (1) to Martha OMOHUNDRO, bond 22 Feb 1796 and (2) to Winifred L. PAYNE (dau. of James PAYNE), bond 31 Dec 1804 (MLBWC:34); Winifred L. (PAYNE) JENKINS mar. (2) Chas. MOTHERSHEAD, WC, bond 27 Nov 1811 (MLBWC:47); on the mot. of Chas. MOTHERSHEAD & Winifred his wife who was Winifred JENKINS wid. & admx. of Jn. B. JENKINS, ord. that they settle their admin. of the est. of Jn. B. JENKINS, 22 Feb 1819 (WC OB 1819-23:13); on the mot. of Chas. MOTHERSHEAD commissioners aptd. to settle Winifred MOTHERSHEAD's (formerly Winifred JENKINS) gdnship. acct. with James & Mary JENKINS orphans of Jn. B. JENKINS, 23 Aug 1824 (WC OB 1823-27:111); [Sabby] JENKINS is poss. Sebina B. JENKINS who mar. Gerard A. SANFORD, WC, bond 18 Oct 1820 (MLBWC:61)]

JENKINS, Smith; PO Sep 1815, T 20 Oct 1815; 23 Oct 1815. WC; INV, $391.00. (WC RI 10:29)
[Smith JENKINS, son of Rich. JENKINS, mar. Jemima WASHINGTON, WC, bond 5 Dec 1792 (MWO:200)]

JESPER, Daniel & Catharine; PO 1 Oct 1804, T 6 Dec 1805; 1 Sep 1806
RC; DIV of slaves of the est. of Daniel JESPER & Catharine JESPER dec'd between Catharine JESPER orphan of William JESPER dec'd by her gdn. George MITCHELL, George JESPER, Thomas STEPHENS in right of his wife Mary Ann dec'd by his attorney in fact Peter TEMPLE and Daniel JACKSON as gdn. to his children Luke, John, Catharine and George; the value of each party's portion was £165. (RC AB 3:173)
[The births of 2 children of Daniel & Catharine JESPER are rec. in the NFPR: Thomas b. 24 Mar 1764 & Edward b. 16 Jun 1777 (NFPR:105); Daniel JESPER, in his will (RC 8 Nov 1778-1 Feb 1779), named his wife Catharine and sons Thos., Dan., Wm., Geo. & Edw. (RC WB 7:335); Thos. STEPHENS mar. Mary Ann JESPER, RC, bond 17 Dec 1796 (MRC:194)]

JESPER, George; 6 Aug 1821
RC; Mary JESPER orphan of George JESPER chose Warner L. TAPSCOTT as her gdn. (RC OB 25:189)

JESPER, George; PO 3 Dec 1821, T 2 Apr 1825; 2 May 1825
RC; DIV of Negroes belonging to the est: Sally & child Maria, Nanny, Elijah, Guy & blind girl Mary, Joe, Ned, Frances, Elijah Jr.; allotted to Peggy E. JESPER as her dower (Elijah, Ned, Frances), to Polly JESPER (Nanny), to

Daniel JESPER (Joe, Elijah Jr.), to Edward JESPER (Guy, Mary), to Thomas JESPER (Sally & child Maria). (RC AB 4:172)
[Geo. JESPER mar. Peggy WALL, RC, bond 21 Jul 1813 (MRC:105); Peggy E. JESPER, wid. of Geo. JESPER, Dan. JESPER, Thos. JESPER, Polly & Edw. JESPER, the last three named infants by their next friend Daniel JESPER, compl., against Rich. STREET, sheriff, and admr. of Geo. JESPER's est.; Peggy E. JESPER aptd. gdn. to her son Edw. JESPER orphan of Geo. JESPER, 3 Dec 1821 (RC OB 25:218, 222); Rich. SAUNDERS aptd. gdn. to Edw. JESPER orphan of Geo. JESPER, 7 Jun 1824 (RC OB 26:207); Manus ROWAN pltf. against Dan. JESPER, Martin HILL & Polly his wife who was Polly JESPER, Thos. JESPER & Edw. JESPER heirs of Geo. JESPER, 3 Oct 1825 (RC OB 27:7); Martin HILL mar. Mary JESPER, RC, bond Dec 1823 (MRC:93); Peggy (WALL) JESPER mar. (2) Edmund N. NORTHEN, RC, bond 21 Oct 1822 (MRC:148, RC OB 27:156); settlement of Rich. SAUNDERS' acct. of his gdnship. of Edw. JESPER orphan of Geo. JESPER, 8 May 1827 (RC OB 27:160)]

JESPER, Richard; 5 Feb 1821
RC; Elizabeth JESPER orphan of Richard JESPER chose James BRAGG as her gdn. (RC OB 25:106)
[Ann JESPER, Polly JESPER, Eliz. BRAGG who was Eliz. JESPER, complts., against Alice JESPER, Harriet JESPER & Jn. JESPER infants of Rich. JESPER dec'd by their gdn. Geo. SAUNDERS, 5 Nov 1821 (RC OB 25:211)]

JETT, Catharine; PO 22 Aug 1808, T 1 Oct 1808; 23 Jan 1809
WC; settlement of Peter JETT & Ben STEWARD's executorship acct. of the est. of Catharine JETT dec'd and also Catharine JETT's executorship acct. of the est. of Thomas JETT dec'd; the balance of £307.7 was allotted to William BROWN, William Jett BROWN admr. of E. JETT & Opie LINDSAY the persons entitled to the same under the wills of the decedants. (WC RI 9:80)
[This is Cath. JETT who mentioned in her will (WC 7 Nov 1786 – 27 Feb 1787) land in KGC and daus. Betty & Frances JETT and Ann BROWN; Peter JETT was named ex. (WC DW 16:379 and 17:35); she may have been the wid. of Wm. JETT who with his wife Katherine was named in the will of Willoughby NEWTON (WC 7 Dec 1766 – 26 May 1767) (WC DW 17:461)]

JETT, Elizabeth; T 5 Feb 1799; 24 Feb 1800
WC; INV £954.17.6; includes the following Negroes: Ben, [Jerrard], Bill [TUXON], John, Bill CYRUS, Tom, Moses, Jacob, Aimey (sick), Hannah, Patt, [Kate], Sharlot, Paul, Easter, Sarah. (WC RI 8:42)

JETT, Jeremiah B.; T 4 Jan 1815; 27 Feb 1815
WC; INV, $4159.26, includes Negroes Solomon (a blacksmith with tools), young fellows John & James, James Pratt, boy Payton, Frank (woman with 3 children Harriot, Robin & Lucy), Judy & her child Thornton, Sarah (old woman), young girl Emeline, old woman Peg worth nothing. (WC RI 9:431)
[Jeremiah B. JETT died intest. around 1814; he seems to have left two children, a son William who prob. died young and a dau. Mary Ann Piper who mar. Dr. Ferdinando FAIRFAX on 11 Jan 1831 (WCCP:35, MLBWC:22); Dan. CARMICHAEL aptd. gdn. of Mary & Wm. JETT orphans of Jeremiah B. JETT, 22 May 1815 (WC OB 1814-18:125); Jas. JETT relinquished his right of admin. on the est. of Jeremiah B. JETT, 28 Nov 1814 (WC OB 1814-18:84)]

JETT, Sucky; 24 Mar 1808; 22 Jul 1822
WC; WILL; rest of est. after debts paid to dau. Catherine HODGE; dau. Catherine extx; WITS: Wm. Storke JETT Jr., Wm. Storke JETT. (WC DW 24:341)

JETT, Thomas; PO Jun 1801; 26 Jul 1802. WC; INV, £39.11.6. (WC RI 8:171)

JETT, Thomas H.; T 16 Dec 1823; 10 Jan 1825
NC; INV, [m]; includes the following Negroes: young men John & Reuben; boys Solomon & Joe, old women [Billy], Lucy & Nanny; girl Dinah. (NC RB 24:112)

JETT, William & Elizabeth; T 2 Feb 1803; 13 Jun 1803
NC; INV, [m]; includes Negroes Jessee, Judah, [Phoeby--*but crossed out*]. (NC RB 17:3)

JEWELL, James; T 2 Mar 1819; 25 Oct 1819. WC; INV, [m]. (WC RI 10:430)

JOHNSON, Osmond; father of Evelina and Harriet d. intest. in 1825. (WC CC 1825-001)

JOHNSON, Samuel; T 25 Mar 1816; 25 Mar 1816
WC; DIV of slaves; James & Peter to Henry JOHNSON; Benjamin & Jack to George JOHNSON who mar. Nancy; Aaron & Nancy to Elizabeth JOHNSON; Isaac & Dick, Bennett the only remaining legatee mention[ed] in the residuary clause of the will having died and also previous to the death of Nancy who mar. George JOHNSON; specific sum of $572 was div. as follows: to George JOHNSON who mar. Nancy a full sis. to Bennett, $127.11 1/9, to Elizabeth JOHNSON also a full sis, $127.11 1/9, to Henry a full bro., $127.11 1/9, to Harriott JOHNSON a half sis., $63.55 5/9, to William JOHNSON a half bro., $63.55 5/9, to Samuel a half bro, $63.55 5/9. (WC RI 10:50)
[Eliz. & Hen. JOHNSON, orphans of Sam. JOHNSON, chose Thos. JOHNSON as their gdn., 24 Oct 1814 (WC OB 1814-18:78)]

JOHNSON, Samuel Sr.; 24 Mar 1802; 27 Sep 1802
WP, WC; WILL; dau. Harriet JOHNSON; son William; young children: Samuel, Burnett, Nancy, Betsy & Henry; friends James MUSE & William NELSON exors; WITS: Susannah SHORT, Jn. MUSE, Thos. MUSE. (WC DW 20:383)

JOHNSTON, Margaret; 12 Sep 1810; 25 Mar 1811
WC; WILL; son George JOHNSTON house & lot w/o I now reside; sons Thomas JOHNSTON, Birkett JOHNSTON, James JOHNSTON; son Thomas JOHNSTON ex.; WITS: Danl. CARMICHAEL; COD: 1 Mar 1811; cow & desk to son William JOHNSTON; Wit: Jn. MULLANY. (WC DW 22:191)

JOHNSTON, Margaret; T 26 Mar 1811; Apr 1811. WC; INV, [m]. (WC RI 9:236)

JONES, Abner; 24 Aug 1795; 2 Mar 1807
RC; WILL; bro. Thomas JONES (under 21) all land w/o I now live containing 130 ac.; niece Elizabeth COATS dau. of James COATS; friend George SISSON exor.; WITS: Jn. SMITH, Martin SISSON, Randal SISSON; [first proved 7 Apr 1800 but ord to lie for further proof]. (RC WB 9:307)
[Abner JONES was prob. the son of David & Mary JONES; he was b. in NFP 13 Mar 1765; his sis. Lucy, b. in NFP 27 Jan 1768 is no doubt the Lucy JONES who mar. James COATES, RC, bond 3 Mar 1792 (NFPR:109, MRC:40)]

JONES, Catesby; T 28 Jul 1802; 11 Oct 1802
NC; INV, [m]; includes timber for a brig at Mr. [Rul's] in Westmoreland; "schooner Betsy, which Mr. William FORBES was to furnish the rig[g]ing; he was to keep the vessel untill she had paid for the rig[g]ing by her freights. She was delivered to Mr. FORBES September 1799. I suppose there must have been freights sufficient to pay for the rig[g]ing as it is three years in September since Mr. FORBES had the vessell." Phil WHITE DS for William NELMS shff. (NC RB 16:467)

JONES, Caty; 11 Dec 1799; 1 Jun 1801. RC; INV; £20.15.[?]. (RC WB 9:148)

JONES, Charles; PO 5 Oct 1801, T 27 Nov 1802; 7 Feb 1803
RC; DIV of Negroes among John JONES (received George, Mary, John, Sophia, Rachel, Jesse, Moses, Dennis, James, Jeremiah, & [Sanney]) & William BOON who mar. Elenor JONES (received Gumby, Nelly, Jacob, Joan, Jenny, Silvy, Phillis, Samuel, Betty, Hannah & 2 children. (RC AB 3:99)

JONES, Edward; PO 6 Apr 1801, T 8 Apr 1801; 6 Jul 1801
RC; DIV of est. among: the reps. of Winifred JONES, William BARBER who mar. Elizabeth JONES, the reps. of Lucy JONES who mar. Daniel BROWN, the reps. of Margarett JONES who mar. George NORTHEN. (RC AB 3:48)
[Edward JONES seems to have had two wives, (1) Jane WILLIAMS who was the mother of Winifred and (2) Barbara BAKER who was the mother of Elizabeth (b. 1751), Lucy (b. 1753), and Margaret (b. 1756)(MWO:204, SSPR:108-109); in his will (RC 5 Oct 1756 - 2 Apr 1759) he named his wife Barbary, daus. Eliz., Winifred, Lucy & Margaret (RC WB 6:148); Wm. BARBER mar. Eliz. JONES, dau. of Edw. JONES (d. 1759) RC, by 1767; Dan. BROWN mar. Lucy JONES, RC, by 6 Apr 1801; Geo. NORTHEN mar. Margaret JONES, RC, by 1767 (MRC:9, 25, 148; RC WB 9:107)]

JONES, Eppa; 4 Dec 1820
RC; Rich. CLAUGHTON gdn. of John W. & Eliza H. JONES orphans of Eppa JONES; court ord. the Negroes which were devised by John JONES to the heirs of Eppa JONES to be div. between Priscilla L. JONES and the sd. John W. and Eliza H. JONES. (RC OB 25:92)
[Epaphroditus JONES, son of John and Hannah JONES, mar. Sally Lewis CLAUGHTON, RC, bond 14 Dec 1798 (MRC:108)]

JONES, George; T 6 Dec 1821; 14 Jun 1824
NC; INV; [also a second INV T 14 [Nov]]. (NC RB 23:508, 511)

JONES, Griffin; 4 Apr 1820
RC; Mary C. JONES, wid. of Griffin JONES, to admin. the est. of Richard STOTT. (RC OB 24:419)
[Mary C. STOTT, wid., mar. Griffin JONES, RC, bond 24 Jun 1816 (MRC:108)]

JONES, John Sr.; 26 Dec 1815; 1 Jan 1816
RC; WILL; land w/o I now live & Negroes Doll & small boy Ned to son George JONES; plant. adj Richard STREET & James PULLEN and Negro boy George & his bro. James to son Willis; 3 children of dec'd son Eppa JONES: Priscilla, John W., & Betsy to have Negro woman Lucy & her child Jere; dau. Betsy HEADLEY to have 2 Negro girls Hanah & Sarah; heirs of dau. Nancy HEADLEY to have 2 small Negro girls Leannah & Moriah; dau. Milly DAMERON to have one Negro girl Marjory & a boy Peter; 3 grown up Negroes Solomon, Edmund, & Nelson to be hired out yearly; Negro woman Jane to son George; little Negroes not mentioned above to be eq. div. among my children namely George JONES, Willis JONES, Betsy HEADLEY, Milly DAMERON, & the heirs of Eppa JONES (Priscilla, John & Betsy JONES); George JONES, Willis JONES & Griffin HEADLEY exors; WITS: Griffin HEADLEY, Jn. DOUGLAS Jr., Sam. BEARCROFT. (RC WB 9:499)
[Jn. JONES was a son of Ambrose & Eliz. (HAYDON) JONES (MWO:203; RC WB 7:431); his birth on 20 Jun 1747 was recorded in the SSPR (SSPR:118); Eliz JONES mar. Randal HEADLEY, RC, bond 31 Dec 1799; Nancy JONES mar. Wm. HEADLEY, RC, bond 16 Jan 1805; Milly JONES mar. Wm. DAMERON, Jr., RC, bond 10 Apr 1809 (MRC:48, 92)]

JONES, John; PO 5 Feb 1816; 7 Jul 1817

RC; INV; $5139.41, includes the following Negroes: Doll, Jane, Lucy, Solomon, [Edmund], Pricilla, Sarah, Hannah, Nelson, George, Mariah, Marjory, Leannah, Peter, Ned, Rachel, Mahaley, James, Mary, Jera. (RC WB 9:560)

JONES, John; PO 5 Feb 1816, T 3 May 1817; 7 Jul 1817
RC; DIV of est. among George JONES (Negroes Doll, Ned, Jane, Rachel, Mahala), Eppa JONES' heirs (Lucy & Jerry), Elizabeth HEADLEY (Sarah & Hannah, Edmond), Nancy HEADLEY (Mariah, Leanah), Willis JONES (George, James, Mary, Solomon), Milly DAMERON (Marjorum, Peter, Nelson). (RC AB 3:422)

JONES, John; PO 4 Dec 1820, T 26 Dec 1820; 5 Feb 1821
RC; DIV of Negroes devised by John JONES to the heirs of Eppa JONES dec'd between Priscilla L. JONES (Jerry), John W. JONES (Lucy) & Elizabeth H. JONES (Polly & Ann). (RC AB 3:701)

JONES, Lewis; 29 Aug 1799; 17 Feb 1800
LC; WILL; wife Milly during her widowhood the use of my Negroes Hannah, Mima & Abraham; after wife's death or remarriage, Negroes to go to dau. Sally JONES; to son Loftis' eldest son, whose name at present I do not know, my sword, gun and all that pertain to her [sic]; 5 shillings to son Lewis JONES; money in the house to wife; residue of est. to be div. into 3 eq. parts, one part to wife & the other 2 parts to be eq. div. among 4 daus. Judith, Molly, Lucy & Sally; wife extx.; WITS: Jos. CARTER Jr., Jn. LAWRY. (LC WB 28:39)
[Lewis JONES mar. Milley CHILTON, a dau. of Wm. CHILTON (d. LC bef 1791), LC, before Oct 1790 (MLBLC:43, LC WB 22:307); he served as a lieutenant in the Virginia State Navy during the Revolutionary War; his wid. Milly was receiving a pension of $360 per year in 1839; his dau. Mary or Molly married [fnu] ROGERS and was apparently a resident of EC in 1838; his son Loftis had a dau. Malinda who was a resident of Washington by 1839 and married [fnu] DAVIS (VS1776 III:1016); Patty JONES orphan of Lewis JONES chose Peter TANKERSLEY as her gdn, 15 Dec 1800 (LC Orders 21 1799-1800:201); Patty JONES orphan of Lewis JONES chose Moses GEORGE as her gdn., 20 Sep 1802 (LC Orders V 1802-03:194); Moses GEORGE was the gdn. of Patty JONES orphan of Lewis JONES, 16 Apr 1805, but these three records may not be for this Lewis JONES (LC OB 1804-05:332)]

JONES, Lewis; 20 Sep 1802
LC; Lewis JONES d. intestate; ord. to sell his slave Peter and div. the proceeds between John MASON who mar. Sally JONES & Patty JONES the legal reps. of sd. Lewis JONES. (LC Orders V 1802-03:194)
[Patty JONES orphan of Lewis JONES chose Peter TANKERSLEY as her gdn, 15 Dec 1800 (LC Orders 21 1799-1800:201); Patty JONES orphan of Lewis JONES chose Moses GEORGE as her gdn., 20 Sep 1802 (LC Orders V 1802-03:194); Moses GEORGE was the gdn. of Patty JONES orphan of Lewis JONES, 16 Apr 1805 (LC OB 1804-05:332); Jn. MASON, son of Alley MASON, mar. Sally JONES, LC, bond 12 Apr 1802 (MLBLC:51)]

JONES, Loftis; T 19 Nov 1802; 13 Dec 1802. NC; INV, [m]. (NC RB 16:484)
[Wm. JONES orphan of Loftis JONES chose Moses LUNSFORD as his gdn., NC 12 Jan 1819 (NC OB 1816-20:320)]

JONES, Mary; 2 Sep 1805
RC; Nunc. will; on 11 Jul 1805, Mary COATS, wife of Thomas COATS, deposed that sometime during the latter part of last winter or early in the spring, Mary JONES, a blind woman of a sickly habit, ancient and very

infirm, sent for her and told her that a heifer belonging to the sd. JONES should go to her grson. Henry Taylor DRAKE; on 11 Jul 1805, Nancy CARR of LP deposed that she was present at James DRAKE's on 25 Jan 1805 when Mary JONES, a very ancient, sickly, blind, and infirm woman in her last illness declared that she wanted James DRAKE to hold fast of her property what he had and that she wanted James DRAKE's son Richard Fendall DRAKE to have her bed and that Mary JONES departed this life the day after making this declaration. (RC WB 9:258)
[A Jas. DRAKE mar. Jenny JONES, WC, bond 2 Jan 1793 (MLBWC:20)]

JONES, Polly; PO 12 Nov 1810; 10 Jun 1811
NC; INV, $758.60; included one large schooner and one small schooner (each worth $200). (NC RB 19:58)
[Polly JONES was the wid. of Jos. JONES who in his will (NC 2 Sep 1803 - 14 Jan 1811) left her his whole est. including two boats, "one a scuner and the other a slup;" in Polly JONES' nunc. will which was sworn on 24 Oct 1810, she asked that her est. be div. into 4 parts for Catesby JONES, Rich. JONES, Stephen HAYNIE and Wm. SWIFT (NC RB 18:501, 514); Polly JONES died on 25 Oct 1810 (NC OB 1807-11:217)]

JONES, Robert; 14 Feb 1798; 21 Jul 1800
LC; WILL; my land & plant. w/o I now live to dau. Betty RICH during her life; at dau's death land to be eq. div. between my two grsons Robert RICH & James JONES (both under 21); wife Eve JONES & dau. Betty RICH to have use of whole est; at wife's death est. to be eq. div. between daus. Betty RICH & Eve JONES; sons Robert JONES & William JONES to have only 1 shilling; friends Capt George DAVENPORT & Henry HAZARD exors.; WITS: Alex. MARSH, Rodham LUNSFORD. (LC WB 28:41)

JONES, Robert; PO 12 May 1812, T 24 Sep 1812; 12 Oct 1812
NC; settled Martin HAYNIE's acct. of his gdnship. of the orphans of Robert JONES dec'd & possessed Silas SNOW who mar. Nancy JONES with his wife's proportion of Robert JONES' est. and with his wife's proportion of Samuel & Susannah JONES' part of Robert JONES' est. & possessed Elizabeth BETTS who was Elizabeth JONES one of the heirs of Robert JONES with her proportion of Samuel & Susannah JONES' part of Robert JONES' est, the sd. Samuel & Susannah being dead. (NC GA 1788-1824:305)
[Martin HAYNIE was gdn. of Betty, Nancy & Sam. JONES orphans of Robt. JONES, 12 Mar 1810 (NC OB 1807-11:158); Silas SNOW mar. Nancy JONES, NC, bond 2 Feb 1809; Elizabeth JONES mar. Elisha BETTS, wid, NC, bond 11 Jul 1804 (MLBNC:9, 93)]

JONES, Samuel; PO 10 Jul 1815, T 24 Jul 1815; 14 Aug 1815
NC; INV, [m]; includes only Negro boy William; William was appraised in the est. of Robert CROCKET through a mistake of the appraisers. (NC RB 20:173)
[The est. of Sam. JONES was ord. to be admin. by Thos. J. HAYES, NC, 10 Jul 1815 (NC OB 1811-1816:349)]

JONES, Samuel; PO 10 Nov 1823; 13 Jun 1825. NC; INV, [m]. (NC RB 24:257)

JONES, Sanford; PO 2 Jun 1800, T 20 Jun 1800; 1 Jun 1807
RC; DIV of 214-ac. tract adj Totuskey Mill Pond among the widow (52 ac), Molley JONES (54 ac), Melinda JONES (54 ac) & Sanford JONES. (RC AB 3:184)
[Totuskey Mill Pond must have been located at Totuskey Mill (also known as Hammock's, Wither's and Moore's Mill) on Mill Branch between Haynesville and Emmerton (Miller:62, 102)]

JONES, Sanford; T 19 Feb 1814; 1 Apr 1814
RC; DIV of land between Sanford JONES & Mary JONES. (RC AB 3:315)

JONES, Sarah; 15 May 1824; 22 Nov 1824
WC; WILL; to dau. Kitty JONES all the prop. whereof I die possessed & all my interest in the est. of my bro. John JONES dec'd; 2 bros Charles & Feilder JONES exors; WITS: J[ames]. JETT, Jn. REDMAN, Bend. JOHNSON. (WC DW 25:123)

JONES, Vincent; 6 Oct 1820; 2 Mar 1824
RC; WILL; one third of est. to wife Patty JONES during her lifetime; to sons Richard Burgess JONES & George Saunders JONES all land in RC after allotting to my wife Martha [sic] JONES one third of sd. land; wife's third to son Vincent JONES at her death; dau. Susannah shall equally share & inherit her eq. & proportionable share with the rest of my girls in case that she or her representative will not bring as a claim against my est. a bond which I gave to James SCATES for the benefit of my dau. Susannah and in case she should bring this claim she shall not inherit any other part of my est; balance of pers. est. including Negroes to be sold and eq. div. between my girl children: [Juletey], [Shilotte] Temple, Mary Ann, & Martha [Julinah] JONES; friends Joseph BELFIELD & Joshua REAMY exors.; WITS: Wm. MOTHERSHEAD, Thos. JENKINS, Jas. BROWN. (RC WB 10:37)
[Vincent JONES mar. Martha JENKINS, WC, bond 30 May 1814 (MLBWC:37); Thos. SANDERS & Susanna his wife, pltfs., vs. Charlotte T. JONES, Mary Ann JONES, Martha [S.] JONES, Rebecca M. JONES & Vincent JONES and Nicholas QUESENBURY & [m] his wife, defts.; Dominick BENNEHAN aptd. gdn. to infant children Charlotte, Mary Ann, Martha, Rebecca & Vincent JONES. 4 Apr 1826 (RC OB 27:52); Thos. SANDERS mar. Susanna JONES, RC, bond 22 Sep 1819; Nich. QUESENBURY mar. Martha JONES, RC, bond 25 Jul 1825 (MRC:165, 179); Thos. R. BARNES aptd. gdn. to Vincent JONES orphan of Vincent JONES, 5 Jun 1827 (RC OB 27:169)]

JONES, Vincent; T 11 Mar 1824; 6 Jun 1825. RC; INV, $836.22; includes Negro Hannah. (RC WB 10:78)

JONES, Violet; 16 Jun 1806
LC; Overseers of the Poor to bind out John JONES orphan of Violet JONES. (LC Orders D22 1805-08:193)
[Overseers of the Poor to bind out [Monroe] JONES son of Violet JONES to Ellyson CURRIE, 21 Jun 1813 (LC Orders 24:156)]

JONES, Walter (Dr.); PO 11 Mar 1816; 14 Jul 1817
NC; INV of slaves, NC; $6250.00; includes the following Negroes: Reuben, Dennis, Charles, Davy, Mary Ann, Sarah & child, Mima, Pressy & her child Mary Ann, Barbara, Sophy, Tilda, Jim, Jack, Venus, Eliza, Nelly, Charity, Joe, William, Robert, Melinda, Stephen. (NC RB 21:213)
[In his will (NC 11 Jan 1816 - 11 Mar 1816), Dr. Walter JONES named his children Eliz. CURRIE, Ann PECK, Maria JONES, Lucius JONES, Walter JONES, and Frederick JONES (NC RB 20:362); Billy late slave of Dr. Walter JONES, emancipated in his will, granted permission to reside in NC, NC 12 Jan 1819 (NC OB 1816-20:322)]

JONES, Walter (Dr.); PO 5 Jan 1817, T 14 Jan 1817; 14 Jun 1821
NC; DIV of slaves; Lot 1 (Charles, Sarah & child Nelly, Jim, Jack) to Lucius JONES; Lot 2 (Dennis, Barbary, Charity, Joe, William) to Maria JONES; Lot 3 (Davy, Mime, Robert, Stephen, Melinda, Venus) to Ellyson CURRIE in right of Elizabeth CURRIE; Lot 4 (Reuben, Sophy, Tilda, Eliz, Prissey & child Mary Ann) to John PECK in right of Ann PECK; Mime for herself & her

children waived the right to choose to whom she would belong & Mary Ann waived the right of choosing to whom Eliza would belong; Mary Ann for herself chose Anne PECK for her mistress. (NC RB 21:221)
[Ellyson CURRIE mar. Eliz. F. JONES, dau. of Walter JONES, NC, bond 14 Dec 1812; Jn. PECK, of RC, mar. Anne JONES, dau. of Walter JONES, NC, bond 18 Jun 1812 (MLBNC:25, 81)]

JONES, Walter (Dr.); [m]; 11 Jun 1821. NC; INV, [m]. (NC RB 22:574)

JONES, Walter (Dr.); T 25 Nov 1823
NC; DIV of Hayfields Tract among Miss Maria JONES (rec'd the house lot), E[lyson] CURRIE (rec'd the meadow lot), Mrs Anna PECK (rec'd the mill lot), and Mr. CURRIE. (NC RB 23:418)
[The Hayfields Tract was located in northern NC between Hyacinth and Gibeon Church (Miller:64)]

JONES, William; PO 8 Sep 1806, T 27 Nov 1806; 8 Dec 1806
NC; INV, £90.13.0. (NC RB 17:487)
[In his will (NC 21 Jul 1806 - 8 Sep 1806), Wm. JONES of SSP named his dau. Nancy JONES and son Sam. JONES; he also left legacies to his wife and the rest of his children [nfi] (NC RB 17:460); Thos. JONES was aptd. gdn. of Sally JONES orphan of Wm. JONES, NC, 15 Nov 1814 (NC OB 1811-15:259); Albert G. PLUMMER aptd. gdn. of Sally JONES orphan of Wm. JONES, NC 13 May 1822 (NC OB 1820-25:195, 313)]

Judy [free Negro]; 23 Sep 1807; 4 Apr 1808
RC; WILL; all pers. est. & all land given to me by my friend & master John FAWCETT to friend Joseph SCATES; old woman Sarah & her husband Will may continue on my sd. land & work the same free from rent during the period of the sd. Sarah's natural life; friend Thomas JONES exor.; WITS: Wm. BOWING, Geo. NEWMAN, Jesse BOWING. (RC WB 9:319)
[This Jn. FAWCETT (d. RC, 1802) is prob. the one named as an ex. of the will of Geo. Lee TURBERVILLE (d. RC 1798) (RC WB 9:91); *see also Jn. FAWCETT above*]

JYLES, William; 1775; [m]
WC; WILL; £15 to dau. Betty; £8 to dau. Anne; three children Eliz., Anne & Winne JYLES; Thomas CHILTON exor.; wits: Jn. MOXLEY, Abraham WEAVER, Job WIGLEY. (WC Unrec Wills 1755-1800 #15)
[This must be the Wm. JYLES who is named as a s-i-l in the will of Adam WEAVER (WC, 30 Nov 1770 - 25 Jun 1771) (WC DW 15:131)]

KEENE, Thomas; the son of Newton and Sarah (EDWARDS) KEENE mar. Ann McADAM, dau. of Jos. McADAM, bef. 20 Apr 1785; he had four children by Ann: Sarah Gaskins, Betsy McAdam, Ann, and Janetta. (NC CC 1805-030)
[Further details on the children of Thos. KEENE are provided by a subsequent CC: Sarah Gaskins KEENE mar. Thos. OLDHAM, NC, bond 4 Dec 1805; Betsy McAdam KEENE mar. Bushrod M. BEACHAM, NC, bond 26 Jan 1808; Ann KEENE mar. (1) Wm. [L.] GARNER, NC, bond 10 May 1815 and (2) Albert G. PLUMMER, NC, bond 31 Mar 1821; and Janetta KEENE mar, Chas DAMERON, wid., NC, bond 17 Apr 1822; he also seems to have had a son Jn. N. G. T. E. KEENE (MLBNC:6, 25, 40, 78. 83; NC CC 1821-002)]

KEEVE, James; PO 12 Jan 1818, T 27 Jan 1818; 14 Dec 1818
NC; Negro Samuel belonging to James KEEVE dec'd was sold to Griffin H. FOUSHEE for $410; proceeds less commission of $21 div. among Samuel M. BLUNDON (received 1/3); Hiram CORBELL gdn. to Leroy KEEVE & Sally KEEVE (received the other two thirds). (NC RB 21:558)

KEEVE, Thomas; PO 12 Feb 1816, T 29 Feb 1816; 11 Mar 1816
NC; allotted to Martin BLUNDON & Judith his wife her dower in the est. of her late husband Thomas KEEVE; BLUNDON rec'd Negroes Quanna and boy Randle and land adj. Sally [HAYES], Little Cove, and Hely WILDY. (NC RB 20:381; OB 1816-20:8)
[In MLBNC, p. 11 the bond of Martin M. BLUNDON dated 3 Jan 1816 Judith KEEVE's name is incorrectly recorded as Judith KEENE, wid; and on p. 62 the marriage bond of Thos. KEEVE, Jr. to Judith CORBELL, 8 Jun 1809, Thomas' name is incorrectly listed as "KEENE;" since there were both KEENE and KEEVE families in NC at the same time, great care must be taken to distinguish between them; in his will (NC 18 Oct 1814 - 14 Nov 1814) Thos. KEEVE names his oldest son Leroy, his next oldest son James and daus. Sally and Eliz. as well as his aunt Sally HAYES; he mentions his wife & mother but does not name them (NC RB 20:76); Hiram CORBELL was aptd. gdn. of Leroy, Sally & Jas. KEEVE orphans of Thos. KEEVE, NC, 14 Jul 1817 (NC OB 1816-20:157); Hiram HARDING aptd. gdn. of Leroy KEEVE orphan of Thos. KEEVE, 13 Feb 1826 (NC OB 1825-30:67)]

[KEEVE], Thomas; PO 14 Mar 1815; 8 Sep 1817
NC; INV, $2657.42 1/2; includes the following Negroes: Samuel, Joanna & child Hannah, Salley (girl), Silva & child Henry, John (a boy), Huldy (girl), Easter & child Randolph, Anne (girl), Alice. (NC RB 21:237)

KELLUM, Elizabeth; T 30 Oct [?]; 11 Aug 1823. NC; INV, $68.59. (NC RB 23:353)

KELLUM, Elizabeth; T 30 Oct 1821; 8 Sep 1823 NC INV. (NC RB 23:360)

KELLUM, William L.; PO 8 Sep 1806, T 26 [Sep 1806]; 8 Jun 1807
NC; INV, £294.12.6; includes Negroes old woman Rachel and young woman Lucey. (NC RB 17:533)
[In his will (NC 14 Sep 1804 - 10 Feb 1806), Wm. Lattimore KELLUM named his wife Ann and children Jn. Liston KELLUM, Wm. KELLUM, Rich. KELLUM, Ann KELLUM and Molley KELLUM (NC RB 17:379)]

KELLY, James; PO 21 Apr 1795; 21 Sep 1795
LC; INV, £366.0.6; includes Negroes: [James], Joseph, [Ted], Lucy, Nanny, Sam, Harry. (LC EB 24:49)

KELLY, James; 15 Feb 1798; 7 Jun 1802.
LP, RC; WILL; wife Susannah; youngest sons Alexander Doniphan & Spicer the land w/o I now live with the tenement BALDERSON lives on & the mill thereunto annexed to be eq. div; dau. Elizabeth OLIFF; grson. James PAINE son of Richard PAINE; dau. Molly ASBURY; 4 sons: John, James, Alexander, & Spicer; sons John & Alexander exors; [no wits]; will presented by Hen. SISSON, Griffin GARLAND & Jas. KELLY Jr. (RC WB 9:173)
[Jas. KELLY (1737-1802) was the son of Alexander KELLY (d. 1754) & Eliz. WILLSON; he mar. his cousin Susan WILLSON (b. 1741); Hen. ASBURY mar. (2) Sally Maulden KELLY, RC, bond 17 Feb 1792; Thos. OLIVE mar. Eliz. KELLY, RC, bond 4 Nov 1793; Rich. PAYNE mar. Susannah KELLY, RC, bond 1 Mar 1790 (MRC:5, 110, 111, 151, 155)]

KELLY, James; PO Jun 1806; 7 Jul 1806
RC; admin. acct. by John KELLY & Alexander D. KELLY mentions R. PAYNE gdn. of James PAYNE, grdau. Susanna W. ASBURY & grchil who were the children of Thomas OLIVE, John KELLY, James KELLY, Alexander D. KELLY & Spicer W. KELLY. (RC AB 3:159)

KELLY, James; PO 20 Feb 1809; 18 Dec 1809

LC; INV, [m]; includes Negroes: James, Joe, Sam, Harry, Nancy, Beck, Winny, [?]. (LC EB 27:65)

KELLY, James Jr.; PO May 1815, T 2 Jan 1819; 5 Jun 1820
RC; DIV of land (along Rappahannock Creek) among 5 heirs including Jonas HINSON & Polly his wife. (RC AB 3:689)
[This is Jas. KELLY, Jr. who mar. Mary DYE, RC, bond 6 Aug 1792 (MRC:111); on the mot. of Jn. MARKS & Caty his wife that that part of the land in this county whereof Jas. KELLY died seized which was assigned to Mary KELLY the wid. of the sd. KELLY has lately come by descent from the sd. Jas. KELLY who died intestate to Nancy BOWEN, Caty MARKS, Polly HINSON & Betsey KELLY, an infant, children and heirs of sd. Jas. KELLY; Jonas & Polly HINSON were residents of Ky. at this time; 4 Mar 1823 (RC OB 26:37); Jesse BOWING mar. Nancy KELLY, dau. of Molly KELLY, WC, 24 Mar 1810 (MLBWC:7); Jonas HINSON mar. Polly KELLY, dau. of Molly KELLY, WC, bond 30 Jul 1810 (MLBWC:31); a mar. between Jn. MARKS and Catherine MARKS [sic], bond 15 Jan 1821, is listed in MLBWC:43; can this be an error for Catherine KELLY?; the court certified that Nancy BOWEN wife of Jesse BOWEN, Cath. MARKS wife of Jn. MARKS and Eliz. JENNINGS wife of Jn. JENNINGS are the only surviving heirs of Mary KELLY the wife of Jas. KELLY who was the dau. of Fauntleroy DYE dec'd except Polly HINSON the wife of Jonas HINSON dec'd who removed to the state of Kentucky about 15 years ago, 2 May 1825 (RC OB 26:305), however a Jonas HINSON was the head of a household in RC in the 1820 census.]

KELLY, James Sr. 5 Dec 1803. RC; INV. (RC WB 9:218)

KELLY, John; 4 Feb 1815; 6 Mar 1815
LP, RC; WILL; all land to son John KELLY; dau. Kittey M. KELLY; dau. Julia KELLY; land & [slave] Sam to be hired out to support children; 3 friends James SCATES, Daniel SANDERS, & William SANDERS exors; WITS: Hudson MORRIS, Eliza H. CLAYTOR, Robt. JENKINS. (RC WB 9:465)

KELLY, John; [m]; 5 Aug 1817. RC; INV, $343.32. (RC WB 9:565)

KELLY, Sally; 10 Feb 1821; 1 Jul 1822
RC; WILL; mother Mary KELLY; sis. Elizabeth; son Reuben KELLY; sis. Caroline; friend John MARKS ex.; WITS: Enoch FINCH, Jos. N. JONES, Jesse BOWING. (RC WB 9:726)

KELLY, Spicer W.; 7 Mar 1803; 6 Jun 1803
RC; WILL; bro. James; bro. Alexander D.; sis. Elizabeth OLIFF; nephew James PAYNE; nieces Susannah W. ASBURY & Susannah W. KELLY (dau. of bro. John KELLY); bro. John ex; WITS: Jn. McCORMICK, Wm. THOMPSON, Wm. KELLY, Reuben KELLY; RC WB 9:212)
[Spicer KELLY was a son of Jas. KELLY (d. RC 1802) of LP (*see above*); his sis. Eliz. mar. Thos. OLIFF, RC, bond 4 Nov 1783 (RC WB 9:173; MWO:268)]

KELSICK, Mary; PO Jul 1806; 2 Feb 1808
RC; settlement of John WEATHERS' acct. as curator and admin. of the est. of Mary KELSICK dec'd and div. the sd. est. among William MORGAN in behalf of his wife who was Isabella B. KELSICK, Eleanor B. THORNTON, John WEATHERS in behalf of his wife who was Rebecca B. KELSICK. (RC AB 3:198)
[Wm. MORGAN mar. Isabella Barber (KELSICK) LAWSON, the wid. of Rich. LAWSON and dau. of Younger & Mary (BARNES) KELSICK, between 1792 and 1806; Jn. WEATHERS mar. Rebecca Beckwith KELSICK, RC, bond 4 Jan 1790 (MRC:115, 138, 225)]

KEM, Amy; 9 Oct 1815; 16 Feb 1818

LC; WILL; grson. Hiram CHILTON; d-i-l Lucy KEM; grdau. Sally Kirk CHILTON; residue of est. to dau. Elizabeth CHILTON during her life; at dau's death residue to be eq. div. among all her children except Hiram & Sally Kirk; friend Spencer GEORGE & grson. Hiram CHILTON exors; WIT: Spencer GEORGE. (LC WB 28:186)
[This is Amy the wid. of (1) Wm. DAVIS (d. LC bef. Feb 1785) and (2) Jos. KEM; her dau., Eliz., by Wm. DAVIS, mar. Andrew CHILTON, LC, bond 23 Dec 1788 (MRC:73, 211)]

KEM, Amy; PO 16 Feb 1818; 20 Apr 1818
LC; INV at the house of Andrew CHILTON, $78.43. (LC EB 27:421)

KEM, Burgess Kirk; 17 Sep 1816
LC; Enoch GEORGE aptd. gdn. to Jn., [Roxa], Lucy, & Susan KEM orphans of Burgess K. KEM. (LC Orders 24:336)
[Burgess Kirk KEM was the son of Amy and Jos. KEM, who named him in his will (LC 25 Jul 1790 - Feb 1791) (LC EB 22:294); David EDWARDS aptd. gdn. to Jn., Roxalana or Roxey, Lucy, and Susannah KEMM orphans of Burgess K. KEMM, 16 Jun 1823 (LC OB 25:379); *see also LC CC 1818-001*]

KEM, Henry; PO 21 Apr 1795 T 4 May 1795; 21 Jun 1796. LC; INV, £31.13.0. (LC EB 24:17)

KEM, Henry; PO 17 Feb 1800, T 27 Mar 1800; 20 Oct 1800. LC; distribution of est. among creditors. (LC EB 24:126)

KEM, Henry; PO 18 Jun 1804; 17 Sep 1804
LC; DIV of money belonging to the est, £5.14.3 between Mrs. Elizabeth MARSH, the wid., in her own right & as the gdn. of Polly KEM orphan of the dec'd; there was no gdn. for Elizabeth KEM the other orphan; the amount of money due the sd. est. in the hands of the ex. of Maj. James EWELL was not provided to the clerk of the court, but it appeared that £7.3.4 was due from EWELL's est. (LC EB 24:278)
[Betty KEM mar. Wm. MARSH, LC, 26 Jan 1796 (MWO:235); Betsey KEM orphan of Hen. KEM chose Moses ROBINSON as her gdn.; the heirs of Hen. KEM included Eliz. KEM, Polly KEM by the sd. Eliz. her gdn. and Betsy KEM by Moses ROBINSON her gdn., 18 Feb 1805 (LC OB 1804-05:281)]

KEM, Henry; PO 16 Apr 1806, T 24 May 1806; 15 Sep 1806
LC; sale of land and DIV of proceeds between Moses ROBINSON gdn. to Betsy KEM orphan of Henry KEM & Elizabeth MARSH gdn. to Polly KEM. (LC EB 24:372)

KEM, James; 18 May 1810
NC; Jane, Mary & Sally KEM were recognized as sisters and only heirs of James KEM late a private in the 5th US Regiment of infantry. (NC OB 1807-11:187)

KEM, John; PO 10 Jul 1809; 9 Oct 1809
NC; possessed Jane KEMM with a bond of $26.50 which appears to be her proportionable part of the lands of her late father John KEMM. (NC RB 18:241)
[James KEM for himself and as gdn. of Polly, Jane & Sally KEM heirs of Jn. KEM brought suit to sell the lands of Jn. KEM (NC OB 1807-11:53); Jane KEM to be allotted her proportion of the sale of the lands of her late father Jn. KEM, NC 10 Jul 1809 (NC OB 1807-11:113)]

KEM, Joseph; Mar 180[7]
LC; list of all the slaves that Amy KEM holds as dower in the est. of her dec'd husband Joseph KEM: Harry (age 70), Joseph (10), [?] (7), Harry (3),

[Bass] (12), Jacob (2), Milly (45), Sarahann (28), Sally (25), [Mareah] (14), Wilmouth (12), [Delia] (5), [Hannah] (18). (LC EB 27:63)
[Jos. KEM, in his will (LC 25 Jul 1790 - Feb 1791), named his wife Amy, his son Burgess Kirk KEM (under 21), his daus. Susanna KEM (under 20) & Molly THOMPSON, his s-i-l Rich. DAVIS, his d-i-l Judith DAVIS and his sis. Sukey KEM (LC WB 22:294)]

KEM, Lucy; T 30 May 181[5]; 17 Mar 1817. LC; INV. (LC EB 27:359)

KENDALL, William; 12 Dec 1804; 27 Apr 1807
WC; WILL; wife Peggy use of whole est. during widowhood; son John Spilman KENDALL one Negro boy when 21; son William Fisher KENDALL Negro boy Edward when 21; whole est. to be div. between two sons; wife, Samuel KENDALL, & William [BOWLER] exors; WITS: Jas. MORRIS, Jas. KENDALL, Jessee KENDALL. (WC DW 21:341)

KENDALL, William; T 9 Nov 1808; Oct 1811
WC; INV, £834.1.10; includes Negroes Charles, lad Daniel, boys Baylor & Edmond, Hester, Fanny, girl Caty, Peggy & 2 children (say her own), Viary & child Nisa; Samuel MOTHERSHEAD mar. Margaret the wid. of William KENDALL. (WC RI 9:298)
[Sam. MOTHERSHEAD mar. Margaret KENDALL, WC, bond 19 Apr 1808 (MLBWC:47; WC Orders 1807-10:177)]

KENNAN, John; 1 Jan 1821
RC; Samuel MISKELL aptd. gdn. of Lefever KENNAN orphan of John KENNAN. (RC OB 25:96)
[Wm. KENNAN orphan of Jn. KENNAN chose Edmnd NORTHEN as his gdn., 7 Oct 1822 (RC OB 25:339); Lefever CANNON by Sam. MISKELL his next friend & gdn., Wm. CANNON by Edmund NORTHEN his next friend, compl. vs. Eliza CANNON now Eliza NORTHEN, 3 Feb 1823 (RC OB 26:23); Lefevre KENNON mar. Eliz. MISKELL, RC, bond 25 Jun 1828 (MRC:112)]

KENNER, [fnu]; PO 10 Dec 1821, T 25 Jan 1822; 10 Jun 1822
NC; as a result of a suit, John COLES, pltf., against Brereton KENNER, Winder KENNER, Jane KENNER & Elizabeth HARCUM, defts.; Jos. EDWARDS aptd. gdn. to Jane KENNER & Catherine ROBINSON aptd. gdn. to Elizabeth HARCUM both infants; commissioners & surveyor aptd. to survey and div. lands among pltf. & defts.; John COLES rec'd 108 ac.; Elizabeth HARCUM rec'd 35 ac; Jane KENNER rec'd 58 ac.; Mrs. KENNER's dower land on Bridge Neck amounted to 208 ac. (NC RB 23:166)
[The land in question was held in right of Mary KENNER the grandmother of Brereton and Winder KENNER; Jane KENNER is a sis. of Brereton & Winder and Mary HARCUM the mother of Eliz. was another sis. (NC CC 1821-003); Mary P. KENNER, ward of V. HARCUM, mar. Vincent HARCUM, NC, bond 9 Dec 1811 (MLBNC:46); Miller:16 locates Bridge Neck south of the Little Wicomico River in the Fairfields District of NC]

KENNER, John B.; 15 May 1819; 12 Jul 1819
SSP, NC; WILL; all est. to wife Sarah KENNER; at wife's death to be eq. div. among dau. Elizabeth LAMKIN's children; in case my son John D. KENNER should come here again he shall be paid $30 and no more; wife Sarah extx.; WITS: Sam. B. BLACKWELL. (NC RB 22:80)
[Jn. B. KENNER mar. Sarah DOWNING, dau. of Jn. & Hannah (FALLIN) DOWNING, NC, lic. 11 Oct 17[77] (MRC:212); Eliz. KENNER mar. Chas. LAMKIN, NC, bond 8 Apr 1815 (MLBNC:65); on the mot. of Jn. KENNER ord. that Rich. KENNER, Eliz. KENNER & Sally KENNER be summoned to show cause why the lands of Jn. B. KENNER should not be sold and

proceeds div., NC 15 May 1825 (NC OB 1820-25:456); Jn. B. KENNER & Sarah his wife and his children Jn. D. and Eliz. KENNER sued for a div. of the Negroes which descended to Hannah SHEARMAN (sis. of Sarah KENNER and wife of Martin SHEARMAN) from her father Jn. DOWNING; the Negroes were: Mima (old), Joe (much afflicted), Winny, Letty, girl Phebe (in Louisa Co. with J. DOWNING), boy Charles (age 3 afflicted with ricketts), boy Tom (very likely) and boy Lewis (mulatto) (NC CC 1818-006)]

KENNER, Rodham; PO 9 Jan 1813, T 4 Nov 1815; 28 Nov 1815
WC; statement of slaves pursuant to the provisions & directions of the act. of the V[irginia] Legislature passed the 9th Jany 1813 entitled an act concerning slaves by Rodham KENNER who has within the last two weeks removed into the State of Virginia from Kentucky with a [view] & bona fide intention of becoming a resident to wit: Anthony about 60, Bob a mulatto about 30, & [Will] a boy about 10; KENNER swore that the slaves had not been brought into the Commonwealth for the purpose of sale or with intent to evade the laws of the Commonwealth to prevent the further importation of slaves or in any manner contrary to the provisions of the sd. act concerning slaves. (WC RI 10:38)

KENNER, Rodham; 2 Mar 1818; 25 Jan 1819
WC; WILL; all my est. to sis. Judith KENNER of East Tennessee; my old Negro woman Nancy to be set free; sis. Judith extx; WITS: Jn. BAYNE, Rich BAYNE; [Judith KENNER of the state of East Tennessee declined to act as extx. and William B. POPE was granted a certificate to obtain letters of admin. with the will annexed]. (WC DW 23:440, RI 10:334)

KENNER, Rodham; 18 Dec 1818; 12 Jul 1819
NC; tract of land known as Kennersley which descended from the late Rodham KENNER to his 2 daus. Rebecca FLANNERY & the late Mrs Susan THORNTON; dividing line is confirmed; WITS: Benj. TURNER, Jn. MIDDLETON, Jn. TIFFEE [finally recorded 11 Jun 1821]. (NC RB 22:571) [Rebecca KENNER mar. Michael FLANNERY, *see above*]

KENNER, Rodham; [m]; 23 Aug 1819
WC; INV, [m]; includes Negroes James, Bob, William. (WC RI 10:400)

KENNER, Winder (Col.); PO 8 Apr 1805; 14 Jun 1805
NC; allotment of dower in land to the wid. Mary KENNER; tract was located near the head of Sloop Landing Cove, and Rock Hole Creek. (NC RB 17:292) [This is Winder KENNER, son of Winder KENNER (d. NC 1762) who mar. Mary BALL, dau. of Col. Spencer BALL of LC, lic. Mar 1764 (MWO:212); Miller:136 locates Rock Hole Creek in East central NC south of Smith Point.]

KENNER, Winder; PO 10 May 181[3], T 19 Oct 1813; 14 Feb 1814
NC; Sarah KENNER wid. of Winder KENNER allotted her dower in the tract of land in Brereton's Neck it being land sold by sd. KENNER to John GORDON. (NC RB 19:506)
[Winder KENNER mar. Sarah DOWNING (dau. of Sarah DOWNING), NC, bond 11 Oct 1790 (MWO:213; NC CC 1809-007); this may be the Winder KENNER who was the father of Mary B. KENNER (who mar. Valentine HARCUM, NC, bond 9 Dec 1811), Brereton, Winder and Janetta KENNER (MLBNC:46; NC CC 1813-008)]

KENT, Daniel; PO 18 Mar 1811; 21 May 1811
LC; INV, $523.79; includes [Negro] James; John C. KENT admr. (LC EB 27:85)

KENT, Daniel; T 15 Jul 1811, Filed 15 Jul 1811; 15 Jul 1811

LC; list of all the slaves that has come to my possession by allotment of my dower of the slaves of the est. of Daniel KENT, /s/ Mary KENT: Molly (age 30), Sarah (33), Harriett (5). (LC EB 27:129)
[This is prob. the Dan. KENT who mar. Mary HUNTON, LC, bond 8 Jul 1809 (MLBLC:44)]

KENT, Jesse; PO 19 Dec 1814, T 4 Jan 1815; 15 Jul 1816. LC; INV, $46.05. (LC EB 27:339)

KENT, John C.; T 25 Dec 1812; 14 May 1821. NC; INV, [m]. (NC RB 22:520)
[The est. of Jn. C. KENT was ord. to be admin. by Sam M. SHEARMAN & Rich. TOWELL, NC, 14 Dec 1812 (NC OB 1811-1816:133); Thos. Y. HUNTON was aptd. gdn. of Dan. & Jas. M. KENT orphans of Jn. C. KENT, NC, 9 Oct 1815 (NC OB 1811-15:382); Jasper STOTT aptd. gdn. of Dan. & Madison KENT orphans of Jn. C. KENT, NC 10 Sep 1821 (NC OB 1820-25:139); allot Archibald HINTON & Nancy his wife her dower in the lands of Jn. C. KENT, NC 10 Sep 1821 (NC OB 1820-25:139); settlement with Susan HUNTON admx. of Thos. HUNTON the acct. of his gdnship. with Madison & Dan. KENT, 21 May 1822 (LC OB 25:303)]

KENT, Lodiwick; PO 19 Dec 1814, T 4 Jan 1815; 15 Jul 1816
LC; INV, $65.25; includes seven lots of tools. (LC EB 27:341)
[This may be the Lody W. KENT who mar. Caty BROOKS, LC, bond 19 Mar 1810 (MLBLC:45)]

KENT, Thomas; T 5 Mar 1815; 12 Jun 1815
NC; INV; includes Negroes Nancy, Fanny & child Fanny, boys William & Spencer, girl Mahala, boy Nelson, girls Mary & Judith and a schooner called the "Ann" with all her rigging valued at $261. (NC RB 20:147)
[In his will (NC 6 Nov 1814 - 9 Jan 1815), Thos. KENT named his wife Eliz., son Warner KENT, and daus. Louisa Ingram KENT & Salley Carter KENT (NC RB 19:597)]

KENT, William; 3 Aug 1793; 15 Jun 1807.
WP, NC; WILL; whole est. to wife Julian KENT; at wife's death est. to be eq. div. between 2 sons Billy Brown KENT & Rodham KENT; rest of children one shilling apiece and no more; friend Richard LUNSFORD & David [PALMER] exors; WITS: Asa SWANSON, Jn. TARKELSON, Wm. GOODRIDGE. (LC WB 28:101)

KENT, William; PO 13 Mar 1821; 11 Mar 1822
NC; INV, [m]; includes Negroes Isaac, Daniel, Billy, James, John, Spencer, Nelson, Sucky, Milly, Winney & child Susan, Delia & child Emanuel, Amy, Anna. (NC RB 23:111)

KENT, William; PO 16 Aug 1824; 21 Mar 1825. LC; INV, [m]. (LC EB 29:403)

KENT, William Jr.; Jun 1812; 13 Nov 1820
NC; WILL; whole est. to wife Elizabeth; at wife's death or remarriage, son William to have all my land; balance of est. to be eq. div. among my daus; [no ex. named]; WITS: Jn. GIBSON, Peter TANKERSLEY, Charles KELLEY; [admin with the will annexed granted Cyrus HAYNIE, 9 Jun 1828]. (NC RB 22:433)

KESTERSON, Elizabeth; T 22 Jan 1792; 10 Feb 1792
NC; Elizabeth KESTERSON gdn. to her 2 daus. Nancy & Elizabeth B. KESTERSON. (NC GA 1788-1824:116)

KESTERSON, Elizabeth; PO 13 Jan 1812, T 14 Jan 1812; 13 Jul 1812
NC; INV, [m]; div. of est. among James TIGNOR, Eunice BRIDGMAN, Elijah BLUNDON, & Elizabeth B. KESTERSON (each rec'd HHF worth $9.16 1/4). (NC RB 19:221)

[In her will (NC 23 May 1811 - 13 Jan 1812), Eliz. KESTERSON named her dau. Eliz. Berry KESTERSON, her grsons. Addison & Lemuel KESTERSON, her grdau. Polly KESTERSON, daus. Winifred BLUNDON, Eunice BRIDGEMAN, Nancy TIGNOR, and sons Jas. & Wm. KESTERSON (NC RB 19:139); Jas. TIGNOR mar. Nancy KESTERSON, NC, bond 12 Feb 1803; Eunice KESTERSON mar. Jos. BRIDGEMAN, NC, bond 22 Dec 1788 (MLBNC:12, 101)]

KESTERSON, James; T 10 Dec 1818; 22 Nov 1820. LC; INV $822.9[8 1/2]. (LC EB 29:49)

KESTERSON, James; PO 14 Aug 1820; 14 May 1821
NC; DIV of proceeds of sale of land belonging to the heirs of James KESTERSON; land was purchased by William A. KESTERSON & proceeds were payable to Kitty KESTERSON gdn. to the heirs to be div. among the orphans: William H. KESTERSON, Henrietta B. KESTERSON, Felicia C. KESTERSON & James B. KESTERSON. (NC RB 22:530)
[Jas. KESTERSON mar. two women named Kitty, (1) Kitty Chinn CARTER dau. of Jos. CARTER, LC, bond 4 Feb 1801 and (2) Kitty CHOWNING, LC, bond 16 Apr 1804 (MLBLC:45); Kitty KESTERSON aptd. gdn. to Wm., Henrietta, Felicia & Jas. KESTERSON orphans of Jas. KESTERSON, 16 Nov 1818 (LC OB 25:22); mot. of Kitty KESTERSON gdn. of Wm. H., Henrietta B., Felicia C. and Jas. B. KESTERSON orphans of Jas. KESTERSON to sell tract of land, NC 14 Aug 1820 (NC OB 1820-25:49)]

KESTERSON, William; PO 13 Jan 1812, T 15 Jan 1812; 9 Mar 1812
NC; INV & DIV of est. among Eliza B. KESTERSON (rec'd Epharam and lad Peter), James TIGNOR (rec'd Judith & Spencer), Unis BRIDGMAN (rec'd Polly & Solomon), Elijah BLUNDON (rec'd Jane & Sam). (NC RB 19:153)
[This is prob. Wm. KESTERSON the son of Eliz. KESTERSON and bro. of Eliza. B. KESTERSON, Nancy TIGNOR, and Eunice BRIDGEMAN (NC RB 19:139)]

KEW, John; T 30 Oct 1806; 22 Jun 1806
WC; INV, £122.4.6; includes Negro Celia & child. (WC RI 9:19)
[This is poss. the Jn. KEW who mar. Mary PURSLEY, WC, bond 9 May 1800 (MLBWC:37); Jn. PURSLEY was aptd. gdn. to defend the infant children of Jn. KEW dec'd to wit: Jn. H. KEW & Leanna KEW on a motion to sell the land of their father, 25 Feb 1811 (WC Orders 1810-13:82); Leanna KEW mar. Washington G. MARINER, WC, bond 25 Jan 1812 (MLBWC:43) *NB: But this would make Leanna only about 11 years old when she mar. if she was a dau. of Jn. KEW & Mary PURSLEY; perhaps Mary was a second wife.*]

KEW, Margaret; T 15 Feb 1811; Apr 1811. WC; INV, £88.11.0; includes Celia & child Hannah. (WC RI 9:242)

KIDD, Frances C.; 29 Jun 1818; 21 Jan 1822
LC; WILL; whole est. to dau. Alcinda Martin WOODY; John CHOWNING ex; WITS: Thos. MYERS, Wm. PAYNE. (LC WB 28:222)
[This is Frances TAPSCOTT, wid. of Rich. TAPSCOTT, who mar. Benj. KIDD, LC, bond 1 Aug 1798 (MLBLC:45, 73); Alcinda KIDD orphan of Benjamin KIDD chose Jn. LUNSFORD as her gdn., 16 Feb 1818 (LC Orders 24:414); Alcinda KID mar. Thos. WOODY, LC, bond 21 Feb 18[1]8 (MLBLC:80)]

KING, Samuel; T 25 Jul 182[1]; Jul 1823. WC; INV, $241.86. (WC RI 11:373)
[This may be the Sam. KING who mar. Sarah WROE the dau. of Jn. WROE (d. RC 1794) (RC DB 19:138)

KIRK, Anthony; PO 17 Sep 1798; 17 Jun 1799

LC; INV, [m]; includes Negroes George, Moses, Joe, John, Gabriel, Jean, Beck, Mima & child, Judith, Unis, Rachel. (LC EB 24:97)
[Anthony KIRK d. intest. in 1792 leaving a wid., Eliz., and two small children, Nancy Westley and Eliz.; his wid. d. in 1798; his dau. Eliz. mar. Jabez HUBBARD and his sis. Catherine mar. Chas. BRENT (LC CC 1810-007); Eliz. KIRK mar. Jabez HUBBARD, LC, bond 6 Jan 1808; Catherine KIRK mar. Chas. BRENT, LC, bond Dec 1791 (MLBLC:7, 39); Wm. KIRK aptd. gdn. of Eliz. KIRK orphan of Anthony KIRK, 17 Jun 1805 (LC Orders W 1804-05:398); Wm. KIRK aptd. gdn. of Nancy KIRK orphan of Anthony KIRK, 17 Sep 1805 (LC Orders D22 1805-08:60)]

KIRK, George; 20 Apr 1818
LC; Elizabeth KIRK orphan of George KIRK chose One[siphoras] HARVEY as her gdn. (LC Orders 24:426)

KIRK, James; T 19 Jan 1806; 10 Sep 1806
LC; list of slaves held for life by Mary KIRK, wid.: Hannah (70 years), Richard (52), Thomas (22), Jenny (24), Jess (17), Daniel (14), Hannah (12), James (20), Molly (5), Fanny (1). (LC EB 24:345)

KIRK, Mary; 10 Jan 1815; 17 Jul 1815.
WCP, LC; WILL; est. to be eq. div. between five friends: Eppa NORRIS, Rawleigh DUNAWAY, Susannah DUNAWAY, Caty KEMM, Ann THRAILKIL; friends Eppa NORRIS & James ROBINSON exors; WITS: Jas. ROBINSON Jr., Jas. KELLY, Nancy ROBINSON. (LC WB 28:165)

KIRK, Randal; 12 Apr 1791; May 1792
WC; WILL; wife Elizabeth my land during her natural life; at wife's death to son Thomas KIRK on condition he will pay £10 apiece to his brothers & sisters, otherwise land to be sold and proceeds eq. div. between all children: Thomas, Randal Robertson, Jesse Nelson McCarty, Benedict Middleton and Mary Sisson KIRK; William HARRISON, Elizabeth KIRK & Thomas KIRK exors; WITS: Thos. MIDDLETON, Elijah WILLIAMS, Sam. HARRISON. (WC Unrec Wills 1755-1800 #40)

KIRK, Sarah Ann; T 24 Jan 1815; 21 Nov 1815. LC; INV. (LC EB 27:265)

KIRK, William; 19 Sep 1820; 16 Oct 1820
LC; WILL; third part of all my est. to wife Nancy D. KIRK during her life; at wife's death to be eq. div. among my children James KIRK, John KIRK, William KIRK, Harriett KIRK & Betsey KIRK & my grchildren William H. SYDNOR & Ann Mary SYDNOR; plant. where I now live including the mill to be div. between sons James & William; land devised to me by the late John STEPTOE & still & worm to son John KIRK; Negro girl Ann to dau. Harriett; Negro girl Judith to dau. Betsey; Negro woman Hannah now in the possession of William SYDNOR to grchildren William H. & Ann Mary SYDNOR; Negroes [Ransend] & Janette in the hands of son James for the benefit of dau. Nancy REVEER (wife of John REVEER); daus. Harriett & Betsey to have a home while single; $400 to educate son William; William's est. to be under the care of son James until he is 21; son James ex.; WITS: Ralph EDMONDS, Jn. HALL, Ephraim SPRIGGS; COD: son James to have Negro man Daniel (the carpenter) for his trouble carrying out my will; [same wits]. (LC WB 28:210)
[Wm. SYDNOR mar. Mary KIRK, dau. of Wm. KIRK, LC, bond 11 Feb 1817 (MLBLC:72); Nancy KIRK mar. Jn. W. REVERE, LC, bond 16 Jul 1804 (MLBLC:62); Eliz. KIRK orphan of Wm. KIRK chose Jas. KIRK for her gdn., 20 Nov 1820 (LC OB 25:172)]

KIRK, William; PO 21 Nov 1820, T 11 Dec 1820; 19 Feb 1821

LC; INV, $11,320.84; includes Negroes Moses, Roger, Daniel (carpenter, legacy to James KIRK), Jack, Tom (the miller), Randall, Daniel, Joseph, Armistead, Ben, [Sandra], [Randsome] (legacy to Mrs. Ann [REVERE], [Tom], Lewis, Ben (a boy), James, Isaac, Charles, Phillis, Nanney, [Mass], Jenney, [Angick], Charity, [Ammeny], Ann (legacy to Harriet KIRK), Keziah, Janette (legacy to Ann REVIRE), Judith (legacy to Elizabeth KIRK), Lucinda, Sally, Suckey, Hannah (legacy to William H. & Ann M. SYDNOR, [name unclear], Maria, [Prittanie], [Selva], Lucy, [Clarkey], Milly; PO 18 Dec 1820 the commissioners met on 28 Dec 1820 at the house of William KIRK and div. the Negroes among Ann KIRK the wid. (rec'd Old Jack, Tom the miller, Armstead, Keziah, Silva, Lucy, Charles, Winney, Sally, Tom, Mass, [Anzick], [?]), James KIRK (rec'd Ben, Amony, Phillis), John KIRK (rec'd Ben, Lucinda, Isaac), William SYDNOR gdn. to William H. & Ann M. SYDNOR (rec'd Joe, Sucky, Lucy, and Maria), William SAUNDERS who mar. Harriet KIRK (rec'd ?, Milly, [Prittanie], Roger], Elizabeth KIRK (rec'd Lewis, Jenny, Charity & Moses) and William H. KIRK (rec'd Randal, Charity, [James]), Ann REVERE (rec'd Randsome & Janette). (LC EB 29:61, 64)
[Wm. SAUNDERS mar. Harriett KIRK, LC, bond 23 Nov 1820 (MLBLC:65, 72)]

KIRKHAM, Alfred; T 28 Sep 1822; 11 Nov 1822
NC; INV, only item was a sloop called the "More Grog" valued at $70. (NC RB 23:252)

KIRKHAM, Vincent; 8 Apr 1822; 13 May 1822
NC; WILL; to mother Elizabeth BARNS one Negro woman Esther & her 4 children Peter, Samuel, Nancy & John; at mother's death Ester & increase to go to half bro. and half sisters, Lindsey, Nancy, Eliza & Jane BARNS; Stephen BARNS ex; WITS: Geo. C. ASHBURN, Lindsey BARNS; [probate granted to Stephen BARNS 13 Aug 1822]. (NC RB 23:153)
[Eliz. KIRKHAM wid. mar. Stephen BARNES, wid, NC, bond 4 May 1818 (MLBNC:5)]

KNIGHT, John; 14 Mar 1814
NC; Zephaniah KNIGHT orphan of Jn. chose Seth LUNSFORD as his gdn. (NC OB 1811-15:221)

KNOTT, Elender; 11 Apr 1786; [m]
WC; of Yeocomico; WILL; two Negro girls Dinah & Sillar to sis. Eliz. McCLANAHAM; b-i-l James McCLANAHAM to be ex. and pay all debts; WITS: Jn. CRITCHER, Andrew MORGAN. (WC Unrec Wills 1755-1800 #30)
[This is poss. Elenor WEST, dau. of Jn. WEST (d. NC 1759) and sis. of Sarah JEFFRIES (d. NC 1768), who mar. [James] KNOTT bef. 4 Jan 1759 (MWO:216)]

KNOTT, James C.; PO 8 Jul 1805, T 3 Aug [1805]; 14 Apr 1806
NC; INV, £465.11.9; includes Negroes Billy, Bob, Minor. (NC RB 17:398)
[Jas. KNOTT, wid., mar. Molly WALKER, wid., NC, bond 31 May 1791 (MLBNC:65); in his will (NC 20 Nov 1804-11 Feb 1805), Jas. C. KNOTT of SSP named his wife Molly KNOTT, his bro. Wm. (and William's wife Eliz.), his children Rich., Wm., Jas. & Polly, and his wife's dau. Eliz. W. WALKER (NC RB 17:258; NC CC 1829-007); Rich. KNOTT, the orphan of James C. KNOTT, chose Wm. ANDERSON as his gdn., NC, 14 May 1811 (NC OB 1807-11:255); as of 14 Mar 1815, Molly KNOTT had been dead more than 3 months (NC OB 1811-15:294)]

KNOTT, James C.; PO 12 Aug 1822, Oct 1822; 10 May 1824

NC; div. of lands of James C. KNOTT dec'd among the heirs: Richard KNOTT, Elizabeth WALKER, and an unidentified heir who rec'd Lot 3. (NC RB 23:456)

KNOTT, Molley; PO 14 Mar 1815; 8 Jan 1816
NC; has been dead more than 3 mos. and no one has applied to admin. her est.; sheriff was aptd. to admin. the est. and he could find no est. to admin. (NC RB 20:334)
[This is poss. Molly the wid. of James C. KNOTT (*see above*)]

KNOTT, Richard; T 28 Aug 1823; 8 Aug 1825
NC; INV, [m]; includes following Negroes: Isaac, Ann, & small boy Henry. (NC RB 24:294)
[This is prob. Richard KNOTT the son of Jas. C. KNOTT (*see above*)]

LACKEY, John; PO 12 Jan [1808], T 18 Feb 1808; 13 Jun 1808
NC; INV at the house of Mrs. Mary LACKEY, [m]. (NC RB 17:632)
[Jn. LACKEY mar. Mary CONWAY, wid., NC, bond 24 Sep 1799 (MLBNC:65)]

LAMBERT, James; 10 Apr 1803; 5 Dec 1803
RC; WILL; sis. Milly LAMBERT, sis. Molly HAYBURN; nephew James LAMBERT; George son of Charles HAYBURN; Joshua STONE; Betsy DOBYNS; friend George SISSON & nephew James LAMBERT exors; WITS: Wm. CLARK, Wm. SAMFORD. (RC WB 9:226)
[Jas. LAMBERT was the son of Wm. & Mary LAMBERT; the births of six children of Wm. & Mary are recorded in the NFPR: John (1741), William (1743), Mary Ann (1745), James (1750), Joanna (1756), and Milly (1757) (NFPR:113)]

LAMBERT, James; 6 Feb 1804. RC; INV. (RC WB 9:231)

LAMBERT, James; T 24 Mar 1815; 4 Aug 1817. RC; INV, $107.69. (RC WB 9:564)

LAMKIN, Ashton; PO 25 Mar 1806; 26 Jan 1807
WC; INV of Negroes includes Bett & child William, Beck, Haney, Reuben, Sisle, Old Jane, Hannah & child Spencer, Bill, Ozman, Jack, Dol appraised at £598; these were div. between Hannah M. LAMKIN & Willis GARNER who mar. Fanny G. LAMKIN. (WC RI 9:11)
[This is prob. the Ashton LAMKIN who mar. Hannah MIDDLETON, dau. of Robt. MIDDLETON, bef. 23 Jul 1777 (MWO:217); Willis GARNER mar. Frances LAMKIN, WC, bond 25 Nov 1805 (MLBWC:25)]

LAMKIN, Charles; PO 8 Jun 1812; 8 Mar 1813
NC; Chancery suit, James BEACHAM & Jane his wife, complts. against Polly LAMKIN, deft.; Thomas TAYLOR aptd. gdn. to the deft. an infant; commission ord. to div. the land between the parties acc. to the will of Charles LAMKIN; each claimant rec'd 35 1/2 ac. on the main road from Lewis LAMKIN's to the NC Court House. (NC RB 19:355)
[In his will (NC 23 [m] 1802 - 12 Apr 1803), Chas. LAMKIN named his son Chas. and daus. Jane & Polly LAMKIN (NC RB 16:542); Jas. BEACHAM mar. Jane LAMKIN, ward of Sam. HILTON, NC, bond 13 Jan 1807 (MLBNC:6)]

LAMKIN, George; [m]; 9 Jun 1801
NC; INV, £584.9.2; includes following Negroes Daniel, Sam, Ben, Nell, Reubin, Nelson, Lila, Nance, Siller. (NC RB 16:265)
[This is prob. Geo. LAMKIN who mar. Rebecca HUDNALL, dau. of Jos. HUDNALL of SSP (d. NC 1801-1802), NC, lic. 18 Sep 17[77] (MWO:218); in his will (NC 7 Apr 1800 - 8 Sep 1800), Geo. LAMKIN of SSP named his wife

Rebecah, and children Griffin, Chas. A., Mary F., Matthew, and Joseph LAMKIN; his bro. Matthew LAMKIN was one of his exors. (NC RB 16:173]

LAMKIN, Griffin; T 16 Dec 1822; 11 Mar 1823

NC; INV; includes Negroes Ben, boy James, Nelly, Felicia & child, Ellen, [Cannis]. (NC RB 23:289)

[Griffin LAMKIN was the son of Geo. LAMKIN of SSP (d. NC, 1800) (NC RB 16:173); he mar. Mary HAGGEMONS, NC, bond 8 Feb 1817 (MLBNC:65)]

LAMKIN, Lewis Jr.; 12 Jan 1818.

NC; Charles BELL aptd. gdn. of Malinda, James L. and Lewis ap Lewis LAMKIN orphans of Lewis LAMKIN, Jr. (NC OB 1816-20:212; OB 1825-30:276)

[Lewis LAMKIN Jr. mar. Griffithello (CLAUGHTON) BARNES, dau. of Jn. CLAUGHTON and wid. of Edw. BARNES, NC, bond 29 Oct 1811 (MLBNC:4, 65); in his will (NC 25 Jul 1813 - 14 Mar 1814), Lewis LAMKIN of SSP names his wife Griffithello and children Malinda Ann, James Lewis and Lewis ap Lewis; his friend Chas. BELL was ex. (NC RB 19:523); settle Chas. BELL's gdnship. of Linsey [sic], Jas., & Lewis LAMKIN orphans of Lewis LAMKIN and also Chas. L. BELL's gdnship. of Wm. M. BELL orphan of Thos. [BELL], 9 Feb 1829 (NC OB 1825-30:332)]

LANGLEY, William G.; PO 8 Dec 1806, T 20 Dec 1806; 8 Jun 1807

NC; INV, includes Negroes Job, woman Britanne, girls Fillis & Druciller. (NC RB 17:537)

LANGLEY, William G.; PO 12 Sep 1808, T 26 Nov 1808; 12 Feb 1810.

NC; INV, $926.25; includes Negroes Job, Britannia & child Ellen, girls Phillis & Druciller. (NC RB 18:316)

LANSDELL, Thomas; T 28 Apr 1815; 14 Jun 1824

NC; INV; includes Negroes Manuel, Daniel, Billey WIGGINS, Winny WIGGINS, Winney & child Elizabeth, Hiram, Rachel & child [sic] Lewis & Charlotte, Delila, Linsey, Charles, Judith, Betty, Nancy, Mime, Spencer, Mariah & child Moses, Jeremiah, Patty, Lee (since dead), Shadrick. (NC RB 23:498)

[This is prob. Thos. LANSDELL, wid., who mar. Mary BLACKWELL, NC, 18 Sep 1812 (MLBNC:66); the est. of Thos. LANSDELL was ord. to be admin. by Mary LANSDELL & Sam. BLACKWELL, NC, 13 Mar 1815 (NC OB 1811-1816:287); Thos. HUGHLETT was aptd. gdn. of Jn. M. and Thos. H. LANSDELL orphans of Thos. LANSDELL, NC 8 Sep 1817 (NC OB 1816-20:179); Jn. M. LANSDELL chose Rich. MITCHELL as his gdn. and sd. Rich. was also aptd. gdn. of Thos. H. LANSDELL orphans of Thos. LANSDELL, NC 12 Jan 1819 (NC OB 1816-20:320)]

LATTIMORE, Charles; PO 11 Oct 1802, T 28 Oct 1802; 12 Sep 1803

NC; INV, £60.7.6; includes Negroes Stephen, Joshua, Rawley, Levina & youngest child, Letty & child, Winney & child Job, Pleasant, Siner, Phillis, Mary, Sally, William; Elizabeth LATTIMORE extx. (NC RB 17:45)

[This is prob. Chas. LATTIMORE, Jr. who mar. Ruth SYDNOR, dau. of Anthony & Eliz. SYDNOR, NC, 9 Jun 1783 (MWO:220); in his will (NC 23 May 1802 - 11 Oct 1802), Chas. LATTIMORE of WicP named his wife Betsy and daus. Suckey & Sarah LATTIMORE and daughter's uncle Jn. SYDNOR (NC RB 16:464)]

LATTIMORE (LATTERMORE), Elizabeth; T 24 Jan 1815; 10 Mar 1817

NC; INV, $1886.90; includes Negro man Able, Syner, Pleasant, Ellen (child), Margery & child Delia, James. (NC RB 21:155)

[This is Eliz. BALL who mar. Chas. LATTIMORE, NC, bond 10 Aug 1795 (MLBNC:66); in her will (NC 1 Nov 1814 - 9 Jan 1815), she named her d-i-l Susan HUDNALL, neices Hannah PINCKARD, dau. of Cyrus PINCKARD, Sarah Lattimore BALL & Hannah G. BALL, bros. Thos. BALL & Jos. BALL, Seinthia BALL, dau. of Wm. BALL, and Eliz. Ann BALL, dau. of David BALL (NC RB 19:586); Suckey LATTIMORE mar. Warner HUDNALL, NC, bond 8 Jun 1812; Cyrus PINCKARD mar. (1) Alice BALL (dau. of David BALL), NC, bond 14 Nov 1796 (MLBNC:56, 82)]

LATTIMORE, William; 14 Jun 1819.

NC; Charles LATTIMORE chose Thomas SHEARMAN as his gdn. and the sd. SHEARMAN is aptd. gdn. to William LATTIMORE orphans of William LATTIMORE. (NC OB 1816-20:363)

[This is prob. the Wm. LATTIMORE who mar. Winifred (SHEARMAN) HURST the wid. of Kemp HURST on 13 Dec 1796 (MWO:221; NC CCs 1803-002 and 1809-018)]

LAWRENCE, Jane; 26 Sep 1808

WC; Overseers of the Poor to bind William Stuart LAWRENCE orphan of Jane LAWRENCE to James DOZIER, carpenter. (WC Orders 1807-10:204)

LAWSON, Daniel; 14 Mar 1814; 2 May 1814

LP, RC; WILL; wife Mary LAWSON; part of the tract w/o I now live lying on the north of a line beginning at the mouth of the branch between my residence & John GARLAND's & running a southwesternly course till it strikes the main road leading from the mouth of Totuskey and 3 slaves Job, Old Easter, & boy Jerry to neice Rebecca ALLISON; at her death to go to dau. Betsey DOBYNS; old free Judy, the wife of my fellow Bradley, should be permitted to remain on & occupy the small house and have the use of so much land as I have heretofore permitted her to cultivate during her life; rest of est. to dau. Betsey DOBYNS; s-i-l Thomas DOBYNS exor; WITS: Vin BRAMHAM, Vincent GARLAND. (RC WB 9:459)

[This is Dan. LAWSON, Sr. who mar. Mary GARLAND, RC, bond 25 Jun 1783; Betsy LAWSON mar. Thos. DOBYNS, dau. of Daniel LAWSON, Sr., RC, bond 5 Nov 1811 (MRC:56, 115); in MRC:115 two marriages are listed for Daniel LAWSON Junior; the first marriage, to Mary GARLAND, should prob. be for Daniel LAWSON Senior; Totuskey Creek arises west of Rainswood and empties into the Rappahannock River between Accaceek Point and Waverly Point (Miller:158)]

LAWSON, Daniel Jr.; 28 Sep 1812; 7 Dec 1812

RC; WILL; all est. to wife & she to be extx; Wit: Thos. P. SMITH. (RC WB 9:411)

[Dan. LAWSON Jr. mar. Catherine WILLIAMS, dau. of Thaddeus & Catherine (CORRIE) WILLIAMS, RC, bond 9 Jan 1809 (MRC:115)]

LAWSON, Epaphroditus; 21 Jul 1800

LC; Epaphroditus LAWSON orphan of Epaphroditus LAWSON chose Thomas JAMES as his gdn. (LC Orders 21 1799-1801:128)

LAWSON, Henry; 29 May 1800; 20 Jun 1803

LC; WILL; to wife Esther LAWSON one third of whole est; at wife's death her third to be eq. div. between my children: Thomas LAWSON, William LAWSON, Winnefred Kirk LAWSON, Sally Chinn LAWSON, Susannah Mitchell LAWSON, and Fanny LAWSON; all land & plant. w/o I now live & Negro Joe to son Henry Chinn LAWSON; Negro Letty to dau. Winnefred Kirk LAWSON; Negro Maria to dau. Sally Chinn LAWSON; wife Esther &

sons Henry Chinn & Thomas LAWSON exors; WITS: Augustine CARTER, Rawleigh TAPSCOTT, Martin SHEARMAN. (LC WB 28:72)
[Hen. LAWSON mar. Esther CHINN, LC, bond 21 Oct 1768 (MWO:221); Thos. LAWSON orphan of Hen. LAWSON chose Hen. C. LAWSON his gdn. and Wm. LAWSON orphan of Hen. LAWSON chose Esther LAWSON his gdn., 20 Jun 1803 (LC Orders V 1802-03:367)]

LAWSON, Henry; PO 19 Dec 1803; 20 Feb 1804
LC; DIV of est. among: the wid., Thomas LAWSON, William LAWSON, Winifred K. LAWSON, Sarah C. LAWSON, Susanna M. LAWSON, Fanny LAWSON. (LC EB 24:265)

LAWSON, John; 19 Apr 1794; 1[6] Feb 1795.
CCP, LC; in case I should die without an heir all my est. to wife Mary Tunstall LAWSON; William DEGGE admr; WITS: Wm. DEGGE, Geo. BRENT. (LC WB 28:12)
[Jn. LAWSON mar. Mary Tunstall [DEGGES], LC, bond 20 Jan 1794 (MLBLC:47, MWO:222)]

LAWSON, John; 16 Feb 1795; 20 Jul 1795
LC; INV, £283.10.6; includes Negroes: Fanny & child Mariah, Leannah, Milley, Betty, boy Sam, Sam, girl Jane. (LC EB 24:42)

LAWSON, William; PO 21 Jun 1802; 20 Sep 1802
LC; DIV of est. among: Anthony LAWSON, Betty LAWSON, Ann LAWSON. (LC EB 24:212)
[Eliz. LAWSON orphan of Wm. LAWSON chose Hen. C. LAWSON her gdn., 20 Jun 1803 (LC Orders V 1802-03:367); Ann LAWSON orphan of Wm. LAWSON chose Wm. SMITHER for her gdn., 17 Dec 1804 (LC OB 1804-05:267); on the mot. of Sam. WILLIAMS gdn. of Betsy LAWSON ord. that Hen. C. LAWSON be summoned to show cause why he has not settled his admin. of the est. of Wm. LAWSON, 16 Jun 1823 (LC OB 25:378)]

LAWSON, William; 3 Dec 1814; 15 May 1815
LC; WILL; "I do hereby certify that I was present when William LAWSON received a wound from the British on the third of this instant of which wound he died in or about four hours after he received the same, during that time he desired me to tell his brother Henry C. LAWSON that if he died & which he said there was no doubt of to have him buried in Richmond County along side of his wife and have the graves inclosed and to have his little daughter's grave inclosed that is buried in his grave yard also and for his dau. that's now living to remain with her aunt Mrs Eleanor WILLIAMS and at her death for Amelia GLASCOCK to take her and that [if] his dau. should die before she arrives to the age of sixteen years that it is his wish and desire that his bro. Henry C. LAWSON shall have every thing that he may possess, he also said that he gave Thomas Lee LAWSON son of Henry C. LAWSON his bridle and saddle and his mare if he cured her and observed that she was appraised to sixty dollars, also a five dollar hat he had paid for at Mr WADDEY's, he also desired me to tell his brother Henry C. LAWSON that Mr. Thomas MASON owed him twelve dollars for a cow and calf he sold him also that Mr John THOMSON had his pockett book with thirty dollars in it and his purse with three dollars in silver and that his chest of tools is at Mr GLASCOCK's, given under my hand this 4th day of December 1814." Benjamin GEORGE; [will proved by oaths of Benj. GEORGE & Jn. THOMSON.]. (LC WB 28:163)
[LAWSON may have been killed following the seizure of Tappahannock on 3 December 1814 by British naval forces.]

LAWSON, William; 4 Feb 1822
RC; Samuel WILLIAMS aptd. gdn. to Malissa G. LAWSON orphan of William LAWSON. (RC OB 25:239)

LAYCOCK, Jeremiah; 25 Apr 1814
WC; ord. that Mathew LAYCOCK orphan of Jeremiah LAYCOCK be bound to John BAILEY. (WC OB 1814-18:51)
[Jeremiah LAYCOCK mar. Eliz. KENNER, WC, bond 23 Sep 1794 (MLBWC:39)]

LEE, Baldwin M.; 27 Sep 1804; 25 Feb 1822
of Leesville, WC; WILL; that part of the Smithfield Tract in EC, which I shall be entitled to at the death of my mother Susanna LEE, to my bro. John P. LEE; all the rest of my property, lands & Negroes to my sis-in-law Mary J. LEE; Mrs Mary J. LEE, John P. LEE & George W. LEE exors; COD: brother George W. LEE removed as executor; desire to do something by will for the four children recommended to my care by my bro. John P. LEE, to wit: Catherine SMITH, Florinda SMITH, John & William SMITH but I find some difficulty in doing so at this time, I leave them to the care of my sis-i-l believing she will do them justice; Mrs. LEE has the entire control and disposition of my est; 10 Sep 1821; WITS: Jn. REDMAN, Benj. T. STEWART, Chris. J. COLLINS, Dan. CARMICHAEL. (WC DW 24:250)
[Baldwin M. LEE d. at his residence in WC on 7 Feb 1822 after a painful & protracted illness. (*Baltimore Patriot & Mercantile Advertiser*, 19 Feb 1822, p. [3])]

LEE, Baldwin M.; T 20 Oct 1822; [30 Oct 1822]
WC; INV; includes several books & Negroes Edmund, John, Owen, Billy, Stewart, Winney, Patty, Nancy, Peter, John taylor, Milly (chargeable), Davy, Frank, Jerry, Bob, Henry, Kitt (sold for $425). (WC RI 11:316)

LEE, Charles; PO 18 Apr 1803, T 20 Jun 1803; 20 Jun 1803
LC; DIV of est. of Charles LEE late of Middlesex Co. which was devised to the children of Robert McTYRE dec'd and the est. of Robert McTYRE Sr. dec'd which was also devised to the sd. legatees; legatees were: Williamson GARNER, Frizel McTYRE, George H. POPE, Charles Lee McTYRE, William McTYRE, Jane McTYRE, Benjamin CUNDIFF. (LC EB 24:242)

LEE, Elenor Ann; [m]; 23 Nov 1818
Late of Charles Co., Md; she left to the Rev. Benjamin CONTEE now dec'd & to his children the following Negroes in WC, and as it may be necessary to remove them to Md & as Mr. Phillip A. L. CONTEE, ex. of Benjamin CONTEE, is obliged to account for said Negroes to the Orphan's Court in Md, he wishes them registered in the Clerk's Office of WC & certified by the clerk: Charles (aged 50), Jack (25), Armstrong (22), Louisa (18), Gracee (16), Leland (12), Suckey (1), Mimey (13), Polly (13), Prudence (12), Hesekiah (13), Guy (9), Hampton (4), Nancey (2), Mariah (5), John (2), [Lusina] (6 mos.). (WC RI 10:324)

LEE, George; T 13 Sep 1806; 18 Sep 1806
LC list of slaves held in right of his wife as her dower: Joe (age 38), Daniel (34), John (13), Sally (18), Hannah (36), Ellen (9), Charles (4), James (4), Daniel (2), Maria (8), male child of Hannah just bornd. (LC EB 24:347)

LEE, George Fairfax; 3 Dec 1804; 24 Dec 1804
WC; WILL; to be decently interred in Mount Pleasant Garden where wife & children are without pomp or parade; Hugh QUINLAN to pay debts; amount due by William CHELTON of Loudon Co. and all lands in Loudon Co. to Hugh QUINLAN; Tasker QUINLAN son of Hugh the full amount of

the debt due by his uncle John Tasker CARTER; rest of est. to bro. Lancelot; 5 guineas to bro. William and 5 guineas to sis. for mourning rings; no ex.named; WITS: Allen S. DOZIER, Chas. C. RICE, Rich. B. JOHNSON, Nelson R. DOZIER. (WC DW 21:213)
[Geo. Fairfax LEE was the eldest son of Geo. LEE (d. WC 1762) (WC DW 14:91); Hugh QUINLAN (given as "QUINTON" in MLBWC) mar. (1) Anne Tasker PECK, the dau. of Robt. & Frances (TASKER) CARTER and wid. of Jn. PECK, WC, bond 20 Apr 1796 and (2) Judith Brereton THOMPSON, WC, bond 23 Aug 1803 (MWO:291, MLBWC:56); Mount Pleasant was part of the Machodoc tract in WC east of Hague belonging to the Lee Family (Miller:105)]

LEE, John; PO 24 Jan 1803; 25 Apr 1803
WC; DIV & APP of slaves at Bushfield; slaves valued at £3395; list of slaves with ages made 20 Apr 1803: Duke (32), Simon (26), Ewell (30), Billy (22), Allick (26), Ozmond (21), Edmond (21), Spencer (40), Reubin (54, infirm in the knee), Tom (35), [Nacey] (40, infirm in the head), West (40), Sam (45), Daniel (50, hired in Alexandria), Old Moses (48), Johnny (38), Little Moses (18), Jerry (37), Natt (65), Little Ben (30, infirm), Old Phil (75, infirm), [Stupart] (13), Dick (10), Little Duke (10), Jimmy (10), Isaac (10), Daniel (7), Ben (6), Little West (5), Sanders (4), George (4), Eliza (16), Bridgett (16), Letty (18), Sarah (14), Leanah (14), Dinah (14), Sillah (12), Judy (12), Dolley (8), Rose (8), Luckey (8), Winney (5), Polley (5), Kesiah (5), Milly (30), Davy (2), Frank (6 mos), Peggy (28) with [Haney] (3) & Jonah (6 mos); Barbara 30 with Billy (1); Ruth (30) with Aron (3); Sarah (30) with Salley (2); Nancy (25) with Eliza (8 mos); Margary (23) with Sam (18 mos); Suckey (23) with Sally (2 mos); Betty (26) with Spencer (3); Lucy (25) with Tom (4); Winney (35); Christian (38) with Letty (5); Nelly (40) with Johnny (7); Old Winney (60); Nanny (granney) (60); Nanny (75); Lucy (75); Solomon (son of Frankey dec'd, 7 mos); Divison No 1 to Richard B. LEE, Division No. [2 ?] was divided into 2 eq. parts to Baldwin M. LEE & John P. LEE admins of Philip LEE dec'd & next friend to Molly LEE, Susanna LEE & Philicia LEE daus. of Philip LEE; Lot No. 2 to be div. into four eq. parts, one to Baldwin M. LEE (admr. of John P. LEE & next friend to the aforesd., one part to Letice WHITING, one part to Archebal DENHOLM's father & gdn. to Elizabeth DENHOLM & the other part to Paul MICOU. (WC RI 8:212)

LEE, Kendall; 11 Oct 1819
NC; Mary LEE aptd. gdn. of Edward, Wm. H., Sarah E., Kendall, Jn. L. and Geo. G. LEE orphans of Kendall LEE. (NC OB 1816-20:396)
[In his will (NC 30 Mar 1815 - 9 Oct 1815) Kendall LEE mentioned his wife and children but did not name them (NC RB 20:279); Kendall LEE mar. Mary NUTT, ward of Jn. CRALLE, NC, bond 3 Mar 1796 (MLBNC:67)]

LEE, Margaret Matilda; only child of Henry LEE esq., d. at Stratford, WC on 13 Oct 1820 (*Daily National Intelligencer*, 20 Oct 1820, p. [3])

LEE, Philip; PO Nov 1803, T 4 Jun 1804; 27 Aug 1804
WC; DIV of est. among widow Mary J. LEE & 3 daus.: Mary S. LEE, Susanna [H]. LEE, Philicia Sally LEE; the Negroes were div. as follows: Susanna H. LEE rec'd Lot 1 (Duke, O. Sam, Jonathan, Maria & child Caroline, Smith, Nancy, O. Bridget, Zarah, G. Hannah, G. Caty, Tom, Jerry & Milly), Philicia S. LEE rec'd Lot 2 (Moses, Old Moses, Isaac, Margery & child Sam, G. Milly, G. Dolly, G. Harriett, G. Phill, G. Ben & Austin, G. Sarah, G. Priscilla, George), Mary S. LEE rec'd Lot 3 (G. Sam, Stewart, S. Beck & child Fanny,

Ruth & ch[ild] Aaron, Lucy, O. Lucy, Daniel, Scilla, Anthony, Criss, Dolly). (WC RI 8:463, 466)

[Jn. P. LEE and Baldwin M. LEE aptd. gdn. of Molly LEE, Susanna LEE and Felicia LEE, orphans of Phillip LEE, WC, 24 Jan 1803 (WC Orders 1801-04:343); Baldwin M. LEE is gdn. of Mary LEE, Susannah LEE & Philicia LEE orphans of Philip LEE, 28 Mar 1808 (WC OB 1807-10:150); Mary S. LEE, eldest dau. of Philip LEE dec'd, mar. Jas. C. ANTHONY of Richmond at Leesville, WC, on 15 Jul 1808 (*Richmond Enquirer*, 5 Aug 1808 p. [3]); Court noted that a mistake was made when Baldwin M. LEE & Jn. P. LEE were entered as guardians to the children of Philip LEE; it should have been just Baldwin M. LEE who was the children's gdn., 27 Apr 1818 (WC OB 1814-18:377)]

LEE, Philip; PO Oct 1804; 26 Nov 1804

WC; DIV of Negroes: Lot 1, Susannah H. LEE: Beck & child Nancy, Rippon, Little George (sometimes called Mary's George), Anne; Lot 2, Philicia S. LEE: Angelina & child Henry, George son of Angelina, O. Mary, Harriot, Caty; Lot 3, Mary S. LEE: Hannah & child Spencer, George the son of Hannah, William son of Hannah, Little Mary, Mary Aggy's dau. (WC RI 8:511)

LEE, Richard; 24 Jan 1803

WC; Rich. B. LEE admr. of Rich. LEE dec'd was gdn. of Molly LEE, Lettice LEE and Ricardia LEE daus. of Rich. LEE dec'd. (WC Orders 1801-04:343)

[Rich. LEE, of Lee Hall, in his will (WC 16 Feb 1790 – 23 Feb 1795) left his est. to his son Richard who d.s.p an infant; the unchristened child mentioned in his will was Polly who mar. Thomas JONES; the dower land was allotted to Willoughby NEWTON who mar. LEE's wid. Sally (WC bond 23 May 1796); after his will was written he had two other children Lettice and Ricarda, but he d. without changing his will (WC DW 19:79; WC CC 1806-006; MLBWC:50); Lettice LEE, orphan of Richard LEE, chose Thos. JONES as her gdn., WC 27 Oct 1806 (WC Orders 1804-07:424); suit in chancery, Thos. JONES & Polly his wife who was Polly the dau. of Rich. LEE against Lettice LEE & Ricarda LEE, children of Rich. LEE; WC 30 Oct 1806 (WC Orders 1804-07:436); Ricardia LEE orphan of Rich. LEE chose Jn. Augustine SMITH as her gdn, 28 Aug 1809 (WC Orders 1807-10:390); *see also WC CC 1803-006*]

LEE, Richard; 10 Oct 1822; 10 May 1824

NC; WILL; wife, unmarried daus. and son's wid. & child (should she have one) to live together as one family during the lifetime of my wife and enjoy my est; after death of wife my ex. to sell land and div. the money between my children & the child my son's wid. is now big with; after wife's death the Negroes left to her & female children by her grfather Thomas HURST to be eq. div. between my children and the child my son's wid. is big with; if my daus. refuse to comply with this section of my will then I revoke the second section as to my daus. and give the whole of my est. to the child my son's wid. is big with; friend Joseph BALL of Ditchly ex; WITS: Jos. BALL Jr., Thomas. K. HURST, K. HURST, Wm. SYDNOR; COD: 25 Oct; prop. that falls to my grchild. Elizabeth Martha LEE out of my est. to continue in the hands of Jos. BALL of Ditchly until the child marries or is of age. (NC RB 23:459)

[Rich. LEE, son of Col. Chas. & Sarah (HULL) LEE, mar. Eliz. HURST, dau. of Thos. & Eliz. (HUDNALL) HURST, NC, bond 21 Mar 1795 (MWO:224)]

LEE, Richard; T 11 Dec 1824; 13 Jun 1825. NC; INV, [m]; includes Negro boy James. (NC RB 24:243)

LEE, Sarah; [n.d.]; 19 Jun 1815

LC; Nunc. will of Sarah LEE wid. of Thomas LEE by the oaths of Elizabeth CURRELL & Milly HUGHLETT who said that Sarah LEE died on 26 Feb 1815 and was well in her senses and desired that her son John H. LEE should have all her est. and that the sd. John H. LEE may be put in the care of Dolly CURRELL and to live with her his lifetime & Dolly CURRELL to be well paid for keeping her "poor child." (LC WB 28:164)
[This is prob. Sally HILL who mar. Thos. LEE, LC, bond 23 Jun 1802 (MLBLC:47, *see Thos. LEE below*)]

LEE, Thomas; Dec 1812
LC: list of the dower slaves belonging to Sarah LEE wid. of Thomas LEE: Sprigg (about 21), Daniel (about 14), Pegga (child), Pegga (27), [child (about 14 mos)], Rachel (about 30), Mahaly (about 10), Fanny (about 45), Charles (4). (LC EB 27:129)
[Thos. LEE mar. Sally HILL, LC, bond 23 Jun 1802 (MLBLC:47); Sally LEE aptd. gdn. to Jn. Hill LEE orphan of Thos. LEE, 17 Jun 1811 (LC Orders 24:22); commissioners aptd. to div. that part of the est. of Thos. LEE dec'd which was allotted to his wid. Sarah LEE dec'd among the legal reps. and settle the gdnship. acct. of Sarah LEE with Jn. H. LEE orphan of Thos. LEE and possess Hen. C. LAWSON his present gdn. with his est., 20 Jun 1815 (LC Orders 24:238-239)]

LEE, Thomas Ludwell; 25 May 1812
WC; on the mot. of William BRENT Jr. & Winifred his wife, who was Winifred LEE to summon John D. ORR who mar. Lucinda L. LEE, Mary Elliott ORR, Eleanor Lucinda ORR & Thomas Ludwell ORR, the children of the above-named Lucinda L., Fanny LEE extx. of Thomas Ludwell LEE, St. Leger Landon CARTER & Elizabeth his wife who was Elizabeth Ludwell LEE, Mary Elliott LEE, Fanny Carter LEE, Ann Lucinda LEE, Catherine Tayloe LEE & Ann Carter LEE, the children of the sd. Thomas Ludwell LEE, Daniel C. BRENT who mar. Anne Fenton LEE, Thomas Ludwell Lee BRENT, Adelaede BRENT, Eleanor Carroll BRENT, Mary Aylett BRENT & George Lee BRENT, which last five and the pltfs. William BRENT and the children of the before-named Ann Fenton BRENT, Patrick H. DOUGLAS and Eveline Byrd his wife who was the wid. of George LEE and the children of the sd. George LEE, if any be left, all of which parties are the descendants & distributees of Mary LEE dec'd, a sis. of Dr. George STEPTOE dec'd to show cause why a tract in WC called Sandy Point should not be sold. (WC Orders 1810-13:238)
[This case involves descendants of Thos. Ludwell LEE of Bellview, Stafford Co. (son of Thos. LEE & Hannah Harrison LUDWELL, d. 1778) and his wife Mary AYLETT (dau. of Wm. AYLETT & Eliz. ESKRIDGE who mar. 2 Dr. James STEPTOE); Thos. Ludwell & Mary LEE had six children: Thos. Ludwell Jr. (d. 1807) who mar. Frances "Fanny" CARTER, Wm. Aylett (d. young), Geo. (d. 1802) who mar. Eveline Byrd BEVERLY (who mar. 2 Dr. Patrick H. DOUGLAS), Ann Fenton who mar. Daniel Carroll BRENT, Lucinda who mar. Jn. D. ORR and Rebecca; Thos. Ludwell LEE Jr.& his wife Frances had five children: Eliz. Ludwell who mar. St. Leger L. CARTER, 1808, Winifred Beale who mar. Wm. BRENT, 1810., Mary Elliott, Fanny Carter, Ann Lucinda, Catherine Tayloe, & Ann Carter; Dan. C. & Anne Fenton BRENT had five children: Thos. Ludwell Lee, Adelaede, Eleanor Carroll, Mary Aylett & Geo. Lee; Jn. D. & Lucinda L. ORR had three children: Mary Elliott, Eleanor Lucinda & Thos. Ludwell

(<http://en.wikipedia.org/wiki/Thomas_Ludwell_Lee> accessed 10 Aug 2012]

LEFEVER, Nathaniel; 29 Jul 1802
WC; Overseers of the Poor to bind out Francis, Phineas and Fanny LEFEVER orphans of Nathaniel LEFEVER. (WC Orders 1801-04:298)
[Phineas LEFEVER mar. Abby PEED dau. of Alisay PEED, WC, bond 8 Mar 1813 (MLBWC:39)]

LELAND, Ann Henrietta (Miss.); T 22 Jan 1802; 9 Jan 1809
NC; INV, £340.15.6; includes Negroes Letty, Polly, Eady, Lucy, Maria, Sally, Joe, Suckey; DIV of est; Lot 1 (Letty) drawn by John CRALLE, Lot 2 (Polly) drawn by Mrs. NUTT's heirs, Lot 3 (Eady) drawn by John LELAND's heirs, Lot 4 (Lucy) drawn by Miss Susan LELAND, Lot 5 (Maria) drawn by Miss Sally LELAND, Lot 6 (Sally) drawn by Charles LELAND, Lot 7 (Suckey) drawn by Miss Lucy LELAND; [the INV & DIV were presented 7 Jan 1809]. (NC RB 18:91)
[This is Ann Henrietta dau. of Jn. LELAND of WicP (d. NC 1778) (NC RB 10:285); the est. of Ann H. LELAND was ord. to be admin. by Chas. LELAND, NC, 14 Dec 1801 (NC Minute Book 1801-1805:71); Mary LELAND mar. (1) Jn. HAYNIE, NC, lic. 26 Dec 1770 and (2) Jn. CRALLE, NC bond 18 Feb 1793 (MWO:92, 174); Mrs. NUTT is prob. Martha NUTT another dau. Jn. LELAND (MWO:266); Jos. A. CARTER in right of his wife Eliza C. who was the only child of Wm. D. NUTT dec'd a son of Martha NUTT a sis. of Ann H. LELAND is entitled to a portion of the est. of Ann H. LELAND who d. intest w/o issue (NC CC 1820-015)]

LELAND, Charles; T 22 March 1815; [10] Jun 1816
NC; INV, $4613.78 3/4 which includes $637.78 3/4 cash in the desk and Negroes George, Jack, Massey & 4 children, half of Negro woman Liddy & 2 children, Ben, Clary, Liday, Suckey, and bonds worth $2503.74. (NC RB 20:523)
[Lucy LELAND & Sam. Am. LELAND orphans of Chas. LELAND chose Thos. TOWLES as their gdn. and the sd. TOWLES is aptd. gdn. of Hen. T. & Lucius C. LELAND, NC, 13 Nov 1820 (NC OB 1820-25:65)]

LELAND, Charles; PO 8 Feb 1819, T 9 Aug 1819; 9 Aug 1819
NC; DIV of Negroes between the est. of Charles LELAND (received Henry) dec'd & Samuel A. M. LELAND (received Lydia & Michael). (NC RB 22:99)

LELAND, Charles; T 30 Mar 1818; 10 Jul 1820
NC; INV, $4977.50; includes many books & Negroes appraised Jan 1819: Jack, George, Ben, James, John (boy), George (boy), [Massie] & young child Ken, Dall (supposed to be idiotic), Lydia, Sukey, Clara, Nancy, joint interest with Sam LELAND in Negro woman Lydia & her boy Henry, Michael. (NC RB 22:374)

LELAND, Charles; T Jan 1819; 9 Oct 1820
NC; INV, $4977.50; includes Negroes: Jack, George, Ben, James, John (boy), George (boy), Massir & young child Kendall (supposed to be [ideotic]), Lydia, Sukey, Clara, Nancy, a joint interest with Sam. LELAND in Negro woman Lydia & her boy Henry, Michall; the foregoing was an INV & discovery of all the goods and chattels of my testator (Charles LELAND unadministered by Henry L. GASKINS late his executor) by Thomas TOWLES admr. with the will annexed. (NC RB 22:407)

LELAND, Charles; PO 10 Apr 1821 T 23 Apr 1821; 14 May 1821

NC; DIV of slaves of est. of Charles LELAND to John L. CHINN in right of his wife who was Lucy LELAND (Jack, Massy, & Young George) & Charles H. LELAND (Ben & Lydia). (NC RB 22:525)
[Jn. L. CHINN, wid, mar. Lucy E. LELAND, NC, bond 12 Feb 1821 (MLBNC:17)]

LELAND, Charles; PO 12 Nov 1825, T 29 Dec 1825; 9 Jan 1826
NC; DIV of Negroes of the est. of Charles LELAND dec'd and Sarah BALL dec'd; Negroes of Charles LELAND were: George (an old man), Charles (a small boy), Nancy (young woman), Sukey & infant Lucy, Clary & infant Betsey, Henry (a young man), Steptoe (a small boy), & Griffin (a very small boy); Negroes of Sarah BALL were: Matilda (an old woman) & Delia (a girl); div. as follows: Lot 1 (George, Clary & infant, Charles, Steptoe) to Leucius LELAND, Lot 2 (George [sic], Henry, Delia) to Samuel A. M. LELAND, Lot 3 (Sukey & infant, Griffin, Nanny) [no name of recipient given]. (NC RB 24:379)
[Sam. LELAND chose Jn. D. LELAND as his gdn. and the sd. Jn. is also aptd. gdn. of Hen. & Lucius LELAND, NC 14 May 1822 (NC OB 1820-25:202)]

LELAND, John; PO 21 Dec 1801, T 26 Dec 1801; 15 Feb 1802
LC; DIV of est. among: Baldwin M. LELAND, Maria LELAND, John L. LELAND, Leroy P. LELAND. (LC EB 24:179)
[Leroy P. LELAND orphan of Jn. LELAND chose Baldwin M. LELAND his gdn. and sd. Baldwin is aptd. gdn. of Maria LELAND also an orphan of sd. Jn. LELAND, 21 Dec 1801 (LC Orders 21 1799-1801:365)]

LELAND, John D. & C. H.; PO May 1818, T 9 Jun 1818; 14 Sep 1818
NC; sale of Negro lad John, the prop. of John D. & C. H. LELAND, for $667; proceeds minus commission of $30 div. between John D. LELAND & Sally BALL as gdn. to Charles H. LELAND. (NC RB 21:489)

LELAND, Lucy; 1815; 13 Oct 1817
NC; WILL; £25 of the money due me from my bro. Charles LELAND to nephew Charles Henry LELAND; neice Lucy LELAND; nephew John D. LELAND; nephew Samuel A. M. LELAND half of the woman Lydia & her two children Henry & Michael; nephew Henry Towles LELAND my Negro boy Squire; nephew Lucius Cary LELAND Negro girl Sarah Ann; rest of est. consisting of the following Negroes: Suck, Fanny, Betty, Tom & William to nephew John D. LELAND but to remain in the hands of my bro. until nephew is 21 or marries; my relation Henry L. GASKINS & my bro. Charles LELAND exors; WITS: Eliza L. BRENT, Chas. LELAND; [admin with the will annexed granted to Charles Henry LELAND 11 Apr 1825]; NC RB 21:263)
[Lucy LELAND was a dau. of Jn. LELAND (d. NC 1778) and the sis. of Sarah LELAND, Martha NUTT, Ann Henrietta LELAND & Susannah LELAND (d. NC 1804) and Charles LELAND (d. NC 1815) who named her as gdn. to his infants (NC RB 10:285, RB 17:161, RB 20:33)]

LEMOINE, Feriol; 17 May 1819
LC; Feriol LEMOINE aptd. gdn. of his children Feriol, Josephine & Moreau LEMOINE. (LC OB 25:53)
[This is prob. Feriol LEMOINE who mar. Fanny MITCHELL, LC, bond 24 Aug 1803 (MLBLC:48); Frances Josephine LEMOINE dau. of F. LEMOINE Sr. mar. Jn. H. HARDING, LC, bond 27 Dec 1827; Fereal LEMOINE Jr. was sec. (MLBLC:35); Feriol LEMOINE d. intestate leaving a wid. Frances B. LEMOINE and the following children: Feriol, Moreau, Frances J. the wife of J. H. HARDING and Louisa now the wife of A. [S.] WILLIS; since the death

of Feriol LEMOINE, Moreau LEMOINE died leaving a wid. and two children: Frances Ellen and Virginia LEMOINE (LC CC 1837-002)]

LEMOINE, Peter; T 3 Dec 1812; 20 Dec 1812
LC; INV, £90.12.4 3/4 or $302.6 1/4; includes many different kinds of cloth & sewing supplies. (LC EB 27:131)

LENDRUM, Thomas; 10 Jan 1811; 22 Jul 1811
WC; WILL; wife Margaret Storke LENDRUM; after her death pers. est. to be eq. div. between surviving children; land to be sold for 2 annual payments and to be div. as aforesaid between the surviving children viz. the money arising from the sale of the land, I hereby give & confirm to Dr. COLLINS, Barbary & her increase forever; Dr. Christopher J. COLLINS ex. & wife extx; WITS: Jn. PIERCE, Dan. BRISCOE, Nelson CRIDLIN. (WC DW 22:212) [Acc. to a chancery document recorded in Henrico Co., 8 May 1834, Dr. Thomas LANDRUM died leaving six children: Thomas W., Elizabeth (married COLLINS), Lucy E., Harriet, John B., and Margaret LANDRUM; Dr. LANDRUM was the son of Parson LANDRUM of KGC; he served as a surgeon's mate on the *Tempest* and the *Tartar* in the Virginia State Navy during the Revolutionary War (see: <http://www.rivahresearch.com/westmorelandcty/vitals/resources/military/jamesluttrell.htm> accessed 11 Aug 2012 and VS1776 II:923-930)]

LEVY, Ezekiel; 15 Aug 1812; 4 Jan 1813
RC; WILL; to be buried in my garden alongside my dau. Hannah; Thomas MITCHELL to make my coffin plain & be paid $10; only that part of the funeral ceremony may be read over me as begins with "man that is born of a woman," to the conclusion of the Lord's Prayer omitting the fighting of wild beasts at Ephesus in short the whole of Saint Paul's Epistle to the Corinthians; plant. I now live on bought of John HAMMOND & Thomas WILLIAMS to dau. Matilda (under 18) also mill & land bought of George MISKEL as trustee of Thomas WILLIAMS; being at this time in a bargain with Dr. [*first name missing*] SMITH of New York or his agent Mr. Daniel CARMICHAEL for a tract of land lying in Cherry Point called the Old Quarter & other land adjoining it supposed to be about 400 ac, should that purchase be made, tract to dau. Matilda; Negroes Sam called the Barber, George the [Ginner], Zachariah, Bill, Bob, Sally & her children Minna & Bob, Jane & her 4 children Henry, Cate, Joan & Jude & my old woman Molly; Negroes Sam the Blacksmith, Cyrus, George, Joseph, Williamson, Peggy & her 3 children Billy, Lucy, & Levina, and woman Charity to dau. Fanny TOMLIN & after her death to be eq. div. between my two grchildren Robert & Ezekiel Levy TOMLIN; furniture & HH goods to dau. Fanny & Moore F. TOMLIN; 200 ac. near Thomas's Ordinary & half of land in Luzerne Co., Pennsylvania & Negro Moses & his wife [Merella] & child Hugh to grson. Robert TOMLIN; 350 ac. in the Fork purchased of Brown & Donoway & Negroes Willoughby, Betty & her boy & half of land in Luzerne Co., Pa. to grson. Ezekiel Levy TOMLIN; share of stock in the Virginia bank for the education of the poor children in Farnham Par; $75 to my little companion Richard T. McKENNY; Smollets History of England complete to friend Henry M. DOBYNS; my violin & music book to grson. Ezekiel Levy TOMLIN hoping he will be a musician & not a jig player; all my Hebrew books to the congregation of the City of Richmond; all my French books to grson. Ezekiel Levy TOMLIN; $12 mourning ring to dearly beloved friend of nearly 40 years Aaron LEVY; little Negro Charlotte to serve dau. Fanny TOMLIN until 18 when she is to be free (her age to be computed from 3 Dec

1806 when she was born); friends Col. Vincent BRAMHAM, John Y. CHINN, & Henry M. DOBYNS exors; Dr. John Y. CHINN to be testamentary guardian to dau. Matilda; WITS: A. BEALE, Wm. ALDERSON Sr., Danl. L. McCARTY, Jn. REDMAN, Danl. FLINN; COD: will was executed before I left home to go to the Springs in 1812; if tract in Cherry Point is not purchased, dau. Matilda to have $1500 in silver or good bonds; 23 Sep 1812. (RC WB 9:414)

[Ezekiel LEVY mar. Frances SYDNOR, RC, bond 28 Sep 1787 (MWO:225); Frances M. LEVY mar. Moore F. TOMLIN, son of Robt. & Susanna (FAUNTLEROY) TOMLIN, RC, bond 23 Apr 1805; Matilda F. LEVY mar. Jn. BURKE of WC, RC, bond 27 Jun 1815 (MRC:31, 217)]

LEWIS, Ann; 22 Jan 1785; May 1791

WC; WILL; son William LEWIS; dau. Nancy LEWIS; [no ex. named]; WITS: Sam. RUST, Wm. BRAN[N]. (WC Unrec Wills 1755-1800 #39)

[An Ann HALL, dau. of Leasure HALL (d. WC 1772), mar. Wm. LEWIS, son of Jas. & Hannah LEWIS of NC, bef. 3 Aug 1769 (MWO:227, WC DW 15:211)]

LEWIS, Charles; T 29 Oct 1818; 18 Oct 1819. LC; INV, [m]; includes 6 lots of tools. (LC EB 27:502)

LEWIS, Griffin; d. intestate leaving the following children: Samuel, Jordan and John; John had also d. before 1818 leaving two inf. children: Robert and Appia. (NC CC 1818-005)

[Griffin LEWIS was prob. the son of Willoughby LEWIS (d. NC 1803); he d. in NC c. 1814 and his est. was admin. by Sam. LEWIS (NC OB 1811-1816:274)]

LEWIS, James; [31 Mar 1823]; 12 May 1823

NC; Nunc. will of James LEWIS of NC & Upper St. Stephen's Par who died on Monday 31 Mar 1823; all est. left to his wife Susan LEWIS; Baldwin M. LELAND & Lucy P. LELAND made oath on 1 Apr 1823 that this is a correct statement. (NC RB 23:312)

[This may be James LEWIS who mar. Susanna CLARK, RC, bond 7 Feb 1810 (MRC:118)]

LEWIS, Jane; PO Aug 1811; 4 Nov 1817. RC; INV, £83.15.0. (RC WB 9:586)

LEWIS, John; PO 14 Oct 1800, T 24 Oct 1800; 13 Apr 1801. NC; INV, [m]. (NC RB 16:231)

[In his will (NC 21 Jan 1798-14 Oct 1800), Jn. LEWIS of SSP named his daus. Hannah LEWIS, Sarah LEWIS, Lunna WILLIAMS and grson. Wm. Brady LEWIS (NC RB 16:187)]

LEWIS, John; T. 30 Oct 1806; 1 Dec 1806. RC, INV, £103.19.6, includes Negro girls Siller & Mary. (RC WB 9:300)

LEWIS, John; PO 9 Nov 1812, T 30 Dec 1812; 11 Sep 1815

NC; based on suit by Lewis LAMKIN & wife & others, complts. [against] Thomas BRANN & Phebe his wife & others, tract of land was div. into 3 eq. parts; Thomas BRANN & Phebe his wife rec'd one third and were ord. to sell the remaining two thirds; BRANN & wife rec'd 5 ac. on Monday's Point which included the store houses etc. on the point; the two thirds containing 70 ac. was purchased by William HENDERSON for $700. (NC RB 20:233)

[NC, CC 1812-006 sheds more light on this record: Lewis LAMKIN & Griffithello his wife, Thos. BELL & Ann his wife, Pemberton CLAUGHTON Jr. & Jane G. CLAUGHTON, Jas. CLAUGHTON, Peter G. McCLANAHAN & Frances his wife, Rich. CLAUGHTON, Wm. BENNETT & Phoebe his wife, Priscilla, Betsy & Jn. JONES by Eppa JONES their gdn. & next friend sued to have a tract of land left by Jn. LEWIS sold and the proceeds divided among his next of kin; Griffithello LAMKIN, Ann BELL, Pemberton CLAUGHTON & Jane CLAUGHTON are children of Nancy CLAUGHTON who was Nancy LEWIS a sis. of Jn. LEWIS late of Monday's Point; Jas. CLAUGHTON, Frances McCLANAHAN, Rich. CLAUGHTON & Phoebe BENNETT are children of Priscilla CLAUGHTON who was Priscilla LEWIS; Priscilla, Betsy & Jn. JONES are children of Sally JONES who was Sally CLAUGHTON a dau. of Priscilla LEWIS another sis. of Jn. LEWIS; Jn. LEWIS d. prob. in Jan 1812 without issue leaving the above individuals and another sis. Phoebe BRANN; *see also: Edward BARNES, Jn. CLAUGHTON & Lewis LAMKIN above*)

LEWIS, John; PO 1 May 1815; 6 Nov 1815. RC; INV, £48.18.3. (RC WB 9:485)

LEWIS, Samuel; PO 17 Feb 1812, T 8 Aug 1812; 21 Sep 1812
LC; an absenter and seems to be dead; INV, $985; includes Negroes Ann & child Moses, Charlotte, girl Sukey; DIV among legal reps: Lot 1 (Ann & child Moses) to Thomas JAMES in right of his wife who is own aunt to sd. Samuel LEWIS, Lot 3 (Sukey) to Timothy McNAMARA in right of his son Timothy who is the only heir of his mother Mary McNAMARA dec'd who was own aunt to sd. Samuel LEWIS, Lot 2 (Charlotte) to Epaphroditus & John C. LAWSON heirs of Epaphroditus LAWSON dec'd who was own uncle to sd. Samuel LEWIS. (LC EB 27:128)
[Timothy McNAMARA, mariner, mar. Mary LAWSON, LC, bond 15 Jul 1807 (MLBLC:50)]

LEWIS, William; 22 Nov 1819; 14 Feb 1820
NC; WILL; my three daus. Frances, Rebeccah & Judith to have my land as long as Frances lives; at her death land to be sold and the proceeds eq. div. amongst the whole of my children: James, Nancy DOUGLAS, William, Rebeccah, Judith & Joseph; sons James & William LEWIS exors; WITS: Griffin HEADLEY, Randal LEWIS, Thomas LEWIS; James & William LEWIS refused to be exors. & William R. FALLIN granted certificate to obtain letters of admin. with the will annexed. (NC RB 22:231)
[Nancy LEWIS mar. Wm. DOUGLAS of RC, NC, bond 17 Oct 1805 (MLBNC:31); Jas. DIXON mar. Judith LEWIS, NC, bond 29 Dec 1824 (MLBNC:29); on the mot. of Wm. LEWIS, ord. that Jos. LEWIS, Nancy DOUGLAS, Jas. DIXON & Judith his wife, and Geo. LEWIS be summoned to show cause why lands of Wm. LEWIS should not be sold, 13 Mar 1827 (NC OB 1825-30:153)]

LEWIS, Willoughby; PO 11 Mar 1803, T 25 Mar 1803; 13 Jun 1803
NC; INV, [m]. (NC RB 16:544)
[In his will (NC 23 Dec 1802-14 Mar 1803), Willoughby LEWIS named his sons Wm., Willoughby & Griffin, his wife Hanie, daus. Bette & Alice LEWIS, and grson. Jn. LEWIS son of Jeremiah LEWIS (NC RB 16:527)]

LIGHTFOOT, Lisha; 29 Aug 1800; 7 Dec 1807
RC; WILL; son Thomas LIGHTFOOT & his wife Milley use of my land & plant. upon paying such legacies as shall be here mentioned; granddau. Betey [Gusil] LIGHTFOOT £20 when 21 or married; granddau. Nancy LIGHTFOOT bed $ £10 when 21 or married; all land & plant. to grson. John Numan Brockenbroy LIGHTFOOT; son Thomas LIGHTFOOT & Leroy DOBYNS exors; WITS: Geo. NASH, Jessey GARNER, Jn. GARNER. (RC WB 9:315)
[Lisha LIGHTFOOT was Alice ALGAR dau. of Sam. & Mary ALGAR who mar. Daniel LIGHTFOOT ca. 1740; Daniel & Alice had at least the following

children: William (b 1745), Betty (b. 1750), Samuel (b. 1752), Thomas (b. 1755); Daniel LIGHTFOOT d in RC 26 Mar 1755 (RC WB 6:80; NFPR:117; MRC:119)]

LITTRELL, Richard Sr.; T 13 May 1818; 13 Sep 1819
NC; INV, [m]; includes Negroes Aaron, Seller. (NC RB 22:114)

LITTRELL, Sally; 1 Oct 1804. RC INV. (RC WB 9:245)

LITTRELL, Sarah; PO Oct 1804, T 19 Feb 1805; 6 Jun 1805
RC; DIV of est. between Thomas ELMORE in right of his wife, John LITTRELL & the orphans of Richard LITTRELL dec'd; each party received £8.7.0. (RC AB 3:136)
[Thos. ELMORE mar. Mary Ann LITTRELL, NC, bond 28 May 1796 (MLBNC:36)]

LITTRELL, Thomas; T 30 Apr 1815; 9 Oct 1815. NC; INV, $141.71 1/2. (NC RB 20:281)
[The est. of Thos. LITTRELL was ord. to be admin. by Jas. B. DODSON, NC, 11 Apr 1815 (NC OB 1811-1816:311)]

LITTRELL, Thomas; PO 15 Aug 1815, T 14 Jun 1817; 14 Jul 1817
NC; DIV of lands among the heirs; to Melinda the piece of land formerly the prop. of [Nathaniel THOMAS] dec'd & the home house to the other child Juliett reserving to the wid. her dower. (NC RB 21:221)

LITTRELL, William; 17 Feb 1800; 5 Dec [1803]
Farnham Par, RC; WILL; mother Patience LITTRELL shall have all my part of my father's est. during her life; at her death to go to my bro. John LITTRELL; George JONES ex; WITS: Thos. ELMORE, [Hen.] ELMORE. (RC WB 9:225)
[Wm. LITTRELL was the son of Moses & Patience LITTRELL; he was b in NC 4 Jul 1778; he had two bros., John (b. 1780) & Leroy (b. 1783) and three sisters: Sarah (b. 1776), Betty (b. 1787) & Mary Ann (b. 1773) (SSPR:102, 103); Moses LITTRELL d. bef 8 Feb 1796 (NC OB 1796-97:4)]

LITTRELL, William; 1 Oct 1804. RC INV. (RC WB 9:246)

LOCKE, Joseph; 17 Dec 1821
LC; admin. of the est. of Joseph LOCKE dec'd granted to James KIRK. (LC OB 25:274)

LOCKE, Stephen; 17 May 179[6]; 18 Jul 1803
LC; sale of land & div. of proceeds among the wid., Sally LOCK and children: John, Polly, William, Nancy, Leroy, Lucinda; Joseph LOCKE, bro. of Stephen, was the admr. (LC EB 24:248, LC CC 1796-009)
[Stephen LOCK was the gdn. of the orphans of Thos. WEST, LC, 1785 (LC WB 22:94); Jos. LOCKE admin. the est. of Stephen LOCKE, NC, 11 Feb 1794 (NC OB 1790-1795:398)]

LONGWITH, Burgess; 4 Jun 1814; 1 Jun 1818.
LP; RC; WILL; remainder of est. after debts are paid to be eq. div. between grson.s George & Fleet (sons of my son William LONGWITH); Eppa WEATHERS ex.; WITS: Vin. SHACKLEFORD, Jn, WEATHERS. (RC WB 9:603)
[Burgess LONGWITH mar. Jane FERGUSON, RC, bond 16 Oct 1795 (MRC:120; RC OB 24:225)]

LONGWITH, John; 19 Jun 1799; 17 Sep 1804
LC; WILL; Negroes Charles, Charlotte, Joseph, & Patt to dau. Judith DOGGETT; after death of dau. and her husband John DOGGETT Negroes to be eq. div. among their heirs; Negro girl Easter to granddau. Judith Pinckard DOGGETT; if granddau. has no heirs, Easter to go to son John LONGWITH;

Negro Tom to dau. Alley MASON and after her death to her son John MASON; all my land to son John LONGWITH and after his death to his son John LONGWITH; Negroes Will, Isaac, Robin, Cloe & Old Sarah to son John; son John LONGWITH ex; WITS: Wm. GIBSON, Sam. M. SHEARMAN, Dale C. EDWARD; COD. dtd. 29 Mar 1804; Negro Sarah shall be set free at my death; WIT: Wm. GIBSON. (LC WB 28:84)
[Judith LONGWITH mar. Jn. DOGGETT, Jr., LC, bond 17 Aug 1795; Alley LONGWITH, dau. of Jn., mar. Jn. MASON, LC, bef. 19 Jun 1799 (MWO:237); Jn. MASON, son of Alley MASON, mar. Sally JONES, LC, bond 12 Apr 1802 (MLBLC:22, 51); Jn. LONGWITH orphan of Jn. LONGWITH chose Jn. HUNT as his gdn., 20 Oct 1817 (LC Orders 24:384); *NB: it is not clear which Jn. LONGWITH is the father*]

LONGWITH, John; PO 15 Oct 1804; 17 Jun 1805
LC; INV, [*value unclear*]; includes Negroes Solomon, Chloe, Robin. (LC EB 24:319)

LONGWITH, John; 20 Jul 1818
LC; Peter BEANE Jr. aptd. gdn. to William, Esther & Mahala LONGWITH orphans of John LONGWITH. (LC OB 25:8)

LOWE, Richard; 7 Jul 1804; 24 Jun 1805
WC; all est. to nephew Richard BATTEN; WITS: Stephen BAILEY. (WC DW 21:180)

LOWE, Samuel; T. 29 Nov 1814; 9 Jan 1815. NC; INV, $200.52. (NC RB 19:600)

LOWE, Sanford; PO 8 [Aug] 1813; 12 Jun 1815
NC; INV, $578.10; includes Negro girl Alsy. (NC RB 20:142)
[Sanford LOWE seems to have had 3 wives: (1) Lucy TRASCE, wid. of Jas. TRASCE, NC, bond 11 Aug 1800; (2) Eliz. LANSDELL, dau. of Jn. LANSDELL, NC, bond 11 Jun 1804, and (3) Lucy BALL, ward of Edw. ROGERS, NC, bond 28 Apr 1807 (MLBNC:70, 102); his wid. Lucy (BALL) LOWE mar. 2nd Sam. BLUNDON, NC, bond 22 May 1815 (MLBNC:11; NC OB 1816-20:60)]

LOWE, Sanford; PO 13 Aug 1822, T 25 Nov 1822; 13 Jan 1823
NC; settlement of Joseph DOULIN's acct. of gdnship. of Thomas LOWE and div. of the est. among the heirs: Lemuel LOWE, Thomas LOWE, Brittanie LOWE, Polly S. LOWE, Lucy BLUNDON; returned on 13 Jan 1823 but ord. to lie for exception; finally rec 14 Jul 1823. (NC RB 23:339)
[Jn. LANSDELL aptd. gdn. of Lemuel LOWE, NC 10 Jul 1815 (NC OB 1811-15:351); Jn. LANSDELL aptd. gdn. of Thos. LOWE orphan of Sanford LOWE, NC 10 Jun 1822 (NC OB 1820-25:217)]

LOWRY, Elizabeth; T 28 Aug 1817; 17 Nov 1817
LC; DIV of Negroes mentioned in a deed recorded in LC court 20 Sep 1802 at Davises Warehouse by subscribers mutually chosen by George B. OLIVER trustee for Elizabeth LAWRY & children, Polly S. LAWRY & Thomas NEWGENT in right of his wife Fanny who was Fanny LAWRY; Negroes were div. among: Polly S. LAWRY, Thomas NEWGENT in right of his wife Fanny, Lucy LAWRY, James LAWRY, John LAWRY, William LAWRY. (LC EB 27:399)
[This is Betty HILL, dau. of Eliz. HILL (d. LC, 1796) and wid. of Jn. LOWRY (*see Eliz. HILL above*); Thos. NEWGENT mar. Fanny LOWRY, LC, bond 15 May 1815 (MLBLC:54)]

LOWRY, John Jr.; PO 15 Oct 1821, T 23 Nov 1821; 17 Dec 1821
LC; sold Negro woman Ellen the prop. of John LOWRY Jr. and paid to Lewis HAMMONDS in right of his wife Lucy who was Lucy LOWRY $85.83 with

interest from 28 Aug 1817 making the sum of $107.60 being money due from sd. John LOWRY Jr. to the sd. Lucy in the div. of the Negroes of John LOWRY Sr dec'd; also paid John LUNSFORD $43.34 with interest making $54.31 being the sum due from John LOWRY Jr in the div. aforesd. to William LOWRY who has died and which is heired by his father John LOWRY Sr and given up by him in a schedule to satisfy a debt which was due a Mr. WARREN of Norfolk and which was to go into the hands of John LUNSFORD his agent. (LC EB 29:152)
[Acc. to MLBLC:35, Lewis HAMMOND[S] mar. Lucy HAMMOND [sic], LC, bond 16 Oct 1820, but the above rec. suggests that Lucy's surname might be an error for Lucy LOWRY; on the mot. of Jn. LUNSFORD ord. that Wm. ORRILL & Polly his wife, Fanny NEWGENT who was Fanny LOWRY, Lewis HAMMONDS & his wife Lucy, Jas. & Jn. LOWRY be summoned to show cause why the lands conveyed in trust by Jn. LOWRY for their benefit should not be sold for an eq. division, 21 May 1822 (LC OB 25:303, 331); Wm. ORRILL mar. Polly Simmonds LOWRY, LC, bond 11 Dec 1817; Fanny LOWRY mar. Thos. NEWGENT, LC, bond 15 May 1815 (MLBLC:54, 56)]

LOWRY, Mary; [m]; 18 Jan 1802
LC; Nunc. will; will was contested by John LOWRY & Elizabeth GARNER; will was declared valid by LC court; Mary LOWRY left her Negro woman Charlotte [& James] to Fanny CUNDIFF. (LC WB 28:59)

LUCAS, Nathaniel; 17 Mar 1815; 28 Oct 1816
WC; WILL; all est. to wife Ellanor LUCAS and after her death to be eq. div. amongst all my children lawfully begotten; [no ex. named]; WITS: Thos. POOR, Spencer LUCAS. (WC DW 23:225)
[This is prob. Nathaniel LUCAS who mar. Nelly LAWRENCE, WC, bond 31 May 1791 (MLBWC:40); a Nathaniel LUCAS, mulatto, was living with his wife Nelly and children Meredith, Alcey, and Fanny on Wm. FITZHUGH's land in WC in 1801 (Paul Heinegg, *Free African Americans of North Carolina, Virginia and South Carolina from the Colonial Period to About 1820*, Baltimore: Clearfield, Vol. II, 5th Ed., 2005, p. 785.)]

LUCAS, Spencer; T 13 Jan 1819; 22 Feb 1819. WC; INV, $251.94. (WC RI 10:358)
[A Spencer LUCAS mar. Jane YARDLEY, WC, bond 27 May 1810 (MLC WC:40)]

LUNSFORD, Elizabeth; PO 11 Mar 1816; 8 Sep 1817. NC; INV, $69. (NC RB 21:256)

LUNSFORD, John; 10 Nov 1815; 18 Dec 1815
LC; WILL; land to son John LUNSFORD; if son dies without heirs land to be sold and money eq. div. among 3 daus: Sally, Anna & [Pina]; Negro girl Maria to dau. Sally; daus. to have one twelve months education with some good proper school mistress; son John LUNSFORD & s-i-l Moses LUNSFORD exors; WITS: Spencer GEORGE, Wm. LUNSFORD. (LC WB 28:173)
[Moses LUNSFORD mar. Sally LUNSFORD, dau. of Jn. LUNSFORD, LC, bond 8 Jan 1811 (MLBLC:49); Jn. LUNSFORD aptd. gdn. to Anna & Piney LUNSFORD orphans of Jn. LUNSFORD, 19 Feb 1816 (LC Orders 24:283)]

LUNSFORD, John; PO 3 Apr 1816; 19 Aug 1822
LC; DIV of Negroes among Moses LUNSFORD in right of his wife Sally (Emmanuel, Sinah & Stafford), John LUNSFORD (Jesse, Jenney & child), Anna LUNSFORD (Spencer, Daphney, Isaac), [Pianna] LUNSFORD (Jacob, Charity & Melinda); each child's proportion was valued at $677.50. (LC EB 29:224)

LUNSFORD, John (Capt.); T 2Jan 1816; [17 Nov 1823]
LC; INV, [m]; includes Negroes Jessee, Emmanuel, Spencer, Jacob, Charity, Daphney, Jane & child, [Syne], Mariah, Winney, Malinda, Rose, Isaac, Stafford. (LC EB 29:298)

LUNSFORD, Lewis; PO 10 Sep 1798; 12 Apr 1802
NC; DIV of slaves among the wid. (her dower) (rec'd Beck & child Peggy, Sarah, Armistead, Dick), Harriet LUNSFORD (rec'd Mitchell & Mary Anne), Hiram LUNSFORD (rec'd Ann & Polly), Mariah LUNSFORD (rec'd Emanuel-a blacksmith), Darius W. LUNSFORD (rec'd Mary & child Lucy & Rose); Elizabeth W. LUNSFORD the admx. mar. Elisha CARTER and also received the blacksmith tools and all the books. (NC RB 16:357)
[Lewis LUNSFORD mar. Eliz. Waddey DAMERON, NC, 15 Mar 1787 (MWO:232); Eliz. W. LUNSFORD, wid., mar. (2) Elisha CARTER, NC, bond 1 Sep 1797 (MLBNC:15); *see also NC CC 1805-015*]

LUNSFORD, Lewis; PO 8 Oct 1804; 14 Jan 1811
NC; DIV of land among his children, Lot 1 (77 ac) to Hariot LUNSFORD, Lot 2 (92 2/5 ac) to Bartholomew DAMERON Sr. as gdn. for Hiram LUNSFORD, Lot 3 (82 1/4 ac) to Bartholomew DAMERON Sr. as gdn. for Darias W. LUNSFORD, Lot 4 (61 1/2 ac) to Bartholomew DAMERON Sr. as gdn. for Mariah LUNSFORD; div. was made at the request of Elisha CARTER who mar. the relict of the sd. dec'd & Bartholomew DAMERON Sr. (NC RB 18:502; see also NC CC 1805-015)

LUNSFORD, Lynton; 15 Mar 1816; 20 May 1816
LC; INV; includes Negroes: Wilmoth, Isaac, Luesia, Solomon; [a second INV was taken on 7 Apr 1816; it listed the same slaves with the exception of Isaac]. (LC EB 27:297, 298)
[Linton LUNSFORD mar. Frankey CARTER, dau. of Jas. CARTER, LC, bond 18 Aug 1803 (MLBLC:49)]

LUNSFORD, Richard; [m]; 8 May 1815
NC; 136-ac. tract of land belonging to LUNSFORD sold to Walter NUTT for $116.10 and proceeds div. among Walter NUTT, Sally LUNSFORD, Nancy LUNSFORD, Nelley LUNSFORD, William LUNSFORD, & Mary LUNSFORD. (NC RB 20:132

LUNSFORD, Richard; PO 12 Nov 1816; 12 Aug 1817
NC; sale of Negroes Ellen & child the prop. of Mary LUNSFORD dec'd orphan of Richard LUNSFORD and div. of proceeds among Edward C. PITMAN gdn. to William LUNSFORD, Walter NUTT as gdn. to Sally, Nancy & Nelly LUNSFORD, and Walter NUTT [in his own right]; chancery suit, 8 Jul 1816; Edward C. PITMAN gdn. & next friend of William & Mary LUNSFORD heirs of Richard LUNSFORD dec'd, pltfs. against Walter NUTT & Elizabeth his wife & Sarah, Nancy & Nelly LUNSFORD also heirs of sd. Richard LUNSFORD defts; lands lately held as dower by the wid. of Richard LUNSFORD to be sold; land & 2 Negroes Nancy & Milly were sold and proceeds div. among Edward C. PITTMAN gdn. to William LUNSFORD, Sally LUNSFORD, Walter NUTT gdn. to Nelly & Nancy LUNSFORD, and Walter NUTT [in his own right]. (NC RB 21:227; OB 1816-20:53; NC CC 1813-012)
[Walter NUTT mar. Eliz. S. LUNSFORD, dau. of Rich. LUNSFORD, LC, bond 28 Feb 1809 (MLBLC:78); Ann LUNSFORD orphan of Rich. LUNSFORD chose Moses LUNSFORD as her gdn., 11 May 1818 (NC OB 1816-20:252)]

LUNSFORD, Tarpley; PO 13 Jun 1803, T 14 Jul 1803; 10 Dec 1804

NC; his land sold to Cyrus HARDING and proceeds div. between Richard DUNAWAY and Thomas HURST gdn. of Joseph & James LUNCEFORD. (NC RB 17:241)
[In his will (NC [m]-9 Feb 1801), Tarpley LUNSFORD named his sons Jos. & Jas., his dau. Nancy LUNSFORD, and wife Jane (NC RB 16:224); Rich. DUNAWAY mar. Nancy LUNCEFORD, NC, bond 23 Feb 1801 (MLBNC:32)]

LUTTRELL, William; 23 Oct 1815
WC; James LUTTRELL orphan of William LUTTRELL chose John MULLINS as his gdn. and John LUTTRELL another orphan of William chose William DOLEMAN as is gdn.; Keziah LUTTRELL was the wid. and admx. of William. (RC OB 1814-18:188, 189)
[Wm. LITTRELL mar. Keziah MARMADUKE, WC, bond 17 Jul 1801 (MLBWC:40); Keziah LUTTRELL wid. & admx. of Wm. LUTTRELL aptd. gdn. to Francis & Wm. LUTTRELL orphans of Wm. LUTRELL, 28 Nov 1815 (WC OB 1814-18:195)]

LYELL, Dozier; 27 Mar 1827
WC; ord. that Fanny JOHNSON, wife of Benedict JOHNSON, who was formerly Fanny LYELL, be summoned to say whether she will take admin. on the est. of Dozier LYELL unadministered by William JOHNSON. (WC OB 1823-27:360)
[Dozier LYELL mar. Fanny SMITH, dau. of Peggy SMITH, WC, bond 22 Aug 1811; Fanny (SMITH) LYELL mar. (2) Benedict JOHNSON, WC, bond Jan 1827 (MLBWC:35, 40)]

LYELL, John; PO 5 Oct 1801, T 8 Dec 1801; 6 Oct 1806
RC; DIV of est. (which includes slaves Gavin, Joan, Lucy, Judith, Jack, Daniel & Winney and bonds worth £62.10.0) among: John LYELL, Joseph LYELL, Thomas LYELL, Elizabeth LYELL, Francis ATWELL, Samuel LYELL, Hutson LYELL, Dozier LYELL, Robert LYELL; each received est. worth £43.3.4. (RC AB 3:176)

LYELL, Joseph; PO Jun 1808; 5 Dec 1808
RC; INV, £181.12.0, est. was formerly administered by Nancy LYELL, dec'd. (RC WB 9:341)
[This is prob. the Jos. LYELL who mar. Nancy DALE, RC, bond 12 May 1798 (MRC:121)]

LYELL, Joseph; PO Dec 1808; 6 Feb 1809
RC; settlement of Samuel LYELL's admin. acct. of Joseph LYELL's est. and div. of est. between his legal reps.: Lucy LYELL, Ann LYELL (her gdn. was John LYELL). (RC AB 3:212)

LYELL, Joseph; PO Jun 1809; 6 Jun 1809
RC; INV, £1057.4.2 1/2 plus £1290.53.0 in bonds. (RC WB 9:353)

LYELL, Joseph; PO 3 Jun 1816; 6 Oct 1817
RC; Negro Elijah was hired out in 1813, 1814, 1815 & 1816 by Samuel LYELL gdn. of Lucy LYELL after the death of his ward in 1813 from which time Ann LYELL was entitled to him as the sis. & heir of sd. Lucy; settled acct. of John LYELL gdn. of Ann LYELL; proceeds of improper hire to be paid to John LYELL as gdn. (RC AB 3:442)

MAHANES, Charles; 18 Dec 1809
LC; Chancery suit, Thomas HARVEY, pltf., against Molly MAHANES, wid. of Charles MAHANES and Judith H[ughlett] MAHANES, Betsy C. MAHANES, William MAHANES, Janetta MAHANES, Polly MAHANES

and Charles M. MAHANES heirs of Charles MAHANES) (LC Orders B23 1808-11:140; LC CC 1812-011)
[Chas. MAHANES, son of Meredith MAHANES of LC, mar. Mary ANGEL, NC, bond 12 Jan 1795 (MLBNC:72)]

MAHANES, Meredith; 30 Mar 1802; 19 Oct 1807
LC; WILL; 60 ac. of land adj. the place w/o he now lives to son Charles MAHANES; three sons Samuel, Lewis & John MAHANES; £25 for education of son John; wife Nancy MAHANES; at wife's death land & plant. to be eq. div. between three sons Samuel, Lewis & John; at wife's death pers. est. to be eq. div. between three daus. Sinah SIMMONDS, Emley & Judith MAHANES; wife Nancy, John SIMMONDS & Cyrus PINCKARD exors; WITS: Wm. YERBY, Mary YERBY, Jn. BEAN, Wm. [F.] YERBY. (LC WB 28:104)
[A Meredith MAHANES mar. Eliza CURTIS, NC, lic. 1 Oct 1767 (MWO:233); Tarpley WEBB, son of Jas. WEBB, was bound to a Meredith MAHANES on 16 Jun 1768 to learn to read and write and the trade of a tailor (LC OB 18:55); Jn. SIMMONDS mar. Sinah [MAHANES]. dau. of Meredith, LC, bond 8 Apr 1799 (MLBLC:68)]

MAHANES, Merideth; PO 24 Nov 1807; 20 Jun 1809. LC; INV, £390.15.7. (LC EB 27:53)

MALEY, James; PO 14 Sep 1818, T 1 Oct 1818; 9 Nov 1818
NC; Chancery suit between John MALEY & Melinda LITTRELL an inf. by the sd. John MALEY her gdn. & next friend, pltfs. against Willoughby HARRISON & Mary his wife, defts.; land sold to John MALEY and Negro Peter sold to Griffin FOUSHEE and Negro George sold to Willoughby HARRISON; bonds delivered to John MALEY & Willoughby HARRISON. (NC RB 21:520)
[This is the Jas. MEALEY who mar. Winifred HAYNIE, dau. of Hezekiah HAYNIE, NC, bef. 16 May 1788 (MWO:243); Willoughby HARRISON mar. Mary MEALY, dau. of James MEALY, NC, bond 29 Nov 1798 (MWO:169); acc. to NC CC 1818-002, Jas. MALEY d. leaving a will which named his wife Winnefred, and his children: Wm., Jn., Mary, Jas., and Hannah; Wm. & Jas. d.s.p. intestate; Hannah mar. a LITTRELL and had a child Malinda; Malinda LITTRELL was the dau. of Thos. LITTRELL & Hannah MEALEY who were mar. in NC, bond 22 Jan 1807 (MLBNC:47, 69)]

MALEY, James; 1 Oct 1818; 9 Nov 1818
NC; land adjoining Coan Mill belonging to James MALEY, the father of John MALEY & Melinda LITTRELL which has since been in the possession & occupation of his wid. Winefred MALEY lately dec'd, was sold to John MALEY. (NC RB 21:524)
[Miller:31 tentatively locates Coan Mill on Coan Mill Stream which flows into the Coan River that arises near Heathsville and flows northward into the Potomac.]

MALEY, James; T 1 Oct 1818; 12 Jul 1819. NC; INV, $99.50. (NC RB 22:77)

MALEY, Winnifred; 3 Apr 1816; 9 Nov 1818
NC; WILL; all stock of cattle, hogs & sheep, tight casks, & stands, plant. utensils being the prop. that I have raised since the death of my husband I give to my son John MALEY & Mary HARRISON to be eq. div; $5 to granddau. Malinda LITTRELL; [no ex. named]; WITS: Jn. HALL, Jn. OLDHAM. (NC RB 21:525)
[This is Winifred HAYNIE the wid. of Jas. MALEY (*see above*)]

MARKS, John; PO 7 Dec 1795, T 13 Jan 1796; 3 Sep 1799

RC; DIV of proceeds of sale of Negroes Paul, Bill, Guy, [Molly], Winney, Boson, Judy & child Tom; each claiment [none identified except the children of Susanna CRASK] to receive £33.0.3 1/4. (RC AB 3:2)

[Jn. MARKS Sr. in his will (RC 23 Mar 1786 - 4 Apr 1791), named his wife Hannah and children James, Betty BRUCE, Frances BRAGG, Penelope CARTER, Mary WILSON, Hannah BRUCE, Sarah CRASK, Susannah CRASK, William, John, Elias, Fennell (RC WB 8:94); Sarah MARKS, dau. of Jn. MARKS, Sr., mar. Vincent CRASK, RC, bef. 22 Apr 1784 (MWO:93); Betty MARKS mar. [Wm.] BRUCE bef. 12 Nov 1783; Frances MARKS mar. [Jn.] BRAGG, bef. 23 Mar 1786; Penelope MARKS mar. [fnu] CARTER bef. 23 Mar 1786; Mary MARKS mar. Daniel WILSON, RC, bond 19 Jan 1773; Hannah MARKS mar. Benj. BRUCE bef. 23 Mar 1786; Susannah MARKS mar. [fnu] CRASK bef. 2 Mar 1786 (MWO:47, 56, 66, 93, 381)]

MARMADUKE, Joseph; T 10 Feb 1818; 22 Feb 1818. WC; INV, $279.29. (WC RI 10:244)

MARMADUKE, Joseph; T 5 Feb 1818; 25 Jan 1819. WC; INV, $279.28 3/4. (WC RI 10:325)

[Eliz. MARMADUKE orphan of Jos. MARMADUKE chose Wm. M. WALKER as her gdn., 28 Jan 1822 (WC OB 1819-23:344)]

MARMADUKE, Sarah; [3] Aug 1804; 22 Oct 1804

WC; WILL; son Vincent MARMADUKE; dau. Elizabeth McCLANAHAM; son Meredith M. MARMADUKE; son-in-law John HUNTER; son Vincent & John McCLANAHAM exors; WITS: Edw. PORTER, Hannah [m]; a COD. dtd. 21 Sep 1804 gave her son Meredith half of tobacco crop and 10 barrels of corn; rest of crop to be eq. div. among son Vincent, John McCLANAHAM, John HUNTER & Meredith M. MARMADUKE; Wit. Edw. PORTER. (WC DW 21:109)

[This is prob. Sarah SANFORD the wife of Vincent MARMADUKE, (*see below*)]

MARMADUKE, Sarah; PO 22 Mar 1819, T 25 Mar 1820; 27 Mar 1820

WC; DIV of est. among: Vincent MARMADUKE, Meredith M. MARMADUKE, John MACLANAHAN, John HUNTER's est. (WC RI 10:484)

MARMADUKE, Vincent; 25 Mar 1811

WC; it appearing to the court that Vincent MARMADUKE died sometime in the year 1791 intestate seized in fee simple of a small tract of about 100 ac. ... leaving four children: Molly, Vincent, Betsey, and Meredith; Molly has died leaving five children by John HUNTER her husband: James, John, Nancy, Sally, & Samuel HUNTER, infants; Betsey mar. John McCLANAHAN. (WC Orders 1810-13:87)

[Vincent MARMADUKE's wife may have been Sarah SANFORD dau. of Wm. SANFORD (d. WC 1784) as Wm. SANFORD named a dau. Sarah MARMANDUKE [sic] in his will (WC DW 16:212, 17:99); *see also Sarah MARMADUKE above*]

MARMADUKE, Vincent; [PO 22 Mar 1819, T 25 Mar 1820]; 27 Mar 1820

WC; INV, $1056 (deduct $83.34 for a Negro girl Kenner sold under an execution after being allotted to V. MARMADUKE); DIV of Negroes among widow (received Jack & Milly as dower), John HUNTER (Jerry), Vincent MARMADUKE (Patty), John MACLANAHAN (Jenny), Meredith M. MARMADUKE (Bettey). (WC RI 10:483

MARSH, Charles; 3 Dec 1811; 9 Mar 1818

WicP, NC; WILL; all est. I lend to my wife Nancy MARSH; if she should marry she is to have only her thirds; after wife's death land to be sold & money eq. div. amongst my children: Walter, Charles, Elizabeth, & Rebecca; wife & friend George BARRETT or George DAMERON exors; WITS: Wm. HARDING, Geo. DAMERON, Margaret SEEBRE. (NC RB 21:368)
[Chas. MARSH mar. Nancy DAMERON, NC, bond 29 May 1801 (MLBNC:73); on the mot. of Walter MARSH ord. that Chas., [Elizabeth] and Rebecca MARSH be summoned to show cause why lands of Chas. MARSH dec'd should not be sold, 10 Dec 1827 (NC OB 1825-30:223); Rebecca MARSH chose Walter MARSH as her gdn., 14 Jan 1828 (NC OB 1825-30:228)]

MARSH, Charles; T 27 Mar 1818; 12 Oct 1818. NC; INV, $220.64 1/4. (NC RB 21:508)

MARSH, Edward; PO 14 May 1810, T 5 Dec 1810; 14 Jan 1811. NC; INV, £75.9.9. (NC RB 18:503)
[In his will (NC 7 Apr 1797 - 14 May 1810), Edward MARSH names his wife Judith and five children: Rosten Conner, Nancy Davis, Katharen, Ailcy, & Judith; his bro. Alexander was an ex. (NC RB 18:390); the name is given as "Edwin" in Lewis & Booker's will abstracts of NC, but it is clearly "Edward" in this record]

MARSH, Edward; 14 Jun 1819
NC; Mahala MARSH orphan of Edward MARSH chose Morris JONES as her gdn. (NC OB 1816-20:364)
[Mahala MARSH mar. Morris JONES, NC, bond 14 Jun 1819 (MLBNC:62)]

MARSH, Gideon; PO 9 Dec 1811, T 17 Dec 1811; 14 Jun 1813. NC; INV, $203.15. (NC RB 19:406)
[In his will (NC 12 Aug 1796 - 9 Dec 1811), Gideon MARSH of WicP named his wife (*but not by name*), his sons Gideon Hammons, Jn. Glover, Lanzey Denny, Griffin & Bobbey, his dau. Betsy, and his son Gideon's grmother. Mary WALKER (NC RB 19:126); there are at least 3 marriages for men named Gideon MARSH in NC: (1) to Molly BARNES in NC, 1775, (2) to Nancy PERCIFULL, NC, bond 12 Sep 1785, and (3) to Nancy BOYD, prob the wid. of Robt. BOYD, NC, bond 11 May 1795 (MWO:235)]

MARSH, Gideon H.; PO 13 Jun 1808, T 23 Nov 1808; 12 Jun 1809
NC; INV, £253.13.5 1/2; includes Negroes Sally & child Steptoe, Amy, Thomas, John. (NC RB 18:173)
[Poss. Gideon Hammons MARSH son of Gideon MARSH (d. NC 1811) (NC RB 19:126)]

MARSH, Joseph; PO 11 Jan 1808; 12 Jun 1809
NC; INV, £5.17.4 1/2; includes 6 gallons sour country made wine and 4 1/2 gallons of vinegar. (NC RB 18:170)
[The est. of Jos. MARSH was ord. to be admin. by Wm. HARDING, NC, 11 Jan 1808 (NC OB 1807-1811:19)]

MARTIN, Hannah; 23 Sep 1807; 20 Feb 1815
LC; WILL; silk rug to grdau. Louisa Martin SHEARMAN; grdau. Kitty Ann Martin BRENT; dau. Caty BRANAN; interest in some Negroes & prop. now in the poss of Bettey SCHOFIELD of Amherst Co. if alive which belonged to the est. of my father William MITCHELL dec'd which sd. SCHOFIELD holds as dower prop. being at one time wid. of my dec'd father; this interest I lend to my friend Sam M. SHEARMAN for the use of my dau. Caty BRANAN; WITS: Hugh BRENT, Augusten HUGHLETT. (LC WB 28:154)

[Hannah MITCHELL, dau. of Wm. MITCHELL, mar. Wm. MARTIN, LC, bond 16 Aug 1782 (MWO:236, MLBLC:51); Caty MARTIN mar. Spencer BRANAN, RC, bond 22 Dec 1794 (MRC:23)]

MARTIN, Jacob; 30 Jan 1810; 24 Dec 1810.
WP, WC; WILL; I have strong reasons to believe that I am justly entitled to between 40 & 50 ac. of land now in the possession of James MUSE, if sd. land should be recovered by my ex. I give it to my grdau. Elizabeth MILLER; rest of est. to grdau. Ann Benger HIPKINS; friends James MILLER & Joseph COX exors; WITS: Jas. MILLER, Sam. LEWIS, Robt. G. ROBB. (WC DW 22:388)
[A Jacob MARTIN was named heir and devisee of Jn. MARTIN; WC, 27 Jul 1802 (WC Orders 1801-04:262); Margaret MARTIN, the dau. of Capt Jacob MARTIN, mar. William Aug. HIPKINS, WC, bond 10 Jun 1799 (MLBWC:31)]

MARTIN, Mary Ann; 26 Aug 1787; Aug 1791
WC; WILL; whole est. to dau. Sarah [LOVE]; dau. to be extx.; WITS: Jn. BERKLEY, [Jos.] MONROE. (WC Unrec Wills 1755-1800 #40)

MARTIN, William; 16 Dec 1799
LC; Nancy MARTIN orphan of William MARTIN chose Hugh BRENT as her gdn. (LC Orders (21) 1799-1801:69)
[Wm. MARTIN mar. Hannah MITCHELL, LC, bond 16 Aug 1782 (MLBLC:51; LC Orders 21 1799-1801:79); Settlement of the gdnship. acct. of Geo. BRENT & Martin SHEARMAN with Nancy & Alice MARTIN orphans of Wm. MARTIN returned, 20 Jan 1800 (LC Orders 21 1799-1801:71); Alice dau. of Wm. MARTIN mar. Hugh BRENT, RC, bond 30 Nov 1799 and Nancy her sis. mar. Sam. M. SHEARMAN, LC, bond 5 Oct 1801 (LC CC 1802-012; MLBLC:67; MWO:49); acc. to a LC chancery suit, Wm. MARTIN Sr. d. leaving a wid. Hannah and several children including Jn., his eldest, who was born bef. the marriage of Wm, and Hannah, and Wm., and several others born after the marriage (LC CC 1797-005)]

MASON, John; PO 19 Oct 1795; 15 Feb 1796
LC; INV, £9.3.7; on 15 Feb 1796 the report of the allotment of Margaret FAULKNER's dower in the est. of her late husband John MASON was returned & ord. to be rec.; DIV of est. among Margaret MASON, John MASON (his gdn. was James BUSK), Sarah MASON. (LC EB 24:7)
[Jn. MASON mar. Margaret EDWARDS, dau. of Elisha EDWARDS, NC, 4 Jan 1789 (MWO:237)]

MASON, John; 10 Aug 1798; 17 Jun 1799
LC; WILL; land & plant. to wife Alley during her widowhood; at wife's death or remarriage land & plant. to son John MASON; wife to be extx.; WITS: Jas. CARTER, Spencer WATTS. (LC WB 28:29)
[Jn. MASON mar. Alley LONGWITH, dau. of Jn. LONGWITH, bef. 10 Aug 1798 (MWO:237)]

MASON, John; PO 17 Jun 1799; 19 Jul 1802. LC; INV, £42.11.5. (LC EB 24:201)

MASON, John; 18 Jun 1804
LC; Peter TANKERSLEY was the gdn. of Judith FLOWERS who was Judith MASON lately his ward. (LC OB 1804-05:151)
[Jn. MASON must have mar. a TAPSCOTT since, in her will (LC 16 Dec 1790 - 17 Jan 1791) Mary TAPSCOTT names, among others, her dau. Mrs. MASON and her dau. Judith and her grchil. Molly, Solomon & Judith MASON (LC WB 22:286); Jn. FLOWER[S] mar. Judith MASON, LC, bond 18 Apr 1803 (MLBLC:28); settle with Peter TANKERSLEY the acct. of his

gdnship. of Judith FLOWERS who was Judith MASON and possess Jn. FLOWERS the husband of sd. Judith with her est., 19 Sep 1803 (LC Orders V 1802-03:437); on the mot. of Jn. FLOWERS ord. that Thos. MASON, Solomon MASON, Wm.MASON & Polly MASON be summoned to show cause why Negro slave Solomon belonging to the est. of Jn. MASON should not be sold and the proceeds div., LC 15 Oct 1804 (LC OB 1804-05:232)]

MASON, John; 20 Mar 1820
LC; Overseers of the Poor to bind out Elizabeth MASON orphan of John MASON to Royston HUGHLETT. (LC OB 25:112)

MASON, Solomon;
LC; d. intest. between 1802 and 1807 leaving no father or mother but the following siblings: Judith (who mar. John FLOWERS, LC, bond 18 Apr 1803), William, Thomas, and Mary (LC CC 1819-040; MLBLC:28)

MASSEE, Barbara; 10 Nov 1814;
WC; WILL; s-i-l Joseph BARTLETT to be ex; son Roy MASSEE; dau. Lewsetty JOHNSON; s-i-l John MOTHERSHEAD; dau. Alsey BARTLETT; WITS: Jn. NEALE, Campbell TEET. (WC DW 23:56)
[Lucetta MASSEY mar. Rich. B. JOHNSON, WC, bond 30 Aug 1799; Jn. MOTHERSHEAD mar. Celia MASSEY, WC, bond 19 Aug 1801 (MLBWC:36, 47)]

MATHANY, John; T 23 Sep 1803; 25 Jun 1804
WC; INV, £96.11.0; includes Negro Lucy; DIV with allotments to dau. Nancy MATHANY & son William MATHANY. (WC RI 8:426)
[Jn. MATHANY was prob. the son of Thos. MATHANY (d. WC 1803) (*see below*); he mar. Winney BARECROFT (who may have been his 1st wife), WC, bond 9 Mar 1787 (MLBWC:44)]

MATHANY, Thomas; 12 Apr 1803; 25 Sep 1803.
CP, WC; WILL; son Daniel Negro man [Jinny] & Negro woman Peg; grson. William Barecroft MATHANY Negro man Harry & Negro girl Nancy; grdau. Nancy MATHANY Negro girl Bell; dau. Nancy NEALE's children Daniel, Thomas, & Betsy Negro lad James, Negro woman Sarah, and Sarah's dau. Linda; grdau. Nancy WHITE Negro man Abram; son Daniel exor; WITS: David [WARDROBE], Geo. MOORE; WC DW 20:486

MATHANY, Thomas; [m]; 28 Nov 1803
WC; INV, £649.14.0; includes Negroes: Jerry, Henry, James, Margaret, Sarah & child, Betty, Nancy, Sindey, Abraham. (WC RI 8:369)

MATHEWS, John; T 25 Mar 1806; 26 May 1806.
of Federal Farm, WC, INV, £2374.14.0. (WC RI 8:614)
[Miller:49 identifies Federal Farm as a tract near Hinnom which is north of Peirce Creek]

MAUND, John James; PO 1820, T 20 Dec 1820; 28 Aug 1821
WC; INV & DIV of Nominy Hall Tract containing 2739 ac; div. among Dr. ARNEST, the children of Dr. ARNEST by his former wife Harriett MAUND, Henry MAUND, Thomas MAUND; est. was worth $16,586. (WC RI 11:112)
[John James MAUND mar. Harriett Lucy CARTER, dau. of Robt. & Frances (TASKER) CARTER, in Aug 1789 (MWO:239); the wid. and children of John James MAUND were named in a suit to confirm title of Spencer BALL to a 790-ac. tract of land called Toomey's Tract on Craigs Cr. in Botetourt Co.; they were: Harriett Lucy MAUND, wid., and children Nancy Martin, Robt. Carter, Jn. Jas., Thos. Martin, Geo. Carter, Hen. Lee Newton and Julia; WC, 23 Jul 1804 (WC Orders 1804-07:57); Dr. ARNEST was John ARNEST of Baltimore who mar. Anne Martin MAUND the dau. of H. L. MAUND, WC,

bond 16 Jan 1810. (MLBWC:2); Ann ARNEST, consort of Dr. Jn. ARNEST, late of Baltimore, died on 23 May 1818 in WC in her 29th year (*Baltimore Patriot & Mercantile Advertiser*, 4 Jun 1818, p. [2]); Nancy Martin MAUND, Robert Carter MAUND, Jn. Jas. MAUND, Thos. Martin MAUND, Geo. Carter MAUND, Hen. Lee Newton MAUND, and Julia MAUND are infant children of Jn. Jas. MAUND, 23 Oct 1809 (WC Orders 1807-10:408); Jn, J. MAUND d. on 6 Sep. 1818 in WC in his 26th year; Miss. Julia C. MAUND of WC, d. on 5 Oct 1818 in her 17th year (BDBN:77, 78)]

McADAM, Joseph & John; 7 Mar 1822; 11 Mar 1822
NC; P of A; Robert NUTT & Charlotte M. NUTT, Thomas TAYLOR & Martha C. TAYLOR, John McADAM & Louisa McADAM, Thomas BROWN & Elizabeth BROWN, Thomas OLDHAM & Sally G. E. his wife, Elizabeth McA. BEACHAM, Albert G. PLUMMER & Ann his wife and Janetta KEENE appointed Allen LATHA[M] & Benjamin G. LEONARD as their attornies to recover all the lands they are entitled to under Joseph McADAM & John McADAM, both now dec'd, and which they were entitled to receive for their bounty in land from the state of Virginia for their services during the Revolutionary War in the Virginia Line or Continental Establishment or which they had purchased from others entitled thereto; WITS: Rich. H. GASKINS, Thos. E. HARDING, Rich. HUDNALL (as to first 8); R. CLAUGHTON, Jn. MIDDLETON, Iz. ANDERSON (as to 6 last). (NC RB 22:631)
[The people in this record are descendants of Dr. Jos. McADAM (d. NC 1785) who had sons Jn., Chas., and Geo. Thos. and daus. Sarah C., Janette, Ann, Martha & Charlotte; Sarah C. mar. [Edwin] CONWAY bef. 1785; Janette mar. Wm. BROWN, NC, 1771; Ann mar. Thos. KEENE NC, bef. 1785 and Charlotte mar. (1) Thos. TAYLOR, bef. 1788 and (2) Robt. NUTT, NC, after 1791; Martha (d. NC 1794) did not marry; Jn. & Chas. d.s.p.; Sarah E. the dau. of Thos. GASKINS & wid. of Geo. Thos. McADAM mar. (2) David BALL, NC, 1795 (NC RB 15:9; MWO:55, 86, 209, 346); Martha C. TAYLOR (mar. Thos. TAYLOR, NC, bond 10 Nov 1817), Louisa BALL, dau. of David (mar. Dr. JN. McADAM, NC, bond 27 Dec 1814), Sarah KEENE (mar. Thos. OLDHAM, NC, bond 4 Dec 1805), Betsy McA. KEENE, dau. of Thos. (mar. Bushrod McF. BEACHAM, NC, bond 26 Jan 1808), and Ann, wid. of Wm. S. GARNER (mar. Albert G. PLUMMER, NC, bond 31 Mar 1821, all seem to be granddaus. of Dr. Jos. McADAM (MLBNC:6, 71, 78, 83, 99); Jn. McADAM served 3 years as a lieutenant in the Continental Line and his bro. Joseph (d. c. 1777) was a surgeon's mate in the Virginia Continental Line (VS1776 II:834); for info on Charlotte McADAM see NC OB 1807-11:16; to the satisfaction of the court Thos. BROWN is an heir of Jn. McADAM who was a capt. in the Virginia Line and one of the heirs of Jos. McADAM a surgeon in the Virginia Line, NC 10 Feb 1823 (NC OB 1820-25:266); the court believes that Doctor Jn. McADAM is the only heir at law of his father Geo. Thos. McADAM, NC 9 Jun 1823 (NC OB 1820-25:300)]

McCARTY, Ann B.; T 7 Jan 1824; 5 Dec 1825. RC; INV, $386.05 1/4. (RC WB 10:91)

McCARTY, Charles T.; 7 Dec 1801
RC INV; includes following slaves: Mingo, Marcus, Harry, Solomon, Little Harry, Charlotte, Mary, Anne, Matilda, Jane, Myrna, Lucy. (RC WB 9:161)
[This is prob. Charles Travers McCARTY, son of Maj. Chas. Barber & Winifred (TARPLEY) McCARTY, who mar. Apphia Fauntleroy TOMLIN, RC, bond 12 Jan 1796 (MRC:123)]

McCARTY, Daniel ; 27 Apr 1800; 22 Jun 1801.
of Pope's Creek, WC; WILL; wife Margaret; overseer Pope TIFFEY; if he has no children all est. to wife & her heirs supposed child Thomas POPE to be supported by est. until 21 and to be educated and learn a decent trade; [no wits]. (WC DW 20:220)
[Daniel McCARTY mar. Margaret ROBINSON, dau. of Wm. ROBINSON, WC, bond 2 Sep 1797 (MWO:239); Margaret (ROBINSON) McCARTY mar. (2) Rich. STEWART, WC, bond 27 Jul 1802 (MLBWC:67); Margaret McCARTY was the wid. of Daniel McCARTY, and his two orphans under 21 were named as Ann R. and Elizabeth, WC, 29 Jul 1802 (WC Orders 1801-04:299); Ann R. McCARTY mar. Maj. Hen. LEE at Pope's Creek, WC, on 8 Apr 1817 (*Washington City Weekly Gazette*, 12 Apr 1817, p. 561)]

McCARTY, Daniel; PO Mar 1803; 15 Jun 1803
WC £5201; allot to the defendant that part of the est. of Daniel McCARTY which is devised to Margaret the wife of the defendant Richard by the will of the sd. Daniel McCARTY; one third of the Negroes: Foreman Harry, Titus, Cuped, Ned, Billy, Phil, Bob, Edmond, Daniel, Bill, Cul[b]y [Jun.], Nacey, Old Sam, Lucy, Mach, Henny, Patty, Bob Jun. Leannah, Bob Sen. Sall Sen. Judy, Clarissa, Jerry, Mariah, Jane, Winny, Mary, Sam, Nancy, Sally, Charlotte, Pheby, Old Jane, Old Alice, Bridget, Madge, Isaac, Frank, infant (9 mos), infant (3 mos), Sally, infant (1 mo); Foreman Adam & Emanuel, Gawin & Tom, Peter & Jerry, [James] & Prince, Billy & Peter, Reubin & Anthony Sen., Jesse & Joshua, George & Aron, Frank & [Celly], Harry & Charles, John & Anthony Jun., James & Daniel, Old James & Nick, Anthony & Nell, Alice & Amy, Judy & Silla, Patience Jun. & Jane, Jane & Moll, Lucy & Mary, Minny & Milly, Dinah & Rachel, Cate & Peggy, Sall Jun. & Sall, Adam & George, [Eady] & Hannah, [Jane] & [Leannah], [?]bba & Fanny, Giles & [Lees] (carpenters). Joe & Charles (carpenters), Mary & Beck, Dinah & Letty, Maneah & Lucinda, Hetty & Aggy, Lybria & Patience, Sebinah & W[enia], Old Jane & London, Beck & Winney, Osmond & Cate, [?] (smith) & Jane, Margery & infant, Betty & Patt, Pinder & infant, 2 infants, Lewis (3 yrs); Pope TIFFY overseer; likewise allotted to the defendent the house plant. with two thirds of the land (305 ac) on the west side of the road leading by Mattox Church beginning on the east side of the main road leading from Mattox Bridge to Westmoreland Courthouse. (WC RI 8:237)
[Giles (carpenter, age c. 35) and Jerry (age c. 35) ran away from the est. of Dan. McCARTY in Jun 1811 (*Alexandria Gazette*, 10 Jul 1811, p. [1] and 8 Jan 1812, p. [1]; Miller:2 identifies Mattox Church as Appomattox Church located on the Potomac just below the mouth of Mattox Creek]

McCARTY, Daniel the Younger; T 22 Nov 1817; 24 Nov 1817
WC; settlement of the guardianship acct. & admin.acct. of Richard STUART of the children & est. of Daniel McCARTY the Younger dec'd; McCARTY died in 1800 leaving wid. & two daus.; each dau. was entitled by his will to an eq. portion of his est. after the allotment of that part devisied to his wife; in 1802 Richard STUART mar. McCARTY's wid. at which time the children were very young, Anne the oldest being 5 and Elizabeth not quite 3; Ann was about to be married in 1817; McCARTY's wid. died and the daus. were placed with their grandmother Mrs. Margaret ROSE where they lived from that time until they went to Philadelphia for the purpose of finishing their education. (WC RI 10:225)
[Eliz. McCARTY orphan of Dan. McCARTY chose Hen. LEE as her gdn., 24 Nov 1817 (WC OB 1814-18:348)]

McCARTY, Daniel L.; 6 Apr 1813; 3 Jul 1815
NFP, RC; WILL; enough of est. to be sold to pay debts; remainder of est. to wife Ann B. McCARTY during her widowhood; son Madison & dau. Elizabeth Ann; exors. to act as testamentary guardians to children; Negroes & other property to which I shall be entitled to at the death of my m-i-l Judith G. McCARTY from the est. of my father; wife, b-i-l Thomas YERBY, relation William McCARTY, & friend George SAUNDERS exors; WITS: Rich. STREET, Jeremiah NORTHEN, Isaac [SMITH]. (RC WB 9:482)
[Daniel L. McCARTY mar. Ann B. YERBY, RC, bond 26 Aug 1806 (MRC:123); Robt. W. McCARTY aptd. gdn. to Madison, Ann & Maria McCARTY inf. children of Dan. L. McCARTY dec'd, 4 Jan 1825 (RC OB 26:264); Wm. McCARTY aptd. in place of Robt. W. McCARTY, dec'd, as gdn. to Madison, Ann, & Maria McCARTY inf. children of Dan. L. McCARTY, 2 Jan 1827 (RC OB 27:128)]

McCARTY, Dennis; 30 Jul 1803; 3 Dec 1804
NFP, RC; WILL; wife Elizabeth; dau. Juliet (when 18); son Albert; son William to receive the forest tract purchased of Frederick DOBYNS (when 21); son George the land and plant. w/o I now live at the death of my wife and also the profits of Farnham Bridge (when 21) he keeping up the bridge agreeable to my contract with the court after that period; wife to be extx & friends John M. YERBY & Bartholomew McCARTY exors; WITS: Jas. D. SYDNOR, Lawson DOBYNS, Dan. L. McCARTY; [Cod dtd. 30 Jul 1803] (RC WB 9:247)
[Dennis McCARTY mar. Eliz. Woodbridge YERBY, RC, bond 3 Dec 1790 (MWO:239); a court case suggests that Dennis McCARTY had more children than are named in his will; Wm. D. McCARTY, Geo. Y. McCARTY, Albert McCARTY, Augustine NEALE & Juliet Ann his wife, Geo. YERBY, an infant by Geo. SAUNDERS his next friend, and Judith G. McCARTY, compl., vs. Wm. G. YERBY, 3 Feb 1823 (RC OB 26:22); Augustine NEALE mar. Juliet Ann McCARTY, dau. of Eliz. McCARTY, RC, bond 21 Dec 1815 (MRC:144); Jn. YERBY mar. Eliz. D. McCARTY, ward of Judith G. McCARTY, RC, bond 17 Jun 1805 (MRC:238)]

McCARTY, Fanny; 10 Nov 1793; 20 Oct 1794
LC; Fanny McCARTY, dau. of Col. Thaddeus McCARTY (d. LC 1787), d. in 1794 and left a will (*not included in Lee: 1959*) in which she devised her whole est. to her half-sis. Mary Chinn MATTHEWS wife of John MATTHEWS. (NC CC 1801-011)
[Col. Thaddeus McCARTY in his will (LC 25 Oct 1787 - 17 Dec 1787), named his sons Jas. Ball & Frederick and daus. Mildred Smith, Sally, Nancy, Eliz., Mary Chinn and Fanny (LC WB 22:159); Mildred Smith McCARTY d. intest in 1793 leaving a bro. Jas. Ball McCARTY and a sis. Sarah McCARTY of the whole blood and four sis. of the half blood: Mary Chinn, Nancy Lawson, Eliz. Purkins and Fanny (NC CC 1801-011, 1805-028); Mary Chinn McCARTY mar. Jn. MATTHEWS bef. 12 Jun 1797 (MWO:237)]

McCARTY, Frances; 10 Nov 1793; 20 Oct 1794
CCP, LC; Negro girl Frank to bro. James Ball McCARTY; sis. Mary Chinn McCARTY; bro. James Ball McCARTY & cousin Bartholomew McCARTY exors; WITS: Fanny BALL, Jas. BALL. (LC WB 28:6

McCARTY, Sarah; PO Jun 1798; 20 Jan 1800
LC; INV, £247.2.6; includes Negroes: Peter (old), Harry, Lucy, Lydia; DIV of balance of est. at the house of Severe GALLE among: Mary C. MATHEWS (sis. of the half blood), Ann CUTHBERT (sis. of the half blood), Maria

[CRAINE] (sis. of the half blood), James McCARTY (bro. of the whole blood), Mary EDWARDS (half blood by mother) being her part of the profits arising from the est. of William BRUMLEY dec'd. (LC EB 24:107, 108) [Sarah McCARTY was the dau. of Col. Thaddeus McCARTY (d. LC, 1787) (LC WB 22:159); she received a legacy in the will of Wm. BRUMLEY (d. LC, 1793) (LC WB 22:358)]

McCARTY, Sydnor; PO 5 Jun 1820; 4 Sep 1820
RC; INV, $1749.29, includes following Negroes: Lucy, Daniel, Mary, Judy, girl Lucinda, boy Frank, girl Eve (subject to fits). (RC WB 9:667) [Sydnor McCARTY, bro. of Bartholomew McCARTY, mar. Eliz. W. HUNTON, RC, bond 27 Sep 1809 (MRC:124); Eliz. W. McCARTY aptd. gdn. to her son Jn. McCARTY the orphan of Sydnor McCARTY, RC, 3 May 1819 (RC OB 24:329); Thos. Y. HUNTON aptd. gdn. of Jn. McCARTY Jr. orphan of Sydnor McCARTY, 1 May 1820 (RC OB 25:6); Foushee G. TEBBS aptd. gdn. of Jn. McCARTY orphan of Sydnor McCARTY, 7 Nov 1820 (RC OB 25:81)]

McCARTY, Tarpley; PO Nov 1818, T 1 Jan 1819; 4 Sep 1820
RC; DIV of Negroes among B. McCARTY's heirs (Sam, William, Molly), Robert W. McCARTY & Winnefred his wife (Susan & child Scilla, Joe), John McCARTY Jr., son of Sydnor McCARTY, (Moses Senr., Livinia), Frances A. SMITH & Charles M. SMITH and John McCARTY Sr. (RC AB 3:698) [Tarpley McCARTY mar. Catharine TOMLIN, dau. of Robt. & Susanna (FAUNTLEROY) TOMLIN, RC, bond 30 Mar 1803 (MRC:124); div. of Negroes and other pers. prop. of Tarpley McCARTY into 5 parts: (1) Jn. McCARTY, (2) Jn. McCARTY son of Sydnor McCARTY dec'd, (3) Robt. McCARTY & wife Winefred T. dau. of Chas. T. McCARTY dec'd, (4) Frances A. SMITH & Chas. McCarty SMITH children of Winefred SMITH dec'd who was Winefred McCARTY, (5) Robt. W. McCARTY, Manus ROWAN & Fanny P. his wife & Bartholomew McCarty TOMLIN, Robt. W. & Frances P. were children of Bartholomew McCarty TOMLIN who was a grson. of Bartholomew McCARTY lately dec'd; RC, 2 Nov 1818 (RC OB 24:220, 275); Winifred T. McCARTY mar. Isaac SMITH, RC, bond 27 Oct 1814 (MRC:189); Manus ROWAN mar. Fanny P. McCARTY, RC, bond 5 Aug 1816 (MRC:174)]

McCARTY, William; 19 Jul 1801; 6 Jun 1803
RC; WILL; wife; son Daniel (under 21); dau. Ailcy [*several lines mutilated*]; wife, bro. Dennis McCARTY & George YERBY exors; [no wits]. (RC WB 9:213)

McCARTY, William; PO Jan 1806; 2 Jun 1806
RC; DIV of slaves among: John M. YERBY in right of his wife Elizabeth, Daniel L. McCARTY and five others not further identified. (RC AB 3:157) [Jn. M. YERBY mar. Eliz. D. McCARTY, RC, bond 17 Jun 1805 (MRC:238)]

McCARTY, William; PO 1 Nov [1813], T 31 Dec 1813; 7 Mar 1814
RC; valuation of slaves belonging to the est. of William McCARTY dec'd; includes Daniel, Abraham, Harry, Hampton, George, Chichester, Robin, Armistead, Milly an old woman, Criss, Matilda, Manuel son of Criss; these slaves were div. into 4 lots; Louisa H. McCARTY, a dau., drew Lot 1. (RC AB 3:300)

McCARTY, William; PO 7 Jan 1822, T 5 Apr 1825; 7 Jun 1825
RC; allotment to Henry W. TEBBS in right of his wife Nancy of his proportion of the Negroes undivided belonging to the est. of William McCARTY dec'd; TEBBS was also to receive $100 from Mrs. Judith G. McCARTY the extx. (RC AB 4:175)

[This is Wm. McCARTY who mar. Judith YERBY, RC, bond 24 Dec 1798 (MRC:124); Hen. Wm. TEBBS of Middlesex Co., son of Foushee G. TEBBS, mar. Nancy Y. McCARTY, dau. of Judith G. McCARTY, RC, bond 15 Dec 1821 (MRC:207)]

McCAVE, John; 13 Dec 1819
NC; Betsy McCAVE orphan of John McCAVE chose Paul JONES as her gdn. (NC OB 1816-20:414)

McCLANAHAN, Daniel; 27 Jul 1801
WC; Margaret McCLANAHAN aptd. gdn. to Anne & Elizabeth R. McCLANAHAN orphans of Daniel M. McCLANAHAN. (WC Orders 1801-04:76)
[Marg. McCLANAHAN was admx. with the will annexed of Dan. McCLANAHAN and gdn. to his infant daus. Ann Robinson and Betsy McCLANAHAN, WC, 22 Mar 1802 (WC Orders 1801-04:209)

McCLANAHAN, James; PO 9 Oct 1809; 11 Dec 1809
NC; allottment of dower in slaves of James McCLANAHAN to Elizabeth McCLANAHAN (rec'd Dinah & Betty), residue of slaves div. among William J. McCLANAHAN (Sam & Adam), Richard McCLANAHAN (Luce) Peter G. McCLANAHAN (Sall). (NC RB 18:268)
[This is prob. the James McCLANAHAN whose est. was ord. to be admin. by Wm. CLAUGHTON; 10 Sep 1798; his wid. Eliza McCLANAHAN refused to admin. on her husband's est. (NC Fiduciary Bonds 1797-1801 cited in Lewis & Booker, 1964:49)]

McCLANAHAN, Jane; 4 Jan 1803; 24 Jun 1803.
CP, WC; WILL; cousin Benedeck LAMKIN use of all Negroes until bro. Wm. McCLANAHAN & nephew Peter McClanahan BARNES reach 21; bro. William 4 Negroes: Winney, Davy, Reubin, & Molly; nephew Peter McClanahan BARNES Negro boy Isaack; cousin Benedeck exor.; WITS: Levi HILLYARD, Smith KING, Peter Rust LAMKIN. (WC DW 20:469)
[Peter McClanahan BARNES was prob. the son of Edw. BARNES who mar. Alice McCLANAHAN, NC, bond 28 Oct 1797; in the bond Alice McCLANAHAN was identified as a dau. of Jane McCLANAHAN (MLBNC:4)]

McCLANAHAN, Thomas; PO 14 Apr 1806, T 20 May 1806; 13 Oct 1806
NC; INV, £488.8.2; includes Negroes Sam & Moses. (NC RB 17:467)
[This is prob. the Thos. McCLANAHAN who mar. Eliz. BARNES, NC, bond 5 Mar 1800 (MLBNC:71); in his will (NC 29 Jan 1806 - 14 Apr 1806), Thos. McCLANAHAN of SSP named his wife Betsy and 3 children: Jas. McCLANAHAN, Nancy Dale McCLANAHAN & Peter Lamkin McCLANAHAN (NC RB 17:395)]

McCLANAHAN, Thomas; 13 Nov 1809
NC; Samuel BARNES aptd. gdn. to Nancy D. McCLANAHAN orphan of Thomas McCLANAHAN. (NC OB 1807-11:132)
[Randall R. KIRK was aptd. gdn. to Jas. and Peter L. McCLANAHAN, orphans of Thos. McCLANAHAN, NC, 14 Dec 1812 (NC OB 1811-15:137); Randall R. KIRK mar. Eliz. McCLANAHAN (prob. the wid. of Thos.), NC, bond 4 Jan 1808 (MLBNC:65)]

McCLANAHAN, William; PO 11 Jul 1803, T 31 Dec 1803; 11 Jun 1804
NC; DIV of the prop. of William McCLANAHAN dec'd, whose gdn. was Thomas McCLANAHAN, between Thomas McCLANAHAN (received Negroes Sam & Moses) & Samuel BARNES Jr. gdn. of Peter M. BARNES (received 166 ac. & Negro Hannah). (NC GA 1788-1824:229)

McCLANAHAN, William; PO 24 Nov 1806; 27 Jun 1808. WC; INV, £79.16.5 3/4. (WC RI 9:52)

McCURDY, Samuel; T 23 Dec 1814; 14 Aug 1815

NC; INV, includes Negroes Bob, boy Abraham, Sally & child Caroline, Nancy & child Steptoe, Charlott & child Mahala, Rachel & child Alfred, Milley & children Luisa & Linzey, [Marthen] & children John & Charlott, girl Harriett, boys Hiram & Robert, girl Milinda, Grace. (NC RB 20:181)

[Sam. McCURDY had a store in Northumberland Courthouse in partnership with [fnu] McCAUSLAND; the partnership was dissolved in the fall of 1797 (*Federal Gazette & Baltimore Daily Advertiser*, 16 Feb 1798, p. [1])]

McCURDY, Samuel; PO 12 Nov 1816, T 20 Dec 1816; 10 Mar 1817

NC; Chancery suit, Edward N. CLOPPER & Grace his wife, late Grace McCURDY extx of Hugh McCURDY dec'd, complts. against Thomas H. JETT admr. with the will annexed of Samuel McCURDY dec'd and John C. W. McCURDY, William J. McCURDY, Fleming B. McCURDY and Diana H. McCURDY infants heirs & devisees of the [sd.] Samuel McCURDY by Thomas H. JETT their gdn. specifically appointed to defend them in this suit defts; defts to pay complts. £1195.11.9 Maryland currency of the value of £956.9.4 farthing Virginia currency with interest (NC RB 21:150)

[Sam. McCURDY mar. Hannah K. HUDNALL, NC, bond 21 Aug 1801 (MLBNC:72); in his will (NC 28 Oct 1814-12 Dec 1814), he named his wife Hannah and his children Eliz., Hugh, Ann, Jn. C. W., Wm. T., Fleming B. and Dianna H. and Polly Hudnall; his children Eliz., Hugh & Ann rec'd all his interest to property in Ireland (NC RB 19:571); Wm. HARDING & Sally his wife, Steptoe TAYLOR & Polly his wife vs. Jn., Fleming & Diana McCURDY infants ... to sell land descended to them from Hannah McCURDY, 11 Feb 1822 (NC OB 1820-25:173); Wm. HARDING aptd. gdn. of Diana McCURDY orphan of Sam. McCURDY, NC 12 Aug 1822 (NC OB 1820-25:227)]

McFARLANE, Elizabeth; 2 Nov 1760; 23 Sep 1800.

CP, WC; WILL; 3 daus. Mary, Jane, Anne (their father was Thomas McFARLANE); son Francis WRIGHT ex; WITS: Hannah HARRIS, Dan. TIBBS, Aston LAMKIN, Dan. TIBBS Jr., Willoughby NEWTON, Francis CALLIS, Benedict MIDDLETON, Sam. RUST, Benj. MIDDLETON, Thos. MOORE, Lewis CHASTAIN, Jeremiah HARRISON, Jos. [HAZEL]. (WC DW 20:160)

[Thos. McFARLANE mar. Eliz. the wid. of Rich. WRIGHT (d. WC 1741); he d. in WC in the fall of 1755 leaving his wife and 4 daus: Mary, Jane, Ann, & Hannah; he also left legacies to Eliz. COX & Francis WRIGHT (his stepson) (WC DW 11:26, DW 12:302)]

McGINNIS, Nicholas; 7 May 1821

RC; Mary WATSON who was Mary McGINNIS, wid. of Nicholas McGINNIS, has dower right to 4 Negroes bel. to the est. of Nicholas McGINNIS: Sarah, Baley, Grace & Wm., but Mary is of unsound mind. (RC OB 25:130)

[Mary McGINNIS, wid., mar. Jn. WATSON, RC, bond 6 Sep 1790 (MRC:224); on the mot. of Rich. STRAUGHAN who has purchased the dower interest of Mary WATSON who was MAGINNIS in slaves allotted to the sd. Mary as dower in her former husband's est.; Jn. SCATES purchased the remainder of one of the distributees of the sd. MAGINNIS in the sd. slaves, ord. that the other distributees Nath. MAGINNIS, Beckham KELLY & Sucky his wife, Nicholas MAGINNIS & Jn. MAGINNIS be summoned to court to show cause why the dower slaves should not be sold, 27 Aug 1821 (WC OB 1819-23:300); Beckham KELLY mar. Susanna McGINNIS, RC, bond 9 Jan 1797 (MRC:111)]

McGURK, John; T 1 Feb 1823; 12 Jan 1824. NC INV. (NC RB 23:401)

McGUIRE, John; WC; d. c. 5 Jun 1782 leaving a wid. Ann who mar. (2) William MORTON and a dau. Elizabeth who mar. George McKENNEY (WC CC 1795-001)

[Eliz. McGUIRE mar. Geo. McKENNEY, WC, bond 29 Jul 1791 (MLBWC:42)]

McKENNEY, Presley; T 9 Sep 1815; 22 Feb 1819. WC; INV, [$]214.97. (WC RI 10:351)

[This is poss. Presley McKENNEY, Jr. who mar. Nancy McKENNEY, WC, bond 30 Jul 1797 (MLBWC:241)]

McKENNY, Ellis [G.]; 26 Jun 1820

WC; Letty McKENNY aptd. gdn. to Judith & Polly McKENNY and Susan ANTHONY late Susan McKENNY; John YEATMAN made oath that Ellis [G.] McKENNY who died in the service of the US was the bro. of the above-named Judith & Polly McKENNY and Susan ANTHONY late Susan McKENNY and that they are his only legal heirs and descendants. (WC OB 1819-23:160)

[Susannah McKENNY mar. Wm. ANTHONY, WC bond 26 Oct 1819 (MLBWC:2)]

McKILDOE, Robert; 1802

WC; Robert McKILDOE died intestate in WC in 1799 leaving children William, Robert, James and Margaret and a wid. Elizabeth (who mar. 3rd Wm. Robertson DOZIER); Geo. THOMPSON was appointed gdn. to Margaret McKILDOE; in 1803, Robert & William McKILDOE, sons of Robert, sold a 66-ac. tract of land in WC on the south side of the main road from Hutt's Old Mill to Westmoreland Court House that had belonged to their father. (WC Orders 1801-04:200, DB 20:470, 481; WC CC 1802-017)

[admin. of the est. of Robt. McKILDOE granted Sam. TEMPLEMAN, 27 May 1799 (WC Orders 1799-1801:6); Robt. SANFORD aptd. gdn. of Robt. & Jas. McKILDOE, 26 Jan 1801 (WC Orders 1799-1801:401); the land of Robt. McKILDOE who died intestate was divided among Eliz. DOZIER the wid. of Robt. McKILDOE who received one third as dower and Wm., Jas. and Margaret the children of sd. Robt., WC, 22 Mar 1802 (WC Orders 1801-04:207); Peggy S. McKILDOE mar. Sam. LYELL, WC bond 8 Dec 1807 (MLBWC:41); the wid. Elizabeth was prob. Elizabeth SANFORD whom he mar. in WC, bond 3 Jun 1796 and who was a wid. at the time and certainly not his first wife (MLBWC:42); however, acc. to WC CC 1819-007 Eliz. who mar. Robt. McKILDOE was the wid. of Rich. SHACKLEFORD, Jr. and mar. (3) Wm. R. DOZIER; Miller:71 locates Hutt's Mill in WC on Templeman Run near its confluence with Nomini Creek.]

McKILDOE, William; 24 Apr 1820

WC; a certif. from Mary McKILDOE, wid. & rel. of William McKILDOE, of her relinquishment of right to admin. on the est. of her dec'd husband. (WC OB 1819-23:142)

[Wm. McKILDOE mar. Polly SELF, dau. of Wm. SELF, WC, c. 26 Oct 1803 (MLBWC:42)]

McNAMARA, John; PO 20 Oct 1823, 28 Dec 1823; 19 Jul 1824

LC; DIV of Negroes to Sarah McNAMARA wid. of John (Cyrus, Old Daniel, George, Dillah also Solomon as heir of her son William & son of sd. John McNAMARA), to Sarah McNAMARA dau. of sd. John (Young Daniel,

Sarah, Robert & Harriet), to Thomas Lee LAWSON gdn. of Henry McNAMARA (Charles, Letty & her child Daniel, Frederick); John HALL was gdn. to Sarah E. McNAMARA. (LC EB 29:345)
[This is prob. the Jn. McNAMARA who mar. Salley M. GIBSON, WC, bond 13 Jan 1817 (MLBLC:50); Hen. L. McNAMARA orphan of Jn. McNAMARA chose Thos. L. LAWSON as his gdn., 15 Dec 1823 (LC OB 26:13)]

McNAMARA, Timothy; 6 Nov 1823; 16 Feb 1824
LC; WILL; use of third of my two plants. in this co including the whole of the dwelling house where I now live & third of my Negroes to wife as long as she remains my widow; wife to care for two daus; plant, including Cherry Point, where I now live to dau. Frances; my plant. in this co in the neck called Georgetown to dau. Mary; Richard BRENT; ex. to sell house and lot in Fredericksburg and schooner; friend Ralph EDMONDS ex. & gdn. to two daus; WITS: Jas. POLLARD, Thos. L. LAWSON, Isaac CURRELL Jr.; COD. dtd. 23 Jan 1824 - land I purchased from Benjamin GEORGE by deed dtd. 21 Jan 1824 to dau. Mary Lawson McNAMARA; ex. to pay $5 to assist in [taring] & underpinning the meeting house near the White Stone; a head & foot stone with the ages & date of death to be placed at the graves of myself, wife & my two sons; friend William STORKE of NC joint ex.; WITS: Jn. HUNT, Benj. GEORGE. (LC WB 28:245)
[There are at least 3 marriages for a Timothy McNAMARA in the LC records: (1) Timothy McNAMARA, mariner, mar. Mary LAWSON, bond 5 Aug 1796, (2) Timothy McNAMARA mar. Frances LAWSON, bond 15 Jul 1807, and (3) Timothy McNAMARA mar. Eliza L. BRENT, bond 20 Nov 1820 (MLBLC:50)]

McNAMARA, Timothy (Capt.); PO 19 Jul 1824, T 31 Aug 1824; 15 Nov 1824
LC; DIV of slaves among: the wid. rec'd her dower (Jesse, Dick, Suckey, Spencer, Mirah, Sally, Sam), Frances McNAMARA (rec'd Bob, Jacob, Catharine, Charles, Nancy, Moses), and Mary McNAMARA (rec'd Roda, Isaac, Levina, Judith, Albert, Richard, Sprigg, Abraham); each one rec'd slaves worth $1285. (LC EB 29:362

McNAUGHTON, Daniel; T 23 Dec 1814; 15 May 1815; LC INV. (LC EB 27:197)

McNAUGHTON, Duncan (Rev.); T 19 Jun 1809; 15 May 1810
NC [m]; includes many books (among them a biographical dictionary, Hermes Plays, set of encyclopedias, 8 volumes of *The Spectator*, Sheridan's lectures, an English grammar, a 'Gallic Bible,' History of Women, and 4 volumes on medicine). (NC RB 18:400)
[McNAUGHTON was a native of Perthshire, Scotland; he served as rector of St. Stephen's Parish, NC beginning in 1802; his years there were filled with controversy when the Overseers of the Poor tried to sell two of the glebe lands (Fairfield and Cherry Point) belonging to the parish; judging from the book "Gallic bible" in his inventory, McNAUGHTON may have been able read Scot's Gaelic; he died in NC on 16 May 1809 (2 Munf 513); his est. was ord. to be admin. by Jn. THOMSON, NC, 12 Jun 1809 (NC OB 1807-1811:110); McNAUGHTON's tombstone is located on Cherry Point near the Glebe Mansion (NNVHM Vol. IX, No. 1, p. 837)]

McNEAL, James; 25 Aug 1801
WC; Mary McNEAL aptd. gdn. to John R. McNEAL, Harriet McNEAL, and Jean McNEAL orphans of James McNEAL. (WC Orders 1801-04:138)
[Jas. McNEIL mar. Mary DOLEMAN a dau. of [fnu] MOXLEY and wid. of Wm. DOLEMAN (d. WC 1784), WC, 19 May 1785 (MWO:242); Harriet McNEIL mar. Jas. H. BAILEY, WC, bond 16 Sep 1807 (MLBWC:3); Jane

McNEIL orphan of Jas. McNEIL chose Jn. REDMAN as her gdn., 24 Apr 1815 (WC OB 1814-18:113)]

McTYRE, Charles L.; T 3 May 1811; 17 Jun 1811. LC; INV, £16.2.9. (LC EB 27:87) [Chas. L. McTYRE mar. Eliz. DAVENPORT, LC, 15 Oct 1795 (WMHM 18:3 p. 176); Eliz. (DAVENPORT) McTYRE seems to have mar. (2) Wm. BRADBURY, LC, bond 6 Dec 1811 and (3) Edw. PINCKARD, LC, bond 2 Nov 1813 (MLBLC:7, 50, 59; LC CC 1822-003)]

McTYRE, Elizabeth; 17 Apr 1790; 21 Feb 1791
CCP, LC; WILL; land I now live on to son Robert McTYRE; after son's death, land to his son Charles Lee; Frances MORGAN; grdau. Hannah DAVIS; dau. Frances YERBY; dau. Katty DAVIS; Mary MEREDITH; son John McTYRE 1 shilling; grson. Robert McTYRE 1 shilling; to son [Frizrell] McTYRE Negroes [Cox], Betty & her 2 children Rawleigh & Lucy; s-i-l John DAVIS; dau. Catharine DAVIS; grdaus. [Ann] & Frances DAVIS; Mary MEREDITH; rest of est. to daus. Frances YERBY & Katty DAVIS; my black colt to my Negro woman Winny; friend Ozwald NEWBY Sr., Abner PALMER & son Robert McTYRE exors; WITS: Jas. [W.] BALL, Robt. CLARK, Judith CLARK; will was further & fully proved on 21 Apr 1795. (LC WB 28:14)
[This is Eliz. FRIZELL, dau. of Francis(co) FRIZELL, who mar. Robt. McTYRE (d. LC 1775) in 1733 (MWO:242, LC WB 20:83, WB 22:303); Caty McTYRE mar. Jn. DAVIS, LC, bond 30 Dec 1766; Frances McTIRE, dau. of Robt. McTIRE, mar. Wm. YERBY, LC, bond 17 Apr 1753 (MLBLC:20, 81)]

McTYRE, Fanny (Mrs.); PO 20 Jun 1803; 18 Jul 1803. LC; INV, [m]. (LC EB 24:242)

McTYRE, Robert; 18 Nov 1799
LC; Charles McTYRE, William C. McTYRE and Fanny wife of George H. POPE are heirs of Robert McTYRE dec'd. (LC Orders (21) 1799-1801:59)
[Fanny McTIRE mar. Geo. POPE, LC, bond 24 Mar 1796 (MLBLC:60); [Jenny] Lee McTYRE orphan of Robt. McTYRE chose Wm. B. KENT as her gdn., 19 Dec 1803 (LC Orders V 1802-03:506); Joanna ROBINSON extx. of Jesse ROBINSON, pltf., against Chas. L. McTYRE, Wm. C. McTYRE, Geo. H. POPE & Fanny his wife, Williamson GARNER & Charlotte his wife, Frizell McTYRE and Wm. B. KENT & Jane L. his wife, which sd. Chas. L., Wm. C., Fanny, Charlotte, Frizell & Jane L. are sons and daus. and coheirs of Robt. McTYRE, defts., in debt (LC Orders D22 1805-08:313); Williamson GARNER mar. Charlotte McTYRE LC, bond 24 Mar 1802; Wm. B. KENT mar. Jenny Lee McTYRE, LC, bond 22 Dec 1803 (MLBLC:29, 45); *see also LC CC 1810-016 which also identifies Jn. McTYRE as a bro. to Robt. McTYRE*]

McTYRE, William C.; PO 15 Jan 1821, T Feb 1821;[19] Mar 1821
LC; assigned to Alice McTYRE her dower in the slaves (Young Lucy, child Peter) and div. the balance of the slaves among the four children: John (girl Jenny), Nancy C. who mar. David BUCHAN (boy Henry), Sarah L. (Juliet, Old Lucy) & Fanny McTYRE (girl Mary). (LC EB 29:71)
[Wm. C. McTYRE mar. Alice POPE, RC, bond 13 Feb 1798 (MRC:126); Nancy C. McTYRE mar. David BUCHAN, poss. as his 2nd wife, LC, bond 7 Dec 1819 (MLBLC:10); [Alcy] McTYRE aptd. gdn. to Jn., Nancy, Sally & Fanny McTYRE orphans of Wm. C. McTYRE, 18 Jan 1819 (LC OB 25:37); Ailcy McTYRE aptd. gdn. to Nancy McTYRE orphan of Wm. McTYRE, 15 Nov 1819 (LC OB 25:92); it appearing to the court that the land of which Wm. C. McTYRE died seized is not of the value of $300 to each of the heirs, therefore ord. that Alice McTYRE, David BUCHAN & Nancy his wife, Fanny & Sally McTYRE by Alice McTYRE their mother and next friend be summoned to

show cause why sd. land should not be sold and proceeds divided, 21 Oct 1822 (LC OB 25:336)]

MEATH, Jesse; PO 12 Apr 1808; 13 Feb 1809

NC; sale of Negroes Hannah, Henna, & Matilda mentioned in a suit Elijah MOORE & Nancy his wife, Fanny MEATH by William BARNES her gdn, Kitty Jackson MEATH by Elijah MOORE her gdn, Thaddeus MEATH by Bennedict LAMKIN his gdn. & Jesse MEATH by John CRALLE Jr. his gdn. against John CRALLE Jr admr. de bonis non with the will annexed of Jesse MEATH dec'd; possessed Elijah MOORE & Nancy his wife with their proportion (she being of the whole blood) which is £40.3.4 1/2 and William BARNES with his ward's proportion, also £40.3.4 1/2; possessed Elijah MOORE gdn. to Kitty J. MEATH, Thaddeus MEATH by Bennedict LAMKIN his gdn. and John CRALLE Jr. gdn. to Jesse MEATH who are of the half blood with their respective proportions which are £20.1.8 1/4 each. (NC RB 18:115)

[Elijah MOORE's wife was prob. Nancy MEATH the dau. of Jesse MEATH; however there is also a marriage for an Elijah MOORE to a Nancy CLARKE, RC, bond 8 Mar 1786 (MRC:136); in his will (NC 23 Jun 1806-14 Jul 1806), Jesse MEATH names his sons Thadias Jackson and Jessey and his daus. Nancey, Kittey Jackson, Fanney, Polley & Haney (NC RB 17:446); Royston BETTS, Jr. was aptd. gdn. of Kitty J. MEATH orphan of Jesse MEATH, NC, 10 Nov 1817 (NC OB 1816-20:196); Kitty J. MEATH chose Benedict LAMKIN as her gdn., NC 8 Nov 1819 (NC OB 1816-20:403); *see also NC CC 1808-003*]

MEATH, Jesse; PO 9 May 1815, T 15 Jul 1815; 11 Mar 1816

NC; land which MEATH died seized & possessed sold to Vincent BARNES and proceeds div. among Elijah MOORE & Nancy his wife, Benedict LAMKIN gdn. to Thomas J. MEATH [sic], and Elijah MOORE as gdn. to Kitty J. MEATH. (NC RB 20:389)

MEREDITH, Anna; T 5 May 1806; 10 Sep 1806

LC; list of Negroes that Anna MERIDITH got for her third: Jacob (between 40 & 50), Phillis (between 20 & 30), [Minger] (7), Davy (5), Daniel (1). (LC EB 24:346)

MEREDITH, Catharine; PO 22 Nov 1820; 16 Apr 1821. LC INV. (LC EB 29:89)

MEREDITH, John; 24 May 1794; 21 Sep 1795

LC; WILL; all est. to wife Mary except the graveyard; if wife marries she may be thirded and the rest of my est. be eq. div. amongst my three daus. Ann, Hannah, & Betsy MEREDITH; wife Mary extx. under the direction of my friends Col. James GORDON & Peter [BEATIE] whom I appoint as trustees; WITS: Wm. MEREDITH, Geo. WARWICK, Jn. RICE. (LC WB 28:18)

[Jn. MEREDITH mar. Mary DILLARD, LC, bond 13 Dec 1782 (MLBLC:51)]

MEREDITH, John; PO 25 Sep 1796; 15 Feb 1796

LC; INV, £169.14.0; includes Negroes: Moses, girl Jona, boys Manuel & George. (LC EB 24:7)

MEREDITH, William; 1 Mar 1808; 19 Apr 1808

LC; WILL; est. already given to children John, William, Frances F. PULLEN & Thomas; rest of est. to be kept together in the possession of wife during her life or until she should marry for the support & maintenance of wife & children Robert, Nancy & Caroline & for the support, maintenance & education of my children Joseph & Hannah; Negro [Battron] to son John; Negro Henry to son William; Negro Willis to dau. Frances F. PULLEN; plant. w/o I now live to son John; Negro Solomon to son Robert after the death or marriage of his mother; wife & friend & b-i-l William YERBY Jr. &

friend Richard BERRYMAN exors; WITS: Chas. EDMONDS, Lucy [NUTT], Rich. BERRYMAN, Hugh BRENT. (LC WB 28:106)

[Frances Frizel MEREDITH mar. Thaddeus PULLEN, wid, LC, bond 16 Oct 1797 (MLBLC:61); Nancy MEREDITH orphan of Wm. MEREDITH chose Rich. BERRYMAN as her gdn., 20 May 1811 (LC Orders 24:15); according to information extracted from the Thomas Meredith Papers at the Maryland Historical Society, Wm. MEREDITH mar. Caty YERBY; his son Thomas moved to Baltimore where he became a partner in William Meredith & Co. in 1807 (see <http://www.werelate.org/wiki/Genealogical_Information_Abstracted_from_the_Thomas_Meredith_Papers> for more on Thomas MEREDITH]

MEREDITH, William; T 8 Jul 1808; 18 Jul 1808
LC; INV, £813.2.0; includes Negroes Daniel, Solomon, Saunders, George, boy Stephen, Nell, Nanny, Patty, girl Matilda. (LC EB 27:32)

MEREDITH, William; PO 20 Nov 1820; 15 Jan 1821
LC; DIV made at the house of Maj. John MEREDITH of the Negroes of the late William MEREDITH among the following children: Joseph MEREDITH (Saunders), Hannah MEREDITH (Priscilla & Solomon), Thomas MEREDITH (James & Daniel), Mrs. C. SHEARMAN (Dianna, Jacob, Peggy), Mrs. A. CORBIN (Mimy), Mrs. F. PULLIN's heirs (Harry & Davy), William MEREDITH's heirs (Polly). . (LC EB 29:52)

[Caroline MEREDITH mar. Jos. SHEARMAN, LC, bond 2 Mar 1819; Nancy MEREDITH mar. Gawin CORBIN, LC, bond 20 May 1811 (MLBLC:16, 67); admin. de bonis non of the est. of Wm. MEREDITH granted to Jn. MEREDITH and he is aptd. gdn. of Hannah & Jos. MEREDITH, 20 Nov 1820 (LC OB 25:172)]

MEREDITH, William; PO 20 Nov 1820, T 14 Dec 1820; 16 Apr 1821
LC; APP, $1894.07; includes Negroes Daniel (aged about 60), Jacob (68), Sanders (40), Mima (29), Patty (33), boys Solomon (10) & Henry ([9]), girl Diana (4), infants David & Pegg, girl Matilda (a legacy to Ann Y. CORBIN), Mahala (a legacy to Caroline SHEARMAN), boy James (a legacy to Thomas MEREDITH), girl Cillar (a legacy to Hannah MEREDITH). (LC EB 29:88)

MERRYMAN, Thomas; PO Feb 1805; 16 Apr 1805. LC; INV, £8.10.4. (LC EB 24:311)

[A Thos. MERRYMAN mar. Milly DAVIS, dau. of Jos. DAVIS, LC, bond 1 Aug 1803 (MLBLC:51); Milly MERRYMAN was the wid. of Thos. MERRYMAN and Thos. was his son, 19 Apr 1808 (LC Orders 22D 1805-08:464; LC CC 1819-004)]

MIDDLETON, Benedict; 28 Jan 1822
WC; on the mot. of Benedict WRIGHT, ord. that Sam. [J.] BOOTH & Polly his wife, Benedict D. WRIGHT, Betsy CLARK, Judy CLARK & William WRIGHT be summoned to show cause why a sale & div. should not be had of 4 slaves the title to which slaves they derive from Benedict MIDDLETON. (WC OB 1819-23:347)

[On the mot. of Rich. STRAUGHAN, assignee & [?] of Benedict MIDDLETON, ord. that Martha OLDHAM, Jane WROE, Benedict LAMKIN, Wm. WRIGHT, Benedict WRIGHT, Sam. J. BOOTH & Polly his wife, Betsy CLARK & Judy CLARK be summoned to show cause why a Negro woman slave named Lucy and her children devised to the sd. parties from Benedict MIDDLETON should not be sold, 24 Jun 1822 (WC OB 1819-23:431); Martha MIDDLETON, wid., mar. Nath. OLDHAM, WC bond 4 Apr 1793

(MLBWC:51); Sam. J. BOOTH mar. Mary W. WRIGHT, WC bond 27 Jun 1817 (MLBWC:7)]

MIDDLETON, Benjamin; 7 Dec 1790; [m]
WC; WILL; all est. to Robert MIDDLETON son of William MIDDLETON and grson. of Fleet COX Sr.; if he dies before age 21 or leaves no heirs est. to go to John MIDDLETON son & grson. of the above-named MIDDLETON & COX; [no ex. named]; WIT: Peter Presley COX. (WC Unrec Wills 1755-1800 #39)
[Wm. MIDDLETON mar. Molly COX dau. of Fleet COX, 4 Dec 1777 (MWO:245)]

MIDDLETON, Benjamin; 28 Jul 1802
WC; Jos. BROWN mar. Mary MIDDLETON dau. of Benj. MIDDLETON and is the ex. of Jane MIDDLETON a dau. of sd. Benj. and gdn. of Lettice and Hannah daus. of sd. Jane; Eliz. KIRK and Alice SELF are also daus. of Benj. MIDDLETON; [fnu] KING is a dau. of Alice SELF. (WC Orders 1801-04:273)
[Jane Middleton SELF, dau. of Hen. SELF, mar. Smith KING, Jr., WC, bond 12 Jan 1790 (MLBWC:38)]

MILES, George; 30 Nov 1818; 3 Aug 1819
RC; WILL; girl Hannah and two thirds of my est. to wife Hannah MILES; my girl Phillis to my neice Fanny Ellen WELFORD; my girl Alcy to my neice [Avalinn] WELFORD; rest of est. to bro. Thomas MILES who is not to sell or hire any of sd. property out of the neighborhood; if bro. should die all the Negroes which comes to his part to go to the heir of my wife & should she die without heir then the Negroes in her possession to go to the two eldest daus. of Lewis BURREL[L] of Richmond, Fanny & Ann Eliza; no ex; WITS: Thos. T. REYNOLDS, H[orace] WELLFORD, Jn. DAVIS; [Will was originally brought to court on 8 Dec 1818, but was not admitted to record until 3 Aug 1819]. (RC WB 9:620)
[Geo. MILES mar. Hannah HOW, RC, bond 24 Apr 1817 (MRC:132); Fanny Ellen WELFORD, dau. of Horace WELFORD, mar. Walter F. JONES and moved to Petersburg (WCCP:66)]

MILES, George; T 3 Sep 1819; 4 Oct 1824
RC; INV, $4781.06 1/4; includes Negroes: Jack, Sam (blind), Joe, Edmund, [Harry], [Dennis] (old). [Seany], Sally, Mary, Peggy, Lucy, John, Henry, Phillis, Alecy, Hannah. (RC WB 10:54)

MILLAR, Stephen; 12 Dec 1805; 15 Sep 1806
LC; WILL; my land to wife Maryann MILLAR; son Rodham MILLAR; after wife's death land to be sold & money eq. div. among my four children: Elizabeth MILLAR, Rodham MILLAR, Thomas MILLAR, & Robert MILLAR; wife extx; WITS: Wm. MEREDITH, Geo. WALE, Jas. GAINES. (LC WB 28:96)

MILLER, Ann M.; [m]; 18 Mar 1822
LC; DIV of $666.54 3/4 among the heirs of Ann M. MILLER: Spencer GEORGE admr. of Sarah E. GEORGE dec'd mother of Ann M. [MILLER], Mary Ann MILLER (whole blood), Virginia MILLER (whole blood), Warren W. C. GEORGE (half blood), Charles D. GEORGE (half blood). (LC EB 29:203)
[Ann M. MILLER was the dau. of Peter H. MILLER (d. LC 1811) (*see below*)]

MILLER, Elizabeth H.; PO 18 Nov 18[??], T 7 Feb 1818; 16 Feb 1818
LC; DIV among legal reps: Spencer GEORGE in right of his wife, Mary Ann MILLER, Ann M. MILLER, to Virginia P. MILLER; Spencer GEORGE was gdn. to Mary Ann, Ann M., and Virginia P. MILLER. (LC EB 27:404)

MILLER, Jacob; 8 Apr 1818; 27 Apr 1818
WC; D of G; for natural love & affection to Lucinda NEALE alias MILLER and my son William S. MILLER of sd. co. tract of land in WC I purchased of the heirs of Daniel CARTER willed to him by Joseph BARKER also all my personal property; WITS: Patsey WASHINGTON, Jn. S. HEAD, Aleck SANDERS. (WC DW 23:363)
[Jacob MILLER mar. Lucinda NEALE, wid. of Rodham NEALE, WC, bond 15 Nov 1815 (MLBWC:45, WCCP:6)]

MILLER, John; PO 14 May 1816; 10 Jun 1816
NC; has been dead more than 3 mos. and no person applying for the admin. of his est, ord. that Samuel CRALLE sheriff of this county take the est. into his hands and make sale of so much thereof as shall be perishable for the payment of debts; sheriff could find no est. to admin. (NC RB 20:485)

MILLER, John Jr.; T 15 Sep 1807; 14 Nov 1809
NC; INV, $838.24; includes Negroes Billy and Winney and a large collection of books (among them were Bailey's Dictionary, Ferguson's astronomy, Gibson's surveying, Rollin's ancient history, *The Federalist*, Virginia Debates, Reeve's Histroy of the English Law, Revision of the Laws of 1769 & Goldsmith's Animated Nature). (NC RB 18:256)
[The will of Jn. MILLER was ord. to be admin. by Peter H. MILLER, NC, 14 Sep 1807 (NC Minute Book 1805-1807:255); Jn. MILLER Jr. gave notice that he was relinquishing his law practice in the county courts of NC and LC and the district court of NC and transferring his law business to Stokeley TOWLES, esq. of LC, 31 Dec 1807 (*Richmond Enquirer*, 5 Jan 1808, p. [4])]

MILLER, John Jr.; [m]; [12 Feb 1810]
NC; INV of bonds, notes, exors. & accounts to be considered as a continuation of an inv heretofore returned (includes a very long list of these documents). (NC RB 18:306)

MILLER, John Sr.; 28 Feb 1809; 16 Oct 1809
LC; WILL; to son Peter H. MILLER all the land I possess in this county with its appurtenances comprehending the mill I lately purchased of the heirs of George NORRIS dec'd & also the following Negroes: Phoebe & her son Jonathan, Sophia, Aaron, Charles, & Prescilla & the desk & book case that was formerly the property of my son John; to dau. Nancy LANGSDALE the following Negroes: Winny, Daniel, Billy WIGGENS & his wife Winney, Rachel & her children & Betty & the desk that was her mother's; son Thomas MILLER having been absent for about two years & I do not know whether he is dead or alive; if he is alive I leave to him in the hands of my exors. all the land I possess in NC during his life and after his death to his heirs; if he does not return or lacks heirs, largest plant. in NC to my grson. John LANGSDALE; my other plant. in NC to my son Peter; to son Thomas whenever he shall return the following Negroes: Esther & her children, Young George, Lucy & Henry; if son Thomas does not return or have heirs, Esther & her children to go to dau. Nancy & Young George, Lucy & Harry to my son Peter; $100 to Joseph Addison CARTER the son of my friend Joseph CARTER Jr; residue of est. to be eq. div. between three children Thomas, Peter & Nancy except Old George whom I give to my son Peter; son Peter & s-i-l Thomas LANGSDALE exors.; WITS: Jos. CARTER Jr, [Edward] DUNTON, Wm. SIMMONDS. (LC WB 28:111)
[Ann MILLER mar. Thos. LANSDALE, LC, bond 28 Jan 1803 (MLBLC:46); *see also LC CC 1815-001*]

MILLER, John Sr.; PO 16 Oct 1809, T 20 Dec 1809; 18 Feb 1811

LC; INV of est. in NC, $1526; includes Negroes William WIGGINS & his wife Wendy, Rachel, Delilah, Lindsay, Charles, Daniel, Winney, Betty. (LC EB 27:78)

MILLER, John Sr.; PO 16 Oct 1809, T 7 Nov 1809; 16 Mar 1812
LC; INV, [m]; includes Negroes: Phebe, Jonathan, Sophia, Aaron, Charles, Presilla, Old George, Easther, Isaac, Griffin, Anthony, Young George, Lucy, Harry, Old Mima, Mark.; at the house of Benjamin LANSDELL, INV of est. in NC includes Negroes William WIGGINS & his wife Winny, Rachell, Delilah, Lindsey, Charles, Daniel, Winny, Betty. (LC EB 27:103, 105)

MILLER, Peter H.; 19 May 1811; 17 Jun 1811
LC; WILL; est. to be kept together during wife's widowhood or as daus. may marry or come of age; daus. to receive education; friends William KERBY Sr., William KIRK, Peter BEANE & Spencer GEORGE exors; WITS: Jos. CARTER Jr., Wm. NEWBY, Thos. LANSDELL. (LC WB 28:114)

MILLER, Peter H.; T 17 Oct 1811; 18 Jan 1813
LC; INV, [m]; includes many bonds & Negroes: [George], Aaron, Charles, Armestead, Beck, Davy, Jonathan, Robert, Lee, Daniel, Phebe, Peggy, Siller, Sopha, Amey, Eliza. (LC EB 27:134)

MILLER, Peter H.; PO 15 Jun 1815; 21 Nov 1815
LC; DIV among legal reps: the widow Sarah [E.] MILLER (received her dower), Spencer GEORGE in right of his wife Sarah E. GEORGE (received Negroes Aaron, Jack, Siller, Lee), Virginia P. MILLER (Eliza, Davey, Phebe, Stephen) by her gdn, Polly Ann MILLER (Amy, Sophia, Albert), Nancy M. MILLER (Daniel, Jonathan, George), Elizabeth H. MILLER (Emanuel, Charles); also div. the est. of Sally MILLER another orphan of Peter H. MILLER. (LC EB 27:271)
[Peter H. MILLER son of Jn. MILLER Sr. mar. Sally Everett NEWBY, LC, bond 23 Dec 1800; Sally E. MILLER mar. (2) Spencer GEORGE, LC, bond 15 Apr 1815 (MLBLC:31, 52; LC OB 25:274); div. of the est. of Sally MILLER dec'd infant orphan of Peter H. MILLER among her legal reps.; Spencer GEORGE aptd. gdn. to Mary Ann, Nancy Morris, Eliz. Hunton & Virginia Patros MILLER orphans of Peter H. MILLER, 19 Jun 1815 (LC Orders 24:236, 344); settlement with Spencer GEORGE of his gdnship. with Mary Ann, Ann M. and Virginia P. MILLER orphans of Peter H. MILLER, 20 Dec 1819 (LC OB 25:102); on the mot. of Spencer GEORGE father of Warren W. C. GEORGE & Chas. D. GEORGE it is ord. that Mary Ann & Virginia P. MILLER be summoned to show cause why the lands of which Ann M. MILLER died seized except those which she derived from her father should not be sold and the proceeds divided, 18 Sep 1820 (LC OB 25:162); *see also NC CC 1815-023 and LC CC 1815-004*]

MILLER, Peter H.; PO 21 Jan 1822, T 8 Mar 1822; 18 Mar 1822
LC; DIV of slaves assigned to Mrs. Sarah E. GEORGE dec'd late the wid. of Peter H. MILLER as her thirds under his will among: Sally MILLER, Elizabeth MILLER, Ann M. MILLER, Spencer GEORGE admr. of Sarah E. GEORGE, Mary Ann MILLER, Virginia P. MILLER, Warren W. C. GEORGE (half blood), Charles D. GEORGE (half blood); under the will of Peter H. MILLER his 5 children had a vested interest in the thirds assigned to his wid. The div. of the thirds is therefore first made among 5; three of the children having died before their mother, 2 before and 1 after the birth of their half brother Warren W. C. GEORGE & Charles D. GEORGE, their several parts according to the time of their death is divided among the surviving sisters & mother in the two cases and among the 2 surviving

sisters of the whole blood the mother & the 2 brothers of the half blood in the third case, that is to say: to Mary Ann MILLER, to Virginia P. MILLER, to Spencer GEORGE admr. of Sarah E. GEORGE dec'd, to Warren W. C. GEORGE, to Charles D. GEORGE. (LC EB 29:183)

MILLER, Thomas; T 22 Jun 1813 & 10 Nov 1813; 14 Feb 1814. NC; INV, [m]. (NC RB 19:490)

MILLER, Thomas; PO 10 May [1824], T 19 Jul 1824; 9 Aug 1824
NC; land of which Thomas MILLER died seized sold to Jn. GEORGE for $370.80; proceeds div. among the heirs: Jasper STOTT who mar. Polly MILLER, Rawleigh D. CARTER gdn. to Virginia P. MILLER, and Addison HALL gdn. to Thomas H. LANSDELL & John M. LANSDELL. (NC RB 24:17)
[Thos. MILLER, bro. of Peter H. MILLER of LC d. in 1813 unmarried and without issue; Mary Ann, Nancy Maurice, Eliz. Newton and Virginia [Petross] MILLER are children of Peter H. MILLER a bro. of Thos. and Nancy the wife of Thos. H. LANSDELL is a sis. of sd. Thos.; another sis., Sally, has died since the decease of Thos. (NC CC 1815-023); Jasper STOTT mar. Mary Ann MILLER, LC, bond 11 Nov 1822 (MLBLC:70); on the mot. of Jasper STOTT ord. that Virginia P. MILLER & Thos. H. LANSDELL & Jn. M. LANSDELL be summoned to show cause why real estate of Thos. MILLER should not be sold and the proceeds div. among the heirs, NC 9 Mar 1824 (NC OB 1820-25:358)]

MILLS, William; 21 Oct 1757; 28 Mar 1758; WC; his housekeeper Easter ELLIOTT; William [m]. (WC DW 13:137)
[*omitted by Fothergill*]

MINOR, Elliott S.; 1820; 27 Dec 1824
WC; WILL; whole est, except my Negro boy slave Billy, to my sis. Fanny; if sis. has no heirs, est. to go to friend Mrs. Eliza Maria JONES the wife of Mr. John W. JONES; to Beverley the supposed son of my bro. Daniel MINOR dec'd now resident in our family my Negro boy Billy; I desire my friend John W. JONES to take into his charge & protection the sd. Beverley & Billy & after the sd. Beverley shall have received some information in the English language that my sd. friend may place them out to some trade; friends Richard T. BROWN & John W. JONES exors; WIT: Wm. A. SPARK. (WC DW 25:133)
[Acc. to a chancery suit, Eliza M. JONES vs. John C. BEALE & ux. &c, filed in 1833 and discontinued in 1857 in WC, Fanny MINOR mar. John C. BEALE, WC, bond 19 Dec 1826 (WCCP:161; MLBWC:5)]

MINOR, John; PO 9 Feb 1807, T 9 Apr 1807; 14 Apr 1807
NC; DIV of est, Lot 1 (William NORRIS & William EDWARDS claims), Lot 2 (James SMITH, Richard WATKINS, Jesse MEATH, Daniel WINSTEAD claims), Lot 3 (James WINSTEAD, Joseph J. MONROE, Samuel McCURDY, John SEWARD claims), Lot 4 (Daniel WINSTEAD claim), Lot 5 (NELMS & BALL claims), Lot 6 (William BALL claim), Lot 7 (Armistead CURRIE claim), Lot 8 (Edward BARNES claim), Lot 9 (William B. LEWIS claim for benefit of John SYDNOR), Lot 10 (Charles FALLIN claim), Lot 11 (John MILLER Jr. claim), Lot 12 (Samuel McCURDY claim), Lot 13 (John SEWARD claim), Lot 14 (James FORRESTER claim), Lot 15 (William HUMPHRY claim), Lot 16 (Joseph J. MONROE claim); the claims were to be paid by several individuals including James WINSTEAD and Jane C. MINOR [it is not clear if any of the persons making claims are heirs]. (NC RB 17:520)

[Jn. MINOR married Jane C. OLDHAM, dau. of Wm. & Ann OLDHAM, around 1799; Jane C. (OLDHAM) MINOR mar. (2) Thos. HEADLEY in Dec 1805; at that time she was a wid. with two daus. Sally and Eliza; Sally & Eliz. MINOR orphans of Jn. MINOR chose Edw. OLDHAM their gdn., 12 Jan 1818 (NC OB 1816-20:215); Sally MINOR mar. J. T. CARTER in NC in 1820 and Eliza mar. Dan. RIGGS before 1829 (*see Sam. OLDHAM below*).]

MISKELL, George; 13 Jan 1816; 5 Feb 1821
NFP, RC; WILL; land known by the name of William's & [Gupton's] to my grson. George HENDERSON; Catharine JESPER at the age of 21 to have the priviledge of taking or refusing the land which I now hold & which was conveyed to me by George JESPER; Negro boy [Tom] to grson. George HENDERSON; Negroes Traverse, Nanny, Peg, & Joe to be eq. div. between the children of my dau. Magdaline HENDERSON; s-i-l William HENDERSON; Negroes Manuel, Milly, Darkey, Parthena, Criss & her four children, also Spencer & Charlotte to eq. div. between the children of my dau. Elizabeth STREET; s-i-l Richard STREET; carpenters Joe & Manuel to finish the house for s-i-l Richard STREET; Negroes Nanny, Mary & two children Squire & Simon, George (a fellow), Jerry, Newman, & Jack, Levinia and Judith to dau. Catharine MISKELL; $700 from the sale of Negroes Hannah & Rodham to granddau. Nancy MISKELL when she is 21; faithful & trusty servant Simon to have liberty to select his mistress among my children; sons-i-l Richard STREET & William HENDERSON to be exors; WITS: Geo. SAUNDERS, Edw. NORTHEN, Miskell SAUNDERS, Meredith HUDSON; COD dtd. 28 Sep 1819: legacy to grdau. Nancy is revoked and Negro Hannah to go to children of dau. Elizabeth STREET & Rodham to go to dau. Catharine; no charge to be made against grdau. Nancy for board; carpenter Joe to go to dau. Catharine and Newman to go to children of dau. Magdaline; Negro girl Hannah to granddau. Mary HENDERSON; WITS: Meredith HUDSON, A. BRYANT, Geo. SAUNDERS. (RC WB 9:678)
[Rich STREET mar. Eliz. MISKELL, RC, bond 14 Sep 1807; Wm. HENDERSON mar. Magdalene MISKELL, RC, bond 25 Jul 1809 (MRC:93, 198)]

MISKELL, Newman; PO 2 Jan 1815; 5 Dec 1825
RC; INV; includes Negroes: Daniel, Joe, George, Presley, Fanny & child Ozmund, Ann, Mariah, Winney, Hannah & child Ellen, Nancy, Judah, Matilda, John, Jacob, Sarah. (RC WB 10:94)
[Newman MISKELL mar. Jane BEACHAM, RC, bond 17 Dec 1811 (MRC:133); Jane BEACHAM was the ward of Thos. BEACHAM, NC, 13 Jan 1812 (NC OB 1811-15:39); Jane MISKELL, wid. of Newman, mar. (2) Thos. G. TARPLEY, RC, bond 22 Nov 1815 (MRC:204); Newman and Jane MISKELL had at least one child, Nancy (RC Orders 1814-16:58); Wm. HENDERSON aptd. gdn. to Nancy MISKELL orphan of Newman MISKELL, 5 Feb 1821 (RC OB 25:104); on the mot. of Miskell SAUNDERS and Catharine his wife, ord. that Wm. HENDERSON & Magdalene his wife, Rich. STREET & Eliz. his wife, and Nancy MISKELL an infant of Newman MISKELL dec'd be summoned to show cause why the land of which Sarah SAUNDERS died seized should not be sold, 4 Feb 1822 (RC OB 25:239)]

MISKELL, William; [5] Jan 1803; 5 Dec 1803
RC; WILL; wife Winifred all my tract of land; after her death or remarriage to go to son Samuel; if he has no heirs, to son William; daus. Sarah, Polly Smith; son Henry; four children: Sarah, Samuel, Polly Smith, and William;

bro. George, Daniel JACKSON, Winifred MISKELL, & son Samuel exors; WITS: Geo. NASH, Dan. DOBYNS Jr., Luke JACKSON. (RC WB 9:225) [The births of Sally (28 May 1780) & William (24 Oct 1786) to William & Winney MISKELL are recorded in the NFPR (NFPR:131); Sarah MISKELL mar. Geo. T. GARLAND, RC, bond 29 Oct 1803; Polly Smith MISKELL mar. Jesse DOBYNS, RC, bond 29 Jul 1807 (MRC:55, 75)]

MISKELL, William; T 19 Dec 1803; 3 Jun 1805
RC INV; £366.7.9; includes the following Negroes: Milly, Peggy, Letty, Mary, Hannah, Joseph, [V]iley, Austin. (RC WB 9:249)

MITCHEL, David; 14 Jan 1775; [m].
CP, WC; WILL; whole est. to John Brown STEEL; if STEEL should die before age 21 and have no heirs, est. to go to William WROE; William WROE & John MOORE exors; WITS: Rich. WROE, [Absolom] WROE. (WC Unrec Wills 1755-1800 #16)

MITCHELL, [George]; 16 Apr 1821
LC; George MITCHELL aptd. gdn. to Elizabeth Jane MITCHELL & William Gibson MITCHELL. (LC OB 25:209)
[Eliz. Jane and Wm. Gibson are prob. children of Geo. MITCHELL]

MITCHELL, Daniel H.; T 1 Jan 1824; 15 Mar 1824
LC; DIV of Negro Joe amongst the heirs of Daniel H. MITCHELL to whom James MITCHELL in his last will devised the sd. Negro; Joe was sold to Joseph W. CHINN for $350 and the proceeds minus a commission of $21 were divided up among Elenor B. MITCHELL (mother of Daniel), Frances MITCHELL (a sis.), Meredith M. MITCHELL (a bro.), Joseph R. MITCHELL & Thomas M. S. MITCHELL (half-bros.). (LC EB 29:312)

MITCHELL, Dorothy; 27 Sep 1822; 18 Nov 1822
LC; WILL; son John; if son dies his wife to have use of his est. as long as she remains his widow; grdau. Dorothy L. DEGGE & grson. James M. DEGGE; s-i-l Bidkar GEORGE; son William; bro. John T. DEGGE; grdau. Mary GEORGE; grdau. [Jane E.] GEORGE; dau. Mary T. GEORGE; s-i-l Bidkar GEORGE ex; WITS: Spencer GEORGE. [*NB: This will was very difficult to read*]. (LC WB 28:233)
[Capt. Bedkar GEORGE mar. Mary DEGGE, LC, bond 5 May 1815 (MLBLC:30)]

MITCHELL, Dorothy; PO 18 Nov 1822, T 13 Dec 1822; 16 Dec 1822. LC; INV, $404.36 1/2. (LC EB 29:240)

MITCHELL, Elenor B.; T 18 Dec 1823; 15 Mar 1824. LC; INV, [m]. (LC EB 29:317)

MITCHELL, Henry M.; PO 11 Aug 1813; 17 Mar 1817. LC; INV at Mrs. Elenor BRENT's; includes Negroes Lindsey & [Denny]. (LC EB 27:361)

MITCHELL, Henry M.; T 29 Dec 1819; 17 Jul 1820
LC; INV, $837; includes Negroes Lindsey, Domeny, Lucy, Charles (a child), Adam, Sam; after widow's dower was allotted the remainder was div. between his two children Frances Eleanor Bromley MITCHELL & James Hains Brent MITCHELL; James has since died leaving a wid. & child Frances. (LC EB 29:31)
[Hen. M. MITCHELL mar. Eliz. BRENT, LC, bond 7 Dec 1808 (MLBLC:52); Eliz. (BRENT) MITCHELL mar. (2) Thos. SHEARMAN, LC, bond 17 Dec 1817 (MLBLC:67LC OB 25:36); Thos. SHEARMAN aptd. gdn. of Frances B. MITCHELL orphan of Hen. M. MITCHELL, 15 Jun 1818 (LC OB 25:3); Dan. P. MITCHELL aptd. gdn. of Frances B. MITCHELL orphan of Hen. M. MITCHELL, 15 Oct 1821 (LC OB 25:257)]

MITCHELL, James; 21 May 182[0]; 21 Jul 1823

LC; WILL; debts to be paid out of my est. that came to me out of the est. of William BRENT my wife's father; plant. to wife Eleanor during her life or widowhood also following Negroes: James, Judy, Alice, Winney & Frank and [Louise] Judy's children; girl Mahala to dau. Frances M. MITCHELL; Negro Joe to son Daniel H. MITCHELL; three children Frances M., Meredith M. & Daniel; after wife's death son Meredith M. MITCHELL to have my plant. but if Meredith dies before he arrives to lawful age land & plant. to son Joseph R. MITCHELL; Negroes that came to me out of the est. of Joseph SHEARMAN my first wife's father to be eq. div. between my two sons Joseph R. & Thomas M. [J.] MITCHELL; bro. Daniel MITCHELL & two friends Eppa NORRIS & Rawleigh DUNAWAY exors; WITS: Thaddeus MITCHELL, Geo. M. MITCHELL, Eliz. SHEARMAN. (LC WB 28:234) [Jas, MITCHELL mar. (1) Susanna P. SHEARMAN, dau. of Susanna SHEARMAN, LC, bond 23 Sep 1801 and (2) Eleanor B. BRENT, LC, bond 13 Dec 1809 (MLBLC:52); Jos. & Thos. MITCHELL were sons of Susan P. MITCHELL, 17 Jun 1822 (LC OB 25:312); Jas. MITCHELL aptd. gdn. to Jos. R. & Thos. M. [J.] MITCHELL, 15 Jul 1822 (LC OB 25:316, 317); Dan. P. MITCHELL aptd. gdn. to Frances & Meredith M. MITCHELL orphans of Jas. MITCHELL, 15 Dec 1823 (LC OB 26:11)]

MITCHELL, James; PO 21 Jul 1823, T 4 Nov 1823; 15 Mar 1824
LC; INV, [m], includes Negroes James, Winney, Joe, Judy & child Luesa, Eve & child Charles, girls Frankey, Jane, & Mahala, boys Harry & George, Alice, girl Patty, Sinah & child Julia, boys Eppa & Opie, girl Milly. (LC EB 29:315)

MITCHELL, Mary (Mrs.); PO 17 Jul 1809; 20 Nov 1809; LC; INV, [*value unreadable*]. (LC EB 27:63)

MITCHELL, Priscilla; 24 Apr 1821; 5 May 1823
RC; WILL; to son Richard Tasker MITCHELL my tenement or tract of land on Bull Run in Prince William Co called Cancer Farm attaching thereto Lot[s] No. 12 & 13 to make it a compleat farm; to dau. Harriet Bladen WEIR the land I bought of Barnes BECKWITH in RC & my land that joins your bro. Richard Tasker MITCHELL and that is across the road and the farm that Robert KINCHELOW leased; I request that William J. WEIR let Travers & his wife Judah & Louisa live on your farm called Malebrow that I purchased of Mr. BECKWITH as long as they live paying cotton for rent; I leave my Baltimore property & my bank stock to my dear Harriet B. WEIR; I give my grson. Robert M. FORBES my land on Sandy Point in WC; if he should die without an heir the land to go to her [sic] uncle Robert Bladen MITCHELL; I give half my land called Frying Pan tract to my grdau. Louisa Carter FORBES; I leave my servant Mary free & her children to live on Harriet's land paying her rent; Mary's children, Fanny, William & Anthony, to serve Harriet until 25; son Carter MITCHELL; dau. Julia Landon BAILEY; my servant Travers free and his wife Judah; to son Robert Bladen MITCHELL one half of my Frying Pan tract; [no ex. named]; [no WITS]; [John W. BELFIELD swore that will was signed by MITCHELL & Carter MITCHELL was granted letters of admin. with the will annexed. (RC WB 10:17) [This is Priscilla CARTER, dau. of Robt. & Frances (TASKER) CARTER, who mar. Robt. MITCHELL, RC, Mar 1782 (MWO:247, *see below*); Frances T. MITCHELL, dau. of R[obert] MITCHELL, mar. Wm. FORBES, RC, bond 29 Oct 1803; Julia L. MITCHELL of Grove Mount mar. Jn. BAILEY of WC, RC, bond 10 Dec 1817; Harriet B. MITCHELL, dau. of Robt. & Priscilla (CARTER) MITCHELL, mar. Wm. J. WEIR of EC, in RC, 18 Sep 1817 (MRC:6, 70, 227)]

MITCHELL, Richard; 23 Oct 1815; 20 Oct 1817
WCP; WILL; LC; all land I purchased of Ann WARWICK & Negro girl Amy, boy Harry, girl Mariah, & boys Martin & Johnson to Judy [COSSEY]; her son James [COSSEY]; if Judy [COSSEY] marries or takes up with any man after my death she is to have only one third of what is before mentioned & that for her life only; if I do not build a house for her on the land I have given her, my ex. is to build her a good frame house 14 feet by 20 for a dwelling house; to dau. Fanny B. LEMOINE following Negroes: Daniel, Jim, Joseph, Easter, Tab, Eliza, Mary & Patty; to son William B. MITCHELL my land & plant. on Morattico Creek & my land and plant. w/o I now live called "Deep Creek" & the following Negroes: Ned, Charles, Shadrack, Judy, Criss & Nancy; son is to pay $500 each to my grchil. Feriol LEMOINE, [More] LEMOINE, & Josephine LEMOINE; son Robert died without heirs leaving a widow; James [COSSEY] to be sent to school to learn reading, writing & arithmatic as far as the rule of 3; son William B. MITCHELL ex; WITS: C[hichester]. TAPSCOTT, Thos. G. ROBERTSON, Eppa LAWSON. (LC WB 28:183)
[Rich. MITCHELL served as a midshipman in the Va. State Navy during the Revolutionary War (VS 1776 I:37); Fanny MITCHELL mar. Feriol LEMOINE, LC, bond 24 Aug 1803 (MLBLC:48); Miller:103 describes Morattico Creek as arising southeast of Farnham Creek in RC and flowing southeasterly joining Lancaster Creek near its mouth and then flowing into into the Rappahannock River.]

MITCHELL, Richard; PO 20 Oct 1817, T 25 Nov 1817; 16 Mar 1818
LC; INV, $9274.51; includes Negroes: Bill, Natus, Daniel, Charles, James, Travis, Harry, Spencer, Martin, Jesse, Johnson, Joe, William, Judy, Buck, Criss, Esther, Molly, Suckey, Penny & 2 children, Nancy, Anna & 2 children, Tab, Eliza, Mary, Fanny, Polly, Maria. (LC EB 27:408)

MITCHELL, Richard; PO 19 Nov 1821, 3 Jan 1822; 18 Mar 1822
LC; INV of est. left by Richard MITCHELL to Juda CAUSEY, includes Negroes Harry, Johnson, Anna, Maria, Delia; est. was div. among Juda CAUSEY (her thirds), Janetta CAUSEY, James CAUSEY. (LC EB 29:187)

MITCHELL, Richard; 20 Nov 1820; 21 Mar 1821
LC; WILL; all the dower in the est. of her former husband John DEGGE to wife Polly; land & plant. w/o he now lives to son James MITCHELL; land & plant. w/o he now lives to son Thaddeus MITCHELL; land & plant. I lately bought of Onesephorus HARVEY to son John Westley MITCHELL; all my Negroes now in her possession to dau. Fanny PICKERING; at her death sd. Negroes to be eq. div. between dau. Peggy & dau. Fanny; Negroes Milly & Malinda to dau. Betsey HAYS; Negro woman Rachel & her child Sinah & $100 to grdau. Fanny [Bromley] MITCHELL when she comes of age or marries; my 3 Negro men [*1 word unclear*], Spencer & Jesse to son Daniel P. MITCHELL; Negro woman [*1 word unclear*] to son John [W]estley MITCHELL; Negro boy Adam to grson. Meredith MUSE; son Daniel ex; WITS: [J.] TOWLES, Stephen CHILTON Jr. (LC WB 28:211)
[Jn. DEGGE mar. Polly BRENT, LC, bond 17 Jul 1809 (MLBLC:21); Eliz. MITCHELL mar. Thos. J. HAYS, LC, bond 15 Jun 1812 (MLBLC:37)]

MITCHELL, Richard; PO 20 Mar 1821, T 18 Jun 1821; 15 Jul 1822
LC; INV, $644.00; includes Negroes Rachal, Sarah, Adam, James; APP of pers. est. in NC made 4 Jun 1821, $2250.00; includes Negroes Billey, boys John & Isaac, girls Mary & Emsey, old woman Milly, woman Malinda (pregnant), girl Jane, woman Siller & child Janettee. (LC EB 29:212)

MITCHELL, Robert; 10 May 1808; 5 Sep 1808
RC; WILL; use of dwelling house and land near L. BELFIELD's, Chinquopin Island, & Packet's Gut & land called "Dean's" & one third of Negroes to wife; son Robert Bladen MITCHELL land I purchased of Marmaduke B. BECKWITH, part of that tract on the south side of the road leading from Robert BISPHAM's mill to Cat Point Ferry, which I purchased of Matthew T. FORD, & the tract called "Dyas" purchased of Richard B. ALEXANDER & his father John; son Carter MITCHELL tract of land purchased of Richard BRUER; son Richard Tasker MITCHELL tract of land purchased of Matthew T. FORD on the north side of the new road leading from Robert BISPHAM's mill to Cat Point ferry, 2 tracts in RC & NC which were devised to me by my uncle Richard MITCHELL & tract of land in Prince William Co. called "Cancer Farm;' dau. Fanny [FORBES]; other seven children; four daus. Julia Landon, Sop[h]ia Fairfax, Olivia Ann, & Harriet Bladen; Negroes Travers & his wife Judy to wife; sons Robert Bladen MITCHELL, Carter MITCHELL & Richard Tasker MITCHELL exors. [*a very detailed will*]. (RC WB 9:333) [Robt. MITCHELL mar. Priscilla CARTER the dau. of Robert & Frances (TASKER) CARTER in Mar 1782 (MWO:247); Cat Point Creek flows into the Rappahannock River in north central RC.]

MITCHELL, Robert; T. 14 Mar 1815; 1 Apr 1816. RC; INV, $1141.33. (RC WB 9:514)

MITCHELL, Robert; PO Sep 1808; 2 Apr 1821.
RC; INV; [value m., but very large], includes the following Negroes: Travers & Louisa (bequeathed to Mrs. MITCHELL); Newman, Tom, Dennis, Delesear; Daniel, Rebecca & child; Nancy Sr., Tab, Nancy Jr., Sinah, Mary, Matilda, Betsy, Anthony; Jesse Sr., Siller; George Sr., Sarah, Hannah, George, Ellen, Sally, Dominick, [Levina]; George PURSE; Sicily, Amy & children, Aaron, Easter, Peter; Peter Sr., Nanny, Charles; Jack, Ellen & child, Billy, Isaac, John, Joe; Sarah & child, Nick, Lewis, Eliza; Sally Sr., Peggy Sr. & child, Phebe, John; Barbara, Suky; Winey & child, George, Betsey; Dennis, Spencer, Shadrack, Lucy, Fanny, Peggy Jr; Harry, Alice, Saul, Christopher, George; Martin, Milly, Liddy, Simon, Dennis; Dick, Jesse, Molly & child, Sinah Sr., Solomon, Tim, Richmond, Armistead [*NB: the names listed above were grouped with a line under the last name in a group; this has been replaced by a semi-colon; no explanation of the groupings was evident*]. (RC WB 9:682)

MITCHELL, Robert; PO 6 Oct 1823, T 26 Dec 1823; 7 Jun 1824
RC; DIV of slaves held by Priscilla MITCHELL, his wid, dec'd in her lifetime among William J. WEIR in right of his wife who was Harriett MITCHELL (received John Newman, 34; Edward, 18; Hannah, 24; Thornton, 3; Louisa, 3; old woman Nanny, 50 & infirm), Robert B. MITCHELL (Tom W. Fell, 32; Dennis Jr., 17, Henry an infant of Nelly; Criss, 8; old woman Milly, 70); Carter MITCHELL (Dennis, 30; William, 14; Sarah, 1; Lizzy, 10); William MAXWELL ex. of John MAXWELL dec'd and an admr. of Olivia A. MAXWELL who was Olivia A. MITCHELL (Billy, 29; Jacob, 17; Fanny, 22; Mary Fanny's child, 4; Frankey, 5); Presley COX in right of his dec'd wife who was Sophia MITCHELL ([Delesieur], 28; Louis, 10; Judith, 16; Judith's child an infant; Celia, 6; Francis, 5); Richard T. MITCHELL (Isaac, 25; John, 6; Lucy, 30; Fanny Lucy's infant; Ellen, 45; Moore, 8; Henry, 5); Louisa & Robert FORBES children of William FORBES dec'd in right of their dec'd mother who was Frances T. MITCHELL (George, 20; Barnaby, 12; Barbara, 27; Elizabeth Barbara's infant; Mima, 11; Maria Aimy, 38; Scipio, 3); John BAILEY in right of his wife who was Julia MITCHELL (Joe, 20; Peggy, 22;

Sam P's child; George a carpenter, 45; Sarah George's wife, 40; Eliza infant of sarah; Rebecca, 3; David, 3; Stewart, 2; Siller, 45; Billy an old man 65). (RC AB 4:120)
[Presley COX, of WC, mar. Sophia F. MITCHELL, RC, bond 11 Jan 1810; Wm. FORBES mar. Frances T. MITCHELL, RC, bond 29 Oct 1803 (MRC:45, 70)]

MITCHELL, Robert; PO Feb 1809; 7 Jun 1824
RC; DIV of slaves belonging to the est. as presented by Carter MITCHELL ex. of sd. Robert MITCHELL; to Mrs. MITCHELL the Negroes Newman, Tom, Dennis, Delesieur, Amy & 2 children, Fanny, Lucy, Peggy, Helen & child, Billy, Isaac, John, Joe, George, Sarah & child, Hannah, Nelly, George, Sally, Peter & Nanny, Milly & Barbary, Jesse & wife, Dennis; to Robert Bladen MITCHELL the Negroes Daniel, Becky & child Laura, Kit, Nick, Betsey, George; to Carter MITCHELL the Negroes Jack, Molly & child, Peter, Adam, Easter; to William FORBES the Negroes Sinah & child, Judy, George & wife, Saul, Tab & boy Anthony; to R. Tasker MITCHELL the Negroes [Dominie], Lavina, Shadric, Peggy, Phebe, John & Reubin, Eliza; to Harriet MITCHELL the Negroes Dick, Winny & child, Spencer, Charles, Betsy; to Julia MITCHELL the Negroes Jessee, Nancy, Matild [sic], Harry, Alice & child, Old Sinah & child; to Sophia MITCHELL the Negroes Martin, Milly & child, Simon, Armistead, Lydia; to Olivia MITCHELL the Negroes Dennis, Mary, Solomon, old Cecilia, Tom, Lewis. (RC AB 4:121)

MITCHELL, William; 12 Feb 1803; 18 Jun 1804
CCP, LC; WILL; plant. on which I now reside containing about 300 ac. to wife Mary MITCHELL; after wife's death plant. to go to son Richard MITCHELL; dau. Mary to live with son Richard as long as she remains single; other tract of land known as Kennedy's containing about 286 ac. to son George MITCHELL; son George to have the privilege of cutting hay off the marshes annexed to the land I have given to my son Richard & of pasturing his cattle upon the same; [Negroes] Anthony, Harry & Nell to wife; Negro woman Lucy & her children, Negro fellow James who is now living with him & Negro boy called [Bond] who is at present with me and £100 to enable him to pay for the land he has purchased in NC to son William; to dau. Nancy a Negro girl called Ellen & a boy called Moses; remainder of est. to be div. into 4 eq. parts, one part to go to dau. Judith NORRIS; other parts to son George, son Richard & dau. Nancy; Negroes Hannah & Lee now with James NORRIS to go to dau. Judith NORRIS; friend Joseph CARTER Jr. & sons William & Richard exors; WITS:Abner PALMER, Wm. BRENT, Rich. MITCHELL, Wm. BOATMAN Sr., Reubin BARRICK. (LC WB 28:80)
[Wm. MITCHELL mar. Mary MILLER, LC, bond 24 Nov 1769 (MWO:247); Judith MITCHELL, dau. of Wm. MITCHELL Sr., mar. Jas. NORRIS, LC, bond 10 Mar 1792 (MLBLC:54)]

MITCHELL, William; PO 18 Feb 1805; 16 Sep 1805
LC; DIV of Negroes among: the widow, Richard MITCHELL, Judith NORRIS, Nancy MITCHELL, George M. MITCHELL. (LC EB 24:328)

MITCHELL, William; PO 18 Jun 1804, T 29 Aug 1804; 21 Oct 1805
LC; INV, £1262.1.6; includes Negroes: Henry, Anthony, Daniel, Simon, Ned, Moses, Ben, Nanny, Nelly, Old Nanny, Winny & child, Lucy & child Mima, Letty & two children, Mary, Jenny, Lewis, Alice, Jack, Ellen. (LC EB 24:331)

MITCHELL, William; PO 18 Dec 1809, T 28 Dec 1809; 19 Feb 1810

LC; INV & DIV of slaves allotted to Mrs. Mary MITCHELL dec'd for her dower who was wid. of William MITCHELL: Harry, Antony, Ned, Winny & 2 children Jacob & Daniel, Mary, [Nelly], [Jenny], [Lewis], Shadrack; $1989.97; div. among: James NORRIS in right of his wife Judith, George MITCHELL, Richard MITCHELL, Thaddeus MITCHELL in behalf of his two children Maryann & Nancy MITCHELL. (LC EB 27:69)

MITCHELL, William; PO 11 Sep 1815, T 20 Sep 1815; 8 Apr 1816
NC; INV taken at the house of [N]elly S. MITCHELL, $2732.871 includes Negroes Dick, Sinah & child Daniel, Lettice [& child] Lettice, Esther & child Tom, George, Winney, Salley, girl Sinah, Marjarom, Milley, boy Dick. (NC RB 20:421)
[The est. of Wm. MITCHELL was ord. to be admin. by Nelly MITCHELL, NC, 11 Sep 1815 (NC OB 1811-1816:376)]

MITCHELL, William; PO 11 Nov 1822; 9 Dec 1822
NC; allotment of slaves belonging to the est. of William MITCHELL dec'd: to Nelly S. MITCHELL, the wid, by consent of parties (Dick-an old man, George, Sally, Letty-an old woman, Eliza-a small girl); Lot 1 to William C. MITCHELL (Dick-a boy, Sinah, Letty, [Boston]); Lot 2 to Th. N. BELL (Daniel-a boy with a sprained arm, Margery, Darkey, Sinah-old woman), Lot 3 to John MITCHELL (Thadeus, Easter & child Easter, Milley, Tomze; William MITCHELL left one other child, Nancy, who has died without issue & un-married since the death of the sd. William MITCHELL died intestate; the wid. released all her right and interest in the portion of the est. of her dec'd dau. Nancy to her surviving children: Elizabeth BELL late Elizabeth MITCHELL, William C. & John MITCHELL. (NC RB 23:260)
[Wm. MITCHELL mar. Nelly S. DAWSON, NC, bond 9 Jan 1799; Nelly S. MITCHELL aptd. gdn. of Betsy, Nancy, Wm. & Jn. MITCHELL, NC 12 Nov 1821 (NC OB 1820-25:146); Eliz. MITCHELL, ward of Nelley MITCHELL, mar. Thos. V. BELL, NC, bond 29 Jul 1822 (MLBNC:8, 74)]

MONGER, Francis A.; T 30 Dec 1817; 28 Jun 1819
WC; INV, $2432; includes Judah (an old woman), Jessey, Jane, [Luckey], Nancy, Edy, Harriott, Linday, Ausban, Leeah. (WC RI 10:388)
[Francis A. MUNGER mar. Susanna CRITCHER, WC, bond 24 Sep 1816 (MLBWC:48); Susan (CRITCHER) MONGER mar. (2) Wm. C. CHANDLER, WC, bond 6 Jan 1821 (MLBWC:12); admin. acct. of Susan MONGER now Susan CHANDLER with the est. of Francis A. MONGER returned, 27 May 1822 (WC OB 1819-23:397)]

MONROE, Andrew (Col.); 21 Mar 1783; 24 Feb 1784
WC; inv. at the house of John MONROE (his son); included 40 slaves valued at £1928. (WC Unrec Wills 1755-1800 #26)

MONROE, Austin; T. 15 Dec 1814; 6 Feb 1816. RC; INV, $36.50. (RC WB 9:507)

MONROE, Benjamin; 1 May 1809; 25 Sep 1809
WC; WILL; all ready money to wife Elizabeth MONROE; all est. to wife during her life or widowhood then tract of land that my grfather. John PIPER gave to me to nephew William W. MONROE, also tract I bought of John MONROE, one other tract that I bought of John M. SMITH, and tract I bought of George MONROE w/o I now live with the following Negroes: Roger, Elizabeth, Ben, young Billy, Aaron, Thornley, Tom, Jenks, Cary, Letty, Cornelia, Molley, Betsey, old [Patt], Mary, George, Henry, Peter, Charles, Reuben & young Tom also one dozen silver tablespoons and all my blacksmith's tools; nephew Jesse MONROE the following Negroes: Polly, Nathan, Nancy, Sally, Winney, Hannah, Peggy, Hampton, Edmund & Cary

[sic]; niece Alsey YEATMAN dau. of David MONROE the following Negroes: Salley & her young child Salley Ann, Pattey & her young child Robin, Lucinda, Suckey, Isaac, Sinah, & old Bill; lend to niece Betsey SMITH dau. of David MONROE six Negroes: Fanny, Caty, James, John, Frank, & Jane & after her death to be eq. div. between her 2 daus. Rachel C. SMITH & Mary M. SMITH; rest of est. to be eq. div. among David MONROE's four children: Jesse MONROE, William W. MONROE, Betsey SMITH & Alsey YEATMAN; wife extx; WITS: Christ. J. COLLINS, Jas. MUSE, Rich. THOMPSON, Rich. MONROE. (WC DW 21:540)

[Jn. & Ann (QUISENBERRY) PIPER were the parents of Rachel PIPER who mar. Wm. MONROE, WC, bef 12 Aug 1759 (MWO:248); Alice MONROE mar. Hen. L. YEATMAN, WC, bond 8 Aug 1808 (MLBWC:78); Betsy MONROE, dau. of David MONROE, mar. Wm. M. SMITH, WC, bond 9 Jul 1793 (MLBWC:66)]

MONROE, Benjamin; PO 25 Sep 1809; 26 Feb 1810
WC; INV, £2992.9.7; includes Negroes Thomas JINKS, Benjamin, Peter (a blacksmith), Bill Jr., Bill Sr., Thomas Jr., Nathan, Patt (old), Mary, George, Henry, Charles, Cornelia, Polley (a child), Nancy, Warner, Salley, Winney, Hannah, Peggy, Hampton, Edmond, [Cary], Lilley, Lilley Ann, Patty, Robin, Lucinda, Susanna, Isaac, Sinah, Fanney, Caty, James, John, Frank, Jane; slaves were worth £2255.0.0. (WC RI 9:161)

MONROE, Benjamin; T 6 Jun 1823; 23 Jun 1823. WC; INV, $456.48. (WC RI 11:370)

MONROE, David; PO 24 Mar 1817, T 30 Apr 1817; [m]
WC; INV, $2828.06 3/4; includes Negroes Pompy, Susannah, Reuben & Henry (devised to Elizabeth SMITH; sold by the testator previous to his death), Malinda, Rose, Nancey, John, Thornton, Old Winney. (WC RI 10:308)

MONROE, David; 21 Jan 1815; 24 Mar 1817
WC; WILL; son William all the Negroes that he has had out of my est. & likewise the $250 he received of me for selling my Negroes & the $800 that I lent him; five Negroes--Pompy, Susannah, Rheuben, Harry, & Malindy-- to wait upon my dau. Betsy SMITH; all land on the north side of a line from my good spring an east course to the old head of Mattox Road to dau. Betsy; $250 in the care of my son Jesse for dau. Betsy; $100 to sis. Martha; all land on the south side of the above line to son Jesse; Jesse also to have all the Negroes he has had out of my est. together with three other Negroes Rose, Nancy, & John; [no ex. named] [no wits] [will proved by oaths of Jas. JETT & Daniel CARMICHAEL]; WC DW 23:247)

[NB: *David's dau. Alice is missing from this will, see Benj. MONROE above*]

MONROE, Elizabeth; late of WC dec'd; Daniel CARMICHAEL of WC was aptd. gdn. of her inf. son George E. MONROE; by 1814 George had removed to Fayette Co., Kentucky and chosen Ludwell CARY of that county as his gdn. (WC CC 1814-005)

MONROE, Elizabeth; 29 May 1816; 2 Feb 1818.
RC (but residing in WC); WILL; tract of land in RC known as Cold Hill to Gallatin PLUMMER on condition that when he is 21 he pay $200 to his sis. Anne PLUMMER her heirs or assigns and $200 to my neice Anne GRAHAM her heirs or assigns (all of WC); my Negro Margery to my neice Mary Elizabeth GRAHAM to be sold and the money applied to the purchase of another Negro for her; to bro. John MIDDLETON all the property he now has in his possession belonging to me; $200 to my sis. Anne PLUMMER as above and to my neice Anne GRAHAM $200 as above; residue of est. to my

bro. John MIDDLETON for the proper use and behoof only of my mother Mary PLUMMER; William MIDDLETON, John MIDDLETON, and John GRAHM exors; WITS: Jane YEATMAN, Mary W. WRIGHT, Nath. OLDHAM. (RC WB 9:599)
[Mary PLUMMER was Mary COX, dau. of Fleet COX, who mar. (1) Wm. MIDDLETON, WC, 4 Dec 1777 and (2) Thos. PLUMMER, WC, bond 7 Mar 1795 (MWO:245, 284)]

MONROE, Elizabeth; 6 Jul 1822; May 1823
WC; WILL; to bro. Samuel MARSHALL $300 in bonds; to Benjamin MONROE son of Jesse MONROE; neice Betsey SMITH; clothes to the slaves that wait on me in my sickness; William W. SMITH's two daus. Rachel C. & Mary M.; to the slaves belonging to the est. of Benjamin MONROE I give as follows: to old Tom, Peter, John, Hampton, Winney, Fanny, Mary, Nancy & Patty $60 apiece; to Nathan, James, George, Charles, Bill, Sinah, [Cornely], & Jane $40 apiece; to Peggy, Hannah, Frank & [Warnner] $25 apiece; Sally & Lilleann $10 apiece; to Wallis $5; remainder of est. to my bro. Samuel MARSHALL; bro. Samuel, Joseph FOX & Richard MONROE; WITS: John T. SMITH, Henry BOW[COCK]. (WC DW 24:482)

MONROE, Elizabeth; T 6 Jun 1823; 23 Jun 1823. WC; INV. (WC RI 11:372)

MONROE, Elliott; 19 Jan 1798; 27 Feb 1800
WC; WILL; wife; son Spence; dau. Elizabeth MONROE; youngest son not yet baptized; child wife is pregnant with; friends Beckwith BUTLER & John WASHINGTON exors; Wit: Jn. CAMPBELL. (WC DW 20:89)
[Elliott MONROE mar. Susannah DAVIS, WC, bond 1 Aug 1795 (MLBWC:45); Jn. STROTHER aptd. gdn. to Eliz. & Geo. MONROE, orphans of Elliott MONROE, WC 28 Mar 1803 (WC Orders 1801-04:348)]

MONROE, Elliott; PO 28 May [1810], T 16 Jun 1810; 26 Nov 1810
WC; DIV of Negroes between John JONES who mar. Elizabeth MONROE (received Cyner & infant, Beck, Winney, Anthony, [Planter], Peggy, Elijah & [Auguss], Dany, Will) & George MONROE (received Mima, Sally, James, Evelina, Sarah & infant, Letty, Betsy, Peggy, Phebe, James, Bill--yellow fellow). (WC RI 9:223)

MONROE, George; 9 May 1781
WC; Div. of est. among the wid., William MONROE, Mary MONROE, Sarah MONROE, George MONROE, John MONROE and Nancy MONROE. (WC Unrec Wills 1755-1800 #22)
[*NB: this document is damaged and very difficult to read*]

MONROE, Jemima; 22 Dec 1785; 25 Apr 1786
WC; WILL; est. to be sold and half of the cash to dau. Elizabeth MONROE; the other half to son William MONROE; Benjamin MONROE and son William exors; WITS: Francis BERRYMAN, Jn.BUTLER. (WC Unrec Wills 1755-1800 #29; DW 16:306, DW 17:30)

MONROE, John; 17 Jan 1807; 2 Feb 1807
RC; WILL; all est. to wife; bro. William MONROE to advise wife; all my children; wife to be extx; Wit: Thos. P. SMITH. (RC WB 9:305)

MONROE, William; 29 May 1781
WC; DIV of slaves; Jemimah (the wid.) received Philip, Dal, Jean, Little Jean, Tom; John MONROE (heir-at-law) received Aaron, Billy, Anne; William MONROE received Sam, Hannah, Billy; [Mary] MONROE received Little Dal, Aime; Sally MONROE received Poll, Milly, Moses; Betsy MONROE received Roger and Winny. (WC Unrec Wills 1755-1800 #23)

[This may be Wm. MONROE who mar. Jemima SMITH in KGC, 2 Apr 1746 (MWO:248)]

MONROE, William; T 8 Feb 1799; 22 Jul 1805
WC; INV, £420.18.4; includes Negroes Milley, boy Charles, boy James, boy Daniel, boy Jack. (WC RI 8:557)

MONTAGUE, Winifred Griffin; 13 May 1804; 7 Jul 1806
RC; WILL; daus. Wilalmira W. HAYNIE & Harriett MONTAGUE; son Thomas T.; friend Mr. James WILLIAMS ex. & dau. Wilalmira extx; [no WITS named; proved by Barth. McCARTY & Thos. WALKER]. (RC WB 9:291)
[This is Winifred Griffin TARPLEY who mar. (1) Wm. WEBB (d. RC 1765) and (2) Jas. MONTAGUE of Middlesex Co., RC, bond 20 Nov 1771 (RC WB 6:391; MRC:135, 226-227); Wilalmira WEBB mar. Holland HAYNIE, 17 Sep 1781 (MWO:173); *in MWO:173 it was incorrectly stated that Wilalmira mar. (2) Cap. Jas. MONTAGUE*]

MOOKLAR, William; PO 25 Sep 1797; 26 Feb 1805
WC; INV, £190.12.8; includes Negro Will. (WC RI 8:528)
[Wm. MOOKLAR mar. Sally ATTWELL, dau. of Mary ATWELL, WC, bond 20 Dec 1791 (MLBWC:45)]

MOON, Mary; PO 9 Aug 1819; 13 Aug 1821. NC; INV, $260.75. (NC RB 22:603)

MOON, Mary; PO 12 Jun 1820, T 14 Jul 1821; 12 Nov 1821
NC; balance of est. in hands of the admr. William TREAKLE div. among the heirs: Joseph MOON, Robert MOON, Mary MOON, Cyrus MOON; each rec'd $35.04. (NC RB 23:28)

MOON, William; PO 9 Jan 1815, T 18 Jan 1815; 11 Dec 1815. NC; INV, $170.70. (NC RB 20:314)

MOON, William; PO 12 May 1817, T 25 Jan 1819; 8 Feb 1819
NC; settlement of William W. APPLEBY's admin.acct. of the est. of William MOON; wid. [nfi] entitled to 1/3 or $114.21; remainder div. among 10 legal reps: John WILKINS, Richard WHEELER, William MOON, Polley MOON, Suky MOON, Thomas MOON, Joseph MOON, Robert MOON, Mary MOON, & Cyrus MOON. (NC RB 21:582)

MOON, William; PO 12 May 1817; 15 Jun 1825
NC; DIV of est. on 25 Jan 1819; widow entitled to one third or $114.21; balance divided among 10 people: John WILKINS, Richard WHEELER, William MOON, Polly MOON, Suky MOON, Thomas MOON, Joseph MOON, Robert MOON, Mary MOON, Cyrus MOON (each received $22.84). (NC RB 24:239)
[Jn. WILKINS mar. Nancy MOON, NC, bond 1 Mar 1816; Rich. WHEELER, wid, mar. Hannah MOON, NC, bond 5 Jan 1815 (MLBNC:107, 109); Wm. KIRKHAM was aptd. gdn. of Sukey MOON orph. of Wm. MOON, NC, 8 May 1815 (NC OB 1811-15:316); Rich. WHEELER aptd. gdn. of Mary & Cyrus MOON and Wm. J. MOON aptd. gdn. of Robt. MOON, NC 18 Mar 1820 (NC OB 1820-25:3)]

MOORE, Haberne; 20 Jul 1821; 6 May 1822
RC; WILL; wife Nancy; wife to be extx; WITS: [not named, but one was Augustine NEALE]. (RC WB 9:713)

MOORE, James (Col.); PO 14 Jun 1813, T 3 Nov 1813; 15 Aug 1815
NC; INV at Northumberland House, late the mansion of Col. James MOORE, $1779.53. (NC RB 20:196)
[The est. of Jas. MOORE was ord. to be admin. by Thos. TOWLES, NC, 14 Jun 1813 (NC OB 1811-1816:174); the tombs of Col. Jas MOORE ("an officer

of the Revolutionary army who departed this life May 20th 1813 aged 56 years"), his wife Sarah ("who departed this life Dec. 1st 1814 aged 47 years"), and Thos. TOWLES ("born 16 of December 1785 died April 5th 1822") are in the Northumberland House cemetery (NNVHM Vol. IX, No. 1, p. 843); Col. Jas. MOORE d. at his residence in NC on 20 May 1813, he entered the army at age 18 in the Pennsylvania Line and served under Gen. Anthony Wayne (*Daily National Intelligencer*, 11 Jun 1813, p. [3]; Miller:114 identifies Northumberland House as a large tract in NC on the banks of Cod Creek north of Heathsville.]

MOORE, James G.; 2 Jun 1823
RC; Patty wife of Thos. SUTTON was Patty MOORE only heir of James G. MOORE. (RC OB 26:63)
[Jas. G. MOORE mar. Ann JONES, RC, bond 17 Dec 1791 (MRC:137); Thos. SUTTON mar. Patsey MOORE, RC, bond 29 Mar 1823 (MRC:200)]

MOORE, Jeduthan; PO 12 Jul 1814; 8 May 1815. NC; INV, $1171.1[8]. (NC RB 20:106)
[Jeduthun MOORE was a bro. of Thos. MOORE (d. NC 1801); in his will (NC [m]-11 Jul 1814) Jeduthun MOORE named his eldest dau. Betsy MOORE, wife Betty MOORE, dau. Polley MOORE, son Nathan MOORE, grson. Jedisa (or Jededisa) Moore DAVIS and s-i-l Linsey DAVIS (NC RB 16:205, RB 19:558)]

MOORE, John; 6 Dec 1807; 6 Jun 1808
RC; WILL; all my property to my wife Mary MOORE; after wife's death est. to be eq. div. between my s-i-l Thomas SHIRLEY & my d-i-l Jane SHIRLEY, my dau. Sarah MOORE & my son Austin MOORE; wife to be extx.; WITS: Geo. T. GARLAND, Thos. DOZIER, Newby BARRICK. (RC WB 9:325)
[Jn. MOORE mar. Mary SHIRLEY in NC on 9 Nov 1792 (MWO:250); Henry W. HEADLEY was appointed admr. de bonis non with the will annexed of Jn. MOORE unadministered by Mary MOORE dec'd (RC DB 20:68)]

MOORE, John; T. 15 Feb 1816; 6 Jan 1817. RC; INV, $195.09. (RC WB 9:542)

MOORE, John; PO 14 Jun 1824; 9 Aug 1824
NC; sale of lands belonging to the heirs of John MOORE dec'd on 26 Jun 1824 for $734 to Linszey DAVIS; proceeds allotted to John W. MOORE, Thomas H. MOORE, Harriett MOORE, Rusha MOORE, Kitty MOORE, Richard MOORE; Thomas, Harriett, Kitty, Rusha & Richard are under 21. (NC RB 24:26)
[Jn. MOORE d. intest. in 1823 leaving the following children: Jn. W., Thos. H., Harriet, Rusha, Kitty and Rich, and no wid. (NC CC 1824-005); if all the recs. are for the same individual, then Linszey DAVIS was mar. at least 6 times; one of these marriages was to Thirza MOORE, NC, bond 20 Apr 1811, Jeduthun MOORE gave consent for Thirza (MLBNC:27); Lindsay DAVIS is gdn. of Harriet, Rusha & Cath. MOORE orphans of Jn. MOORE, 12 Dec 1825 (NC OB 1825-30:58)]

MOORE, Judith; 1 Jun 1779; [m]
CP, WC; WILL; est. I am now possessed with by the death of my husband Elijah MOORE instead of my choosing my thirds I only chose a child's part which part to be eq. [div.] amongst my children Losson, George and William MOORE; James HARRISON & George HARRISON of NC exors. and also gdns. for my three sons and see that their whole est. be ... kept in the hands of the aforementioned exors. until sons shall arrive of lawful age to chose gdns. for themselves; WITS: Wm. MIDDLETON, Hen. SELF, [m] SHORT. (WC Unrec Wills 1755-1800 #19)

MOORE, Nancy (Mrs.); PO 8 May 1815; 12 Feb 1816. NC; INV, [m]. (NC RB 20:344)

MOORE, Sarah (Mrs.); PO 12 Dec 1814, T 21 Dec 1814; 9 Oct 1815. NC; INV taken at Northumberland House, $1563.80. (NC RB 20:256)

MOORE, Vincent; PO 22 Feb 1819, T 12 Mar 1819; 22 Mar 1819. WC; INV, $142.87 1/2. (WC RI 10:360)

MORGAN, Andrew; PO Mar 1815, T 10 Mar 1815; 6 Feb 1816
RC; sale of tract of land & 2 Negroes belonging to est; proceeds of sale, $1022.15, div. among John MORGAN in his own right & as gdn. to Eliza BURCH, Vincent MORGAN, William MORGAN in right of his wife Nancy, Fanny MORGAN, Peter MORGAN in his own right & as gdn. to Jilison B. BURCH, F. [G.] TEBBS as assigned gdn. to Winny, Jane & Morgan JACKSON. (RC AB 3:371)
[Jilson or Gilson B. BURCH, who must have been the father of the "Jilison" B. BURCH & Eliza BURCH, mentioned above, mar. Lucy MORGAN, dau. of Andrew & Winifred MORGAN, RC, bond 4 Sep 1797 (MWO:58); "Jilison" or Gilson B. BURCH, the younger, mar. Susan S. NORTHEN, RC, bond 17 Dec 1833 (MRC:30); Lucy (MORGAN) BURCH (who was dec'd bef Aug 1814) mar. (2) Daniel JACKSON, RC, bond 9 Dec 1806 (MRC:101); Wm. MORGAN mar. Nancy MORGAN, RC, bond 9 Apr 1801 (MRC:138)]

MORGAN, Daniel; T 26 Apr 1800; 26 May 1801
WC; INV in Amherst Co, £180.0.0; includes Negroes Jacob (about 18), Mimey (about 12); INV PO 24 Mar 1800, old Ben, Daniel, Natt, Sall, Little Sall, Jenny & her child Caroline, Little George, Suckey, Haney, Little Ben, Betty & her child Molly, Billy, Little Billy son of Dinah, Judy, Hannah, George, Dinah & her 2 children Dinah & Judy, Anne, James, Nelly, Abram, Samuel, Sawney. (WC RI 8:131

MORGAN, Fanny; T 13 Mar 1822; 2 Aug 1824. RC; INV, [m]. (RC WB 10:44)
[This is prob. the Fanny MORGAN who mar. Peter MORGAN, RC, bond 1 Nov 1809 (MRC:138)]

MORGAN, Peter N.; [m]; R. 6 May 1816. RC; INV, [m]. (RC WB 9:528)

MORGAN, Peter [N.]; T 13 Nov 1816; 1 Feb 1819. RC; INV, [m]; RC WB 9:618)
[Wm. R. SHACKLEFORD aptd. gdn. to Peter MORGAN son of Peter MORGAN, 4 Mar 1822 (RC OB 25:251); settlement of Wm. R. SHACKLEFORD's gdnship. acct. of Peter MORGAN orphan of Peter N. MORGAN, 6 Feb 1827 (RC OB 27:141)]

MORGAN, William; 26 Feb 1811; 1 Apr 1811
RC; WILL; all worldly goods to son Andrew MORGAN; if he die bef 21 to go to wife Patty MORGAN; friend Martin SISSON exor; WITS: Reuben CLARKE, Thos. [P.] SMITH. (RC WB 9:393)
[Wm. MORGAN mar. Patty PULLY, RC, bond 11 Feb 1807 (MRC:138)]

MORGAN, Winefred; T 4 Mar 1818; 1 Feb 1819
RC; DIV of est. among John MORGAN, Vincent MORGAN, William MORGAN in behalf of his wife Nancy, Fanny MORGAN, the heirs of Lucy MORGAN (each heir received $50.71 2/5), John MORGAN was admr. de bonis non; further div. of the est. of Winefred MORGAN & Peter MORGAN was div. among the same heirs. (RC AB 3:656)
[This is Winifred PURCELL, dau. of Tobias PURCELL & Mary Ann MURRAY, who mar. Andrew MORGAN, c. 1771 (MRC:137)]

MORRIS, Bethlehem; 3 Mar 1802; 7 Jun 1802.
LP, RC; WILL; whole est. to s-i-l John FONES & Jane his wife; John FONES ex; WITS: Jn. EIDSON, Jos. FONES, Sam. RYALS. (RC WB 9:173)

MORRIS, Hudson; 21 Dec 1817; 5 Nov 1817
RC; WILL; all land that came to me by my wife and that I bought to be eq. div. between my three children Caty T. MORRIS, Pollyan MORRIS, & Nancy MORRIS; widow to have my plant. during her widowhood and at her death to my son John MORRIS and when he is of age to have a good horse and saddle; if wife is pregnant, that child should have as much money as the land one of my daus. gets is worth; friend Abraham WHITE & widow exors; WITS: Billey SANDERS, Jas. PRATT, Fanny THOMPSON. (RC WB 9:567) [Hudson MORRIS mar. Sally NASH, dau. of Mary PRATT, RC, bond 4 Aug 1806 (MRC:138); Wm. [P.] REAMY who mar. Cath. MORRIS a dau. of Hudson MORRIS dec'd, Mary MORRIS, Jn. [F.] MORRIS, Nancy MORRIS and Julia MORRIS infants by Dan. SAUNDERS their gdn. and next friend, pltfs., against Sarah MOTHERSHEAD admx. of Hudson MORRIS, deft., in chancery, 3 Dec 1827 (RC OB 27:187); Sally MORRIS (wid.) mar. Wm. MOTHERSHEAD, RC, bond 9 Mar 1821 (MRC:140); Wm. REAMY mar. Cath. MORRIS, dau. of Sally MOTHERSHEAD wife of Wm. MOTHERSHEAD, WC, bond 26 Mar 1827 (MLBWC:57); gdnship. accts. of Wm. MOTHERSHEAD & wife to Cath., Mary, Jn. F., Nancy & Julia MORRIS orphans of Hudson MORRIS returned, 4 Mar 1828 (RC OB 27:199)]

MORRIS, John; T 22 Apr 1800; 30 Jul 1801. WC; INV, £67.7.0. (WC RI 8:134) [Mrs. Eliz. JOHNSON, formerly Eliz. MORRIS, admx of the est. of Jn. MORRIS, WC, 27 Apr 1801 (WC, Orders 1801-04:36); Eliz. MORRISS mar. Jas. JOHNSON, WC, bond 23 Mar 1801 (MLBWC:36); Eliz. may be Eliz. McKAVE who mar. Jn. MORRIS, WC, bond 16 Apr 1795 (MWO:251)]

MORRIS, John; PO 17 Sep 1804; 18 Feb 1805. LC; INV, £1.7.6. (LC EB 24:304)

MORRIS, John; 4 Jan 1819
RC; Spencer MILLER mar. Mahala MORRIS the wid. and admx. of Jn. MORRIS. (RC OB 24:304)
[Spencer MILLER mar. Mahala MORRIS (the wid. of Jn. MORRIS -- whom she mar. in RC, bond 6 Aug 1798 -- and dau. of Jn. KELLY), WC, bond 26 May 1817; she seems to have been his 2nd wife; he mar. (1) Nancy B. MOXLEY, WC, bond 20 Dec 1815 and (3) Frances JAMES, WC, bond 10 Jul 1820 (MLBWC:45; MRC:138); Mahala (KELLY, MORRIS) MILLER had died by 1 Nov 1819 when Spencer MILLER was admr. of her est. (RC OB 24:383); Joshua REAMY was gdn. to Jas., Wm. R. and Jn. MORRIS, orphans of John (RC OB 24:399); Wm. R. MORRIS, compl., vs. Jas. MORRIS, Eliza. MORRIS, Jn. MORRIS, Mahala MORRIS, Vincent MORRIS & Lemuel MORRIS infants; their gdn. was Joshua REAMY, 5 Feb 1821 (RC OB 25:108); Overseers of the Poor of LP ord. to bind out Jn. MORRIS orphan of Jn. MORRIS to Joshua REAMY, 4 Feb 1822 (RC OB 25:238); Wm. SETTLE aptd. gdn. to Martha, Vincent & Lemuel MORRIS orphans of Jn. MORRIS, 6 May 1822 (RC OB 25:285); Martha MORRIS orphan of Jn. MORRIS chose Moore F. BROCKENBROUGH as her gdn., 7 Aug 1826 (RC OB 27:92); Joshua REAMY aptd. gdn. to Vincent & Lemuel MORRIS orphans of Jn. MORRIS, 6 Feb 1827 (RC OB 27:139)]

MORRIS, William; PO Jul 1811; Nov 1811
RC; INV, £1107.19.2 1/2, includes Negroes: Harry, young man Joe, woman Rocksey, Cate, Nelly & young child, Betty, girls Suckey, Jane, Lucy, Rachel, Caty, Peggy, Molly, & Fanny, boys Jesse, Solomon, Tom & Reuben. (RC WB 9:398)

MORRISON, Jesse; 25 Aug 1808; 13 Oct 1817

NC; WILL; to sis. [H]etty HUMPHRIES two Negroes Agga & Marina; trusty friend and relative Joseph MORRISON ex.; WITS: Sam. BLACKWELL, Wm. MORRISON. (NC RB 21:264)
[Hetty HUMPHRIES is prob. Hatha MORRISON who mar. Geo. HUMPHRIES, NC, bond 24 Dec 1804 (MLBNC:57)]

MORRISON, John; 1 Sep 1820; 9 Oct 1820
NC; Thomas JACQUES of NC made oath that he has been acquainted with the family of John MORRISON dec'd late of Somerset Co., Md for several years past and that he did not know of either a bro. or sis. living except Sally MORRISON who is the only lawful heir of sd. MORRISON & who executed a P of A to Peter NELMS of NC. (NC RB 22:406)

MORRISON, Joseph; 10 Mar 1820; 13 Nov 1820
NC; WILL; half of est. to wife Hannah C. MORRISON during her life; $40 & silver watch to son Washington N. MORRISON when he is 21; $20 to step-dau. Malindy W. MORRISON; Negro Jerry and rest of est. to be sold & proceeds eq. div. among my children Washington N. MORRISON, Parthanny N. MORRISON, Betsy Smith MORRISON, Maryann J. W. MORRISON, Hannah MORRISON & Eliza MORRISON; friend William JETT ex; WITS: W. DARNABY; [Wm. JETT relinquished his executorship and a certif. was granted him for obtaining letters of admin. with the will annexed was granted]. (NC RB 22:434)
[Jos. MORRISON mar. Hannah MORRISON, wid., RC, bond 14 Apr 1802; Hannah was prob Hannah WOOLLARD (dau. of Samuel WOOLLARD, d. RC 1786) the wid. of Wm. MORRISON who d. in RC bef. 2 Jun 1800 (MRC:138, RC WB 7:535, WB9:132)]

MORRISON, Nancy; PO 1[3] Mar 1815; 10 Jun 1816. NC; INV, $177.45 1/2. (NC RB 21:5)
[The est. of Nancy MORRISON was ord. to be admin. by Jos. MORRISON, NC, 13 Mar 1815 (NC OB 1811-1816:288)]

MORRISON, Richard; T 15 Nov 1799; 14 Jul 1800
NC; INV; includes Negroes Moses, Chloe, Rebecca, Agnes, Grace, Delila, girl Lucy, boys Joseph, Robert & Samuel, girls Phoebe & Marina. (NC RB 16:144)
[In his will (NC 2 Mar 1799-8 Apr 1799), Rich. MORRISON desired his est. to be eq. div. between his children, but he did not name any of them (NC RB 15:586)]

MORRISON, Richard; 9 Jan 1826
NC; on the mot. of Hiram FORBUSH & Lucy his wife, ord. that Walter, Thomas & William MORRISON infant children of Richard MORRISON be summoned to show cause why lands of sd. Richard should not be sold. (NC OB 1825-30:59)
[Hiram FORBUSH mar. Lucy MORRISON, NC, bond 14 Apr 1825 (MLBNC:38); Wm. W. APPLEBY aptd. gdn. of Wm. MORRISON orphan of Rich. MORRISON, 13 May 1828 (NC OB 1825-30:261)]

MORRISON, William; PO 7 Oct 1799; 2 Jun 1800. RC; INV, £11.1.6. (RC WB 9:132)

MORRISON, William; PO 11 Jul 1811; 13 Jul 1812. NC; INV, [m]; includes Negro Chloe. (NC RB 19:227)
[The est. of Wm. MORRISON was ord. to be admin. by Jos. MORRISON, 11 Feb 1811 (NC OB 1807-1811:230)]

MORSE, Ebenezer; 17 Jul 1811; [m] Sep 1811
WC; WILL; sisters Polly & Nancy MORSE 7 ac. tract of land adj Mr. Henry TAPSCOTT; third of corn to be deducted for Stephen BAILEY for rent of this

place; no ex. named; WITS: Hen. PACKER, Hannah MINOR, [F]anny MINOR, Job SELF. (WC DW 22:216)
[This man's surname also appears as MOSS; he was prob. the Ebenezer MOSS or MORSE who mar. Nancy (or Ann) SELF the wid. of Moses SELF (WC CC 1810-009); there is an error in MWO:314 for Moses SELF; he could hardly have made an application for a pension in 1819 since he died in 1794; there were several Ebenezer MOSSes or MORSEes on the Northern Neck at this time.]

MORSE, Sheldon; 23 Sep 1811
WC; Richard OMOHUNDRO aptd. gdn. of Lucy MORSE orphan of Sheldon MORSE. (WC Orders 1810-13:172)
[Although the surname seems to be "MORSE," this is almost certainly Sheldon or Shelton MOSS who d. in LC in 1801 (*see below*)]

MORTON, James; T 30 Jan 1799; 4 Feb 1799
RC; DIV of Negroes Harry, Will, Phillis & her child John said to be born since the death of James MORTON, Beck, Thom & Sam between William HOBLEINE [also given as HOBBURNE] as gdn. for William Morton CLARKE & William REYNOLDS in behalf of his wife Hannah. (RC AB 3:5)
[Wm. REYNOLDS mar. Hannah MORTON, WC bond 24 Dec 1793 (MWO:295)]

MORTON, John; PO Jun 1803; 4 Nov 1817. RC; INV, £40.1.6. (RC WB 9:586)

MOSS, John A.; 1 Nov 1819
RC; Lucinda MOSS was the wid. of John A. MOSS. (RC OB 24:381)
[Jn. A. MOSS of NC mar. Lucinda BEALE dau. of Rich. BEALE, RC, bond 5 Oct 1808 (MRC:139); Lucinda (BEALE) MOSS mar. (2) Wm. McCARTY, RC, bond 20 Sep 1820 (MRC:124); Wm. McCARTY aptd. gdn. of Rich. Hen. MOSS & Harriet MOSS orphans of Jn. A. MOSS, 1 Oct 1821 (RC OB 25:204)]

MOSS, Sheldon; 18 Jul 1801; 19 Oct 1801
LC; WILL; Negro boy Billy to son John Allen MOSS; Negro girl Jeany to dau. Peggy when she reaches 18 or marries; either to my dau. Margaret or to my dau. Elizabeth which either of them that will give the best price for her shall own her on paying the other the one half of her value at the end of 12 months; NB: this extra donation is made to make up unto my daus. a small legacy left them by their uncle Henry ALLEN, dec'd; residue of est. to be eq. div. amongst my surviving children; son John A. MOSS & my dau. Elizabeth MOSS exors; WITS: Thos. WEST, F[ortunatus] DAVENPORT, Leroy NUTT. (LC WB 28:56)
[Ann D. MOSS & [Dianna] A. A. MOSS orphans of Sheldon MOSS chose Fleming BATES as their gdn., 21 Dec 1807 (LC Orders 22D 1805-08:431); the will of Margaret Tabb MOSS, Petersburg, Va., 17 Nov 1803 – 3 Dec 1804 names her sisters Nancy, Diana and Lucy; her friend and relation Mrs. Mary CLAUSEL, her uncle Hen. ALLEN and her father Sheldon MOSS (NC CC 1813-010)]

MOSS, Sheldon; PO 16 Feb 1807, T 16 Dec 1807; 18 Mar 1811
LC; INV, £1094.9.; includes Negroes Ned, Alice & child, boy Benjamin, boy Anthony, boy Paul, Judy, Jane & child, Nanny, [?], Hannah, boy Billy, boy John, Beck, Betty; John A. MOSS ex; DIV of Negroes among: Lucy MOSS, Sheldon MOSS, Ann [?] MOSS, Fleming BATES, Richard OMOHUNDRO, John A. MOSS, Donald MOSS, Margaret T. MOSS, 14 Mar 1811. (LC EB 27:79, 80)
[Fleming BATES mar. Mary MOSS, NC, bond 20 Jul 1803; Rich. OMOHUNDRO mar. Eliza MOSS, NC, 10 Jan 1807 (MLBNC:6, 79)]

MOTHERSHEAD, Charles; 4 Oct 1817; 23 Feb 1818
WC; WILL; being on a bed of sickness; my land in WC to bro. Daniel MOTHERSHEAD and after his death to his son Charles; all slaves to bro. Daniel and they are not to be hired out but kept together; box of new china that I lately purchased to bro. Daniel's dau. Betsy; my riding mare to Richard COLLINS; pair of boots to James L. MOTHERSHEAD; $100 for repairs of Nominy Meeting House; William MOTHERSHEAD; $30 to Miss Libby WILLSON to be paid out of the corn in [Jos.] TEMPLEMAN's hands; James L. MOTHERSHEAD ex; WITS: Robt. FAUNTLEROY, Hen. SISSON. (WC DW 23:360)

MOTHERSHEAD, Charles C.; PO Jan 1818, T 11 Feb 1818; 25 May 1819
WC; INV, [m]; includes Negroes boy Cupit, Liddy & child, girl Sophey, boy Luis, girl [Abhyline] & Julyann. (WC RI 10:373)

MOTHERSHEAD, George; T 28 jun 1815; 23 Oct 1815. WC; INV, $346.41. (WC RI 10:31)

MOTHERSHEAD, John; 26 Oct 1822; 2 Dec 1822
RC; WILL; dau. Sally RYALLS; dau. Polly BARTLETT, dau. Betsy BARTLETT; dau. Susan MOTHERSHEAD; dau. Alice MOTHERSHEAD; dau. Lucy MOTHERSHEAD; dau. Julia MOTHERSHEAD; son William MOTHERSHEAD so much of the plant. w/o I now live together with the houses beginning at the corner ash between Vincent JONES & John BALDERSON & from sd. corner ash to a black heart cherry tree standing in the wheat lot and from thence to a large red oak stump formerly a line between this and the land now occupied by Steward FRANKLIN; to son James MOTHERSHEAD balance of the tract of land w/o I now live togethr with a part of the tract of land called Loin's beginning at a white oak below where Abraham WHITE formerly lived and running a straight line to a chestnut tree with the top broken off in James MORRIS's line; to son Richard MOTHERSHEAD all the rest of my land; three sons William, James, & Richard exors; WITS: M. C. HARVEY, Hen. BARTLETT, Ann JONES; COD: I give to my son James MOTHERSHEAD instead of what I have given him in the above will the balance of the tract of land w/o I now live together with a part of the tract called Loin's beg. at a white oak below where Abraham WHITE formerly lived running down the cool spring branch to a large ditch and down the sd. ditch to a bridge & from the sd. bridge to Morriss's line [same date & WITS]. (RC WB 10:5)
[Polly MOTHERSHEAD, dau. of John, mar. Thos. BARTLETT, WC, bond 4 Jan 1815 (MLBWC:5); Julia MOTHERSHEAD orphan of Jn. MOTHERSHEAD chose Rich. MOTHERSHEAD as her gdn., 26 Mar 1827 (WC OB 1823-27:355)]

MOTHERSHEAD, John; T Dec 1822; 7 Jun 1824. RC; INV, $347.72. (RC WB 10:41)

MOTHERSHEAD, Nathaniel; 17 Jan 1815; 27 Feb 1815
WC; WILL; three children of William MOTHERSHEAD dec'd: Uriah, Mary & Anne; three Negroes Charles, Paul, & [Boson]; son Daniel MOTHERSHEAD; half of land son Daniel lives on for the benefit of the three children of William MOTHERSHEAD; son Charles MOTHERSHEAD to manage all my affairs; WITS: Jas. H. MOTHERSHEAD, W[illiam] L. MOTHERSHEAD, Campbell TEET. (WC DW 23:68)

MOTHERSHEAD, Nathaniel; T 7 Apr 1815; 24 Jul 1815. WC; INV, $169.55. (WC RI 9:460)

MOTHERSHEAD, Nathaniel; T 21 May 1815; 4 Nov 1817

RC; INV; $2109.00, includes Negroes: Old Frances, Hanner, Winney, Amay, Adam, Job, Judy, Daniel. (RC WB 9:578)

MOTHERSHEAD, Richard; 16 Apr 1811; 29 Oct 1811

WC; WILL; wife Isabella; dau. Lucy; son George; dau. Moriah a Negro girl named Cate; son Henry to be educated; after wife's death or remarriage est. to be eq. div. between my children: Lucy, George, Moriah & Henry MOTHERSHEAD; [no ex. named]; WITS: Wm. KING, Wm. SPURLING, Jn. MOTHERSHEAD; COD: I appoint Mr. Geo. CHRISTOPHER my ex; WITS: Wm. KING, Wm. SPURLING; Jn. MOTHERSHEAD. (WC DW 22:232) [By Dec 1811, Isabella MOTHERSHEAD had married a BEALE, prob. Samuel BEALE who was appointed gdn. to Maria and Samuel MOTHERSHEAD, orphans of Richard; she also renounced the provision made for her by her former husband Richard MOTHERSHEAD, insisting upon her dower or thirds (WC Orders 1810-13:192); Isabella MOTHERSHEAD aptd. gdn. of Lucetta MOTHERSHEAD, 28 Oct 1811 (WC Orders 1810-13:174); Sam. BEALE aptd. gdn. of Maria & Sam. MOTHERSHEAD orphans of Rich. MOTHERSHEAD, 23 Dec 1811 (WC Orders 1810-13:192); Geo. MOTHERSHEAD orphan of Rich. MOTHERSHEAD chose Thos. BARBOUR as his gdn., 22 Mar 1813 (WC Orders 1810-13:293); Maria MOTHERSHEAD orphan of Rich. MOTHERSHEAD chose Thos. BARBER as her gdn., 28 Nov 1814 (WC OB 1814-18:85); Thos. BARBER aptd. gdn. of Hen. MOTHERSHEAD orphan of Rich. MOTHERSHEAD, 26 Feb 1816 (WC OB 1814-18:205); Geo. MOTHERSHEAD was the gdn. of Hen. MOTHERSHEAD orphan of Rich. MOTHERSHEAD, 4 Feb 1822 (RC OB 25:239, 303)]

MOTHERSHEAD, Richard; [m]; 28 Feb 1820

WC; Negroes belonging to the est. of Richard MOTHERSHEAD dec'd: Milley (40 years old), Nancy dau. of Milley (1 1/2), Sarah (31), Cate dau. of Sarah (8), Harry son of Sarah (5), Sam son of Sarah (2); div. of est. after taking out Sarah for the widow's dower and Cate the dau. of Sary which was a legacy left to dau. Mariah; boy Henry to Thomas BARBER in right of his wife, Sam to George MOTHERSHEAD, Milly to Mariah MOTHERSHEAD, and Nancy to Henry MOTHERSHEAD. (WC RI 10:452) [Thos. BARBER mar. Lucy MOTHERSHEAD, dau. of Isabella MOTHERSHEAD, WC, bond 6 Nov 1811 (MLBWC:4)]

MOTHERSHEAD, Samuel; 4 Jun 1823; 28 Jul 1823

WC; WILL; after debts are paid, rest of est. to Elias MOTHERSHEAD; Josias HAZARD ex; WITS: Jn. BEDDOO, Thomas [J.] MOTHERSHEAD. (WC DW 24:520)

MOTHERSHEAD, William; T. 7 Apr 1815; 24 Jul 1815

WC; INV, $555; includes Negroes Molly & Boson. (WC RI 9:461) [This is prob. the Wm. MOTHERSHEAD who mar. Sary MOTHERSHEAD, WC, 17 Jan 1809 (MLBWC:47); Sally MOTHERSHEAD aptd. gdn. to Moriah, Mary & Ann MOTHERSHEAD orphans of Wm. MOTHERSHEAD, 25 Mar 1816 (WC OB 1814-18:212)]

MOTT, Moseley; 1801

NC; Moseley MOTT d. intest. in 1801; his sisters Jane B. WEBB the wife of Homer WEBB and Sally MOTT and bro. Charles were his heirs; Homer WEBB Jr. was aptd. gdn. to Sally and Charles MOTT; Moseley was the son of Moseley MOTT who in his will (NC 2 Apr 1793 – 14 Oct 1793), named only his present wife Sally, his sons George and William and dau. Jean Betts; the slaves belonging to his est. were div. on 8 Sep 1800 among Sally MOTT (rec'd Nance, Aaron & Tom), Homer WEBB (rec'd Lucy & Moses), Charles MOTT (rec'd Solomon & Peggy) and Moseley MOTT (rec'd Chloe & Emanuel); Homer WEBB mar. Jane (Jean or Jenny) B. MOTT, NC, bond 22 May 1799; Sally MOTT, the wid. of Moseley, mar. Elijah HARRISON, NC, bond 16 Apr 1795 (NC CC 1802-015; NC RB 14:716; MLBNC:47, 106)

MOTT, James; PO 8 Sep 1817, T 11 Apr 1818; [m]
NC; on motion of Joseph MOTT gdn. to Elizabeth, Randolph, & John MOTT orphans of James MOTT dec'd who died intestate by William HARDING his agent prop. belonging to James MOTT was sold; land was sold to Robert M. MARSH for $263 and Negro Rachel was sold to Josias INGRAM and proceeds minus commission were paid to Joseph MOTT to be div. among the heirs. (NC RB 21:509; OB 1811-15:393; OB 1816-20:177)

MOTT, Thomas; 13 Oct 1795; 15 Feb 1796
LC; WILL; all land in NC to eldest son Joseph MOTT when he arrives to 20 years; land son Joseph heirs by his mother on the Eastern branch of Corotomon to be made over to his sis. Frances MOTT when he comes of age in law; use of all lands in LC to wife Elizabeth MOTT until my children by her come of age or marry & then she is to have one third of the land I now live on & an eq. portion of my pers. est. with her children during her life; land w/o I now live to my son Thomas MOTT; child wife is now pregnant with to have tract of land purchased of Capt. Henry HINTON; Negro fellow Charles to wife; Negro Stephen & a child I bargained for out of the est. of Thomas [REID's] est; wife extx; WITS: Wm. YERBY, Jn. CUNDIFF, Thos. PALMER. (LC WB 28:1)
[Peter BEANE aptd. gdn. of Frances & Jas. MOTT orphans of Thos. MOTT, 21 Jan 1800 (LC Orders 21 1799-1801:77, Orders V 1802-03:255)]

MOTT, Thomas; PO 16 Oct 1798 & 17 Dec 1798; 15 Jul 1799
LC; INV at the house of Betty MOTT extx. & DIV of est. among: James SUTTON gdn. to Joseph MOTT orphan of sd. Thomas MOTT (received Negroes Lucy & Sarah) and several others nfi. (LC EB 24:100)

MOXLEY, Alexander; PO 27 Dec 1813, T 1 Jan 1814; 28 Mar 1814
WC; DIV of est. between Ann MOXLEY the wid. & Charles TALLIAFERRO who mar. Susan MOXLEY (dau. & only child to the sd. Alexander); Ann MOXLEY received Tom, Old Milley, Charlotte's child Mary; Charles TALLIFERRO received Jenny, Betsey, Washington, Robert, Billy, Sarah, Charlotte. (WC RI 9:417)
[Alex. MOXLEY mar. Nancy QUISENBURY, dau. of Nicholas QUISENBURY, WC, bond 13 Jan 1789; Chas. TALLIAFERRO mar. Susanna MOXLEY, WC, bond 31 Jan 1812 (MLBWC:47, 69)]

MOXLEY, Augustine; WC; Caty the wife of Augustine MOXLEY is the only dau. and heir at law of Edward MOXLEY late of WC; Edward MOXLEY's wid. mar. Thomas STONE and had three children by him: Daniel, Edward, and Joseph. (WC CC 1795-002)
[In MWO:254, the wife of Augustine MOXLEY was tentatively identified as Caty STONE; the above record confirms that she was actually Caty MOXLEY; Augustine MOXLEY in his will (WC 9 Jun 1797 – 28 Aug 1797) named his wife Caty, his nephews Robt. SANFORD, Jn. son of Wm. MOXLEY, Willoughby SANFORD, Elijah SANFORD; Edw. son of Thos. STONE; nieces Fanny SCRIMER {sic}, Betsy DODD, and Pinney WEAVER; goddau. Caty Moxley Pope SANFORD; Sam. son of Jane MOXLEY, Alfred son of niece Pinney WEAVER, and sis. Elinor SANFORD (WC DW 19:264);

Pinney WEAVER is prob. Penny SANFORD who mar. Jn. WEAVER, WC, bond 24 Mar 1792 (MLBWC:74)]

MOXLEY, Daniel; T 9 Mar 1818; 4 Jan 1825
RC; INV, [m]; includes Negroes: Rawleigh, Penny, Maria & her infant, Sally, [Henry]. (RC WB 10:60)

MOXLEY, Daniel; 27 Dec 1822; 4 Jan 1825
RC; APP of Negroes Rawleigh, Maria, boy Joe, girls Hannah & Judy, boy Lazarus, Sally, girl Eliza, boy Henry; DIV between Lucy MOXLEY (received Henry, Judy), Joseph Edward MOXLEY (Hannah, Eliza), Anne B. MOXLEY (Sally, Joe) & James MOXLEY (Rawleigh, Maria, Lazarus). (RC AB 4:161)
[Augustine NEALE aptd. gdn. to Nancy & Jas. B. MOXLEY orphans of Dan. MOXLEY, 5 Nov 1822 (RC OB 26:6)]

MOXLEY, Harriet; 30 Jun 1818; 10 Aug 1818
NC; WILL; to niece Eliza Nelms HUNT all my interest in the land of my late mother Elizabeth MOXLEY w/o John HUNT now lives & all the rest of my est; friend John HUNT ex; WITS: Peggy MOXLEY, Jn. DAWSON, Wm. JETT. (NC RB 21:474)
[Eliza Nelms HUNT may have been the dau. of Jn. HUNT who mar. Maria MOXLEY, dau. of Daniel MOXLEY, NC, bond 24 Dec 1807 (MLBNC:58)]

MOXLEY, Richard; 23 Dec 1799
WC; Henry ASBURY & Sally his wife to settle their admin. acct. on the est. of Richard MOXLEY. (WC Orders 1799:1801:166)
[Hen. ASBURY mar. Sally MOXLEY (wid.) WC, bond 9 Apr 1796 (MLBWC:2); Sally MOXLEY was prob. Sally SISSON who mar. Rich. MOXLEY, WC, bond 16 Mar 1789 (MLBWC:48); Martin SISSON aptd. gdn. of Eliz. MOXLEY orphan of Rich. MOXLEY, 23 Dec 1799. (WC Orders 1799:1801:166)]

MOXLEY, Robert; T 17 May 1803; 29 May 1804
WC; INV, £555.8.7; includes Negroes Betty & child, Sall & her child Amy, Edmond, Molly, Charlotte, Lett, Peter (a lad), Payton (a lad). (WC RI 8:422)
[Robt. MOXLEY d. intest. leaving three daus. as his heirs: Lucy, Eliz., and Nancy. (WC CC 1818-003, 1831-002)]

MOXLEY, Robert; PO Aug 1805 & Sep 1807, T 10 Dec 1808; 4 Jul 1809
WC; new DIV of est. among legal reps, Negro boy John which formerly fell to John R. McNEIL who mar. Lucy one of the children of Robert MOXLEY now belongs to Nancy MOXLEY another of the children; McNEIL refuses to give up the Negro. (WC RI 9:[138])
[Jn. McNEIL mar. Lucy MOXLEY, WC, poss. in 1807 (MLBWC:43); Eliz. MOXLEY orphan of Robt. MOXLEY, chose Benj. BRAMHAM her gdn., WC 26 Aug 1805 (WC Orders 1804-07:292); Nancy MOXLEY chose Jn. R. McNEIL as her gdn., 23 Dec 1811 (WC Orders 1810-13:192); Jn. R. McNEIL & wife Lucy, Eliz. MOXLEY, and Nancy MOXLEY brought suit against Christopher MOXLEY, admr. of Robt. MOXLEY, who refused to give an acct. of the est.; Eliz. and Nancy were both under 21 in Jun 1818 (WC OB 1814-18:402, WC CC:1831-002)]

MOXLEY, Rodham; PO 25 Jan 1819; 24 Jan 1820
WC; INV, $7726.87; includes Negroes Griffin, David, [Preston], Jesse, Charles, Henry, Sciller & child Caroline, Nancy & child Mary, Henrietta & child Corban, girl Edie, boys Cyrus, Isaac & Daniel. (WC RI 10:442)
[Rodham MOXLEY mar. Mary WELDON, WC, bond 8 Jul 1810 (MLBWC:48); Wm. H. SANFORD aptd. gdn. to Rich., Rodney [sic] & Anne MOXLEY orphans of Rodham MOXLEY, 27 Mar 1820 (WC OB 1819-23:124);

on the mot. of Wm. H. SANFORD & Mary his wife admr. & admx. of Rodham MOXLEY, ord. that they settle up their admin. acct. and that Wm. H. SANFORD settle up his gdnship. accts. of Ann, Rich. & Rodham MOXLEY orphans of Rodham MOXLEY, 26 Jul 1824 (WC OB 1823-27:99); Wm. H. SANFORD mar. Mary S. MOXLEY, WC, bond 7 Jun 1819 (MLBWC:62)]

MOZINGO, Edward; PO Mar 1801, T 8 Feb 1802; 5 Apr 1802
RC; DIV of est. among Pierce MOZINGO, Thomas CROOKHORN for his wife Hannah, James BARRETT for Sarah TOMS, John MOZINGO for his sis. Rebecca, James BARRETT for his wife Mary, Pierce MOZINGO for his sis. Winefred, Edward MOZINGO. (RC AB 3:85)
[Thos. CROOKHORN mar. Hannah MOZINGO, dau. of Edw. MOZINGO, RC, bond 17 Feb 1793; Jas. BARRETT mar. Mary MOZINGO, dau. of Edw. MOZINGO, bef. 29 Mar 1794 (MWO:30, 94)]]

MOZINGO, Edward; [m]; 2 Mar 1818
RC; WILL; son Joseph to the care of Samuel TEMPLEMAN Sr. until age 21 and he is to be schooled; all land to son Joseph; all timber to Samuel TEMPLEMAN to keep the cider casks in repair; rest of property to be eq. div. between daus. [S]ibby & Lucy; Samuel TEMPLEMAN Sr. to be guardian to dau. Lucy until she is 21; WITS: Marcus C. HARVEY, Sam. TEMPLEMAN Jr. (RC WB 9:602)
[Augustine SANFORD aptd. gdn. to Jos. MOZINGO orphan of Edw. MOZINGO, 26 Nov 1822 (WC OB 1819-23:502)

MOZINGO, Edward; T 14 Jan 1818; 7 Feb 1820. RC; INV, $87.75. (RC WB 9:647)

MOZINGO, John; T. 13 Feb 1807; 6 Apr 1807. RC; INV, £24.16.0. (RC WB 9:308)

MOZINGO, John; 31 Aug 1820; 2 Oct 1820
RC; WILL; wife Elinor MOZINGO one third part of my est; after her death est. is to be eq. div. between my children: Thomas, Pierce, Christopher, & Hannah MOZINGO and my grandchildren: the heirs of my dau. Nancy THOMAS, Daniel, Ellen, John & William THOMAS (the children of William THOMAS); Susan BROWN formerly the wife of my son John MOZINGO dec'd; Caty PECURE and Betsy BARROTT; Negro man Luis to be sold; friend Capt. Joseph BELFIELD & son Pierce MOZINGO exors; WITS: Matthew V. YEATMAN, Levi YEATMAN, Thos. YETMAN Jr.; COD: sons Pierce & Christopher MOZINGO to have title to the land w/o I now reside during the term of lease which I hold; wife to have her full thirds of the land which I now lease consisting of 50 ac. adjoining my house and 50 on the Beaver dams bordering on the Pantico Swamp which land was mortgaged to old Mr. CARTER for 99 years and the time has expired & without they can show their right I leave fee simple interest to my sons Thomas, Pierce, Christopher & my dau. Nancy THOMAS' heirs & my dau. Hannah MOZINGO [same date and wits] (RC WB 9:671)
[Wm. THOMAS mar. Nancy MOZINGO, dau. of Jn. MOZINGO, RC, bond 6 Jan 1800 (MRC:208); Miller:7 locates Beaverdam Creek in RC arising as the east branch of Brockenbrough Creek between Foneswood and Singerly; Pantico Swamp must be located on or near Pantico Run which Miller:121 locates on the border between RC and WC.]

MOZINGO, John; T 29 Sep 1820; 4 Aug 1823
RC; INV, $817.59 1/2; includes Negro man Lewis & old Negro woman [not named]. (RC WB 10:27)

MOZINGO, Richard; 28 Mar 1814

WC; Sarah MOZINGO orphan of Richard MOZINGO chose William L. MOTHERSHEAD as her gdn. (WC OB 1814-18:13)

MOZINGO, Samuel; PO Mar 1813, T 15 Apr 1813; 23 Aug 1813. WC; INV, $224.08. (WC RI 9:376)

MULLINS, John; 24 Jan 1820
WC; William M. WALKER aptd. gdn. to John & William MULLINS orphans of John MULLINS; Polly MULLINS orphan of John MULLINS chose James MULLINS as her gdn. (WC OB 1819-23:100, 124)
[On the mot. of Wm. M. WALKER gdn. of Jn. & Wm. MULLINS orphans of Jn. MULLINS, ord. that Jas. MULLINS settle his admin. on the est. of Jn. MULLINS, 26 May 1823 (WC OB 1819-23:558)]

MULLINS, John; [m]; 28 Aug 1821
WC; INV, $1649.96; includes a large stock of various kinds of cloth. (WC RI 11:103)

MURREN, George; 8 Jan 1824; 3 Feb 1824
RC; WILL; to son Thompson MURREN my houses & lot at Richmond Court House which I purchased of Col. John TAYLOE & my Negro boy Martin & $100; to Priss (a free woman of color) $100 in consideration of her attention to me & in lieu of any wages she may be entitled to, but in case she should make any charge for her service the sd. sum of $100 is not to be paid her; balance of est. to be eq. div. between my two sisters Sueanna & Sarah MURREN whom I left in Londonderry in the north of Ireland & my bro. Thomas MURREN; rest of est. to be sold; suits to be immediately brought for sums of money due me and money arising be paid to John McKIM or Samuel McDONALD of Baltimore for the purpose of their disposing of it as I have before mentioned to my sis. & bro; friend Col. Moore F. BROCKENBROUGH & son Thompson MURREN exors; WITS: E. E. BUCKNER, Dan. GARLAND, W. Y. WEATHERS. (RC WB 10:30)
[A William Thompson MURREN of RC mar. Mary McPHERSON of Fredericksburg on 19 Jan 1826 (MRC:142)]

MUSE, Daniel; T 19 Mar 1803; 10 Sep 1804
NC; INV, [m]; includes Negro woman Rachel. (NC RB 17:200)

MUSE, Daniel; 14 Jul 1819; 26 Jul 1819
NC; WILL; reaffirms deed of 29 Apr 1819 which transferred to Peyton DREW of Richmond all right, title, & interest in all & every property real or personal to which I may be entitled as the son & heir-at-law of Daniel MUSE dec'd of NC; since the conveyance cannot be reduced to possession by the sd. DREW because the same hath not been specifically conveyed which could not be done at the time of executing the sd. deed because of the confused state in which my affairs and the affairs of the sd. Daniel MUSE Sr. dec'd were at that time; appoints DREW his attorney; WITS Jn. DAVENPORT, Wm. DABNEY, Wm. R. MILLER. (NC RB 22:110)

MUSE, James; 1 May 1811; 23 Mar 1812
WC; WILL; est. of bro. Thomas MUSE; nephew William MUSE Negroes: Isaac, Sebinnah & old Sarah & 10 head of sheep; dwelling house and all cleared land on that tract purchased of William W. MONROE to my bro. John MUSE; all lands in WC to nephew Elliott MUSE; Elliott MUSE exor.; WITS: G. PAYNE, Jas. E. BUTLER, Jas. JETT. (WC DW 22:259)

MUSE, Nicholas; [m]; 25 Aug 1802
WC; INV; includes Negroes Charley, Joshua, Phil, Peggy, boys Janney, Aron, Charley. (WC RI 8:180)

MUSE, Nicholas; 1 Nov 1799; 25 Jun 1804.

WP, WC; WILL; wife Ann use of plant. in the Barrens called Winter Harbour; son William land in Potomac River w/o I now live,Negroes Phill, Charles & Aaron, and he is to provide for son John; son Thomas land in the Barrens after death of wife and Negroes [Josua,] & [Peg]; son Elliot Negroes James & Charles the youngest son of [Peg]; bros. James & Thomas MUSE & son William exors; WITS: Wm. A. WASHINGTON, Jas. NEVISON, Wm. RICE. (WC DW 21:45)
[Nicholas MUSE mar. Anne THOMPSON, wid., WC, bond 27 Jan 1791 (MWO:257)]

MUSE, Richard (Capt.); Sep 1797; 26 Jan 1801
WC; INV, £842.6.4; includes the following Negroes: Ceasar, Male, Crummele, Jacob, Frank, Sarah, Spencer, Clary, Charlotte, Lucy, Milley, Joe, Philishia, Willis, Maria. (WC RI 8:109)

MUSE, Samuel; 22 Dec 1800
WC; John [ASHBY] aptd. gdn. of Thomas MUSE orphan of Samuel MUSE. (WC Orders 1799-1801:395)
[The est. of Sam. MUSE was div. among Sukey, Thos., Nancy, and Lewis S. MUSE, 2 Jan 1799 (WWCV:202)]

MUSE, Thomas; 27 Feb 1810; 23 Apr 1810
WC; WILL; slave Ceasar to sis. Ann Piper HUNTER; Negro woman Charlotte to bro. Lewis Smith MUSE; money due by my guardian John ASHLEY from hiring out the said Negroes to be eq. div. between bro. & sis; [no ex. named]; WITS: Henry G. [LOTUZ], Mary CARVER, Jn. PEIRCE Jr. (WC DW 22:81)
[This is Thos. MUSE the son of Samuel MUSE and Mary SMITH and grson. of Thos. MUSE and Ann PIPER (MWO:257)]

MUSE, Thomas; 13 Mar 1810; 25 Jun 1810
WP, WC; WILL; wife Frances Negroes Charlotte, Leddy, Milley, [Horice], George, China & Joe & 2 trunks, feather bed & bed furniture that I got by her in lieu of her dower; wife also to get use of Negroes: Letty, Nancy, James, [Minna], & Williams also use of dwelling house & land adj. bro. James MUSE, the head of my old mill pond & William W. MONROE; son Thomas S. MUSE following Negroes: Big Mary, Willis, James, Williams, Little Mary, Judah, Easther, Betsey, Winney, Lucy, Aron, Daniel, Old Phill, Dall, Scipio, & Frederick; son-in-law Stephen JETT following Negroes: Young Phill, Elias, James Cox [sic], Frank, Matilda, James Junr., John, Old Sin, Virgin, & Philicia; grdau. Betsey JETT dau. of James JETT following Negroes: Letty, Nancy, Kessia, Joe, Matthew, Scipio & her young child; grdau. Nancy JETT the followinf Negroes: Ethelinda & Minna; grson. John JETT Negro boy Henry; rest of est. to be eq. div. among son Thomas MUSE, Stephen JETT, grdau. Betsey JETT & wife Frances; bro. James MUSE, Frances MUSE & Stephen JETT exors; WITS: Chris. HOLLINS, Jn. MUSE, Wm. W. MONROE. (WC DW 22:100)
[Frances MUSE renounced the provisions for her in this will on 22 Jun 1810 (WC DW 22:99-100); Stephen JETT mar. Eliz. D. MUSE, dau. of Thos. MUSE, WC, bond 13 May 1805 (MLBWC:35); Jas. JETT mar. Nancy MUSE, dau. of Thos. MUSE, WC, bond 25 Feb 1805 (MLBWC:35); Thos. S. MUSE orphan of Thos. MUSE chose Jas. JETT as his gdn., 28 Oct 1811 (WC Orders 1810-13:175); *see also WC CC 1812-004*]

MUSE, Thomas; PO Jul 1810 T Jan 1811; 25 Feb 1811. WC; INV of est. in Fauquier Co., $690. (WC RI 9:227)

MUSE, Thomas; PO 23 Mar 1812, T 10 Apr 1812; 25 Jan 1813

WC; DIV of est; to Frances MUSE (now Frances BERRYMAN) out of the Negroes named in the residuary clause of the will Charlotte & George, out of Thomas S. MUSE part [?], Willis, Aaron & Phill, out of the est. of Stephen JETT's part Elias & Philitia, out of Nancy JETT's part $90, leaving a boy named Henry bequeathed to John JETT (an infant without gdn.) undivided; to Thomas L. MUSE Negroes William, Big Mary, Little Mary, Judy, Easter, Betsey, Winney, Lucy, Daniel, Frederick, Polly, Lidia & Joe; to the est. of Stephen JETT dec'd Young Phill, James, Old Linn, Virgin, Alexander, Horace & [Chinea]; to Nancy JETT Ethelinda; to Betsy JETT Lilly, Nancy, Milly & Alfred. (WC RI 9:366)

[Chancery suit, Frances MUSE & Thos. N. BERRYMAN who mar. sd. Frances, complts., vs. Thos. L. MUSE, Betsy JETT, Jas. JETT, Nancy JETT, Jn. JETT and Stephen JETT admr. of Thos. MUSE dec'd; Stephen JETT to pay £54 to the complts. and allott Frances her dower, 23 Mar 1812 (WC Orders 1810-13:203)]

MUSE, William; 7 Dec 1811; 23 Mar 1812.

WP, WC; WILL; bro. Thomas MUSE plant. on Popes Creek in WC; if bro. dies without lawful heir to my nephew Douglas MUSE son of my bro. Elliott MUSE; bros Thomas & Elliott MUSE exors; WITS: J. JETT, Thos. S. MUSE, Jn. MUSE. (WC DW 22:260)

[Popes Creek flows into the Potomac River in northeastern WC.]

MYERS, George F.; 10 Feb 1824; 15 Mar 1824

LC; WILL; half of plant. w/o I now live to my sis. Julia GEORGE; if sis. Amanda COLES has a son who lives to age 21 the other half of sd. plant. to him; for want of a son to Amanda whole plant. to sis. Julia; to Miss Mary SMITH who lives in the family at present for her particular attention to me in my [illness] $100; residue of est. after debts paid to be eq. div. among sisters Julia GEORGE, Amanda COLES & bro. William MYERS; [no ex. named]; WITS: Chas. H. LELAND, Wm. PULLEN Wm. KIRKHAM, Raw. DUNAWAY; COD dtd. 10 Feb 1824: at the death of Mrs Elizabeth BASYE I shall be entitled to a certain portion of the est. of Elismond BASYE dec'd in consequence of my having married his dau. & as I wish to settle disputes that may occur I give my right & title & interest to sd. est. upon the conditions that Mrs. Elizabeth BASYE & the heirs of Elismond BASYE will give up to my sisters Julia GEORGE, Amanda COLES & bro. William MYERS an award of about $211 which is the award of Addison HALL, George WEBB & Rawleigh DUNAWAY who were appointed to settle the accts between Elizabeth BASYE & myself; friend Richard P. COLES to qualify as my ex; [same wits.]; LC WB 28:248)

[Geo. F. MYERS mar. Nancy BASYE, LC, bond 11 Dec 1820; Julia GEORGE is prob. Nancy Julia MYERS, dau. of Thos. MYERS, who mar. Enock GEORGE, LC, bond 11 Dec 1816; Amanda MYERS mar. Rich. P. COLES, LC, bond 19 Jun 1821 (MLBLC:15, 30, 53)]

MYERS, George F.; PO 15 Mar 1824, T 19 Mar 1824; 19 Jul 1824

LC; INV, $1030.33 1/2; includes Negroes Nathaniel, Williamson, Edie. (LC EB 29:345)

MYERS, Thomas; 4 Dec 1792; 15 Jun 1795

LC; WILL; all land to grson. Thomas MYERS; Negro boy Elijah & his mother Ailce to grson. George ARMS; remainder of est. to be div. into 3 eq. parts, one for grson. Thomas MYERS, one for the children of my late dau. Jane ARMS (Elizabeth GEORGE, Molly NORRIS, Sally ARMS, William ARMS & George ARMS), & the other third for the children of my late dau.

Behetheland CLAUGHTON (William CLAUGHTON, Pemberton CLAUGHTON, Elizabeth CANNON, Mary CRAWLEY & Jane CLAUGHTON); grson. Thomas MYERS & friend Joseph CARTER Jr. exors; WITS: Augustus CARTER, Job CARTER, Jos. CARTER Jr., Jos. STEPHENS, Thos. HATHAWAY. (LC WB 28:15)

[Jane MYERS, dau. of Thos. MYERS, mar. [Wm.] ARMES well bef. 2 Jul 1785; Eliz. Linton ARMS mar. Wm. GEORGE, LC, bond 2 Jul 1785; Molley ARMS mar. Eppey NORRIS, LC, bond 21 Nov 1789; Behetheland MYERS, dau. of Thos. MYERS, mar. Pemberton CLAUGHTON well bef. 18 Feb 1788; Mary CLAUGHTON mar. Samuel CRALLE, LC, 19 Sep 1786 (MWO:17, 79, 93, 146, 265)]

MYERS, Thomas; 21 Feb 1818; 16 Apr 1821

LC; WILL; all my land that I now live on to son George; all money due me including the money due me from [Isiah HAINS] of the state of Georgia to son William; all the Negroes in my possession to my children George, William, Nancy [Julia] & [Anne] as well as those that I may be entitled to at the death of Mrs. Ann ROGERS that came from or may come from the est. of Charles ROGERS dec'd; to my children Mary Ann [Yerby] and Elizabeth Maria all the Negroes that I am possessed of that came by their mother; residue of est. to be eq. div. among my children, to wit: George, William, Nancy Julia, Amanda, Mary Ann Yerby and Elizabeth Mariah; son George and s-i-l Enoch GEORGE ex.; WITS: J[ohn] CHOWNING, Geo. WEBB, John S. CHOWNING. (LC WB 28:215)

[This is prob. the Thos. MYERS who mar. (1) Peggy ROGERS, LC, bond 23 Feb 1796 and (2) Mary Ann HARRIS, LC, bond 20 Jul 1807 (MLBLC:54); Enoch GEORGE mar. Nancy Julia MYERS, dau. of Thos. MYERS, LC, bond 11 Dec 1816, prob. as his second wife (MLBLC:30); in 1825 Raw. W. DOWNMAN, sheriff of the county, administered the est. of Thos. MYERS which was unadministered by Geo. F. MYERS; Mary Ann MYERS, wid. & rel. of Thos. MYERS, and Nancy Julia GEORGE formerly Nancy Julia MYERS, Wm. MYERS, Mary Ann Y. MYERS and Eliz. MYERS children of Thos. MYERS ask to have surplus money divided (LC CC 1825-007)]

MYERS, Thomas; 16 Apr 1821

LC; Amanda MYERS chose Rawleigh DUNAWAY as her gdn.; Mary Ann MYERS aptd. gdn. to Mary Ann Yerby and Elizabeth Mariah MYERS orphans of Thomas MYERS. (LC OB 25:204)

[Thos. MYERS mar. Mary Ann HARRIS, LC, bond 20 Jul 1807; Amanda MYERS mar. Rich. P. COLES, LC, bond 19 Jun 1821; Eliz. M. MYERS mar. Wm. H. KIRK, LC, bond 9 Aug 1830; Mary Ann Y. MYERS mar. Chas. ROGERS, LC, bond 2 Feb 1827 (MLBLC:15, 46, 54, 64); settlement with Mary Ann MYERS the acct. of her gdnship with Mary Ann & Eliz. MYERS, 21 Jun 1824 (LC OB 26:48)]

MYERS, Thomas; PO 16 Apr 1821, T 10 May 1821; 21 Jan 1822

LC; INV, $14,025.85 1/4; includes Negroes Williamson, Charles, Solomon, Dennis, Sinah & child Maria, Sellah & child Henry, Fanny & child Polly, Letty, Edith, Charlotte, Tab (old), Charles, Lindsey, Ralph, Frederick, George, Martha & child Mima, Matilda & child Jennetta, Easter & child Rose, Delia (Martha's child), Bridget (Martha's child), Emala (Easter's child), Maria (Easter's child), Old Easter, Sampson alias Spencer, Joe, Lindsey (a joiner), Shadrack, Griffin, Elijah, Emsey, Eliza, John, Ralph, Natt, Henry, Daniel, Adam, Old Harry, Robbin, Cyrus, Leroy, Jenny, Nell, Letty, Judy &

child Milly, Milly & child Fanny, Lucinda, Old Winney; the slaves were worth a total of $12,561. (LC EB 29:153)

MYERS, Thomas; 19 Mar 1822
LC; [COD to will of Thomas MYERS list of Negroes advanced my son: Griffin, Elijah, Lett, Emrey, Elisey, John; [total value $2850]; [presented to county court; opinion of court was that sd. paper shall not be recorded as a codicil to the will of Thomas MYERS; from which sd. opinion George Y. MYERS admr. with the will annexed of Thomas MYERS prayed an appeal to the next Superior Court of law; Superior Court, 5 Sep 1823; George F. MYERS (appellant) against William MYERS (appellee); Superior Court decided that codicil was valid and ordered that the appellant recover against the appellee his costs; on 15 Sep 1823 County Court ordered the COD to be recorded]. (LC WB 28:238)

NASH, George; 19 May 1813; 27 Apr 1818
WP, WC; WILL; whole est. to wife Sarah NASH; [no ex. named]; WITS: Wm. MITCHEL, Thos. NASH, Jas. NASH, Geo. NASH. (WC DW 23:364)
[There is an undated bond in WC for a marriage between Geo. NASH & Sally MITCHELL (MLBWC:49)]

NASH, James; T 5 Apr 1819; 25 Mar 1822. WC; INV. (WC RI 11:161)

NASH, John; 5 Dec 1803. RC; INV. (RC WB 9:222)

NASH, Richard; PO 8 Sep 1810; R. 6 May 1816. RC; INV, [m]. (RC WB 9:520)

NASH, William; 6 Feb 1815; 27 Feb 1815
WC; Patty ALVERSON & George T. SPILMAN, both of WC, made oath that William NASH who died at his own house in the sd. county on the fifth day of the present month, did call on them on the 4th of sd. month to bear witness that it was his desire that his wife Sally should have the whole of his est. for the benefit of herself & his two daus. Susannah & Jenny NASH and that if his two sons Thomas & James NASH who had left him should return they should be entitled to only one shilling apiece. (WC DW 23:66)

NASH, Winder; 27 Oct 1807
WC; the Overseers of the Poor to bind out James NASH, Thornton NASH, Winder Kenner NASH & John NASH orphans of Winder NASH to Rodham NEALE. (WC Orders 1807-10:83)
[This is prob. the Winder NASH who mar. Sally ALVERSON, WC, bond 7 Jun 1788 (MLBWC:50)]

[NEAL], James; T 17 Aug 1819; 14 Feb 1820. NC; INV, [m]. (NC RB 22:212)

NEALE, Daniel; T 21 Apr 1818; 25 Oct 1819
WC; INV [$130.86]; includes several kinds of saws and carpenter's tools. (WC RI 10:433)

NEALE, James; T 8 Nov 1808; 28 Aug 1809
WC; INV, [m]; includes Negro man [Peter]. (WC RI 9:149)
[This may be the Jas. NEALE whose orphan Polly had Jas. SORRELL as her gdn., 23 Dec 1811 (WC Orders 1810-13:193)]

NEALE, Joseph; 21 Sep 1802; 24 Jan 1803
WC; WILL; after debts are paid rest of est. to be eq. div. between bro. Benedict & children of late bro. Edward; father Jeremiah NEALE exor; WITS: Jas. A. THOMPSON, Timothy HARRINGTON, Geo. WHITELOCK. (WC DW 20:447)

NEALE, Nancy; 24 Nov 1820; 4 Nov 1824
RC; WILL; to son Augustine NEALE (otherwise called Austin) my Negro man called John MAIDEN; if son die without issue, Negro to be held for benefit of dau. Mary Steward SAUNDERS wife of George SAUNDERS; to

my grand nephew James Bramham MOXLEY my Negro woman Mina for his education until he arrives at 21; grson. Austin Neale SAUNDERS son of my sd. dau. Mary S. SAUNDERS my Negro woman Maria & her son William for his education until he arrives at 21; Negroes Sam, Wallase, George, Jenny & [Letty] to be hired out for benefit of dau. Mary S. SAUNDERS; nephew Philip A. BRAMHAM; son Augustine, nephew Philip A. BRAMHAM & friend William Y. STURMAN exors; WITS: Elenor Ann BRAMHAM, W. Y. STURMAN, Mary S. BRAMHAM [will was presented on 6 Aug 1821 [sic], but rec. on 4 Nov 1824]. (RC WB 10:50)
[Mary S. NEALE mar. George SAUNDERS, RC, bond 17 Feb 1819 (MRC:180)]

NEALE, Presley; T 22 Oct 1799; 16 Jun 1800
LC; INV, £202.6.4; includes Negroes: Harry, girl Jane. (LC EB 24:111)
[This must be Presley NEALE Jr.; Presley NEALE Sr. aptd. gdn. to Betsy Carter NEALE & Presley NEALE orphans of Presley NEALE Jr., 21 Oct 1799 (LC Orders (21) 1799-1801:56)]

NEALE, Presley; PO 19 Oct 1807, T 11 Nov 1807; 15 Feb 1808
LC; INV; £300; includes Negroes: Esther, Mimy, Winny, Nancy, Samuel, David, Jack. (LC EB 27:28)

NEALE, Presley; 26 Feb 1810
WC; settlement of the gdnship. account of Presley NEALE of his gdnship. of Betsy Carter NEALE orphan of Presley NEALE. (WC Orders 1807-10:444)
[This is poss. Presley NEALE who mar. who mar. Sally JACKSON, WC, bond 21 Dec 1786 (MLBWC:50)]

NEALE, Presley; 21 Jan 1815; 27 Feb 1815
WP, WC; WILL; house & plant. w/o I now live to wife Mary NEALE; after her decease to be div. as follows: my Negro man Will to son John NEALE; Negro girl Sucky to dau. Nancy PAYNE; all land to be div. between my two sons Daniel NEALE & Richard NEALE in the following manner: beginning at Saw Pit Bottom & running up the eastern branch to POPE's line, the lower part to Daniel NEALE, the upper part together with the houses to Richard NEALE; Negro man Daniel & girl Judith to son Daniel; servant Negro Peter and all my farming, carpenter's & joiner's tools to son Richard; dau. Franky NEALE to have use & full possession of her choice of the back rooms in my dwelling house & also my weaving house loom & all the weaving gear & two Negro girls Sarah & Mary; $10 to granddau. Betsey Carter NEALE; children of Rodham NEALE whatever his est. may be indebted to mine; Negro woman [Sibb's] youngest child to be sold & the money applied to pay debts; sons John & Richard and wife Mary exors; WITS: Aleck SANDERS, Geo. QUISENBERRY, [W.] REAMEY. (WC DW 23:69)
[This is prob. Presley NEALE who mar. Mary, dau. of Ann CARTER, bef. 5 Jan 1789 (MWO:260); Anne NEALE mar. James PAYNE, WC, bond 18 Dec 1798 (MLBWC:53)]

NEALE, Presley; PO 16 Jan 1815, T 21 Jan 1815; 20 May 1816. LC; INV, $84.31 1/2. (LC EB 27:331)

NEALE, Presley; 17 May 1819
LC; Polly S. NEALE aptd. gdn. of William Y. NEALE orphan of Presley NEALE. (LC OB 25:53)
[This is Presley NEALE who mar. Polly GEORGE, LC, bond 29 Jan 1812 (MLBLC:54)]

NEALE, Presley (the Elder); PO 16 Jan 1815, T 21 Jan 1815; 17 Apr 1815

LC; DIV of est. between Thomas MYERS (Committee for Rodham NEALE) & Joseph CARTER Jr. (admr. of Presley NEALE the Younger); the tract of land to be div. was located near the head of Harrises Creek. (LC EB 27:195) [Miller:63 locates Harrises Creek in LC on the peninsula between the mouth of Corrotoman River and Carter Creek]

NEALE, Richard; 21 Aug 1800; 5 Jan 1801
RC; WILL; daus. Elizabeth CALLIS, Margaret GARNETT, Judith MATTHEWS, Susannah BOWLERE (or BOULWARE), & Hannah Shapleigh NEALE; grson. Richard Neale CALLIS (under 21); Henry GARNETT & Richard N. CALLIS exors; [no wits]. (RC WB 9:141)
[Rich. NEALE was the son of Maj. Rich. NEALE and Judith SHAPLEIGH; he mar. (1) Catherine FAUNTLEROY between 1742 & 1744 and (2) Ann (HEADLEY) REYNOLDS widow of John REYNOLDS in the spring of 1762; Eliz. NEALE mar. Robt. CALLIS, RC; Margaret NEALE mar. Capt. Hen. GARNETT, RC, bond 17 Sep 1765; Judith NEALE mar. Edw. MATTHEWS bef. 1791 (MRC:32, 76, 144; RC DB 12:354, 357; WB 6:262; MWO:238)]

NEALE, Richard; 19 Aug 1817; 24 Nov 1817
WC; WILL; land left to me by my father Presley NEALE to Presley NEALE son of my bro. John NEALE during his life, if he die without heir land to go to John NEALE son of John NEALE; after the death of Samuel TEMPLEMAN the silver watch marked on the back "PN" to Presley NEALE; one half of the land I purchased of Richard CARTER to be eq. div. between Thomas P. NEALE & Ann NEALE (children of Rodham NEALE); at the death of my mother Mary NEALE I am by my father's will entitled to a Negro man Peter which sd. Negro Peter I give to my bro. John NEALE provided he gives Thomas NEALE son of Rodham NEALE sufficient schooling for a workman & binds him to learn a good & useful trade; all my joiners and carpenters tools to Presley NEALE son of John; remaining est. to be eq. div. between my sisters Nancy PAYNE & Frankey NEALE, but if sis. Frankey NEALE ever marries Jacob A. REMMY I give the whole of the remainder of my est. to Nancy PAYNE; bro. John NEALE ex; WIT: Sam. TEMPLEMAN, Jn. REDMAN, Jn. HARVEY; WC DW 23:314

NEALE, Rodham; T 6 Apr 1813; Sep 1813. WC; INV, [m]; includes Negro Dick. (WC RI 9:378)
[This is prob. the Rodham NEALE whose wid., Lucy or Lucinda, mar. Jacob MILLER, *see above* (WCCP:6)]

NEALE, Rodham; PO 15 Oct 1817; 9 Nov 1818. NC; INV, $45.50. (NC RB 21:540)

NEALE, Rodham; PO 16 Mar 1819, T 12 May 1819; 17 May 1819
LC; INV, [m]; includes Negro boy Davy & Old Ester. (LC EB 27:480)

NEALE, Rodham; PO 20 Jun 1820, T 21 Jul 1820; 16 Oct 1820
LC; DIV of $564.62 1/2 in hands of Thomas MYERS admr. among George WEBB who mar. Polly NEALE, Elizabeth NEALE, Thomas MYERS, [Junah] HAINES. (LC EB 29:53)
[Geo. WEBB mar. Polly L. NEALE, LC, bond 15 Mar 1820 (MLBLC:78)]

NEALE, Thomas; PO 3 May 1813; 7 Feb 1814
RC; INV, £262.16.4, includes Negro boys George & [Tornton]; young Negro man Jesse. (RC WB 9:446)
[Acc. to a chancery suit in WC, Thos. NEALE died in 1813 leaving an only child Mira; Mira NEALE mar. Elliott POPE, WC, bond 26 Oct 1826; John NEALE, the grfather. of Mira died intestate leaving a wid, Mary, and children Thomas (the father of Mira), James NEALE, and Hannah NEALE who mar. Chas. BARNES, WC, bond 5 Nov 1806 (WCCP:30; MLBWC:4, 54);

Mary NEALE aptd. gdn. to Elmyrah NEALE orphan of Thos. NEALE, 28 Oct 1816 (WC OB 1814-18:266); on the mot. of Elliott POPE, ord. that the admin. of Mary NEALE settle the gdnship. acct. of sd. Mary with her ward Maria NEALE, now Maria POPE, 27 Feb 1827 (WC OB 1823-27:349); Elliott POPE mar. Mira NEALE, WC, bond 26 Oct 1826 (MLBWC:54)]

NELMS, Aaron; 20 Jul 1822; 12 Jul 1824
NC; WILL; to grdau. Elizabeth NELMS, dau. of my son Richard NELMS, all my land in NC adj the lands of Mrs. Catherine NELMS, Col. William JETT & others; if she should die without issue I give the land to my grson. William Henry NELMS, son of my son Richard NELMS; grson. William HUDNALL son of my dau. Nancy NELMS; [no ex. named]; WITS: Hiram BLACKWELL, Mary DAMERON, Philip TIGNOR, Lucrecia TIGNOR. (NC RB 24:10

NELMS, Eben; PO 11 Jan [1802], T 18 Aug 1802; 11 Oct 1802
NC; INV, £1462.0.6; includes Negroes Henry, Simon, James, Solomon, Molly, William, Aaron, Cooper, George, Winney, Sam, Isaac, Jenny, Massey, Grace, Esther, Mary, Hiram, Maria, Winney's child not named. (NC RB 16:463)
[In his will (NC 21 Nov 1801-11 Jan 1802), Eben NELMS named his two unmarried children Edwin & Hannah NELMS (NC RB 16:329)]

NELMS, Edwin; T 24 Nov 1814; 12 Dec 1814
NC; INV, $5644.99; includes Negroes two old men named Bill, Aron, George (a miller), James, Saul, Winney, Esther, Maria, Jane & young child Amey, Judith, boys Spencer, Simon, Isaac, Nace & Peter, girls Fanney, Mary, Massey, Agey, Molley, Lucy, old woman [Milney]. (NC RB 19:567)

NELMS, Edwin; 15 Apr 1828
NC; on the mot. of Presley NELMS, by his next friend Catharine NELMS (wid. of Edwin NELMS), ord. to div. the lands of Edwin NELMS dec'd between Edwin NELMS and the sd. Presley NELMS, sons of Edwin NELMS dec'd. (NC OB 1825 - 30:250)

NELMS, Richard; T 26 Nov 1824; 10 May 1825. NC; INV, $149.29. (NC RB 24:194)

NELMS, William; PO 11 Nov 1822; 14 Jun 1824
NC; INV; includes Negroes Sarah, boy Shadrick, Salley. (NC RB 23:494)

NELSON, William; 27 Jan 1800
WC; settle Mary NELSON's gdnship. accts. on the estates of John, Elizabeth & Nancy NELSON orphans of William NELSON. (WC Orders 1799-1801:177)
[In his will (WC 3 Mar 1796 - 25 Apr 1796) Wm. NELSON named his wife Mary, his daus. Frances HORE, Susanna WICKLIFF and Jane NELSON, son William and three youngest children Betsy, Nancy & Jn. (WC DW 19:169); Frances NELSON mar. Jas. HORE, WC, bond 9 Jun 1790 (MWO:185); Susannah NELSON mar. Chas. WICKLIFF, WC, bond 10 Feb 1789 (MWO:375); Jas. HOOE & Frances his wife, Chas. WICKLIFF & Susannah his wife, Jn. HARVEY & Jane his wife and Wm. NELSON as ex. and heirs of Wm. NELSON ord. to be summoned to show cause why Negro boy Tom should not be sold, 27 Jan 1800 (WC Orders 1799-1801:177); *NB: The name of the husband of Frances NELSON was transcribed by both Fothergill (1925) and Nottingham (1928) as "James HORE" yet it certainly looks like "James HOOE" in the record of 27 Jan 1800.*]

NEWBY, James; PO 18 Jul 1791; 21 Jun 1796
LC; INV, £997.[?].4; includes Negroes: Ile of White, Archibald, Dick, Ben, Hannah, Sarah, Mima, Bel & child Fanny, Sally, [Biddicame], Patty, Priscilla,

Bob, [Fantantire], Tabby, Letty, Ruth, Nathaniel, Philis, Godfrey. (LC EB 24:18)

NEWBY, James; [m]; 15 Apr 1799

LC; DIV of that part of the est. as was willed to his son Dennis NEWBY among: John NEWBY's est, William NEWBY, James NEWBY, Joseph WALKER, Cyrus NEWBY. (LC EB 24:92)

[Jos. WALKER mar. Jane NEWBY, LC, bond 5 Jan 1796 (MLBLC:76)]

NEWBY, John; PO 15 [Oct] 1802; 16 Sep 1805

LC; DIV of proceeds from selling 2 slaves to Sarah Ann NEWBY between: John HATHAWAY & Elizabeth NEWBY. (LC EB 24:327)

[this is the Jn. NEWBY who mar. Eliz. HUNTON dau. of Thos. HUNTON, LC, bond 30 Dec 1772 (MLBLC:54); in his will (LC 8 Jan 1794 - 17 Feb 1794), Thos. HUNTON named, among others, his dau. Eliz. NEWBY and grchil. Eliz. NEWBY, Jean Pollard NEWBY & Jn. NEWBY (LC WB 22:410); Jn. HATHAWAY mar. Jenny P. NEWBY dau. of Eliz. NEWBY, LC, bond 28 Dec 1801 (MLBLC:36); Jn. PASQUIT mar. Eliz. NEWBY, LC, bond 2 Oct 1797 (MLBLC:57); ord. that Eliz. NEWBY in her own right & as gdn. of Jn. NEWBY, Jn. HATHAWAY & Jane P. his wife, and Jn. HATHAWAY as gdn. of Hen. PASQUETH be summoned to show cause why Negro slaves Sarah & her child Geo. belonging to the est. of Jn. NEWBY dec'd should not be sold and the proceeds div. among his reps., LC 17 Sep 1804 (LC OB 1804-05:226);]

NEWBY, Oswald; PO 16 Jun 1800, T 2 Jul 1800; 19 Jul 1813

LC; INV; includes Negroes: boy Nelson, girls Sally & Judy, Davy, girl Mary, Milly, boy Pete, boy George, Abram, James & Darkey, boy John; DIV of Negroes among: Richard NORRIS, Abraham NEWBY, Prichard NEWBY, Joseph FICKLIN, Larkin PEMBERTON, Thomas FLINT, John SHACKLEFORD, William NEWBY taken 22 Dec 1800. (LC EB 27:155)

[Rich. NORRIS mar. Sarah Ann NEWBY, LC, bond 11 Jan 1791 (MLBLC:55)]

NEWBY, Oswald; PO 21 Nov 1808; 17 Apr 1809

LC; INV, £473.11.0 & DIV of est. of Oswald NEWBY which was assigned to Sarahann NEWBY dec'd, his wid., as her dower; DIV among: William NEWBY, Joseph FICKLIN in right of his wife Esther, Prichard NEWBY, Larkin PEMBERTON in right of his wife Molly, Thomas FLINT in right of his wife Priscilla, John SHACKLEFORD for the benefit of his dau, and Edward NEWBY's heirs. (LC EB 27:48)

[Jos. FICKLIN mar. Easter NEWBY, LC, bond 3 Feb 1781; Larkin PEMBERTON mar. Mary NEWBY, LC, bond 7 Oct 1788; Thos. FLINT mar. Priscilla NEWBY, LC, bond 30 Aug 1797 (MLBLC:27, 28, 58)]

NEWBY, Sarah Ann; PO Nov 1818; Dec 1818

LC; INV, [m]; includes Negroes: Sarah, Mary, George, girls Eliza & Lucinda, old man Peter considered of no value. (LC EB 27:442)

NEWBY, Sarahann; 13 Jul 180[2]; 21 Nov 1808

LC; WILL; Negro girl Mary to son [Prichard] NEWBY; to grdau. Sarahann P. N. FLINT first child of Negro Mary; rest of est. to be eq. div. among son Prichard NEWBY & my grchil. Robert T. FICKLIN, Sally E. MILLER, Robert N. NORRIS, Robert PEMBERTON, Oswald PEMBERTON to have one share between them, [Irena] SHACKLEFORD & Sarahann P. N. FLINT; rest of wearing apparel to be eq. div. among daus. Esther FICKLIN, Mary PEMBERTON, Sarahann NORRIS, [Siller FLINT], & Irena SHACKLEFORD; clothing to Negro woman Dorcas; clothing to my maid [Brittannia]; grson. Wm. NEWBY; grdau. Nancy NEWBY; son Prichard NEWBY ex; WITS: Sillar

FLINT, Sally ROSSON, Fanny BRENT; COD dtd. 17 Jun 1808: son Prichard NEWBY to have whole est. during his life; at son's death est. to be eq. div. between my grdaus. bearing my name: Sally E. MILLER, Sarahann P. N. FLINT, Sarahann NORRIS & Sarahann PEMBERTON; same WITS. (LC WB 28:109)

[Sarahann was the wid. of Oswald NEWBY (*see above*)]

NEWBY, Sarahann (Mrs.); PO 21 Nov 1808; 17 Apr 1809

LC; INV, £249.2.6.; includes Negroes: Sarah, Mary, George, Peter. (LC EB 27:48)

NEWBY, William; 5 Feb 1815; 20 Mar [1815]

LC; WILL; to my dau. Sarah E. MILLER my Negro woman Peggy RICH & $150 for rebuilding her mill; to my son William P. NEWBY all the land I now possess with the following Negroes Jacob, Mark & Mary; to dau. Nancy M. WALL the following Negroes Fortunatus, Patty, Tab, Hannah, Rachel, & Fanny; son William P. NEWBY ex; WITS: Thos. G. ROBERTSON, Jn. BEANS, Jn. BEANS, Jr. (LC WB 28:157)

[William NEWBY served 3 years as a carpenter in the Virginia State Navy during the Rev. War (VS1776 I:5); Sally Everett NEWBY mar. Peter H. MILLER, son of Jn. MILLER, LC, bond 23 Dec 1800; Nancy M. NEWBY mar. Rich. WALL, LC, bond 28 Jan 1815 (MLBLC:52, 76); Nancy M. WALL, wid., mar. (2) Thos. RAINS, NC, bond 4 Sep 1820 (MLBNC:85); William P. NEWBY was a resident of Culpeper Co., Va. by 1838 (VS1776 I:6)]

NEWBY, William; T 24 Mar 1815; 17 Jul 1815

LC; INV; includes slaves (legacy to William P. NEWBY): Jacob, Mac, Mary; (legacy to Nancy M. WALLS [sic]): Natus, Patty & child, Tab, Hannah, Rachel, Fanny; Dick, Judy, Solomon, Peter. (LC EB 27:236)

NEWBY, William; T 21 Nov 1818; 20 Mar 1820

LC; INV, [m]; includes Negroes Peter, Dick, Judy, Ellick. (LC EB 29:11)

NEWMAN, James B.; 1 Aug 1825

RC; Joseph, Ann, Martha, George, Arsione, Fanny & Mary infant children of James B. NEWMAN, dec'd, represented by Thomas DOBYNS their next friend, pltfs., vs. Joseph PALMER coroner and admr. of William NASH. (RC OB 26:338; OB 27:6)

NEWMAN, William; 7 Jun 1825

RC; William NEWMAN of this county died intest. and no one appearing to take admin. on his est., ord. that the coroner of RC Jos. PALMER dispose of his est. (RC OB 26:318)

NEWSOM (NEASOM), Elizabeth; 1807 - 1811

LC; Elizabeth NEWSOM was the dau. of Samuel NEWSOM, grdau. of Robert & Bethlehem (JONES) NEWSOM, and half sis. on her father's side of Rachel BROWN and Esther CHRISTIAN; her est. was the subject of a large and complicated CC in LC; Elizabeth, who lived for several years with her uncle Jeremiah NEWSOM, was apparently handicapped; several deponents claimed that she "was often helpless and unable to feed or dress herself," that "she was afflicted with fits," and could not use her right hand or foot; after the death intestate of Elizabeth, Rachel BROWN and her husband Spencer and Polly CHRISTIAN only child of Esther CHRISTIAN sued over the slave Thisbe (whom they claimed was purchased by Jeremiah NEWSOM with money that belonged to Elizabeth) and her children and grandchildren (Palmer, Betty, Manuel, Billy, Bass, Hannah, Dick, Sarah, Peter, Fanny, and Billy); the children of Jeremiah NEWSOM's son Robert (Polly R., George,

Eppa L. and Catherine L.) and Robert's wid. Mary "Molly or Polly" the wife of Rich. STOTT were also parties to the suit (LC CC 1811-010)

NEWSOM (NEASOME), Eppa L.; 3 Aug 1814; 4 Dec 1815
RC; WILL; all lands & tenements in RC & personal est. to wife Frances, i.e., that land in which I am in possession as also the reversion in that part which was allotted to my late father's widow now Mrs. STOTT & which third part is now held by Leroy DOBYNS; [no exors]; WITS: Rich. EFFORD, Lancelot B. CORBIN, Thos. SYDNOR Jr. (RC WB 9:492)
[Epaphroditus Lawson NEWSOM was a son of Robt. & Caty NEWSOM (*see below*); he mar. Fanny PALMER, RC, bond 7 Jun 1813 (MRC:145); "Mrs. STOTT" is apparently Mary "Polly" C. NEWSOM who mar. (1) Robt. NEASOM, RC, bond 1 Sep 1798 and (2) Rich. STOTT, LC, bond 9 Jul 1804 (MLBLC:70, 145)]

NEWSOM (NEASOME), Eppa L.; PO 4 Dec 1815; 7 Feb 1820
INV, RC; $1831.97, includes the following Negroes: [Vila] & child Harry, Manuel, George, Sukey, Pay & Eliza. (RC WB 9:653)

NEWSOM, Jeremiah; PO 11 Nov 1811, T 22 Nov 1811; 8 Mar 1813. NC; INV, £35.3.2. (NC RB 19:342)
[Jeremiah NEWSOM was the son of Robt. and Bethlehem (JONES) NEWSOM and bro. of Robt. NEWSOM (LC WB 14:9); the est. of Jeremiah NEWSOM was ord. to be admin. by Wm. SMITHERS, NC, 11 Nov 1811 (NC OB 1811-1816:26)]

NEWSOM (NEASOM), Polly R.; PO 4 Jul 1815; 6 Feb 1816
RC; DIV of two slaves; Charles & Milly were sold for $920 and the money, less $46 commission, was div. among Mary STOTT (the mother of the dec'd), Richard STOTT, Betsey STOTT, reps. of Eppa L. NEASOM, Catharine DOBYNS wife of William DOBYNS. (RC AB 3:343)
[Polly was a dau. of Robt. NEWSOM (*see below*); Wm. DOBYNS mar. Caty L. NEASOM, ward of L. R. DOBYNS, RC, bond 5 Dec 1807 (MRC:56)]

NEWSOM (NEASOM), Robert; T 8 Dec 1803; 1 Jul 1805
RC; INV, £945.9.4; includes the following Negroes: Charles, Perimas, Emanuell, Will, [Gratio], boy [Bass], Bettey & 2 small children, Silvey, Hannah, Fanney, Thesby, girl Milly, girl Sarah. (RC WB 9:253)

NEWSOM (NEASOM), Robert; PO Dec 1804, T 29 Dec 1804; 1 Apr 1805
RC; DIV of slaves among: Eppa L. NEASOM, Catharine L. NEASOM, Polly [C.] NEASOM, & George R. NEASOM. (RC AB 3:135)
[Caty Lawson NEWSOM (b. 5 Sep 1788) and Epaphroditus Lawson NEWSOM (b. 18 Mar 1786) were children of Robert & Caty (LAWSON) NEWSOM of NFP; the birth of a third child to Robt. & Caty, Rachel Davenport (b. 29 Apr 1781), was also rec. in the NFPR (NFPR:138; MWO:262); in a partially readable document a CC between Eppa L. NEWSOM, Wm. DOBYNS & Caty L. his wife against Hen. R. DOBYNS gdn. for Polly R. NEWSOM and Lucy DOBYNS involved the div. of property of Eppa LAWSON, RC, 4 Sep 1809 (RC Orders 1809-10:18)]

NEWSOM, Robert; 18 Oct 1809
LC; Chancery suit; Spencer BROWN & Rachel his wife and Polly CHRISTIAN, pltfs., against Eppa L. NEASOM & Catherine NEASOM by their gdn. Leroy DOBYNS, Henry M. DOBYNS, Polly NEASOM & George NEASOM by their gdn. Henry M. DOBYNS, Richard STOTT & Molly his wife who was Molly NEASOM, Ezekiel LEVY admr. of Robert NEASOM, James TUNE, George DAVIS and James [CURRELL] who has mar.

Catherine L. NEASOM one of the aforesd. parties. (LC Orders D22 1805-08:410; Orders B23 1808-11:125)
[Spencer BROWN mar. Rachel NEWSOM, Rich. STOTT mar. Polly C. NEWSOM, LC, bond 9 Jul 1804 (MLBLC:70); *see also Elizabeth NEWSOM above*]

NEWSOM, Robert; 5 Sep 1825
RC; settlement of Milton S. GLASCOCK's gdnship. acct. of Polly R. NEWSOM orphan of Robert NEWSOM. (RC OB 25:4)

NEWTON, Willis; 22 Jun 1812
WC; Mrs. Sally NEWTON, wid. of Willis NEWTON, aptd. gdn. of Jn. Maund NEWTON, Eliza NEWTON, Willis NEWTON, Thos. Fisher NEWTON, and Agnes NEWTON orphans of sd. Willis NEWTON. (WC Orders 1810-13:249)
[This must be Willoughby NEWTON, *see below*]

NEWTON, Willoughby; 28 May 1812; 22 Jun 1812
WC; WILL; property to be eq. div. between my children by John MURPHY Jr., George WHITELOCK, & Peter COX Esq.; wife [Sally] & friend Dr. J. Augustine SMITH exors; WITS: Sarah BERRYMAN. (WC DW 22:290)
[Willoughby NEWTON mar. Sally LEE, wid., WC, bond 23 May 1796 (MWO:263); commissioners aptd. to settle the gdnship. accts. of Sally NEWTON with her wards: Jn. P. NEWTON, dec'd, Eliza B. NEWTON now Eliza B. MURPHY, Willoughby NEWTON, Thos. NEWTON and Agnes NEWTON orphans of Willoughby NEWTON, 24 Nov 1823 (WC OB 1823-27:23, 33); Eliza B. NEWTON mar. Dr. Robt. MURPHY, at Lee Hall, WC, on 21 May 1818, bond 18 May 1818 (MLBWC:48, *Alexandria Gazette & Daily Advertiser*, 4 Jun 1818, p. [2])]

NEWTON, Willoughby; [m]; 28 Nov 1814
WC; list of dower Negroes belonging to the est. allotted to Mrs. NEWTON: Ned (30 years old), Billy Blundell (40), Betty (70), Sam (22), Becky (30), James (11), Ellick (8), Bettey (6), Fanney (1), Rachel (49), Bettey (28), Letty (1), Felitia (7), Joe (5), Winney (12). (WC RI 9:429)

NEWTON, Willoughby; PO 1812, T 3 Jan 1813; 24 Apr 1815
WC; INV, [m], includes a large number of books (among which are Cicero's Life, 15-vol History of England, Fuller's Pharmacopoeia, Love's Art of Surveying, a French dictionary, Elements of Agriculture, Dictionary of English & Latin Phrases) and Negroes Billy Blundell (aged 45), Ned (35), Dick (30), Marquis (30), [Oaks] Billy (40), Charles (45), [?]ey (70), Winney (55), Zara (55), Betty (65), Dinah (55, disabled), Rachel (50), Nancey (13), Winney (11), Cordelia (10), Rose (9), Franky (6), Becky (22), James (13), Ellick (9), Letty (1), Lucy (22), George (12), John (10), Margaret (4), Jeffrey (2), Letty (35), Winney (6), James (5), [Akey] (4), Charles (2), Betty (27), Sam (21), Felicia (4), Joe (2). (WC RI 9:435)

NICKEN, Amos; PO 8 Jun 1807; 8 Feb 1808; NC; INV, [m]. (NC RB 17:610)
[In his will (NC 6 Apr 1807-8 Jun 1807) Amos NICKENS [sic] named his son Amos, his wife Sally, and his grson. Darius NICKENS (NC RB 17:529); Sally NICKENS may be the sis. of Jn. PINN who named her in his will (NC 9 Jul 1785 – 9 Jun 1792) (unrecorded will abstracted in NCVW 1793-1816:80)]

NICKEN, Bartley; 20 Dec 1804; 16 Apr 1805
CCP, LC; WILL; house where my father now lives to [Uriell] NICKEN son of Robert NICKEN; £12 in cash to Elizabeth NICKEN dau. of John NICKEN; Richard NICKEN ex.; WITS: Peter TANKERSLEY, Wm. BRENT, Hollon DAMERON. (LC WB 28:89)

NICKEN, Bartley; PO 10 Apr 1805; 17 Jun 1805. LC; INV, £18.7.9. (LC EB 24:321)

NICKEN, Peter; 19 Dec 1826

LC; Overseers of the Poor to bind Peter NICKEN to Hancock HAYNIE to learn the trade of a wheelwright. (LC OB 26:225)

NICOLL, William Henry; 10 Jul 1820; 14 Aug 1820

NC; WILL; to wife Harriot Vaulx NICOLL all my est; at wife's death all est. to son Walter Augustus NICOLL; as soon after my death as they think proper my exors. to sell all or part of my est. in NC & buy US bank stock or some other stock from which an annual interest will be obtained; Abimael Youngs NICOLL of New Brunswick, New Jersey to be gdn. to son Walter Augustus NICOLL and the sd. Abimael & Thomas TOWLES of NC exors; [no wits. but will proved by Sam BLACKWELL & Fleming BATES]. (NC RB 22:382)

[Abimael Youngs NICOLL served as Adjutant General and acting Inspector General of the U.S. Army from 1807 to 1812; Harriet Vaulx NICOLL was Harriet V. CONWAY of NC who mar. Wm. H. NICOLL, esq. aid-de-camp to Maj. Gen. Ripley in Washington on 7 May 1818 (*City of Washington Gazette*, 9 May 1818, p. [3])]

NICOLL, William H.; PO 14 Aug 1820, T 29 Nov 1820; 14 Jan 1822

NC; INV at Cupids, $7802.88; includes Negroes Shadrach, [Peniss] [sic], Bacchus, William, Williamson, George, John, Doctor, Solomon, Moses, Harrison, Alice & 4 small children Isaac, Phillis, Winney & Stanley, [Fama] & 3 small children Tom, Lucinda & Janetta, Sally & 2 small children Judy & Louis, Violet & small child Ned, Joanna, Grace, Old Sally, Old Peggy (a charge) and a number of books. (NC RB 23:73)

[Cupids may refer to a tract of land located in Hull Neck north of Edwardsville in NC. (Miller:37)]

NICOLL, William [H.]; 12 Jul 1824. NC, INV, $12,895.27. (NC RB 24:3)

NORRIS, George; 18 Oct 1809

LC; Chancery suit; John NORRIS, James L. NORRIS, Nancy NORRIS and Hannah NORRIS, pltfs., against Elizabeth NORRIS, Judith NORRIS, Sally NORRIS and Nelson NORRIS, infants under 21, by the sd. Elizabeth NORRIS their gdn., re. dower and div. of lands. (LC Orders B23 1808-11:120)

[Eliz. NORRIS was the wid. of Geo. NORRIS, who d. intest, and Eliz., Jn., Jas. L., Nancy, Hannah, Judith, Sally and Nelson were his children; Eliz. the wid. may be Eliz. LEDFORD who mar. Geo. NORRIS, LC, bond 3 Aug 1770 (LC CC 1805-014; MLBLC:54); on 10 Mar 1796 before his death, Geo. NORRIS gave a 150-ac. tract of land to his children Eliz. & Jn.; Eliz. mar. Geo. C. DUNAWAY, LC, bond 16 Oct 1797 and d. in Dec 1801; in her will Eliz. DUNAWAY gave the 150 ac. to her bro. James L. NORRIS if he would give the land left him by his father to his bro. Jn. NORRIS; on 24 Apr 1802 Mary DUNAWAY, Chattin DUNAWAY, Thos NEWGENT & Judith his wife and Martin CARTER & Milly his wife released their claims to the 150-ac tract to Jas. L. and Jn. NORRIS (LC CC 1806-001; MLBLC:24)]

NORRIS, Ann M.; T 10 Mar 1821; 19 Mar 1821

LC; DIV of est. in the hands of the admr. Rawleigh DUNAWAY, $99.94 1/2, between Nelly DOZIER & Nancy M. NORRIS. (LC EB 29:71)

[Ann is the wid. of Martin NORRIS (*see below*); Nelly NORRIS mar. Rich. T. DOZIER, LC, bond 1 Jan 1808 (MLBLC:23)]

NORRIS, Hannah; 15 Jan 1812; 15 Jun 1812

LC; WILL; all my land to my mother; [no ex. named]; WITS: Jas. L. NORRIS, Sally NORRIS, Judith NORRIS. (LC WB 28:131)

NORRIS, James; 20 Feb 1807; 15 Jun 1812
LC; WILL; all land w/o I now live containing 215 ac. & Negroes Peter, Stephen, Aaron, Matilday, Judith & Anna to son John NORRIS; Negroes: Big George, Charles, Lewis, Mitchell & Rose to son Opie NORRIS; I lend to my son James NORRIS my plant. in RC containing 134 ac. & & Negroes Little George, Cyrus, Joe & Daniel; after his death land to my grson. Richard NORRIS (the son of James NORRIS); Negroes to be eq. div. between his [James] children; to dau. Judeth [or Judah] NORRIS during her life Esther, Fielding, Mahala, Peter, Pope & Lucinday; to grson. Charles FALLIN when he arrives at 21 the following Negroes Charlotte, Leroy & Griffin; son John NORRIS ex; WITS: Rawleigh DUNAWAY, Thos. BEANE, Marah [or Mary] STONEHAM. (LC WB 28:134)
[This is prob. the James NORRIS who mar. Judith MITCHELL, dau. of Wm. MITCHELL, Sr., LC, bond 10 Mar 1792 (MWO:265); Nancy NORRIS, Jr. mar. Wm. FALLIN, LC, bond 6 Jan 1805 (MLBLC:27)]

NORRIS, James; T 15 Dec 1812; 19 May 1817
LC; INV, $[2464.19]; includes Negroes: Peter, Stephen, George, Charles, Aaron, Cyrus, George, Lewis, Fielding, Daniel, Leroy, Joe, Peter, Pope, Griffin, Henry, Anna, Judy, Esther, Jenny, Charles, Ailcy, Matilda, Mahala, Lucinda, Rachel, Mary, Mitchell, Rose. (LC EB 27:375)

NORRIS, John; 13 May 1816
NC; William GARLINGTON aptd. gdn. of John H. NORRIS orphan of John NORRIS. (NC OB 1816-20:38)
[This is prob. the Jn. NORRIS who mar. Susanna GARLINGTON dau. of Lucy GARLINGTON, NC, bond 8 Aug 1803 (MLBNC:78); Susannah GARLINGTON was the dau. of Wm. & Lucy GARLINGTON and sis. of Polly, Wm., Nancy & Lucy GARLINGTON (NC CC 1820-013); on the mot. of Jas. L. NORRIS gdn. of Jn. H. NORRIS orphan of Jn. NORRIS ... to lay off the sd. Jn. H. NORRIS' interest in the lands of which his grandfather Wm. GARLINGTON died seized, NC 14 Oct 1822 (NC OB 1820-25:240)]

NORRIS, John; 17 Oct 1825
LC; Olivia NORRIS aptd. gdn. to John, Charles C., [Opie], & Joseph NORRIS orphans of John NORRIS. (LC OB 26:146)
[Jn. NORRIS mar. Olivia CARPENTER, LC, bond 17 Jun 1816 (MLBLC:55)]

NORRIS, Joseph; PO Jan 1798; 19 Feb 1798
LC; INV (includes Negroes Harry, Letty, Shadrick, Charlotte) & DIV of est. among: Eppey NORRIS, Septimus NORRIS, John PALMER, Thaddeus NORRIS,William NORRIS, Richard NORRIS, John KELLY. (LC EB 24:72)
[Jn. PALMER mar. Mary NORRIS, LC, bond 19 Jun 1796; Jn. KELLY mar. Sarah NORRIS, LC, bond 5 Jan 1792 (MLBLC:44, 57)]

NORRIS, Martin; PO 17 Oct 1803; 17 Apr 1804
LC; INV; includes Negroes Ned, boy Moses, woman Darkey, Mima, girl Sarah. (LC EB 24:267)

NORRIS, Martin; PO 21 Jan 1811, T 8 Jan 1812; 20 Apr 1812
LC; DIV of Negroes (Moses, Ned, Sarah, Darkey, Linda, Mima, Patty) among: the widow (her dower), Rawleigh NORRIS, Nancy M. NORRIS, Nelly DOZIER, Robert M. NORRIS. (LC EB 27:109)
[Martin NORRIS mar. Nancy MERCER, dau. of Isaac MERCER (d. LC 1779), LC, bef. 17 May 1781 (MWO:265); he served as a lieutenant in the Virginia State Line during the Rev. War (VS1776 I:7); Martin NORRIS d. intest. leaving a wid., Nancy, and five children Nelly DOZIER, Nancy Martin, Rawleigh, Thos., and Robt. Martin NORRIS; Rawleigh NORRIS and Thos.

NORRIS d. during the lifetime of their mother (LC CC 1817-008); Nelly NORRIS mar. Rich. T. DOZIER, LC, bond 1 Jan 1808 (MLBLC:23); Nancy Martin NORRIS orphan of Martin NORRIS chose Ann NORRIS as her gdn. and sd. Ann is aptd. gdn. to Robt. Martin NORRIS also an orphan of Martin NORRIS, 16 Dec 1811; Nancy M. NORRIS mar. Wm. D. RAINS, LC, bond 31 Dec 1821 (MLBLC:62) (LC Orders 24:54)]

NORRIS, Rawleigh; PO 20 Nov 1815; 18 Dec 1815
LC; INV; includes Negro girl Harriott. (LC EB 27:275)
[Nelly DOZIER brought suit against Nancy M. NORRIS & Robert M. NORRIS to show cause why land of Rawleigh NORRIS should not be sold and proceeds distributed among heirs, 1 Dec 1817 (RC OB 24:164)]

NORRIS, Sarah; PO Jan 1798); [19 Feb 1798]. LC; INV, £132.12.9. (LC EB 24:73)

NORRIS, William; 25 Oct 1821; 10 Dec 1821
NC; WILL; est. after debts paid to wife Winney NORRIS; unless wife has a lawful heir, at her death est. to be eq. div. between bro. James NORRIS' heirs & Martin NORRIS; Richard HEADLEY & William ROUTT exors; WITS: Edw. OLDHAM, Alpheus BARNES, Jn. MALEY, Griffin HEADLEY. (NC RB 23:50)
[Edw. BARNES mar. Winifred NORRIS, wid. & admx. of the est. of Wm. NORRIS, NC, bond 1 Feb 1825 (MLBNC:4; NC OB 1825-30:110)]

NORRIS, William; PO 9 Dec 1822, T 13 Mar 1823; 12 May 1823
NC; INV; includes Negroes Winney, Tom, Jacob, Bill, Sarah, child Jane, girls Lucy, Matilda & Winney, boys James, Hiram, Septimus, Presley, Griffin & Jacob. (NC RB 23:302)

NORTHEN, George; PO 7 Apr 1800, T 4 Sep 1801; 7 Sep 1801
RC; DIV of est. among the claimants: Edward J. NORTHEN, Edmond NORTHEN, Polly NORTHEN, Barbara B. NORTHEN, Samuel NORTHEN, Abner DOBYNS Jr in right of his wife Winifred. (RC AB 3:53)
[Geo. NORTHEN mar. Margaret JONES, dau. of Edw. JONES, RC, after 1767 (MWO:266); Abner DOBYNS mar. Winifred NORTHEN, dau. of Geo & Margaret (JONES) NORTHEN, RC, bond 14 Nov 1798 (MRC:54)]

NORTHEN, James; T. 9 Feb 1813; 1 Jul 1815. RC; INV, $2903.75 1/2. (RC WB 9:532)

NORTHEN, James; PO 8 Dec 1818, T 21 Jan 1819; 6 Apr 1819
RC; DIV of est. among wid, Catharine G. NORTHEN (received Negroes Samuel, Milly & Fanny), Catharine M. NORTHEN (Ede & Harry), William NORTHEN (James & Sue), William THRIFT (Sam), Peter NORTHEN (Billy). (RC AB 4:21)
[Jas. NORTHEN mar. Catharine Gwinn SMITH, RC, bond 22 Dec 1800 (MRC:148); Cath. G. SMITH was a sis. of Thos. P. SMITH who mar. Sarah L. DOBYNS (wid. of Charles and dau. of Leroy & Lucy DOBYNS), and Sarah S. SMITH who mar. Jn. CLAUGHTON of NC (MRC:39, 55, 191; RC OB 24:201); Catharine G., Thos. P., & Sarah S. were children of Wm. SMITH (d. RC 1786) (RC WB 7:528); Wm. THRIFT mar. Jane NORTHEN, RC, bond 12 Nov 1818 (MRC:215); Peter NORTHEN, Wm. NORTHEN and Cath. NORTHEN by their next friend Thos. DOBYNS & Wm. THRIFT & Jane his wife who was Jane NORTHEN, compl. vs. Cath. G. NORTHEN, wid., and others to sell slaves belonging to the est. held by the def. Cath. G. NORTHEN as dower in the est. of Jas. NORTHEN dec'd., 7 Jul 1823 (RC OB 26:76)]

NORTHEN, Margarett; PO Jun 1801, T 4 Jun 1801; 5 Jul 1801
RC; DIV of the est. of Edward JONES allotted to Margarett NORTHEN dec'd among the children of the sd. Margarett: Edward J. NORTHEN, Abner

DOBYNS who mar. Winifred NORTHEN, Barbra B. NORTHEN, Edmond NORTHEN, Samuel NORTHEN, Polly NORTHEN. (RC AB 3:49)
[Edw. JONES was the father of Margaret who mar. Geo. NORTHEN between 1767 & 1774 (MWO:266, WRC:186)]

NORTHEN, Peter; 2 Jun 1817
RC; William, Jeremiah, George, Edmond N., and Elias NORTHEN and Jane the wife of Richard L. SHACKLEFORD are heirs of Peter NORTHEN. (RC OB 24:103)
[Rich. L. SHACKLEFORD mar. Jane NORTHEN, RC, bond 11 Jan 1814 (MRC:185); Capt. Peter NORTHEN mar. Jane dau. of James & Sarah Ann ALDERSON bef. 1774; they had 9 children: James, Sarah Ann, Wm., Jeremiah, Edmund N., Geo., Elias, Jane, and Peter Smith; *for additional information see MRC:148-149 and MWO:266*]

NUTT, Ann (Mrs.); PO 13 Feb 1815, T 23 Feb 1815; 11 Apr 1815
NC; INV, [m]; includes Negro Sukey. (NC RB 20:58)
[Report of settlement of gdnship. acct. of Ann NUTT on the est. of Nancy Y. NUTT her ward and possessing W. KIRK the present gdn. with the est., 17 Apr 1815 (LC Orders 24:222)]

NUTT, Henry; PO 19 Jan 1801; 20 Apr 1801
LC; INV, [£428], includes a very large stock of various kinds of cloth & the schooner "William & Henry." (LC EB 24:143)

NUTT, Leroy; T 4 Sep 1806; 10 Sep 1806
LC; list of slaves held by Leroy NUTT in right of his wife: Robin (age 45), Jack (25), James (14), Hannah (38), David (9), Lavina (2), Matilda (1). (LC EB 24:346)

NUTT, Moseley; PO 13 Jul 1801; 12 Sep 1803
NC; INV, £3035.14.2; includes Negroes Archebel, Caleb, Eppey, Isaac, Solomon, Hirum, Milley, Mim, Silvey, Molley, Levina, Fanney, Polley, Lucinda, Siller, Mark, Rickard, Robard, Charles, John, Nathan, Jesse, Mima, Nelly, Hannah, Lucy, Ailce, Polley, Andrew, Jobe, Spencer, Leroy, Winne, Jane, Ruth, [Fame], Malinda, Nancy, Samuel, Absolom, Easter, Clary, Clark, Rachel, Ezekiel, George, Keziah, Mark, Solomon, Moses. (NC RB 17:41)
[Moseley NUTT mar. Sarah GARLINGTON, dau. of Wm. GARLINGTON, NC, 1767 (MWO:266); in his will (NC 1 Apr 1801-14 Apr 1801) Moseley NUTT named his sons William & Walter, his dau. Judith CHILTON and his bro. Rich. NUTT (NC RB 16:343); Judith NUTT mar. Jesse CHILTON, NC, bond 22 Dec 1796 (MWO:73); *see also NC CC 1805-031*]

NUTT, Moseley; PO 13 Jul 1801; 12 Sep 1803
NC; DIV of est. among [Richard] NUTT for Walter NUTT (rec'd Negroes Silvy, Clarke, Lucinda, Polly CARTER & her youngest child Clary, Archer, Cales, Absolom, Samuel, Hyrum, and Milly; Jesse CHILTON (all the Negroes left to his wife as mentioned in her father's will: Nell & Jesse, Hannah, Patty & Nathan, Alice, Dick, Bob, John, Lucy, Charles & Yellow Myma and Negroes that were not legacies: Solomon, Rachel, Levina, Ezekiel) and [Richard] NUTT for William NUTT (rec'd legacy Negroes Fame, Ruth, Malindy & Siller, Winney & her child Nancy, Andrew, Mark, Spencer, Isaac, Leroy & Jane; Negroes that were not legacy: Jemima, Casiah, George, Anne). (NC RB 17:43)

NUTT, Richard; PO 9 Mar 1812; 14 Feb 1814
NC; Chancery suit between Colin NUTT, Thomas YERBY & Delia his wife, John PULLIN & Carmen his wife, Rushworth NUTT and Austin NUTT, John NUTT & Ann NUTT by Ann NUTT their mother & gdn. and the sd.

Ann NUTT in her own right, Leroy NUTT, Caroline C. NUTT, Conway NUTT, [Olivia] Ann D. NUTT & [*blank*] NUTT children of Leroy NUTT dec'd by Alice T. NUTT their mother and next friend pltfs. against Onesiphorus HARVEY adrm. of Richard NUTT Jr. dec'd & Onesiphorus HARVEY & Emily his wife, defts.; ord. that the lands in Fluvanna [Co.] to which Richard NUTT Jr. dec'd had a vested right under the will of Richard NUTT Sr. dec'd be div. so as to give Colin NUTT & Rushworth NUTT, Delia YERBY, Carmen PULLIN and Emily HARVEY each half portion and to Leroy NUTT and the other children of Leroy NUTT dec'd one half portion to be div. among them and to Austin NUTT, John NUTT and Ann NUTT Jr. each whole portions. (NC RB 19:507)

[Rich. NUTT, wid., mar. Nancy the dau. of Nancy YERBY and [fnu] KELLY and wid. of Wm. ROEBUCK, NC, bond 2 Mar 1791 (MWO:266, 302; LC CC 1800-002); in his will (NC 25 May 1811-14 Oct 1811), Rich. NUTT [Sr.] of WicP named his wife Nancy and his children: Leroy NUTT, Rich. NUTT, Austin NUTT, Nancy NUTT, Jn. NUTT, Rush NUTT, Collin NUTT, Emmy HARVEY, Carmin PULLIN & Delia YERBY (NC RB 19:107); Thos. YERBY mar. Delia NUTT, NC, bond 7 Jan 1805; Jn. PULLIN mar. Carmen NUTT, NC, bond 1 Aug 1808; Onesiphorus HARVEY mar. Emily NUTT, NC, bond 25 Jun 1800 (MLBNC:47, 84, 113); Nancy NUTT orphan of Rich. NUTT chose Wm. KIRK as her gdn.; settlement with Geo. BARROCK admin. of Ann NUTT dec'd who was gdn. to Nancy NUTT orphan of Rich. NUTT, 20 Feb 1815 (LC Orders 24:215); *see also NC OB 1811-15:48 and CC 1812-014*]

NUTT, Richard; PO 9 Dec 1811; 14 Mar 1815

NC; commissioners met at the store of William HARDING and div. the Negroes left by sd. Richard NUTT to his wid. during her life and possessed each heir or their reps. with their part; all the other Negroes belonging to the est. were formerly div. and put in the possession of the reps.; Lot 1 for Miss Nancy NUTT (Negro fellow Simon) left in the hands of O. HARVEY, Lot 2 for One. HARVEY (Sillar), Lot 3 for Delia YERBY (Lavina), Lot 4 for [Augustus] NUTT (Lucy) put in the possession of Griffin EDWARDS his gdn., Lot 5 for John NUTT (Eady) put in the possession of Maj. William KIRK his gdn., Lot 6 for Doctor Rushworth NUTT (Tomsy) in the hands of One. HARVEY the ex. for him, Lot 7 for Collin NUTT (Daniel) dec'd left in the hands of One. HARVEY the ex., Lot 8 for Mrs. Carmine PULLIN (Betty), Lot 9 for Richard NUTT Jr. dec'd left in the hands of Ones. HARVEY the ex. (NC RB 20:34)

[Jn. NUTT orphan of Rich. NUTT chose Rushworth NUTT as his gdn., 18 Aug 1817 (LC Orders 24:384); *NB: it is not clear which Rich. NUTT is the father of this Jn. NUTT*]

NUTT, Richard Sr.; PO 9 Dec 1811; 11 Jan 1813

NC; INV, $12976.14, and DIV of est; Mrs. NUTT rec'd Negroes Jacob, Simon, Sillar, Lavina, Lucy, Eady, Tomsay, Daniel (Judale's son), Bill & three fourths of the HH & KF and plant. utensils; Leroy NUTT rec'd Yellow Winney (a legacy); Rushworth NUTT rec'd the following Negroes in the Mississippi Territory: John, Frederick, Cate, Jackson, Willis; Mrs. Emma HARVEY rec'd Betty, Peter, Patty, Spencer, Darkey, Elijah; Delia YERBY rec'd Wilmouth, Mitchell, Emanuel, Sarah, Lewis (Siner's child), Winney; Carmine PULLIN rec'd Solomon, Moses, Betty (Siner's child), Josua, Agga, Spencer; Collin NUTT rec'd Shadrack (a legacy) & the following Negroes in the Mississippi Territory: James, Isaac, Griffin, Sally, one fourth of the HH & KF and plant. utensils and one half of the casks, tubs & barrels; Richard

NUTT Jr. dec'd rec'd a number of books as a legacy and the following Negroes Armstead, Suckey, Harry, [Janey], [Fanie]; Nancy Y. NUTT rec'd Charles, Mariah, Polly, Rose; Austin NUTT rec'd [Joe], Milley, Frederick, Matilda; John NUTT rec'd James as a legacy and Solomon, John, Fanny, Daniel, Siner. (NC RB 19:289)
[A Negro named Shadrack, age c. 30, belonging to Rich. NUTT of NC was advertised as a runaway in Jan 1806 (Richmond *Enquirer*, 1 Feb 1806, p. [1]); Nancy NUTT was gdn. to Austin, Nancy and Jn. NUTT, orphans of Rich. NUTT; NC, 9 Dec 1811 (NC OB 1811-15:33); Rush NUTT was the head of a household in Jefferson Co., Miss. in the 1820 census.]

NUTT, Sally; PO 8 Feb 1808; 12 Jun 1809
NC; sale of land of which Sally NUTT died seized and div. of proceeds among claimants; 31 1/2 ac. purchased by William J. McCLANAHAN (one of the claimants) for $99.40 and $89.37 div. among John DOWNING Sr. ($9.93) who mar. Betsy NUTT half sis. to the dec'd Sally NUTT, Kendall LEE who mar. Mary NUTT half sis. to the sd. dec'd rec'd $9.93 which is discounted with William J. McCLANAHAN & Thomas E. NUTT by consent it being in part for money due from Mary NUTT (now Mary LEE) to Elizabeth F. NUTT (now McCLANAHAN) in the div. of their father's est. with 13 years interest and partly the sd. Kendall's proportion of the money the dec'd Sally NUTT fell indebted to Thomas E. NUTT in the aforesaid div. with interest as aforesaid amounting (it appears) to more than his proportion of the net proceeds of the sale of the dec'd's land, to Thomas E. NUTT bro. to the dec'd (a bond for $19.86), possessed William J. McCLANAHAN in behalf of his wife Elizabeth F. sis. to the dec'd Sally NUTT with $19.86, to Sarah NUTT gdn. to Robert NUTT (bro. to sd. dec'd) a bond for $19.86, to Richard SELDEN gdn. to Eliza NUTT orphan of William D. NUTT dec'd half bro. to sd. dec'd Sally NUTT for $7.68. (NC RB 18:172)
[Kendall LEE mar. Mary NUTT, ward of Jn. CRALLE, NC, bond 3 Mar 1796 (MLBNC:67); Eliz. F. NUTT mar. Wm. J. McCLANAHAN, NC, bond 8 Dec 1807 (MLBNC:71); Eliz. C. NUTT mar. Jos. A. CARTER, LC, bond 28 Oct 1817 (MLBLC:12); *see also NC OB 1807-11:22 and Col. Wm. NUTT below*]

NUTT, Walter; PO 8 Dec 1823; 9 Aug 1824. NC; INV, [m]. (NC RB 24:25)

NUTT, William (Col.);
NC; William NUTT d. intest. leaving a wid. Sarah and the following children: Elizabeth the wife of Jn. DOWNING, William D., Henry L., Mary wife of Kendall LEE, Thomas E., Betsy F. and Robert; William D. NUTT d. intest. leaving one child Eliza and Henry L. NUTT d. intest. leaving two daus. Mary and Eliza; Mary and William D. NUTT were siblings of the whole blood and Eliz. DOWNING, Thomas E. NUTT, Betsy F. NUTT and Robert NUTT were siblings of the half blood (NC CC 1822-001)
[It is not entirely clear to me how to organize this family based on this CC; I believe that Wm. D. NUTT and Henry L. Nutt were children of the unknown first wife of Col. Wm. NUTT and that Eliz DOWNING, Mary LEE, Thos. E., Besty F. McCLANAHAN, Robt., and poss. Sally who must have d. well before this suit were children of Sarah EDWARDS the second wife of Col. NUTT; however if Eliz. DOWNING wife of Jn. DOWNING Sr. and Mary LEE the wife of Kendall LEE are indeed daus. of Col. NUTT's second wife whom he mar. in 1785, how could they have mar. in 1780 and 1796 respectively? perhaps Col. NUTT was mar. three times; I cannot explain daus. named Elizabeth and Betsy; Betsy F. NUTT must be the Elizabeth Fauntleroy NUTT named as a granddau. in the will of Eliz. EDWARDS (NC

18 Feb 1797 – 12 Jun 1797) (NC RB 15:382); Wm. NUTT mar. (2?) Sarah EDWARDS, NC, lic. 5 Mar 1785 (MWO:267); Eliz. NUTT mar. Jn. DOWNING, NC, lic. 31 Oct 1780 (MWO:113); *see also Sally NUTT above*]

NUTT, William D.; PO 19 Nov 1800; 16 Feb 1801
LC; INV, £924.12.7; includes Negroes: Baccus, Phill, Tom, Ned, Peter, Jack, Joe, Tom (little), Simon, Winny, Peggy, Hannah. (LC EB 24:133)
[Eliz. the wife of Rich. SELDEN was Eliz. NUTT admx. of Wm. D. NUTT, 16 Sep 1805 (LC Orders D22 1805-08:54); Eliz. NUTT mar. Rich. SELDEN, LC, bond 14 Jun 1803 (MLBLC:66); *see also LC CC 1805-011*]

OLDHAM, Ann; PO 10 Dec 1804, T 1 Dec 1805; 9 Dec 1805. NC; INV, £28.3.9. (NC RB 17:352)
[The est. of Ann OLDHAM was ord. to be admin. by James OLDHAM, NC, 13 Feb 1804 (NC MB 1801-1805:196)]

OLDHAM, George; 1 Apr 1822; 9 Sep 1822
NC; WILL; remaining prop. after debts paid to wife Margaret OLDHAM for the benefit of her and the children that remain with her; after wife's death prop. to be eq. div. between my two children Margaret & Sally B. OLDHAM & grson. Richard EDWARDS; friend Thomas BERRY ex.; WITS: Sam. BERRY, Griffin EDWARDS; Thos. BERRY relinquished his right of executorship and a cert. was granted him for obtaining letters of admin. on the est. with the will annexed. (NC RB 23:217)
[This is prob. the Geo. OLDHAM, the son of Jas. OLDHAM, who mar. Peggy BERRY, NC, bond 26 Sep 1788 (MWO:267); Margaret OLDHAM, orphan of Geo. OLDHAM, chose Jn. ROBINSON as her gdn., 14 Nov 1825 (NC OB 1825-30:46); Rich. EDWARDS is no doubt a child of Judith OLDHAM, dau. of Geo., who mar. Griffin EDWARDS, NC, bond 14 Dec 1818 (MLBNC:33)]

OLDHAM, George; PO 9 Sep 1822; 13 Jun 1825. NC; INV, [m]. (NC RB 24:253)

OLDHAM, James; T 10 Apr 1815; 12 Jun 1815
NC; INV; includes only a debt due from the United States of $24.52; George OLDHAM admin. (NC RB 20:147)

OLDHAM, John; PO 12 Dec 1803, T 13 Dec 1803; 13 Feb 1804
NC; INV, £347.5.6; includes Negroes Ruth, Ruth [sic], Andrew, Catherine, Mariah, Jude. (NC RB 17:119)
[In his will (NC 19 Apr 1803-12 Dec 1803), Jn. OLDHAM of SSP named his siblings Jas., Thos., Jane C. MINOR, Nancy OLDHAM & Edw. OLDHAM, he also left a legacy to his mother but did not name her (NC RB 17:93)]

OLDHAM, John; PO 8 Oct 1811; 13 Mar 1811
NC; INV; Rich. CLAUGHTON could not find any est. to admin. (NC RB 19:11)

OLDHAM, Samuel; 17 May 1819
LC; Chichester TAPSCOTT aptd. gdn. of Susan Chinn OLDHAM & Elizabeth Shearman OLDHAM orphans of Samuel OLDHAM. (LC OB 25:53)
[This is prob. Sam. OLDHAM who mar. Ann SHEARMAN, LC, bond 2 Feb 1803 (MLBLC:56); commission aptd. to settle with Dominick BENNEHAN the acct. of his admin. of the est. of Ann OLDHAM dec'd and settle with BENNEHAN the acct. of his gdnship. with Susan C. & Eliz. S. OLDHAM, 16 Oct 1826 (LC OB 26:211); 121-ac. tract of land in LC which descended to Eliz. S. OLDHAM & Susan C. OLDHAM who mar. Robt. SCOTT from their mother, Ann OLDHAM, to be sold and proceeds div. between Robt. SCOTT & wife and Eliz. S. OLDHAM, 19 Dec 1826 (LC OB 26:224-225)]

OLDHAM, Samuel; 13 May 1829

NC; on the motion of Thomas OLDHAM, Edward OLDHAM and Nancy MASON ord. that Daniel RIGGS & Elizabeth his wife, John T. CARTER & Sally his wife, William HEADLEY & James HEADLEY be summoned to show cause why the lands of Samuel OLDHAM should not be sold. (NC OB 1825-30:356)
[Jn. T. CARTER mar. Sarah M. MINOR, NC, bond 29 Dec 1820 (MLBNC:15; Sam. OLDHAM, of RC, was a son of James OLDHAM; he died underage and without issue; Edw. OLDHAM, Nancy (OLDHAM) MASON and Jane (OLDHAM, MINOR) HEADLEY were siblings of Jas. OLDHAM and aunts and uncle of Sam. OLDHAM; Edw. OLDHAM was the father of Jas., Jane, Edw. & Rich. OLDHAM; Jane OLDHAM mar. (1) Jn. MINOR c. 1799 and (2) Thos. HEADLEY, 1805 and had Sarah MINOR who mar. Jn. T. CARTER, Eliz. MINOR who mar. Dan. RIGGS, Wm. HEADLEY & Jas. HEADLEY (NC CC 1831-002)]

OLDHAM, Thomas; 25 Nov 1823; 12 Jan 1824
NC; WILL; my land & Negro James to dau. Lucy SELF; Negro woman Winney to dau. Gracy S. DAMERON; Negro man Stephen to dau. Nancy HEADLEY; Negro man William to grson. Leroy O. DAMERON; Negro man John & all est. not before mentioned to be sold & proceeds eq. div. between 3 children Gracy S. DAMERON, Nancy HEADLEY & Lucy SELF; friends Walter SELF & Richard HEADLEY exors; WITS: Sam. CRALLE, Darius G. CRALLE, Jn. KING. (NC RB 23:402)
[Lucy OLDHAM mar. Walter SELF, NC, bond 17 Jul 1809; Gracey Smith OLDHAM mar. Christopher DAMERON, NC, bond 16 Aug 1792; Nancy OLDHAM mar. Rich. HEADLEY, NC, bond 30 May 1808 (MLBNC:25, 52, 91)]

OLDHAM, Thomas; T 17 Jan 1824; 14 Mar 1825
NC; INV, $1520.38; includes the following Negroes: Winney, John, Stephen, William, James. (NC RB 24:168)

OLDHAM, William; PO 14 Jan 1800, T 24 Jan 1800; 9 Dec 1800
NC; INV, [m]; includes Negroes Sam Sr., Sam Jr., James, Jesse, Adam, Solomon, Nelson, Cate & child Mariah, Polly, Charles, Manuel, Peter, Tom ASTON, Mansfield, Lucy & child Ciller, Fanny, Jude. (NC RB 16:198)
[The est. of Wm. OLDHAM was ord. to be admin. by Jas. OLDHAM, Jn. OLDHAM & Jn. MINOR, NC, 9 Dec 1799 (NC Fiduciary Bonds 1797-1801); Jenny C. MINOR was gdn. to Nancy OLDHAM and Thos. OLDHAM in a suit against Jas. OLDHAM admr. of Wm. OLDHAM, 30 Nov 1804 (NC CC 1805-003)]

OLDHAM, William; PO 13 Mar 1810; 13 Mar 1811
NC William OLDHAM, inspector, having been dead more than 3 months and no one applied for administration of his est.; no est. could be found to administer. (NC RB 19:12; OB 1807-11:161)

OLDHAM, William; 9 Mar 1823; 1[6] Jun 1823
LC; WILL; whole est. to wife Frances so long as she remains my widow; if wife marries she is to have one third; the other two thirds to dau. Cordelia Catherine; friend John CHOWNING ex; WITS: Jn. B. ROANE, Spencer BROWN, Leroy CHOWNING. (LC WB 28:232)
[Wm. OLDHAM mar. Frances BLAKEY, LC, bond 23 Jul 1817; Cordelia C. OLDHAM mar. Leroy CHOWNING, LC, bond 18 Nov 1839 (MLBLC:14, 56)]

OLDHAM, William; T 9 Dec 1823; 15 Mar 1824

LC; INV, $909.46; included Negroes Ned, O. George, Henry, Old Tom, Phill, George, Sam, Bob, James, Mimy & child Stephen, Lucy & child Martha, Dinah, Patty, Arlana, Spencer. (LC EB 29:321)

OLDHAM, William Sr.; 19 Dec 1790; 12 Apr 1791
NC; WILL; son William OLDHAM land w/o I now live; dau. Fanney Lawson OLDHAM; wife Nancy OLDHAM; Robt. EDWARDS & William OLDHAM exors; WITS: Wm. NORRIS, Peter C. RICE, John OLDHAM. (NC RB 14:424)
[Wm. OLDHAM mar. Nancy DOBYNS, RC, bond 29 Apr 1786 (MWO:268); Merryman PAYNE, wid., mar. Nancy OLDHAM, wid. of Wm. OLDHAM Sr., NC, bond 23 Aug 1792 (MLBNC:80; NC CC 1800-010); Fanny Lawson OLDHAM d.s.p (NC CC 1800-010, 1811-014)]

OLIFF, Charles; of WC was found dead on the Bank of Goose Creek, Loudoun Co., Va. about three miles above the bridge. (*Genius of Liberty*, 21 Jul 1818, p. [2])

OLIFF, James; 1811 – 1817
WC; James OLIFF d. intest. in 1795 leaving Thomas, Ann, John Davis, George, Charles, and James his only children and heirs at law. (WC CC 1817-017)

OLIFF, Sarah; 23 Aug 1799; 26 Nov 1799
WC; WILL; dau. Anne; sons John D. and George; grdau. Lucy OLIFF; exors. George OLIFF & Anne OLIFF. (WC DW 20:35)

OLIVER, Tapscott; 5 Sep 1807; 21 Sep 1807
LC; WILL; whole est. to Mary my former faithful old woman slave but now freed by my deed of emancipation dtd. 22 Mar 1806 recorded in the district court 2 Apr the same year; friend Griffin EDWARDS ex.; WITS: Ezekiel HAYDON, Fortunatus GEORGE. (LC WB 28:102)
[Tapscott OLIVER mar. Winifred LUNSFORD, LC, bond 21 Mar 1780 (MLBLC:56)]

OLIVER, Tapscott; PO 21 Sep 1807; 19 Oct 1807. LC; INV, $145.09; Griffin EDWARDS ex. (LC EB 27:23)

OLIVER, Thomas; T 24 Nov 1810; 21 Sep 1812
LC; INV, includes Negroes: Moses, Jenny & child, Phillis, Dinah & child, Samuel, Cate, Betty, Daniel, Harriott, George. (LC EB 27:123)
[Matthew H. OLIVER orphan of Thos. OLIVER chose Geo. [P.] OLIVER as his gdn., Hannah OLIVER was the wid. of Thos., 19 Dec 1811 (LC Orders B23 1808-11:233); *NB: it is not certain that this Thos. OLIVER is the one whose inv, is rec. above*; a Thos. OLIVER mar. an unknown woman, LC, bond 17 Aug 1802 (MLBLC:56); Hannah OLIVER, wid. of Thos., mar. Bede HUGHLETT, LC, bond 7 Jan 1813 (MLBLC:39); Hannah (OLIVER) HUGHLETT was gdn. to Jn. & Alcy Hughlett OLIVER orphans of Thos. OLIVER, 21 Jun 1813 (LC Orders 24:158); Geo. P. OLIVER aptd. gdn. to Jn. D. & Alice C. OLIVER orphans of Thos. OLIVER replacing Hannah (OLIVER) HUGHLETT, 19 Jul 1813 (LC Orders 24:161); ord. that Geo. P. OLIVER be summoned to render an acct. of his gdnship. & an inv. of Jn. D. OLIVER & Alice H. OLIVER orphans of Thos. OLIVER his wards, 16 Sep 1816 (LC Orders 24:334, 336)]

OMOHUNDRO, John; 27 Apr 1795; 22 Nov 1802
WC; WILL; to be buried at Thos. OMOHUNDRO's by his wife; all land to son John OMOHUNDRO along with 3 slaves: Kate, Suckey, Nancy, a dictionary and arithmatic books; dau. Clarinda OMOHUNDRO a slave named Nell; Maj. Walker MUSE, William OMOHUNDRO, and son John to

be exors; WITS: Thos. OMOHUNDRO, Wm. OMOHUNDRO. (WC DW 20:403)

OMOHUNDRO, John; PO 23 Mar 1812; 26 Aug 1816. WC; INV, £13.10.2. (WC RI 10:87)

OMOHUNDRO, Martha; 3 Jun 1806; 25 Aug 1806.
CP, WC; WILL; grson. Marks CRASK; grdau. Sebina JENKINS; whole est. to be eq. div. among four sons: William CRASK, Thomas OMOHUNDRO, William OMOHUNDRO & Richard OMOHUNDRO; four sons exors.; WITS: Nancy BAILEY, [Gracy] BULGER. (WC DW 21:268)
[This is prob. Martha CRASK, the wid. of Wm. CRASK, who mar. Thos. OMOHUNDRO bef. 9 Nov 1779 (MWO:268)]

OMOHUNDRO, Martha; T 27 Feb 1808; 27 Nov 1809
WC; INV, £61.3.6; DIV of est. among Thomas OMOHUNDRO, William CRASK, William OMOHUNDRO. (WC RI 9:160)

OMOHUNDRO, Thomas; 4 May 1820; 26 Jun 1820
WC; WILL; to dau. Martha OMOHUNDRO the plant. w/o I now live with an eq. portion of all my pers. est; to dau. Ann OMOHUNDRO all my tract of land in the fork of Hutt's Mill Pond in WC with an eq. portion of all my pers. est; if both daus. die without heirs my whole est. to my six nephews: Thomas OMOHUNDRO, William OMOHUNDRO, Richard OMOHUNDRO, John OMOHUNDRO (sons of [my] bro. William OMOHUNDRO and Edward B. OMOHUNDRO & Richard OMOHUNDRO (sons of my bro. Richard OMOHUNDRO; bros William & Richard exors; WITS: Thos. [S]. DAVIS, Thos. M. JENKINS, Tarpley BRYANT. (WC DW 24:98)
[Martha OMOHUNDRO mar. Francis LINTHICUM, WC, bond 10 Jan 1829 and Ann OMOHUNDRO mar. Thos. Wm. HUTT, WC, bond 24 Jul 1827 (MLBWC:33, 40; WCCP:20); Rich. OMOHUNDRO aptd. gdn. of Martha & Ann orphans of Thos. OMOHUNDRO, 28 Apr 1823 (WC OB 1819-23:553; OB 1823-27:227); Hutt's Mill was located in WC on Templeman Run (formerly Cos Cos Creek) near its confluence with Nomini Creek (Miller:71)]

OPIE, Leroy (Maj.); a native of NC; paymaster of the US Army for the district of Virginia and North Carolina, died on 30 Oct 1819 in an accident on his return from Wilmington, North Carolina leaving a wid. and child. (*American Beacon and Norfolk & Portsmouth Daily Advertiser*, 6 Nov 1819, p. [3])

OPIE, Lindsey; 17 Jun 1799
LC; Jennetta OPIE orphan of Lindsey OPIE chose John S. BALL as her gdn. (LC Orders (21) 1799-1801:2)

OPIE, Thomas; T 2 Jul 1799; 15 Oct 1799
NC; INV, [m]; includes Negroes Joe, Mark, James, Harry, William, Daniel, David, Griffin, Cloe & child, Salley & child, Fanny & child, Nell, Milley, Letty & child, Bob & Solomon together, Harriett, Fielding & Washington together, Presley & Dennis together, Jane, Edmand, Mima & Leviner, Easter & [Massy]. (NC RB 16:14)
[In his will (NC 10 Jul 1798-10 Dec 1798), Thos. OPIE named his bro. Hierome Lindsy OPIE & sisters Sally PARKER, Suanna OPIE and Leroy & Jane OPIE (nfi) (NC RB 15:541); Septimus D. CLARK mar. Jane, also called Janetta, McAdam OPIE a sis. of Thos. OPIE who had been aptd. her gdn. on 12 Apr 1795 (NC CC 1816-012)]

OVERSTREET, Bartlett; 20 Feb 1804
LC; William Jason OVERSTREET orphan of Bartlett OVERSTREET chose Jonathan WILDER as his gdn. (LC Orders W 1804-05:10)

[*This man's name is also given as "Bartley OVERSTREET"* (ALCW:239)]

OWENS, Elizabeth; PO 10 Feb 1800; 13 Apr 1801

NC; INV of est. presented by William REIGNS ex., £141.14.8; DIV among William REIGNS in behalf of his children (rec'd Negro Dick), Rawleigh REIGNS in behalf of his child. (NC RB 16:228)

[In her will (NC 30 Oct 1799-10 Feb 1800), Eliz. OWENS names her neices Molly & Betsy REIGNES and Nancy REIGNES (nfi) (NC RB 16:54)]

PACKETT, William R.; T 13 Feb 1816; 5 Sep 1825. RC; INV, $117. (RC WB 10:84)

PAGE, Bernard (The Rev.); 16 May 1803

LC; The Rev. Bernard PAGE inducted as rector of Christ Church Parish on 20 Jul 1795, d. at the house of Gilbert CURRELL about 1 Oct 1795 intestate; admin. on this est. granted to Gilbert CURRELL on 21 Oct 1795; sd. Bernard PAGE was about 60, a tall man about 6' high; it appears to the court that he was an Englshman as he said and had relations in England. (LC Orders V 1802-03:321)

[The Rev. Bernard had an interesting history. He was ordained in London in 1772 and sent to Pennsylvania where he was the first Episcopal minister of Wyoming. He moved about to several other churches in New York before ending up in Virginia where he was at Christ Church in Alexandria and in Shepherdstown. (see also: Sheldon Reynolds, Esq., "The Rev. Bernard Page, A. M. First Episcopal Minister of Wyoming," A.D. 1771, *Proceedings and Collections of the Wyoming Historical and Geological Society* Vol. II, Pt. 1, (1886), pp. 206-216 and Bishop William Meade, *Old Churches, Ministers and Families of Virginia*, 2 vols., Philadelphia, 1857, repr. Baltimore: Genealogical Publishing Company, 1966)]

PAGE, Thomas T.; 2 Feb 1824

RC; Thomas T. PAGE chose Milly PAGE as his gdn. and sd. Milly PAGE is aptd. gdn. to Judith F., Robt. C. & Wm. Hen. PAGE orphans of Thos. T. PAGE. (RC OB 26:144)

[Can this be the Thos. T. PAGE who d. in Prince William Co., Va in 1823? In his will (Pr. Wm. Co. 13 Jun 1822 – 7 Jul 1823) he mentions his wife and children but does not name them (Pr. Wm. Co. WB M:31); Judith F. PAGE mar. Wm. W. LYELL, RC, bond 5 Jul 1828 (MRC:122)]

PAGE, William; PO 25 Apr 1814; 27 Jun 1814

WC; INV, $1651.74, includes Negroes boy Rheubin & Frank, girls Nancy, Letty & Fanney. (WC RI 9:425)

PAGE, William; PO Apr 1814, T 6 May 1815; [22 May 1815]

WC; DIV of est. among the distributees: Elizabeth PAGE (the wid.), James [HOWSTON], and John PAGE. (WC RI 9:444)

PALMER, Abner; 26 Jun 1807; 19 Oct 1807

LC; WILL; use of half the land I now live on (adj. land of Joseph B. DOWNMAN dec'd) to wife Nancy PALMER; Negro man Tom & Negro woman Winney to wife; all land and plant. w/o I now live to son Armistead J. PALMER reserving one half for his mother's use during her life; Negro girl [Menerly] to son Armistead; Negro boy Moses to dau. Sally PALMER; 1 shilling to dau. Betsy BRENT; Negro woman Silvia to grsons William B. BRENT & Albert H. BRENT; Negro girl Rose to dau. Apphia PALMER; Negro boy Leroy to dau. Winnefred James DUNAWAY; friend John CARPENTER & son Armistead exors; WITS: Jas. NORRIS Jr., Judith NORRIS, Jn. CARPENTER, Maryann DODSON. (LC WB 28:103)

[Abner PALMER mar. Nancy BOATMAN, dau. of Robt. & Apphia BOATMAN, bef. 25 Sep 1771 (MWO:271); Winny James PALMER mar. Opie DUNAWAY, LC, bond 20 Sep 1802 (MLBLC:24)]

PALMER, Abner; 19 Dec 1808
LC; INV, £624.4.3.; includes Negroes: Tom, Moses, Winny, [Silly], Rose, [Lett], Minerva. (LC EB 27:43)

PALMER, Benjamin; 1 [Jun] 1821); [?] Jun 1821
LC; WILL; whole est. to wife Molley as long as she remains my wid.; plant. w/o I now live to son William during his life; if son should have no heirs land to go to daus. Delia & Polly; rest of est. to be sold and proceeds eq. div. between sons Joshua & William & daus. Delia & Polly; grchildren by dau. Sy[bil]; wife Molly extx; WITS: Jn. WADDEY, Thos. J. TALLEY, Anne WARWICK, E. PERCIFULL, Rich. PAYNE. (LC WB 28:217)
[Benj. PALMER mar. Mary GEORGE (poss. as his second wife), LC, bond 27 Feb 1817 (MLBLC:57); Benj. PALMER served as a pvt. and poss. later a corporal in the artillery during the Rev. War; he died 12 Jun 1821 (LC OB 25:40; HRVR:601, PR1835:714)]

PALMER, Benjamin; PO 16 Jul 1821); [21] Sep 1821. LC; INV, [m]. (LC EB 29:115)

PALMER, John; 17 Oct 1804; 17 Dec 1804
LC; WILL; all prop. to wife Mary PALMER; wife extx; WITS: Geo. ARMS, Jn. RICE, Jas. ADAMS. (LC WB 28:87)
[This is prob. Jn. PALMER who mar. Mary NORRIS, LC, bond 19 Jun 1796 (MLBLC:57)]

PALMER, John; PO 21 May 1811, T 28 Nov 1811; 21 Mar 1814
LC; real & pers. est. of John PALMER orphan of Thomas PALMER was sold for $430.83 & div. among: Thomas CARTER in right of his wife who was the mother of sd. John PALMER, Robert D. PALMER in right of his wife a sis. to sd. John PALMER, Joseph DALE in right of his wife another of sd. John PALMER's sisters, Judith PALMER also a sis. in the hands of Thomas CARTER her gdn, and Thomas CARTER's two children by his present wife which sd. children is half blood to the dec'd John PALMER. (LC EB 27:172; Orders 24:14)
[Thos. CARTER mar. Judah PALMER, LC, bond 18 Nov 1799; Robt. D. PALMER mar. Dolly J. PALMER, LC, bond 21 Dec 1807 (MLBLC:12, 57); Jos. DALE mar. Chloe PALMER, RC, bond 6 Nov 1809 (MRC:48)]

PALMER, John; 10 Nov 1828
NC; ord. the div. of the property heretofore conveyed by John PALMER to his dau. Lucy PALMER and his son John PALMER (now dead) between Jesse MAITH who has mar. the sd. Lucy PALMER and the sd. John PALMER [sic]. (NC OB 1825-30:316)
[Jesse MAITH mar. Lucy PALMER, NC, bond 21 Nov 1827 (MLBNC:72)]

PALMER, Joseph; PO 14 Feb 1814; 9 Jan 1815
NC; INV, $1478.38; includes Negroes Mark, girl Jane, boy Kendell, girls Fillis & Siner. (NC RB 19:598)
[The est. of Jos. PALMER was ord. to be admin. by Geo. BARRETT, NC, 14 Feb 1814 (NC OB 1811-1816:211); Jn. PALMER the orphan of Jos. PALMER chose Wm. HARDING as his gdn., NC, 12 Dec 1814 (NC OB 1811-15:267)]

PALMER, Robert D.; 6 Nov 1818; 21 Dec 1818
WicP, LC; WILL; $1 to s-i-l Samuel STONUM; use of all est. to wife Dolly J. PALMER during her widowhood or single life; use of tract of land where my dwelling house now stands to son Robert D. PALMER; if he has no heirs

tract to be eq. div. between my son Thomas D. PALMER & dau. Milly D. PALMER; use of one half of the land I purchased of Thomas WEBB & land I purchased of the sale of John TALLEY dec'd to my son Thomas D. PALMER; use of the other half of the sd. land to dau. Milly D. PALMER; use of my man Spencer to son Thomas D.; my woman Charlotte to dau. Milly D.; my woman [*1 word unclear*] to son Robert D.; to the heirs of my dau. Elizabeth R. STONUM $150 after the death of my wife; wife to have 3 children educated; wife & Jas. ROBINSON exors; WITS: Thos, CARTER, Chas. J. YERBY, Benj. PALMER. (LC WB 28:193)

[Robt. D. PALMER appears to have been married twice: (1) to Milly CUNDIFF, dau. of Rich. & Susanna CUNDIFF, LC, bond 22 Aug 1797 and (2) to Dolly J. PALMER, LC, bond 21 Dec 1807 (MLBLC:57); Robt. PALMER aptd. gdn. to his dau. Betsy Robert PALMER, 17 Oct 1803 (LC Orders V 1802-03:451); Sam. STONUM mar. Eliz. R. PALMER, LC, bond 3 Dec 1817 (MLBLC:70); Dolly J. PALMER wid. of Robt. mar. Thos. T. ATWELL, LC, bond 21 Jul 1823 (MLBLC:2)]

PALMER, Robert D.; T 12 Jan 1819; 19 Apr 1819
LC; INV, [m]; includes Negroes: Spencer, Charlotte, [Orah]. (LC EB 27:470)

PALMER, Thomas; PO 20 Jan 1800; 20 Feb 1809
LC; DIV of Negroes at the house of Thomas CARTER among legal reps: Judith (widow), Chloe PALMER, [Doretha] PALMER, John PALMER, Thomas PALMER. (LC EB 27:46)

[Thos. PALMER mar. Judith CUNDIFF, dau. of Jn. CUNDIFF, LC, bond 29 Jul 1785 (MWO:272); Thos. PALMER d. intest. in 1795 or 1796 leaving a wid. Judith and children Dolly J., Chloe, Jn. and Judith; his wid. Judith mar. (2) Thos. CARTER (LC CC 1811-014); Thos. CARTER mar. Judah PALMER, LC, bond 18 Nov 1799 (MLBLC:12); Jn. PALMER orphan of Thos. PALMER chose Thos. CARTER as his gdn. and sd. CARTER is aptd. gdn. of Thos. & Judith PALMER also orphans of Thos. PALMER, 21 Sep 1807 (LC Orders D22 1805-08:404); Thos. CARTER was gdn. of Thos. PALMER orphan of Thos. PALMER; on the mot. of Thos. CARTER gdn. of Thos. PALMER, dec'd, ord. that Jos. DALE & Chloe his wife, Robt. D. PALMER & Dolly his wife, Jn. PALMER & Judith PALMER by the sd. Thos. CARTER their gdn. and the sd. Thos. CARTER & Judith his wife be summoned to show cause why the lands and slaves of sd. Thos. PALMER orphan of Thos. PALMER Sr. should not be sold, 16 Jul 1810 (LC Orders 23B 1808-11:205); Jos. DALE mar. Chloe PALMER, RC, bond 6 Nov 1809 (MRC:48); Dolly J. PALMER orphan of Thos. PALMER chose Robt. D. PALMER as her gdn., 21 Dec 1807 (LC Orders 22D 1805-08:431); Robt. D. PALMER mar. Dolly J. PALMER, LC, bond 21 Dec 1807 (MLBLC:57); Judith PALMER orphan of Thos. PALMER chose Robt. D. PALMER as her gdn., 16 Oct 1815 (LC Orders 24:265)]

PALMER, Thomas; PO 21 Sep 1807; 20 Feb 1809
LC; DIV of est. among John PALMER , [?] PALMER, Chloe PALMER, Thomas PALMER, Judith PALMER. (LC EB 27:47)

PALMER, Thomas; PO 20 Aug 1810, T 28 Nov 1811; 21 Mar 1814
LC; DIV of proceeds of sale of pers. est. of Thomas PALMER orphan of Thomas PALMER among Thomas CARTER in right of his wife who was the mother of the above orphan, Robert D. PALMER in right of his wife one of the sd. orphan's sisters, Joseph DALE in right of his wife another of sd. orphan's sisters, Judith PALMER another sis. in the hands of her gdn. Thomas CARTER, and Thomas CARTER's two children by his present wife which children is half blood in the aforementioned orphan. (LC EB 27:171)

PALMER, William Sr.; 17 Mar 1812; 4 Oct 1813
NFP, RC; WILL; all prop. except the land w/o my son William PALMER now lives to wife Elizabeth during her life; at death of my wife land including land purchased of Rawleigh DALE to be eq. div. between sons Charles & Joseph PALMER (both unmarried); $100 to dau. Nancy POPE; $100 to dau. Caty DOBYNS; $100 to dau. Sally PALMER the wife of Mr. Armstead PALMER; $100 to be eq. div. between grdaus Sally & Elizabeth PALMER daus. of my son Jn. PALMER dec'd; $100 each to daus. Elizabeth & Fanny PALMER; Negro woman Winny to dau. Caty DOBYNS; wife, Thaddeus POPE, William PALMER & Joseph PALMER exors; WITS: Hen. M. DOBYNS, Jn. GORDON, Rich. M. GLASCOCK. (RC WB 9:433)
[Ann "Nancy" PALMER mar. Thaddeus POPE, RC, bond 7 Jan 1795; Caty PALMER mar. Daniel DOBYNS Jr.; Sally PALMER, dau. of William PALMER Sr., mar. Armistead J. PALMER of LC, RC, bond 26 Dec 1808 (MRC:54, 153, 160)]

PALMER, William Sr.; PO 3 Nov 1821, T 4 Nov 1822; 5 May 1823
RC; DIV of land devised by William PALMER's will to his two sons Charles & Joseph PALMER. (RC AB 4:58)

PARK, James; [m]; 27 Jun 1803. WC; INV, £4901.4.3. (WC RI 8:235)
[This is prob. the James PARK whose storehouse at Broadfield two miles from Mattox Bridge in WC was advertised for lease by Townsend S. DADE (*Alexandria Advertiser*, 15 Jan 1808, p. [3])]

PARK, James; PO Sep 1802, T 4 Dec 1802; 26 Feb 1805. WC; INV, £442.3.0. (WC RI 8:530)

PARKER, Alexander; 25 Mar 1821; 26 Mar 1821
WC; manumission of Negro woman slave Louisa; WITS: Jn. W. JONES. (WC DW 24:149)

PARKER, Alexander; 14 Jul 1821; 26 Nov 1821
WC; WILL; to son Henry PARKER all my tract of land on Yeocomico Neck w/o I now live; to dau. Eliza Maria JONES my tract of land called Ellersly w/o she now lives and also a Negro girl Lavinia now in her possession; to dau. Harriett PARKER £800 to be paid in Negroes and also one Negro girl of her choice; wife [unnamed]; all residue of property to son Henry PARKER; son Henry & John W. JONES exors; WIT: Jn. [S.] TAPSCOTT. (WC DW 24:224)
[General Alexander PARKER as a captain commanded the 3rd Company of the 2d Virginia Regiment in September 1775; he participated in fighting at Great Bridge, Brandywine, Germantown, Waxhaws, and Ogeechee Creek; Alexander's bro. Col. Richard PARKER was killed in South Carolina. (WCCP:40); Col. Alexander PARKER mar. Eliz. REDMAN, wid., WC, bond 18 Mar 1790 (MLBWC:52); Alex. PARKER d. in 1821; Eliz. PARKER, his wid., & Hen. PARKER, his son, were legatees; Hen. PARKER d. bef. 1838; the distributees of Hen. PARKER were Judith, his wid., who mar. (2) Charles B. TURNER in 1838 and his daus. Maria E. & Henrietta PARKER (WCCP:128); for more on this PARKER Family, see *Virginia Citizen* (Irvington, Va.) 25 Nov 1904, p. 1; Miller:175 locates Yeocomico Neck in WC between Bonum Creek and the Yeocomico River.]

PARKER, Alexander; 8 Sep 1821; 22 Apr 1822
WC; by a contract between PARKER & Richard T. BROWN dtd. 14 Apr 1821, PARKER agreed to relinquish all his right to the dower est. in both land & Negroes, which his wife had in her former husband's (Henry Sisson REDMAN) est. & by the sd. agreement did covenant with the sd. BROWN

that his wife should ratify & approve the sd. relinquishment, now Elizabeth PARKER releases all manner of right of dower unto the sd. Richard T. BROWN & his wife Lucy; WITS: Jn. MURPHY, Jn. CAMPBELL, J. W. JONES; MEMO: Henry PARKER states that he has received full satisfaction of the $1176, that being the amount of valuation of the Negroes legally the dower property of Elizabeth PARKER in the est. of her first husband Henry Sisson REDMAN & against any claim which from her the within deed was executed in a credit given to an execution which issued on 22 May 1821 on a decree pronounced in the City Court [of Fredericksburg] on 3 Apr 1821 wherein Richard T. BROWN & Lucy his wife were pltfs. & Alex. PARKER & Elizabeth his wife & others were defts. & Alex. PARKER & Elizabeth his wife were pltfs. & Richard T. BROWN & Lucy his wife were defts.; all of which complain in an indorsation made on the back of the sd. execution so issued as aforesd. (WC DW 24:283)

PARKER, John; 25 Jan 1819
WC; James JETT aptd. gdn. to Thomas & Elizabeth PARKER orphans of John PARKER; John A. PARKER one of the infant distributees of John PARKER has Thomas Y. STURMAN as his gdn. (WC OB 1819-23:7)
[The wid. of Jn. PARKER was Elizabeth, 22 Mar 1819 (WC OB 1819-23:19)]

PARKER, John; PO 23 Feb 1824; 28 Feb 1825
WC; DIV of est. among Richard B. PARKER (Mima, Maria), James M. PARKER (Nelson), John H. PEAKE (Turner, Janney), Thomas PARKER (Martha, Emily), John A. PARKER (Richard, Frankey). (WC RI 11:504)
[Wm. H. PARKER aptd. gdn. of Rich. B. PARKER orphan of Jn. PARKER, 22 Apr 1811 (WC Orders 1810-13:94); Jas. PARKER orphan of Jn. PARKER chose Col. Alex. PARKER as his gdn., 24 May 1813 (WC Orders 1810-13:304); Jn. H. PEAKE mar. Eliz PARKER, WC, bond 10 Jun 1823 (MLBWC:53; WC OB 1823-27:38); Thos. PARKER orphan of Jn. PARKER chose Jn. A. PARKER as his gdn., 28 Apr 1823 (WC OB 1819-23:551)]

PARKER, John (Capt.); T 9 Aug 1810; 22 Feb 1819. WC; INV, £479.2.9. (WC RI 10:345)

PARKER, Toulson; PO 8 Jun 1801, T 18 Aug 1802; 13 Sep 1802
NC; DIV of est. in the hands of John S. ELLISTON as admr. to Seth BLUNDEN an admr. to Toulson PARKER; each legal rep's part was £3.3.9 3/4; John CORBELL was possessed with his legal part of the same. (NC RB 16:440)
[In his will (NC 9 Feb 1795-14 Nov 1796) Toulson PARKER named his daus. Sally BLUNDON, Polly HARCUM, Betsy KENNER, Charlotte PARKER & Nancy PARKER, son Wm. PARKER, grdau. Jane P. PICKREN, Spencer M. PICKREN, Rich. KENNER, Seth BLUNDON, Wm. HARCUM and bro. Jn. DAUGHITY (NC RB 15:331); Seth BLUNDON mar. Sally PARKER, NC, bef. 9 Feb 1795; Wm. HARCUM mar. Polly PARKER, NC, bond 12 Apr 1790; Rich. KENNER mar. Eliz. PARKER, NC, bond 30 Nov 1790; Spencer Mottram PICKREN mar. Jean PARKER, dau. of Toulson PARKER, NC, bond 10 Jun 1788 (MWO:44, 164, 212, 280)]

PASQUETT, John; 17 Apr 1804
LC; Wm. HATHAWAY aptd. gdn. of Henry PASQUETT orphan of John PASQUETT. (LC OB 1804-05:72)
[Poss. the Jn. PASQUIT who mar. Eliz. NEWBY, LC, bond 2 Oct 1797 (MLBLC:57)]

PASQUITH, William; 10 Jan 1820

NC; Eliz. & William PASQUITH chose Holland SPRIGGS their gdn. and the sd. Holland SPRIGGS is aptd. gdn. of James, Austin & Noah PASQUITH orphans of William PASQUITH. (NC OB 1816-20:419)

PAYNE, George; 23 Aug 1824

WC; John PAYNE aptd. gdn. to John, James & Eliza PAYNE orphans of George PAYNE. (WC OB 1823-27:109)

[Thos. MASTIN aptd. gdn. to Jn., Jas., & Eliza children of Geo. PAYNE, 23 Aug 1825 (WC OB 1823-27:216); Dan. PAYNE aptd. gdn. to Jas. H. & Eliza Ann PAYNE orphans of Geo. PAYNE, 27 Mar 1826 (WC OB 1823-27:255)]

PAYNE, James; [m]; 27 Sep 1802

WC; INV, £489.1.6.; includes Negroes George, Bobb, Edey, Esther, Criss, Lucina, Mary. (WC RI 8:183)

PAYNE, James; T 25 Jan 1805; 24 Jun 1804

WC; DIV of slaves, to the wid. Ann PAYNE: Bet & Lucy; [Old Dorice &] George to Sally & Ursley PAYNE children by the last wife; Ester to Winney PAYNE the oldest child by the first wife; Edy & her 2 children Mary & William to Molly & Nancy PAYNE children by the first wife jointly between them. (WC RI 8:554)

[The wives of James PAYNE were: (1) Ann HUNTER, WC, bond 27 Dec 1786 and (2) Anne NEALE, WC, bond 18 Dec 1798 (MWO:275); chancery suit; Jn. B. JENKINS & Winifred his wife who was formerly Winifred PAYNE dau. & coheir of James PAYNE, who d. intestate in Feb. 1802, against Nancy PAYNE, Sally PAYNE, Ursula PAYNE and Molly PAYNE infants under 21 who are children and heirs of sd. James PAYNE by their gdns. Ann PAYNE, the wid. of James, and [Samuel] HUNTER to sell land of James and div. proceeds eq., 28 Oct 1806 (WC Orders 1804-07:427; WC CC 1806-004); Jn. B. JENKINS mar. Winifred L. PAYNE, WC bond 31 Dec 1804 (MLBWC:34); on the mot. of Rich. NEALE ord. that the Master Commissioner do settle the gdnship. acct. of Ann PAYNE on the est. of Sarah & Ursley PAYNE orphans of Jas. PAYNE, 22 Jul 1816 (MC OB 1814-18:249); Ursula PAYNE mar. Geo. LAMKIN, WC bond 10 Jan 1822 (MLBWC:38)]

PAYNE, James; T 3 Jan 1807, T 11 Aug 1807; 24 Aug 1807

WC; DIV; land sold at auction to Mrs. Ann PAYNE for £126 which was then div. among the children of James PAYNE: Samuel HUNTER gdn. of Nancy & Molly PAYNE, Mrs. Ann PAYNE gdn. of Sarah & U[r]sala PAYNE & John B. JENKINS who mar. Winney PAYNE. (WC RI 9:24)

[Jn. B. JENKINS mar. Winifred L. PAYNE, WC, bond 31 Dec 1804 (MLBWC:34)]

PAYNE, James; 23 Jan 1809

WC; Samuel HUNTER was gdn. of Molly PAYNE & [Nancy] PAYNE orphans of James PAYNE; est. of James PAYNE to be div. between them. (WC Orders 1807-10:255)

PAYNE, James; PO 23 Jan 1809; 28 Jan 1811

WC; DIV of Negroes between Molly PAYNE (girl Mary, boys Daniel & William) and Nancy PAYNE (Edy, boy William). (WC RI 9:227)

PAYNE, Jesse; 20 Nov 1822

LC; John PAYNE aptd. gdn. to Edward & Richard PAYNE orphans of Jesse PAYNE. (LC OB 25:344)

PAYNE, John; 20 Jun 1803

LC; Elizabeth PAYNE orphan of John PAYNE chose Thomas SHELTON her gdn. (LC Orders V 1802-03:365)

PAYNE, John Sr.; 21 Apr 1824; 23 Aug 1824

WC; WILL; sons John & Daniel & dau. Elizabeth to pay one third of any balance of debts; to son John all the lands in Irish Neck known by the name of Wroes which I purchased of WASHINGTON & also all the land I purchased of Thomas HILL, my interest in the bridge over Mattox Creek and my pocoson land near Leeds together with the land I purchased of Anthony PEYTON and the tobacco warehouse & the land on which it stands & the following Negroes Matilda, Charlotte, Charlot sis. of Matilda, Molly, Jury, Nancy, Dick, Phebe, Bet, Nanny & [Cull]; to son Daniel my tract of land called the Glebe, my tract of land purchased of my bro. William and the following Negroes: Winny, Judy & her children except for Solomon; to dau. Elizabeth MASTIN all my lands in RC & my forest lands in WC called The Cottage & the following Negroes: Charity, Anthony, Joe, Milly, Nelly, Mimy, [Buddy], Solomon, [Tally], William, Daniel, James, Jimmy, Rachael & Susan; to grson. James PAYNE all the land I purchased of Elliott MUNROE and the lands I bought of John WASHINGTON now in the occupation of his mother also to my grson. James & his sis. Eliza to be div. between them a Negro woman named Edy and a Negro man Emanuel and the money that I have from time to time advanced for their father's est; since grdau. received no land, grson. James is to pay her $1,000 within 3 years after she is mar. or becomes of age; sons John & Daniel & s-i-l Thomas MASTIN exors; WITS: Law. WASHINGTON, S. OLDHAM, Matthew DEATLEY, Robt. S. HIPKINS. (WC DW 25:80)

[Thos. MARTIN [prob. an error for MASTIN] mar. Eliz. C. PAYNE, WC, bond 27 Nov 1820 (MLBWC:44); a chancery suit filed in 1846, revealed that Eliz. MASTIN wid. of [Thos.] MASTIN mar. (2) John P. DAVIS, WC, bond 22 Aug 1836, and died in 1844 (WCCP:78); Miller:73 identifies Irish Neck as an earlier name for Colonial Beach]

PAYNE, Merryman; 9 Jun 1810; 20 Mar 1815

LC; WILL; use of my plant. w/o I now live to wife Nancy during her life; to son William PAYNE my plant. on the river and part of the neck beg. at the head of Overstreet's Cove by a straight line to the land of William GEORGE; after death of my wife the land w/o I now live to son William PAYNE; remainder of est. to wife and at her death to be eq. div. amongst my 4 daus: Kitty PAYNE, Betsy PAYNE, Lucy PAYNE & Nelly PAYNE; friends Joseph CARTER, John CHOWNING, & my son William PAYNE exors; WITS: J[ames] TOWLES, Geo. BROOKS. (LC WB 28:156)

[This is prob. Merryman PAYNE who mar. (1) Frances JOHNSON, Fauquier Co., 26 Feb 1786 and (2) Nancy OLDHAM, dau. of Thos DOBYNS and wid. of Wm. OLDHAM, NC, 23 Aug 1792 (MRC:155); Eliza J. PAYNE orphan of Merryman PAYNE chose Wm. OLDHAM as her gdn. and sd. OLDHAM is aptd. gdn. to Lucy Stephen PAYNE & Nelly PAYNE orphans of sd. dec'd, 20 Mar 1815 (LC Orders 24:218, OB 25:81, 108)]

PAYNE, Merryman; PO 20 Mar 1815; 19 Aug 1816

LC; INV; includes [Negroes]: James, Stephen, Emanuel, Joseph, Robin, Hannah, Betty & child Caroline, Letty & child George, Maria & child Fanny, Dolly, Dilcey, Jenny; DIV of Negroes between: Miss Lucy, Miss Nelly, Miss Betsey, Mrs. Kitty BISCOE. (LC EB 27:345, 347)

PAYNE, Sally; 21 Apr 1823

LC; admin. of the est. of Sally PAYNE granted to Edward PAYNE. (LC OB 25:364)

[This is Sally DAVENPORT who mar. Edw. PAYNE, LC, bond 12 Nov 1795 (MLBLC:57)]

PAYNE, William; PO 20 Jan 1817, T 21 Jan 1817; 17 Mar 1817. LC INV. (LC EB 27:362)
[Geo. H. PAYNE aptd. gdn. to Nancy, William, James & Sarah orphans of Wm. PAYNE, 20 Jan 1817 (LC Orders 24:345); Thos. TAYLOR aptd. gdn. to Sally B. PAYNE orphan of Wm. PAYNE, 15 Dec 1823 (LC OB 26:12); admin. of all & singular the goods and chattels, rights & credits of Wm. PAYNE (son of Wm. PAYNE dec'd, is granted to Rich. PAYNE; Rich. PAYNE aptd. gdn. to Jas. & Sally B. PAYNE, 17 Jan 1825 (LC OB 26:96)]

PEACHEY, William; 30 Jul 1798; 6 Sep 1802
RC; WILL; requests rector to preach a sermon on the Sunday following his death upon the words, "Not dead, but gone before;" dau. ARMISTEAD, dau. NICHOLSON; son William Travers; son's late bro. Samuel; dec'd bro. Thomas Griffin; eldest grchild. Elizabeth B. ARMISTEAD; daus. Winifred & Susannah; s-i-l John NICHOLSON; William EUSTACE of LC who has obtained a prohibiting decree against my sis. EUSTACE for the descendants of a slave woman; Samuel Peachey MENZIES; grson. John NICHOLSON Jr.; son William Travers & s-i-l John NICHOLSON & friend Rawleigh COLSTON exors; friend John MINOR to be ex. for the sole purpose of closing my executorship of the late Henry ARMISTEAD's est; notes that his dau. Winifred ARMISTEAD died on 18 Dec 1798; her est. to go to her daus.; [no wits named, but will was presented by Jn. CAMPBELL, Peter TEMPLE, & Bartholomew McCARTY]. (RC WB 9:182)
[Wm. PEACHEY was the son of Capt. Sam. & Winifred (GRIFFIN) PEACHEY; he mar. twice, (1) Million GLASCOCK, 1748 & (2) Elizabeth Griffin COLSTON, 1761 (NFPR:144, 145; MRC:155-156; MWO:277); Wm. PEACHEY's dau. Winifred mar. Hen. ARMISTEAD in RC, bond 14 Dec 1774; she was a widow by 1789 ((MLB RC1; MRC:4; MWO:17); his dau. Susanna mar. John NICHOLSON in RC 26 Apr 1789 (MLB RC; MRC:147; MWO:264); Wm. PEACHEY's sis. Alice Corbin mar. Jn. EUSTACE in RC 6 Oct 1743 (NC RB 4:244; NFPR:60, MRC:65-66; MWO:126); Samuel Peachey MENZIES was Wm. PEACHEY's nephew, the son of his sis. Phebe who mar. Adam MENZIES, 1752 (MWO:243)]

PEACHEY, William; PO 6 Sep 1802; 4 Oct 1802
RC INV; $5708.09 1/2; [inv contains a long list of books & maps & the following Negroes: Damon (very aged & infirm), Big Winney, Little Winney, Amay, Lucy, Fortune, Charles, Charlotte, Ben, Marcia & infant Bob, Alice, Robin, Cyrus, Patty, Manuel, Mansfield, [Mingo], Norah, Edmund, Atholinda, Criss, [Daved], Billy, Rawleigh, Marcus, Octavia, Solomon, Aggy, John, Nofelia, Tom, Sarah. (RC WB 9:191

PEACHEY, William T.; 1 Jun 1807. RC; INV, £178.6.0. (RC WB 9:310)

PEAKE, John (Dr.); PO 27 Dec 1813, T 2 Jan 1816; 25 Mar 1822
WC; INV, $5384.09; includes Negroes Tom, Belinda, Henna, Mima, Celia, Nicholas, William, Henry, Lucy, [Tasco], James, Esther, Cyrus, Austin, Sancho, Jack, Daniel, Ben; on 2 Jan 1816 the following slaves were valued & div: Thom, Sancho, Jack, Nicholas, William, Henry, Henney, Belinda, Celia, Jemima, Esther, Esther's children (Cyrus, Austin, Henry), Lucy, Celia's children (Harriott, Matilda, Tasker), Jemima's children (Jim, Sally, Marcia); slaves div. among wid., Robert B. MITCHELL in right of his wife, Emanuel PECK in right of his wife, Miss Sally PEAKE, John H. PEAKE, Miss Mary PEAKE. (WC RI 11:147, 153)
[Catherine PEAKE orphan of Jn. PEAKE chose Catherine PEAKE as her gdn. and sd. Catherine was aptd. gdn. of Sally R. and Mary Eliz. PEAKE, 28 Oct

1811 (WC Orders 1810-13:174); Humphry PEAKE aptd. gdn. of Jn. Hamden PEAKE, 28 Oct 1811 (WC Orders 1810-13:175); Emanuel PICK [sic] mar. Catherine PEAKE, WC, bond 22 May 1816 (MLBWC:53)]

PECK, John; PO 1 Jun 1795; 6 Jan 1800
RC; INV, £1051.8.1; includes the following slaves: Peter, Nanny, Billy, Sook, Charlotte, Nancy, Frank, Beck, Rose, Sam, Solomon, Milly, Jane, Alexander, Lucy, Letty, Abba, James, Rachel, Enouch, Moses, Betty, Criss, Frank, George, Mary, Caty, George, Patty, Tom; Sarah, Immanuel. (RC WB 9:128)

PECK, John; PO 28 Dec 1812, T 6 Jan 1813; 26 Apr 1813
WC; DIV of Negroes and other pers. est. at the Coles Point Plant; to John PECK (Frankey & her children, Sam, Solomon, Judy, [Dallas] & Tom, Moses, Kitty, Sam and Nelson, Criss & Maria-her child, Old Betty); to Emanuel PECK (Enoch, Moses, Letty, Suckey & her children, Charlott, Nancy, Eady, Edmond & Henry, Sally & her children Fanny, Jenny, Emanuel & Betsey; to Harriott PECK (Rachell & her children Lucy & Betsey, Frank, Beck & her child Solomon, Mary, James, Rose & her children Sam & Matilda, Milly & her children, Jery, Polly, Tom & Nancy. (WC RI 9:371)
[Jn. PECK, of New Jersey, mar. Ann Tasker CARTER, dau. of Robert and Frances (TASKER) CARTER, 6 Jan 1785 (MWO:277); Ann T. (CARTER) PECK mar. (2) Hugh QUINLAN, WC, bond 20 Apr 1796 (MLBWC:56); Wm. FORBES qualified as gdn. of Jn. C. PECK & Emanuel PECK orphans of Jn. PECK, 23 Jan 1809 (WC Orders 1807-10:255); Emanuel PECK orphan of Jn. PECK chose Jn. TURBERVILLE as his gdn., 23 Mar 1812 (WC Orders 1811-13:195); the real est. belonging to Ann PECK in NC was div. among her heirs: Harriet PECK, Jn. C. PECK, Emanuel PECK, and Tasker C. QUINLAN, NC, 11 Jan 1813 (NC OB 1811-15:142); see also WC CC 1811-004 and NC CC 1814-004; Miller:32 locates Coles Point Neck or Coles Neck in WC as a neck of land extending north from Gardner Creek between Lower Machodoc Creek and the Potomac River]

PECK, John C.; T 4 Feb 182[1]; 6 Jan 1823
RC; INV, $1087.01 1/2; INV of slaves in RC, $2276.00, RC; Betty, Mary Ann, Reuben, Moses, Daniel, Sophia, Sam, Wilson, Eliza, Glasgow, Frankey, Old Frankey, William; INV taken at Ragged Point, WC on 13 Feb 1823 & rec 5 May 1823, $129.19 1/2; Anna PECK, admx. (RC WB 10:18, 23, 24)
[Jn. C. PECK was a son of Jn. PECK, 23 Jan 1809 (WC Orders 1807-10:255); Ann C. PECK aptd. gdn. to her children: Lucy, Walter, Alice L. & Harriet E. PECK orphans of Jn. C. PECK, 6 Jan 1823 (RC OB 26:17); Harriet PECK was named gdn. to Lucy J., Alice [S.], Walter J., and Elizabeth H. children of Jn. C. PECK dec'd, 7 Oct 1833 (RC OB 28:186); Lucy Jones PECK mar. Francis JONES of Gloucester Co., Va., RC, bond 10 Aug 1832 (MRC:108)]

PECURE, William; 26 Jun 1820
WC; Youel DAVIS made oath that Susan PECURE is next of kin to William PECURE who died in the US service. (WC OB 1819-23:160)
[Susanna PECURE mar. Youell DAVIS, WC c. Aug 1821 (MLBWC:18)]

PEED, Philip; T 17 Sep 1806; 24 Nov 1806. WC; INV, [m]; includes Negro Bob. (WC RI 8:627)

PEOPLES, Harriet; 26 Apr 1812
WC; Mary PEOPLES orphan of Edmund and Harriet PEOPLES chose Lovell HARRISON as her gdn. (WC Orders 1810-13:229)
[Harriet PEOPLES was the dau. of Lovell & Hannah (FOOTMAN) HARRISON; in her will (WC 6 Nov 1791 - 26 Mar 1792), Hannah HARRISON named her dec'd husband Lovell HARRISON, her daus.

Hannah HARRISON, Harriet PEOPLES, Mary Lovell, and Ann Muse and her sons Alexander & Joseph (MWO:169; WC DW 18)]

PERCIFULL, Elijah; 1 Jan 1814; 18 Sep 1815
LC; WILL; to dau. Polly PERCIFULL Negro girl Judith on her paying her bros. Robert & Neddy PERCIFULL £4 each; land to be sold and proceeds eq. div. amongst my children John [Y.] PERCIFULL, Robert PERCIFULL, Neddy PERCIFULL, Thomas PERCIFULL, Judith who mar. Thomas POTTS, Betsy who mar. TAPSCOTT, Ruth who mar. William SIMS, Polly PERCIFULL, Sally PERCIFULL, Rebeckah PERCIFULL, [&] Caty PERCIFULL; following Negroes given to children: Daniel to dau. Judith, Nancy to son Robert, boy Leroy to son John; heirs of dau. Nancy who mar. Gideon MARSH to have 20 shillings and no more; Thomas POTTS & John Y. PERCIFULL exors; WITS: Cornelius SULLIVAN, Robt. D. PALMER, Benj. PALMER. (LC WB 28:169)
[Judah Tayloe PERCIFULL mar. Thos. POTTS, both residents of NC at the time, LC, bef. 17 Oct 1797 (MWO:287); Ruthie PERCIFULL mar. Wm. SIMS, LC, bond 25 Jun 1804; Nancy PERCIFULL mar. Gideon MARSH, LC, bond 12 Sep 1785 (MLBLC:50, 68); Rebeckah PERCIFULL orphan of Elijah PERCIFULL chose Jn. SAMPSON as her gdn. and Sally PERCIFULL orphan of same chose Robt. D. PALMER as her gdn., 20 Nov 1815 (LC Orders 24:267-268, LC OB 25:13); Jn. Y. PERCIFULL aptd. gdn. to Thos. PERCIFULL and Robt. PERCIFULL aptd. gdn. to Caty PERCIFULL orphans of Elijah PERCIFULL, 18 Dec 1815 (LC Orders 24:274); Caty PERCIFULL orphan of Elijah PERCIFULL chose Ben. WADDEY for her gdn., 18 Dec 1820 (LC OB 25:181)]

PERCIFULL, Elijah; T 24 Nov 1815; 19 Mar 1816
LC; INV; inludes Negroes: James, Emanuel, Easter, Ciller, Edey, Judith, Violett, Fanny, Hannah, Jerry, Mary; DIV of est, PO 18 Dec [1815], among: Rebecca PERCIFULL, Edward PERCIFULL, Caty PERCIFULL, Robert PERCIFULL, Polly PERCIFULL, William SIMS heirs, John Y. PERCIFULL, Thomas PERCIFULL, Sarah PERCIFULL, Thomas POTTS, Elizabeth TAPSCOTT; Thomas POTTS & John Y. PERCIFULL exors. (LC EB 27:292, 296)

PERCIFULL, Elijah; PO 21 Jun 1819; 16 Aug 1819
LC; possessed Edward PERCIFULL gdn. to William SIM's orphans with their portion of Elijah PERCIFULL's (dec'd) est. (LC EB 27:489)

PERCIFULL, Eppa A.; 19 Apr 1802
LC; Jenny PERCIFUL orphan of Eppa A. PERCIFUL chose Rich. SELDEN as her gdn. replacing Mary JOPES. (LC Orders V 1802-03:58)
[The est. of Eppa A. PERCIFUL was appraised in 1789 (LC WB 22:207)]

PERCIFULL, John; T 15 Sep 1820; 17 Dec 1821. LC; INV, [m]. (LC EB 29:145)

PERCIFULL, John Y.; 9 Apr 1820; 19 Jun 1820
LC; WILL; son Elijah [sic] John Y. PERCIFULL to have all my land; dau. Catharine Margaret K. PERCIFULL to have liberty to live in my house undisturbed until she may think proper to marry; remainder of est. to dau; bro. Edward PERCIFULL ex; WITS: Wm. HARDING, Benj. PALMER, Thos. M. OWENS. (LC WB 28:206)

PERKINS, Elizabeth; 15 Feb 1819
LC; George PERKINS granted admin. on the est. of his late wife Elizabeth PERKINS. (LC OB 25:39)
[This is presumably Elizabeth CRAINE who mar. Geo. PERKINS, NC, bond 28 Feb 1790 (MLBNC:81)]

PEYTON (PAYTON), Anne; 8 Apr 1801; 22 Mar 1802
WC; WILL; granddau. Betsy PAYTON all lands in WC bought of grson. Anthony PAYTON also land she holds in her own right w/o she now lives; William Starke JETT & grson. Anthony PAYTON exors; WITS: Vincent BARRACK, Reubin GREEN, Mary E. PAYTON, John PAYNE. (WC DW 20:326)

PEYTON (PAYTON), Anthony; 26 Feb 1788; [m]
WC; WILL; wife Ann PAYTON use of the plant. w/o I now live; after her death use of plant. to grdau. Anne STONE and after her death to grson. Beckwith JETT; slaves Moses, his wife Jeane & Will to grdau. Ann BERKLEY; old plant. as far as the Mill Run and Negroes Dick, Lucy & Fanny to grson. Anthony PAYTON; Negroes Tom, Peter, Winny & Lott to grdau. Anne STONE; Negroes Jeane, Davey & Aron to grdau. Ann PAYTON; Negroes Old Harry & Old Judah to grson. Wm. JETT; Negroes Rose & Paul now in her possession with two fellows Ben & Jim to grdau. Elizabeth HUDNALL; land on the east side of my mill with my mill which land I purchased of Robt. VAULX & Rich. STEELE with Negroes Kitt & Milly to grson. George PAYTON; Negroes Jack, George & Judah to grson. Burkett JETT; James MUSE, William PAYNE & John BERKLEY exors; WITS: Jesse [JETT], Wm. JETT, Walter JAMES, Wm. PAYTON. (WC Unrec Wills 1755-1800 #36)

PEYTON, Anthony; 25 Sep 1815; 23 May 1825
WC; WILL; of the Town of Leeds, $100 to my nephew George DRAKE; my house & lots in Leeds which were sold by commissioners to George FITZHUGH & purchased of him by me to my wife Elizabeth; William S. JETT Sr. ex; WITS: Robt. R. HODGE, Jn. P. HUNGERFORD, Alex. HODGE. (WC DW 25:184)
[Anthony PEYTON mar. Betsy HUDNALL, WC, bond 26 Jan 1790 (MLBWC:52)]

PEYTON, Betsy; 2 May 1825; 23 May 1825
WC; WILL; lot & houses thereon now in the occupancy of Henry D. STARK to my nephew William J. STONE; residue of my prop. to be sold and proceeds used for the benefit of my nephew William J. STONE's children; Dr. George R. PITTS ex; WITS: Wm. ANDERSON, Wm. DEATLEY, Jn. M. MARMADUKE; in a COD gifts are made to John M. MARMADUKE & Mrs. Susan DEATLEY; WITS: Wm. ANDERSON, Eliza H. STONE. (WC DW 25:183)
[This is prob. Betsy the wid. of Anthony PEYTON (*see above*)]

PEYTON, John; 19 May 1806; 23 Jun 1806
WC; WILL; nephew John PEYTON Jr. use of 1/2 of all my land during his life and after his death to his son William Henry PEYTON; other half of land to nephew James PEYTON; rest of property to be eq. div. among nieces Lucy PEYTON, Emily PEYTON, Alice PEYTON & nephew John PEYTON's two sons William Henry PEYTON & Charles; my Chicksaw filly to nephew John Peyton CLAXTON; nephews John PEYTON & James PEYTON exors; WITS: Thos. N. BERRYMAN, Lucy GREEN, Peggy NEWMAN, Sam. HUNTER. (WC DW 21:257)
[Jn. PEYTON Jr. d. intest leaving only 4 slaves -- Davy (about 45 or 50), Dan. (about 45 or 50), Milly (about 25) and an infant -- and 4 children -- Wm. H. PEYTON (now of age), Chas. W. PEYTON, Mary E. PEYTON and Jn. A. PEYTON infants under 21 -- he also left 300 ac. of very poor land in WC; equal div. could not be made so land and slaves to be sold, 27 Oct 1823 (WC

1823-27:9; WC CC 1823-004); Dan. CARMICHAEL aptd. gdn. to Chas. W. and Jn. A. PEYTON orphans of Jn. PEYTON, 28 Mar 1825 (WC OB 1823-27:152)]

PEYTON, John; PO 23 Jun 1806; 27 Oct 1806. WC; INV, £197.1.6. (WC RI 8:626)

PEYTON, John; T 15 Apr 1812; 27 May 1816
WC; INV, [m]; includes Negroes Davey, Jacob, Daniel, Milly (girl about 14), Peggy (an old woman 70). (WC RI 10:61)

PHILLIP, John; PO 13 Nov 1815; 8 May 1822
NC; INV included only 1 silver watch worth $20. (NC RB 23:128)
[The est. of Jn. PHILLIPS [sic] was ord. to be admin. by Randall R. KIRK, NC, 13 Nov 1815 (NC OB 1811-1816:389)]

PHILLIPS, Bryant; [m]; 6 Oct 1806
RC; WILL; wife Ann land I now live on & part of land I bought of John BRYANT beg. at the Horse Pond & Negro man Daniel; at wife's death or remarriage above land to go to youngest son Bryant PHILLIPS; rest to be eq. div. bet Nancy, Jane, & Milly PHILLIPS; all other lands & tracts called Wilson's & Alderson's to be eq. div. bet my children James, Betsy, Sally & John PHILLIPS; Peter NORTHEN, Richard BENNEHAN, Eppa NORRIS, & Raw DUNAWAY exors; WITS: Rawleigh HAZARD, Jane LAMPKIN, Jane PULLEN. (RC WB 9:298)
[This is prob. Bryant PHILLIPS who mar. Nancy STONUM, RC, bond 22 Dec 1794 (MRC:158); Jn. PHILLIPS orphan of Bryant chose Jn. B. STRAUGHN as his gdn., RC, [7 Aug 1808] (RC Orders 1809-10:13)]

PHILLIPS, Bryant; T. 26 Jan 1808; 4 Apr 1808
RC; INV; £373.9.7 1/2, includes Negroes Judith & Daniel. (RC WB 9:320)

PHILLIPS, Bryant; PO Apr 1808, T 2 Jan 1809; 4 Dec 1809
RC; DIV of acct. balances among the 4 children of Mrs Ann PHILLIPS and the four eldest children of Bryant PHILLIPS; the following people were named to receive proportions: James PHILLIPS, John C. STRAUGHAN, George N. STONUM and Joseph REDMAN gdn. to John PHILLIPS; Sally PHILLIPS was named as now Sally STRAUGHAN. (RC AB 3:229)
[Geo. N. STONUM mar. Eliz. PHILLIPS, RC, bond 23 Dec 1807; Sally PHILLIPS mar. John C. STRAUGHAN, of NC, RC, bond 19 Nov 1806 (MRC:196, 197)]

PHILLIPS, George; T 18 Aug 1795; 11 Oct 1802
NC; INV, £65.14.3; includes Negro girl Suky. (NC RB 16:472)

PICKERING, William; 11 Aug 1823
NC; William HUGHLETT aptd. gdn. of Noah & Joseph PICKERING orphans of William PICKERING. (NC OB 1820-25:313)
[Wm. HUGHLETT, wid., mar. Judith PICKERING, NC bond 26 May 1823 (MLBNC:57); Wm. HUGHLETT & Judith his wife and sd. HUGHLETT as gdn. of Noah & Jos. PICKERING and Spencer PICKERING are heirs and distributees of Wm. PICKERING, NC 11 Aug 1823 (NC OB 1820-25:315)]

PICKREN, Presley; 12 Aug 1816
NC; Thomas JAQUES aptd. gdn. of Orange PICKREN orphan of Presley PICKREN; Shapleigh P. GILL aptd. gdn. of George & Samuel PICKREN orphans of Presley PICKREN and Thomas PICKREN aptd. gdn. of Presley PICKREN orphan of Presley PICKREN; on the motion of Joseph MORRISON gdn. of Nancy PICKREN, Thomas PICKREN & Sally his wife late Sally PICKREN & dau. of Presley PICKREN, Thomas JAQUES gdn. of Orange PICKREN, Shapleigh P. GILL gdn. of George and Samuel PICKREN and the sd. Thomas PICKREN gdn. of Presley PICKREN which sd. Nancy,

Sally, Orange, George, Samuel, and Presley are children & heirs of Presley PICKREN dec'd to show cause why lands of Presley PICKREN should not be sold etc. (NC OB 1816-20:74, 75)

[Presley PICKREN was the son of Geo. PICKREN Sr. (d. NC 1800) (NC RB 16:186); he had 3 wives: (1) Sally CHILTON, NC bond 17 Feb 1790; (2) Eliz. HAYNIE, wid., NC, bond 27 Feb 1798; (3) Hannah HUMPHRIES, NC, bond 11 Mar 1808 (MLBNC:81); his est. was admin. by Benedict BURGESS, 13 Nov 1815 (NC OB 1811-16:154); Overseers of the Poor of Upper SSP bound Orange PICKREN to Thos. JAQUES to learn the trade of a blacksmith, NC 13 Nov 1820 (NC OB 1820-25:67)]

PICKREN, Spencer M.; PO 9 Sep 1816; 14 Oct 1816. NC; INV, $[96,67]. (NC RB 21:93)

[Spencer Mottram PICKREN mar. Jean PARKER dau. of Toulson PARKER, NC, bond 10 Jun 1788 (MLBNC, NC RB 15:331)]

PICKREN, William; PO 18 May 1810, T 25 May 1810; 9 Jul 1810

NC; allottment to the wid. Lucy PICKREN of her thirds of the land of William PICKREN; included 28 ac, houses and about 1/3 of the orchard. (NC RB 18:425)

[This is prob Wm. PICKREN Jr. who mar. Lucey HAYNIE, NC, bond 12 Dec 1794 (MLBNC:82); in a chancery suit in Jun 1810, Lucy PICKREN was named next friend of [Lucy,] Wm., Spencer, Judith, Noah, and Joseph PICKREN (NC CC 1820-006)]

PICKREN, William; PO 12 Mar 1810; 10 Sep 1810. NC; INV, $51.09. (NC RB 18:459)

[The est. of Wm. PICKREN was ord. to be admin. by Sam. DAVIS, NC, 12 Mar 1810 (NC OB 1807-1811:157)]

PIERCE, John; 26 May 1817

WC; John PIERCE aptd. gdn. to Lovel & Nancy PIERCE orphans of John PIERCE. (WC OB 1814-18:302)

PIERCE, Joseph; PO 27 Aug 1798; 24 [m]

WC; DIV, £619.0.0; includes the following [Negroes]: Cupit (to serve 5 yrs from 5 Jun 1798 to 5 Jun 1803), Jeremiah (to serve 5 yrs from 5 Jun 1798 to 5 Jun 1803), Cate (to serve 5 yrs from 5 Jun 1798 to 5 Jun 1803), George (to serve 5 yrs from 5 Jun 1798 to 5 Jun 1803), Moor (to serve 8 yrs from 5 Jun 1798 to 5 Jun 1806), Lucy (to serve 9 yrs from 5 Jun 1798 to 5 Jun 1807), Jenny (to serve 9 yrs from 5 Jun 1798 to 5 Jun 1807), Jack (to serve 12 yrs from 5 Jun 1798 to 5 Jun 1810), Suckey (to serve 15 yrs from 5 Jun 1798 to 5 Jun 1813), Solomon (to serve 15 yrs from 5 Jun 1798 to 5 Jun 1813), Phillis (to serve 18 yrs from 5 Jun 1798 to 5 Jun 1816), [Mozina] (to serve 19 yrs from 5 Jun 1798 to 5 Jun 1817), Nelly (to serve 19 yrs from 5 Jun 1798 to 5 Jun 1817), Nancy (to serve 20 yrs from 5 Jun 1798 to 5 Jun 1818), Winney (to serve 24 yrs from 5 Jun 1798 to 5 Jun 1822), Silas (to serve 26 yrs from 5 Jun 1798 to 5 Jun 1824), Elisha (to serve 29 yrs from 5 Jun 1798 to 5 Jun 1827), Hannah (to serve 28 yrs from 5 Jun 1798 to 5 Jun 1826), Lucy dau. of Jenny (to serve 30 yrs from 5 Jun 1798 to 5 Jun 1828), Daniel son of Lucy (to serve 30 yrs from 5 Jun 1798 to 5 Jun 1828), Peggy dau. of Jenny (to serve 30 yrs from 5 Jun 1798 to 5 Jun 1828); Negroes to be div. between 5 children: Ransdell PIERCE, Thomas HILL, William GREENLAW, Peggy PIERCE, Fanny PIERCE. (WC RI 8:79)

[Thos. HILL mar. Martha PIERCE, dau. of Jos. PIERCE, WC, bond 7 Jun 1787; Wm. GREENLAW mar. Sally Randall PIERCE, WC, bond 13 Apr 1796 (MWO:155, 180)]

PIERCE, Richard; 25 Mar 1816

WC; it appears to the court that John PIERCE is father and heir at law of Richard PIERCE. (WC OB 1814-18:209)

PILSBURY, John; Mar 1803; 23 May 1803

WC; INV, £436.4.0; incudes Negroes Daniel, Cate & 3 children, Billy, Frank, Jane & 2 children. (WC RI 8:227)

[This is prob. Jn. PILSBURY who mar. Sally SCOTT, dau. of Thos. SCOTT, WC, bond 26 Oct 1786 (MWO:282); Sam. HARRISON aptd. gdn. of Eliz., Nancy, Jn. & Thos. PILLSBURY orphans of Jn. PILLSBURY, 22 Jun 1807 (WC Orders 1807-10:30); on the mot. of Wm. GILBERT ord. that Sam. HARRISON gdn. of Mary [McGUIN] formerly Mary PILLSBURY, Nancy PILLSBURY, Thos. PILLSBURY, and Jn. PILLSBURY orphans of Jn. PILLSBURY be summoned to court in a case of debt, 26 Jun 1809 (WC Orders 1807-10:357)]

PINCKARD, Ann; 18 Sep 1815

LC; Overseers of the Poor to bind out Griffin PINCKARD orphan of Ann PINCKARD to Charles BAILEY. (LC Orders 24:259)

PINCKARD, Cyrus; 10 Sep 1827

NC; Eliz. & Thomas PINCKARD orphans of Cyrus PINCKARD chose Jane PINCKARD as their gdn. (NC OB 1825-30:202)

[Cyrus PINCKARD mar. twice, (1) to Alice BALL, dau. of David BALL, NC, bond 14 Nov 1796 and (2) to Jane HURST, NC, bond 12 Feb 1810 (MLBNC:82); Cyrus was the father of at least one child, a dau. Hannah who was named as a neice by Betsy (BALL) LATTIMORE in her will (NC 1 Nov 1814 - 9 Jan 1815) (NC RB 19:586)]

PINCKARD, Elizabeth; PO 12 Oct 1812; 10 May 1813

NC; INV, £58.13.8 1/4. (NC RB 19:383)

[The est. of Eliz. PINCKARD was ord. to be admin. by Cyrus PINCKARD, NC, 12 Oct 1812 (NC OB 1811-1816:114)]

PINCKARD, John; 20 Oct 1806

LC; Overseers of the Poor to bind out John, George and Cyrus orphans of John PINCKARD. (LC Orders D22 1805-08:237)

PINCKARD, Robert; PO 11 Jan 1813, T 14 Jan 1813; 8 Feb 1813

NC; DIV of dower slaves of the late Eliza PINCKARD among the heirs of Robert PINCKARD as follows: Lot 1, Lott & Nanny, to John WADDY, Lot 2, Absolom, to George W. YERBY, Lot 3, Sam, to the children of John [sic] UPSHUR by Charlotte PINCKARD dau. of sd. Robert PINCKARD, Lot 4, boy Joe, to Cyrus PINCKARD. (NC RB 19:330)

[This is prob. the Robt. PINCKARD who mar. Eliz. DAMERON, wid., NC, 13 Mar 1765 (MWO:282); the est. of Robt. PINCKARD was ord. to be admin. by Eliz. PINCKARD, NC, 10 Oct 1785 (NC OB 1783-1785:394); Jn. WADDY mar. Molly PINCKARD, NC, bond 14 Dec 1801; Geo. W. YERBY mar. Eliz. PINCKARD, dau. of Eliz. PINCKARD, NC, bond 5 Apr 1789; Jas. [sic] UPSHUR mar. Charlotte PINCKARD, NC, bond 20 May 1796 (MLBNC:103, 104, 113)]

PINCKARD, Thomas; 16 Mar 1794; 21 Dec 1795

LC; should Mrs. PINCKARD still refuse relinquishing her dower in the land lately sold Capt. B. C. SPILLER sufficient allowance be made him for such refusal out of the bonds that may be unpaid and due for the payment of the same; rest of est. to be div. between my son Thomas PINCKARD and dau. Alice Griffin PINCKARD so that Alice Griffin PINCKARD have just half as much as her bro. Thomas; friends Col. Thomas GASKINS, William EUSTACE, Charles LELAND & Henry Lee GASKINS exors. & gdns. of my son Thomas PINCKARD and give him a good education even to the last penny he may be worth; dau. Alice to live with her mother; sis. Ann LEE; [no wits listed, but will proved by oaths of Gilbert CURRELL & Wm. GIBSON]. (LC WB 28:23)

[Ann LEE is poss. Ann GASKINS, who was identified in MWO as the dau. of Thos. GASKINS of WP, NC, who mar. (1) Thos. PINCKARD, 1761, NC and (2) Rich. Hen LEE, NC, bef. 8 Dec 1783; however her mention in this record as "sister" raises some doubts about this identification (MWO:224, 282)]

PINCKARD, Thomas; 14 Jul 1813; 23 May 1814.

CP, WC; WILL; being in good health and sound mind and memory, not knowing how soon I may be called off in defense of my country and fall in so doing; my watch to John Leroy CHINN the oldest son of my aunt Eliza SEWARD; all wearing apparel to Mr. William CHOWNING, Jr; remaining property to Thomas Griffin SEWARD; asks that Thomas SEWARD (with the consent of his father) change his name to PINCKARD when he is 21; John SEWARD of LC ex; [no wits named]; [will brought to court by the Rev. John SEWARD and proved by Wm. Young STURMAN and two of the court]. (WC DW 23:27)

[Thos. PINCKARD is prob. the son of Thos. PINCKARD who mar. Ann Corbin GRIFFIN, dau. of Maj. Leroy & Alice (CURRIE) GRIFFIN, LC, 19 Jun 1784 MRC:159, MWO:282); Eliz. SEWARD is Eliz. GRIFFIN, dau. of Maj. Leroy & Judith (BALL) GRIFFIN and wid. of Jos. CHINN, who mar. (2) Jn. SEWARD, LC, bond 3 Sep 1806 (MWO:75, MLBLC:66)]

PINCKARD, Thomas; T 14 Mar 1815; 28 Jun 1819. WC; INV, [m]. (WC RI 10:388)

PINN, Aaron; 16 Mar 1819

LC; Betsy PINN orphan of Aaron PINN chose John LEWIN as her gdn., 16 Mar 1819. (LC OB 25:44)

[This is prob. Aaron PINN who mar. Mary Kelly WEAVER, LC, bond 3 Mar 1794 (MLBLC:59)]

PITMAN, Jessey; 26 Oct 1822; 11 Nov 1822

NC; all est. to wife Lucy PITMAN; [no ex]; WITS: Robt. FORESTER, Jas. ANDERSON, Deller PITMAN. (NC RB 23:247

PITMAN, Lee; 8 Jun 1802; 22 Nov 1802.

CP, WC; WILL; wife Charlotty all land including tract purchased of Maj. Geo. GARNER in Ragged Point Neck and adj. tract bought of Willis GARNER also tract bought of the est. of Daniel CRABB; if wife dies lands to go to nephew William PITTMAN son of Mitchel PITMAN dec'd; after William's death, lands to go to William GARNER orphan of Vincent GARNER; dower slaves in the est. of Vincent GARNER dec'd to wife during her life; wife & Reston B. [COVINTON] exors; WITS: Sidney SETTLE, Sam. BEALE Jr., Thos. BEALE. (WC DW 20:401)

[Lee PITMAN mar. Lottey GARNER, WC, bond 7 Dec 1795 (MLBWC:54); Charlotte PITMAN had mar. (2)Thos. STOWERS, by 28 May 1804 (WC Orders 1804-07:9); Ragged Point is located in WC; it is the northeasternmost point of Coles Neck (Miller:131)]

PITMAN, Lee; T 7 May 1803; May 1803. WC; INV, £78.6.0. (WC RI 8:228)

PITMAN, Michael; 19 Dec 1808

LC; Overseers of the Poor to bind out Robert PITMAN orphan of Michael PITMAN. (LC Orders B23 1808-11:8)

PITMAN, Susanna; T 20 Jun 1809; 12 Feb 1810

NC; INV, $273.32; includes old woman Molley. (NC RB 18:331)

[Susanna PITMAN was prob. the wid. of Wm. PITMAN (*see below*); the est. of Susanna PITMAN was ord. to be admin. by Aug[ustine] PITMAN, NC, 12 Jun 1809 (NC OB 1807-1811:109)]

PITMAN, Thomas; PO Jun 1815; 17 May 1824
LC; INV, [m]; includes Negroes George, Winney, Jenny, Sarah, Manuel, Young George, David, Betsy, Mary. (LC EB 29:336)
[Ord. that Isaac, Nancy, Thos., Judith & Caty PITMAN be summoned to show cause why the lands of which Thos. PITMAN died seized should not be sold and the proceeds div. among his legal heirs, 21 Feb 1825 (LC OB 26:103)]

PITMAN, William; PO 8 Jun 1801, T 22 Oct 1801; 14 Jun 1802
NC; INV, £415.1.11; includes Negroes Daniel, Fanny, Mary; DIV of est. among Sukey PITMAN (rec'd Daniel), William PITMAN (possessed Sukey PITMAN his gdn. with Negro woman Fanny bequeathed to William in the will of the deceased), Ewell WEBB & Caty his wife, Augustine PITMAN, Thomas PITMAN, Robert FORRESTER & Sally his wife. (NC RB 16:397)
[In his will (NC 20 Jul 1799-13 Apr 1801), Wm. PITMAN named his youngest son Wm. PITMAN, his father Thos. PITMAN, and his other children Salley PITMAN, Augustine PITMAN, Caty WEBB, and Thos. PITMAN (NC RB 16:264); Ewell WEBB mar. Caty PITMAN, dau. of Wm. PITMAN, NC, bond 10 Feb 1795 (MWO:368); Robt. FORRESTER mar. Sally PITMAN, NC, bond 20 Jan 1802 (MLBNC:38)]

PITMAN, William; PO 18 Nov 1816; 17 Mar 1817. LC INV. (LC EB 27:361)

PITMAN, William; 21 Sep 1818
LC; sale of the lands of Lee Monroe & Sally PITMAN orphans of William PITMAN to deliver proceeds to their gdn. Eppa HILL. (LC OB 25:18)
[Lee Monroe PITMAN is prob. Leroy M. PITMAN who mar. Roxy KEMM, LC, bond 29 Dec 1825 and Margaret EATON, LC, bond 20 Aug 1828 (MLBLC:60); on the mot. of Warren, Eliz. & Wm. PITMAN by their next friend Jas. BRENT ord. that Monroe & Sally PITMAN be summoned to show cause why lands of Wm. PITMAN dec'd should not be sold; Eppa HILL is aptd. gdn. of Monroe & Sally to defend them in ths motion, 16 Nov 1818 (LC OB 25:25); ord. that Jas. BRENT Jr. gdn. of Warren & Eliz. PITMAN orphans of Wm. PITMAN pay to Judith ASHBURN $8 for Warren and $12 for Eliz. for their support the present year, 19 Jun 1820 (LC OB 25:139, 210)]

PITT, Marcellus; PO 12 Jan 1824; 10 May 1824. NC INV. (NC RB 23:462)
[Marcellus PITTS [sic], wid., mar. Margaret GILL, NC, bond 9 Dec 1820 (MLBNC:82)]

PITTS, David H.; T 18 Mar 1815; 1 May 1815. RC; INV, $62.60. (RC WB 9:472)

PLUMMER, Fleet B.; 19 Feb 1825; 7 Mar 1825
RC; to niece Mary PLUMMER, dau. of John PLUMMER, my Negro girl Judy; to William DUDLEY orphan of John DUDLEY, my Negro boy Nelson; to my bro. Albert Gallatin PLUMMER all the rest of my est; my bros. Col. William Middleton & Albert G. PLUMMER exors; WITS: Rob. P. HEADLEY, Thos. H. HEADLEY. (RC WB 10:67)
[This is prob. Fleet B. PLUMMER, son of Thos. PLUMMER, who mar. Eliza B. BALL, wid., RC, bond 6 Sep 1816 (MRC:159)]

PLUMMER, Richard; 7 Sep 1818
RC; Mary the wid. of Richard PLUMMER, John PLUMMER, Benjamin C. PLUMMER, & Fleet B. PLUMMER were next of kin to Robert MITCHELL dec'd. (RC OB 24:263)

PLUMMER, Thomas; 1 Apr 1822

RC; Sarah Ann J. PLUMMER orphan of Thomas PLUMMER chose William MIDDLETON as her gdn. (RC OB 25:273)

POLK, Charles Peale; 14 Feb 1822; 9 May 1822
RC; WILL; tract of land called Mount Pleasant to wife Ellen Ball POLK; dau. Ellen POLK (under 21); daus. Elizabeth E, POLK, Anne M. POLK, & Caroline POLK; sons Daniel P. POLK, Edward POLK, Franklin POLK & Columbus POLK; friends John Y. CHINN, Samuel WILLIAMS, & John SEWARD exors; WITS: Wm. Lee BALL, Underhill [DORMAN], Alph HYATT, Noble MONTAGUE. (RC WB 9:724)
[Chas. Peale POLK, of the city of Washington, mar. Ellen B. DOWNMAN, RC, bond 23 Dec 1816 (MRC:160)]

POLK, Charles Peale; PO Aug 1822; 7 Feb 1825. RC; INV, [m]. (RC WB 10:62)

POLLARD, James; 12 Feb 1803; 18 Apr 1803
LC; WILL; est. to remain together for benefit of wife Lucy POLLARD and all unmarried children until wife's death or marriage; my plant. w/o I now live to son William POLLARD; son Thomas POLLARD all the land I bought of George BRENT, John STEPTOE, & [Nathaniel] GORDON and also my Negro boy Jacob; son James POLLARD my land at the place called The Cross Roads & my Negro boy [Dick]; to dau. Ann POLLARD my two Negro girls Hagar & Rachall; to dau. Lucy POLLARD my two Negro girls Winny [GRANT] & Mary; after death or marriage of wife balance of est. to be eq. div. among children William POLLARD, Thomas POLLARD, Ann POLLARD, James POLLARD, & Lucy POLLARD; dau. Mary HUNTON has already received her proportion of est; mortgage that James [HARVEY] Esq. holds on the land given to my son Thomas to be paid; two sons William & Thomas exors; WITS: Martin SHEARMAN, Robt. C. [?], Rebecca M. GEORGE. (LC WB 28:67)
[Mary POLLARD, dau. of James, mar. Jn. W. HUNTON, LC, bond 15 May 1794 (MWO:193)]

POLLARD, James; PO 18 Apr 1803, T 17 Nov 1803; 19 Dec 1803
LC; INV, [m]; includes Negroes: Nat, Anthony, Miles, Nelson, Jacob, Judy, Winny, Sillar, Winny GRANT, Hagar, Mary, Rachel. (LC EB 24:255)

POLLARD, James; 20 Jan 1813; 16 Feb 1813
LC; WILL; tract of land called Cross Roads in LC left to me by my father James POLLARD dec'd to sis. Lucy POLLARD; Negro man Nelson to nephew John W. [HUNTON] son of my sis. Mary; Negro man Natt & Negro woman Judy with balance of est. to nephew James POLLARD son of my bro. William POLLARD; bro. William POLLARD & friend Samuel M. SHEARMAN exors; WITS: Sam. M. SHEARMAN, Rich. BERRYMAN, Rich. T. HINTON. (LC WB 28:140)

POLLARD, Mary; 3 Feb 1819; 18 Mar 1822
LC; WILL; to grson. Thornley B. TANKERSLEY all the est. prop. & possessions which I have in my possession & he is to be ex; WITS: Wm. KELLEY, Chas. KELLEY, Addison HALL. (LC WB 28:225)

POLLARD, William; 30 Jun 1816; 20 Oct 1817
LC; WILL; wife Nancy Hall POLLARD and son James POLLARD to be supported by the profits of my est.; after wife's death or marriage est. to son James; friends Capt. Henry C. LAWSON and Peter BEANE, Sr., to be gdns. to son James; my only motive for appointing my son gdns. is that he has arrived to that period of life which will and does require some other person to govern and manage him more than a loving and tender mother he being the only child; wife to be extx; [no wits listed, but will proved by oaths of

Ralph EDMONDS & Wm. T. YERBY]; COD, 30 Jun 1816: If son James POLLARD claims any thing of my est. on account of the little est. given him by his uncle James POLLARD dec'd he shall forfeit what I have given him. (LC WB 28:185)
[Wm. POLLARD mar. Nancy A. [sic] GEORGE, LC, bond 21 Aug 1797, (MLBLC:60)]

POLLARD, William; PO 16 Nov 1818; 19 Apr 1819. LC ; INV, [m]. (LC EB 27:468)

POMROY, John; 24 Jun 1805
WC; Elizabeth PUMROY orphan of John PUMROY chose Vincent EDMONDS her gdn. (WC Orders 1804-07:274)

POOLEY, William; [T 30 Oct 1800]; 8 Apr 1805. NC; INV, £117.1.1 ½. (NC RB 17:268)
[The est. of Wm. POOLEY was ord. to be admin. by Peter WILKINS, NC, 14 Oct 1800 (NC Fiduciary Bonds 1797-1801)]

POOLEY, William; [m]; 8 Jul 1816. NC; INV, $22.69. (NC RB 21:22)
[This may be the Wm. POOLEY who mar. Emsey WHEELER, dau. of Moses WHEELER (d. NC 1795), NC, bond 20 Nov 1811 (MLBNC:83, NC RB 15:138); Emsey and Wm. POOLEY apparently had no children as none are mentioned in the will of Emsey POOLEY (NC 29 Sep 1813 - 13 Mar 1815) (NC RB 20:14)]

POOR, Charles; 31 Oct 1798; 24 May 1799
WC; WILL; dau. Frances WEAVER, wife of Frederick, 20 shillings; dau. Mary ANNADELL wife of David 1 shilling; son Thomas residue and he to be ex; WITS: Thos. HUTT, Nathaniel MOTHERSHEAD. (WC DW 20:5; (Frederick WEAVER mar. Frances POOR, dau. of Chas. POOR, bef. 31 Oct 1798 (MWO:368); Mary POOR mar. David ANNADELL (or ANNODALE), WC, bond 26 Aug 1794 (MLBWC:2)]

POPE, Austin; PO Apr 1800; 23 Mar 1801. WC; INV, £96.2.6. (WC RI 8:115)
[An Austin POPE mar. Fanny YEATMAN, WC, bond 7 Aug 1793 (MLBWC:54) and an Austin POPE was the overseer for Isaac POLLACK (of Georgetown, Md.) in WC; there are several letters from him to Newton BERRYMAN in WC CC 1802-016]

POPE, Elijah; PO 11 May 1818; 9 Dec 1822. NC INV. (NC RB 23:263)
[Ann POPE, wid. of Elijah POPE, mar. Chas. DAMERON, NC, bond 3 May 1819 (MLBNC:25); allott to Chas. DAMERON & Ann his wife her thirds of the pers. est. of her late husband Elijah POPE; Chas. DAMERON aptd. gdn. of Ann POPE orphan of Elijah POPE, NC 18 Dec 1819 (NC OB 1816-20:417; OB 1820-25:235)]

POPE, George H.; 2 Sep 1822
RC; Fortunatus, Leroy, William, Betsy, Nancy, Maria & Sally POPE who are infants (except Fortunatus) of George H. POPE dec'd by Fortunatus POPE their next friend, compl., vs. Fanny POPE def. (RC OB 25:331)
[This is prob. Geo. POPE who mar. Frances MacTYRE, RC, bond 22 Mar 1796 (MWO:285); Jn. POPE aptd. gdn. to Margaret, Wm., & Sally POPE orphans of Geo. H. POPE; Nancy POPE aptd. gdn. to Sally, Jos. & Nancy POPE orphans of Geo. H. POPE, 1 Sep 1823 (RC OB 26:108); Leroy POPE orphan of Geo. H. POPE chose Jos. P. DAVENPORT as his gdn., 5 Jan 1824 (RC OB 26:136); settle Wm. C. WHEELER's gdnship. of Maria M. POPE now the wife of Thos. BLACKERBY, 8 Oct 1827. (NC OB 1825-30:207)]

POPE, Humphry; 6 Oct 1817

RC; WILL; Susan, wife of Thomas BRYANT, Westley, Thomas, Mary, Rebecca and William POPE were heirs of Humphry POPE. (RC OB 24:146) [Susanna POPE mar. Thos. L. BRYANT, RC, bond 7 Feb 1815 (MRC:29); Thos. BRYANT aptd. gdn. of Rebecca POPE & Wm. E. POPE orphans of Humphry POPE, 1 May 1820 (RC OB 25:6); Thos. POPE chose Miskell SAUNDERS as his gdn. and sd. SAUNDERS is aptd. gdn. to Mary E. POPE orphans of Humphry POPE, 6 Aug 1821 (RC OB 25:187)]

POPE, John; May 1797

WC; acc. to a chancery suit, John POPE made his will in Nov 1784 and named his children Elliott, William Ransdell, John and Thomas. (WC CC 1804-015, DW 16:253, DW 17:31)

[In WWCV, p. 180, Fothergill mistakenly gives Jn. POPE's sons as "Elliott, William, Ransdell, John and Thomas."]

POPE, John F.; [m]; 8 Jun 1812

NC; one third part of his land (99 ac. with dwelling house) & Negroes Peter (an old man), Milley, [Owill] (a boy) & Winney (an old woman) allotted to Hiram RAINS who mar. sd. POPE's wid. (NC RB 19:198)

POPE, John F.; PO 9 Jan 1815; 11 Apr 1815

NC; DIV of slaves among the heirs: [Cynthia] POPE (rec'd Aron), William POPE (rec'd Isaac), Elizabeth POPE (rec'd [Nanson] & Elizabeth), Nicholas POPE (rec'd Britania & [Vison]). (NC RB 20:59)

[Jn. Fleet POPE was the eldest son of Nicholas POPE (d. NC 1777) (NC RB 10:176); he mar. Frances FALLIN, NC, bond 20 Mar 1797 (MLBNC:83); in his will (NC 22 Feb 1808-14 Nov 1808), Jn. F. POPE of WicP, named his children Jn. POPE, Nicholas POPE, William POPE, Eliz. POPE and a dau. (Cynthia) not yet baptized; he also left one third of his est. to his wife but did not name her (NC RB 18:57); Frances POPE, wid. of John F. POPE, mar. Hiram RAINS, son of Wm. RAINS, NC, bond 23 Apr 1811 (MLBNC:85); Hiram RAINS was aptd. gdn. of Eliz., Jn. F., Wm., and Cynthia orphans of Jn. F. POPE, NC, 8 Feb 1813 (NC OB 1811-15:147); *for more on this family, see VS1776 I:323-325*]

POPE, Lawrence; 4 May 1810; 27 Aug 1810

WP, WC; WILL; dau. Fanny EDWARDS all the money due me from the est. of William EDWARDS dec'd also all his est. I purchased after his death in 1807; grson. Henry Lewis POPE $100 due me from his father Austin POPE's est; dau. Jane QUESENBURY a Negro woman Sarah and one seventh part of property given to my wife during her life; daus. Suckey POPE, Sally POPE, Caty POPE (all under 18); all lands to be eq. div. among 3 sons Lawrence Berry POPE, Elliot POPE, & John POPE (all under 21); wife Penny POPE to educate six children I have by her: Suckey, Sally, Caty, Lawrence B., Elliott & John; wife, s-i-l George QUESENBURY, & nephew and friend Pope TIFFY exors; WITS: Gerrard McKENNEY, Wm. QUESENBURY, Jn. H. DOLEMAN, Jn. LAWRENCE. (WC DW 22:117)

[Frankey POPE mar. the Rev. Wm. EDWARDS, WC, bond 3 Dec 1790 (MLBWC:21); Jane Carter POPE mar. Geo. QUESENBURY, WC, bond 27 Nov 1809 (MLBWC:56); Lawrence POPE orphan of Lawrence POPE chose Jn. W. HUNGERFORD as his gdn., 22 Jul 1816 (WC OB 1814-18:250); Jn. POPE, born 31 May 1807, son of Lawrence POPE sued Rich. BAYNE, his gdn. in WC in 1835; in the suit the children of Lawrence are given as Jane QUISENBERRY, Lawrence B. POPE, Elliot POPE, Sally JONES and John POPE (WCCP:23); there was also another dau., Susan, who mar. Rich. BAYNE (WCCP:23, 46, 48); Jn. POPE orphan of Lawrence POPE chose Rich. BAYNE as his gdn., 22 Jul 1822 (WC OB 1819-23:443)]

POPE, Lawrence; PO 27 Aug 1810; 23 Mar 1812
WC; INV, $4627.90; includes Negroes Bascoe, George, Solomon, Guss, boys Philip, Ripon, Thornton & Bob, Polly & Spencer, girls Ebey, Guly, Rachel, Chaney & Cate, Suck, Sarah. (WC RI 9:314)

POPE, Penelope; 19 Aug 1817; 20 Aug 1817.
WC; D of G; to her two daus. Ellen BAYNE & Fanney DOLEMAN one half of the tract of land in RC given her by her mother Hannah QUESENBURY by D of G dtd. 10 Jul 1817; WIT: Rodham KENNER, Campbell TEET, Thos MILLER, Josiah HAZARD. (WC DW 23:332)
[Penelope POPE was the dau. of Nicholas QUISENBURY and the wid. of (1) Jacob VIGOR and (2) Lawrence POPE; she mar. POPE as his 3rd wife, WC, bond 22 Nov 1793 (MLBWC:54; MWO:285, 361); Frances Bayne VIGAR mar. Jn. H. DOLEMAN, WC, bond 10 Jun 1805 (MLBWC:20)]

PORTER, Hudson; 1 Dec 1802; 28 Feb 1803
WC; WILL; nephew Henry GREGGS $100 when 21; rest of est. to bro. Edward PORTER and he to be exor.; WITS: Wm. PORTER, Jn. YEATMAN, Thos. YEATMAN. (WC DW 20:432)

PORTER, John; 9 Aug 1811.
Bourbon Co., Kentucky, January Court 1810, Catharine PORTER wid. & rel. of John PORTER declared that she would not accept of the provision made for her by the last will & test. of her sd. dec'd husband and that she will receive such part and share of her sd. husband's est. the law hath in that case. (WC DW 22:231)

PORTER, William; [m]; [m]
WC; DIV of est; balance due the est. of Wesley PORTER in the hands of the admr. $122.90 1/2; Lewis PORTER's proportion of William PORTER's est. in the hands of the adm $80.27 1/2; deduct from the above for Elliott PORTER's interest in that portion of the Negroes that Lewis PORTER was intitled to from William PORTER's est. $32.08 1/2; the balance ($171,09 1/2) div. among: Sampson PORTER, William PORTER, Nancy PORTER, Fanny PORTER & Polly PORTER all of the whole blood & Elliott PORTER of the half blood. (WC RI 11:215)
[Sampson PORTER orphan of Wm. PORTER chose Edw. PORTER as his gdn., 26 Feb 1816 (WC OB 1814-18:206)]

PORTER, William (Capt.); T 4 May 1820; 27 Dec 1824
WC; INV; includes Negroes Ben, Margarette, Dinah, Leah, Sisson, Osman, Annanias, James, Cilia, Sarah. (WC RI 11:487)
[Acc. to a chancery suit filed in WC in 1835, Wm. PORTER was the son of Dempsey PORTER, and he died in 1820 leaving all of his est. to his nephew Dempsey P. GILBERT (the son of Wm. GILBERT & Elenor PORTER) who was living in Kentucky at the time (WCCP:36; WC DW 19:201)]

PORTER, William D.; Mar 1810
RC; land of William D. PORTER was div. between the est. of John PORTER dec'd and Jemima DEATLEY. (RC Orders 1809-10:39)
[Jemima DEATLEY seems to have been a resident of Bourbon Co., Ky. in 1818 when she sold a tract of land known as The Horsehead located in RC and NC to Jn. KING (RC DB 20:472); Jemima DEATLEY was the head of a large household in Carlisle, Nicholas Co., Ky in the 1820 census; she may have been the wife of Jn. DEATLEY who was the head of a household in Bourbon Co., Ky in the 1810 census]

PORTER, William Sr.; 30 Aug 1806; 24 Nov 1806.

CP, WC; WILL; son Elliott PORTER that part of my land lying on the SW of the new road from Crabb's Cross Roads to Richmond Court House & joining the land of William PORTER of Kentucky containing 73 ac, my Negro man James & 1/8 part of livestock and furniture; dau. Nancy PORTER $100; dau. Fanny PORTER $100; dau. Mary PORTER $100; all money is out in bonds; daus. to have interest from their legacies annually until they come of age or marry and then to have the legacies; rest of est. to wife Mary PORTER; at her death or remarriage and then sons Wesly, Lewis, Sampson & William to have all est. on the NE side of the new road from Crabb's Cross Roads to Richmond Court House containing 282 1/2 ac. to be eq. div; my part of the lot & house William EDWARDS and myself purchased of John PORTER to be sold; rest of est. to be eq. div. among all children except Elliott; wife & son Elliott exors; WITS: Jn. YEATMAN Sr., Wm. McCLANAHAM, Wm. EDWARDS. (WC DW 21:284)
[Armstrong McKENNY aptd. gdn. to Mary PORTER orphan of Wm. PORTER; Sampson & Wm. PORTER, also orphans of Wm., chose McKENNY for their gdn., 28 Mar 1815 (WC OB 1814-18:108)]

POTTS, Thomas; 25 Aug 1795; 19 Oct 1795
LC; WILL; Negro woman Mima to wife during her widowhood; if wife marries sd. Mima to return and be div. as directed; Negro boy Billie to sons William & Robert; Negroes Tom & [Ansy] other children John POTTS, James POTTS, Bartley POTTS, Patty BISCOE & Hannah POTTS; friends Thomas MYERS, Joseph CARTER & Peter BEANE exors; WITS: Jas. EWELL, Jn. CHOWNING, Martin GEORGE, Thos. MERRYMAN. (LC WB 28:20)
[Thos. DAVIS mar. Hannah orphan of Thos. POTTS bef. 20 Jul 1801 (LC Orders 21 1799-1801:275); Wm. POTTS orphan of Thos. POTTS chose Jn. POTTS as his gdn. and sd. Jn. is also aptd. gdn. to Robt. POTTS orphan of sd. dec'd., 17 Jan 1803 (LC Orders V 1802-03:256); settlement with Jn. POTTS the acct. of his gdnship. of Robt. POTTS orphan of Thos. POTTS and sell the slave William belonging to the est. of Thos. POTTS and div. the proceeds between Wm. & Robt. POTTS, 15 Mar 1813 (LC Orders 24:144)]

POTTS, Thomas; T 5 Nov 1795; 20 Feb 1797. LC; INV, £345.10.5. (LC EB 24:52)

POWER, James; PO 9 Jan 181[4]; 10 Jun 1816. NC; INV, $86.37 1/2. (NC RB 21:14)
[James POWER is prob. the son of Jos. POWER of SSP (d. NC 1801) (*see below*); his est. was ord. to be admin. by Jn. McCAVE, NC, 9 Jan 1814 (NC OB 1811-1816)]

POWER, Joseph; PO 12 Oct 1801, T 20 Nov 1801; 13 Jun 1803. NC; INV, [m]. (NC RB 17:5)
[In his will (NC 23 Apr 1801-12 Oct 1801), Jos. POWER of SSP named his wife Betty, his son James POWER, and his daus. Winnifred, Sally, Betty & Beckey POWER (NC RB 16:298)]

POWER, Mary (Mrs.); T 17 Dec 1814; 15 Aug 1815. NC; INV, [m]; includes Negro Stephen. (NC RB 20:195)
[In her will (NC 7 Oct 1802-15 Nov 1814), Mary POWERS [sic] of SSP named her sons Wm. & Jn. POWERS and dau. Eliz. FRANCE (NC RB 20:89); Eliz. POWER mar. Wm. FRANCE, NC, bond 1 Dec 1800 (MLBNC:40)]

POWER, Sarah; 9 Jan 1815
NC; Nunc. WILL; Ann S. KIRK and John LOWRY deposed that Sarah POWER who died at her place of residence last November in her last illness bequeathed her property to Betty POWER. (NC OB 1811-15:273)

PRICE, John; 4 Apr 1788; Oct 1788

WC; WILL; use of plant. to wife Ann PRICE; at her death to go to bro. William PRICE; bro. William PRICE ex.; WITS: Wm. WILSON, Jn. WOOD, Nathaniel KING. (WC Unrec Wills 1755-1800 #37)

PRIDHAM, Christopher; 11 Jan 1822; 5 Dec 1825
RC; WILL; to dau. Caty PRIDHAM the use of my land in NC during her life & a Negro girl Lucy, but if Caty has no heirs, William Rust Pridham PROCTOR (under 18) to have Negro Lucy; for love & affection I have for John Middleton Pridham PROCTOR believing him to be my son, I give him part of the land that lies in WC being the land that joins the land of Samuel CRALLE & the land that I hold in NC and also Bill, Winney & three children; but for want of heirs or selling or offering for sale sd. land or Negroes, William Rust Pridham PROCTOR to have above land & Negroes; land left to dau. Caty PRIDHAM shall descend to John Middleton Pridham PROCTOR at her death; to William Rust Pridham PROCTOR all the land I hold in RC and the land in WC not before given & also the following Negroes: Tom, Rachel & two children, Phillis & Lee, Betsy & two children, [?], Harriet, & George; to Elizabeth PROCTOR for the services rendered and she shall be comfortably maintained out of my est. so long as she behaves herself and continues to live with & take care of William Rust Pridham PROCTOR [but on failure] of either, William Rust Pridham PROCTOR to have what was devised to her; all est. to continue as it is until William Rust Pridham PROCTOR arrives to the age of 18 then all est. not before mentioned shall be eq. div. between John Middleton Pridham PROCTOR and William Rust Pridham PROCTOR; Elizabeth PROCTOR & John Middleton Pridham PROCTOR exors; WITS: Sam. CRALLE, Jn. PROCTOR, Abraham PROCTOR (RC WB 10:101)
[This is prob. the Christopher PRIDHAM who mar. Katharine LONGWORTH, RC, bond 19 May 1783 (MRC:162)]

PRITCHETT, Rodham; PO 8 Dec 1800, T 1 Jan 1802; 14 Jun 1802
NC; INV of Negroes, £285.0.0; includes Adam, Bett, Jude, Ellin, Cillar, Winney; DIV of est. among Rodham PRITCHET (rec'd Adam), John PRITCHET (rec'd Bett), Samuel C. PRITCHET (rec'd Jude), Polly PRITCHET (rec'd Ellin), Susan PRITCHET (rec'd Cillar & Winney). (NC RB 16:392)

PRITCHETT, Rodham; PO Jun 1801, T 26 Nov 1806; 1 Dec 1806
RC; DIV of lands adj John DODSON dec'd & James DODSON between John PRITCHETT & Rodham PRITCHETT. (RC AB 3:181)

PROSSER, Samuel; 7 Jul 1824; 12 Dec 1825
NC; WILL; Miss Lucy ROUTT to have the use of all my Negroes: Mark, Rachel & Eliza for the maintenance of my children until they come of age or marry provided she remain single; if she should marry all the prop. except the Negroes to be sold and disposed of as follows: dau. Judith Roebuck PROSSER to have $100; at the age [sic] or marriage of my son Richard Sydnor PROSSER & my dau. Priscilla Parkinson PROSSER the above-named Negroes should be eq. div. between them; balance of est. to be eq. div. among my three children Judith R., Richard S. & Priscilla P.; William ROUTT ex; WITS: Thos. HUGHLETT, Sam. WALKER; [Wm. ROUTT having removed from the state, certificate for obtaining letters of admin. was granted to Thos. HUGHLETT;; admin. with the will annexed was granted to Lucy PROSSER 12 May 1829]; NC RB 24:371)
[Sam. PROSSER was prob the Sam. PROSSER who mar. Nancy Robuck BOOTH, dau. of Jn. & Winnifred BOOTH, NC, bond 15 Dec 1807 (MLBNC:84)]

PUGH, Lewis; 1 Dec 1801; 4 Oct 1802
RC; WILL; wife; son William G. (under 21); wife & George MOORE exors; WITS: Abner HOWE, Wm. HARRISON. (RC WB 9:190)

PULLEN, Addaline; PO 17 Dec 1821, T 1 Jan 1822; 19 Feb 1822
LC; sale of Negroes (Jesse & Molly for $672) at Lancaster Courthouse which Addaline PULLEN died seized; proceeds after commission deducted was $631.68 and was div. among Addaline PULLEN's heirs: Westley KIRK, Richard PAYNE gdn. to N. B. PULLEN, Jonathan PULLEN, John MEREDITH gdn. to William PULLEN, William GEORGE gdn. to Frances GEORGE; all except Frances GEORGE received $140.37 1/2; Frances GEORGE rec'd $70.18. (LC EB 29:173)
[Addaline PULLEN was the dau. of Thaddeus PULLEN (see below)]

PULLEN, Andrew; 7 Aug 1820
RC; Daniel WILSON aptd. gdn. of James PULLEN orphan of Andrew PULLEN. (RC OB 25:46)

PULLEN, Catharine; PO 19 Jan 1818 & 17 Mar 1818, T 19 Mar 1818; 15 Jun 1818
LC; DIV of proceeds of sale of slave Sarah among William GEORGE in right of his wife Frances, Westley KIRK in right of his wife Betsy who was Betsy PULLEN, Enoch GEORGE gdn. of Jonathan PULLEN, William GEORGE gdn. of William PULLEN, Addaline PULLEN & Nancy PULLEN; in a former div. Catharine PULLEN was due money from the div. of Negroes of Thaddeus PULLEN dec'd by Jonathan PULLEN her bro. (LC EB 27:427)
[Wm. GEORGE mar. Fanny PULLEN, LC, bond 6 Mar 1817 (MLBLC:32)]

PULLEN, Hannah; PO 16 Nov 1816; 5 May 1817
RC; INV, $2650.00, includes the following Negroes: John, Harry, Winny, Sarah, Armistead, Daniel, Jesse, Frank, Spencer, Lucinda, Tab. (RC WB 9:559)

PULLEN, Henry; 17 Jun 1816
LC; Betsy PULLEN orphan of Henry PULLEN chose George PULLEN as her gdn.,; LC Orders 24:313

PULLEN, Jesse; PO 1802, T 15 Feb 1804; 2 Apr 1804
RC; legacies paid to following legatees by admr. Everard PULLEN: Joshua BOING Sr., William BOING, James JENNINGS. (RC AB 3:131)
[Jesse PULLEN mar. Peggy FISHER, RC, bond 1 Dec 1788 (MRC:163)]

PULLEN, John; 20 Oct 1814; 19 Jun 1815
LC; WILL; all est. to wife [Carmin] PULLEN during her life; if wife is pregnant and has a boy, I give him the plant. where I now live & my dau. Elizabeth PULLEN must be made equal with my other prop; [no ex. or wits named]. (LC WB 28:165)
[Jn. PULLEN mar. Carmen NUTT, dau. of Rich. NUTT (d. NC 1811), NC, bond 1 Aug 1808 (MLBNC:84, *see Rich. NUTT above*)]

PULLEN, John; PO 19 Jun 1815, T 20 Dec 1815; 21 Aug 1816
LC; INV; includes [Negroes]: Joe, Billy, Mitchell, Joshua, Spencer, John, Moses, Cate, Aggy, Cordelia, Betty. (LC EB 27:348)

PULLEN, John; PO 20 Oct 1823; 16 Aug 1824
LC; sale of land of John PULLEN dec'd to Caroline SHEARMAN for $551.50 and div. of proceeds among Richard PAYNE gdn. of Nancy B. PULLEN, John MEREDITH gdn. of William PULLEN and Westley KIRK. (LC EB 29:349)

PULLEN, Jonathan; PO 15 Sep 1800, T 29 Oct 1800; 19 Jan 1801. LC; INV, $498.20. (LC EB 24:130)

PULLEN, Leroy; T 29 Sep 1812; 11 Apr 1814

NC; INV, £997.6.3; includes Negroes Frank, Jeremiah, Daniel, Rose, Hiram, Sarah, Richard, Diner, Mark, Isac, Absolum, Davide. (NC RB 19:538) [In his will (NC 11 Jun 1810-8 Jun 1812), Leroy PULLEN of SSP named his son Thos. PULLEN & dau. Eliz. BOOTH. (NC RB 19:201)]

PULLEN, Thaddeus; PO 19 Jul 1809; 15 Oct 1810
LC; INV, \$2162.62; includes Negroes: Bob, Chriss, Hannah, Alcy, Sarah, John, Ann, Manuel, Davy. (LC EB 27:75)

PULLEN, Thaddeus; PO 17 Feb 1817; 19 Jan 1818
LC; DIV of slaves to Frances GEORGE the late wid. of the sd. Thaddeus PULLEN, Westley KIRK in right of his wife Elizabeth who was Elizabeth PULLEN, Enoch GEORGE gdn. to Jonathan PULLEN, William GEORGE gdn. to William PULLEN, William GEORGE as gdn. to Catharine PULLEN, William GEORGE as gdn. to Addaline M. PULLEN, William GEORGE as gdn. to Nancy B. PULLEN. (LC EB 27:399)
[Thaddeus PULLEN mar. (1) Nancy FIENDLEY, LC, bond 4 May 1793 and (2) Frances Frizell MEREDITH, LC, 26 Oct 1797 (MLBLC:61, MWO:290); Fanny (MEREDITH) PULLEN mar. Wm. GEORGE, LC, bond 6 Mar 1817 (MLBLC:32; LC OB 24:413); Betsy PULLEN orphan of Thad. PULLEN chose Westley KIRK as her gdn., 19 Feb 1816 (LC Orders 24:283); on the mot. of Westley KIRK who mar. Eliz. PULLEN, ord. that Jonathan PULLEN, Wm. PULLEN, Cath. PULLEN & Nancy B. PULLEN & Adeline BUTLER be summoned to show cause why the lands of Thad. PULLEN should not be sold for a div. of the proceeds, 20 Jan 1817 (LC Orders 24:346, 348); Jonathan PULLEN orphan of Thad. PULLEN chose Enoch GEORGE as his gdn., 20 Jan 1817 (LC OB 24:347); Frances F. PULLEN aptd. gdn. to Wm., Caty, Adeline M. and Nancy B. PULLEN orphans of Thad. PULLEN, 20 Jan 1817 (LC OB 24:349); settlement with Wm. GEORGE the acct. of hus gdnship. with Wm., Adeline & Nancy B. PULLEN orphans of Thad. PULLEN, 17 Jan 20 (LC OB 25:104); Rich. PAYNE aptd. gdn. to Adeline, Nancy & Wm. PULLEN orphans of Thad. PULLEN, 21 Feb 1820 (LC OB 25:108, 109); on the mot. of Rich. PAYNE gdn. to Nancy B. PULLEN ord. that Wm. PULLEN by Jn. MEREDITH his gdn. & Westley KIRK and Betsy his wife be summoned to show cause why the lands of Jn. PULLEN should not be sold and the proceeds eq. div. among his heirs, 18 Aug 1823 (LC OB 25:393)]

PULLEN, Thaddeus; PO 1820, ; 17 Apr 1820
LC; DIV of Negroes which F. F. GEORGE who was Frances F. PULLEN wid. & rel of Thaddeus PULLEN died seized & possessed as her dower in his est. among: Wesley KIRK in right of his wife Elizabeth who was Elizabeth PULLEN (Negro Bob), Jonathan PULLEN (boy Jerry), William PULLEN (boy Henry), Addaline PULLEN (girl Mary), Nancy B. PULLEN (Alice). (LC EB 29:15)

PULLEN, Thomas; PO 15 Feb 1814; 10 Mar 1823
NC; INV; includes Negroes [Jery], Chichester, Daniel, girl Lavina, Frankey, girl Rose, boy Hiram, girl Salley and a "Buffalow heifer."; NC RB 23:280)
[Thos. PULLEN mar. Nancy CUNDIFF, NC, bond 11 Feb 1813 (MLBNC:84); in his will (NC 28 Aug 1813-14 Feb 1814), Thos. PULLEN named his wife Nancy and dau. Rocksey PULLEN; he also freed his "old woman Frank" (NC RB 19:503)]

PULLEN, William; PO 19 Dec 1814; 18 Mar 1816
LC; INV, \$114.62; James BALL admr. (LC EB 27:289)
[Mary PULLEN orphan of Wm. PULLEN chose Wm. PULLEN as her gdn.; Jn. PULLEN orphan of Wm. chose Jas. BALL as his gdn, 19 May 1817 (LC

OB 25:364); Thad. MITCHELL aptd. gdn. to Sam. Montgomery PULLEN orphan of Wm. PULLEN, 15 Jun 1818 (LC OB 25:1); Overseers of the Poor to bind out Sam. [M.] PULLEN orphan of Wm. PULLEN to Thad. MITCHELL, 16 Sep 1822 (LC OB 25:332)]

PURSELL, Edward M.; 4 Oct 1819
RC; the distributees of the est. of Edw. M. PURSELL were: Rawleigh HAZARD & Eliz. his wife, William F. DAVIS & Letty his wife, Fortunatus POPE & Fanny his wife, George R. PURSELL & Sally his wife, Hannah PURSELL, Joseph R. PURSELL, John PURSELL, the children of Edward PURSELL and the children of Jeremiah THRIFT & Peggy his wife. (RC OB 24:378)
[Raw. HAZARD mar. Eliz. R. PURSELL, RC, bond 15 Mar 1817; Wm. F. DAVIS mar. Letty R. PURSELL, RC, bond 23 Mar 1818; Fortunatus POPE mar. Frances R. PURSELL, RC, bond 8 Dec 1817 (MRC:52, 91, 160)]

PURSELL, George; 16 Apr 1810; 2 Jul 1810
RC; WILL; all my est. to wife Sarah; [slaves] George & Liz to be hired out by the ex.and to receive half of the hire for their own use; old Nanny that I left free should continue on the land where she now is; my store house to be sold; rent of £25 per annum paid half yearly for my tavern that Mr. John WEATHERS now has rented for 5 years; at wife's death est. to be eq. div. amongst my 10 children; wife & son William exors; WITS: Chas. BELL, Jonathan BECKWITH, Jas. NORTHEN. (RC WB 9:371)
[Sarah PURSELL, Geo. PURSELL, Fanny PURSELL, Nancy PURSELL, and Sarah PURSELL as gdn. ad litem to Stephen PURSELL, Lee PURSELL, Sally PURSELL, Philip PURSELL, Lewis PURSELL, and Benj. PURSELL were heirs of Geo PURSELL dec'd (RC OB 24:304)]

PURSELL, George; T 3 Jun 1811; 7 Jun 1813
RC; INV, £575.19.3, includes following slaves: George, Tom, Leze, Nancey, Winney, Sharlott, Lucy, Molly. (RC WB 9:426)

PURSELL, James; T 26 Jan 1802; 1 Feb 1802
RC; DIV of est. between William HAMMACK (received Milly & child) & John PURSELL (received Hannah & Lucy). (RC AB 3:80)
[Wm. HAMMOCK mar. Betsy PURSLEY dau. of Mary PURSLEY, WC, bond 13 Nov 1797 (MLBWC:28)]

PURSELL, John; 5 Oct 1801. RC INV; £26.11.3. (RC WB 9:158)

PURSLEY, John; 22 Jul 1816
WC; John PURSLEY a resident of WC proved by the oath of John LAWRENCE that he is the son of Elizabeth PURSLEY bro. [sic] of John PURSLEY who entered in the US service as a soldier under Walter BERRYMAN, a lt. of artillery, in the year 1813 or 14 during the late war and that he is consequently the nephew of the sd. John PURSLEY and the only heir which sd. John PURSLEY died at Ft. Washington on the Potomac in the year 1814 or 15. (WC OB 1814-18:249)
[The court certified that Jn. PURSLEY was the legal rep. of Jn. PURSLEY who died at Ft. Washington in 1814 or 15, 24 Nov 1817 (WC OB 1814-18:357); *PURSLEY is apparently a variant of PURCELL*]

PURSLEY, John; 4 Jun 1821
RC; Joseph [J.] PURSLEY & Elizabeth PURSLEY orphans of John PURSLEY chose Joseph DALE as their gdn. and he is aptd. gdn. to James & Mary PURSLEY also orphans of sd. John. (RC OB 25:162)
[This is no doubt the Jn. PURSLEY who mar. Polly DALE, RC, bond 10 Jul 1802 (MRC:165); Jn. PURSLEY d. seized & possessed of an 80 ac. tract in WC

leaving four inf. children: Betty, Jas., Mary and Jos. and a wid. Mary (WC CC 1821-015); Jos. PURSLEY an inf. by Jos. DALE his next friend compl. against Mary PURSLEY wid. of Jn. PURSLEY and Betsy PURSLEY, Jas. PURSLEY and Mary PURSLEY infants, defts., in chancery to sell land, 27 Feb 1821 (WC OB 1819-23:228)]

QUESENBURY, Ann; 16 Feb 1808; 28 Mar 1808
WC; WILL; my Negro man Stephen to Gen. John HUNGERFORD because he prefers him for his master; my Negro man George to Lawrence POPE; my Negro girl Sarah to Susannah [m]; John JETT of this county; rest of est. to friend Caty DEEN; [no ex. named]; WITS: Jn. THOMPSON, Jas. ELLIOTT, Jas. FISHER. (WC DW 21:558)

QUESENBURY, Hannah; 10 Jul 1817; 28 Jul 1817
WC; D of G; to daus. Penelope POPE, wid. of Lawrence POPE, & Nancy MOXLEY wid. of Alexander MOXLEY a tract of land in RC adj. the lands of Joshua REMMY containing 150 ac. to be eq. div. between them; WITS: Rich. BAYNE, Jn. BAYNE, Jacob A. REAMY. (WC DW 23:302)
[Hannah was the wid. of Nicholas QUESENBURY, *see below*]

QUESENBURY, Nicholas; 10 Jun 1802; 28 Oct 1816
WC; WILL; wife Hannah QUESENBURY during her widowhood the land that was Butler's, the land that was Bartlett's, and the land that my bro. James QUESENBURY gave me; son George QUESENBURY; my part of the Negroes now in the possession of Ann QUESENBURY, being her thirds of the Negroes that belonged to my bro. James, to be eq. div. amongst my three daus, Penny POPE, Nancy MOXLEY, Catie RIGG; Sarah & her children to dau. Penny POPE; land that was Pannel's with Milley & her children to dau. Nancy MOXLEY; land called Black Neck with Pat & her children to dau. Catie RIGG; [no ex. named]; WITS: Newton BERRYMAN, Wm. BUTLER, Alick SANDERS, Wm. QUESENBURY. (WC DW 23:215)
[Penelope QUESENBURY mar. (1) Jacob VIGOR and (2) Lawrence POPE (as his 3rd wife), WC, bond 22 Nov 1793; Nancy QUESENBURY mar. Alex. MOXLEY, WC, bond 13 Jan 1789; Catherine QUESENBURY mar. Jonathan RIGG, WC, bond 22 Feb 1794 (MWO:254, 285, 297, 361)]

QUINLAIN, Judith; T 8 Oct 1806; 27 Oct 1806; WC; INV. (WC RI 8:624)
[Could this be Judith Brereton THOMPSON who mar. Hugh QUINLAN, poss. as his 2nd wife, WC, bond 23 Aug 1803 ? (MLBWC:56); in both marriages of Hugh QUINLAN in MLBWC:56 his name is given as "QUINTON."]

QUINLAN, Ann; PO 4 Jun 1798; 7 Jul 1800. RC; INV. (RC WB 9:134)
[This is Anne Tasker (CARTER) PECK, dau. of Robt. & Frances (TASKER) CARTER and wid. of Jn. PECK, who mar. Hugh QUINLAN, WC, bond 20 Apr 1796 (MWO:291); Chancery suit, Jn. C. PECK & Emanuel PECK inf. under 21 by Geo. WHITLOCK their next friend and Tasker Carter QUINLAN an inf. under 21 by Carter MITCHELL his gdn. vs. Harriet PECK to div. the lands of Anne QUINLAN dec'd (WC Orders 1810-13:28)]

RAINS, Hiram; 11 Dec 1815
NC; Hiram RAINS has been dead more than 3 months. (NC OB 1811-15:395)
[Hiram RAINS, son of Wm. RAINS, mar. Frances POPE, wid., NC, bond 23 Apr 1811 (MLBNC:85)]

RAINS, William; PO 13 Feb 1815; 8 Jan 1816. NC; INV, [m]; includes u/i Negro man. (NC RB 20:332)

RALPH, Robert F.; T 29 Nov 1814; 27 Feb 1815

WC; INV, £25.16.6; includes pay received when in service of [R.] E. BROWN $17.41 (= £5.2.6). (WC RI 9:430)

REAMY, Joshua; T 17 Nov 1821); [11] Mar 1824. RC; INV, $1674.71 1/2. (RC WB 10:39)

REAMY, Joshua; PO Jun 1822; 7 Jun 1824
RC; DIV of est. among Berryman REAMY, Daniel MOTHERSHEAD in right of his wife Caty A., John CARPENTER in right of his wife Nancy C., Josiah HAZARD in right of his wife Fanny S., James REAMY, Jacob A. REAMY, Susannah C. CARPENTER's children (Elizabeth C., William R., Nancy R., Bethiah A., Lucy, John), William REAMY's children (Albert J., [Adelade T]., Adeline L., Delia F., Colista E., George W. H., Henry J., Milton H., [Spazmoth] B.). (RC AB 4:118)
[Jn. CARPENTER mar. Nancy REAMY, WC, bond 13 Feb 1818 (MLBWC:12); Jn. C. CARPENTER aptd. gdn. to [Barmoth] B. REAMY orphan of Wm. REAMY; Berryman REAMY aptd. gdn. to Geo. H. REAMY orphan of Wm. REAMY, Thos. MILLER aptd. gdn. to Adelade R., Delia F., [Catula] E. and Milton H. REAMY orphans of Wm. REAMY, 2 Dec 1822 (RC OB 26:12); the name given above as "Colista E." and "Catula E." is given in MLBWC as "Carlisle E." who mar. Hen. BARTLETT, WC, bond 11 Nov 1828 (MLBWC:4)]

REAMY, Joshua Sr.; 20 Jul 1820; 1 Oct 1821
RC; WILL; dau. Nancy C. CARPENTER; [dau] Fanny L. HAZARD; son James REAMY; son Jacob A. REAMY; granddau. Aldalade T. REAMY one feather bed & furniture which she generally sleeps on provided she marries to my liking or lives with me as long as I may live; two other grandchildren that live with me George W. H. REAMY and [?] when they come of age; heirs of dau. Lucy MILLER (if any); remaining est. to be eq. div. between my children now living: Bereman REAMY, Catey A. MOTHERSHEAD, Nancy C. CARPENTER, Fanny L. HAZARD, James REAMY, Jacob A, REAMY, and the children of Susanna C. CARPENTER and son William REAMY dec'd; sons Bereman and James exors; WITS: Robt. SANDERS, Jas. NASH, Jas. COATS. (RC WB 9:710)
[Fanny Lewis REAMY mar. Josiah HAZARD, WC, bond 22 Mar 1803 (MLBWC:30)]

REAMY, William; 5 Jan 1824
RC; Overseers of the Poor of LP ord. to bind George W. H. REAMY orphan of William REAMY to Berryman REAMY. (RC OB 26:140)
[Geo. W. H. REAMY mar. Eliz. HUTT, WC, bond 25 Jan 1836 (MLBWC:57); Adeline REAMY orphan of Wm. REAMY chose Dan. MOTHERSHEAD as her gdn. and MOTHERSHEAD is also aptd. gdn. of Hen. REAMY, 27 Jun 1825 (WC OB 1823-27:187); Adeline REAMY mar. Thos. SANFORD, WC, bond 15 Feb 1834 (MLBWC:62)]

REDMAN, Caleb; PO 11 Sep 1815, T 4 Sep 1817; 13 Oct 1817
NC; Chancery suit, George HAYES & Maria his wife pltfs. against Janetta, Cyrus & James REDMAN; defts. are infants under 21 and court appointed Cyrus SUTTON their gdn. to defend them in this suit; commissioners appointed to div. the lands unbequeathed by the will of Caleb REDMAN dec'd among the parties entitled thereto; each heir received 22 1/2 ac. as follows: Lot 1 to James REDMAN, Lot 2 to Junetta REDMAN, Lot 3 to Cyrus REDMAN, Lot 4 to George HAYES who mar. Maria REDMAN. (NC RB 21:265; NC CC 1815-028)

[Caleb REDMAN mar. Dolly REDMAN, NC, bond 13 Feb 1797 (MLBNC:85); in his will (NC 16 Dec 1812-15 Nov 1814), Caleb REDMAN named his sons James & Cyrus and his daus. Debba Mariah & Janetty; he also mentioned his wife but did not name her (NC RB 20:93); Maria REDMAN mar. Geo. HAYES, NC, bond 9 Jan 1815 (MLBNC:51); Geo. HAYES was aptd. gdn. to [Janetta], Cyrus and Jas. REDMAN orphans of Caleb REDMAN, NC, 8 May 1815 (NC OB 1811-15:315); in his will Caleb REDMAN emancipated his slave George alias George REDMAN after his wife's death and George was granted permission to reside within NC, 9 Sep 1816 (NC OB 1816-20:89); Wm. HARDING Jr. aptd. gdn. of James REDMAN and Matthew HUDSON aptd. gdn. of Cyrus REDMAN, orphans of Caleb REDMAN, NC 8 Feb 1819 (NC OB 1816-20:330); Cyrus REDMAN aptd. gdn. of Jas. REDMAN orphan of Caleb REDMAN, 13 Nov 1826 (NC OB 1825-30:125)]

REDMAN, John; PO Mar 1805; 27 May 1805
WC; INV, £114.1.6; includes Negroes Lucy, Nancy. (WC RI 8:543)

REDMAN, John; T 12 Mar 1822; 25 Mar 1822
WC; INV, $9234.44; includes Negroes Reuben, Sarah, Sarah, Lucinda, Mildred, Patsey, Winney, Elizabeth, Maria, Judah, Lucius, Battaille, William, Henry, James, Adam, Turner, Richard, Alice, Hannah, Philicia, Hester, Sarah, Lucy, Rachael, Elizabeth, Lewis, Adam, Lucy, Robin, Mary, Winney (blind & old), Robin, Charles, Fanny, Aaron, John. (WC RI 11:166)
[Jn. CAMPBELL aptd. gdn. to Jn. M., Thos. J., Fred. B., Cath., and Benj. S. REDMAN orphans of Jn. REDMAN, 23 Sep 1822 (WC OB 1819-23:478); commissioners aptd. on 24 Nov last to settle the; admin. acct. of Jn. CAMPBELL with the est. of Jn. REDMAN as also the gdnship. acct. of sd. CAMPBELL with his wards, Jn. Milton, Thos. Jett, Catherine, Benj. S. and Fred. B. REDMAN 5 of the children of sd. REDMAN, 23 Feb 1824 (WC OB 1823-27:36); on the mot. of Marshall RUST & his wife Augusta, which Augusta is one of the children of Jn. REDMAN dec'd, ord. that Jn. Milton, Thos. Jett, Cath., Fred. B. and Benj. S. REDMAN infant children of Jn. REDMAN be summoned to show cause why real est. in WC which their sd. father died seized should not be sold, 23 Jan 1826 (WC OB 1823-27:242)]

REDMAN, Joseph; PO 4 Dec 1811; 7 Dec 1812
RC; INV, £1532.1.0, includes Negroes: Andrew, Phillip, Jack, Lucy, Peter, Jacob, Arthur, [Thad], Dennis, Shadrack, Jere, Moses, Manuel, George, Harrey, Daniel, Winney & child Spencer, Mariah, Lucinda, Armistead, Jesse, Milley, James, Rawleigh (lame), Lydda, Old Lucy. (RC WB 9:411)

REDMAN, Joseph Sr.; 27 Feb 1811; 1 Jul 1811
NFP, RC; WILL; 10 Negroes: Jack, Lucy, Armstead, Jess, Winny, Harry, Daniel, Mariah, Lucinda, Spencer to dau. Hannah PULLEN; 160 ac. purchased of William & John POPE to dau. Hannah; plant. w/o I now live containing 220 ac. & 3 Negroes: Andrew, Fill, & Manuell to son Joseph REDMAN Jr.; Negro George to dau. Lettuce PURCELL; 2 Negroes: Peter & Dennis to children of son Solomon REDMAN; 7 Negroes: Jacob, Arthur, Paul, Shadrake, Jerry, Leddy, & Lucy to son John REDMAN; balance of est. to be eq. div. amongst all my children; sons Joseph & John exors; WITS: Thaddeus BRYANT, Wm. STONUM, Sinah LEWIS. (RC WB 9:393)
[Hannah REDMAN mar. Jonathan PULLEN, RC, bond 6 Feb 1797; Letty REDMAN mar. Edw. M. PURSELL, RC, bond 22 Feb 1781 (MRC:164)]

REDMAN, Salley; [m]; [m] Mar 1812

CP, WC; WILL; sis. Frances ROBINSON Negro woman Mimy & Betty & child Sam; niece Sally M. ROBINSON; bro. Solomon REDMAN & sis. Frances ROBINSON exors; WITS: Solomon REDMAN. (WC DW 22:252) [Frances REDMAN mar. Solomon ROBINSON, WC, bond 13 Mar 1797 (MLBWC:59)]

REDMAN, Solomon; PO 4 Jan 1796; 6 Apr 1801
RC; INV; includes the following slaves: Sue, Judy & child [Perrimus]. (RC WB 9:144)

REDMAN, Solomon; [m] Jan 1822; 23 Jun 1823
WC; WILL; to wife Salley [A.] REDMAN during her life the plant. w/o I now live & two Negroes Tom & Roger also the dower Negroes that is allotted for her dower belonging to the est. of James ROBINSON dec'd namely Meredith, Sam, Milly & Lucy; to dau. Ann RICE two Negroes Levina & Jenny; to son William REDMAN my tract of land called Traveller's Rest; to son Vincent REDMAN my tract of land w/o I now live after the death of my wife & one Negro Old Dick; to son John REDMAN my tract of land called The Mushpot & one Negro young Moses; to dau. Martha F. REDMAN two Negroes Isaac & Phill; to dau. Mary P. REDMAN two Negroes [Johnson] & Young Dick; to child wife is now pregnant with two Negroes Charles H. & Henry provided that the child should be born alive; rest of est. to be eq. div. between all children; friend Robert BAILEY ex; WITS: Thos. STOWERS, Jn. REDMAN, Jn. CRENSHAW. (WC DW 24:514)
[Sally A. REDMAN, was prob. Sally A. CRENSHAW, the dau. of David CRENSHAW, who mar. James ROBINSON, WC, in 1812; she mar. (2) Solomon REDMAN, who was prob. a wid. at the time, WC, bond 25 Apr 1821 (MLBWC:57, 59); Ann RICE is prob. Nancy R. REDMAN who mar. (1) Thos. B. RICE, WC, bond 19 Feb 1819 and (2) Jn. M. BRANSON, WC, bond 17 Mar 1828 (MLBWC:8, 58; WCCP:8); the unborn child was Sarah A. F. REDMAN; Sally REDMAN (wid. of Sol. REDMAN) aptd. gdn. to Mary, Susan & Fanny ROBINSON orphans of James ROBINSON and also to Sarah Ann REDMAN orphan of Sol. REDMAN, 24 Nov 1823 (WC OB 1823-27:18); Sol. S. HUTT aptd. gdn. to Jn. & Mary P. REDMAN orphans of Sol. REDMAN; Thos. S. RICE aptd. gdn. to Martha F. REDMAN also an orphan of Sol. REDMAN, 22 Nov 1824 (WC OB 1823-27:131); the only Traveler's Rest listed in Miller:159 is that near Horse Head in NC.]

REDMAN, Solomon; PO 25 Oct 1824; 2 Feb 1825
WC; DIV of Negroes among Thomas RICE (Roger, small girls Polly, Judy & Harriott), John REDMAN (Old Tom, girl [Sofa], girl Denis, small boy Tom), Mary P. REDMAN (Jinny, Henretta), Sarah Ann REDMAN (Lucy & child Judith), Martha REDMAN (Hanah & child). (WC RI 11:[505])

REDMAN, William; 7 Sep 1781; 26 Sep 1799
WC; WILL; wife Kesiah; after wife's death or marriage to be eq. div. between children; exors. wife, Wm. RICE, Jn. RICE; WITS: Wm. MONROE Sr., Lovill HARRISON, Jeremiah CLAXTON. (WC DW 20:55)
[Wm., Stewart, Vincent, Solomon, Mary, Nancy and Jn. are children of Wm. REDMAN the Elder (WC Orders 1801-04:261; CCs 1801-006 and 1802-009)]

REDMAN, William; [m]; 24 Aug 1801
WC; INV, £489.9.0; includes Negroes Cate, Alce, Winney, boys Moses, Aron, David & Ben. (WC RI 8:135)

REDMAN, William; T 15 Nov 1804; 22 Apr 1805
WC; INV, £4423; includes Negroes Phil, Suckey & child, Lucy & child, Cillar, Ben, Levin[a]. (WC RI 8:536)

REDMAN, William; 26 Jul 1819; 23 Aug 1819
WC; DIV of Negroes among Spence HUTT in right of his wife Mary who was Mary REDMAN (received Phill, Levina, Moses, Edy), William REDMAN (Ben, Suckey, Mima, Mima [sic]), and John REDMAN (Silla, Lucy, James, Peggy, Lucy). (WC RI 10:402)
[Wm. & Polly REDMAN orphans of Wm. REDMAN chose Solomon REDMAN as their gdn., 26 Oct 1818 (WC OB 1814-18:414); report of the settlement of Sol. REDMAN's gdnship. accts. of the orphans of Wm. REDMAN ret.; the report contains several accts. including accts. with Mary P. REDMAN, Jn. REDMAN and Wm. REDMAN (WC OB 1823-27:52)]

REESE, Daniel; 28 Dec 1814; 15 May 1815
LC; WILL; whole est. to s-i-l Griffin WILLIAMS; [no ex. named]; WITS: Jn. HAGGAMOND, Thos. N. LAWSON, David H. JAMES. (LC WB 28:162)
[Daniel REES mar. Alice WILLIAMS, who was the wid. of Peter WILLIAMS at the time, LC, bond 25 Dec 1809; Dan. REESE was described as a "stranger & seafaring man" in an 1811 chancery suit (MLBLC:62; LC CC 1811-006)]

REVEER, Bushrod; 19 Apr 1803
LC; settle the gdnship. acct. of Charles EDWARDS dec'd with John W. REVEER orphan of Bushrod REVEER. (LC Orders V 1802-03:310)

REVERE, Ailsey; 12 Oct 1813; 20 Feb 1815
LC; WILL; one flax wheel etc. to dau. Betsy REVERE; son Thomas REVERE; daus. Nancy, Sally, Ailsey & the heirs of Jane to have one shilling each; son Thomas ex; WITS: Raw. DUNAWAY, Thaddeus GOODRIDGE, [Joel] REVERE. (LC WB 28:155)

REVERE, James; 30 Nov 1815; 16 Dec 1816
CCP, LC; WILL; to son James REVERE the plant. w/o he now lives known by the name of Shop Lands with the following Negroes Ned, Emmanuel & Denny also my large shop tools; the plant. I now live on to son Joel REVERE with the following Negroes Sam, [Melay], & Rachel and my small shop tools; to my son Cyrus REVERE the following Negroes Betty, Solomon, Priscilla & Molly; to dau. Polly the following Negroes Letty, Maria & [Simon]; my Negro woman [Cumfort] to son Cyrus & dau. Polly; to the two children of my dec'd son William REVERE $150 to be paid at the day they arrive to lawful age or marriage ($100 to the male & $50 to the females; son James ex; WITS: Thos. G. ROBERTSON, Wm. DOWNMAN. (LC WB 28:180)
[Sally REVERE was aptd. gdn. of Joel & Betsy REVERE orphans of Wm. REVERE (prob. the dec'd son of Jas.), NC, 13 Nov 1815 (NC OB 1811-15:387); rep. on the sale & div. of the slave devised by James REVERE to Cyrus REVERE & Polly DUDLEY and also of the sale & div. of the slave Harry devised by sd. Jas. REVERE to Joel, Cyrus & Jas. REVERE & Polly DUDLEY, 18 May 1818 (LC Orders 24:430)]

REVERE, James; PO 16 Dec [1816], T 19 Dec 1816; 21 Apr 1817
LC; INV; includes Negroes: Comfort, Ned, Letty, Emanuel, Sam, Betty, Rachel, Solomon, Maria, Priscilla, Molley, Dennis, Amelia, Simon, Henry; DIV of est. T 20 Dec 1816 among: Joel REVERE, Cyrus REVERE, James REVERE, Polly DUDLEY's orphans. (LC EB 27:373, 373a)

REVERE, James; PO 19 Jan 1818, T 2 mar. 1818; 20 Apr 1818
LC; APP of 3 slaves devised by James REVERE to Polly DUDLEY; slaves were then sold and the proceeds div. among the heirs of sd. Polly DUDLEY dec'd: Peggy DUDLEY, James DUDLEY, William DUDLEY, Thomas DUDLEY, Ann DUDLEY; each heir received $169.40 which was delivered to John ROGERS gdn. to sd. orphans. (LC EB 27:416)

REVERE, John; 15 Mar 1803; 17 Dec 1804.
CCP, LC; WILL; I lend to my grson. Riveer SEBREE all my land so long as he lives; at his death to return to his lawful heir; grson. Riveer SEBREE to have five year's schooling & £5; remaining part of my est. to be eq. div. between two grsons Riveer & John SEBREE; Robert M. ROBERTSON & Thomas REVERE exors; WITS: Thos. REVERE, Robt. M. ROBERTSON, Andrew ROBERTSON. (LC WB 28:86)
[Riveer & Jn. SEBREE are prob. children of Delilah REVIER who mar. Jesse SEBREE, LC, bond 26 Sep 1796 (MWO:313)]

REVERE, John; PO 17 Dec 1804; 18 Feb 1805. LC; INV, £14.14.2. (LC EB 24:304)

REVERE (RIVERE), Johnson; PO 20 Oct 1800, T 15 Nov 1800; 19 Jan 1801
LC; INV, £286.9.5; includes Negroes: Sillar, Polly, Edward, Millicent. (LC EB 24:127)
[Jenny REVEER orphan of Johnson REVEER chose Thos. REVEER as her gdn., 15 Dec 1800 (LC Orders 21 1799-1801:200)]

REVERE, Peter; [m]; 21 Jun 1802
LC; WILL; whole est. to wife Hannah REVERE; at wife's death, land to return to son Isaac; dau. Betty NIGHT; rest of pers. est. to be eq. div. among rest of my children; James BUSH & Peter BUSH exors; WITS: Wm. REVERE Jr., Eppey NORRIS, Jas. ROBINSON, Thaddeus GOODRIDGE. (LC WB 28:62)
[Peter REVERE was the son of John REVERE (d. LC, 1787); Hannah REVERE was prob a dau. of James BUSH; Elizabeth RIVERE mar. John KNIGHT, LC, bond 24 Nov 1785 (MWO:216, 298)]

REVERE, William; 12 Oct 1802; 16 Apr 1804
CCP, LC; WILL; wife Mary use of my land & plant. w/o I now live & also the land & plant. w/o my bro. James REVERE; at wife's death lands & plant. to bro. James REVERE; James NORRIS & William GOODRIDGE exors; WITS: Jos. BALL, Jas. BALL, Wm. Lee BALL. (LC WB 28:77)

REVERE, William; PO 13 Feb 1815; 12 Jun 1815. NC; INV, [m]. (NC RB 20:138)

REYNOLDS, Reuben; 13 Mar 1815; 25 Dec 1815.
CP, WC; WILL; whole est. to wife Elizabeth REYNOLDS and her heirs descending from her mother's side; wife to be extx; WITS: Wm. BRICKEY, Hannah HARRISON. (WC DW 23:139)
[Reubin RAYNOLDS mar. Elizabeth THOMAS, WC, bond 5 Sep 1804 (MLBWC:58)]

REYNOLDS, William; [m]; May 1818
WC; INV. $1317.75; includes Negroes Fillis, girl Rachel, boys James, Adam & Jerry, girl Amy. (WC RI 10:263)
[Wm. REYNOLDS d. intest. leaving five children: James M., Sally, Thos., Wm., and Jn. WC CC 1820-005); Wm. HAZARD aptd. gdn. to Thos. G. REYNOLDS, Jn. G. REYNOLDS & Wm. B. REYNOLDS orphans of Wm. REYNOLDS, 27 Mar 1820 (WC OB 1819-23:121); on the mot. of Sally REYNOLDS, ord. that Wm. HAZARD settle his admin. acct. on the est. of Wm. REYNOLDS and also his gdnship. accts. of Thos., Wm. & Jn. REYNOLDS orphans of Wm. REYNOLDS; Jn. REYNOLDS chose Sally REYNOLDS as his gdn., 22 May 1826 (WC OB 1823-27:259, 264); gdnship. accts. of Wm. HAZARD with Thos. G., Wm. B., Jn. G., and Wm. REYNOLDS ret., 24 Jul 1826 (WC OB 1823-27:289)]

RICE, Charles; PO 11 Mar 1813, T 24 Mar 1813; 9 Aug 1813. NC; INV, £70.0.6. (NC RB 19:427)

RICE, Charles; T 17 Apr 1812; 14 Feb 1814. NC; INV, $175.90. (NC RB 19:472)

[The est. of Chas. RICE, Jr. was ord. to be admin. by Rich. WALL, NC, 13 Apr 1812 (NC OB 1811-1816:67)]

RICE, Charles L.; 13 Oct 1823

NC; it appears to the satisfaction of the court by evidence of Richard RICE that Charles L. RICE formerly of this county who enlisted in the service of the US during the late war with Great Britain and who has departed this life left no child, that he was never married and that his only heir at law is his mother Nancy LITTLE now residing in this county. (NC OB 1820-25:327)

RICE, Isaac; PO 14 Dec 1813, T 3 Apr 1815; 8 May 1815

NC; DIV of est. acc to his will among Milley RICE the wid. (rec'd Solomon, Tignor, Hannah, Fanney & child Tom, Masse, Alice, Darkey); Isaac HAYNIE (rec'd Charles for his son Isaac HAYNIE), Edward HUMPHLETT (rec'd Argyle), John RICE (rec'd Nancy), Betsy GEORGE (rec'd Dolley); second div. among the heirs: Isaac HAYNIE for his son (rec'd Simon & Siner), Joseph RICE (rec'd Daniel & Siller), Edward HUMPHLETT (rec'd Molley & James), Betsy GEORGE (rec'd Rachal & Jere), John RICE (rec'd Lucy, Polley & Sarah). (NC RB 20:121)

[Isaac RICE, wid., mar. Milley BURRASS, wid., NC, bond 15 Mar 1792 (MLBNC:86); in his will (NC 30 Nov 1799-14 Dec 1813), Isaac RICE of SSP named his wife Milley, his sons Joseph & John, and his daus. Judith CORBELL, Winnifred HAYNIE and Betty GEORGE (NC RB 19:463); Judith RICE mar. Rich. S. CORBELL, wid., NC, bond 8 Jul 1790; Winefred RICE mar. Isaac HAYNIE as his first wife, NC, bond 25 Jul 1795; Eliz. RICE mar. Balah or Balam GEORGE, NC, bond 13 Jun 1793 (MWO:88, 145, 173); Edward HUMPHLETT seems to have mar. Judith (RICE) CORBELL as her 2nd husband, NC, bond 21 Sep 1803 (MLBNC:58)]

RICE, Isaac; PO 14 Dec 1813; 8 May 1815

NC; INV, [m]; includes Negroes Daniel, Charles, Solomon, Simon, Argyle, Tignor, Jery, Siner, Sarah, Siller, Fanny & child Thomas, Lucy, Hannah, Nancy, Dolley, Rachel, Molley, Darky, Massa, James, girls Alice & Polly. (NC RB 20:123)

RICE, James; 22 Apr 1817; 23 Jun 1817

WC; WILL; Negro boy Henry to son John Tayloe RICE; Negro Polly to son Steptoe Tayloe RICE; Negro girl Elizabeth to dau. Mary Tayloe RICE; Negroes Esther, Dennis, Toney & Charlotte that came to me by their mother to be eq. div. between sons John & Steptoe & dau. Mary; Negroes Frankey, Bill, Sam, John, Lucy, Nanney & Prue (these being the Negroes come to me by their mother) to sons Thomas & Janus RICE and daus. Sally ROBINSON & Jemima RICE; land & houses to be rented out and the money arising therefrom by applied to the support and education of my three youngest children John Tayloe RICE, Steptoe Tayloe RICE, & Mary Tayloe RICE (all under 21); I give to my sons John Tayloe RICE & Steptoe Tayloe RICE that part of my land on which the store house stands, the line to begin at the fork of the road at the store house and running along the road leading to Mechodock Neck to William [PALMER's] line then along [PALMER's] line to the road to THOMPSON's line then up the road to the beginning; $15 a year to my nephew Richard SPURLING; if George ROBINSON who mar. my dau. Sally does not give up the Negro Anne that I loaned him then dau. Sally is not to have any part of my est; son Thomas RICE & friend Thomas STOWERS and Solomon REDMAN exors; WITS: Coleman STOWERS, Chas. C. RICE, Solomon REDMAN, Isaac A. NEWTON. (WC DW 23:282)

[James RICE mar. Margaret BROWN, WC, bond 1 Jan 1789 (MLBWC:58); Jemima RICE orphan of Jas. RICE chose Geo. GLASCOCK as her gdn., 27 Oct 1817 (WC OB 1814-18:345); Jas. RICE orphan of Jas. RICE chose Geo. ROBINSON as his gdn. and ROBINSON was aptd. gdn. to Mary RICE also an orphan of Jas.; Thos. RICE aptd. gdn. to Jn. T. RICE and Steptoe T. RICE orphans of Jas. RICE, 24 Nov 1817 (WC OB 1814-18:356)]

RICE, James; T 7 Nov 1817; 27 May 1822. WC; INV, $1726.66. (WC RI 11:178)

RICE, John Sr.; T 16 Feb 1816; 8 Apr 1816
NC; INV, [m]; div. of est. PO 13 Feb 1815 made at the house of William WALKER the admr.; balance of $529.74 div. among Joseph BOOTH gdn. to William, Hiram & Walter BOOTH and as gdn. to Harriett BOOTH. (NC RB 20:413, 419)
[In his will (NC 8 Jan 1815-13 Feb 1815), John RICE Sr. named his wife Hannah, his son George, his dau. Nancy WALKER, and his grchil. Wm. BOOTH, Hiram BOOTH, Walter BOOTH and Hariot BOOTH (NC RB 19:621)l Sally RICE mar. Jos. BOOTH, NC, bond 26 Dec 1803; Nancy RICE mar. Wm. WALKER, NC, bond 25 Jul 1797(MLBNC:11, 105)]

RICE, Milly; 27 Jun 1818; 9 Nov 1818
NC; WILL; grchild Jesse BURRIS son of my son Jesse BURRIS; son William BURRIS; [no ex. named]; WITS: Wm. GORDON, Eliza H. GORDON. (NC RB 21:527)
[Milly BURRIS was a wid. when she mar. Isaac RICE (*see above*) in NC, bond 15 Mar 1792 (MLBNC:86)]

RICE, Peter C.; 28 Mar 1818; 14 Dec 1818
NC; WILL; all lands to be sold; rest of est. to wife during her life and she is to give sons as they respectively reach lawful age a Negro boy; daus. to receive a [Negro] girl; my watch to the Rev. Samuel L. STRAUGHAN; my shaving case to Richard CLAUGHTON; Richard CLAUGHTON & William ROUTT exors; WITS: Wm. WALKER, Wm. FRENCH Sr., Rich. ROUTT [admon. of est. with the will annexed granted Walter RICE, 9 Jun 1828]. (NC RB 21:545)

RICE, Peter C.; T 29 Dec 1818; 8 Feb 1819
NC; INV, [m]; includes the following Negroes: old women Chloe, Dinah, & Letty; Rose & child Felicia, Peter, Moses, girl Matilda, Cordelia, boys Corbell, Henry & James; girl Janetta (small), Stephen (small), boy William. (NC RB 21:585)

RICE, Richard; 31 Jan 1795; 2 Apr 1799
NFP, RC; WILL; to my son Thomas SHERLY born before wedlock my land in NC formerly belonged to Robert SIBBLES; should son Thomas die without heir his part of my est. to his sis. Anna Rust SHERLY being born before wedlock; to my son Richard RICE land where I now live; if son Richard should die without heir his part of my est. to be eq. div. between his sisters Judah & Sally; whole est. to be kept together until son Richard RICE comes of age; remaining est. to be eq. div. between William, Darcus, Winney Fred RICE, Thomas & Anna R. SHERLEY being born before wedlock, Richard, Judah & Salley RICE; Anna R. SHERLEY to have Sharlot and Judah to have Patt and Salley to have Fanny; William FORESTER, Thomas SHERLEY & Richard RICE exors; [no wits]. (NC DCO:353)
[Rich. RICE mar. (as his 2nd wife ?) Judith SHIRLEY c. 1776 (MWO:296); Sarah "Sally" RICE mar. Jn. MALEY, NC, bond 23 Dec 1799 (MLBNC:72, NC RB 18:6)]

RICE, Richard; PO 4 Apr 1799; 2 Sep 1799

[RC]; APP; includes Negroes: Lette, Sharlot, Sam, Patt, Fanne, George, Easter, Mime, Ben (a charge). (NC DCO:357)

RICE, Richard; PO 10 Jun 1799; 9 Sep 1799
NC; DIV of pers. est. of Richard RICE dec'd acc. to will & div. of land between William RICE (rec'd 70 ac. on main road adj. John JONES), Isaac CALTON who mar. one of the heirs of sd. dec'd (rec'd 70 ac), Richard RICE (rec'd land adj Wm. HEADLEY), Sally RICE and Judah RICE (rec'd land adj Sam. HUDSON); div. was contested by Thomas SHEARLY & Ann EFFORD and supported by William RICE; court ord. the report to be recorded. (NC RB 16:7)
[Ann EFFORD is Anna Rust (SHEARLY) RICE who mar. Wm. EFFORD, RC, bond 1 Apr 1795 (MWO:123)]

RICE, Richard; PO 10 Jun 1799; 13 Jun 1808
NC; DIV of pers. est. among William RICE (rec'd Negro Sam), Thomas RICE (rec'd George), Isaac CARLTON (rec'd [Jeke] & child), Richard RICE (rec'd Easter), [Henry] HEFFORD (rec'd Sharlott), Sally RICE (rec'd Fanny), Judith RICE (rec'd Patt). (NC RB 17:623)

RICE, Sarah; T 22 Nov 1817; 18 Aug 1818. NC, INV, [m]. (NC RB 21:466)

RICE, Sarah Ann; 19 Feb 1814; 18 Nov 1817
SSP, NC; WILL; to my nephew William WAY $40; all lands & residue of est. to Susanna HILL; William WAY & Susanna HILL exors; WITS: Peter C. RICE, Jn. HALL, Jas. [NEALE]. (NC RB 21:282)
[Sarah Ann RICE was a dau. of Jn. RICE and sis. of Isaac, Wm., Jn., Betty and Sarah Anne RICE and Winnifred WAY, Anne LUTTRELL and Susanna HILL; Wm. WAY was prob. the son of Winnifred RICE the second wife of Rich. WAY (NC RB 14:582, RB 15:20, 160, RB 20:79, 157; MWO:368)]

RICE, William; PO 11 Jun [1792], T 4 Jul 1792; 8 Oct 1792
NC; DIV of the estates of Sarah & Lucy RICE orphans of William RICE between them; Sarah received Negroes Winny, Fanny & child John, Simon & Rody; Lucy received Letty, George, James & Charles; Thomas WALKER was their gdn. (NC GA 1788-1824:70)

RICHARDS, Ann; 11 Sep 1812; 3 Jan 1814.
LP, RC; WILL; children Susannah & William; grson. Rawley RICHARDS; WITS: Vincent REYNOLDS, Jas. BEALE, Hannah C. MORRISON. (RC WB 9:440)
[Ann RICHARDS was the head of a household in the 1810 census of RC. Included in her household were 1 male 16 - 20, 2 females 0 - 1, 2 females 10 - 16, 2 females 20 - 26, one female 26 - 45 and 1 slave.]

RICHARDS, Ann; PO 8 Jan 1814; 5 Dec 1815. RC, INV, $148.50. (RC WB 9:495)

RICHARDSON, Mourning; 25 Dec 1815
WC; Daniel CARMICHAEL aptd. gd. of John, William & Eliza. RICHARDSON orphans of Mourning RICHARDSON. (WC OB 1814-18:197)
[Mourning RICHARDSON mar. Byron TRIPLETT, WC, bond 12 Jul 1799 (MLBWC:58); in the case of Francis TRIPLETT, pltf., against RICHARDSON and others, Dan. CARMICHAEL was aptd. gdn. to Jn. F. RICHARDSON, Wm. F. RICHARDSON & Eliz. RICHARDSON, infants, and Wm. COGHILL was aptd. gdn. to the inf. defts. R. COGHILL & Wm. COGHILL, 22 May 1820 (WC OB 1819-23:147); Francis TRIPLETT mar. Eliza M. RICHARDSON, WC, bond Dec 1828 (MLBWC:72)]

RICHARDSON, Sarah; WC; petitioned the court for relief from her husband George RICHARDSON for ill treatement, Jan 1794 (WC CC 1794-007)

RICHARDSON, Thomas A.; T 23 Nov 1814; 11 Jul 1815. NC; INV, $117.37 1/2. (NC RB 20:153)
[The est. of Thos. A. RICHARDSON was ord. to be admin. by Edw. G. RICHARDSON, NC, 15 Nov 1814 (NC OB 1811-1816:257)]

ROBB, Frances; 7 Oct 1794; 15 Sep 1800.
CCP, LC; WILL; my plant. w/o I now live & my Negro fellow Richard commonly called Dick to grdau. Frances ROBB; grdau. extx; WITS: Eliz. CHILTON, Andrew CHILTON, Wm. EDWARDS. (LC WB 28:43)
[If this is Frances BUCKLES who mar. James ROBB, LC, bond 9 Jan 1733, then she lived a very long life (MLBLC:63)]

ROBB, John M.; PO 21 May 1822; 17 Nov 1823
LC; INV of est. in the possession of the admr. B. M. WALKER, $137.75. (LC EB 29:294)

ROBERTS, John; Oct 1791; 18 Jun 1792
LC; WILL; Negro Henry HALL to grson. Isaac PITMAN; Negro boy Baley [WILLIAMS] to grson. Cyrus ROBERTS; the use of my land and all the rest of my est. to wife Mary ROBERTS during her life or widowhood; after wife's death or marriage land to grson. John ROBERTS; rest of est. to be eq. div. among my grchil. John ROBERTS, Cyrus ROBERTS, Sally W. ROBERTS, Sukey A. ROBERTS; friend William EUSTACE & William MEREDITH exors; WITS: Jn. STEPTOE, Wm. GEORGE, Wm. [POLLARD]. [exors refused to qualify; Molly ROBERTS granted certif. of admin. with the will annexed; further proved 21 Oct 1793]. (LC WB 28:94)
[Isaac PITMAN is prob. the son of Polly ROBERTS who mar. Thos. PITMAN, LC, bond 30 Mar 1786 (MLBLC:60)]

ROBERTS, John; 20 Oct 1806
LC; John ROBERTS orphan of John ROBERTS chose William POLLARD as his gdn. (LC Orders D22 1805-08:230)

ROBERTS, John, Jr.; 20 Jul 1807. LC; d. intest.; sheriff to sell his est., 20 Jul 1807. (LC Orders D22 1805-08:370)

ROBERTS, Mary; 20 Jul 1807. LC; d. intest.; sheriff to sell her est., 20 Jul 1807. (LC Orders D22 1805-08:370)

ROBERTSON, Andrew; 22 Feb 1795; 20 Apr 1795
LC; WILL; plant. I live on containing between 500 & 500 ac. bought of John SMITHER, George HEALE & James & Agnes ROBINSON to son Robert Munroe ROBERTSON; my plant. called Crumps containing 300 ac. bought of George HEALE & Lindsey OPIE to son Thomas Glascock ROBERTSON; my lands bought of George HEALE & John GOODRIDGE on north side of [Wooddy] Swamp containing about 500 ac. to be eq. div. between two sons Duncan Forbes ROBERTSON & Andrew ROBERTSON; £300 each & a Negro to wait on them to four daus. Margaret, Ann Ball, Priscilla & Elizabeth Harriet when they marry or at age 21; all my medicine, physical, chirurgical books & instruments to be eq. div. between son George & s-i-l James EWELL Jr.; bond of Col. GORDON's, dec'd, worth £115 to son George; wife Ann ROBERTSON; wife, s-i-l James EWELL & son Munro ROBERTSON exors; WITS: Sally HARDING, Johnson RIVEER, Leroy EWELL. (LC WB 28:13)
[Dr. James EWELL, Jr. mar. Margaret ROBERTSON, LC, bond 30 Nov 1794 (MLBLC:26); Duncan Forbes ROBERTSON orphan of Andrew ROBERTSON chose Spencer BALL as his gdn., 15 Sep 1800 (LC Orders 21 1799-1801:159); Andrew ROBERTSON orphan of Andrew ROBERTSON chose Wm. MONTAGUE as his gdn., 20 Oct 1800 (LC Orders 21 1799-1801:164); *see also LC CC 1820-067*]

ROBERTSON, Andrew; T 4 Jan 179[6]; 15 Feb 1796
LC; INV, £1356.16.6; includes Negroes: Mark, David, Dick, Billy, Rawleigh, James, Lewis, Solomon, Moses, [?], Burges, Isaac, Aaron, Letty, Sue, Winney, Tab, Judy, Betty, Alice, Esther, Polly, [Nan], [Dina], Charlotte, Clairy. (LC EB 24:1)

ROBINSON, George; 20 Dec 1801; 22 Mar 1802.
WP, WC; WILL; all est. to son George; neighbor John PAYNE exor; WITS: Jas. MUSE, Wm. STONE. (WC DW 20:336)

ROBINSON, James; T 27 Dec 1804; 28 Oct 1805
WC; INV, £411.17.0; includes Negroes: Sarah, Lettice & child George, Siller & young child, boys Spencer & Fielding. (WC RI 8:585)

ROBINSON, James; 26 Nov 1821
WC; Solomon REDMAN aptd. gdn. to Mary, Susan & Fanny ROBINSON orphans of James ROBINSON. (WC OB 1819-23:334)
[This may be the James ROBINSON who mar. Sally A. CRENSHAW, dau. of David CRENSHAW, WC, shortly after 27 Dec 1812 (MLBWC:59); on the mot. of Ethelwald SANFORD & Sally his wife, ord. that Master Commissioner GRAHAM settle the gdnship. of Sol. REDMAN with the sd. Sally ROBINSON, 23 Jun 1823 (WC OB 1819-23:573)]

ROBINSON, Jeremiah; PO 14 May 1822, T 2 Aug 1822; 9 Sep 1822
NC; Samuel WILDY, Wade G. BEATLEY & Jane his wife and Sally and Winney WILDY infants under 21 by Samuel WILDY their gdn. & next friend complts against Betsy & John ROBINSON infants under 21 defts; James ROBINSON apptd special gdn. to the defts; commissioners & surveyor apptd to lay off and div. lands belonging to William WILDY & Jeremiah ROBINSON in 7 eq. parts and allot to the defts 3 parts out of which to assign to Sally ROBINSON wid. of Jeremiah ROBINSON dec'd her dower; est. was div. among: James ROBINSON gdn. to John ROBINSON ($178.30 5/9), Samuel WILDY gdn. to Sally & Winnefred WILDY ($178.30 2/9), Samuel WILDY in part ($89.15 1/2) and Wadey G. BEETLY in right of his wife ($89.15 1/2); each legal rep. to receive $89.15. (NC RB 23:218)
[Jeremiah ROBINSON d. intest. leaving a wid. Sally and two children Betsy and Jn. (NC CC 1822-008); *see also William WILDY below*]

ROBINSON, John; 16 Sep 1818; 9 Nov 1818
NC; WILL; to my mother-in-law all which may be [*1 wd unclear*] from my father's est; all wearing apparel to William FORBUSH; [no ex. named]; WITS: Wm. KIRKHAM, Thos. FORBUSH. (NC RB 21:523)

ROBINSON, John; PO [4] May 1818; 12 Jun 1820. NC; INV, [m]; includes 1 Negro boy. (NC RB 22:352)

ROBINSON, Solomon; 6 Jun 1799; 26 Aug 1799
WC; WILL; daus. Anne HUTT, Keziah STOWERS, Molly McCLANAHAM, Hannah MOXLEY; son Solomon; dau. Fanny REDMAN; son James; wife Franky; land to be div. between sons; exors. wife and friends Wm. HUTT, Thos. STOWERS, Wm. EDWARDS; WITS: Wm. HUTT, Geo. THOMSON, Jn. McCLANAHAN, Wm. EDWARDS. (WC DW 20:52)
[Ann ROBINSON mar. Gerard HUTT, WC, bond 16 Jan 1787 (MWO:195; in MLBWC:32, the groom's name is given as "HULL" but it is certainly "HUTT"); Keziah ROBINSON mar. Thos. STOWERS, WC, bond 18 Jul 1793; Hannah ROBINSON mar. Jeremiah MOXLEY, WC, bond 23 May 1796; Frances ROBINSON mar. Solomon REDMAN, WC, bond 11 May 1799; a Solomon ROBINSON mar. Frances REDMAN, WC, bond 13 Mar 1797 (MLBWC:48, 57, 68); Solomon ROBINSON aptd. gdn. of Jas. ROBINSON

orphan of Solomon ROBINSON, 26 Aug 1799 (WC Orders 1799-1801:103); Solomon REDMAN aptd. gdn. of Sally ROBINSON orphan of Solomon ROBINSON, 22 Dec 1800 (WC Orders 1799-1801:395); Molly ROBINSON and her husband Jn. McCLANAHAN reportedly moved to Georgia or Carolina (WC CC 1807-002); a Jn. McCLANAHAN was the head of a household in Greenville Co., South Carolina in the 1810 census.]

ROBINSON, Solomon; PO Aug 1799; 28 Apr 1800. WC; INV; $6203.37. (WC RI 8:46)

ROBINSON, Solomon; 15 Jan 1804; 26 Mar 1804.
CP, WC; WILL; wife Ursula (Ursley) P. Negroes Roger, Sinah & Peter; son John James ROBINSON Negroes Ned & Sam & 2/3's of land on Nomony Creek; dau. Nancy Spence ROBINSON other 1/3 of land on Nomony Creek; wife, Samuel TEMPLEMAN, John LYALL & Thomas HUTT exors; WITS: Wm. PORTER Jr., Jn. LYELL, Thomas HUTT. (WC DW 21:13)
[Jas. ROBINSON orphan of Solomon chose Solomon REDMAN as his gdn., WC 26 Mar 1804 (WC Orders 1804-07:41); Ursula P. ROBINSON was aptd. gdn. to Jn. Jas. ROBINSON and Nancy Spence ROBINSON orphans of Sol. ROBINSON WC 24 Jan 1806 (WC Orders 1804-07:335); the acct. of the gdnship. of Thos. STOWERS with his wards Nancy & Jn. ROBINSON orphans of Solomon ROBINSON returned, 26 May 1823 (WC OB 1819-23:558)]

ROBINSON, Solomon; PO 28 Apr 1806; 23 Jun 1806.
WC; INV; includes Negroes Nedd, Roger, Sam, Dinah & her child Peter, boy Tom. (WC RI 8:618)

ROBINSON, William; PO 26 Jan 1807, T 20 Feb 1807; 24 Aug 1807
WC; INV, £206.6.6; includes Negroes Judy, boy Meredith, girls Heby & Charlotte, infant Elliott. (WC RI 9:22)
[This may be the Wm. ROBINSON who mar. Sally McKINNEY, WC, bond 13 Mar 1802 (MLBWC:59); Gerrard McKINNEY, who was sec. for the above mar. bond, and Armstrong McKINNEY were children of Gerrard McKINNEY who d. in WC 1784; they had a sis. named Sarah (WC DW 16:249, DW 17:23); Armstrong McKINNEY aptd. gdn. of Chas. & Thos. ROBINSON orphans of Wm. ROBINSON, 27 May 1812 (WC Orders 1810-13:247)]

ROCK, Francis; PO 19 Jun 1797; 21 Sep 1801
LC; DIV of est. among: Mrs. Judith ROCK, John ROCK, Charles ROCK, Alexander ROCK, William ROCK, Thomas ROCK, Polly ROCK; each distributee rec'd £9. (LC EB 24:160)
[Francis ROCK, son of Constantine ROCK, mar. Judith DODSON around 1773; he may have had another child, Winifred, born around 1788, who mar. Wm. BARECROFT (MLBNC:5)]

ROGERS, Ann; 1 Sep 1817; 15 Jun 1818
LC; WILL; whole est. to son William H. ROGERS; also any dividend & proportion that may fall to my share in the unsettled estates of my two dec'd bros. Henry TAPSCOTT & Martin TAPSCOTT; some years ago in the lifetime of my dec'd dau. Nancy ROGERS I gave to my children a Negro man Daniel to be sold & div. among them, but sd. dau. Nancy died soon after & before such division; whole sum to son William H. ROGERS; [no ex. named]; WITS: C. TAPSCOTT, Wm. S. DOGGETT; COD dtd. 1 Sep 1817: half only of what I may receive of Henry & Martin TAPSCOTT's est. I give to my son William H. ROGERS; the other half to be eq. div. by giving the half of sd. balance it being a fourth of the whole to my dau. Hannah

CHILTON & the other fourth to be div. between the children of my dec'd dau. Peggy MYERS. (LC WB 28:188)
[This is Ann TAPSCOTT dau. of Henry TAPSCOTT (d. LC 1781) who mar. Charles ROGERS, LC, bef. 15 Apr 1777 (MWO:302, *see below*); Hannah ROGERS mar. Merryman CHILTON, LC, bond 8 Feb 1805; Peggy ROGERS mar. Thos. MYERS, LC, bond 23 Feb 1796 (MLBLC:13, 54)]

ROGERS, Charles; PO 18 Sep 1797, T 13 Oct 1797; 16 Oct 1797
LC; INV, £189.1.9; includes Negroes Emanuel, Ned, Winny. (LC EB 24:67)

ROGERS, Charles; PO 21 Nov 1814, T 8 Jan 1815; 20 Feb 1815
LC; DIV of Negroes among: Thomas MYERS, Merryman CHILTON, William A. ROGERS. (LC EB 27:194a)

ROGERS, Charley; PO 21 Dec 1818, T 4 Jan 1818; 15 Feb 1819
LC; INV & DIV of slaves (exclusive of those slaves that were given up in the lifetime of Ann ROGERS dec'd), div. was made among William H. ROGERS, Merryman CHILTON who mar. Hannah ROGERS & Thomas MYERS who mar. Peggy ROGERS made 8 Jan 1815; div. of Nancy ROGERS dec'd part of her dec'd father's est; slaves of Nancy ROGERS allotted to John ROGERS & Charles ROGERS sons of Charles ROGERS dec'd the Younger. (LC EB 27:460)
[*See also LC CC 1801-002*]

ROGERS, Edward; PO 11 Mar 1816; 13 May 1816
NC; allotted to William BRIDGEMAN & wife Sally her dower in the est. of her late husband Edward ROGERS; included 27 2/3 ac. tract of land adj. John HULL's orphans, land that Spencer THOMAS leased of Edward ROGERS, James SMITH, and Hull's Creek and 4 ac. of woodland. (NC RB 20:443)
[Edw. ROGERS mar. Sally BALL, ward of Rich. BALL, NC, bond 5 Jun 1804 (MLBNC:89); Wm. BRIDGEMAN mar. Sally ROGERS, wid., NC, bond 13 Sep 1813 (MLBNC:12; NC RB 20:101); Harriet ROGERS orphan of Edw. ROGERS chose Wm. BRIDGMAN as her gdn., and BRIDGMAN is aptd. gdn. of Betsy ROGERS and Lucretia ROGERS orphans of Edw. ROGERS, NC 9 Jun 1823 (NC OB 1820-25:297); Eliz. ROGERS chose Elisha FALLIN as her gdn. and the sd. FALLIN is aptd. gdn. of Lucretia ROGERS orphans of Edw. ROGERS, NC 9 Aug 1824 (NC OB 1820-25:403)]

ROGERS, Jane; PO 22 Nov 1795; 17 Jun 1799
LC; INV, £40; includes Negro Dick. (LC EB 24:95)
[Chancery suit: Jn. ROGERS, Thos. MYERS & Peggy his wife, Hannah ROGERS, Nancy ROGERS and Wm. H. ROGERS, infants under 21 by Ann ROGERS their next friend, complts. against Wm. CHOWNING & Jn. CHOWNING admrs. of Jane ROGERS, ord. that the complts. recover of the defs. the Negro slave Dick, 22 Aug 1799 (LC Orders (21) 1799-1801:35, 288); Thos. MYERS mar. Peggy ROGERS, LC, bond 23 Feb 1796 (MLBLC:54)]

ROGERS, John (Capt.); T 16 Dec 1800; 8 Jun 1801
NC; INV, [m]; includes Negroes David, Stephen, Solomon, Rose, boy George, William TOMBSY and several named books. (NC RB 16:244)
[Thos. S. ROGERS orphan of Jn. ROGERS chose Jn. ROGERS as his gdn., 20 Jan 1806 (LC Orders D22 1805-08:108), *NB: not certain that Thos. S. is the son of this Jn. ROGERS*]

ROGERS, William; [m]; 22 May 1815. WC; INV, $209.09. (WC RI 9:441)
[Eliz. ROGERS, wid., and Wm. ROGERS, son, relinquish right of admin. on est. of Wm. ROGERS, dec'd, 25 Apr 1814 (WC OB 1814-18:49)]

ROSE, John; 18 Mar 1802; 25 Apr 1803

WC; WILL; all est. to wife during her widowhood; bro. Alexander & sis. have deeded their parts of land inherited from bro. Dr. Robert ROSE in order to sell the land; req. that land be sold and money div. among bro. and 2 sisters; dau. Mildred & son [Charles] Walter (both under 21); dau. to have Gallasway, Hannah, Rachel, Lucy, Charity; s-i-l William ROBINSON (under age) tracts called Tracy & Turnbull's as dower lands for his mother for her life 87 ac. on lower side of Mattox [Creek] and on the White Oak Swamp; son Walter land w/o I now live & all the slaves; 2 daus-in-law Anne W. ROSE & Margaret McCARTY; 1500 ac. in Kentucky deeded to him by Burgess BALL on 8 May 1794 to be sold; wife, Dr. Henry ROSE, William ROBINSON and friend Lawrence BERRY of King Geo. [Co.] to be exors; no wits. (WC DW 20:448)

[Jn., Alexander, and Dr. Robt. ROSE were sons of Chas. ROSE (d. WC 1761) (WC DW 14:26); Dr. Robt. ROSE served as a surgeon of the Continental Line for 8 years during the Revolutionary War; he d. in WC in 1793 unmarried leaving two bros. and two sisters: Jn., Alexander, Catherine ROSE, and Molly HODGE (prob the wife of Thos. HODGE) (VS1776 III:1139, MWO:183); Hen. ROSE, Wm. ROBINSON & Laurence BERRY aptd. gdns. to Mildred ROSE and Chas. [W.] ROSE, orphans of Jn. ROSE, WC, 26 Apr 1803 (WC Orders 1801-04:368); Miller:169 locates White Oak Swamp in WC between Colonial Beach and Oak Grove poss. on Monroe Creek.]

ROUT, Sarah; 19 Apr 1798; 15 Sep 1800.

CCP, LC; WILL; one shilling to son Lewis LAMPKIN; Negro man Peter & all the remainder of est. to dau. Patty ROUT; James ROBB ex; WITS: Jas. BALL, Geo. [STAMPER], Sinah LEWIS. (LC WB 28:44)

ROY, John C.; 5 Jun 1820

RC; Kemp EVANS aptd. gdn. of John W. ROY and Ann ROY orphans of John C. ROY. (RC OB 25:33)

[This is John Corrie ROY of King & Queen Co. who mar. Eliz. Corrie WILLIAMS, dau. of Thaddeus & Catharine WILLIAMS, RC, bond 29 Nov 1804 (MRC:174); Kemp EVANS & Catharine his wife in chancery vs. Jn. W. ROY & Ann ROY, infants, to div. the dower lands & Negroes of which the late Catharine WILLIAMS, wid. of Thaddeus WILLIAMS, died seized into two eq. parts one to EVANS and the other to Jn. & Ann ROY, 3 Jul 1820 (RC OB 25:36); Kemp EVANS mar. Catharine LAWSON (dau. of Thaddeus & Catharine WILLIAMS & wid. of Dan. LAWSON Jr), RC, bond 5 Jan 1815 (MRC:66, 115)]

RUAIK, Samuel; 20 Nov 1826

LC; on the mot. of Lawson HATHAWAY ord. that the est. of Samuel RUAIK be committed to the hands of Daniel MITCHELL, sheriff of this county, who is to dispose thereof. (LC OB 26:216)

RUST, Elizabeth; PO Nov 1804, T 4 Feb 1807; 26 Oct 1807

WC; DIV of proceeds of sale of slaves (Judah, Bob & Phillis) of Elizabeth RUST between the brothers & sisters of Elizabeth RUST: Fanny RUST, John RUST, Sally RUST, Peter RUST, James RUST & Susanna RUST; proceeds were received by Stephen BAILEY admr. of James RUST Jr. & John RUST and George RUST as gdn. of Peter RUST, Susanna RUST & Fanny RUST and as agent for Sally RUST. (WC RI 9:31)

RUST, Elizabeth H.; 15 Nov 1818; 21 Dec 1818

LC; WILL; ex. to pay $400 to Mrs. Olivia DOWNMAN as a small token of my sincere love & gratitude for the parental like love & affection which she has manifested towards me; if she dies before the payment can be made, money to be eq. div. among her heirs; Miss Sarah DOWNMAN of Morattico to be paid $200 as a small token of my love & gratitude for the sister like attention she has always paid me; all the rest of my est. to my bro. Benjamin D. RUST & he to be ex; WITS: Wm. Lee BALL, Robt. WOODDY, J[as.] [K.] BALL. (LC WB 28:191)

RUST, Elizabeth H.; T 8 Jun 1821; 18 Jun 1821. LC; INV; no est. was presented. (LC EB 29:109)

RUST, George; [m]; 28 Apr 1800
WC; WILL; my part of my father's est. to bro. John RUST; sis. Fanny; bro. Peter; sisters Betsy & Sally; [no exors. or wits; pres in court by Jn. Jas. MAUND]. (WC DW 20:123)
[Fanny, Sally, Peter and Susanna RUST infants under 21 by Jn. RUST their gdn. sued Stephen BAILEY, admr. with the will annexed, of Geo. RUST to divide his est; Negro Judy who was devised to Betsy RUST, sis. of the pltfs., by Geo. RUST was to be sold and the proceeds div. eq. among Fanny, Jn., Sally, Peter, Jas., and Susanna RUST, WC 26 Nov 1804 (WC Orders 1804-07:169, WC CC 1804-014)]

RUST, George; 23 Nov 1818
WC; On the mot. of Elis HUDNAL who mar. Sally RUST orphan of Geo. RUST, ord. that Thos. STOWERS & Jas. COX who rep. the est. of Col. Geo. GARNER dec'd do state and settle an acct. of the sd. GARNER's gdnship of Sam., Geo., Edw. & Sally RUST orphans of Geo. RUST. (WC OB 1814-18:420)
[Ellis HUDNALL mar. Saley RUST, NC, bond 6 Feb 1816 (MLBNC:55)]

RUST, George N.; T 14 Jun 1800; 26 Jan 1801
WC; INV at the Island, RC; £253.12.0; includes Negroes Judy, Dick, Tom. (WC RI 8:112)

RUST, George N.; PO Aug 1804, T 31 Oct 1801; 24 Jun 1804
WC; INV, £303.4.0; includes Negroes Tom, Dick (a legacy to Sally RUST), Tom (a legacy to Eliza alias Betsey RUST), Negroes allotted to Geo. N. RUST out of his father's est. which he left as legacies to John RUST & Fanny RUST: James & George. (WC RI 8:551)

RUST, James; T 14 Jun 1800; 23 feb 1801
WC; INV at the Island, RC; £425.1.0; includes Negroes James, Will, [Aca], Hannah, Easter, Mary; second inv. taken 7 Jun 1800, £481.0.6; includes Negroes Tom, Jane, Lett, Fillace, Bob, George, Sall, Charlotte, Sophia, Jude. (WC RI 8:113)

RUST, James; T 31 Oct 1804; 24 Jun 1804
WC; INV & DIV, £913.1.8; includes Negroes James, Bill, [Akey], Bob, Sally, Moll, George, Jude, Frank, Charlotte, Hannah, Lett, Filla[?], Tom; to be div. into 7 parts: George N. RUST, Eliza RUST, Sally RUST. Peter RUST, Sukey RUST & Fanny RUST. (WC RI 8:546)

RUST, Jeremiah; PO Oct 1801, T 30 Dec 1801; 28 Feb 1804
WC; DIV of Negroes; found that the greater part of the Negroes belonging to the sd. est. are now in Frederick Co; list of Negroes in WC: George, Rose, Sall (her child), Joe (her child), Daniel (her child), Felicia & Drusilla (twins, her children); worth £950; DIV among Thomas RUST (George, Harry, Sall, Little Abraham), Sally RUST (Big Abraham, Big Daniel, Lucy & Sam her child), Molly RUST alias MILLER (Jacob, Baker, Beck, Little Peg) & Betsey RUST (Anthony, Joe, Little Daniel, Rose, Felix, Drucilla). (WC RI 8:373)
[Jos. MILLER mar. Mary RUST a dau. of Jeremiah RUST, WC, 28 Dec 1801 (WC Orders 1801-04:195)]

RUST, John; PO Feb 1805, T 2 Mar 1805; [26 Aug 1805]

WC; INV, £240.18.8; includes Negroes [Akey], James, Frank, Fillace. (WC RI 8:566)

RUST, Peter; T 25 Oct 1810; 7 Jan 1811. RC; INV, [m]. (RC WB 9:379)
[This is prob. Peter RUST who mar. Eliz. Ball DOWNMAN, dau. of Geo. DOWNMAN, WC, bond 28 Dec 1793 and was the father of Eliz. H. and Benj. D. RUST (MWO:306; RC DB 20:337; NC RB 21:444)

RUST, William L.; 4 May 1819
RC; Mary RUST was aptd. gdn. to Henry T. RUST orphan of William L. RUST. (RC OB 24:335)
[This may be the Wm. RUST who mar. Mary TILLERY, RC, bond 18 Jan 1812 (MRC:175)]

RUST, Youel; T 13 Apr 1801; 28 May 1804
WC; INV, £1066.8.0; includes Negroes Andrew, Harry, Spencer, Reubin, Judy, George, Phillice, Doll, Nelly, Hannah, Winney, Jenny, Liddy, Lithe. (WC RI 8:504)
[Eliz. RUST qualified as admx. of Youel RUST, WC, 23 Mar 1801 (WC Orders 1801-04:26); a suit to div. the est. of Youel RUST among the wid. Elizabeth and children Jane, Polly, Merideth M. HACKNEY and wife Eliz., Sam. RUST and Wm. RUST was filed in WC, 23 Oct 1804 (WC Orders 1804-07:108)]

RYALS, James; [m]; 4 Jun 1804. RC; INV. (RC WB 9:235)

SALLARD, Simon; T 3 Feb 1803; 1 Jun 1807
RC; DIV of slaves between Benjamin BRANHAM & Capt. Samuel W. HIPKINS. (RC AB 3:190)
[Capt. Sam. William HIPKINS mar. Jane SALLARD, prob. a dau. of Simon SALLARD, RC, bond 25 Jul 1796 (MWO:182)]

SAMPSON, George; 18 Jan 1798; 16 Apr 1798
LC; WILL; all the money that I put in trade with him to my bro. Joseph SAMPSON; sis. Nancy SAMPSON; bro. John SAMPSON; sis. Ann SULLIVAN; bro. Joseph SAMPSON ex; WITS: Jn. CLUTTON, Geo. CLUTTON, Robt. FORSTER. (LC WB 28:28)
[Ann SULLIVAN was a dau. of Jos. SAMPSON of WicP (d. NC 1782); she had mar. [fnu] SULLIVAN bef 7 Oct 1782 (MWO:337)]

SAMPSON, George; PO Apr 1798; T 11 Sep 1798; 17 Jun 1799. LC; INV, $246.99. (LC EB 24:95)

SAMPSON, George; [14] Nov 1821; 13 May 1822
WicP, NC; WILL; plant. where I now reside containing 122 ac. to my dau. Judith W. SAMPSON; land I purchased of Walter [NUTT] containing 200 ac. to son Thornton SAMPSON; Negro man Cyrus to dau. Elizabeth SAMPSON; Negro man Isaac to dau. Lucy SAMPSON; Negro boy Warner left in the hands of son Thomas for dau. Nancy POPE; son Thornton & friend William BASYE exors; WITS: Thos. S. SYDNOR, Augustine PITMAN, Jn. BOOTH. (NC RB 23:152)
[Nancy SAMPSON mar. Thos. POPE, NC, bond 22 Dec 1817(MLBNC:83)]

SAMPSON, George; PO 11 Nov 1822, T 20 Dec 1822; 10 Nov 1823
NC; INV, $1500.25; includes Negroes Isaac, Cyrus, Winney, boy James. (NC RB 23:379)

SAMPSON, John; 19 Jun 1809
LC; Overseers of the Poor to bind out William SAMPSON orphan of John SAMPSON to Burgess S. [MOORE]. (LC Order Book 23A (Minutes) 1808-11:(unpaged)

SAMPSON, Joseph; 25 Apr 1800; 21 Feb 1803

LC; WILL; all est. to wife Nancy SAMPSON; at wife's death or remarriage est. to be eq. div. between children: Martin, Polly, Joseph, Nancy, Hiram & George SAMPSON; wife Nancy & friends John & Benjamin [LANSDELL] exors; WITS: Wm. B. BEANE, Jesse LANSDELL, Lucy SWANSON; LC WB 28:66)

[Jos. SAMPSON prob. mar. Nancy BEAN, dau. of Peter BEAN (d. NC, 1787), bef. 7 Jun 1785 (MWO:308)]

SAMPSON, Joseph; PO 21 Feb 1803; 18 Apr 1803. LC; INV,£786.19.[?]. (LC EB 24:234)

SANDERS (SAUNDERS), Hundley; PO 6 Jan 1817, T 7 Jan 1817; 7 Aug 1820 RC; DIV of Negroes among Ruth SAUNDERS (the wid.), Edward SAUNDERS (James), Elisabeth SAUNDERS (Ralph), William SAUNDERS (Squire), Henry SAUNDERS (Easter), Robert SCOTT (Dafney), Thomas SAUNDERS (Winney), Richard S. SAUNDERS (Sam). (RC AB 3:688)

[Robt. SCOTT mar. Catherine SAUNDERS, dau. of Hundley SAUNDERS, RC, bond 7 Feb 1815 (MRC:182); Ruth SAUNDERS was appt. gdn. to Eliz. & Harry SAUNDERS, orphans of Hundley and Thos. SAUNDERS & Edw. SAUNDERS, also orphans of Hundley, chose Wm. SAUNDERS as their gdn., 6 Jan 1817 (RC OB 24:62); Hen. SAUNDERS orphan of Hundley SAUNDERS chose Wm. SAUNDERS as his gdn. and sd. William is aptd. gdn. of Eliz. SAUNDERS, 6 Nov 1820 (RC OB 25:75); Edw. SAUNDERS orphan of Hundley SAUNDERS chose Robt. SCOTT as his gdn., 7 May 1821 (RC OB 25:120); the lands of Hundley SAUNDERS were div. among Ruth SAUNDERS, the wid., Robert SCOTT & Catherine his wife, Wm. SAUNDERS, Rich. SAUNDERS, Thos. SAUNDERS, Edw. SAUNDERS, Hen. SAUNDERS, & Betsy SAUNDERS (RC OB 24:265-266); Robt. SCOTT mar. Catherine SAUNDERS dau. of Hundley, RC bond 7 Feb 1815 (MRC:182); Eliz. SAUNDERS orphan of Hundley SAUNDERS chose Thos. SAUNDERS as her gdn, 7 Mar 1825 (RC OB 26:284)]

SANDERS, William; PO 6 Nov 1820; 6 Aug 1821. RC; INV, $91.45. (RC WB 9:709)

SANDERS, William Sr.; 1 Nov 1816; 6 Nov 1820

LP, RC; WILL; plant. that was my father's to son Billy SANDERS and my Negro man Moses after the death of my wife; wife Ann SANDERS during her natural life and no longer my Negro man Moses on condition that she renounces all claims against my est. on account of Negroes Nan & Peter one of whom is dead & the other sold; son Daniel SANDERS the plant. w/o he now lives & my Negro boy Reuben; my granddau. Susannah SANDERS; my grandchildren Richard Burges JONES, George Sanders JONES, Julily JONES, & Vincent JONES children of Vincent & Rebecca JONES; plant. called Thomases (being part of the land I purchased of James BEALE) & my Negro boy Aaron to son Allen SANDERS; land I bought of Daniel SANDERS & my Negro girl Jane; remainder of est. to be sold and proceeds eq. div. between my four sons Billy, Daniel, Allen, & James; Richard BARNES & my son Daniel exors; WITS: Abraham WHITE, Robt. JINKINS. Jas. BROWN. (RC WB 9:674)

[Daniel son of William & Ann SANDERS was born 19 Jan 1782; he died intest. on 20 May 1832 (Sanders Family Bible); he was the father of Susan (who married Samuel M. NEWMAN, RC, bond 22 Apr 1833), Dorathea L. (who married Theodorick N. BALDERSON, St. Mary's Co., Md, 12 Oct 1838), Mary C., and Charles A. SANDERS (RC Loose Papers. Box #1, CCs at

Rule); Rebecca SANDERS, dau. of Wm., mar. Vincent JONES, RC, bond 3 Jul 1797 (MRC:110)]

SANDY, Thomas; PO 23 Nov 1818; 22 Mar 1819
WC; settlement of guardianship acct. of dec'd Thomas SANDY with his children: James SANDY, Thomas SANDY, Lucinda SANDY, Henry SANDY, and John A. SANDY. (WC RI 10:361)
[Thos. SANDY aptd. gdn. of his children: Jas., Thos., Hen., Jn. A. and Lucy SANDY, 25 Nov 1810 (WC Orders 1810-13:187); David GREENLAW aptd. gdn. of Thos. SANDY orphan of Thos. SANDY, 23 Dec 1816 (WC OB 1814-18:272); ord. that Wm. GREENLAW admr. of Thos. SANDY, settle the gdnship. acct. of Thos. SANDY upon the estates of Jas., Thos., Lucinda, Hen., and Jn. SANDY children of the sd. Thos. SANDY dec'd, 27 Jan 1817 (WC OB 1814-18:275); Lucinda SANDY orphan of Thos. SANDY chose Wm. B. LEWIS as her gdn., NC, 10 Mar 1818 (NC OB 1816-20:238)]

SANFORD, Allen; 29 Dec 1800; 26 Jan 1801
WC; Nunc. WILL; SANFORD died 25 Dec 1800; he requested that Jn. SANFORD should receive £3 for his child; sworn to by Rachel WEAVER & Wm. McKINNEY; WITS: Wm. SPARK, Wm. OMOHUNDRO. (WC DW 20:178)

SANFORD, Augustine; T 15 Nov 1822; 22 Sep 1823. WC; INV. (WC RI 11:380)

SANFORD, Charles; 26 Jun 1818; 26 Oct 1818
WC; WILL; I lend to my wife Sibbella SANFORD during her widowhood the plant. I now live on and the plant. I bought of Mr. STARKS for the use of herself & my two children Fanny Fairfax SANFORD & Charles Henry SANFORD together with Negroes Nelson, Lewis, Frank, Joseph, Peter, young Susannah, [Gilmore], Arch, Griffin, old Lucy, young Lucy, old Susannah & Rachel; son William all my plant. utensils & the plant. that was MOXLEY['s]; my money to be put in bank for 10 years & the interest applied to repairing the building[s] on the three plantations; to dau. Lucy LYELL the Negroes Nel, Marcus, Patty, Betsey, Reuben & Letty; to son William the plant. that was my father;s also part of the plant. w/o I now live and the Negro Ben; friend John PAYNE & wife Sibbella SANFORD exors; in case PAYNE should die before he finishes his executorship, friend James JETT to replace him; WITS: Wm. M. WALKER, Vincent MARMADUKE. (WC DW 23:414)
[If this is the Chas. SANFORD who mar. Sabina ROSE, WC, bond 22 Sep 1800, then he must have had an earlier wife who was the mother of Lucy (MLBWC:61); Lucy SANFORD mar. Jn. LYELL, WC, bond 8 Dec 1796 (MLBWC:40); [S]ibby SANFORD aptd. gdn. to Chas. H. & Fanny Fairfax SANFORD orphans of Chas. SANFORD, 23 Nov 1818 (WC OB 1814-18:421)]

SANFORD, Charles; T 19 & 21 Jan 1819; 25 Apr 1821
WC; INV, [m]; includes Negroes Nelson, Francis, Peter, Joseph, Lucy, Susannah, Rachel, Lucy, boy Benjamin, girl Letty, boy Griffin, girl Susanna, boy Gilmore, boy Archibald. (WC RI 11:49)

SANFORD, Elijah; 22 May 1815
WC; Peggy SANFORD aptd. gdn. to Lucinda & Matilda infant orphans of Elijah SANFORD. (WC OB 1814-18:121)
[Elijah SANFORD mar. Peggy SANFORD, WC, bond 30 Aug 1811 (MLBWC:61)]

SANFORD, Eleanor; PO [1805]; 23 Oct 1815. WC; INV, £50.12.0. (WC RI 10:27)

SANFORD, George; 19 Aug 1812; 22 May 1815

CP, WC; WILL; son John SANFORD; daus. Susan SANFORD, Kitty SANFORD, Nancy THOMAS, Hannah SANFORD, Molly SANFORD, Jane SANFORD, Fanny SANFORD; grson. John SANFORD to have five years schooling; [no ex. named]; WIT: Solomon REDMAN. (WC DW 23:101)

SANFORD, Hannah; 20 Sep 1811; 27 Feb 1815
CP, WC; WILL; Isaac N. ANGEL; balance of property to nephew William L. SANFORD; [no ex. named]; WIT: Jane HARRISON. (WC DW 23:62)

SANFORD, Jemima; PO 24 Nov 1802; 22 Mar 1802
WC; INV & DIV; Negroes Henry, Jacob, Isaac, Nancy, Rachel, Jesse, Luckey worth £305.0.0 allotted as follows: John WEAVER's lot, William McKENNEY's lot, Willoughby SANFORD's lot, Allen SANFORD's est. (WC RI 8:160)
[Wm. McKENNEY mar. Caty SANFORD, WC, bond 12 Jan 1797; John WEAVER mar Penny SANFORD, WC, bond 24 Mar 1792 (MLBWC:42, 74)]

SANFORD, John; T 10 Dec 1802; 6 Oct 1803
WC; INV; £65.12.6; includes Negro Jude & 2 children to serve 4 years. (WC RI 8:363)

SANFORD, John; 23 Oct 1815
WC; Gerard SANDFORD orphan of John SANDFORD chose Samuel TEMPLEMAN as his gdn. and TEMPLEMAN is aptd. gdn. of Fanny & [Kitty] SANDFORD orphans of John. (WC OB 1814-18:186)
[Jn. SANFORD d. intest. leaving a wid. Anna and children Gerard, Fanny and Kitty (WC CC 1815-003)]

SANFORD, Patrick; children of Patrick SANFORD are: Elizabeth, Frances, Nancy, Peggy, Patrick Spence, and Samuel; Frances "Frankey" SANFORD mar. William FRANKS, WC, bond 27 Feb 1797 and Elizabeth SANFORD mar. Henry FRANKS, WC, bond 31 Jan 1787; in a deed of gift dtd 21 Oct 1789, Patrick SANFORD gave his sons Samuel and Patrick S. a tract of land named Liberty Hall (MLBWC:23, WC CC 1802-003)

SANFORD, Reuben; WC; Ann the wife of Reuben SANFORD was the wid. of (1) Jeremiah HALL and (2) John MORGAN. (WC CC 1791-007)

SANFORD, Robert; PO 28 Dec 1812; 27 Jun 1813
WC allot Susannah SANFORD her dower in the Negroes belonging to the est. & div. the residue agreeable to decree between Alawitha JETT & Robert SANFORD; Susannah received Harry, Betty, Patty, Milly, Sampson, Rose; Robert SANFORD received George Sr., Silvey, Jenney, Thomas, Mary, Lucy, Betsey, Daniel; Alawitha JETT received George Jr., Letty, Cupid, Lucy, Hannah, Peter, Harriott. (WC RI 9:374, 376a)
[Acc. to a chancery suit filed in WC in 1838, Robt. SANFORD died intest. bef. Mar 1812 leaving a wid., Susanna, and two children Robt. & Alawitha (or Alswitha); he also had a 500-ac. tract called "Walnut Farm;" Alawitha SANFORD mar. Jas. JETT (WCCP:38); a Robt. SANFORD mar. Susannah FOX, WC, bond 20 Jul 1807, but if this is the Robt. SANFORD in this record, it must have been at least a second marriage (MLBWC:62)]

SANFORD, Sabra (Mrs.); 31 Jul 1802; 6 Aug 1802
WC; nunc. WILL; James A. THOMPSON for his trouble in caring for her; remainder to her two sisters who live near Mr. Wm. PARKER. (WC DW 20:376)
[She died on the morning of 1 Aug 1802]

SANFORD, Thomas; William BUTLER was gdn. to Ursula, Patty, and Caty SANFORD orphans of Thomas SANFORD, Oct 1796 (WC CC 1797-003)

SANFORD, Thomas; T 18 Aug 1804; 27 Aug 1804. WC; INV, £16.14.9. (WC RI 8:446)

SANFORD, William; PO 14 Aug 1810; 12 Nov 1810
NC; acct. of sales of pers. est. by Royston BETTS for Thomas HURST, $5.57. (NC RB 18:491)

SANFORD, William; 25 Mar 1812
WC; Chancery suit, William SANFORD, Jeremiah SANFORD, John BULGER & Mary his wife, Daniel MARMADUKE ex. of Daniel MARMADUKE & Sarah MARMADUKE pltfs. vs. Charles SANFORD ex. of Wm. SANFORD. (WC Orders 1810-13:226, 267)
[In his will (WC 31 May 1782 - 30 Mar 1784) Wm. SANFORD names his wife Barbara, his sons Chas., Rich., Wm., & Jeremiah, and his daus. Mary BULGER and Sarah MARMADUKE (WC DW 16:212, DW 17:99); Dan. MARMADUKE mar. Sarah MINOR, wid. of Wm. MINOR, bef Dec 1773; she must have been Sarah SANFORD and mar. (1) Wm. MINOR (MWO:234); by 1814, the chancery suit was Wm. SANFORD, Jeremiah SANFORD, Thos SANFORD, Wm. SANFORD, Dan. MARMADUKE, admr. of Dan. MARMADUKE dec'd, & Sarah MARMADUKE and Jn. BULGER & Mary his wife, compl. against Chas. SANFORD, ex. of Wm. SANFORD, 28 Nov 1814 (WC OB 1814-18:84; CC 1814-004)]

SANFORD, Willoughby; 28 Apr 1800
WC; Willoughby SANFORD orphan of Willoughby SANFORD chose Thos. STOWERS as his gdn. (WC Orders 1799-1801:207)

SCATES, Bartlett; PO 6 Jun 1808; 4 Nov 1817. RC; INV, £111.16.6. (RC WB 9:582)
[A Bartlett SCATES mar. Susanna JONES, RC, bond 2 Aug 1802 (MRC:181); Jn. B. SCATES was the orphan of Bartlett SCATES, RC, 4 May 1818 (RC OB 24:205)]

SCATES, Joseph; PO 6 Jun 1814; 4 Nov 1817; RC; INV, £197.7.0. (RC WB 9:595)

SCHOFIELD, Fortunatus; 20 Feb 1804
LC; Ellen BROWN is gdn. of Alcy SCHOFIELD and William KIRK is gdn. of Lilly Green SCHOFIELD orphans of Fortunatus SCHOFIELD. (LC Orders W 1804-05:13)
[Lilly SCHOFIELD orphan of Fortunatus SCHOFIELD chose Wm. KIRK as her gdn., 18 Oct 1802 (LC Orders V 1802-03:211); chancery suit, Abraham CARTER, pltf., against Wm. KIRK gdn. to Lilly G. SCHOFIELD, Eleanor BROWN gdn. to Alice SCHOFIELD, Jacob CURRELL & Lucy his wife, Sam. ALFORD & Nancy his wife and Wm BROWN, defts., 15 Feb 1808 (LC Orders 22D 1805-08:444); Nancy, Lilly G., and Alice were daus. of Fortunatus SCHOFIELD; Lucy SCHOFIELD who mar. Jacob CURRELL, LC, bond 24 Jul 1790, and Fortunatus were grandchildren of Wm. SCHOFIELD of Amherst and Rockbridge Co.; Lilly G. SCHOFIELD mar. (1) Jos. WALKER, LC, bond 16 Nov 1807 and (2) Griffin ASHBURN, LC, bond 22 Mar 1815; Eleanor BROWN was prob. the mother of Fortunatus and Lucy (see CCs LC 1819-013 and Rockbridge Co. 1813-007; MLBLC:1, 76; MWO:96)]

SCHOFIELD, Henry; T 4 May 1815; 20 May 1816
LC; INV, [m]; includes one small Negro girl named Jenney. (LC EB 27:317)

SCHOFIELD, John; [n.d.]; 20 May 1816
LC; WILL; to the care of Thomas SCHOFIELD in case of any accident should happen me you will find in the hands of John [HUNT] by his receipts in my pocket book also in Ralph EDMONDS $100 and some odd dollars, also in my pocket book bond on Thomas SAYLER for $100 dollars with interest; also one bond [of] William POLLARD $15; you will find this in care of

Thomas CROSLEY, [Freds.] also with Capt. John WILLIAMS you will find receipt in favor of me for $500 dollars and the bonds in Isaac A. [KINGSON] in Baltimore you will receive this and divide between your children and bro. Henry and finally if my silver watch should ever reach you this is for your son John SCHOFIELD and if he should die give it to Henry SCHOFIELD the offspring ... do this as my wish; my beds you know where they at [*sic*] Mr. William KELLY's; pay the same attention and you will oblige your friend and loving brother; /s/ John SCHOFIELD. (LC WB 28:177)

SCHOFIELD, John; T 12 Apr 1817; 16 Nov 1818. LC; INV, $64. (LC EB 27:441)

SCRIMGER, Charity; T 17 May 1815; 5 Dec 1815. RC; INV, $237.72 1/2. (RC WB 9:496)

[*This is the wid. of Walter J. SCRIMGER below*]

SCRIMGER, John; PO 5 Jul 1819; 1 Oct 1821. RC; INV, $99.14 1/2.; RC WB 9:712

SCRIMGER, Walter J.; 27 Oct 1803; 2 Apr 1804

RC; WILL; wife Charity land & plant; 3 daus: Elizabeth, Catherine, & Nancy; son James (when of age); wife Charity & son William exors; WITS: Geo. PURCELL, Geo. PURCELL [sic]. (RC WB 9:233)

[Walter James SCRIMGER prob. mar. Charity BERRICK, RC, bef 18 Apr 1794; bride was prob. a dau. of Geo. BERRICK (MWO:312); the land of which Charity SCRIMGER died seized was to be div. among Thos. J. SCRIMGER, Jas. SCRIMGER, Jn. SCRIMGER (who resided out of state), Nancy PACKETT wife of Henry, Eliz. ALDERSON wife of Jn., Cath. SCRIMGER, and Wm. SCRIMGER (infant son of Wm. SCRIMGER), RC, 5 Nov 1815 (RC Orders 1814-16:50); Nancy SCRIMGER mar, Hen. PACKETT, RC, bond 7 Sep 1807 (MRC:152); Eliz. SCRIMGER mar. Jn. ALDERSON, RC, bond 26 Dec 1812 (MRC:1)]

SCRIMGER, William; T 10 Dec 1813; 4 Nov 1817. RC; INV, $330.82. (RC WB 9:582)

SCURLOCK, George; PO 3 Jun 1799; 7 Jul 1800. RC; INV, £48.18.[?]. (RC WB 9:136)

SEBREE, Henry B.; 19 Jan 1825; 21 Feb 1825

LC; WILL; land w/o I now live to son Austin SEBREE; my land on the Eastern Branch & my schooner to be sold; balance of est. after debts paid to wife Elizabeth SEBREE; Addison HALL & William GILMOUR exors; WITS: Jn. LAWRY, Jn. E. LAWRY; [COD:] son Austin to have my Negro Frank; [will finally proved by additional oath of Jasper STOTT on 21 Mar 1825]; LC WB 28:256)

[Acc. to Miller:43, there are Eastern Branches of Carter Creek, the Corrotoman River, and Morattico Creek.]

SEBREE, James; PO 13 Nov 1804, T 20 Nov 1804; 14 Jan 1805

NC; INV, £137.10.3; DIV of est. among James SEBREE the admr., William SEBREE, Capt. Joshua COCKARELL, Elizabeth BEATLEY, Nancy SEBREE, Rhoda SEBREE (each rec'd £22.18.4 1/2). (NC RB 17:242, 243)

[Jas. SEBREE mar. Eliz. LINKHORN, dau. of Wm. LINKHORN (d. NC 1770) bef. 17 Apr 1770 (MWO:313); in his will (NC 13 Jan 1785-14 Feb 1785), Jas. SEBREE named his wife. Elizabeth and dau. Chloe WHEELER; he mentions, but did not name other children (NC RB 12:396); Sally SEBREE mar. Joshua COCKRELL, poss. as his 3rd wife, NC, bond 13 Feb 1797 (MWO:81)]

SEBREE, James; PO 10 Feb 1806, T 1 Mar 1806; 14 Jul 1806

NC; settlement of James SEBREE's acct. of his; admin. of the est. of James SEBREE dec'd and div. of est. among Cloe WHEELER (legacy by will) and the legal reps: Elizabeth BEETLEY, James SEBREE, William SEBREE, Jesse

WALKER, Joshua COCKRELL, Thomas W. GOFF (each rep. rec'd £6.16.6). (NC RB 17:444)
[Chloe SEBREE mar. [fnu] WHEELER bef. 13 Jan 1785 (MWO:372); Jesse WALKER mar. Rhoda SEBREE, NC, bond 21 Dec 1805; Thos. GOFF mar. Nancy SEBRELL [sic], NC, bond 26 Jan 1805 (MLBNC:43, 104)]

SEBREE, James; PO 14 Dec 1813; 14 Mar 1814. NC; INV, [m]. (NC RB 19:529)

SEBREE, James; PO 10 Jul 1815, T 21 Aug 1815; 9 Oct 1815
NC; INV, [m]; allotted Linzey DAVIS in right of his wife Nancy who was Nancy SEBREE one third of est. including 25 ac. tract on Cupit's Creek. (NC RB 20:272, 275; OB 1811-15:348)
[Jas. SEBREE mar. Nancy WALKER, ward of Thos. BERRY, NC, bond 10 May 1802 (MLBNC:90); Linszey DAVIS, wid., Nancy SEBRELL [sic], wid., NC, bond 10 Mar 1814 (MLBNC:27); Cupid's or Cubitt Creek is located in northeast NC between Hull Neck and Mob Neck (Miller:37)]

SEBREE, John; T 15 Apr 1809; 13 Aug 1810. NC; INV, [m]. (NC RB 18:438)

SEBREE, John; PO 15 Mar 1819; 17 May 1819. LC; INV, $521.13 3/4. (LC EB 27:481)

SEBREE, John; PO 20 Dec 1819, T 20 Jan 1820; 21 Feb 1820
LC; DIV of $547.91 in the hands of the admr. Eppa NORRIS among the wid. (her dower), and the following heirs: Moses, Travis, Robert, Thomas, Elizabeth C., Sarah Ann, David & Joseph SEBREE (each rec'd $45.68); Edward C. PITMAN was gdn. for Travis SEBREE; Cornelius SULLIVANT was gdn. for Robert, Thomas, Elizabeth C., Sarah Ann, David & Joseph SEBREE. (LC EB 21:8)
[[Wm.] SULLIVANT aptd. gdn. of Robt., Thos., Sarah Ann, Eliza Chinn, David & Jos. SEBREE orphans of Jn. SEBREE, 15 Mar 1819 (LC OB 25:43); Travers SEBREE orphan of Jn. SEBREE chose Edw. C. PITMAN as his gdn., 17 May 1819 (LC OB 25:54); ord. that Moses, Travis, Robt., Thos., Sarah Ann, Eliz. Chinn, David, and Jos. SEBREE orphans of Jn. SEBREE be summoned to show cause why the lands of which the sd. Jn. SEBREE d. seized & possessed in this county should not be sold, 21 Jun 1819 (LC OB 25:66, OB 25:82)]

SEBREE, William; T 26 Nov 1816; 16 Mar 1818. LC; INV, $113.25. (LC EB 27:410)

SEBREE, William; 6 Sep 1818; 4 Nov 1818
NC; WILL; third part of all I possess to wife Elizabeth SEBREE; what I had lent to my dau. Lucy EDWARDS previous to her death to her child; balance of est. to be eq. div. between my 3 children: Elizabeth, Polly, & William SEBREE; friend John COTTRELL ex. & guardian to 3 children; WITS: Linszey DAVIS, Jos. WALKER. (NC RB 21:522)
[This is prob. Wm. SEBREE who mar. Eliz. ANGELL, NC, bond 26 Dec 1792 (MLBNC:90); Lucy SEBREY mar. Griffin EDWARDS Jr., NC, bond 28 Nov 1816 (MLBNC:33)]

SEBREE, William; PO 9 Nov 1818; 14 Dec 1818. NC; INV, [m]. (NC RB 21:562)

SEBREE, William; 15 Feb 1820; 14 Aug 1820
SSP, NC; WILL; $10 to dau. Elizabeth SEBREE; all rest of est. to s-i-l Charles ELMORE & dau. Sally ELMORE; s-i-l Charles ELMORE & friend Chichester DOBYNS exors; WITS: Wm. BARECROFT, Jas. PEARCE; [on the motion of Elizabeth SEBREE will was held for probate until the next court term; at session on 9 May 1820, Chichester DOBYNS relinquished his executorship and the court ruled that the will was not the will of William SEBREE and should be withheld from the record; Elizabeth SEBREE who opposed the record of the will was to recover her costs against Charles ELMORE who

offered the same for record; ELMORE appealed; on 11 Sep 1820 the Superior Court of Law of NC reversed the 9 May decision and ord. the will to be rec.]. (NC RB 22:399)
[Sally SEBREE mar. Chas. ELMORE, wid, NC, bond 6 Sep 1819 (MLBNC:35); this may be Wm. SEBREE who served as a pvt. in the Virginia Line during the Rev. War and who d. on 16 Feb 1820 (PR1835:725)]

SEBREE, William; PO 7 Dec 1822, T 13 Mar 1823; 14 May 1823
NC; DIV of balance of est. from John COTTRELL his ex; div. among John LANSDELL Jr. gdn. to Betsy & Polly SEBREE two of the heirs & William SEBREE. (NC RB 23:316)
[On the mot. of Linsey DAVIS, ord. to div. the est. of Betsy SEBREE dec'd, orphan of Wm. SEBREE, among her heirs, 12 Sep 1825 (NC OB 1825-30:41)]

SELF, Alice; 6 Nov 1799; 26 Jul 1819
WC; WILL; all my est. to my five grandchildren Benjamin KING, George KING, Henry Newton KING, Alice Middleton KING, & William Smith KING to be eq. div. among them at the death of their father & mother, that is to say the land that fell to me by my father Benjamin MIDDLETON's will; friend Benedict LAMKIN & Smith KING Jr. exors; WITS: Bened. WRIGHT, Robt. HUDSON, Bend. LAMKIN; [proved Nov 1802 but lodged for further proof]. (WC DW 23:502)
[Jane Middleton SELF, dau. of Hen. SELF, mar. Smith KING, Jr., WC, bond 12 Jan 1790 (MWO:214); *see Benj. MIDDLETON above*]

SELF, Mathias; T 1 Aug 1803; 11 Jun 1804. NC; INV, [m]; includes Negro Peter. (NC RB 17:164)
[Mathias SELF, son of James SELF, mar. Nancy COLE, NC, lic. 11 Aug 1773 (MWO:314)]

SELF, Samuel A.; T 21 Mar 1815; 1 May 1815. RC; INV, $68.96. (RC WB 9:474)

SETTLE, Thomas; PO Jun 1808; 27 Feb 1809
WC; INV, $2239.32; includes Negroes Bandy, Charles, Cyrus, Lett, Jane & child Lucy, boy Robbin, girl Frankey, Lett & child, girl Winny, boy Sam, Salley, girl Rose, girl Nancey. (WC RI 9:179)
[This is Thos. SETTLE bro. of Reuben SETTLE; he also had a sis. Sidney who mar. Sam. LAMKIN, a sis. Charlotte who mar. Fleet LAMKIN (WC, bond 30 Dec 1795), a half bro. Matthew COURTNEY and a half sis. Mary W. COURTNEY who mar. Thos. MATHANEY, WC, bond 26 Apr 1806 (WCCP:2, MLBWC:38, 44)]

SHACKLEFORD, Clement; 4 Mar 1817
RC; INV, £1084.2.10; includes slaves George, Davy, Newman, Pyramus, Grace & child, [Jone], Nancy & child, Molly, Sam, Ned, Sarah, Synah, Abram, Solomon, Dick, Hannah, [Sylva], Simon, Old Sarah, Winney, Patt and a number of books including several on midwifery. (RC WB 9:545)
[This is prob. the Clement SHACKLEFORD who mar. Mary Lawson REDMAN, dau. of Vincent REDMAN, RC, bond 23 May 1798 (MRC:184)]

SHACKLEFORD, Elizabeth B.; 2 Feb 1816; 8 Mar 1816
RC; WILL; niece Elizabeth B. BALL all right, title & interest in the est. of my husband William SHACKLEFORD dec'd; if Elizabeth B. BALL should die without heirs, est. to be eq. div. among my sister Katherine NORTHERN's children; niece Elizabeth B. BALL to be extx.; WITS: Thos. Y. REYNOLDS, G. MARREN, Sam. B. KELSICK; [signed "Betsy B. SHACKLEFORD"]. (RC WB 9:513)
[Elizabeth Brereton SMITH mar. Wm. SHACKLEFORD, RC, bond 9 Jun 1801; Catharine Gwinn SMITH mar. James NORTHEN, RC, bond 22 Dec

1800 (MRC:148, 185); Elizabeth B. and Catharine G. SMITH were daus. of William SMITH (d. RC 1786) (RC WB 7:528)]

SHACKLEFORD, [Richard]; T 31 Dec 1798; 5 Oct 1801
RC; DIV of slaves between Clement (received boy Simon, Joan & child Ben, Hannah, old woman Sarah) & Vincent SHACKLEFORD (received Newman, Sarah, George, Nancy, Dinah). (RC AB 3:77)

SHACKLEFORD, Richard; PO 5 Oct 1807, T 1 Jan 1808; 4 Jan 1808
RC; DIV of legacy bequeathed by the late Richard SHACKLEFORD to the children of his son Richard SHACKLEFORD dec'd namely John SHACKLEFORD & Nancy L. SHACKLEFORD. (RC AB 3:194)

SHACKLEFORD, Vincent; 17 Nov 1819; 5 Jun 1820.
of Cobham Park, LP, RC; WILL; I relinquish to James SCRIMGER all the right, title, or interest that I have in the land that the sd. SCRIMGER purchased of Edmund N. NORTHEN; to my sis-i-l Mary L. SHACKLEFORD and her three youngest children: William, John & James the Negro woman [Joyce] and other articles purchased by me at the sale of the est. of my bro. Clement SHACKLEFORD and left on the plant.; exors. to sell my lots & houses at Richmond Courthouse & my full proportion of the land which descended to me by my mother and that also which was devised to me by my father; Negro man Sam & his wife & children and my Negro man Bob, should he come in or be recovered (he being at present a runaway) be sent off and sold; rest of est. to be kept together for the support of my wife & the support and education of my children; friend Moore T. BROCKENBROUGH Esq. to be guardian to all my children; my sword that was taken from me and returned when taken prisoner at Farnham Church to Moore BROCKENBROUGH Esq.; Dr. Austin BROCKENBROUGH or some other doctor or surgeon to extract the ball now in my right leg and deliver it to my wife in the hope and confidence that she by the indelible impression to be made by such memento may instill the strongest and most lasting principles of courage and patriotism in the young and tender minds of our mutual offspring; friends John CAMPBELL Esq. & Mr. Baldwin M. LEE both of WC and my worthy friend and neighbor Col. Vincent BRAMHAM of RC exors; WITS: Emanuel PECK, Alfred DODSON, Rich. L. SHACKLEFORD, Robt. B. MITCHELL. (RC WB 9:662)
[In a letter to the Clerk of the RC Court dtd. "Western Leesville, Aug 30, 1820" Baldwin M. LEE writes that he is unable to comply with SHACKLEFORD's request for him to be an ex. of his est. (RC WB 9:670); Vincent SHACKLEFORD was a captain of artillery in the 41st Regiment of Virginia Militia; he was wounded in the skirmish between that unit and British forces at Farnham Church on 6 December 1814; he served as a delegate to the state legislature in 1812 (*Rich. Enq.*, 14 Apr 1812); acc. to an article in the *Petersburg Daily Courier* (21 Dec 1814) Capt. SHACKLEFORD "with about sixty of the artillerists, encountered four hundred of the enemy with the utmost intrepidity; that he gave them several fires with his two pieces, and drove them from the plain. Eventually capt. S. was wounded and taken prisoner – the enemy paroled him with complements on his conduct." The *Rich. Enq.* of 24 December 1814 reported that the British had lost 15 killed and 31 wounded while Capt. Shackleford's men lost only 2 wounded and "our militia never gave an inch." Acc. to <http://familytree maker.genealogy.com/users/s/h/a/William-O-Shackleford/GENE1-0040.html>, accessed 16 Jul 2012, Vincent Lyne SHACKLEFORD was the son of Rich. and Eliz. SHACKLEFORD; he mar. Lucy Roane

BROCKENBROUGH dau. of Moore Fauntleroy BROCKENBROUGH, RC, bond 19 Dec 1806, and had six children: Moore, Thos. Roane, Virginia, Eliza M., Lyne, and Vincent.]

SHEARMAN, Ann; PO 21 Oct 1793, T 24 Oct 1793; 17 Dec 1798
LC; INV, £547,14.2; includes Negroes: Simon, Harry, Will, Billy, Dorcus, Milly & Letty, Charlotte, Sam, Fanny, James, Tabitha, Mariah, Jesse, Immanuel, Dick, Jack. (LC EB 24:84)

SHEARMAN, Joseph; 18 Jan 1800; 16 Jun 1800
LC; WILL; to wife Susan SHEARMAN the land & plant. w/o I now live; at wife's death land to be sold and proceeds eq. div. among all my children: Nancy, Thomas, Joseph, Sarah Mitchell, & Susanna Payne; to dau. Nancy SHEARMAN my two Negroes Sarah & Butler; wife to have one third of balance of est. during her life; est. to be div. by friends Joseph CHINN, Richard MITCHELL, John CARPENTER, & Bartho. CHINN; wife to be extx; WITS: C. TAPSCOTT, Martin SHEARMAN, Martin TAPSCOTT. (LC WB 28:40)
[Jos. SHEARMAN mar. Susanna CHINN, sis. of Robt. CHINN, LC, bond 10 Mar 1768 (MLBLC:67); Susanna Payne SHEARMAN orphan of Jos. SHEARMAN chose Susanna SHEARMAN as her gdn., 16 Jun 1800 (LC Orders 21 1799-1801:123)]

SHEARMAN, Joseph; PO 15 Jan 1800; 15 Sep 1800
LC; INV, £1930.8.4; includes Negroes: Charles, Daniel, James, Lindsey, Andrew, Anthony, Perymus, Harry, Burgess, Butler, Travis, Eppey, Opie, Old Nan, Phillis, Alice & child Chloe, Cate & child Billy, Hannah, Sarah, Hannah, Sinah, Polly, Maria, Isabella, Levina, Letty. (LC EB 24:123)

SHEARMAN, Joseph; PO 15 Dec 180[0], T 30 Dec 1800; 16 Feb 1801
LC; INV & DIV of Negroes Charles, Daniel, James, Lindsay, Andrew, Perrimus, Burges, Butler, Traverse, Eppy, Opie, Nan, Phillis, Alce & child Polly, Cate & child Billy, Sarah, Young Hannah, Sinah, Isabell, Levina, Letty among: the widow, Sarah M. SHEARMAN, Joseph SHEARMAN, Susanna P. SHEARMAN, Thomas SHEARMAN, Nancy SHEARMAN. (LC EB 24:132)

SHEARMAN, Joseph; T Jan 1806; 10 Sep 1806
LC; List of Negro slaves held by dower by Susanna SHEARMAN wid. of Joseph: Daniel (about 30 years), Perimus (18), Opie (14), Nan (58), Cate (45), Hannah (25), Lavina (10), Letty (7), Hethy (5), [Roena] (1), Billy (5), Sam (3). (LC EB 24:345)

SHEARMAN, Joseph; T 31 Mar 1820; 17 Dec 1821
LC; INV, $2214.75; includes Negroes Daniel, David, Peggy & child Margaret, Philice, Hetty. (LC EB 29:148)
[A Jos. SHEARMAN mar. Caroline MEREDITH, LC, bond 2 Mar 1819 (MLBLC:67); Caroline SHEARMAN aptd. gdn. to Jos. SHEARMAN, 21 May 1821 (LC OB 25:209)]

SHEARMAN, Louisa M.; 5 Feb 1825; 21 Mar 1825
LC; WILL; sis. Ann D. SHEARMAN; bro. Thomas W. M. SHEARMAN; sis. Hannah Mariah SHEARMAN; friend Maj. John MEREDITH ex; WITS: [Leea] HINTON, Jas. BRENT, Eliz. F. H. BRENT. (LC WB 28:255)

SHEARMAN, Martin; 18 Sep 1811; 20 Jun 1814
LC; WILL; to my bro. Ezekiel G. SHEARMAN my land & plant. w/o I now live & the following Negroes: Joseph, Billy (the cartman), Samuel, Daniel (the carpenter), Sinah, Apphia, Mahaly & Amy; to nephews Ellis L. B. TAPSCOTT & John M. S. TAPSCOTT my land & plant. at or near the mouth of Musqueato Creek to be eq. div; Negroes Billy (called Billy TAPSCOTT),

Thomas [SPRIGGS], [Arcigna] & Morgan to have their freedom; $20 per year to [Arcigna] for 20 years should she live so long; bro. Ezekiel G. SHEARMAN & my old & valuable friend Maj. William KIRK exors; WITS: Sam. M. SHEARMAN, Jas. GIBSON; COD dtd. 30 Dec 1813: dear & valuable relation Polly TAPSCOTT for her particular care to my domestic concerns since the death of my wife shall have & enjoy the use of a part of my land & plant. given to my bro; the part which is for Polly TAPSCOTT is bounded as follows, beg at a beach about two or three hundred yards above my wind mill thence running through the middle of a marsh up its different courses to the main road called the Ferry Road from thence by my line which is a ditch to the river from thence along the river shore to the beginning which bounds will include my dwelling house & orchard & also the use of my Negro man Joseph & woman Sinah; exors. to pay Polly TAPSCOTT $150 a year; WITS: Sam. M. SHEARMAN, Jas. GIBSON. (LC WB 28:148)
[Mosquito Cr. is located in southeastern LC; it flows into the Rappahannock Riv. (Miller:104)]

SHEARMAN, Martin; PO 21 Nov 1814, T 4 Jul 1815; 21 Aug 1815
LC; DIV of slaves among his legatees agreeably to his will: E. G. SHEARMAN, John M. TAPSCOTT, Ellis L. B. TAPSCOTT. (LC EB 27:246)

SHEARMAN, Martin; T 25 Oct 1814; 16 Jun 1817
LC; INV; includes Negroes: Daniel the Carpenter, Billey the priest, Harry, Daniel, Sprigg, Abram, Domine (dead), Billey, James, Lewis, Malinda, Nelson, Morgan, Sam, Agga, Fanny, Lucy, Sinah & child Joseph, Alpha, Matilda, Lucinda, Syphax, Sillar, Araiana, Mahala, Winney, Billey; [all of the slaves were appraised at between $60 and $400 except the last Billey who was appraised at 1 cent]. (LC EB 27:382)

SHEARMAN, Samuel M.; 14 Jan 1815; 20 Mar 1815
LC; WILL; I lend to my wife Nancy SHEARMAN all my est. as long as she remains my wid. except the prop. I have lately purchased from the est. of Hugh BRENT dec'd now in the poss of Mrs. BRENT; land I bought from Suttons should be sold to pay debts; as to the plant. on Nantepison Neck I wish that to go to my son Thomas William Martin SHEARMAN; [no ex. named]; WITS: Jane SUTTON, Robt. PERCIFULL, Ralph EDMONDS. (LC WB 28:159)
[Sam. M. SHEARMAN mar. Nancy MARTIN, LC, bond 5 Oct 1801 (MLBLC:67); Sam. M. SHEARMAN seems to have had at least three other children; Jn. HUNT was aptd. gdn. of Thos. Wm. Martin SHEARMAN & Hannah Mariah SHEARMAN and Lavina Martin SHEARMAN & Ann Downing SHEARMAN chose Jn. MEREDITH as their gdn., 16 Apr 1821 (LC OB 25:204); settlement with Jn. MEREDITH the acct. of his gdnship. with Lavina M. & Ann D. SHEARMAN orphans of Sam. M. SHEARMAN, 17 Feb 1823 (LC OB 25:353); Nantepoison or Antipoison Neck is located in LC between Tabbs Creek and Antipoison Creek (Miller:2)]

SHEARMAN, Samuel M.; T 28 Mar 1815; 17 Jul 1815
LC; INV, includes Negroes: Shadrack, Butler, Meshack, Ransom, Daniel, Grace, Dinah, Fanny, Letty, Reuben, Peggy (badly burnt), Vilet, Drusilla, Jesse, Felix, David, Hiram, Judith, Nelly, Polly. (LC EB 27:244)

SHEARMAN, Susannah; PO 19 Mar 1821, T Apr 1821; 21 Jan 1822
LC; DIV of Negroes which Susannah SHEARMAN held as her dower in the est. of her dec'd husband Joseph SHEARMAN as follows: Lot 1 ([Rien?], Sarah, Perrymus) to Sarah M. MITCHELL's children; Lot 2 (Opie, Mima) to James MITCHELL's children; Lot 3 (Levina, Eppa, Fanny Edwards) to

Thomas SHEARMAN; Lot 4 (Hannah & child, Burgess, Daniel, Della) to Ann OLDHAM; Lot 5 (Hetty & child Letty, Aaron, Kate, Sam) to Joseph SHEARMAN's child. (LC EB 29:165)
[Susanna P. SHEARMAN, dau. of Susanna SHEARMAN, mar. James MITCHELL, LC, bond 23 Sep 1801; Ann SHEARMAN mar. Sam. OLDHAM, LC, bond 2 Feb 1803 (MLBLC:52, 56; *see also Joseph SHEARMAN above*)]

SHEARMAN, Susannah; T 31 Mar 1821; 20 May 1822. LC INV. (LC EB 29:199)

SHEARMAN, Susannah; PO 19 Mar 1822, T 31 Mar 1821; 17 Jun 1822. LC; INV, $72.74 1/2. (LC EB 29:199)

SHEARMAN, Thomas; PO 1821, T 31 Dec 1821; 20 May 1822
LC; INV; includes Negroes Phillis, Hannah, Levina, girl Fanny, boy Adam. (LC EB 29:200)
[This is prob. Eliz. MITCHELL who mar. Thos. SHEARMAN, LC, bond 17 Dec 1817 (MLBLC:67); Eliz. SHEARMAN aptd. gdn. to Susannah P. & Jos. W. B. SHEARMAN orphans of Thos. SHEARMAN, 15 Jul 1822 (LC OB 25:316, 317)]

SHEARMAN, Winifred G.; PO 18 Aug 1817, T 7 Jan 1818; 16 Feb 1818
LC; INV, $1125; includes Negroes Matilda, George, Sirius, Mary. (LC EB 27:406)

SHELTON, Henry; PO 24 Sep 1795; 17 Oct 1796
LC; INV, £452.16.0; includes Negroes: Anthony, Fanny, Dinah, Lucy, [Mimy], Ralph, Sarah, Sally, John, Ellen, George, Cate. (LC EB 24:28)

SHELTON, Henry; PO 18 Oct 1802; 22 Feb 1803
LC; INV, includes Negroes: Anthony, Ralph, George, Fanny & child [Page Monroe], Mima & child Isaac, Sarah, Sally, Cate, John, Diner, Kendall, Ellen, Mariah, Mahaly; DIV of est. among: Anthony LAWSON who mar. Ann SHELTON, John FLOWERS gdn. for Charles W. SHELTON, John FLOWERS gdn. for Sally SHELTON. (LC EB 24:231)
[Ann SHELTON mar. Anthony LAWSON, LC, bond 19 Jul 1802 (MLBLC:46); Jn. FLOWERS aptd. gdn. of Polly & Chas. SHELTON orphans of Hen. SHELTON; Lucy STREET aptd. gdn. of Thos. & Maria SHELTON orphans of Hen. SHELTON 20 Sep 1802 (LC Orders V 1802-03:187, 188)]

SHELTON, Thomas; 25 Jul 1806; 15 Dec 1806
LC; WILL; all land to wife Catharine SHELTON during her life or widowhood but she is not to sell or give any timber off the sd. land for any purpose & not to clear any land nor cut any timber down more than barely enough for the use of the plant. & she is also to keep the apple orchard under a fence so as the trees are not barked; at wife's death or marriage land to go to son Thomas Barton SHELTON provided he lives to age 21; if he does not, land to go to son John Payne SHELTON; after wife's death pers. est. to be eq. div. among four children: John Payne SHELTON, Kitty SHELTON, Judith Newton Payne SHELTON, and [F]enette SHELTON; son Thomas Burton to be schooled; prop. now in possession of Mrs. Bridgett WATTS belonging to her children in which I have two parts I leave as above; friends Capt. John CHOWNING & William BISCOE exors; WITS: Alex. MARSH, Wm. HATHAWAY, Wm. GEORGE, Wm. OLDHAM. (LC WB 28:99)
[Thos. SHELTON mar. Caty PAYNE, dau. of Bridget PAYNE, LC, bond 22 Apr 1790 (MLBLC:67); Overseers of the Poor in the Upper District to bind out Thos. Barton SHELTON orphan of Thos. SHELTON, 19 Jan 1807 (LC Orders D22 1805-08:281)]

SHELTON, Thomas; PO 15 Dec 1806; 19 Jun 1809. LC; INV, £59.7.6 1/2. (LC EB 27:53)

SHIRLEY, George; 9 Jan 1826

NC; on the mot. of William HEADLEY & Sally his wife, ord. that John, George, Robert, Betsy, Daniel & James SHIRLEY and John LEWIS & Polly his wife be summoned to show cause why the lands of George SHIRLEY should not be sold. (NC OB 1825-30:61)

[Wm. HEADLEY mar. Sally SHEARLEY, NC, bond 3 Jan 1816, Geo. SHEARLEY gave consent for Sally; Jn. LEWIS mar. Polly SHEARLEY, bond 21 Dec 1819, consent by Geo. SHEARLEY (MLBNC:52, 68); Geo. & Eliz. SHIRLEY chose Sally SHIRLEY as their gdn. & the sd. Sally is aptd. gdn. of Dan. & Jas. SHIRLEY, 13 Feb 1826 (NC OB 1825-30:66)]

SHIRLEY (SHERLEY), Peter; PO 1 Jan 1816; 2 May 1825. RC; INV, [m]. (RC WB 10:73)

SHIRLEY (SHERLEY), Thaddeus; T 12 Nov 1823; 2 May 1825. RC; INV, $202.12. (RC WB 10:75)

[Thaddeus SHIRLEY mar. Betsy R. JEFFRIES, RC, bond 15 Apr 1816 (MRC:186)]

SHORT, John; PO Jun 1800; 6 Oct 1800. RC; INV, £23.0.9. (RC WB 9:137)

SHORT, Landman; 12 Oct 1799; Sep 1800

WC; WILL; wife Susannah to enjoy all prop. during her widowhood; stepson Kennedy; if wife should die or remarry, prop. to be eq. div. between three children [Landmon Mitchel, James Kennedy, and Thomas]; William Stork JETT and Baldwin LEE Esq. exors.; WITS: Robt. [CURRIN], Harriett JOHNSON, Fanny CANNADAY. (WC Unrec Wills 1755-1800 #46)

[Landman SHORT mar. Susannah TAIT, WC, bond 28 My 1793 (MLBWC:65); Hen. WASHINGTON was aptd. gdn. to Landman, Thos., and Jas. SHORT orphans of Landman SHORT; WC 28 May 1804 (WC Orders 1804-07:9)]

SHORT, Landman; [m]; 25 Jun 1804. WC; INV; includes Negro girl Hannah. (WC RI 8:429)

SHORT, Thomas; T 24 Jun 1808; 15 Aug 1808

LC; INV; includes one half of schooner "Eagle." (LC EB 27:38)

[Eliz. & Nancy SHORT orphans of Thos. SHORT chose Thos. JAMES as their gdn.; Rich. BENJAMIN aptd. gdn. to Thos. & Lydia orphans of Thos. SHORT, 19 Dec 1808 (LC Orders B23 1808-11:7); Moses SHORT orphan of Thos. SHORT chose Jn. SAMPSON as his gdn., 20 Feb 1809 (LC Orders B23 1808-11:14); Nancy SHORT orphan of Thos. SHORT chose Luke ASHBOURNE as her gdn., 18 Sep 1809 (LC Orders B23 1808-11:115); Thos. SHORT orphan of Thos. SHORT chose Rich. TOWELL as his gdn.; Rich. BERRYMAN was his former gdn.; Overseers of the Poor in the Lower District to bind out Thos. SHORT to Rich. TOWELL, 20 Sep 1813 (LC Orders 24:166); Letty SHORT orphan of Thos. SHORT chose Nathan SPRIGGS as her gdn., 20 Sep 1813 (LC Orders 24:166); settlement of Nathan SPRIGGS gdnship. acct. with Lydia SHORT orphan of Thos. SHORT, 15 Jun 1818 (LC OB 25:3)]

SIMES, Sally; [m]; 14 Apr 1807. NC; INV, £27.1.1 1/2. (NC RB 17:521)

[The est. of Sally SIMS was ord. to be admin. by Rich. SWANN, NC, 12 Jan 1807 (NC MB 1805-1807:196)]

SIMKINS, William; 3 Feb 1803; 25 Apr 1803

WC; WILL; dau. Sally (the dau. of Mrs. Jane BENNETT then LEFAVOUR) $150 to be put in the hands of Mr. Baldwin M. LEE for her benefit; rest of est.

to his father; if father dies to be div. among bros. & sisters; friend Baldwin M. LEE to be exor.; WITS: Wm. RICE, Thos. ROWAND. (WC DW 20:458)
[Jane LEFEVRE mar. Robt. BENNETT, WC, bond 26 Jul 1800 (MLBWC:6)]

SIMKINS, William; 1[6] Jul 1803; 2[?] Jul 1803. WC; INV, £44.16.9 1/2. (WC RI 8:245)

SIMMONS, Charles; PO 20 Mar 1815, T 22 Mar 1815; 17 Jul 1815
LC; INV; includes slaves: Peter, Jesse, Lavina & child, Beck & child, William, Amos, Thomas, Obediah, Richard, Judith. (LC EB 27:242)
[Lucy T. SIMMONDS aptd. gdn. to Chas. & Polly SIMMONDS orphans of Chas. SIMMONDS, 19 Feb 1816 (LC Orders 24:285); Chas. SIMMONDS mar. Lucy T. GEORGE, LC, bond 21 Jan 1811 (MLBLC:68)]

SIMMONS, James; T 1 Dec 1808; 18 Nov 1811
LC; INV, £357.16.11; includes Negroes: Joe, Judy & child Lucy, John, [Giles], Beck & child Tom, William [LEE], Amos [BRENT]. (LC EB 27:95)

SIMMONS, William; T 24 [m] 1815; 17 Jul 1815
LC; INV; includes slaves: Moses, Billy, Willis, Old Judy, Young Judy, Winny, Siller, John, Spencer, Esther, Rawleigh, Nanny, Jane, Clary, Lucinda. (LC EB 27:239)

SIMMONS, William; PO 20 Dec 1824, T 27 Dec 1824; 21 Feb 1825
LC; allottment of dower of Frances SIMMONS in Negroes (Moses, Judith, Nanny, Spencer, Agathy, Caty) & residue div. among heirs: James SIMMONS (Billy, Polly), Frances SIMMONS (Willis, Lucinda), Cyrus SIMMONS (John, Jack), William SIMMONS (Esther, Clary), Benjamin M. WALKER in right of his wife Lucy who was Lucy SIMMONS (Priscilla, Winny). (LC EB 29:391)
[Wm. SIMMONS mar. Frances ROBB, LC, bond 17 Aug 1801 (MLBLC:68); Lucy SIMMONS mar. Benj. M. WALKER, LC, bond 2 Jan 1822 (MLBLC:76); Frances & Wm. SIMMONS chose Frances SIMMONS for their gdn. and sd. Frances is aptd. gdn. to Jas. SIMMONS, 20 Dec 1824 (LC OB 26:90)]

SIMMS, Franklin; 25 Aug 1803; 26 Jan 1806
WC; WILL; whole est. to wife Sukey; after her death to be eq. div. among children; sons Benjamin & Richard exors; WITS: Wm. Storke JETT, Sam. JOHNSTON, Spencer BETTISWORTH. (WC DW 21:234)
[*Alexander SIMMS (d. WC 1745) named a Franklin SIMMS in his will, but it is not clear if Franklin was his son (WC DW 10:168)*]

SIMPSON, Thomas; 25 May 1767, [m]
WC; WILL; late of WC but now of Whitehaven in the county of Cumberland, Great Britain; lands, Negroes, goods, ships, wares, and merchandises to be sold; wife Mary (dau. of Thomas SMITH) if she has no issue by me; John SMITH who was under the care and tuition of William [and Magdalen] JACKSON in WC when I left the colony in 1765 £500 when 21; Nancy SAUL under the care and tuition of Charles BENNETT & his wife in WC when I left the colony in 1765 £300; [Isabella] SMITH dau. of Mary SMITH who formerly lived with me in Virginia but now of Whitehaven £300 when 21; nephew John SIMPSON £5; nephew Joseph [SIMPSON] £50; nephew Thomas [SIMPSON] £100; niece Bettsey [SIMPSON] £50; rest of est. to bro. John SIMPSON; if wife has issue by me remainder of est. to go to that child when 21; wife Mary and bro. John SIMPSON exors; WITS: Jn. MALLESON, J. F. WARD. (WC CC 1791-011)
[A Magdalen JACKSON was named as a grandchild in the will of Hannah DEMOVEL (WC, 8 Sep 1744 – 25 Sep 1744); a Magdalene JACKSON (wid. of Christopher M. JACKSON, d. WC 1749)in her will (WC 11 Aug 1766 – 24

Nov 1767) named her sons Sam. Rust, Julius Augustine, Thaddeus, and Christopher M. JACKSON (WWCV:117, 127, 159)]

SIMS, Sally; 14 Jan 1811
NC; Cuthbert SIMS to be possessed with his part of the est. of Sally SIMS. (NC OB 1807-11:225)
[This is prob. the Sally SIMS whose est. was admin. by Rich. SWANN (NC Minute Book 1805-07:196)]

SIMS, William; PO 11 Mar 1816, T 20 Mar 1816; 13 May 1816
NC; INV, [m]. (NC RB 20:457)
[On the mot. of Peter COLLISON and his wife Susan who was Susan SIMS, the sheriff to admin. the est. of Wm. SIMS, 26 May 1817 (WC OB 1814-18:300) *NB: it is not certain that this Wm. SIMS is the one whose inv. was rec. in NC in May 1816*; Susan SIMMS mar. Peter COLOSON, WC, bond 11 Jan 1811 (MLBWC:14); Edw. PERCIFULL aptd. gdn. to Thos., Winny, Harriett & Jas. SIMS orphans of Wm. SIMS, 21 Jun 1819 (LC OB 25:66, 364)]

SIMS, Winnifred; PO 14 Nov 1808; 9 Jul 1810. NC; INV, [m]. (NC RB 18:421)
[The est. of Winifred SIMS was ord. to be admin. by Wm. SIMS, NC, 14 Nov 1808 (NC OB 1807-1811:72)]

SISSON, Elizabeth; T 15 Feb 1816; 2 Nov 1818 RC; INV, [m]. (RC WB 9:608)

SISSON, George; 8 Jun 1810; 2 Jul 1810
RC; WILL; wife Mary Stewart SISSON all my land on the west side of the main road leading to the Folly Neck bound by the land of William BERNETT, the heirs of Benj. SMITH & Totuskey Creek; after her death or remarriage to be eq. div. between 4 sons: George SISSON, Archibald SISSON, Hiram Steward SISSON, & Henry SISSON; dau. Eliza Redman SISSON rest of land on east side of the sd. Folly Road; son Martin SISSON and wife exors; WITS: Robt. G. TOMLIN, Wm. MISKELL, Jn. REDMAN Jr. (RC WB 9:371)
[Geo. SISSON mar. Mary S. REDMAN, WC, bond 26 Jun 1797; Mary S. REDMAN must have been at least a 2nd wife since George's son Martin was old enough to be his ex.and to have mar. Caty MOXLEY in Nov 1797 (MWO:320); Miller:52 locates Folly Neck on the Rappahannock River between Totuskey Creek and Richardson Creek in RC.]

SISSON, George; PO 2 Jul 1811; 4 Nov 1817. RC; INV, $23.72 1/2. (RC WB 9:596)

SISSON, Henry; PO 6 Jan 1818, T 7 Feb 1818; 2 Nov 1818
RC; Negroes belonging to the est. were sold & proceeds ($2363.36) div. among the legal reps. of sd. SISSON: Edward SPENCE who mar. Sally SISSON (one of the orphans of William SISSON) and as gdn. of Ann SISSON (another orphan of William SISSON), Charles MUSE as gdn. for William R. & Elizabeth SISSON (orphans of William SISSON), Martin SISSON's orphans (Enoch FINCH as gdn. of George SISSON), William WALKER as gdn. of Jemima SISSON, A. M. KENNEY in right of Lewellen PORTER, Enoch FINCH in right of his wife who was Elizabeth MOXLEY, Mary NEALE gdn. of Mira NEALE orphan of Patty NEALE who was Patty HART and the reps. of Elizabeth BRAGG who was Elizabeth HART), Mrs. BRAGG survived her grandfather Henry SISSON but has since died leaving a husband and child. (RC AB 3:637)
[Edward SPENCE mar. Sally SISSON, WC, bond 11 Dec 1809; Enoch FINCH mar. Eliz. Muse MOXLEY, WC, bond 21 Dec 1807; Patsy HART mar. Thos. NEALE, WC, bond 20 Dec 1805 (MLBWC:[23], 50, 66); Eliz. HART mar. Wm. K. BRAGG, RC, bond 16 Nov 1808 (MRC:22); Wm. M. WALKER's gdnship.

acct. with Jemima SISSON who mar. Jas. MULLINS ret. to court, 28 Jul 1823 (WC OB 1819-23:584)]

SISSON, Martin; 24 May 1813
WC; Geo. SISSON orphan of Martin SISSON chose Wm. SETTLE as his gdn. (WC Orders 1810-13:305)
[Martin SISSON mar. Nancy (HARRIS) SYDNOR, wid. of Giles SYDNOR, RC, bond 10 Apr 1802 (MRC:188, 201; RC OB 25:3); Jemimah SISSON orphan of Martin SISSON chose Wm. M. WALKER as his gdn., 22 May 1815 (WC OB 1814-18:129); Geo. SISSON orphan of Martin SISSON chose Enoch FINCH as his gdn., 22 Jul 1816 (WC OB 1814-16:250); Randall SISSON orphan of Martin SISSON chose Miskell SAUNDERS as his gdn. and sd. SAUNDERS is aptd. gdn. to Fanny SISSON orphan of sd. Martin, 7 Jan 1822 (RC OB 25:228); settlement of Miskell SAUNDERS' acct. of his gdnship. of Fanny SISSON orphan of Martin SISSON, 7 Aug 1827 (RC OB 27:180)]

SISSON, William; [m] Jan 1804; 28 May 1804
WC; WILL; wife Peggy to have use of all lands and to maintain four children: Sally, Eliza, William, & Ann; son William (under 15) to have tract adj to Westmoreland Courthouse; daus. are under 18; wife extx; WITS: Jn. WATTS, Martin SISSON. (WC DW 21:27)
[Wm. SISSON mar. Peggy MUSE, WC, bond 16 Dec 1789 (MLBWC:65); Peggy SISSON mar. (2) Gerard McKENNEY, WC, bond 10 Feb 1807 (MLBWC:42; WC Orders 1804-07:483; Orders 1807-10:196); Sally & Eliza SISSON orphans of Wm. SISSON chose Chas. [MUSE] as their gdn. and MUSE was aptd. gdn. of Wm.& Ann SISSON, 25 Oct 1809 (WC Orders 1807-10:434)]

SISSON, William; PO 28 Aug 1806, T 28 Aug 1806; 24 Nov 1806. WC; INV, £300.10.3; includes Negroes James, Patty. (WC RI 9:1)

SISSON, William; PO 26 Sep 1808, T 2 Jan 1809; 23 Jan 1809. WC; INV, £295.5.7; includes Negroes James & Patty. (WC RI 9:73)

SLACUM, George; T 22 Feb [1812]; 12 May 1812. NC; INV, $85.52 3/4. (NC RB 19:184)
[The est. of Geo. SLACUM was ord. to be admin. by Lewis LAMKIN, Jr., NC, 12 Feb 1810 (NC OB 1807-1811:152)]

SMEAD, Charles; 20 Jul 1813; 3 Jan 1814
NFP, RC; WILL; wife Sarah T. SMEAD all land & property in Ohio also all my bonds; wife to be extx; WITS: Eliz. SMITH, Maria H. SMITH, Sarah U. TEACKLE. (RC WB 9:439)

SMITH, Alice; 30 Jul 1803; 28 Nov 1803
WP, WC; WILL; niece Eliza Ball [HARVEY] Negro woman Patty & her youngest child Levina; bro. John HARVEY Negro boy Constanton; nephew Octavious HARVEY; bro. John exor; WITS: Jos. FOX Jr., Jas, HARVEY. (WC DW 20:497)

SMITH, Ann; 22 Jul 1808; 28 May 1810
WC; WILL; Nancy JOHNSTON dau. of Dennis JOHNSTON; livestock to be eq. div. between Nancy JOHNSTON & Hannah JOHNSTON daus. of Dennis & Levinah JOHNSTON; friend Dennis JOHNSTON exor.; WITS: Jn. BRICKEY, Wm. BRICKEY. (WC DW 22:94)

SMITH, Benjamin; [7] Oct 1802
RC INV; £1100.11.8; includes the following Negroes: Lancaster, Daniel, Harry, Simon, Bob, Abraham, Job, Appia, Frank, Alexander, Betty dau. of [Norah], Nanny, Old Judith, Alce, Ellener, Heathey, Dick, Cate, June & child, Norah & child, Lucy & child. (RC WB 9:188)

SMITH, Benjamin; PO Dec 1801; 6 Jun 1803
RC; DIV of slaves among: Colston SMITH, John SMITH, Sydnor SMITH, Elizabeth SMITH, Benjamin SMITH, Mariah SMITH, William SMITH, Susannah SMITH. (RC AB 3:107)
[Susan SMITH had mar. James YOUNG and was a resident of Fredericksburg, Va. by Apr 1819 (RC DB 20:597)]

SMITH, Benjamin P.; PO 28 Oct 1816, T 28 Nov 1816; 28 Jul 1817
WC; INV of est. produced by Mrs. Judith SMITH admx.; $6660.86; includes Negroes Abram, Isaac, Reuben, David, Peter, William, Thomas, Benjamin, Walker; Cary Sr., Milly, Hany, Cary Jr., girls Letty, Rachael, Molly, Caty, Malinda, Hanah & Virgin. (WC RI 10:115)

SMITH, Benjamin P.; PO 28 Jan 1822, T 26 Apr 1822; 27 May 1822
WC; DIV of Negroes (Isaac, Cary & Patsey, Haney, Davy, Letty, Betsey & [George], Reuben, Polly, Milly, Peter, Ben, Virginia, Walker, Reuben Sr., Hannah, Caty, Cary, Betty, Malinda, Tom) among Maria SMITH (now Maria BOWCOCKS), John [T.] SMITH, William SMITH, James SMITH, Henry P. SMITH, and Margaret P. SMITH. ; WC RI 11:203; OB 1819-23:342)
[Maria, Jn., & Wm. SMITH orphans of Benj. P. SMITH chose Judith SMITH as their gdn. and she is aptd. gdn. to Jas., Hen. & Margaret also orphans of Benj. P. SMITH, 22 Feb 1819 (WC OB 1819-23:12, 392); Maria SMITH mar. Hen. P. BOWCOCK, WC, bond 21 Jan 1822 (MLBWC:7); Jessee MONROE is gdn. of Jas., Hen. Pope and Margaret P. SMITH orphans of Benj. P. SMITH, 22 Nov 1824 (WC OB 1823-27:133); Wm. SMITH aptd. gdn. of Jas., Hen. P. and Marg. P. SMITH orphans of Benj. P. SMITH, 25 Sep 1826 (WC OB 1823-27:323)]

SMITH, Charity; PO 20 Jul 1807, T 13 Aug 1807; 18 Jan 1808. LC; INV, [m]. (LC EB 27:26)
[Charity SMITH d. intest.; sheriff to sell her est., 20 Jul 1807 (LC Orders D22 1805-08:370)]

SMITH, Elizabeth; 31 Jan 1807; 23 Mar 1807
WC; WILL; dau. Elizabeth M. SMITH Negro woman Rachel; son Richard A. SMITH; rest of est. to be eq. div. among all my children; sis. Mary NELSON extx; WITS: Thos. BERRYMAN, Jas. PEYTON. (WC DW 21:321)
[Elizabeth and her sis. Mary seem to have been HARRISONS; Eliz. HARRISON mar. Sam. SMITH, WC, 13 May 1791; Mary HARRISON mar. Wm. NELSON, WC, bond 31 Aug 1791 (MLBWC:50, 66)]

SMITH, Elizabeth; T 9 Jul 1807; 24 Aug 1807. WC; INV, £58.6.6; includes 1 old Negro woman. (WC RI 9:21)

SMITH, Elizabeth; T 20 Feb 1811; May 1811
WC; DIV of est. in hands of Mary NELSON extx; est. was div. among the orphans Jane BUNOUF (formerly Jane SMITH), Mary H. W. SMITH, Richard A. SMITH & Elizabeth M. SMITH. . (WC RI 9:246)

SMITH, Frances; PO 7 Dec 1818, T 11 Feb 1819; 5 Dec 1825
RC; INV; includes Negroes worth $7400: Betty, Henry (Betty's child), Caty (William Caty's child), Milly (Criss Milly's child), Ned, David, Betsy, James, Easter, Amey, Sophia (Amey's child), Mary, Nancy, Henry, George. (RC WB 10:97)

SMITH, [Francis]; 7 Jun 1825
RC; David C. BELFIELD & Mariah his wife who was Mariah B. SMITH and Alice L. SMITH, pltfs. vs. Lettice SMITH & Francis G. W. M. B. SMITH infants by their gdn. Lettice L. SMITH to div. land into 4 eq. parts. Report of div. of land of Letty L. SMITH between her children David C. BELFIELD in

right of his wife who was Maria B. SMITH, Frances G. M. B. SMITH and Letty L. SMITH, 5 Jun 1826 (RC OB 27:76)
[This record seems to be for the division of land that had belonged to Benj. RUST (d. EC 1787) in RC; RUST named his wife Lettice Lee RUST and children (but not identified) in his will; she seems to have mar. (2) Francis SMITH; Maria B. SMITH mar. David C. BELFIELD, EC, 12 Aug 1824 (MOREC:217); several accounts on the internet refer to a Lettice NUPHIS who mar. Francis SMITH; the surname NUPHIS comes from a manuscript on the WEBB Family. I believe that NUPHIS is an error for RUST (RC OB 26:315); Benj. RUST served as a lt. in the Va. State Navy during the Rev. War; by 1832, Lettice SMITH was certified by the EC Court as the sole surviving heir of Benj. RUST; for more on Benj. and Lettice RUST, see petition in the Archives Dept. Va. State Library; see also <http://listlva.lib.va.us/cgi-bin/wa.exe?A2=VA-ROOTS;445d1967.1207>, <http://listlva.lib.va.us/cgi-bin/wa.exe?A2=VA-ROOTS;e8538a3b.1207>, and <http://listlva.lib.va.us/cgi-bin/wa.exe?A2=VA-ROOTS;fdfa74f3.1207> all accessed 30 Oct 2012]

SMITH, Francis; 2 Aug 1824
RC; Maria Belfield SMITH orphan of Francis SMITH chose John W. BELFIELD as her gdn. (RC OB 26:220)

SMITH, George W.; PO 23 Feb 1823; 26 Apr 1824. WC; INV; includes numerous legal books. (WC RI 11:[439])

SMITH, Isaac; 4 Jan 1815; 7 Nov 1815
RC; WILL; whole est. to wife, also use & profits of my plant. called Woodlawn so long as I may be entitled to it under my father's will while she remains my widow; whenever wife is dispossessed of Woodlawn she may have the use of Moratico during her widowhood; if wife has a child by me that comes to age she is to have use of half with other half going to child; friends Bartho. McCARTY & William D. McCARTY exors; WITS: Eliz. SMITH, Fanny P. McCARTY, Robt. W. McCARTY. (RC WB 9:487)
[This is prob. the Isaac SMITH who mar. Winifred T. McCARTY, the ward of Robt. S. HIPKINS, RC, bond 27 Oct 1814 (MRC:189); it appears to the court that Winefred T. McCARTY, late wife of Robt. W. McCARTY which sd. Winefred was Winifred SMITH admx. with the will annexed of Isaac SMITH, is now dead; Robt. W. McCARTY and Catherine SMITH summoned to court to see if they will take admin. of sd. Isaac SMITH's est., 7 Oct 1822 (RC OB 25:342); Winifred T. SMITH, wid., mar. Robert W. McCARTY, RC bond 1 Apr 1816 (MRC:124)]

SMITH, James; 22 Jun 1822; 14 Mar 1825
NC; WILL; all est. to son James M. SMITH; if he die without issue, exors. to sell whole est. and proceeds dispersed as follows: $5000 to Samuel BLACKWELL, Fleming BATES, & Izates ANDERSON as trustees for the benefit of education in NC; $500 to each ex.; rest of est. to be eq. div. between my bro. William SMITH's three sons: James, Robert & William; my bro's place of residence is [Cahery] near [*1 word unclear*] Limavady; son James & friends Samuel BLACKWELL, Fleming BATES & Izates ANDERSON exors; [no WITS listed, but will was proved by Jn. GRINSTEAD, Wm. ROUTT, & Griffin H. FOUSHEE]. (NC RB 24:180)
[Limavady is a town in Co. Londonderry, Northern Ireland; a James SMITH was the compl. in a suit against Eliz. B. BAKER, Virginia LAKE (or BAKER), Walter BAKER & Sam. BLACKWELL in NC in 1810; Eliz. BAKER, Virginia

LAKE and Walter BAKER were not residents of the state at that time (*Richmond Enquirer*, 9 Jan 1810, p. [4]); *see also Corban BAKER above*]

SMITH, James; 13 Nov 1826
NC; Betsy, John & Barbara SMITH orphans of James SMITH chose William W. APPLEBY as their gdn. (NC OB 1825-30:125)

SMITH, John (Capt.); PO 31 Jul 1798; 1 Oct 1804
RC; INV; £1213.14.6; includes the following Negroes: Tom, Moses, George, Squire, Isaac, Sam, Billy, Stephen, Dall, Alice, Milly, Lucy, Fanny & child James, Norah, Criss, Nancey, Mahaly, Betty, Letty, Robin. (RC WB 9:240)

SMITH, John Jr. (Capt.); T 27 Sep 1806; 3 Jul 1809
RC; INV, £1232.3.6, includes following slaves: Alice, Letty & child, girl Mahala, Moses, Isaac, Tom, George, Sam, boy Robin, boy Bil, boy [Jim], boy Peter, man [Squire], woman Dall, Milly, girl Nancy, girl Mary, girl Frankey, girl Judy, girl Nelly, girl Rachel. (RC WB 9:357)

SMITH, John M.; T Dec 1817; 16 Dec 1822
LC; DIV of Negroes among Baldwin SMITH (Juba, Peter, Ellick, Polly, Sinah, Sidney & Nancy, Nelly), Mary B. SMITH (Adam, Davy, Randall, Betty & John, Julia, Lucinda, Peggy. Sillah), Ailcy SMITH (Jerry, Sam, Martha, Fanny, Jenny, Sarah, Isabell, Grandison), value of each heir's share was $2330. (LC EB 29:239)
[This is John Matthews SMITH who mar. Sarah CHINN, LC, bond 20 Sep 1791 (MLBLC:68); Alice SMITH orphan of Jn. M. SMITH chose Rich. SELDEN as her gdn.; Jn. Y. CHINN aptd. gdn. to Baldwin & Mary B. SMITH orphans of Jn. M. SMITH; Jn. Y. CHINN granted admin. on the est. of Sary Y. SMITH, 18 Aug 1817 (LC OB 24:385); Mary B. SMITH mar. Aldea A. GLASCOCK, RC, bond 8 Oct 1822 (MRC:78; LC OB 26:12)]

SMITH, John M.; T 4 Mar 1815; 16 Oct 1824
LC; INV, [m]; includes Negroes James, Juba, Adam, Peter, Ellick, Davy, Eppy, Sam, Isabella, Sucky, Betty & child Peggy, Sidney & child Nancy, Nelly, Sinah, Martha, Margery, Polly, Fanny, Winney, Randall, Harriott, Julia, Sarah, Lucinda, Jinny, Jerry. (LC EB 29:356)

SMITH, Judith; T 14 Dec 1820; 27 May 1822. WC; INV, $791.06. (WC RI 11:196)

SMITH, Lucetta; 16 Oct 1810; 28 Nov 1814
WC; WILL; dau. Elizabeth SMITH called Elizabeth STROTHER the use of my land in KGC which I purchased of John STROTHER; to daus. Nancy SMITH called Nancy STROTHER and Jane SMITH called Jane STROTHER all my lands in WC; son Benjamin P. SMITH; dau. Lucy NEALE; dau. Mary OWENS; rest of est. to be eq. div. among daus. Elizabeth SMITH, Nancy SMITH, and Jane SMITH; WITS: Alex. BERRYMAN, [Weeks] BERRYMAN. (WC DW 23:55)
[This is Lucetta WEEKS, dau. of Benj. WEEKS, who mar. Wm. SMITH of KGC bef 2 Dec 1782 (MWO:325); however, Lucetta seems to have had a number of children by John STROTHER of KGC (see <http://records.ancestry.com/ John_Strother_records.ashx?pid=194019> accessed 18 Jul 2012)]

SMITH, Lucetta; 27 Jan 1817
WC; on the mot. of Joseph G. JEWETT who mar. Nancy one of the daus. of Lucetta SMITH dec'd, ord. to div. the est. devised by the sd. Lucetta to her two daus. the sd. Nancy and Jane who mar. Ritchie ADKINS. (WC OB 1814-18:275)

[Joseph G. JEWETT mar. Nancy STROTHER, 15 Aug 1815; Ritchie ATKINS mar. Jane STROTHER, bond 5 Feb 1816 (MLBWC:3); *see Lucetta SMITH above*]

SMITH, Lucy (Mrs.); 3 Jul 1809. RC; INV, £343.11.0. (RC WB 9:359)

SMITH, Mary; 29 Mar 1800; 6 Apr 1801.
Wakefield, RC; WILL; sons John & William Colston; grdaus. Betty Brereton GARLAND & Sarah Gwynn GARLAND; father Thomas PLUMMER; sons & friend Benjamin Newton GARLAND exors; WITS: Dan. LAWSON, Eliz. ENGLISH, Sarah ENGLISH, Griffin GARLAND, Thos. P. SMITH. (RC WB 9:145)
[Mary SMITH was the wid. of Wm. SMITH Gent., d. RC, 1786 (RC WB 7:528)]

SMITH, Mary; 21 Nov 1801; 24 Jan 1803
WC; WILL; sis. Susanna LEE of Essex my mulatto fellow Abel; three nieces Mary LEE, Susanna LEE & Philecia LEE (all under 21) daus. of my nephew Philip LEE dec'd my Negro woman Mary alias Moll and her children Aggy, Hannah, Beck, Angelina, Prue, Mary, George, and Peter; nephew Baldwin M. LEE my books of accounts, bonds, notes, bills & debts; rest of est. to be eq. div. among nephews John P. LEE, Baldwin M. LEE, & George W. LEE and my niece Susanna LEE dau. of my sister Susanna LEE of Essex; nephews & niece to be exors; WITS: J. S. CARTER, Stephen MOORE, Gerard McKENNEY, Reubin McKENNEY. (WC DW 20:418)
[The LEE nieces and nephews are the children of John, son of Philip LEE, and Susanna (SMITH) LEE. Jn. LEE d. in EC in the spring of 1777 and named only a son Hancock LEE in his will. *Edmund Jennings Lee, Lee of Virginia, 1642-1892: Biographical and Genealogical Sketches of the Descendants of Colonel Richard Lee*, Philadelphia: Franklin Printing Co., 1895, pp. 161-164.)

SMITH, Peggy; 16 Dec 1805
LC; Overseers of the Poor to bind out Spencer CURRELL orphan of Peggy SMITH dec'd to Edward CURRELL. (LC Orders D22 1805-08:103)

SMITH, Peter; PO 11 Jan 1813; 8 Feb 1813. NC; INV, $206.06. (NC RB 19:321)
[Lucy SMITH was aptd. gdn. of Nancy, Hannah, Wm. & Polly SMITH orphans of Peter SMITH, NC, 11 Mar 1816 (NC OB 1816-20:11; Lucy SMITH was prob. Lucy CROWDER who mar. Peter SMITH, NC, bond 17 Jan 1798 (MLBNC:93)]

SMITH, Samuel; 13 May 1802; 28 Jun 1802
WC; WILL; wife Elizabeth; four little children: Jane SMITH, Mary Harrison [Wood] SMITH, Richard Alexander SMITH, and Elizabeth Mathew SMITH; wife & friend Harrison BURGESS exors; WITS: Wm. NELSON, Mary NELSON. (WC DW 20:352)
[Sam. SMITH mar. Eliz. HARRISON, WC, bond 13 May 1791 (MLBWC:66)]

SMITH, Samuel; T 22 Oct 1803; 25 Oct 1803. WC; INV, £82.12.0. (WC RI 8:357 [sic] prob. should be 257)

SMITH, Sarah; T 10 Dec 1817; 16 Oct 1824. LC; INV, [m]. (LC EB 29:358)

SMITH, Stephen; 3 Nov 1803; 18 Jun 1804
LC; WILL; profits of my est. to wife Charity & dau. Hannah and to heirs of dau.; if dau. die without heirs profits of est. to be put in the hands of the presiding elder of the district of the White Marsh Methodist Society for their use & benefit of the Episcopal Church of Methodist; friend[s] William YERBY & William MEREDITH exors; WITS: Jn. HALL, Chas. BRENT. (LC WB 28:83)

SMITH, Stephen; PO 18 Jun 1804; 17 Sep 1804; LC; INV, [m]. (LC EB 24:273)

SMITH, William W. ; 14 Apr 1824; 26 Apr 1824
WC; WILL; all est. to wife during her life; dau. Rachel Clementine MONROE; dau. Mary SMITH; remainder of est. to be eq. div. between son William W. Monroe SMITH & dau. Eliza T. SMITH; s-i-l James S. MONROE & John T. SMITH exors; WITS: John B. FANT, Jas. S. GREEN, Jesse MONROE; [in a relinquishment dtd. 14 Apr 1824, James [S.] MONROE of Culpeper Co., Va & John T. SMITH of WC relinquish all right, title, etc. to the property left to Rachel Clementine SMITH & Mary M. now wives of the sd. James [S.] MONROE & John T. SMITH by the will of David MONROE dec'd to William W. Monroe SMITH and Eliza T. SMITH; WITS: Jesse MONROE, Jn. B. FANT.] (WC DW 25:54)
[Rachel C. SMITH mar. Jas. L. [sic] MONROE, WC, bond 18 Feb 1822; John T. SMITH mar. Mary M. SMITH, dau. of Wm. W. SMITH, WC, bond 25 Dec 1822 (MLBWC:45, 66)]

SMITHER, George; [m] 1811; 17 Jun 1811
LC; WILL; wife Nancy F. SMITHER; son Robert SMITHER; son to be well educated; if son die before age 21 whole est. to wife; if wife & son die est. to go to children of bro. William SMITHER; wife & friend Joseph BALL of Ditchley exors; WITS: Wm. POLLARD, Jn. HALL. (LC WB 28:115)
[This is prob. Geo. SMITHER who mar. Ann F. SPILLER, LC, bond 14 Jan 1805 (MLBLC:68); Robt. SMITHER orphan of Geo SMITHER chose Wm. F. RUST as his gdn., NC 14 Jan 1822 (NC OB 1820-25:170); Ann F. SMITHER wid. of Geo. mar. Jas. B. GALLOWAY, LC, bond 9 Dec 1812 (MLBLC:29; LC Orders 24:205)]

SMITHER, George; PO 17 Jun 1811, T 22 Jun 1811; 16 Sep [1811]
LC; INV, $3387.49 1/3; includes Negroes: Roger, Phill, John, Israel, Letty, Philis, Suckey, Sally, Judy, Betty, Minerva, Mariah, Fanny, Billy, Agga. (LC EB 27:91)

SMITHER, Lancelot; 15 Mar 1808
NC; Peter [G.] RICE aptd. gdn. to Priscilla & Lancelot SMITHER heirs of Lancelot SMITHER; NC OB 1807-11:29)
[Lancelot SMITHER, son of Gabriel & Wilmoth SMITHER, was born in NFP, RC 21 Oct 1758; he mar. Nancy PRITCHETT, dau. of Rodham PRITCHETT, NC, bond 8 Feb 1785 (NFPR:172; MWO:325); Nancy (PRITCHETT) SMITHER mar. (2) Philip WHITE (NC CC 1813-004) could this be the marriage recorded in MLBNC as Philip WHITE, wid. & Ann SMITH [sic], wid., NC, bond 7 Mar 1808? (MLBNC:108); *for more information on Lancelot SMITHER and his siblings, see NC CC 1806-001*]

SMITHER, Thomas; PO 19 Apr 1803; 20 Feb 1804
LC; INV, £227.5.6; includes Negroes: Letty, Edy, Darcus, Enzy, Judith; DIV of est. between: George SMITHER & William SMITHER. (LC EB 24:264)

SMITHER, William; 21 Feb 1811; 15 Jul 1811
LC; WILL; use of est. to wife Elizabeth SMITHER and she is to maintain the children; at wife's marriage or decease son Thomas SMITHER to have messuage or tenement w/o I now live; all prop. in Negroes to two daus. Elizabeth SMITHER & Judith SMITHER; if wife be pregnant that child to share est. with daus; wife extx; WITS: Sam. SPENCER, David PARMELE, Jn. FLOWERS, Geo. WALE. (LC WB 28:117)
[This is prob. Wm. SMITHER who mar. Eliz. LAWSON, LC, bond 5 Aug 1803 (MLBLC:68); Isaac HURST aptd. gdn. to Thos., Judith & Milly Ann SMITHER orphans of Wm. SMITHER, 18 Oct 1819 (LC OB 25:86)]

SMITHER, William; PO 15 Jul 1811, T 23 Aug 1811; 16 Sep [1811]

LC; INV; includes Negroes: Solomon, Spencer, Siller, Jefferson, Suckey. (LC EB 27:91)

SMITHER, William; PO 15 Nov 1819, T 27 Nov 1819; 2[0] Mar 1820
LC; INV, $1792.56 1/2; includes Negroes Solloman, Spencer, Sylla, Jefferson, Suckey. (LC EB 29:12)

SNOW, Charles; PO 11 Nov 1822; 9 Jul 1823
NC; land belonging to the heirs of Charles SNOW dec'd was sold to Willis INGRAM for $207 and proceeds div. among: Sally SNOW, Elizabeth SNOW, William SNOW & Charles SNOW. (NC RB 23:322; OB 1820-25:200)

SOMERVILLE, William C.; 27 Nov 1826
WC; William C. SOMERVILLE dead for more than 3 mos. and no one came forward to admin. his est.; sheriff to admin. the est. (WC OB 1823-27:333)
[This is prob. Wm. C. SOMERVILLE, of Charles Co., Md., who purchased Stratford from Hen. Lee III in 1822; SOMERVILLE was from Maryland and the bro. of Hen. V. SOMERVILLE, Esq. of Baltimore. He died at La Grange, the home of the Marquis de Lafayette near Paris, in January 1826 on his way to take the post of charge d'affairs to the court of Sweden. He was buried at Courpalay near La Grange on 19 Jan 1826 (Paul C. Nagel, *The Lees of Virginia: Seven Generations of an American Family*,1996. New York:Oxford University Press, p. 215; *Richmond Enquirer*, 24 Mar 1826, p. [4], *Boston Commercial Gazette*, 30 Mar 1826, p. [1], 6 Apr 1826, p. [1], *American Mercury*, 4 Apr 1826, p. [2])]

SORRELL, James; T Dec 1800; 28 Sep 1801
WC; INV, £458.0.0; includes Negroes Abraham, Adam, Peter, Gawin; DIV: widow's proportion, John SORREL's proportion, Elizabeth NEALE's proportion, Thomas SORREL's proportion, James SORREL's proportion. (WC RI 8:139)
[This is prob. James SORRELL who mar. Martha ATWELL, dau. of Jn. ATWELL (d. WC 1770), WC, between Apr 1770 and Nov 1790 (MWO:326)]

SORRELL, James; PO 24 Jan 1806, T18 Dec 1806; 23 Jan 1809. WC; INV, £38.1.0. (WC RI 9:83)

SORRELL, Thomas; 17 Jan 1788; 6 Apr 1796
of CP, WC; WILL; 622-ac. tract of land & all my Negroes: Harry, Jeremiah, David, Solomon, Charles, Sarah, Kate, Peg, Jone, Natt, Ralph, Rachel, Leroy, Daingerfield, Hannah, Nan, Henry to wife Million SORRELL; after wife's death above to return to my worthy friend Col. George GLASCOCK of RC; only one shilling to bro. James SORRELL; god son Mitchell HUNT; wife Million & friend Col. George GLASCOCK exors; [no wits]; [appeal by George GLASCOCK from a judgment of the County Court of WC dtd. 23 Mar 1795; DC reversed the WC Court judgment]. (NC DCO:335)
[Thos. SORRELL mar. Million GLASCOCK, dau. of Gregory GLASCOCK, RC, bond 20 Oct 1770 (MRC:192)]

SORRELL, Thomas A.; 22 Jun 1811; 23 Dec 1811
WC; WILL; land bought of Peter RUST to be sold to pay debts; bro. James SORREL; wife Anne one third of est. during her life and at her death to go to son Attwell SORREL; son Attwell to get rest of est.; if bro. James SORREL receives the legacy herein bequeathed, it will be considered by myself & him in full for any claim whatever that he may have against me as admr. of my father James SORREL dec'd or against me on any accompt whatever; friend Thomas STOWERS to be guardian to my son Attwell & exor; WITS: Jeremiah JEFFRIES, Jn. C. SELF, Peter N. RUST. (WC DW 22:242)

[Thos. A. SORRELL mar. Nancy ATTWELL, dau. of Wm. ATTWELL, WC, bond 18 Aug 1807 (MLBWC:66)]

SOUTH, John; 13 Dec 1791; 4 Sep 1792
WC; WILL; to William SANFORD son of Winifred SANFORD 5 Negroes: Sam, Sall, Pat, Rose, George, Negro Willoughby; gun & shoe buckles to William CRENSHAW son of David CRENSHAW; Ann CRENSHAW; Negro Pender to my dau. Ann McCLANAHAN; Negro Mary to grdau. Ann McCLANAHAN; Negro Charlot to grdau. Magdalen McCLANAHAN; Negro Solomon to grson. Richard McCLANAHAN; Negro David to grson. Thomas McCLANAHAN; Negro Jerry to grdau. Jemima McCLANAHAN; Negro Rachel to grdau. Elizabeth McCLANAHAN; large Bible & other books to William SANFORD; friend David CRENSHAW & William SANFORD exors; WITS: Presley SELF, Wm. FEAGIT, Geo. WILKERSON. (NC DCO:288)

SOUTH, John; PO Sep 1792 T 13 Sep 1792; 1 Apr 1793
WC; INV; includes Negroes: Sam, Pender, Sally, Patt, Rachel, Rose, George, Mary, Willoughby, Davy, Jerry, Charlotte, Solomon. (NC DCO:319)

SPARK, Alexander; 25 Feb 1783
WC; WILL; plant. in Gloucester Co. called [Marlow's] to James; land near the Bristol Mine in WC to William; Negroes to be eq. div. amongst the three [sic]; four Negroes living with Betty DAVIS: Sam & Hannah & two children to [*1 word unclear*] & her dau. [Betty] DAVIS; Negro formerly called Rose changed to Fanny to Grace FISHER the natural dau. of Thomas SHADRICK's wife for life and at her death to go to James & Sophia children of the sd. Grace. (WC Unrec Wills 1755-1800 #25)
[*This will was incomplete; at the end there were three names, possibly wits.: Thos. SMITH, Rich. PARKER, Doctor [?]; SPARK died before Rich. PARKER could complete drawing up the will; the notes for a will were admitted to record and Thomas THOMSON was granted a certificate of admin.; on the outside of the bundle containing this will the following note was written, "Recorded in 1783 and the Record Book wherein it was recorded being stolen it is again admitted to record in 1801 by ord. of court;"* an Alexander SPARK mar. Eliz. LAWSON, dau. of Thos. LAWSON, RC, bond 21 Nov 1765 (MWO:327); Wm. SPARK, of St. Thomas Par., Jamaica, in his will (WC 1 Jan 1764 - 25 Aug 1767) mentioned his bro. Alex. SPARK of WC (WC DW 14:490, 16:59); the Bristol Iron Mines were located along Bristol Mine Run which originates on the WC - KGC line and flows south into the Rappahannock River (Miller:16)]

SPARK, William; 25 May 1802; 28 Jun 1802
WC; WILL; wife; infant son; est. from marriage with my wife to revert to her provided that she within 6 months of arriving to the age of 21 convey by deed the water grist mill to my son; bro. James SPARK exor; WITS: Alex. PARKER, Maria BARNETT, Eliza SIMPSON. (WC DW 20:350)
[This is prob. the Wm. SPARKS [sic] who mar. Lucy REDMAN, WC, bond 6 Jan 1801; Lucy mar. (2) Rich. T. BROWN, WC, bond 27 Mar 1806 (MLBWC:9, 66); Wm. SPARKE orphan of Wm. SPARKE chose Rich. T. BROWN as his gdn., 27 Apr 1818 (WC OB 1814-18:378)]

SPENCE, Thomas; 22 Oct 1821; 24 Jun 1822
WC; WILL; having given to my son William as much of my est. as I can afford to give either of my other children I therefore desire that his children have no part of my est. in any event; I release to my son Thomas SPENCE all the rents of the land now in his possession; to my dau. Kitty a Negro girl Maria; to my dau. Jamimah a Negro girl Malinda; dau. Jane Newton a Negro

girl Peggy; I confirm to dau. HUNGERFORD the gift of the Negro Eliza; rest of est. I lend to my wife; wife & sons Thomas, Edward & Alexander exors; WITS: Jn. [?] SMITH, M. A. HARVEY, Jn. CAMPBELL. (WC DW 24:334) [Several chancery suits give information on the heirs of Thos. SPENCE; his children are named as: William, Thomas, Edward, Alexander and John SPENCE, Isabella who mar. (1) Geo. FIELD and (2) Wm. M. WALKER, Elizabeth B. who mar. Jas. BARKLEY, Amelia, Catherine who mar. Geo. R. PITTS, Jamima who mar. Wm. M. DAMERON, and Jane N. (WCCP:17, 26); Amelia SPENCE mar. Hen. HUNGERFORD, WC, bond 12 Mar 1818 (MLBWC:32)]

SPILLER, Ann; PO Nov 1812, T 18 Dec 1812; 18 Jan 1813. LC INV. (LC EB 27:132)

SPILLER, Benedictus; PO 15 Jul [1805]; 16 Sep 1805

LC; INV (consisted entirely of books and included a Latin dictionary and grammar), $89.25; the admr. was Benjamin SPILLER. (LC EB 24:326)

SPILLER, Benjamin C.; 26 Mar 1801; 20 Jul 1801

LC; WILL; est. to remain undivided for the use of wife Ann SPILLER & the support of my children (who is to pay no rent); should one of my daus., Susanna, Ann Frazier, Grace and Rockseylany marry before the death of wife, she shall have her portion of my est; Negro woman Hannah to wife; 1000 ac. of land in Kentucky part of my 4000 ac. of military land granted to me for my services to the Commonwealth during the last war to my sons William & Hickman SPILLER; my dwelling plant. w/o I now live which I purchased of Thomas PINCKARD to son Benedictus SPILLER provided that he pay to his bro. James SPILLER when he shall come of age £250; if son James should die before he comes of age, £250 to be paid to son Patrick SPILLER; all the land I purchased of Hudson MUSE & the mill I bought of William EUSTACE to my son Benjamin SPILLER after the death of my wife; my land in NC I purchased of Thomas HULL to my son Patrick SPILLER after the death of my wife; 1000 ac. in Kentucky to my son James SPILLER; should my exors. recover the land that is in dispute between Peter TANKERSLEY & myself it should be eq. div. between my sons Benedictus & Benjamin; son Benedictus & friends William KIRK & John CARPENTER exors; WITS: Martin SHEARMAN, Walt. JONES, [Lorimer] CHOWNING, Thos. JAMES, Jn. STEPTOE, Jn. FLOWERS; COD dtd. 11 Apr 1801, friend Martin SHEARMAN added to exors. (LC WB 28:50)
[A Capt. Benj. SPILLER received 4000 ac. on 1 Mar 1783 for 3 years infantry service in the Continental Line; his name also appears as a capt. on the pay roll of the 2nd Va. Regt. under Col. Gregory Smith (RWR:116, 152, 533); Susanna SPILLER orphan of Benj. [B.] SPILLER chose Martin SHEARMAN as her gdn., 21 Sep 1801 (LC Orders 21 1799-1801:321); Ann SPILLER orphan of Benj. [B.] SPILLER chose Ann SPILLER for her gdn., LC 17 Dec 1804 (LC OB 1804-05:267); Chancery suit, Rich. MITCHELL & Dolly his wife who was Dolly DEGGE surviving admx. of Jn. DEGGE, pltfs., against Chas. LELAND ex. of Thos. PINCKARD, Elias EDMONDS & Martin SHEARMAN, Wm. KIRK & Jn. CARPENTER surviving exors. of Benj. C. SPILLER, Ann SPILLER, Wm. SPILLER, & Hickman SPILLER, Susanna [HURST], Benj. SPILLER. Geo. SMITHER & Ann Frazer his wife, Grace SPILLER, Roxalana SPILLER, Patrick SPILLER & Jas. SPILLER, defts. (LC Orders D22 1805-08:341; Orders 24:35); Benj. C. SPILLER was the son of Wm. SPILLER of King William Co., Va. (http://spotisadog.wordpress.com/2010/05/25/will-of-benjamin-c-spiller-died-1801-lancaster-county-virginia/ and http://spotisadog.wordpress.com/ 2010/06/23/more-on-benjamin-c-

spiller-and-children/ accessed 12 Feb 2012); Susanna SPILLER mar. Warner HURST, LC, bond 15 Oct 1801; Ann Frazer SPILLER mar. Geo. SMITHER, LC, bond 14 Jan 1805; Grace SPILLER mar. Ralph EDMONDS, LC, bond 24 Mar 1809; Roxelana SPILLER mar. Jn. HUGHLETT, LC, bond 10 Dec 1808 (MLBLC:25, 39, 40, 68); there is an error in MLBLC:39 and MWO:190; the year of marriage for Roxelana SPILLER should be 1808 and not 1708); Jas. SPILLER orphan of Benj. C. SPILLER chose Martin SHEARMAN as his gdn., 21 Sep 1812 (LC Orders 24:117); Jas. SPILLER orphan of Benj. C. SPILLER chose Jas. HURST as his gdn., 18 Apr 1814 (LC Orders 24:185, 199); *see also LC CCs 1819-031 and 1819-042*]

SPILLER, Benjamin C.; PO 19 Sep 1803; 19 Dec 1803
LC; allotted to Warner HURST who mar. Susanna SPILLER all his wife's part of the est. of Benjamin C. SPILLER; includes Negroes Armistead, Caty & child [Decima], Delphia & Sarah. (LC EB 24:257)
[Warner HURST mar. Susan SPILLER, LC, bond 15 Oct 1801 (MLBLC:40); Roxalana SPILLER orphan of Benj. C. SPILLER chose Benj. SPILLER as her gdn., 21 Nov 1808; possess Jn. HUGHLETT who mar. Roxalana SPILLER one of the legatees of Benj. C. SPILLER with her proportion of the sd. decedant's est., 16 Jan 1809 (LC Orders B23 1808-11:1, 9); Geo. SPILLER orphan of Benj. C. SPILLER chose Elias EDMONDS as his gdn., 20 Mar 1809 (LC Orders B23 1808-11:15); Elias EDMONDS aptd. gdn. to Jas. SPILLER orphan of Benj. SPILLER, 18 Oct 1809 (LC Orders B23 1808-11:125)]

SPILMAN, James; PO 21 Oct 1811; 17 Feb 1812. LC; INV, $25.37. (LC EB 27:99)

SPILMAN, Joshua; [m]; 15 Feb 1802
LC; INV, $203.19; PO 15 Feb 1802, est. acct. of Barbara HUGHLETT, who was Barbara SPILMAN admx. of Joshua SPILMAN, was settled and est. was div. among the legal reps: M. TAPSCOTT, A. STARK, Eliza SPILMAN, William SPILMAN, Gilbert SPILMAN, George SPILMAN, James SPILMAN, Joshua SPILMAN and Lucinda SPILMAN, div. recorded 19 Jul 1802. (LC EB 24:175, 208; Orders V 1802-03:12)
[Joshua SPILMAN, wid., mar. (2?) Barbary DAMERON, wid., LC, bond 6 Feb 1794; Barbara SPILMAN mar. (3?) Ephraim HUGHLETT, LC, bond 21 May 1801; Mary SPILMAN mar. Jn. TAPSCOTT, LC, bond 8 Sep 1786 (MLBLC:39, 69, 72); possess Thos. JAMES gdn. of Lucinda SPELMAN with her proportion of the est. of Joshua SPELMAN, 15 Dec 1806 (LC Orders D22 1805-08:277)]

SPRIGGS, Nathan; 20 Jan 1817
LC; Nathan SPRIGGS aptd. gdn. to his children Polly, Winny, [Dedamia], & Nathan SPRIGGS. (LC Orders 24:346)

STAMPER, Leonard; 5 Jul 1813; 24 Nov 1817.
of LC; WILL; 37 1/2 ac. tract in Middlesex Co. which I heired by my father to bro. John; if I dispose of this tract in my lifetime, bro. John to have $80; to bro. William his bond for £21.5 due 1 Sep 1807; to bro. Samuel his bond for $55.25 due 29 Dec 1810 and all my books which list of may be found on my day book of creditor & debtor; I release my bro. Samuel from payment of a receipt for a bond of $18 which was due me by William N. KIDD & put into his hands for collection the sd. KIDD went off without paying it; two nephews John & George CARDWELL $40 each; niece Frances STAMPER dau. of Nelson STAMPER $50; half my wearing apparel to bro. Nelson; goddau. Lucy PAYNE dau. of Merryman PAYNE $40 to be prudently laid out for her education; to R. W. DOWNMAN Esq. $100 for his trouble in acting on this instrument; no bonds which I do or may hold to be brought

suit on in less than 12 months after my decease; all the rest of my money which is about $1000 to be laid out in bank stock or in such a manner as it may be called in at the expiration of 10 years and the interest arising therefrom to be given to the poor of Middlesex & Lancaster cos. & the rest be div. as follows: $100 to bro. William, $100 to sis. Elizabeth CARDWELL, $100 to bro. John, $50 to bro. Samuel, $50 to bro. Nelson, and $20 to the Protestant minister who preaches my funeral sermon; R. W. DOWNMAN & William L. BALL Gent. exors; he does not think wits. necessary; P.S. I had formerly left Amelia DOWNMAN a legacy but upon after circumstancy [sic] think proper to erase it & leave her nothing. [proved by the oaths of Jn. REDMAN & Thos. S. MUSE.] (WC DW 23:311)

STEPHENS, Joseph; PO Oct 1797, T 25 Oct 1797; 18 Jun 1798
LC; INV, £318.12.7; includes Negroes: Hercules, James, Pleasant, Jenny, Fanny, Suky, Sally. (LC EB 24:76)

STEPHENS, Joseph; T 21 Dec 1798; 17 Jun 1799
LC; INV of est. unadministered by Charlotte STEPHENS, [m]; includes Negroes: Hercules, James, Jinny, Pleasant, Fanny, Sukey, Sally. (LC EB 24:96) [Jos. STEPHENS mar. Charlotte BRENT, LC, bond 15 Mar 1782 (MLBLC:70)]

STEPHENS, Joseph; PO 15 Dec 1806, T 21 Jan 1807; 21 Dec 1807
LC; DIV of est. among: Richard STEPHENS, William STEPHENS, Joseph STEPHENS, George STEPHENS; Hugh BRENT & Martin BRENT admrs. (LC EB 27:24)
[Geo. P. STEPHENS orphan of Jos. STEPHENS chose R. STEPHENS as his gdn. and settle with Hugh BRENT former gdn. of Geo. P. STEPHENS, 21 Sep 1812 (LC Orders 24:118)]

STEPHENS, Mark; T 18 Jun 1801; 7 Apr 1806. RC; INV, £20.19.0. (RC WB 9:279)

STEPHENS, Mary Ann; T. 3 Nov 1806; 1 Dec 1806. RC; INV, £107.0.2 1/2; includes Negro woman Milly. (RC WB 9:300)
[This is prob. Mary Ann JESPER, dau. of Thos. (d. RC 1797) & Ann JESPER, who mar. Thos. STEPHENS, RC, bond 17 Dec 1796 (MWO:331)]

STEPHENS, Thomas; 14 Apr 1806; 2 Jun 1806
NFP, RC; WILL; all est. to sis. Elizabeth BROWN & bro. William RUICK; friend George JESPER; friends Hundley SAUNDERS & Edward SAUNDERS exors; WITS: Thos. DOBYNS, Sam. MISKELL. (RC WB 9:283)

STEPHENS, Thomas; T 17 Nov 1806; 7 Mar 1814. RC; INV, [m]. (RC WB 9:448)

STEPTOE, Elizabeth; 1 Sep 1801; 26 Oct 1802
WC; WILL; friend Kesiah PENDERGRASS 50 ac. on Windsor Plant.; mentions Aunt STURMAN; Sally NEWTON; Alice JONES; Mary PARKER; Ransdell PIERCE; b-i-l James STEPTOE the family bible and family pictures; Henry NEALE son of Penelope MOXLEY; Margaret WILKERSON; Saul and his wife Letty; Robin & Absolom; Preston; Nanny who nursed both my dear children; [Jugurtha] commonly called Garth & Milly; little girl called [Leal] that now waits upon me to serve Miss Peggy PIERCE until 18 and then liberated; Mr. Elijah RANSDELL of Kentucky if he should come to WC; John WICKHAM of Richmond; Elder Henry TOLER 50 ac. of Windsor and £10 annually as long as he continues pastor of Nomini Baptist Church; boy called Cupid to serve TOLER until 25 and then set free; little boy called Dennis to serve Elder Andrew BROADDUS until 30 and then liberated; friend and bro. in Christ Samuel [TEMPLEMAN] remainder of land at Windsor; desires that Cesar, Saul, Preston, Absolom, Robin, Aunt Lettie, Nanny & [Minne] be set free as soon as possible; old Negroes who are without a home and incapable of getting one to live on the land at Windsor

support; £10 for furnishing Nomini Meeting House or building another; Sam. TEMPLEMAN to be ex.and he is to have a plain tombstone erected to the memory of son Edward STEPTOE (age 13 years & 3 mos.) whose remains lie in Georgetown, Maryland and to enclose the family graveyard at Yeocomico Church if not with brick or stone with a good post and railings done by Saul & Tom; if TEMPLEMAN die bef. executing terms of will then Elder Hen. TOLER to succeed him; Ransdell PIERCE to succeed TOLER if necessary; WITS: Sally NEWTON, Angelica COLLINS, Willoughby NEWTON. (WC DW 20:392)

[This is prob. Eliz. the wid. of Dr. Geo. STEPTOE who named his wife Eliz. and son Edward and mentioned an unborn child in his will (WC 22 Jan 1783 - 27 May 1784) (WC DW 16:218, DW 17:11); Eliz. was the dau. of Edw. & Eliz. (STURMAN) RANSDELL and wid. of (1) James DAVENPORT; she mar. Geo. STEPTOE bet. 1777 and 1784 (MWO:331); the Windsor plant. mentioned here is prob the tract located in Montross, WC (Miller:173); Miller:175 locates the 1706 Yeocomico Church at Tucker Hill north of Kinsale in WC.]

STEPTOE, Elizabeth; T 14 Dec 1802; 28 Feb 1804

LC; INV, £2716.6.0; includes Negroes Old Addam (age 80), Old Beck (80), Saul (50), Letty (55) wife to Saul, Old Winney (55), Jugarthy (25), Tom forty (40), Will SMITH (35), Nanny (27), Frank (23) son of Nanny (hired up the country), Beck (15) dau. of Nanny, Sam (12) a son of Nanny, Betty Steptoe (4) dau. of Nanny; Yellow Letty (32) dau. of Cate, Isabella (4) her dau, Samuel (2) her son; Preston (16) son of Cate, Jonathan (14) son of Cate, James (11) son of Cate; Flora (27) dau. of Cate, Ned (6) son of Flora, Fan[n]y (5) dau. of Flora, Daniel (3) son of Cate, Kittey (1) dau. of Cate; Old Robbin (55), Old Preston (48); Old Mary (46), Absolom (40) purchased by Mrs. STEPTOE since the death of Dr. STEPTOE, Old Molly (49), Barbara (32) her dau; Billy (25) son of Moll, Lean[der] (22) son of Moll, Hannah (20) dau. of Moll; Cesar (14) son of Barbara, Harriot Baker (8) dau. of Barbara, James (2) Wm. STEPTOE's son [sic]; Dennis Monroe (4) son of Ha[nnah], William Robinson (2) son of Ha[nnah]; [Memey] (45), Esther (26), Clarissa (23), Alice (6) dau. of Clarissa, Cupit (4) son of Esther, Richard (3) Parker's son, Salina (2) [dau. of Parker]; Solomon (1) son of Clarissa, Sylvia (30) Mary's dau, George (12) her son, Leah (10) dau. of [Mary], Prince (6) son of [Mary], Cyrus (4) son of [Mary], Lucy (19) Mary's dau, Milly (25) Mary's dau, Mary Ann (5) Mary's dau, Sally Ransdell (1) Mary's dau. (WC RI 8:377)

STEPTOE, John; 24 Dec 1804; 18 Nov 1805

LC; WILL; if wife Betsy Martin STEPTOE should have a child within 9 months of my decease all my est. to that child whether male or female; if wife does not have a child within 9 months, she is to have the following Negroes: George WOOD, Daniel, Hannah, David, Peggy, and Page MONROE; Negro woman Amy in consequence of her faithful service should be manumitted and set free and have a home in my dwelling plant. during her natural life; friend William KIRK; land & plant. to wife; at wife's death land & plant. to friend William KIRK; wife & William KIRK exors; WITS: Martin SHEARMAN, Wm. MEREDITH, Spencer GEORGE, Jn. THRALL. (LC WB 28:93)

[Jn. STEPTOE mar. Elizabeth Martin GEORGE, LC, bond 12 Dec 1786 (MLBLC:69)]

STEPTOE, John; T 21 Nov 1805; 10 Sep 1806

LC; list of all Negroes devised to Betsy M. STEPTOE by John STEPTOE: Roger (50 years), George (41), Bob (15), Billy (11), Leroy (6), Sarah (60), Milly (55), Charity (38), Jennetta (3), Amanda (1), Betsy (1). (LC EB 24:345)

STEPTOE, John Esq.; PO 18 Nov 1805, T 28 Nov 1805; 17 Jul 1809
LC; INV, £1284.12.11; includes Negroes: George [W???], Daniel, Roger, Bob, David, Billy, [Page], [?], Peggy, Charity, Milley, Sarah, Janett, Amanda, Betty, Hannah, Amy, George. (LC EB 27:57, 58)

STEWART, John; 8 Dec 1819; 28 Feb 1820
of Traveller's Rest, WC; WILL; two sons Benjamin F. STEWART & William Price STEWART; wife Frances STEWART; four children Benjamin F. STEWART, William Price STEWART, Sarah PAYNE, & Jane Elizabeth McKENNY; Negroes James, Bill, Fanny, Maria, Daniel, Mary & Beverly to wife; friends John CAMPBELL Esq. and Baldwin M. LEE and sons Benjamin F. & William Price and wife exors; WITS: William Starke JETT, Wm. COGHILL, Rich. POTTS Jr., Jn. S. WILKINSON, Wm. BERKLEY, Chas. HAYDEN, Baldwin M. LEE. (WC DW 24:38)
[Sarah STEWARD [sic] mar. Meredith PAYNE, WC, bond 7 Nov 1811; Jane STEWARD [sic] mar. Armstrong McKENNY, WC, bond 12 Aug 1813 (MLBWC:42, 53); Col. Jn. STEWART, age 52, d. of the gout on 12 Dec 1819 at his seat in WC; he left a wid. and four small children (BDBN:108, *Baltimore Patriot & Mercantile Advertiser*, 20 Dec 1819, p. [2])]

STEWART, John (Col.); T 9 Sep 1820, 17 Oct 1820; [m]
WC; INV of the est. at his residence called Traveller's Rest where he died, $2454.95; includes Negroes Fanny, young Negro woman Maria & her two children Mary & William, boys Daniel & Beverly; INV at his plant. called White Point on the Potomac in WC, $4426.28; includes Negroes Tom, James, Davy, Abram, Robin, Letty, Sarah, Winny & child, Hannah, Henry, Lucinda. (WC RI 11:113)
[The only Traveler's Rest identified by Miller:159 is located in NC near Horse Head; she identifies three White Points in WC (Miller:169)]

STONE, John; 19 Aug 1802; 28 Mar 1803.
CP, WC; WILL; entire est. to wife Martha STONE and she to be extx.; WITS: Jn. BROWN Sr., Wm. H. HALL, Wm. McKILDOE. (WC DW 20:440)

STONE, John; Mar 1803; 23 May 1803. WC; INV, £109.11.0. (WC RI 8:226)

STONE, Martha; T 16 Jan 1821; 22 Oct 1821
WC; INV, $1607.46; includes Negroes Margua (age 36), Lucey (17), Maria (15), Clarey (10), Eliza (8), Fanny (6), Nancy (2). (WC RI 11:127)

STONE, Martha; PO 25 Dec 1820, T 16 Jan 1821; 28 Jan 1822
WC; INV, $1607.46; DIV of slaves among William B. STONE, the first & oldest child, (Maria child of Margarey, Clarey child of Margary), Richard MOTHERSHEAD in right of his wife (Lucy child of Margary, Fanny), John SUTTON in right of his wife (Margarey, Nancey her child, Eliza her child); at her death Martha STONE held two tracts of land, 46 ac. in RC and 65 ac. in WC. (WC RI 11:134)
[Martha STONE was the wid. of Jn. STONE (d. WC 1803) (WC DW 20:440); Rich. MOTHERSHEAD mar. Mary STONE, WC, bond 27 Dec 1820; Jn. SUTTON mar. Martha STONE, WC, bond 31 Aug 1819 (MLBWC:47, 69)]

STONEHAM, John; 18 Feb 1805
LC; James NORRIS was gdn. of Betsey STONEHAM orphan of John STONEHAM. (LC OB 1804-05:280)
[This must be the Jn. STONUM who mar. Nanny NORRIS in LC bef. 20 Mar 1782 (MWO:334); div. of proceeds of the sale of the slaves Lucy, Sam, Billy

and Lucy's child at the breast, £135.11, among Jn., Jane, Peggy, Nancy, Betsy and Molly the children of Jn. STONUM dec'd and the grandchilden of Jn. NORRIS (d. LC 1789) who left them a legacy, LC, 1 May 1799 (LC CC 1799-002; LC WB 22:225)]

STONUM, Mary; 13 May 1806; 7 Jul 1806
RC; WILL; son George STONUM one feather bed & furniture but not to take it away from this place until he shall settle himself; dau. Betsy JESPER; rest of est. to dau. Susanna STONUM; at her death to go to her children if any; dau. Susanna extx; WITS: Jn. SMITH, Jane HARRISON. (RC WB 9:292)
[This is Mary the wid. of Geo. STONUM; the births of three daus. of Geo. & Mary STONUM were rec. in the NFPR: Susanna (b. 21 Jan 1777), [fnu] (b. 16 May 1778) and Nancy (b. 1 Sep 1781) (NFPR:177); Eliz. STONUM, orphan of Geo. STONUM, mar. Rich. JESPER, RC, bond 30 Dec 1793 (MRC:105)]

STONUM, Mary; PO 7 Jul 1806; 6 Sep 1813. RC; INV, $127.75. (RC WB 9:431)

STONUM, Peggy; 18 Jan 1800; 21 Sep 1801.
CCP, LC; WILL; all est. to aunt Nancy NORRIS; uncle Martin NORRIS & friend Eppey NORRIS exors; WITS: Alex. MARSH, Jesse ROBINSON. (LC WB 28:55)
[Peggy STONUM was the dau. of Jn. STONUM who mar. Nanny NORRIS, dau. of Jn. NORRIS (d. LC 1789); Martin NORRIS was the son of Jn. NORRIS and the bro. of Nanny NORRIS; he mar. Nancy MERCER, dau. of Isaac MERCER (d. LC 1779), LC, bef. 17 May 1781 (LC WB 22:225, MWO:265, 334)]

STONUM, Richard; PO Sep 1799; 16 Jun 1800
LC; INV, £96.5.3 1/2; includes Negro Joe & a parcel of smith's tools. (LC EB 24:112)

STORKE, John; T 15 Mar 1813; 24 Jan 1820
WC; INV at Mattox, £1259.8.9; includes many kinds of cloth and Negro Davy. (WC RI 10:435)

STOTT, Eleanor; 7 Feb 1804; 3 Sep 1804
RC; WILL; father Leroy STOTT plant. during his life & after his death to sis. Nancy STOTT; at sis. death to go to Luke HANKS; m-i-l [Pegey] STOTT; father & Luke HANKS exors; WITS: Spencer BRANNAN, Saley STOTT, Gudith NEW[GAN], Pegey STOTT. (RC WB 9:237)
[Eleanor (b. 2 Dec 1781) was a dau. of LeRoy & Ann STOTT (NFPR:177); she had a sis. Nancy (b. 2 Jan 1788); LeRoy mar. (2) Peggy NEWGENT (RC, bond 30 Mar 1796) (MWO:335); Luke HANKS mar. Levina STOTT, dau. of Jn. STOTT, RC, bond 4 Jan 1792 (MWO:163)]

STOTT, Elizabeth; 29 Aug 1782; 21 Feb 1791
LC; WILL; Negro girl Sinah to grdau. Easter SHEARMAN; Negro boy John [PIERCE] to grdau. Frances HUNTON; Negro girl Nancy to grdau. Elizabeth Barber HUNT; Negro girl Sarah to grdau. Susanna POPE; Negro girl Lucy to great grdau. Elizabeth Barber HUNTON; remainder of est. to be eq. div. between my children William, Charles, George, Elizabeth, Frances & the children of my dau. Mary SHEARMAN dec'd; son George HUNT & s-i-l John POPE exors; Jas. BALL, Jas. BALL Jr., Fanny BALL; COD dtd. 14 Jun 1785: if son William HUNT makes any demand against my est. I revoke any legacy given him; WITS: Jas. BALL Jr., Fanny BALL, Raw. DOWNMAN. [Caveat entered by Wm. HUNT & will was left until April for probat when recording was postponed, "and the late clerk having failed to record the said will, it is now recorded agreeably to the former order of court"]. (LC WB 28:17)

[Eliz. STOTT was apparently mar. to a HUNT bef. her marriage to [fnu] STOTT; she had at least two children by HUNT: Mary HUNT who mar. Martin SHEARMAN, Jr. LC, bond 7 Jan 1762 and Wm. HUNT (MWO:317)]

STOTT, John; 3 Feb 1817. RC; died intest.; sheriff to; admin. his small est. (RC OB 24:70)

STOTT, Oliver; 3 Nov 1812; 2 Aug 1813
RC; all the Negroes in the possession of Mr. Thomas ROCK & wife to my dau. Jane ROCK; profits of est. to wife Mary until my last child Thaddeus arrives to the age of 16; 3 daus. Sally, Elizabeth, & Charity Ann STOTT; all lands to 3 sons Joel S., Oliver S., & Thaddeus C. STOTT; 6 last children: Sally C. STOTT, Elizabeth O. STOTT, Joel STOTT, Oliver STOTT, Charity Ann STOTT, & Thaddeus C. STOTT; Richard BENEHAN, Luke HANKS, & Thaddeus BRYANT exors; WITS: Jas. STOTT, [Ewl.] HANKS, Eppa STOTT. (RC WB 9:430)
[This is prob. Oliver STOTT who mar. Mary COELMAN, dau. of Thos. & Betty COELMAN, RC, bond 28 Jan 1797 (MRC:197)]

STOTT, Richard; 18 Jan 1802
LC; Richard STOTT, John MORRIS & Catherine his wife, and Mary STOTT are heirs & reps. of Richard STOTT. (LC Orders V 1802-03:3)
[Jn. MORRIS mar. Caty STOTT, age 20, RC, bond 1 Jul 1798 (MRC:138); acc. to LC CC 1812-006 Rich. STOTT d. intestate leaving a wid. Ann, who mar. (2) Thos. MASON, and 4 children: Mary, Rich., Cath. (who mar. Jn. MORRIS), and Jn.; Thos. MASON, wid., mar. Nancy STOTT, wid., LC, 30 Apr 1796 (MWO:237); *see also LC CC 1803-014*]

STOTT, Richard; 5 Jun 1821
RC; the court decided that Molly STOTT was a child of Richard STOTT and is legally entitled to an eq. proportion of a pension due Richard STOTT the whole of which pension having been received by Thomas DOBYNS gdn. to Richard & Elizabeth STOTT two of the children of the sd. Richard. (RC OB 25:162)

STOTT, Robert; PO Mar 1813; 5 Nov 1817. RC; INV, $175.84 1/2. (RC WB 9:568)

STOTT, Thomas; T 5 May 1796; 19 Dec 1796
LC; INV, [m]; includes Negroes David, Jane, Easter, Lucy, Charles, Dolly, Fanny, Sarah, Roger, Jude, Feeby. (LC EB 24:37)

STOTT, William; [m]; 17 Feb 1817
LC; WILL; whole est. to wife; if wife remarries est. to be eq. div. among my children; son Jasper STOTT; rest of children Elizabeth, Sarah, Maple [sic], William & Archibald; [no ex. named]; WITS: Griffin CHILTON; [will proved by oaths of Thos. CARTER & Wm. T. YERBY]. (LC WB 28:183)
[Sarah STOTT orphan of Wm. STOTT chose Jasper STOTT for her gdn., 18 Dec 1820 (LC OB 25:181)]

STOTT, William; T 27 Feb 1817; 21 Feb 1820
LC; INV, [m]; includes Negroes Dominy, Richard, Esther & child Ellin, Eve. (LC EB 29:1)

STOWERS, Richard; PO Nov 1806; 26 Jan 1807. WC; INV, £130.12.0; includes Negro Jack. (WC RI 9:8)

STRAUGHAN, Samuel L.; 3 Oct 1820; 13 Aug 1821
NC; WILL; wife Betsey T. to have the use of all my est; at her death or remarriage exors. to sell all perishable part of est, hire out the servants & rent the land until a final division becomes necessary either by the marriage or arrival to age 21 of either of my children; faithful servant Phillis to be liberated & set free from servitude & application be made to the court of this

county to permit her to remain in this state; two boys Fielding & Joseph to be hired out from year to year & proceeds applied to the support & tuiting of my younger children especially Samuel L. who I wish well educated; my library of books to son Samuel L.; my surveying instruments & all my books on that subject to my step-son Robert ALEXANDER; my watch to my friend Walter RICE; each of my children Sally S., Alice J., Mary P., Martha, Elizabeth, Jane L. & Samuel L. to have an eq. div. of my est; friends Eppa [NORRIS], Richard H. GASKINS & Rawleigh DUNAWAY exors; WITS: Jos. RICE, Wm. WALKER, Nancy WALKER. (NC RB 22:594)
[Sam. L. STRAUGHAN mar. Betsy T. ALEXANDER, wid., NC, bond 30 Jul 1804 (MLBNC:95); The Rev. Sam. STRAUGHAN, a Baptist minister, d. in July 1821 at his residence in NC in his 38th year; he had been confined with a pulmonary complaint for 12 months (*Baltimore Patriot & Mercantile Advertiser*, 13 Jul 1821, p. [2])]

STRAUGHAN, Samuel L.; PO 1 Aug 1821; 12 Nov 1821
NC; INV, $1212.[??]; includes [slaves] Fielding, Isaih, Fillis and a set of surveying instruments as well as a proportionable part of Hiram STRAUGHAN's est. now in the hands of John C. STRAUGHAN in Kentucky. (NC RB 23:22)

STRAUGHAN, Samuel Lamkin; 11 Dec 1809
NC; slaves bel. to the est. of Samuel L. STRAUGHAN dec'd to be sold and proceeds div. among John C. STRAUGHAN, Samuel L. STRAUGHAN, James L. STRAUGHAN, and John C STRAUGHAN as gdn. of Jane L. and Hiram L STRAUGHAN/; NC OB 1807-11:147)
[Sam. Lamkin STRAUGHAN was born 6 Feb 1759, a son of Rich. & [Jane LAMKIN] STRAUGHAN; he mar. Phoebe LEWIS, dau. of Jas. & Priscilla (RANDOLPH) LEWIS, NC, lic. 25 Oct 1779 - 25 Apr 1780 (MWO:335); the births of the following children to Sam. L. and Phoebe STRAUGHAN were rec. in the SSPR: Jn. Corbin, b. 21 Oct 1781, Sam. Lamkin, b. 30 Jul 1783, James Lewis, b. 6 Nov 1785, Rich., b. 28 May 1787, Jean Lewis, b. 6 Feb 1791 (SSPR:91, 92); Nath. OLDHAM was aptd. gdn. of Jn. C. STRAUGHAN, Sam. L. STRAUGHAN & Jas. L. STRAUGHAN, 27 Jan 1800 (WC Orders 1799:1801:176); Jn. C. STRAUGHAN was aptd. gdn. to Sam. L. STRAUGHAN, Jas. L. STRAUGHAN, Rich. STRAUGHAN, Jane L. STRAUGHAN and Hannah [sic] L. STRAUGHAN, WC 27 Jun 1803 (WC Orders 1801-04:406); in her will (NC 12 Jun 1812-12 Oct 1812), Jane LEWIS named Jn. C., Sam. L., Jas. L., Jane L., and Hierome STRAUGHAN as heirs (NC RB 19:264); *see also NC CCs 1809-017 and 1809-024*]

STREET, Henry; PO 18 Feb 1799; 15 Apr 1811
LC; INV; includes Negroes valued at $4880: Ned, Abram, Charles, Billy, James, Ralph, Nathan, John, Davy, Lewis, Jack, Dick, Armistead, June, Alice & child Nelly, Sally & child Matilda, Harlow, Polly, [Fanny], Scillah; DIV of est. between: Lucy STREET (wid.) and Thomas STREET, 21 Dec 1810. (LC EB 27:82)

STREET, Henry; [m]; 15 Jul 1811
LC; INV & DIV of slaves that were allotted to Lucy STREET dec'd as her dower, Lot 1 (Abraham, Polly, [?]) to Thomas STREET, Lot 2 (Ralph, Nathan, June) to W. T. YERBY in behalf of his wife Maria. (LC EB 27:88)

STREET, Lucy; 6 Feb 1811; 19 Mar 1811
LC; WILL; son Thomas STREET; relation John CHOWNING Jr. the use of the Negro boy Nathan for the present year; rest of est. to dau. Maria YERBY;

son Thomas, s-i-l William T. YERBY & relation John CHOWNING Jr. exors; WITS: Jn. BEAN, Sarah D. SPRIGGS. (LC WB 28:113)
[This is the wid. of Hen. STREET, d. LC c. 1799 (*see above*)]

STREET, Lucy; [m]; 17 Aug 1812. LC; INV. (LC EB 27:117)

STREET, Richard; 22 Oct 1822; 3 Oct 1825
RC; WILL; whole est. to wife Elizabeth STREET during her life; after wife's death est. to be eq. div. among daus: Elizabeth STREET, Susannah M. STREET, Maria STREET, Catharine STREET & Frances STREET; wife Elizabeth extx; [no WITS]. (RC WB 10:87)
[Rich. STREET mar. Eliz. MISKELL, RC, bond 14 Sep 1807 (MRC:198)]

STROTHER, Margarett; 11 Feb 1799; 26 Aug 1799
WC; WILL; grson. Jn. UNDERWOOD £100; dau. Eliz. MUSE residue and she to be extx. WITS: Thos. HUTT, Jn. ESKRIDGE, Jas. HACKNEY. (WC DW 20:48)

STUCKY, Job; 21 Jun 1799; 6 Jan 1800. RC; INV, £45.8.3. (RC WB 9:125)
[In his will (RC 13 Dec 1798-3 Jun 1799), Job Sims STUCKY names his wife Mary or Molly, and dau. [Bennerama]; the births of 2 daus. to Job STUCKY are recorded in the NFPR: Griffin Warmouth (b. 1782) and Hannah (b. 1781) (MWO:186)]

STURMAN, Foxhall; 26 Aug 1817
WC; William Y. STURMAN aptd. gdn. to Mary Ann & Elizabeth W. L. STURMAN inf. orphans of Foxhall STURMAN. (WC OB 1814-18:344)
[This is prob. Foxhall STURMAN the son of Elliott STURMAN (d. WC 1792) (WCW:193); Foxhall STURMAN mar. Eliz. NEALE, WC bond 2 Dec 1810 (MLBWC:68)]

SUGGITT, John; PO 7 Oct 1799; 7 Sep 1801
RC; DIV of est. of John SUGGITT among the claimants: Edward B. JONES in his own right, Newman B. BARNES as gdn. to Williamson P. JONES & Fanny JONES. (RC AB 3:53)
[Edward JONES, a minister, mar. Hannah SUGGITT, RC, bond 27 May 1775 (MRC:107)]

SULLIVANT, Ahimaz; T 25 May 1815; 22 May 1816. LC INV. (LC EB 27:336)

SULLIVANT, Charles; 20 Jul 1807
LC; it appears to the court that the land of which Charles SULLIVANT died seized and possessed in this county intestate will not exceed the value of $100 to each of his reps. it is ord. that Martin CARTER & Sarah his wife, William BROWN Jr. by his father and next friend, William BROWN, William ROBINSON & Nancy his wife, William DODSON Jr. by his father & next friend, William DODSON and Joseph SULLIVANT heirs & reps. of sd. Charles SULLIVANT be summoned to show cause why the land should not be sold. (LC Orders 22D 1805 - 08:368)
[Martin CARTER mar. Sally CRAIN, LC, bond 17 Feb 1807 (Sally was Sally SULLIVANT who mar. (1) Isaac CRAIN, LC, bond 24 Aug 1787); Wm. ROBINSON mar. Nancy SULLIVANT, LC, bond 24 Jan 1797 (MLBLC:12, 17, 64); William BROWN is prob. the Wm. BROWN who mar. Peggy HAYDON, wid., LC, bond 19 Dec 1796 (Peggy was Peggy SULLIVANT, dau. of Judith SULLIVANT, who had mar. (1) Wm. HAYDON, LC, bond 14 Mar 1792); Wm. DODSON is prob. the Wm. DODSON who mar. Sabra SULLIVANT, LC, bond 30 Jun 1803 (MLBLC:21)]

SULLIVANT, Dennis; PO 10 Oct 1803, T 23 Aug 1805; 15 Oct 1805
NC; DIV of pers. est. among the reps: Betty SULLAVANT, Thomas SULLAVANT. Salley SULLAVANT, John SULLAVANT, Nancy

SULLAVANT, Francis SULLAVANT in the hands of Cornelius SULLAVANT, Cornelius SULLAVANT in his own hands (each rep. rec'd £7.3.5 1/2). (NC RB 17:345)

SULLIVANT, John; PO 15 Jul 1793; 20 Jun 1796
LC; INV, £242.19.4; includes Negroes Will, Sam, Judith, Tom. (LC EB 24:14)

SULLIVANT, John; 16 Sep 1799
LC; Charles WEBB & Nancy [sic] his wife are admrs. of est. of John SULLIVANT. (LC Orders (21) 1799-1801:46)
[This is prob. Jn. SULLIVANT who mar. Mary NICHOLS, LC, bond 2 Jul 1779 (MLBLC:71); Mary (NICHOLS) SULLIVANT mar. (2) Chas. WEBB, LC, bond 6 Jun 1795 (MLBLC:78); LC CC 1804-015 confirms that Chas. WEBB's wife was Mary the wid. of Jn. SULLIVAN]

SULLIVANT, John; 21 Feb 1803
LC; on the mot. of Hill W. HUTCHINGSON ord. that Molly SULLIVANT, John SULLIVANT, and Thomas SULLIVANT, by Michael WILDER his gdn. be summoned to show cause why the slaves Sam, Judy, [Spencer], & Daniel belonging to the est. of John SULLIVANT should not be sold. (LC Orders V 1802-03:260)
[Michael WILDER aptd. gdn. to Thos. SULLIVANT orphan of Sally SULLIVANT, 21 Feb 1803 (LC Orders V 1802-03:261); Hill W. HUTCHINSON mar. Molly PEARSON, LC, bond 8 Jan 1805 (MLBLC:41)]

SULLIVANT, Joseph; PO 31 May 1822; 8 Jul 1822
NC; after examination, SULLIVAN was declared a person of unsound mind and that he should be restrained from going at large; for want of room he could not be received into the public hospital for the maintainance and care of persons of unsound mind in the city of Williamsburg; he was directed to be confined in the NC jail; his est. was inventoried and valued at $50 a year; it included 200 ac. of land. (NC RB 23:186)
[On the mot. of Rich. SULLIVAN, ord. that Polly, Peggy, Judith & Jos. SULLIVAN heirs and distributees of Jos. SULLIVAN be summoned to show cause why lands of sd. Jos. SULLIVAN should not be sold, 9 Aug 1825 (NC OB 1825-30:34); Polly SULLIVAN mar. Isaac B. MARSH (as his 1st wife), NC, bond 3 Jan 1828 (MLBNC:73); settle Rich. SULLIVAN's acct. of his gdnship. of Polly SULLIVAN now MARSH (NC OB 1825-30:243); the first hospital in the US solely for the treatment of mentally ill persons was opened in Williamsburg in 1773 (for more information on this hospital, see <http://www.history.org/almanack/places/hb/hbhos.cfm>, accessed 7 Jan 2013]

SULLIVANT, William; T 28 Dec 1814; 16 Oct 1815; LC; INV, $88.87; Thomas SULLIVANT admr. (LC EB 27:258)

SULLIVANT, William; PO 16 Oct 1815, 22 Nov 1816; 20 May 1816
LC; DIV of proceeds of sale of land among following heirs: Elizabeth KELLUM, Judith SULLIVANT, Sarah SULLIVANT, Molly SULLIVANT, Thomas SULLIVANT, and the heirs of [Ahimez] SULLIVANT. (LC EB 27:313)
[The marriage of Wm. KELLUM to Petsey [sic] SULLIVANT, bond 29 Oct 1803, is listed in MLBNC:63; ord. that Eliz. KELLAM, Judith SULLIVANT, Polly SULLIVANT, Sarah SULLIVANT, Thos. SULLIVANT, Nancy SULLIVANT & Jn. SULLIVANT; Thos. SULLIVANT, Polly SULLIVANT & Nancy SULLIVANT children of [Ahimaz] SULLIVANT be summoned to show cause why land of which Wm. SULLIVANT died seized & possessed should not be sold, 19 Dec 1814 (LC Orders 24:210)]

SUTTON, Amey; [m]; 25 Oct 1802
WC; INV, £35.7.0, presented by Susanna WESTON, admx. (WC RI 8:18[7]) [Amey SUTTON was the wid. of Jacob SUTTON, WC, 24 Aug 1801 (WC Orders 1801-04:128)]

SUTTON, Cyrus; 18 Mar 1814; 11 Sep 1815
NC; deed of manumission to Winney (age 35) to be free 1 Mar 1817, Lucy (9) to be free 1 Mar 1825, Moses (7) to be free 1 Mar 1832, Isaac (5) to be free 1 Mar 1834, Stephen (3) to be free 1 Mar 1836, James (19) to be free 1 Mar 1820; the issue of the aforesd. females born after the date of these presents shall be free, if males at 25 and if females at 21. (NC RB 20:244)

SUTTON, Cyrus; 8 Feb 1819; 12 Jul 1819
NC; WILL; use of est. to wife while she remains my wid.; wife to keep all my children and at any rate to give them a common education & lern them how to get an honest living; in case any of my children should marry & get a family, if wife should see proper to let them have any property, let 2 or 3 men of discretion be called on to appraise it and let them account for it at the general division; all slaves to be free agreeable to a bill of emansepation [sic] recorded in Northumberland Court in the following manner: Lucy to be free the 1st day of March 1825, Moses the 1st day of March 1832, Isaac the 1st day of March 1834, Stephen the 1st day of March 1836, James the 1st day of March 1820 & the issue of the females that may hereafter be born if males at 25 if females at 21; land to be div. between 3 oldest sons Henry, Cyrus & William, James [sic] and if either of my eldest sons should die underage & without heirs I give this land to Warner & the balance of my est. to be eq. div. between my other [3] children: Warner, Sally, Ann [*NB: It isn't clear if this dau's name is Sally or Sally Ann*] & Judith; friend William HARDING ex; WITS: Jn. R. HARRISON, Jesse CROWDER. (NC RB 22:78)
[Cyrus SUTTON was the son of James SUTTON (d. NC 1812) of WicP (NC RB 19:148); Hen. SUTTON aptd. gdn. of Sally & Judith SUTTON orphans of Cyrus SUTTON, 12 Mar 1827 (NC OB 1825-30:148)]

SUTTON, George; PO Jun 1803, T 8 Jul 1803; 26 Mar 1804. WC; INV, £39.1.0. (WC RI 8:396)
[Moses SELF was aptd. gdn. to Sally SUTTON orphan of Geo. SUTTON, WC, 28 Nov 1803 (WC Orders 1801-04:485)]

SUTTON, James; 14 Dec 1818; Hiram HARDING aptd. gdn. of John C. SUTTON orphan of James SUTTON. (NC OB 1816-20:315)
[Thos. BLACKWELL aptd. gdn. of Jn. C. SUTTON orphan of Jas. SUTTON, NC 14 Jan 1822 (NC OB 1820-25:170); Jn. C. SUTTON mar. Dianna H. McCURDY, ward of Wm. HARDING, Jr., NC, bond 29 Sep 1831 with the consent of Thos. BLACKWELL gdn. of John (MLBNC:96)]

SUTTON, James; [m]; 28 Aug 1821
WC; INV, $725.50; includes Negro woman [nfi] and a number of carpenter's tools including several different kinds of planes, saws, and augers. (WC RI 11:101)

SUTTON, James; PO 22 Aug 1824, T 8 Sep 1824; 27 Sep 1824
WC; INV; includes Negroes [Feby] (woman), Maria, Harry, girls Matildy & Sarah, boys Sam & Robert, girl Easter, Natt (a legacy to Elizabeth SUTTON & delivered some years since). (WC RI 11:452)

SUTTON, James (Capt.); [m]; 11 Mar 1822
NC; INV of Negroes, $5875; includes James, Parker, Frank, Lile, Siner, Fanny, Sally, boys George, David, Steptoe, Jerry, Griffin, Spencer, William & James, girls Rachel (big), Emsy, Mary, Rachel (small), & Ginny; thirds of

Negroes of Mrs. James SUTTON: James, Frank, Lile, Siner, Rachel, Emsy. (NC RB 23:115)

SUTTON, James (Capt.); [m]; 11 Mar 1822
NC; INV, [m]; includes Negroes James, Parker, Frank, Lile, Fanny, Siner, Sally, boys George, David, Steptoe, Jerry, Griffin, Spencer, William,& James, girls Rachel, Emsy, Mary, Rachel & Ginny. (NC RB 23:150)

SUTTON, James M.; 19 Aug 1816; 23 Dec 1816
WC; WILL; all est. & plant. given me by my father w/o he now resides in WC to wife Elizabeth SUTTON; friends William NELSON & Daniel CARMICHAEL; WITS: J. STEWART, Jas. REAMY, Ann NELSON. (WC DW 23:241)

SUTTON, James Sr.; 15 Sep 1818; 23 Nov 1818
WC; WILL; wife Frances SUTTON to have the whole of my est. during her widowhood except the part given my dau. Elizabeth SUTTON which I desire she may receive immediately on my decease; dau. Elizabeth a Negro man [Nat]; son Vincent SUTTON all my lands & still; dau. Frances SUTTON [Negroes] Pheba, Robert, & Sam; dau. Tracy M. SUTTON a Negro girl Maria; dau. Lucy SUTTON a Negro girl Sarah; son John SUTTON two Negroes Harry & Easter; three grandchildren [John] SUTTON, Susan SUTTON & Mary SUTTON $100 to be eq. div. among them; wife, son Vincent, & Richard T. BRANN exors; WITS: Wm. DOZIER, Jas. ROWLES. (WC DW 23:426)
[Jas. SUTTON mar. Frances WHITE, wid, WC, bond 3 Oct 1786 (MLBWC:69); Jeremiah SMITH mar. Fanny SUTTON, WC, bond 3 Feb 1824 (MLBWC:66, WC OB 1823-27:47)]

SUTTON, Jesse; 22 Aug 1803
WC; Elizabeth & Sibella SUTTON orphans of Jesse SUTTON chose Susanna WESTON as their gdn. (WC Orders 1801-04:445, Orders 1807-10:174)
[Susanna WESTON may be the same Susanna who with her dau. Ann was named in the will of Jn. WASHINGTON (WC 7 Apr 1794 – 22 Jun 1795) (WC DW 19:108)

SUTTON, Moses; PO 12 Dec 1796; 10 Jan 1804
NC; INV, £480.0.5; includes Negroes Sollomon, Dick GRANT, Isaac, [u/i woman], Jean & child, girl Luke a legacy, boy Daniel. (NC RB 17:113)

SUTTON, Moses; PO 13 Oct 1812, T 8 Feb 1813; 8 Feb 1813
NC; Chancery suit, Elismond BASYE, Thomas WEBB & Judith his wife who was Judith BASYE, Epaphroditus FIELDING & Mary his wife who was Mary BASYE, George SAMPSON & Elizabeth his wife who was Elizabeth BASYE & Jesse BASYE pltfs. against Caty SUTTON deft.; deft. still in default; ord. that she pay $932.97 with interest from 14 Oct 1811; if she defaults, lands of Moses SUTTON to be sold and proceeds applied to satisfying the decree; on 29 Dec 1812 land was sold to Elismond BASYE for $560. (NC RB 19:333)
[Moses SUTTON mar. at least three times; he was a wid. when he mar. Eliz. PITMAN, NC, bond 3 Mar 1791; his next wife was Caty PITMAN, wid., NC, bond 11 Jan 1793; his first wife may have been Dolly PALMER whom a Moses SUTTON mar. in NC, bond 28 Feb 1763 (MWO:338); In his will (NC 19 Apr 1796-12 Dec 1796) Moses SUTTON of WicP named his wife (nfi), his sons Jn., Thos., Wm., Rich., and Jas. SUTTON and Griffin, Cyrus, Salley, and Jeduthun PITMAN (NC RB 15:329); Thos. WEBB mar. Judith BASYE, LC, bond 30 Sep 1786 (MLBLC:78); Caty PITMAN was Caty WEBB who mar. Jeduthun PITMAN, LC, bond 29 Mar 1783 (MLBLC:60)]

SUTTON, Nancy Meeks; 19 Mar 1803; 28 Nov 1803
WC; WILL; whole est. to infant dau. Sally; if she dies without heirs, Negro woman Nelly & her child Betsy to bro. William PACKETT & sis. Betsy PACKETT; uncle William BRICKEY exor; WITS: Jane REYNOLDS, Nancy BRICKEY, Wm. BRICKEY; Wm. BRICKEY renounced the executorship 26 Mar 1803. (WC DW 20:501)
[Ann Meeks PACKETT was a niece of Ann MEEKS (d. WC 1784) (WC DW 16:233, 17:14); this looks suspiciously like the Nancy PACKETT who mar. Geo. SUTTON, WC, bond 1 Nov 1811, but the date of the bond, if correct, is incompatible with the date of her will. (MLBWC:69)]

SUTTON, Samuel; PO 21 Dec 1801; 18 Jan 1802. LC; INV at the house of Thomas CARTER, £5.14.0. (LC EB 24:169)

SUTTON, Thomas; T 9 Dec 1812; 25 Sep 1815
WC; INV, £244.0.3; includes Negroes Frank, Jack, Lucy & child Nancy. (WC RI 10:24)
[Thos. FRANKLIN mar. a dau. of Thos. D. SUTTON dec'd, 27 Feb 1815 (WC OB 1814-18:97); a mar. bond is rec. in WC for Thos. FRANKLIN & Harriet SUTTON on 9 Feb 1814 (MLBWC:24); Jn. BROWN aptd. gdn. of Nancy & Sally SUTTON orphans of Thos. D. SUTTON, 26 Feb 1816, WC OB 1814-18:205)]

SUTTON, William Sr.; 15 Aug 1815; 26 May 1821
WC; WILL; to son William SUTTON Jr. land w/o I now live together with my hand mill; granddau. Sibella CONNELLEE dau. of Maria CONNELLEE; remainder of est. to be eq. div. among Sarah BRUCE, Frankey McKENNEY, Richard SUTTON, William SUTTON Jr. & John B. WALKER; son William SUTTON Jr. ex; WITS: Jn. BROWN, Marcius C. HARVEY, Sam. TEMPLEMAN [in a codicil SUTTON gives his son William permission to improve his land]. (WC DW 24:169)
[Salley SUTTON mar. Hen. BRUCE, RC, bond 12 Aug 1786 (MRC:27); Frankey McKENNEY is prob. Frances SUTTON who mar. Gerard McKENNEY, Jr., WC, bond 24 Dec 1799 (MLBWC:42)]

SWANN, Joseph; PO 13 Feb 1815; 8 May 1815. NC; INV, [m]. (NC RB 20:117)
[Jos. SWANN is prob. the son of Rich. SWANN & Judy JONES and grson. of Sarah JONES of SSP (d. NC 1798) who named her dau. Judith SWAN and grsons. Jos., Rich. & Wm. SWANN in her will (NC 21 Jan 1798-10 Sep 1798) (NC RB 15:505; MLBNC:97)]

SWANN, Richard; PO 18 Mar 1815; 14 Jun 1819. NC; INV. $87.29. (NC RB 22:69)
[Rich. SWANN is prob. the son of Rich. SWANN & Judy JONES and grson. of Sarah JONES of SSP (d. NC 1798) who named her dau. Judith SWAN and grsons. Jos., Rich. & Wm. SWANN in her will (NC 21 Jan 1798-10 Sep 1798) (NC RB 15:505; MLBNC:97)]

SWANSON, Asa; PO 8 Jun 1807; 14 Sep 1807. NC; INV, [m]. (NC RB 17:569)
[Asa SWANSON married twice, (1) Eliz. BARECROFT, NC, lic. 14 Jul 1785 and (2) Betty H. GARTON, NC, bond 8 Jul 1791 (MWO:339); he was sec. for Jn. SWANSON to admin. the est. of Jn. SWANSON, NC, 14 Feb 1791 (NC OB 1790-1795:63); his est. was ord. to be admin. by Wm. HARDING, NC, 8 Jun 1807 (NC MB 1805-1807:239)]

SWANSON, Asa; PO 13 Feb 1809, T 31 Mar 1809; 9 Jul 1810
NC; his lands sold and proceeds div. among William HARDING as gdn. to Lucy, Cyrus & Molley SWANSON, George SWANSON, Sukey SWANSON; [Thomas MILLER also signs Sukey SWANSON's receipt for £10.1 for her part of her father's land]. (NC RB 18:428)

SWANSON, Jesse; PO 10 Jan 1804; 15 Oct 1805
NC; INV, [m]; est. layed off for dower of Judith SWANSON the wid. and Cyrus HARDING gdn. to Maria SWANSON the orphan of Jesse SWANSON was possessed with her est. (NC RB 17:343)
[Jesse SWANSON was the son of Stephen SWANSON of WicP (d. NC 1794) (NC RB 15:59); he mar. Judith GASTON, NC, bond 22 Nov 1794 (MLBNC:97)]

SYDNOR, Anthony; PO 13 May 1816); [8] Sep 1817
NC; INV, [m]; includes the following Negroes: Isaac, Billy, Geophery, Solomon, Rawleigh, Aaron, John, Moses, Diana, Grace, Teresa & child [Rosa], Phebe, Agga, Betty, Charlotte. (NC RB 21:229)
[Anthony SYDNOR mar. Eliz. CHOWNING 10 Jan 1788; they had the following children: Fortunatus (b. 1788), Wm. (b. 1791), Thos. Sharp (b. 1793), Sarah (b. 1797), Eliz. Chowning (b. 1799); Eliz. C. SYDNOR mar. Dandridge COX, 7 Jan 1824 (BNCHS vol. IX, no. 1:68); in his will (NC 8 Mar 1815-13 May 1816), Anthony SYDNOR named his wife Elizabeth and children Wm. SYDNOR, Sarah SYDNOR, Eliz. Chowning SYDNOR, Thos. Sharp SYDNOR, and Fortunatus SYDNOR (NC RB 20:459); Eliz. C. SYDNOR orphan of Anthony SYDNOR chose Wm. SYDNOR as her gdn., NC 8 Nov 1819 (NC OB 1816-20:399)]

SYDNOR, Anthony; T 2 Jun 1819; 12 Aug 1823
NC; INV; includes Negroes Isaac WIGGIN, Billy, Godfrey, Rawleigh, Sollomon, Aaron, John WIGGIN, Moses, Dianna, Grace, Tereze & child Peter, Phebe, Agathy & child Daniel, Roxalany, [Ormacinda]. (NC RB 23:343)

SYDNOR, Anthony; PO 10 Nov 1823, T 29 Dec 1823; 12 Jan 1824
NC; settlement of William SYDNOR & Thomas S. SYDNOR's acct. of their executorship of the will & admin. of the est. of Anthony SYDNOR dec'd; distributed among Thomas S. SYDNOR agent for Fortunatus SYDNOR, Thomas S. SYDNOR, John CHRISTOPHER who mar. Sarah SYDNOR and Elizabeth C. SYDNOR; each distributee rec'd $53.81. (NC RB 23:400)
[Jn. CHRISTOPHER mar. Sally SYDNOR, NC, 10 May 1820 (MLBNC:17)]

SYDNOR, Eppa; T 8 Dec 1803; 13 Nov 1806
NC; INV; includes Negroes girl Lett, Nan & child, Spencer, Esther. (NC RB 17:481)
[Thos. SYDNOR Jr. was aptd. gdn. to Wm. & Judith SYDNOR, orphans of Eppa SYDNOR, RC, 5 Apr 1819, but it is not clear if it was this Eppa SYDNOR (RC OB 24:323)]

SYDNOR, Fauntleroy; [m]; 16 Jan 1797
LC; INV, £194.14.6; PO 19 Sep 1796, DIV of estates of James SYDNOR, dec'd & Fauntleroy SYDNOR, dec'd as follows: Mrs. E. SYDNOR (Lot 6: Hannah), George SYDNOR (Lot 5: Phoebe), Moore SYDNOR (Lot 1: George), William CHICHESTER (Lot 7: Maria [& Bida...]), William SYDNOR (Lot 3: Joe), Fanny SYDNOR (Lot 4: Tom), Samuel SYDNOR (Lot 2: Sarah); each Lot was worth £58.1.2 1/2. (LC EB 24:40)

SYDNOR, George; PO 15 Oct 1798; 15 Jul 1799
LC; INV & DIV of Negroes among: D. P. CHICHESTER in right of his wife Catharine, Fanny SYDNOR, Samuel G. SYDNOR, Ellen SYDNOR, William F. SYDNOR. (LC EB 24:101, 103)
[Catharine SYDNOR, a dau. of Wm. SYDNOR & Ellen FAUNTLEROY, mar. Dodridge Pitt CHICHESTER (1773 – 1833); she d. 16 Jan 1801 age 34; she and her husband are buried in the Chichester Family Cemetery, Lorton, Fairfax

Co., Va. (<http://www.findagrave.com/cgi-bin/fg.cgi?page=gr&GRid=43838744> accessed 20 Jul 2012.]

SYDNOR, Giles; PO 1 Dec 1800; 6 Feb 1804
RC; INV; £1034.0.6; includes the following Negroes: Prince, Adam, James, Joe, Charles, Simon, David, boy Tom, Isaac, [Sem], Molly, Milly, Betty, Alse, Janney, Nell. (RC WB 9:227)
[A Giles SYDNOR, b. 8 Aug 1753, was the son of Epaphroditus SYDNOR (d. RC 1756) (NFPR:180, RC WB 6:86); a Jiles [sic] SYDNOR was the father of a dau. born in NFPR in 1783 (NFPR:180); and a Giles SYDNOR mar. Nancy HARRIS, RC, bond 7 Apr 1795 (MRC:201); it is probable, but not certain, that these three Giles were the same person; Nancy the wid. of Giles SYDNOR mar. Martin SISSON, RC, bond 10 Apr 1802 (MRC:188; RC OB 24:415)]

SYDNOR, James; PO 19 Sep 1796; 16 Jan 1797
LC; INV, £211.14.0; includes Negroes: George, Sarah, Joe, Maria. (LC EB 24:39)

SYDNOR, James D.; 3 Jun 1813; 2 Aug 1813
NFP, RC; WILL; plant. in the forest formerly held by my aunt Ann DOWNMAN supposed to contain 300 ac. & plant. in the Fork of Totuskey formerly held by my father to sis. Nancy SYDNOR; plant. w/o I now reside to sis. Dewanna SYDNOR; uncle Rawleigh DOWNMAN may stay on this plant. during the single life of my sis. Dewanna; Negroes to be eq. div. between sisters Nancy & Dewanna; uncle Rawleigh DOWNMAN, relation Sydnor S. DAVIS, & friend Rawleigh William DOWNMAN of LC exors; WITS: Geo. SAUNDERS, Jn. GARDNER, Wm. HAMMOCK, G. DAVIS. (RC WB 9:429)
[James Downman SYDNOR, b. 12 Dec 1777, was the son of Anthony & Eliz. (DOWNMAN) SYDNOR (NFPR:180)]

SYDNOR, James D.; T 22 Oct 1813; 7 Mar 1815
RC; INV, $5780.90, includes following Negroes: Old Sam, Rodham, Archibald, Isaac, Sucky old, [Lew], Criss, Darkey, Adam, Israel, Davis, George. (RC WB 9:466)

SYDNOR, John; PO Oct 1808; 5 Jun 1809. RC; INV, £364.5.0. (RC WB 9:350)

SYDNOR, John; PO Jun 1809, T 5 Feb 1810; 7 Mar 1810
RC; DIV of Negroes remaining after satisfying the sum mentioned in the will of John SYDNOR between Moore F. TOMLIN in right of his wife Fanny M. TOMLIN (Williamson, Alice), Matilda LEVY (Jane & her 2 children Jane & Cate, Molly). (RC AB 3:234)

SYDNOR, John ; 10 Aug 1807; 3 Oct 1808
RC; WILL; dwelling plant. to son John SYDNOR & land on the south side of the meanders of the Drinking Swamp & Negroes Priss, Mary, Vincent, Billy, Betty, Simon, Bob, Tom, Venie, [Greasher], Zachariah, Jack, Judy, Nanny, Delilah, Beck & her child Spencer; son Samuel SYDNOR all land lying between the main road leading from the Horsehead to Totuskey Bridge & the meanders of the Drinking Swamp except the land I purchased of John DONAWAY also my Negro slaves Jeremiah, Harry, Pheby, Milly, Hannah, Levina & Malinda; all my lands lying between the main road leading from the Horsehead to Totuskey Bridge & the Marshy Swamp & the land I purchased of John DONAWAY to Milly SYDNOR during her life; at her death to go to grson. John SYDNOR; if he has no heir to go to grson. Epa SYDNOR; Milly SYDNOR to have the use of Negroes Tom, Winny, Dall, Dick, Joe, & Isaac (a boy) during her life & at her death to be eq. div. between her children; if Ezekiel LEVY or his heirs, exors. or admins. pay to

my est. £82.14.9 with interest from 8 Nov 1794 I desire that the Negroes I lent his wife be eq. div. between my two grdaus Fanny M. TOMLIN & Matilda LEVY; if the sum is not paid, Negroes to be sold; [COD] I have omitted mentioning my son Tom in my will but it want [sic] because I forgot him. (RC WB 9:337)

[Moore F. TOMLIN mar. Frances M. LEVY, RC, bond 23 Apr 1805 (MRC:217); Frances & Matilda were daus. of Ezekiel LEVY (d. RC, 1813); the slaves devised by Jn. SYDNOR to his grdaus. Fanny M. TOMLIN and Matilda LEVY were ord. to be divided, RC, [Mar 1810] (RC Orders 1809-10:39); Drinking Swamp arises east of Haynesville in RC and flows southwesterly into Totuskey Creek (Miller:42); the Marshy Swamp forms part of the border between NC, WC and RC north of Village (Miller:94); there was a place called the Horsehead, not included in Miller, near Village and may be the spot where the Marshy Swamp has its origin.]

SYDNOR, Margaret; 20 Mar 1820

LC; admin. on the est. of Margaret Slate late the wife of William SYDNOR is granted to sd. SYDNOR. (LC OB 25:111)

[This is Margaret S. BRENT who mar. Wm. SYDNOR, LC, bond 10 Mar 1813 (MLBLC:72)]

SYDNOR, Milly (Mrs.); 5 Nov 1810; 5 Nov 1810.

RC; Nunc. WILL; William DOWNMAN deposed that Milly SYDNOR wished dau. Elizabeth to have the bed & furniture willed to her by old Mr. Sydnor which she had never received & a cow; dau. Milly to have a bed & furniture & a cow and calf; dau. Judith Lucinda to have bed curtain, bedstead & furniture, her case of drawers & 2 cows and a calf; grdau. Milly Ball DOWNMAN; son William to have black walnut armchair that bel. to his grfather. Williamson BALL; $4 owed to Billy CLARK; 4/ or 4/6 to HEN[D]ERSON; Elizabeth DOWNMAN gave essentially the same deposition; Ellen B. DOWNMAN, sis. of William, said that Milly SYDNOR told her, it was but little she had to give, but what she had it was her wish for her daus. to have it; that her sons could do without it or was not deserving of anything from her. (RC WB 9:378)

[This is Mildred "Milly" BALL, the dau. of Capt. Williamson BALL, who mar. Eppa SYDNOR between 1776 and 1784 (MRC:201)]

SYDNOR, Moore; 3 May 1797; 15 Jan 1795

LC; WILL; all Negroes & stock to be kept on my plant. during the life of my mother; should my mother die before my sis. Fanny arrives to the age of 21 or marries, my est. to be kept in the situation alluded to until she is 21 or marries; plant. to be under the direction of my bro. George; pers. est. to be eq. div. between all my brothers & sisters; after sis. comes of age or marries land to go to bro. George; if he has no child land & plant. to go to bro. Samuel Griffin SYDNOR; 10 guineas to cousin Hannah MITCHELL; bros. George & Samuel exors; WITS: Geo. CAMPBELL, Jos. MOTT, Tabitha MOTT; COD [same date as will]: I give my bro. George my right & claim to that part of my dec'd bro. James' est. which I have not received & cannot receive until the death of my mother provided he will pay off all claims which may appear to be due from me to my dec'd father's est, but if he will not, I give all my right title etc. to part of my dec'd bro. James' est. to be eq. div. between my sisters Caty CHICHESTER & Fanny provided D. P. CHICHESTER will relinquish all claims he may have against me [same wits.] (LC WB 28:27)

SYDNOR, Moore; PO 15 Oct 1798;

LC; INV of est. unadministered by George SYDNOR his ex., [m]; includes Negroes: Glasgow, George, Moses, Adam, Jenny, [Jerry]. (LC EB 24:103)

SYDNOR, William; 20 Nov 1820

LC; William SYDNOR aptd. gdn. of William H. & Mary K. SYDNOR his children. (LC OB 25:172)

SYDNOR, William Fauntleroy;

LC; William F. SYDNOR d. in Apr 1796 leaving children Richard, William, Anne and Samuel B.; William F. was the son of William (d. LC 1794) and Ellen (FAUNTLEROY) SYDNOR and bro. of Moore, Fauntleroy, Samuel G., Caty (mar. Doddridge Pitt CHICHESTER), Fanny, George and James SYDNOR (LC CC 1802-001; LC WB 22:248, WB 28:27)

[Wm. F. SYDNOR mar. Sarah CHINN dau. of Robt. & Eliz. (BELFIELD) CHINN, LC, bond 30 Nov 1785 (MWO:341)]

TAITE, Anne; 7 Oct 1777; [m]

NC; WILL; clothes & wearing apparel to be eq. div. between friends Mrs. Margaret SINCLAIR & Miss Betsy WAUGHOP; grson. William GRAHAM son of my dau. Anne GRAHAM to pay debts; all lands claimed by me in LC under the will of & deed of my late bro. William KEENE as also all other lands claimed by me under all other persons as well within the county of Lancaster as elsewhere; since there may arise some dispute about part of the land in LC by me held under my late bro. William KEENE as I imagined to be entailed upon my dau. Betsy CAMPBELL & my grson. John GRAHAM for settling of which I earnestly beg and desire that my sd. dau. Betsy CAMPBELL & her heirs & my grson. John GRAHAM out of the respect they have ever shown to me may out of their own free good will cause a good & faithful and sufficient faith in the law to be made of the sd. land as thought to be entailed unto my sd. grson. William GRAHAM son of my dec'd dau. Anne GRAHAM; Negroes Jacob, Winney, Bett, Sam, John, William, Margary, Phillis, Sam, & George to grson. William GRAHAM; great grson. William GRAHAM son of my grson. John GRAHAM; great grdau. Nancey GRAHAM; friend Miss Betsy BONUM; grson. William GRAHAM, friend Rodham KENNER & Lindsey OPIE exors; WITS: Alex. CUNNINGHAM, Jn. WARDEN, Griffin FAUNTLEROY, Geo. H. OPIE, Eliz. OPIE. (NC DCO:325)

[This may be Anne COUTANCEAU, dau. of Peter COUTANCEAU & Anne (THERRIOTT) KEENE, who was b. c. 1703 and mar. (1) Wm. METCALF c. 1722 and (2) Wm. TAITE; although it is poss. that she was a dau. of Anne THERRIOTT by her first husband Wm. KEENE (MWO:209); she was the mother of Anne METCALF (1723-1750, mar. Jn. GRAHAM 1741) and Betty METCALF (b. 1725/6, mar. Wm. CAMPBELL 1747-1748) (MWO:64, 90, 209, 341; NC OB 1699-1713:438)]

TALLEY, John; 10 Aug 1816; 19 Aug 1816

LC; WILL; est. to be kept together in the possession of my wife Darkey TALLY; at wife's death est. to be sold and proceeds eq. div. amongst my children Thomas J. TALLY, John TALLY, James [TALLY], [Molly] WEBB, Nancy P. TALLY; the children of my son George TALLY to have one eighth part; the children of my son Champion to have one eighth part; the children of [my] son Moses to have one eighth part; to s-i-l Joseph DUNAWAY one cent and no more; sons James & Thomas J. TALLY exors; WITS: Rich. PAYNE, [N.] SPRIGGS, Edw. PERCIFULL. (LC WB 28:178)

[Mary TALLEY mar. Thos. WEBB, LC, bond 4 Feb 1797 (MLBLC:78)]

TALLEY, John; 19 May 1817; 18 Aug 1817. LC INV. (LC EB 27:389)

TALLEY, John; PO 15 Dec 1817, T 22 Dec 1817; 16 Feb 1818

LC; DIV of est. at the house of James TALLEY (admr. with the will annexed) among: the children of George TALLEY, John TALLEY, Thomas J. TALLEY, Molly WEBB wife of Thomas WEBB, James TALLEY, Champion TALLEY's children, Moses TALLEY's children, Nancy TALLEY. (LC EB 27:405)

TALLEY, Moses; PO 10 May 1815; 11 Sep 1815
NC; INV, $103.25; Eleanor TALLEY admr. (NC RB 20:216)
[Moses TALLEY, of NC, mar. Ellin MAITH, RC, bond 10 Nov 1806 (MRC:203); the est. of Moses TALLEY was ord. to be admin. by Ellen M. TALLEY, NC, 8 May 1815 (NC OB 1811-1816:314)]

TANKERSLEY, Peter; T 5 Oct 1812; 15 Feb 1813. LC; INV. (LC EB 27:140)
[Peter TANKERSLEY d. intest. in 1812 leaving seven children: Rich., Jas. R., Thornley B., Wm., Emily, Jane, and Beverly TANKERSLEY; Rich. & Jas. R. TANKERSLEY were not inhabitants of Virginia in 1819 (LC CC 1820-058)]

TAPSCOTT, Ezekiel; T 28 Nov 1799; 20 Apr 1801
LC; INV, £200.10.10; includes Negroes: Margaret, boy James, girl Lucy. (LC EB 24:140)
[Polly TAPSCOTT orphan of Ezekiel TAPSCOTT chose Nathan SPRIGGS as her gdn., 20 Jan 1800 (LC Orders 21 1799-1801:72); Jn. TAPSCOTT was aptd. gdn. of Harriett TAPSCOTT and Jas. TAPSCOTT orphans of Ezekiel TAPSCOTT, 20 Feb 1804 (LC OB 1804-05:12); it appears to the court that the lands of Ezekiel TAPSCOTT are not worth more than $100 and it is ord. that Jn. TAPSCOTT gdn. of Jas. TAPSCOTT & Harriet TAPSCOTT and Hen. SCHOFIELD and Polly his wife be summoned to show cause why lands should not be sold and proceeds div., 17 Jun 1805 (LC OB 1804-05:399); Hen. SCHOFIELD mar. Polly TAPSCOTT, LC, bond 26 Dec 1803 (MLBLC:65); Jas. TAPSCOTT orphan of Ezekiel TAPSCOTT chose Jn. CUNDIFF the Younger as his gdn. (LC Orders D22 1805-08:290)]

TAPSCOTT, Henry; 18 May 1802
LC; Chancery suit: John TAPSCOTT complt. against Mary TAPSCOTT & Rawleigh TAPSCOTT exors. of Henry TAPSCOTT, Henry TAPSCOTT, Martin TAPSCOTT, Chichester TAPSCOTT, Joseph TAPSCOTT, Polly TAPSCOTT, Sally TAPSCOTT, Betsy TAPSCOTT, William GEORGE admr. of Richard TAPSCOTT, Ann ROGERS & Jospeh CARTER surviving exors. of Charles ROGERS and Martin SHEARMAN and Alice his wife to settle the est. of Henry TAPSCOTT. (LC Orders V 1802-03:88)
[This is prob. Hen. TAPSCOTT who mar. Mary SHEARMAN (a dau. of Martin SHEARMAN), LC, bond 11 Feb 1758 (MLBLC:72; LC WB 20:15); in his will (LC 29 Dec 1777 - 19 Apr 1781), Hen. TAPSCOTT of CCP named his sons Hen., Raw., Wm., Martin, Chichester, Rich., Jos. and Sam TAPSCOTT, his daus. Sarah, Betsy, and Polly TAPSCOTT, Ann ROGERS, Alice TAPSCOTT, and an unborn child (prob. Jn. S. TAPSCOTT); he mentions his wife, but does not name her; in the div. of his est. in 1789, she is identified as Mary TAPSCOTT (LC WB 20:190); Ann TAPSCOTT mar. Chas. ROGERS, LC, bef. 29 Dec 1777 (LC WB 22:393, MWO:302); Alice TAPSCOTT mar. Martin SHEARMAN (son of Martin SHEARMAN), LC, bond 23 Feb 1784 (MWO:317);a LC CC identifies Rich., Rawleigh, Martin, Alice, Chichester, Sarah, Jos., Polly, and Betsy as children of Hen. TAPSCOTT by one wife and Jas., Hen., Wm., and Ann as children by another wife; it is not clear which children were full siblings of Jn. S. and Sam. (LC CC 1819-019)]

TAPSCOTT, John; PO 20 Jul 1807; 19 Oct 1807

LC; INV, $2331.14; includes Negroes: Gaby, Sarah, Mary, Fanny, Sinah, Spencer, Abraham, Jane, Maria, Judy, Darias, [Simon], Venus, Rachel. (LC EB 27:22)

TAPSCOTT, John; PO 18 Dec 1809,T 14 Jul 1810; 16 Jul 1810
LC; partial DIV of est; Lot 5 to George WEBB in right of his wife Alice one of the heirs and Lot 7 to Henry TAPSCOTT son of John and another of the heirs. (LC EB 27:75)
[Geo. WEBB mar. Alice TAPSCOTT, LC, bond 23 Dec 1808 (MLBLC:78); Hen. TAPSCOTT orphan of Jn. TAPSCOTT chose Nathan SPRIGGS as his gdn., 19 Feb 1810 (LC Orders 23B 1808-11:148)]

TAPSCOTT, John; PO 16 Feb 1818; T 15 Apr 1821; 16 Apr 1821
LC; DIV of slaves among John TAPSCOTT (Negro Sarah & child), Lawson GEORGE (Simon), Robert TAPSCOTT (Venus), Nancy TAPSCOTT (Jane), Richard TAPSCOTT (Emanuel, Lisha, Rachel, Agatha). (LC EB 29:87)
[Lawson GEORGE mar. Lucy TAPSCOTT, LC, bond 24 Sep 1817 (MLBLC:30); Rich. TAPSCOTT orphan of Jn. TAPSCOTT chose Mary TAPSCOTT for his gdn. and sd. Mary is aptd. gdn. to Jn. & Robt. TAPSCOTT also orphans of Jn., 16 Feb 1818 (LC Orders 24:415)]

TAPSCOTT, John Sr.; PO 17 May 1824, T 1 Jun 1824; 21 Jun 1824
LC; DIV of est. held by his wid. Mary TAPSCOTT dec'd and also the estates of John TAPSCOTT Jr. dec'd, Richard TAPSCOTT dec'd & Nancy TAPSCOTT dec'd [among] George WEBB gdn. to his children (Amanda, Amy), George BRENT in right of his wife Catharine (Sinah, Hannah, Anny, Billy), Lawson GEORGE in right of his wife Lucy (Lily, Henry, Sally), Henry TAPSCOTT (Emanuel, Felicia, Edy) & Robert TAPSCOTT (Tom, Aggy, Spencer), the legal heirs of the four estates above mentioned being of lawful age & present agreed & directed us to divide the sd. 4 estates by throwing these all together; Rachel an old woman went to Henry TAPSCOTT who received $11.23 for keeping her during her life. (LC EB 29:337)
[Geo. WEBB mar. Alice TAPSCOTT, LC, bond 23 Dec 1808; Geo. BRENT Jr. mar. Catherine TAPSCOTT, LC, bond 29 Aug 1816; Lawson GEORGE mar. Lucy TAPSCOTT, LC, bond 24 Sep 1817 (MLBLC:7, 30, 78)]

TAPSCOTT, Joseph;
LC; d. intest.; his wid. Ann M. mar. William ALDERSON (LC CC 1806-017)
[Jos. TAPSCOTT mar. Ann M. CHINN, RC, bond 19 Dec 1793 (MWO:343)]

TAPSCOTT, Martin; 21 Oct 1800; 2 Apr 1805
WC; WILL; Milley (a Negro woman) to be sold if needed to pay debts; son Henry Brereton TAPSCOTT at school in order to obtain a good English education is to make or call my sis. Alice SHEARMAN's his home which I hope will not be disagreable to her & Mr. Martin SHEARMAN; whole est. to son Henry Brereton TAPSCOTT; if son dies without heirs all of the Negroes he dies possessed of given by me shall be emancipated and set free agreable to the act of assembly made in that case; bro. Henry TAPSCOTT to be supported out of my est. during his life as usual; 4 or 5 of my Negro boys as near the age of my son Henry Brereton TAPSCOTT as can be found to be bound out to some profitable [trade] until they are 21; if son dies without heir all the young Negroes that the law cannot emancipate owing to their minority shall be bound to some profitable trade; my Negro woman Levinia to be emancipated & set free agreable to an instrument of writing in her possession given by me dtd. 28 Apr 1794 with a N.B. to it; no APP of my est. to be made but each ex. to take a private INV and keep a copy; let the ages of the Negroes be put down in the INV; bros. Henry TAPSCOTT & Chichester

TAPSCOTT & friends Martin SHEARMAN & Maj. George GARNER exors. & gdns of my son; [no wits.]. (NC DCO:396)
[A long CC in WC provides details on Martin TAPSCOTT and his family; his son, Henry B., died before age 21 and without issue; at the time of his death, he left four uncles of the whole blood: Rawleigh, Jos., Chichester & Jn. TAPSCOTT, four aunts of the whole blood: Alice, Polly, Sally & Betsey TAPSCOTT, two uncles of the half blood: Jas. & Hen. TAPSCOTT, and one aunt of the half blood: Ann TAPSCOTT; Betsey TAPSCOTT mar. Ezekiel SHEARMAN (LC, bond 14 Jul 1808) and Ann TAPSCOTT mar. a ROGERS (WC CC 1854-07 abstracted in WCCP:137-140; MLBLC:67); Alice TAPSCOTT mar. Martin SHEARMAN, LC, bond 23 Feb 1784 (MLBLC:67)]

TAPSCOTT, Martin (Maj.); T 28 Dec 1804; 26 Feb 1805
WC; INV; includes Negroes George (26 years old), Dennis (25), Joe (23), Aleck (20), Patrick (17), Anna (16), Dunkin (14), Leanna (10), Carmichael (9), John (5), Zanobia (3), Juliet (2), Lavinia (43), Williamson (18), Tom (16), Joe (8), Bob (5), Silius (14), Agga (11), Matilda (7), Molly (20), Leo (5), George (50), Daniel (45), Rawleigh (47), Bob (33), Milly (20), [Heny] (2), Anna (3 mos), Sukey (40), Edwin (4), Isaac (3), Polly (7 mos), Glascow (in the possession of Gerr'd HUTT said to be sold when aged about 9 still at Mr. BOWAND's). (WC RI 8:52[1])

TAPSCOTT, Polly; [m]; 21 Sep 1818
LC; DIV of proceeds of sale of slaves (Dianna, Nancy, Leannah, Winny) among Chichester TAPSCOTT, Sarah TAPSCOTT, Ezekiel G. SHEARMAN in right of his wife Betsy who was Betsy TAPSCOTT, John S. TAPSCOTT, the heirs of Rawleigh TAPSCOTT dec'd and the heirs of Joseph TAPSCOTT of whole blood and also Ann ROGERS who was Ann TAPSCOTT, Williams TAPSCOTT & the heirs of James TAPSCOTT dec'd of half blood. (LC EB 27:437)
[This is apparently Polly the dau. of Hen. & Mary (SHEARMAN) TAPSCOTT (*see above*); Ezekiel G. SHEARMAN mar. Betsey TAPSCOTT, LC, bond 14 Jul 1808 (MLBLC:67]

TAPSCOTT, Richard; 16 Sep 1806; 15 Jun 1807
LC; INV, £80; includes Negroes Jack in the possession of John TAPSCOTT & Tabitha in the poss of James TAPSCOTT. (LC EB 27:18)
[This Rich. TAPSCOTT is apparently a son of Hen. TAPSCOTT (*see above*) who in his will (LC 29 Dec 1777 - 19 Apr 1781) named his wife Mary, sons Hen., Rawleigh, Wm., Martin, Chichester, Rich., Jos. and Sam., and daus. Sarah, Betsy & Polly TAPSCOTT, Ann ROGERS, and Alice TAPSCOTT and an unborn child (LC WB 20:190); Rich. TAPSCOTT mar. Frances GEORGE, dau. of Frances GEORGE, LC, bond 14 Aug 1789 (MLBLC:73); Rich. TAPSCOTT d. intest. around 1794 leaving his wid. Frances and a son Sam. who d. soon after his father; he was also the father of a dau. Polly who d. when about 4; Frances TAPSCOTT, wid., mar. Benj. KIDD of Middlesex Co., LC, bond 1 Aug 1798 (LC CC 1819-019; MLBLC:45); a list of Henry's children and their descendents was given in a LC document concerning the division of Rich. TAPSCOTT's slaves: it appearing to the court that the slaves of which Rich. TAPSCOTT died seized & possessed in this county intestate cannot be div. in kind among his legal reps., on the mot. of Rawleigh TAPSCOTT, ord. that Robert, James, Albion & Warner TAPSCOTT, heirs of Jas. TAPSCOTT, dec'd also Louisa, Baker, Newton, Caroline & Chichester TAPSCOTT infants & heirs of the sd. Jas. TAPSCOTT by Martin SHEARMAN their gdn., Benj. KIDD & Frances his wife, Hen. TAPSCOTT,

Ann ROGERS, Wm. TAPSCOTT, Martin SHEARMAN & Alice his wife, Ezekiel G. SHEARMAN & Betsy his wife, Sarah TAPSCOTT, also Robt. & Jos. TAPSCOTT infants & heirs of Jos. TAPSCOTT dec'd by the sd. Martin SHEARMAN their gdn., and Chichester TAPSCOTT, Polly TAPSCOTT and Jn. S. TAPSCOTT the other heirs and reps. of Rich. TAPSCOTT be summoned to show cause why the slaves should not be sold, 21 Nov 1808 (LC Orders B23 1808-11:4)]

TARKELSON, Joseph; T 24 Dec 1795; 21 Jan 1799
LC; INV, £45.13.6; DIV of est. among: Tarkle TARKLESON, Elizabeth TARKLESON, William TARKLESON. (LC EB 24:86)

TARKLESON, Tarkle; PO 25 Feb 1814; 17 Jul 1815. LC; INV, £3.8.6. (LC EB 27:243)

TARPLEY, Thomas; 5 Nov 1814; 4 Dec 1815
NFP, RC; WILL; to be buried near dear departed children and their mother; son Thomas Griffin Peachey TARPLEY; son William Henry TARPLEY; dau. Charlotte Phillipina; dau. Frances Ann; dau. Catherine A. M. HALL; dau. Eliza HATCH; Negro woman to 2 daus. Charlotte P. & Frances Ann; land to be sold; exors. friend Bartho. McCARTY & son Thomas G. P. TARPLEY; WITS: Meredith HUDSON, Aug[ustine] NEALE, Jn. N. ROOTES; Cod (6 Nov 1814): books to be div. between sons Thomas & William; WITS: Aug. NEALE, Jn. N. ROOTES. (RC WB 9:491)
[Eliza TARPLEY mar. Jos. HATCH of Richmond City, RC, bond 25 Jun 1811 (MRC:90)]

TARPLEY, Thomas; T 21 Dec 1815; 4 Nov 1817. RC; INV, $483.60. (RC WB 9:570)

TATE, James; 23 May 1803
WC; Kenedy TATE and Sally TATE orphans of James TATE chose Henry WASHINGTON as their gdn. (WC Orders 1801-04:370)
[Sally TATE mar. Hen. DEATLEY, WC, bond 9 Aug 1804 (MLBWC:19); Kenedy TATE, orphan of James, chose Wm. DISHMAN as his gdn., WC 27 Oct 1806 (WC Orders 1804-07:424); suit in chancery; Hen. DEATLEY & Sally his wife against Kenedy TATE by Wm. DISHMAN his gdn. which Kenedy and Sally are children of Jas. TATE to div. the land of Jas. TATE, WC 23 Mar 1807 (WC Orders 1804-07:485)]

TATE, William; 27 Feb 1815. WC; John NEALE aptd. gdn. to Henry TATE, William TATE and Campbell TATE orphans of William TATE. (WC OB 1814-18:94)

TAYLOE, John Jr.; T 8 Jul 1824; 2 Aug 1824
RC; INV taken at Mount Airey, $2417.50; includes Negroes: Nancy, John, Letty, Salley, Billey, Winney, Archey, John. (RC WB 10:43)

TAYLOE, William; PO 9 Jan 1815, T 28 Jan 1815; 14 Feb 1820
NC; INV, [m]; includes Negroes: Lazarus, Sam, Jack, Mark, Jesse, Milley, Mary, Leisha; INV of TAYLOE's est. at Laurel Grove in WC, taken 3 Mar 1815 includes Negroes: Joe, Sylva, Rachel, Phillace, Maria, Lewis, Daniel, Rose, Sukey, James, Nancy, [Isaac], Sinah for 1 year. (NC RB 22:221)

TAYLOR, Elizabeth; 12 Dec 1815; 20 Jan 1817
LC; WILL; to be buried by the grave of my husband; to Nancy PAYNE (the dau. of my nephew William PAYNE dec'd) my Negro Alford; my Negro woman Amey to be sold and the money from the sale to be eq. div. amongst the other three children of sd. William PAYNE namely William PAYNE, James PAYNE, & Sally PAYNE; sis. Lucy EDWARDS; my nephew William

BELL of Fauquier Co. ex; WITS: Rich. PAYNE, Mariah PAYNE, Milley Y. BOATMAN; [will presented in court by Geo. H. PAYNE]. (LC WB 28:182) [Eliz. TAYLOR is prob. the second wife of Thos. TAYLOR, *see below*)

TAYLOR, Elizabeth; PO 20 Jan 1817; 17 Apr 1817
LC; INV, $680.02 1/2; includes Negroes: boy Alfred, woman Amey. (LC EB 27:369)

TAYLOR, Isaac; 13 Jul 1818; Lee TAYLOR orphan of Isaac TAYLOR chose Thomas TAYLOR as gdn. (NC OB 1816-20:270)

TAYLOR, James; 11 Sep 1826
NC; Herod BETTS aptd. gdn. to Thomas & Frederick TAYLOR orphans of James TAYLOR. (NC OB 1825-30:117)
[This is prob. the James R. TAYLOR who mar. Henrietta BETTS, NC, bond 30 Mar 1813 (MLBNC:98)]

TAYLOR, Moses; PO 10 Apr 1797; 12 Jul 1802
NC; INV, £333.13.3; includes Negroes Bob, William, Cabel, Ben. (NC RB 16:425)
[In his will (NC 14 Mar 1797-10 Apr 1797), Moses TAYLOR named his wife Eliz. S. TAYLOR and childen Geo. B., Steptoe, Fanny, & Mary B. TAYLOR; and mentioned land inherited from his mother Judith TAYLOR (NC RB 15:371)]

TAYLOR, Thomas; 25 Dec 1813; 19 Dec 1814
LC; WILL; eight Negroes Jesse, Joe, Aggy, Nanny, Emma, Alford, Letty & her child to wife Elizabeth TAYLOR; rest of Negroes to be eq. div. between two daus: Charlotte M. TAYLOR & Martha TAYLOR; my lands to be div. into 3 parts allowing my forest plant. as one of the divisions & wife to have her choice of the divisions & at her death her part of land to go to dau. Martha; dau. Sarah Ann PAYNE to have her choice in one of the other lots; dau. Charlotte McAdam TAYLOR to have other third; William TAYLOR & John CARPENTER exors; [no wits. listed, but will proved by oaths of Jos. CARTER Jr. & Rawleigh DUNAWAY]; LC WB 28:151)
[Thos, TAYLOR mar. (1) Charlotte McADAM, dau. of Jos. McADAM, bef. 1 Jan 1788; he seems to have mar. (2) Eliz. who may have been a wid. PAYNE (MWO:346; *see above*); Martha Conway TAYLOR orphan of Thos. TAYLOR chose Robt. NUTT as her gdn., 19 Dec 1814 (LC Orders 24:210, OB 25:36)]

TAYLOR, Thomas; T 3 Apr 1815; 15 Feb 1819
LC; INV, [m]; includes Negroes: John, Charles, Jesse, boy Alford, Charlotte, Emma, girls Betsey, Juliett, and Polly, boys Armistead & Henry. (LC EB 27:453)

TAYLOR, William; 26 May 1823
WC; Robert BAILEY aptd. gdn. to John J., David B., and Sally N. TAYLOR, orphans of William TAYLOR, who came to court and chose BAILEY as their gdn. (WC OB 1819-23:563)
[David B. TAYLOR mar. Fanny P. BAILEY, WC, bond 13 Dec 1826 (MLBWC:70)]

TEAGUE, Newman [A.]; 6 Jun 1809. RC; INV, £30.15.6 1/2. (RC WB 9:352)
[Newman B. TEAGUE mar. Rose MINTER, RC, bond 13 feb 1799 (MRC:206)]

TEET, William; T 20 Dec 1814; 22 Dec 1815. WC; INV, $258.68. (WC RI 10:42)

TELLIS, David J.; PO 13 Jul 1815; 14 May 1816. NC; INV, [m]; includes Negro Jesse. (NC RB 20:477)
[The est. of David J. TELLIS was ord. to be admin. by Thos. BELL, NC, 13 Feb 1815 (NC OB 1811-1816:276)]

TELLIS, Rodham; PO 12 Mar 1811; 9 Sep 1811

NC; INV, $53.68; includes several blacksmith tools bellows, 2 anvils, 2 vises, 5 hammers, punches, chisels, mandrils. (NC RB 19:98)
[Rodham TELLIS seems to have mar. twice, (1) Betsy JONES, dau. of Izabel HARRISON (wid. of (1) Jos. FISHER and (2) (fnu) JONES), RC, bond 22 May 1788 (MRC:207, MWO:168) and (2) Susanna COOKMAN, wid., NC, bond 13 Feb 1804 (MLBNC:99); there is also evidence of another wife as the birth of Patty Baley to Rodham & Hannah TELLIS is rec. in the SSPR 29 Sep 1786 (SSPR:96); in his will (NC 13 Dec 1810-12 Mar 1811), Rodham TELLIS of SSP named his children Patty FISHER, David, Nancy & William; his wid. Susannah TELLIS refused to qualify to admin. her husband's est. (NC RB 19:9)]

TEMPLE, Peter; 20 Nov 1807; 4 Jul 1808
RC; WILL; exors. to sell tract of land near Farnham Church; slaves Nancy, Ballinda & her child Fanny, Polly, Joe, Lucy, Nelson & Winney and her child to be hired out; dau. Frances ("Francy," under 21); asks dau. to release to her bro. John (under 21) her right to land which has descended from her mother to herself & her bro; son Philip (under 21); son John Samuel TEMPLE tract of land in Naylor's Hole Neck called Waterview and half of my slaves; son Philip TEMPLE all land in Middlesex Co. and half my slaves; son Philip also to have slaves of his uncle Williamson FAUNTLEROY which are held in dower by his grandmother Judith FAUNTLEROY; friend Miss Letty Lee FAUNTLEROY; bro. John TEMPLE; friend John CAMPBELL; Col. James BALL of LC, bro. John TEMPLE, Joseph BALL of NC, Samuel TEMPLEMAN & John CAMPBELL of WC exors; WITS: Chas. SMITH, Thos. PINCKARD, Geo. SAUNDERS; Cod: 17 Jan 1808, in the event of death of Mrs. Judith FAUNTLEROY & Miss Lettice L. FAUNTLEROY, bro. John TEMPLE to take guardianship of dau. Frances Ann; friend Bartholomew McCARTY added to exors; WITS: Anna JONES, Thos. SYDNOR. (RC WB 9:327)
[Peter TEMPLE mar. Louisa FAUNTLEROY, RC, bond 2 Feb 1800 (MRC:207); Louisa was a dau. of John FAUNTLEROY (d. testate RC, 1798) & Judith (BALL) GRIFFIN (MRC:68; RC WB 9:89); on the mot. of Frances Ann MATTHEWS admx. of Philip TEMPLE dec'd by her attorney Wm. A. WRIGHT ord. that Eliz. F. CAMPBELL admx. with the will annexed of Jn. CAMPBELL late gdn. of Jn. S. & Philip TEMPLE dec'd orphans of Peter TEMPLE settle an acct. of sd. Jn. CAMPBELL's gdnship. of Jn. S. & Philip TEMPLE, 3 Mar 1828 (RC OB 27:197)]

TEMPLE, Peter; T Jul 1808; 4 Nov 1817
RC; INV, £1492.18.0, taken at the Waterview Plant; includes the following Negroes: Nancy (50), Isaac (40), Winney (45), Sina (10), Isaac (8), Francis (5), Billy (3), Aron (35), Pattey (27), Aron (37), John (18), Jack (18), Jane (20), Lette (20), Billey (4), James (13), Billey (12), Davey (12). (RC WB 9:592)

TEMPLE, Peter; T 31 Mar 1818; 7 Feb 1820
RC; INV; $11,347.87, taken at Waterview; includes the following Negroes: Old Isaac NEWTON, Young Isaac NEWTON, John CAROLINE, John, Jack BLUE, Bill, James, Harry, Frederick, Charles, Betty, Winney, Letty, Jenny, Peggy & child Fanny, Sarah, Franky, Bill NEWTON, Bill, Peter, Dennis, George, Betsey, Betsey [sic], Polly, Polly (a child), Lucy, Milley (infirm). (RC WB 9:642)

TEMPLE, Peter; T 14 Dec 1819; 7 Feb 1820; INV, RC; includes the following Negroes: John, Yellow James, John PIN, Jack, Charles, James, Isaac (young), Henry, Billy, Billy (younger), Isaac (old), boy Billy, Peggy & child Fanny, Sinah & child Winney, Franky, Letty & child Milly, Polly, Dennis, Winny,

Betsey (blk), Betsy (yellow), Peter, George, Polly (young), old Betty, Lucy. (RC WB 9:645)

TEMPLE, Peter; T 7 Oct 1822; 7 Oct 1822

RC; DIV of slaves between John S. TEMPLE (received John RED, age 36; Letty, 40; Billy, 16; Polly, 10; Dennis, 9; Milly, 6; Billy, son of Isaac NEWTON, 16; John BLUE, 33; Betsy, yellow, 13; Lucy, 9; Fanny, 5; George, 8; Charles, 23) & Philip TEMPLE (received James, 30; Sinah, 25; Polly, dau. of James, 8; Winny, 5; Newton, 3; Sarah Ann, 5 mos; Isaac NEWTON, 50; Winny 52; Franky, 20; Peter, 11; Betsy, black, 12; Billy SOMERSET, 25; John PINN, 21; Betty PINN, 60). (RC AB 4:51)

TEMPLEMAN, Thomas; 28 Sep 1801

WC; Anne TEMPLEMAN wid. of Thomas TEMPLEMAN. (WC Orders 1801-04:157)

[Thos. TEMPLEMAN mar. Ann SANFORD, dau. of Willoughby SANFORD, bef. 5 Dec 1785 (MWO:347)]

THOMAS, Ann; 5 Oct 1801. RC INV; £10.10.6. (RC WB 9:160)

THOMAS, Beckham; T 22 Apr 1820; 22 May 1820. WC; INV, $143.50. (WC RI 10:503)

[This is prob. the Becham THOMAS who mar. Nelly ANTHONY, NC, bond 5 Jul 1813 (MLBNC:71)]

THOMAS, James; PO Feb 1807; 14 Oct 1811

NC; INV, £70.13.9; includes a "buffelow" steer and a pair of "specticles."; NC RB 19:103)

[In his will (NC 7 Dec 1806-13 Jan 1807), Jas. THOMAS named his wife Ellen and asked that his land be sold after his wife's death from child to child as they grow up, but he did not name any children (NC RB 17:501)]

THOMAS, James; 7 Sep 1818

RC; a free Negro; died intest.; sheriff to admin. his est. (RC OB 24:262)

THOMAS, John; PO 13 Jul 1802; 12 Dec 1803

NC; DIV of est. among Elizabeth THOMAS dau. of William THOMAS dec'd, Lewis LAMKIN for Judeth his wife, John THOMAS, Spencer THOMAS, Francis THOMAS, Charlote THOMAS & Catey THOMAS (each rec'd £12.3.4 1/2); the reps. of Winney Ann THOMAS who was the rep. of John THOMAS dec'd are entitled to the sums as follows: Salley WINTER, Thomas BEEN for Catey his wife, Jessey SEBREY, William SWAIN for Charlotte his wife, Fanney SEBREY & Eppey SEBREY (each rec'd £2.0.7 1/2). (NC RB 17:90)

[Thos. BEAN mar. Catey WINTERS [sic], NC, bond 21 Oct 1796 (MLBNC:7)]

THOMAS, Rodham; PO 22 Mar 1824, T 20 May 18[2]4; 20 Sep 1824

LC; INV, $29.33 1/2; includes set of blacksmith tools. (LC EB 29:352)

THOMAS, Sally; PO 9 Jun 1806, T 27 Jan 1807; 9 Feb 1807

NC; INV at house of Daniel WINSTEAD's; est. contained only Negro Daniel (£90) and £37.17.10 1/2 in cash. (NC RB 17:505)

[In her will (NC 16 Aug 1803-12 Sep 1803), Sally THOMAS left Negro boy Daniel to her mother Mary WINSTEAD; at mother's death to be eq. div. between bros. Geo & Haynie WINSTEAD; Daniel WINSTEAD was her f-i-l (NC RB 17:62)]

THOMPSON, Archibald; 13 Jul 1812

NC; Frances THOMPSON to be allotted her dower in the lands of her late husband, Archibald THOMPSON. (NC OB 1811-15:99)

[Archibald THOMPSON mar. Frances HUDNALL, NC, bond 21 Jan 1808 (MLBNC:100)]

THOMPSON, Elizabeth; 11 Oct 1816; 28 Jul 1817
WC; WILL; all property to be eq. div. amongst my children; if son Thomas shall receive payment for his property destroyed by the British then he is to have only one fourth of my property, the other three fourths to be eq. div. between my dau. Betsy & my son George THOMPSON; exors. to make good deeds for my lots sold in Alexandria; $100 to be eq. div. between my sis. Sally & my neice Emily GRIFFITH; whereas I alone qualified as extx. of the will of my husband Dr. George THOMPSON & John MURPHY, & Charles LELAND were my only securities ... if either of my children or their legal reps. shall at any time claim or demand, recover or receive of either of my sd. securities any sum of money for or on account of the securityship, then the sd. child in so doing shall forfeit all benefit & advantage of the proportion hereby given such child or children by this will; as soon as my children arrive at the age of 21 they are to give to my sd. securities full & complete exoneration & discharge for and on account their liability aforesaid for me as extx of my sd. husband; friends John MURPHY of WC & Henry L. GASKINS of NC to be exors; WITS: Anne MURPHY, Emily C. GRIFFITH, Robt. MURPHY. (WC DW 23:301)
[This is Eliz. GRIFFITH the dau. of The Rev. Dr. David GRIFFITH (d. Philadelphia Aug 1789) and Hannah COLVILLE (d. Alexandria Nov 1811) and the wid. of Dr. Geo. THOMPSON (d. WC, 1804) (*see below*); several CCs provide information on the family of the Rev. DR. GRIFFITH (*Philadelphia Mercury*, 8 Aug 1789, p. [4]; *The Times and District of Columbia Advertiser*, 3 Dec 1800, p. [3]; *Alexandria Gazette*, 8 Mar 1809, p. [4]); the *Alexandria Herald* (25 Oct 1816, p. [3]) noted the death of Eliza THOMPSON relict of Dr. Geo. THOMPSON at her residence, Oakville, in WC on 10 Oct 1816; NB: It is not clear how she could have died on 10 Oct yet written her will on 11 Oct.]

THOMPSON, Elizabeth (Mrs.); T 26 Dec 1816; 27 Apr 1818; WC; INV, [m]. (WC RI 10:247)

THOMPSON, Elizabeth Griffith; 20 May 1824; 25 Apr 1825
WC; WILL; to dispose of all the est. of which I am in possession or to which I am in any manner entitled under the will of my dec'd father; the family of slaves, Polly & her 3 children, to be sold and money to be applied to the payment of the debt due to my gdn. Mr. John MURPHY & should that not be sufficient to discharge the debt due by my dec'd bro. George W. THOMPSON & myself, exors. are directed to sell any other part of my prop; residue of my est. to my aunt Sally Windslow GRIFFITH & should the claim I have against the govt. or under the treaty with Great Britain for depredations on prop. during the late war be recovered I likewise devise the same to my sd. aunt; Dr. Robert MURPHY of WC & Sally W. GRIFFITH of Alexandria exors; WITS: Jas. D. KERR, A. ADDISON, [Camls.] GRIFFITH, Jn. P. McGUIRE; [will was proved in the Orphans Court of Alexandria County on 9 Feb 1825]. (WC DW 25:168)
[This is the dau. of Dr. Geo. THOMPSON & Eliz. GRIFFITH, *see above and below*]

THOMPSON, Frances; 3 Apr 1823; 9 Feb 1824
NC; WILL; all land in NC & Negro woman Letty to dau. Maryann H. THOMPSON; if dau. should die before age 21 & leave no heirs, land to go to nephew John JETT & Negro woman Letty to go to Judith H. JETT; William BASYE & Joseph BASYE exors; WITS: Royston BETTS, Jane HARDING, Sally H. LEDFORD; [Wm. & Jos. BASYE relinquished their right of

executorship and Wm. HUDNALL, sheriff, appointed admr.]. (NC RB 23:422)
[This is prob. Frances HUDNALL who mar. Archibald THOMPSON, NC, bond 21 Jan 1808 (MLBNC:100)]

THOMPSON, George; 3 Feb 1803; 26 Mar 1804
WC; WILL; Negro woman Sally to wife Eliza; if she remarries to take her thirds out of tract called Pierce's where she is to remove to live; the family to hold or work any part of the Nomony Tract which has been improved for 30 odd years by my father; son Charles THOMSON alias BRIARLY (under 21) Negro boy Edward & two girls Polly & Betty (all of them children of Sylla) also boy Landon and he is to have a good English education; son Thomas THOMPSON tract of land called Nomony w/o I now live & tract over the ferry known as Liberty Hall and, if child wife is now pregnant with be a girl, the tract called by some Pierce's but called by the family Oakville, also Negroes: Spencer, Big Daniel, Little Daniel, James the son of Violet, William his bro, Sam the son of Spencer & Sally, Anthony the Ferryman, Marcus, Harry, & James the fellow purchased of Col. HALL at a sheriff's sale also Nancy (Anthony's wife), Sophy, Patty, Harriet the dau. of Nancy, Ariana, Isaac & Charles; also ferry boat to son Thomas; son Thomas to be sent to Princeton College or some other of equal fame; dau. Elizabeth Griffith THOMPSON Negroes: Aaron, Osmond, William, [Bennet,] Moses, Sally (the dau. fo Anthony & Nancy), Sylla & her dau. Nancy also £500; child wife is now pregnant with Negroes Adam, Gilbert, Jack, Glasco, Caroline, Fanney, & Charles; wife's youngest bro. Colvil GRIFFITH schooling & to be put with Charles LELAND to study law; wife & John MURPHY, Charles LELAND, & Henry Lee GASKINS exors; codicil dated "Charleston" 28 Mar 1803 to friend Geo. WHITELOCK [*extensive details of legacies to living children & child wife was pregnant with*]. (WC DW 21:5)
[This is prob. Dr. Geo. THOMPSON (*see Eliz. THOMPSON, above*); Liberty Hall tract was located in WC near Nomini Bridge (Miller:86)]

THOMPSON, George (Dr.); T 12 Apr 1804; 27 Aug 1804
WC; INV, £2870.15.0; includes Negroes Anthony, Gilbert, Billy CONNET, Aaron, Little Daniel, Spencer, Adam, Moses, Glasco, Jack, Marcus, Little James, William, Big James, Big Daniel, Sam, Toby, Sam COLE, Sally, Sciller, Edward, Polly, Betty, Nancy, Antony, Letty, Sucky, Nancy, Harriott, Sally, Sharlott, James BURK, Sophia, Charles; Caroline, Abraham; Old Letty, Isaac, Areanna, Landron, Fanny. (WC RI 8:443)

THOMPSON, Joseph; 28 Feb 1804
WC; Hugh QUINLAN was aptd. gdn. to Joseph THOMPSON orphan of Joseph THOMPSON. (WC Orders 1801-04:494)

THOMPSON, Judith; 26 Apr 1802
WC; DIV of the dower Negroes of the late Mrs. Judith THOMPSON which she held as the dower of Patrick SPENCE dec'd. (WC Orders 1801-04:213)
[Judith SPENCE, wid. of Patrick SPENCE, mar. Dr. Thomas THOMPSON bef. 31 Dec 1784 (MWO:350)]

THOMPSON, Judith (Mrs.); [m]; 22 Nov 1802
WC; DIV of dower slaves between George THOMPSON who was entitled to half & the est. of Samuel SANFORD & Lawrence SANFORD entitled to the other half; includes Negroes Asman, Judith (girl), Mariah (girl), Lucinda, [Mintas], James; Samuel SANFORD in his will left Samuel TEMPLEMAN one of his exors. who qualified thereto in sd. will he leaves the Negroes that might fall to him of sd. dower to be eq. div. between his bros. Patrick Spence

& Lawrence which Negroes are by the sd. will to be free at the age of 35. (WC RI 8:191)

[In his will (proved in WC on 6 Sep 1797) Sam. SANFORD of Baltimore, Md. named his bros. Edw., Lawrence & Patrick Spence. (WC DW 19:301)]

THOMPSON, Margaret; 16 Oct 1790; [m]

WP, WC; WILL; dau. Jane HENNAGE; s-i-l George HENNAGE who intends to live with me the ensuing year; rest of est. to be div. between sons Baldwin JOHNSON, Isaac JOHNSON and dau. Jane HENNAGE; [no ex. named]; WITS: Peter JETT, Jn. JETT. (WC Unrec Wills 1755-1800 #38)

THOMPSON, William; 27 Jul 1801

WC; Richard THOMPSON, Elizabeth L. THOMPSON and Maria THOMPSON (an infant under 21) brought suit against William THOMPSON; all were children of William THOMPSON. (WC Orders 1801-04:79)

THORNTON, Presley; 24 Apr 1815

WC; John Tayloe LOMAX & Charlotte his wife, Arthur W. THORNTON, Presley THORNTON and Virginia THORNTON are heirs of Presley THORNTON, dec'd. (WC OB 1814-18:112)

[This is Presley THORNTON (d. Genessee, NY, 1807) the son of Presley THORNTON (d. NC, 1770); he mar. Eliz. THORNTON in 1783 and had three children: Charlotte Belson, who mar. Jn. Tayloe LOMAX 25 Jul 1805, Arthur William and Presley. *Genealogy of the Virginia Family of Lomax*, Chicago: Rand McNally & Co., 1913, pp. 52-53; NC RB 19:68)

THRALL, Ellen; 15 Jul 1822

LC; on the mot. of Thos. L. LAWSON & Wickliff GEORGE ord. that James THRALL, Robert EVANS & Alice T. his wife, John REEVES & Lucy his wife be summoned to show cause why the lands of which Helen [sic] THRALL died seized should not be sold and the proceeds divided. (LC OB 25:316)

[This is Ellen GEORGE who mar. Jn. THRALL, LC, bond 2 Feb 1780; Robt. EVANS mar. Alcy T. CARTER, LC, bond 3 May 1819 (MLBLC:26); ord. that Jas. THRALL, Robt. EVANS who mar. Eliz. CARTER formerly Eliz. THRALL, Jn. REEVES who mar. Lucy MASON formerly Lucy THRALL, Sally T. THRALL orphan of Thos. THRALL & Nancy THRALL orphan of Jn. THRALL Jr. be summoned to show cause why the land which Jn. THRALL held in right of his wife Ellen should not be sold for a div. among the sd. Ellen's heirs, 16 Sep 1822 (LC OB 25:331, 346)]

THRALL, John; PO 19 May 1817, T 25 Jun 1817; 21 Apr 1818

LC; INV, $1133; includes Negroes Daniel & Peter. (LC EB 27:423)

THRALL, John; PO 21 Sep 1818; 19 Jun 1820

LC; INV; $75; includes only "one Negro woman Jane." (LC EB 21:28)

THRALL, Thomas; PO 17 Jan 1814, T 25 Mar 1817; 16 Mar 1818

LC; INV; includes Negroes: Davy, Siner. (LC EB 27:408)

[Thos. THRALL mar. Rebecca M. GEORGE, LC, bond 1 Feb 1809 (MLBLC:74); Rebeckah wife of Jn. S. STOTT was the wid. of Thos. THRALL, 17 Jun 1816 (LC Orders 24:315); Jn. S. STOTT mar. Rebeckah M. THRALL, LC, bond 1 Jun 1816 (MLBLC:70); Wickliff GEORGE aptd. gdn. to Lilly Tarpley THRALL orphan of Thos. THRALL, 15 Apr 1822 (LC OB 25:295)]

THRALL, William; 21 Apr 1818

LC; court certifies that John THRALL now residing in this county is the father and heir at law of William THRALL dec'd, formerly of this county. (LC Orders 24:429)

THRIFT, George; 1800; 6 Jul 1801

RC; INV, £592.9.[?]; includes the following slaves: Philis, Sam, Jerry, John, Jesse. (RC WB 9:151)

THRIFT, Samuel; PO 26 Nov ; 27 Jan 1800
WC; INV, [m]; includes the following Negroes: Guy, Sarah, Nancy, Hannah. (WC RI 8:39)

THRIFT, Samuel; PO 23 Jan 1809, T 10 Feb 1809; 26 Mar 1810
WC; DIV of est. at the house of Francis SELF between Francis SELF who mar. Ann THRIFT his wife (rec'd Sarah & Dick) & Jeremiah THRIFT (rec'd Jude & Jane) the only heirs. (WC RI 9:182)
[Francis SELF mar. Ann THRIFT, WC, bond 20 Sep 1806 (MLBWC:64); Sam. BEALE was aptd. gdn. to Jeremiah THRIFT the orphan of Sam. THRIFT, WC, 24 Aug 1801 (WC Orders 1801-04:132); Newyear BRANSON was aptd. gdn. to Ann and Jeremiah THRIFT orphans of Sam. THRIFT, WC 26 Mar 1804 (WC Orders 1804-07:42); Frances [sic] SELF gdn. of Jeremiah THRIFT and Ann SELF formerly THRIFT moved to div. the est. of Sam. THRIFT between the sd. orphans, 23 Jan 1809 (WC Orders 1807-10:257)]

THROP, William & Hannah; PO 9 Jul 1810, T 25 Sep 1810; 11 Feb 1811
NC; possessed James THROP with the est. of William & Hannah THROP and examined John COCKARELL's acct. of his; admin. on the est. of Richard THROP dec'd; COCKARELL had £35.16.9 which was turned over to James THROP. (NC RB 18:523)

TICER, Lewis; 8 Oct 1821
NC; Isaac HAYNIE aptd. gdn. of [Coms.] TICER orphan of Lewis TICER. (NC OB 1820-25:144)
[Lewis TICER mar. Nancy HAYNIE, NC, bond 12 Feb 1810 (MLBNC:100)]

TIDWELL, Anna Barbara; 20 Oct 1784; 28 Mar 1786
WC; three daus. Hannah TIDWELL, Barbara TIDWELL & Betsy MUSE; son Joseph SANFORD; dau. Becky DOZIER Negro woman Kate during her life and then to go to her dau. Sarah DOZIER; Thomas MUSE & Richard DOZIER exors; WITS: Barbara SANFORD, Ursula Presley GORDON. (WC Unrec Wills 1755-1800 #28; DW 16:397, DW 17:176)
[This is Anna Barbara MUSE, dau. of Wm. & Mary (POPE) MUSE, who mar. (1) Jos. SANFORD bef. May 1744 and (2) Jn. TIDWELL after 1751 (MWO:352); Rebecca SANFORD mar. Rich. DOZIER bef. 21 Feb 1769 (MWO:116); Eliz. TIDWELL mar. Thos. MUSE, bef. 29 Sep 1783 (MWO:257)]

TIDWELL, William Carr; Jan 1774; 9 Mar 1774.
CP, WC; WILL; to be buried by beloved wife; all land & slaves to son Reuben TIDWELL; if son should die without heirs to three neices Hannah, Elizabeth & Barbary TIDWELL; Negro girl Jambo to Rebecca NEWTON dau. of friend Richard JACKSON; land given by my father Robert TIDWELL; good friends Joseph LANE, Richard JACKSON & John ROCHESTER exors; WITS: Peter McCLANAHAN, Jn. NORTHEN, Geo. JACKSON. (WC Unrec Wills 1755-1800 #11)
[Wm. Carr TIDWELL was the son of Robt. TIDWELL who in his will (WC 27 Sep 1757 – 28 Jul 1761) named his wife Hannah, som Wm. Carr, dau. Eliz., granddau. Hannah TIDWELL, son Jn. and Kath. JENKINS (nfi) (WC DW 14:48)]

TIFFEY, Pope; [m]; 28 Oct 1811
WC; WILL; half of all est. to wife; after her death to be eq. div. among my children; other half to be eq. div. among my children; [no ex. or wits]. (WC DW 22:229)

[Pope TIFFEY mar. Eliz. VIGAR, WC, bond 24 Aug 1801 (MLBWC:72); Eleanor TIFFEY aptd. gdn. of Susan P. TIFFEY orphan of Pope TIFFEY; Jn. REDMAN aptd. gdn. of Sarah, Rich., Mary, Betsy & Jn. TIFFEY orphans of Pope TIFFEY, 23 Mar 1812 (WC Orders 1810-13:202; OB 1814-18:355); Jn. BAYNE mar. Ellen TIFFEY, WC bond 28 Nov 1814 (MLBWC:5); Hen. A. RILEY & Sally his wife, Mary, Eliz., Nancy, Rich., Jn., and Susan TIFFEY infant children of Pope TIFFEY by Jn. REDMAN their gdn. & next friend, complts. against Jn. BAYNE & Ellen his wife, defts.; ord. that one half of the land that Pope TIFFEY devised to his children be sold., 29 May 1821 (WC OB 1819-23:255); Rich. TIFFEY orphan of Pope TIFFEY chose Dan. CARMICHAEL as his gdn., 26 Aug 1822; Mary & Eliz. TIFFEY orphans of Pope TIFFEY also chose CARMICHAEL as their gdn., 28 Oct 1822 (WC OB 1819-23:454, 486)]

TIFFEY, Pope; PO 25 Dec 1820, T 30 Dec 1820; 22 Jul 1822
WC; list & DIV of Negroes among the orphan children of Pope TIFFEY; Boatswain (about 21), Alice (18), Lizzy & her child Aimey, William son to Lizzy (4 or 5), Caty (about 45), Peggy (about 13), Adam (about 10), Barbary (about 8), Harry (about 6); div. among Richard TIFFEY, Elizabeth TIFFEY, Mary TIFFEY, Susan TIFFEY (Mrs. BAYNE gdn.), Henry RILEY who mar. Sally TIFFEY, John TIFFEY. (WC RI 11:239)
[Hen. A. RILEY mar. Sarah TIFFEY, WC, bond 6 Dec 1820 (MLBWC:59)]

TIGNOR, James; 3 Apr 1818; 12 Oct 1818
NC; WILL; plant. w/o I now live & two Negroes Spencer & Judah to wife Nancy TIGNOR during her life or widowhood; at wife's death sd. land to dau. Delia TIGNOR; also to dau. Delia Negro girl Mary; to dau. Betsy TIGNOR Negro boy Sam; at wife's death Negro woman Judah to dau. Betsy TIGNOR; friend Thomas J. HAYES ex; WITS: Royston B. COVINGTON, Wm. PROSSER. (NC RB 21:513)
[Jas. TIGNOR mar. Nancy KESTERSON, NC, bond 12 Feb 1803 (MLBNC:101)]

TIGNOR, Philip; PO 11 Dec 1807; 13 Feb 1809
NC; INV, [m]; includes Negroes old woman Letty, Sharlot, George, boys Isaac & Leroy, girls Anny & Mary, boys George, [Isarel], & Henry. (NC RB 18:102)
[Philip TIGNOR mar. Molly MOTT, NC, c. 14 Sep 1778 (MWO:353); in his will (NC 11 Dec 1799-13 Jan 1806), Philip TIGNOR of SSP named his wife Molly and his son James; he had other children who are not named (NC RB 17:387)]

TIGNOR, Philip; 9 Dec 1811
NC; Mary TIGNOR, orphan of Philip, chose Matthew HUDSON as her grdn. (NC OB 1811-15:34)
[This is prob. Philip TIGNOR who mar. Molly MOTT (*see above*); Mary TIGNOR, ward of Matthew HUDSON, mar. Matthew HUDSON, NC, bond 9 Dec 1811 (MLBNC:54)]

TIGNOR, Philip; T 29 Dec 1824; 11 Jul 1825
NC; INV, $3036.10; includes following Negroes: Sharlotte & child Dealia, Isaac, Lee, Ann, Mary & child Warner, boys Henry Jr, Henry Sr., Israel, George, Samuel, Washington, Hiram. (NC RB 24:274)

TIGNOR, Philip; 29 Dec 1824; 11 Jul 1825
NC; DIV of slaves among Samuel BLUNDON's heirs (Isaac & child Dealia), Matthew HUDSON (Lee & boy Henry Jr.), James TIGNOR's heirs (Ann & boy Washington), Patty TIGNOR's est. (Henry & man [sic] Sharlott), Phillip

TIGNOR's heirs (boys Israel & Samuel), John PROSSER (George & boy Warner), Elizabeth HAYNIE (Mary & boy Hiram); NC RB 24:273)
[Sam. BLUNDON, wid., mar. Judith TIGNOR, NC, bond 1 Feb 1805; Jn. PROSSER mar. Salley TIGNOR, NC, bond 6 Jun 1810; Eliz. TIGNOR mar. Sam. HAYNIE, NC, bond 8 Feb 1819 (MLBNC:11, 50, 84)]

TIGNOR, Polly; 22 Jan 1825; 13 Jul 1825
NC; DIV of Negroes bel. to est; $349.94 div. among: Matthew HUDSON for his wife's part, John PROSSER for his wife's part, William TIGNOR, Thomas TIGNOR, Liddleton COCKARILL for his wife's part, William HARDING Jr. as admr. of Philip TIGNOR dec'd & as gdn. for Elizabeth TIGNOR, John McCURDY for his wife's (Delia TIGNOR) part, Thomas TIGNOR as gdn. to Lucy & Elijah BLUNDON; NC RB 24:272)
[Polly TIGNOR was the wife of Philip TIGNOR (*see above*); Jn. McCURDY mar. Cordelia TIGNOR, ward of B. BURGESS, NC, bond 11 Mar 1824 (MLBNC:84, 71)]

TIGNOR, William; 6 Apr 1801. RC; INV; £38.16.3. (RC WB 9:143)

TIGNOR, William; PO 8 Sep 1817; 12 Jan 1818
NC; Div of land among the heirs [nfi]. (NC RB 21:347)
[This is prob. Wm. TIGNOR who, in his will (NC [m] - 9 Jan 1815), named his wife Sally, grsons. Wm. Bennet TIGNOR & Jn. TIGNOR, dau. Nancy TIGNOR and son Phillip TIGNOR (NC RB 19:605)]

TILLERY, Jobe; 30 Apr 1807; 4 Mar 1811
NFP, RC; WILL; land to dau. Nancy TILLERY during her life; at her death to go to dau. Mary TILLERY; rest of est. to be eq. div. between Nancy TILLERY, Mary TILLERY and Lucy SMITH orphan of Elizabeth TILLERY; dau. Milly SCURLOCK 10 shillings; friend Joseph WOOLLARD Sr. & Nancy TILLERY exors; WITS: H. W. HEADLEY, Rawleigh DOWNMAN, Joseph WOOLLARD; [Annotation:; admin. with the will annexed committed to Wm. Forrester ... 7 Oct 1816]. (RC WB 9:392)
[Mary TILLERY, dau. of Job, mar. Wm. RUST, RC, bond 18 Jan 1812 (MRC:175; RC OB 24:36)]

TODD, Henry; 2 Jan 1813; 1 Mar 1813
NFP, RC; WILL; bro. Peter TODD; $10 to Thaddeus SHIRLEY; $100 due from George HARRIS in the hands of Martin SISSON with the rest of my est. to be eq. div. between my 2 bros. John & Peter TODD & they are to be exors; WITS: Wm. FORESTER, Edmund R. JEFFRIES. (RC WB 9:419)

TODD, Henry; PO 1 Mar 1813; 6 Nov 1815. RC; INV, £36.6.9. (RC WB 9:484)

TOLEMAN, Joseph; T 5 May 1795; 15 Feb 1796. LC; INV, [m]. (LC EB 24:10)

TOMLIN, Eleanor; PO 6 Jan 1800; 7 Apr 1800
RC; INV of 11 Negro slaves, £490.0.0; includes the following slaves: John, lads Sam & Humphrey; Jane & two children Moses & William; Moll & two children John & Tom; Peter, Lucy. (RC WB 9:130)

TOMLIN, Eleanor; PO 6 Jan 1800, T 7 Jan 1800; 7 Apr 1800
RC; DIV of the slaves of the est. of Eleanor TOMLIN dec'd between Bartholomew McCARTY (Humphrey & Sam), Catharine TOMLIN (Moll & 2 children John & Tom), Apphia F. McCARTY (Jenny & 2 children Moses & William), Moore F. TOMLIN (Lucy & Peter) & Susanah TOMLIN (John). (RC AB 3:29)
[Bartholomew McCARTY mar. Eliz. TOMLIN. RC, bond 28 Apr 1788; Chas. Travers McCARTY mar. Apphia Fauntleroy TOMLIN, RC, bond 12 Jan 1796; Eliz., Apphia, Catharine, Moore and Susannah TOMLIN were children of Robt. (d. RC, 1795) & Susannah (FAUNTLEROY) TOMLIN (RC WB 9:19;

MWO:238, 239); Eleanor must be the dau. called "Nelly" in Robt. TOMLIN's will.]

TOMLIN, George H.; T 7 Apr 1803; 5 Dec 1803
RC INV; £1292.16.0; includes the following Negroes: Sam, Tom, Luke, Peter; Molly, Suckey, Peg, Beck, Sukey, Sarah, Vilet; children lately born: Molly's child Betsey, Beck's child Cillar, Suckey's child. (RC WB 9:221)

TOMLIN, George H.; PO 2 Jun 1817, T 27 May 1818; 6 Jul 1818
RC; DIV of the est. in the hands of B. OLIVER Jr. admr. amongst the distributees: B. OLIVER Jr. & Lucy his wife (whole blood), Williamson B. TOMLIN (whole blood), Williamson P. JONES admr. of Judith his wife (half blood), B. OLIVER Jr. admr. of John W. TOMLIN (half blood), Williamson B. TOMLIN admr. of Bartholomew McCarty TOMLIN (half blood). (RC AB 3:617)
[Benj. OLIVER, Jr. of Hanover Co., Va., mar. Lucy Harrison TOMLIN, dau. of Col. Walker & Priscilla (BALL) TOMLIN bef. 1818; Williamson P. JONES mar. Judith L. TOMLIN, dau. of Col. Walker TOMLIN, RC, bond 11 Jan 1804 (MRC:110, 151)]

TOMLIN, Moore F.; 21 Mar 1815; 7 Nov 1815
LP, RC; WILL; Negroes Elles & her 2 children Sally & Leah and Charlotte to wife Fanny; plant. at Farnham Church purchased of William ALDERSON and the land called Rainses on Totuskey may be sold along with livestock for the support of wife & children; land in WC called [T....] & slaves Joe, Dick & Peter may remain in possession of wife; youngest son Henry Walker; b-i-l Bartholomew McCARTY, nephew Robert W. McCARTY & friend John [BURKE] exors; WITS: Matilda F. LEVY, Horace WELLFORD, Fanny P. McCARTY; RC WB 9:488)
[Moore F. TOMLIN, the son of Robt. & Susanna (FAUNTLEROY) TOMLIN, mar. Frances M. LEVY, dau. of Ezekiel LEVY, RC, bond 23 Apr 1805 (MRC:217); Lemuel L. YERBY mar. Frances "Fanny" TOMLIN, wid., RC, bond 19 Jan 1821 (MRC:239; RC OB 25:231)]

TOMLIN, Robert; PO Jun 1797, T 3 Oct 1797; 5 Jun 1799
RC; slaves of Robert TOMLIN were div. into 4 lots for his 4 children; his dau. Catharine TOMLIN drew Lot 3; Lot 1 - Job, Tom, Sarah & child, Rose & child, Isaac, Judy, Fanny, Old Peter; Lot 2 - James, Frank, Mary, Betty, Charity, George, Levina, Criss; Lot 3 - Godfrey, Nassau, Mary Ann & child, Molly & child, Grace, Suckey, Carpt. Solomon, Joe; Lot 4 - John, Sam, Jenny & child, Humphrey, Lucy, Old Moll, Little Peter, Little Tom; PO 3 Dec 1798, Lot 1 was drawn by Susanna TOMLIN, Lot 2 was drawn by Moore TOMLIN, and Lot 3 (formerly Lot 4) was drawn by Elenor TOMLIN on 2 Jan 1799. (RC AB 3:7)
[Robt. TOMLIN, son of Robt. & Winifred (WEBB) TOMLIN, mar. Susanna FAUNTLEROY, dau. of Col. Moore & Eliz. (MITCHELL) FAUNTLEROY, RC, c. 1770 (MWO:354)]

TOMLIN, Robert Giberne (Dr.); 13 Aug 1811; 1 Jun 1812
NFP, RC; WILL; Negro girl Barbara the dau. of Judy to Fanny P. McCARTY; £200 Virginia money to my bro. Williamson B. TOMLIN; all my surgical instruments to my friend Dr. John W. [B.] GRAY of Tappahannock; Negroes Judy & her 3 youngest children & Little Frank to be sold; all my land, Negroes & prop. to my son Bartholomew McCarty TOMLIN; wife Eloisa T. TOMLIN to have control of prop. during her life; house servant Frank to have his freedom and the land I purchased of George SISSON & wife, but if wife wishes he may remain as a servant to her she giving him such

compensation as she shall think necessary during her life; Bartholomew McCARTY, my bro. John W. TOMLIN & Williamson B. TOMLIN, my b-i-l Williamson P. JONES & my friend George SAUNDERS exors; WITS: Geo. PANE, Tarpley McCARTY, Jn. M. YERBY; COD 1: 17 Aug 1811 to Bartholomew McCARTY son of Bartholomew McCARTY when 21 the proportion of the claim to which I am entitled due from Thomas SYDNOR to my father's est; each ex.to have a $5 mourning ring; John SEWARD to have $40 for performing my funeral ceremony; Robert McCARTY to have my writing desk; WITS: Jn. M. YERBY, Geo. TUNE; COD 2: 30 Sep 1811, bequest to Dr. GRAY revoked since my bro. Williamson B. TOMLIN seems now determined to pursue the study of physic I give him all my sd. instruments & my [electric] machine; WITS: Archelus DALE, B. McCARTY. (RC WB 9:404)

[Robt. G. TOMLIN, son of Col. Walker & Sarah (FAUNTLEROY) TOMLIN, mar. Eloisa T. McCARTY, dau. of Bartholomew & Eliz. (TOMLIN) McCARTY, RC, bond 26 Sep 1805 (MRC:217); sometime before the death of Jn. W. TOMLIN, he, together with Wm. B. TOMLIN, Bartholomew M. TOMLIN and Lucy the wife of Benj. OLIVER became entitled to c. 600 ac. of land in LC and c. 60 ac. in RC by the death of Judith L. JONES and Jn. W. TOMLIN and Robt. G. TOMLIN died leaving large landed estates and many slaves but not enough to cultivate the lands as well as considerable debt; to pay off this debt, Margaret W. TOMLIN, the wid. of Jn. W. TOMLIN, on behalf of her six inf. children, Benj. OLIVER, admr. of Jn. W. TOMLIN, and Williamson B. TOMLIN, admr. of Robt. G. TOMLIN & gdn. of Bartholomew M. TOMLIN the only child and heir of Robt. G. TOMLIN petitioned the Virginia General Assembly to sell these lands; the Committee for the Courts of Justice recommended that the lands be sold, 24 Dec 1818 (*Journal of the House of Delegates of the Commonwealth of Virginia,* Richmond: Thomas Ritchie, 1818, p. 66); Judith L. JONES was the dau. of Col. Walker TOMLIN and the wife of Williamson P. JONES whom she mar. in RC, bond 11 Jan 1804 (MRC:110); the presence of an "electric machine" among the medical equipment of Dr. TOMLIN is interesting. Electrical therapy was used to treat various illnesses since the mid-18th century.]

TOMLIN, Walker; PO 1 Feb 1802, T 20 Mar 1802; 5 Apr 1802
RC; DIV of land & slaves of which Walker TOMLIN died possessed in fee simple among: John Walker TOMLIN, Judith L. TOMLIN, Robert G. TOMLIN, Williamson B. TOMLIN, Lucy H. TOMLIN & George H. TOMLIN children of the sd. Walker TOMLIN; John W. TOMLIN received land in King William Co.; Judith L. TOMLIN received land in RC & LC; Robert G. TOMLIN received land in RC; Williamson B. TOMLIN received land in RC; Lucy H. TOMLIN received land in RC; George H. TOMLIN received land in RC. (RC AB 3:80)

TOMLIN, Walker (Col.); 15 Feb 1802; 5 Apr 1802
RC; Newcastle; INV mentions his other plants: Hickory Thicket, Cobham Park, Newington, Stanley Hall, Rose Hill, Suggitt's & plant. on Currotomen in LC; includes following slaves at Newcastle: Charles (45), Michael (45), Tobey (32), John (28), George (badly grown, 18), Noah (15), [Cuffee] (well grown, 14), Paul (well grown, 10); very old Joan, very old Nanney, Molly (40), Milly (35), Betty (33), Peg (35), Sarah (25), Mary (30), Ellen (28), Charlotte (28), Phoeby (23), Sukey (23), Betty (well grown, 13), Eve (well grown, 13), Fanny (same size of Eve, 11), [Clarisa] (12), Lucy (12); Solomon (7), [Claibert] (7), Joe (7), Billy (7), [?] (5), Cyrus (5), Frank (5), Joe (5),

Dudley (3), David (3), [Haven] (3); Patty (8), Barbara (8), Sillah (8), Hannah (8), Mima (7), Judy (7), Maria (5), Polly (5), Amey (3), Abba (3), Charity (2 yrs 3 mos), Milly (2 yrs 3 mos), Nanney (2 yrs 3 mos), Rhoda (6 mos), Jacob (12 mos), Winney (12 mos), Reuben (12 mos), Tobey (12 mos), Bob (12 mos); at Hickory Thicket: Sam (45), Luke (22), John (22), Cyphas (20); Martha (45), Suckey (18), Lyddy (24), Molly (35); Ned (14), Peter (13), Alfred (8), Porteus (4), Billy (9 mos); Pleasant (11), Charity (well grown 9), Pleasant (6), Mary (5); Lyddy's children (8 days); at Stanley Hall: Phill (34), Andrew (25), Jacob (24), Frank (16); Violet (36), Judy (28), Leanna (19), Charlotte (16), Winney (delicate, 22), Jane (15), Suckey (13), Barbara (well grown, 13), Agga (well grown, 12), Beck (small, 24); Moses (6), Daniel (small, 6), Harry (7), James (2), Frank (2); Nance (small, 18 mos), Esther (small & infirm, 2), Mary (1); at Rose Hill, Carpenters: David (60), George (52), Manuel (49), Glasgow (very infirm); men: Adam (45), Adam Jr. (21), Cyrus (18); women: Barbara (54), Nance (45, infirm), Jane (45), Lucy (40), Grace (28), Amey (31), Lucinda (22, infirm), Sylla (27, delicate); boys: Planter (16), Esau (16, fittified), Tom (12), Noah & Travis (11 each), Plato (5), John (4 1/2), Bob (4); Spencer (4), David (9 mos), William (2); girls: Fanny (11), Maria (11 1/2), Suckey (9), Agnis (7 1/2), Eliza (6 1/2), Sinah (5), Penelope (2), Anna [Smith's] (18 mos); at Suggetts: Charles (21); Lydda (17), Lissa (18), Lydda (16); Daniel (10), Sam (6); plant. on Corotomon in LC, 12 Mar 1802: Davy (38), Andrew (26), Tom (21), Humphrey (16), Winney (34), Sarah (25, unlikely), Rachel (20), Barbara (16), boys Jesse (11), Job (10) & Billy (18 m), girls Lavina (12), Cate (12), Nelly (8), Rosalina (8), Molly (4), Matilda (3), Milly (4). (RC WB 9:165)

TOMLIN, Walker; PO 4 Nov 1816, T 27 May 1818; 6 Jul 1818

RC; settle the acct. of John W. TOMLIN as admr. of his dec'd father Walker TOMLIN which was presented by Benjamin OLIVER Jr. admr. of John W. TOMLIN dec'd; a balance of £2589.8.9 1/2 is due sd. John W. TOMLIN; Explanatory Note: The different distributees of the est. of Col. Walker TOMLIN dec'd will [therefore] have to refund to John W. TOMLIN's est. in the following proportion: Robert G. TOMLIN dec'd, Williamson P. JONES who mar. Judith L. TOMLIN, Williamson B. TOMLIN, Benjamin OLIVER Jr. who mar. Lucy H. TOMLIN, George H. TOMLIN dec'd, John W. TOMLIN. (RC AB 3:634)

[Jn. W. TOMLIN was gdn. to Williamson B. TOMLIN, Lucy H. TOMLIN, and Geo. H. TOMLIN orphans of Walker TOMLIN, RC, 6 Jul 1818 (RC OB 24:234)]

TOULSON, James; PO 12 Jun 1809; 9 Jul 1810

NC settlement of Shapleigh WADDEY's (dec'd, Shapleigh N. WADDEY ex.) acct. of est. of James TOULSON; James CONWAY ward of Richard TOULSON to receive £36.9.1; Richard TOULSON rec'd his full proportion of the est. (NC RB 18:426)

[The est. of Jas. TOULSON was ord. to be admin. by Rich. TOULSON & Shapleigh WADDY, NC, 12 Mar 1798 (NC Fiduciary Bonds 1797-1801); a Richard TOULSON was living at the mouth of Great Wicomico Creek in 1812 (*Alex. Daily Advertiser*, 25 May 1812, p. [3])]

TOULSON, John; PO 13 Dec 1802, T 13 Jan 1803; 13 Jun 1803

NC; INV, [£510.0.0]; includes Negroes Grace, Peter, Peggy, Bob, [F]ame, Billy, Sally, Hannah, Jenney, Sam, Jesse, Violet; DIV of est. among DAUGHITY's children (rec'd Grace, Peter, Peggy), Ro[bert] TOULSON (Tame, Billy, Sally, Jesse), James CONWAY (rec'd Bob, Violet), Shapleigh WADDY (rec'd Hannah, Janny, Sam). (NC RB 16:548)

[The est. of Jn. TOULSON was ord. to be admin. by Shapleigh WADDY, 13 Dec 1802 (NC Minute Book 1801-1805:141); DAUGHITY is prob. the u/i husband of Betty TOULSON, dau. of Thos. TOULSON (d. NC 1794); James CONWAY mar, Nancy TOULSON, dau. of Thos. TOULSON (d. NC 1794); Shapleigh WADDY mar. Molley TOULSON, dau. of Thos. TOULSON (d. NC 1794) (NC RB 15:32, MWO:101, 362); Shapleigh WADDY admr. of Jn. TOULSON dec'd to div. that part of his est. to which Nancy C. GOODE & Rebecca DAUGHITY are entitled, NC 12 Sep 1808 (NC OB 1807-11:61)]

TOULSON, Thomas; T 15 Dec 1809; 11 Feb 1811. NC; INV, £172.3.8 3/4. (NC RB 18:524)

[The est. of Thos. TOULSON was ord. to be admin. by Cyrus SUTTON, NC, 10 Oct 1809 (NC OB 1807-1811:131)]

TOULSON, Thomas; PO 12 Feb 1810; 11 Mar 1811

NC; settlement of Cyrus SUTTON's acct. of his admin. of the est. of Thomas TOULSON; wid. Jane TOULSON possessed with her dower (£53.14) and each legal rep., Mary MOON (wife of William MOON), Thomas TOULSON, Catesby TOULSON, Newton TOULSON, Alcy TOULSON, & Richard TOULSON entitled to £17.18; William MOON was gdn. to Catesby & Newton TOULSON; Jane TOULSON was gdn. to Alcy & Richard TOULSON; Thomas TOULSON was of full age. (NC RB 19:2)

[This is prob. Thos. TOULSON, wid., who mar. Jane NEALE, NC, bond 15 Apr 1805 (MLBNC:101); Wm. MOON mar. Molly TOULSON, dau. of Thos. TOULSON, NC, bond 6 Jun 1804 (MLBNC:74); Catesby TOULSON chose Wm. MOON as his gdn. and MOON was also aptd. gdn. of Newton TOULSON; Catesby and Newton were orphans of Thos. TOULSON; Jane TOULSON was aptd. gdn. of Alice and Rich. TOULSON, also orphans of Thos., NC, 13 Nov 1809 (NC OB 1807-11:131)]

TOWELL, Richard; 18 Aug 1823

LC; settle with Bernard T. PHILLIPS & Sarah his wife who was Sarah TOWELL admx. of Richard TOWELL the acct. of their admin. of the est. of sd. dec'd. (LC OB 25:394)

[Rich. TOWELL mar. Sally HINTON, LC, bond 24 Sep 1811; Sarah (HINTON) TOWELL mar. (2) Bernard PHILLIPS, LC, bond 2 Apr 1823 (MLBLC:59, 74)]

TOWLES, Henry; 25 Sep 1791; 16 Dec 1799

LC; WILL; tract of land called Poplar Point to my son Henry TOWLES; plant. w/o I now live to my son Stokeley TOWLES; land James W. BALL & myself had of Rawleigh TAPSCOTT as also Moses the Negro we had of him to be sold & my half of the proceeds paid to Mrs. Hannah BAILEY & Mr. WILLIAMSON for their claims against me; wife; rest of est. after debts paid to be eq. div. among my six children Elizabeth Martin, Sarah, James, Fanny, Tom and Oliver; b-i-l M. Gilbert CURRELL and my son Stokeley exors; [no wits. named, but will was proved by oaths of Peter BEANE, Jn. CARPENTER and Oswald NEWBY]. (LC WB 28:38)

[This is prob. the Hen. TOWLES who mar. Judith HAYNES, LC, bond 19 May 1768 (MLBLC:74); Frances TOWLES orphan of Hen. TOWLES chose Stokeley TOWLES as her gdn; Thos. TOWLES orphan of Hen. TOWLES chose Judith TOWLES as his gdn., Judith TOWLES is the wid. of Hen., 16 Dec 1799 (NC Orders (21) 1799-1801:70); CC, Hen. TOWLES, Stokeley TOWLES, Chas. LELAND & Sarah his wife, pltfs., aganst James TOWLES & Thos. TOWLES and Oliver TOWLES by the sd. James TOWLES their gdn. re. the sale of mulatto slave Charlotte and div. of proceeds, 18 Oct 1809 (LC

Orders B23 1808-11:120; CC 1809-010); Chas. LELAND, wid., mar. Sarah TOWLES, LC, bond 13 Dec 1797 (MLBLC:48); Poplar Point is prob. located in southeastern LC near Poplar Neck (see Miller:127)]

TOWLES, Henry; 16 Dec 1799; 16 Dec 1799
LC; Judith TOWLES wid. & rel. declares that she will not take or accept the provision made for her in the will of Henry TOWLES & demands that part of the est. to which she is entitled by law; WITS: Eliz. LOVELL, Chas. LELAND. (LC EB 24:104)

TOWLES, Henry; PO Dec 1799; 19 Jan 1801
LC; DIV of Negroes among: Oliver TOWLES, Charles LELAND, James TOWLES, Thomas TOWLES, Fanny TOWLES; each rec'd $488.40. (LC EB 24:131)

TOWLES, Henry (Col.); PO 15 Oct 1804, T 6 Jun 1806; 15 Sep 1806
LC; INV of the est. in bonds, judgments, clerk's fees, etc., £840.3.6; DIV of est. among: Charles LELAND in right of his wife Sarah, James TOWLES, Porteus TOWLES in right of his wife Frances, Thomas TOWLES, Oliver TOWLES; DIV of slaves allotted to Mrs. Judith TOWLES for her dower among the legatees of Col. Henry TOWLES, [same legatees as above]. (LC EB 24:349, 363)
[Chas. LELAND, wid., mar. Sarah TOWLES, LC, bond 13 Dec 1797; Porteus TOWLES mar. Frances TOWLES, LC, bond 18 Feb 1802 (MLBLC:48, 74)]

TOWLES, James; Filed 30 Nov 1810;
LC; list of Negroes held by James TOWLES during the life of the present wife of Thomas CARTER: Meshack (age about 36), Sarah his wife (about 32), [Ame] a girl, Sarah a child about 2. (LC EB 27:129)

TOWLES, James; 27 Jul 1819; 21 Aug 1820
LC; WILL; one third of est. to wife Felicia; after her death est. to be eq. div. between sons John & Henry; if sons die without heirs before age 21 est. to be eq. div. among my bros. Henry & Thomas TOWLES & the children of my sisters Sarah LELAND & Frances TOWLES; friend Porteus TOWLES & bro. Thomas TOWLES exors. & gdns. of my children; COD dtd. 5 Aug 1820 appoints Col. John CHOWNING an additional ex; WITS: B. H. WALKER, Kitty KESTERSON. (LC WB 28:207)
[This is the son of Hen. & Judith TOWLES (*see above and below*); Jas. TOWLES mar. Felicia CHOWNING, LC, bond 8 Oct 1807 (MLBLC:74)]

TOWLES, James; PO Sep 1820, T 23 Nov 1820; 15 Jul 1822
LC; INV, [m]; includes Negroes Aaron, Tom, Henry, John (weaver), joint interest with W. YERBY's est. in Edmund the miller, [Phill], Anna, Silvia, Rose, Caty, Violet, Siller. (LC EB 29:205)

TOWLES, Judith; 19 Jun 1802; 15 Oct 1804
LC; daus. Sarah LELAND & Frances TOWLES; sons Thomas & Oliver TOWLES; residue of est. to be div. among my children: Henry, Stokely, Sarah, James, Thomas & Oliver; sons Thomas & Oliver to have twice as much of the residue as any one of my other last-mentioned children; friend Capt. John CHOWNING, Charles LELAND, & son James TOWLES exors; WITS: Mary WILSON, Jn. S. CHOWNING. (LC WB 28:85)
[This is Judith (HAYNES) TOWLES wid. of Hen. TOWLES (*see above and MLBLC:74*)]

TOWLES, Judith (Mrs.); T 3 Oct 1804; 15 Sep 1806
LC; INV at the house of Porteus TOWLES Esq, $1049.90. (LC EB 24:364)

TOWLES, Mary W.; PO 19 Sep 1814, T 9 Nov 1814; 15 May 1815
LC; INV; includes Negroes: Ciller, Hellen, James. (LC EB 27:198)

TOWLES, Oliver; PO 16 Nov 1812, T 22 Dec 1812; 18 Jan 1813
LC; INV; includes Negroes: Tom, Phillis, Sam, Nancy, William, Tom. (LC EB 27:133)

TOWLES, Oliver; PO 15 May [1816]; 20 Apr 1818
LC; INV at the house of John EDWARDS late the dwelling house of Oliver TOWLES, $1561.57; includes Negroes: [Jim], Tom, Sam, Billy, Nancy, Phillis. (LC EB 27:422)
[Oliver TOWLES mar. Margaret YERBY, only dau. of Wm. YERBY, LC, bond 14 Jun 1809; Jn. EDWARDS mar. Margaret TOWLES, the wid. of Oliver, LC, bond 27 Oct 1814 (MLBLC:25, 74); Thos. TOWLES was the bro. of Oliver TOWLES, 21 Nov 1814 (LC Orders 24:206); on the mot. of Chas. W. N. LELAND ord. that Wm. H. TOWLES, Wickliff GEORGE who mar. Maria F. TOWLES, Jas. S. TOWLES, Porteus TOWLES & Oliver TOWLES children of Porteus TOWLES dec'd, Jn. L. CHINN & Lucy his wife who was Lucy LELAND, Sam. A. M. LELAND, Hen. T. LELAND, Lucia C. LELAND, Jn. TOWLES & Mary W. B. TOWLES be summoned to show cause why the lands of which Oliver TOWLES died seized should not be sold and the proceeds div. among his heirs, 19 Jul 1824 (LC OB 26:56-57)]

TOWLES, Porteus; 5 Mar 1821; 21 May 1821
LC; WILL; to my son William K. TOWLES land w/o I now live; balance of est. after debts paid to be eq. div. amongst my other children: Mary, James S., Porteus & Oliver; friend John CHOWNING ex; WITS: Wm. KIRKHAM, Wm. [?], Archalus DODSON. (LC WB 28:216)
[Wm. BLAKEMORE aptd. gdn. to Jas., Porteus & Oliver TOWLES orphans of Porteus TOWLES, 19 Nov 1821 (LC OB 25:261)]

TOWLES, Porteus; T 4 Dec 1821; 18 Mar 1822
LC; INV, $594.82; includes Negroes Aaron, Richmond, Charles (old), Sollomon, Sam (young), Charles, Joe, Billy, Daniel, O[ld] Sam, Flora, Fanny, Matilda, Caty (sold by admr.), Nancy, Phillis, Nany, O[ld] Juda. (LC EB 29:175)

TOWLES, Porteus; T 19 Aug 1822; 21 Oct 1822
LC; DIV of slaves among Oliver TOWLES (Aaron, Joe, Judy old, Nancy), Porteus TOWLES (Richmond, Sam old, Matilda), James TOWLES (old Charles, Sam young, Daniel old, Fanny), Mary TOWLES (Solomon, Charles young, Nanny old, Phillis). (LC EB 29:237)

TOWLES, Stokeley; 27 Sep 1811; 20 Apr 1812
LC; WILL; use of whole est. to wife Mary Wallace during her life; at wife's death or marriage whole est. to dau. Mary Wallace Ball; Negroes Siller & her two children Holley & James to wife; if wife remarries wife to have no benefit under this will until she executes a deed of release of right of dower in the land I sold my mother in Corotoman to the person legally entitled to the same who is at present Porteus TOWLES; if dau. should survive her mother but leave no heirs the est. that I got by my wife to be div. eq. between Ann HIPKINS wife of Robert S. HIPKINS, Cyrus BALL, Judith E. LEE wife of William L. LEE & Sarah BALL & the balance of est. to be eq. div. between my brothers & sisters; wife & Col. James BALL exors; if wife desires ex. may sell Negro Charlotte; [no wits, but will proved by oaths of Ellyson CURRIE & William T. YERBY]. (LC WB 28:128)
[Stokely TOWLES, son of Col. Hen. & Judith (DIGGS) TOWLES, mar. Mary W. BALL, LC, bond 21 Jan 1799 (MLBLC:74, MWO:355); Robt. HIPKINS mar. Ann BALL, LC, bond 22 Jan 1800; Wm. L. LEE mar. Judith E. BALL, LC, bond 27 Dec 1809 (MLBLC:38, 47); Thos. TOWLES aptd. gdn. of Mary

W. B. TOWLES orphan of Stokeley TOWLES, NC 11 Dec 1820 (NC OB 1820-25:69); Jn. L. CHINN aptd. gdn. of Mary W. B. TOWLES orphan of Stokeley TOWLES, NC 13 May 1822 (NC OB 1820-25:198); Mary W. B. TOWLES orphan of Stokely TOWLES chose Dan. CARMICHAEL as her gdn., 2 Feb 1824 (RC OB 26:145)]

TOWLES, Stokeley; [m]; 16 May 1814
LC; INV, $3869.00 1/2; includes Negroes Aaron, Joe, Charles, Molly, Beck, Winney, King, Mary, Caty, John, Ned, Lucinda, Delphia, Jesse, Judith. (LC EB 27:174)

TOWLES, Stokeley (Maj.); PO 1814; T 7 Apr 1814; 16 May 1814
LC; DIV of Negroes among his children: Porteus TOWLES, Elizabeth TOWLES, Thomas TOWLES, Mildred ELLIS, Stokeley TOWLES, William TOWLES, Rawleigh TOWLES, Nancy TOWLES, Caty TOWLES. (LC EB 27:176)

TOWLES, Stokeley; PO 20 Apr 1812, T 28 Apr 1812; 15 Aug 1814
LC; INV in LC (a very large est. including a many books mainly on legal subjects but also a French grammar) and Negroes: Shardick, Anthony, Armstead, Fielding, Daniel, James, Spencer, Charlotte, Ellen, Siller, Judah, Annica, Mary Ann; INV in NC, T 25 Jun 1812. (LC EB 27:185, 188)

TOWLES, Stokeley; T 8 Nov 1814; 19 Jun 1815
LC; INV of est. unadministered by his late extx. Mary W. TOWLES, taken at Broomfield; includes Negroes: Shadrack, Fielding, Armistead, Anthony, Daniel, Spencer, Charlotte, Annica, Mary Ann, Judah, Charlotte's young child, Solomon, Pluto, Hannah; $4310.70; also an INV of judgments, bonds, bills, acceptances & accounts due the est. (LC EB 27:215, 219)

TOWLES, Thomas; 21 Sep 1820; 13 May 1822
NC; WILL; wife Margaret D. TOWLES to have use of whole est. during her life or widowhood for her own support & the education & support of our mutual offspring James Moore, Thomas, Sally & Margaret TOWLES; at wife's death or marriage the farm where I now live called Snowden and my interest in the head of the river mill seat & Hog Island to my son James M. TOWLES; the farm called Dameron's (where Robert J. DAMERON & his wife Alice are tenants for life) on the Chesapeake Bay to son Thomas; the farm near the courthouse called Oakley & the lot near it that I purchased of John H. FALLIN & Coan Mill to dau. Sally; my lands on Boyd's swamp to dau. Margaret; friend Fleming BATES ex; [no WITS]. (NC RB 23:149)
[Thos. TOWLES mar. Margaret D. MOORE, dau. of Jas. MOORE, NC, bond 1 Oct 1807 (MLBNC:102); Miller:67 identifies Hog Island as a neck of land in NC between Judith Sound & the Potomac River.]

TOWNSEND, Elizabeth; PO 12 Jun 1815, T 20 Jun 1816; 10 Jun 1816
NC; INV, $56.82. (NC RB 20:485)
[The est. of Eliz. TOWNSEND was ord. to be admin. by Jeremiah ROBINSON, NC, 12 Jun 1815 (NC OB 1811-1816:339); this may be Betty the wid. of Haynie TOWNSEND who, in his will (NC 28 Apr 1802 – 12 Jul 1802), named his wife Betty and children Edwin, Winifred Haynie, Sally Edwards, Betsy and Jn. (NC RB 16:421)]

TRACIE, John; PO 14 Apr 1795; 14 Jul 1800
NC; INV, £161.14.6; includes Negroes boy Vincent, girl Sharlotte. (NC RB 16:142)
[The est. of Jn. TRACIE was ord. to be admin. by Wm. CLAUGHTON, NC, 8 Dec 1794 (NC OB 1790-1795:494)]

TRAVERS, Thomas A.; T 11 Jun 1800; 10 Jan 1804

NC; INV; includes schooner rigging & furniture and Negroes Eve, Phillis, boy Cesar, girl Silvia and boy Toney. (NC RB 17:103)
[Thos. A. TRAVERS mar. Alice NEALE but died w/o issue; his est. was ord. to be admin. by Alice R. TRAVERS & Thos. FALLIN, NC, 14 May 1800 (NC Fiduciary Bonds 1797-1801); Alice R. TRAVERS, wid., mar. Wm. P. COX, NC, bond 23 Dec 1800 (MLBNC:22; NC CCs 1801-009 and 1812-015); Thos. A., Matthew, Ann, Louisa, Hen. H., and Wm. B. were children of Wm. & Rebecca TRAVERS (NC OB 1796-97:1, RB 17:229; CC 1814-017); Ann TRAVERS mar. Jas. MORGAN and Louisa seems to have mar. a Hen. TRAVERS; I suspect that this latter marriage is the one recorded in MLBNC for Hen. TRAVERS & "Terasa" TRAVERS, bond 21 Jun 1790 (NC CCs 1805-007 and 1814-017, MLBNC:102)]

TREAKLE, James; 11 Sep 1815
NC; Betsy and James TREAKLE are orphans of James. (NC OB 1811-15:375)

TREAKLE, William; T 28 Mar 1815; 9 Dec 1816
NC; DIV; to Nancy TREAKLE, wid, Negro woman Molley, girl Ginney, boy [Samuel]; allotted to Richard NELMS who mar. Nancy TREAKLE (the wid.) one third of the land, viz. all the land on the right of the road leading down Brereton Neck bordering on Cockerell's Creek, that tract known by the name of [Tarry's] or boat landing with a sufficient part of the timber in the swamp to support the two small places which we judge equal [and one] third part of all the land belonging to the est. of William TREAKLE dec'd and not having time to go through the business having met at the Lower Methodist Meeting House this 2nd day of Nov 1816 & find that the admrs have paid Richard NELMS $131.64 that being his full proportion of the balance of the est. as also the above balance of $13.33 1/3 cents; we find that the act of sales amounts to $941.31. And the admrs. acct. against the est. of William TREAKLE dec'd for money paid by them for which vouchers has been shown us to our satisfaction [amount] to the sum of $600.60 including the admrs. commission at the rate of one percent and which being deducted from the amount of sales as also Richard NELMS part leaves a balance of $209.[06] to be divided between the balance of the heirs which is done as follows: to Jesse CROWDER, to William TREAKLE, to Royston HARRISON, to James TREAKLE, to John TREAKLE, to Elizabeth A. TREAKLE; 9 Nov 1816. (NC RB 21:119)
[Wm. TREAKLE mar. at least 3 times, (1) unknown, (2) Eliz. HAYES, NC, bond 10 Oct 1791 and (3) Nancy BROWN, wid., NC, bond 29 Dec 1814; Nancy (BROWN) TREAKLE mar. Rich. NELMS, NC, bond 29 Aug 1815 (MLBNC:77, 102); Jesse CROWDER mar. Susanna TREACLE, dau. of Wm., NC, bond 21 Oct 1805; Royston HARRISON mar. Polly TREAKLE, ward of Royston HARRISON, NC, bond 15 Mar 1815 (MLBNC:24, 47); in his will (NC 3 Feb 1815-13 Mar 1815), Wm. TREAKLE named his sons Wm., Jas., & Jn. and daus. Sukey CROWTHER, Polly, & Betsy Ann (NC RB 20:24); Wm. HARDING aptd. gdn. of Jas. TREAKLE orphan of Wm. TREAKLE, NC 14 Jan 1822 (NC OB 1820-25:170); on the mot. of Jesse CROWDER for himself and as gdn. of Betsy Ann TREAKLE ord. that Jas. TREAKLE, Jn. TREAKLE, Royston HARRISON, Wm. CROWDER, Jesse CROWDER Jr., and Jn. CROWDER heirs of Wm. TREAKLE be summoned to show cause why lands of sd. Wm. TREAKLE should not be sold and proceeds div. among the sd. heirs, NC 11 Aug 1823 (NC OB 1820-25:314, 325); Miller:15 & 32 locates Brereton's Neck in NC prob. the southern portion of present Bull Neck along the Chesapeake Bay and Cockrell Creek in east central NC between Cockrell

Neck and Bull Neck flowing southeast into the Great Wicomico River at Fleeton.]

TREAKLE, William; PO 13 Mar 1815; 11 Sep 1815
NC; INV, [m]; includes Negroes boy Peter, Molley & child George, girl Gin, boy Israel, old woman Judah, girls Judah, Mary, & Salley. (NC RB 20:217)

TREAKLE, William; PO [7] Dec 1816, T 11 Jul 1817; 14 Jul 1817
NC; sale of Negro boys Peter & George for $706 and DIV of proceeds among heirs: Jesse CROWTHER, Jesse CROWTHER as gdn. to Betsy Ann TREAKLE, John HARRISON as gdn. to Juliet TREAKLE, William TREAKLE, William TREAKLE as gdn. to John TREAKLE, Royston HARRISON. (NC RB 21:224)
[Royston HARRISON aptd. gdn. of Jn. TREAKLE orphan of Wm. TREAKLE, NC 13 Aug 1821 (NC OB 1820-25:127)]

TREAKLE, William; PO 12 Feb 1821; 11 Mar 1822
NC; INV, [m]; includes a Negro girl belonging to John TREAKLE of whom he was gdn. (NC RB 23:116)

TRIPLETT, William; WC; d. intest. c. 1794 leaving a wid. who d. long before 1820 and three children: Francis his only son and daus. Byron and Fairfax; Byron mar. Mourning RICHARDSON, WC bond 12 Jul 1799, and had three children: John F., William F., and Elizabeth; Fairfax mar. William COGHILL and had two children Elizabeth and William. (WC CC 1820-006, 1823-002, 1827-005; MLBWC:58)

TROPP, Richard; PO 11 Dec 1809; 14 May 1810. NC; INV, £65.7.1 1/2. (NC RB 18:388)
[This man's name is usually spelled 'THROP;' the est. of Rich. THROP was ord. to be admin. by Jn. COCKARILL, NC, 11 Dec 1809 (NC OB 1807-1811:146)]

TUCKER, Thomas; [nd]
NC; Thomas TUCKER died seized & possessed of a water grist mill leaving the following children: Rebecca (who mar. Francis BIRD), Molly (who mar. John HOOPER), Harriet (who mar. George HEADLEY), James, Thomas, Selah, John, Fanny, Ann, and Benjamin; in an undated CC Francis & Rebecca BIRD, John & Molly HOOPER, George & Harriet HEADLEY, James TUCKER, Thomas TUCKER and Selah TUCKER brought suit against John, Fanny, Ann and Benjamin TUCKER asking that the mill be sold and the proceeds distributed among the heirs. (NC CC 1111-006)
[Harriet TUCKER, dau. of Thos. TUCKER, mar. Geo. HEADLEY, NC, bond 16 Feb 1814 (MLBNC:52)]

TUCKER, Thomas; T 23 Feb 1819; 14 Feb 1820. NC; INV, $111.97 1/2. (NC RB 22:218)

TULLY, Matthew; 22 Sep 1806
WC; Hannah TULLY, wid. of Matthew TULLY, aptd. gdn. of [Nancy] Turner TULLY the orphan of Matthew. (WC Orders 1804-07:421)
[Matthew TULLY was admr. to Mary MUNDAY, and he mar. Hannah the only child and heir of Mary (WC CC 1795-004)]

TUNE, George D.; 1 Sep 1821; 5 Aug 1823
RC; WILL; to sis. Judith D. TUNE a Negro girl Mary; to son Steptoe Travis TUNE the following Negroes: Robin & Winney; rest of est. & land to wife as long as she remains single; after her death to son Steptoe; if son die without heir, his legacy to children of my sis. Elizabeth GORDON; friend Miskell SAUNDERS ex; WITS: Edw. B. FOSTER, Miskell SAUNDERS, Nancy H.

TUNE; [Miskell SAUNDERS refused to qualify as an ex; certif. granted to wid. Patsey. F. TUNE to obtain letters of admin] ; RC WB 10:29)
[Geo. Davenport TUNE was the son of Kestor (or Castor) TUNE; he was b. in early 1781 and prob. mar. twice, (1) Eliz. HAMMOCK, RC, bond 1 Feb 1808 and (2) Patty F. BRYANT, RC, bond 11 Dec 1815 (NFPR:190; MRC:219); Eliz. TUNE, dau. of Castor TUNE, mar. Jn. GORDON, RC, bond 8 Jul 1795 (MRC:79)]

TUNE, James; 7 Jan 1822
RC; On the mot. of Lewis TUNE admr. of James TUNE, ord. that Dewanna TUNE, Sally TUNE, Mary TUNE, Richard SAUNDERS & Catherine his wife who was Catherine TUNE orphan of William TUNE be summoned to court to show cause why the slaves which James TUNE died seized should not be sold; same ord. on mot. of Lewis TUNE admr. of Sarah TUNE to show cause why the land and slaves of Sarah TUNE should not be sold. (RC OB 25:234)
[Catherine TUNE mar. Rich. S. SAUNDERS, RC, bond 14 Nov 1821 (MRC:181); on the mot. of Rich. SAUNDERS & Cath. his wife by Aug. NEALE their attorney, ord. that Lewis TUNE, Dewanna TUNE, Sally TUNE, Molly TUNE & Thos. HOWE & Sally his wife who was Sally TUNE and Joshua STONE & Nancy his wife who was Nancy TUNE be summoned to show cause why the slaves of Jas. TUNE should not be sold; 6 Jan 1823 (RC OB 26:20; *Rich. Enq.* 23 Jan 1823:[3]); Sally TUNE mar. Thos. HOWE, RC, bond 22 Dec 1821 (MRC:98); Joshua STONE mar. Ann TUNE, wid., RC, bond 5 Feb 1805 (MRC:196)]

TUNE, James; T 21 Dec 1815; 6 May 1822. RC; INV, $956.6[3]. (RC WB 9:714)

TUNE, Joannah; 20 Oct 1825; 7 Nov 1825
RC; WILL; I lend to my sis. Sarah TUNE during her life one Negro man James, one Negro woman Hannah & one Negro girl Maria; I lend to my sis. Mary SAUNDERS during her life one Negro man Stephen, one Negro woman Fanny and one Negro girl Mary; I lend to my sis. Catharine SAUNDERS one Negro a Solomon, Negro boys Ned, Bill, & George,and one Negro woman Morgana; to my niece Sarah HOW Negro girl Ann; all my est. real & pers. to my niece Mary Elizabeth SAUNDERS; Richard SAUNDERS ex; WITS: Leannah CHILTON, Frances NEASOME; [offered for probate on 7 Nov 1825, but Thomas SAUNDERS in right of his wife Mary contested the will]. (RC WB 10:99)
[Mary TUNE mar. Thos. SAUNDERS, RC, bond 1 Nov 1824; Catharine TUNE mar. Rich. S. SAUNDERS, RC, bond 14 Nov 1821 (MRC:181); Joannah, Mary and Catharine TUNE were daus. of Sam. & Sarah TUNE]

TUNE, Sarah; 16 Mar 1814; 6 May 1822
NFP, RC; WILL; wid. of Samuel TUNE; four daus. Joanna, Sally, Molly, & Catharine; granddau. Sally BARNES; son Lewis TUNE; friend Bartho. McCARTY & son Lewis exors; WITS: Fedelia A. JEFFRIES, Matilda JEFFRIES, B. McCARTY; ["Sally BARNES" was interlined before will was signed]. (RC WB 9:712)
[The four daus. Joannah, Mary, Sally and Caty, received legacies from the est. of Peter BARNES, *see above*]

TUNE, Sarah; T 7 Dec [1815]; 6 May 1822. RC; INV, $471.20 ½. (RC WB 9:716)

TURBERVILLE, Gawin C.; [m]; 28 Nov 1814
WC; list of Negroes belonging to the est: [Sipno], Baker, Henry; Sucky; Be[ck] & 3 children Rachel (12), Winney (10), Frances (8); Juliett & 2 children (1 & 4 years old). (WC RI 9:429

TURBERVILLE, George Lee; 25 Jun 1810

WC; John TURBERVILLE, Eliza T. TURBERVILLE who mar. Reuben BEALE and Martha TURBERVILLE who mar. Robert BEALE are the heirs of Maj. George Lee TURBERVILLE. (WC Orders 1807-10:546)
[Geo. Lee Turberville of Epping was the son of Jn. TURBERVILLE of Hickory Hill who d. in WC in 1799 by which time Geo. Lee was also dec'd (WC DW 20:75); in his will (RC 8 Oct 179[5] - 2 Apr 1798), Geo. Lee TURBERVILLE named his son John (under 16), daus. Eliza Tayloe & Martha Felicia (RC WB 9:91); Eliza Tayloe TURBERVILLE mar. Reuben BEALE, WC, 28 Apr 1800 (MWO:33); Martha Filecia TURBERVILLE of RC mar. Robt. BEALE of Madison Co., RC, bond 1 Aug 1802 (MRC:12); Martha TURBERVILLE, relict of the late Geo. TURBERVILLE d. 20 Nov 1809 at Pecatone, WC (*Alexandria Gazette*, 26 Jan 1810, p. [3])]

TURBERVILLE, John; 21 Mar 1799; 26 Aug 1799 and 1 Nov 1799
CP, WC; WILL; to be bur. next to first wife Martha in garden at Hickory Hill; grson. John TURBERVILLE all lands I was possessed of at the time I wrote his father of his intended mar. w/ Miss Eliz. Tayloe CORBIN of Buckingham including Negroes already given him: Lewis, Ambrose, Abberdeen, Thom, Gawin, Sam, Prince, Charity, Hampshire, Little Hampshire, Archey, Sampson, James, David, George, Billey, Bob, Kess, Betty, Rachel, Moll, Sarah, Grymes, [Set], Sue, Joe, Phillis, Moses, Billey, Abraham, Francis & Eve; son Geo. Lee TURBERVILLE dec'd; dau. Martha Corbin TURBERVILLE land in Loudoun now Fairfax Co. and Negroes Felicia with her child, Charles, Jesse, [Hanson], Sally, [Sidae], Sally and [Sidae's] children at Landon Plant., Sandy, Jack, and Nancy and Sampson at Falls Plant., also Harry's dau. Babbara at Hiccory Hill; son Troilus Lewins TURBERVILLE to build house for dau. Martha with not less than two rooms on a floor (single story), cellars under it with brick or stone chimney, a kitchen, a meat house, a dairy and an overseer's house or cabin; wife Anne to have following slaves Jesse the driver, Prue, Harriett, Jenny (Abraham's wife) and children Harry, Milly, and Isaac's son Baker and Nat and his children and all the other house servants; carpenter Billey and Armstead to be included in my dearest wife's dower also that old carpenter Jack, young carpenter Jack, carpenter Billey the younger and [molato ?] Billey all working at the carpenter's trade be included in my son Troilus Lewins' part of the Negroes also Siller and her children and Sarah the dairy maid and her children with Isaac his wife and all his children be included in my son Troilus Lewins' part of the Negroes; grson. Philip JONES son of dau. Letitia Corbin JONES to have 300-ac. tract in Loudon Co.; grson. Catesby JONES to receive 600-ac. tract; grson. Roger JONES; grdaus, Elizabeth Lee JONES, Sally Skelton JONES, and Martha Corbin JONES to each receive £500 money of Virginia; dau. JONES to receive £500 to support grson. Eusebius JONES; wife and friends John MURPHY, Corbin WASHINGTON and nephew George Richard TURBERVILLE exors.; COD. As soon as son Troilus reaches age 21 he is to qualify as an ex. and gdn. to grandchildren. (WC DW 20:75)
[Jn. TURBERVILLE's second wife was Ann BALLENTINE, wid., whom he mar. in WC, bond 19 Dec 1792 (MLBWC:72); the court decided that each of the distributees proportion of the land in WC purchased by Jn. TURBERVILLE dec'd since 1782 was less than $100 and ord. that Mottrom BALL & Martha his wife, Reuben BEALL & Eliz. his wife, Robt. BEALL & Martha F. his wife, Eliz. L. JONES, Roger JONES, Thos. ap Catesby JONES & Philip JONES infants by Jeykill JONES their gdn., Wm. GORDON & Martha T. his wife, Hen. W. BALL, Catesby Jones BALL & Lettice BALL infants by

Wm. GORDON their gdn. be summoned to show cause why land should not be sold, 22 Jun 1812 (WC Orders 1810-13:254); Reuben BEALL mar. Eliza Tayloe TURBERVILLE, WC, bond 28 Apr 1800 (MLBWC:5); Robt. BEALE mar. Martha Filecia TURBERVILLE, RC, bond 1 Aug 1802 (MRC:12); Wm. GORDON mar. Martha T. JONES, ward of Jekyll JONES, NC, bond 11 Aug 1810 (MLBNC:43); Catesby JONES mar. Lettice Corbin TURBERVILLE, WC, bond 29 Dec 1778 (MWO:203); in a chancery suit, Mottrom BALL & Martha his wife, Philip JONES, Catesby JONES, Eliz. L. JONES, Roger JONES, Wm. GORDON & Martha T. his wife and Catesby BALL & Letice BALL, complts. against Jn. MURPHY ex. of Jn. TURBERVILLE, def., the court ord. the def. to surrender to the complts. all the RE Jn. TURBERVILLE died seized of having in regard to the right of dower of Ann the wid.; Philip JONES, Catesby JONES, Eliz. L. JONES, Roger JONES, Wm. GORDON & Martha T. his wife, and Catesby BALL & Lettice BALL are heirs of Eusebius JONES; Martha Corbin BALL is mother of Mottrom 26 Mar 1816 (WC OB 1814-18:220; CC 1818-001); Martha wife of Robt. BEALE and Eliz. T. wife of Reubin BEALE are sisters of Jn. TURBERVILLE, 24 Nov 1817 (WC OB 1814-18:357); Miller:66 locates the Hickory Hill tract in WC about 7 miles east of Templemans Crossroads]

TURBERVILLE, John; T Nov 1799; 23 Jun 1800
Late of Hickory Hill, WC, INV; £4296.18.10 & £3961.4.9; includes the following Negroes: Abraham, boy Moses, Nancy & 3 children Judy, Betty & Suckey; Janey & 4 children Patty, Letty, Celia, Hesiah; Suckey & 3 children Silly, Edmund & Sina; Milly & child Silvey; Priscilla & 4 children Nancy, Flora, Billey & Anthony; Harriott & child Sarah; Sarah & child Daniel; girl Franky; girls Nancy & Livinia; girls Jane & Barbara; boy Henry; boy Sammy; Henry, Betty, Jesse, Billey (carpenter), Alexander, Nathaniel, Prue; at plant. called the Narrows: Eugene, Suckey, Susanna, Peggy, Alice, Abraham, Nancy, Cate, Cate, Beckey, Mary, Mary, Andrew, boy Charles; INV of TURBERVILLE's Falls Quarter known as Woodberry in Fairfax Co. & at the plant. formerly in Loudon Co. now in Fairfax Co known as [Hilway], T 25 Nov 1799, includes the following Negroes: carpenter John, Arthur, [Lacy], Billy, Bob, Armstead, Jack, Solomon, Sandy, Harry, [?], Old Nan, Jemima, Scilla, Betty, Letty, Suckey & her child, [Dirty] & her child, Sinah, Carey, Nancy, Old Pat, Old Suckey, Frank, boy Abraham, Randall, children: Charity, Elce, Thaddeus, Moses, Charles, Patty, Winney, James, Billey, Easter, Billey; at the Upper Place: Isaac, Charles, David, Jesse, Sampson, Billey, Jack, Tom, Hanson, James, Adam, [Baka], Ellick, Dominick, [Tilia], Daniel, Harriot, [Kizey], Sally, Sharlott, Lidda, Barbary, Frank, Randal, Sarah. (WC RI 8:63)

TURBERVILLE, John; [m]; 23 Mar 1818
WC; DIV of Negroes; [actually a list of Negroes with their ages and values] Prue (17) & child, Mariah (11), Billy (21), Abraham (54), Moses (45), Edmund (19), Fanny (14), John (12), Nelly & child Dawson, Spencer (9), Emmily (6), Levinia (3), Sarah [m], Sally (13), Patty (9), Daniel (22), Billy (54), George (20), Sam (19), Levinia (18), Dick (10), Joshua (5), [Ewell] (7), Eley (10), Nan (8), Prue [m]. (WC DW 23:347)

TURBERVILLE, John (Maj.); [m]; 25 May 1819
WC; DIV of real est. including the mill into 2 equal moities; the whole of the Hickory Hill Tract containing 2223 ac. was allotted into 3 distinct tracts, that part called Avery's containing 861 ac, that part containing 256 ac. & the H. Hill mansion house and that part which lies on the southeast side of the road

by H. Hill gate to the mill containing 1106 ac. and the Narrows containing 860 ac, and the tract called Parham and the mill & mill seat; land was div. between Maj. Robert BEALE (received Parham, Avery's, the mill & mill seat, and the H. Hill house tract) in right of his wife Martha who was Martha F. TURBERVILLE a sis. of sd. Maj. John TURBERVILLE and Reubin BEALE (received the Narrows & the H. Hill tract on the southeast side of the road leading to the mill) as gdn. to his children in right of his late wife Eliza Tayloe who was Eliza Tayloe TURBERVILLE another sis. of Maj. John TURBERVILLE. (WC RI 10:382)

[Robt. BEALE mar. Martha F. TURBERVILLE (one of three children – Eliza T., Martha F. and Jn. -- of Geo. Lee TURBERVILLE, *see above*); Maj. Jn. TURBERVILLE d. intest. in Nov 1815 (WC CC 1816:004)]

TURBERVILLE, John Maj.; [m]; 24 Mar 1818

WC; INV, [m], includes Negroes Abraham (blacksmith about 55), John (about 12), Dick (about 12), Nancy (about 9), Sarah (very old), William (about 19), Prue (about 15), Billy (a carpenter about 57), Prue (very old), Joshua (about 2), Ewel (between 2 and 3), Sally (about 10), Maria (about 9), Patty (about 6), Daniel (about 20), Sam (about 14), Edmund, George, Marilla (old & afflicted), Lavinia, Fanny (about 10), Alice (between 6 and 7), Spence (6), Moses (house servant), Nelly (about 30), Emily (about 4, badly grown), Lavinia (infant). (WC RI 10:237)

TURBERVILLE, Martha; 13 Nov 1809; 26 Feb 1810

WC; WILL; son Gawin Corbin TURBERVILLE; I place in the hands of Thomas STOWERS (in trust) for the use of my dau. Hannah Lee BASEY all livestock, wearing apparel & all rents on my dower property in Fairfax Co; none of the above property which is placed in the hands of Thomas STOWERS shall not in no instance be subject to the payments of any debts created either by Hannah Lee BASEY or her husband previous to their marriage or at any period thereafter; [no ex. named]; WITS: Thos. COVINGTON, Isbel LONG; [added in margin: 1819 Feby Ch M. T's will further proved and will put with papers; that court certificate not recorded here, there being no room]. (WC DW 22:23)

[Hannah Lee TURBERVILLE, dau. of Martha TURBERVILLE, mar. Thos. Pope BASYE, WC, bond 15 May 1804 (MLBWC:5); will of Martha TURBERVILLE finally proved 22 Feb 1819 (WC OB 1819-23:16)]

TURBERVILLE, Martha; T 31 Aug 1810; 23 Mar 1813. WC; INV, £89.14.4 [= $299 ?]. (WC RI 9:368)

TURNER, Charles; T 1 Mar 1803; 12 Dec 1803

NC; INV, [m]; includes Negroes Ben, Nan, boy Dorsey, Ellen, boys Christopher & Joe. (NC RB 17:93)

TURNER, James; T 4 Mar 1812; 11 Aug 1812. NC; INV, $193.86. (NC RB 19:238)

[The est. of James TURNER, who had been dead more than 3 mos., was ord. to be admin. by the sheriff, 10 Feb 1812 (NC OB 1811-1816:44)]

VANLANDINGHAM, [Francis]; PO [m]; 14 Oct 1816. NC; INV, [m]. (NC RB 21:95)

[This is prob. Francis VANLANDINGHAM who, in his will (NC 26 Apr 1816-13 May 1816), named his wife Sally, son Joel and daus. Lucy & Nancy VANLANDINGHAM and Hannah SMITH; he also named Jn. ROCK & his heirs as legatees (NC RB 20:464); Hannah VANLANDINGHAM mar. Benj. O. SMITH, wid., NC, bond 23 Oct 1815 (MLBNC:92); Jn. ROCK mar. Catherine VANLANDINGHAM, dau. of Francis, NC, bond 18 Jul 1809 (MLBNC:88)]

VANLANDINGHAM, Richard; 6 Dec 1813; 25 Jun 1814
NC; John MORRISON assigns over to Randal HEADLEY all rights, claims, etc. in right of his wife Rebecca who was Rebecca VANLANDINGHAM in the est. of her father Richard VANLANDINGHAM dec'd. (NC RB 19:467)
[Geo. COOKMAN was gdn. of Rebecca VANLANDINGHAM now wife of Jn. MORRISON, NC, 14 Dec 1813 (NC OB 1811-15:208)

VANLANDINGHAM, Thomas; T 25 Jun 1812; 12 Aug 1812. NC; INV, [m]. (NC RB 19:239)

VASS, Alexander (Dr.); of EC was the admr. of his late wife Millicent who was Millicent CHICHESTER the dau. of Richard and Anne (GORDON) CHICHESTER b. in LC 13 Mar 1765; she was also the grdau. of James GORDON the Elder who named her in his will (LC 6 Jan 1767 – 18 Feb 1768) (LC CC 1798-001; LC WB 18:105;
http://freepages.genealogy.rootsweb.ancestry.com/~duffy/reports/gordon/rr01_003.htm, accessed 26 Oct 2012)

VENIE, George; 2 Sep 1817; 3 Nov 1817
NFP, RC; WILL; whole est. to friend George MISKELL and he is named ex.; WITS: Rich. STREET, Merideth HUDSON. (RC WB 9:566)

VIGOR, Jacob; 22 Oct 1810
WC; Nelly VIGOR orphan of Jacob VIGOR chose George QUESENBERRY as her gdn. (WC Orders 1810-13:51)
[This is prob. Jacob VIGOR who mar. Penelope QUISENBERRY dau. of Nicholas QUISENBERRY (MWO:361)]

VIGOR, Sarah; 2 Jan 1810; 22 Oct 1810
WC; WILL; greatgrson. John Beane TIFFEY all lands in WC and elsewhere & the following Negroes: Charles (a young man), Jessee (a boy of about 10), and Jenny (a girl of 10 or 12); grdau. Frances DOLEMAN a young Negro woman Charlotte; grdau. Eleanor VIGOR Negro girl Aggy & loom; great grdau. Mary Pope TIFFEY Negro Bob; great grdau. Sarah TIFFEY; all money & crop on hand at my death to be eq. div. between children of Pope TIFFEY that he had by my grdau. Elizabeth TIFFEY, Eleanor VIGOR, & the children of my grdau. Frances DOLEMAN; rest of Negroes to be eq. div. between the children of Pope TIFFEY that he had by my grdau. Elizabeth TIFFEY, William VIGOR, Eleanor VIGOR, & Frances DOLEMAN; Pope TIFFEY, John PAYNE, & George QUESENBURY exors; Rich. STUART, Pope TIFFEY. (WC DW 22:139)
[This is no doubt Sarah BAYNE, dau. of Mathew BAYNE (d. WC 1771), who mar. Wm. VIGOR well bef. Mar 1767; in his will (WC [m] - 31 Mar 1767), Wm. VIGOR named his wife Sarah and dau. Frances; he also had 6 sons but did not name them (MWO:361; WC DW 14:425; DW 15:122); Frances Bayne VIGOR mar. (1) John H. DOLEMAN, WC, bond 10 Jun 1805 and (2) Rich. CRASK, WC, bond 19 Nov 1818 (MLBWC:17, 20); *see WCCP:135-136 for more on the DOLEMAN family*]

VIGOR, Sarah; PO 22 Oct 1810; 24 Dec 1810
WC; INV; includes Negroes Bob, Charles, boy Jesse, girls Charlotte & Agnes. (WC RI 9:224)

WADDY, Catharine; PO 21 Mar 1814, T 14 Jul 1814; 18 Jul 1814
LC; INV, $846.02 1/2; includes Negroes: Henry, Sam, Judith; DIV between: Richard PAYNE & Benjamin WADDY. (LC EB 27:183)
[Rich. PAYNE mar. Maria WADDY, NC, bond 12 Sep 1808 (MLBNC:80)]

WADDY, George P.; PO 9 Nov 1812; 8 Mar 1813

NC; INV, £949.2.9; includes Negroes David, Eady & child David, Janny & child Jesse, Alice, Eunice, girl Lucy, boy Moses, girls Mariah, Nanney, & Letty, boy Dennis, girl Sally, boys Sharack & Mark, Winney. (NC RB 19:349) [Geo. P. WADDY was the nephew of Wm. WADDY (*see below*); his est. was ord. to be admin. by Eliz. WADDY, 9 Nov 1812 (NC OB 1811-1816:125); Eliz. & Margaret WADDY chose Eliz. WADDY as their gdn. and sd. Eliz. was aptd. gdn. of Jane WADDY orphans of Geo. P. WADDY, NC, 9 Nov 1818 (NC OB 1816-20:300); on the mot. of Thos. L. P. JAMES & wife, ord. that Marg. P., Jane E. and Jn. M. WADDY, the heirs and Eliz. WADDY the wid. of Geo. P. WADDY be summoned to show cause why land of Geo. P. WADDY should not be sold, 10 May 1825 (NC OB 1825-30:4); Thos. JAMES, son of Thos. JAMES mar. Eliz. WADDY, ward of Eliz. WADDY, NC, bond 9 Nov 1818 (MLBNC:60)]

WADDY, James; PO 10 Jul 1809, T 11 Aug 1809; 14 Aug 1809
NC; allotted Catherine WADDY, the wid., one third of the chattels of the sd. decedant (she having been possessed of her dower in the Negroes previously by consent of the parties); also allotted Richard PAYNE who mar. Maria WADDY one of the children of the sd. James WADDY with the Negroes Neroe, Lewis, Lidia & Judith, to Benjamin WADDY one other of the reps. with the Negroes Fanney, Ester and lads Joe & Harry; Richard PAYNE & Benjamin WADDY each received tracts of 111 ac. (NC RB 18:204)
[The est. of Jas. WADDY was ord. to be admin. by his wid. Catherine WADDY, 10 Apr 1797 (NC Minute Book 1793-1797); Rich. PAYNE mar. Maria WADDY, NC, bond 12 Sep 1806; Geo. P. WADDY gave consent for Maria (MLBNC:80); Maria WADDY chose Geo. P. WADDY as her gdn. and he was also gdn. to Benj. WADDY; Maria and Benj. were orphans of Jas. WADDY; 12 Sep 1808 (NC OB 1807-11:61, 114)]

WADDY, Margaret (Mrs.); PO 8 Jan 1798; 11 Apr 1803
NC; DIV of est. between Caty WADDY for the orphans of James WADDEY (rec'd Betty, Joseph, Lewis, Esther, Harry) and George P. WADDY (rec'd Nan, Billy, Unity, Jacob, Emanuel). (NC RB 16:535)

WADDY, Margaret (Mrs.); PO 9 Jan 1797; 13 Jun 1803
NC; INV, $1319.13; includes Negroes Nan, Betty, boys Billy & Lewis, girl Unity, boy Joe, girl Esther, boys Jacob, Emanuel, & Harry. (NC RB 16:555)
[The est. of Margaret WADDY was ord. to be admin. by Geo. P. WADDY (NC OB 1796-1797:101)]

WADDY, Shapleigh; PO 11 Nov 1805; 11 Sep 1809
NC; INV, £844.18.11; includes cowper's tools & Negroes Jacob, Lazarus, Judea (very much afflicted), boy Bob, girl Easther, boy Joe, Nancy & child Tom, girls Hannah, Charlotte, Sally, Chloe, & Jane, boys Emanuel & Sam, girl Milley. (NC RB 18:217)
[Shapleigh WADDY, son of Benj. & Judith (NEALE) WADDY, mar. Molly TOULSON, dau. of Thos. TOULSON, bef. 3 Apr 1794 (MWO:362); in his will (NC 15 Nov 1804-10 Jun 1805), Shapleigh WADDY named his wife Molly and sons Shapleigh N. & Alexander WADDY; he mentions his daus. but does not name them (NC RB 17:286); in her will (NC 15 Oct 1812-13 Feb 1815), Mary "Molly" WADDY, the wid. of Shapleigh WADDY, names daus. Susannah & Nancy WADDY and Peggy HUDNALL, s-i-l Jn. HUDNALL, son Shapleigh N. WADDY, and bro. Rich. TOULSON (NC RB 19:620); a Shapleigh WADDY was a midshipman in the Virginia State Navy for three years (VS1776 III:1221); Jacob, known as "Wildcat" Jacob, a slave of Shapleigh WADDY was found guilty of hogstealing, NC 10 Oct 1808 (NC

OB 1807-11:67); Susanna WADDY seems to have mar. Jas. S. ELLISTON by 10 Nov 1817 (NC OB 1816-20:195)]

WADDY, Shapleigh; T 12 Dec 1811; 12 May 1812
NC; DIV of 367-ac. tract of land on branches of Little Wiccomico River & adj Capt. Wm. NELMS; Shapleigh N. WADDY chose the part south of the main road. (NC RB 19:184)

WADDY, Shapleigh; PO 14 Nov 1814; 14 Mar 1815
NC; DIV of est. after John HUDNALL the admr. sold the girl Easther to pay the debts of the sd. WADDY; Mrs. Sally WADDY rec'd boy Bob, John HUDNALL rec'd Emanuel, Miss Susan WADDY rec'd Lazarus, and Miss Nancy WADDY rec'd girl Mariah. (NC RB 20:31)
[Jn. HUDNALL, ward of Thos. HARVEY, mar. Margaret B. WADDY, NC, bond 11 Sep 1809 (MLBNC:55)]

WADDY, Shapleigh N.; PO 9 Jan 1815; 13 Feb 1815
NC; INV, $741.66 1/4. (NC RB 20:18)
[Shapleigh N. WADDY was the son of Shapleigh & Mary "Molly" (TOULSON) WADDY (*see above*); his est. was ord. to be admin. by Wm. ESKRIDGE, NC, 9 Jan 1814 (NC OB 1811-1816:272); Jn. NELMS aptd. gdn. of Ann, Alexander, Margaret, and Shapleigh WADDY orphans of Shapley WADDY, NC, 8 Dec 1817 (NC OB 1816-20:211); Shapleigh N. WADDY mar. Sally EDWARDS, ward of Wm. EDWARDS, NC, bond 19 Nov 1808 (MLBNC:104)]

WADDY, William; PO 14 Oct 1805, T 25 Feb 1806; 15 Apr 1806
NC; INV, £676.14.6; includes Negroes Anthony, Frederick, Silva & child Frederick, girl Kisiah, boy Milton, girls Mahala & Patience, boy Robin. (NC RB 17:402)

WADDY, William; PO 8 Dec 1806, T 7 Feb 1807; 14 Apr 1807
NC; slaves Anthony, Frederick & Sylva sold for £231 and Martha H. WADDY was possessed with £57.15 in bonds being her proportion of the sum; William JONES was possessed with the balance being his and his wife's part and Lucy C. WADDY & Elizabeth H. WADDY's parts; JONES was their gdn. (NC RB 17:519)
[In his will (NC 22 Jun 1805-14 Oct 1805), Wm. WADDY named his daus. Patty H. WADDY, Lucy C. WADDY, Betsy H. WADDY & Maryann JONES, his wife Mary S., and his s-i-l Wm. JONES, and his nephew Geo. P. WADDY (NC RB 17:325); Wm. JONES mar. Mary Ann WADDY, NC, bond 8 Apr 1799 (MLBNC:62)]

WADDY, William; PO 8 Dec 1806, T 14 Nov 1806; 13 Jul 1807
NC; INV, £658.14.9; includes Negroes Anthony, Frederick, Silva & child Frederick, girl Kesiah, boy Milton, girls Mehala & Patience, boy Robin. (NC RB 17:562)

WAIDE, Richard; 14 May 1821
NC; Henry S. GASKINS aptd. gdn. of Delia A. WAIDE orphan of Richard WADE. (NC OB 1820-21:98)
[This is prob. the Rich. WAIDE who mar. Alice ANGELL, dau. of Wm. ANGELL, NC, bond 4 Jan 1808 (MLBNC:104); Delia Ann WAIDE, ward of Hen. S. GASKINS, mar. Jn. CLAUGHTON, NC, bond 2 Jan 1826 (MLBNC:18)

WAIDE, William; 10 Jun 1816
NC; Lilly WAIDE orphan of William WAIDE chose Joseph DESHIELDS as her gdn. (NC OB 1816-20:54)

WALE, George; 6 Jul 1810; 20 Nov 1815

LC; WILL; after debts are paid my mother Winney WALE to have use of all remained of my est; after mother's death whole est. to be eq. div. between my cousins Joseph SPRIGGS son of Ephraim SPRIGGS & Nathan SPRIGGS son of Nathan SPRIGGS; Nathan SPRIGGS ex; WITS: Eppa LAWSON, Jn. HUTCHINGS, Jn. HUNT. (LC WB 28:170)

[Winney WALE was Winifred SPRIGGS who mar. Lawson WALE, LC, bond 15 May 1783 (MLBLC:76); Lawson WALE (d. LC 1785), the father of this Geo. was a son of Geo. WALE the Elder who in his will (LC 13 Mar 1767 – 20 Aug 1767) named his wife Sarah, sons Geo., Jn., Lawson and Wm. and daus. Caty, Maryann, Joanna and Sarah; Geo. WALE d. intestate without issue; Catherine mar. Wm. BRENT and also d.s.p.; Joanna mar. [fnu] LEWIS; Sarah mar. Zachariah BARR, NC, 2 Jun 1776 and Mary mar. Jas. HUDNALL and had moved to Buckingham Co., Va. by 1797; Jn. WALE is prob. the Jn. WALE orphan of Geo. WALE who was bound to Wm. LAWSON in 1773 to learn the trade of shop joiner and house carpenter; Jn. WALE went to sea in the US Navy during the Rev. War, his ship was captured, he was never heard of again and was declared dead (LC WB 18:87; WB 22:10; LC OB 15:349; LC CCs 1795-002, 1796-004, 1810-021, 1810-022; MWO:29, 188)]

WALE, George; PO 20 Nov 1815, T 23 Nov 1815; 19 Feb 1816
LC; INV; includes Negroes: Armestead, Harry. (LC EB 27:280)

WALKER, Anna; T 11 Apr 1811; Jul 1811. WC; INV, £46.6.[11]. (WC RI 9:255)

WALKER, Betsy; 13 Oct 1823
NC; Thos. COOKMAN aptd. gdn. of Betsy WALKER orphan of Betsy WALKER. (NC OB 1820-25:325)

WALKER, Edmund; Edmund WALKER d. intest. c. 1795 (his inv. showing a worth of £53.14 was taken in Nov 1795) leaving an only son who d. an inf. and a 135-ac. tract in NC; his wid. Sarah "Sally" mar. (2) Francis VANLANDINGHAM, wid., NC, bond 17 Nov 1795; he also had two siblings: George WALKER, and Samuel WALKER (MLBNC:103; NC CC 1806-006)

[Sam. WALKER was dec'd by 1803 leaving the following children: Edmund, Nancy (who mar. Ewell SELF), Fanny, Wm., and Benedict; NC CC 1806-006 also suggests relationships between Ann WALKER who mar. Daniel MOORE, Reuben MOORE, Walker MOORE, [fnu] CRASK and his wife Polly, and Geo. LAVENDER and his wife Nancy]

WALKER, Frances; PO Jun 1812; 26 Apr 1813. WC; INV, [m]. (WC RI 9:372)

WALKER, George; 10 Jan 1810; 28 Feb 1814
WC; WILL; land I purchased of Ransdel PIERCE acting as trustee for Templeman [G. BROWN] to nephew Benedict WALKER; Benedict WALKER to be ex.; WITS: Rodham HALL, Thos. YEATMAN, W. R. PACKETT. (WC DW 23:10)

WALKER, Jesse; PO 9 Jan 1815; 12 Jun 1815
NC; INV, $1178.64 1/4; includes Negroes boy Ezekel & Harris & girl Emzy. (NC RB 20:149)

[In his will (NC 8 Oct 1814-9 Jan 1815), Jesse WALKER named his wife Rhoda, and children Winder George, Jesse and Lucy WALKER (NC RB 19:584)]

WALKER, John; PO 11 Dec 1809; 12 Feb 1810
NC; allotted her dower in land of John WALKER to the wid. Salley E. WALKER; land was adj land of Robert CHRISTOPHER and on main road to Northumberland Courthouse. (NC RB 18:322)

[Jn. WALKER mar. Sally E. PITMAN, dau. of Caty SUTTON, NC, bond 15 Dec 1808 (MLBNC:104); Caty SUTTON was Caty WEBB who mar. (1) Jeduthun PITMAN, LC, bond 29 Mar 1783 (MLBLC:60) and (2) Moses SUTTON, NC, bond 28 Feb 1793 (MLBNC:96); the est. of Jn. WALKER was ord. to be admin. by Wm. HUGHLETT, NC, 10 Oct 1809 (NC OB 1807-1811:135)]

WALKER, John; PO May 1810, T 31 May 1811; 8 Feb 1813
NC; land bel. to John WALKER was sold on 13 Dec 1810 to Sally E. WALKER for £21.11; proceeds seem to have been div. among William HUGHLETT who mar. Elizabeth WALKER one of the heirs of John WALKER, Burnett JONES [sic] who mar. Leannah WALKER another of the heirs, Benjamin WALKER another of the heirs, Benj. LANSDELL as gdn. to Thomas WALKER an infant and also an heir. (NC RB 19:337)
[Wm. HUGHLETT mar. Eliz. WALKER, NC, bond 29 Jan 1799 (MLBNC:57); *see Wm. HUGHLETT above.*]

WALKER, Joseph D.; PO 19 Jun 1809, T 30 Jun 180[9]; 17 Jul 1809. LC; INV, [m]. (LC EB 27:62)

WALKER, Richard; PO 10 Dec 1798; 9 Dec 1799
NC; INV, [m]; includes Negroes Dick, Will, George, Lucy. (NC RB 16:30)
[In his will (NC 13 Nov 1798-10 Dec 1798), Rich. WALKER named his sons Benj., Jn. & Thos. and daus. Leaner & Eliz. WALKER (NC RB 15:546)]

WALKER, Richard; PO 14 Jan 1799, T 13 Aug 1802; 13 Sep 1802
NC; DIV of est; each rep. to receive £87.6.0 1/4; Henry CUNDIFF, ex. of Richard WALKER delivered legacies to Benjamin JONES who mar. Leaner WALKER, to Matthew LAMKIN gdn. to John WALKER, and to Benjamin LANSDELL gdn. to Thomas WALKER orphan of Richard WALKER (also rec'd Negro girl Lucy). (NC RB 16:455)

WALKER, Risden; 14 Jun 1824
NC; Leroy DAVIS aptd. gdn. of William WALKER orphan of Risden WALKER. (NC OB 1820-25:398)
[This man's first name has also been recorded as Risdon and Reiden; he was the son of Wm. WALKER (d. NC 1802) (NC RB 16:372); Risdon WALKER mar. Molly Hurst DAVIS, ward of Lindsay DAVIS, NC, bond 20 Nov 1805 (MLBNC:104)]

WALKER, Sally E.; PO 11 May 1812; 8 Jun 1812. NC; INV, [m]. (NC RB 19:213)

WALKER, Samuel; PO Aug 1804; 24 Nov 1806; WC. INV, £57.18.3. (WC RI 9:5)

WALKER, Thomas; 6 Jan 1823
RC; Jn. CLARKE was chosen by Myra L. WALKER orphan of Thos. WALKER as gdn. (RC OB 26:18)
[Eliz. WALKER orphan of Thos. WALKER chose Fleet B. PLUMMER as her gdn., 5 Jan 1824 (RC OB 26:139)]

WALKER, William; 1 Apr 1823; 8 Nov 1824
SSP, NC; WILL; use of all est. to wife Nancy WALKER during her life or widowhood; the whole of my land to my sons John & William WALKER to be eq. div; to my single daus. at my death one bed & furniture or $30 cash; all remaining est. to be div. into 5 parts for Nancy WALKER, Lucy WALKER, Hannah WALKER, Fanny WALKER, & Betsy DUGLAS's children; Joseph RICE & Robert ALEXANDER exors; WITS: Wm. FORESTER. (NC RB 24:67)
[This is prob. Wm. WALKER who mar. Nancy RICE, NC, bond 25 Jul 1797; Elizabeth WALKER, dau. of Wm. WALKER, mar. Edw. DOUGLASS, NC, bond 14 Dec 1818 (MLBNC:31, 105)]

WALKER, William; 18 Nov [1824]; 10 Jan 1825. NC; INV, [$419.20]. (NC RB 24:141)

WALL, Edward; 26 Nov 1810; 7 Jun 1813
RC; WILL; whole est. to wife Margaret during her life & after her death to be eq. div. amongst the whole of my children; wife to be extx; WITS: Edmund R. JEFFRIES, Rich. H. HOGAN, Thos. HOGAN. (RC WB 9:427)
[Rich. WALL was gdn. to Jn. R. WALL orphan of Edw. WALL (RC OB 24:373; NC CC 1834-004)]

WALL, Edward; T 12 Oct 1813; 4 May 1814
RC; INV, $1626.77, includes black men Bob, John, and John [sic]. (RC WB 9:456)

WALL, Thaddeus; PO 13 Sep 1824, T 19 Feb 1825; 13 Jun 1825
NC; sale of land of which Thaddeus WALL died seized & possessed to Richard HEADLEY for $51.50; proceeds div. among the heirs: John R. WALL (rec'd $8.63), Edmond NORTHEN in right of his wife Peggy (rec'd $2.16), Bartholomew DODSON in right of his wife Elizabeth (rec'd $4.61), William M. HALL (rec'd $2.16), James R. RICE in his own right (rec'd $4.31), Elizabeth & Lucy HALL (rec'd $2.16 each). (NC RB 24:264)
[Peggy WALL mar. (1) Geo. JESPER, RC, bond 21 Jul 1813 and (2) Edmond NORTHEN, RC, bond 21 Oct 1822 (RC OB 27:156, MRC:105, 148); Bartholomew DODSON mar. Eliz. N. RICE, ward of Rich. WALL, NC, bond 22 Apr 1819 (MLBNC:30); on the mot. of Jn. R. WALL in his own right and as attorney in fact for Edw. WALL, Jas. W. RICE, Bartholomew DODSON & Eliz. his wife ord. that Edmund NORTHERN & Peggy his wife, Wm. M. HALL, Peggy HALL, Eliz. HALL and Lucy HALL be summoned to appear in court to show cause why the lands of Thaddeus WALL should not be sold for a distribution to the heirs, 10 Aug 1824 (NC OB 1820-25:406)]

WAPLE, George N.; [m]; 2 Nov 1812
RC; WILL; wife Rebecca; daus. Maria & [Henney]; wife to be extx. & keep est. together until children come of age or marry; WITS: Sam. B. KELSICK, Jn. EIDSON. (RC WB 9:410)
[A George N. WAPLE was recorded as the head of a household in RC in the 1810 census; his household included one male 0 - 16, one male 26 - 45, 2 females 0 - 10, a female 16 - 20 and 42 slaves (1810 Census Richmond Co., Va.]

WAPLE, George N.; PO 4 Nov 1812; 1 Nov 1813. RC; INV, $244.50. (RC WB 9:435)

WARD, John; 2 Apr 1816; 23 Mar 1818
WC; WILL; $1.00 to my daughter whose name I do not know which I had by my last wife and who moved from this county to some part in the west of this state some 8 or 10 years ago with her mother; a Negro woman Sarah & her four children: Joshua, Joseph, Charles & Catherine to dau. Jane Garrett WARD; all the rest of my est. to sd. dau. Jane; friend Daniel CARMICHAEL ex; WIT: Thos. N. BERRYMAN, Wm. DISHMAN, Geo. G. BARAK. (WC DW 23:349)

WARD, John; T 7 Mar 1818; 28 Jun 1819
WC; INV; includes Negroes Joshua (young man), Joe, Sarah, Cate, Charles (a boy). (WC RI 10:389)

WARD, Richard; T 5 Nov 1814; 14 May 1816. NC; INV, [m]. (NC RB 20:480)

WARDROBE, David; 10 Dec 1811; 23 Dec 1811.
CP, WC; WILL; wife Polly WARDROBE one Negro girl Jane; John CRITCHER one silver watch; Susannah CRITCHER; friend John B.

MURPHY all my books & bookcase & surveying compass & chain; balance of est. to wife; household & kitchen furniture to be sold and money eq. div. among wife, John CRITCHER & Susannah CRITCHER; John & Susannah CRITCHER are under age and unmarried; John MURPHY & John B. MURPHY exors; WITS: Chas. S. ASKINS, Alfred C. ASKINS. (WC DW 22:240)
[David WARDROBE mar. Polly MEZICK, WC, bond 17 May 1811 (MLBWC:73); Jn. & Susanna CRITCHER are children of Jn. CRITCHER (d. WC 1806) (*see above*)]

WARDROBE, David; T 10 Jan 1812; 25 May 1812
WC; INV, [$4948.25]; includes Negroes Frank, Anthony, Glasgow, Emanuel, Parker, Lucy, Susan, Cambridge, Charles, Betty, Judy, Patty, Maria, Milly, Isbell, Filicia, Winney, Sally, Sampson, Thomas, Joseph, [Lidey], Jane. (WC RI 9:329)

WARDROBE, Polly; 12 Dec 1821; 22 Aug 1825
WC; WILL; my land & a Negro woman Patty to my bro. John MEZECK; at his death land to go to his son Joseph MEZECK; Elizabeth MEZECK; Negro girl Sally to Eliza L. CRITCHER; Negro boy Robin to John CRITCHER Jr.; Negro boy John to nephew Joseph MEZECK; to my bro. Benjamin COURTNEY Negro woman Judith; to neice Nancy COURTNEY Negro girl Felicia and at Nancy's death Felicia & her increase to her three bros: John, Linsey & Thomas COURTNEY; Negro girl Milly to my 3 nephews John, Linsey & Thomas COURTNEY; bros. John MEZECK & Benjamin COURTNEY exors; WITS: Jn. CRITCHER, Jn. S. TAPSCOTT, Catharine GARNER. (WC DW 25:205)
[This is Polly MEZICK whose marriage to David WARDROBE (*see above*) lasted less than a year (MLBWC:73)]

WARDROBE, Polly; T 2 Nov 1822; 25 Aug [1823]
WC; INV, $2357.24; includes Negroes Anthony, Judith & child, Patty, Milly, Felicia, Robert, Sally, John. (WC RI 11:[404])

WARING, Epaphroditus Lawson (Dr.) (WEARING); 27 Apr 1821; 26 May 1821
WC; WILL; to bro. Horace WEARING all my interest in the dower right of my father's est. and also my interest in my bro. Francis G. WEARING's est; all est. to my wife; if wife has a child after my death, est. to be eq. div; bro. Robert Payne WEARING, friend Henry WEARING & wife exors; WITS: Jn. REDMAN, Ann S. BUTLER, Silas SHORT. (WC DW 24:168)
[This is Eppaphroditus Lawson WARING who mar. Elizabeth BANKHEAD, WC, bond 30 Oct 1817 (MLBWC:73)]

WARING, Epaphroditus Lawson; 23 Feb 1824
WC; On the mot. of Henry T. GARNETT & Eliza his wife who is extx. of E. L. WARING, commissioners aptd. to settle the acct. of GARNETT & wife admin. on the est. of sd. WARING. (WC OB 1823-27:35; Epaphroditus Lawson WARING mar. Eliz. BANKHEAD, WC, bond 30 Oct 1817; Eliza L. (BANKHEAD) WARING mar. (2) Hen. T. GARNETT, WC, bond 12 Oct 1822 (MLBWC:24, 73); Dr. Epaphroditus Lawson WARING of Mattox Bridge, WC, d. on 1 May 1821; he was a member of the Protestant Episcopal church (*Rich. Enq.* 25 May 1821, p. [3])]

WARWICK, Benjamin; T 29 Feb 1816; 17 Mar 1817. LC INV. (LC EB 27:366)
[Ben. WARWICK mar. Charlotte GEORGE, LC, bond 25 Jan 1792 (MLBLC:77); admin. on the est. of Ben. WARWICK unadmin. by Charlotte WARWICK granted to Jas. WARWICK, 19 Feb 1816 (LC Orders 24:285);

Griffin WARWICK orphan of Benj. WARWICK chose Enoch GEORGE as his gdn., 19 Aug 1816 (LC Orders 24:323)]

WARWICK, Philip; PO 16 Feb 1807; 13 Jun 1807

LC; INV of est. presented by George CAMPBELL his admr., £19.4.0; includes old Negro man Harry & old Negro woman Winney. (LC EB 27:15)

WASHINGTON, George; 24 Feb 1810; 27 Jul 1812

WC; WILL; sis. Frances WASHINGTON 3 Negroes Jude, Thomas & Aleck; sis. Elizabeth WASHINGTON 2 Negroes Sophia & Munkey; remaining est. to be eq. div. between my four sisters & Elizabeth SANFORD the dau. of my sis. Ann SANFORD; Robert RANDALL & sis. Frances WASHINGTON exors; [no wits named]; [will was proved by the oath of Thomas M. WASHINGTON on 24 Aug 1812]. (WC DW 22:308)

[On the mot. of Robt. RANDALL & Martha his wife who stated that Geo. WASHINGTON died seized of a tract of land in WC having heirs the sd. Martha RANDALL, Alice B. GARNER wife of Spencer GARNER, Frances wife of Jn. UNDERWOOD, Eliz. WASHINGTON and Eliz. SANFORD an inf. dau. of Ann SANDFORD dec'd; heirs ord. to appear in court to show cause why land should not be sold, 27 May 1817 (WC OB 1814-18:308); Robt. RANDALL mar. Marthey WASHINGTON, WC bond 25 Oct 1787 (MWO:292); Spencer GARNER mar. Alice Bailey WASHINGTON, WC bond 6 Mar 1798 (MLBWC:24); Jn. UNDERWOOD mar. Frances WASHINGTON, WC bond 27 Jan 1813 (MLBWC:73); Ann WASHINGTON mar. Reubin SANFORD, WC bond 11 Dec 1799 (MLBWC:62)]

WASHINGTON, Hannah; [m]; 26 Apr 1801

of Bushfield, Cople Par, WC; WILL; son Bushrod WASHINGTON livestock and furniture; grdau. Anne Aylett ROBINSON furniture and household goods; grson. Richard Henry Lee WASHINGTON silver plate; legacy from bro. in law General WASHINGTON; dau. in law Hannah WASHINGTON; should grson. Rich. Hen. Lee WASHINGTON die bef. 21 his legacy to go to infant grson. Corbin WASHINGTON or his bros. John Augustine & Bushrod Corbin WASHINGTON; friend Mary HARRINGTON wife of Dr. Timothy; grdaus. June Mildred WASHINGTON & Mary Lee WASHINGTON; grson. Bushrod WASHINGTON son of William Augustine WASHINGTON; son Bushrod and Wm. ROBINSON who mar. grdau. Anne Aylett WASHINGTON exors. [*This is a very long and detailed will, mentioning specific bequests; in it Hannah WASHINGTON expresses her fear of premature burial and how she wishes to avoid it.*] (WC DW 20:211)

[This is Hannah BUSHROD, the wid. of John Augustine WASHINGTON who d. in WC in 1787; in his will, written in 1784, John Augustine WASHINGTON names his sons Bushrod & Corbin, his dau. Jenny the wife of Wm. Augustine WASHINGTON, his dau. Mildred, and his granddau. Ann Aylette WASHINGTON and his bro. Gen. Geo. WASHINGTON (WC DW 18); Anne Aylett WASHINGTON mar. Wm. ROBINSON, WC, bond 8 Oct 1800 (MLBWC:59); Bushrod WASHINGTON later became a Supreme Court Justice (for more information, see John A. Wayland *The Washingtons and Their Homes*, Berryville, Va: Virginia Book Co, 1973.)]

WASHINGTON, John; 3 Jul 1785; 26 Jun 1787

WC; WILL; wife Constant; unborn child; son William Henry WASHINGTON; son Thomas Lund WASHINGTON; dau. Sarah HARPER; dec'd son Robert Townshand; seven children: John Terett, William Henry, Thomas Lund, Robert Pitt, George, Louisa Fassaker, Nancy Constantia & unborn child; wife & friend William FITZHUGH of Chatham & nephew

Henry WASHINGTON exors; WITS: Jn. [R?], Alexander [SOMERVAIL]. (WC Unrec Wills 1755-1800 #31; DW 16:335; DW 17:118)
[NB: There is an error in the abstract by Fothergill (WWCV:186); the son's name is "Thomas Lund WASHINGTON" not "Robert Lund WASHINGTON"]

WASHINGTON, John; 12 Sep 1798; 25 Mar 1805
WP, WC; WILL; son George WASHINGTON all est. in Caroline Co. which he possessed in 1794; whole est. in WC. to wife; son George Negroes Kate, Jonathan & Bell after death of wife; grdau. Caty Storke WASHINGTON Negro Jenny; son John WASHINGTON rest of est. after death or remarriage of wife; wife and two sons exors; WITS: Jas. MUSE, Mary Ann MUSE, Geo. BUCKNER. (WC DW 21:159)

WASHINGTON, John Jr.; 8 Sep 1802; 25 Apr 1803
WC; WILL; bro. George WASHINGTON a Negro boy Simon & a bay horse; niece Caty Stork WASHINGTON seven Negroes: Peg, Alice, Telly, Lucy, Charity, Siller & Judy; father John WASHINGTON four Negroes: Gabriel, Fanny, George & Ben; bro. George WASHINGTON to be exor.; WITS: Jas. MUSE, Thos. HILL. (WC DW 20:447)

WASHINGTON, William A.; PO 1810; Oct 1811
WC; INV, $26,792.83; includes Negroes Hannah (age 25), Charles (9), Lucy (7), Joshua (2), Griffin (husband of Hannah, 30); Dinah (35), Hannah (7), Lewis (3), Peg (22), Milly (7), Harry (5), Ninah (2); Cary (55), James (husband to Cary, 60, died 12 Feb at Haywood) [Cary & James were for sale at Port Royal on 15 Jan 1811], General (20), West (17), Brooks (15), Matilda (10); Fanny (22), Mary (young), Edmund (5); Charity (30), Warner (6), Billy (2), Spencer (husband to Charity, 25); [Lisey] (40), Fortune (16), Adam (14), Barrott (7), Jenny (5), Jeffrey (40), Nancy (32), Walker (16), Melinda (7), Anna (2); Ned (40), Comfort (25), Caty (8), Delphia (1); Sally (28), Jack (10); [Lotty] (20), Aaron (young), George (3); [Kessey] (21), Tunstal (m); Old Darcus (55); Judy (40), Eve (7); Caty (50), Sall (16) & young child Thomas; Celia (18), Adam (18), Henry (4); Suckey (57), Thornton (10), Frank (21), Peter (16), Nelson (14); Nancy (27), Eliza (10), Joshua (6), William (4); Tom (42), Moll (40); Mark (45), Phill (14), Willis (10), Prince (10); Sarah (36), James (17), Archibald (15), Thomas (13); Cornelia (6); Sam (13); Solomon (28); Reuben (27); Gus (21); Oliver (19); James (30); Charles (30); Big Daniel (50); Isaac (50); Basco (36); Arthur (60); [Lewie] (53); Joshua (36); Daniel (26, blacksmith); Billy (60, blacksmith); Dick (35); Ben (16); Winny (60); Andrew (36, workman), Ceasar (36, workman) [*names separated by semicolons seemed to be grouped together*]. (WC RI 9:282)

WASHINGTON, William Augustine; 12 Jul 1810; 17 Oct 1810
of Georgetown in the District of Columbia; WILL; son Bushrod all lands in WC which I purchased of Henry WASHINGTON & James MARYE bounded by the land purchased by James MARYE at the Schoolmaster's donation in Washington Par., the white marsh the western branch of Bridge Creek, the Barrens, the Montrose land, the lands of the late John ROSE, the late Anthony PEYTON, T. N. BERRYMAN, & Robert HIPKINS, lands left by John ROSE to his son Walter in Mattox Neck; son George Corbin lands at the beginning of Bridge Creek adj land I purchased of John Hooe WASHINGTON called Indian Town, the great quarter or Wise's Field, Blenheim, Pea Hill which I bought of John H. WASHINGTON, the Ruins where Capt. John PEYTON now lives, Popes Creek, William MUSE & Potomac River; son George Corbin 105 ac. called "Jonathans" purchased by

my father of HIGDON, also 200 ac. near Pea Hill, Blenheim, Gravelly Run, Pope SMITH's land; mentions legacies devised to sons Bushrod & George Corbin by their uncle the late General George WASHINGTON; deceased dau. Ann ROBINSON; wife Sarah land and servant woman Jenny & her husband David also Negro woman Sarah that I purchased of John TAYLOE Esq.; after wife's death her lands to be eq. div. between dau. Sarah Tayloe & son William Augustine; wife, son George Corbin & friend Robert BEVERLEY exors; appoints wife guardian to dau. Sarah Tayloe & son William Augustine both of whom are unmarried and under age; WITS: Charlotte FITZHUGH, Cha. WORTHINGTON, F. S. KEY. (WC DW 22:165) [Wm. Augustine WASHINGTON mar. three times: (1) Jane "Jenny" WASHINGTON, dau. of Col. Jn. Augustine WASHINGTON, WC, bond 25 Sep 1777; (2) Mary LEE, dau. of Rich. Hen. LEE, WC, bond 4 Jul 1792; and (3) Sarah "Sally" TAYLOE, dau. of Jn. & Rebecca (PLATER) TAYLOE, 11 May 1799 (MWO:366); he was the father of nine children: Hannah B., Augustine, Anne A., Bushrod, Corbin A., George C., Sarah T., Lawrence, and William A.; Wm. A. WASHINGTON was aptd. gdn. to his infant children Bushrod and George, WC 27 Jun 1803 (WC Orders 1801-04:406); Sarah WASHINGTON was gdn. of her children Sarah & Wm. A. WASHINGTON, 25 May 1812 (WC Orders 1810-13:234); the Ruins was apparently the name of a plantation in WC; Miller:137 has a Ruin Branch which flows from WC into RC and empties into Cat Point Creek.]

WATSON, John; PO Jul 1808; 6 Feb 1809. RC; INV, £4.10.0. (RC WB 9:343)

WATTS, [Joseph]; 19 Feb 1821
LC; John & Joseph WATTS orphans of [Joseph] WATTS chose Thomas M. [OWENS] for their gdn. (LC OB 25:192)

WATTS, Bridget; T [1] May 1809; 19 Jun 1809
LC; DIV of bonds from the sale of Negroes among: James KESTERSON admr. of Thomas SHELTON dec'd Edward PAYNE's proportion of the above which the sd. SHELTON bought of the sd. PAYNE, Caty SHELTON in her own right, Spencer BROWN in right of his wife Judith, William GEORGE son of William in right of his wife Behethaland, Elizabeth PAYNE. (LC EB 27:51; Orders 22D 1805-08:461)
[Judith, Catharine and Behethaland PAYNE were daus. of Jn. PAYNE (d. LC 1788) (LC WB 22:193); Bridget PAYNE mar. Jn. WATTS, LC, bond 25 Jan 1797; Spencer BROWN mar. Judith PAYNE, LC, bond 17 May 1802, Wm. GEORGE mar. Behethaland N. PAYNE, LC, bond 11 Apr 1806 (MLBLC:9, 32, 77)]

WATTS, John; 31 Jan 1802; 19 Apr 1802
LC; WILL; land I now live on to be sold after my children come of age & the money eq. div. among them; Negroes not to be sold; two Negroes Siller & Amey to son Spencer WATTS; to son William L. WATTS Negro woman Rachel that was given him by his grfather. John LONGWITH; Negro woman Sukey to my dau. Polly WATTS; Negro woman Fanny to dau. Lucinda WATTS; Negro George to continue on the plant. this year & finish the crop & if there should be money wanting to pay my debts he may be sold, but if the money should not be wanting then he is to stay on the plant. & work to maintain the children & school them & at a future day he is to be sold; friends John LONGWITH & Spencer WATTS exors; WITS: Wm. GIBSON, Fanny PITMAN, Mary PEARSON, Jn. HALL, Jn. HUTCHING. (LC WB 28:61)

[This is Jn. WATTS who mar. a dau. of Jn. LONGWORTH of LC (MWO:367); Wm. WATTS orphan of Jn. WATTS chose Ephraim SPRIGGS as his gdn., 19 Sep 1803 (LC Orders V 1802-03:437)]

WATTS, Spencer; 18 Sep 1815

LC; Overseers of the Poor to bind out John & Joseph WATTS orphans of Spencer WATTS. (LC Orders 24:259)

[Spencer WATTS prob. mar. Betsy BUTLER; the consent is dated 30 Mar 1801 (MLBLC:77)]

WATTS, William L.; 8 Nov 1815; 20 Nov 1815

LC; WILL; all est. to sis. Lucy WATTS; friend John BISCOE ex; WITS: Robt. BISCOE, Polly BISCOE. (LC WB 28:170)

[This is William Longworth WATTS, son of Jn. WATTS (d. LC 1802) *see above*]

WAY, John; PO 13 Jun 1796; 14 Oct 1799

NC; INV, £333.11.6; includes Negroes James, Peter, Letty, and boy Dick. (NC RB 16:13)

[This is prob. Jn. WAY who mar. Sally SUTTON, NC, bond 14 Feb 1791 (MWO:367); in his will (NC 15 Jan 1796-13 Jun 1796), Jn. WAY of SSP named his wife Sally Lansdell WAY, his b-i-l Wm. WAY and father Rich. WAY (NC RB 15:285)]

WEATHERS, George; 12 Mar 1807; 6 Dec 1813.

LP, RC; WILL; wife Mary William; 3 children William (under 21), Peggy Armstead & Polly Ellen WEATHERS; 2 Negroes James & Will to son William; 2 Negroes Daniel & Fanny to dau. Peggy Armstead (when 18); 2 Negroes [Danah] & Jeremy to dau. Polly Ellen (when 18); land purchased of James SAMFORD to be eq. div. between my 3 sons: Vincent, George, & Eppa WEATHERS; wife & 3 sons John, Vincent & Eppa exors; WITS: Clemt. SHACKLEFORD, Jn. YEATMAN Jr., Susanna THOMAS. (RC WB 9:436)

[Geo. WEATHERS mar. Mary SANDY, RC, bond 8 May 1790 (MRC:224); Vincent WEATHERS was dec'd by 7 Oct 1816; he had four children: Lucy, Vincent, Betsy & Letty (RC OB 24:42)]

WEATHERS, John; 22 Jun 1822; 7 Oct 1822.

LP, RC; WILL; to wife Rebecca B. WEATHERS the Negroes Billy & his wife Joan, Grace & Betty also my stock of hogs which I have at Smithfield in LC; at wife's death Negroes & all property given her to be eq. div. between three children Addison WEATHERS, Malvina WEATHERS, & Juliet Ann WEATHERS; son William Y. WEATHERS; dau. Isabella K. AMORY $150 which my s-i-l Thomas C. AMORY received from Richard LAWSON for the sale of land; dau. Eleanor JEFFRIES; dau. Catherine STURMAN; to son Addison WEATHERS Negro girl Betsy; to dau. Malvina WEATHERS Negro girl Peggy & Joan's youngest child Dennis; to dau. Juliet Ann WEATHERS two Negro girls Mary & Martha; wife to have care of the property devised to children Addison, Malvina & Juliet Ann (all of whom are under age); land which was my father's & which I purchased near this place with a small piece which I also purchased of Charles L. CARTER adj. thereto to be sold & the proceeds thereof with the interest in the est. of George PURSELL dec'd which I purchased of George R. PURSELL to be eq. div. among all my children; son William Younger WEATHERS and two s-i-l Thomas C. AMORY & William Young STURMAN exors; WITS: Geo. SAUNDERS, Thos. T. REYNOLDS, Jn. FERGUSON; COD dtd. 29 Jun 1822: property devised to wife to be eq. div. among children Addison, Malvina & Juliet Ann at wife's death or remarriage [same WITS]; [exors refused to qualify;

William Y. WEATHERS & William R. JEFFRIES granted letters of admin. with the will annexed]. (RC WB 10:2)
[Jn. WEATHERS mar. Rebecca Beckwith KELSICK, RC, bond 4 Jan 1790; Thos. C. AMORY, of Gloucester Co., Va., mar. Isabella K. WEATHERS, RC, bond 8 Oct 1818; Wm. R. JEFFRIES mar. Eleanor WEATHERS, RC, bond 24 Dec 1818; Wm. Y. STURMAN mar. Catherine WEATHERS, RC, bond 21 Feb 1821 (MRC:3, 103, 198-199, 225); Addison WEATHERS orphan of Jn. WEATHERS chose Wm. Y. WEATHERS as his gdn.; Rebecca WEATHERS aptd. gdn. to Malvina & Juliet Ann orphans of Jn. WEATHERS, 5 Jul 1824 (RC OB 26:213)]

WEATHERS, John; T 9 Dec 1822; 3 Feb 1823
RC; INV, $1054.15; includes Negroes Betty (old woman), Peggy (girl). (RC WB 10:14)

WEATHERSPOON, William; T 20 Mar 1802; 28 Apr 1806. WC; INV. (WC RI 8:611)
[This is prob. the Wm. WEATHERSPOON who mar. Joyce BUTLER, WC, bond 25 May 1790 (MLBWC:75)]

WEAVER, Benjamin; 13 Jul 1812; 17 Nov 1812
LC; WILL; being much advanced in years; use of my lands to my nieces Elizabeth & Jenny WEAVER; at their deaths to be eq. div. among the male issues of Jenny WEAVER should she have more than one son, if not to the son alone, but should she leave daus. and no sons then the land to be eq. div. among the daus.; my bed & bible to my niece Jenny WEAVER; James BALL of Ditchley ex; WITS: Geo. S. LEE, Arthur LEE, Jos. BALL. (LC WB 28:137)

WEAVER, Benjamin; PO 17 Nov 1812, T 28 Dec 1812; 17 Mar 1817; LC INV. (LC EB 27:367)

WEAVER, Calep; [m] Dec 1814; 22 May 1815
WC; WILL; sis. Elizabeth ANTON; balance of my money remaining in the hands of Burdit ESKRIDGE to bro. John WEAVER [who is under age]; [no ex. named; WITS: Jas. L. MOTHERSHEAD, Elishe WHITE, Burditt ESKRIDGE]. (WC DW 23:99)

WEAVER, Darkey; 23 Jul 1820; 21 Aug 1820
LC; WILL; grson. John Weaver BELL; grson. James BELL; grdau. Nancy BELL; rest of est. to son Coleman BELL; friend James BRENT ex; WITS: Jas. BRENT, Jane BRENT, Spencer GEORGE Jr., B. M. WALKER. (LC WB 28:208)
[This is Dorcus BELL who mar. Jn. WEAVER, LC, bond 10 Jun 1789, *see below*; Coleman BELL was apparently a s-i-l who had mar. Agga WEAVER, LC, bond 26 Dec 1806 (MLBLC:5, 78)]

WEAVER, John; 6 Nov 1809; 20 Feb 1815
LC; WILL; all est. to wife Darkey WEAVER; after death of wife whole est. to grson. John BELL; if grson. does not have issue, est. to James BELL; wife to give sow & gun to Samuel BELL; wife extx; WITS: Jn. DOGGETT, Betsey BELL, Chas. BRENT. (LC WB 28:162)

WEAVER, John; 25 May 1824
WC; admin. on the est. of John WEAVER granted to James L. MOTHERSHEAD by consent of James ANTHONY who mar. a sis. of sd. John WEAVER. (WC OB 1823-27:56)
[Jas. ANTHONY mar. Fanny WEAVER, WC, bond 6 Sep 1816 (MLBWC:2); Fanny WEAVER was prob. a dau. of Thos. WEAVER, q.v.; a Jn. WEAVER was aptd. gdn. to his son Elford WEAVER, 26 Jan 1801 (WC Orders 1799-1801:402)]

WEAVER, Thomas; 26 Jun 1815

WC; Thos. SPENCE Sr. aptd. gdn. to John WEAVER orphan of Thomas WEAVER; Fanny WEAVER another orphan of Thomas, chose SPENCE as her gdn., and Daniel SANFORD aptd. gdn. to Letty WEAVER an orphan of Thomas. (WC OB 1814-18:156-157)

WEAVER, William; PO 27 Feb 1815, T 3 Mar 1815; Mar 1818. WC; INV, [m]. (WC RI 10:259)
[Jn. BRYANT aptd. gdn. to Anne & Wm. orphans of Wm. WEAVER; Wm. DOLEMAN aptd. gdn. to Polly WEAVER orphan of Wm. WEAVER, 24 Apr 1815 (WC OB 1814-18:116)]

WEAVER, Zechariah; 28 Mar 1825
WC; on the mot. of James WEAVER, Jeremiah SANFORD & Harriet his wife (who was Harriet WEAVER), Benjamin WEAVER, which sd. James, Harriet & Benjamin were children of Zechariah WEAVER dec'd, James MULLINS, John MULLINS, George H. SISSON & Polly his wife and William MULLINS by William M. WALKER his gdn., which sd. James, John, Polly & William are children of Ann MULLINS the wife of John MULLINS dec'd and also a dau. of Zechariah WEAVER, ord. the sale of the tract of about 15 ac. in WC whereof the sd. Zechariah WEAVER died seized and possessed. (WC OB 1823-27:154)
[Zechariah WEAVER was a son of Adam WEAVER (d. WC 1771) (WC DW 15:131); Harriet WEAVER mar. Jere. SANFORD, WC, c. Oct 1809; Ann WEAVER mar. Jn. MULLINS, WC, bond 3 Oct 1806; Mary MULLINS mar. Geo. H. SISSON, WC, bond 15 Nov 1820 (MLBWC:48, 61, 65)]

WEBB, [George]; 18 Jul 1826
LC; Julia WEBB chose William H. TOWLES as her gdn.; Milton WEBB chose John CHOWNING as his gdn.; Albert WEBB chose William WEBB as his gdn. (LC OB 26:197)
[This is Geo. WEBB who mar. (1) Alice TAPSCOTT, dau. of Jn. & Mary TAPSCOTT, LC, bond 23 Dec 1808 and (2) Polly L. NEALE, LC, bond 15 Mar 1820 (MLBLC:78); on the mot. of Wm. H. TOWLES ord. that Julia, Albert, Milton, Maria, Geo. H. & Jas. WEBB be summoned to show cause why the lands of which Polly L. (Geo. WEBB's wife) died seized should not be sold and the proceeds be eq. div. among the legal heirs, 20 Nov 1826 (LC OB 26:213); court decided that the two Negroes Amanda & Amy belonging to Julia, Albert, Milton & Maria WEBB orphans of Geo. WEBB which they heired from their grandmother Mary TAPSCOTT could not be div. in kind and should be sold and the proceeds div. among the sd. parties, 20 Nov 1826 (LC OB 26:216)]

WEBB, Charles; 17 Mar 1812; 20 Apr 1812
LC; WILL; Negro boy John & the youngest child of Sucky to son George WEBB; Negro boy George & girl Sarah to son Griffen WEBB; Negro woman Sucky & her son Bob & $150 (to educate him) to son William WEBB; my Negro man Simon to remain on the plant. w/o I now live until the end of the present year at which time I give him his freedom so as to exonerate him from my heirs; John CHOWNING ex; WITS: Wm. NEWBY, Jn. BISCOE. (LC WB 28:127)
[Jn. CHOWNING Jr. aptd. gdn. to Wm. WEBB orphan of Chas. WEBB, 16 Nov 1812 (LC Orders 24:124); Geo. WEBB & Jn. CHOWNING as gdn. of Wm. WEBB orphans of Chas. WEBB are entitled to a tract of land of which Griffin WEBB died possessed, 20 Oct 1817 (LC Orders 24:396); ord. that Jn. CHOWNING gdn. of Wm. WEBB orphan of Chas. WEBB bind his sd. ward

to Jn. POPE house joiner & carpenter until he is 21, 16 Aug 1819 (LC OB 25:75)]

WEBB, Charles; T 27 Nov 1812; 15 Feb 1813
LC; INV; includes Negroes: Simon, boy John, George, Robert, Suckey, Sarah, Harriott. (LC EB 27:146)

WEBB, Ewell; PO 12 Jun 1815; 8 Jul 1816. NC; INV, [m]. (NC RB 21:35)
[Ewell WEBB was the son of Homer WEBB (d. NC 1795) (NC RB 15:213); Wm. P. WEBB, Jane WEBB, and Mary WEBB orphans of Ewell WEBB chose Jane WEBB as their gdn., 8 Jun 1829 (NC OB 1825-30:359) *NB: it is not certain that these Ewell WEBBs are the same person*]

WEBB, George; 17 Jul 1826
LC; Wickliff GEORGE aptd. gdn. of Horrice, James & Polly WEBB orphans of George WEBB. (LC OD 26:196)

WEBB, Giles; PO 10 Nov 1823; 10 May 1824
NC; INV, [m]; includes Negroes Mary & child Sally, boy James, girls Mariah & Jane. (NC RB 23:468)
[Giles WEBB was the son of Cuthbert WEBB (d. NC 1797) (NC RB 15:360); he seems to have mar. twice, (1) Ann MARSH, NC, bond 12 Jan 1818 and (2) Frances S. ALEXANDER, NC, bond 23 Nov 1821 (MLBNC:106)]

WEBB, Griffin; T 14 Sep 1815; 19 Feb 1816. LC INV. (LC EB 27:277)

WEBB, Homer; 8 Jun 1818
NC; Homer WEBB enlisted in the service of the US in the late war and was honorably discharged on 21 Mar 1815; he left the following persons nearest of kin and legal heirs: Hanna RICE, Roxa RICE and Peter W. RICE children of Betsy RICE dec'd who was Betsy WEBB sis. of the whole blood to sd. Homer WEBB; the sd. Betsy having been the wife of George RICE; Patsy HEADLEY and Delia HEADLEY children of Sally HEADLEY dec'd a paternal half sis. to sd. Homer WEBB; the sd. Sally having married with Eppa HEADLEY dec'd and Nancy MOORE a paternal half sis. to the sd. WEBB who married Cyrus MOORE. (NC OB 1816-20:266)
[Eliz. WEBB mar. Geo. RICE, NC, bond 3 Feb 1802 (MLBNC:86); Sally WEBB mar. Eppa HEADLEY, NC, bond 10 Dec 1804 (MLBNC:52); Nancy WEBB mar. Cyrus MOORE, NC, 10 Jun 1805 (MLBNC:74)]

WEBB, Isaac; 7 Nov 1826
RC; on mot. of Virginia & Elizabeth WEBB inf. children of Isaac WEBB by Thomas T. REYNOLDS their gdn. and next friend against William ALDERSON & Nancy his wife who was another child of Isaac WEBB to sell the lands of Isaac WEBB. (RC OB 27:126)
[This is prob. the Isaac WEBB who mar. Eliz. KIRK, RC, bond 6 Oct 1800 (MRC:226); Wm. ALDERSON mar. Ann WEBB, RC, bond 2 Jul 1816 (MRC:2)]

WEBB, James; T 26 Jul 1813; 3 Jan 1814
RC; INV, [m], but included $506.96 in cash and $401.67 in bonds due and Negroes: Sam, Thadius, Joe, George, Caroline, Charlotte, Apphia, Jane, Hannah. (RC WB 9:441)

WEBB, John; John WEBB of NC purchased a tract of land from Yarrett HUGHLETT by deed of 6 Nov 1742; WEBB married and had three daus. and d. intest.; the eldest d. in his lifetime; the other two, Ann and Sarah, were living at the time of his death; Ann mar. Noah RODGERS and had one child, Francis, who survived his parents and d. intest.; Sarah mar. Jn. VANLANDINGHAM before she was 21 and had several children (Ewell, Maryann, Joanne and Francis VANLANDINGHAM); Jn.

VANLANDINGHAM d. in 1782 and his wife Sarah d. in 1786; in May 1804 the VANLANDINGHAM children, Ewell, Maryann and Joanna sued Jn. HEATH, Wm. BALL, Robt. CHRISTOPHER and Wm. MITCHELL over the tracts of land which they claimed by purchase; although the bottom of the complaint was mutilated, it seems that Ann RODGERS took possession of the land after the death of her father and that it had been div. up into several parcels; the defendants seem to be claiming that Ann was entitled to the land since Sarah was illegitimate; in a dep. dtd. 15 Aug 1804, MITCHELL claimed that Sarah (WEBB) VANLANDINGHAM was illegitimate; in a dep. of the same date, Jn. CHRISTOPHER said that his father bought the land in question from Jn. RODGERS and his wife nearly 59 years earlier and also that Sarah WEBB was illegitimate; however, Thos. COLEMAN who was the clerk of SSP for many years and kept the parish register locked up provided an extract from the SSPR that, "Sarah WEBB dau. of John was born 4 Oct 1741;" Winifred MEALLY deposed that her mother, Sarah, was a bastard child, and Rich. GRINSTEAD, age 68, deposed that he heard that Dan. MEALEY "kept the mother of her the sd. Sarah during the lifetime of him the sd. John WEBB;" Francis VANLANDINGHAM said that he never heard that his mother was illigitimate; Sarah SMITHER deposed that her father was John WEBB and that she was born on 4 Oct 1741; on page 161 of the SSPR the births of Eliz. (29 Jan 1739), Sarah (4 Oct 1741), Lucretia (3 Jan 1746) and Jn. (22 Feb 1748) are recorded adjacent to one another. (NC CC 1812-003)

WEBB, John; T 3 Dec 1796; 8 Sep 1800
NC; INV taken at the house of Thomas WEBB in Mecklenburg [Co.], Va. £115.16.0; includes Negro man Andrew. (NC RB 16:167)
[The est. of Jn. WEBB was ord. to be admin. by Thos. JOHNSON, NC, 12 Sep 1796 (NC OB 1796-1797:67)]

WEBB, John F.; 16 Nov 1819; 14 Aug 1820
NC; WILL; land to wife until my son John Nutt WEBB is 21; dau. Sarah Yerby WEBB; after debts paid rest of my prop. to be eq. div. between the rest of my children; [no ex. named]; WITS: Hiram HARDING, B. BURGESS. (NC RB 22:389)
[This is prob. Jn. Flint WEBB the son of Isaac WEBB of SSP (d. NC 1815) (NC RB 20:49)]

WEBB, Richard; 6 Feb 1823; 5 May 1823
RC; WILL; to son William WEBB the tract of land where I now live known as Mill Wood reserving to my wife one third of the same during her natural life; if son William die without heirs sd. land to go to my dau. Elizabeth WEBB; to dau. Elizabeth a Negro boy Frank, Negro girls Hannah & Matilda, and Negro boys John & Tom; rest of property to be appraised & valued as soon as son William is 21 and to be eq. div. between son William & dau. Elizabeth; friend Joseph DALE & son William exors; WITS; Rich. DURRETT, W. T. DAVIS, Jas T. CLEMENTS. (RC WB 10:25)

WEBB, Richard; T 12 Sep 1823; 7 Feb 1825
RC; INV, $4443.00; includes Negroes: George, Juba, Fenton, Jupiter, Bill, Norah, Billy, Mary, Charles [& Amey, Betty's children], Nancy, Lucy, Judah, Joe, Frank, Hannah, Matilda, John, Tom. (RC WB 10:64)

WEBB, Samuel; PO 11 Mar 1822; 10 Jun 1822. NC; INV, [m]. (NC RB 23:160)
[Max. HAYNIE aptd. gdn. to Jn. WEBB orphan of Sam. WEBB, 8 Oct 1827 (NC OB 1825-30:209)]

WEBB, Tarpley; 18 Jul 1803

LC; Nancy Dameron WEBB orphan of Tarpley WEBB chose Moses GEORGE her gdn. (LC Orders V 1802-1803:380)

WEBB, William; [m]; 10 Feb 1800

NC; INV, [m].; includes Negroes Moses, Rody, George, Solomon, Criss, [Venson], Siller, Easter. (NC RB 16:64)

[The est. of Wm. WEBB was ord. to be admin. by Homer WEBB Jr.; Eliz. E. WEBB refused admin. on her husband's est., NC, 9 Dec 1799 (NC Fiduciary Bonds 1797-1801)]

WEBB, William; 5 May 1824; 14 Jun 1824

NC; WILL; all land to son William B. WEBB; youngest dau. Nancy G. WEBB to be boarded 3 years out of my est; all pers. est. to be eq. div. between my 4 children: Eliza WEBB, Winnefret WEBB, Ann WEBB & Nancy G. WEBB; friend William W. APPLEBY ex; WITS: Linszey DAVIS, Lucy [LOE], Jn ROBINSON; [Wm. W. APPLEBY relinquished his executorship & a certificate was granted him for obtaining letters of admin. with the will annexed.]; NC RB 23:478

WEBB, Winifred (Miss); PO 14 Aug 1815; [m]

NC; INV at the house of Mrs Sally HAYNIE, $3240, $1120; includes the following Negroes: Newman (a man), Sam, Jacob, Newman (a boy), Harry (a boy), John (a boy), [Butche], Lucy & her child James, Silvy, [Massay]. (NC RB 21:235)

[In her will (NC 20 Sep 1814-14 Aug 1815), Winnifred WEBB named her sisters Sally HAYNIE & Eliz. ESKRIDGE and her nephew Wm. ESKRIDGE (NC RB 20:177)]

WEBSTER, William; [1804]. RC; INV. (RC WB 9:233)

WEBSTER, William; 23 Sep 1802; 4 Jul 1803

RC; WILL; manumitts Negro man slave named Sam & leaves him the plant. during his life; sis. Elizabeth CRAWFORD to have use of the house on the sd. plant. with a garden, cotton patch, & firewood & and to have the plant. at the death of Negro Sam; mentions Mary PACKETT & her dau. Betsy PACKETT; Negro servant Sam to receive his wearing apparel, gun & rest of pers. prop; George PURCELL & Henry HARFORD exors; WITS: Jn. DAVIS, Hen. CRUDSON. (RC WB 9:217)

WEEDON, Sarah; 16 Jul 1812; 7 Jun 1813

LP, RC; WILL; Negro girl to dau. Frances HINSON; Negro man Paul to son Thomas WEEDON; 3 grchil. [Bethire] WEEDON, Martha WEEDON & Thomas WEEDON Jr.; son Thomas WEEDON exor; WITS: Dan. MOXLEY, Robt. JENKINS, Frances MOXLEY, Mary GARLAND. (RC WB 9:428)

[Fanny WEEDON, dau. of Sarah WEEDON, mar. Jennings HINSON, WC, bond 25 Jun 1803 (MLBWC:31)]

WEEDON, Thomas; PO Jan 1783; 26 Apr 1804. WC; INV, £49.14.6. (WC RI 8:398)

WEEKS, Benjamin Pope ; T 11 Nov 1801; [m] 1801

WC; INV, £1207 (for the slaves); includes Negroes Old Dick, Young Dick, Darcy, Parker, Oldest Winney, Harrard, Nell, Alexander, Billy, Thornton, Peggy, Sophia, Allin, Dinah, Hannah, Sauny, Y[oungest] Winney, Grace, Easter, Nancy & Simon her child, Jerry, Patt, [Lirra], Alfred, John. (WC RI 8:145)

[Benj. P. WEEKS mar. Mary SMITH, WC, bond 28 Nov 1796 (MWO:371); acc. to a WC CC, Benj. P. WEEKS d. ca. 1802 leaving a wid., Mary, a son, Wm. (who d. an inf. ca. 1804), and sisters Mary Elliott (who mar. Jn. PEYTON), Eliz. (who mar. Vincent BARRACK), Margaret (who mar. Edw. DAVIS) and Jane (who mar. [fnu] CURRAN); Jane CURRAN had a son Elliott; Edward

DAVIS was a resident of EC (WC CC 1807-008, 1819-006); Mary WEEKS, the wid. of Benj. P. WEEKS, mar. Fielding OWENS, WC, bond 26 Aug 1801 (MLBWC:52; Orders 1801-04:320); Edw. DAVIS mar. Margaret WEEKS, EC, 1808 (IMORECV:75); Vincent BARROCK mar. Eliz. WEEKS, WC, bond 11 Dec 1800; Jn. PEYTON mar. Mary WEEKS, WC, bond 19 Sep 1798 (MLBWC:4, 52); slaves of Benj. P. WEEKS allotted to the wid. to be div., 2/3 to the def. Jn. HARVEY and 1/3 to Wm. W. OWENS an inf. by Dan. CARMICHAEL his gdn. and next friend, 25 Oct 1819 (WC OB 1819-23:86; WC CC 1858-02); Benj. P. WEEKS also left an unbaptised inf. child, called Wm. WEEKS or Wm. Edmonson WEEKS, who d. underage (WC CC 1805-005)]

WEEKS, Benjamin Pope; PO 24 Feb 1806, T 24 Aug 1807; 24 Aug 1807
WC; sale of two tracts of land formerly belonging to WEEKS, one in WC (sold to Thomas N. BERRYMAN for £121) & one in RC (sold to Daniel CARMICHAEL for £20.1); proceeds div. among Vincent BARROCK (rec'd £33.15.3), John PEYTON (rec'd £73.10.6), and E. & Margaret DAVIS (rec'd £33.5.3). (WC RI 9:25)

WEEKS, Mary; 17 Oct 1797; 23 Aug 1802
WC; WILL; nephew Weeks BERRYMAN plant. on [Popes] Creek; Benjamin Pope SMITH plant. at head of Popes Creek; Mary Elliot WEEKS; friend John PAYTON now living with me the plant. I purch. of Mr. William A. HIPKINS called "The Ruins;" slaves to have choice of choosing master or mistress among sisters or sisters' children: Celia BERRYMAN, [Lucetta] SMITH, Alexander BERRYMAN, Weeks BERRYMAN, Benjamin Pope SMITH or [Lucy] SMITH; remainder of est. to be eq. div. between sisters Celia BERRYMAN, [Lucetta] SMITH and Thos. N. BERRYMAN; friend Thos. Newton BERRYMAN & Jn. PAYTON exors; WITS: Wm. Aug. WASHINGTON, Jeremiah CLAXTON, Wm. MUSE. (WC DW 20:375) [Celia WEEKS, dau. of Benj. WEEKS (d. WC 1784), mar. (1) Wm. BUTLER (d. WC 1784) and (2) Thos. Newton BERRYMAN, WC, c. 25 Nov 1786 (MWO:39); Lusetta WEEKS, dau. of Benj. WEEKS, mar. Wm. SMITH of KGC, bef. 2 Dec 1782 (MWO:325); *see also WC CC 1802-008*]

WEEKS, Mary; [m]; 28 Mar 1803
WC; INV; includes Negroes: Ben, Jack, Tom, Charles, Ashton (legacy), Sall, boys Dick, Daniel, & Will, Rachel, boys Joshua & George, girls Dinah & Mariah, Hannah, boy Thornton. (WC RI 8:195)

WEEKS, Mary; [7] Feb 1803; 28 Mar 1803
WC; DIV of est. to Celia BERRYMAN the slaves Hannah, Thornton & George; to Weeks BERRYMAN the slaves Rachel & Daniel; to Alexander BERRYMAN the slaves Daniel & Joshua; to Thomas [N.] BERRYMAN the slaves Tom & Will; to Pope SMITH the slaves Jacob & Maria; to Lucy SMITH the slaves Dick & Sarah; to Lusetta SMITH the slaves Ben & Charles. (WC RI 8:206)

WEEKS, William; 24 Feb 1806
WC; chancery suit; John PAYTON & Mary Elliot his wife, Vincent BARRICK & Elizabeth his wife, Edward DAVIS (of EC) & Margaret his wife and Elliot CURRIE sued Fielding OWENS & Mary his wife; Mary Elliot PEYTON, Margaret DAVIS, and Elizabeth BARRICK are sis. of Benjamin P. WEEKS and heirs of William WEEKS an infant who died c. 1804 the son of Benjamin P. WEEKS dec'd who died c. 1802 leaving 112 ac. in WC and 100 ac. in RC and a wife Mary who mar. Fielding OWENS; Elliott CURRIE is the son of Jane CURRIE who was also a sis. of Benjamin. (WC Orders 1804-07:341)

[Jn. PAYTON mar. Mary WEEKS, WC bond 19 Sep 1798 (MLBWC:52); Vincent BARROCK mar. Eliz. WEEKS, WC bond 11 Dec 1800 (MLBWC:4)]

WELCH, Betsy; T 15 May 1819; 13 Sep 1819. NC; INV, $111.57 1/2. (NC RB 22:120)

WELCH, Elizabeth; 5 May 1819; 10 May 1819
SSP, NC; WILL; all my land to be eq. div. between two daus. Judith HAYNIE & Nancy HAYNIE; sis. Nancy DAVIS; friends Mackcimilian HAYNIE & Alexander HAYNIE exors; WITS: Wm. HUGHLETT, Thos. DAVIS. (NC RB 22:53)
[Maximillion HAYNIE mar. Judith WELCH, dau. of Betty WELCH, NC, bond 25 Feb 1788 (MLBNC:50); Alexander HAYNIE mar. Nancy WELCH, dau. of Betty WELCH, NC, bond 12 Dec 1791 (MLBNC:48); Judith WELCH is prob. the Judith, dau. of Jn. & Bette WELCH, born 23 Dec 1771 (SSPR:127)]

WELDON, George; 10 Mar 1814; 27 Feb 1815
WC; WILL; wife Leanner; dau. Mary MOXLEY; dau. Elizabeth TRUE; four sons & two daus. not above named; WITS: Reuben BRIANT, Jn. DODD. (WC DW 23:65)
[Mary WELDON mar. Rodham MOXLEY, WC, bond 8 Jul 1810; Eliz. WELDON mar. Wm TRUE, WC, bond 29 Dec 1808 (MLBWC:48, 72)]

WEST, Joseph; PO 16 Dec 1820; 17 Jan 1825. LC; INV, $101.56 1/2. (LC EB 29:388)

WEST, Thomas; 4 Oct 1813; 20 Feb 1815
LC; WILL; after debts are paid balance of est. consisting of Kentucky land, Negroes, stock, HH & KF, bonds, accounts, money & my two cotton machines one in which the late Mr. Sto[ckley] TOWLES & myself were in partnership which now is repairing, the other which is fixed in Capt. R. G. HIPKINS' mill in which we are also partners I give to my dau. Mary by Chloe VAUGHAN but in case she should have one or more children by me then such of my est. that my sd. dau. would have provided that I have no other child should be eq. div. among them severally; if they leave no heirs I give it to my nephews & nieces the children of my bro. John WEST; [Chloe] VAUGHAN to be frugally supported out of my est. during her good conduct & single life; child Mary & others if any to be educated; my silver watch & breast pin to my friend William T. YERBY; friend Wm. T. YERBY ex.; WITS: Walter B. WADDY, Griffin CHILTON. (LC WB 28:153)
[Chloe VAUGHN seems to have been Chloe HUBBARD who mar. Jn. VAUGHN, LC, bond 1 Apr 1805 (MLBLC:75)]

WEST, Thomas; T 17 Jul 1820; 23 May 1821
LC; settlement of William T. YERBY's admin. acct. of Thomas WEST & the gdnship. accts. of sd. YERBY with Mary WEST & Elizabeh WEST; John CHOWNING was the admr. with the will annexed of William T. YERBY dec'd who was ex. of Thomas WEST dec'd by 16 Apr 1821. (LC EB 29:100)
[Settlement with Jn. CHOWNING admr. of Wm. Y. YERBY dec'd gdn. of Mary & Eliz. adopted children and orphans of Thos. WEST the acct. of the sd. YERBY's gdnship. of the sd. orphans, 19 Jun 1820 (LC OB 25:138)]

WEYMOUTH, Thomas; 16 Jun 1806
LC; Thomas WEYMOUTH d. leaving a small est. in the county; no one appeared to admin. it; sheriff ord. to dispose of the est. (LC Orders D22 1805-08:193)

WHEELER, Elizabeth; 10 Sep 1825; 10 Oct 1825
NC; WILL; my land at the ferry landing to niece Elizabeth Spilman COCKARILL (under 21) being all the land I possess containing 104 ac; if

niece die before age 21 & without children, I give land to sis. Judith COCKARILL during her life & after her death to nephew Thomas COCKARILL; to bro. William WHEELER $150; $50 to sis. Judeth COCKARILL; b-i-l John COCKARILL ex; WITS: Willis INGRAM, Jn. McADAM, Rebecca MARSH. (NC RB 24:363)
[Judith WHEELER, dau. of Thomas WHEELER, mar. John COCKARILL, NC, bond 22 Dec 1817 (MLBNC:18)]

WHEELER, Maurice; PO Apr 1799; 17 Jun 1799
LC; DIV of land among: Luke ASHBURN who mar. Betty WHEELER, Moses WHEELER, John COX gdn. to Nanny Harrison COX grdau. to sd. Maurice. (LC EB 24:100)
[There are two appraisals for the est. of Maurice WHEELER, one rec. on 21 Oct 1784 and the other on 21 Apr 1788 (LC WB 22:53, 176); Elisabeth WHEELER mar. Luke ASHBURNE, LC, bond 6 Jan 1787; Jn. COX mar. Mary WHEELER, LC, bond 15 Jun 1789 (MLBLC:1, 17)]

WHEELER, Moses; 22 Apr 1806
LC; Dempsey TREACLE aptd. gdn. of Betsy WHEELER orphan of Moses WHEELER. (LC Orders D22 1805-08:138)
[Moses WHEELER mar. Martha WILLIAMS, dau. of Peter WILLIAMS, LC, bond 30 May 1799; Martha (WILLIAMS) WHEELER mar. (2) Dempsey TREACLE, son of Rich. TREACLE, LC, bond 10 Oct 1805 (MLBLC:74, 79); Luke ASHBOURNE apd. gdn. to Betsy WHEELER orphan of Moses WHEELER, 19 Jun 1820 (LC OB 25:139)]

WHEELER, Thomas; T 22 Nov 1819; 1[2] Jun 1820. NC; INV, $438.24 1/2. (NC RB 22:334)

WHITE, Benjamin; PO 4 Jan 1819; 1 Feb 1819. RC; INV, $36.1 1/4. (RC WB 9:613)
[Mary WHITE aptd. gdn. to Zachariah, Sam. & Wm. WHITE, RC, 6 Oct 1817 (RC OB 24:147)]

WHITE, John; 14 Nov 1814; 27 Feb 1815
WC; WILL; wife Elishe WHITE all my est; wife is not to sell or traffic away my Negro woman Poll or her increase; after wife's death Poll to be able to chose her master from among all my children: Sharlotty B. WHITE, [Wilesth] WHITE, Gra[n]vill WHITE, Thomas WHITE, and Henry WHITE; WITS: Jas. MOTHERSHEAD, Ales MOTHERSHEAD, Meredith [?]. (WC DW 23:59)
[Jn. WHITE mar. Elisha MOTHERSHEAD, WC, bond 25 Mar 1799 (MLBWC:75)]

WHITE, John; T 18 Mar 1815; 22 May 1815. WC; INV, [m]. (WC RI 9:447)

WHITE, John G.; T 7 Dec 1818; 1 Feb 1819
RC; INV, [m], includes the following Negroes: John, Molly (& her child Oscar), Frederick, Peggy, Henry, Jenny. (RC WB 9:614)
[A Jn. G. WHITE mar. Amelia A. T. GLASCOCK, RC, bond 7 Dec 1816 (MRC:230)]

WHITE, John M.; PO Dec 1805; 2 Jun 1806. RC; INV, £300.17.1 3/4. (RC WB 9:285)

WHITE, Seleashea; PO 17 Jul 1816; 1 Feb 1819; RC; INV, £3.7.0. (RC WB 9:611)
[Seleashea WHITE was the wife of Zachariah WHITE whom she mar. bef. 28 Jul 1761; she was a dau. of Benj. WALKER of CP, WC (MWO:374)]

WHITE, William; 2 Oct 1806; 24 Aug 1807
WC; WILL; laboring under a severe sickness; son William WHITE tract and he is to maintain wife; rest of est. to be eq. div. among the whole of my children; WITS: Thos. LENDRUM, Jessee JETT. (WC DW 21:363)

WHITE, Zachariah; T 9 Apr 1801; 7 Oct 1805
RC; INV, slaves appraised at £460.0.0, includes the following Negroes: Pat, Rose dau. of Pat, Suckey & unnamed girl child, Billy son of Suckey, Sam son of Suckey, George son of Pat, Lucy dau. [Pat ?], Jesse son of Suckey, Molly dau. of [Suckey], Edmond son of Pat, Glasgow son of Suckey. (RC WB 9:263)

WILCOX, Anthony; left his wife Phebe with two infant children in WC in mid-1817 taking his eldest son Henry, age about 7, with him; he was seen in Norfolk around September 1819. (*American Beacon & Norfolk & Portsmouth Daily Advertiser*, 14 Oct 1819, p. [4])

WILCOX, James; 7 Jun 1824
RC; Martin HILL aptd. gdn. to Elizabeth & John WILCOX orphans of James WILCOX. (RC OB 26:206)

WILDER, Judith; 17 Feb 1800, T 13 Jun [1800]; 15 Dec 1800
LC; INV at the house of Newman WILDER, £4.8.6. (LC EB 24:126)

WILDER, Michael; 24 Nov 1824; 20 Dec 1824
LC; WILL; wife to have land during her life & at her death to be div. between my two sons James & Nathaniel; $100 to son Michael; balance of est. to wife and at her death to be div. between my five children; [no ex. named]; WITS:W. B. WADDEY, Dan. P. MITCHELL Jr., Jesse GEORGE. (LC WB 28:254)
[Jn. ROBERTS mar. Mary A. WILDER, who was either the wid. or a dau. of Michael WILDER, LC, bond 1 Dec 1825 (MLBLC:63, LC OB 26:170)]

WILDER, Michael; PO 20 Dec 1824; 14 Jan 1825. LC; INV, [m]. (LC EB 29:380)

WILDER, Newman; 18 Apr 1803
LC; Newman WILDER d. intest. possessed of a small est. on which no person will administer; ord. that the sheriff dispose of the est. (LC Orders V 1802-03:318)
[This must be the Newman WILDER who mar. Nancy GEORGE, LC, bond 1794 (MLBLC:79)]

WILDY, Jane; 9 Mar 1815; 13 Dec 1819
NC; WILL; Negroes Peter, Isaiah, Moses, Rose, George, Winny, Mary, John, Young Pricilla, Old Pricilla, Isaac, Jerry, Stephen, Robert, Rachel & all the remainder of my slaves to my half bro Izates ANDERSON; Izates ANDERSON to pay my niece Elizabeth WILDY, dau. of my bro. Hely WILDY, $20 a year until it amounts to $200; Izates ANDERSON to purchase a Negro boy slave around 15 years old & convey him to William DAUGHITY son of my sis. Elizabeth DAUGHITY & he is to also purchase a Negro girl around 10 years old and convey her to my niece Jane DAUGHITY dau. of my sd. sis; my cousin Polly HUDNALL; Izates ANDERSON ex; WITS: Sam. KERCHEVAL, Eliz. HUCHIN, Sam. BERRY. (NC RB 22:167)
[Jane WILDY was a dau. of Jos. & Judith (HARDING) WILDEY who mar. in NC in Dec 1757; Jos. WILDEY d in NC in 1769; Judith (HARDING) WILDEY mar. 2nd Jn. ANDERSON, NC, lic. 7 Dec 1774; Izates ANDERSON the son of Jn. & Judith ANDERSON was b in SSP 7 Feb 1779 (NC RB 7:443, MWO:15, 376, SSPR:6)]

WILDY, Joseph; PO 16 Dec 1812, T 28 Dec 1812; 12 Jul 1813
NC; DIV of Negroes willed by Joseph WILDY dec'd to Judith WILDY late Judith ANDERSON; Lot 1 (Saul & Alice) drawn by Walter & Izates ANDERSON heirs of John ANDERSON who purchased from William COLES who mar. Sally WILDY; Lot 2 (Sinah & child Winny & Sally) drawn by Thomas BETTS who mar. with Molly WILDY; Lot 3 (Vincent, [T]ina & child) drawn by Izates ANDERSON who purchased from William WILDY;

Lot 4 (Spencer, Sarah, Winny - old, Emma) drawn by Izates ANDERSON who purchased from Jane WILDY, Lot 5 (Suck, Jenny) drawn by James DAUGHITY who mar. Elizabeth CONWAY formerly Elizabeth WILDY; Lot 6 ([Jun] - sold by Hele WILDY) drawn by Hele WILDY. (NC RB 19:421)
[Jas. DAUGHITY, wid., mar. Betsey CONWAY, wid., NC, bond 17 Feb 1800 (MLBNC:26); for more on the family of Jas. DAUGHITY, see VS1776 III:1098]

WILDY, William; T 29 Oct 1807; 11 Jan 1808. NC; INV, [m]. (NC RB 17:602)

WILDY, William; 16 Jun 1814; 13 Oct 1817
SSP, NC; WILL; land to be eq. div. between three sons: Jere, James & William; to dau. Rebeckah BETTS Negro woman Abigail & her two children & a Negro girl [Jenney]; to dau. Betsy DOWNING $1.00; balance of est. to be eq. div. between Jere, James, Polly, Mariah, Nancy, Sally, & William WILDY; [no ex. named]; WITS: Iz[ates]. ANDERSON, Jane WILDY; [Royston BETTS Jr. was granted a letter of admin]. (NC RB 21:257)
[Rebecca WILDY mar. Tellus BETTS, NC, bond 28 Jan 1809; Eliz. A. WILDY mar. Edw. DOWNING, wid., NC, bond 18 Apr 1814 (MLBNC:9, 31); allot to Sally WILDY wid. of Wm. WILDY and [gdn. ?] of Jere., Mariah, Nancy & Sally WILDY four of the children of the sd. Wm. her thirds in his est., 12 Jul 1824 (NC OB 1820-25:401)]

WILDY, William; T 20 Dec 1817; 10 May 1819
NC; INV, [m]; include Negroes: Adam, Spencer, Hammond (a lad), Saul (a lad), Moses (small boy), Molley (woman & boy child [petified]), Plesant, Peggy, [Trusey] (girl), Agnes (small girl), [Senor] (small girl), Suckey (small girl at the breast). (NC RB 22:29)

WILDY, William; PO 2 Jul 1824; 11 Oct 1824
NC; settlement of Royston BETTS' acct. of his; admin. of the est. of William WILDY; balance div. among the wid. Sarah WILDY, Jeremiah WILDY (son & heir), Maria WILDY, Ann WILDY & Sarah WILDY (daus & heirs), James WILDY and William WILDY; div. of slaves among the wid. (rec'd Adam, Spencer, Pleasant & Milly), Maria WILDY (rec'd [Hammond]), Jeremiah WILDY (rec'd [Trecy] & Mariah), Nancy WILDY (rec'd Agnes, Sinah & Dinah), Sarah WILDY (rec'd Peggy & Sukey), James WILDY (rec'd Solomon), William WILDY (rec'd James, Lucy & Eliza); Jeremiah WILDY was gdn. to Sally & James WILDY. (NC RB 24:61)

WILDY, William Jr.; PO 12 Jul 1819, T 21 Aug 1819; 13 Sep 1819
NC; DIV of proceeds of sale of Negro Daniel among the heirs: John LANSDELL Jr., William WILDY, William WILDY as attorney for John WILDY, Jeremiah ROBINSON as gdn. to Sally & Winefred WILDY, Joseph DOULIN as gdn. to Samuel WILDY, Wady G. BEETLY. (NC RB 22:117; OB 1807-11:227)
[Wm. WILDY d. intest. leaving seven children: Sam., Jane BEETLY, Sally, Winny, Wm., Jn., and Hannah LANSDELL (NC CC 1822-008); Jn. LANSDELL Jr. mar. Hannah T. WILDY, NC, bond 19 May 1812; Wadey G. BEATLEY mar. Jane WILDEY, NC, bond 9 Feb 1818 (MLBNC:7, 66); Winefred & Sally WILDER orphans of Wm. WILDY chose Jn. ROBINSON as their gdn., NC, 11 Nov 1822 (NC OB 1820-25:243)]

WILKERSON, John; 19 Aug 1810; 27 Feb 1815
WC; of KGC; WILL; wife Sarah WILKERSON all of my est; my lands, except a small parcel lying in the fork of James MUSE's mill pond, to be eq. div. between my four sons: Isaac WILKERSON, John S. WILKERSON, Reuben N. WILKERSON, and Austin WILKERSON; sons who receive land adjacent to Joseph HUTT, William RODGERS, BAILEY's, and Jane WILKERSON to be

furnished with timber from the track w/o I now live; at death of wife all Negroes, stock, household & kitchen furniture to be eq. div. between Isaac WILKERSON, John S. WILKERSON, Reuben N. WILKERSON, Austin WILKERSON, & Leannah FRANK; dau. Leannah FRANK small tract of land on the west side of James MUSE's mill pond; dau. Nancy Noel [?] one shilling and nothing more of my property shall she inherit; son Isaac WILKERSON & John FRANK Sr. exors; WITS: Geo. PINKARD, Rich. REYNOLDS, Stephen MARDERS, Robt. WILKERSON, Jn. SPILMAN. (WC DW 23:60)

[Austin WILKERSON mar. Susanna BRENNON, WC, bond 29 Jan 1823 (MLBWC:76); there are numerous records of WILKERSON marriages in KGC including that of Isaac WILKERSON and Mary Ann MARDERS, bond 7 Feb 1815 (KGCVM:17)]

WILKERSON, John; T 6 Jun 1815; 26 Feb 1816
WC; INV, [m]; includes Negroes: Matthew, Milley, girls Peggy, Carline, Mary, boy Joseph; boys Augustine & Lewis, woman & child, girls Nancy, Sarah, Kisey & Sharlot. (WC RI 10:46)

WILKINS, Haynie; PO 10 Jun 1816; 13 Jan 1817
NC; INV, $554.53; includes Negro boy [Louis]. (NC RB 21:128)

WILKINS, Haynie; PO 13 Jan 1817; 20 Nov 1817
NC; sale of Negro boy Lewis belonging to the est. of Haynie WILKINS dec'd and div. of proceeds to the several heirs: John WILKINS, William WILKINS, and Winnifred WILKINS gdn. to Dolly WILKINS, Haynie WILKINS, Elen WILKINS and Millindy WILKINS. (NC RB 21:286)

WILKINS, Haynie; PO 13 Jan 1817, T 18 Feb 1817; 14 Dec 1818
NC; Winnifred WILKINS allotted her third part of the est. of her late husband Haynie WILKINS; she received $184.07 and 20 3/4 ac. of land near Abraham's Cove and adj John S. FALLIN & Thos. HUDNALL. (NC RB 21:559)

[Haynie WILKINS mar. Winney HAYNIE, dau. of Jn. & Peggy HAYNIE, NC, bond 23 Feb 1791 (MLBNC:109)]

WILKINS, Haynie; PO 13 Mar 1820, T 7 Apr 1820; 12 Jun 1820
NC; as the result of a court case John WILKINS, William WILKINS, Hezekiah HAYNIE & Dolly his wife against Winifred WILKINS rel. & wid. of Haynie WILKINS, Ellen WILKINS & Matilda WILKINS (infants under 21 & orphans of Haynie WILKINS dec'd) by Winifred WILKINS their gdn, the land belonging to the heirs of Haynie WILKINS was sold to Dr. Hiram HARDING. (NC RB 22:339; NC CC 1820-003)

[Hezekiah HAYNIE mar. Dolly WILKINS, NC, bond 13 Jan 1817 (MLBNC:49)]

WILKINS, Peter; PO 13 Mar 1815; 14 Aug 1815. NC; INV, [m]. (NC RB 20:167)
[This is prob. the Peter WILKINS named as s-i-l by Jn. WHEELER in his will (NC 27 Aug 1794-13 Oct 1794) (NC RB 15:106); he may have been Peter WILKINS son of Jn. & Ann WILKINS, 31 Dec 1761 (SSPR:164); the est. of Peter WILKINS was ord. to be admin. by Willis. J. WILKINS, NC, 13 Mar 1815 (NC OB 1811-1816:289); the heirs of Peter WILKINS seem to have been Willis J., Alice, Hannah, Ann and Walter WILKINS, NC, 11 Sep 1815 (NC OB 1811-15:370); Roy BETTS aptd. gdn. of Ann F. & Walter W. WILKINS orphans of Peter WILKINS, NC 13 Dec 1819 (NC OB 1816-20:414)]

WILKINSON, William; PO 12 Nov [1821]; 13 Jan 1823. NC INV. (NC RB 23:271)

WILLIAMS, Benjamin; PO 8 May 1815; 8 May 1820. NC; INV, $241.17. (NC RB 22:274)

[The est. of Benj. WILLIAMS was ord. to be admin. by Wm. ROCHESTER, NC, 8 May 1815 (NC OB 1811-1816:316); Francis HOLLIDAY aptd. gdn. of Ben. & Ellen WILLIAMS orphans of Ben. WILLIAMS, NC 8 May 1820 (NC OB 1820-25:18)]

WILLIAMS, Catharine; 11 Jan 1820; 8 Aug 1820
RC; WILL; dau. Elizabeth ROY; grson. John Wiley ROY; granddau. Ann Catherine ROY; $4 out of my est. to be paid to my woman Fanny which I borrowed from her; dau. Catherine EVANS; WITS: Griffin G. DUDLEY, Sally TUNE. (RC WB 9:668)
[This is Catherine CORRIE dau. of Jn. CORRIE of EC who mar. Thaddeus WILLIAMS bef. 1787; Eliz. Corrie WILLIAMS mar. Jn. Corrie ROY of King & Queen Co., son of Beverley ROY, RC, bond 29 Nov 1804; Catherine WILLIAMS, dau. of Catherine WILLIAMS, mar. (1) Dan. LAWSON, Jr., RC, bond 9 Jan 1809 and (2) Kemp EVANS, RC, bond 5 Jan 1815 (MRC:66, 115, 174, 232)]

WILLIAMS, Edward C.; T 21 Apr 1821; 14 May 1821. NC; INV, $19.50. (NC RB 22:524)

WILLIAMS, Elijah; 22 Nov 1816; 9 Dec 1816
SSP, NC; WILL; land in RC to Robert H. HALL; John C. DAWSON; Samuel WILLIAMS; Henry S. DAWSON; Calvert WILLIAMS [a female]; two friends Thomas BEACHAM & Pemberton CLAUGHTON exors; WITS: Luke DAMERON, Sam. DAWSON, Judith KENT. (NC RB 21:122)

WILLIAMS, Elizabeth; 20 Oct 1821; 25 Mar 1822
WC; WILL; to my neice Alice WEAVER one Negro girl named Jenny; to my nephew Henry WEAVER all the balance of my property including five Negroes Polly, Harriett, Ben, Daniel, & George; nephew Henry WEAVER ex; WITS: Chas. MUSE, Wm. MUSE, Catherine MUSE, Nancy HENAGE. (WC DW 24:273)
[This is the dau. of Rachel WILLIAMS (d. WC 1815) (*see below*)]

WILLIAMS, James; PO 13 Mar 1815; 11 Dec 1815
NC; INV, $500.57 1/2; includes u/i Negro man. (NC RB 20:311)
[The est. of Jas. WILLIAMS was ord. to be admin. by Geo. OLDHAM, 13 Mar 1815 (NC OB 1811-1816:289)]

WILLIAMS, James; PO 11 Dec 1815, T 29 Dec 1815; 8 Jan 1816
NC; settled George OLDHAM's acct. of his admin. of the est. and div. of $246.69 among the legal reps.: Betsy WILLIAMS, James WILLIAMS, Aron WILLIAMS, Nancy WILLIAMS, Sally WILLIAMS, John WILLIAMS. (NC RB 20:328)

WILLIAMS, Nancy; 10 Mar 1811; 7 Oct 1811
RC; WILL; sis. Barbary NEASOM and her children; Negro man Billy to be sold; money lent to William NEASOM I give to him & he is to be exor; WITS: Luke JACKSON, Samuel W. NEASOM. (RC WB 9:397)
[Barbara WILLIAMS mar. Wm. NEWSOM, RC, bond 4 Dec 1786 (MRC:146)]

WILLIAMS, Nancy; T 30 Nov 1811; 2 Dec 1811. RC; INV, [$]918.13. (RC WB 9:402)

WILLIAMS, Peter; 19 Feb 1812; 20 Apr 1812
LC; WILL; all est. to my daus. Judith & Molley for one year after my death; afterwards debts to be paid and then whole est. to be eq. div. among all my children: heirs of my son Peter, Elizabeth, Pattey, Judith, Molley & Suckey; friends John HUNT & Thomas JAMES exors; WITS: Thos. JAMES, Jn. HUNT, Jas. BRENT Sr. (LC WB 28:127)

WILLIAMS, Peter; PO 15 Jun 1812, T 13 Aug 1812; 17 Aug 1812. LC; INV; includes Negro Bill. (LC EB 27:115)

WILLIAMS, Peter; PO 19 Oct 1819; [20 Dec 1819]
LC; DIV of slaves; Negroes Jack, Roxy & Betty were sold and Negro Winney was given to the widow. (LC EB 27:511)

WILLIAMS, Peter Jr.; PO 13 Feb 1819; 20 Jun 1820
LC; DIV of est. as follows: to the wid. her dower ($66.05), to Griffin WILLIAMS his part including his part of his grandfather's est. making together $86.18, to George H. HUTCHINGS gdn. to Alice WILLIAMS, Peter WILLIAMS & James C. WILLIAMS (each due $86.18). (LC EB 21:28)
[This is prob. Peter WILLIAMS who mar. Alcy CONNOLLY dau. of Patrick CONNOLLY, LC, bond 25 Sep 1792 (MLBL:80); Alice (CONNOLLY) WILLIAMS mar. (2) Dan. REES[E], LC, bond 25 Dec 1809 (MLBLC:62); acc. to LC CC 1811-006, Dan. REESE was "a stranger and seafaring man;" Alice REESE to settle the accts. of her admin. of the est. of Peter WILLIAMS; Geo. H. HUTCHINGS aptd. gdn. to James, Peter & Alice WILLIAMS orphans of Peter WILLIAMS, 15 Feb 1819 (LC OB 25:40); ord. that Griffin & Alcy WILLIAMS, Peter & James WILLIAMS by Geo. H. HUTCHINGS their gdn. & next friend & Alice REESE late Alice WILLIAMS by summoned to show cause why the slaves of which Peter WILLIAMS Jr. d. seized & possessed may not be sold to divide the proceeds, 16 Aug 1819 (LC OB 25:74, OB 25:81)]

WILLIAMS, Peter Sr.; PO 15 Feb 1813, T 25 Jan 1814; 16 May 1814
LC; DIV of pers. est. (bonds worth $592.56) at Kilmarnock among: Dempsey TREAKLE in right of his wife, Elizabeth SHORT, John HUTCHINGS for the heirs of Peter WILLIAMS Jr. dec'd, John TOALMAN in right of his wife, Molly WILLIAMS, Judith WILLIAMS. (LC EB 27:176)
[Dempsey TREAKLE, son of Rich. TREAKLE, mar. Martha WHEELER, dau. of Peter WILLIAMS and wid. of Moses WHEELER (whom she mar. in LC, bond 30 May 1799), LC, bond 10 Oct 1805 (MLBLC:74, 78); Jn. TOLEMAN mar. Susanna WILLIAMS, LC, bond 15 Dec 1808 (MLBLC:74)]

WILLIAMS, Rachel; 22 Jan 1813; 28 Aug 1815
WC; WILL; one Negro woman called Jenny to grchildren Henry WEAVER, Lucinda WEAVER & Alice WEAVER; I give $300 now in the hands of Robert S. HIPKINS on interest in the following manner: $100 to son William WILLIAMS, $100 to dau. Elizabeth WILLIAMS, $100 to be eq. div. between my grchildren Henry, Lucindy & Alice WEAVER; dau. Elizabeth WILLIAMS extx; WITS: Newton BERRYMAN, Mary BUTLER, Ritchie ALSOP. (WC DW 23:110)

WILLIAMS, Sarah [S.]; PO Feb 1802; [3 Jun 1805]
RC; APP & DIV of the est. of Sarah L. WILLIAMS at the house of Chichester TAPSCOTT; 1 lot for Chichester TAPSCOTT, 1 lot for Thaddeus WILLIAM's children, 1 lot for Samuel WILLIAMS. (RC WB 9:251)
[Sarah S. WILLIAMS was a dau. of Sam. (d. RC 1777) & Betty WILLIAMS; her sis. Betty mar. Chichester TAPSCOTT (RC bond 23 Dec 1792) (MWO:342); in her will (RC 1 Apr 1786-2 Apr 1787) Sarah S. WILLIAMS named her mother Betty A., her sisters Winifred DOBYNS & Betsy A. WILLIAMS, her bros. Thaddeus & David and her nephew Samuel WILLIAMS (RC WB 7:538)]

WILLIAMS, Sarah S.; T 3 Aug 1805; 4 May 1818
RC; DIV of £117.16.1 3/4 among Thaddeus WILLIAMS' children, David WILLIAMS' son & Chichester TAPSCOTT's children. (RC AB 3:535)

WILLIAMS, Thaddeus; PO 6 Jan 1800; 1 Oct 1804
RC; INV; £1348.13.1; includes the following Negroes: [Sein], Matt, Solomon, Newman, Charles, Bristol, Anthony, Simon, Sam, Isaac, boys Adam, Billy, & Dangerfield, girls Frank & Lucy, small boy Jim, twins Judah & Seth, Mary & child, Fanny & child, Lett, small boy Tom, Joe. (RC WB 9:238

WILLIAMS, Thad[deus]; T 3 Feb 1798; 7 Jul 1806
RC; INV, £1108.10.11. (RC WB 9:295)
[Thaddeus WILLIAMS was a son of Sam. (d. RC 1777) & Betty Anne WILLIAMS and bro. of Sarah S. WILLIAMS (RC WB 7:273)]

WILLIAMS, Thaddeus; PO 1 May 1804 & 2 Sep 1805; 4 Sep 1809
RC; APP & DIV of slaves among the wid. Catharine WILLIAMS (Anthony, Joe, Fanny, Frankey, Bristoe, Lilly, Sarah, Newman), John C. ROY & Elizabeth C. his wife (Sam, Charles, Tom, Lucy, James, David, Judy, Tim) and Catharine WILLIAMS (Simon, Isaac, Dangerfield, Mary & child, Emanuel, Matt, Polly); T 30 Oct 1805 in pursuance of 2 orders & a suit in chancery between Elizabeth C. WILLIAMS an infant under 21 by Richard L. REDMAN her next friend (who afterwards mar. John C. ROY) and Catharine WILLIAMS wid. of Thaddeus WILLIAMS dec'd & gdn. to Catharine WILLIAMS; PO 7 Oct 1805 the slaves devised to Elizabeth C. WILLIAMS (who mar. John C. ROY) (rec'd Molly) & Catharine WILLIAMS (rec'd Charity) jointly by Winnefred DOBYNS dec'd, T 30 Oct 1805; rec 4 Dec 1809. (RC AB 3:222, 231)
[Thaddeus WILLIAMS mar. Catherine CORRIE, dau. of Jn. CORRIE of EC, Va., bef. 1787 (MWO:379); Catherine the wife of Kemp EVANS of EC, Va. was a co-heir of Thaddeus WILLIAMS (RC DB 20:630)]

WILLIAMS, Thomas; T 28 May 1800; 9 Jun 1800. NC; INV, [m]. (NC RB 16:115)
[The est. of Thos . WILLIAMS was ord. to be admin. by Geo. WILLIAMS, NC, 14 Apr 1800 (NC Fiduciary Bonds 1797-1801)]

WILLIAMS, Thomas; Oct 1809
RC; Thomas WILLIAMS aptd. gdn. to Polly, John, and Joseph N. the orphans of Thomas WILLIAMS. (RC Orders 1809-10:[26])

WILLIAMS, Thomas; PO 12 Feb 1810, T 2 May 1810; 9 Jul 1810
NC; INV, $244.95; includes Negro Judah. (NC RB 18:425)
[The est. of Thos . WILLIAMS was ord. to be admin. by Hiram BLACKWELL, NC, 12 Feb 1810 (NC OB 1807-1811:154); Spencer M. PICKREN was aptd. gdn. of Rich. S. and Eliz. WILLIAMS orphans of Thos. WILLIAMS, NC, 8 Feb 1813 (NC OB 1811-15:146)]

WILLIAMS, Thomas; PO May 1811; Aug 1811. WC; INV, $241.26. (WC RI 9:276)

WILLIAMS, William; 15 Jul 1814; 24 Jun 1816
WC; WILL; whole of est. to wife during her widowhood until my two children Matthias Turner WILLIAMS & Mary Turner WILLIAMS arrive at the age of 21; friends Solomon REDMAN & Thomas STOWERS exors; WITS: Geo. B. SMITH, Robt. MIDDLETON. (WC DW 23:207)
[This is prob. the William WILLIAMS who mar. Margaret T. BRANSON, dau. of Newyear BRANSON, WC, bond 14 Jan 1805 (MLBWC:76); she mar. (2) Charles MUSE bef. Aug 1817 (WC OB 1814-18:342, 354, 358, 378, 381); ord. that Peggy MUSE formerly Peggy WILLIAMS be summoned to next court to say whether she will take upon herself the gdnship. of her son Matthew WILLIAMS, 26 Aug 1817 (WC OB 1814-18:342); Vincent T. BRANN aptd. gdn. to Matthew WILLIAMS orphan of Wm. WILLIAMS, 24 Nov 1817 (WC OB 1814-18:354)]

WILLIAMS, William; PO 24 Jun 1816; Mar 1817

WC; INV, $1006.25; includes Negroes Winney & child, boy Joe. (WC RI 10:103)

WILLIAMS, [William]; 26 Aug 1816

WC; Joice WILLIAMS wid. of William WILLIAMS aptd. gdn. to Elijah and Griffin WILLIAMS orphans of William WILLIAMS. (WC OB 1814-18:252) [There is a problem with the identity of the father of Elijah & Griffin WILLIAMS; while he is identified as William here, the obituary of Elijah WILLIAMS claims that "[Elijah] was born in Westmoreland County in the year 1803. His father, Thomas Williams, died when he was quite young ...." (*Religious Herald*, 13 Dec 1866, p. 199). The Griffin WILLIAMS named as the bro. of Elijah is called Thomas G. WILLIAMS in later records, probably for Thomas Griffin WILLIAMS; could the father of Elijah and Thomas G. have been "Thomas William WILLIAMS"? Another problem with this family is the identity of the wife of William or Thomas William WILLIAMS. In this record she is named as Joice, but when she died she was called Jane (WC OB 1827-31:230, 231, 244) She is no doubt Jane [Joice] GARNER who mar. Thomas WILLIAMS, WC bond 23 Dec 1805 (MLBWC:76); Elijah WILLIAMS' tombstone in the cemetery at Gibeon Baptist Church in NC gives his birth as 1803 which may be an error.]

WILLIAMSON, Walter; 18 Jun 1801; 23 Oct 1815

late of KGC but now at Popes Creek in WC; WILL; Sukey & her child & her sis. Lucy to my niece Mildred Washington ROSE; rest of est. to my nephew Charles Walter ROSE [both Mildred & Charles were under age]; friend John ROSE of Montrose ex; WITS: Robt HALL, Pope TIFFEY. (WC DW 23:138)

WILSON, Daniel; 14 Feb 1799; 7 Jan 1802. RC, INV; [m]. (RC WB 9:171)

WILSON, Edward; 3 Jun 1823

RC; Henry WILSON, about 18 or 19, orphan of Edward WILSON cannot come to court but wishes to chose Joseph FONES as his gdn. (RC OB 26:69)

WILSON, Elias; 15 Oct 1801; 6 Feb 1804

RC; WILL; 3 children: Chilton, Salley, & Betty; desires that Elisha BARTLETT Sr. or his heirs shall receive only 1 shilling of the est; children of his dec'd son Daniel; Daniel MARMADUKE & Chilton WILSON exors; WITS: Hen. WILSON, Abraham WHITE, Jas. MARKS. (RC WB 9:230)

WILSON, Elias; PO Feb 1804; 1 Oct 1804

RC; INV; includes the following Negroes: Winney, Jane, Harry, Abram, Paul, Billy, Joe, girls Lyddia, Sarah, Reah, woman Milly. (RC WB 9:242)

WILSON, Garland; PO May 1818, T 30 May 1818; 2 Nov 1818

RC; Negro boy Billy belonging to the est. of Garland WILSON was sold at White's Tavern for $620; the proceeds were div. among Allen P. WILSON & [Libba] WILSON of the old blood and Henry P. WILSON & Maria WILSON of the half blood. (RC AB 3:645)

WILSON, James; 3 Aug 1818

RC; James WILSON d. in the service of the US Army under Capt. CARTER; he left three children: James, Polly, and Sally and a wid., Sally, who mar. William WILSON. (RC OB 24:242; OB 25:273, 276)
[Moore F. BROCKENBROUGH is gdn. to Jas., Polly, & Sally WILSON orphans of James WILSON, 6 May 1822 (RC OB 25:287)]

WILSON, Molley; 2 Jan 1812; 20 Jul 1812.

CCP, LC; WILL; land & plant. w/o I now live to dau. Betsey [Bowss] WILSON; if dau. should die without heirs land to be sold & money eq. div. between three sons Cyrus WILSON, Darious WILSON, & William WILSON;

[no ex. named]; WITS: Wm. KIRK, Thos. KENT, Eppa [LUNES]. (LC WB 28:132)

WILSON, Morton; PO 7 Jun 1800; 7 Feb 1803.
RC, INV; [m]; includes the following Negroes: Canaday (a Negro boy), Winney (a Negro girl), George, Tom, Dick (small boy), Dublin (small boy), Aron, Reubin (boy), Moses, Rose (girl), Mary, Patience, Jenney & child Silvey, Milly & child Polly, Mima & child Lewis, Betty (old woman). (RC WB 9:208)

WILSON, Morton; PO Jan 1804; 1 Oct 1804
RC INV; includes the following Negroes: Jemima & child, Winny & child, Hannah, Milly & child, Jane, Betty, Patience & child, Sally, Samuel, Polly, Silvy, Rose, Dick, Dublin, Kenady, Moses, Aaron, George, Mary & child, Reuben, Bill. (RC WB 9:243)

WILSON, Morton; PO Feb 1804, T 24 Apr 1804; 1 Dec 1806
RC; DIV of est. among Eleanor WILLSON, James WILLSON, Richard WILLSON, Henry WILLSON & Martha WILLSON. (RC AB 3:180)
[Morton WILSON mar. Eliz. FORD, RC, bond 9 Jul 1753 (MRC:233); in his will (RC 29 Jun 1797-1 Jul 1799) he named his wife Eliz., daus. Eleanor & Martha, and sons Thos. Ford, James, Rich., & Hen. (RC WB 9:117)]

WILSON, Shelton; PO May 1818, T 30 May 1818; 2 Nov 1818
RC; DIV; Negroes Lydia & child, Mary & Chloe, girls Hetha & Jenny belonging to the est. of Shelton WILSON were sold at White's Tavern for $1792; the proceeds were div. among the reps. of Elizabeth WILSON dec'd the sis. of Chelton [sic] WILSON (entitled to 1/4), William WILSON son of Elizabeth WILSON (entitled to 1/8), Allen, Sibba, Henry & Maria (children of Edward WILSON dec'd and grchildren of Elizabeth WILLSON; each entitled to 1/4 of 1/8), the reps. of Sally WEEDEN the sis. of Chelton WILLSON (entitled to 1/4), Thomas WEEDEN son of Sally WEEDEN dec'd (entitled to 1/8), Eppa J. HINSON who mar. Fanny WEEDEN dau. of Sally WEEDEN dec'd (entitled to 1/8), the reps. of Penelope BARTLETT dec'd the sis. of Chilton WILSON dec'd entitled to 1/4, Sally, John, Elijah, Caty, Isaac, Joseph, Becky & Penelope children of Penelope BARTLETT dec'd (entitled to 1/8 of 1/4), Thomas MOSS son of Sally & grson. of Penelope BARTLETT dec'd (entitled to 1/8 of 1/4), the reps. of John BARTLETT (entitled to 1/8 of 1/4), Eliza [sic] BARTLETT son of Penelope BARTLETT (entitled to 1/8 of 1/4), Caty PULLEN dau. of Penelope BARTLETT (entitled to 1/8 of 1/4), Isaac BARTLETT son of Penelope BARTLETT (entitled to 1/8 of 1/4), John BARTLETT son of Joseph & grson. of Penelope BARTLETT (entitled to 1/8 of 1/4), Daniel WILLSON who mar. Becky WILSON dau. of Penelope BARTLETT (entitled to 1/8 of 1/4), Alexander NASH who mar. Penelope BARTLETT dau. of Penelope BARTLETT (entitled to 1/8 of 1/4), the reps. of Daniel WILLSON dec'd (entitled to 1/4), Lucy, Rebeccah, David, Polly, James & Nancy children of Daniel WILLSON dec'd (each entitled to 1/6 of 1/4), Polly WILLSON dau. of Lucy WILSON dec'd & grdau. of Daniel WILLSON (entitled to 1/6 of 1/4), Joseph PULLEN, Evalina PULLEN & James PULLEN children of [m] PULLEN who mar. Rebecca WILSON dec'd who was the dau. of Daniel WILSON dec'd (each entitled to 1/8 of 1/4), Daniel WILSON son of Daniel WILSON dec'd (entitled to 1/6 of 1/4), Reuben SANFORD who mar. Polly WILSON dau. of Daniel WILLSON dec'd (entitled to 1/6 of 1/4), Polly WILSON, Sally WILLSON & James WILSON children of James WILSON dec'd who was a son of Daniel WILSON dec'd (each entitled to 1/8 of 1/4), Samuel R. JONES who mar.

Nancy WILSON dau. of Daniel WILSON dec'd (entitled to 1/6 of 1/4). (RC AB 3:646)
[Shelton (Chelton or Chilton) WILSON was a son of Elias WILSON (*see above*); Rebecca WILSON mar. Andrew PULLEN, WC, bond 7 Mar 1804; Mary "Polly" WILSON mar. Reuben SANFORD, WC, bond 4 Nov 1812; Nancy WILSON mar. Sam. R. JONES (in MLBWC, the groom is identified as "Samuel R. FONES," but in this rec. it is clearly "JONES"), WC, bond 26 Oct 1815; Becky BARTLETT mar. Daniel WILSON f RC, WC, bond 20 Oct 1806 (MLBWC:[23], 55, 62, 76)]

WILSON, William; T 23 Nov 1814; 20 May 1816. LC; INV, $91.83. (LC EB 27:314)

WINDSOR, William; 19 Nov 1803; 28 Feb 1804
WC; WILL; all est. after debts paid to wife Susan[nah]; friend Henry BOOCOCK exor; WITS: Thos. WEAVER, Rich. STEEL, Joshua BUTTS. (WC DW 21:1)

WINDSOR, William; PO Feb 1804, T 10 Mar 1804; 28 May 1804
WC; INV, £75.7.0.; includes one half of the schooner "Philicity" valued at £50. (WC RI 8:403)

WINSTEAD, Daniel; 15 Nov 1814
NC; Jn. FULKS was aptd. gdn. of Wm. and Dan. WINSTEAD orphans of Dan. WINSTEAD. (NC OB 1811-15:260)
[Dan. WINSTEAD mar. Mary THOMAS, wid. of David THOMAS, 13 Jan 1786; they had six children: Geo. (b. 1786), Hannah (b. 1791), Haynie (b. 1793), Susanna (b. 1795), Dan. (b. 1801), and Wm. Christopher (b. 1803) (see Register of Wicomico Baptist Church in BNCHS vol. III no. 1:49); in his will (NC 15 Oct 1814 - 14 Nov 1814) Daniel WINSTEAD of SSP named his wife Mary and children Geo., Hannah FULKS, Suckey DAMERON, Harry, Daniel and Wm. (NC RB 20:78); Hannah WINSTEAD mar. Jn. FULKS, NC, bond 30 Oct 1813 (MLBNC:40); Dan. WINSTEAD orphan of Dan. WINSTEAD chose Alex. ROCK as his. gdn., NC 13 Aug 1821 (NC OB 1820-25:124)]

WINSTEAD, George; T 1 Sep 1819; 12 Mar 1821. NC; INV, $408.50 1/2. (NC RB 22:498)

WINSTEAD, John; 15 May 1827
NC; Huldah M. NEWSOM who was formerly Hulda M. WINSTEAD involved in sale of lands of John WINSTEAD. (NC OB 1825-30:168)
[Hulda WINSTEAD mar. Alexander NEWSOM, wid., NC, bond 9 Apr 1825 (MLBNC:77)]

WINSTEAD, Samuel; T 9 Jul 1808; 12 Sep 1808. NC; INV, [m]. (NC RB 18:33)
[The est. of Sam. WINSTEAD was ord. to be admin. by the sheriff, NC, 13 Jun 1808 (NC OB 1807-1811:53)]

WINSTEAD, Samuel S.; T 24 Nov 1821; 8 Apr 1822. NC; INV, $30.19. (NC RB 23:131)

WOOD, Joseph; [PO 12 Apr 1804], T 11 Mar 1811; 8 Apr 1811
NC; William WOOD acknowledged that he rec'd of Thomas BETTS, his gdn., the sum of £25 in full for his part of his father, Joseph WOOD's est. which he claimed by John ALMON's will. (NC RB 19:18)
[Jn. ALMON, in his will (NC 25 Jan 1792-14 Sep 1795) left Joseph WOOD two Negroes (NC RB 15:203)]

WOOD, Samuel; 28 Feb 1803
WC; the lands devised by Sam. WOOD to his son Sam. WOOD, dec'd, and which have descended from the son to Hethy, Molly, Nelly, Frances, Gideon and Thos. WOOD, to be sold and the proceeds divided. (WC Orders 1801-04:348)

[Sam. WOOD, in his will (WC 2 Dec 1793-28 Oct 1794) named his wife Pheba and daus. Nelly, Frances and Hester (WC DW 19:75); Frances WOOD mar. Dan. BURGESS, WC, bond 4 Mar 1796 (MLBWC:10); Sam. WOOD the younger d. an inf.; Frances WOOD, Gideon WOOD, Thos. WOOD, and Nelly JOHNSON wife of Jn. G. JOHNSON were siblings of the whole blood of sd. Sam. WOOD the younger; Hetty the wife of Reuben KENNEDY and Molly the dec'd wife of Dan. BURGESS were sisters of the half blood (WC CC 1804-008)]

WOOD, William; 3 Jun 1823
RC; on the motion of John WOOD by Joseph W. CHINN, his attorney, ord. that the sheriff of this county take into his hands the est. of William WOOD dec'd, a free person of color, and administer the same. (RC OB 26:67)

WOODY, Thomas; 25 May 1818; 15 Jun 1818
LC; WILL; if wife Alcinda has a child in 9 mos from this date I give the whole of my est. after deducting one third to her child & the other third to her the sd. Alcinda WOODY; but should she have no child I then give her the use of one third part of my est; balance of est. to bro. Robert WOODY; bro. Robert ex; WITS: Geo. WEBB, Jn. HUTCHINGS. (LC WB 28:187)
[Thos. WOODY mar. Alcinda KID, LC, bond 21 Feb 18[1]8 (MLBLC:80); Alcinda WOODY mar. (2) Rich. A. STEPHENS, LC, bond 29 Nov 1822 (MLBLC:70)]

WORMLEY, John; mar. Frances "Fanny" BOND, LC, bond 19 Aug 1784; Jn. WORMLEY d. in 1785; Frances (BOND) WORMLEY mar. (2) Nathaniel BURWELL, LC, bond 20 Apr 1786 and (3) Griffin GARLAND, LC, bond 16 May 1791; in his will (LC 26 Sep 1784 – 16 Jun 1785) Jn. WORMLEY named his wife Frances and his nephews Robt. Wormley CARTER & Jn. WORMLEY (MLBLC:10, 29, 80; LC WB 22:76; LC CC 1823-002)
[Nath. BURWELL d. in LC in late 1789 or early 1790 (LC WB 22:253)]

WORNUM, Thomas; PO 14 Jul 1800; 9 Sep 1800
NC; DIV of est. between the legal reps: William WORNUM Jr. (rec'd Sarah, Fanny & Joe) and Samuel WORNUM (rec'd Winney & George). (NC RB 16:179)

WORNUM (WORNOM), William; PO 9 Jan 1815, T 16 Jan 1815; 13 Feb 1815
NC; INV, $4111.81; includes Negroes Moses, Kendal, Argell, Richard, Jemimah, Letty, Ellender, Esther, Judah, Izrael, Peggy, Joseph, Sallimon, Isaac. (NC RB 19:609)
[In his will (NC 18 Nov 1811-9 Jan 1815), Wm. WORNUM of SSP named his sons Thos. & Wm. WORNUM and daus. Nancy MOORE, Rebeckah DAVIS (and her 3 children Betsy, Thos., & Molly) and "sons" Jn. DAVIS & Linsey DAVIS (NC RB 19:588)]

WORNUM (WORNOM), William; PO 13 Feb 1815, T 17 Feb 1815; 13 Feb 1815
NC; DIV of est. in the hands of Thomas WORNOM ex. of the will among Thomas WORNOM (rec'd Negroes Richard, Easter, Peggy, Isaac), John MORE (rec'd Argell, Ellender, Joseph), Lynzy DAVIS gdn. to his 3 children (rec'd Moses, Jeremiah, Izrael, Solomon), and Benedic BURGESS gdn. of Alsey WORNOM orphan of William WORNOM (rec'd Kendall, Letty, Judith). (NC RB 20:6)
[Linzey DAVIS mar. Rebecca WORNOM, dau. of Wm. WORNUM, NC, bond 20 Jan 1802; Rebecca was dead by 1811 when DAVIS mar. the second of his three wives (MLBNC:27); Jn. MOORE, wid., mar. Nancy WORNUM, dau. of Wm. WORNUM, NC, bond 4 Apr 1801 (MLBNC:75)]

WORNUM, William Jr.; PO 11 Mar 1816, T 12 Jul 1816; 12 Aug 1816

NC; in suit of Milley WORNUM against Benedict BURGESS admr. of William WORNUM Jr. dec'd & Alice WORNUM (an infant under 21) Commissioners allotted dower (which included Negro man Kendal & a small Negro child, and 22 ac. of land) in the est. of William WORNUM, Jr. dec'd to Thomas GEOFF who mar. Millicent WORNUM the late wid. (NC RB 21:63)
[Wm. WORNUM, Jr. mar. Milley ROBERSON, NC, bond 15 Aug 1812; Thos. GEOFF, wid., mar. Millicent C. WORNUM, wid., NC, bond 30 May 1816 (MLBNC:42, 112); the est. of Wm. WORNUM, Jr. was ord. to be admin. by Benedict BURGESS, NC, 13 Feb 1815 (NC Order Book 1811-1816:277); Wm. WORNUM d. in 1814 and his father, Wm. WORNUM Sr., d. a few days before his son in 1814 (NC CC 1816-001)]

WRIGHT, John; PO Dec 1794; 6 Dec 1824
RC; INV, [m] & DIV; lands divided: Plantation called McKenny's valued at £8 per year, Mansion House at £14 per year, Eskridge's at £6 per year; Mansion House & dower Negroes Martin, Thaddeus, Kiziah, & Mima allotted to the widow; Thomas WRIGHT was allotted George, Winny & child, Phoebe & a mulatto girl Sarah MAIDEN; George DAVIS was allotted Solomon, Charles & Clary; John WRIGHT was allotted Sam, Sylvia, Bob & Joan; the disposition of the free mulatto Cyrus is not clear. (RC WB 10:58)
[A George DAVIS mar. an Elizabeth WRIGHT in RC, bond May 1795 (MRC:50)]

WRIGHT, Johnson W.; PO Jan 1803, T 8 Feb 1803; [26 Aug 1804]
WC; INV, £290.2.7 1/2; includes Negroes Rose, Mag, Fry. (WC RI 8:509)

WRIGHT, Molly Fleet; 8 May 1812; 27 Jul 1812.
CP, WC; WILL; bro. Richard WRIGHT all my interest in the land belonging to my father's est. provided he pays his sis. Sary Ellen WRIGHT one half the value of the sd. interest; sis. Eliza WRIGHT one Negro girl Hannah; sis. Fanney WRIGHT one Negro boy Spencer; bro. Richard WRIGHT exor; WITS: Benedict LAMKIN, Nath'l OLDHAM, Charlotte ATTWELL. (WC DW 22:292)
[This is the dau. of Presley WRIGHT (d. WC bef. Mar 1812) (*see below*)]

WRIGHT, Presley; PO 27 Mar 1809; 24 Apr 1809
WC; INV, £943.12.8 1/4; includes Negroes Antony, James, Joe, Willis, Ned, Siner, Nell, Luce, Hannah, Daniel, Spencer. (WC RI 9:139)

WRIGHT, Presley; PO 23 Mar 1812; 26 Aug 1812
WC; DIV of est. among legal reps: Richard WRIGHT, Sarah WRIGHT, Eliza WRIGHT, Presley WRIGHT, George M. WRIGHT, John WRIGHT, Frances WRIGHT, and Mary F. WRIGHT. (WC RI 9:338)
[Presley WRIGHT chose Rich. WRIGHT as his gdn.; Rich. WRIGHT aptd. gdn. of Eliza & Fanny WRIGHT orphans of Presley WRIGHT; Jn. WRIGHT chose Geo. WRIGHT as his gdn., 23 Mar 1812 (WC Orders 1810-13:197, 198); Geo. M. WRIGHT aptd. gdn. to Eliza WRIGHT orphan of Presley WRIGHT in the room of Rich. WRIGHT, 23 Jun 1817 (WC OB 1814-18:313); Geo. M. WRIGHT aptd. gdn. to Frances WRIGHT orphan of Presley WRIGHT, 22 Jun 1818 (WC OB 1814-18:397)]

WRIGHT, Presley; Jun 1818; 24 Apr 1820
WC; Div of land; Lot 1 (the mansion house) drawn by Eliza WRIGHT; Lot 2 drawn by Frances WRIGHT; Lot 3 drawn by Eleanor SMITH; Lot 4 drawn by John WRIGHT; Lot 5 drawn by Eleanor SMITH; Lot 6 drawn by Sarah WRIGHT; Lot 7 drawn by Eleanor SMITH; Lot 8 drawn by Eleanor SMITH. (WC DW 24:59)

WRIGHT, Thomas R.; PO 4 Apr 1796; 2 Mar 1801
RC; INV, £246.14.[6]; includes the following slaves: George, Pheby, Winey & child, Milley. (RC WB 9:142)

WROE, John; PO Jul 1794; 6 Feb 1804
RC; INV; [m]; includes the following Negroes: Cloe, Winny & child Sarah; Letty, Easter, James, Polly, [Joan]. (RC WB 9:228)
[This is Jn. WROE who d. in RC in 1794; in his will (RC 9 Jan 1794-7 Jul 1794) he named his 9 children: Hannah MIDDLETON, Betty, Jane, Nancy, Alice, John, Samuel, Nathaniel & Sarah (RC WB 9:5); Hannah mar. Jn. MIDDLETON, WC, bond 29 Jan 1788 (MLBWC:45); Hannah and Jn. were residents of North Carolina by Nov 1800 (RC DB 17:439); Nancy WROE mar. Rawleigh BRYANT (RC DB 17:439); Sarah WROE mar. Sam. KING of WC, RC, bond 9 Mar 1802 (MRC:113, RC DB 19:136); see also NC CC 1801-008 which suggests that Jn. WROE had another son, Peter, his eldest;]

WROE, William; 18 Jan 1781; 27 Nov 1781
WP, WC; WILL; son Original WROE received land and Negro Dick; son William WROE received land in Culpeper Co.; rest of est. to wife; six children: William, Katherine, Elenor, Rebeckah, Jinny & [Gracey]; wife and son Original exors; WITS: Jn. [TANCILL], Hen. [ROE], Dan. KELLEY. (WC Unrec Wills 1755-1800 #24)

YEATMAN, James; 24 Jun 1822
WC; Nancy YEATMAN aptd. gdn. to her children: Eliza. A., Henry A., Alfred J., Amelia S., Nancy B., Thomas[,] John & Catherine M. YEATMAN orphans of James YEATMAN. (WC OB 1819-23:428)

YEATMAN, Jennings A. (Mrs.); age about 40 d. giving birth to quadruplets on 16 Oct 1822 near WC Courthouse; one child was stillborn. (*Baltimore Patriot & Mercantile Advertiser*, 29 Oct 1822, p. [2])
[Jennings A. YEATMAN mar. Caty SANFORD, who must have been his second wife, WC, bond 25 Jun 1823 (MLBWC:78)]

YEATMAN, John; [T 9 Jan 1811]; 23 Mar 1812
WC; INV, £633.15.6, includes Negroes Tom, unnamed woman & children, Jane & child Polly, Nell, Fanny, Maria, Cordeally, John, Eliza. (WC RI 9:313)

YEATMAN, John Sr.; 28 Mar 1811; 27 May 1811
WC; WILL; 50 ac. of land over the creek on Nomony & 10 or a dozen up here that wife can dispose of as she pleases; I wish this to be plainly understood that if my wife gives or conveys the said land or any part thereof in any manner whatever to any of the favorite grand children, that it is to be considered as their father's or mother's [*1 word unclear*] proportionable part of my other property except the dollar above mentioned. If she should not give, sell or convey the sd. land or any part thereof to any of her children or grandchildren more than another, and let all her children receive their proportionable parts of the said land, then it is my will and desire after her death that all my estate both real and personal be equally divided among all her children. But she is by no means at liberty to sell, lend, convey, or give to one child or grandchild more than another any part of my estate; dau. Elizabeth SANFORD; my grand-children whose fathers are dead is [sic] only to receive their fathers' proportionable part of my est. to be eq. div. among them; wife extx., sons Thomas, John, and James exors; WITS: Jas. B. NEWMAN, Wm. NEWMAN. (WC DW 22:210)
[Jn. YEATMAN Sr. was the father of: Wm. YEATMAN, Jesse B. YEATMAN, Elizabeth YEATMAN, John YEATMAN, and James YEATMAN and the grandfather of Jn. B., Thos. W. & Wm. S. (sons of Wm. YEATMAN), Lucy,

Patty, Benj. & Jos. (children of Jesse B. YEATMAN), Nancy, Eliz., Susan & Wm. (children of Eliz. SANFORD), and Eliz. Anney Austin, Alfred, Amelia, Nancy, Thos. & Susan (children of Jas. YEATMAN); his wid. Susan relinquished her right to 75 ac. on Nominy Creek part of the land called Harrises in 1821 (WC CC 1821-024); Eliz. YEATMAN mar. Wm. S. SANFORD, WC, bond 27 May 1799 (MLBWC:62)]

YEATMAN, Susanna; 15 Feb 1819; 23 Mar 1819
WC; relinquishes all her rights, etc. of 3 Negroes left to her by the will of her dec'd husband John YEATMAN of WC as follows: Maria, Nan & Sophia to be eq. div. among his heirs acc to the devise of his will; WITS: Samson PORTER, Thos. OHARROW. (WC RI 10:359)
[This may be Susanna BAKER, dau. of Wm. BAKER, who mar. Jn. YEATMAN bef. 29 May 1765 (MWO:388)]

YEATMAN, Thomas; 4 Apr 1808; 26 Nov 1810.
WP, WC; WILL; dau. Patty SANFORD & her children all the property already received of mine & what she may receive of mine after the date of this writing (which will be seen in my pocket book in acct. also I lend to her & her children one Negro woman Sembo; dau. Fanny POPE 5 Negroes: Moll, Siller, George, Bett & an infant boy by Siller and all the property she purchased at her dec'd husband Austen POPE's est; dau. Sally THOMPSON all the property & cash that she and her husband Richard THOMPSON has rec'd of mine & further 3 Negroes: Moriah, Millinda, & Horrace; dau. Lucy NORTHEN 2 Negroes: Nan & Phil & some livestock; son Meredith YEATMAN 1 Negro woman Daphney; rest of est. to be eq. div. among my 5 sons: John YEATMAN, Thomas M. YEATMAN, Griffin YEATMAN, Meredith YEATMAN & Henry L. YEATMAN; sons Meredith and Henry L. exors; thus I am in hopes this aforesd. instrument of writing will be fairly understood by my dear children & that when justly consider'd will find I have not been partial to any but impartial to all; WITS: Walkr. MUSE, Sophia MUSE. (WC DW 22:158)
[Patty YEATMAN mar. Edw. SANFORD, WC, bond 24 Nov 1787; Fanny YEATMAN mar. Austin POPE, WC, bond 7 Aug 1793; Sally YEATMAN mar. Rich. THOMPSON, WC, bond 25 Jun 1798 (MLBWC:54, 71, 310); Lucy Robinson YEATMAN mar. Wm. NORTHEN, 1798 (MWO:266)]

YEATMAN, Thomas; PO 27 Jun 1813, T 27 Nov 1813; 28 Mar 1814. WC; INV, $52.50. (WC RI 9:418)

YEATMAN, William; 22 Apr 1811
WC; John B. YEATMAN & Thomas W. YEATMAN chose James YEATMAN as their gdn. and the sd. James is aptd. gdn. of William S. YEATMAN all the orphans of William YEATMAN. (WC Orders 1810-13:11)

YEATMAN, William; 9 May 1816; 1 Jul 1816
LP, RC; WILL; all est. to wife Mary; after her death or remarriage land to son Matthew YEATMAN except tract on which my son Thomas YEATMAN now lives or small corner of land below his house to Edward MOZINGO's line likewise my son Matthew is to let his bro Robert live with him and to keep him from want as he is partly a cripple; remainder of est. to be eq. div. between my four sons Thomas, Robert, Matthew and John H. YEATMAN; wife Mary to be extx. and should she shortly remove out of this world son Thomas to execute will; WITS: Wm. BROWN, Jn. MOZINGO. (RC WB 9:530)
[Wm. YEATMAN mar. Nancy (MORRIS) BROWN, wid. of Thos. BROWN, RC, bond 3 Sep 1804 (MRC:26, 238); Nancy YEATMAN, wid. of Wm.

YEATMAN, was the mother of Matthew, Mary and Alice YEATMAN who were all under 14, RC, 3 Nov 1817 (RC OB 24:153)]

YEATMAN, William; PO 2 Oct 1820; 2 Apr 1821. INV, RC, [m]. (RC WB 9:701)

YEATMAN, William; T 7 Feb 1821; 2 Apr 1821
RC; div. of est. in the hands of the rep. John H. YEATMAN among: Thomas YEATMAN, Ann YEATMAN (wid. of William) in right of her infant children by the sd. William, & John H. YEATMAN. (RC AB 3:712

YERBY, Charles; PO 9 Oct 1809, T 4 Jul 1810; 9 Jul 1810
NC; one fourth of the mill known as Curtis's Mill belonging to Charles YERBY sold for $37.50; proceeds div. among Cyrus COPPEDGE in right of his wife Elizabeth, John YERBY orphan of [Chs.] YERBY dec'd, Cyrus COPPADGE as gdn. for Thomas & Charles YERBY orphans of Charles YERBY. (NC RB 18:424)
[In his will (NC 15 Feb 1794-13 Oct 1794), Chas. YERBY named his wife Judith, his dau. Betsey, and his sons John, Thomas and Charles (NC RB 15:100); Thos. HARVEY was gdn. of Thos. YERBY orphan of Chas. YERBY, 23 May 1805 (LC OB 1804-05:383); Cyrus COPPAGE mar. Eliz. YERBY, ward of Thos. HARVEY, NC, bond 13 Jan 1806 (MLBNC:21); Cyrus COPPEDGE gdn. of Thos. & Chas. YERBY orphans of Chas. YERBY and Jn. YERBY heirs of Chas. YERBY (NC OB 1807-1811:127); Judith, the wid. of Chas. YERBY, seems to have remarried twice, (2) James CARTER of Amherst Co., NC, bond 9 Dec 1799 and (3) Geo. BRENT, wid., NC, bond 13 Feb 1802 (MLBNC:12, 15, NC CC 1804-015)]

YERBY, Delia; 16 May 1820; 16 May 1820
LC; memo of the dower Negroes of Delia YERBY now Delia WADDY: Armistead, Lewis, Patt, Mary & her child Jud[y]; /s/ John WADDY. (LC EB 21:27)
[Delia YERBY mar. (2) John WADDY, LC, bond 20 Sep 1819 (MLBLC:76)]

YERBY, George; PO Mar 1817; 8 Apr 1817
RC; INV; included Negroes Elijah, Lewis, Tom, Alick, Malissa; Negroes appraised at $2200.00; Foushee [G.] TEBBS admr. de bonis non. (RC WB 9:553)

YERBY, George W.; PO 20 Dec 1824, T 3 Jan 1825; 17 May 1825
LC; DIV of Negroes among Eliza YERBY (Fanny & child Mitchell, Absolom, Shadrick, Frederick, Nancy), Joseph YERBY (Cyrus, Pleasant & child Rosanna, Harry, Willis, Betty), Lemuel YERBY (Daniel, Dennis, Jane, Hannah, Mahala, Eady), Ellison YERBY (Mark, Hannah & child Charles, Mary & child Winney, Winney, George, Armstead), David YERBY (Joe, Isaac, Emily, Juley, Siller, Darkey). (LC EB 29:434)

YERBY, John; T 22 Jul 1792; 21 Sep 1795
LC; INV, [m]; includes Negroes: Old Roger, Mingo, Nanny, Winney, Solomon, Aaron, Abraham, George, Moses, Jenny, Peter (little), Hannah, Joanna & child George, Judith, Sarah, Mima, Venus, Cate, Nanny, Grace, Simon, Dennis, [Sawny], James, Jesse, Fanny, Peggy, Oliver, Kitt, Amy, [Sam], Charlotte & a young child, Sillah, George, Darkey, Tom; DIV of est. among: Mary HUBBARD's reps., reps. of Elizabeth YERBY, Ann BRENT, reps. of Hannah EDWARDS, Thomas YERBY. (LC EB 24:44)
[John YERBY, Mary HUBBARD, Eliz. YERBY, Ann BRENT, Hannah EDWARDS, & Thos. YERBY were children of Thos (d. LC 1756) & Hannah (d. LC 1761) YERBY; Mary YERBY mar. Jos. HUBBARD, LC, bef. 20 Mar 1756, Ann YERBY mar. [Thos.] BRENT, LC, bef. 20 Mar 1756, Hannah

YERBY poss. mar. Jn. EDWARDS, LC, bef. 20 Mar 1756 (LC WB 15:252, WB 16:145, 231; MWO:50, 122, 187)]

YERBY, John; PO 22 Feb 1792; 20 Oct 1801

LC; DIV of est. at the house of Jn. YERBY and on 22 Nov 1796 at the house of Peter TANKERSLEY among: First Division: Mary HUBBARD's reps., William BOATMAN, Ann BRENT, Hannah EDWARDS, Thomas YERBY; Second Division: Reps. of Hannah EDWARDS, Ann BRENT, William BOATMAN, reps. of Mary HUBBARD. (LC EB 24:164)

YERBY, John M.; 16 Oct 1812; 7 Dec 1812

NFP, RC; all land to be eq. div. among 3 sis. Judith G. McCARTY, Elizabeth McCARTY & Nanny YERBY; sis., William L. BALL & Augustine NEALE exors; WITS: Dan. L. McCARTY, Geo. SAUNDERS, Thos. MITCHELL, Feriol LEMOIN. (RC WB 9:410)

[Jn. M. YERBY & his sisters were children of Geo. YERBY (d. RC, 1793) (RC WB 8:157); they were the children of his first marriage; he had two children by his 2nd marriage to Eliz. Rust GARLAND IN 1790 but he did not name them in his will (MRC: 238); Judith YERBY mar. Wm. McCARTY, RC, bond 24 Dec 1798 (MRC:124)]

YERBY, John M. (Maj.); PO 7 Dec 1812; 3 May 1813

RC; INV, [m], includes the following slaves: Lee, Dennis, Sally, Old Rachel, Judah, Ellen, Louisa, Travers, Jerry, Squire, Juva, Rachel (girl), Margery & child. (RC WB 9:424)

YERBY, John M. (Maj.); T Dec 1812; 7 Aug 1817

RC; DIV of Negroes & land of which Maj. John M. YERBY died seized & possessed among: Mrs. Judith G. McCARTY (Travas, Ellen, Louisa, Juba; 216 ac. next to Glascock's Mill Stream, 49 ac. of White Oak Swamp land), Miss Nancy YERBY (Lee, Dennis, Margery & child, Judah; all the houses & land around the houses 159 ac., 49 ac. of White Oak Swamp), Mrs. Elizabeth McCARTY (Jerry, Squire, Sally, Rachel; 216 ac. of the lower field, 49 ac. of swamp). [Note. Old woman Rachel being considered past work was permitted to choose her mistress & she chose Mrs. J. G. McCARTY]. (RC AB 3:435)

YERBY, John W.; 4 May 1824

RC; John W. YERBY late soldier in the svc. of the US died leaving no father, mother, wife, child or children but only three sis. and one bro.: (1) Margaret F. YERBY who mar. William D. McCARTY; she died during the year 1815 leaving one child [Aylin] Y. McCARTY who has recently died; (2) Apphia [F.] YERBY who mar. Geo. Y. McCARTY who died in 1823 leaving one child George A. McCARTY; (3) Ann B. McCARTY who was Ann B. YERBY wid. of Daniel L. McCARTY who died in 1823 leaving three children (infants): Madison, Elizabeth Ann & Maria McCARTY; and (4) Thomas YERBY. (RC OB 26:195)

[Margaret F. YERBY mar. Wm. D. McCARTY, RC, bond 7 Dec 1813; Apphia F. YERBY mar. Geo. Y. McCARTY, RC, bond 13 Jun 1815; Ann B. YERBY mar. Dan. L. McCARTY, RC, bond 26 Aug 1806 (MRC:123, 125, 125)]

YERBY, Margaret; 7 Jun 1805; 17 Sep 1805

LC; WILL; $10 to grdau. Margaret BEANE; pewter & other things that I gave her & which she now has to be considered as John BEANE Jr.'s property; my three Virginia cloth gowns to be div. among my three Negro wenches; remainder of est. to be eq. div. among my five children or their children; sis. Margaret KIRK; dau-i-l Mary YERBY; son William YERBY ex; WITS: Thos. CARTER, Judith CARTER. (LC WB 28:90)

YERBY, Margaret; PO 17 Sep 1805, T 15 Nov 1805; 16 Dec 1805
LC; INV at the house of William YERBY, £20.5.[6]. (LC EB 24:333)

YERBY, Mary; 10 Jul 1822; 21 Jul 1823
LC; WILL; sis. Catherine YERBY if she should outlive me; [no ex. named]; WITS: Sharpley SCHOFIELD, Thos. SCHOFIELD. (LC WB 28:234)

YERBY, Thomas; PO 9 Dec 1805, T 2 Jan 1806; 10 Feb 1806
NC; INV at the house of William YERBY includes Negroes Isaac, Jane, Amos, Milley & child, Janetta, Nancy, Patience, Halley, Maryann & DIV of est. among: Lot 1 William PARROTT (rec'd Isaac & Patience), Lot 2 John BEANE (rec'd Jane, Nancy & Halley), Lot 3 Charles YERBY's orphans (rec'd Amos), Lot 4 William YERBY (rec'd Maryann), Lot 5 for Benjamin LINTON, Moses LINTON (rec'd Milley & child), Lot 6 for Benjamin LINTON, Moses LINTON (rec'd Janetta). (NC RB 17:383)
[Will PARROTT, Jr. mar. Judith YERBY, NC 26 Feb 1774 (MWO:273)]

YERBY, Thomas; PO Sep 1808; 6 Jun 1809
RC; DIV of slaves among Aphia YERBY (Lewis, John, Allen, Ameny & child Peggy, Sally, Nailor's Hole Hannah), John YERBY (Tom, Isaac, Bob, Rachel & child Fanny, Milly & Travis, Old Jack), Thomas YERBY (Bill, George, Solomon, Charlotte & child Sarah, Lucinda, Daniel), [Beggy] YERBY (Elijah, Prince, Juba, Sukey & 2 children Priscilla & Kate, Esther, Old Phillis), Daniel L. McCARTY (Aaron, Davy, Matilda, Nancy, Hannah). (RC AB 3:218)
[Dan. L. McCARTY & Ann B. his wife who was Ann B. YERBY, Jn. W. YERBY an infant under 21 by Jn. M. YERBY his gdn, Margaret YERBY also an infant under 21 by Dan. L. McCARTY her gdn. sued Thos. and Apphia YERBY infants under 21 by Wm. GIBSON their gdn. to div. the lands of Thos. YERBY dec'd, RC, 4 Sep 1809 (RC Orders 1809-10:21); Dan. L. McCARTY mar. Ann B. YERBY, RC, bond 26 Aug 1806 (MRC:123)]

YERBY, Thomas; 2 Oct 1809
RC; INV, £2027.14.3, includes following slaves: Jack, Isaac, James, Aron, George, Davy, Margaret, boy George, Bill, child Winny, Daniel, Samuel, Peter, Milly, boy Tom, girl Hannah, Phillis, Charlotte, Lucinda, Bob, Appleby, Hannah, Betty, Elijah, Lewis, Bill, Prince, Tom, [Amny], Allen, Juby, Susanna, Matilda, Rachel, Nancy, Spencer, John L., Sally, Solomon, Janny (old), Doll (old), Violet (old). (RC WB 9:361)

YERBY, Thomas; PO 20 Mar 1815, T 7 Apr 1815; 21 Aug 1815
LC; INV; includes Negroes: Isaac, Solomon, Armistead, Hannah, Sarah, Maryann, Winney, Patty, Tonus, Jesse, Lewis, Emanuel, James, George, Milly, Cate, Olivia (Maryann's child), Griffin. (LC EB 27:248)

YERBY, Thomas; PO 20 Feb 1815, T 25 Feb 1815; 19 Feb 1816
LC; INV, $1731.54; includes Negroes: Stephen, Joshua, Anthony, Judith, Hulday, Mary. (LC EB 27:284)

YERBY, Thomas; 21 Oct 1816
LC; Delia YERBY aptd. gdn. to William, Henry & Mary YERBY orphans of Thomas YERBY. (LC Orders 24:339, OB 25:75, OB 26:81)
[Delia YERBY mar. (2) Jn. WADDY, LC, bond 20 Sep 1819 (MLBLC:76, LC CC 1820-065); Chas. J. YERBY replaced Delia YERBY as gdn. of Wm., Hen., & Mary YERBY, 18 Oct 1819 (LC OB 25:86, 237)]

YERBY, William; 13 Mar 1813; 20 Apr 1813
LC; WILL; to son William T. YERBY the plant. w/o he now lives & all lands west of the road that leads from Cabbin Swamp to the Girls Bridge Swamp & the Negroes Solomon, Nelson, Cate & her 4 youngest children now in his possession, Ephraim, Jane & Harry the plasterer; to son Charles J. YERBY

my dwelling house & all my land east of the road that leads from the Cabin Swamp to the Girls Bridge Swamp & the Negroes Richard, Benjamin, Samuel, Lucy & child, Charity & her three youngest children, John & Chloe; to dau. Margaret TOWLES the following Negroes: Moses or value sold to Richard STEPHENS for £100, Rose & her 3 youngest children now with her, Frederick, Gilbert, Nancy, Amos, Jude & her child; grson. Henry W. TOWLES; balance of est. to be eq. div. between 4 children: Thomas YERBY, William T. YERBY, Margaret TOWLES, & Charles J. YERBY; two sons Thomas & William exors; WITS: Wm. TAYLOR, Jn. DOGGETT, Wm. STOTT, Rich. CUNDIFF; [COD, same date, mentions a deed of trust made some years past by Charles BELL for 3 Negroes & some other prop.]. (LC WB 28:141)

[Margaret YERBY mar. Oliver TOWLES, LC, bond 14 Jun 1809 (MLBLC:74); Chas. J. YERBY orphan of Wm. YERBY chose Jn. CHOWNING Jr. as his gdn., 18 Oct 1813 (LC Orders 24:170); Miller:20 locates Cabin Swamp in LC northeast of Lancaster Courthouse]

YERBY, William; PO 20 Apr 1813; 20 Jun 1815

LC; INV, [m]; includes Negroes: Isaac, Spencer, Rose, Ephram, Nelson, Chloe, Richard, Solomon, Jude, Moses, Hannah, Lucy & child, Elijah, Charity, Jane, Benjamin, Cate, Henry, Samuel, Mary Ann, Frederick, Jesse, Gilbert, John, Daniel, Nancy, Amy, Primus, Thomas, Elias, Eddey, Patty, Milley, Patty, Hulda, Charlotte, James, Robert, Mariah, Cate dau. of Mary Ann, John son of Jude, Griffin, Polly. (LC EB 27:226)

YERBY, [William]; 17 Aug 1824

LC; William YERBY & Mary B. YERBY chose Opie BEANE for their gdn.; settlement with John WADDY the acct. of his gdnship. with William & Mary YERBY. (LC OB 26:64)

[There is a marriage rec. for Wm. YERBY and Cordelia M. CHILTON, LC, bond 23 Feb 1729 [sic] with Fauntleroy N. CHILTON sec. in MLBLC:81; since Fauntleroy N. CHILTON was married in 1824, the year of this marriage must be in error; Cordelia M. CHILTON was a dau. of Jesse CHILTON, *see above*; Mary B. YERBY mar. Hiram STONHAM, LC, bond 10 Apr 1828, Opie BEANE was sec. (MLBLC:70); *see also Delia YERBY above*]

YERBY, William T.; Apr 1818; 21 Jun 1819

LC; WILL; whole est. to wife Maria for her support & the support of her children by me until they are 21 & schooled; son William Henry YERBY to have $500 more than the rest; Sp[encer] GEORGE & Col. John CHOWNING exors; as my papers. are very confused I give them $100 more if one qualify the whole; if both, $50 each; excuse the above being in haste and very sick; the exors. will find a great many little memorandums abt $300 bond, act[ns] L. GEORGE $80, J. A. CARTER abt $125 apply to Sp. GEORGE; [no wits listed, but proved by the oaths of Chas. J. YERBY & Benj. M. WALKER. (LC WB 28:196)

[Wm. T. YERBY's wife was Maria STREET dau. of Hen. & Lucy STREET, *see above*]

YERBY, William T.; T 22 Sep 1819; 18 Oct 1819

LC; INV, [$7568.25]; includes Negroes: Nelson, Charles, James, John, Nathan, Elias, Richard, Armistead, Henderson, Robert, Milly, Keziah, Felicia, Caty, [Huldy], [Rocillana], Priscilla, Butler, Nancy, Edmond (at the mill, half his value). (LC EB 27:501)

YOPP, Betty; PO 19 Nov 1804; 15 Jul 1805

LC; INV at the house of Ann NUTT, £20.9.6 1/4. (LC EB 24:322)

YOPP, Maryann; 3 Feb 1805; 16 Jun 1806
LC; WILL; all est. I now possess & all that I may heir from my mother Elizabeth YOPP or from my father William YOPP to my sis. Chloe LUNSFORD; friend & sis. Chloe LUNSFORD extx; WITS: Wm. YERBY, Wm. J. YERBY, Jn. YERBY. (LC WB 28:95)
[See Wm. YOPP, below]

YOPP, Samuel; 16 Feb 1807
LC; Sarah & Polly YOPP orphans of Samuel YOPP chose Elias EDMONDS as their gdn. (LC Orders D22 1805-08:290)
[This is Sam. YOPP son of Sam. YOPP of CCP who named his son Sam., grdaus. Alice, Salley & Polly YOPP, and daus. Amey YOPP, Ann HUBBARD & Salley WILDER in his will (LC 12 Oct 1793 - 21 Oct 1793) (LC WB 22:295); Geo. SPILMAN mar. Alice YOPP, LC, bond 23 May 1808 (MLBLC:69; LC Orders 24:14); Sally YOPP mar. Spencer WILDER, LC, bond 30 May 1789 and moved to Georgia (MWO:376; LC CC 1808-006)]

YOPP, William; PO 17 Dec 1804; 15 Jul 1805
LC; DIV of proceeds of Negro Harry's sale among reps. of William YOPP: Judith HUBBARD, Ann NUTT, Maryann YOPP. [William] YOPP, Chloe LUNCE [sic], Charles YOPP, Ann YOPP gdn. to Louisa YOPP; another div. of the proceeds of sale of slave Harry among heirs was recorded on 20 Jan 1806; the heirs in this rec were given as: Judith HUBBARD, Nancy NUTT, Chloe LUNSFORD, [Molly] YOPP, Nancy NUTT as gdn. to Louisa YOPP orphan of Betsy YOPP; the commissioners decided that the bonds which were the portions of the heirs William & Charles YOPP would be safer in the office of the commissioners. (LC EB 24:325, 335)
[Wm. YOPP seems to have d. bef. Apr 1787; two divisions of his est. are recorded: 21 Apr 1788, among Betty YOPP (wid.), Stephen LOCKE gdn. of Wm., Cloe & Chas. YOPP, Mary Ann YOPP, Jas. NUTT & Wm. HUBBARD (sons-in-law), Sarah Ann YOPP and Betty YOPP (LC WB 22:177); 21 Sep 1789, among Mrs. Betty YOPP (wid.), Jas. NUTT, Wm. HUBBARD, Maryann YOPP, Wm. YOPP, Cloe YOPP, Chas. YOPP, Betty YOPP (LC WB 22:221); Ann NUTT aptd. gdn. of Louisa YOPP orphan of Eliz. YOPP, 17 Dec 1804 (LC OB 1804-05:268); Judith YOPP mar. Wm. HUBBARD, LC, bond 3 Jan 1785 (MLBLC:39); Chloe YOPP mar. Epaphroditus LUNSFORD, LC, bond 5 Aug 1795 (MLBLC:49); Nancy NUTT ord. to apply $15 to the support of her ward Louisa YOPP orphan of Betsy YOPP, 20 Apr 1807 (LC Orders D22 1805-08:319)]

YOUNG, Alexander; T Jun 1810; Nov 1811
WC; INV; £34.14.0; includes a brown buffalo cow & calf. (WC RI 9:305)

APPENDIX 1

Major Virginia Estate Laws

A law passed in December 1792 reduced various earlier laws concerning wills and estates into one. For the complete law relating to wills, see Samuel Shepherd, *The Statutes at Large of Virginia from October Session 1792, to December Session 1806, Inclusive*, Vol. I, New York: AMS Press, Inc., pp. 88-99. Among the provisions included were :

1. Every person over 21 to have the right to devise "all the estate, right, title and interest in possession, reversion or remainder, which he hath ... in lands, tenements or hereditaments, or annuities or rents charged upon or issuing out of them...."
2. Widows retained their dower rights.
3. A will made when the testator had no children did not affect those born afterwards.
4. No nuncupative will shall be established, unless it be made in the time of the last sickness of the deceased at his habitation, or where he hath resided for ten days next preceding, except where the deceased is taken sick from home and dies before he returns to such habitation, nor where the value exceeds thirty dollars, unless it be proved by two witnesses.
5. Any soldier in actual military service, or any mariner or seaman being at sea, may dispose of his chattels as he might heretofore have done.
6. The county court has the power to hear and determine all causes, matters, suits and controversies testamentary, arising within its jurisdiction. A will shall be proved in the county wherein a testator has a mansion house or known place of residence.
7. When a will is exhibited to be proved the court having jurisdiction may proceed immediately to receive the probat thereof and grant a certificate of such probat. If the will is not contested within seven years the probat shall be forever binding. If anyone contests the validity of the will by a bill in chancery within seven years, the verdict of a jury trial shall be final between the parties.
8. All persons named as executors in a will shall, after the copy thereof has been admitted to record, be entitled to a probat of the said will. Where there are no executors named or if all of the executors refuse the executorship, the court shall have power and authority to hear and determine the right of administration, and to grant a certificate for obtaining letters of administration, with the will annexed.
9. If the executors named in the will refuse executorship, the court may receive the proof of the will and grant a certificate for obtaining letters of administration with the same annexed to the person to whom administration would have been granted if there had been no will of the deceased.
10. When a widow shall not be satisfied with the provisions made for her by the will of her husband, she may, within one year from the time of his death, declare that she will not take or accept the provision and renounce all benefit which she might claim by the will; she will then be entitled to one-third part of the slaves whereof her husband died possessed, which she shall hold during her life and she may be entitled to such share of his other personal estate as if he had died intestate

11. Every court granting a certificate for a probate or administration shall nominate three or more appraisers in every county or corporation where any of the personal estate of the decedent shall be to view and appraise all the personal estate produced to them and return such appraisement to the court; which appraisement, if signed by the executor or administrator, may be considered as an inventory of such part of the estate as had heretofore come to his hands. Each appraiser shall be entitled to fifty cents per day for his attendance to be paid by the executor or administrator, and charged to the estate.
12. Executors and administrators to sell at public sale all such goods of their testator or intestate, specific legacies excepted, as are liable to perish, be consumed, or rendered worse by keeping.

Another act passed in December 1792 concerned the course of descent when a person died intestate. The descent passed first to his children, then to his father, then to his mother, brothers and sisters and their descendants. Provisions were also made if the decedent was an infant.

APPENDIX 2

Records Checked

Lancaster County
Estate Book 24 1796-1806
Estate Book 27 1806-1819
Estate Book 29 1820-1825
Order Books 1799 - 1827
Will Book 28 1795-1839
Wills 1795-1819
Chancery Cases 1795-1825

Northumberland County
District Court Orders etc. 1789-1825
Fiduciary Bonds 1797 - 1801
Guardianship Accounts 1 1788-1824
Order Books 1807-1830
Record Book 16 1799-1803
Record Book 17 1803-1808
Record Book 18 1808-1811
Record Book 19 1811-1815
Record Book 20 1815-1816
Record Book 21 1816-1819
Record Book 22 1819-1822
Record Book 23 1822-1824
Record Book 24 1824-1826
Chancery Cases 1795-1835

Richmond County
Account Book 3
Account Book 4
Order Books 1809-1832
Will Book 9 1794-1822
Will Book 10 1822-1846

Westmoreland County
Deeds & Wills 20 1799-1803
Deeds & Wills 21 1804-1808
Deeds & Wills 22 1809-1813
Deeds & Wills 23 1814-1819
Deeds & Wills 24 1819-1823
Deeds & Wills 25 1824-1828
Orders 1799-1827
Records & Inventories 8 1799-1806 [NB. There is a problem with the page numbers in this book; at some point after page 245 the numbers change to the 300s so that what is probably page 257 is actually numbered 357.]
Records & Inventories 9 1806-1815
Records & Inventories 10 1815-1820
Records & Inventories 11 1820-1825

APPENDIX 3

Surname Variants

Often one surname had several spelling variants. The list below gives some of these variants.

ABBEY	Abbay
ALDERSON	Alverson
ALFORD	Alfred
ALGAR	Aylgar
ALMOND	Almon, Ammon
ANNADALE	Annidal, Anadale, Annandale, Annodale
APPLEBY	Apleby, Applebe
ARMES	Arms
ASHBURN	Ashbern
ASTON	Asten, Astin
ATWELL	Atwill
BAILEY	Baley, Bayley
BARECROFT	Bearcroft, Barcroft
BARRICK	Barrack, Barrock, Berrick
BARRETT	Barrot, Barriott
BASYE	Basey, Baysie, Bassye
BATTEN	Battin
BAYNE	Baine, Bane
BEANE	Been
BEATLEY	Beetley, Beetly (May be confused with DEATLEY)
BENNEHAM	Benniham, Bennehan, Beanham
BERRICK	Barrick
BEVANS	Bevins, Beavens
BIRKETT	Burkett
BISCOE	May be confused with BRISCOE
BLACKERBY	Blakerby, Blackeby, Blackerly
BLACKMORE	Blakemore
BLOMFIELD	Broomfield
BLUNDON	Blundell, Blundall
BOWEN	Bowing, Bowin, Boing, Boin
BOYLE	Boile
BRAMHAM	Branham
BROCKENBROUGH	Brockenbroy
BRUCE	Bruse
BRUMLEY	Bromley, Brombley, Brounley
BRYANT	Bryan, Briant
BUCHAN	Buckhann
BURK	Burt
BURWELL	Burrell ?
BUTLER	Boteler
CALVERT	Colvert
CAMPBELL	Cammell, Camell
CAUSEY	Cossey
CAVENDER	May be confused with LAVENDER

CHARLETON	Chorton
CHILTON	Chelton, Shelton
CHITWOOD	Chetwood
CLAYTON	Claughton (may be confused with CLAYTOR or CLATOR)
COCKARILL	Cockrell, Cockarill, Cockall
COLEMAN	Coelman
COLLINS	Collin, Collings
CONNALLY	Conerly, Conolly, Conally, Connellee, Conoly, Connelly
CRALLE	Crawley
CRITCHER	Crutcher
CROWDER	Crowther, Crouther
CURTIS	Curtice, Cirtis
DAUGHITY	Daughety, Dorety
DEGGE	Degges
DODSON	Dotson
DOGGETT	Doggitt, Doged, Dagod
DOUGLAS	Douglass, Dougliss, Dugles
DOULIN	Dooling, Dulin
DUNAWAY	Donoway
EFFORD	Hefford, Hereford, Helford, Jefford
ELLIOTT	Ellit
ERSKINE	Areskin, Ersking
EWELL	Euel, Youel, Youell
FANN	Fenn
FEAGITT	Feagett, Figgot, Figot, Figget
FINDLEY	Fendla, Fendlea, Fendly, Fenly, Fendley, Fiendley
FOWKE	Fooke
FRISTOE	Fristow, Frestow
FULKS	Faulks, Folks, Fowke, Fooke
GASKINS	Gaskings
GATHINGS	Gaythings, Gathins
GAYTON	Gaydon
GILES	Jyles
GOLDSBOROUGH	Goldsbury, Goldsberry
GOODRIDGE	Goodrich
HABRON	Hebron, Heabron, Hayburn, Harborn, Habborn, Habern
HAGGOMAN	Haggamond, Haggemons
HALE	Haile, Hail, Heale
HAMMACK	Hammock
HAMMOND	Hammon, Hamon
HARDWICK	Hardidge, Hardage
HOGAN	Hogans
HOW	Howe
HUDSON	Hodson, Hutson
HUGHES	Huse
HUNTON	May be confused with HINTON or HUNTER
HUTT	May be confused with HULL or HILL
INGOE	Inger
JASPER	Jesper
JEFFRIES	Jeffrys, Geffreys, Gefferys
JENNINGS	Genings

JESPER	Jasper
KEEVE	May be confused with KEENE
KEM	May be confused with KEW
KENNAN	Cannan, Cannon (May be confused with KENNER)
KENNEDY	Cannaday
KEYSER	Keaser, Keasor, Keiser, Keisor, Keysor
LANSDALE	Langsdale, Lansdell
LATTIMORE	Lattermore
LAYCOCK	Leacock, Leecock, Lacock
LONGWITH	Longworth
LONGWORTH	Longwith
LOWE	Loe
LOWRY	Lawry
LUNSFORD	Lunceford
LUTTRELL	Littrell, Littrall, Littrill, Luttrill, Lutterell, Litterell
MAIDEN	Maden
MAITH	Meath, Math
MASSEY	Massee
McGINNIS	Maginnis
McGUIRE	Mackgyer, Mackgyar, McGuier
McINDREE	McKindree
McKAY	Maccay
McKILDOE	McKeldo, McKildo, McKelder
MEALEY	Mealy, Maley
MONGER	Munger
MORROW	Murrah, Murray, Murrow, Murow
MOSS	Morse
MOTHERSHEAD	Modiset
NASH	Knash
NEWGENT	Nugent
NEWSOM	Neasom, Neasome, Neasum
OLIFF	Eliff, Olive
PASQUITH	Pasqueth, Pasquett, Pasquit
PAYTON	Peyton, Patton, Patten
PECK	Pick, Peake
PICKREN	Pickron, Pickring, Pickering
PIERCE	Peirce, Pearse
PRIDHAM	Bridham
PUGH	Pew, Pue
PULLEN	Pullin
PURCELL	Pursell, Pussell; probably Pursley
RAINS	Reigns, Raines
RAWLINGS	Rawllings, Rawlins, Rolens
REAMY	Ramey, Remmy
REYNOLDS	Raynolds, Rennolds
RIVEER	Reveer, Revere, Rever, Raveer, Revier, Revire
RUICK	Reuick
SANDERS	Saunders
SANFORD	Samford, Sandford
SCHOFIELD	Scofield, Scofill
SCOTT	Scutt

SCRIMGER	Schrimsher, Scrimiger, Scrimsher
SEAMONS	Seamans, Seamon, Seamons, Seamar
SEBREE	Sebrey, Sebrell, Seebre, Seabry, Sebra
SETTLE	Suttle
SHIRLEY	Shearley, Shurley, Sherley
SIMMONS	Simonds, Simmonds
SIMMS	Sims, Simes, Syms
SPENDERGRASS	Pendergrass
STEWART	Steward, Stuart
STONUM	Stoneham
SULLIVAN	Sullavant, Sullivant, Sullevent, Sullvent
TATE	Taite
TELLIS	Telles, Tealis
THRELKILL	Threlkeld
THROP	Tropp
TOULSON	Toleson
TRACEY	Trasce, Tracie
TUNE	Toon(e)
VENEY	Venie, Veeney, Venea
VIGOR	Vigar, Viger
WEATHERS	Withers
WEBLIN	Webling
WEYMOTH	Warmoth
WHELDON	Weldon
WILKINSON	Wilkerson
WILSON	Willson
WROE	Roe, Rowe
YEATS	Yates
YERBY	Yearby

Several family names have variants with a final –s. Among the most common are: Cole – Coles, Degge – Degges, Hammond – Hammonds, Hogan – Hogans, Nicken – Nickens, and Power – Powers.

APPENDIX 4

Nicknames and Given Name Variants

Nicknames are found frequently in these records. Women and slaves were far more likely than men to be called by a nickname. There were also numerous spelling and pronunciation variants of given names. These reflect colloquial pronunciations and non-standard spellings. The following list gives some of the nicknames and given name variants encountered in this book.

Ailce - Alice
Alcey – Alice
Barbary – Barbara
Bartlett - Bartley
Betsy – Elizabeth
Betty – Elizabeth
Briney – Sabrina
Caty – Catherine
Charlotty – Charlotte
Darkey – Dorcus
Dolly – Dorothy
Ellen – Eleanor
Emmy – Emily, Emma
Emsey – Emily, Emma
Eppa, Eppy - Epaphroditus
Fanny – Frances
Frankey – Frances
Hely, Heli – Helkiah
Heney – Henrietta
Hetty – Hester
Janey – Jane
Jenny – Jane
Judy – Judith
Katty – Catherine
Kitty – Catherine
Letty – Lettice
Lisha - Alice
Lotty, Lotte – Charlotte
Lody – Lodiwick
Lucrecy – Lucretia
Matilday - Matilda
Milly – Mildred, Melia
Milley - Millicent
Molly - Mary
Nancy - Anne
Nanny - Nancy
Peggy - Margaret
Penny - Penelope
Polly – Mary
Randal – Randolph
Roxy – Roxalana
Rush(a) - Rushworth
Sally – Sarah
Sary - Sarah
Sibbella – Sibyl
Sibb - Sibyl
Suckey, Sukey - Susan
Susan - Susannah
Tomsy – Thomasin
Winny – Winifred

APPENDIX 5

County Families

By 1800, many families had spread out of their home counties into adjacent counties or further afield out of the Northern Neck and westward into the western counties and Kentucky or southward into the Carolinas. However there were still strong associations between certain families and Northern Neck counties. Out of the more than 600 family names in this book, the following were strongly associated with a single county:

Lancaster County: ARMES, BOND, BRENT, CHILTON, CHINN, CHOWNING, CURRELL, DEGGE, DOGGETT, DUNAWAY, GEORGE, GIBSON, HATHAWAY, HILL, HINTON, HUNTON, KIRK, LOWRY, MEREDITH, MYERS, NEWBY, NORRIS, PERCIFULL, POLLARD, REVERE, SHEARMAN, SHELTON, SIMMONS, SMITHER, TOWLES.

Northumberland County: ALEXANDER, ANDERSON, BARNES, BEACHAM, BEATLEY, BLACKERBY, BLUNDON, CHRISTOPHER, CLAUGHTON, COCKARILL, COLES, CONWAY, CORBELL, CRALLE, DOWNING, GASKINS, HALL, HARCUM, HARVEY, HAYES, HAYNIE, HENRY, HUDNALL, HURST, KNOTT, LELAND, MARSH, MOON, OLDHAM, RICE, TIGNOR, WILDY, WINSTEAD.

Richmond County: ALDERSON, ALLOWAY, BAKER, BALDERSON, BARTLETT, BELFIELD, BRUCE, BRYANT, DOBYNS, FAUNTLEROY, GARLAND, HAZARD, JESPER, KELLY, MOZINGO, NEWSOM, PURSELL, TOMLIN, TUNE.

Westmoreland County: ATWELL, BABER, BRINNON, HUTT, MARMADUKE, MONROE, MUSE, OMOHUNDRO, PEYTON, PORTER, REDMAN, SANFORD, THOMPSON, TURBERVILLE, WASHINGTON.

APPENDIX 6

Frequency of White's Names

The frequencies of first names used by white residents of the Northern Neck differ from those of slaves as the following lists, based on a sample of 2000 names, will show. The 20 most common women's first names were:

> Elizabeth, Anne, Mary, Sarah, Nancy, Hannah, Judith, Frances, Catharine, Margaret, Sally, Winifred, Susanna, Lucy, Jane, Alice, Polly, Eleanor, Molly, Amy.

The 20 most common men's first names were:

> John, Thomas, George, Richard, William, Charles, Joseph, Samuel, Benjamin, Daniel, Henry, Robert, Peter, James, Jesse, Edward, David, Nicholas, Vincent, Presley.

A number of men's and women's names occur rarely. Among these are: Anjaletta, Bethire, Champion, Cotance, Devereaux, Dounda, Epaphroditus (also Eppa, Eppy), Fortunatus, Helkiah (also Heli, Hely), Kestor (also Castor), Original, Risdon (or Reiden), Tarkle, Theodorick, Theophilus, Tunstall, Wilalmira, Wilseth. These names, with the possible exception of Epaphroditus, seem to be limited to specific families or groups of related families.

Seventy two occurrences of family names used as first names have been identified in this study. The most common of these were: Griffin (28 occurrences), Rodham and Presley (15 occurrences each), Ewell/Youell (13 occurrences), Williamson (11 occurrences), Sydnor, Addison and Fleet (8 occurrences each), Lindsey and Newton (7 occurrences each), Steptoe, Lawson, and Winder (6 occurrences each). Less common were: Thornton, Bartlett/Bartley, Travers, Tarpley, Behethaland, Willoughby, and Washington (5 occurrences each), Monroe, Newman, Fauntleroy, Harrison, and Wesley (4 occurrences each), Tasker, Chichester, Chatham, Hudson, Mottrom, Coleman, Hancock, and Shipley (3 occurrences each), Berryman, Fleming, Kenner, Middleton, Beckwith, Merryman, Chattin/Chatwin, Townsend, Fielding, Peyton, Corbin, Sanford, and Madison (2 occurrences each), and Miskell, Hundley, Riveer, Landmon, Belfield, Newby, Bushrod, Mountjoy, Champe, templeman, Price, Ludwell, Sisson, Downing, Underhill, Ramey, Toulson, Broaddus, Haynes, Burditt, Wickliff, Barnett, Colville, Brereton, Dozier, and Frizell (one occurrence each). There were many more occurrences of family names used as middle names.

APPENDIX 7

Slave Names

Using a sample of over 4,000 slave names the following statistics have been extracted. The 20 most common men's first names were:

James, George, Daniel, Isaac, Samuel, Billy, Tom, David, John, Harry, Moses, Peter, Joe, Charles, William, Solomon, Spencer, Henry, Jack, Dick.

The 20 most common women's names were:

Winifred (including Winney), Betty, Hannah, Sarah, Nancy, Lucy, Fanny, Sally, Mary, Polly, Charlotte, Milly, Patsy, Sukey, Maria, Letticia (including Lettice, Letty), Priscilla (including Cilla, Priss, Sillar), Catharine, Esther, Rachel.

Of interest are eight slave names of possible African origin that occur in this sample. These are: Cuffee (possibly Akan), Genge (possibly Luba), Guly, Gumby, Juba, Konoko, Manay (possibly Samba Leko or Benin), Quanna (possibly Kono), Shurya, and Sembo.

Slaves were beginning to use family names during this period, and we find the following surnames among slaves:

ASHTON,Charles and Nelson
ASTON,Tom
BAKER, Harriet
BIRD, Jenny
BLUE, Jack and John
BLUNDELL, Billy
BRENT, Amos
BURK, James
BURN, George
BUTTON, Peter
CAROLINE, John
CASSITY, Ann and Betty
COLE, Sam
CONNET, Billy
CRANK, Sam
CYRUS, Bill
GRANT, Dick and Winny
HARRISON, Winny
JINKS, Thomas
KEY, James
LEE, William
LEWIS, Billy and George
MONROE, Dennis
NEALE, John
NEWTON, Bill, Isaac and Old Isaac
PINN, Betty, John and Tignor
POPE, Peter
PURSE, George
RANSDELL, Sally
ROBINSON, William
SAUNDERS, James
SMITH, Will
SOMERSET, Billy
STEPTOE, Betty
TOMBSY, William
TRACY, Joe
TUXON, James and Bill
UMPHRY, Cate
WIGGIN(S), Betty, Billy, Isaac, John, Nancy, William and Winny
WIGHAM, Will
WILDY, Winney
WILLIS, Billy and Jack

The earliest use of a family name by a slave in this material was Betty CASSITY owned by William DAVIS of LC in 1798. The names ASTON, ASHTON, BAKER, BLUNDELL, BRENT, COLE, HARRISON, BURN, GRANT, LEE, LEWIS, MONROE, NEALE, NEWTON, POPE, RANSDELL, ROBINSON, SAUNDERS, SMITH, STEPTOE, and WILDY were also used by white families. For a study of free

African-Americans in Virginia, see <www.freeafrican americans.com / Virginia_NC.htm>.

APPENDIX 8

Manumission of Slaves

Forty three wills in this collection contain provisions for the manumission of slaves. These manumissions seem to be motivated by genuine kindness and the desire to reward faithful service. A few other wills stopped short of actual manumission, but directed that slaves be allowed to choose their future masters or mistresses. Manumission during the period covered by this book was governed by the 1792 act to authorize the manumission of slaves which set forth conditions on manumission. The law read, in part:

> That it shall hereafter be lawful for any person, by his or her last will and testament, or by any other instrument in writing, under his or her hand and seal, attested and proved in the county court by two witnesses, or acknowledged by the party in the court of the county where he or she resides to emancipate and set free, his or her slaves, or any of them, who shall thereupon be entirely and fully discharged from the performance of any contract entered into during servitude, and enjoy as full freedom as if they had been particularly named and freed by this act.
>
> That all slaves so set free, not being in the judgment of the court, of sound mind and body, or being above the age of forty-five years, or being males under the age of twenty-one, or females under the age of eighteen years, shall respectively be supported and maintained by the person so liberating them, or by his or her estate; and upon neglect or refusal so to do, the court of the county where such neglect or refusal may be, is hereby empowered and required, upon application to them made, to order the sheriff to distrain and sell so much of the person's estate as shall be sufficient for that purpose. *Provided also,* That every person by written instrument in his life time, or if by last will and testament, the executors of every person freeing any slave, shall cause to be delivered to him or her, a copy of the instrument of emancipation, attested by the clerk of the court of the county, who shall be paid therefor, by the person emancipating, five shillings, to be collected in the manner of other clerk's fees. Every person neglecting or refusing to deliver to any slave by him or her set free, such copy, shall forfeit and pay ten pounds, to be recovered with costs in any court of record, one half thereof to the person suing for the same, and the other to the person to whom such copy ought to have been delivered. It shall be lawful for any justice of the peace to commit to the gaol of his county, any emancipated slave travelling out of the county of his or her residence without a copy of the instrument of his or her emancipation, there to remain till such copy is produced and the gaoler's fees paid.

For the complete text of the law, see William Waller Hening, *The Statutes at Large; Being a Collection of all the Laws of Virginia from the First Session of the Legislature in the Year 1619,* Vol. XI, Richmond: George Cochran, 1823, pp. 39 – 40.

A law passed in 1806 required emancipated slaves to leave the state.

> If any slave hereafter emancipated shall remain within this Commonwealth more than 12 months after his or her right to freedom shall have accrued, he or she shall forfeit all such right, and may be apprehended and sold by the overseers of the poor of any county or corporation in which he or she shall be found for the benefit of the poor of such county or corporation.[1]

---

[1] Shepherd Vol. III, pp. 251-253.

However an emancipated slave could apply to the county court for permission to remain in the county. There are examples among the records abstracted here of the court granting this permission as well as refusing to grant it.

SELECT BIBLIOGRAPHY
and Abbreviations

ac. acres
acc. according
acct(s). account(s)
adj. adjacent, adjoining
admin. administer, administered; administration
admr . administrator
admx. administratrix
ALCW Lee, Ida J. 1959, ***Abstracts Lancaster County, Virginia, Wills 1653 – 1800***. Richmond, Va.: The Dietz Press, Inc.
aptd. appointed
atty. attorney
b. born
BDBN Barnes, Robert W. 2011, ***Biographical Data from Baltimore Newspapers 1817 – 1819.*** Baltimore: Clearfield
beg. beginning
bel. belonging
b-i-l. brother-in-law
BNCHS ***Bulletin of the Northumberland County Historical Society,*** Heathsville, Va., 1964 – 2010.
bro. brother
bet. between
CC chancery case
CCP Christ Church Parish, Lancaster County
cod. codicil
complt(s). complainant(s)
CORBIN Stanard, W. G. 1920-23. The Corbin Family. ***VMHB*** 28:281-283, 370-373; 29:124-128, 243, 374-382, 520-526; 30:80-85, 309-318, 403-407; 31:80-83, 170.
CP Cople Parish, Westmoreland County
d. died
D of G. deed of gift
d-i-l. daughter-in-law
dau(s). daughter(s)
DC District Court
dec'd deceased
deft(s). defendents
dep. deposition
div. division, divid(ed)
d.s.p. decessit sine prole "died without issue"
dtd dated
EC Essex County
eq. equal
eq. div. equally divided
est. estate
ex(ors). executor(s)
extx. executrix
f-i-l father-in-law
fnu first name unknown
FP Farnham Parish, RC
gdn(s). guardian(s)
gdnship. guardianship
grdau. granddaughter

grfath. grandfather
grson. grandson
HHF household furniture
HH & KF household & kitchen furniture
HRVR John H. Gwathmey. 1938. ***Historical Register of Virginians in the Revolution. Soldiers . Sailors . Marines, 1775 – 1783***. Baltimore: Genealogical Publishing Company (reprinted several times)
husb. husband
IMORECV Eva Eubank Wilkerson. 1983. ***Index to Marriages of Old Rappahannock and Essex Counties, Virginia 1655 – 1900***. Baltimore: Genealogical Publishing Co.
inf. infant (child under 21)
INV inventory (also includes appraisals)
KGC King George County
KGCVM Elizabeth Nuckols. 1995. ***King George County Virginia Marriages, Vol. I, Marriage Bonds Book 1 1786 – 1850.*** Athens, GA: Iberian Publishing Co.
King J. Estelle Stewart King. 1986. ***Abstracts of Wills, Administrations, and Marriages of Fauquier County, Virginia 1759 – 1800***. Baltimore: Genealogical Publishing Co.
LC Lancaster County
LCVMB Ida J. Lee. 1972 ***Lancaster County, Virginia, Marriage Bonds, 1652-1850***. Baltimore: Genealogical Publishing Co.
LCWB28 Mary Ball Washington Museum and Library. 1975. ***Lancaster County, Virginia, Will Book 28.*** Lancaster, Va.
lic. (marriage) licence
lnu last name unknown
LP Lunenburg Parish, Richmond County
LPR Lunenburg Parish Register (included in NFPR)
LVA Library of Virginia, Richmond
[m] missing
mar. married
MB Minute Book
MC Middlesex County
Meade Meade, William (Bishop). 1966 ***Old Churches Ministers and Families of Virginia,*** Baltimore: Genealogical Publishing Co. (2 volumns)
Miller Miller, Mary R. 1983 ***Place-Names of the Northern Neck of Virginia,*** Richmond: Virginia State Library
MLBLC Nottingham, Stratton. 1927, 1996 ***The Marriage License Bonds of Lancaster County, Virginia from 1701 to 1848.*** Baltimore: Clearfield Co., Inc
MLBNC Nottingham, Stratton. 1928, 1975 ***The Marriage License Bonds of Westmoreland County, Virginia from 1786 to 1850.*** Baltimore: Genealogical Publishing Co., Inc.
MLBWC Nottingham, Stratton. 1928, 1975 ***The Marriage License Bonds of Westmoreland County, Virginia From 1786 to 1850.*** Baltimore: Genealogical Publishing Co., Inc.
mot. motion
MWO Headley, Robert K. 2003 ***Married Well and Often. Marriages of the Northern Neck of Virginia 1649-1800.*** Baltimore: Genealogical Publishing Co., Inc.
NC Northumberland County
NCHS Northumberland County Historical Society, Heathsville.
NCVCR Walczyk, Gail M. 2001 ***Northumberland County, Virginia Church Records of Births and Deaths 1650-1810.*** Coram, NY: Peter's Row.
NCVW 1770-1793 Lewis, James F. and J. Motley Booker, M.D. ***Northumberland County Virginia, Wills 1770-1793 and Administrations 1770-1790*** Callao, Va.: Walker's Printing Service.

NCVW 1793-1816 Lewis, James F. and J. Motley Booker, M.D. ***Northumberland County Virginia, Wills 1793-1816 and Administrations 1790-1816*** Callao, Va.: Walker's Printing Service.

Nelson Nelson, John Kendall 2001 ***A Blessed Company: Parishes, Parson, and Parishoners in Anglican Virginia, 1690-1776.*** Chapel Hill & London: The University of North Carolina Press.

nfi not further identified

NFPR King, George H. S. 1966 ***The Registers of North Farnham Parish 1663 – 1814 and Lunenburg Parish 1783 – 1800 Richmond County, Virginia.*** Fredericksburg, Va. [references to NFPR and LPR are to pages in this book]

NNVHM ***Northern Neck of Virginia Historical Magazine.***

nunc. nuncupative will (oral will)

OB Order Book

ord. ordered

pers. est. personal estate

plant. plantation

pltf(s). plaintif(s)

PO per order (date the court ordered the action to be taken)

P of A power of attorney

poss. possibly

PR1835 ***The Pension Roll of 1835, Vol. II.*** Baltimore: Clearfield Company [*reprinted several times*]

pres. presented

prob. probably

prop. property

RC Richmond County

RE real estate

rec. recorded (date the document was recorded in court)

rec'd received

rel. relict

rep(s). representative(s)

req. requests

ret. returned (the date the document was delivered to court)

Rich. Enq. *Richmond Enquirer*

RWR Brumbaugh, Gaius Marcus 1967, 1995. ***Revolutionary War Records, Virginia.*** Baltimore: Genealogical Publishing Co., Inc.

SAL Hening, William Waller. 1809-23. ***The Statutes at Large; Being a Collection of All the Laws of Virginia, from the First Session of the Legislature, in the Year 1619,*** Richmond, Va.: Samuel Pleasants, 13 volumes.

sd. said

sec. security

Shepherd Shepherd, Samuel. *Statutes at Large of Virginia, from October Session 1792, to December Session 1806, inclusive, in Three Volumes, (New Series) Being a Continuation of Hening.* Richmond: Samuel Shepherd, 1836.

s-i-l. son-in-law

sis. sister

sis-i-l sister-in-law

SSP St. Stephen's Parish, Northumberland County

SSPR St. Stephen's Parish Register (references to pages of the SSPR are to pages in the original; see: VCA3 and NCVCR)

T taken (date the inventory or appraisement was actually made)

test. testament

VCA3 Fleet, Beverley 1938, 1961 **Virginia Colonial Abstracts Vol. III Northumberland Co. Record of Births 1661-1810**. Baltimore: Genealogical Publishing Co.

VS1776 Burgess, Louis A. 1927, 1994 **Virginia Soldiers of 1776.** Baltimore: Genealogical Publishing Co., Inc., 3 vols.

WB will book

WC Westmoreland County

WCCP Lee, Elizabeth Nuckols 2004 ***Westmoreland County Virginia Loose Chancery Papers vol. 1: 1804-1864***. Athens, GA: New Papyrus Publishing Co. [The title of this book is somewhat misleading; it contains only selected chancery cases from WC. The LVA Website contains scanned images of many more chancery cases for this time period]

w/o whereon

WicP Wicomico Parish, Northumberland County

wid. widow, widower

wit(s). witness(es)

WP Washington Parish, Westmoreland County

WRC Headley, Robert K. 1983 ***Wills of Richmond County, Virginia 1699-1800***. Baltimore: Genealogial Publishing Co, Inc.

WWCV Fothergill, Augusta B. 1973 ***Wills of Westmorland County, Virginia 1654-1800***. Baltimore: Genealogical Publishing Co., Inc.

INDEX

Names of testators and other main entries are not included in the index since they are in alphabetical order. A name that appears more than once on a page is entered only once in the index. Several common names have been abbreviated, e.g., Jn. for John, Robt. for Robert, and Raw. for Rawleigh. All variants of a name have been indexed so be sure to check them. For example if you are looking for an Elizabeth check Eliz., Eliza, Betty, Bett., Betsy, Bettey, Betsey, Liz., and Lizzy. Several general categories have been indexed; these include counties, states, tracts of land (including plantations), places (if no state is named, the place is in Virginia), churches, emancipation, slaves, doctors, creeks, swamps, necks of land, commercial entities, and military organizations and events.

CPSIA information can be obtained at www.ICGtesting.com
Printed in the USA
LVOW06s0023120214
373286LV00011B/195/P

9 780806 319858